BY MAYA ANGELOU

AUTOBIOGRAPHIES

I Know Why the Caged Bird Sings

Gather Together in My Name

*Singin' and Swingin' and Gettin'
Merry Like Christmas*

The Heart of a Woman

*All God's Children Need
Traveling Shoes*

A Song Flung Up to Heaven

Mom & Me & Mom

ESSAYS

*Wouldn't Take Nothing for My
Journey Now*

Even the Stars Look Lonesome

Letter to My Daughter

POETRY

*Just Give Me a Cool Drink of Water
'fore I Diiie*

*Oh Pray My Wings Are Gonna Fit
Me Well*

And Still I Rise

Shaker, Why Don't You Sing?

I Shall Not Be Moved

On the Pulse of Morning

Phenomenal Woman

A Brave and Startling Truth

Amazing Peace

Mother

His Day Is Done

CHILDREN'S BOOKS

*Poetry for Young People:
Maya Angelou*

*My Painted House, My Friendly
Chicken, and Me*

Kofi and His Magic

MAYA'S WORLD SERIES

Angelina of Italy

Izak of Lapland

Mikale of Hawaii

Renée Marie of France

PICTURE BOOKS

Love's Exquisite Freedom

Now Sheba Sings the Song

Life Doesn't Frighten Me

COOKBOOKS

Hallelujah! The Welcome Table

Great Food, All Day Long

COLLECTIONS

*The Collected Autobiographies of
Maya Angelou*

Celebrations

Rainbow in the Cloud

Maya Angelou: The Complete Poetry

THE COLLECTED AUTOBIOGRAPHIES
OF MAYA ANGELOU

THE COLLECTED AUTOBIOGRAPHIES OF MAYA ANGELOU

THE MODERN LIBRARY

NEW YORK

2004 Modern Library Edition

Compilation copyright © 2004 by Random House, Inc.

I Know Why the Caged Bird Sings copyright © 1969, copyright renewed 1997
by Maya Angelou

Gather Together in My Name copyright © 1974, copyright renewed 2002
by Maya Angelou

Singin' and Swingin' and Gettin' Merry Like Christmas copyright © 1976
by Maya Angelou

The Heart of a Woman copyright © 1981 by Maya Angelou

All God's Children Need Traveling Shoes copyright © 1986 by Maya Angelou

A Song Flung Up to Heaven copyright © 2002 by Maya Angelou

Each of the six works contained in this book was published individually
by Random House, an imprint of The Random House Publishing Group,
a division of Random House, Inc.

Owing to limitations of space, permission acknowledgments appear on page 1172.

LIBRARY OF CONGRESS CATALOGING-IN-PUBLICATION DATA

Angelou, Maya.
The collected autobiographies of Maya Angelou / Maya Angelou.
p. cm.
Contents: I know why the caged bird sings—Gather together in my name—Singin'
and swingin' and getting' merry like Christmas—The heart of a woman—All God's
children need traveling shoes—A song flung up to heaven.
ISBN 0-679-64325-7
1. Angelou, Maya—Childhood and youth. 2. Authors, American—Homes and
haunts—Arkansas. 3. Angelou, Maya—Homes and haunts—Arkansas.
4. Authors, American—20th century—Biography. 5. Entertainers—United
States—Biography. 6. African American families—Arkansas. 7. African
American authors—Biography. 8. Arkansas—Social life and customs. I. Title.
PS3551.N464Z466 2004
818'.5409—dc22 2004046665
[B]

Modern Library website address:
www.modernlibrary.com

*This collection gratefully acknowledges the gifts of all
of my ancestors. It is dedicated to my great-grandchildren,*
CAYLIN NICOLE JOHNSON
and
BRANDON BAILEY JOHNSON.

Contents

I Know Why the Caged Bird Sings

1

Gather Together in My Name

223

Singin' and Swingin' and Gettin' Merry Like Christmas

385

The Heart of a Woman

619

All God's Children Need Traveling Shoes

881

A Song Flung Up to Heaven

1053

I KNOW WHY
THE CAGED BIRD SINGS

This book is dedicated to My Son,
GUY JOHNSON,
and all the Strong Black Birds of Promise
Who Defy the Odds and Gods
and Sing Their Songs

ACKNOWLEDGMENTS

I thank my mother, VIVIAN BAXTER, *and my brother,* BAILEY JOHNSON, *who encouraged me to remember. Thanks to the* HARLEM WRITERS' GUILD *for concern and to* JOHN O. KILLENS *who told me I could write. To* NANA KOBINA NKETSIA IV *who insisted that I must. Lasting gratitude to* GERARD PURCELL *who believed concretely and to* TONY D'AMATO *who understood. Thanks to* ABBEY LINCOLN ROACH *for naming my book.*

A final thanks to my editor at Random House, ROBERT LOOMIS, *who gently prodded me back into the lost years.*

"What you looking at me for?
I didn't come to stay..."

I hadn't so much forgot as I couldn't bring myself to remember. Other things were more important.

"What you looking at me for?
I didn't come to stay..."

Whether I could remember the rest of the poem or not was immaterial. The truth of the statement was like a wadded-up handkerchief, sopping wet in my fists, and the sooner they accepted it the quicker I could let my hands open and the air would cool my palms.

"What you looking at me for...?"

The children's section of the Colored Methodist Episcopal Church was wiggling and giggling over my well-known forgetfulness.

The dress I wore was lavender taffeta, and each time I breathed it rustled, and now that I was sucking in air to breathe out shame it sounded like crepe paper on the back of hearses.

As I'd watched Momma put ruffles on the hem and cute little tucks around the waist, I knew that once I put it on I'd look like a movie star. (It was silk and that made up for the awful color.) I was going to look like one of the sweet little white girls who were everybody's dream of what was right with the world. Hanging softly over the black Singer sewing machine, it looked like magic, and when people saw me wearing it they were going to run up to me and say, "Marguerite [sometimes it was 'dear Marguerite'], forgive us, please, we didn't know who you were," and I would answer generously, "No, you couldn't have known. Of course I forgive you."

Just thinking about it made me go around with angel's dust sprinkled over my face for days. But Easter's early morning sun had shown the dress to be a plain ugly cut-down from a white woman's once-was-purple throwaway. It was old-lady-long too, but it didn't hide my skinny legs, which had been greased with Blue Seal Vaseline and powdered with the Arkansas red clay. The age-faded color made my skin look dirty like mud, and everyone in church was looking at my skinny legs.

Wouldn't they be surprised when one day I woke out of my black ugly dream, and my real hair, which was long and blond, would take the place of the kinky mass that Momma wouldn't let me straighten? My light-blue eyes were going to hypnotize them, after all the things they said about "my daddy must of been a Chinaman" (I thought they meant made out of china, like a cup) because my eyes were so small and squinty. Then they would understand why I had never picked up a Southern accent, or spoke the common slang, and why I had to be forced to eat pigs' tails and snouts. Because I was really white and because a cruel fairy stepmother, who was understandably jealous of my beauty, had turned me into a too-big Negro girl, with nappy black hair, broad feet and a space between her teeth that would hold a number-two pencil.

"What you looking..." The minister's wife leaned toward me, her long yellow face full of sorry. She whispered, "I just come to tell you, it's Easter Day." I repeated, jamming the words together, "Ijustcometotellyouit'sEasterDay," as low as possible. The giggles hung in the air like melting clouds that were waiting to rain on me. I held up two fingers, close to my chest, which meant that I had to go to the toilet, and tiptoed toward the rear of the church. Dimly, somewhere over my head, I heard ladies saying, "Lord bless the child," and "Praise God."

My head was up and my eyes were open, but I didn't see anything. Halfway down the aisle, the church exploded with "Were you there when they crucified my Lord?" and I tripped over a foot stuck out from the children's pew. I stumbled and started to say something, or maybe to scream, but a green persimmon, or it could have been a lemon, caught me between the legs and squeezed. I tasted the sour on my tongue and felt it in the back of my mouth. Then before I reached the door, the sting was burning down my legs and into my Sunday socks. I tried to hold, to squeeze it back, to keep it from speeding, but when I reached the church porch I knew I'd have to let it go, or it would probably run right back up to my head and my poor head would burst like a dropped watermelon, and all the brains and spit and tongue and eyes would roll all over the place. So I ran down into the yard and let it go. I ran, peeing and crying, not toward the toilet out back but to our house. I'd get a whipping for it, to be sure, and the nasty children would have something new to tease me about. I laughed anyway, partially for the sweet release; still, the greater joy came not only from being liberated from the silly church but from the knowledge that I wouldn't die from a busted head.

If growing up is painful for the Southern Black girl, being aware of her displacement is the rust on the razor that threatens the throat.

It is an unnecessary insult.

CHAPTER 1

When I was three and Bailey four, we had arrived in the musty little town, wearing tags on our wrists which instructed—"To Whom It May Concern"—that we were Marguerite and Bailey Johnson Jr., from Long Beach, California, en route to Stamps, Arkansas, c/o Mrs. Annie Henderson.

Our parents had decided to put an end to their calamitous marriage, and Father shipped us home to his mother. A porter had been charged with our welfare—he got off the train the next day in Arizona—and our tickets were pinned to my brother's inside coat pocket.

I don't remember much of the trip, but after we reached the segregated southern part of the journey, things must have looked up. Negro passengers, who always traveled with loaded lunch boxes, felt sorry for "the poor little motherless darlings" and plied us with cold fried chicken and potato salad.

Years later I discovered that the United States had been crossed thousands of times by frightened Black children traveling alone to their newly affluent parents in Northern cities, or back to grandmothers in Southern towns when the urban North reneged on its economic promises.

The town reacted to us as its inhabitants had reacted to all things new before our coming. It regarded us a while without curiosity but with caution, and after we were seen to be harmless (and children) it closed in around us, as a real mother embraces a stranger's child. Warmly, but not too familiarly.

We lived with our grandmother and uncle in the rear of the Store (it was always spoken of with a capital *s*), which she had owned some twenty-five years.

Early in the century, Momma (we soon stopped calling her Grandmother) sold lunches to the sawmen in the lumberyard (east Stamps) and the seedmen at the cotton gin (west Stamps). Her crisp meat pies and cool lemonade, when joined to her miraculous ability to be in two places at the same time, assured her business success. From being a mobile lunch counter, she set up a stand between the two points of fiscal interest and supplied the workers' needs for a few years. Then she had the Store built in the heart of the Negro area. Over the years it became the lay center of activities in town. On Saturdays, barbers sat their customers in the shade on the porch of the Store, and troubadours on their ceaseless crawlings through the South leaned across its benches and sang their sad songs of The Brazos while they played juice harps and cigar-box guitars.

The formal name of the Store was the Wm. Johnson General Merchandise Store. Customers could find food staples, a good variety of colored thread, mash for hogs, corn for chickens, coal oil for lamps, light bulbs for the wealthy, shoestrings, hair dressing, balloons, and flower seeds. Anything not visible had only to be ordered.

Until we became familiar enough to belong to the Store and it to us, we were locked up in a Fun House of Things where the attendant had gone home for life.

———

Each year I watched the field across from the Store turn caterpillar green, then gradually frosty white. I knew exactly how long it would be before the big wagons would pull into the front yard and load on the cotton pickers at daybreak to carry them to the remains of slavery's plantations.

During the picking season my grandmother would get out of bed at four o'clock (she never used an alarm clock) and creak down to her knees and chant in a sleep-filled voice, "Our Father, thank you for letting me see this New Day. Thank you that you didn't allow the bed I lay on last night to be my cooling board, nor my blanket my winding sheet. Guide my feet this day along the straight and narrow, and help me to put a bridle on my tongue. Bless this house, and everybody in it. Thank you, in the name of your Son, Jesus Christ, Amen."

Before she had quite arisen, she called our names and issued orders, and pushed her large feet into homemade slippers and across the bare lye-washed wooden floor to light the coal-oil lamp.

The lamplight in the Store gave a soft make-believe feeling to our world which made me want to whisper and walk about on tiptoe. The odors of onions and oranges and kerosene had been mixing all night and wouldn't be disturbed until the wooded slat was removed from the door and the early morning air forced its way in with the bodies of people who had walked miles to reach the pickup place.

"Sister, I'll have two cans of sardines."

"I'm gonna work so fast today I'm gonna make you look like you standing still."

"Lemme have a hunk uh cheese and some sody crackers."

"Just gimme a coupla them fat peanut paddies." That would be from a picker who was taking his lunch. The greasy brown paper sack was stuck behind the bib of his overalls. He'd use the candy as a snack before the noon sun called the workers to rest.

In those tender mornings the Store was full of laughing, joking, boasting and bragging. One man was going to pick two hundred pounds of cotton, and another three hundred. Even the children were promising to bring home fo' bits and six bits.

The champion picker of the day before was the hero of the dawn. If he prophesied that the cotton in today's field was going to be sparse and stick to the bolls like glue, every listener would grunt a hearty agreement.

The sound of the empty cotton sacks dragging over the floor and the murmurs of waking people were sliced by the cash register as we rang up the five-cent sales.

If the morning sounds and smells were touched with the supernatural, the late afternoon had all the features of the normal Arkansas life. In the dying sunlight the people dragged, rather than their empty cotton sacks.

Brought back to the Store, the pickers would step out of the backs of trucks and fold down, dirt-disappointed, to the ground. No matter how much they had picked, it wasn't enough. Their wages wouldn't even get them out of debt to my grandmother, not to mention the staggering bill that waited on them at the white commissary downtown.

The sounds of the new morning had been replaced with grumbles about cheating houses, weighted scales, snakes, skimpy cotton and dusty rows. In later years I was to confront the stereotyped picture of gay song-singing cotton pickers with such inordinate rage that I was told even by fellow Blacks that my paranoia was embarrassing. But I had seen the fingers cut by the mean little cotton bolls, and I had witnessed the backs and shoulders and arms and legs resisting any further demands.

Some of the workers would leave their sacks at the Store to be picked up the following morning, but a few had to take them home for repairs. I winced to picture them sewing the coarse material under a coal-oil lamp with fingers stiffening from the day's work. In too few hours they would have to walk back to Sister Henderson's Store, get vittles and load, again, onto the trucks. Then they would face another day of trying to earn enough for the whole year with the heavy knowledge that they were going to end the season as they started it. Without the money or credit necessary to sustain a family for three months. In cotton-picking time the late afternoons revealed the harshness of Black Southern life, which in the early morning had been softened by nature's blessing of grogginess, forgetfulness and the soft lamplight.

CHAPTER 2

When Bailey was six and I a year younger, we used to rattle off the times tables with the speed I was later to see Chinese children in San Francisco employ on their abacuses. Our summer-gray pot-bellied stove bloomed rosy red during winter, and became a severe disciplinarian threat if we were so foolish as to indulge in making mistakes.

Uncle Willie used to sit, like a giant black Z (he had been crippled as a child), and hear us testify to the Lafayette County Training Schools' abilities. His face pulled down on the left side, as if a pulley had been attached to his lower teeth, and his left hand was only a mite bigger than Bailey's, but on the second mistake or on the third hesitation his big overgrown right hand would catch one of us behind the collar, and in the same moment would thrust the culprit toward the dull red heater, which throbbed like a devil's toothache. We were never burned, although once I might have been when I was so terrified I tried to jump onto the stove to remove the possibility of its remaining a threat. Like most children, I thought if I could face the worst danger voluntarily, and *triumph,* I would forever have power over it. But in my case of sacrificial effort I was thwarted. Uncle Willie held tight to my dress and I only got close enough to smell the clean dry scent of hot iron. We learned the times tables without understanding their grand principle, simply because we had the capacity and no alternative.

The tragedy of lameness seems so unfair to children that they are embarrassed in its presence. And they, most recently off nature's mold, sense that they have only narrowly missed being another of her jokes. In relief at the narrow escape, they vent their emotions in impatience and criticism of the unlucky cripple.

Momma related times without end, and without any show of emotion, how Uncle Willie had been dropped when he was three years old by a woman who was minding him. She seemed to hold no rancor against the baby-sitter, nor for her just God who allowed the accident. She felt it necessary to explain over and over again to those who knew the story by heart that he wasn't "born that way."

In our society, where two-legged, two-armed strong Black men were able at best to eke out only the necessities of life, Uncle Willie, with his starched shirts, shined shoes and shelves full of food, was the whipping boy and butt of jokes of the underemployed and underpaid. Fate not only disabled him but laid a double-tiered barrier in his path. He was also proud and sensitive. Therefore he couldn't pretend that he wasn't crippled, nor could he deceive himself that people were not repelled by his defect.

Only once in all the years of trying not to watch him, I saw him pretend to himself and others that he wasn't lame.

Coming home from school one day, I saw a dark car in our front yard. I rushed in to find a strange man and woman (Uncle Willie said later they were schoolteachers from Little Rock) drinking Dr. Pepper in the cool of the Store. I sensed a wrongness around me, like an alarm clock that had gone off without being set.

I knew it couldn't be the strangers. Not frequently, but often enough, travelers pulled off the main road to buy tobacco or soft drinks in the only Negro store in Stamps. When I looked at Uncle Willie, I knew what was pulling my mind's coattails. He was standing erect behind the counter, not leaning forward or resting on the small shelf that had been built for him. Erect. His eyes seemed to hold me with a mixture of threats and appeal.

I dutifully greeted the strangers and roamed my eyes around for his walking stick. It was nowhere to be seen. He said, "Uh...this

this...this...uh, my niece. She's...uh...just come from school." Then to the couple—"You know...how, uh, children are...th-th-these days...they play all d-d-day at school and c-c-can't wait to get home and pl-play some more."

The people smiled, very friendly.

He added, "Go on out and pl-play, Sister."

The lady laughed in a soft Arkansas voice and said, "Well, you know, Mr. Johnson, they say, you're only a child once. Have you children of your own?"

Uncle Willie looked at me with an impatience I hadn't seen in his face even when he took thirty minutes to loop the laces over his high-topped shoes. "I...I thought I told you to go...go outside and play."

Before I left I saw him lean back on the shelves of Garret Snuff, Prince Albert and Spark Plug chewing tobacco.

"No, ma'am...no ch-children and no wife." He tried a laugh. "I have an old m-m-mother and my brother's t-two children to l-look after."

I didn't mind his using us to make himself look good. In fact, I would have pretended to be his daughter if he wanted me to. Not only did I not feel any loyalty to my own father, I figured that if I had been Uncle Willie's child I would have received much better treatment.

The couple left after a few minutes, and from the back of the house I watched the red car scare chickens, raise dust and disappear toward Magnolia.

Uncle Willie was making his way down the long shadowed aisle between the shelves and the counter—hand over hand, like a man climbing out of a dream. I stayed quiet and watched him lurch from one side, bumping to the other, until he reached the coal-oil tank. He put his hand behind that dark recess and took his cane in the strong fist and shifted his weight on the wooden support. He thought he had pulled it off.

I'll never know why it was important to him that the couple (he said later that he'd never seen them before) would take a picture of a whole Mr. Johnson back to Little Rock.

He must have tired of being crippled, as prisoners tire of penitentiary bars and the guilty tire of blame. The high-topped shoes and the cane, his uncontrollable muscles and thick tongue, and the looks he suffered of either contempt or pity had simply worn him out, and for one afternoon, one part of an afternoon, he wanted no part of them.

I understood and felt closer to him at that moment than ever before or since.

———

During these years in Stamps, I met and fell in love with William Shakespeare. He was my first white love. Although I enjoyed and respected Kipling, Poe, Butler, Thackeray and Henley, I saved my young and loyal passion for Paul Lawrence Dunbar, Langston Hughes, James Weldon Johnson and W.E.B. Du Bois' "Litany at Atlanta." But it was Shakespeare who said, "When in disgrace with fortune and men's eyes." It was a state with which I felt myself most familiar. I pacified myself about his whiteness by saying that after all he had been dead so long it couldn't matter to anyone any more.

Bailey and I decided to memorize a scene from *The Merchant of Venice,* but we realized that Momma would question us about the author and that we'd have to tell her that Shakespeare was white, and it wouldn't matter to her whether he was dead or not. So we chose "The Creation" by James Weldon Johnson instead.

CHAPTER 3

Weighing the half-pounds of flour, excluding the scoop, and depositing them dust-free into the thin paper sacks held a simple kind of adventure for me. I developed an eye for measuring how full a silver-looking ladle of flour, mash, meal, sugar or corn had to be to push the scale indicator over to eight ounces or one pound. When I was absolutely accurate our appreciative customers used to admire: "Sister Henderson sure got some smart grandchildrens." If I was off in the Store's favor, the eagle-eyed women would say, "Put some more in that sack, child. Don't you try to make your profit offa me."

Then I would quietly but persistently punish myself. For every bad judgment, the fine was no silver-wrapped Kisses, the sweet chocolate drops that I loved more than anything in the world, except Bailey. And maybe canned pineapples. My obsession with pineapples nearly drove me mad. I dreamt of the days when I would be grown and able to buy a whole carton for myself alone.

Although the syrupy golden rings sat in their exotic cans on our shelves year round, we only tasted them during Christmas. Momma used the juice to make almost-black fruit cakes. Then she lined heavy soot-encrusted iron skillets with the pineapple rings for rich upside-down cakes. Bailey and I received one slice each, and I carried mine around for hours, shredding off the fruit until nothing was left except the perfume on my fingers. I'd like to think that my desire for pineapples was so sacred that I wouldn't allow myself to steal a can (which was possible) and eat it alone out in the garden, but I'm certain that I must have weighed the possibility of the scent exposing me and didn't have the nerve to attempt it.

Until I was thirteen and left Arkansas for good, the Store was my favorite place to be. Alone and empty in the mornings, it looked like an unopened present from a stranger. Opening the front doors was pulling the ribbon off the unexpected gift. The light would come in softly (we faced north), easing itself over the shelves of mackerel, salmon, tobacco, thread. It fell flat on the big vat of lard and by noontime during the summer the grease had softened to a thick soup. Whenever I walked into the Store in the afternoon, I sensed that it was tired. I alone could hear the slow pulse of its job half done. But just before bedtime, after numerous people had walked in and out, had argued over their bills, or joked about their neighbors, or just dropped in "to give Sister Henderson a 'Hi y'all,' " the promise of magic mornings returned to the Store and spread itself over the family in washed life waves.

Momma opened boxes of crispy crackers and we sat around the meat block at the rear of the Store. I sliced onions, and Bailey opened two or even three cans of sardines and allowed their juice of oil and fishing boats to ooze down and around the sides. That was supper. In the evening, when we were alone like that, Uncle Willie didn't stutter or shake or give any indication that he had an "affliction." It seemed that the peace of a day's ending was an assurance that the covenant God made with children, Negroes and the crippled was still in effect.

———

Throwing scoops of corn to the chickens and mixing sour dry mash with leftover food and oily dish water for the hogs were among our evening chores. Bailey and I sloshed down twilight trails to the pig pens, and standing on the first fence rungs we poured down the unappealing concoctions to our grateful hogs. They mashed their tender pink snouts down into the slop, and rooted and grunted their satisfaction. We always grunted a reply only half in jest. We were also grateful that we had concluded the dirtiest of chores and had only gotten the evil-smelling swill on our shoes, stockings, feet and hands.

Late one day, as we were attending to the pigs, I heard a horse in the front yard (it really should have been called a driveway, except that there was nothing to drive into it), and ran to find out who had come riding up on a Thursday evening when even Mr. Steward, the quiet, bitter man who owned a riding horse, would be resting by his warm fire until the morning called him out to turn over his field.

The used-to-be sheriff sat rakishly astraddle his horse. His nonchalance was meant to convey his authority and power over even dumb animals. How much more capable he would be with Negroes. It went without saying.

His twang jogged in the brittle air. From the side of the Store, Bailey and I heard him say to Momma, "Annie, tell Willie he better lay low tonight. A crazy nigger messed with a white lady today. Some of the boys'll be coming over here later." Even after the slow drag of years, I remember the sense of fear which filled my mouth with hot, dry air, and made my body light.

The "boys"? Those cement faces and eyes of hate that burned the clothes off you if they happened to see you lounging on the main street downtown on Saturday. Boys? It seemed that youth had never happened to them. Boys? No, rather men who were covered with graves' dust and age without beauty or learning. The ugliness and rottenness of old abominations.

If on Judgment Day I were summoned by St. Peter to give testimony to the used-to-be sheriff's act of kindness, I would be unable to say anything in his behalf. His confidence that my uncle and every other Black man who heard of the Klan's coming ride would scurry under their houses to hide in chicken droppings was too humiliating to hear. Without waiting for Momma's thanks, he rode out of the yard, sure that things were as they should be and that he was a gentle squire, saving those deserving serfs from the laws of the land, which he condoned.

Immediately, while his horse's hoofs were still loudly thudding the ground, Momma blew out the coal-oil lamps. She had a quiet, hard talk with Uncle Willie and called Bailey and me into the Store.

We were told to take the potatoes and onions out of their bins and knock out the dividing walls that kept them apart. Then with a tedious and fearful slowness Uncle Willie gave me his rubber-tipped cane and bent down to get into the now-enlarged empty bin. It took forever before he lay down flat, and then we covered him with potatoes and onions, layer upon layer, like a casserole. Grandmother knelt praying in the darkened Store.

It was fortunate that the "boys" didn't ride into our yard that evening and insist that Momma open the Store. They would have surely found Uncle Willie and just as surely lynched him. He moaned the whole night through as if he had, in fact, been guilty of some heinous crime. The heavy sounds pushed their way up out of the blanket of vegetables and I pictured his mouth pulling down on the right side and his saliva flowing into the eyes of new potatoes and waiting there like dew drops for the warmth of morning.

CHAPTER 4

What sets one Southern town apart from another, or from a Northern town or hamlet, or city high-rise? The answer must be the experience shared between the unknowing majority (it) and the knowing minority (you). All of childhood's unanswered questions must finally be passed back to the town and answered there. Heroes and bogey men, values and dislikes, are first encountered and labeled in that early environment. In later years they change faces, places and maybe races, tactics, intensities and goals, but beneath those penetrable masks they wear forever the stocking-capped faces of childhood.

Mr. McElroy, who lived in the big rambling house next to the Store, was very tall and broad, and although the years had eaten away the flesh from his shoulders, they had not, at the time of my knowing him, gotten to his high stomach, or his hands or feet.

He was the only Negro I knew, except for the school principal and the visiting teachers, who wore matching pants and jackets. When I learned that men's clothes were sold like that and called suits, I remember thinking that somebody had been very bright, for it made men look less manly, less threatening and a little more like women.

Mr. McElroy never laughed, and seldom smiled, and to his credit was the fact that he liked to talk to Uncle Willie. He never went to church, which Bailey and I thought also proved he was a very courageous person. How great it would be to grow up like that, to be able to stare religion down, especially living next door to a woman like Momma.

I watched him with the excitement of expecting him to do anything at any time. I never tired of this, or became disappointed or disenchanted with him, although from the perch of age, I see him now as a very simple and uninteresting man who sold patent medicine and tonics to the less sophisticated people in towns (villages) surrounding the metropolis of Stamps.

There seemed to be an understanding between Mr. McElroy and Grandmother. This was obvious to us because he never chased us off his land. In summer's late sunshine I often sat under the chinaberry tree in his yard, surrounded by the bitter aroma of its fruit and lulled by the drone of flies that fed on the berries. He sat in a slotted swing on his porch, rocking in his brown three-piece, his wide Panama nodding in time with the whir of insects.

One greeting a day was all that could be expected from Mr. McElroy. After his "Good morning, child," or "Good afternoon, child," he never said a word, even if I met him again on the road in front of his house or down by the well, or ran into him behind the house escaping in a game of hide-and-seek.

He remained a mystery in my childhood. A man who owned his land and the big many-windowed house with a porch that clung to its sides all around the house. An independent Black man. A near anachronism in Stamps.

Bailey was the greatest person in my world. And the fact that he was my brother, my only brother, and I had no sisters to share him with, was such good fortune that it made me want to live a Christian life just to show God that I was grateful. Where I was big, elbowy and grating, he was small, graceful and smooth. When I was described by our playmates as being shit color, he was lauded for his velvet-black skin. His hair fell down in black curls, and my head was covered with black steel wool. And yet he loved me.

When our elders said unkind things about my features (my family was handsome to a point of pain for me), Bailey would wink at me from across the room, and I knew that it was a matter of time before he would take revenge. He would allow the old ladies to finish wondering how on earth I came about, then he would ask, in a voice like cooling bacon grease, "Oh Mizeriz Coleman, how is your son? I saw him the other day, and he looked sick enough to die."

Aghast, the ladies would ask, "Die? From what? He ain't sick."

And in a voice oilier than the one before, he'd answer with a straight face, "From the Uglies."

I would hold my laugh, bite my tongue, grit my teeth and very seriously erase even the touch of a smile from my face. Later, behind the house by the black-walnut tree, we'd laugh and laugh and howl.

Bailey could count on very few punishments for his consistently outrageous behavior, for he was the pride of the Henderson/Johnson family.

His movements, as he was later to describe those of an acquaintance, were activated with oiled precision. He was also able to find more hours in the day than I thought existed. He finished chores, homework, read more books than I and played the group games on the side of the hill with the best of them. He could even pray out loud in church, and was apt at stealing pickles from the barrel that sat under the fruit counter and Uncle Willie's nose.

Once when the Store was full of lunchtime customers, he dipped the strainer, which we also used to sift weevils from meal and flour, into the barrel and fished for two fat pickles. He caught them and hooked the strainer onto the side of the barrel where they dripped until he was ready for them. When the last school bell rang, he picked the nearly dry pickles out of the strainer, jammed them into his pockets and threw the strainer behind the oranges. We ran out of the Store. It was summer and his pants were short, so the pickle juice made clean streams down his ashy legs, and he jumped with his pockets full of loot and his eyes laughing a "How about that?" He smelled like a vinegar barrel or a sour angel.

After our early chores were done, while Uncle Willie or Momma minded the Store, we were free to play the children's games as long as we stayed within yelling distance. Playing hide-and-seek, his voice was easily identified, singing, "Last night, night before, twenty-four robbers at my door. Who all is hid? Ask me to let them in, hit 'em in the head with a rolling pin. Who all is hid?" In follow the leader, naturally he was the one who created the most daring and interesting things to do. And when he was on the tail of the pop the whip, he would twirl off the end like a top, spinning, falling, laughing, finally stopping just before my heart beat its last, and then he was back in the game, still laughing.

Of all the needs (there are none imaginary) a lonely child has, the one that must be satisfied, if there is going to be hope and a hope of wholeness, is the unshaking need for an unshakable God. My pretty Black brother was my Kingdom Come.

———

In Stamps the custom was to can everything that could possibly be preserved. During the killing season, after the first frost, all neighbors helped each other to slaughter hogs and even the quiet, big-eyed cows if they had stopped giving milk.

The missionary ladies of the Christian Methodist Episcopal Church helped Momma prepare the pork for sausage. They squeezed their fat arms elbow deep in the ground meat, mixed it with gray nose-opening sage, pepper and salt, and made tasty little samples for all obedient children who brought wood for the slick black stove. The men chopped off the larger pieces of meat and laid them in the smokehouse to begin the curing process. They opened the knuckle of the hams with their deadly-looking knives, took out a certain round harmless bone ("it could make the meat go bad") and rubbed salt, coarse brown salt that looked like fine gravel, into the flesh, and the blood popped to the surface.

Throughout the year, until the next frost, we took our meals from the smokehouse, the little garden that lay cousin-close to the Store and from the shelves of canned foods. There were choices on the shelves that could set a hungry child's mouth to watering. Green beans, snapped always the right length, collards, cabbage, juicy red tomato preserves that came into their own on steaming buttered biscuits, and sausage, beets, berries and every fruit grown in Arkansas.

But at least twice yearly Momma would feel that as children we should have fresh meat included in our diets. We were then given money—pennies, nickels, and dimes entrusted to Bailey—and sent to town to buy liver. Since the whites had refrigerators, their butchers bought the meat from commercial slaughterhouses in Texarkana and sold it to the wealthy even in the peak of summer.

Crossing the Black area of Stamps which in childhood's narrow measure seemed a whole world, we were obliged by custom to stop and speak to every person we met, and Bailey felt constrained to spend a few minutes playing with each friend. There was a joy in going to town with money in our pockets (Bailey's pockets were as good as my own) and time on our hands. But the pleasure fled when we reached the white part of town. After we left Mr. Willie Williams' Do Drop Inn, the last stop before whitefolksville, we had to cross the pond and adventure the railroad tracks. We were explorers walking without weapons into man-eating animals' territory.

In Stamps the segregation was so complete that most Black children didn't really, absolutely know what whites looked like. Other than that they were different, to be dreaded, and in that dread was included the hostility of the powerless against the powerful, the poor against the rich, the worker against the worked for and the ragged against the well dressed.

I remember never believing that whites were really real.

Many women who worked in their kitchens traded at our Store, and when they carried their finished laundry back to town they often set the big baskets down on our front porch to pull a singular piece from the starched collection and show either how graceful was their ironing hand or how rich and opulent was the property of their employers.

I looked at the items that weren't on display. I knew, for instance, that white men wore shorts, as Uncle Willie did, and that they had an opening for taking out their "things" and peeing, and that white women's breasts weren't built into their dresses, as some people said, because I saw their brassieres in the baskets. But I couldn't force myself to think of them as people. People were Mrs. LaGrone, Mrs. Hendricks, Momma, Reverend Sneed, Lillie B, and Louise and Rex. Whitefolks couldn't be people because their feet were too small, their skin too white and see-throughy, and they didn't walk on the balls of their feet the way people did—they walked on their heels like horses.

People were those who lived on my side of town. I didn't like them all, or, in fact, any of them very much, but they were people. These others, the strange pale creatures that lived in their alien unlife, weren't considered folks. They were whitefolks.

CHAPTER 5

"Thou shall not be dirty" and "Thou shall not be impudent" were the two commandments of Grandmother Henderson upon which hung our total salvation.

Each night in the bitterest winter we were forced to wash faces, arms, necks, legs and feet before going to bed. She used to add, with a smirk that unprofane people can't control when venturing into profanity, "and wash as far as possible, then wash possible."

We would go to the well and wash in the ice-cold, clear water, grease our legs with the equally cold stiff Vaseline, then tiptoe into the house. We wiped the dust from our toes and settled down for schoolwork, cornbread, clabbered milk, prayers and bed, always in that order. Momma was famous for pulling the quilts off after we had fallen asleep to examine our feet. If they weren't clean enough for her, she took the switch (she kept one behind the bedroom door for emergencies) and woke up the offender with a few aptly placed burning reminders.

The area around the well at night was dark and slick, and boys told about how snakes love water, so that anyone who had to draw water at night and then stand there alone and wash knew that moccasins and rattlers, puff adders and boa constrictors were winding their way to the well and would arrive just as the person washing got soap in her eyes. But Momma convinced us that not only was cleanliness next to Godliness, dirtiness was the inventor of misery.

The impudent child was detested by God and a shame to its parents and could bring destruction to its house and line. All adults had to be addressed as Mister, Missus, Miss, Auntie, Cousin, Unk, Uncle, Buhbah, Sister, Brother and a thousand other appellations indicating familial relationship and the lowliness of the addressor.

Everyone I knew respected these customary laws, except for the powhitetrash children.

Some families of powhitetrash lived on Momma's farm land behind the school. Sometimes a gaggle of them came to the Store, filling the whole room, chasing out the air and even changing the well-known scents. The children crawled over the shelves and into the potato and onion bins, twanging all the time in their sharp voices like cigar-box guitars. They took liberties in my Store that I would never dare. Since Momma told us that the less you say to whitefolks (or even powhitetrash) the better, Bailey and I would stand, solemn, quiet, in the displaced air. But if one of the playful apparitions got close to us, I pinched it. Partly out of angry frustration and partly because I didn't believe in its flesh reality.

They called my uncle by his first name and ordered him around the Store. He, to my crying shame, obeyed them in his limping dip-straight-dip fashion.

My grandmother, too, followed their orders, except that she didn't seem to be servile because she anticipated their needs.

"Here's sugar, Miz Potter, and here's baking powder. You didn't buy soda last month, you'll probably be needing some."

Momma always directed her statements to the adults, but sometimes, Oh painful sometimes, the grimy, snotty-nosed girls would answer her.

"Naw, Annie..."—to Momma? Who owned the land they lived on? Who forgot more than they would ever learn? If there was any justice in the world, God should strike them dumb at once!—"Just give us some extry sody crackers, and some more mackerel."

At least they never looked in her face, or I never caught them doing so. Nobody with a smidgen of training, not even the worst roustabout, would look right in a grown person's face. It meant the person was trying to take the words out before they were formed. The dirty little children didn't do that, but they threw their orders around the Store like lashes from a cat-o'-nine-tails.

When I was around ten years old, those scruffy children caused me the most painful and confusing experience I had ever had with my grandmother.

One summer morning, after I had swept the dirt yard of leaves, spearmint-gum wrappers and Vienna-sausage labels, I raked the yellow-red dirt, and made half-moons carefully, so that the design stood out clearly and masklike. I put the rake behind the Store and came through the back of the house to find Grandmother on the front porch in her big, wide white apron. The apron was so stiff by virtue of the starch that it could have stood alone. Momma was admiring the yard, so I joined her. It truly looked like a flat redhead that had been raked with a big-toothed comb. Momma didn't say anything but I knew she liked it. She looked over toward the school principal's house and to the right at Mr. McElroy's. She was hoping one of those community pillars would see the design before the day's business wiped it out. Then she looked upward to the school. My head had swung with hers, so at just about the same time we saw a troop of the powhitetrash kids marching over the hill and down by the side of the school.

I looked to Momma for direction. She did an excellent job of sagging from her waist down, but from the waist up she seemed to be pulling for the top of the oak tree across the road. Then she began to moan a hymn. Maybe not to moan, but the tune was so slow and the meter so strange that she could have been moaning. She didn't look at me again. When the children reached halfway down the hill, halfway to the Store, she said without turning, "Sister, go on inside."

I wanted to beg her, "Momma, don't wait for them. Come on inside with me. If they come in the Store, you go to the bedroom and let me wait on them. They only frighten me if you're around. Alone I know how to handle them." But of course I couldn't say anything, so I went in and stood behind the screen door.

Before the girls got to the porch I heard their laughter crackling and popping like pine logs in a cooking stove. I suppose my lifelong paranoia was born in those cold, molasses-slow minutes. They came finally to stand on the ground in front of Momma. At first they pretended seriousness. Then one of them wrapped her right arm in the crook of her left, pushed out her mouth and started to hum. I realized that she was aping my grandmother. Another said, "Naw, Helen, you ain't standing like her. This here's it." Then she lifted her chest, folded her arms and mocked that strange carriage that was Annie Henderson. Another laughed, "Naw, you can't do it. Your mouth ain't pooched out enough. It's like this."

I thought about the rifle behind the door, but I knew I'd never be able to hold it straight, and the .410, our sawed-off shotgun, which stayed loaded and was fired every New Year's night, was locked in the trunk and Uncle Willie had the key on his chain. Through the fly-specked screen-door, I could see that the arms of Momma's apron jiggled from the vibrations of her humming. But her knees seemed to have locked as if they would never bend again.

She sang on. No louder than before, but no softer either. No slower or faster.

The dirt of the girls' cotton dresses continued on their legs, feet, arms and faces to make them all of a piece. Their greasy uncolored hair hung down, uncombed, with a grim finality. I knelt to see them better, to remember them for all time. The tears that had slipped down my dress left unsurprising dark spots, and made the front yard blurry and even more unreal. The world had taken a deep breath and was having doubts about continuing to revolve.

The girls had tired of mocking Momma and turned to other means of agitation. One crossed her eyes, stuck her thumbs in both sides of her mouth and said, "Look here, Annie." Grandmother hummed on and the apron strings trembled. I wanted to throw a handful of black pepper in their faces, to throw lye on them, to scream that they were dirty, scummy peckerwoods, but I knew I was as clearly imprisoned behind the scene as the actors outside were confined to their roles.

One of the smaller girls did a kind of puppet dance while her fellow clowns laughed at her. But the tall one, who was almost a woman, said something very quietly, which I couldn't hear. They all moved backward from the porch, still watching Momma. For an awful second I thought they were going to throw a rock at Momma, who seemed (except for the apron strings) to have turned into stone herself. But the big girl turned her back, bent down and put her hands flat on the ground—she didn't pick up anything. She simply shifted her weight and did a hand stand.

Her dirty bare feet and long legs went straight for the sky. Her dress fell down around her shoulders, and she had on no drawers. The slick pubic hair made a brown triangle where her legs came together. She hung in the vacuum of that lifeless morning for only a few seconds, then wavered and tumbled. The other girls clapped her on the back and slapped their hands.

Momma changed her song to "Bread of Heaven, bread of Heaven, feed me till I want no more."

I found that I was praying too. How long could Momma hold out? What new indignity would they think of to subject her to? Would I be able to stay out of it? What would Momma really like me to do?

Then they were moving out of the yard, on their way to town. They bobbed their heads and shook their slack behinds and turned, one at a time:

"'Bye, Annie."

"'Bye, Annie."

"'Bye, Annie."

Momma never turned her head or unfolded her arms, but she stopped singing and said, "'Bye, Miz Helen, 'bye, Miz Ruth, 'bye, Miz Eloise."

I burst. A firecracker July-the-Fourth burst. How could Momma call them Miz? The mean nasty things. Why couldn't she have come inside the sweet, cool store when we saw them breasting the hill? What did she prove? And then if they were dirty, mean and impudent, why did Momma have to call them Miz?

She stood another whole song through and then opened the screen door to look down on me crying in rage. She looked until I looked up. Her face was a brown moon that shone on me. She was beautiful. Something had happened out there, which I couldn't completely understand, but I could see that she was happy. Then she bent down and touched me as mothers of the church "lay hands on the sick and afflicted" and I quieted.

"Go wash your face, Sister." And she went behind the candy counter and hummed, "Glory, glory, hallelujah, when I lay my burden down."

I threw the well water on my face and used the weekday handkerchief to blow my nose. Whatever the contest had been out front, I knew Momma had won.

I took the rake back to the front yard. The smudged footprints were easy to erase. I worked for a long time on my new design and laid the rake behind the wash pot. When I came back in the Store, I took Momma's hand and we both walked outside to look at the pattern.

It was a large heart with lots of hearts growing smaller inside, and piercing from the outside rim to the smallest heart was an arrow. Momma said, "Sister, that's right pretty." Then she turned back to the Store and resumed, "Glory, glory, hallelujah, when I lay my burden down."

CHAPTER 6

Reverend Howard Thomas was the presiding elder over a district in Arkansas that included Stamps. Every three months he visited our church, stayed at Momma's over the Saturday night and preached a loud passionate sermon on Sunday. He collected the money that had been taken in over the preceding months, heard reports from all the church groups and shook hands with the adults and kissed all small children. Then he went away. (I used to think that he went west to heaven, but Momma straightened me out. He just went to Texarkana.)

Bailey and I hated him unreservedly. He was ugly, fat, and he laughed like a hog with the colic. We were able to make each other burst with giggling when we did imitations of the thick-skinned preacher. Bailey was especially good at it. He could imitate Reverend Thomas right in front of Uncle Willie and never get caught because he did it soundlessly. He puffed out his cheeks until they looked like wet brown stones, and wobbled his head from side to side. Only he and I knew it, but that was old Reverend Thomas to a tee.

His obesity, while disgusting, was not enough to incur the intense hate that we felt for him. The fact that he never bothered to remember our names was insulting, but neither was that slight, alone, enough to make us despise him. But the crime that tipped the scale and made our hate not only just but imperative was his actions at the dinner table. He ate the biggest, brownest and best parts of the chicken at every Sunday meal.

The only good thing about his visits was the fact that he always arrived late on Saturday nights, after we had had dinner. I often wondered if he tried to catch us at the table. I believe so, for when he reached the front porch his little eyes would glitter toward the empty dining room and his face would fall with disappointment. Then immediately, a thin curtain would fall over his features and he'd laugh a few barks, "Uh, huh, uh, huh, Sister Henderson, just like a penny with a hole in it, I always turns up."

Right on cue every time, Momma would answer, "That's right, Elder Thomas, thank the blessed Jesus, come right in."

He'd step in the front door and put down his Gladstone (that's what he called it) and look around for Bailey and me. Then he opened his awful arms and groaned, "Suffer little children to come unto me, for such is the Kingdom of Heaven."

Bailey went to him each time with his hand stretched out, ready for a manly handshake, but Reverend Thomas would push away the hand and encircle my brother for a few seconds. "You still a boy, buddy. Remember that. They tell me the Good Book say, 'When I was a child I spake as a child, I thought as a child, but when I became a man, I put away childish things.' " Only then would he open his arms and release Bailey.

I never had the nerve to go up to him. I was quite afraid that if I tried to say, "Hello, Reverend Thomas," I would choke on the sin of mocking him. After all, the Bible did say, "God is not mocked," and the man was God's representative. He used to say to me, "Come on, little sister. Come and get this blessing." But I was so afraid and I also hated him so much that my emotions mixed themselves up and it was enough to start me crying. Momma told him time after time, "Don't pay her no mind, Elder Thomas, you know how tender-hearted she is."

He ate the leftovers from our dinner and he and Uncle Willie discussed the developments of the church programs. They talked about how the present minister was attending to his flock, who got married, who died and how many children had been born since his last visit.

Bailey and I stood like shadows in the rear of the Store near the coal-oil tank, waiting for the juicy parts. But when they were ready to talk about the latest scandal, Momma sent us to her bedroom with warnings to have our Sunday School lesson perfectly memorized or we knew what we could expect.

We had a system that never failed. I would sit in the big rocking chair by the stove and rock occasionally and stamp my feet. I changed voices, now soft and girlish, then a little deeper like Bailey's. Meanwhile, he would creep back into the Store. Many times he came flying back to sit on the bed and to hold the open lesson book just before Momma suddenly filled the doorway.

"You children get your lesson good, now. You know all the other children looks up to you all." Then, as she turned back into the Store Bailey followed right on her footsteps to crouch in the shadows and listen for the forbidden gossip.

Once, he heard how Mr. Coley Washington had a girl from Lewisville staying in his house. I didn't think that was so bad, but Bailey explained that Mr. Washington was probably "doing it" to her. He said that although "it" was bad just about everybody in the world did it to somebody, but no one else was supposed to know that. And once, we found out about a man who had been killed by whitefolks and thrown into the pond. Bailey said the man's things had been cut off and put in his pocket and he had been shot in the head, all because the whitefolks said he did "it" to a white woman.

Because of the kinds of news we filched from those hushed conversations, I was convinced that whenever Reverend Thomas came and Momma sent us to the back room they were going to discuss whitefolks and "doing it." Two subjects about which I was very dim.

On Sunday mornings Momma served a breakfast that was geared to hold us quiet from 9:30 A.M. to 3 P.M. She fried thick pink slabs of home-cured ham and poured the grease over sliced red tomatoes. Eggs over easy, fried potatoes and onions, yellow hominy and crisp perch fried so hard we would pop them in our mouths and chew bones, fins and all. Her cathead biscuits were at least three inches in diameter and two inches thick. The trick to eating catheads was to get the butter on them before they got cold—then they were delicious. When, unluckily, they were allowed to get cold, they tended to a gooeyness, not unlike a wad of tired gum.

We were able to reaffirm our findings on the catheads each Sunday that Reverend Thomas spent with us. Naturally enough, he was asked to bless the table. We would all stand; my uncle, leaning his walking stick against the wall, would lean his weight on the table. Then Reverend Thomas would begin. "Blessed Father, we thank you this morning..." and on and on and on. I'd stop listening after a while until Bailey kicked me and then I cracked my lids to see what had promised to be a meal that would make any Sunday proud. But as the Reverend droned on and on and on to a God who I thought must be bored to hear the same things over and over again, I saw that the ham grease had turned white on the tomatoes. The eggs had withdrawn from the edge of the platter to bunch in the center like children left out in the cold. And the catheads had sat down on themselves with the conclusiveness of a fat woman sitting in an easy chair. And still he talked on. When he finally stopped, our appetites were gone, but he feasted on the cold food with a non-talking but still noisy relish.

In the Christian Methodist Episcopal Church the children's section was on the right, cater-cornered from the pew that held those ominous women called the Mothers of the Church. In the young people's section the benches were placed close together, and when a child's legs no longer comfortably fitted in the narrow space, it was an indication to the elders that that person could now move into the intermediate area (center church). Bailey and I were allowed to sit with the other children only when there were informal meetings, church socials or the like. But on the Sundays when Reverend Thomas preached, it was ordained that we occupy the first row, called the mourners' bench. I thought we were placed in front because Momma was proud of us, but Bailey assured me that she just wanted to keep her grandchildren under her thumb and eye.

Reverend Thomas took his text from Deuteronomy. And I was stretched between loathing his voice and wanting to listen to the sermon. Deuteronomy was my favorite book in the Bible. The laws were so absolute, so clearly set down, that I knew if a person truly wanted to avoid hell and brimstone, and being roasted forever in the devil's fire, all she had to do was memorize Deuteronomy and follow its teaching, word for word. I also liked the way the word rolled off the tongue.

Bailey and I sat alone on the front bench, the wooden slats pressing hard on our behinds and the backs of our thighs. I would have wriggled just a bit, but each time I looked over at Momma, she seemed to threaten, "Move and I'll tear you up," so, obedient to the unvoiced command, I sat still. The church ladies were warming up behind me with a few hallelujahs and Praise the Lords and Amens, and the preacher hadn't really moved into the meat of the sermon.

It was going to be a hot service.

On my way into church, I saw Sister Monroe, her open-faced gold crown glinting when she opened her mouth to return a neighborly greeting. She lived in the country and couldn't get to church every Sunday, so she made up for her absences by shouting so hard when she did make it that she shook the whole church. As soon as she took her seat, all the ushers would move to her side of the church because it took three women and sometimes a man or two to hold her.

Once when she hadn't been to church for a few months (she had taken off to have a child), she got the spirit and started shouting, throwing her arms around and jerking her body, so that the ushers went over to hold her down, but she tore herself away from them and ran up to the pulpit. She stood in front of the altar, shaking like a freshly caught trout. She screamed at Reverend Taylor. "Preach it. I say, preach it." Naturally he kept on preaching as if she wasn't standing there telling him what to do. Then she screamed an extremely fierce "I said, preach it" and stepped up on the altar. The Reverend kept on throwing out phrases like home-run balls and Sister Monroe made a quick break and grasped for him. For just a second, everything and everyone in the church except Reverend Taylor and Sister Monroe hung loose like stockings on a washline. Then she caught the minister by the sleeve of his jacket and his coattail, then she rocked him from side to side.

I have to say this for our minister, he never stopped giving us the lesson. The usher board made its way to the pulpit, going up both aisles with a little more haste than is customarily seen in church. Truth to tell, they fairly ran to the minister's aid. Then two of the deacons, in their shiny Sunday suits, joined the ladies in white on the pulpit, and each time they pried Sister Monroe loose from the preacher he took another deep breath and kept on preaching, and Sister Monroe grabbed him in another place, and more firmly. Reverend Taylor was helping his rescuers as much as possible by jumping around when he got a chance. His voice at one point got so low it sounded like a roll of thunder, then Sister Monroe's "Preach it" cut through the roar, and we all wondered (I did, in any case) if it would ever end. Would they go on forever, or get tired out at last like a game of blindman's bluff that lasted too long, with nobody caring who was "it"?

I'll never know what might have happened, because magically the pandemonium spread. The spirit infused Deacon Jackson and Sister Willson, the chairman of the usher board, at the same time. Deacon Jackson, a tall, thin, quiet man, who was also a part-time Sunday school teacher, gave a scream like a falling tree, leaned back on thin air and punched Reverend Taylor on the arm. It must have hurt as much as it caught the Reverend unawares. There was a moment's break in the rolling sounds and Reverend Taylor jerked around surprised, and hauled off and punched Deacon Jackson. In the same second Sister Willson caught his tie, looped it over her fist a few times, and pressed down on him. There wasn't time to laugh or cry before all three of them were down on the floor behind the altar. Their legs spiked out like kindling wood.

Sister Monroe, who had been the cause of all the excitement, walked off the dais, cool and spent, and raised her flinty voice in the hymn, "I came to Jesus, as I was, worried, wounded, and sad, I found in Him a resting place and He has made me glad."

The minister took advantage of already being on the floor and asked in a choky little voice if the church would kneel with him to offer a prayer of thanksgiving. He said we had been visited with a mighty spirit, and let the whole church say Amen.

On the next Sunday, he took his text from the eighteenth chapter of the Gospel according to St. Luke, and talked quietly but seriously about the Pharisees, who prayed in the streets so that the public would be impressed with their religious devotion. I doubt that anyone got the message—certainly not those to whom it was directed. The deacon board, however, did appropriate funds for him to buy a new suit. The other was a total loss.

Our presiding elder had heard the story of Reverend Taylor and Sister Monroe, but I was sure he didn't know her by sight. So my interest in the service's potential and my aversion to Reverend Thomas caused me to turn him off. Turning off or tuning out people was my highly developed art. The custom of letting obedient children be seen but not heard was so agreeable to me that I went one step further: Obedient children should not see or hear if they chose not to do so. I laid a handful of attention on my face and tuned up the sounds in the church.

Sister Monroe's fuse was already lit, and she sizzled somewhere to the right behind me. Elder Thomas jumped into the sermon, determined, I suppose, to give the members what they came for. I saw the ushers from the left side of the church near the big windows begin to move discreetly, like pallbearers, toward Sister Monroe's bench. Bailey jogged my knee. When the incident with Sister Monroe, which we always called simply "the incident," had taken place, we had been too astounded to laugh. But for weeks after, all we needed to send us into violent outbursts of laughter was a whispered "Preach it." Anyway, he pushed my knee, covered his mouth and whispered, "I say, preach it."

I looked toward Momma, across that square of stained boards, over the collection table, hoping that a look from her would root me safely to my sanity. But for the first time in memory Momma was staring behind me at Sister Monroe. I supposed that she was counting on bringing that emotional lady up short with a severe look or two. But Sister Monroe's voice had already reached the danger point. "Preach it!"

There were a few smothered giggles from the children's section, and Bailey nudged me again. "I say, preach it"—in a whisper. Sister Monroe echoed him loudly, "I say, preach it!"

Two deacons wedged themselves around Brother Jackson as a preventive measure and two large determined-looking men walked down the aisle toward Sister Monroe.

While the sounds in the church were increasing, Elder Thomas made the regrettable mistake of increasing his volume too. Then suddenly, like a summer rain, Sister Monroe broke through the cloud of people trying to hem her in, and flooded up to the pulpit. She didn't stop this time but continued immediately to the altar, bound for Elder Thomas, crying "I say, preach it."

Bailey said out loud, "Hot dog" and "Damn" and "She's going to beat his butt."

But Reverend Thomas didn't intend to wait for that eventuality, so as Sister Monroe approached the pulpit from the right he started descending from the left. He was not intimidated by his change of venue. He continued preaching and moving. He finally stopped right in front of the collection table, which put him almost in our laps, and Sister Monroe rounded the altar on his heels, followed by the deacons, ushers, some unofficial members and a few of the bigger children.

Just as the elder opened his mouth, pink tongue waving, and said, "Great God of Mount Nebo," Sister Monroe hit him on the back of his head with her purse. Twice. Before he could bring his lips together, his teeth fell, no, actually his teeth jumped, out of his mouth.

The grinning uppers and lowers lay by my right shoe, looking empty and at the same time appearing to contain all the emptiness in the world. I could have stretched out a foot and kicked them under the bench or behind the collection table.

Sister Monroe was struggling with his coat, and the men had all but picked her up to remove her from the building. Bailey pinched me and said without moving his lips, "I'd like to see him eat dinner now."

I looked at Reverend Thomas desperately. If he appeared just a little sad or embarrassed, I could feel sorry for him and wouldn't be able to laugh. My sympathy for him would keep me from laughing. I dreaded laughing in church. If I lost control, two things were certain to happen. I would surely pee, and just as surely get a whipping. And this time I would probably die because everything was funny—Sister Monroe, and Momma trying to keep her quiet with those threatening looks, and Bailey whispering "Preach it" and Elder Thomas with his lips flapping loose like tired elastic.

But Reverend Thomas shrugged off Sister Monroe's weakening clutch, pulled out an extra-large white handkerchief and spread it over his nasty little teeth. Putting them in his pocket, he gummed, "Naked I came into the world, and naked I shall go out."

Bailey's laugh had worked its way up through his body and was escaping through his nose in short hoarse snorts. I didn't try any longer to hold back the laugh, I just opened my mouth and released sound. I heard the first titter jump up in the air over my head, over the pulpit and out the window. Momma said out loud, "Sister!" but the bench was greasy and I slid off onto the floor. There was more laughter in me trying to get out. I didn't know there was that much in the whole world. It pressed at all my body openings, forcing everything in its path. I cried and hollered, passed gas and urine. I didn't see Bailey descend to the floor, but I rolled over once and he was kicking and screaming too. Each time we looked at each other we howled louder than before, and though he tried to say something, the laughter attacked him and he was only able to get out "I say, preach." And then I rolled over onto Uncle Willie's rubber-tipped cane. My eyes followed the cane up to his good brown hand on the curve and up the long, long white sleeve to his face. The one side pulled down as it usually did when he cried (it also pulled down when he laughed). He stuttered, "I'm gonna whip you this time myself."

I have no memory of how we got out of church and into the parsonage next door, but in that overstuffed parlor, Bailey and I received the whipping of our lives. Uncle Willie ordered us between licks to stop crying. I tried to, but Bailey refused to cooperate. Later he explained that when a person is beating you you should scream as loud as possible; maybe the whipper will become embarrassed or else some sympathetic soul might come to your rescue. Our savior came for neither of these reasons, but because Bailey yelled so loud and disturbed what was left of the service, the minister's wife came out and asked Uncle Willie to quiet us down.

Laughter so easily turns to hysteria for imaginative children. I felt for weeks after that I had been very, very sick, and until I completely recovered my strength I stood on laughter's cliff and any funny thing could hurl me off to my death far below.

Each time Bailey said "Preach it" to me, I hit him as hard as I could and cried.

CHAPTER 7

Momma had married three times: Mr. Johnson, my grandfather, who left her around the turn of the century with two small sons to raise; Mr. Henderson, of whom I know nothing at all (Momma never answered questions directly put to her on any subject except religion); then finally Mr. Murphy. I saw him a fleeting once. He came through Stamps on a Saturday night, and Grandmother gave me the chore of making his pallet on the floor. He was a stocky dark man who wore a snap-brim hat like George Raft. The next morning he hung around the Store until we returned from church. That marked the first Sunday I knew Uncle Willie to miss services. Bailey said he stayed home to keep Mr. Murphy from stealing us blind. He left in the middle of the afternoon after one of Momma's extensive Sunday dinners. His hat pushed back off his forehead, he walked down the road whistling. I watched his thick back until he turned the bend by the big white church.

People spoke of Momma as a good-looking woman and some, who remembered her youth, said she used to be right pretty. I saw only her power and strength. She was taller than any woman in my personal world, and her hands were so large they could span my head from ear to ear. Her voice was soft only because she chose to keep it so. In church, when she was called upon to sing, she seemed to pull out plugs from behind her jaws and the huge, almost rough sound would pour over the listeners and throb in the air.

Each Sunday, after she had taken her seat, the minister would announce, "We will now be led in a hymn by Sister Henderson." And each Sunday she looked up with amazement at the preacher and asked silently, "Me?" After a second of assuring herself that she indeed was being called upon, she laid down her handbag and slowly folded her handkerchief. This was placed neatly on top of the purse, then she leaned on the bench in front and pushed herself to a standing position, and then she opened her mouth and the song jumped out as if it had only been waiting for the right time to make an appearance. Week after week and year after year the performance never changed, yet I don't remember anyone's ever remarking on her sincerity or readiness to sing.

Momma intended to teach Bailey and me to use the paths in life that she and her generation and all the Negroes gone before had found, and found to be safe ones. She didn't cotton to the idea that whitefolks could be talked to at all without risking one's life. And certainly they couldn't be spoken to insolently. In fact, even in their absence they could not be spoken of too harshly unless we used the sobriquet "They." If she had been asked and had chosen to answer the question of whether she was cowardly or not, she would have said that she was a realist. Didn't she stand up to "them" year after year? Wasn't she the only Negro woman in Stamps referred to once as Mrs.?

That incident became one of Stamps' little legends. Some years before Bailey and I arrived in town, a man was hunted down for assaulting white womanhood. In trying to escape he ran to the Store. Momma and Uncle Willie hid him behind the chifforobe until night, gave him supplies for an overland journey and sent him on his way. He was, however, apprehended, and in court when he was questioned as to his movements on the day of the crime, he replied that after he heard that he was being sought he took refuge in Mrs. Henderson's Store.

The judge asked that Mrs. Henderson be subpoenaed, and when Momma arrived and said she was Mrs. Henderson, the judge, the bailiff and other whites in the audience laughed. The judge had really made a gaffe calling a Negro woman Mrs., but then he was from Pine Bluff and couldn't have been expected to know that a woman who owned a store in that village would also turn out to be colored. The whites tickled their funny bones with the incident for a long time, and the Negroes thought it proved the worth and majesty of my grandmother.

CHAPTER 8

Stamps, Arkansas, was Chitlin' Switch, Georgia; Hang 'Em High, Alabama; Don't Let the Sun Set on You Here, Nigger, Mississippi; or any other name just as descriptive. People in Stamps used to say that the whites in our town were so prejudiced that a Negro couldn't buy vanilla ice cream. Except on July Fourth. Other days he had to be satisfied with chocolate.

A light shade had been pulled down between the Black community and all things white, but one could see through it enough to develop a fear-admiration-contempt for the white "things"—whitefolks' cars and white glistening houses and their children and their women. But above all, their wealth that allowed them to waste was the most enviable. They had so many clothes they were able to give perfectly good dresses, worn just under the arms, to the sewing class at our school for the larger girls to practice on.

Although there was always generosity in the Negro neighborhood, it was indulged on pain of sacrifice. Whatever was given by Black people to other Blacks was most probably needed as desperately by the donor as by the receiver. A fact which made the giving or receiving a rich exchange.

I couldn't understand whites and where they got the right to spend money so lavishly. Of course, I knew God was white too, but no one could have made me believe he was prejudiced. My grandmother had more money than all the powhitetrash. We owned land and houses, but each day Bailey and I were cautioned, "Waste not, want not."

Momma bought two bolts of cloth each year for winter and summer clothes. She made my school dresses, underslips, bloomers, handkerchiefs, Bailey's shirts, shorts, her aprons, house dresses and waists from the rolls shipped to Stamps by Sears and Roebuck. Uncle Willie was the only person in the family who wore ready-to-wear clothes all the time. Each day, he wore fresh white shirts and flowered suspenders, and his special shoes cost twenty dollars. I thought Uncle Willie sinfully vain, especially when I had to iron seven stiff starched shirts and not leave a cat's face anywhere.

During the summer we went barefoot, except on Sunday, and we learned to resole our shoes when they "gave out," as Momma used to say. The Depression must have hit the white section of Stamps with cyclonic impact, but it seeped into the Black area slowly, like a thief with misgivings. The country had been in the throes of the Depression for two years before the Negroes in Stamps knew it. I think that everyone thought that the Depression, like everything else, was for the whitefolks, so it had nothing to do with them. Our people had lived off the land and counted on cotton-picking and hoeing and chopping seasons to bring in the cash needed to buy shoes, clothes, books and light farm equipment. It was when the owners of cotton fields dropped the payment of ten cents for a pound of cotton to eight, seven and finally five that the Negro community realized that the Depression, at least, did not discriminate.

Welfare agencies gave food to the poor families, Black and white. Gallons of lard, flour, salt, powdered eggs and powdered milk. People stopped trying to raise hogs because it was too difficult to get slop rich enough to feed them, and no one had the money to buy mash or fish meal.

Momma spent many nights figuring on our tablets, slowly. She was trying to find a way to keep her business going, although her customers had no money. When she came to her conclusions, she said, "Bailey, I want you to make me a nice clear sign. Nice and neat. And Sister, you can color it with your Crayolas. I want it to say:

> 1 5 lb. can of powdered milk is worth 50¢ in trade
> 1 5 lb. can of powdered eggs is worth $1.00 in trade
> 10 #2 cans of mackerel is worth $1.00 in trade."

And so on. Momma kept her store going. Our customers didn't even have to take their slated provisions home. They'd pick them up from the welfare center downtown and drop them off at the Store. If they didn't want an exchange at the moment they'd put down in one of the big gray ledgers the amount of credit coming to them. We were among the few Negro families not on relief, but Bailey and I were the only children in the town proper that we knew who ate powdered eggs every day and drank the powdered milk.

Our playmates' families exchanged their unwanted food for sugar, coal oil, spices, potted meat, Vienna sausage, peanut butter, soda crackers, toilet soap and even laundry soap. We were always given enough to eat, but we both hated the lumpy milk and mushy eggs, and sometimes we'd stop off at the house of one of the poorer families to get some peanut butter and crackers. Stamps was as slow coming out of the Depression as it had been getting into it. World War II was well along before there was a noticeable change in the economy of that near-forgotten hamlet.

———

One Christmas we received gifts from our mother and father, who lived separately in a heaven called California, where we were told they could have all the oranges they could eat. And the sun shone all the time. I was sure that wasn't so. I couldn't believe that our mother would laugh and eat oranges in the sunshine without her children. Until that Christmas when we received the gifts I had been confident that they were both dead. I could cry anytime I wanted by picturing my mother (I didn't quite know what she looked like) lying in her coffin. Her hair, which was black, was spread out on a tiny little white pillow and her body was covered with a sheet. The face was brown, like a big O, and since I couldn't fill in the features I printed M O T H E R across the O, and tears would fall down my cheeks like warm milk.

Then came that terrible Christmas with its awful presents when our father, with the vanity I was to find typical, sent his photograph. My gift from Mother was a tea set—a teapot, four cups and saucers and tiny spoons—and a doll with blue eyes and rosy cheeks and yellow hair painted on her head. I didn't know what Bailey received, but after I opened my boxes I went out to the backyard behind the chinaberry tree. The day was cold and the air as clear as water. Frost was still on the bench but I sat down and cried. I looked up and Bailey was coming from the outhouse, wiping his eyes. He had been crying too. I didn't know if he had also told himself they were dead and had been rudely awakened to the truth or whether he was just feeling lonely. The gifts opened the door to questions that neither of us wanted to ask. Why did they send us away? and What did we do so wrong? So Wrong? Why, at three and four, did we have tags put on our arms to be sent by train alone from Long Beach, California, to Stamps, Arkansas, with only the porter to look after us? (Besides, he got off in Arizona.)

Bailey sat down beside me, and that time didn't admonish me not to cry. So I wept and he sniffed a little, but we didn't talk until Momma called us back in the house.

Momma stood in front of the tree that we had decorated with silver ropes and pretty colored balls and said, "You children is the most ungrateful things I ever did see. You think your momma and poppa went to all the trouble to send you these nice play pretties to make you go out in the cold and cry?"

Neither of us said a word. Momma continued, "Sister, I know you tender-hearted, but Bailey Junior, there's no reason for you to set out mewing like a pussy cat, just 'cause you got something from Vivian and Big Bailey." When we still didn't force ourselves to answer, she asked, "You want me to tell Santa Claus to take these things back?" A wretched feeling of being torn engulfed me. I wanted to scream, "Yes. Tell him to take them back." But I didn't move.

Later Bailey and I talked. He said if the things really did come from Mother maybe it meant that she was getting ready to come and get us. Maybe she had just been angry at something we had done, but was forgiving us and would send for us soon. Bailey and I tore the stuffing out of the doll the day after Christmas, but he warned me that I had to keep the tea set in good condition because any day or night she might come riding up.

CHAPTER 9

A year later our father came to Stamps without warning. It was awful for Bailey and me to encounter the reality one abrupt morning. We, or at any rate I, had built such elaborate fantasies about him and the illusory mother that seeing him in the flesh shredded my inventions like a hard yank on a paper chain. He arrived in front of the Store in a clean gray car (he must have stopped just outside of town to wipe it in preparation for the "grand entrance"). Bailey, who knew such things, said it was a De Soto. His bigness shocked me. His shoulders were so wide I thought he'd have trouble getting in the door. He was taller than anyone I had seen, and if he wasn't fat, which I knew he wasn't, then he was fat-like. His clothes were too small too. They were tighter and woolier than was customary in Stamps. And he was blindingly handsome. Momma cried, "Bailey, my baby. Great God, Bailey." And Uncle Willie stuttered, "Bu-Buh-Bailey." My brother said, "Hot dog and damn. It's him. It's our daddy." And my seven-year-old world humpty-dumptied, never to be put back together again.

His voice rang like a metal dipper hitting a bucket and he spoke English. Proper English, like the school principal, and even better. Our father sprinkled *er*s and even *errer*s in his sentences as liberally as he gave out his twisted-mouth smiles. His lips pulled not down, like Uncle Willie's, but to the side, and his head lay on one side or the

---

other, but never straight on the end of his neck. He had the air of a man who did not believe what he heard or what he himself was saying. He was the first cynic I had met. "So er this is Daddy's er little man? Boy, anybody tell you errer that you er look like me?" He had Bailey in one arm and me in the other. "And Daddy's baby girl. You've errer been good children, er haven't you? Or er I guess I would have er heard about it er from Santa Claus." I was so proud of him it was hard to wait for the gossip to get around that he was in town. Wouldn't the kids be surprised at how handsome our daddy was? And that he loved us enough to come down to Stamps to visit? Everyone could tell from the way he talked and from the car and clothes that he was rich and maybe had a castle out in California. (I later learned that he had been a doorman at Santa Monica's plush Breakers Hotel). Then the possibility of being compared with him occurred to me, and I didn't want anyone to see him. Maybe he wasn't my real father. Bailey was his son, true enough, but I was an orphan that they picked up to provide Bailey with company.

I was always afraid when I found him watching me, and wished I could grow small like Tiny Tim. Sitting at the table one day, I held the fork in my left hand and pierced a piece of fried chicken. I put the knife through the second tine, as we had been strictly taught, and began to saw against the bone. My father laughed a rich rolling laugh, and I looked up. He imitated me, both elbows going up and down. "Is Daddy's baby going to fly away?" Momma laughed, and Uncle Willie too, and even Bailey snickered a little. Our father was proud of his sense of humor.

For three weeks the Store was filled with people who had gone to school with him or heard about him. The curious and envious milled around and he strutted, throwing *er*s and *errer*s all over the place and under the sad eyes of Uncle Willie. Then one day he said he had to get back to California. I was relieved. My world was going to be emptier and dryer, but the agony of having him intrude into every private second would be gone. And the silent threat that had hung in the air since his arrival, the threat of his leaving someday, would be gone. I wouldn't have to wonder whether I loved him or not, or have to answer "Does Daddy's baby want to go to California with Daddy?" Bailey had told him that he wanted to go, but I had kept quiet. Momma was relieved too, although she had had a good time cooking special things for him and showing her California son off to the peasants of Arkansas. But Uncle Willie was suffering under our father's bombastic pressure, and in mother-bird fashion Momma was more concerned with her crippled offspring than the one who could fly away from the nest.

He was going to take us with him! The knowledge buzzed through my days and made me jump unexpectedly like a jack-in-the-box. Each day I found some time to walk to the pond where people went to catch sun perch and striped bass. The hours I chose to go were too early or late for fishermen, so I had the area to myself. I stood on the bank of the green dark water, and my thoughts skidded like the water spiders. Now this way, now that, now the other. Should I go with my father? Should I throw myself into the pond, and not being able to swim, join the body of L.C., the boy who drowned last summer? Should I beg Momma to let me stay with her? I could tell her that I'd take over Bailey's chores and do my own as well. Did I have the nerve to try life without Bailey? I couldn't decide on any move, so I recited a few Bible verses, and went home.

Momma cut down a few give-aways that had been traded to her by white women's maids and sat long nights in the dining room sewing jumpers and skirts for me. She looked pretty sad, but each time I found her watching me she'd say, as if I had already disobeyed, "You be a good girl now. You hear? Don't you make people think I didn't raise you right. You hear?" She would have been more surprised than I had she taken me in her arms and wept at losing me. Her world was bordered on all sides with work, duty, religion and "her place." I don't think she ever knew that a deep-brooding love hung over everything she touched. In later years I asked her if she loved me and she brushed me off with: "God is love. Just worry about whether you're being a good girl, then He will love you."

I sat in the back of the car, with Dad's leather suitcases, and our cardboard boxes. Although the windows were rolled down, the smell of fried chicken and sweet potato pie lay unmoving, and there wasn't enough room to stretch. Whenever he thought about it, Dad asked, "Are you comfortable back there, Daddy's baby?" He never waited to hear my answer, which was "Yes, sir," before he'd resume his conversation with Bailey. He and Bailey told jokes, and Bailey laughed all the time, put out Dad's cigarettes and held one hand on the steering wheel when Dad said, "Come on, boy, help me drive this thing."

After I got tired of passing through the same towns over and over, and seeing the empty-looking houses, small and unfriendly, I closed myself off to everything but the kissing sounds of the tires on the pavement and the steady moan of the motor. I was certainly very vexed with Bailey. There was no doubt that he was trying to butter up Dad; he even started to laugh like him, a Santa Claus, Jr., with his "Ho, ho, ho."

"How are you going to feel seeing your mother? Going to be happy?" he was asking Bailey, but it penetrated the foam I had packed around my senses. Were we going to see Her? I thought we were going to California. I was suddenly terrified. Suppose she laughed at us the way he did? What if she had other children now, whom she kept with her? I said, "I want to go back to Stamps." Dad laughed, "You mean Daddy's baby doesn't want to go to St. Louis to see her mother? She's not going to eat you up, you know."

He turned to Bailey and I looked at the side of his face; he was so unreal to me I felt as if I were watching a doll talk. "Bailey, Junior, ask your sister why she wants to go back to Stamps." He sounded more like a white man than a Negro. Maybe he was the only brown-skinned white man in the world. It would be just my luck that the only one would turn out to be my father. But Bailey was quiet for the first time since we left Stamps. I guess he was thinking too about seeing Mother. How could an eight-year-old contain that much fear? He swallows and holds it behind his tonsils, he tightens his feet and closes the fear between his toes, he contracts his buttock and pushes it up behind the prostate gland.

"Junior, cat's got your tongue? What do you think your mother will say, when I tell her her children didn't want to see her?" The thought that he *would* tell her shook me and Bailey at the same time. He leaned over the back of the seat—"My, it's Mother Dear. You know you want to see Mother Dear. Don't cry." Dad laughed and pitched in his seat and asked himself, I guess, "What will she say to that?"

I stopped crying since there was no chance to get back to Stamps and Momma. Bailey wasn't going to back me up, I could tell, so I decided to shut up and dry up and wait for whatever seeing Mother Dear was going to bring.

St. Louis was a new kind of hot and a new kind of dirty. My memory had no pictures of the crowded-together soot-covered buildings. For all I knew, we were being driven to Hell and our father was the delivering devil.

Only in strict emergencies did Bailey allow me to speak Pig Latin to him in front of adults, but I had to take the chance that afternoon. We had spun around the same corner, I was sure, about fifty times. I asked Bailey, "Ooday ooyay inkthay isthay is our atherfay, or ooday ooyay inkthay atthay eeway are eeingbay idkay appednay?" Bailey said, "My, we're in St. Louis, and we're going to see Mother Dear. Don't worry." Dad chuckled and said, "Oohay oodway antway ootay idkay appnay ooyay? Ooday ooyay inkthay ooyay are indlay ergbay ildrenchay?" I thought that my brother and his friends had created Pig Latin. Hearing my father speak it didn't startle me so much as it angered. It was simply another case of the trickiness of adults where children were concerned. Another case in point of the Grownups' Betrayal.

To describe my mother would be to write about a hurricane in its perfect power. Or the climbing, falling colors of a rainbow. We had been received by her mother and had waited on the edge of our seats in the overfurnished living room (Dad talked easily with our grandmother, as whitefolks talk to Blacks, unembarrassed and unapologetic). We were both fearful of Mother's coming and impatient at her delay. It is remarkable how much truth there is in the two expressions: "struck dumb" and "love at first sight." My mother's beauty literally assailed me. Her red lips (Momma said it was a sin to wear lipstick) split to show even white teeth and her fresh-butter color looked see-through clean. Her smile widened her mouth beyond her cheeks beyond her ears and seemingly through the walls to the street outside. I was struck dumb. I knew immediately why she had sent me away. She was too beautiful to have children. I had never seen a woman as pretty as she who was called "Mother." Bailey on his part fell instantly and forever in love. I saw his eyes shining like hers; he had forgotten the loneliness and the nights when we had cried together because we were "unwanted children." He had never left her warm side or shared the icy wind of solitude with me. She was his Mother Dear and I resigned myself to his condition. They were more alike than she and I, or even he and I. They both had physical beauty and personality, so I figured it figured.

Our father left St. Louis a few days later for California, and I was neither glad nor sorry. He was a stranger, and if he chose to leave us with a stranger, it was all of one piece.

CHAPTER 10

Grandmother Baxter was a quadroon or an octoroon, or in any case she was nearly white. She had been raised by a German family in Cairo, Illinois, and had come to St. Louis at the turn of the century to study nursing. While she was working at Homer G. Phillips Hospital she met and married Grandfather Baxter. She was white (having no features that could even loosely be called Negroid) and he was Black. While she spoke with a throaty German accent until her death, he had the choppy spouting speech of the West Indians.

Their marriage was a happy one. Grandfather had a famous saying that caused great pride in his family: "Bah Jesus, I live for my wife, my children and my dog." He took extreme care to prove that statement true by taking the word of his family even in the face of contradictory evidence.

The Negro section of St. Louis in the mid-thirties had all the finesse of a gold-rush town. Prohibition, gambling and their related vocations were so obviously practiced that it was hard for me to believe that they were against the law. Bailey and I, as newcomers, were quickly told by our schoolmates who the men on the street corners were as we passed. I was sure that they had taken their names from Wild West Books (Hard-hitting Jimmy, Two Gun, Sweet Man, Poker Pete), and to prove me right, they hung around in front of saloons like unhorsed cowboys.

We met the numbers runners, gamblers, lottery takers and whiskey salesmen not only in the loud streets but in our orderly living room as well. They were often there when we returned from school, sitting with hats in their hands, as we had done upon our arrival in the big city. They waited silently for Grandmother Baxter.

Her white skin and the pince-nez that she dramatically took from her nose and let hang free on a chain pinned to her dress were factors that brought her a great deal of respect. Moreover, the reputation of her six mean children and the fact that she was a precinct captain compounded her power and gave her the leverage to deal with even the lowest crook without fear. She had pull with the police department, so the men in their flashy suits and fleshy scars sat with church-like decorum and waited to ask favors from her. If Grandmother raised the heat off their gambling parlors, or said the word that reduced the bail of a friend waiting in jail, they knew what would be expected of them. Come election, they were to bring in the votes from their neighborhood. She most often got them leniency, and they always brought in the vote.

St. Louis also introduced me to thin-sliced ham (I thought it a delicacy), jelly beans and peanuts mixed, lettuce on sandwich bread, Victrolas and family loyalty. In Arkansas, where we cured our own meat, we ate half-inch slabs of ham for breakfast, but in St. Louis we bought the paper-thin slices in a strange-smelling German store and ate them in sandwiches. If Grandmother never lost her German accent, she also never lost her taste for the thick black German *Brot*, which we bought unsliced. In Stamps, lettuce was used only to make a bed for potato salad or slaw, and peanuts were brought in raw from the field and roasted in the bottom of the oven on cold nights. The rich scents used to fill the house and we were always expected to eat too many. But that was a Stamps custom. In St. Louis, peanuts were bought in paper bags and mixed with jelly beans, which meant that we ate the salt and sugar together and I found them a delicious treat. The best thing the big town had to offer.

When we enrolled in Toussaint L'Ouverture Grammar School, we were struck by the ignorance of our schoolmates and the rudeness of our teachers. Only the vastness of the building impressed us; not even the white school in Stamps was as large.

The students, however, were shockingly backward. Bailey and I did arithmetic at a mature level because of our work in the Store, and we read well because in Stamps there wasn't anything else to do. We were moved up a grade because our teachers thought that we country children would make our classmates feel inferior—and we did. Bailey would not refrain from remarking on our classmates' lack of knowledge. At lunchtime in the large gray concrete playground, he would stand in the center of a crowd of big boys and ask, "Who was Napoleon Bonaparte?" "How many feet make a mile?" It was infighting, Bailey style.

Any of the boys might have been able to beat him with their fists, but if they did, they'd just have had to do it again the next day, and Bailey never held a brief for fighting fair. He taught me that once I got into a fight I should "grab for the balls right away." He never answered when I asked, "Suppose I'm fighting a girl?"

We went to school there a full year, but all I remember hearing that I hadn't heard before was, "Making thousands of egg-shaped oughts will improve penmanship."

The teachers were more formal than those we knew in Stamps, and although they didn't whip students with switches, they gave them licks in the palms of their hands with rulers. In Stamps teachers were much friendlier, but that was because they were imported from the Arkansas Negro colleges, and since we had no hotels or rooming houses in town, they had to live with private families. If a lady teacher took company, or didn't receive any mail or cried alone in her room at night, by the weeks' end even the children discussed her morality, her loneliness and her other failings generally. It would have been near impossible to maintain formality under a small town's invasions of privacy.

St. Louis teachers, on the other hand, tended to act very siditty, and talked down to their students from the lofty heights of education and whitefolks' enunciation. They, women as well as men, all sounded like my father with their *ers* and *errers*. They walked with their knees together and talked through tight lips as if they were as afraid to let the sound out as they were to inhale the dirty air that the listener gave off.

We walked to school around walls of bricks and breathed the coal dust for one discouraging winter. We learned to say "Yes" and "No" rather than "Yes, ma'am," and "No, ma'am."

Occasionally Mother, whom we seldom saw in the house, had us meet her at Louie's. It was a long dark tavern at the end of the bridge near our school, and was owned by two Syrian brothers.

We used to come in the back door, and the sawdust, stale beer, steam and boiling meat made me feel as if I'd been eating mothballs. Mother had cut my hair in a bob like hers and straightened it, so my head felt skinned and the back of my neck so bare that I was ashamed to have anyone walk up behind me. Naturally, this kept me turning quickly as if I expected something to happen.

At Louie's we were greeted by Mother's friends as "Bibbie's darling babies" and were given soft drinks and boiled shrimp. While we sat on the stiff wooden booths, Mother would dance alone in front of us to music from the Seeburg. I loved her most at those times. She was like a pretty kite that floated just above my head. If I liked, I could pull it in to me by saying I had to go to the toilet or by starting a fight with Bailey. I never did either, but the power made me tender to her.

The Syrian brothers vied for her attention as she sang the heavy blues that Bailey and I almost understood. They watched her, even when directing their conversation to other customers, and I knew they too were hypnotized by this beautiful lady who talked with her whole body and snapped her fingers louder than anyone in the whole world. We learned the Time Step at Louie's. It is from this basic step that most American Black dances are born. It is a series of taps, jumps and rests, and demands careful listening, feeling and coordination. We were brought before Mother's friends, there in the heavy saloon air, to show our artistry. Bailey learned easily, and has always been the better dancer. But I learned too. I approached the Time Step with the same determination to win that I had approached the time tables with. There was no Uncle Willie or sizzling pot-bellied stove, but there was Mother and her laughing friends, and they amounted to the same thing. We were applauded and given more soft drinks and, more shrimp, but it was to be years later before I found the joy and freedom of dancing well.

———

Mother's brothers, Uncles Tutti, Tom and Ira, were well-known young men about St. Louis. They all had city jobs, which I now understand to have been no mean feat for Negro men. Their jobs and their family set them apart, but they were best known for their unrelenting meanness. Grandfather had told them, "Bah Jesus, if you ever get in jail for stealing or some such foolishness, I'll let you rot. But if you're arrested for fighting, I'll sell the house, lock, stock, and barrel, to get you out!" With that kind of encouragement, backed by explosive tempers, it was no wonder they became fearsome characters. Our youngest uncle, Billy, was not old enough to join in their didoes. One of their more flamboyant escapades has become a proud family legend.

Pat Patterson, a big man, who was himself protected by the shield of a bad reputation, made the mistake of cursing my mother one night when she was out alone. She reported the incident to her brothers. They ordered one of their hangers-on to search the streets for Patterson, and when he was located, to telephone them.

As they waited throughout the afternoon, the living room filled with smoke and the murmurs of plans. From time to time, Grandfather came in from the kitchen and said, "Don't kill him. Mind you, just don't kill him," then went back to his coffee with Grandmother.

They went to the saloon where Patterson sat drinking at a small table. Uncle Tommy stood by the door, Uncle Tutti stationed himself at the toilet door and Uncle Ira, who was the oldest and maybe everyone's ideal, walked over to Patterson. They were all obviously carrying guns.

Uncle Ira said to my mother, "Here, Bibbi. Here's this nigger Patterson. Come over here and beat his ass."

She crashed the man's head with a policeman's billy enough to leave him just this side of death. There was no police investigation nor social reprobation.

After all, didn't Grandfather champion their wild tempers, and wasn't Grandmother a near-white woman with police pull?

I admit that I was thrilled by their meanness. They beat up whites and Blacks with the same abandon, and liked each other so much that they never needed to learn the art of making outside friends. My mother was the only warm, outgoing personality among her siblings. Grandfather became bedridden during our stay there, and his children spent their free time telling him jokes, gossiping with him and showing their love.

Uncle Tommy, who was gruff and chewed his words like Grandfather, was my favorite. He strung ordinary sentences together and they came out sounding either like the most profane curses or like comical poetry. A natural comedian, he never waited for the laugh that he knew must follow his droll statements. He was never cruel. He was mean.

When we played handball on the side of our house, Uncle Tommy would turn the corner, coming from work. He would pretend at first not to see us, but with the deftness of a cat he would catch the ball and say, "Put your minds where your behinds are, and I'll let you on my team." We children would range around him, but it was only when he reached the steps that he'd wind up his arm and throw the ball over the light post and toward the stars.

He told me often, "Ritie, don't worry 'cause you ain't pretty. Plenty pretty women I seen digging ditches or worse. You smart. I swear to God, I rather you have a good mind than a cute behind."

They bragged often about the binding quality of the Baxter blood. Uncle Tommy said that even the children felt it before they were old enough to be taught. They reminisced over Bailey's teaching me to walk when he was less than three. Displeased at my stumbling motions, he was supposed to have said, "This is *my* sister. *I* have to teach her to walk." They also told me how I got the name "My." After Bailey learned definitely that I was his sister, he refused to call me Marguerite, but rather addressed me each time as "Mya Sister," and in later more articulate years, after the need for brevity had shortened the appellation to "My," it was elaborated into "Maya."

We lived in a big house on Caroline Street with our grandparents for half the year before Mother moved us in with her. Moving from the house where the family was centered meant absolutely nothing to me. It was simply a small pattern in the grand design of our lives. If other children didn't move so much, it just went to show that our lives were fated to be different from everyone else's in the world. The new house was no stranger than the other, except that we were with Mother.

Bailey persisted in calling her Mother Dear until the circumstance of proximity softened the phrase's formality to "Muh Dear," and finally to "M'Deah." I could never put my finger on her realness. She was so pretty and so quick that even when she had just awakened, her eyes full of sleep and hair tousled, I thought she looked just like the Virgin Mary. But what mother and daughter understand each other, or even have the sympathy for each other's lack of understanding?

Mother had prepared a place for us, and we went to it gratefully. We each had a room with a two-sheeted bed, plenty to eat and store-bought clothes to wear. And after all, she didn't have to do it. If we got on her nerves or if we were disobedient, she could always send us back to Stamps. The weight of appreciation and the threat, which was never spoken, of a return to Momma were burdens that clogged my childish wits into impassivity. I was called Old Lady and chided for moving and talking like winter's molasses.

Mother's boyfriend, Mr. Freeman, lived with us, or we lived with him (I never quite knew which). He was a Southerner, too, and big. But a little flabby. His breasts used to embarrass me when he walked around in his undershirt. They lay on his chest like flat titties.

Even if Mother hadn't been such a pretty woman, light-skinned with straight hair, he was lucky to get her, and he knew it. She was educated, from a well-known family, and after all, wasn't she born in St. Louis? Then she was gay. She laughed all the time and made jokes. He was grateful. I think he must have been many years older than she, but if not, he still had the sluggish inferiority of old men married to younger women. He watched her every move and when she left the room, his eyes allowed her reluctantly to go.

CHAPTER 11

I had decided that St. Louis was a foreign country. I would never get used to the scurrying sounds of flushing toilets, or the packaged foods, or doorbells or the noise of cars and trains and buses that crashed through the walls or slipped under the doors. In my mind I only stayed in St. Louis for a few weeks. As quickly as I understood that I had not reached my home, I sneaked away to Robin Hood's forest and the caves of Alley Oop where all reality was unreal and even that changed every day. I carried the same shield that I had used in Stamps: "I didn't come to stay."

Mother was competent in providing for us. Even if that meant getting someone else to furnish the provisions. Although she was a nurse, she never worked at her profession while we were with her. Mr. Freeman brought in the necessities and she earned extra money cutting poker games in gambling parlors. The straight eight-to-five world simply didn't have enough glamor for her, and it was twenty years later that I first saw her in a nurse's uniform.

Mr. Freeman was a foreman in the Southern Pacific yards and came home late sometimes, after Mother had gone out. He took his dinner off the stove where she had carefully covered it and which she had admonished us not to bother. He ate quietly in the kitchen while Bailey and I read separately and greedily our own Street and Smith pulp magazine. Now that we had spending money, we bought the illustrated paperbacks with their gaudy pictures. When Mother was away, we were put on an honor system. We had to finish our homework, eat dinner and wash the dishes before we could read or listen to *The Lone Ranger*, *Crime Busters* or *The Shadow*.

Mr. Freeman moved gracefully, like a big brown bear, and seldom spoke to us. He simply waited for Mother and put his whole self into the waiting. He never read the paper or patted his foot to radio. He waited. That was all.

If she came home before we went to bed, we saw the man come alive. He would start out of the big chair, like a man coming out of sleep, smiling. I would remember then that a few seconds before, I had heard a car door slam; then Mother's footsteps would signal from the concrete walk. When her key rattled the door, Mr. Freeman would have already asked his habitual question, "Hey, Bibbi, have a good time?"

His query would hang in the air while she sprang over to peck him on the lips. Then she turned to Bailey and me with the lipstick kisses. "Haven't you finished your homework?" If we had and were just reading—"O.K., say your prayers and go to bed." If we hadn't—"Then go to your room and finish ... then say your prayers and go to bed."

Mr. Freeman's smile never grew, it stayed at the same intensity. Sometimes Mother would go over and sit on his lap and the grin on his face looked as if it would stay there forever.

From our rooms we could hear the glasses clink and the radio turned up. I think she must have danced for him on the good nights, because he couldn't dance, but before I fell asleep I often heard feet shuffling to dance rhythms.

I felt very sorry for Mr. Freeman. I felt as sorry for him as I had felt for a litter of helpless pigs born in our backyard sty in Arkansas. We fattened the pigs all year long for slaughter on the first good frost, and even as I suffered for the cute little wiggly things, I knew how much I was going to enjoy the fresh sausage and hog's headcheese they could give me only with their deaths.

Because of the lurid tales we read and our vivid imaginations and, probably, memories of our brief but hectic lives, Bailey and I were afflicted—he physically and I mentally. He stuttered, and I sweated through horrifying nightmares. He was constantly told to slow down and start again, and on my particularly bad nights my mother would take me in to sleep with her, in the large bed with Mr. Freeman.

Because of a need for stability, children easily become creatures of habit. After the third time in Mother's bed, I thought there was nothing strange about sleeping there.

One morning she got out of bed for an early errand, and I fell asleep again. But I awoke to a pressure, a strange feeling on my left leg. It was too soft to be a hand, and it wasn't the touch of clothes. Whatever it was, I hadn't encountered the sensation in all the years of sleeping with Momma. It didn't move, and I was too startled to. I turned my head a little to the left to see if Mr. Freeman was awake and gone, but his eyes were open and both hands were above the cover. I knew, as if I had always known, it was his "thing" on my leg.

He said, "Just stay right here, Ritie, I ain't gonna hurt you." I wasn't afraid, a little apprehensive, maybe, but not afraid. Of course I knew that lots of people did "it" and that they used their "things" to accomplish the deed, but no one I knew had ever done it to anybody. Mr. Freeman pulled me to him, and put his hand between my legs. He didn't hurt, but Momma had drilled into my head: "Keep your legs closed, and don't let nobody see your pocketbook."

"Now, I didn't hurt you. Don't get scared." He threw back the blankets and his "thing" stood up like a brown ear of corn. He took my hand and said, "Feel it." It was mushy and squirmy like the inside of a freshly killed chicken. Then he dragged me on top of his chest with his left arm, and his right hand was moving so fast and his heart was beating so hard that I was afraid that he would die. Ghost stories revealed how people who died wouldn't let go of whatever they were holding. I wondered if Mr. Freeman died holding me how I would ever get free. Would they have to break his arms to get me loose?

Finally he was quiet, and then came the nice part. He held me so softly that I wished he wouldn't ever let me go. I felt at home. From the way he was holding me I knew he'd never let me go or let anything bad ever happen to me. This was probably my real father and we had found each other at last. But then he rolled over, leaving me in a wet place and stood up.

"I gotta talk to you, Ritie." He pulled off his shorts that had fallen to his ankles, and went into the bathroom.

It was true the bed was wet, but I knew I hadn't had an accident. Maybe Mr. Freeman had one while he was holding me. He came back with a glass of water and told me in a sour voice, "Get up. You peed in the bed." He poured water on the wet spot, and it did look like my mattress on many mornings.

Having lived in Southern strictness, I knew when to keep quiet around adults, but I did want to ask him why he said I peed when I was sure he didn't believe that. If he thought I was naughty, would that mean that he would never hold me again? Or admit that he was my father? I had made him ashamed of me.

"Ritie, you love Bailey?" He sat down on the bed and I came close, hoping. "Yes." He was bending down, pulling on his socks, and his back was so large and friendly I wanted to rest my head on it.

"If you ever tell anybody what we did, I'll have to kill Bailey."

What had we done? We? Obviously he didn't mean my peeing in the bed. I didn't understand and didn't dare ask him. It had something to do with his holding me. But there was no chance to ask Bailey either, because that would be telling what we had done. The thought that he might kill Bailey stunned me. After he left the room I thought about telling Mother that I hadn't peed in the bed, but then if she asked me what happened I'd have to tell her about Mr. Freeman holding me, and that wouldn't do.

It was the same old quandary. I had always lived it. There was an army of adults, whose motives and movements I just couldn't understand and who made no effort to understand mine. There was never any question of my disliking Mr. Freeman, I simply didn't understand him either.

For weeks after, he said nothing to me, except the gruff hellos which were given without ever looking in my direction.

This was the first secret I had ever kept from Bailey and sometimes I thought he should be able to read it on my face, but he noticed nothing.

I began to feel lonely for Mr. Freeman and the encasement in his big arms. Before, my world had been Bailey, food, Momma, the Store, reading books and Uncle Willie. Now, for the first time, it included physical contact.

I began to wait for Mr. Freeman to come in from the yards, but when he did, he never noticed me, although I put a lot of feeling into "Good evening, Mr. Freeman."

One evening, when I couldn't concentrate on anything, I went over to him and sat quickly on his lap. He had been waiting for Mother again. Bailey was listening to *The Shadow* and didn't miss me. At first Mr. Freeman sat still, not holding me or anything, then I felt a soft lump under my thigh begin to move. It twitched against me and started to harden. Then he pulled me to his chest. He smelled of coal dust and grease and he was so close I buried my face in his shirt and listened to his heart, it was beating just for me. Only I could hear the thud, only I could feel the jumping on my face. He said, "Sit still, stop squirming." But all the time, he pushed me around on his lap, then suddenly he stood up and I slipped down to the floor. He ran to the bathroom.

For months he stopped speaking to me again. I was hurt and for a time felt lonelier than ever. But then I forgot about him, and even the memory of his holding me precious melted into the general darkness just beyond the great blinkers of childhood.

———

I read more than ever, and wished my soul that I had been born a boy. Horatio Alger was the greatest writer in the world. His heroes were always good, always won, and were always boys. I could have developed the first two virtues, but becoming a boy was sure to be difficult, if not impossible.

The Sunday funnies influenced me, and although I admired the strong heroes who always conquered in the end, I identified with Tiny Tim. In the toilet, where I used to take the papers, it was tortuous to look for and exclude the unnecessary pages so that I could learn how he would finally outwit his latest adversary. I wept with relief every Sunday as he eluded the evil men and bounded back from each seeming defeat as sweet and gentle as ever. The Katzenjammer kids were fun because they made the adults look stupid. But they were a little too smart-alecky for my taste.

When spring came to St. Louis, I took out my first library card, and since Bailey and I seemed to be growing apart, I spent most of my Saturdays at the library (no interruptions) breathing in the world of penniless shoeshine boys who, with goodness and perseverance, became rich, rich men, and gave baskets of goodies to the poor on holidays. The little princesses who were mistaken for maids, and the long-lost children mistaken for waifs, became more real to me than our house, our mother, our school or Mr. Freeman.

During those months we saw our grandparents and the uncles (our only aunt had gone to California to build her fortune), but they usually asked the same question, "Have you been good children?" for which there was only one answer. Even Bailey wouldn't have dared to answer No.

CHAPTER 12

On a late spring Saturday, after our chores (nothing like those in Stamps) were done, Bailey and I were going out, he to play baseball and I to the library. Mr. Freeman said to me, after Bailey had gone downstairs, "Ritie, go get some milk for the house."

Mother usually brought milk when she came in, but that morning as Bailey and I straightened the living room her bedroom door had been open, and we knew that she hadn't come home the night before.

He gave me money and I rushed to the store and back to the house. After putting the milk in the icebox, I turned and had just reached the front door when I heard, "Ritie." He was sitting in the big chair by the radio. "Ritie, come here." I didn't think about the holding time until I got close to him. His pants were open and his "thing" was standing out of his britches by itself.

"No, sir, Mr. Freeman." I started to back away. I didn't want to touch that mushy-hard thing again, and I didn't need him to hold me any more. He grabbed my arm and pulled me between his legs. His face was still and looked kind, but he didn't smile or blink his eyes. Nothing. He did nothing, except reach his left hand around to turn on the radio without even looking at it. Over the noise of music and static, he said, "Now, this ain't gonna hurt you much. You liked it before, didn't you?"

I didn't want to admit that I had in fact liked his holding me or that I had liked his smell or the hard heart-beating, so I said nothing. And his face became like the face of one of those mean natives the Phantom was always having to beat up.

His legs were squeezing my waist. "Pull down your drawers." I hesitated for two reasons: he was holding me too tight to move, and I was sure that any minute my mother or Bailey or the Green Hornet would bust in the door and save me.

"We was just playing before." He released me enough to snatch down my bloomers, and then he dragged me closer to him. Turning the radio up loud, too loud, he said, "If you scream, I'm gonna kill you. And if you tell, I'm gonna kill Bailey." I could tell he meant what he said. I couldn't understand why he wanted to kill my brother. Neither of us had done anything to him. And then.

Then there was the pain. A breaking and entering when even the senses are torn apart. The act of rape on an eight-year-old body is a matter of the needle giving because the camel can't. The child gives, because the body can, and the mind of the violator cannot.

I thought I had died—I woke up in a white-walled world, and it had to be heaven. But Mr. Freeman was there and he was washing me. His hands shook, but he held me upright in the tub and washed my legs. "I didn't mean to hurt you, Ritie. I didn't mean it. But don't you tell...Remember, don't you tell a soul."

I felt cool and very clean and just a little tired. "No, sir, Mr. Freeman, I won't tell." I was somewhere above everything. "It's just that I'm so tired I'll just go and lay down a while, please," I whispered to him. I thought if I spoke out loud, he might become frightened and hurt me again. He dried me and handed me my bloomers. "Put these on and go to the library. Your momma ought to be coming home soon. You just act natural."

Walking down the street, I felt the wet on my pants, and my hips seemed to be coming out of their sockets. I couldn't sit long on the hard seats in the library (they had been constructed for children), so I walked by the empty lot where Bailey was playing ball, but he wasn't there. I stood for a while and watched the big boys tear around the dusty diamond and then headed home.

After two blocks, I knew I'd never make it. Not unless I counted every step and stepped on every crack. I had started to burn between my legs more than the time I'd wasted Sloan's Liniment on myself. My legs throbbed, or rather the insides of my thighs throbbed, with the same force that Mr. Freeman's heart had beaten. Thrum...step... thrum...step...STEP ON THE CRACK...thrum...step. I went up the stairs one at a, one at a, one at a time. No one was in the living room, so I went straight to bed, after hiding my red-and-yellow-stained drawers under the mattress.

When Mother came in she said, "Well, young lady, I believe this is the first time I've seen you go to bed without being told. You must be sick."

I wasn't sick, but the pit of my stomach was on fire—how could I tell her that? Bailey came in later and asked me what the matter was. There was nothing to tell him. When Mother called us to eat and I said I wasn't hungry, she laid her cool hand on my forehead and cheeks. "Maybe it's the measles. They say they're going around the neighborhood." After she took my temperature she said, "You have a little fever. You've probably just caught them."

Mr. Freeman took up the whole doorway, "Then Bailey ought not to be in there with her. Unless you want a house full of sick children." She answered over her shoulder, "He may as well have them now as later. Get them over with." She brushed by Mr. Freeman as if he were made of cotton. "Come on, Junior. Get some cool towels and wipe your sister's face."

As Bailey left the room, Mr. Freeman advanced to the bed. He leaned over, his whole face a threat that could have smothered me. "If you tell…" And again so softly, I almost didn't hear it—"If you tell." I couldn't summon up the energy to answer him. He had to know that I wasn't going to tell anything. Bailey came in with the towels and Mr. Freeman walked out.

Later Mother made a broth and sat on the edge of the bed to feed me. The liquid went down my throat like bones. My belly and behind were as heavy as cold iron, but it seemed my head had gone away and pure air had replaced it on my shoulders. Bailey read to me from *The Rover Boys* until he got sleepy and went to bed.

That night I kept waking to hear Mother and Mr. Freeman arguing. I couldn't hear what they were saying, but I did hope that she wouldn't make him so mad that he'd hurt her too. I knew he could do it, with his cold face and empty eyes. Their voices came in faster and faster, the high sounds on the heels of the lows. I would have liked to have gone in. Just passed through as if I were going to the toilet. Just show my face and they might stop, but my legs refused to move. I could move the toes and ankles, but the knees had turned to wood.

Maybe I slept, but soon morning was there and Mother was pretty over my bed. "How're you feeling, baby?"

"Fine, Mother." An instinctive answer. "Where's Bailey?"

She said he was still asleep but that she hadn't slept all night. She had been in my room off and on to see about me. I asked her where Mr. Freeman was, and her face chilled with remembered anger. "He's gone. Moved this morning. I'm going to take your temperature after I put on your Cream of Wheat."

Could I tell her now? The terrible pain assured me that I couldn't. What he did to me, and what I allowed, must have been very bad if already God let me hurt so much. If Mr. Freeman was gone, did that mean Bailey was out of danger? And if so, if I told him, would he still love me?

After Mother took my temperature, she said she was going to bed for a while but to wake her if I felt sicker. She told Bailey to watch my face and arms for spots and when they came up he could paint them with calamine lotion.

That Sunday goes and comes in my memory like a bad connection on an overseas telephone call. Once, Bailey was reading *The Katzenjammer Kids* to me, and then without a pause for sleeping, Mother was looking closely at my face, and soup trickled down my chin and some got into my mouth and I choked. Then there was a doctor who took my temperature and held my wrist.

"Bailey!" I supposed I had screamed, for he materialized suddenly, and I asked him to help me and we'd run away to California or France or Chicago. I knew that I was dying and, in fact, I longed for death, but I didn't want to die anywhere near Mr. Freeman. I knew that even now he wouldn't have allowed death to have me unless he wished it to.

Mother said I should be bathed and the linens had to be changed since I had sweat so much. But when they tried to move me I fought, and even Bailey couldn't hold me. Then she picked me up in her arms and the terror abated for a while. Bailey began to change the bed. As he pulled off the soiled sheets he dislodged the panties I had put under the mattress. They fell at Mother's feet.

CHAPTER 13

In the hospital, Bailey told me that I had to tell who did that to me, or the man would hurt another little girl. When I explained that I couldn't tell because the man would kill him, Bailey said knowingly, "He can't kill me. I won't let him." And of course I believed him. Bailey didn't lie to me. So I told him.

Bailey cried at the side of my bed until I started to cry too. Almost fifteen years passed before I saw my brother cry again.

Using the old brain he was born with (those were his words later on that day) he gave his information to Grandmother Baxter, and Mr. Freeman was arrested and was spared the awful wrath of my pistol-whipping uncles.

I would have liked to stay in the hospital the rest of my life. Mother brought flowers and candy. Grandmother came with fruit and my uncles clumped around and around my bed, snorting like wild horses. When they were able to sneak Bailey in, he read to me for hours.

———

The saying that people who have nothing to do become busybodies is not the only truth. Excitement is a drug, and people whose lives are filled with violence are always wondering where the next "fix" is coming from.

The court was filled. Some people even stood behind the churchlike benches in the rear. Overhead fans moved with the detachment of old men. Grandmother Baxter's clients were there in gay and flippant array. The gamblers in pin-striped suits and their makeup-deep women whispered to me out of blood-red mouths that now I knew as much as they did. I was eight, and grown. Even the nurses in the hospital had told me that now I had nothing to fear. "The worst is over for you," they had said. So I put the words in all the smirking mouths.

I sat with my family (Bailey couldn't come) and they rested still on the seats like solid, cold gray tombstones. Thick and forevermore unmoving.

Poor Mr. Freeman twisted in his chair to look empty threats over to me. He didn't know that he couldn't kill Bailey ... and Bailey didn't lie ... to me.

"What was the defendant wearing?" That was Mr. Freeman's lawyer.

"I don't know."

"You mean to say this man raped you and you don't know what he was wearing?" He snickered as if I had raped Mr. Freeman. "Do you know if you were raped?"

A sound pushed in the air of the court (I was sure it was laughter). I was glad that Mother had let me wear the navy-blue winter coat with brass buttons. Although it was too short and the weather was typical St. Louis hot, the coat was a friend that I hugged to me in the strange and unfriendly place.

"Was that the first time the accused touched you?" The question stopped me. Mr. Freeman had surely done something very wrong, but I was convinced that I had helped him to do it. I didn't want to lie, but the lawyer wouldn't let me think, so I used silence as a retreat.

"Did the accused try to touch you before the time he or rather you say he raped you?"

I couldn't say yes and tell them how he had loved me once for a few minutes and how he had held me close before he thought I had peed in the bed. My uncles would kill me and Grandmother Baxter would stop speaking, as she often did when she was angry. And all those people in the court would stone me as they had stoned the harlot in the Bible. And Mother, who thought I was such a good girl, would be so disappointed. But most important, there was Bailey. I had kept a big secret from him.

"Marguerite, answer the question. Did the accused touch you before the occasion on which you claim he raped you?"

Everyone in the court knew that the answer had to be No. Everyone except Mr. Freeman and me. I looked at his heavy face trying to look as if he would have liked me to say No. I said No.

The lie lumped in my throat and I couldn't get air. How I despised the man for making me lie. Old, mean, nasty thing. Old, black, nasty thing. The tears didn't soothe my heart as they usually did. I screamed, "Ole, mean, dirty thing, you. Dirty old thing." Our lawyer brought me off the stand and to my mother's arms. The fact that I had arrived at my desired destination by lies made it less appealing to me.

Mr. Freeman was given one year and one day, but he never got a chance to do his time. His lawyer (or someone) got him released that very afternoon.

In the living room, where the shades were drawn for coolness, Bailey and I played Monopoly on the floor. I played a bad game because I was thinking how I would be able to tell Bailey how I had lied and, even worse for our relationship, kept a secret from him. Bailey answered the doorbell, because Grandmother was in the kitchen. A tall white policeman asked for Mrs. Baxter. Had they found out about the lie? Maybe the policeman was coming to put me in jail because I had sworn on the

Bible that everything I said would be the truth, the whole truth, so help me, God. The man in our living room was taller than the sky and whiter than my image of God. He just didn't have the beard.

"Mrs. Baxter, I thought you ought to know. Freeman's been found dead on the lot behind the slaughterhouse."

Softly, as if she were discussing a church program, she said, "Poor man." She wiped her hands on the dishtowel and just as softly asked, "Do they know who did it?"

The policeman said, "Seems like he was dropped there. Some say he was kicked to death."

Grandmother's color only rose a little. "Tom, thanks for telling me. Poor man. Well, maybe it's better this way. He *was* a mad dog. Would you like a glass of lemonade? Or some beer?"

Although he looked harmless, I knew he was a dreadful angel counting out my many sins.

"No, thanks, Mrs. Baxter. I'm on duty. Gotta be getting back."

"Well, tell your ma that I'll be over when I take up my beer and remind her to save some kraut for me."

And the recording angel was gone. He was gone, and a man was dead because I lied. Where was the balance in that? One lie surely wouldn't be worth a man's life. Bailey could have explained it all to me, but I didn't dare ask him. Obviously I had forfeited my place in heaven forever, and I was as gutless as the doll I had ripped to pieces ages ago. Even Christ Himself turned His back on Satan. Wouldn't He turn His back on me? I could feel the evilness flowing through my body and waiting, pent up, to rush off my tongue if I tried to open my mouth. I clamped my teeth shut, I'd hold it in. If it escaped, wouldn't it flood the world and all the innocent people?

Grandmother Baxter said, "Ritie and Junior, you didn't hear a thing. I never want to hear this situation nor that evil man's name mentioned in my house again. I mean that." She went back into the kitchen to make apple strudel for my celebration.

Even Bailey was frightened. He sat all to himself, looking at a man's death—a kitten looking at a wolf. Not quite understanding it but frightened all the same.

In those moments I decided that although Bailey loved me he couldn't help. I had sold myself to the Devil and there could be no escape. The only thing I could do was to stop talking to people other than Bailey. Instinctively, or somehow, I knew that because I loved him so much I'd never hurt him, but if I talked to anyone else that person might die too. Just my breath, carrying my words out, might poison people and they'd curl up and die like the black fat slugs that only pretended.

I had to stop talking.

I discovered that to achieve perfect personal silence all I had to do was to attach myself leechlike to sound. I began to listen to everything. I probably hoped that after I had heard all the sounds, really heard them and packed them down, deep in my ears, the world would be quiet around me. I walked into rooms where people were laughing, their voices hitting the walls like stones, and I simply stood still—in the midst of the riot of sound. After a minute or two, silence would rush into the room from its hiding place because I had eaten up all the sounds.

In the first weeks my family accepted my behavior as a post-rape, post-hospital affliction. (Neither the term nor the experience was mentioned in Grandmother's house, where Bailey and I were again staying.) They understood that I could talk to Bailey, but to no one else.

Then came the last visit from the visiting nurse, and the doctor said I was healed. That meant that I should be back on the sidewalks playing handball or enjoying the games I had been given when I was sick. When I refused to be the child they knew and accepted me to be, I was called impudent and my muteness sullenness.

For a while I was punished for being so uppity that I wouldn't speak; and then came the thrashings, given by any relative who felt himself offended.

———

We were on the train going back to Stamps, and this time it was I who had to console Bailey. He cried his heart out down the aisles of the coach, and pressed his little-boy body against the window pane looking for a last glimpse of his Mother Dear.

I have never known if Momma sent for us, or if the St. Louis family just got fed up with my grim presence. There is nothing more appalling than a constantly morose child.

I cared less about the trip than about the fact that Bailey was unhappy, and had no more thought of our destination than if I had simply been heading for the toilet.

CHAPTER 14

The barrenness of Stamps was exactly what I wanted, without will or consciousness. After St. Louis, with its noise and activity, its trucks and buses, and loud family gatherings, I welcomed the obscure lanes and lonely bungalows set back deep in dirt yards.

The resignation of its inhabitants encouraged me to relax. They showed me a contentment based on the belief that nothing more was coming to them, although a great deal more was due. Their decision to be satisfied with life's inequities was a lesson for me. Entering Stamps, I had the feeling that I was stepping over the border lines of the map and would fall, without fear, right off the end of the world. Nothing more could happen, for in Stamps nothing happened.

Into this cocoon I crept.

For an indeterminate time, nothing was demanded of me or of Bailey. We were, after all, Mrs. Henderson's California grandchildren, and had been away on a glamorous trip way up North to the fabulous St. Louis. Our father had come the year before, driving a big, shiny automobile and speaking the King's English with a big city accent, so all we had to do was lie quiet for months and rake in the profits of our adventures.

Farmers and maids, cooks and handymen, carpenters and all the children in town, made regular pilgrimages to the Store. "Just to see the travelers."

They stood around like cutout cardboard figures and asked, "Well, how is it up North?"

"See any of them big buildings?"

"Ever ride in one of them elevators?"

"Was you scared?"

"Whitefolks any different, like they say?"

Bailey took it upon himself to answer every question, and from a corner of his lively imagination wove a tapestry of entertainment for them that I was sure was as foreign to him as it was to me.

He, as usual, spoke precisely. "They have, in the North, buildings so high that for months, in the winter, you can't see the top floors."

"Tell the truth."

"They've got watermelons twice the size of a cow's head and sweeter than syrup." I distinctly remember his intent face and the fascinated faces of his listeners. "And if you can count the watermelon's seeds, before it's cut open, you can win five zillion dollars and a new car."

Momma, knowing Bailey, warned, "Now Ju, be careful you don't slip up on a not true." (Nice people didn't say "lie.")

"Everybody wears new clothes and have inside toilets. If you fall down in one of them, you get flushed away into the Mississippi River. Some people have iceboxes, only the proper name is Cold Spot or Frigidaire. The snow is so deep you can get buried right outside your door and people won't find you for a year. We made ice cream out of the snow." That was the only fact that I could have supported. During the winter, we had collected a bowl of snow and poured Pet milk over it, and sprinkled it with sugar and called it ice cream.

Momma beamed and Uncle Willie was proud when Bailey regaled the customers with our exploits. We were drawing cards for the Store and objects of the town's adoration. Our journey to magical places alone was a spot of color on the town's drab canvas, and our return made us even more the most enviable of people.

High spots in Stamps were usually negative: droughts, floods, lynchings and deaths.

Bailey played on the country folks' need for diversion. Just after our return he had taken to sarcasm, picked it up as one might pick up a stone, and put it snufflike under his lip. The double entendres, the two-pronged sentences, slid over his tongue to dart rapier-like into anything that happened to be in the way. Our customers, though, generally were so straight thinking and speaking that they were never hurt by his attacks. They didn't comprehend them.

"Bailey Junior sound just like Big Bailey. Got a silver tongue. Just like his daddy."

"I hear tell they don't pick cotton up there. How the people live then?"

Bailey said that the cotton up North was so tall, if ordinary people tried to pick it they'd have to get up on ladders, so the cotton farmers had their cotton picked by machines.

For a while I was the only recipient of Bailey's kindness. It was not that he pitied me but that he felt we were in the same boat for different reasons, and that I could understand his frustration just as he could countenance my withdrawal.

I never knew if Uncle Willie had been told about the incident in St. Louis, but sometimes I caught him watching me with a far-off look in his big eyes. Then he would quickly send me on some errand that would take me out of his presence. When that happened I was both relieved and ashamed. I certainly didn't want a cripple's sympathy (that would have been a case of the blind leading the blind), nor did I want Uncle Willie, whom I loved in my fashion, to think of me as being sinful and dirty. If he thought so, at least I didn't want to know it.

Sounds came to me dully, as if people were speaking through their handkerchiefs or with their hands over their mouths. Colors weren't true either, but rather a vague assortment of shaded pastels that indicated not so much color as faded familiarities. People's names escaped me and I began to worry over my sanity. After all, we had been away less than a year, and customers whose accounts I had formerly remembered without consulting the ledger were now complete strangers.

People, except Momma and Uncle Willie, accepted my unwillingness to talk as a natural outgrowth of a reluctant return to the South. And an indication that I was pining for the high times we had had in the big city. Then, too, I was well known for being "tender-hearted."

Southern Negroes used that term to mean sensitive and tended to look upon a person with that affliction as being a little sick or in delicate health. So I was not so much forgiven as I was understood.

CHAPTER 15

For nearly a year, I sopped around the house, the Store, the school and the church, like an old biscuit, dirty and inedible. Then I met, or rather got to know, the lady who threw me my first life line.

Mrs. Bertha Flowers was the aristocrat of Black Stamps. She had the grace of control to appear warm in the coldest weather, and on the Arkansas summer days it seemed she had a private breeze which swirled around, cooling her. She was thin without the taut look of wiry people, and her printed voile dresses and flowered hats were as right for her as denim overalls for a farmer. She was our side's answer to the richest white woman in town.

Her skin was a rich black that would have peeled like a plum if snagged, but then no one would have thought of getting close enough to Mrs. Flowers to ruffle her dress, let alone snag her skin. She didn't encourage familiarity. She wore gloves too.

I don't think I ever saw Mrs. Flowers laugh, but she smiled often. A slow widening of her thin black lips to show even, small white teeth, then the slow effortless closing. When she chose to smile on me, I always wanted to thank her. The action was so graceful and inclusively benign.

She was one of the few gentlewomen I have ever known, and has remained throughout my life the measure of what a human being can be.

Momma had a strange relationship with her. Most often when she passed on the road in front of the Store, she spoke to Momma in that soft yet carrying voice, "Good day, Mrs. Henderson." Momma responded with "How you, Sister Flowers?"

Mrs. Flowers didn't belong to our church, nor was she Momma's familiar. Why on earth did she insist on calling her Sister Flowers? Shame made me want to hide my face. Mrs. Flowers deserved better than to be called Sister. Then, Momma left out the verb. Why not ask, "How *are* you, *Mrs.* Flowers?" With the unbalanced passion of the young, I hated her for showing her ignorance to Mrs. Flowers. It didn't occur to me for many years that they were as alike as sisters, separated only by formal education.

Although I was upset, neither of the women was in the least shaken by what I thought an unceremonious greeting. Mrs. Flowers would continue her easy gait up the hill to her little bungalow, and Momma kept on shelling peas or doing whatever had brought her to the front porch.

Occasionally, though, Mrs. Flowers would drift off the road and down to the Store and Momma would say to me, "Sister, you go on and play." As I left I would hear the beginning of an intimate conversation. Momma persistently using the wrong verb, or none at all.

"Brother and Sister Wilcox is sho'ly the meanest—" "Is," Momma? "Is"? Oh, please, not "is," Momma, for two or more. But they talked, and from the side of the building where I waited for the ground to open up and swallow me, I heard the soft-voiced Mrs. Flowers and the textured voice of my grandmother merging and melting. They were interrupted from time to time by giggles that must have come from Mrs. Flowers (Momma never giggled in her life). Then she was gone.

She appealed to me because she was like people I had never met personally. Like women in English novels who walked the moors (whatever they were) with their loyal dogs racing at a respectful distance. Like the women who sat in front of roaring fireplaces, drinking tea incessantly from silver trays full of scones and crumpets. Women who walked over the "heath" and read morocco-bound books and had two last names divided by a hyphen. It would be safe to say that she made me proud to be Negro, just by being herself.

She acted just as refined as whitefolks in the movies and books and she was more beautiful, for none of them could have come near that warm color without looking gray by comparison.

It was fortunate that I never saw her in the company of powhite-folks. For since they tend to think of their whiteness as an evenizer, I'm certain that I would have had to hear her spoken to commonly as Bertha, and my image of her would have been shattered like the un-mendable Humpty-Dumpty.

One summer afternoon, sweet-milk fresh in my memory, she stopped at the Store to buy provisions. Another Negro woman of her health and age would have been expected to carry the paper sacks home in one hand, but Momma said, "Sister Flowers, I'll send Bailey up to your house with these things."

She smiled that slow dragging smile, "Thank you, Mrs. Henderson. I'd prefer Marguerite, though." My name was beautiful when she said it. "I've been meaning to talk to her, anyway." They gave each other age-group looks.

Momma said, "Well, that's all right then. Sister, go and change your dress. You going to Sister Flowers's."

The chifforobe was a maze. What on earth did one put on to go to Mrs. Flowers' house? I knew I shouldn't put on a Sunday dress. It might be sacrilegious. Certainly not a house dress, since I was already wearing a fresh one. I chose a school dress, naturally. It was formal without suggesting that going to Mrs. Flowers' house was equivalent to attending church.

I trusted myself back into the Store.

"Now, don't you look nice." I had chosen the right thing, for once.

"Mrs. Henderson, you make most of the children's clothes, don't you?"

"Yes, ma'am. Sure do. Store-bought clothes ain't hardly worth the thread it take to stitch them."

"I'll say you do a lovely job, though, so neat. That dress looks pro-fessional."

Momma was enjoying the seldom-received compliments. Since everyone we knew (except Mrs. Flowers, of course) could sew compe-tently, praise was rarely handed out for the commonly practiced craft.

"I try, with the help of the Lord, Sister Flowers, to finish the inside just like I does the outside. Come here, Sister."

I had buttoned up the collar and tied the belt, apronlike, in back. Momma told me to turn around. With one hand she pulled the strings and the belt fell free at both sides of my waist. Then her large hands were at my neck, opening the button loops. I was terrified. What was happening?

"Take it off, Sister." She had her hands on the hem of the dress.

"I don't need to see the inside, Mrs. Henderson, I can tell…" But the dress was over my head and my arms were stuck in the sleeves. Momma said, "That'll do. See here, Sister Flowers, I French-seams around the armholes." Through the cloth film, I saw the shadow approach. "That makes it last longer. Children these days would bust out of sheet-metal clothes. They so rough."

"That is a very good job, Mrs. Henderson. You should be proud. You can put your dress back on, Marguerite."

"No ma'am. Pride is a sin. And 'cording to the Good Book, it goeth before a fall."

"That's right. So the Bible says. It's a good thing to keep in mind."

I wouldn't look at either of them. Momma hadn't thought that taking off my dress in front of Mrs. Flowers would kill me stone dead. If I had refused, she would have thought I was trying to be "womanish" and might have remembered St. Louis. Mrs. Flowers had known that I would be embarrassed and that was even worse. I picked up the groceries and went out to wait in the hot sunshine. It would be fitting if I got a sunstroke and died before they came outside. Just dropped dead on the slanting porch.

There was a little path beside the rocky road, and Mrs. Flowers walked in front swinging her arms and picking her way over the stones.

She said, without turning her head, to me, "I hear you're doing very good school work, Marguerite, but that it's all written. The teachers report that they have trouble getting you to talk in class." We passed the triangular farm on our left and the path widened to allow us to walk together. I hung back in the separate unasked and unanswerable questions.

"Come and walk along with me, Marguerite." I couldn't have refused even if I wanted to. She pronounced my name so nicely. Or more correctly, she spoke each word with such clarity that I was certain a foreigner who didn't understand English could have understood her.

"Now no one is going to make you talk—possibly no one can. But bear in mind, language is man's way of communicating with his fellow man and it is language alone which separates him from the lower animals." That was a totally new idea to me, and I would need time to think about it.

"Your grandmother says you read a lot. Every chance you get. That's good, but not good enough. Words mean more than what is set down on paper. It takes the human voice to infuse them with the shades of deeper meaning."

I memorized the part about the human voice infusing words. It seemed so valid and poetic.

She said she was going to give me some books and that I not only must read them, I must read them aloud. She suggested that I try to make a sentence sound in as many different ways as possible.

"I'll accept no excuse if you return a book to me that has been badly handled." My imagination boggled at the punishment I would deserve if in fact I did abuse a book of Mrs. Flowers'. Death would be too kind and brief.

The odors in the house surprised me. Somehow I had never connected Mrs. Flowers with food or eating or any other common experience of common people. There must have been an outhouse, too, but my mind never recorded it.

The sweet scent of vanilla had met us as she opened the door.

"I made tea cookies this morning. You see, I had planned to invite you for cookies and lemonade so we could have this little chat. The lemonade is in the icebox."

It followed that Mrs. Flowers would have ice on an ordinary day, when most families in our town bought ice late on Saturdays only a few times during the summer to be used in the wooden ice-cream freezers.

She took the bags from me and disappeared through the kitchen door. I looked around the room that I had never in my wildest fantasies imagined I would see. Browned photographs leered or threatened from the walls and the white, freshly done curtains pushed against themselves and against the wind. I wanted to gobble up the room entire and take it to Bailey, who would help me analyze and enjoy it.

"Have a seat, Marguerite. Over there by the table." She carried a platter covered with a tea towel. Although she warned that she hadn't tried her hand at baking sweets for some time, I was certain that like everything else about her the cookies would be perfect.

They were flat round wafers, slightly browned on the edges and butter-yellow in the center. With the cold lemonade they were sufficient for childhood's lifelong diet. Remembering my manners, I took nice little lady-like bites off the edges. She said she had made them expressly for me and that she had a few in the kitchen that I could take home to my brother. So I jammed one whole cake in my mouth and the rough crumbs scratched the insides of my jaws, and if I hadn't had to swallow, it would have been a dream come true.

As I ate she began the first of what we later called "my lessons in living." She said that I must always be intolerant of ignorance but understanding of illiteracy. That some people, unable to go to school, were more educated and even more intelligent than college professors. She encouraged me to listen carefully to what country people called mother wit. That in those homely sayings was couched the collective wisdom of generations.

When I finished the cookies she brushed off the table and brought a thick, small book from the bookcase. I had read *A Tale of Two Cities* and found it up to my standards as a romantic novel. She opened the first page and I heard poetry for the first time in my life.

"It was the best of times and the worst of times . . ." Her voice slid in and curved down through and over the words. She was nearly singing. I wanted to look at the pages. Were they the same that I had read? Or were there notes, music, lined on the pages, as in a hymn book? Her sounds began cascading gently. I knew from listening to a thousand preachers that she was nearing the end of her reading, and I hadn't really heard, heard to understand, a single word.

"How do you like that?"

It occurred to me that she expected a response. The sweet vanilla flavor was still on my tongue and her reading was a wonder in my ears. I had to speak.

I said, "Yes, ma'am." It was the least I could do, but it was the most also.

"There's one more thing. Take this book of poems and memorize one for me. Next time you pay me a visit, I want you to recite."

I have tried often to search behind the sophistication of years for the enchantment I so easily found in those gifts. The essence escapes but its aura remains. To be allowed, no, invited, into the private lives of strangers, and to share their joys and fears, was a chance to exchange the Southern bitter wormwood for a cup of mead with Beowulf or a hot cup of tea and milk with Oliver Twist. When I said aloud, "It is a far, far better thing that I do, than I have ever done..." tears of love filled my eyes at my selflessness.

On that first day, I ran down the hill and into the road (few cars ever came along it) and had the good sense to stop running before I reached the Store.

I was liked, and what a difference it made. I was respected not as Mrs. Henderson's grandchild or Bailey's sister but for just being Marguerite Johnson.

Childhood's logic never asks to be proved (all conclusions are absolute). I didn't question why Mrs. Flowers had singled me out for attention, nor did it occur to me that Momma might have asked her to give me a little talking to. All I cared about was that she had made tea cookies for *me* and read to *me* from her favorite book. It was enough to prove that she liked me.

Momma and Bailey were waiting inside the Store. He said, "My, what did she give you?" He had seen the books, but I held the paper sack with his cookies in my arms shielded by the poems.

Momma said, "Sister, I know you acted like a little lady. That do my heart good to see settled people take to you all. I'm trying my best, the Lord knows, but these days..." Her voice trailed off. "Go on in and change your dress."

In the bedroom it was going to be a joy to see Bailey receive his cookies. I said, "By the way, Bailey, Mrs. Flowers sent you some tea cookies—"

Momma shouted, "What did you say, Sister? You, Sister, what did you say?" Hot anger was crackling in her voice.

Bailey said, "She said Mrs. Flowers sent me some—"

"I ain't talking to you, Ju." I heard the heavy feet walk across the floor toward our bedroom. "Sister, you heard me. What's that you said?" She swelled to fill the doorway.

Bailey said, "Momma." His pacifying voice—"Momma, she—"

"You shut up, Ju. I'm talking to your sister."

I didn't know what sacred cow I had bumped, but it was better to find out than to hang like a thread over an open fire. I repeated, "I said, 'Bailey, by the way, Mrs. Flowers sent you—' "

"That's what I thought you said. Go on and take off your dress. I'm going to get a switch."

At first I thought she was playing. Maybe some heavy joke that would end with "You sure she didn't send me something?" but in a minute she was back in the room with a long, ropy, peach-tree switch, the juice smelling bitter at having been torn loose. She said, "Get down on your knees. Bailey, Junior, you come on, too."

The three of us knelt as she began, "Our Father, you know the tribulations of your humble servant. I have with your help raised two grown boys. Many's the day I thought I wouldn't be able to go on, but you gave me the strength to see my way clear. Now, Lord, look down on this heavy heart today. I'm trying to raise my son's children in the way they should go, but, oh, Lord, the Devil try to hinder me on every hand. I never thought I'd live to hear cursing under this roof, what I try to keep dedicated to the glorification of God. And cursing out of the mouths of babes. But you said, in the last days brother would turn against brother, and children against their parents. That there would be a gnashing of teeth and a rendering of flesh. Father, forgive this child, I beg you, on bended knee."

I was crying loudly now. Momma's voice had risen to a shouting pitch, and I knew that whatever wrong I had committed was extremely serious. She had even left the Store untended to take up my case with God. When she finished we were all crying. She pulled me to her with one hand and hit me only a few times with the switch. The shock of my sin and the emotional release of her prayer had exhausted her.

Momma wouldn't talk right then, but later in the evening I found that my violation lay in using the phrase "by the way." Momma explained that "Jesus was the Way, the Truth and the Light," and anyone who says "by the way" is really saying, "by Jesus," or "by God" and the Lord's name would not be taken in vain in her house.

When Bailey tried to interpret the words with: "Whitefolks use 'by the way' to mean while we're on the subject," Momma reminded us that "whitefolks' mouths were most in general loose and their words were an abomination before Christ."

CHAPTER 16

Recently a white woman from Texas, who would quickly describe herself as a liberal, asked me about my hometown. When I told her that in Stamps my grandmother had owned the only Negro general merchandise store since the turn of the century, she exclaimed, "Why, you were a debutante." Ridiculous and even ludicrous. But Negro girls in small Southern towns, whether poverty-stricken or just munching along on a few of life's necessities, were given as extensive and irrelevant preparations for adulthood as rich white girls shown in magazines. Admittedly the training was not the same. While white girls learned to waltz and sit gracefully with a tea cup balanced on their knees, we were lagging behind, learning the mid-Victorian values with very little money to indulge them. (Come and see Edna Lomax spending the money she made picking cotton on five balls of ecru tatting thread. Her fingers are bound to snag the work and she'll have to repeat the stitches time and time again. But she knows that when she buys the thread.)

We were required to embroider and I had trunkfuls of colorful dishtowels, pillowcases, runners and handkerchiefs to my credit. I mastered the art of crocheting and tatting, and there was a lifetime's supply of dainty doilies that would never be used in sacheted dresser drawers. It went without saying that all girls could iron and wash, but the finer touches around the home, like setting a table with real silver, baking roasts and cooking vegetables without meat, had to be learned elsewhere. Usually at the source of those habits. During my tenth year, a white woman's kitchen became my finishing school.

Mrs. Viola Cullinan was a plump woman who lived in a three-bedroom house somewhere behind the post office. She was singularly unattractive until she smiled, and then the lines around her eyes and mouth which made her look perpetually dirty disappeared, and her face looked like the mask of an impish elf. She usually rested her smile until late afternoon when her women friends dropped in and Miss Glory, the cook, served them cold drinks on the closed-in porch.

The exactness of her house was inhuman. This glass went here and only here. That cup had its place and it was an act of impudent rebellion to place it anywhere else. At twelve o'clock the table was set. At 12:15 Mrs. Cullinan sat down to dinner (whether her husband had arrived or not). At 12:16 Miss Glory brought out the food.

It took me a week to learn the difference between a salad plate, a bread plate and a dessert plate.

Mrs. Cullinan kept up the tradition of her wealthy parents. She was from Virginia. Miss Glory, who was a descendant of slaves that had worked for the Cullinans, told me her history. She had married beneath her (according to Miss Glory). Her husband's family hadn't had their money very long and what they had "didn't 'mount to much."

As ugly as she was, I thought privately, she was lucky to get a husband above or beneath her station. But Miss Glory wouldn't let me say a thing against her mistress. She was very patient with me, however, over the housework. She explained the dishware, silverware and servants' bells. The large round bowl in which soup was served wasn't a soup bowl, it was a tureen. There were goblets, sherbet glasses, ice-cream glasses, wine glasses, green glass coffee cups with matching saucers, and water glasses. I had a glass to drink from, and it sat with Miss Glory's on a separate shelf from the others. Soup spoons, gravy boat, butter knives, salad forks and carving platter were additions to my vocabulary and in fact almost represented a new language. I was fascinated with the novelty, with the fluttering Mrs. Cullinan and her Alice-in-Wonderland house.

Her husband remains, in my memory, undefined. I lumped him with all the other white men that I had ever seen and tried not to see.

On our way home one evening, Miss Glory told me that Mrs. Cullinan couldn't have children. She said that she was too delicate-boned. It was hard to imagine bones at all under those layers of fat. Miss Glory went on to say that the doctor had taken out all her lady organs. I reasoned that a pig's organs included the lungs, heart and liver, so if Mrs. Cullinan was walking around without those essentials, it explained why she drank alcohol out of unmarked bottles. She was keeping herself embalmed.

When I spoke to Bailey about it, he agreed that I was right, but he also informed me that Mr. Cullinan had two daughters by a colored lady and that I knew them very well. He added that the girls were the spitting image of their father. I was unable to remember what he looked like, although I had just left him a few hours before, but I thought of the Coleman girls. They were very light-skinned and certainly didn't look very much like their mother (no one ever mentioned Mr. Coleman).

My pity for Mrs. Cullinan preceded me the next morning like the Cheshire cat's smile. Those girls, who could have been her daughters, were beautiful. They didn't have to straighten their hair. Even when they were caught in the rain, their braids still hung down straight like tamed snakes. Their mouths were pouty little cupid's bows. Mrs. Cullinan didn't know what she missed. Or maybe she did. Poor Mrs. Cullinan.

For weeks after, I arrived early, left late and tried very hard to make up for her barrenness. If she had had her own children, she wouldn't have had to ask me to run a thousand errands from her back door to the back door of her friends. Poor old Mrs. Cullinan.

Then one evening Miss Glory told me to serve the ladies on the porch. After I set the tray down and turned toward the kitchen, one of the women asked, "What's your name, girl?" It was the speckled-faced one. Mrs. Cullinan said, "She doesn't talk much. Her name's Margaret."

"Is she dumb?"

"No. As I understand it, she can talk when she wants to but she's usually quiet as a little mouse. Aren't you, Margaret?"

I smiled at her. Poor thing. No organs and couldn't even pronounce my name correctly.

"She's a sweet little thing, though."

"Well, that may be, but the name's too long. I'd never bother myself. I'd call her Mary if I was you."

I fumed into the kitchen. That horrible woman would never have the chance to call me Mary because if I was starving I'd never work for her. I decided I wouldn't pee on her if her heart was on fire. Giggles drifted in off the porch and into Miss Glory's pots. I wondered what they could be laughing about.

Whitefolks were so strange. Could they be talking about me? Everybody knew that they stuck together better than the Negroes did. It was possible that Mrs. Cullinan had friends in St. Louis who heard about a girl from Stamps being in court and wrote to tell her. Maybe she knew about Mr. Freeman.

My lunch was in my mouth a second time and I went outside and relieved myself on the bed of four-o'clocks. Miss Glory thought I might be coming down with something and told me to go on home, that Momma would give me some herb tea, and she'd explain to her mistress.

I realized how foolish I was being before I reached the pond. Of course Mrs. Cullinan didn't know. Otherwise she wouldn't have given me the two nice dresses that Momma cut down, and she certainly wouldn't have called me a "sweet little thing." My stomach felt fine, and I didn't mention anything to Momma.

That evening I decided to write a poem on being white, fat, old and without children. It was going to be a tragic ballad. I would have to watch her carefully to capture the essence of her loneliness and pain.

The very next day, she called me by the wrong name. Miss Glory and I were washing up the lunch dishes when Mrs. Cullinan came to the doorway. "Mary?"

Miss Glory asked, "Who?"

Mrs. Cullinan, sagging a little, knew and I knew. "I want Mary to go down to Mrs. Randall's and take her some soup. She's not been feeling well for a few days."

Miss Glory's face was a wonder to see. "You mean Margaret, ma'am. Her name's Margaret."

"That's too long. She's Mary from now on. Heat that soup from last night and put it in the china tureen and, Mary, I want you to carry it carefully."

Every person I knew had a hellish horror of being "called out of his name." It was a dangerous practice to call a Negro anything that could be loosely construed as insulting because of the centuries of their having been called niggers, jigs, dinges, blackbirds, crows, boots and spooks.

Miss Glory had a fleeting second of feeling sorry for me. Then as she handed me the hot tureen she said, "Don't mind, don't pay that no mind. Sticks and stones may break your bones, but words . . . You know, I been working for her for twenty years."

She held the back door open for me. "Twenty years. I wasn't much older than you. My name used to be Hallelujah. That's what Ma named me, but my mistress give me 'Glory,' and it stuck. I likes it better too."

I was in the little path that ran behind the houses when Miss Glory shouted, "It's shorter too."

For a few seconds it was a tossup over whether I would laugh (imagine being named Hallelujah) or cry (imagine letting some white woman rename you for her convenience). My anger saved me from either outburst. I had to quit the job, but the problem was going to be how to do it. Momma wouldn't allow me to quit for just any reason.

"She's a peach. That woman is a real peach." Mrs. Randall's maid was talking as she took the soup from me, and I wondered what her name used to be and what she answered to now.

For a week I looked into Mrs. Cullinan's face as she called me Mary. She ignored my coming late and leaving early. Miss Glory was a little annoyed because I had begun to leave egg yolk on the dishes and wasn't putting much heart in polishing the silver. I hoped that she would complain to our boss, but she didn't.

Then Bailey solved my dilemma. He had me describe the contents of the cupboard and the particular plates she liked best. Her favorite piece was a casserole shaped like a fish and the green glass coffee cups. I kept his instructions in mind, so on the next day when Miss Glory was hanging out clothes and I had again been told to serve the old biddies on the porch, I dropped the empty serving tray. When I heard Mrs. Cullinan scream, "Mary!" I picked up the casserole and two of the green glass cups in readiness. As she rounded the kitchen door I let them fall on the tiled floor.

I could never absolutely describe to Bailey what happened next, because each time I got to the part where she fell on the floor and screwed up her ugly face to cry, we burst out laughing. She actually wobbled around on the floor and picked up shards of the cups and cried, "Oh, Momma. Oh, dear Gawd. It's Momma's china from Virginia. Oh, Momma, I sorry."

Miss Glory came running in from the yard and the women from the porch crowded around. Miss Glory was almost as broken up as her mistress. "You mean to say she broke our Virginia dishes? What we gone do?"

Mrs. Cullinan cried louder, "That clumsy nigger. Clumsy little black nigger."

Old speckled-face leaned down and asked, "Who did it, Viola? Was it Mary? Who did it?"

Everything was happening so fast I can't remember whether her action preceded her words, but I know that Mrs. Cullinan said, "Her name's Margaret, goddamn it, her name's Margaret." And she threw a wedge of the broken plate at me. It could have been the hysteria which put her aim off, but the flying crockery caught Miss Glory right over her ear and she started screaming.

I left the front door wide open so all the neighbors could hear. Mrs. Cullinan was right about one thing. My name wasn't Mary.

CHAPTER 17

Weekdays revolved on a sameness wheel. They turned into themselves so steadily and inevitably that each seemed to be the original of yesterday's rough draft. Saturdays, however, always broke the mold and dared to be different.

Farmers trekked into town with their children and wives streaming around them. Their board-stiff khaki pants and shirts revealed the painstaking care of a dutiful daughter or wife. They often stopped at the Store to get change for bills so they could give out jangling coins to their children, who shook with their eagerness to get to town. The young kids openly resented their parents' dawdling in the Store and Uncle Willie would call them in and spread among them bits of sweet peanut patties that had been broken in shipping. They gobbled down the candies and were out again, kicking up the powdery dust in the road and worrying if there was going to be time to get to town after all.

Bailey played mumbledypeg with the older boys around the chinaberry tree, and Momma and Uncle Willie listened to the farmers' latest news of the country. I thought of myself as hanging in the Store, a mote imprisoned on a shaft of sunlight. Pushed and pulled by the slightest shift of air, but never falling free into the tempting darkness.

In the warm months, morning began with a quick wash in unheated well water. The suds were dashed on a plot of ground beside the kitchen door. It was called the bait garden (Bailey raised worms). After prayers, breakfast in summer was usually dry cereal and fresh milk. Then to our chores (which on Saturday included weekday jobs)— scrubbing the floors, raking the yards, polishing our shoes for Sunday

(Uncle Willie's had to be shined with a biscuit) and attending to the customers who came breathlessly, also in their Saturday hurry.

Looking through the years, I marvel that Saturday was my favorite day in the week. What pleasures could have been squeezed between the fan folds of unending tasks? Children's talent to endure stems from their ignorance of alternatives.

After our retreat from St. Louis, Momma gave us a weekly allowance. Since she seldom dealt with money, other than to take it in and to tithe to the church, I supposed that the weekly ten cents was to tell us that even she realized that a change had come over us, and that our new unfamiliarity caused her to treat us with a strangeness.

I usually gave my money to Bailey, who went to the movies nearly every Saturday. He brought back Street and Smith cowboy books for me.

One Saturday Bailey was late coming back from the Rye-al-toh. Momma had begun heating water for the Saturday-night baths, and all the evening chores were done. Uncle Willie sat in the twilight on the front porch mumbling or maybe singing, and smoking a ready-made. It was quite late. Mothers had called in their children from the group games, and fading sounds of "Yah... Yah... you didn't catch me" still hung and floated into the Store.

Uncle Willie said, "Sister, better light the light." On Saturdays we used the electric lights so that last-minute Sunday shoppers could look down the hill and see if the Store was open. Momma hadn't told me to turn them on because she didn't want to believe that night had fallen hard and Bailey was still out in the ungodly dark.

Her apprehension was evident in the hurried movements around the kitchen and in her lonely fearing eyes. The Black woman in the South who raises sons, grandsons and nephews had her heartstrings tied to a hanging noose. Any break from routine may herald for them unbearable news. For this reason, Southern Blacks until the present generation could be counted among America's arch conservatives.

Like most self-pitying people, I had very little pity for my relatives' anxiety. If something indeed had happened to Bailey, Uncle Willie would always have Momma, and Momma had the Store. Then, after all, we weren't their children. But I would be the major loser if Bailey turned up dead. For he was all I claimed, if not all I had.

The bath water was steaming on the cooking stove, but Momma was scrubbing the kitchen table for the umpteenth time.

"Momma," Uncle Willie called and she jumped. "Momma." I waited in the bright lights of the Store, jealous that someone had come along and told these strangers something about my brother and I would be the last to know.

"Momma, why don't you and Sister walk down to meet him?"

To my knowledge Bailey's name hadn't been mentioned for hours, but we all knew whom he meant.

Of course. Why didn't that occur to me? I wanted to be gone. Momma said, "Wait a minute, little lady. Go get your sweater, and bring me my shawl."

It was darker in the road than I'd thought it would be. Momma swung the flashlight's arc over the path and weeds and scary tree trunks. The night suddenly became enemy territory, and I knew that if my brother was lost in this land he was forever lost. He was eleven and very smart, that I granted, but after all he was so small. The Bluebeards and tigers and Rippers could eat him up before he could scream for help.

Momma told me to take the light and she reached for my hand. Her voice came from a high hill above me and in the dark my hand was enclosed in hers. I loved her with a rush. She said nothing—no "Don't worry" or "Don't get tender-hearted." Just the gentle pressure of her rough hand conveyed her own concern and assurance to me.

We passed houses which I knew well by daylight but couldn't recollect in the swarthy gloom.

"Evening, Miz Jenkins." Walking and pulling me along.

"Sister Henderson? Anything wrong?" That was from an outline blacker than the night.

"No, ma'am. Not a thing. Bless the Lord." By the time she finished speaking we had left the worried neighbors far behind.

Mr. Willie Williams' Do Drop Inn was bright with furry red lights in the distance and the pond's fishy smell enveloped us. Momma's hand tightened and let go, and I saw the small figure plodding along, tired and old-mannish. Hands in his pockets and head bent, he walked like a man trudging up the hill behind a coffin.

"Bailey." It jumped out as Momma said, "Ju," and I started to run, but her hand caught mine again and became a vise. I pulled, but she yanked me back to her side. "We'll walk, just like we been walking, young lady." There was no chance to warn Bailey that he was danger-ously late, that everybody had been worried and that he should create a good lie or, better, a great one.

Momma said, "Bailey, Junior," and he looked up without surprise. "You know it's night and you just now getting home?"

"Yes, ma'am." He was empty. Where was his alibi?

"What you been doing?"

"Nothing."

"That's all you got to say?"

"Yes, ma'am."

"All right, young man. We'll see when you get home."

She had turned me loose, so I made a grab for Bailey's hand, but he snatched it away. I said, "Hey, Bail," hoping to remind him that I was his sister and his only friend, but he grumbled something like "Leave me alone."

Momma didn't turn on the flashlight on the way back, nor did she answer the questioning Good evenings that floated around us as we passed the darkened houses.

I was confused and frightened. He was going to get a whipping and maybe he had done something terrible. If he couldn't talk to me it must have been serious. But there was no air of spent revelry about him. He just seemed sad. I didn't know what to think.

Uncle Willie said, "Getting too big for your britches, huh? You can't come home. You want to worry your grandmother to death?" Bailey was so far away he was beyond fear. Uncle Willie had a leather belt in his good hand but Bailey didn't notice or didn't care. "I'm going to whip you this time." Our uncle had only whipped us once before and then only with a peach-tree switch, so maybe now he was going to kill my brother. I screamed and grabbed for the belt, but Momma caught me. "Now, don't get uppity, miss, 'less you want some of the same thing. He got a lesson coming to him. You come on and get your bath."

From the kitchen I heard the belt fall down, dry and raspy on naked skin. Uncle Willie was gasping for breath, but Bailey made no sound. I was too afraid to splash water or even to cry and take a chance of drowning out Bailey's pleas for help, but the pleas never came and the whipping was finally over.

I lay awake an eternity, waiting for a sign, a whimper or a whisper, from the next room that he was still alive. Just before I fell exhausted into sleep, I heard Bailey: "Now I lay me down to sleep, I pray the Lord my soul to keep, if I should die before I wake, I pray the Lord my soul to take."

My last memory of that night was the question, Why is he saying the baby prayer? We had been saying the "Our Father, which art in heaven" for years.

For days the Store was a strange country, and we were all newly arrived immigrants. Bailey didn't talk, smile or apologize. His eyes were so vacant, it seemed his soul had flown away, and at meals I tried to give him the best pieces of meat and the largest portion of dessert, but he turned them down.

Then one evening at the pig pen he said without warning, "I saw Mother Dear."

If he said it, it was bound to be the truth. He wouldn't lie to me. I don't think I asked him where or when.

"In the movies." He laid his head on the wooden railing. "It wasn't really her. It was a woman named Kay Francis. She's a white movie star who looks just like Mother Dear."

There was no difficulty believing that a white movie star looked like our mother and that Bailey had seen her. He told me that the movies were changed each week, but when another picture came to Stamps starring Kay Francis he would tell me and we'd go together. He even promised to sit with me.

He had stayed late on the previous Saturday to see the film over again. I understood, and understood too why he couldn't tell Momma or Uncle Willie. She was our mother and belonged to us. She was never mentioned to anyone because we simply didn't have enough of her to share.

We had to wait nearly two months before Kay Francis returned to Stamps. Bailey's mood had lightened considerably, but he lived in a state of expectation and it made him more nervous than he was usually. When he told me that the movie would be shown, we went into our best behavior and were the exemplary children that Grandmother deserved and wished to think us.

It was a gay light comedy, and Kay Francis wore long-sleeved white silk shirts with big cuff links. Her bedroom was all satin and flowers in vases, and her maid, who was Black, went around saying "Lawsy, missy" all the time. There was a Negro chauffeur too, who rolled his eyes and scratched his head, and I wondered how on earth an idiot like that could be trusted with her beautiful cars.

The whitefolks downstairs laughed every few minutes, throwing the discarded snicker up to the Negroes in the buzzards' roost. The sound would jag around in our air for an indecisive second before the balcony's occupants accepted it and sent their own guffaws to riot with it against the walls of the theater.

I laughed, too, but not at the hateful jokes made on my people. I laughed because, except that she was white, the big movie star looked just like my mother. Except that she lived in a big mansion with a thousand servants, she lived just like my mother. And it was funny to think of the whitefolks' not knowing that the woman they were adoring could be my mother's twin, except that she was white and my mother was prettier. Much prettier.

The movie star made me happy. It was extraordinary good fortune to be able to save up one's money and go see one's mother whenever one wanted to. I bounced out of the theater as if I'd been given an unexpected present. But Bailey was cast down again. (I had to beg him not to stay for the next show.) On the way home he stopped at the railroad track and waited for the night freight train. Just before it reached the crossing, he tore out and ran across the tracks.

I was left on the other side in hysteria. Maybe the giant wheels were grinding his bones into a bloody mush. Maybe he tried to catch a boxcar and got flung into the pond and drowned. Or even worse, maybe he caught the train and was forever gone.

When the train passed he pushed himself away from the pole where he had been leaning, berated me for making all that noise and said, "Let's go home."

One year later he did catch a freight, but because of his youth and the inscrutable ways of fate, he didn't find California and his Mother Dear—he got stranded in Baton Rouge, Louisiana, for two weeks.

CHAPTER 18

Another day was over. In the soft dark the cotton truck spilled the pickers out and roared out of the yard with a sound like a giant's fart. The workers stepped around in circles for a few seconds as if they had found themselves unexpectedly in an unfamiliar place. Their minds sagged.

In the Store the men's faces were the most painful to watch, but I seemed to have no choice. When they tried to smile to carry off their tiredness as if it was nothing, the body did nothing to help the mind's attempt at disguise. Their shoulders drooped even as they laughed, and when they put their hands on their hips in a show of jauntiness, the palms slipped the thighs as if the pants were waxed.

"Evening, Sister Henderson. Well, back where we started, huh?"

"Yes, sir, Brother Stewart. Back where you started, bless the Lord." Momma could not take the smallest achievement for granted. People whose history and future were threatened each day by extinction considered that it was only by divine intervention that they were able to live at all. I find it interesting that the meanest life, the poorest existence, is attributed to God's will, but as human beings become more affluent, as their living standard and style begin to ascend the material scale, God descends the scale of responsibility at a commensurate speed.

"That's just who get the credit. Yes, ma'am. The blessed Lord." Their overalls and shirts seemed to be torn on purpose and the cotton lint and dust in their hair gave them the appearance of people who had turned gray in the past few hours.

The women's feet had swollen to fill the discarded men's shoes they wore, and they washed their arms at the well to dislodge dirt and splinters that had accrued to them as part of the day's pickings.

I thought them all hateful to have allowed themselves to be worked like oxen, and even more shameful to try to pretend that things were not as bad as they were. When they leaned too hard on the partly glass candy counter, I wanted to tell them shortly to stand up and "assume the posture of a man," but Momma would have beaten me if I'd opened my mouth. She ignored the creaks of the counter under their weight and moved around filling their orders and keeping up a conversation. "Going to put your dinner on, Sister Williams?" Bailey and I helped Momma, while Uncle Willie sat on the porch and heard the day's account.

"Praise the Lord, no, ma'am. Got enough left over from last night to do us. We going home and get cleaned up to go to the revival meeting."

Go to church in that cloud of weariness? Not go home and lay those tortured bones in a feather bed? The idea came to me that my people may be a race of masochists and that not only was it our fate to live the poorest, roughest life but that we liked it like that.

"I know what you mean, Sister Williams. Got to feed the soul just like you feed the body. I'm taking the children, too, the Lord willing. Good Book say, 'Raise a child in the way he should go and he will not depart from it.' "

"That's what it say. Sure is what it say."

———

The cloth tent had been set on the flatlands in the middle of a field near the railroad tracks. The earth was carpeted with a silky layer of dried grass and cotton stalks. Collapsible chairs were poked into the still-soft ground and a large wooden cross was hung from the center beam at the rear of the tent. Electric lights had been strung from behind the pulpit to the entrance flap and continued outside on poles made of rough two-by-fours.

Approached in the dark the swaying bulbs looked lonely and purposeless. Not as if they were there to provide light or anything meaningful. And the tent, that blurry bright three-dimensional A, was so foreign to the cotton field, that it might just get up and fly away before my eyes.

People, suddenly visible in the lamplight, streamed toward the temporary church. The adults' voices relayed the serious intent of their mission. Greetings were exchanged, hushed.

"Evening, sister, how you?"

"Bless the Lord, just trying to make it in."

Their minds were concentrated on the coming meeting, soul to soul, with God. This was no time to indulge in human concerns or personal questions.

"The good Lord give me another day, and I'm thankful." Nothing personal in that. The credit was God's, and there was no illusion about the Central Position's shifting or becoming less than Itself.

Teenagers enjoyed revivals as much as adults. They used the night outside meetings to play at courting. The impermanence of a collapsible church added to the frivolity, and their eyes flashed and winked and the girls giggled little silver drops in the dusk while the boys postured and swaggered and pretended not to notice. The nearly grown girls wore skirts as tight as the custom allowed and the young men slicked their hair down with Moroline Hairdressing and water.

To small children, though, the idea of praising God in a tent was confusing, to say the least. It seemed somehow blasphemous. The lights hanging slack overhead, the soft ground underneath and the canvas wall that faintly blew in and out, like cheeks puffed with air, made for the feeling of a country fair. The nudgings and jerks and winks of the bigger children surely didn't belong in a church. But the tension of the elders—their expectation, which weighted like a thick blanket over the crowd—was the most perplexing of all.

Would the gentle Jesus care to enter into that transitory setting? The altar wobbled and threatened to overturn and the collection table sat at a rakish angle. One leg had yielded itself to the loose dirt. Would God the Father allow His only Son to mix with this crowd of cotton pickers and maids, washerwomen and handymen? I knew He sent His spirit on Sundays to the church, but after all that was a church and the people had had all day Saturday to shuffle off the cloak of work and the skin of despair.

Everyone attended the revival meetings. Members of the hoity-toity Mount Zion Baptist Church mingled with the intellectual members of the African Methodist Episcopal and African Methodist Episcopal Zion, and the plain working people of the Christian Methodist Episcopal. These gatherings provided the one time in the year when all of those good village people associated with the followers of the Church of God in Christ. The latter were looked upon with some suspicion because they were so loud and raucous in their services. Their explanation that "the Good Book say, 'Make a joyful noise unto the Lord, and be exceedingly glad' " did not in the least minimize the condescension of their fellow Christians. Their church was far from the others, but they could be heard on Sunday, a half mile away, singing and dancing until they sometimes fell down in a dead faint. Members of the other churches wondered if the Holy Rollers were going to heaven after all their shouting. The suggestion was that they were having their heaven right here on earth.

This was their annual revival.

Mrs. Duncan, a little woman with a bird face, started the service. "I know I'm a witness for my Lord...I know I'm a witness for my Lord, I know I'm a witness..."

Her voice, a skinny finger, stabbed high up in the air and the church responded. From somewhere down front came the jangling sound of a tambourine. Two beats on "know," two beats on "I'm a" and two beats on the end of "witness."

Other voices joined the near shriek of Mrs. Duncan. They crowded around and tenderized the tone. Handclaps snapped in the roof and solidified the beat. When the song reached its peak in sound and passion, a tall, thin man who had been kneeling behind the altar all the while stood up and sang with the audience for a few bars. He stretched out his long arms and grasped the platform. It took some time for the singers to come off their level of exaltation, but the minister stood resolute until the song unwound like a child's playtoy and lay quieted in the aisles.

"Amen." He looked at the audience.

"Yes, sir, amen." Nearly everyone seconded him.

"I say, Let the church say 'Amen.' "

Everyone said, "Amen."

"Thank the Lord. Thank the Lord."

"That's right, thank the Lord. Yes, Lord. Amen."

"We will have prayer, led by Brother Bishop."

Another tall, brown-skinned man wearing square glasses walked up to the altar from the front row. The minister knelt at the right and Brother Bishop at the left.

"Our Father"—he was singing—"You who took my feet out the mire and clay—"

The church moaned, "Amen."

"You who saved my soul. One day. Look, sweet Jesus. Look down, on these your suffering children—"

The church begged, "Look down, Lord."

"Build us up where we're torn down... Bless the sick and the afflicted..."

It was the usual prayer. Only his voice gave it something new. After every two words he gasped and dragged the air over his vocal cords, making a sound like an inverted grunt. "You who"—grunt—"saved my"—gasp—"soul one"—inhalation—"day"—humph.

Then the congregation, led again by Mrs. Duncan, flew into "Precious Lord, take my hand, lead me on, let me stand." It was sung at a faster clip than the usual one in the C.M.E. Church, but at that tempo it worked. There was a joy about the tune that changed the meaning of its sad lyrics. "When the darkness appears, and the night draweth near and my life is almost gone..." There seemed to be an abandon which suggested that with all those things it should be a time for great rejoicing.

The serious shouters had already made themselves known, and their fans (cardboard advertisements from Texarkana's largest Negro funeral home) and lacy white handkerchiefs waved high in the air. In their dark hands they looked like small kites without the wooden frames.

The tall minister stood again at the altar. He waited for the song and the revelry to die.

He said, "Amen. Glory."

The church skidded off the song slowly. "Amen. Glory."

He still waited, as the last notes remained in the air, staircased on top of each other. "At the river I stand—" "I stand, guide my feet—" "Guide my feet, take my hand." Sung like the last circle in a round. Then quiet descended.

The Scripture reading was from Matthew, twenty-fifth chapter, thirtieth verse through the forty-sixth.

His text for the sermon was "The least of these."

After reading the verses to the accompaniment of a few Amens he said, "First Corinthians tells me, 'Even if I have the tongue of men and of angels and have not charity, I am as nothing. Even if I give all my clothes to the poor and have not charity, I am as nothing. Even if I give my body to be burned and have not charity it availeth me nothing. Burned, I say, and have not charity, it availeth nothing.' I have to ask myself, what is this thing called Charity? If good deeds are not charity—"

The church gave in quickly. "That's right, Lord."

"—if giving my flesh and blood is not charity?"

"Yes, Lord."

"I have to ask myself what is this charity they talking so much about."

I had never heard a preacher jump into the muscle of his sermon so quickly. Already the humming pitch had risen in the church, and those who knew had popped their eyes in anticipation of the coming excitement. Momma sat tree-trunk still, but she had balled her handkerchief in her hand and only the corner, which I had embroidered, stuck out.

"As I understand it, charity vaunteth not itself. Is not puffed up." He blew himself up with a deep breath to give us the picture of what Charity was not. "Charity don't go around saying 'I give you food and I give you clothes and by rights you ought to thank me.' "

The congregation knew whom he was talking about and voiced agreement with his analysis. "Tell the truth, Lord."

"Charity don't say, 'Because I give you a job, you got to bend your knee to me.' " The church was rocking with each phrase. "It don't say, 'Because I pays you what you due, you got to call me master.' It don't ask me to humble myself and belittle myself. That ain't what Charity is."

Down front to the right, Mr. and Mrs. Stewart, who only a few hours earlier had crumbled in our front yard, defeated by the cotton rows, now sat on the edges of their rickety-rackety chairs. Their faces shone with the delight of their souls. The mean whitefolks was going to get their comeuppance. Wasn't that what the minister said, and wasn't he quoting from the words of God Himself? They had been re-freshed with the hope of revenge and the promise of justice.

"Aaagh. Raagh. I said...Charity. Woooooo, a Charity. It don't want nothing for itself. It don't want to be bossman...Waah...It don't want to be headman...Waah...It don't want to be foreman...Waah...It... I'm talking about Charity...It don't want...Oh Lord...help me tonight...It don't want to be bowed to and scraped at..."

America's historic bowers and scrapers shifted easily and happily in the makeshift church. Reassured that although they might be the low-est of the low they were at least not uncharitable, and "in that great Gettin' Up Morning, Jesus was going to separate the sheep (them) from the goats (the whitefolks)."

"Charity is simple." The church agreed, vocally.

"Charity is poor." That was us he was talking about.

"Charity is plain." I thought, that's about right. Plain and simple.

"Charity is...Oh, Oh, Oh. Cha–ri–ty. Where are you? Wooo... Charity...Hump."

One chair gave way and the sound of splintering wood split the air in the rear of the church.

"I call you and you don't answer. Woooh, oh Charity."

Another holler went up in front of me, and a large woman flopped over, her arms above her head like a candidate for baptism. The emotional release was contagious. Little screams burst around the room like Fourth of July firecrackers.

The minister's voice was a pendulum. Swinging left and down and right and down and left and—"How can you claim to be my brother, and hate me? Is that Charity? How can you claim to be my sister and despise me? Is that supposed to be Charity? How can you claim to be my friend and misuse and wrongfully abuse me? Is that Charity? Oh, my children, I stopped by here—"

The church swung on the end of his phrases. Punctuating. Confirming. "Stop by here, Lord."

"—to tell you, to open your heart and let Charity reign. Forgive your enemies for His sake. Show the Charity that Jesus was speaking of to this sick old world. It has need of the charitable giver." His voice was falling and the explosions became fewer and quieter.

"And now I repeat the words of the Apostle Paul, and 'now abideth faith, hope and charity, these three; but the greatest of these is charity.' "

The congregation lowed with satisfaction. Even if they were society's pariahs, they were going to be angels in a marble white heaven and sit on the right hand of Jesus, the Son of God. The Lord loved the poor and hated those cast high in the world. Hadn't He Himself said it would be easier for a camel to go through the eye of a needle than for a rich man to enter heaven? They were assured that they were going to be the only inhabitants of that land of milk and honey, except of course a few whitefolks like John Brown who history books said was crazy anyway. All the Negroes had to do generally, and those at the revival especially, was bear up under this life of toil and cares, because a blessed home awaited them in the far-off bye and bye.

"Bye and bye, when the morning come, when all the saints of God's are gathering home, we will tell the story of how we overcome and we'll understand it better bye and bye."

A few people who had fainted were being revived on the side aisles when the evangelist opened the doors of the church. Over the sounds of "Thank you, Jesus," he started a long-meter hymn:

"I came to Jesus, as I was,
worried, wounded and sad,
I found in Him a resting place,
And He has made me glad."

The old ladies took up the hymn and shared it in tight harmony. The humming crowd began to sound like tired bees, restless and anxious to get home.

"All those under the sound of my voice who have no spiritual home, whose hearts are burdened and heavy-ladened, let them come. Come before it's too late. I don't ask you to join the Church of God in Christ. No. I'm a servant of God, and in this revival, we are out to bring straying souls to Him. So if you join this evening, just say which church you want to be affiliated with, and we will turn you over to a representative of that church body. Will one deacon of the following churches come forward?"

That was revolutionary action. No one had ever heard of a minister taking in members for another church. It was our first look at Charity among preachers. Men from the A.M.E., A.M.E.Z., Baptist and C.M.E. churches went down front and assumed stances a few feet apart. Converted sinners flowed down the aisles to shake hands with the evangelist and stayed at his side or were directed to one of the men in line. Over twenty people were saved that night.

There was nearly as much commotion over the saving of the sinners as there had been during the gratifying melodic sermon.

The Mothers of the Church, old ladies with white lace disks pinned to their thinning hair, had a service all their own. They walked around the new converts singing,

"Before this time another year,
I may be gone,
In some lonesome graveyard,
Oh, Lord, how long?"

When the collection was taken up and the last hymn given to the praise of God, the evangelist asked that everyone in his presence rededicate his soul to God and his life's work to Charity. Then we were dismissed.

Outside and on the way home, the people played in their magic, as children poke in mud pies, reluctant to tell themselves that the game was over.

"The Lord touched him tonight, didn't He?"

"Surely did. Touched him with a mighty fire."

"Bless the Lord. I'm glad I'm saved."

"That's the truth. It make a whole lot of difference."

"I wish them people I works for could of heard that sermon. They don't know what they letting theyselves in for."

"Bible say, 'He who can hear, let him hear. He who can't, shame on 'em.' "

They basked in the righteousness of the poor and the exclusiveness of the downtrodden. Let the whitefolks have their money and power and segregation and sarcasm and big houses and schools and lawns like carpets, and books, and mostly—mostly—let them have their whiteness. It was better to be meek and lowly, spat upon and abused for this little time than to spend eternity frying in the fires of hell. No one would have admitted that the Christian and charitable people were happy to think of their oppressors' turning forever on the Devil's spit over the flames of fire and brimstone.

But that was what the Bible said and it didn't make mistakes. "Ain't it said somewhere in there that 'before one word of this changes, heaven and earth shall fall away?' Folks going to get what they deserved."

When the main crowd of worshipers reached the short bridge spanning the pond, the ragged sound of honky-tonk music assailed them. A barrelhouse blues was being shouted over the stamping of feet on a wooden floor. Miss Grace, the good-time woman, had her usual Saturday-night customers. The big white house blazed with lights and noise. The people inside had forsaken their own distress for a little while.

Passing near the din, the godly people dropped their heads and conversation ceased. Reality began its tedious crawl back into their reasoning. After all, they were needy and hungry and despised and dispossessed, and sinners the world over were in the driver's seat. How long, merciful Father? How long?

A stranger to the music could not have made a distinction between the songs sung a few minutes before and those being danced to in the gay house by the railroad tracks. All asked the same questions. How long, oh God? How long?

CHAPTER 19

The last inch of space was filled, yet people continued to wedge themselves along the walls of the Store. Uncle Willie had turned the radio up to its last notch so that youngsters on the porch wouldn't miss a word. Women sat on kitchen chairs, dining-room chairs, stools and upturned wooden boxes. Small children and babies perched on every lap available and men leaned on the shelves or on each other.

The apprehensive mood was shot through with shafts of gaiety, as a black sky is streaked with lightning.

"I ain't worried 'bout this fight. Joe's gonna whip that cracker like it's open season."

"He gone whip him till that white boy call him Momma."

At last the talking was finished and the string-along songs about razor blades were over and the fight began.

"A quick jab to the head." In the Store the crowd grunted. "A left to the head and a right and another left." One of the listeners cackled like a hen and was quieted.

"They're in a clench, Louis is trying to fight his way out."

Some bitter comedian on the porch said, "That white man don't mind hugging that niggah now, I betcha."

"The referee is moving in to break them up, but Louis finally pushed the contender away and it's an uppercut to the chin. The contender is hanging on, now he's backing away. Louis catches him with a short left to the jaw."

A tide of murmuring assent poured out the doors and into the yard.

"Another left and another left. Louis is saving that mighty right…" The mutter in the Store had grown into a baby roar and it was pierced by the clang of a bell and the announcer's "That's the bell for round three, ladies and gentlemen."

As I pushed my way into the Store I wondered if the announcer gave any thought to the fact that he was addressing as "ladies and gentlemen" all the Negroes around the world who sat sweating and praying, glued to their "master's voice."

There were only a few calls for R. C. Colas, Dr. Peppers, and Hire's root beer. The real festivities would begin after the fight. Then even the old Christian ladies who taught their children and tried themselves to practice turning the other cheek would buy soft drinks, and if the Brown Bomber's victory was a particularly bloody one they would order peanut patties and Baby Ruths also.

Bailey and I lay the coins on top of the cash register. Uncle Willie didn't allow us to ring up sales during a fight. It was too noisy and might shake up the atmosphere. When the gong rang for the next round we pushed through the near-sacred quiet to the herd of children outside.

"He's got Louis against the ropes and now it's a left to the body and a right to the ribs. Another right to the body, it looks like it was low … Yes, ladies and gentlemen, the referee is signaling but the contender keeps raining the blows on Louis. It's another to the body, and it looks like Louis is going down."

My race groaned. It was our people falling. It was another lynching, yet another Black man hanging on a tree. One more woman ambushed and raped. A Black boy whipped and maimed. It was hounds on the trail of a man running through slimy swamps. It was a white woman slapping her maid for being forgetful.

The men in the Store stood away from the walls and at attention. Women greedily clutched the babes on their laps while on the porch the shufflings and smiles, flirtings and pinching of a few minutes before were gone. This might be the end of the world. If Joe lost we were back in slavery and beyond help. It would all be true, the accusations that we were lower types of human beings. Only a little higher than the apes. True that we were stupid and ugly and lazy and dirty and, unlucky and worst of all, that God Himself hated us and ordained us to be hewers of wood and drawers of water, forever and ever, world without end.

We didn't breathe. We didn't hope. We waited.

"He's off the ropes, ladies and gentlemen. He's moving towards the center of the ring." There was no time to be relieved. The worst might still happen.

"And now it looks like Joe is mad. He's caught Carnera with a left hook to the head and a right to the head. It's a left jab to the body and another left to the head. There's a left cross and a right to the head. The contender's right eye is bleeding and he can't seem to keep his block up. Louis is penetrating every block. The referee is moving in, but Louis sends a left to the body and it's the uppercut to the chin and the contender is dropping. He's on the canvas, ladies and gentlemen."

Babies slid to the floor as women stood up and men leaned toward the radio.

"Here's the referee. He's counting. One, two, three, four, five, six, seven... Is the contender trying to get up again?"

All the men in the store shouted, "NO."

"—eight, nine, ten." There were a few sounds from the audience, but they seemed to be holding themselves in against tremendous pressure.

"The fight is all over, ladies and gentlemen. Let's get the microphone over to the referee... Here he is. He's got the Brown Bomber's hand, he's holding it up... Here he is..."

Then the voice, husky and familiar, came to wash over us—"The winnah, and still heavyweight champeen of the world... Joe Louis."

Champion of the world. A Black boy. Some Black mother's son. He was the strongest man in the world. People drank Coca-Colas like ambrosia and ate candy bars like Christmas. Some of the men went behind the Store and poured white lightning in their soft-drink bottles, and a few of the bigger boys followed them. Those who were not chased away came back blowing their breath in front of themselves like proud smokers.

It would take an hour or more before the people would leave the Store and head for home. Those who lived too far had made arrangements to stay in town. It wouldn't do for a Black man and his family to be caught on a lonely country road on a night when Joe Louis had proved that we were the strongest people in the world.

CHAPTER 20

"Acka Backa, Sody Cracka
Acka Backa, Boo
Acka Backa, Sody Cracka
I'm in love with you."

The sounds of tag beat through the trees while the top branches waved in contrapuntal rhythms. I lay on a moment of green grass and telescoped the children's game to my vision. The girls ran about wild, now here, now there, never here, never was, they seemed to have no more direction than a splattered egg. But it was a shared if seldom voiced knowledge that all movements fitted, and worked according to a larger plan. I raised a platform for my mind's eye and marveled down on the outcome of "Acka Backa." The gay picnic dresses dashed, stopped and darted like beautiful dragonflies over a dark pool. The boys, black whips in the sunlight, popped behind the trees where their girls had fled, half hidden and throbbing in the shadows.

The summer picnic fish fry in the clearing by the pond was the biggest outdoor event of the year. Everyone was there. All churches were represented, as well as the social groups (Elks, Eastern Star,

Masons, Knights of Columbus, Daughters of Pythias), professional people (Negro teachers from Lafayette County) and all the excited children.

Musicians brought cigar-box guitars, harmonicas, juice harps, combs wrapped in tissue paper and even bathtub basses.

The amount and variety of foods would have found approval on the menu of a Roman epicure. Pans of fried chicken, covered with dish-towels, sat under benches next to a mountain of potato salad crammed with hard-boiled eggs. Whole rust-red sticks of bologna were clothed in cheese-cloth. Homemade pickles and chow-chow, and baked country hams, aromatic with cloves and pineapples, vied for prominence. Our steady customers had ordered cold watermelons, so Bailey and I chugged the striped-green fruit into the Coca-Cola box and filled all the tubs with ice as well as the big black wash pot that Momma used to boil her laundry. Now they too lay sweating in the happy afternoon air.

The summer picnic gave ladies a chance to show off their baking hands. On the barbecue pit, chickens and spareribs sputtered in their own fat and a sauce whose recipe was guarded in the family like a scandalous affair. However, in the ecumenical light of the summer picnic every true baking artist could reveal her prize to the delight and criticism of the town. Orange sponge cakes and dark brown mounds dripping Hershey's chocolate stood layer to layer with ice-white coconuts and light brown caramels. Pound cakes sagged with their buttery weight and small children could no more resist licking the icings than their mothers could avoid slapping the sticky fingers.

Proven fishermen and weekend amateurs sat on the trunks of trees at the pond. They pulled the struggling bass and the silver perch from the swift water. A rotating crew of young girls scaled and cleaned the catch and busy women in starched aprons salted and rolled the fish in corn meal, then dropped them in Dutch ovens trembling with boiling fat.

On one corner of the clearing a gospel group was rehearsing. Their harmony, packed as tight as sardines, floated over the music of the county singers and melted into the songs of the small children's ring games.

"Boys, don'chew let that ball fall on none of my cakes, you do and it'll be me on you."

"Yes, ma'am," and nothing changed. The boys continued hitting the tennis ball with pailings snatched from a fence and running holes in the ground, colliding with everyone.

I had wanted to bring something to read, but Momma said if I didn't want to play with the other children I could make myself useful by cleaning fish or bringing water from the nearest well or wood for the barbecue.

I wandered into a retreat by accident. Signs with arrows around the barbecue pit pointed MEN, WOMEN, CHILDREN toward fading lanes, grown over since last year. Feeling ages old and very wise at ten, I couldn't allow myself to be found by small children squatting behind a tree. Neither did I have the nerve to follow the arrow pointing the way for WOMEN. If any grownup had caught me there, it was possible that she'd think I was being "womanish" and would report me to Momma, and I knew what I could expect from her. So when the urge hit me to relieve myself, I headed toward another direction. Once through the wall of sycamore trees I found myself in a clearing ten times smaller than the picnic area, and cool and quiet. After my business was taken care of, I found a seat between two protruding roots of a black walnut tree and leaned back on its trunk. Heaven would be like that for the deserving. Maybe California too. Looking straight up at the uneven circle of sky, I began to sense that I might be falling into a blue cloud, far away. The children's voices and the thick odor of food cooking over open fires were the hooks I grabbed just in time to save myself.

Grass squeaked and I jumped at being found. Louise Kendricks walked into my grove. I didn't know that she too was escaping the gay spirit. We were the same age and she and her mother lived in a neat little bungalow behind the school. Her cousins, who were in our age group, were wealthier and fairer, but I had secretly believed Louise to be the prettiest female in Stamps, next to Mrs. Flowers.

"What you doing sitting here by yourself, Marguerite?" She didn't accuse, she asked for information. I said that I was watching the sky.

She asked, "What for?" There was obviously no answer to a question like that, so I didn't make up one. Louise reminded me of Jane Eyre. Her mother lived in reduced circumstances, but she was genteel, and though she worked as a maid I decided she should be called a governess and did so to Bailey and myself. (Who could teach a romantic dreamy ten-year-old to call a spade a spade?) Mrs. Kendricks could not have been very old, but to me all people over eighteen were adults and there could be no degree given or taken. They had to be catered to and pampered with politeness, then they had to stay in the same category of lookalike, soundalike and beingalike. Louise was a lonely girl, although she had plenty of playmates and was a ready partner for any ring game in the schoolyard.

Her face, which was long and dark chocolate brown, had a thin sheet of sadness over it, as light but as permanent as the viewing gauze on a coffin. And her eyes, which I thought her best feature, shifted quickly as if what they sought had just a second before eluded her.

She had come near and the spotted light through the trees fell on her face and braids in running splotches. I had never noticed before, but she looked exactly like Bailey. Her hair was "good"—more straight than kinky—and her features had the regularity of objects placed by a careful hand.

She looked up—"Well, you can't see much sky from here." Then she sat down, an arm away from me. Finding two exposed roots, she laid thin wrists on them as if she had been in an easy chair. Slowly she leaned back against the tree. I closed my eyes and thought of the necessity of finding another place and the unlikelihood of there being another with all the qualifications that this one had. There was a little peal of a scream and before I could open my eyes Louise had grabbed my hand. "I was falling"—she shook her long braids—"I was falling in the sky."

I liked her for being able to fall in the sky and admit it. I suggested, "Let's try together. But we have to sit up straight on the count of five." Louise asked, "Want to hold hands? Just in case?" I did. If one of us did happen to fall, the other could pull her out.

After a few near tumbles into eternity (both of us knew what it was), we laughed at having played with death and destruction and escaped.

Louise said, "Let's look at that old sky while we're spinning." We took each other's hands in the center of the clearing and began turning around. Very slowly at first. We raised our chins and looked straight at the seductive patch of blue. Faster, just a little faster, then faster, faster yet. Yes, help, we were falling. Then eternity won, after all. We couldn't stop spinning or falling until I was jerked out of her grasp by greedy gravity and thrown to my fate below—no, above, not below. I found myself safe and dizzy at the foot of the sycamore tree. Louise had ended on her knees at the other side of the grove.

This was surely the time to laugh. We lost but we hadn't lost anything. First we were giggling and crawling drunkenly toward each other and then we were laughing out loud uproariously. We slapped each other on the back and shoulders and laughed some more. We had made a fool or a liar out of something, and didn't that just beat all?

In daring to challenge the unknown with me, she became my first friend. We spent tedious hours teaching ourselves the Tut language. You (Yak oh you) know (kack nug oh wug) what (wack hash a tut). Since all the other children spoke Pig Latin, we were superior because Tut was hard to speak and even harder to understand. At last I began to comprehend what girls giggled about. Louise would rattle off a few sentences to me in the unintelligible Tut language and would laugh. Naturally I laughed too. Snickered, really, understanding nothing. I don't think she understood half of what she was saying herself, but, after all, girls have to giggle, and after being a woman for three years I was about to become a girl.

———

In school one day, a girl whom I barely knew and had scarcely spoken to brought me a note. The intricate fold indicated that it was a love note. I was sure she had the wrong person, but she insisted. Picking the paper loose, I confessed to myself that I was frightened. Suppose it was somebody being funny? Suppose the paper would show a hideous beast and the word YOU written over it. Children did that sometimes just because they claimed I was stuck-up. Fortunately I had got permission to go to the toilet—an outside job—and in the reeking gloom I read:

Dear Friend, M.J.
Times are hard and friends are few
I take great pleasure in writing you
Will you be my Valentine?
Tommy Valdon

I pulled my mind apart. Who? Who was Tommy Valdon? Finally a face dragged itself from my memory. He was the nice-looking brown-skinned boy who lived across the pond. As soon as I had pinned him down, I began to wonder, Why? Why me? Was it a joke? But if Tommy was the boy I remembered he was a very sober person and a good student. Well, then, it wasn't a joke. All right, what evil dirty things did he have in mind? My questions fell over themselves, an army in retreat. Haste, dig for cover. Protect your flanks. Don't let the enemy close the gap between you. What did a Valentine do, anyway?

Starting to throw the paper in the foul-smelling hole, I thought of Louise. I could show it to her. I folded the paper back in the original creases, and went back to class. There was no time during the lunch period since I had to run to the Store and wait on customers. The note was in my sock and every time Momma looked at me, I feared that her church gaze might have turned into X-ray vision and she could not only see the note and read its message but would interpret it as well. I felt myself slipping down a sheer cliff of guilt, and a second time I nearly destroyed the note but there was no opportunity. The take-up bell rang and Bailey raced me to school, so the note was forgotten. But serious business is serious, and it had to be attended to. After classes I waited for Louise. She was talking to a group of girls, laughing. But when I gave her our signal (two waves of the left hand) she said good-bye to them and joined me in the road. I didn't give her the chance to ask what was on my mind (her favorite question); I simply gave her the note. Recognizing the fold she stopped smiling. We were in deep waters. She opened the letter and read it aloud twice. "Well, what do you think?"

I said, "What do I think? That's what I'm asking you? What is there to think?"

"Looks like he wants you to be his valentine."

"Louise, I can read. But what does it mean?"

"Oh, you know. His valentine. His love."

There was that hateful word again. That treacherous word that yawned up at you like a volcano.

"Well, I won't. Most decidedly I won't. Not ever again."

"Have you been his valentine before? What do you mean never again?"

I couldn't lie to my friend and I wasn't about to freshen old ghosts.

"Well, don't answer him then, and that's the end of it." I was a little relieved that she thought it could be gotten rid of so quickly. I tore the note in half and gave her a part. Walking down the hill we minced the paper in a thousand shreds and gave it to the wind.

Two days later a monitor came into my classroom. She spoke quietly to Miss Williams, our teacher. Miss Williams said, "Class, I believe you remember that tomorrow is Valentine's Day, so named for St. Valentine, the martyr, who died around A.D. 270 in Rome. The day is observed by exchanging tokens of affection, and cards. The eighth-grade children have completed theirs and the monitor is acting as mailman. You will be given cardboard, ribbon and red tissue paper during the last period today so that you may make your gifts. Glue and scissors are here at the work table. Now, stand when your name is called."

She had been shuffling the colored envelopes and calling names for some time before I noticed. I had been thinking of yesterday's plain invitation and the expeditious way Louise and I took care of it.

We who were being called to receive valentines were only slightly more embarrassed than those who sat and watched as Miss Williams opened each envelope. "Helen Gray." Helen Gray, a tall, dull girl from Louisville, flinched. "Dear Valentine"—Miss Williams began reading the badly rhymed childish drivel. I seethed with shame and anticipation and yet had time to be offended at the silly poetry that I could have bettered in my sleep.

"Margue-you-reete Anne Johnson. My goodness, this looks more like a letter than a valentine. 'Dear Friend, I wrote you a letter and saw you tear it up with your friend Miss L. I don't believe you meant to hurt my feelings so whether you answer or not you will always be my valentine. T.V.'"

"Class"—Miss Williams smirked and continued lazily without giving us permission to sit down—"although you are only in the seventh grade, I'm sure you wouldn't be so presumptuous as to sign a letter with an initial. But here is a boy in the eighth grade, about to graduate—blah, blah, blooey, blah. You may collect your valentines and these letters on your way out."

It was a nice letter and Tommy had beautiful penmanship. I was sorry I tore up the first. His statement that whether I answered him or not would not influence his affection reassured me. He couldn't be after you-know-what if he talked like that. I told Louise that the next time he came to the Store I was going to say something extra nice to him. Unfortunately the situation was so wonderful to me that each time I saw Tommy I melted in delicious giggles and was unable to form a coherent sentence. After a while he stopped including me in his general glances.

CHAPTER 21

Bailey stuck branches in the ground behind the house and covered them with a worn-through blanket, making a tent. It was to be his Captain Marvel hideaway. There he initiated girls into the mysteries of sex. One by one, he took the impressed, the curious, the adventurous into the gray shadows, after explaining that they were going to play Momma and Poppa. I was assigned the role of Baby and lookout. The girls were commanded to pull up their dresses and then he lay on top and wiggled his hips.

I sometimes had to lift the flap (our signal that an adult was approaching) and so I saw their pathetic struggles even as they talked about school and the movies.

He had been playing the game for about six months before he met Joyce. She was a country girl about four years older than Bailey (he wasn't quite eleven when they met) whose parents had died and she along with her brothers and sisters had been parceled out to relatives. Joyce had come to Stamps to live with a widowed aunt who was even poorer than the poorest person in town. Joyce was quite advanced physically for her age. Her breasts were not the hard little knots of other girls her age; they filled out the tops of her skimpy little dresses. She walked stiffly, as if she were carrying a load of wood between her legs. I thought of her as being coarse, but Bailey said she was cute and that he wanted to play house with her.

In the special way of women, Joyce knew she had made a conquest, and managed to hang around the Store in the late afternoons and all day Saturdays. She ran errands for Momma when we were busy in the Store and sweated profusely. Often when she came in after running down the hill, her cotton dress would cling to her thin body and Bailey would glue his eyes on her until her clothes dried.

Momma gave her small gifts of food to take to her aunt, and on Saturdays Uncle Willie would sometimes give her a dime for "show fare."

During Passover week we weren't allowed to go to the movies (Momma said we all must sacrifice to purify our souls), and Bailey and Joyce decided that the three of us would play house. As usual, I was to be Baby.

He strung the tent and Joyce crawled in first. Bailey told me to sit outside and play with my doll baby, and he went in and the flap closed.

"Well, ain't you going to open your trousers?" Joyce's voice was muffled.

"No. You just pull up your dress."

There were rustling sounds from the tent and the sides pooched out as if they were trying to stand up.

Bailey asked, "What are you doing?"

"Pulling off my drawers."

"What for?"

"We can't do it with my drawers on."

"Why not?"

"How are you going to get to it?"

Silence. My poor brother didn't know what she meant. I knew. I lifted the flap and said, "Joyce, don't you do that to my brother." She nearly screamed, but she kept her voice low, "Margaret, you close that door." Bailey added, "Yes. Close it. You're supposed to be playing with our doll baby." I thought he would go to the hospital if he let her do that to him, so I warned him, "Bailey, if you let her do that to you, you'll be sorry." But he threatened that if I didn't close the door he wouldn't speak to me for a month, so I let the end of the blanket fall and sat down on the grass in front of the tent.

Joyce poked her head out and said in a sugary, white-woman-in-the-movies voice, "Baby, you go get some wood. Daddy and I going to light a fire, then I'm going to make you some cake." Then her voice changed as if she was going to hit me. "Go. Git."

Bailey told me after that Joyce had hairs on her thing and that she had gotten them from "doing it" with so many boys. She even had hair under her arms. Both of them. He was very proud of her accomplishments.

As their love affair progressed, his stealing from the Store increased. We had always taken candy and a few nickels and of course the sour pickles, but Bailey, now called upon to feed Joyce's ravening hunger, took cans of sardines and greasy Polish sausage and cheese and even the expensive cans of pink salmon that our family could seldom afford to eat.

Joyce's willingness to do odd jobs slackened about this time. She complained that she wasn't feeling all that well. But since she now had a few coins, she still hung around the Store eating Planter's peanuts and drinking Dr. Pepper.

Momma ran her off a few times. "Ain't you said you wasn't feeling well, Joyce? Hadn't you better get home and let your aunty do something for you?"

"Yes, ma'am." Then reluctantly she was off the porch, her stiff-legged walk carrying her up the hill and out of sight.

I think she was Bailey's first love outside the family. For him, she was the mother who let him get as close as he dreamed, the sister who wasn't moody and withdrawing, and teary and tender-hearted. All he had to do was keep the food coming in and she kept the affection flowing out. It made no difference to him that she was almost a woman, or possibly it was just that difference which made her so appealing.

She was around for a few months, and as she had appeared, out of limbo, so she disappeared into nothingness. There was no gossip about her, no clues to her leaving or her whereabouts. I noticed the change in Bailey before I discovered that she was gone. He lost his interest in everything. He mulled around and it would be safe to say "he paled." Momma noticed and said that he was feeling poorly because of the change in seasons (we were nearing fall), so she went to the woods for certain leaves, made him a tea and forced him to drink it after a heaping spoonful of sulfur and molasses. The fact that he didn't fight it, didn't try to talk his way out of taking the medicine, showed without a glimmer of doubt he was very sick.

If I had disliked Joyce while she had Bailey in her grasp, I hated her for leaving. I missed the tolerance she had brought to him (he had nearly given up sarcasm and playing jokes on the country people) and he had taken to telling me his secrets again. But now that she was gone he rivaled me in being uncommunicative. He closed in upon himself like a pond swallowing a stone. There was no evidence that he had ever opened up, and when I mentioned her he responded with "Joyce who?"

Months later, when Momma was waiting on Joyce's aunt, she said, "Yes ma'am, Mrs. Goodman, life's just one thing right after the other."

Mrs. Goodman was leaning on the red Coca-Cola box. "That's the blessed truth, Sister Henderson." She sipped the expensive drink.

"Things change so fast, it make your head swim." That was Momma's way of opening up a conversation. I stayed mouse-quiet so that I'd be able to hear the gossip and take it to Bailey.

"Now, you take little Joyce. She used to be around the Store all the time. Then she went up just like smoke. We ain't seed hide nor hair of her in months."

"No'm. I shamed to tell you... what took her off." She settled in on a kitchen chair. Momma spied me in the shadows. "Sister, the Lord don't like little jugs with big ears. You ain't got something to do, I'll find something for you."

The truth had to float to me through the kitchen door.

"I ain't got much, Sister Henderson, but I give that child all I had."

Momma said she bound that was true. She wouldn't say "bet."

"And after all I did, she run off with one of those railroad porters. She was loose just like her mammy before her. You know how they say 'blood will tell'?"

Momma asked, "How did the snake catch her?"

"Well, now, understand me, Sister Henderson, I don't hold this against you, I knows you a God-fearing woman. But it seems like she met him here."

Momma was flustered. Such goings on at the Store? She asked, "At the Store?"

"Yes, ma'am. 'Member when that bunch of Elks come over for their baseball game?" (Momma must have remembered. I did.) "Well, as it turned out, he was one of them. She left me a teenincy note. Said people in Stamps thought they were better than she was, and that she hadn't only made one friend, and that was your grandson. Said she was moving to Dallas, Texas, and gone marry that railroad porter."

Momma said, "Do, Lord."

Mrs. Goodman said, "You know, Sister Henderson, she wasn't with me long enough for me to get the real habit of her, but still I miss her. She was sweet when she wanted to be." Momma consoled her with, "Well, we got to keep our mind on the words of the Book. It say, 'The Lord giveth and the Lord taketh away.'"

Mrs. Goodman chimed in and they finished the phrase together, "Blessed be the name of the Lord."

I don't know how long Bailey had known about Joyce, but later in the evening when I tried to bring her name into our conversation, he said, "Joyce? She's got somebody to do it to her all the time now." And that was the last time her name was mentioned.

CHAPTER 22

The wind blew over the roof and ruffled the shingles. It whistled sharp under the closed door. The chimney made fearful sounds of protest as it was invaded by the urgent gusts.

A mile away ole Kansas City Kate (the train much admired but too important to stop in Stamps) crashed through the middle of town, blew its *wooo-wee* warnings, and continued to an unknown glamorous destination without looking back.

There was going to be a storm and it was a perfect night for rereading *Jane Eyre*. Bailey had finished his chores and was already behind the stove with Mark Twain. It was my turn to close the Store, and my book, half read, lay on the candy counter. Since the weather was going to be bad I was sure Uncle Willie would agree, in fact, encourage, me to close early (save electricity) and join the family in Momma's bedroom, which functioned as our sitting room. Few people would be out in weather that threatened a tornado (for though the wind blew, the sky was as clear and still as a summer morning). Momma agreed that I might as well close, and I went out on the porch, closed the shutters, slipped the wooden bar over the door and turned off the light.

Pots rattled in the kitchen where Momma was frying corn cakes to go with vegetable soup for supper, and the homey sounds and scents cushioned me as I read of Jane Eyre in the cold English mansion of a colder English gentleman. Uncle Willie was engrossed in the *Almanac*, his nightly reading, and my brother was far away on a raft on the Mississippi.

I was the first to hear the rattle on the back door. A rattle and knock, a knock and rattle. But suspecting that it might have been the mad wife in the tower, I didn't credit it. Then Uncle Willie heard it and summoned Bailey back from Huck Finn to unlatch the bolt.

Through the open door the moonshine fell into the room in a cold radiance to rival our meager lamplight. We all waited—I with a dread expectancy—for no human being was there. The wind alone came in, struggling with the weak flame in the coal-oil lamp. Pushing and bunting about the family warmth of our pot-bellied stove. Uncle Willie thought it must have been the storm and told Bailey to close the door. But just before he secured the raw wooden slab a voice drifted through the crack; it wheezed, "Sister Henderson? Brother Willie?"

Bailey nearly closed the door again, but Uncle Willie asked, "Who is it?" and Mr. George Taylor's pinched brown face swam out of the gray and into view. He assured himself that we hadn't gone to bed, and was welcomed in. When Momma saw him she invited him to stay for supper and told me to stick some sweet potatoes in the ashes to stretch the evening meal. Poor Brother Taylor had been taking meals all over town, ever since he buried his wife in the summer. Maybe due to the fact that I was in my romanticist period, or because children have a built-in survival apparatus, I feared he was interested in marrying Momma and moving in with us.

Uncle Willie cradled the *Almanac* in his divided lap. "You welcome here anytime, Brother Taylor, anytime, but this is a bad night. It say right here"—with his crippled hand he rapped the *Almanac*—"that November twelfth, a storm going to be moving over Stamps out of the east. A rough night." Mr. Taylor remained exactly in the same position he had taken when he arrived, like a person too cold to readjust his body even to get closer to the fire. His neck was bent and the red light played over the polished skin of his hairless head. But his eyes bound me with a unique attraction. They sat deep in his little face and completely dominated the other features with a roundness which seemed to be outlined in dark pencil, giving him an owlish appearance. And when he sensed my regarding him so steadily his head hardly moved but his eyes swirled and landed on me. If his look had contained contempt or patronage, or any of the vulgar emotions revealed by adults in confrontation with children, I would have easily gone back to my book, but his eyes gave off a watery nothing—a nothingness which was completely unbearable. I saw a glassiness, observed before only in new marbles or a bottle top embedded in a block of ice. His glance moved so swiftly from me it was nearly possible to imagine that I had in fact imagined the interchange.

"But, as I say, you welcome. We can always make a place under this roof." Uncle Willie didn't seem to notice that Mr. Taylor was oblivious to everything he said. Momma brought the soup into the room, took the kettle off the heater and placed the steaming pot on the fire. Uncle Willie continued, "Momma, I told Brother Taylor he is welcome here anytime." Momma said, "That's right, Brother Taylor. You not supposed to sit around that lonely house feeling sorry for yourself. The Lord giveth and the Lord taketh away."

I'm not sure whether it was Momma's presence or the bubbling soup on the stove which influenced him, but Mr. Taylor appeared to have livened up considerably. He shook his shoulders as if shaking off a tiresome touch, and attempted a smile that failed. "Sister Henderson, I sure appreciate…I mean, I don't know what I'd do if it wasn't for everybody…I mean, you don't know what it's worth to me to be able to…Well, I mean I'm thankful." At each pause, he pecked his head over his chest like a turtle coming out of its shell, but his eyes didn't move.

Momma, always self-conscious at public displays of emotions not traceable to a religious source, told me to come with her and we'd bring the bread and bowls. She carried the food and I trailed after her, bringing the kerosene lamp. The new light set the room in an eerie, harsh perspective. Bailey still sat, doubled over his book, a Black hunchbacked gnome. A finger forerunning his eyes along the page. Uncle Willie and Mr. Taylor were frozen like people in a book on the history of the American Negro.

"Now, come on, Brother Taylor." Momma was pressing a bowl of soup on him. "You may not be hungry, but take this for nourishment."

Her voice had the tender concern of a healthy person speaking to an invalid, and her plain statement rang thrillingly true: "I'm thankful." Bailey came out of his absorption and went to wash his hands.

"Willie, say the blessing." Momma set Bailey's bowl down and bowed her head. During grace, Bailey stood in the doorway, a figure of obedience, but I knew his mind was on Tom Sawyer and Jim as mine would have been on Jane Eyre and Mr. Rochester, but for the glittering eyes of wizened old Mr. Taylor.

Our guest dutifully took a few spoonfuls of soup and bit a semicircle in the bread, then put his bowl on the floor. Something in the fire held his attention as we ate noisily.

Noticing his withdrawal, Momma said, "It don't do for you to take on so, I know you all was together a long time—"

Uncle Willie said, "Forty years."

"—but it's been around six months since she's gone to her rest... and you got to keep faith. He never gives us more than we can bear." The statement heartened Mr. Taylor. He picked up his bowl again and raked his spoon through the thick soup.

Momma saw that she had made some contact, so she went on, "You had a whole lot of good years. Got to be grateful for them. Only thing is, it's a pity you all didn't have some children."

If my head had been down I would have missed Mr. Taylor's metamorphosis. It was not a change that came by steps but rather, it seemed to me, of a sudden. His bowl was on the floor with a thud, and his body leaned toward Momma from the hips. However, his face was the most striking feature of all. The brown expanse seemed to darken with life, as if an inner agitation played under his thin skin. The mouth, opened to show the long teeth, was a dark room furnished with a few white chairs.

"Children." He gum-balled the word around in his empty mouth. "Yes, sir, children." Bailey (and I), used to be addressed so, looked at him expectantly.

"That's what she want." His eyes were vital, and straining to jump from the imprisoning sockets. "That's what she said. Children."

The air was weighted and thick. A bigger house had been set on our roof and was imperceptibly pushing us into the ground.

Momma asked, in her nice-folks voice, "What who said, Brother Taylor?" She knew the answer. We all knew the answer.

"Florida." His little wrinkled hands were making fists, then straightening, then making fists again. "She said it just last night."

Bailey and I looked at each other and I hunched my chair closer to him. "Said 'I want some children.'" When he pitched his already high voice to what he considered a feminine level, or at any rate to his wife's, Miz Florida's, level, it streaked across the room, zigzagging like lightning.

Uncle Willie had stopped eating and was regarding him with something like pity. "Maybe you was dreaming, Brother Taylor. Could have been a dream."

Momma came in placatingly. "That's right. You know, the children was reading me something th'other day. Say folks dream about whatever was on their mind when they went to sleep."

Mr. Taylor jerked himself up. "It wasn't not no dream. I was as wide awake as I am this very minute." He was angry and the tension increased his little mask of strength.

"I'll tell you what happened."

Oh, Lord, a ghost story. I hated and dreaded the long winter nights when late customers came to the Store to sit around the heater roasting peanuts and trying to best each other in telling lurid tales of ghosts and hants, banshees and juju, voodoo and other anti-life stories. But a real one, that happened to a real person, and last night. It was going to be intolerable. I got up and walked to the window.

———

Mrs. Florida Taylor's funeral in June came on the heels of our final exams. Bailey and Louise and I had done very well and were pleased with ourselves and each other. The summer stretched golden in front of us with promises of picnics and fish frys, blackberry hunts and croquet games till dark. It would have taken a personal loss to penetrate my sense of well-being. I had met and loved the Brontë sisters, and had replaced Kipling's "If" with "Invictus." My friendship with Louise was solidified over jacks, hopscotch and confessions, deep and dark, exchanged often after many a "Cross your heart you won't tell?" I never talked about St. Louis to her, and had generally come to believe that the nightmare with its attendant guilt and fear hadn't really happened to me. It happened to a nasty little girl, years and years before, who had no chain on me at all.

At first the news that Mrs. Taylor was dead did not strike me as a particularly newsy bit of information. As children do, I thought that since she was very old she had only one thing to do, and that was to die. She was a pleasant enough woman, with her steps made mincing by age and her little hands like gentle claws that liked to touch young skin. Each time she came to the Store, I was forced to go up to her, while she raked her yellow nails down my cheeks. "You sure got a pretty complexion." It was a rare compliment in a world of very few such words of praise, so it balanced being touched by the dry fingers.

"You going to the funeral, Sister." Momma wasn't asking a question.

Momma said, "You going 'cause Sister Taylor thought so much of you she left you her yellow brooch." (She wouldn't say "gold," because it wasn't.) "She told Brother Taylor, 'I want Sis Henderson's grandbaby to have my gold brooch.' So you'll have to go."

I had followed a few coffins up the hill from the church to the cemetery, but because Momma said I was tender-hearted I had never been forced to sit through a funeral service. At eleven years old, death is more unreal than frightening. It seemed a waste of a good afternoon to sit in church for a silly old brooch, which was not only not gold but was too old for me to wear. But if Momma said I had to go it was certain that I would be there.

The mourners on the front benches sat in a blue-serge, black-crepe-dress gloom. A funeral hymn made its way around the church tediously but successfully. It eased into the heart of every gay thought, into the care of each happy memory. Shattering the light and hopeful: "On the other side of Jordan, there is a peace for the weary, there is a peace for me." The inevitable destination of all living things seemed but a short step away. I had never considered before that dying, death, dead, passed away, were words and phrases that might be even faintly connected with me.

But on that onerous day, oppressed beyond relief, my own mortality was borne in upon me on sluggish tides of doom.

No sooner had the mournful song run its course than the minister took to the altar and delivered a sermon that in my state gave little comfort. Its subject was, "Thou art my good and faithful servant with whom I am well pleased." His voice enweaved itself through the somber vapors left by the dirge. In a monotonous tone he warned the listeners that "this day might be your last," and the best insurance against dying a sinner was to "make yourself right with God" so that on the fateful day He would say, "Thou art my good and faithful servant with whom I am well pleased."

After he had put the fear of the cold grave under our skins, he began to speak of Mrs. Taylor, "A godly woman, who gave to the poor, visited the sick, tithed to the church and in general lived a life of goodliness." At this point he began to talk directly to the coffin, which I had noticed upon my arrival and had studiously avoided thereafter.

"I hungered and you gave me to eat. I was thirsty and you gave me to drink. I was sick and you visited me. In prison, and you left me not. Inasmuch as you have done it unto the least of one of these, you have done it unto Me." He bounded off the dais and approached the velvet gray box. With an imperious gesture, he snatched the gray cloth off the open flap and gazed downward into the mystery.

"Sleep on, thy graceful soul, till Christ calls you to come forth into His bright heaven."

He continued speaking directly to the dead woman, and I half wished she would rise up and answer him, offended by the coarseness of his approach. A scream burst from Mr. Taylor. He stood up suddenly and lengthened his arms toward the minister, the coffin and his wife's corpse. For a long minute he hovered, his back to the church as the instructive words kept falling around the room, rich with promise, full with warnings. Momma and other ladies caught him in time to bring him back to the bench, where he quickly folded upon himself like a Br'er Rabbit rag doll.

Mr. Taylor and the high church officials were the first to file around the bier to wave farewell to the departed and get a glimpse of what lay in store for all men. Then on heavy feet, made more ponderous by the guilt of the living viewing the dead, the adult church marched up to the coffin and back to their seats. Their faces, which showed apprehension before reaching the coffin, revealed, on the way down the opposite aisle, a final confirmation of their fears. Watching them was a little like peeping through a window when the shade is not drawn flush. Although I didn't try, it was impossible not to record their roles in the drama.

And then a black-dressed usher stuck her hand out woodenly toward the children's rows. There was the shifty rustling of unreadiness but finally a boy of fourteen led us off and I dared not hang back, as much as I hated the idea of seeing Mrs. Taylor. Up the aisle, the moans and screams merged with the sickening smell of woolen black clothes worn in summer weather and green leaves wilting over yellow flowers. I couldn't distinguish whether I was smelling the clutching sound of misery or hearing the cloying odor of death.

It would have been easier to see her through the gauze, but instead I looked down on the stark face that seemed suddenly so empty and evil. It knew secrets that I never wanted to share. The cheeks had fallen back to the ears and a solicitous mortician had put lipstick on the black mouth. The scent of decay was sweet and clasping. It groped for life with a hunger both greedy and hateful. But it was hypnotic. I wanted to be off but my shoes had glued themselves to the floor and I had to hold on to the sides of the coffin to remain standing. The unexpected halt in the moving line caused the children to press upon each other, and whispers of no small intent reached my ears.

"Move along, Sister, move along." It was Momma. Her voice tugged at my will and someone pushed from the rear, so I was freed.

Instantly I surrendered myself to the grimness of death. The change it had been able to effect in Mrs. Taylor showed that its strength could not be resisted. Her high-pitched voice, which parted the air in the Store, was forever stilled, and the plump brown face had been deflated and patted flat like a cow's ordurous dropping.

The coffin was carried on a horse-drawn wagon to the cemetery, and all the way I communed with death's angels, questioning their choice of time, place and person.

For the first time the burial ceremony had meaning for me.

"Ashes to ashes and dust to dust." It was certain that Mrs. Taylor was returning to the earth from whence she came. In fact, upon considering, I concluded that she had looked like a mud baby, lying on the white satin of her velvet coffin. A mud baby, molded into form by creative children on a rainy day, soon to run back into the loose earth.

———

The memory of the grim ceremony had been so real to me that I was surprised to look up and see Momma and Uncle Willie eating by the stove. They were neither anxious nor hesitant, as if they knew a man has to say what he has to say. But I didn't want to hear any of it, and the wind, allying itself with me, threatened the chinaberry tree outside the back door.

"Last night, after I said my prayers, I lay down on the bed. Well, you know it's the same bed she died on." Oh, if he'd shut up. Momma said, "Sister, sit down and eat your soup. Cold night like this you need something hot in your stomach. Go on, Brother Taylor. Please." I sat down as near Bailey as possible.

"Well, something told me to open my eyes."

"What kind of something?" Momma asked, not laying down her spoon.

"Yes, sir," Uncle Willie explained, "there can be a good something and there can be a bad something."

"Well, I wasn't sure, so I figured better open 'em, 'cause it could have been, well, either one. I did, and the first thing, I saw little baby angel. It was just as fat as a butterball, and laughing, eyes blue, blue, blue."

Uncle Willie asked, "A baby angel?"

"Yes, sir, and it was laughing right in my face. Then I heard this long moan, 'Agh-h-h-' Well, as you say, Sister Henderson, we been together over forty years. I know Florida's voice. I wasn't scared right then. I called 'Florida?' Then that angel laughed harder and the moan got louder."

I set my bowl down and got closer to Bailey. Mrs. Taylor had been a very pleasant woman, smiling all the time and patient. The only thing that jarred and bothered me when she came in the Store was her voice. Like near-deaf people, she screamed, half not hearing what she was saying and partly hoping her listeners would reply in kind. That was when she was living. The thought of that voice coming out of the grave and all the way down the hill from the cemetery and hanging over my head was enough to straighten my hair.

"Yes, sir." He was looking at the stove and the red glow fell on his face. It seemed as if he had a fire going inside his head. "First I called, 'Florida, Florida. What do you want?' And that devilish angel kept on laughing to beat the band." Mr. Taylor tried to laugh and only succeeded in looking frightened. " 'I want some...' That's when she said 'I want some.' " He made his voice sound like the wind, if the wind had bronchial pneumonia. He wheezed, " 'I want some chi-il-dren.' "

Bailey and I met halfway on the drafty floor.

Momma said, "Now, Brother Taylor, could be you was dreaming. You know, they say whatever you goes to bed with on your mind..."

"No, ma'am, Sister Henderson, I was as wide awake as I am right now."

"Did she let you see her?" Uncle Willie had a dreamy look on his face.

"No, Willie, all I seed was that fat little white baby angel. But wasn't no mistaking that voice... 'I want some children.' "

The cold wind had frozen my feet and my spine, and Mr. Taylor's impersonation had chilled my blood.

Momma said, "Sister, go bring the long fork to take the potatoes out."

"Ma'am?" Surely she didn't mean the long fork that hung on the wall behind the kitchen stove—a scary million miles away.

"I said, go get the fork. The potatoes are burning."

I unwound my legs from the gripping fear and almost tripped onto the stove. Momma said, "That child would stumble over the pattern in a rug. Go on, Brother Taylor, did she say any more?"

I didn't want to hear it if she did, but I wasn't eager to leave the lighted room where my family sat around the friendly fire.

"Well, she said 'Aaah' a few more times and then that angel started to walk off the ceiling. I tell you I was purt' near scared stiff."

I had reached the no man's ocean of darkness. No great decision was called for. I knew it would be torturous to go through the thick blackness of Uncle Willie's bedroom, but it would be easier than staying around to hear the ghoulish story. Also, I couldn't afford to aggravate Momma. When she was displeased she made me sleep on the edge of the bed and that night I knew I needed to be close to her.

One foot into the darkness and the sense of detachment from reality nearly made me panic. The idea came to me that I might never get out into the light again. Quickly I found the door leading back to the familiar, but as I opened it the awful story reached out and tried to grab my ears. I closed the door.

Naturally, I believed in hants and ghosts and "thangs." Having been raised by a super-religious Southern Negro grandmother, it would have been abnormal had I not been superstitious.

The trip to the kitchen and back could not have taken more than two minutes, yet in that time I tramped through swampy cemeteries, climbed over dusty gravestones and eluded litters of night-black cats.

Back in the family circle, I remarked to myself how like a cyclopean eye was the belly of the red-hot stove.

"It reminded me of the time when my daddy died. You know we're very close." Mr. Taylor had hypnotized himself into the eerie world of horrors.

I broke into his reminiscences. "Momma, here's the fork." Bailey had lain down on his side behind the stove and his eyes were shining. He was more fascinated with Mr. Taylor's morbid interest in his story than with the tale itself.

Momma put her hand on my arm and said, "You shaking, Sister. What's the matter?" My skin still rippled from the experience of fear.

Uncle Willie laughed and said, "Maybe she was scared to go in the kitchen."

His high little laugh didn't fool me. Everyone was uneasy at being beckoned into the unknown.

"No sir, I ain't never seen nothing so clear as that little angel baby." His jaws were scissoring mechanically on the already mushy sweet potatoes. "Just laughing, like a house on fire. What you reckon it mean, Sister Henderson?"

Momma had reared back in her rocking chair, a half smile on her face, "If you sure you wasn't dreaming, Brother Taylor..."

"I was as wide awake as I am"—he was becoming angry again—"as I am right now."

"Well, then, maybe it means—"

"I ought to know when I'm asleep and when I'm awake."

"—maybe it mean Sister Florida wants you to work with the children in the church."

"One thing I always used to tell Florida, people won't let you get your words in edgewise—"

"Could be she's trying to tell you—"

"I ain't crazy, you know. My mind's just as good as it was."

"—to take a Sunday school class—"

"Thirty years ago. If I say I was awake when I saw that little fat angel, then people ought to—"

"Sunday school need more teachers. Lord knows that's so."

"—believe me when I say so."

Their remarks and responses were like a Ping-Pong game with each volley clearing the net and flying back to the opposition. The sense of what they were saying became lost, and only the exercise remained. The exchange was conducted with the certainty of a measured hoedown and had the jerkiness of Monday's wash snapping in the wind—now cracking east, then west, with only the intent to whip the dampness out of the cloth.

Within a few minutes the intoxication of doom had fled, as if it had never been, and Momma was encouraging Mr. Taylor to take in one of the Jenkins boys to help him with his farm. Uncle Willie was nodding at the fire, and Bailey had escaped back to the calm adventures of Huckleberry Finn. The change in the room was remarkable. Shadows which had lengthened and darkened over the bed in the corner had disappeared or revealed themselves as dark images of familiar chairs and such. The light which dashed on the ceiling steadied, and imitated rabbits rather than lions, and donkeys instead of ghouls.

I laid a pallet for Mr. Taylor in Uncle Willie's room and crawled under Momma, who I knew for the first time was so good and righteous she could command the fretful spirits, as Jesus had commanded the sea. "Peace, be still."

CHAPTER 23

The children in Stamps trembled visibly with anticipation. Some adults were excited too, but to be certain the whole young population had come down with graduation epidemic. Large classes were graduating from both the grammar school and the high school. Even those who were years removed from their own day of glorious release were anxious to help with preparations as a kind of dry run. The junior students who were moving into the vacating classes' chairs were tradition-bound to show their talents for leadership and management. They strutted through the school and around the campus exerting pressure on the lower grades. Their authority was so new that occasionally if they pressed a little too hard it had to be overlooked. After all, next term was coming, and it never hurt a sixth grader to have a play sister in the eighth grade, or a tenth-year student to be able to call a twelfth grader Bubba. So all was endured in a spirit of shared understanding. But the graduating classes themselves were the nobility. Like travelers with exotic destinations on their minds, the graduates were remarkably forgetful. They came to school without their books, or tablets or even pencils. Volunteers fell over themselves to secure replacements for the missing equipment. When accepted, the willing workers might or might not be thanked, and it was of no importance to the pregraduation rites. Even teachers were respectful of the now quiet and aging seniors, and tended to speak to them, if not as equals, as beings only slightly lower than themselves. After tests were returned and grades given, the student body, which acted like an extended family, knew who did well, who excelled, and what piteous ones had failed.

Unlike the white high school, Lafayette County Training School distinguished itself by having neither lawn, nor hedges, nor tennis court, nor climbing ivy. Its two buildings (main classrooms, the grade school and home economics) were set on a dirt hill with no fence to limit either its boundaries or those of bordering farms. There was a large expanse to the left of the school which was used alternately as a baseball diamond or a basketball court. Rusty hoops on the swaying poles represented the permanent recreational equipment, although bats and balls could be borrowed from the P. E. teacher if the borrower was qualified and if the diamond wasn't occupied.

Over this rocky area relieved by a few shady tall persimmon trees the graduating class walked. The girls often held hands and no longer bothered to speak to the lower students. There was a sadness about them, as if this old world was not their home and they were bound for higher ground. The boys, on the other hand, had become more friendly, more outgoing. A decided change from the closed attitude they projected while studying for finals. Now they seemed not ready to give up the old school, the familiar paths and classrooms. Only a small percentage would be continuing on to college—one of the South's A & M (agricultural and mechanical) schools, which trained Negro youths to be carpenters, farmers, handymen, masons, maids, cooks and baby nurses. Their future rode heavily on their shoulders, and blinded them to the collective joy that had pervaded the lives of the boys and girls in the grammar school graduating class.

Parents who could afford it had ordered new shoes and ready-made clothes for themselves from Sears and Roebuck or Montgomery Ward. They also engaged the best seamstresses to make the floating graduating dresses and to cut down secondhand pants which would be pressed to a military slickness for the important event.

Oh, it was important, all right. Whitefolks would attend the ceremony, and two or three would speak of God and home, and the Southern way of life, and Mrs. Parsons, the principal's wife, would play the graduation march while the lower-grade graduates paraded down the aisles and took their seats below the platform. The high school seniors would wait in empty classrooms to make their dramatic entrance.

In the Store I was the person of the moment. The birthday girl. The center. Bailey had graduated the year before, although to do so he had had to forfeit all pleasures to make up for his time lost in Baton Rouge.

My class was wearing butter-yellow piqué dresses, and Momma launched out on mine. She smocked the yoke into tiny crisscrossing puckers, then shirred the rest of the bodice. Her dark fingers ducked in and out of the lemony cloth as she embroidered raised daisies around the hem. Before she considered herself finished she had added a crocheted cuff on the puff sleeves, and a pointy crocheted collar.

I was going to be lovely. A walking model of all the various styles of fine hand sewing and it didn't worry me that I was only twelve years old and merely graduating from the eighth grade. Besides, many teachers in Arkansas Negro schools had only that diploma and were licensed to impart wisdom.

The days had become longer and more noticeable. The faded beige of former times had been replaced with strong and sure colors. I began to see my classmates' clothes, their skin tones, and the dust that waved off pussy willows. Clouds that lazed across the sky were objects of great concern to me. Their shiftier shapes might have held a message that in my new happiness and with a little bit of time I'd soon decipher. During that period I looked at the arch of heaven so religiously my neck kept a steady ache. I had taken to smiling more often, and my jaws hurt from the unaccustomed activity. Between the two physical sore spots, I suppose I could have been uncomfortable, but that was not the case. As a member of the winning team (the graduating class of 1940) I had outdistanced unpleasant sensations by miles. I was headed for the freedom of open fields.

Youth and social approval allied themselves with me and we trammeled memories of slights and insults. The wind of our swift passage remodeled my features. Lost tears were pounded to mud and then to dust. Years of withdrawal were brushed aside and left behind, as hanging ropes of parasitic moss.

My work alone had awarded me a top place and I was going to be one of the first called in the graduating ceremonies. On the classroom blackboard, as well as on the bulletin board in the auditorium, there were blue stars and white stars and red stars. No absences, no tardinesses, and my academic work was among the best of the year. I could say the preamble to the Constitution even faster than Bailey. We timed ourselves often: "WethepeopleoftheUnitedStatesinorderto formamoreperfectunion..." I had memorized the Presidents of the United States from Washington to Roosevelt in chronological as well as alphabetical order.

My hair pleased me too. Gradually the black mass had lengthened and thickened, so that it kept at last to its braided pattern, and I didn't have to yank my scalp off when I tried to comb it.

Louise and I had rehearsed the exercises until we tired out ourselves. Henry Reed was class valedictorian. He was a small, very black boy with hooded eyes, a long, broad nose and an oddly shaped head. I had admired him for years because each term he and I vied for the best grades in our class. Most often he bested me, but instead of being disappointed I was pleased that we shared top places between us. Like many Southern Black children, he lived with his grandmother, who was as strict as Momma and as kind as she knew how to be. He was courteous, respectful and soft-spoken to elders, but on the playground he chose to play the roughest games. I admired him. Anyone, I reckoned, sufficiently afraid or sufficiently dull could be polite. But to be able to operate at a top level with both adults and children was admirable.

His valedictory speech was entitled "To Be or Not to Be." The rigid tenth-grade teacher had helped him write it. He'd been working on the dramatic stresses for months.

The weeks until graduation were filled with heady activities. A group of small children were to be presented in a play about buttercups and daisies and bunny rabbits. They could be heard throughout the building practicing their hops and their little songs that sounded like silver bells. The older girls (nongraduates, of course) were assigned the task of making refreshments for the night's festivities. A tangy scent of ginger, cinnamon, nutmeg and chocolate wafted around the home economics building as the budding cooks made samples for themselves and their teachers.

In every corner of the workshop, axes and saws split fresh timber as the woodshop boys made sets and stage scenery. Only the graduates were left out of the general bustle. We were free to sit in the library at the back of the building or look in quite detachedly, naturally, on the measures being taken for our event.

Even the minister preached on graduation the Sunday before. His subject was, "Let your light so shine that men will see your good works and praise your Father, Who is in Heaven." Although the sermon was purported to be addressed to us, he used the occasion to speak to backsliders, gamblers and general ne'er-do-wells. But since he had called our names at the beginning of the service we were mollified.

Among Negroes the tradition was to give presents to children going only from one grade to another. How much more important this was when the person was graduating at the top of the class. Uncle Willie and Momma had sent away for a Mickey Mouse watch like Bailey's. Louise gave me four embroidered handkerchiefs. (I gave her three crocheted doilies.) Mrs. Sneed, the minister's wife, made me an underskirt to wear for graduation, and nearly every customer gave me a nickel or maybe even a dime with the instruction "Keep on moving to higher ground," or some such encouragement.

Amazingly the great day finally dawned and I was out of bed before I knew it. I threw open the back door to see it more clearly, but Momma said, "Sister, come away from that door and put your robe on."

I hoped the memory of that morning would never leave me. Sunlight was itself still young, and the day had none of the insistence maturity would bring it in a few hours. In my robe and barefoot in the backyard, under cover of going to see about my new beans, I gave myself up to the gentle warmth and thanked God that no matter what evil I had done in my life He had allowed me to live to see this day. Somewhere in my fatalism I had expected to die, accidentally, and never have the chance to walk up the stairs in the auditorium and gracefully receive my hard-earned diploma. Out of God's merciful bosom I had won reprieve.

Bailey came out in his robe and gave me a box wrapped in Christmas paper. He said he had saved his money for months to pay for it. It felt like a box of chocolates, but I knew Bailey wouldn't save money to buy candy when we had all we could want under our noses.

He was as proud of the gift as I. It was a soft-leather-bound copy of a collection of poems by Edgar Allan Poe, or, as Bailey and I called him, "Eap." I turned to "Annabel Lee" and we walked up and down the garden rows, the cool dirt between our toes, reciting the beautifully sad lines.

Momma made a Sunday breakfast although it was only Friday. After we finished the blessing, I opened my eyes to find the watch on my plate. It was a dream of a day. Everything went smoothly and to my credit. I didn't have to be reminded or scolded for anything. Near evening I was too jittery to attend to chores, so Bailey volunteered to do all before his bath.

Days before, we had made a sign for the Store, and as we turned out the lights Momma hung the cardboard over the doorknob. It read clearly: CLOSED. GRADUATION.

My dress fitted perfectly and everyone said that I looked like a sunbeam in it. On the hill, going toward the school, Bailey walked behind with Uncle Willie, who muttered, "Go on, Ju." He wanted him to walk ahead with us because it embarrassed him to have to walk so slowly. Bailey said he'd let the ladies walk together, and the men would bring up the rear. We all laughed, nicely.

Little children dashed by out of the dark like fireflies. Their crepe-paper dresses and butterfly wings were not made for running and we heard more than one rip, dryly, and the regretful "uh uh" that followed.

The school blazed without gaiety. The windows seemed cold and unfriendly from the lower hill. A sense of ill-fated timing crept over me, and if Momma hadn't reached for my hand I would have drifted back to Bailey and Uncle Willie, and possibly beyond. She made a few slow jokes about my feet getting cold, and tugged me along to the now-strange building.

Around the front steps, assurance came back. There were my fellow "greats," the graduating class. Hair brushed back, legs oiled, new dresses and pressed pleats, fresh pocket handkerchiefs and little handbags, all homesewn. Oh, we were up to snuff, all right. I joined my comrades and didn't even see my family go in to find seats in the crowded auditorium.

The school band struck up a march and all classes filed in as had been rehearsed. We stood in front of our seats, as assigned, and on a signal from the choir director, we sat. No sooner had this been accomplished than the band started to play the national anthem. We rose again and sang the song, after which we recited the pledge of allegiance. We remained standing for a brief minute before the choir director and the principal signaled to us, rather desperately I thought, to take our seats. The command was so unusual that our carefully rehearsed and smooth-running machine was thrown off. For a full minute we fumbled for our chairs and bumped into each other awkwardly. Habits change or solidify under pressure, so in our state of nervous tension we had been ready to follow our usual assembly pattern: the American national anthem, then the pledge of allegiance, then the song every Black person I knew called the Negro National Anthem. All done in the same key, with the same passion and most often standing on the same foot.

Finding my seat at last, I was overcome with a presentiment of worse things to come. Something unrehearsed, unplanned, was going to happen, and we were going to be made to look bad. I distinctly remember being explicit in the choice of pronoun. It was "we," the graduating class, the unit, that concerned me then.

The principal welcomed "parents and friends" and asked the Baptist minister to lead us in prayer. His invocation was brief and punchy, and for a second I thought we were getting back on the high road to right action. When the principal came back to the dais, however, his voice had changed. Sounds always affected me profoundly and the principal's voice was one of my favorites. During assembly it melted and lowed weakly into the audience. It had not been in my plan to listen to him, but my curiosity was piqued and I straightened up to give him my attention.

He was talking about Booker T. Washington, our "late great leader," who said we can be as close as the fingers on the hand, etc.... Then he said a few vague things about friendship and the friendship of kindly people to those less fortunate than themselves. With that his voice nearly faded, thin, away. Like a river diminishing to a stream and then to a trickle. But he cleared his throat and said, "Our speaker tonight, who is also our friend, came from Texarkana to deliver the commencement address, but due to the irregularity of the train schedule, he's going to, as they say, 'speak and run.' " He said that we understood and wanted the man to know that we were most grateful for the time he was able to give us and then something about how we were willing always to adjust to another's program, and without more ado—"I give you Mr. Edward Donleavy."

Not one but two white men came through the door offstage. The shorter one walked to the speaker's platform, and the tall one moved over to the center seat and sat down. But that was our principal's seat, and already occupied. The dislodged gentleman bounced around for a long breath or two before the Baptist minister gave him his chair, then with more dignity than the situation deserved, the minister walked off the stage.

Donleavy looked at the audience once (on reflection, I'm sure that he wanted only to reassure himself that we were really there), adjusted his glasses and began to read from a sheaf of papers.

He was glad "to be here and to see the work going on just as it was in the other schools."

At the first "Amen" from the audience I willed the offender to immediate death by choking on the word. But Amens and Yes, sir's began to fall around the room like rain through a ragged umbrella.

He told us of the wonderful changes we children in Stamps had in store. The Central School (naturally, the white school was Central) had already been granted improvements that would be in use in the fall. A well-known artist was coming from Little Rock to teach art to them. They were going to have the newest microscopes and chemistry equipment for their laboratory. Mr. Donleavy didn't leave us long in the dark over who made these improvements available to Central High. Nor were we to be ignored in the general betterment scheme he had in mind.

He said that he had pointed out to people at a very high level that one of the first-line football tacklers at Arkansas Agricultural and Mechanical College had graduated from good old Lafayette County Training School. Here fewer Amen's were heard. Those few that did break through lay dully in the air with the heaviness of habit.

He went on to praise us. He went on to say how he had bragged that "one of the best basketball players at Fisk sank his first ball right here at Lafayette County Training School."

The white kids were going to have a chance to become Galileos and Madame Curies and Edisons and Gauguins, and our boys (the girls weren't even in on it) would try to be Jesse Owenses and Joe Louises.

Owens and the Brown Bomber were great heroes in our world, but what school official in the white-goddom of Little Rock had the right to decide that those two men must be our only heroes? Who decided that for Henry Reed to become a scientist he had to work like George Washington Carver, as a bootblack, to buy a lousy microscope? Bailey was obviously always going to be too small to be an athlete, so which concrete angel glued to what country seat had decided that if my brother wanted to become a lawyer he had to first pay penance for his skin by picking cotton and hoeing corn and studying correspondence books at night for twenty years?

The man's dead words fell like bricks around the auditorium and too many settled in my belly. Constrained by hard-learned manners I couldn't look behind me, but to my left and right the proud graduating class of 1940 had dropped their heads. Every girl in my row had found something new to do with her handkerchief. Some folded the tiny squares into love knots, some into triangles, but most were wadding them, then pressing them flat on their yellow laps.

On the dais, the ancient tragedy was being replayed. Professor Parsons sat, a sculptor's reject, rigid. His large, heavy body seemed devoid of will or willingness, and his eyes said he was no longer with us. The other teachers examined the flag (which was draped stage right) or their notes, or the windows which opened on our now-famous playing diamond.

Graduation, the hush-hush magic time of frills and gifts and congratulations and diplomas, was finished for me before my name was called. The accomplishment was nothing. The meticulous maps, drawn in three colors of ink, learning and spelling decasyllabic words, memorizing the whole of *The Rape of Lucrece*—it was for nothing. Donleavy had exposed us.

We were maids and farmers, handymen and washerwomen, and anything higher that we aspired to was farcical and presumptuous.

Then I wished that Gabriel Prosser and Nat Turner had killed all whitefolks in their beds and that Abraham Lincoln had been assassinated before the signing of the Emancipation Proclamation, and that Harriet Tubman had been killed by that blow on her head and Christopher Columbus had drowned in the *Santa María*.

It was awful to be Negro and have no control over my life. It was brutal to be young and already trained to sit quietly and listen to charges brought against my color with no chance of defense. We should all be dead. I thought I should like to see us all dead, one on top of the other. A pyramid of flesh with the whitefolks on the bottom, as the broad base, then the Indians with their silly tomahawks and teepees and wigwams and treaties, the Negroes with their mops and recipes and cotton sacks and spirituals sticking out of their mouths. The Dutch children should all stumble in their wooden shoes and break their necks. The French should choke to death on the Louisiana Purchase (1803) while silkworms ate all the Chinese with their stupid pigtails. As a species, we were an abomination. All of us.

Donleavy was running for election, and assured our parents that if he won we could count on having the only colored paved playing field in that part of Arkansas. Also—he never looked up to acknowledge the grunts of acceptance—also, we were bound to get some new equipment for the home economics building and the workshop.

He finished, and since there was no need to give any more than the most perfunctory thank-you's, he nodded to the men on the stage, and the tall white man who was never introduced joined him at the door. They left with the attitude that now they were off to something really important. (The graduation ceremonies at Lafayette County Training School had been a mere preliminary.)

The ugliness they left was palpable. An uninvited guest who wouldn't leave. The choir was summoned and sang a modern arrangement of "Onward, Christian Soldiers," with new words pertaining to graduates seeking their place in the world. But it didn't work. Elouise, the daughter of the Baptist minister, recited "Invictus," and I could have cried at the impertinence of "I am the master of my fate, I am the captain of my soul."

My name had lost its ring of familiarity and I had to be nudged to go and receive my diploma. All my preparations had fled. I neither marched up to the stage like a conquering Amazon, nor did I look in the audience for Bailey's nod of approval. Marguerite Johnson, I heard the name again, my honors were read, there were noises in the audience of appreciation, and I took my place on the stage as rehearsed.

I thought about colors I hated: ecru, puce, lavender, beige and black.

There was shuffling and rustling around me, then Henry Reed was giving his valedictory address, "To Be or Not to Be." Hadn't he heard the whitefolks? We couldn't *be,* so the question was a waste of time. Henry's voice came out clear and strong. I feared to look at him. Hadn't he got the message? There was no "nobler in the mind" for Negroes because the world didn't think we had minds, and they let us know it. "Outrageous fortune"? Now, that was a joke. When the ceremony was over I had to tell Henry Reed some things. That is, if I still cared. Not "rub," Henry, "erase." "Ah, there's the erase." Us.

Henry had been a good student in elocution. His voice rose on tides of promise and fell on waves of warnings. The English teacher had helped him to create a sermon winging through Hamlet's soliloquy. To be a man, a doer, a builder, a leader, or to be a tool, an unfunny joke, a crusher of funky toadstools. I marveled that Henry could go through with the speech as if we had a choice.

I had been listening and silently rebutting each sentence with my eyes closed; then there was a hush, which in an audience warns that something unplanned is happening. I looked up and saw Henry Reed, the conservative, the proper, the A student, turn his back to the audience and turn to us (the proud graduating class of 1940) and sing, nearly speaking,

> "Lift ev'ry voice and sing
> Till earth and heaven ring
> Ring with the harmonies of Liberty…"

It was the poem written by James Weldon Johnson. It was the music composed by J. Rosamond Johnson. It was the Negro national anthem. Out of habit we were singing it.

Our mothers and fathers stood in the dark hall and joined the hymn of encouragement. A kindergarten teacher led the small children onto the stage and the buttercups and daisies and bunny rabbits marked time and tried to follow:

> "Stony the road we trod
> Bitter the chastening rod
> Felt in the days when hope, unborn, had died.
> Yet with a steady beat
> Have not our weary feet
> Come to the place for which our fathers sighed?"

Every child I knew had learned that song with his ABC's and along with "Jesus Loves Me This I Know." But I personally had never heard it before. Never heard the words, despite the thousands of times I had sung them. Never thought they had anything to do with me.

On the other hand, the words of Patrick Henry had made such an impression on me that I had been able to stretch myself tall and trembling and say, "I know not what course others may take, but as for me, give me liberty or give me death."

And now I heard, really for the first time:

> "We have come over a way that with tears
> has been watered,
> We have come, treading our path through
> the blood of the slaughtered."

While echoes of the song shivered in the air, Henry Reed bowed his head, said "Thank you," and returned to his place in the line. The tears that slipped down many faces were not wiped away in shame.

We were on top again. As always, again. We survived. The depths had been icy and dark, but now a bright sun spoke to our souls. I was no longer simply a member of the proud graduating class of 1940; I was a proud member of the wonderful, beautiful Negro race.

Oh, Black known and unknown poets, how often have your auctioned pains sustained us? Who will compute the lonely nights made less lonely by your songs, or the empty pots made less tragic by your tales?

If we were a people much given to revealing secrets, we might raise monuments and sacrifice to the memories of our poets, but slavery cured us of that weakness. It may be enough, however, to have it said that we survive in exact relationship to the dedication of our poets (include preachers, musicians and blues singers).

CHAPTER 24

The Angel of the candy counter had found me out at last, and was exacting excruciating penance for all the stolen Milky Ways, Mounds, Mr. Goodbars and Hersheys with Almonds. I had two cavities that were rotten to the gums. The pain was beyond the bailiwick of crushed aspirins or oil of cloves. Only one thing could help me, so I prayed earnestly that I'd be allowed to sit under the house and have the building collapse on my left jaw. Since there was no Negro dentist in Stamps, nor doctor either, for that matter, Momma had dealt with previous toothaches by pulling them out (a string tied to the tooth with the other end looped over her fist), pain killers and prayer. In this particular instance the medicine had proved ineffective; there wasn't enough enamel left to hook a string on, and the prayers were being ignored because the Balancing Angel was blocking their passage.

I lived a few days and nights in blinding pain, not so much toying with as seriously considering the idea of jumping in the well, and Momma decided I had to be taken to a dentist. The nearest Negro dentist was in Texarkana, twenty-five miles away, and I was certain that I'd be dead long before we reached half the distance. Momma said we'd go to Dr. Lincoln, right in Stamps, and he'd take care of me. She said he owed her a favor.

I knew there were a number of whitefolks in town that owed her favors. Bailey and I had seen the books which showed how she had lent money to Blacks and whites alike during the Depression, and most still owed her. But I couldn't aptly remember seeing Dr. Lincoln's name, nor had I ever heard of a Negro's going to him as a patient. However, Momma said we were going, and put water on the stove for our baths. I had never been to a doctor, so she told me that after the bath (which would make my mouth feel better) I had to put on freshly starched and ironed underclothes from inside out. The ache failed to respond to the bath, and I knew then that the pain was more serious than that which anyone had ever suffered.

Before we left the Store, she ordered me to brush my teeth and then wash my mouth with Listerine. The idea of even opening my clamped jaws increased the pain, but upon her explanation that when you go to a doctor you have to clean yourself all over, but most especially the part that's to be examined, I screwed up my courage and unlocked my teeth. The cool air in my mouth and the jarring of my molars dislodged what little remained of my reason. I had frozen to the pain, my family nearly had to tie me down to take the toothbrush away. It was no small effort to get me started on the road to the dentist. Momma spoke to all the passers-by, but didn't stop to chat. She explained over her shoulder that we were going to the doctor and she'd "pass the time of day" on our way home.

Until we reached the pond the pain was my world, an aura that haloed me for three feet around. Crossing the bridge into whitefolks' country, pieces of sanity pushed themselves forward. I had to stop moaning and start walking straight. The white towel, which was drawn under my chin and tied over my head, had to be arranged. If one was dying, it had to be done in style if the dying took place in whitefolks' part of town.

On the other side of the bridge the ache seemed to lessen as if a whitebreeze blew off the whitefolks and cushioned everything in their neighborhood—including my jaw. The gravel road was smoother, the stones smaller and the tree branches hung down around the path and nearly covered us. If the pain didn't diminish then, the familiar yet strange sights hypnotized me into believing that it had.

But my head continued to throb with the measured insistence of a bass drum, and how could a toothache pass the calaboose, hear the songs of the prisoners, their blues and laughter, and not be changed? How could one or two or even a mouthful of angry tooth roots meet a wagonload of powhitetrash children, endure their idiotic snobbery and not feel less important?

Behind the building which housed the dentist's office ran a small path used by servants and those tradespeople who catered to the butcher and Stamps' one restaurant. Momma and I followed that lane to the backstairs of Dentist Lincoln's office. The sun was bright and gave the day a hard reality as we climbed up the steps to the second floor.

Momma knocked on the back door and a young white girl opened it to show surprise at seeing us there. Momma said she wanted to see Dentist Lincoln and to tell him Annie was there. The girl closed the door firmly. Now the humiliation of hearing Momma describe herself as if she had no last name to the young white girl was equal to the physical pain. It seemed terribly unfair to have a toothache and a headache and have to bear at the same time the heavy burden of Blackness.

It was always possible that the teeth would quiet down and maybe drop out of their own accord. Momma said we would wait. We leaned in the harsh sunlight on the shaky railings of the dentist's back porch for over an hour.

He opened the door and looked at Momma. "Well, Annie, what can I do for you?"

He didn't see the towel around my jaw or notice my swollen face.

Momma said, "Dentist Lincoln. It's my grandbaby here. She got two rotten teeth that's giving her a fit."

She waited for him to acknowledge the truth of her statement. He made no comment, orally or facially.

"She had this toothache purt' near four days now, and today I said, 'Young lady, you going to the Dentist.' "

"Annie?"

"Yes, sir, Dentist Lincoln."

He was choosing words the way people hunt for shells. "Annie, you know I don't treat nigra, colored people."

"I know, Dentist Lincoln. But this here is just my little grandbaby, and she ain't gone be no trouble to you..."

"Annie, everybody has a policy. In this world you have to have a policy. Now, my policy is I don't treat colored people."

The sun had baked the oil out of Momma's skin and melted the Vaseline in her hair. She shone greasily as she leaned out of the dentist's shadow.

"Seem like to me, Dentist Lincoln, you might look after her, she ain't nothing but a little mite. And seems like maybe you owe me a favor or two."

He reddened slightly. "Favor or no favor. The money has all been repaid to you and that's the end of it. Sorry, Annie." He had his hand on the doorknob. "Sorry." His voice was a bit kinder on the second "Sorry," as if he really was.

Momma said, "I wouldn't press on you like this for myself but I can't take No. Not for my grandbaby. When you come to borrow my money you didn't have to beg. You asked me, and I lent it. Now, it wasn't my policy. I ain't no moneylender, but you stood to lose this building and I tried to help you out."

"It's been paid, and raising your voice won't make me change my mind. My policy..." He let go of the door and stepped nearer Momma. The three of us were crowded on the small landing. "Annie, my policy is I'd rather stick my hand in a dog's mouth than in a nigger's."

He had never once looked at me. He turned his back and went through the door into the cool beyond. Momma backed up inside herself for a few minutes. I forgot everything except her face which was almost a new one to me. She leaned over and took the doorknob, and in her everyday soft voice she said, "Sister, go on downstairs. Wait for me. I'll be there directly."

Under the most common of circumstances I knew it did no good to argue with Momma. So I walked down the steep stairs, afraid to look back and afraid not to do so. I turned as the door slammed, and she was gone.

Momma walked in that room as if she owned it. She shoved that silly nurse aside with one hand and strode into the dentist's office. He was sitting in his chair, sharpening his mean instruments and putting extra sting into his medicines. Her eyes were blazing like live coals and her arms had doubled themselves in length. He looked up at her just before she caught him by the collar of his white jacket.

"Stand up when you see a lady, you contemptuous scoundrel." Her tongue had thinned and the words rolled off well enunciated. Enunciated and sharp like little claps of thunder.

The dentist had no choice but to stand at R.O.T.C. attention. His head dropped after a minute and his voice was humble. "Yes, ma'am, Mrs. Henderson."

"You knave, do you think you acted like a gentleman, speaking to me like that in front of my granddaughter?" She didn't shake him, although she had the power. She simply held him upright.

"No, ma'am, Mrs. Henderson."

"No, ma'am, Mrs. Henderson, what?" Then she did give him the tiniest of shakes, but because of her strength the action set his head and arms to shaking

loose on the ends of his body. He stuttered much worse than Uncle Willie. "No, ma'am, Mrs. Henderson, I'm sorry."

With just an edge of her disgust showing, Momma slung him back in his dentist's chair. "Sorry is as sorry does, and you're about the sorriest dentist I ever laid my eyes on." (She could afford to slip into the vernacular because she had such eloquent command of English.)

"I didn't ask you to apologize in front of Marguerite, because I don't want her to know my power, but I order you, now and herewith. Leave Stamps by sundown."

"Mrs. Henderson, I can't get my equipment..." He was shaking terribly now.

"Now, that brings me to my second order. You will never again practice dentistry. Never! When you get settled in your next place, you will be a vegetarian caring for dogs with the mange, cats with the cholera and cows with the epizootic. Is that clear?"

The saliva ran down his chin and his eyes filled with tears. "Yes, ma'am. Thank you for not killing me. Thank you, Mrs. Henderson."

Momma pulled herself back from being ten feet tall with eight-foot arms and said, "You're welcome for nothing, you varlet, I wouldn't waste a killing on the likes of you."

On her way out she waved her handkerchief at the nurse and turned her into a crocus sack of chicken feed.

Momma looked tired when she came down the stairs, but who wouldn't be tired if they had gone through what she had. She came close to me and adjusted the towel under my jaw (I had forgotten the toothache; I only knew that she made her hands gentle in order not to awaken the pain). She took my hand. Her voice never changed. "Come on, Sister."

I reckoned we were going home where she would concoct a brew to eliminate the pain and maybe give me new teeth too. New teeth that would grow overnight out of my gums. She led me toward the drugstore, which was in the opposite direction from the Store. "I'm taking you to Dentist Baker in Texarkana."

I was glad after all that that I had bathed and put on Mum and Cashmere Bouquet talcum powder. It was a wonderful surprise. My toothache had quieted to solemn pain, Momma had obliterated the evil white man, and we were going on a trip to Texarkana, just the two of us.

On the Greyhound she took an inside seat in the back, and I sat beside her. I was so proud of being her granddaughter and sure that some of her magic must have come down to me. She asked if I was scared. I only shook my head and leaned over on her cool brown upper arm. There was no chance that a dentist, especially a Negro dentist, would dare hurt me then. Not with Momma there. The trip was uneventful, except that she put her arm around me, which was very unusual for Momma to do.

The dentist showed me the medicine and the needle before he deadened my gums, but if he hadn't I wouldn't have worried. Momma stood right behind him. Her arms were folded and she checked on everything he did. The teeth were extracted and she bought me an ice cream cone from the side window of a drug counter. The trip back to Stamps was quiet, except that I had to spit into a very small empty snuff can which she had gotten for me and it was difficult with the bus humping and jerking on our country roads.

At home, I was given a warm salt solution, and when I washed out my mouth I showed Bailey the empty holes, where the clotted blood sat like filling in a pie crust. He said I was quite brave, and that was my cue to reveal our confrontation with the peckerwood dentist and Momma's incredible powers.

I had to admit that I didn't hear the conversation, but what else could she have said than what I said she said? What else done? He agreed with my analysis in a lukewarm way, and I happily (after all, I'd been sick) flounced into the Store. Momma was preparing our evening meal and Uncle Willie leaned on the door sill. She gave her version.

"Dentist Lincoln got right uppity. Said he'd rather put his hand in a dog's mouth. And when I reminded him of the favor, he brushed it off like a piece of lint. Well, I sent Sister downstairs and went inside. I hadn't never been in his office before, but I found the door to where he takes out teeth, and him and the nurse was in there thick as thieves. I just stood there till he caught sight of me." Crash bang the pots on the stove. "He jumped just like he was sitting on a pin. He said, 'Annie, I done tole you, I ain't gonna mess around in no niggah's mouth.' I said, 'Somebody's got to do it then,' and he said, 'Take her to Texarkana to the colored dentist' and that's when I said, 'If you paid me my money I could afford to take her.' He said, 'It's all been paid.' I tole him everything but the interest been paid. He said "Twasn't no interest.' I said "Tis now. I'll take ten dollars as payment in full.' You know, Willie, it wasn't no right thing to do, 'cause I lent that money without thinking about it.

"He tole that little snippity nurse of his'n to give me ten dollars and make me sign a 'paid in full' receipt. She gave it to me and I signed the papers. Even though by rights he was paid up before, I figger, he gonna be that kind of nasty, he gonna have to pay for it."

Momma and her son laughed and laughed over the white man's evilness and her retributive sin.

I preferred, much preferred, my version.

CHAPTER 25

Knowing Momma, I knew that I never knew Momma. Her African-bush secretiveness and suspiciousness had been compounded by slavery and confirmed by centuries of promises made and promises broken. We have a saying among Black Americans which describes Momma's caution. "If you ask a Negro where he's been, he'll tell you where he's going." To understand this important information, it is necessary to know who uses this tactic and on whom it works. If an unaware person is told a part of the truth (it is imperative that the answer embody truth), he is satisfied that his query has been answered. If an aware person (one who himself uses the stratagem) is given an answer which is truthful but bears only slightly if at all on the question, he knows that the information he seeks is of a private nature and will not be handed to him willingly. Thus direct denial, lying and the revelation of personal affairs are avoided.

Momma told us one day that she was taking us to California. She explained that we were growing up, that we needed to be with our parents, that Uncle Willie was, after all, crippled, that she was getting old. All true, and yet none of those truths satisfied our need for The Truth. The Store and the rooms in back became a going-away factory. Momma sat at the sewing machine all hours, making and remaking clothes for use in California. Neighbors brought out of their trunks pieces of material that had been packed away for decades in blankets of mothballs (I'm certain I was the only girl in California who went to school in water-marked moiré skirts and yellowed satin blouses, satin-back crepe dresses and crepe de Chine underwear).

Whatever the real reason, The Truth, for taking us to California, I shall always think it lay mostly in an incident in which Bailey had the leading part. Bailey had picked up the habit of imitating Claude Rains, Herbert Marshall and George McCready. I didn't think it at all strange that a thirteen-year-old boy in the unreconstructed Southern town of Stamps spoke with an Englishy accent. His heroes included D'Artagnan and the Count of Monte Cristo and he affected what he thought were their swashbuckling gallantries.

On an afternoon a few weeks before Momma revealed her plan to take us West, Bailey came into the Store shaking. His little face was no longer black but a dirty, colorless gray. As was our habit upon entering the Store, he walked behind the candy counter and leaned on the cash register. Uncle Willie had sent him on an errand to whitefolks' town and he wanted an explanation for Bailey's tardiness. After a brief moment our uncle could see that something was wrong, and feeling unable to cope, he called Momma from the kitchen.

"What's the matter, Bailey Junior?"

He said nothing. I knew when I saw him that it would be useless to ask anything while he was in that state. It meant that he had seen or heard of something so ugly or frightening that he was paralyzed as a result. He explained when we were smaller that when things were very bad his soul just crawled behind his heart and curled up and went to sleep. When it awoke, the fearful thing had gone away. Ever since we read *The Fall of the House of Usher*, we had made a pact that neither of us would allow the other to be buried without making "absolutely, positively sure" (his favorite phrase) that the person was dead. I also had to swear that when his soul was sleeping I would never try to wake it, for the shock might make it go to sleep forever. So I let him be, and after a while Momma had to let him alone too.

I waited on customers, and walked around him or leaned over him and, as I suspected, he didn't respond. When the spell wore off he asked Uncle Willie what colored people had done to white people in the first place. Uncle Willie, who never was one for explaining things because he took after Momma, said little except that "colored people hadn't even bothered a hair on whitefolks' heads." Momma added that some people said that whitefolks had come over to Africa (she made it sound like a hidden valley on the moon) and stole the colored people and made them slaves, but nobody really believed it was true. No way to explain what happened "blows and scores" ago, but right now they had the upper hand. Their time wasn't long, though. Didn't Moses lead the children of Israel out of the bloody hands of Pharaoh and into the Promised Land? Didn't the Lord protect the Hebrew children in the fiery furnace and didn't my Lord deliver Daniel? We only had to wait on the Lord.

Bailey said he saw a man, a colored man, whom nobody had delivered. He was dead. (If the news hadn't been so important, we would have been visited with one of Momma's outbursts and prayers. Bailey was nearly blaspheming.) He said, "The man was dead and rotten. Not stinking but rotten."

Momma ordered, "Ju, watch your tongue."

Uncle Willie asked, "Who, who was it?"

Bailey was just tall enough to clear his face over the cash register. He said, "When I passed the calaboose, some men had just fished him out of the pond. He was wrapped in a sheet, all rolled up like a mummy, then a white man walked over and pulled the sheet off. The man was on his back but the white man stuck his foot under the sheet and rolled him over on the stomach."

He turned to me. "My, he had no color at all. He was bloated like a ball." (We had had a running argument for months. Bailey said there was no such thing as colorlessness, and I argued that if there was color there also had to be an opposite and now he was admitting that it was possible. But I didn't feel good about my win.) "The colored men backed off and I did too, but the white man stood there, looking down, and grinned. Uncle Willie, why do they hate us so much?"

Uncle Willie muttered, "They don't really hate us. They don't know us. How can they hate us? They mostly scared."

Momma asked if Bailey had recognized the man, but he was caught in the happening and the event.

"Mr. Bubba told me I was too young to see something like that and I oughta hightail it home, but I had to stay. Then the white man called us closer. He said, 'O.K., you boys, stretch him out in the calaboose and when the Sheriff comes along he'll notify his people. This here's one nigger nobody got to worry about no more. He ain't going nowhere else.' Then the men picked up corners of the sheet, but since nobody wanted to get close to the man they held the very ends and he nearly rolled out on the ground. The white man called me to come and help too."

Momma exploded. "Who was it?" She made herself clear. "Who was the white man?"

Bailey couldn't let go of the horror. "I picked up a side of the sheet and walked right in the calaboose with the men. I walked in the calaboose carrying a rotten dead Negro." His voice was ancient with shock. He was literally bug-eyed.

"The white man played like he was going to lock us all up in there, but Mr. Bubba said 'Ow, Mr. Jim. We didn't do it. We ain't done nothing wrong.' Then the white man laughed and said we boys couldn't take a joke, and opened the door." He breathed his relief. "Whew, I was glad to get out of there. The calaboose, and the prisoners screaming they didn't want no dead nigger in there with them. That he'd stink up the place. They called the white man 'Boss.' They said, 'Boss, surely we ain't done nothing bad enough for you to put another nigger in here with us, and a dead one at that.' Then they laughed. They all laughed like there was something funny."

Bailey was talking so fast he forgot to stutter, he forgot to scratch his head and clean his fingernails with his teeth. He was away in a mystery, locked in the enigma that young Southern Black boys start to unravel, start to *try* to unravel, from seven years old to death. The humorless puzzle of inequality and hate. His experience raised the question of worth and values, of aggressive inferiority and aggressive arrogance. Could Uncle Willie, a Black man, Southern, crippled moreover, hope to answer the questions, both asked and unuttered? Would Momma, who knew the ways of the whites and the wiles of the Blacks, try to answer her grandson, whose very life depended on his not truly understanding the enigma? Most assuredly not.

They both responded characteristically. Uncle Willie said something like he didn't know what the world was coming to, and Momma prayed, "God rest his soul, poor man." I'm sure she began piecing together the details of our California trip that night.

———

Our transportation was Momma's major concern for some weeks. She had arranged with a railroad employee to provide her with a pass in exchange for groceries. The pass allowed a reduction in her fare only, and even that had to be approved, so we were made to abide in a kind of limbo until white people we would never see, in offices we would never visit, signed and stamped and mailed the pass back to Momma. My fare had to be paid in "ready cash." That sudden drain on the nickel-plated cash register lopsided our financial stability. Momma decided Bailey couldn't accompany us, since we had to use the pass during a set time, but that he would follow within a month or so when outstanding bills were paid. Although our mother now lived in San Francisco, Momma must have felt it wiser to go first to Los Angeles where our father was. She dictated letters to me, advising them both that we were on our way.

And we were on our way, but unable to say when. Our clothes were washed, ironed and packed, so for an immobile time we wore those things not good enough to glow under the California sun. Neighbors, who understood the complications of travel, said goodbye a million times.

"Well, if I don't see you before your ticket comes through, Sister Henderson, have a good trip and hurry back home." A widowed friend of Momma's had agreed to look after (cook, wash, clean and provide company for) Uncle Willie, and after thousands of arrested departures, at last we left Stamps.

My sorrow at leaving was confined to a gloom at separating from Bailey for a month (we had never been parted), the imagined loneliness of Uncle Willie (he put on a good face, though at thirty-five he'd never been separated from his mother) and the loss of Louise, my first friend. I wouldn't miss Mrs. Flowers, for she had given me her secret word which called forth a djinn who was to serve me all my life: books.

CHAPTER 26

The intensity with which young people live demands that they "blank out" as often as possible. I didn't actually think about facing Mother until the last day of our journey. I was "going to California." To oranges and sunshine and movie stars and earthquakes and (finally I realized) to Mother. My old guilt came back to me like a much-missed friend. I wondered if Mr. Freeman's name would be mentioned, or if I would be expected to say something about the situation myself. I certainly couldn't ask Momma, and Bailey was a zillion miles away.

The agony of wonder made the fuzzy seats hard, soured the boiled eggs, and when I looked at Momma she seemed too big and too black and very old-fashioned. Everything I saw shuttered against me. The little towns, where nobody waved, and the other passengers in the train, with whom I had achieved an almost kinfolk relationship, disappeared into a common strangeness.

I was as unprepared to meet my mother as a sinner is reluctant to meet his Maker. And all too soon she stood before me, smaller than memory would have her but more glorious than any recall. She wore a light-tan suede suit, shoes to match and a mannish hat with a feather in the band, and she patted my face with gloved hands. Except for the lipsticked mouth, white teeth and shining black eyes, she might have just emerged from a dip in a beige bath. My picture of Mother and Momma embracing on the train platform has been darkly retained through the coating of the then embarrassment and the now maturity. Mother was a blithe chick nuzzling around the large, solid dark hen. The sounds they made had a rich inner harmony. Momma's deep, slow voice lay under my mother's rapid peeps and chirps like stones under rushing water.

The younger woman kissed and laughed and rushed about collecting our coats and getting our luggage carted off. She easily took care of the details that would have demanded half of a country person's day. I was struck again by the wonder of her, and for the length of my trance, the greedy uneasinesses were held at bay.

We moved into an apartment, and I slept on a sofa that miraculously transformed itself at night into a large comfortable bed. Mother stayed in Los Angeles long enough to get us settled, then she returned to San Francisco to arrange living accommodations for her abruptly enlarged family.

Momma and Bailey (he joined us a month after our arrival) and I lived in Los Angeles about six months while our permanent living arrangements were being concluded. Daddy Bailey visited occasionally, bringing shopping bags of fruit. He shone like a Sun God, benignly warming and brightening his dark subjects.

Since I was enchanted with the creation of my own world, years had to pass before I reflected on Momma's remarkable adjustment to that foreign life. An old Southern Negro woman who had lived her life under the left breast of her community learned to deal with white landlords, Mexican neighbors and Negro strangers. She shopped in supermarkets larger than the town she came from. She dealt with accents that must have struck jarringly on her ears. She, who had never been more than fifty miles from her birthplace, learned to traverse the maze of Spanish-named streets in that enigma that is Los Angeles.

She made the same kinds of friends she had always had. On late Sunday afternoons before evening church services, old women who were carbon copies of herself came to the apartment to share leftovers from the Sunday meal and religious talk of a Bright Hereafter.

When the arrangements for our move north were completed, she broke the shattering news that she was going back to Arkansas. She had done her job. She was needed by Uncle Willie. We had our own parents at last. At least we were in the same state.

There were foggy days of unknowing for Bailey and me. It was all well and good to say we would be with our parents, but after all, who were they? Would they be more severe with our didoes than she? That would be bad. Or more lax? Which would be even worse. Would we learn to speak that fast language? I doubted that, and I doubted even more that I would ever find out what they laughed about so loudly and so often.

I would have been willing to return to Stamps even without Bailey. But Momma left for Arkansas without me with her solid air packed around her like cotton.

Mother drove us toward San Francisco over the big white highway that would not have surprised me had it never ended. She talked incessantly and pointed out places of interest. As we passed Capistrano she sang a popular song that I'd heard on the radio: "When the swallows come back to Capistrano."

She strung humorous stories along the road like a bright wash and tried to captivate us. But her being, and her being our mother, had done the job so successfully that it was a little distracting to see her throwing good energy after good.

The big car was obedient under her one-hand driving, and she pulled on her Lucky Strike so hard that her cheeks were sucked in to make valleys in her face. Nothing could have been more magical than to have found her at last, and have her solely to ourselves in the closed world of a moving car.

Although we were both enraptured, neither Bailey nor I was unaware of her nervousness. The knowledge that we had the power to upset that goddess made us look at each other conspiratorially and smile. It also made her human.

We spent a few dingy months in an Oakland apartment which had a bathtub in the kitchen and was near enough to the Southern Pacific Mole to shake at the arrival and departure of every train. In many ways it was St. Louis revisited—along with Uncles Tommy and Billy—and Grandmother Baxter of the pince-nez and strict carriage was again In Residence, though the mighty Baxter clan had fallen into hard times after the death of Grandfather Baxter some years earlier.

We went to school and no family member questioned the output or quality of our work. We went to a playground which sported a basketball court, a football field and Ping Pong tables under awnings. On Sundays instead of going to church we went to the movies.

I slept with Grandmother Baxter, who was afflicted with chronic bronchitis and smoked heavily. During the day she stubbed out half-finished cigarettes and put them in an ashtray beside her bed. At night when she woke up coughing she fumbled in the dark for a butt (she called them "Willies") and after a blaze of light she smoked the strengthened tobacco until her irritated throat was deadened with nicotine. For the first weeks of sleeping with her, the shaking bed and scent of tobacco woke me, but I readily became used to it and slept peacefully through the night.

One evening after going to bed normally, I awoke to another kind of shaking. In the blunted light through the window shade I saw my mother kneeling by my bed. She brought her face close to my ear.

"Ritie," she whispered, "Ritie. Come, but be very quiet." Then she quietly rose and left the room. Dutifully and in a haze of ponderment I followed. Through the half-open kitchen door the light showed Bailey's pajamaed legs dangling from the covered bathtub. The clock on the dining-room table said 2:30. I had never been up at that hour.

I looked Bailey a question and he returned a sheepish gaze. I knew immediately that there was nothing to fear. Then I ran my mind through the catalogue of important dates. It wasn't anybody's birthday, or April Fool's Day, or Halloween, but it was something.

Mother closed the kitchen door and told me to sit beside Bailey. She put her hands on her hips and said we had been invited to a party.

Was that enough to wake us in the middle of the night! Neither of us said anything.

She continued, "I am giving a party and you are my honored and only guests."

She opened the oven and took out a pan of her crispy brown biscuits and showed us a pot of milk chocolate on the back of the stove. There was nothing for it but to laugh at our beautiful and wild mother. When Bailey and I started laughing, she joined in, except that she kept her finger in front of her mouth to try to quiet us.

We were served formally, and she apologized for having no orchestra to play for us but said she'd sing as a substitute. She sang and did the Time Step and the Snake Hips and the Suzy Q. What child can resist a mother who laughs freely and often, especially if the child's wit is mature enough to catch the sense of the joke?

———

Mother's beauty made her powerful and her power made her unflinchingly honest. When we asked her what she did, what her job was, she walked us to Oakland's Seventh Street, where dusty bars and smoke shops sat in the laps of storefront churches. She pointed out Raincoat's Pinochle Parlor and Slim Jenkins' pretentious saloon. Some nights she played pinochle for money or ran a poker game at Mother Smith's or stopped at Slim's for a few drinks. She told us that she had never cheated anybody and wasn't making any preparations to do so. Her work was as honest as the job held by fat Mrs. Walker (a maid), who lived next door to us, and "a damn sight better paid." She wouldn't bust suds for anybody nor be anyone's kitchen bitch. The good Lord gave her a mind and she intended to use it to support her mother and her children. She didn't need to add "And have a little fun along the way."

In the street people were genuinely happy to see her. "Hey, baby. What's the news?"

"Everything's steady, baby, steady."

"How you doing, pretty?"

"I can't win, 'cause of the shape I'm in." (Said with a laugh that belied the content.)

"You all right, momma?"

"Aw, they tell me the whitefolks still in the lead." (Said as if that was not quite the whole truth.)

She supported us efficiently with humor and imagination. Occasionally we were taken to Chinese restaurants or Italian pizza parlors. We were introduced to Hungarian goulash and Irish stew. Through food we learned that there were other people in the world.

With all her jollity, Vivian Baxter had no mercy. There was a saying in Oakland at the time which, if she didn't say it herself, explained her attitude. The saying was, "Sympathy is next to shit in the dictionary, and I can't even read." Her temper had not diminished with the passing of time, and when a passionate nature is not eased with moments of compassion, melodrama is likely to take the stage. In each outburst of anger my mother was *fair*. She had the impartiality of nature, with the same lack of indulgence or clemency.

Before we arrived from Arkansas, an incident took place that left the main actors in jail and in the hospital. Mother had a business partner (who may have been a little more than that) with whom she ran a restaurant cum gambling casino. The partner was not shouldering his portion of the responsibility, according to Mother, and when she confronted him he became haughty and domineering, and he unforgivably called her a bitch. Now, everyone knew that although she cursed as freely as she laughed, no one cursed around her, and certainly no one cursed her. Maybe for the sake of business arrangements she restrained a spontaneous reaction. She told her partner, "I'm going to be one bitch, and I've already been that one." In a foolhardy gesture the man relieved himself of still another "bitch"—and Mother shot him. She had anticipated some trouble when she determined to speak to him and so had taken the precaution to slip a little .32 in her big skirt pocket.

Shot once, the partner stumbled toward her, instead of away, and she said that since she had intended to shoot him (notice: shoot, not kill) she had no reason to run away, so she shot him a second time. It must have been a maddening situation for them. To her, each shot seemed to impel him forward, the reverse of her desire; and for him, the closer he got to her, the more she shot him. She stood her ground until he reached her and flung both arms around her neck, dragging her to the floor. She later said the police had to untwine him before he could be taken to the ambulance. And on the following day, when she was released on bail, she looked in a mirror and "had black eyes down to here." In throwing his arms around her, he must have struck her. She bruised easily.

The partner lived, though shot twice, and although the partnership was dissolved they retained admiration for each other. He had been shot, true, but in her fairness she had warned him. And he had had the strength to give her two black eyes and then live. Admirable qualities.

———

World War II started on a Sunday afternoon when I was on my way to the movies. People in the streets shouted, "We're at war. We've declared war on Japan."

I ran all the way home. Not too sure I wouldn't be bombed before I reached Bailey and Mother. Grandmother Baxter calmed my anxiety by explaining that America would not be bombed, not as long as Franklin Delano Roosevelt was President. He was, after all, a politician's politician and he knew what he was doing.

Soon after, Mother married Daddy Clidell, who turned out to be the first father I would know. He was a successful businessman, and he and Mother moved us to San Francisco. Uncle Tommy, Uncle Billy and Grandmother Baxter remained in the big house in Oakland.

CHAPTER 27

In the early months of World War II, San Francisco's Fillmore district, or the Western Addition, experienced a visible revolution. On the surface it appeared to be totally peaceful and almost a refutation of the term "revolution." The Yakamoto Sea Food Market quietly became Sammy's Shoe Shine Parlor and Smoke Shop. Yashigira's Hardware metamorphosed into La Salon de Beauté owned by Miss Clorinda Jackson. The Japanese shops which sold products to Nisei customers were taken over by enterprising Negro businessmen, and in less than a year became permanent homes away from home for the newly arrived Southern Blacks. Where the odors of tempura, raw fish and *cha* had dominated, the aroma of chitlings, greens and ham hocks now prevailed.

The Asian population dwindled before my eyes. I was unable to tell the Japanese from the Chinese and as yet found no real difference in the national origin of such sounds as Ching and Chan or Moto and Kano.

As the Japanese disappeared, soundlessly and without protest, the Negroes entered with their loud jukeboxes, their just-released animosities and the relief of escape from Southern bonds. The Japanese area became San Francisco's Harlem in a matter of months.

A person unaware of all the factors that make up oppression might have expected sympathy or even support from the Negro newcomers for the dislodged Japanese. Especially in view of the fact that they (the Blacks) had themselves undergone concentration-camp living for centuries in slavery's plantations and later in sharecroppers' cabins. But the sensations of common relationship were missing.

The Black newcomer had been recruited on the dessicated farm lands of Georgia and Mississippi by war-plant labor scouts. The chance to live in two- or three-story apartment buildings (which became instant slums), and to earn two- and even three-figured weekly checks, was blinding. For the first time he could think of himself as a Boss, a Spender. He was able to pay other people to work for him, i.e. the dry cleaners, taxi drivers, waitresses, etc. The shipyards and ammunition plants brought to booming life by the war let him know that he was needed and even appreciated. A completely alien yet very pleasant position for him to experience. Who could expect this man to share his new and dizzying importance with concern for a race that he had never known to exist?

Another reason for his indifference to the Japanese removal was more subtle but was more profoundly felt. The Japanese were not whitefolks. Their eyes, language and customs belied the white skin and proved to their dark successors that since they didn't have to be feared, neither did they have to be considered. All this was decided unconsciously.

No member of my family and none of the family friends ever mentioned the absent Japanese. It was as if they had never owned or lived in the houses we inhabited. On Post Street, where our house was, the hill skidded slowly down to Fillmore, the market heart of our district. In the two short blocks before it reached its destination, the street housed two day-and-night restaurants, two pool halls, four Chinese restaurants, two gambling houses, plus diners, shoeshine shops, beauty salons, barber shops and at least four churches. To fully grasp the never-ending activity in San Francisco's Negro neighborhood during the war, one need only know that the two blocks described were side streets that were duplicated many times over in the eight- to ten-square-block area.

The air of collective displacement, the impermanence of life in wartime and the gauche personalities of the more recent arrivals tended to dissipate my own sense of not belonging. In San Francisco, for the first time, I perceived myself as part of something. Not that I identified with the newcomers, nor with the rare Black descendants of native San Franciscans, nor with the whites or even the Asians, but rather with the times and the city. I understood the arrogance of the young sailors who marched the streets in marauding gangs, approaching every girl as if she were at best a prostitute and at worst an Axis agent bent on making the U.S.A. lose the war. The undertone of fear that San Francisco would be bombed which was abetted by weekly air raid warnings, and civil defense drills in school, heightened my sense of belonging. Hadn't I, always, but ever and ever, thought that life was just one great risk for the living?

Then the city acted in wartime like an intelligent woman under siege. She gave what she couldn't with safety withhold, and secured those things which lay in her reach. The city became for me the ideal of what I wanted to be as a grownup. Friendly but never gushing, cool but not frigid or distant, distinguished without the awful stiffness.

To San Franciscans "the City That Knows How" was the Bay, the fog, Sir Francis Drake Hotel, Top o' the Mark, Chinatown, the Sunset District and so on and so forth and so white. To me, a thirteen-year-old Black girl, stalled by the South and Southern Black life style, the city was a state of beauty and a state of freedom. The fog wasn't simply the steamy vapors off the bay caught and penned in by hills, but a soft breath of anonymity that shrouded and cushioned the bashful traveler. I became dauntless and free of fears, intoxicated by the physical fact of San Francisco. Safe in my protecting arrogance, I was certain that no one loved her as impartially as I. I walked around the Mark Hopkins and gazed at the Top o' the Mark, but (maybe sour grapes) was more impressed by the view of Oakland from the hill than by the tiered building or its fur-draped visitors. For weeks, after the city and I came to terms about my belonging, I haunted the points of interest and found them empty and un–San Francisco. The naval officers with their well-dressed wives and clean white babies inhabited another time-space dimension than I. The well-kept old women in chauffeured cars and blond girls in buckskin shoes and cashmere sweaters might have been San Franciscans, but they were at most gilt on the frame of my portrait of the city.

Pride and Prejudice stalked in tandem the beautiful hills. Native San Franciscans, possessive of the city, had to cope with an influx, not of awed respectful tourists but of raucous unsophisticated provincials. They were also forced to live with skin-deep guilt brought on by the treatment of their former Nisei schoolmates.

Southern white illiterates brought their biases intact to the West from the hills of Arkansas and the swamps of Georgia. The Black ex-farmers had not left their distrust and fear of whites which history had taught them in distressful lessons. These two groups were obliged to work side by side in the war plants, and their animosities festered and opened like boils on the face of the city.

San Franciscans would have sworn on the Golden Gate Bridge that racism was missing from the heart of their air-conditioned city. But they would have been sadly mistaken.

A story went the rounds about a San Franciscan white matron who refused to sit beside a Negro civilian on the streetcar, even after he made room for her on the seat. Her explanation was that she would not sit beside a draft dodger who was a Negro as well. She added that the least he could do was fight for his country the way her son was fighting on Iwo Jima. The story said that the man pulled his body away from the window to show an armless sleeve. He said quietly and with great dignity, "Then ask your son to look around for my arm, which I left over there."

CHAPTER 28

Although my grades were very good (I had been put up two semesters on my arrival from Stamps), I found myself unable to settle down in the high school. It was an institution for girls near my house, and the young ladies were faster, brasher, meaner and more prejudiced than any I had met at Lafayette County Training School. Many of the Negro girls were, like me, straight from the South, but they had known or claimed to have known the bright lights of Big D (Dallas) or T Town (Tulsa, Oklahoma), and their language bore up their claims. They strutted with an aura of invincibility, and along with some of the Mexican students who put knives in their tall pompadours they absolutely intimidated the white girls and those Black and Mexican students who had no shield of fearlessness. Fortunately I was transferred to George Washington High School.

The beautiful buildings sat on a moderate hill in the white residential district, some sixty blocks from the Negro neighborhood. For the first semester, I was one of three Black students in the school, and in that rarefied atmosphere I came to love my people more. Mornings as the streetcar traversed my ghetto I experienced a mixture of dread and trauma. I knew that all too soon we would be out of my familiar setting, and Blacks who were on the streetcar when I got on would all be gone and I alone would face the forty blocks of neat streets, smooth lawns, white houses and rich children.

In the evenings on the way home the sensations were joy, anticipation and relief at the first sign which said BARBECUE or DO DROP INN or HOME COOKING or at the first brown faces on the streets. I recognized that I was again in my country.

In the school itself I was disappointed to find that I was not the most brilliant or even nearly the most brilliant student. The white kids had better vocabularies than I and, what was more appalling, less fear in the classrooms. They never hesitated to hold up their hands in response to a teacher's question; even when they were wrong they were wrong aggressively, while I had to be certain about all my facts before I dared to call attention to myself.

George Washington High School was the first real school I attended. My entire stay there might have been time lost if it hadn't been for the unique personality of a brilliant teacher. Miss Kirwin was that rare educator who was in love with information. I will always believe that her love of teaching came not so much from her liking for students but from her desire to make sure that some of the things she knew would find repositories so that they could be shared again.

She and her maiden sister worked in the San Francisco city school system for over twenty years. My Miss Kirwin, who was a tall, florid, buxom lady with battleship-gray hair, taught civics and current events. At the end of a term in her class our books were as clean and the pages as stiff as they had been when they were issued to us. Miss Kirwin's students were never or very rarely called upon to open textbooks.

She greeted each class with "Good day, ladies and gentlemen." I had never heard an adult speak with such respect to teenagers. (Adults usually believe that a show of honor diminishes their authority.) "In today's *Chronicle* there was an article on the mining industry in the

Carolinas [or some such distant subject]. I am certain that all of you have read the article. I would like someone to elaborate on the subject for me."

After the first two weeks in her class, I, along with all the other excited students, read the San Francisco papers, *Time* magazine, *Life* and everything else available to me. Miss Kirwin proved Bailey right. He had told me once that "all knowledge is spendable currency, depending on the market."

There were no favorite students. No teacher's pets. If a student pleased her during a particular period, he could not count on special treatment in the next day's class, and that was as true the other way around. Each day she faced us with a clean slate and acted as if ours were clean as well. Reserved and firm in her opinions, she spent no time in indulging the frivolous.

She was stimulating instead of intimidating. Where some of the other teachers went out of their way to be nice to me—to be a "liberal" with me—and others ignored me completely, Miss Kirwin never seemed to notice that I was Black and therefore different. I was Miss Johnson and if I had the answer to a question she posed I was never given any more than the word "Correct," which was what she said to every other student with the correct answer.

Years later when I returned to San Francisco I made visits to her classroom. She always remembered that I was Miss Johnson, who had a good mind and should be doing something with it. I was never encouraged on those visits to loiter or linger about her desk. She acted as if I must have had other visits to make. I often wondered if she knew she was the only teacher I remembered.

———

I never knew why I was given a scholarship to the California Labor School. It was a college for adults, and many years later I found that it was on the House Un-American Activities list of subversive organizations. At fourteen I accepted a scholarship and got one for the next year as well. In the evening classes I took drama and dance, along with white and Black grownups. I had chosen drama simply because I liked Hamlet's soliloquy beginning, "To be, or not to be." I had never seen a play and did not connect movies with the theater. In fact, the only times I had heard the soliloquy had been when I had melodramatically recited to myself. In front of a mirror.

It was hard to curb my love for the exaggerated gesture and the emotive voice. When Bailey and I read poems together, he sounded like a fierce Basil Rathbone and I like a maddened Bette Davis. At the California Labor School a forceful and perceptive teacher quickly and unceremoniously separated me from melodrama.

She made me do six months of pantomime.

Bailey and Mother encouraged me to take dance, and he privately told me that the exercise would make my legs big and widen my hips. I needed no greater inducement.

My shyness at moving clad in black tights around a large empty room did not last long. Of course, at first, I thought everyone would be staring at my cucumber-shaped body with its knobs for knees, knobs for elbows and, alas, knobs for breasts. But they really did not notice me, and when the teacher floated across the floor and finished in an arabesque my fancy was taken. I would learn to move like that. I would learn to, in her words, "occupy space." My days angled off Miss Kirwin's class, dinner with Bailey and Mother, and drama and dance.

The allegiances I owed at this time in my life would have made very strange bedfellows: Momma with her solemn determination, Mrs. Flowers and her books, Bailey with his love, my mother and her gaiety, Miss Kirwin and her information, my evening classes of drama and dance.

CHAPTER 29

Our house was a fourteen-room typical San Franciscan post-Earthquake affair. We had a succession of roomers, bringing and taking their different accents, and personalities and foods. Shipyard workers clanked up the stairs (we all slept on the second floor except

Mother and Daddy Clidell) in their steel-tipped boots and metal hats, and gave way to much-powdered prostitutes, who giggled through their make-up and hung their wigs on the doorknobs. One couple (they were college graduates) held long adult conversations with me in the big kitchen downstairs, until the husband went off to war. Then the wife who had been so charming and ready to smile changed into a silent shadow that played infrequently along the walls. An older couple lived with us for a year or so. They owned a restaurant and had no personality to enchant or interest a teenager, except that the husband was called Uncle Jim, and the wife Aunt Boy. I never figured that out.

The quality of strength lined with tenderness is an unbeatable combination, as are intelligence and necessity when unblunted by formal education. I was prepared to accept Daddy Clidell as one more faceless name added to Mother's roster of conquests. I had trained myself so successfully through the years to display interest, or at least attention, while my mind skipped free on other subjects that I could have lived in his house without ever seeing him and without his becoming the wiser. But his character beckoned and elicited admiration. He was a simple man who had no inferiority complex about his lack of education and, even more amazing, no superiority complex because he had succeeded despite that lack. He would say often, "I been to school three years in my life. In Slaten, Texas, times was hard, and I had to help my daddy on the farm."

No recriminations lay hidden under the plain statement, nor was there boasting when he said, "If I'm living a little better now, it's because I treats everybody right."

He owned apartment buildings and, later, pool halls, and was famous for being that rarity "a man of honor." He didn't suffer, as many "honest men" do, from the detestable righteousness that diminishes their virtue. He knew cards and men's hearts. So during the age when Mother was exposing us to certain facts of life, like personal hygiene, proper posture, table manners, good restaurants and tipping practices, Daddy Clidell taught me to play poker, blackjack, tonk and high, low, Jick, Jack and the Game. He wore expensively tailored suits and a large yellow diamond stickpin. Except for the jewelry, he was a conservative dresser and carried himself with the unconscious pomp of a man of secure means. Unexpectedly, I resembled him, and when he, Mother and I walked down the street his friends often said, "Clidell, that's sure your daughter. Ain't no way you can deny her."

Proud laughter followed those declarations, for he had never had children. Because of his late-arriving but intense paternal sense, I was introduced to the most colorful characters in the Black underground. One afternoon, I was invited into our smoke-filled dining room to make the acquaintance of Stonewall Jimmy, Just Black, Cool Clyde, Tight Coat and Red Leg. Daddy Clidell explained to me that they were the most successful con men in the world, and they were going to tell me about some games so that I would never be "anybody's mark."

To begin, one man warned me, "There ain't never been a mark yet that didn't want something for nothing." Then they took turns showing me their tricks, how they chose their victims (marks) from the wealthy bigoted whites and in every case how they used the victims' prejudice against them.

Some of the tales were funny, a few were pathetic, but all were amusing or gratifying to me, for the Black man, the con man who could act the most stupid, won out every time over the powerful, arrogant white.

I remember Mr. Red Leg's story like a favorite melody.

"Anything that works against you can also work for you once you understand the Principle of Reverse.

"There was a cracker in Tulsa who bilked so many Negroes he could set up a Negro Bilking Company. Naturally he got to thinking, Black Skin means Damn Fool. Just Black and I went to Tulsa to check him out. Come to find out, he's a perfect mark. His momma must have been scared in an Indian massacre in Africa. He hated Negroes only a little more than he despised Indians. And he was greedy.

"Black and I studied him and decided he was worth setting up against the store. That means we were ready to put out a few thousand dollars in preparation. We pulled in a white boy from New York, a good con artist, and had him open an office in Tulsa. He was supposed to be a Northern real estate agent trying to buy up valuable land in Oklahoma. We investigated a piece of land near Tulsa that had a toll bridge crossing it. It used to be part of an Indian reservation but had been taken over by the state.

"Just Black was laid out as the decoy, and I was going to be the fool. After our friend from New York hired a secretary and had his cards printed, Black approached the mark with a proposition. He told him that he had heard that our mark was the only white man colored people could trust. He named some of the poor fools that had been taken by that crook. It just goes to show you how white folks can be deceived by their own deception. The mark believed Black.

"Black told him about his friend who was half Indian and half colored and how some Northern white estate agent had found out that he was the sole owner of a piece of valuable land and the Northerner wanted to buy it. At first the man acted like he smelled a rat, but from the way he gobbled up the proposition, turns out what he thought he smelled was some nigger money on his top lip.

"He asked the whereabouts of the land but Black put him off. He told his cracker that he just wanted to make sure that he would be interested. The mark allowed how he was being interested, so Black said he would tell his friend and they'd get in touch with him. Black met the mark for about three weeks in cars and in alleys and kept putting him off until the white man was almost crazy with anxiety and greed and then accidentally it seemed Black let drop the name of the Northern real estate agent who wanted the property. From that moment on we knew we had the big fish on the line and all we had to do was to pull him in.

"We expected him to try to contact our store, which he did. That cracker went to our setup and counted on his whiteness to ally him with Spots, our white boy, but Spots refused to talk about the deal except to say the land had been thoroughly investigated by the biggest real estate concern in the South and that if our mark did not go around raising dust he would make sure that there would be a nice piece of money in it for him. Any obvious inquiries as to the rightful ownership of the land could alert the state and they would surely push through a law prohibiting the sale. Spots told the mark he would keep in touch with him. The mark went back to the store three or four times but to no avail, then just before we knew he would crack, Black brought me to see him. That fool was as happy as a sissy in a C.C.C. camp. You would have thought my neck was in a noose and he was about to light the fire under my feet. I never enjoyed taking anybody so much.

"Anyhow, I played scary at first but Just Black told me that this was one white man that our people could trust. I said I did not trust no white man because all they wanted was to get a chance to kill a Black man legally and get his wife in the bed. (I'm sorry, Clidell.) The mark assured me that he was the only white man who did not feel like that. Some of his best friends were colored people. In fact, if I didn't know it, the woman who raised him was a colored woman and he still sees her to this day. I let myself be convinced and then the mark began to drag the Northern whites. He told me that they made Negroes sleep in the street in the North and that they had to clean out toilets with their hands in the North and even things worse than that. I was shocked and said, 'Then I don't want to sell my land to that white man who offered seventy-five thousand dollars for it.' Just Black said, 'I wouldn't know what to do with that kind of money,' and I said that all I wanted was to have enough money to buy a home for my old mom, to buy a business and to make one trip to Harlem. The mark asked how much would that cost and I said I reckoned I could do it on fifty thousand dollars.

"The mark told me no Negro was safe with that kind of money. That whitefolks would take it from him. I said I knew it but I had to have at least forty thousand dollars. He agreed. We shook hands. I said it would do my heart good to see the mean Yankee go down on some of 'our land.' We met the next morning and I signed the deed in his car and he gave me the cash.

"Black and I had kept most of our things in a hotel over in Hot Springs, Arkansas. When the deal was closed we walked to our car, drove across the state line and on to Hot Springs.

"That's all there was to it."

When he finished, more triumphant stories rainbowed around the room riding the shoulders of laughter. By all accounts those storytellers, born Black and male before the turn of the twentieth century, should have been ground into useless dust. Instead they used their intelligence to pry open the door of rejection and not only became wealthy but got some revenge in the bargain.

It wasn't possible for me to regard them as criminals or be anything but proud of their achievements.

The needs of a society determine its ethics, and in the Black American ghettos the hero is that man who is offered only the crumbs from his country's table but by ingenuity and courage is able to take for himself a Lucullan feast. Hence the janitor who lives in one room but sports a robin's-egg-blue Cadillac is not laughed at but admired, and the domestic who buys forty-dollar shoes is not criticized but is appreciated. We know that they have put to use their full mental and physical powers. Each single gain feeds into the gains of the body collective.

Stories of law violations are weighed on a different set of scales in the Black mind than in the white. Petty crimes embarrass the community and many people wistfully wonder why Negroes don't rob more banks, embezzle more funds and employ graft in the unions. "We are the victims of the world's most comprehensive robbery. Life demands a balance. It's all right if we do a little robbing now." This belief appeals particularly to one who is unable to compete legally with his fellow citizens.

My education and that of my Black associates were quite different from the education of our white schoolmates. In the classroom we all learned past participles, but in the streets and in our homes the Blacks learned to drop *s*'s from plurals and suffixes from past-tense verbs. We were alert to the gap separating the written word from the colloquial. We learned to slide out of one language and into another without being conscious of the effort. At school, in a given situation, we might respond with "That's not unusual." But in the street, meeting the same situation, we easily said, "It be's like that sometimes."

CHAPTER 30

Just like Jane Withers and Donald O'Connor I was going on a vacation. Daddy Bailey invited me to spend the summer with him in southern California and I was jumpy with excitement. Given our father's characteristic air of superiority, I secretly expected him to live in a manor house surrounded by grounds and serviced by a liveried staff.

Mother was all cooperation in helping me to shop for summer clothes. With the haughtiness San Franciscans have for people who live in the warmer climate, she explained that all I needed were lots of shorts, pedal pushers, sandals and blouses because "southern Californians hardly ever wear anything else."

Daddy Bailey had a girl friend, who had begun corresponding with me some months before, and she was to meet me at the train. We had agreed to wear white carnations to identify each other, and the porter kept my flower in the diner's Frigidaire until we reached the small hot town.

On the platform my eyes skimmed over the whites and searched among the Negroes who were walking up and down expectantly. There were no men as tall as Daddy, and no really glamorous ladies (I had decided that given his first choice, all his succeeding women would be startlingly beautiful). I saw a little girl who wore a white flower, but dismissed her as improbable. The platform emptied as we walked by each other time after time. Finally she stopped me with a disbelieving "Marguerite?" Her voice screeched with shock and maturity. So, after all, she wasn't a little girl. I too, was visited with unbelief.

She said, "I'm Dolores Stockland."

Stunned but trying to be well mannered, I said, "Hello. My name is Marguerite."

Daddy's girl friend? I guessed her to be in her early twenties. Her crisp seersucker suit, spectator pumps and gloves informed me that she was proper and serious. She was of average height but with the unformed body of a girl and I thought that if she was planning to marry our father she must have been horrified to find herself with a nearly six-foot prospective stepdaughter who was not even pretty. (I found later that Daddy Bailey had told her that his children were eight and nine years old and cute as buttons. She had such a need to believe in him that even though we corresponded at a time when I loved the multisyllabic words and convoluted sentences she had been able to ignore the obvious.)

I was another link in a long chain of disappointments. Daddy had promised to marry her but kept delaying until he finally married a woman named Alberta, who was another small tight woman from the South. When I met Dolores she had all the poses of the Black bourgeoisie without the material basis to support the postures. Instead of owning a manor house and servants, Daddy lived in a trailer park on the outskirts of a town that was itself the outskirts of town. Dolores lived there with him and kept the house clean with the orderliness of a coffin. Artificial flowers reposed waxily in glass vases. She was on close terms with her washing machine and ironing board. Her hairdresser could count on absolute fidelity and punctuality. In a word, but for intrusions her life would have been perfect. And then I came along.

She tried hard to make me into something she could reasonably accept. Her first attempt, which failed utterly, concerned my attention to details. I was asked, cajoled, then ordered to care for my room. My willingness to do so was hampered by an abounding ignorance of how it should be done and a fumbling awkwardness with small objects. The dresser in my room was covered with little porcelain white women holding parasols, china dogs, fat-bellied cupids and blown-glass animals of every persuasion. After making the bed, sweeping my room and hanging up the clothes, if and when I remembered to dust the bric-a-brac, I unfailingly held one too tightly and crunched off a leg or two, or too loosely and dropped it, to shatter it into miserable pieces.

Daddy wore his amused impenetrable face constantly. He seemed positively diabolic in his enjoyment of our discomfort. Certainly Dolores adored her outsize lover, and his elocution (Daddy Bailey never spoke, he orated), spiced with the rolling *er*s and *errer*s, must have been some consolation to her in their less-than-middle-class home. He worked in the kitchen of a naval hospital and they both said he was a medical dietician for the United States Navy. Their Frigidaire was always stocked with newly acquired pieces of ham, half roasts and quartered chickens. Dad was an excellent cook. He had been in France during World War I and had also worked as doorman at the exclusive Breakers' Hotel; as a result he often made Continental dinners. We sat down frequently to coq au vin, prime ribs au jus, and cotelette Milanese with all the trimmings. His speciality, however, was Mexican food. He traveled across the border weekly to pick up condiments and other supplies that graced our table as pollo en salsa verde and enchilada con carne.

If Dolores had been a little less aloof, a little more earthy, she could have discovered that those ingredients were rife in her town proper, and Dad had no need to travel to Mexico to buy provisions. But she would not be caught so much as looking into one of the crusty Mexican *mercados,* let alone venturing inside its smelliness. And it also sounded ritzy to say, "My husband, Mr. Johnson, the naval dietician, went over to Mexico to buy some things for our dinner." That goes over large with other ritzy people who go to the white area to buy artichokes.

Dad spoke fluent Spanish, and since I had studied for a year we were able to converse slightly. I believe that my talent with a foreign language was the only quality I had that impressed Dolores. Her mouth was too taut and her tongue too still to attempt the strange sounds. Admittedly, though, her English, like everything else about her, was absolutely perfect.

We indulged in a test of strength for weeks as Dad stood figuratively on the sidelines, neither cheering nor booing but enjoying himself greatly. He asked me once if I "er liked errer my mother." I thought he meant my mother, so I answered yes—she was beautiful and gay and very kind. He said he wasn't talking about Vivian, he meant Dolores. Then I explained that I didn't like her because she was mean and petty and full of pretense. He laughed, and when I added she didn't like me because I was so tall and arrogant and wasn't clean enough for her, he laughed harder and said something like "Well, that's life."

One evening he announced that on the next day he was going to Mexico to buy food for the weekend. There was nothing unusual about his pronouncement until he added that he was taking me along. He filled the shocked silence with the information that a trip to Mexico would give me an opportunity to practice Spanish.

Dolores' silence might have been brought on by a jealous reaction, but mine was occasioned by pure surprise. My father had not shown any particular pride in me and very little affection. He had not taken me to his friends or to southern California's few points of interest. It was incredible that I was to be included in something as exotic as a trip to Mexico. Well, I quickly reasoned, I deserved it. After all, I was his daughter and my vacation fell far short of what I had expected a vacation to be. Had I protested that I would like Dolores to go along, we might have been spared a display of violence and near tragedy. But my young mind was filled with self, and my imagination shivered at the prospect of seeing sombreros, rancheros, tortillas and Pancho Villa. We spent a quiet night. Dolores mended her perfect underwear, and I pretended to read a novel. Dad listened to the radio with a drink in his hand and watched what I now know was a pitiful spectacle.

In the morning, we set out on the foreign adventure. The dirt roads of Mexico fulfilled all my longing for the unusual. Only a few miles from California's slick highways and, to me, tall buildings, we were bumping along on gravel streets that could have competed in crudeness with the worst paths in Arkansas, and the landscape boasted adobe huts or cabins walled with corrugated metal. Dogs, lean and dirty, slunk around the houses, and children played innocently in the nude or near nude with discarded rubber tires. Half the population looked like Tyrone Power and Dolores Del Rio, and the other half like Akim Tamiroff and Katina Paxinou, maybe only fatter and older.

Dad gave no explanation as we drove through the border town and headed for the interior. Although surprised, I refused to indulge my curiosity by questioning him. After a few miles we were stopped by a uniformed guard. He and Dad exchanged familiar greetings and Dad got out of the car. He reached back into the pocket of the door and took a bottle of liquor into the guard's kiosk. They laughed and talked for over a half hour as I sat in the car and tried to translate the muffled sounds. Eventually they came out and walked to the car. Dad still had the bottle but it was only half full. He asked the guard if he would like to marry me. Their Spanish was choppier than my school version but I understood. My father added as an inducement the fact that I was only fifteen years old. At once the guard leaned into the car and caressed my cheek. I supposed that he thought before that I was not only ugly but old, too, and that now the knowledge that I was probably unused attracted him. He told Dad that he would marry me and we would have "many babies." My father found that promise the funniest thing he had heard since we left home. (He had laughed uproariously when Dolores didn't answer my goodbye and I explained as we drove away that she hadn't heard.) The guard was not discouraged by my attempts to get away from his probing hands and I would have squirmed to the driver's seat had not Dad opened the door and got in. After many *adiós*'s and *bonitas* and *espositas* Dad started the car, and we were on our grimy way again.

Signs informed me that we were headed for Ensenada. In those miles, along the twisted roads beside the steep mountain, I feared that I would never get back to America, civilization, English and wide streets again. He sipped from the bottle and sang snatches of Mexican songs as we climbed the tortuous mountain road. Our destination turned out not to be the town of Ensenada, after all, but about five miles out of the city limits. We pulled up in the dirt yard of a *cantina* where half-clothed children chased mean-looking chickens around and around. The noise of the car brought women to the door of the ramshackle building but didn't distract the single-minded activity of either the grubby kids or the scrawny fowls.

A woman's voice sang out, "Baylee, Baylee." And suddenly a claque of women crowded to the door and overflowed into the yard. Dad told me to get out of the car and we went to meet the women. He explained quickly that I was his daughter, which everyone thought to be uncontrollably funny. We were herded into a long room with a bar at one end. Tables sat lopsidedly on a loose-plank floor. The ceiling caught and held my attention. Paper streamers in every possible color waved in the near-still air, and as I watched a few fell to the floor. No one seemed to notice, or if they did, it was obviously unimportant that their sky was falling in. There were a few men on stools at the bar, and they greeted my father with the ease of familiarity. I was taken around and each person was told my name and age. The formal high school "*Cómo está usted?*" was received as the most charming utterance possible. People clapped me on the back, shook Dad's hand and spoke a rat-a-tat Spanish that I was unable to follow. Baylee was the hero of the hour, and as he warmed under the uninhibited show of affection I saw a new side of the man. His quizzical smile disappeared and he stopped his affected way of talking (it would have been difficult to wedge *er*s into that rapid Spanish).

It seemed hard to believe that he was a lonely person, searching relentlessly in bottles, under women's skirts, in church work and lofty job titles for his "personal niche," lost before birth and unrecovered since. It was obvious to me then that he had never belonged in Stamps, and less to the slow-moving, slow-thinking Johnson family. How maddening it was to have been born in a cotton field with aspirations of grandeur.

In the Mexican bar, Dad had an air of relaxation which I had never seen visit him before. There was no need to pretend in front of those Mexican peasants. As he was, just being himself, he was sufficiently impressive to them. He was an American. He was Black. He spoke Spanish fluently. He had money and he could drink tequila with the best of them. The women liked him too. He was tall and handsome and generous.

It was a fiesta party. Someone put money in the jukebox and drinks were served to all the customers. I was given a warm Coca-Cola. The music poured out of the record machine as high-tenored voices wavered and held, wavered and held for the passionate rancheros. Men danced, at first alone, then with each other and occasionally a woman would join the foot-stomping rites. I was asked to dance. I hesitated because I wasn't sure I'd be able to follow the steps, but Dad nodded and encouraged me to try. I had been enjoying myself for at least an hour before I realized it. One young man had taught me how to put a sticker on the ceiling. First, all the sugar must be chewed out of Mexican gum, then the bartender gives a few slips of paper to the aspirant, who writes either a proverb or a sentimental remark on the strip. He takes the soft gum from his mouth and sticks it to the end of the streamer. Choosing a less densely covered area of the ceiling he aims at the spot, and as he throws he lets out a bloodcurdling scream which would not be out of place in a bronco-busting rodeo. After a few squeaky misses, I overcame my reserve and tore my tonsils loose with a yell that would have been worthy of Zapata. I was happy, Dad was proud and my new friends were gracious. A woman brought *chicharrones* (in the South they're called cracklings) in a greasy newspaper. I ate the fried pig skins, danced, screamed and drank the extra-sweet and sticky Coca-Cola with the nearest approach to abandonment I had ever experienced. As new revelers joined the celebration I was introduced as la niña de Baylee, and as quickly accepted. The afternoon sun failed in its attempt to light the room through the single window, and the press of bodies and scents and sounds melted to give us an aromatic and artificial twilight. I realized that I hadn't seen my father for some time. *"Dónde está mi padre?"* I asked my dancing partner. My formal Spanish must have sounded as pretentious to the ears of the paisano as "Whither goeth my sire?" would have sounded to a semiliterate Ozark mountaineer. In any case it brought on a howl of laughter, a bear-crushing embrace and no answer. When the dance was finished, I made my way through the squeeze of the people as unobtrusively as possible. A fog of panic nearly suffocated me. He wasn't in the room. Had he made an arrangement with the guard back at the pass? I would not put it beyond him. My drink had been spiked. The certainty made my knees weak, and dancing couples blurred before my eyes. Dad was gone. He was probably halfway back home with the money from my sale in his pocket. I had to get to the door, which seemed miles and mountains away. People stopped me with *"Dónde vas?"* My response was something as stiff and double meaning as *"Yo voy por ventilarme,"* or "I am going to air out." No wonder I was a big hit.

Seen through the open door Dad's Hudson sat in lonely splendor. He hadn't left me, after all. That meant, of course, that I hadn't been drugged. I immediately felt better. No one followed me into the yard where the late afternoon sun had tenderized the midday harshness. I decided to sit in his car and wait for him since he couldn't have gone far. I knew he was with a woman, and the more I thought about it, it was easy to figure which one of the gay señoritas he had taken away. There had been a small neat woman with very red lips who clung to him avidly when we first arrived. I hadn't thought of it at the time but had simply recorded her pleasure. In the car, in reflection, I played the scene back. She had been the first to rush to him, and that was when he quickly said "This is my daughter" and "She speaks Spanish." If Dolores knew, she would crawl up in her blanket of affectations and die circumspectly. The thought of her mortification kept me company for a long time, but the sounds of music and laughter and Cisco Kid screams broke into my pleasant revengeful reveries. It was, after all, getting dark and Dad must have been beyond my reach in one of the little cabins out back. An awkward fear crept up slowly as I contemplated sitting in the car all night alone. It was a fear distantly related to the earlier panic. Terror did not engulf me wholly, but crawled along my mind like a tedious paralysis. I could roll up the windows and lock the door. I could lie down on the floor of the car and make myself small and invisible. Impossible! I tried to staunch the flood of fear. Why was I afraid of the Mexicans? After all, they had been kind to me and surely my father wouldn't allow his daughter to be ill treated. Wouldn't he? Would he? How could he leave me in that raunchy bar and go off with his woman? Did he care what happened to me? Not a damn, I decided, and opened the flood gates for hysteria. Once the tears began, there was no stopping them. I was to die, after all, in a Mexican dirt yard. The special person that I was, the intelligent mind that God and I had created together, was to depart this life without recognition or contribution. How pitiless were the Fates and how helpless was this poor Black girl.

I made out his shadow in the near gloom and was about to jump out and run to him when I noticed that he was being propelled by the small woman I had seen earlier and a man. He wobbled and lurched but they held him up firmly and guided his staggering toward the door of the *cantina*. Once he got inside we might never leave. I got out of the car and went to them. I asked Dad if he wouldn't like to get into the car and rest a little. He focused enough to recognize me and answered that that was exactly what he wanted; he was a little tired and he'd like to rest before we set out for his place. He told his friends his wishes in Spanish and they steered him to the car. When I opened the front door he said No, he'd lie down on the back seat for a little while. We got him into the car and tried to arrange his long legs comfortably. He began snoring even as we tugged at him. It sounded like the beginning of a deep and long sleep, and a warning that, after all, we were to spend the night in the car, in Mexico.

I thought fast as the couple laughed and jabbered at me in incomprehensible Spanish. I had never driven a car before, but I had watched carefully and my mother was declared to be the best driver in San Francisco. *She* declared it, at least. I was superbly intelligent and had good physical coordination. Of course I could drive. Idiots and lunatics drove cars, why not the brilliant Marguerite Johnson? I asked the Mexican man to turn the car around, again in my exquisite high school Spanish, and it took about fifteen minutes to make myself understood. The man must have asked me if I could drive, but I didn't know the Spanish for the verb "to drive," so I kept repeating *"Sí, sí"* and *"Gracias"* until he got in and headed the car toward the highway. He showed his understanding of the situation by his next action. He left the motor running. I put my foot on the accelerator and clutch, jiggled the gearshift and raised both feet. With an ominous roar we leaped out of the yard.

As we shook onto the shelf of the road the car nearly stalled and I stamped both feet again on the pedal and clutch. We made no progress and an awful amount of noise, but the motor didn't stop. I understood then that in order to go forward I would have to lift my feet off the pedals, and if I did so abruptly the car would shake like a person with St. Vitus Dance. With that complete understanding of the principle of motor locomotion, I drove down the mountainside toward Calexico, some fifty miles away. It is hard to understand why my vivid imagination and tendency toward scariness didn't provide me with gory scenes of bloody crashes on a *risco de Mexico*. I can only think that my every sense was concentrated on steering the bucking car.

When it became totally dark, I fumbled over knobs, twisting and pulling until I succeeded in finding the lights. The car slowed down as I centered on that search, and I forgot to step on the pedals, and the motor gurgled, the car pitched and the engine stopped. A bumbling sound from the back told me that Dad had fallen off the seat (I had been expecting this to happen for miles). I pulled the hand brake and carefully considered my next move. It was useless to think of asking Dad. The fall on the floor had failed to stir him, and I would be unable to do so. No car was likely to pass us—I hadn't seen any motor vehicles since we passed the guard's house early in the day. We were headed downhill, so I reasoned that with any luck we might coast right up to Calexico—or at least to the guard. I waited until I formulated an approach to him before releasing the brake. I would stop the car when we reached the kiosk and put on my siddity air. I would speak to him like the peasant he was. I would order him to start the car and then tip him a quarter or even a dollar from Dad's pocket before driving on.

With my plans solidly made, I released the brake and we began coasting down the slope. I also pumped the clutch and the accelerator, hoping that the action would speed our descent, and wonder of wonders the motor started again. The Hudson went crazy on the hill. It was rebelling and would have leaped over the side of the mountain, to all our destruction, in its attempt to unseat me had I relaxed control for a single second. The challenge was exhilarating. It was me, Marguerite, against the elemental opposition. As I twisted the steering wheel and forced the accelerator to the floor I was controlling Mexico, and might and aloneness and inexperienced youth and Bailey Johnson, Sr., and death and insecurity, and even gravity.

184 · *Maya Angelou*

After what seemed like one thousand and one nights of challenge the mountain began to level off and we started passing scattered lights on either side of the road. No matter what happened after that I had won. The car began to slow down as if it had been tamed and was going to give up without grace. I pumped even harder and we finally reached the guard's box. I pulled on the hand brake and came to a stop. There would be no need for me to speak to the guard since the motor was running, but I had to wait until he looked into the car and gave me the signal to continue. He was busy talking to people in a car facing the mountain I had just conquered. The light from his hut showed him bent from the waist with his upper torso completely swallowed by the mouth of the open window. I held the car in instant readiness for the next lap of our journey. When the guard unfolded himself and stood erect I was able to see he was not the same man of the morning's embarrassment. I was understandably taken aback at the discovery and when he saluted sharply and barked *"Pasa"* I released the brake, put both feet down and lifted them a bit too sharply. The car outran my intention. It leaped not only forward but left as well, and with a few angry spurts propelled itself onto the side of the car just pulling off. The crash of scraping metal was followed immediately by a volley of Spanish hurled at me from all directions. Again, strangely enough, fear was absent from my sensations. I wondered in this order: was I hurt, was anyone else hurt, would I go to jail, what were the Mexicans saying, and finally, had Dad awakened? I was able to answer the first and last concern promptly. Buoyed by the adrenalin that had flooded my brain as we careened down the mountainside, I had never felt better, and my father's snores cut through the cacophony of protestations outside my window. I got out of the car, intending to ask for the *policías,* but the guard beat me to the punch. He said a few words, which were strung together like beads, but one of them was *policías.* As the people in the other car fumbled out, I tried to recover my control and said loudly and too graciously, *"Gracias, señor."* The family, some eight or more people of every age and size, walked around me, talking heatedly and sizing me up as if I might have been a statue in a city park and they were a flock of pigeons. One said *"Joven,"* meaning I was young. I tried to see which one was so intelligent. I would direct my conversation to him or her, but they shifted positions so quickly it was impossible to make the person out. Then another suggested *"Borracho."* Well, certainly, I must have smelled like a tequila farm, since Dad had been breathing out the liquor in noisy respirations and I had kept the windows closed against the cold night air. It wasn't likely that I would explain that to these strangers even if I could. Which I couldn't. Someone got the idea to look into the car, and a scream brought us all up short. People—they seemed to be in the hundreds—crowded to the windows and more screams erupted. I thought for a minute that something awful might have happened. Maybe at the time of the crash…I, too, pushed to the window to see, but then I remembered the rhythmic snores, and coolly walked away. The guard must have thought he had a major crime on his hands. He made moves and sounds like "Watch her" or "Don't let her out of your sight." The family came back, this time not as close but more menacing, and when I was able to sort out one coherent question, *"Quién es?"* I answered dryly and with all the detachment I could summon, *"Mi padre."* Being a people of close family ties and weekly fiestas they suddenly understood the situation. I was a poor little girl thing who was caring for my drunken father, who had stayed too long at the fair. *Pobrecita.*

The guard, the father and one or two small children began the herculean job of waking Dad. I watched coolly as the remaining people paraded, making figure eights around me and their badly bruised automobile. The two men shook and tugged and pulled while the children jumped up and down on my father's chest. I credit the children's action for the success of the effort. Bailey Johnson, Sr., woke up in Spanish. *"Qué tiene? Qué pasa? Qué quiere?"* Anyone else would have asked, "Where am I?" Obviously, this was a common Mexican experience. When I saw he was fairly lucid I went to the car, calmly pushed the people away, and said from the haughty level of one who has successfully brought to heel a marauding car and negotiated a sneaky mountain, "Dad, there's been an accident." He recognized me by degrees and became my pre-Mexican-fiesta father.

"An accident, huh? Er, who was at fault? You, Marguerite? Errer was it you?"

It would have been futile to tell him of my mastering his car and driving it nearly fifty miles. I didn't expect or even need, now, his approbation.

"Yes, Dad, I ran into a car."

He still hadn't sat up completely, so he couldn't know where we were. But from the floor where he rested, as if that was the logical place to be, he said, "In the glove compartment. The insurance papers. Get them and er give them to the police, and then come back."

The guard stuck his head in the other door before I could form a scathing but polite response. He asked Dad to get out of the car. Never at a loss, my father reached in the glove compartment, and took out the folded papers and the half bottle of liquor he had left there earlier. He gave the guard one of his pinch-backed laughs, and descended, by joints, from the car. Once on the ground he towered over the angry people. He took a quick reading of his location and the situation, and then put his arm around the other driver's shoulder. He kindly, not in the least condescendingly, bent to speak to the guard, and the three men walked into the hut. Within easy minutes, laughter burst from the shack and the crisis was over, but so was the enjoyment.

Dad shook hands with all the men, patted the children and smiled winsomely at the women. Then, and without looking at the damaged cars, he eased himself behind the steering wheel. He called me to get in, and as if he had not been helplessly drunk a half hour earlier, he drove unerringly toward home. He said he didn't know I could drive, and how did I like his car? I was angry that he had recovered so quickly and felt let down that he didn't appreciate the greatness of my achievement. So I answered yes to both the statement and the question. Before we reached the border he rolled down the window, and the fresh air, which was welcome, was uncomfortably cold. He told me to get his jacket from the back seat and put it on. We drove into the city in a cold and private silence.

CHAPTER 31

Dolores was sitting, it seemed, in the same place as the night before. Her pose was so similar it was hard to believe she had gone to sleep, eaten breakfast or even patted her firm hairdo. Dad said sportily, "Hello, kid," and walked toward the bathroom. I greeted her: "Hello, Dolores" (we had long dropped the pretense of familial relationship). She responded, briefly but politely, and threaded her attention through the eye of her needle. She was now prudently making cute kitchen curtains, which would soon starchily oppose the wind. Having nothing more to say, I went to my room. Within minutes an argument ensued in the living area that was as audible to me as if the separating walls were muslin sheets.

"Bailey, you've let your children come between us."

"Kid, you're too sensitive. The children, er, my children, can't come between us, unless you let them."

"How can I stop it?"—she was crying—"They're doing it." Then she said, "You gave your daughter your jacket."

"Was I supposed to let her freeze to death? Is that what you'd like, kid?" He laughed. "You would, wouldn't you?"

"Bailey, you know I wanted to like your children, but they ..." She couldn't bring herself to describe us.

"Why the hell don't you say what you mean? You're a pretentious little bitch, aren't you? That's what Marguerite called you, and she's right."

I shivered to think how that revelation would add to her iceberg of hate for me.

"Marguerite can go to hell, Bailey Johnson. I'm marrying you, I don't want to marry your children."

"More pity for you, you unlucky sow. I am going out. Goodnight."

The front door slammed. Dolores cried quietly and broke the piteous whimpers with sniffles and a few dainty nose blows into her handkerchief.

In my room, I thought my father was mean and cruel. He had enjoyed his Mexican holiday, and still was unable to proffer a bit of kindness to the woman who had waited patiently, busying herself with housewifely duties. I was certain that she knew he'd been drinking, and she must have noticed that although we were away over twelve hours, we hadn't brought one tortilla into the house.

I felt sorry and even a little guilty. I had enjoyed myself, too. I had been eating *chicharrones* while she probably sat praying for his safe return. I had defeated a car and a mountain as she pondered over my father's fidelity. There was nothing fair or kind about the treatment, so I decided to go out and console her. The idea of spreading mercy, indiscriminately, or, to be more correct, spreading it on someone I really didn't care about, enraptured me. I was basically good. Not understood, and not even liked, but even so, just, and better than just. I was merciful. I stood in the center of the floor but Dolores never looked up. She worked the thread through the flowered cloth as if she were sewing the torn ends of her life together. I said, in my Florence Nightingale voice, "Dolores, I don't mean to come between you and Dad. I wish you'd believe me." There, it was done. My good deed balanced the rest of the day.

With her head still bent she said, "No one was speaking to you, Marguerite. It is rude to eavesdrop on other people's conversations."

Surely she wasn't so dumb as to think these paper walls were made of marble. I let just the tiniest shred of impudence enter my voice. "I've never eavesdropped in my life. A deaf person would have been hard put not to hear what you said. I thought I'd tell you that I have no interest in coming between you and my father. That's all."

My mission had failed and succeeded. She refused to be pacified, but I had shown myself in a favorable and Christian light. I turned to go.

"No, that's not all." She looked up. Her face was puffy and her eyes swollen red. "Why don't you go back to your mother? If you've got one." Her tone was so subdued she might have been telling me to cook a pot of rice. If I've got one? Well, I'd tell her.

"I've got one and she's worlds better than you, prettier, too, and intelligent and—"

"And"—her voice keened to a point—"she's a whore." Maybe if I had been older, or had had my mother longer, or understood Dolores' frustration more deeply, my response would not have been so violent. I know that the awful accusation struck not so much at my filial love as at the foundation of my new existence. If there was a chance of truth in the charge, I would not be able to live, to continue to live with Mother, and I so wanted to.

I walked to Dolores, enraged at the threat. "I'm going to slap you for that, you silly old bitch." I warned her and I slapped her. She was out of the chair like a flea, and before I could jump back she had her arms around me. Her hair was under my chin and she wrapped her arms, it seemed two or three times, around my waist. I had to push her shoulders with all my strength to unlock the octopus hold. Neither of us made a sound until I finally shoved her back onto the sofa. Then she started screaming. Silly old fool. What did she expect if she called my mother a whore? I walked out of the house. On the steps I felt something wet on my arm and looked down to find blood. Her screams still sailed through the evening air like skipping stones, but I was bleeding. I looked carefully on my arm, but there was no cut. I put my arm back to my waist and it brought fresh blood as I pulled it away. I *was* cut. Before I could fully understand, or comprehend enough to respond, Dolores opened the door, screaming still, and upon seeing me, instead of slamming the door she ran like a mad woman down the stairs. I saw a hammer in her hand, and without wondering if I would be able to take it from her, I fled. Dad's car sat in a yard twice in one day offering magnificent refuge. I jumped in, rolled up the windows and locked the door. Dolores flitted around the car, screaming like a banshee, her face bedizened with fury.

Daddy Bailey and the neighbors he was visiting responded to the screams and crowded around her. She shouted that I had jumped on her and tried to kill her and Bailey had better not bring me back in the house. I sat in the car, feeling the blood slip down to my buttocks as the people quieted and cooled her rage. My father motioned to me to open the window, and when I did he said he would take Dolores inside but I should stay in the car. He would be back to attend to me.

The events of the day swarmed over me and made my breathing difficult. After all the decisive victories of the day my life was to end in sticky death. If Dad stayed a very long time in the house, I was too afraid to go to the door and ask for him, and besides, my feminine training would not allow me to walk two steps with blood on my dress. As I had always feared, no, known, the trials had been for nothing. (The dread of futility has been my lifelong plague.) Excitement, apprehension, release and anger had drained me of mobility. I waited for Fate, the string puller, to dictate my movements.

My father came down the steps in a few minutes and angrily slammed into the car. He sat in a corner of blood and I gave no warning. He must have been pondering what to do with me when he felt the damp on his trousers.

"What the hell is this?" He hunched himself up on a hip and brushed the pants. His hand showed red in the porch's cast-off light. "What is this, Marguerite?"

I said with a coldness that would have done him proud, "I've been cut."

"What do you mean, cut?"

It only lasted a precious minute, but I managed once to see my father perplexed.

"Cut." It was so delicious. I didn't mind draining away into the plaid seat cushions.

"When? By whom?"

Daddy, even in a critical moment, wouldn't say "By who?"

"Dolores cut me." The economy of words showed my contempt for them all.

"How badly?"

I would have reminded him that I was no doctor and therefore was ill equipped to do a thorough examination, but impudence would have diminished my lead.

"I don't know."

He put the car in gear, smoothly, and I enviously realized that although I had driven his car I didn't know how to drive.

I thought we were en route to an emergency hospital, and so with serenity I made plans for my death and will. As I faded into time's dateless night, I would say to the doctor, "The moving finger writes and having writ, moves on..." and my soul would escape gracefully. Bailey was to have my books, my Lester Young records and my love from the next world. I had groggily surrendered myself to oblivion when the car stopped.

Dad said, "O.K., kid, errer let's go."

We were in a strange driveway, and even before I got out of the car he was on the steps of a typical southern California ranch-type house. The doorbell chimed, and he beckoned me up the steps. When the door opened he signaled me to stand outside. After all, I was dripping, and I could see the living room was carpeted. Dad went in but didn't quite close the door, and a few minutes later a woman called to me in a whisper from the side of the house. I followed her into a recreation room, and she asked me where I was hurt. She was quiet and her concern seemed sincere. I pulled off my dress and we both looked into the open flesh on my side. She was as pleased as I was disappointed that the edges of the wound had begun to clot. She washed witch hazel over the rupture and taped me tightly with extra-long Band-Aids. Then we went into the living room. Dad shook hands with the man he'd been talking to and thanked my emergency nurse and we left.

In the car he explained that the couple were his friends and he had asked the wife to look at me. He said he told her if the laceration wasn't too deep he would be grateful if she treated it. Otherwise he'd have to take me to a hospital. Could I imagine the scandal if people found out that his, Bailey Johnson's, daughter had been cut by his lady friend? He was after all a Mason, an Elk, a naval dietician and the first Negro deacon in the Lutheran church. No Negro in the city would be able to hold his head up if our misfortune became common knowledge. While the lady (I never knew her name) dressed my wound he had telephoned other friends and made arrangements for me to spend the night with them. At another strange trailer, in yet another mobile park, I was taken in and given night clothes and a bed. Dad said he'd see me around noon the next day.

I went to bed and slept as if my death wish had come true. In the morning neither the empty and unfamiliar surroundings nor the stiffness of my side bothered me. I made and ate a big breakfast and sat down with a slick magazine to wait for Dad.

At fifteen life had taught me undeniably that surrender, in its place, was as honorable as resistance, especially if one had no choice.

When my father came, with a jacket thrown over the striped cotton uniform he wore as a naval dietician, he asked how I felt, gave me a dollar and a half and a kiss, and said he'd drop by late in the evening. He laughed as usual. Nervous?

Alone, I imagined the owners returning to find me in their house, and realized that I didn't even remember what they looked like. How could I bear their contempt or their pity? If I disappeared Dad would be relieved, not to mention Dolores. I hesitated nearly too long. What would I do? Did I have the nerve to commit suicide? If I jumped in the ocean wouldn't I come up all bloated like the man Bailey saw in Stamps? The thought of my brother made me pause. What would he do? I waited a patience and another patience and then he ordered me to leave. But don't kill yourself. You can always do that if things get bad enough.

I made a few tuna sandwiches, lumpy with pickles, put a Band-Aid supply in my pocket, counted my money (I had over three dollars plus some Mexican coins) and walked out. When I heard the door slam I knew the decision had jelled. I had no key and nothing on earth would induce me to stand around until Dad's friends returned to pityingly let me back in.

Now that I was out free, I set to thinking of my future. The obvious solution to my homelessness concerned me only briefly. I could go home to Mother, but I couldn't. I could never succeed in shielding the gash in my side from her. She was too perceptive not to notice the crusty Band-Aids and my favoring the wound. And if I failed to hide the wound we were certain to experience another scene of violence. I thought of poor Mr. Freeman, and the guilt which lined my heart, even after all those years, was a nagging passenger in my mind.

CHAPTER 32

I spent the day wandering aimlessly through the bright streets. The noisy penny arcades with their gaggle-giggle of sailors and children and the games of chance were tempting, but after walking through one of them it was obvious that I could only win more chances and no money. I went to the library and used a part of my day reading science fiction, and in its marble washroom I changed my bandage.

On one flat street I passed a junkyard, littered with the carcasses of old cars. The dead hulks were somehow so uninviting that I decided to inspect them. As I wound my way through the discards a temporary solution sprang to my mind. I would find a clean or cleanish car and spend the night in it. With the optimism of ignorance I thought that the morning was bound to bring a more pleasant solution. A tall-bodied gray car near the fence caught my eye. Its seats were untorn, and although it had no wheels or rims it sat evenly on its fenders. The idea of sleeping in the near open bolstered my sense of freedom. I was a loose kite in a gentle wind floating with only my will for an anchor. After deciding upon the car, I got inside and ate the tuna sandwiches and then searched the floorboards for holes. The fear that rats might scurry in and eat off my nose as I slept (some cases had been recently reported in the papers) was more alarming than the shadowed hulks in the junkyard or the quickly descending night. My gray choice, however, seemed rat-tight, and I abandoned my idea of taking another walk and decided to sit steady and wait for sleep.

My car was an island and the junkyard a sea, and I was all alone and full of warm. The mainland was just a decision away. As evening became definite the street lamps flashed on and the lights of moving cars squared my world in a piercing probing. I counted the headlights and said my prayers and fell asleep.

The morning's brightness drew me awake and I was surrounded with strangeness. I had slid down the seat and slept the night through in an ungainly position. Wrestling with my body to assume an upward arrangement, I saw a collage of Negro, Mexican and white faces outside the windows. They were laughing and making the mouth gestures of talkers but their sounds didn't penetrate my refuge. There was so much curiosity evident in their features that I knew they wouldn't just go away before they knew who I was, so I opened the door, prepared to give them any story (even the truth) that would buy my peace.

The windows and my grogginess had distorted their features. I had thought they were adults and maybe citizens of Brobdingnag, at least. Standing outside, I found there was only one person taller than I, and that I was only a few years younger than any of them. I was asked my name, where I came from and what led me to the junkyard. They accepted my explanation that I was from San Francisco, that my name was Marguerite but that I was called Maya and I simply had no place to stay. With a generous gesture the tall boy, who said he was Bootsie, welcomed me, and said I could stay as long as I honored their rule: No two people of opposite sex slept together. In fact, unless it rained, everyone had his own private sleeping accommodations. Since some of the cars leaked, bad weather forced a doubling up. There was no stealing, not for reasons of morality but because a crime would bring the police to the yard; and since everyone was underage, there was the likelihood that they'd be sent off to foster homes or juvenile delinquent courts. Everyone worked at something. Most of the girls collected bottles and worked weekends in greasy spoons. The boys mowed lawns, swept out pool halls and ran errands for small Negro-owned stores. All money was held by Bootsie and used communally.

During the month that I spent in the yard I learned to drive (one boy's older brother owned a car that moved), to curse and to dance. Lee Arthur was the only boy who ran around with the gang but lived at home with his mother. Mrs. Arthur worked nights, so on Friday evening all the girls went to his house for a bath. We did our laundry in the Laundromat, but those things that required ironing were taken to Lee's house and the ironing chore was shared, as was everything else.

On Saturday night we entered the jitterbug contest at the Silver Slipper, whether we could dance or not. The prizes were tempting ($25 to first couple, $10 to second and $5 to third), and Bootsie reasoned that if all of us entered we had a better chance. Juan, the Mexican boy, was my partner, and although he couldn't dance any better than I, we were a sensation on the floor. He was very short with a shock of straight black hair that swished around his head when he pivoted, and I was thin and black and tall as a tree. On my last weekend at the yard, we actually won the second prize. The dance we performed could never be duplicated or described except to say that the passion with which we threw each other around the small dance area was similar to the zeal shown in honest wrestling matches and hand-to-hand combat.

After a month my thinking processes had so changed that I was hardly recognizable to myself. The unquestioning acceptance by my peers had dislodged the familiar insecurity. Odd that the homeless children, the silt of war frenzy, could initiate me into the brotherhood of man. After hunting down unbroken bottles and selling them with a white girl from Missouri, a Mexican girl from Los Angeles and a Black girl from Oklahoma, I was never again to sense myself so solidly outside the pale of the human race. The lack of criticism evidenced by our ad hoc community influenced me, and set a tone of tolerance for my life.

I telephoned Mother (her voice reminded me of another world) and asked her to send for me. When she said she was going to send my air ticket to Daddy, I explained that it would be easier if she simply sent my fare to the airline, then I'd pick it up. With the easy grace characteristic of Mother when she was given a chance to be magnanimous she agreed.

The unrestrained life we had led made me believe that my new friends would be undemonstrative about my leaving. I was right. After

I picked up my ticket I announced rather casually that I would be leaving the following day. My revelation was accepted with at least the equal amount of detachment (only it was not a pose) and everyone wished me well. I didn't want to say goodbye to the junkyard or to my car, so I spent my last night at an all-night movie. One girl, whose name and face have melted into the years, gave me "an all-enduring friendship ring," and Juan gave me a black lace handkerchief just in case I wanted to go to church sometime.

I arrived in San Francisco, leaner than usual, fairly unkempt, and with no luggage. Mother took one look and said, "Is the rationing that bad at your father's? You'd better have some food to stick to all those bones." She, as she called it, turned to, and soon I sat at a clothed table with bowls of food, expressly cooked for me.

I was at a home, again. And my mother was a fine lady. Dolores was a fool and, more important, a liar.

CHAPTER 33

The house seemed smaller and quieter after the trip south, and the first bloom of San Francisco's glamour had dulled around the edges. Adults had lost the wisdom from the surface of their faces. I reasoned that I had given up some youth for knowledge, but my gain was more valuable than the loss.

Bailey was much older too. Even years older than I had become. He had made friends during that youth-shattering summer with a group of slick street boys. His language had changed. He was forever dropping slangy terms into his sentences like dumplings in a pot. He may have been glad to see me, but he didn't act much like it. When I tried to tell him of my adventures and misadventures, he responded with a casual indifference which stilled the tale on my lips. His new companions cluttered the living room and halls wearing zoot suits and wide-brimmed hats and dangling long snaky chains hooked at their belts.

They drank sloe gin secretly and told dirty jokes. Although I had no regrets, I told myself sadly that growing up was not the painless process one would have thought it to be.

In one area my brother and I found ourselves closer. I had gotten the knack of public dancing. All the lessons with Mother, who danced so effortlessly, had not borne immediate fruit. But with my newly and dearly bought assurance I could give myself up to the rhythms and let them propel me where they willed.

Mother allowed us to go to the big band dances in the crowded city auditorium. We danced the jitterbug to Count Basie, the Lindy and the Big Apple to Cab Calloway, and the Half Time Texas Hop to Duke Ellington. In a matter of months cute Bailey and his tall sister were famous as those dancing fools (which was an apt description).

Although I had risked my life (not intentionally) in her defense, Mother's reputation, good name and community image ceased, or nearly ceased, being of interest to me. It was not that I cared for her less but that I concerned myself less about everything and everyone. I often thought of the tedium of life once one had seen all its surprises. In two months, I had become blasé.

———

Mother and Bailey were entangled in the Oedipal skein. Neither could do without or do with the other; yet the constrictions of conscience and society, morality and ethos dictated a separation. On some flimsy excuse, Mother ordered Bailey out of the house. On an equally flimsy excuse he complied. Bailey was sixteen, small for his age, bright for any and hopelessly in love with Mother Dear. Her heroes were her friends and her friends were big men in the rackets. They wore two-hundred-dollar Chesterfield coats, Busch shoes at fifty dollars a pair, and Knox hats. Their shirts were monogrammed and their fingernails manicured. How could a sixteen-year-old boy hope to compete with such over-shadowing rivals? He did what he had to do. He acquired a withered white prostitute, a diamond ring on his little finger and a Harris tweed coat with raglan sleeves. He didn't consciously consider the new possessions the open sesame to Mother Dear's vault of acceptance. And she had no idea that her preferences prodded him to such excesses.

From the wings I heard and watched the pavane of tragedy move steadily toward its climax. Interception and even the thought of it was impossible. Easier to plan an obstruction to a sunrise or a hurricane. If Mother was a beautiful woman who exacted the tribute of obeisance from all men, she was also a mother, and "a damn good one." No son of hers was going to be exploited by a used-up white whore, who wanted to milk him of his youth and spoil him for adulthood. Hell, no.

Bailey, for his part, was her son as she was his mother. He had no intention of taking low even from the most beautiful woman in the world. The fact that she happened to be his mother did nothing to weaken his resolve.

Get out? Oh, hell, yes. Tomorrow? What's wrong with today? Today? What about right now? But neither could move until all the measured steps had been negotiated.

During the weeks of bitter wrangling I sat in hopeless wonder. We were not allowed profanity or even obvious sarcasm, but Bailey looped his language around his tongue and issued it out to Mother in alum drops. She threw her "ing bings" (passionate explosions guaranteed to depilate the chest of the strongest man) and was sweetly sorry (only to me) after.

I had been left out of their power/love struggles. It would be more correct to say that since neither needed a claque I was forgotten on the sidelines.

It was a little like Switzerland in World War II. Shells were bursting all around me, souls were tortured and I was powerless in the confines of imposed neutrality—hopes were dying. The confrontation, which brought relief, had come on an ordinary unheralded evening. It was after eleven o'clock, so I left my door ajar, hoping to hear Mother go out, or the creak of Bailey easing up the stairs.

The record player on the first floor volumed up Lonnie Johnson singing, "Tomorrow night, will you remember what you said tonight?" Glasses clinked and voices rubbed each other. A party was shimmering below and Bailey had defied Mother's eleven o'clock curfew. If he made it in before midnight, she might be satisfied with slapping him across the face a few times with her lashing words.

Twelve o'clock came and went at once, and I sat up in bed and laid my cards out for the first of many games of solitaire.

———

"Bailey!"

My watch hands made the uneven V of one o'clock.

"Yes, Mother Dear?" En garde. His voice thrust sweet and sour, and he accented the "dear."

"I guess you're a man... Turn down that record player." She shouted the last to the revelers.

"I'm your son, Mother Dear." A swift parry.

"Is it eleven o'clock, Bailey?" That was a feint, designed to catch the opponent offguard.

"It's after one o'clock, Mother Dear." He had opened up the game, and the strokes from then on would have to be direct.

"Clidell is the only man in this house, and if you think you're so much of a man..." Her voice popped like a razor on a strap.

"I'm leaving now, Mother Dear." The deferential tone heightened the content of his announcement. In a bloodless coup he had thrust beneath her visor.

Now, laid open, she had no recourse but to hurry along the tunnel of her anger, headlong.

"Then Goddammit, get your heels to clicking." And her heels were clicking down the linoleum hall as Bailey tap-danced up the stairs to his room.

When rain comes finally, washing away a low sky of muddy ocher, we who could not control the phenomenon are pressed into relief. The near-occult feeling: The fact of being witness to the end of the world gives way to tangible things. Even if the succeeding sensations are not common, they are at least not mysterious.

Bailey was leaving home. At one o'clock in the morning, my little brother, who in my lonely days of inferno dwelling had protected me from goblins, gnomes, gremlins and devils, was leaving home.

I had known all along the inevitable outcome and that I dared not poke into his knapsack of misery, even with the offer to help him carry it.

I went to his room, against my judgment, and found him throwing his carefully tended clothes into a pillowcase. His maturity embarrassed me. In his little face, balled up like a fist, I found no vestige of my brother, and when, not knowing what to say, I asked if I could help, he answered, "Leave me the shit alone."

I leaned on the doorjamb, lending him my physical presence but said no more.

"She wants me out, does she? Well, I'll get out of here so fast I'll leave the air on fire. She calls herself a mother? Huh! I'll be damned. She's seen the last of me. I can make it. I'll always make it."

At some point he noticed me still in the doorway, and his consciousness stretched to remember our relationship.

"Maya, if you want to leave now, come on. I'll take care of you."

He didn't wait for an answer, but as quickly went back to speaking to his soul. "She won't miss me, and I sure as hell won't miss her. To hell with her and everybody else."

He had finished jamming his shoes on top of his shirts and ties, and socks were wadded into the pillowcase. He remembered me again.

"Maya, you can have my books."

My tears were not for Bailey or Mother or even myself but for the helplessness of mortals who live on the sufferance of Life. In order to avoid this bitter end, we would all have to be born again, and born with the knowledge of alternatives. Even then?

Bailey grabbed up the lumpy pillowcase and pushed by me for the stairs. As the front door slammed, the record player downstairs mastered the house and Nat King Cole warned the world to "straighten up and fly right." As if they could, as if human beings could make a choice.

Mother's eyes were red, and her face puffy, the next morning, but she smiled her "everything is everything" smile and turned in tight little moons, making breakfast, talking business and brightening the corner where she was. No one mentioned Bailey's absence as if things were as they should be and always were.

The house was smudged with unspoken thoughts and it was necessary to go to my room to breathe. I believed I knew where he headed the night before, and made up my mind to find him and offer him my support. In the afternoon I went to a bay-windowed house which boasted ROOMS, in green and orange letters, through the glass. A woman of any age past thirty answered my ring and said Bailey Johnson was at the top of the stairs.

His eyes were as red as Mother's had been, but his face had loosened a little from the tightness of the night before. In an almost formal manner I was invited into a room with a clean chenille-covered bed, an easy chair, a gas fireplace and a table.

He began to talk, covering up the unusual situation that we found ourselves in.

"Nice room, isn't it? You know it's very hard to find rooms now. The war and all...Betty lives here [she was the white prostitute] and she got this place for me...Maya, you know, it's better this way...I mean, I'm a man, and I have to be on my own..."

I was furious that he didn't curse and abuse the Fates or Mother or at least act put upon.

"Well"—I thought to start it—"If Mother was really a mother, she wouldn't have——"

He stopped me, his little black hand held up as if I were to read his palm. "Wait, Maya, she was right. There is a tide and time in every man's life——"

"Bailey, you're sixteen."

"Chronologically, yes, but I haven't been sixteen for years. Anyway, there comes a time when a man must cut the apron strings and face life on his own...As I was saying to Mother Dear, I've come to——"

"When were you talking to Mother...?"

"This morning, I said to Mother Dear——"

"Did you phone her?"

"Yes. And she came by here. We had a very fruitful discussion"—he chose his words with the precision of a Sunday school teacher—"She understands completely. There is a time in every man's life when he must push off from the wharf of safety into the sea of chance...Anyway, she is arranging with a friend of hers in Oakland to get me on the Southern Pacific. Maya, it's just a start. I'll begin as a dining-car waiter and then a steward, and when I know all there is to know about that,

I'll branch out... The future looks good. The Black man hasn't even begun to storm the battlefronts. I'm going for broke myself."

His room smelled of cooked grease, Lysol and age, but his face believed the freshness of his words, and I had no heart nor art to drag him back to the reeking reality of our life and times.

Whores were lying down first and getting up last in the room next door. Chicken suppers and gambling games were rioting on a twenty-four-hour basis downstairs. Sailors and soldiers on their doom-lined road to war cracked windows and broke locks for blocks around, hoping to leave their imprint on a building or in the memory of a victim. A chance to be perpetrated. Bailey sat wrapped in his decision and anesthetized by youth. If I'd had any suggestion to make I couldn't have penetrated his unlucky armor. And, most regrettable, I had no suggestion to make.

"I'm your sister, and whatever I can do, I'll do it."

"Maya, don't worry about me. That's all I want you to do. Don't worry. I'll be okey-dokey."

I left his room because, and only because, we had said all we could say. The unsaid words pushed roughly against the thoughts that we had no craft to verbalize, and crowded the room to uneasiness.

CHAPTER 34

Later, my room had all the cheeriness of a dungeon and the appeal of a tomb. It was going to be impossible to stay there, but leaving held no attraction for me, either. Running away from home would be anticlimactic after Mexico, and a dull story after my month in the car lot. But the need for change bulldozed a road down the center of my mind.

I had it. The answer came to me with the suddenness of a collision. I would go to work. Mother wouldn't be difficult to convince; after all, in school I was a year ahead of my grade and Mother was a firm believer in self-sufficiency. In fact, she'd be pleased to think that I had that much gumption, that much of her in my character. (She liked to speak of herself as the original "do-it-yourself girl.")

Once I had settled on getting a job, all that remained was to decide which kind of job I was most fitted for. My intellectual pride had kept me from selecting typing, shorthand or filing as subjects in school, so office work was ruled out. War plants and shipyards demanded birth certificates, and mine would reveal me to be fifteen, and ineligible for work. So the well-paying defense jobs were also out. Women had replaced men on the streetcars as conductors and motormen, and the thought of sailing up and down the hills of San Francisco in a dark-blue uniform, with a money changer at my belt, caught my fancy.

Mother was as easy as I had anticipated. The world was moving so fast, so much money was being made, so many people were dying in Guam, and Germany, that hordes of strangers became good friends overnight. Life was cheap and death entirely free. How could she have the time to think about my academic career?

To her question of what I planned to do, I replied that I would get a job on the streetcars. She rejected the proposal with: "They don't accept colored people on the streetcars."

I would like to claim an immediate fury which was followed by the noble determination to break the restricting tradition. But the truth is, my first reaction was one of disappointment. I'd pictured myself, dressed in a neat blue serge suit, my money changer swinging jauntily at my waist, and a cheery smile for the passengers which would make their own work day brighter.

From disappointment, I gradually ascended the emotional ladder to haughty indignation, and finally to that state of stubbornness where the mind is locked like the jaws of an enraged bulldog.

I would go to work on the streetcars and wear a blue serge suit. Mother gave me her support with one of her usual terse asides, "That's what you want to do? Then nothing beats a trial but a failure. Give it everything you've got. I've told you many times, 'Can't do is like Don't Care.' Neither of them have a home."

Translated, that meant there was nothing a person can't do, and there should be nothing a human being didn't care about. It was the most positive encouragement I could have hoped for.

———

In the offices of the Market Street Railway Company, the receptionist seemed as surprised to see me there as I was surprised to find the interior dingy and the décor drab. Somehow I had expected waxed surfaces and carpeted floors. If I had met no resistance, I might have decided against working for such a poor-mouth-looking concern. As it was, I explained that I had come to see about a job. She asked, was I sent by an agency, and when I replied that I was not, she told me they were only accepting applicants from agencies.

The classified pages of the morning papers had listed advertisements for motorettes and conductorettes and I reminded her of that. She gave me a face full of astonishment that my suspicious nature would not accept.

"I am applying for the job listed in this morning's *Chronicle* and I'd like to be presented to your personnel manager." While I spoke in supercilious accents, and looked at the room as if I had an oil well in my own backyard, my armpits were being pricked by millions of hot pointed needles. She saw her escape and dived into it.

"He's out. He's out for the day. You might call tomorrow and if he's in, I'm sure you can see him." Then she swiveled her chair around on its rusty screws and with that I was supposed to be dismissed.

"May I ask his name?"

She half turned, acting surprised to find me still there.

"His name? Whose name?"

"Your personnel manager."

We were firmly joined in the hypocrisy to play out the scene.

"The personnel manager? Oh, he's Mr. Cooper, but I'm not sure you'll find him here tomorrow. He's ... Oh, but you can try."

"Thank you."

"You're welcome."

And I was out of the musty room and into the even mustier lobby. In the street I saw the receptionist and myself going faithfully through paces that were stale with familiarity, although I had never encountered that kind of situation before and, probably, neither had she. We were like actors who, knowing the play by heart, were still able to cry afresh over the old tragedies and laugh spontaneously at the comic situations.

The miserable little encounter had nothing to do with me, the me of me, any more than it had to do with that silly clerk. The incident was a recurring dream, concocted years before by stupid whites and it eternally came back to haunt us all. The secretary and I were like Hamlet and Laertes in the final scene, where, because of harm done by one ancestor to another, we were bound to duel to the death. Also because the play must end somewhere.

I went further than forgiving the clerk, I accepted her as a fellow victim of the same puppeteer.

On the streetcar, I put my fare into the box and the conductorette looked at me with the usual hard eyes of white contempt. "Move into the car, please move on in the car." She patted her money changer.

Her Southern nasal accent sliced my meditation and I looked deep into my thoughts. All lies, all comfortable lies. The receptionist was not innocent and neither was I. The whole charade we had played out in that crummy waiting room had directly to do with me, Black, and her, white.

I wouldn't move into the streetcar but stood on the ledge over the conductor, glaring. My mind shouted so energetically that the announcement made my veins stand out, and my mouth tighten into a prune.

I WOULD HAVE THE JOB. I WOULD BE A CONDUC-TORETTE AND SLING A FULL MONEY CHANGER FROM MY BELT. I WOULD.

The next three weeks were a honeycomb of determination with apertures for the days to go in and out. The Negro organizations to whom I appealed for support bounced me back and forth like a shuttlecock on a badminton court. Why did I insist on that particular job? Openings were going begging that paid nearly twice the money. The minor officials with whom I was able to win an audience thought me mad. Possibly I was.

Downtown San Francisco became alien and cold, and the streets I had loved in a personal familiarity were unknown lanes that twisted with malicious intent. Old buildings, whose gray rococo façades housed my memories of the Forty-Niners, and Diamond Lil, Robert Service, Sutter and Jack London, were then imposing structures viciously joined to keep me out. My trips to the streetcar office were of the frequency of a person on salary. The struggle expanded. I was no longer in conflict only with the Market Street Railway but with the marble lobby of the building which housed its offices, and elevators and their operators.

During this period of strain Mother and I began our first steps on the long path toward mutual adult admiration. She never asked for reports and I didn't offer any details. But every morning she made breakfast, gave me carfare and lunch money, as if I were going to work. She comprehended the perversity of life, that in the struggle lies the joy. That I was no glory seeker was obvious to her, and that I had to exhaust every possibility before giving in was also clear.

On my way out of the house one morning she said, "Life is going to give you just what you put in it. Put your whole heart in everything you do, and pray, then you can wait." Another time she reminded me that "God helps those who help themselves." She had a store of aphorisms which she dished out as the occasion demanded. Strangely, as bored as I was with clichés, her inflection gave them something new, and set me thinking for a little while at least. Later when asked how I got my job, I was never able to say exactly. I only knew that one day, which was tiresomely like all the others before it, I sat in the Railway office, ostensibly waiting to be interviewed. The receptionist called me to her desk and shuffled a bundle of papers to me. They were job application forms. She said they had to be filled in triplicate. I had little time to wonder if I had won or not, for the standard questions reminded me of the necessity for dexterous lying. How old was I? List my previous jobs, starting from the last held and go backward to the first. How much money did I earn, and why did I leave the position? Give two references (not relatives).

Sitting at a side table my mind and I wove a cat's ladder of near truths and total lies. I kept my face blank (an old art) and wrote quickly the fable of Marguerite Johnson, aged nineteen, former companion and driver for Mrs. Annie Henderson (a White Lady) in Stamps, Arkansas.

I was given blood tests, aptitude tests, physical coordination tests, and Rorschachs, then on a blissful day I was hired as the first Negro on the San Francisco streetcars.

Mother gave me the money to have my blue serge suit tailored, and I learned to fill out work cards, operate the money changer and punch transfers. The time crowded together and at an End of Days I was swinging on the back of the rackety trolley, smiling sweetly and persuading my charges to "step forward in the car, please."

For one whole semester the streetcars and I shimmied up and scooted down the sheer hills of San Francisco. I lost some of my need for the Black ghetto's shielding-sponge quality, as I clanged and cleared my way down Market Street, with its honky-tonk homes for homeless sailors, past the quiet retreat of Golden Gate Park and along closed undwelled-in-looking dwellings of the Sunset District.

My work shifts were split so haphazardly that it was easy to believe that my superiors had chosen them maliciously. Upon mentioning my suspicions to Mother, she said, "Don't worry about it. You ask for what you want, and you pay for what you get. And I'm going to show you that it ain't no trouble when you pack double."

She stayed awake to drive me out to the car barn at four thirty in the mornings, or to pick me up when I was relieved just before dawn. Her awareness of life's perils convinced her that while I would be safe on the public conveyances, she "wasn't about to trust a taxi driver with her baby."

When the spring classes began, I resumed my commitment with formal education. I was so much wiser and older, so much more independent, with a bank account and clothes that I had bought for myself, that I was sure that I had learned and earned the magic formula which would make me a part of the gay life my contemporaries led.

Not a bit of it. Within weeks, I realized that my schoolmates and I were on paths moving diametrically away from each other. They were concerned and excited over the approaching football games, but I had in my immediate past raced a car down a dark and foreign Mexican mountain. They concentrated great interest on who was worthy of being student body president, and when the metal bands would be removed from their teeth, while I remembered sleeping for a month in a wrecked automobile and conducting a streetcar in the uneven hours of the morning.

Without willing it, I had gone from being ignorant of being ignorant to being aware of being aware. And the worst part of my awareness was that I didn't know what I was aware of. I knew I knew very little, but I was certain that the things I had yet to learn wouldn't be taught to me at George Washington High School.

I began to cut classes, to walk in Golden Gate Park or wander along the shiny counter of the Emporium Department Store. When Mother discovered that I was playing truant, she told me that if I didn't want to go to school one day, if there were no tests being held, and if my school work was up to standard, all I had to do was tell her and I could stay home. She said that she didn't want some white woman calling her up to tell her something about her child that she didn't know. And she didn't want to be put in the position of lying to a white woman because I wasn't woman enough to speak up. That put an end to my truancy, but nothing appeared to lighten the long gloomy day that going to school became.

To be left alone on the tightrope of youthful unknowing is to experience the excruciating beauty of full freedom and the threat of eternal indecision. Few, if any, survive their teens. Most surrender to the vague but murderous pressure of adult conformity. It becomes easier to die and avoid conflicts than to maintain a constant battle with the superior forces of maturity.

Until recently each generation found it more expedient to plead guilty to the charge of being young and ignorant, easier to take the punishment meted out by the older generation (which had itself confessed to the same crime short years before). The command to grow up at once was more bearable than the faceless horror of wavering purpose, which was youth.

The bright hours when the young rebelled against the descending sun had to give way to twenty-four-hour periods called "days" that were named as well as numbered.

The Black female is assaulted in her tender years by all those common forces of nature at the same time that she is caught in the tripartite crossfire of masculine prejudice, white illogical hate and Black lack of power.

The fact that the adult American Negro female emerges a formidable character is often met with amazement, distaste and even belligerence. It is seldom accepted as an inevitable outcome of the struggle won by survivors and deserves respect if not enthusiastic acceptance.

CHAPTER 35

The Well of Loneliness was my introduction to lesbianism and what I thought of as pornography. For months the book was both a treat and a threat. It allowed me to see a little of the mysterious world of the pervert. It stimulated my libido and I told myself that it was educational because it informed me of the difficulties in the secret world of the pervert. I was certain that I didn't know any perverts. Of course I ruled out the jolly sissies who sometimes stayed at our house and cooked whopping eight-course dinners while the perspiration made paths down their made-up faces. Since everyone accepted them, and more particularly since they accepted themselves, I knew that their laughter was real and that their lives were cheerful comedies, interrupted only by costume changes and freshening of make-up.

But true freaks, the "women lovers," captured yet strained my imagination. They were, according to the book, disowned by their families, snubbed by their friends and ostracized from every society. This bitter punishment was inflicted upon them because of a physical condition over which they had no control.

After my third reading of *The Well of Loneliness* I became a bleeding heart for the downtrodden misunderstood lesbians. I thought "lesbian" was synonymous with hermaphrodite, and when I wasn't actively aching over their pitiful state, I was wondering how they managed simpler body functions. Did they have a choice of organs to use, and if so, did they alternate or play favorite? Or I tried to imagine how two hermaphrodites made love, and the more I pondered the more confused I became. It seemed that having two of everything other people had, and four where ordinary people just had two, would complicate matters to the point of giving up the idea of making love at all.

It was during this reflective time that I noticed how heavy my own voice had become. It droned and drummed two or three whole tones lower than my schoolmates' voices. My hands and feet were also far from being feminine and dainty. In front of the mirror I detachedly examined my body. For a sixteen-year-old my breasts were sadly undeveloped. They could only be called skin swellings, even by the kindest critic. The line from my rib cage to my knees fell straight without even a ridge to disturb its direction. Younger girls than I boasted of having to shave under their arms, but my armpits were as smooth as my face. There was also a mysterious growth developing on my body that defied explanation. It looked totally useless.

Then the question began to live under my blankets: How did lesbianism begin? What were the symptoms? The public library gave information on the finished lesbian—and that woefully sketchy—but on the growth of a lesbian, there was nothing. I did discover that the difference between hermaphrodites and lesbians was that hermaphrodites were "born that way." It was impossible to determine whether lesbians budded gradually, or burst into being with a suddenness that dismayed them as much as it repelled society.

I had gnawed into the unsatisfying books and into my own unstocked mind without finding a morsel of peace or understanding.

And meantime, my voice refused to stay up in the higher registers where I consciously pitched it, and I had to buy my shoes in the "old lady's comfort" section of the shoe stores.

I asked Mother.

Daddy Clidell was at the club one evening, so I sat down on the side of Mother's bed. As usual she woke completely and at once. (There is never any yawning or stretching with Vivian Baxter. She's either awake or asleep.)

"Mother, I've got to talk to you…" It was going to kill me to have to ask her, for in the asking wouldn't it be possible that suspicion would fall on my own normality? I knew her well enough to know that if I committed almost any crime and told her the truth about it she not only wouldn't disown me but would give me her protection. But just suppose I was developing into a lesbian, how would she react? And then there was Bailey to worry about too.

"Ask me, and pass me a cigarette." Her calmness didn't fool me for a minute. She used to say that her secret to life was that she "hoped for the best, was prepared for the worst, so anything in between didn't come as a surprise." That was all well and good for most things but if her only daughter was developing into a…

She moved over and patted the bed, "Come on, baby, get in the bed. You'll freeze before you get your question out."

It was better to remain where I was for the time being.

"Mother… my pocketbook…"

"Ritie, do you mean your vagina? Don't use those Southern terms. There's nothing wrong with the word 'vagina.' It's a clinical description. Now, what's wrong with it?"

The smoke collected under the bed lamp, then floated out to be free in the room. I was deathly sorry that I had begun to ask her anything.

"Well?… Well? Have you got crabs?"

Since I didn't know what they were, that puzzled me. I thought I might have them and it wouldn't go well for my side if I said I didn't. On the other hand, I just might not have them, and suppose I lied and said I did?

"I don't know, Mother."

"Do you itch? Does your vagina itch?" She leaned on one elbow and jabbed out her cigarette.

"No, Mother."

"Then you don't have crabs. If you had them, you'd tell the world."

I wasn't sorry or glad not to have them, but made a mental note to look up "crabs" in the library on my next trip.

She looked at me closely, and only a person who knew her face well could have perceived the muscles relaxing and interpreted this as an indication of concern.

"You don't have a venereal disease, do you?"

The question wasn't asked seriously, but knowing Mother I was shocked at the idea. "Why, Mother, of course not. That's a terrible question." I was ready to go back to my room and wrestle alone with my worries.

"Sit down, Ritie. Pass me another cigarette." For a second it looked as if she was thinking about laughing. That would really do it. If she laughed, I'd never tell her anything else. Her laughter would make it easier to accept my social isolation and human freakishness. But she wasn't even smiling. Just slowly pulling in the smoke and holding it in puffed cheeks before blowing it out.

"Mother, something is growing on my vagina."

There, it was out. I'd soon know whether I was to be her ex-daughter or if she'd put me in hospital for an operation.

"Where on your vagina, Marguerite?"

Uh-huh. It was bad all right. Not "Ritie" or "Maya" or "Baby." "Marguerite."

"On both sides. Inside." I couldn't add that they were fleshy skin flaps that had been growing for months down there. She'd have to pull that out of me.

"Ritie, go get me that big *Webster's* and then bring me a bottle of beer."

Suddenly, it wasn't all that serious. I was "Ritie" again, and she just asked for beer. If it had been as awful as I anticipated, she'd have ordered Scotch and water. I took her the huge dictionary that she had bought as a birthday gift for Daddy Clidell and laid it on the bed. The weight forced a side of the mattress down and Mother twisted her bed lamp to beam down on the book.

When I returned from the kitchen and poured her beer, as she had taught Bailey and me beer should be poured, she patted the bed.

"Sit down, baby. Read this." Her fingers guided my eyes to VULVA. I began to read. She said, "Read it out loud."

It was all very clear and normal-sounding. She drank the beer as I read, and when I had finished she explained it in every-day terms. My relief melted the fears and they liquidly stole down my face.

Mother shot up and put her arms around me.

"There's nothing to worry about, baby. It happens to every woman. It's just human nature."

It was all right then to unburden my heavy, heavy heart. I cried into the crook of my arm. "I thought maybe I was turning into a lesbian."

Her patting of my shoulder slowed to a still and she leaned away from me.

"A lesbian? Where the hell did you get that idea?"

"Those things growing on my . . . vagina, and my voice is too deep and my feet are big, and I have no hips or breasts or anything. And my legs are so skinny."

Then she did laugh. I knew immediately that she wasn't laughing at me. Or rather that she was laughing at me, but it was something about me that pleased her. The laugh choked a little on the smoke in its way, but finally broke through cleanly. I had to give a small laugh too, although I wasn't tickled at all. But it's mean to watch someone enjoy something and not show your understanding of their enjoyment.

When she finished with the laughter, she laid it down a peal at a time and turned to me, wiping her eyes.

"I made arrangements, a long time ago, to have a boy and a girl. Bailey is my boy and you are my girl. The Man upstairs, He don't make mistakes. He gave you to me to be my girl and that's just what you are. Now, go wash your face, have a glass of milk and go back to bed."

I did as she said but I soon discovered my new assurance wasn't large enough to fill the gap left by my old uneasiness. It rattled around in my mind like a dime in a tin cup. I hoarded it preciously, but less than two weeks later it became totally worthless.

A classmate of mine, whose mother had rooms for herself and her daughter in a ladies' residence, had stayed out beyond closing time. She telephoned me to ask if she could sleep at my house. Mother gave her permission, providing my friend telephoned her mother from our house.

When she arrived, I got out of bed and we went to the upstairs kitchen to make hot chocolate. In my room we shared mean gossip about our friends, giggled over boys and whined about school and the tedium of life. The unusualness of having someone sleep in my bed (I'd never slept with anyone except my grandmothers) and the frivolous laughter in the middle of the night made me forget simple courtesies. My friend had to remind me that she had nothing to sleep in. I gave her one of my gowns, and without curiosity or interest I watched her pull off her clothes. At none of the early stages of undressing was I in the least conscious of her body. And then suddenly, for the briefest eye span, I saw her breasts. I was stunned.

They were shaped like light-brown falsies in the five-and-ten-cent store, but they were real. They made all the nude paintings I had seen in museums come to life. In a word they were beautiful. A universe divided what she had from what I had. She was a woman.

My gown was too snug for her and much too long, and when she wanted to laugh at her ridiculous image I found that humor had left me without a promise to return.

Had I been older I might have thought that I was moved by both an esthetic sense of beauty and the pure emotion of envy. But those possibilities did not occur to me when I needed them. All I knew was that I had been moved by looking at a woman's breasts. So all the calm and casual words of Mother's explanation a few weeks earlier and the clinical terms of Noah Webster did not alter the fact that in a fundamental way there was something queer about me.

I somersaulted deeper into my snuggery of misery. After a thorough self-examination, in the light of all I had read and heard about dykes and bulldaggers, I reasoned that I had none of the obvious traits—I didn't wear trousers, or have big shoulders or go in for sports, or walk like a man or even want to touch a woman. I wanted to be a woman, but that seemed to me to be a world to which I was to be eternally refused entrance.

What I needed was a boyfriend. A boyfriend would clarify my position to the world and, even more important, to myself. A boyfriend's acceptance of me would guide me into that strange and exotic land of frills and femininity.

Among my associates, there were no takers. Understandably the boys of my age and social group were captivated by the yellow- or light-brown-skinned girls, with hairy legs and smooth little lips, and whose hair "hung down like horses' manes." And even those sought-after girls were asked to "give it up or tell where it is." They were reminded in a popular song of the times, "If you can't smile and say yes, please don't cry and say no." If the pretties were expected to make the supreme sacrifice in order to "belong," what could the unattractive female do? She who had been skimming along on life's turning but never-changing periphery had to be ready to be a "buddy" by day and maybe by night. She was called upon to be generous only if the pretty girls were unavailable.

I believe most plain girls are virtuous because of the scarcity of opportunity to be otherwise. They shield themselves with an aura of unavailableness (for which after a time they begin to take credit) largely as a defense tactic.

In my particular case, I could not hide behind the curtain of voluntary goodness. I was being crushed by two unrelenting forces: the uneasy suspicion that I might not be a normal female and my newly awakening sexual appetite.

I decided to take matters into my own hands. (An unfortunate but apt phrase.)

Up the hill from our house, and on the same side of the street, lived two handsome brothers. They were easily the most eligible young men in the neighborhood. If I was going to venture into sex, I saw no reason why I shouldn't make my experiment with the best of the lot. I didn't really expect to capture either brother on a permanent basis, but I thought if I could hook one temporarily I might be able to work the relationship into something more lasting.

I planned a chart for seduction with surprise as my opening ploy. One evening as I walked up the hill suffering from youth's vague malaise (there was simply nothing to do), the brother I had chosen came walking directly into my trap.

"Hello, Marguerite." He nearly passed me.

I put the plan into action. "Hey." I plunged, "Would you like to have a sexual intercourse with me?" Things were going according to the chart. His mouth hung open like a garden gate. I had the advantage and so I pressed it.

"Take me somewhere."

His response lacked dignity, but in fairness to him I admit that I had left him little chance to be suave.

He asked, "You mean, you're going to give me some trim?"

I assured him that that was exactly what I was about to give him. Even as the scene was being enacted I realized the imbalance in his values. He thought I was giving him something, and the fact of the matter was that it was my intention to take something from him. His good looks and popularity had made him so inordinately conceited that they blinded him to that possibility.

We went to a furnished room occupied by one of his friends, who understood the situation immediately and got his coat and left us alone. The seductee quickly turned off the lights. I would have preferred them left on, but didn't want to appear more aggressive than I had been already. If that was possible.

I was excited rather than nervous, and hopeful instead of frightened. I had not considered how physical an act of seduction would be. I had anticipated long soulful tongued kisses and gentle caresses. But there was no romance in the knee which forced my legs, nor in the rub of hairy skin on my chest.

Unredeemed by shared tenderness, the time was spent in laborious gropings, pullings, yankings and jerkings.

Not one word was spoken.

My partner showed that our experience had reached its climax by getting up abruptly, and my main concern was how to get home quickly. He may have sensed that he had been used, or his disinterest may have been an indication that I was less than gratifying. Neither possibility bothered me.

Outside on the street we left each other with little more than "Okay, see you around."

Thanks to Mr. Freeman nine years before, I had had no pain of entry to endure, and because of the absence of romantic involvement neither of us felt much had happened.

At home I reviewed the failure and tried to evaluate my new position. I had had a man. I had been had. I not only didn't enjoy it, but my normalcy was still a question.

What happened to the moonlight-on-the-prairie feeling? Was there something so wrong with me that I couldn't share a sensation that made poets gush out rhyme after rhyme, that made Richard Arlen brave the Arctic wastes and Veronica Lake betray the entire free world?

There seemed to be no explanation for my private infirmity, but being a product (is "victim" a better word?) of the Southern Negro upbringing, I decided that I "would understand it all better by-and-by." I went to sleep.

Three weeks later, having thought very little of the strange and strangely empty night, I found myself pregnant.

CHAPTER 36

The world had ended, and I was the only person who knew it. People walked along the streets as if the pavements hadn't all crumbled beneath their feet. They pretended to breathe in and out while all the time I knew the air had been sucked away in a monstrous inhalation from God Himself. I alone was suffocating in the nightmare.

The little pleasure I was able to take from the fact that if I could have a baby I obviously wasn't a lesbian was crowded into my mind's tiniest corner by the massive pushing in of fear, guilt, and self-revulsion.

For eons, it seemed, I had accepted my plight as the hapless, put-upon victim of fate and the Furies, but this time I had to face the fact that I had brought my new catastrophe upon myself. How was I to blame the innocent man whom I had lured into making love to me? In order to be profoundly dishonest, a person must have one of two qualities: either he is unscrupulously ambitious, or he is unswervingly egocentric. He must believe that for his ends to be served all things and people can justifiably be shifted about, or that he is the center not only of his own world but of the worlds which others inhabit. I had neither element in my personality, so I hefted the burden of pregnancy at sixteen onto my own shoulders where it belonged. Admittedly, I staggered under the weight.

I finally sent a letter to Bailey, who was at sea with the merchant marine. He wrote back, and he cautioned me against telling Mother of my condition. We both knew her to be violently opposed to abortions, and she would very likely order me to quit school. Bailey suggested that if I quit school before getting my high school diploma I'd find it nearly impossible to return.

The first three months, while I was adapting myself to the fact of pregnancy (I didn't really link pregnancy to the possibility of my having a baby until weeks before my confinement), were a hazy period in which days seemed to lie just below the water level, never emerging fully.

Fortunately, Mother was tied up tighter than Dick's hatband in the weave of her own life. She noticed me, as usual, out of the corner of her existence. As long as I was healthy, clothed and smiling she felt no need to focus her attention on me. As always, her major concern was to live the life given to her, and her children were expected to do the same. And to do it without too much brouhaha.

Under her loose scrutiny I grew more buxom, and my brown skin smoothed and tight-pored, like pancakes fried on an unoiled skillet. And still she didn't suspect. Some years before, I had established a code which never varied. I didn't lie. It was understood that I didn't lie because I was too proud to be caught and forced to admit that I was capable of a less than Olympian action. Mother must have concluded that since I was above out-and-out lying I was also beyond deceit. She was deceived.

All my motions focalized on pretending to be that guileless school-girl who had nothing more wearying to think about than mid-term exams. Strangely enough, I very nearly caught the essence of teenage capriciousness as I played the role. Except that there were times when physically I couldn't deny to myself that something very important was taking place in my body.

Mornings, I never knew if I would have to jump off the streetcar one step ahead of the warm sea of nausea that threatened to sweep me away. On solid ground, away from the ship-motioned vehicle and the smell of hands coated with recent breakfasts, I regained my balance and waited for the next trolley.

School recovered its lost magic. For the first time since Stamps, in-formation was exciting for itself alone. I burrowed myself into caves of facts, and found delight in the logical resolutions of mathematics.

I credit my new reactions (although I didn't know at the time that I had learned anything from them) to the fact that during what surely must have been a critical period I was not dragged down by hopeless-ness. Life had a conveyor-belt quality. It went on unpursued and un-pursuing, and my only thought was to remain erect, and keep my secret along with my balance.

Midway along to delivery, Bailey came home and brought me a spun-silver bracelet from South America, Thomas Wolfe's *Look Home-ward, Angel,* and a slew of new dirty jokes.

As my sixth month approached, Mother left San Francisco for Alaska. She was to open a night club and planned to stay three or four months until it got on its feet. Daddy Clidell was to look after me but I was more or less left on my own recognizance and under the un-steady gaze of our lady roomers.

Mother left the city amid a happy and cheerful send-off party (after all how many Negroes were in Alaska?), and I felt treacherous allowing her to go without informing her that she was soon to be a grandmother.

———

Two days after V-Day, I stood with the San Francisco Summer School class at Mission High School and received my diploma. That evening, in the bosom of the now-dear family home I uncoiled my fearful secret and in a brave gesture left a note on Daddy Clidell's bed. It read: *Dear Parents, I am sorry to bring this disgrace on the family, but I am pregnant. Marguerite.*

The confusion that ensued when I explained to my stepfather that I expected to deliver the baby in three weeks, more or less, was reminiscent of a Molière comedy. Except that it was funny only years later. Daddy Clidell told Mother that I was "three weeks gone." Mother, regarding me as a woman for the first time, said indignantly, "She's more than any three weeks." They both accepted the fact that I was further along than they had first been told but found it nearly impossible to believe that I had carried a baby, eight months and one week, without their being any the wiser.

Mother asked, "Who is the boy?" I told her. She recalled him, faintly.

"Do you want to marry him?"

"No."

"Does he want to marry you?" The father had stopped speaking to me during my fourth month.

"No."

"Well, that's that. No use ruining three lives." There was no overt or subtle condemnation. She was Vivian Baxter Jackson. Hoping for the best, prepared for the worst, and unsurprised by anything in between.

Daddy Clidell assured me that I had nothing to worry about. That "women been gittin' pregnant ever since Eve ate that apple." He sent one of his waitresses to I. Magnin's to buy maternity dresses for me. For the next two weeks I whirled around the city going to doctors, taking vitamin shots and pills, buying clothes for the baby, and except for the rare moments alone, enjoying the imminent blessed event.

After a short labor, and without too much pain (I decided that the pain of delivery was overrated), my son was born. Just as gratefulness was confused in my mind with love, so possession became mixed up with motherhood. I had a baby. He was beautiful and mine. Totally mine. No one had bought him for me. No one had helped me endure the sickly gray months. I had had help in the child's conception, but no one could deny that I had had an immaculate pregnancy.

Totally my possession, and I was afraid to touch him. Home from the hospital, I sat for hours by his bassinet and absorbed his mysterious perfection. His extremities were so dainty they appeared unfinished. Mother handled him easily with the casual confidence of a baby nurse, but I dreaded being forced to change his diapers. Wasn't I famous for awkwardness? Suppose I let him slip, or put my fingers on that throbbing pulse on the top of his head?

Mother came to my bed one night bringing my three-week-old baby. She pulled the cover back and told me to get up and hold him while she put rubber sheets on my bed. She explained that he was going to sleep with me.

I begged in vain. I was sure to roll over and crush out his life or break those fragile bones. She wouldn't hear of it, and within minutes the pretty golden baby was lying on his back in the center of my bed, laughing at me.

I lay on the edge of the bed, stiff with fear, and vowed not to sleep all night long. But the eat-sleep routine I had begun in the hospital, and kept up under Mother's dictatorial command, got the better of me. I dropped off.

My shoulder was shaken gently. Mother whispered, "Maya, wake up. But don't move."

I knew immediately that the awakening had to do with the baby. I tensed. "I'm awake."

She turned the light on and said, "Look at the baby." My fears were so powerful I couldn't move to look at the center of the bed. She said again, "Look at the baby." I didn't hear sadness in her voice, and that helped me to break the bonds of terror. The baby was no longer in the center of the bed. At first I thought he had moved. But after closer investigation I found that I was lying on my stomach with my arm bent at a right angle. Under the tent of blanket, which was poled by my elbow and forearm, the baby slept touching my side.

Mother whispered, "See, you don't have to think about doing the right thing. If you're for the right thing, then you do it without thinking."

She turned out the light and I patted my son's body lightly and went back to sleep.

GATHER TOGETHER

IN MY NAME

This book is dedicated to my blood brother
BAILEY JOHNSON
and to the other real brothers who encouraged me
to be bodacious enough to invent my own life daily:
JAMES BALDWIN
KWESI BREW
DAVID DU BOIS
SAMUEL FLOYD
JOHN O. KILLENS
VAGABOND KING
LEO MAITLAND
VUSUMZI MAKE
JULIAN MAYFIELD
MAX ROACH

A special thanks to my friend
DOLLY MCPHERSON

It was a "come as you are" party and "all y'all come." If you bring your own bottle, you'll be expected to share; if you don't it's all right, somebody will share with you. It was triumph and brotherhood. Everybody was a hero. Hadn't we all joined together to kick the hell out of *der Gruber,* and that fat Italian, and put that little rice-eating Tojo in his place?

Black men from the South who had held no tools more complicated than plows had learned to use lathes and borers and welding guns, and had brought in their quotas of war-making machines. Women who had only known maid's uniforms and mammy-made dresses donned the awkward men's pants and steel helmets, and made the ship-fitting sheds hum some buddy. Even the children had collected paper, and at the advice of elders who remembered World War I, balled the tin foil from cigarettes and chewing gum into balls as big as your head. Oh, it was a time.

Soldiers and sailors, and the few black Marines fresh from having buried death on a sandy South Pacific beach, stood around looking proud out of war-wise eyes.

Black-marketeers had sped around a million furtive corners trying to keep the community supplied with sugar, cigarettes, rationing stamps and butter. Prostitutes didn't even take the time to remove their seventy-five-dollar shoes when they turned twenty-dollar tricks. Everyone was a part of the war effort.

And at last it had paid off in spades. We had won. Pimps got out of their polished cars and walked the streets of San Francisco only a little uneasy at the unusual exercise. Gamblers, ignoring their sensitive fingers, shook hands with shoeshine boys. Pulpits rang with the "I told you so" of ministers who knew that God was on the side of right and He would not see the righteous forsaken, nor their young beg bread. Beauticians spoke to the shipyard workers, who in turn spoke to the easy ladies. And everybody had soft little preparation-to-smile smiles on their faces.

I thought if war did not include killing, I'd like to see one every year. Something like a festival.

All the sacrifices had won us victory and now the good times were coming. Obviously, if we earned more than rationing would allow us to spend during wartime, things were really going to look up when restrictions were removed.

There was no need to discuss racial prejudice. Hadn't we all, black and white, just snatched the remaining Jews from the hell of concentration camps? Race prejudice was dead. A mistake made by a young country. Something to be forgiven as an unpleasant act committed by an intoxicated friend.

During the crisis, black people had often made more money in a month than they had seen in their whole lives. Black men did not leave their wives, driven away by an inability to provide for their families. They rode in public transport on a first-come/first-seated basis. And more times than not were called Mister/Missus at their jobs or by sales clerks.

Two months after V-Day, war plants began to shut down, to cut back, to lay off employees. Some workers were offered tickets back to their Southern homes. Back to the mules they had left tied to the tree on ole Mistah Doo hickup farm. No good. Their expanded understanding could never again be accordioned into these narrow confines. They were free or at least nearer to freedom than ever before and they would not go back.

Those military heroes of a few months earlier, who were discharged from the Army in the city which knows how, began to be seen hanging on the ghetto corners like forgotten laundry left on a backyard fence.

Their once starched khaki uniforms were gradually bastardized. An ETO jacket, plus medals, minus stripes, was worn with out-of-fashion zoot pants. The trim army pants, creases trained in symmetry, were topped by loud, color-crazed Hawaiian shirts. The shoes remained. Only the shoes. The Army had made those shoes to last. And dammit, they did.

Thus we lived through a major war. The question in the ghettos was, Can we make it through a minor peace?

I was seventeen, very old, embarrassingly young, with a son of two months, and I still lived with my mother and stepfather.

They offered me a chance to leave my baby with them and return to school. I refused. First, I reasoned with the righteous seriousness of youth, I was not Daddy Clidell Jackson's blood daughter and my child was his grandchild only as long as the union between Daddy and Mother held fast, and by then I had seen many weak links in their chain of marriage. Second, I considered that although I was Mother's child, she had left me with others until I was thirteen and why should she feel more responsibility for my child than she had felt for her own. Those were the pieces that made up the skin of my refusal, but the core was more painful, more solid, truer. A textured guilt was my familiar, my bedmate to whom I had turned my back. My daily companion whose hand I would not hold. The Christian teaching dinned into my ears in the small town in Arkansas would not be quieted by the big-city noise.

My son had no father—so what did that make me? According to the Book, bastards were not to be allowed into the congregation of the righteous. There it was. I would get a job, and a room of my own, and take my beautiful son out into the world. I thought I might even move to another town and change our names.

During the months when I was tussled with my future and that of my son, the big house we lived in began to die. Suddenly jobless roomers, who lined their solemn trunks with memories before they packed in folds of disappointment, left San Francisco for Los Angeles, Chicago, Detroit, where "they say" jobs were begging for workers. The loud slams of the front doors were heard more seldom, and the upstairs kitchen, where the roomers exercised their cooking privileges, gave fewer and fewer of the exotic aromas which used to send me running to our kitchen for snacks.

The gamblers and prostitutes, black-marketeers and boosters, all those suckerfish who had gotten fat living on the underbelly of the war, were the last to feel the pinch. They had accumulated large masses of money, which never went into a bank, but circulated among their tribe like promiscuous women, and by the nature of their professions, they were accustomed to the infidelity of Lady Luck and the capriciousness of life. I was sorry to see the dancers go—those glamorous women, only slightly older than I, who wore pounds of Max Factor No. 31, false eyelashes and talked out of the sides of their mouths, their voices sliding around cigarettes which forever dangled from their lips. They had often practiced their routines in the downstairs kitchen. The B.S. Chorus. Time steps, slides, flashes and breaks, smoking all the time. I was fairly certain that in order to be a chorus dancer, one would have to smoke.

By no amount of agile exercising of a wishful imagination could my mother have been called lenient. Generous she was; indulgent, never. Kind, yes; permissive, never. In her world, people she accepted paddled their own canoes, pulled their own weight, put their own shoulders to their own plows and pushed like hell, and here I was in her house, refusing to go back to school. Not giving a thought to marriage (admittedly, no one asked me) and working at nothing. At no time did she advise me to seek work. At least not in words. But the strain of her nights at the pinochle table, the responsibility of the huge sums which were kept in the bedroom closet, wore on her already short temper.

In earlier, freer days I might have simply noted and recorded her grumpiness, but now my guilt, which I carried around like a raw egg, fed my paranoia, and I became sure that I was a nuisance. When my baby cried I rushed to change him, feed him, coddle him, to in fact shut him up. My youth and shuddering self-doubt made me unfair to that vital woman.

She took great joy in her beautiful grandchild, and as with most egocentric people, saw his every virtue as a mirror for her own. He had pretty hands... "Well, look at mine." His feet were absolutely straight with high insteps; so were hers. She was not annoyed with me; she was playing the hand life had dealt her as she had always done. And she played it masterfully.

The mixture of arrogance and insecurity is as volatile as the much-touted alcohol and gasoline. The difference is that with the former there is a long internal burning usually terminating in self-destroying implosion.

I would quit the house, take a job and show the whole world (my son's father) that I was equal to my pride and greater than my pretensions.

CHAPTER 1

I was mortified. A silly white woman who probably counted on her toes looked me in the face and said I had not passed. The examination had been constructed by morons for idiots. Of course I breezed through without thinking much about it.

REARRANGE THESE LETTERS: A C T – A R T – A S T

Okay. CAT. RAT. SAT. Now what?

She stood behind her make-up and coiffed hair and manicured nails and dresser-drawers of scented angora sweaters and years of white ignorance and said that I had not passed.

"The telephone company spends thousands of dollars training operators. We simply cannot risk employing anyone who made the marks you made. I'm sorry."

She was sorry? I was stunned. In a stupor I considered that maybe my outsized intellectual conceit had led me to take the test for granted. And maybe I deserved this high-handed witch's remarks.

"May I take it again?" That was painful to ask.

"No, I'm sorry." If she said she was sorry one more time, I was going to take her by her sorry shoulders and shake a job out of her.

"There is an opening, though"—she might have sensed my unspoken threat—"for a bus girl in the cafeteria."

"What does a bus girl do?" I wasn't sure I could do it.

"The boy in the kitchen will tell you."

After I filled out forms and was found uninfected by a doctor, I reported to the cafeteria. There the boy, who was a grandfather, informed me, "Collect the dishes, wipe the tables, make sure the salt and pepper shakers are clean, and here's your uniform."

The coarse white dress and apron had been starched with concrete and was too long. I stood at the side of the room, the dress hem scratching my calves, waiting for the tables to clear. Many of the trainee operators had been my classmates. Now they stood over laden tables waiting for me or one of the other dumb bus girls to remove the used dishes so that they could set down their trays.

I lasted at the job a week, and so hated the salary that I spent it all the afternoon I quit.

CHAPTER 2

"Can you cook Creole?"

I looked at the woman and gave her a lie as soft as melting butter. "Yes, of course. That's all I know how to cook."

The Creole Café had a cardboard sign in the window which bragged: COOK WANTED. SEVENTY-FIVE DOLLARS A WEEK. As soon as I saw it I knew I could cook Creole, whatever that was.

Desperation to find help must have blinded the proprietress to my age or perhaps it was the fact that I was nearly six feet and had an attitude which belied my seventeen years. She didn't question me about recipes and menus, but her long brown face did trail down in wrinkles, and doubt hung on the edges of her questions.

"Can you start on Monday?"

"I'll be glad to."

"You know it's six days a week. We're closed on Sunday."

"That's fine with me. I like to go to church on Sunday." It's awful to think that the devil gave me that lie, but it came unexpectedly and worked like dollar bills. Suspicion and doubt raced from her face, and she smiled. Her teeth were all the same size, a small white picket fence semicircled in her mouth.

"Well, I know we're going to get along. You a good Christian. I like that. Yes, ma'am, I sure do."

My need for a job caught and held the denial.

"What time on Monday?" Bless the Lord!

"You get here at five."

Five in the morning. Those mean streets before the thugs had gone to sleep, pillowing on someone else's dreams. Before the streetcars began to rattle, their lighted insides like exclusive houses in the fog. Five!

"All right, I'll be here at five, Monday morning."

"You'll cook the dinners and put them on the steam table. You don't have to do short orders. I do that."

Mrs. Dupree was a short plump woman of about fifty. Her hair was naturally straight and heavy. Probably Cajun Indian, African and white, and naturally, Negro.

"And what's your name?"

"Rita." Marguerite was too solemn, and Maya too rich-sounding. "Rita" sounded like dark flashing eyes, hot peppers and Creole evenings with strummed guitars. "Rita Johnson."

"That's a right nice name." Then, like some people do to show their sense of familiarity, she immediately narrowed the name down. "I'll call you Reet. Okay?"

Okay, of course. I had a job. Seventy-five dollars a week. So I was Reet. Reet, poteet and gone. All Reet. Now all I had to do was learn to cook.

CHAPTER 3

I asked old Papa Ford to teach me how to cook. He had been a grown man when the twentieth century was born, and left a large family of brothers and sisters in Terre Haute, Indiana (always called the East Coast), to find what the world had in store for a "good-looking colored boy with no education in his head, but a pile of larceny in his heart." He traveled with circuses "shoveling elephant shit." He then shot dice in freight trains and played koch in back rooms and shanties all over the Northern states.

"I never went down to Hang'em High. Them crackers would have killed me. Pretty as I was, white women was always following me. The white boys never could stand a pretty nigger."

By 1943, when I first saw him, his good looks were as delicate as an old man's memory, and disappointment rode his face bareback. His hands had gone. Those gambler's fingers had thickened during the Depression, and his only straight job, carpeting, had further toughened his "moneymakers." Mother rescued him from a job as a sweeper in a pinochle parlor and brought him home to live with us.

He sorted and counted the linen when the laundry truck picked it up and returned it, then grudgingly handed out fresh sheets to the roomers. He cooked massive and delicious dinners when Mother was busy, and he sat in the tall-ceilinged kitchen drinking coffee by the pots.

Papa Ford loved my mother (as did nearly everyone) with a child-like devotion. He went so far as to control his profanity when she was around, knowing she couldn't abide cursing unless she was the curser.

"Why the sheeit do you want to work in a goddam kitchen?"

"Papa, the job pays seventy-five dollars a week."

"Busting some goddam suds." Disgust wrinkled his face.

"Papa, I'll be cooking and not washing dishes."

"Colored women been cooking so long, thought you'd be tired of it by now."

"If you'll just tell me—"

"Got all that education. How come you don't get a goddam job where you can go to work looking like something?"

I tried another tack. "I probably couldn't learn to cook Creole food, anyway. It's too complicated."

"Sheeit. Ain't nothing but onions, green peppers and garlic. Put that in everything and you got Creole food. You know how to cook rice, don't you?"

"Yes." I could cook it till each grain stood separately.

"That's all, then. Them geechees can't live without swamp seed." He cackled at his joke, then recalled a frown. "Still don't like you working as a goddam cook. Get married, then you don't have to cook for nobody but your own family. Sheeit."

CHAPTER 4

The Creole Café steamed with onion vapor, garlic mists, tomato fogs and green-pepper sprays. I cooked and sweated among the cloying odors and loved being there. Finally I had the authority I had always longed for. Mrs. Dupree chose the daily menu, and left a note on the steam table informing me of her gastronomic decisions. But, I, Rita, the chef, decided how much garlic went into the baked short ribs à la Creole, how many bay leaves would flavor the steamed Shreveport tripe. For over a month I was embroiled in the mysteries of the kitchen with the expectancy of an alchemist about to discover the secret properties of gold.

A leathered old white woman, whom Mother found, took care of my baby while I worked. I had been rather reluctant to leave him in her charge, but Mother reminded me that she tended her white, black and Filipino children equally well. I reasoned that her great age had shoved her beyond the pale of any racial differences. Certainly anyone who lived that long had to spend any unused moments thinking about death and the life to come. She simply couldn't afford the precious time to think of prejudices. The greatest compensation for youth's illness is the utter ignorance of the seriousness of the affliction.

Only after the mystery was worn down to a layer of commonness did I begin to notice the customers. They consisted largely of light-skinned, slick-haired Creoles from Louisiana, who spoke a French patois only a little less complicated than the contents of my pots and equally spicy. I thought it fitting and not at all unusual that they enjoyed my cooking. I was following Papa Ford's instructions loosely and adding artistic touches of my own.

Our customers never ate, paid and left. They sat on the long backless stools and exchanged gossip or shared the patient philosophy of the black South.

"Take it easy, Greasy, you got a long way to slide."

With the tolerance of ages they gave and accepted advice.

"Take it easy, but take it."

One large ruddy man, whose name I never knew, allowed his elbows to support him at the twelve-stool counter, and told tales of the San Francisco waterfront: "They got wharf rats who fight a man flat-footed."

"No?" A voice wanted to believe.

"Saw one of those suckers the other night backed a cracker up 'gainst a cargo crate. Hadn't been for me and two other guys, colored guys"—naturally—"he'd of run down his throat and walked on his liver."

Near the steam counter, the soft sounds of black talk, the sharp reports of laughter, and the shuffling feet on tiled floors mixed themselves in odorous vapors and I was content.

CHAPTER 5

I had rented a room (with cooking privileges) in a tall, imposing San Francisco Victorian and had bought my first furniture and a white chenille bedspread. God, but it looked like a field of tiny snow roses. I had a beautiful child, who laughed to see me, a job that I did well, a baby-sitter whom I trusted, and I was young and crazy as a road lizard. Surely this was making it.

One foggy evening on my day off, I had picked up my son and was carrying him home along the familiar streets with the casual ease of an old mother. He snoozed in the angle of my arm, and I thought of dinner, and the radio and a night of reading. Two ex-schoolmates came up the hill toward me. They were of that rare breed, black born San Franciscans. I, cushioned in my maturity, didn't think to further arm myself. I had the arrowproof vest of adult confidence, so I let them approach—easy.

"Let us look at the baby ... I hear he's cute." She was fat with small covetous eyes and was known for having a tiny but pugnacious wit. Her friend, Lily, even as a teen-ager, was old beyond knowing and bored beyond wisdom.

"Yes. They say you made a pretty baby."

I lifted the flap of light blanket from my son's face and shifted myself so that they might see my glory.

"My God, you did that?" The fat one's face broke open into a wounded grin.

Her somber friend intoned, "Jesus, he looks like he's white. He could pass." Her words floated into my air on admiration and wonder. I shriveled that she could say such a terrible thing about my baby, but I had no nerve to cover my prize and walk away. I stood dumbfounded, founded in dumbness.

The short one laughed a crackly laugh and pushed the point between my ribs. "He's got a little nose and thin lips." Her surprise was maddening. "As long as you live and troubles rise, you ought to pay the man for giving you that baby, huh. A crow gives birth to a dove. The bird kingdom must be petrified."

There's a point in fury when one becomes abject. Motionless. I froze, as Lot's wife must have done, having caught a last glimpse of concentrated evil.

"And what did you name him? 'Thank God A-mighty'?"

I could have laid him down there, bunting and all, and left him for someone who had more grace, more style and beauty. My own pride of control would not allow me to show the girls what I was feeling, so I covered my baby and headed home. No good-byes—I left them as if I were planning to walk off the edge of the world. In my room I lay my five months of belongingness on the chenilled bed and sat beside him to look over his perfection. His little head was exactly round and the soft hair curled up in black ripples. His arms and legs were plump marvels, and his torso as straight as a look between lovers. But it was his face with which I had to do.

Admittedly, the lips were thin and traced themselves sparely under a small nose. But he was a baby, and as he grew, these abnormalities would flesh out, become real, imitate the regularity of my features. His eyes, even closed, slanted up toward his throbbing temples. He looked like a baby Buddha. And then I examined his hairline. It followed mine in every detail. And that would not grow away or change, and it proved that he was undeniably mine.

CHAPTER 6

Butter-colored, honey-brown, lemon- and olive-skinned. Chocolate and plum-blue, peaches-and-cream. Cream. Nutmeg. Cinnamon. I wondered why my people described our colors in terms of something good to eat. Then God's prettiest man became a customer at my restaurant.

He sat beside the light-skinned Creoles, and they thinned and paled and disappeared. His dark-brown skin glistened, and the reflected light made it hard to look into my mysterious pots. His voice to the waitress was a thumb poking in my armpits. I hated his being there because his presence made me jittery, but I loathed his leaving and could hardly bear waiting for him to return.

The waitress and Mrs. Dupree called him "Curly," but I thought whoever named him little used their imagination. When he opened the steamy door to the restaurant, surely it was the second coming of Christ.

His table manners pleased me. He ate daintily and slowly as if he cared what he put in his mouth. He smiled at me, but the nervous grimaces I gave him in return couldn't even loosely be called smiles. He was friendly with the customers, the waitress and me, since he always came alone. I wondered why he didn't have girl friends. Any woman would give a pretty to go out with him or rush to sit and talk to him. I never thought he would find me interesting, and if he did, it would be just to tease me.

"Reet." There it was. I acted as if I hadn't heard him.

"Reet. You hear me. Come here."

I have seen bitch dogs in heat sidle sinuously along the ground, tempting, luring. I would like to be able to say I went to him so naturally. Unfortunately not. I draped myself in studied indifference and inched out my voice in disdainful measures.

"Were you speaking to me?"

"Come here, I won't bite." Looking down upon his request, I conceded. If he was beautiful from a distance, up close he was perfection. His eyes were deep-black and slow-lidded. His upper lip arched and fell over white teeth held together in the middle by the merest hint of yellow gold.

"How long you been knowing to cook like that?"

"All my life." I could hardly make the lie leave my tongue.

"You married?"

"No."

"You be careful, somebody's gonna come here and kidnap you."

"Thank you." Why didn't he? Of course he would have had to knock me down, bind and gag me, but I would have liked nothing better.

"You want a soda?"

"No thanks." I turned and went back to the steam table, sweat nibbling above my top lip and under my arms. I wished him away but could feel his gaze on my back. I had spent so many years being people other than myself that I continued to stir and mix, raise and lower burners as if every nerve in my body were not attached to the third stool of the lunch counter.

The door opened and closed and I turned to watch his retreating back, only to find that another customer had left. Automatically I looked for him and met his eyes, solemn on me. I burned at giving myself away.

He nodded me over.

"What time you get off?"

"One o'clock."

"Want me to take you home?"

"I usually go out to see my baby."

"You've got a baby? Somebody must of give it to you for Christmas. A doll baby. How old are you?"

"Nineteen." Sometimes I was twenty, or eighteen. It depended on my mood.

"Nineteen going on seventeen." His smile held no ridicule. Just a smidgen of indulgence.

"Okay. I'll take you to see your baby."

———

He drove his 1941 Pontiac without seeming to think about it. I sat in the corner pushed against the door trying desperately not to watch him.

"Where's the baby's Daddy?"

"I don't know."

"He wouldn't marry you, huh?" His voice hardened in the question.

"I didn't want to marry him." Partly true.

"Well, he's a low-down bastard in my book and needs his ass kicked." I began to love him at that moment.

I shifted to look at him. My avenging angel. Mother and my brother had been so busy being positive and supportive, neither had given any thought to the possibility that I might want revenge. I don't think I had even thought about it before. Now anger was an injection that flooded my body, making me warm and excited.

That's true, he was a low-life bastard. He should have given me a chance to refuse his proposal. Out of my head and into forgetfulness went the memory that I had wilfully initiated my one sexual tryst. My personal reasons and aggressive tactics were conveniently obliterated. Self-pity in its early stage is as snug as a feather mattress. Only when it hardens does it become uncomfortable.

Curly stood in the center of the baby-sitter's living room and said all the mother-liking things: "Sure is a fine baby...Looks just like you...He's gonna be a big one...Check those feet."

Back in the car it never occurred to me to put up resistance when he said we were going to his hotel. I wanted to do what he wanted, so I sat quiet.

As we passed through the hotel lobby, I felt the first stirring of reluctance. Now, wait a minute. What was I doing here? What did he think I was? He hadn't even said he loved me. Where was the soft music that should be playing as he kissed my ear lobe?

He sensed the hesitation and took my hand to guide me down the carpeted hallway. His touch and confidence rushed my doubts. Obviously I couldn't stop now.

"Make yourself comfortable."

He removed his coat and I sat quickly in the one large chair. On the dresser, amid cards and toiletries, stood a bottle of whiskey.

"May I have a drink?" I had never drunk anything stronger than Dubonnet.

"No. I don't think so. But I'll have one." He poured the liquor into a glass he took down from above the face bowl. Water sloshed around and he gulped it down. Then in a moment he stood over me. I wanted to look up at him but my head refused.

"Come here, Reet. Get up." I wanted to, but my muscles had atrophied. I didn't want him to think of me as a dick teaser. A cheat. But my body wouldn't obey.

He bent and took both hands and pulled me upright. He enclosed me in his arms.

"You nearly 'bout as tall as me. I like tall girls." Then he kissed me, softly. And slowly. When he stopped, my body had gone its own way. My heart raced and my knees were locked. I was embarrassed at my trembling.

"Come over to the bed." He patiently pulled me away from the chair.

We both sat on the bed and I could hardly see him, although he was a breath away. He held my face in his large dark hands.

"I know you're scared. That's natural. You're young. But we're going to have a party. Just think of it like that. We're having a love party."

My previous brushes with sex had been just that. Brushes. One violent. The other indifferent, and now I found myself in the hands and arms of a tender man.

He stroked and talked. He kissed me until my ears rang, and he made me laugh. He interrupted his passion to make some small joke, and the second I responded he resumed lovemaking.

I lay crying in his arms, after.

"You happy?" The gold in his mouth glinted like a little star.

I was so happy that the next day I went to a jewelers and bought him an onyx ring with a diamond chip. I charged it to my stepfather's account.

CHAPTER 7

Love was what I had been waiting for. I had done grown-up things out of childish ignorance or juvenile bravado, but now I began to mature. I became pleased with my body because it gave me such pleasure. I shopped for myself carefully for the first time. Searching painstakingly for just the right clothes instead of buying the first thing off the rack. Unfortunately my taste was as new as my interest. Once when

Curly was to take me out to dinner, I bought a smart yellow crepe dress with black roses, black baby-doll shoes, whose straps sank a full inch into my ankles, and an unflattering wide coolie hat with veil. I pinned a small cluster of yellow rose buds on my bosom and was ready for the fray.

He only asked me to remove the corsage.

Curly had said at the beginning of our affair that he had a girl who worked in a San Diego shipyard and her job would be up soon. Then they'd go back to New Orleans and get married. I hastily stored the information in that inaccessible region of the mind where one puts the memory of pain and other unpleasantries. For the while it needn't bother me, and it didn't.

He was getting out of the Navy and only had a couple of months before all his papers would be cleared. Southern upbringing and the terror of war made him seem much older than his thirty-one years.

We took my son for long walks through parks; when people complimented us on our child, he played the proud papa and accepted. At playland on the beach we rode the Ferris wheel and loop-the-loop and gooed ourselves with salt-water taffy. Late afternoons we took the baby back to the sitter and then went to his hotel and one more, or two more, or three more love parties. I never wanted it to end. I bought things for him. A watch (he already had one), a sports coat (too small), another ring, and paid for them myself. I couldn't hear his protestations. I wasn't buying things. I was buying time.

One day after work he took me to the sitter's. He sat and held the baby. His silence should have told me something. Maybe it did, but again I didn't want to know. We left in a quiet mood. He only said, "I want me a boy like that. Just like that."

Since we weren't heading for the hotel, I asked where we were going.

"I'm taking you to your house."

"Why?"

No answer.

He found a parking space a half-block away. The streetlights were just coming on and a soft fog dimmed the world. He reached in the

244 · *Maya Angelou*

back seat and took out two large boxes. He handed them to me and said, "Give me a kiss."

I tried to laugh, to pretend that the kiss was payment for the gifts, but the laugh lied. He kissed me lightly and looked at me long.

"Reet. My girl friend is here and I'll be checking out of the hotel tonight."

I didn't cry because I couldn't think.

"You're going to make some man a wonderful wife. I mean it. These things are for you and the baby. I hate to say good-bye, but I gotta."

He probably said more, but all I remember is walking from the car to my front door. Trying for my life's sake to control the angry lurchings of my stomach. Trying to walk upright carrying the awkward boxes. I had to set down the boxes to find the door key, and habit fitted it into the lock. I entered the hall without hearing him start the car.

Because he had not lied, I was forbidden anger. Because he had patiently and tenderly taught me love, I could not use hate to ease the pain. I had to bear it.

I am certain, with the passage of time, that he loved me. Maybe for the loveless waif I was. Maybe he felt pity for the young mother and fatherless child, and so decided to give us what we both needed for two months. I don't know. I'm only certain that for some reason he loved me and that he was a good man.

The loss of young first love is so painful that it borders on the ludicrous.

I even embarrassed myself. Weeks after Charles left, I stumbled around San Francisco operating in the familiar. The lovely city disappeared in my fog. Nothing I did to food made it interesting to me. Music became a particular aggravation, for every emotional lyric had obviously been written for me alone.

> Gonna take a sentimental journey
> gonna set my heart at ease...

Charles had taken that journey and left me all alone. I was one emotional runny sore. To be buffeted about emotionally was not new, only the intensity and reason were. The new pain and discomfort was physical. My body had been awakened and fed, and suddenly I discovered I had a ravenous appetite. My natural reticence and habit of restraint prevented me from seeking other satisfaction even if it could be found.

I began to lose weight, which, with my height and thinness, I could ill afford to do. The burst of energy which had propelled me into beauty salons and dress shops was now as absent as my gone lover. I longed and pined, sighed and yearned, cried and generally slouched around feeling dismal and bereaved. By eighteen I managed to look run down if not actually run over.

My brother Bailey again was my savior, a role he fulfilled most of my early years.

He returned to the city after some months on an ammunition ship, and came to the restaurant to see me.

"My. What the hell's happened to you?" The way I looked seemed to anger rather than worry him. I introduced him to my employer. She said, "Your brother. He awful little, ain't he? I mean, to be your brother?"

Bailey thanked her smoothly, allowing just the tail of his sarcasm to flick in her face. She never noticed.

"I said, what's the matter with you? Have you been sick?" I held in the tears that wanted to pour into my brother's hands.

"No. I'm okay."

I thought at the time that it was noble to bear the ills one had silently. But not so silently that others didn't know one was bearing them.

"What time do you get off?"

"One o'clock. I'm off tomorrow, so I'm going out to get the baby."

"I'll be back and take you. Then we can talk."

He turned to Mrs. Dupree. "And a good day to you, too, madam." Bailey did little things with such a flourish. He might have been the Count of Monte Cristo, or Cyrano saying farewell to fair Roxanne.

After he had gone, Mrs. Dupree grinned her lips into a pucker. "He's as cute as a little bug."

I busied myself amid the pots. If she thought likening my big brother to an insect would please me, she had another think coming.

———

The baby crawled around the floor of my room as I told Bailey of my great love affair. Of the pain of discovery of pain. He nodded understanding and said nothing.

I thought that while I had his attention I might as well throw in my other sadness. I told him that because my old schoolmates laughed at me, I felt more isolated than I had in Stamps, Arkansas.

He said, "He sounds like a nice guy" and "I think its time for you to leave San Francisco. You could try Los Angeles or San Diego."

"But I don't know where I'd live. Or get a job." Although I was miserable in San Francisco, the idea of any other place frightened me. I thought of Los Angeles and it was a gray vast sea without ship or lighthouse.

"I can't just tear Guy away. He's used to the woman who looks after him."

"But she's not his mother."

"I've got a good job here."

"But surely you don't mean to make cooking Creole food your life's work."

I hadn't thought about it. "I have a nice room here. Don't you think it's nice?"

He looked at me squarely, forcing me to face my fears. "Now, My, if you're happy being miserable, enjoy it, but don't ask me to feel sorry for you. Just get all down in it and wallow around. Take your time to savor all its subtleties, but don't come to me expecting sympathy."

He knew me too well. It was true. I was loving the role of jilted lover. Deserted, yet carrying on. I saw myself as the heroine, solitary, standing under a streetlight's soft yellow glow. Waiting. Waiting. As the fog comes in, a gentle rain falls but doesn't drench her. It is just enough to make her shiver in her white raincoat (collar turned up). Oh, he knew me too well.

"If you want to stay around here looking like death eating a soda cracker, that's your business. There are some rights no one has the right to take from you. That's one. Now, what do you want to do?"

That evening I decided to go to Los Angeles. At first I thought I'd work another month, saving every possible penny. But Bailey said, "When you make up your mind to make a change you have to follow through on the wave of decision." He promised me two hundred dollars when his ship paid off and suggested that I tell my boss that I'd be leaving in a week.

I had never had two hundred dollars of my own. It sounded like enough to live on for a year.

The prospect of a trip to Los Angeles returned my youth to me.

My mother heard my plans without surprise. "You're a woman. You can make up your own mind." She hadn't the slightest idea that not only was I not a woman, but what passed for my mind was animal instinct. Like a tree or a river, I merely responded to the winds and the tides.

She might have seen that, but her own mind was misted with the knowledge of a failing marriage, and the slipping away of the huge sums of money which she had enjoyed and thought her due. Her fingers still glittered with diamonds and she was a weekly customer at the most expensive shoe store in town, but her pretty face had lost its carefree adornment and her smile no longer made me think of day breaking.

"Be the best of anything you get into. If you want to be a whore, it's your life. Be a damn good one. Don't chippy at anything. Anything worth having is worth working for."

It was her version of Polonius' speech to Laertes. With that wisdom in my pouch, I was to go out and buy my future.

CHAPTER 8

The Los Angeles Union Railway Terminal was a marvel of Moorish Spanish glamour. The main waiting room was vast and the ceiling domed its way up to the clouds. Long curved benches sat in dark wooden splendor, and outside its arched doors, palm trees waved in lovely walks. Inlaid blue and yellow tiles were to be found on every wall, arranged in gay and exotic design.

It was easy to distinguish San Franciscans detraining amid the crowd. San Franciscan women always, but always, wore gloves. Short white snappy ones in the day, and long black or white kid leather ones at night. The Southern Californians and other tourists were much more casual. Men sported flowered shirts, and women ambled around or lounged on the imposing seats in cotton dresses which could have passed for brunch coats in San Francisco.

Being from The City, I had dressed for the trip. A black crepe number which pulled and pleated, tucked and shirred, in a warp all its own. It was expensive by my standards and dressy enough for a wedding reception. My short white gloves had lost their early-morning crispness during the ten-hour coach trip, and Guy, whose immensity matched his energy, had mashed and creased and bungled the dress into a very new symmetry. Less than a year old, he had opinions. He definitely wanted to get down and go to that smiling stranger across the aisle, and immediately wanted to be in my lap pulling on the rhinestone brooch which captured and brought light to the collar of my dress.

In spite of the wrinkled dress and in spite of the cosmetic case full to reeking with dirty diapers, I left the train with my son a picture of controlled dignity. I had over two hundred dollars rolled in scratchy ten-dollar bills in my brassiere, another seventy in my purse, and two bags of seriously selected clothes. Los Angeles was going to know I was there.

———

My aunt answered my telephone call.

"Ritie, where are you?"

"We're at the station."

"What we?"

Like all the family she had heard about my pregnancy, but she hadn't seen the result.

"My son and I."

A tiny hesitation, then: "Get a taxi and come out here. I'll pay the cab fare." Her voice didn't ooze happiness at hearing from me, but then, the Baxters were not known to show any emotions. Except violent ones.

Wilshire Boulevard was wide and glossy. Large buildings sat back on tiny little lawns in a privacy that projected money and quiet voices and white folks.

The house on Federal Avenue had a no-nonsense air about it. It was a model of middle-class decorum. A single-story, solidly made building with three bedrooms, good meant-to-last furniture, and samplers on the wall which exhorted someone to "Bless This Home" and warned that "Pride Goeth before a Fall."

The clan had met, obviously called by my aunt, to check out my new addition to the family and give me the benefit of their conglomerate wisdom. My Uncle Tommy sat, wide-spraddled as usual, and grumbled. "Hey, Ritie. Got a baby, I see."

Guy was in my arms and talking, pointing, laughing, so the meaning in his statement was not in the words. He was simply greeting me and saying that although I had a child without benefit of marriage, he for one was not going to ignore either me or the baby.

My family spoke its own mysterious language. The wives and husbands of my blood relatives handed my son around as if they were thinking of adding him to their collection. They removed his bootees and pulled his toes.

"Got good feet."

"Uh huh. High arches."

One aunt ran her hand around his head and was satisfied. "His head is round."

"Got a round head, huh?"

"Sure does."

"That's good."

"Uh huh."

This feature was more than a symbol of beauty. It was an indication of the strength of the bloodline. Every Baxter had a round head.

"Look a lot like Bibbi, doesn't he?" "Bibbi" was the family name for my mother. Guy was handed around the circle again.

"Sure does."

"Yes. I see Bibbi right here."

"Well...but he's mighty fair, isn't he?"

"Sure is."

They all spoke without emotion, except for my Aunt Leah. Her baby voice rose and fell like music played on a slender reed.

"Reetie, you're a woman now. A mother and all that. You'll have two to think of from now on. You'll have to get a job—"

"I've been working as a cook." She shouldn't think I had come to be taken care of.

"—and learn to save your money."

Tommy's wife, Sarah, wrapped my son carefully in his blanket and handed him to me. Aunt Leah stood, a signal that the inspection was over. "What time is your train? Charlie can drive you to the station."

My brain reeled. Had I given the impression that I was going on? Did they say something I missed? "In a few hours. I should be getting back."

We were all shaking hands. Their relief was palpable. I was, after all, a Baxter and playing the game. Being independent. Expecting nothing and if asked, not giving a cripple crab a crutch.

Tom asked, "Need some money, Reet?"

"No thanks. I've got money." All I needed was to get away from that airless house.

My uncles and aunts were childless, except for my late Uncle Tuttie, and they were not equipped to understand that an eighteen-year-old mother is also an eighteen-year-old girl. They were a close-knit

group of fighters who had no patience with weakness and only contempt for losers.

I was hurt because they didn't take me and my child to their bosom,
and because I was a product of Hollywood upbringing and my own
romanticism. On the silver screen they would have vied for me. The
winner would have set me up in a cute little cottage with frangipani
and roses growing in the front yard. I would always wear pretty aprons
and my son would play in the Little League. My husband would come
home (he looked like Curly) and smoke his pipe in the den as I made
cookies for the Boy Scouts meeting.

I was hurt because none of this would come true. But only in part.
I was also proud of them. I congratulated myself on having absolutely
the meanest, coldest, craziest family in the world.

Uncle Charlie, Aunt Leah's husband, never talked much, and on
the way back to that station he broke the silence only a few times.

"You sure got yourself a cute baby."

"Thank you."

"Going on to San Diego, huh?"

I guessed so.

"Well, your father's down there. You won't be by yourself."

My father, who spent his time drinking tequila in Mexico and
putting on high-toned airs in San Diego, would give me a colder reception than the one I'd just received.

I would be by myself. I thought how nice it would be.

I decided that one day I would be included in the family legend.
Someday, as they sat around in the closed circle recounting the fights
and feuds, the prides and prejudices of the Baxters, my name would
be among the most illustrious. I would become a hermit. I would seal
myself off from the world, just my son and I.

I had written a juicy melodrama in which I was to be the star. Pathetic, poignant, isolated. I planned to drift out of the wings, a little
girl martyr. It just so happened that life took my script away and up-
staged me.

CHAPTER 9

"Are you in the life?"

The big black woman could have been speaking Russian. She sat with her back to the window and the sunlight slid over her shoulders, making a pool in her lap.

"I beg pardon?"

"The life. You turn tricks?"

The maid at the hotel had given me the woman's address and said she took care of children. "Just ask for Mother Cleo."

She hadn't asked me to sit, so I just stood in the center of the cluttered room, the baby resting on my shoulder.

"No. I do not." How could she ask me such a question?

"Well, you surely look like a trickster. Your face and everything."

"Well, I assure you, I'm not a whore. I have worked as a chef." How the lowly have become mighty. Ole Creole Kitchen would hitch up its shoulders to know that it once had had a chef—not just a garden-variety cook.

"Well." She looked at me as if she'd soon be able to tell if I was lying.

"How come you got so much powder and lipstick?" That morning I had bought a complete cosmetic kit and spent over an hour pasting my face into a mask with Max Factor's Pancake No. 31. I didn't really feel I had to explain to Mother Cleo, but on the other hand I couldn't very well be rude. I did need a baby-sitter.

"Maybe I put on too much."

"Where do you work?"

It was an interrogation. She had her nerve. Did she think that being called Mother Cleo gave her maternal privileges?

"The Hi Hat Club needs a waitress. I'm going to apply." The make-up was supposed to make me look older. Maybe it only succeeded in making me look cheap.

"That's a good job. Tips can make it a real good job. Let me see the baby."

She got up with more ease than I had expected. When she stretched out her hands a cloud of talcum powder was released. She took the baby and adjusted him down in the crook of her arm. "He's pretty. Still sleeping, huh?"

Mother Cleo metamorphosed in front of me. She was no longer the ugly fat ogre who threatened from her deep chair. Looking down on the infant, she had become the prototype of mother. Her face softened and her voice blurred. She ran stubbly fat fingers around his cap and slid it off.

"I don't usually take them this young. Too much trouble. But he's cute as can be, ain't he?"

"Well, you know—"

"Don't do for you to say so, but still it's true. And you're almost too young to have a baby. I guess your folks put you out, huh?"

She had noticed I wore no wedding ring. I decided to let her think I was homeless. Then I thought, "Let her think nothing. I was homeless."

"Well, I'm going to give you a hand. I'll keep him and I'm going to charge you less than the white ones." I was shocked that she kept white babies. "Lots of white women trust their babies with me rather than they own mothers. There lot of them from the South and they like the idea that they still got a mammy for they children. Can't you just see them? Snotty-nosed little things growing up talking about 'I had a colored mammy.' Huh?" She uglied her face with wrinkles. "But I naturally like children and I make they mommas pay. They pay me good. Don't care how much I like they young 'uns, they don't pay they have to go."

I agreed to her terms and paid her for the first week. Before I left, the baby struggled awake in her arms. She began a rocking motion which didn't lull him. His large black eyes took in the strange face and he began to look around for me. A small cry found its way to the surface before I came into his vision. Once he had assured himself that indeed I was there, he hollered in earnest, angry that I had allowed him to be held by this unknown person, and maybe even a little afraid that I'd given him away. I moved to take him.

"Let him cry." Mother Cleo increased her rocking and bouncing. "He got to get used to it."

"Just let me hold him a second." I couldn't bear his loneliness. I took his softness and kissed him and patted his back and he quieted immediately, as a downpour of rain cuts off.

"You too soft. They all do that till they get used to me." She stood near me and held out her arms. "Give him to me and you go on and get your job. I'll feed him. You bring diapers?"

I nodded to the bag I had dropped beside the door.

"Hush baby, hush baby, hush baby, hush." She had started to croon. I handed the baby to her and right away he began to cry.

"Go on. He'll be all right."

He yelled louder, splitting the air with screams. She contrived a wordless song. His screams were lightning, piercing the dark cloud of her music. I closed the door.

CHAPTER 10

The night club sat on the corner, a one-story building whose purple stucco façade was sprinkled with glitter dust. Inside the dark square room, a bar dimly curved its way from the door to a small dance floor in the rear. Minuscule round tables and chairs jammed against one another, and red bulbs shone down, intensifying the gloom.

The Hi Hat Club had almost too much atmosphere.

Music blared and trembled, competing with the customers' voices for domination of the air. Neither won, except that for a few seconds during the lull between records, the jukebox sat quiet up against the wall, its green and red and yellow lights flickering like an evil robot from a Flash Gordon film.

The customers came mostly from the underworld, though there

was a scattering of young sailors among them. They all jockeyed and shifted, lifting glasses and voices in the thick air, which smelled of Lysol and perfume and bodies, and cigarettes and stale beer. The women were mistresses of decorum. They sat primly at the bar, skirts tucked in, voices quick or silent altogether. On the street they had been as ageless as their profession, but near the posturing, flattering men, they became modest girls. Kittens purring under the strokes.

I watched them and understood. I saw them and envied. They had men of their own. Of course they bought them. They laid open their bodies and threw away their dignity upon a heap of come-filled rubbers. But they had men.

In the late evenings, boosters and thieves wove their paths among the night people, trading, bartering, making contacts and taking orders.

"Got two Roos Bros. suits. Thirty-eight. Black. Pinstripe and nigger-brown. Tag says one-ninety dollars ... they both yours for an ace fifty."

"Gelman shoes. I. Magnin dresses. Your woman'll catch if she wear these threads. For you, four dresses for a deuce."

Depending on the evening's take and the sweet man's mood, the thieves were given money by the pimps which had been given them by the girls which they had saved by lying down first and getting up last.

The waitresses, in a block, were the least interesting of the club's inhabitants. They were for the most part dull married women, who moved among the colorful patrons like slugs among butterflies. The men showed no interest in them, leading me to believe that virtue is safest in a den of iniquity.

I was younger but no more interesting than my colleagues, so the pretty men lumped me with them and ignored us all.

I had no chance to show them how clever I was because wit is communicated by language and I hadn't yet learned theirs. I understood their lack of interest to imply that smart women were prostitutes and stupid ones were waitresses. There were no other categories.

I worked cleaning ashtrays, serving drinks and listening for over a month. My tips were good because I was fast and had a good memory.

"Scotch and milk for you, sir?"

"That's right, little girl, you got a good memory." Though he never saw me, he'd leave a dollar tip.

My first week in San Diego, Mother Cleo had told me she had a room for rent. "I see you a good girl coming over here to see your baby ever day and all, so my husband and me, we ready to let you live here with us. Room'll be fifteen dollars a week. Got a new bedroom suite in it and if you put a rubber sheet on the bed, your baby can sleep with you." So I became a roomer in the home of Mr. Henry and Mrs. Cleo Jenkins.

My life began to move at a measured tempo. I found a modern dance studio where a long-haired white woman gave classes to a motley crew of Navy wives.

I went to work at six (five-thirty to set up tables, get change, arrange my tray with napkins and matches) and was off at two. I shared a ride with a waitress whose husband picked her up every night. I slept late, woke to fix my breakfast around noon and play with my baby.

He amused me. I could not and did not consider him a person. A real person. He was my baby, rather like a pretty living doll that belonged to me. I was myself too young and unformed a human being to think of him as a human being. I loved him. He was cute. He laughed a lot and gurgled and he was mine.

CHAPTER 11

I had begun to look forward to two women coming in every night. They were both just under thirty, and separately they would not have attracted much attention. Johnnie Mae was thin, taller than average, dark-brown-skinned. Her long jaw sagged down, giving her a look of sadness even when she laughed. She wore fuchsia lipstick and most often showed pink smudges on her long white teeth.

Beatrice was plump to ripening. A short yellow woman whose role seemed to be straight man to Johnnie Mae's unfunny but loud humor.

The fact that the pimps and panderers didn't harass them, bespoke the tolerance in the black community for people who chose to lead lives different from the norm. Although they were obviously not sisters, they dressed identically and never spoke to anyone except each other and me.

"Good evening, ladies. Two Tom Collins, I presume." I was a democrat and treated every lady the same.

"Evening, Rita. That's right." They must have spent their free time practicing before mirrors. They sounded alike and even the looks on one face were reflected on the other.

"Got you running this evening, ain't they?" The question did not really need answering. My tray was always filled with fresh drinks, dirty ashtrays or empty glasses.

"When you going to come over to our house?" They smiled at each other, then gave me their sly glances.

"Well, I work all the time, you know."

"Yes, but you have a day off. You say you don't have any friends here."

"I'm thinking about it. That'll be two dollars, please."

Lesbians still interested me, but I no longer felt tenderly protective of them: when I was fifteen I had spent nearly a year concerning myself with society's gross mistreatment of hermaphrodites. I was anxious over the plight of lesbians during the time I was consumed with fear that I might be an incipient one. Their importance to me had diminished in direct relationship to my assurance that I was not.

"Johnnie Mae got something nice for you yesterday."

"Sure did."

"It's a birthday surprise."

"But you don't know my birthday."

"That's how come it's a surprise."

They laughed into each other's laugh and I was forced to join them. Customers at other tables needed my attention, but the two women stayed on the fringes of my mind as I laced myself around the room. They weren't frightening, and they were funny.

"We'll get a bottle of Dubonnet"—Beatrice pronounced it doo

bonnet—"for you and I'll cook. You're off on Sunday. Come over and I'll fry a Sunday bird."

"And we can have a ham."

"Just the three of us? Chicken and ham?" That was a lot of food.

"Nigger ham. A watermelon." Their laughter, crackling, met in the air above the table.

"I take my baby out on Sundays."

They thought about that while I waited on the other customers.

"You can bring him over."

"I'll think about it."

At the bar a thick-waisted waitress who had never invited me to her house curled her upper lip.

"You'd better be careful." She sent a hostile glance to Johnnie Mae's table.

"Why?" I wanted to hear her say it.

"Those women. You know what they are?" Her voice had taken on a sinister depth.

"What?"

"Bull daggers." She smirked her satisfaction at saying the word.

"Oh, really?" I put no surprise in my voice.

"You know about bull daggers, don't you?" Her face showed how her tongue relished the words.

"They dag bulls?" For a second she wasn't sure if I was being smart.

"They love women."

"Oh, is that all? That's all right then. They don't scare me. They can't eat me up." I flounced away, leaving my tray on the bar, and went directly to the table.

"Listen. I'm not a . . . not . . . not a lesbian, and I don't want to be one. Is that all right?"

Their faces closed. Johnnie Mae asked, "Is what all right?"

Suddenly I was ashamed. "I mean, I'd like to come to your house on Sunday. But . . . I mean, I wanted you to know that . . . I don't go that way."

They were silent, wind-up toys whose springs had broken. I wished I could catch the words and swallow them whole.

"I'd like your address." I held out my pencil. Johnnie Mae took it and handed it to Beatrice.

"What time on Sunday?" I had to put something into the emptiness. Beatrice was writing.

"Two o'clock. When we come from church," said Johnnie Mae, handing me the paper.

"Okee dokee. See you then." I wanted to be flippant, to be funny, to say something that would erase the sadness, but I could think of nothing. I got my tray and went back to work.

CHAPTER 12

On the blocks where Saturday-night revelers rambled, Sunday afternoons were given over to the godly. They filled the streets with a mighty thronging, vestiges of a recent contact with God, the Father, lying brightly on a few faces. Most gossiped, shared confidences, checked others' Sunday go-to-meeting clothes, and then spun from the crowd to head homeward.

Growing up, becoming responsible, having to think ahead and assuming the postures of adulthood had certain compensations for me. One that I weekly appreciated was the freedom to sleep late on Sundays. (Somehow the bed was more sensual on that morning than weekdays.) I loved the soul-stirring songs and heartily approved of the minister's passions, but being penned shoulder to shoulder with a rocking crowd of strangers for three hours or more did nothing for my soul.

I maneuvered through the churchgoers, listening for and hearing:

"The Reverend sure spoke today."

"That's the truth, child. He did it today."

"Reverend was talking to my soul this morning."

"Bless your heart. Mine too."

"It's a wonderful thing to go into the house of the Lord."

"That's the truth."

The sounds waved like pretty ribbons and belonged to me. I understood them all. I was a part of that crowd. The fact of my Southern upbringing, the fact of my born blackness meant that I was for the rest of my life a member of that righteous band, and would be whether or not I ever went to church again.

——

The small white house sat squarely in a dirt yard. A few roses tried vainly to grow along a wire fence.

Johnnie Mae opened the door and from her taut smile I knew my blunt words of the other night might have been forgiven, but they were not forgotten.

Beatrice came from the rear of the house and stood beside Johnnie Mae. Both of them talked at once.

"You made it. We didn't think you were going to. We just got back from church. Just changed our clothes." They had changed into matching white T-shirts and pedal pushers.

In Southern towns, the people my grandmother called "worldly" socialized on Saturday night, while the "godly" entertained and were entertained in cool parlors on Sunday. The black people brought that custom north along with their soft speech and remembered recipes. Since my hostesses and I were Southern, I expected to sit at an overloaded table giving fulsome compliments while they plied me with "just one more helping."

"Come in. Take the weight off. Hope you're not starving. I'm just starting to cook." They were as nervous as I. I moved into the tiny room and immediately felt too big for it.

"Thought you were going to bring the baby."

"He was asleep. I'll go back early and take him for a walk." That was going to be my excuse to get away.

"Well, what do you think of our house?" I hadn't had a chance to look around before. I noticed that the walls were bare and there were no books, but furniture they had plenty. A fat, overstuffed rust sofa pressed its matching chair into a corner. Two large chairs, more accidental than incidental, stood pompous against the other wall. Little clear glass lamps, topped with white frilly shades, sat on two end tables. Things took up all the air.

"Come on, see the rest before you sit down." Johnnie Mae's pride carried us into a bedroom while Beatrice went back to the kitchen.

"Have you ever slept in a round bed before?" I hadn't and I hadn't seen one either. It didn't seem appealing, although it was covered with a blue satin spread which matched its curves.

"When Beatrice has her flowers she sleeps in here." I followed her into a monastic cell. A small cot and an old dresser were the room's only furnishings. No lamps, no doilies.

"Her flowers?" I wasn't really so curious as I was uncomfortable.

Johnnie Mae said, "Her monthlies. I don't get them any more. I had an operation. If she wasn't so scared of hospitals, she'd have one too."

"An operation?" I was young, but I was also stupid.

"Had my ovaries and all that mess taken out; Bee ought to get it done too. After all, I'm not about to give her any babies, am I?" She hunched me and winked. I must have returned the wink. I don't know. But I was thinking of the stupidity which got me in the predicament. The big generous unprejudiced spirit which had got me hooked up with two lesbians of heavy humor.

"It's nice. Your house is really very nice. I mean, it reflects your taste and your personalities. I always say, if you want to know a woman, I mean a person, go to their house. It will tell you..." I knew that words, despite the old saying, never fail. And my reading had given me words to spare. I could, and often did to myself or my baby, recite whole passages of Shakespeare, Paul Lawrence Dunbar poems, Kipling's "If," Countee Cullen, Langston Hughes, Longfellow's *Hiawatha*, Arna Bontemps. Surely I had enough words to cover a moment's discomfort. I had enough for hours if need be.

Back on the prickly sofa, Johnnie Mae offered me Dubonnet. I held the glass of thick sweet wine as protection. Thinking she would hesitate to pounce on me if there was a chance I would spill the wine on her furniture, I kept it in front of me like a shield.

"Beatrice, come out here. You're not chained to the stove." She looked at me and raised thick eyebrows. Johnnie Mae had the infuriating habit of making anyone she spoke to into a fellow conspirator. I raised my eyebrows back at her as if I understood her meaning. Beatrice came into the room, a sprinkling of perspiration dotting her face.

"Now, baby, you don't want no black chicken do you?" Beatrice was teasing. Flirting.

"If that chicken gets any darker than you, I'll have to whip your rusty dusty." They were a comedy team. If I had heard that exchange at the club I would have joined their laughter, but perched guarded in the cluttered room, I couldn't find anything funny. I laughed.

"Come here, you sweet thing." Beatrice obeyed and stood like a little chubby girl in front of Johnnie Mae.

"Bend down." Johnnie Mae raised her face and the two women's lips met. I watched and saw their tongues snaking in and out. Except in movies I had never even seen men and women kiss passionately. They pulled apart and looked at me in a practiced gesture. For a second I was too embarrassed to have been caught watching, and in the next second I knew they had wanted me to see. Even after I told them I had no interest in lesbianism, they thought the sight of women kissing would excite me.

I hated their stupidity, but more than that I hated being underestimated. If they only knew, they could strip buck naked and do the Sassy Sue wiggle and I would continue to sit, with my legs crossed, sipping the Dubonnet.

Beatrice's laughter floated over her shoulder as she headed back to the kitchen. Johnnie Mae looked at me and by leering tried to include me in her appreciation.

"Beatrice would make a rabbit hug a hound." She grunted like a pig.

Because laughter seemed to be the safest sport in the house, I laughed and said, "Where do you work? I mean both of you?"

"Right here. Flat on our backs." Nothing embarrassed the woman. "We both take two all-night tricks apiece once a week. Comes to two hundred dollars. We more than get by." She indicated the sofa and chairs. "As you can see."

Lesbian prostitutes! Did they trick with women? I ached to know. How did they pick them up? I had never heard of women hustling other women, but surely they didn't go to bed with men. I fished for a way to put my question.

Johnnie Mae looked around the room, her eyes counting and loving the many pieces of furniture. Her head finished its semicircle and I was back in her vision.

"We're going to have to move, you know?" The question was foolish. Not only did I not know, I didn't care. And if I'd had the chance to think about it, I'd have thought it was a good thing, too.

"The landlord doesn't like us. He's a church deacon, he says. But the real reason is that his son is a faggot. Goes around wearing women's clothes, so the old bastard can't stand gay people." She was happy to grin, thinking of the man's unhappiness. "I told the old bastard so, too." She shrugged her shoulders against the fates. "We'll find another place. I hate to move, though. I mean, we painted this place ourselves." The walls were pea-yellow in the living room. "We called this our honeymoon cottage. Beatrice planted the roses."

I felt there was something I was supposed to say. Something like "You have my deepest sympathy." For some reason, at that moment I thought about Curly and did in fact feel sorry for the two women.

"Niggers make me sick. And nigger men make me sicker than that." She might have been thinking of her landlord, but it seemed she was reading my mind and had the audacity to mean Curly. She would have lost my sympathy, anyway. I hated the word "nigger" and never believed it to be a term of endearment, no matter who used it.

"Now you tell me. We been wondering about you. How come you working as a waitress? You speak such good English, you must have a diploma."

"Yes, I do." Shock pushed my voice out.

"You mean you graduated from high school?"

"Yes."

"And work as a waitress?"

"Well, I can't type or take shorthand or—"

"You remind me of Beatrice." She shouted, "Beatrice. Come here."
I feared I was going to have to sit through the kissing again.
Beatrice stood at the door leading to the living room. "What's on
your mind?"
Johnnie Mae didn't have time for fun. "Bee, Rita's just like you. She
finished high school."
Beatrice, knowing that wasn't such a grand feat said, "Really. Got
your diploma, huh?"
Johnnie Mae answered for me. "Sure she got it. And works as a waitress." I started to explain, but she stopped me. "Beatrice was a WAC. A
corporal." It was hard to believe that all that soft-looking flesh had been
contained in an army uniform. "And when she got out she went to
work. That's where we met. At some rich old woman's house. Bee was
the cook and I was the housekeeper. I took one look at Bee and I have
been keeping her ever since."
Break for peals of laughter.

CHAPTER 13

"Let's have a little grifa before dinner." Johnnie Mae gave an order, not
an invitation. She turned to me.
"You like grifa?"
"Yes. I smoke." The truth was I had smoked cigarettes for over a
year, but never marijuana. But since I had the unmitigated gall to sit
up cross-legged in a lesbian apartment sipping wine, I felt I had the
stamina to smoke a little grifa. Anyway, I was prepared to refuse anything else they offered me, so I didn't feel I could very well refuse
the pot.
Beatrice laid down a Prince Albert can on the table with cigarette
papers.
"Do you want to roll it?" Johnnie Mae was being gracious.

"No thanks. I don't roll very well." I hadn't seen loose tobacco and cigarette papers since I'd left the South, five years earlier. My brother and I used to roll lumpy cigarettes for my uncle on a small hand-cranking machine when he'd run out of ready rolls.

She took the papers and deftly began to sift marijuana. I tried not to appear too curious as the grains of tobacco fell into the cupped paper.

"I'd like to use your bathroom."

"Sure. You know where it is."

I talked to the bathroom mirror. "You have nothing to be nervous about. You'll get out of this. Don't you always get out of everything? Marijuana is not habit-forming. Thousands of people have smoked it. The Indians and Mexicans and it didn't send them mad. Just wash your hands"—which were damp—"and go back to the living room. Keep your cool. Cool."

I inhaled the smoke as casually as if the small brown cigarette I held were the conventional commercial kind.

"No. No. Don't waste the grifa. Hand it here." She dragged the cigarette and made the sound of folks slurping tea from a saucer.

"But I like it my way." Stubborn to the end.

"Well, try it like this." Again the rattling sound.

"All right. I will." I opened my throat and kept my tongue flat so that the smoke found no obstacle in its passage from my lips to my throat. It tore the lining off my tonsils, made my nasal passages burn like red pepper and choked me. While I coughed, gagging, those silly bitches laughed. They would be sitting there with those vapid wrinkles on their faces while I choked to death. Wouldn't they do anything for me? No. Beatrice rescued the joint and sucked in the smoke, puffing out her already fat cheeks to bursting, while her lady love was busily engaged in rolling another stick of tearing fire.

Before the cough stopped shaking me, I had decided I would get even with them. They were lesbians, which was sinful enough, but they were also inconsiderate, stupid bitches. I reached again for the marijuana.

The food was the best I'd ever tasted. Every morsel was an experience of sheer delight. I lost myself in a haze of sensual pleasure, enjoying not only the tastes but the feel of the food in my mouth, the smells, and the sound of my jaws chewing.

"She's got a buzz. That's her third helping."

I looked up to see the two women looking at me and laughing. Their faces seemed to be mostly teeth. White teeth staggering inside dark lips. They were embarrassingly ugly, and yet there was something funny about it. They had no idea that they were so strange-looking. I laughed at their ignorance, and they, probably thinking themselves to be laughing at mine, joined me. When I remembered how they were ready to let me choke to death and how I vowed to get them, the tears rolled down my cheeks. That was really funny. They didn't know what I was thinking and I didn't know what form my revenge would take.

"Let's have some sounds." Beatrice got up from the table. We were by magic back in the murky living room. Johnnie Mae stood putting records on the player. She turned to me as the first record began to play. "You said you're studying how to dance. Do us a dance." Lil Green's voice whined out the sadful lyrics:

> "In the dark, in the dark, I get such a thrill.
>   when you press your fingertips upon my lils."

I couldn't explain that I didn't do dancing alone to music like that. At the studio I did stretches, extensions, pliés and relevés to Prokofiev, Tchaikovsky and Stravinsky.

It was considered normal in gatherings to ask a child or even an adult to entertain. The talented person was expected to share his gift. The singer was asked to "Sing us a little song!" and the person with a gift of memorizing was asked to "Render us a poem!" In my mother's house I had often been called to show what I was studying at dance school. The overstuffed chairs were pulled back and I would dance in the cleared living-room space. I hummed inaudibly and moved precisely from ballet position one straight into a wobbling arabesque. Mother's company would set their highballs down to applaud.

I decided to dance for my hostesses. The music dipped and swayed, pulling and pushing. I let my body rest on the sound and turned and bowed in the tiny room. The shapes and forms melted until I felt I was in a charcoal sketch, or a sepia watercolor.

When the record finished I stopped. The two women sat on the sofa. Made solemn.

"That was good. Wasn't it, baby?"

"Sure was."

"Dance with Beatrice. I don't mind. Go on. Beatrice, dance with Rita."

Again, order was in her voice. The last thing in the world I wanted to do was dance with another woman. Johnnie Mae got up and started the Lil Green song again and Beatrice moved up close to me. She put her arm around my waist and took my left hand as if we were going to waltz. It was crushing. Not only was she fat and soft and a head shorter than I, her big breasts rubbed against my stomach. She stuck her thigh between my knees and we wobbled around the room.

This was the ultimate insult. I would vent my spleen on those thick-headed lecherous old hags. They couldn't do me this way and get away with it.

"That's right, Beatrice, do the dip." The woman did a fancy step and bent back, pulling me with her. I nearly toppled over. Mercifully, the record finished after what seemed one thousand hours and I was allowed to return to the sofa.

"You all look good together. Beatrice can sure dance, can't she? Come here, baby, and give me a kiss."

I got up and made room for Beatrice.

"No. You can stay." She encircled Beatrice, whose face was heavy with submission.

"Have to go to the toilet again." Let the mental machine do its work. In the bathroom an idea bloomed. They were whores. Why not encourage them in their chosen profession? From what I understood, whores can never get enough money, and since they had so little, I dressed my newborn creation carefully and took it back to the living room. I asked if we could turn down the music because I wanted to talk.

"Rita wants to talk." They broke out of their embrace. Nasty things. "I just thought I might be able to help you keep this place. You like it so much and you've made it so cute, it'd be a shame if you lost it."

They nearly became maudlin in their agreement.

"Well, I could rent it, and you could continue to stay."

"You mean you pay the rent and we pay you back."

"No. I'll rent the place in my name, I'll have the lights and gas put in my name. And pay everything. And three nights a week or four nights a week, you all stay here and turn tricks."

Beatrice's silly little voice complained: "You mean to turn our home into a whorehouse?"

Well, whores lived in it and it was a house. "Do you realize if the trade builds up, you can buy a place of your own and fix it just like this?" And they probably would.

"Where would we get the tricks?" Ever-practical Johnnie Mae.

"We'd get white taxi drivers and give them a percentage." My brain was clicking along like a Santa Fe train. A-hooting and a-howling. "They could be told the hours, like between ten and two. Then if every trick is twenty dollars, they get five and we split the fifteen. Seven-fifty for you. Seven-fifty for me."

"We don't want to be whores. I mean, full time." Old big little Beatrice already scared. What did she do in the WACS? Seduce young girls?

"Tricking four days a week isn't full time," I said. "And anyway, if you're successful, you can quit it in six months. Go and buy you a little place. Fact is, you could even get a bigger house." And get even more junk in it.

Johnnie Mae looked at me with suspicion. "When did you figure all that out?"

"Well, I've been wanting to go into business. So I'd been saving my money. I had been thinking in terms of a hamburger stand, but this place is so perfect." And so were they. "If all three of us save, do you realize we could open a restaurant in a year? Beatrice as the chef. You and I as managers."

I was getting to them. "I had a little operation up the coast. A three-girl deal, but I had to close down." Admiration and a little fear showed in their faces. They hadn't bargained for what they were getting.

Johnnie Mae, not wanting to believe what she already believed, asked, "Why were you working as a waitress?"

Should I tell them in order to eat and pay for my son's keep, so they'd throw me down on that uncomfortable sofa and rape me? "I needed a front. Cops after me."

"Cops!" Both of them screamed. Like many weak people they wanted to milk the cow, at the same time denying the smell of bullshit. I saw immediately that I had gone too far.

"Not after me myself. One of my girls, but I wanted to lay a cover for myself."

Beatrice said, "You're awfully young to be in the rackets."

"I've been around, baby." I rolled my eyes to indicate distant and mysterious places. "Well, how does it sound? Say we say Wednesday, Thursday, Friday and Saturday. Then you're free for church on Sunday and—"

"We'd better talk about it."

"I'm off tomorrow and I can get all the business taken care of. No time like the present."

"We only have the two bedrooms. Where will *you* work?"

I almost shouted at the tall woman. Me, turn tricks? What did she think I was? "I'm going to stay on at the restaurant. Shouldn't call attention to myself, you understand. But you won't be alone. I'll have somebody here to watch out for you. Just leave it to me."

I became pompously professional, which was never hard for me, being my father's daughter. "If you'll let me have a tablet and a pen, I'll take the landlord's address."

"Beatrice. Get some paper."

I moved over to the table, shifting the dinner dishes and crumbs out of my way as Johnnie Mae dictated.

"What's this address again?"

She gave it to me and I wrote it over and over on slips of paper.

"What you doing now?" Johnnie Mae wasn't bright, but she'd always be too clever to just go for the okey-doke. I put it in my mind that I'd better keep that in my mind.

"When I leave here, I'm going to start drumming up business," I said. "In a few weeks we'll be thousandaires."

"What?"

"That's just a step from millionaires. Let's have a drink on it." Beatrice poured. The first mouthful nearly sent me reeling. It made contact with the grifa in my brain. For a lightning second I was sober with a clear recollection of what I had done, then blissfully I was high again. An authority in charge of affairs.

I said good-bye, alluded again to the wonderful food and the wonderful future we had in store, and walked out of the house.

I was certain that my heartlessness regarding the women stemmed from a natural need for revenge. After all my soggy sentimentality for the misunderstood, no one could have convinced me that I was merely acting out society's hate for the "other ones."

However, an irony struck me before I reached the little one-foot wire fence that guarded the pavement from the yard. In a successful attempt to thwart a seduction I had ended up with two whores and a whorehouse. And I was just eighteen.

CHAPTER 14

"Good evening, driver."

"Yeah."

"Are there enough houses of ill repute to service the naval personnel?"

"Whaat?"

"I know you're generally paid four dollars on a twenty-dollar customer (I guessed, I didn't know), but if, after Thursday night ten o'clock, you bring clients to this address, you'll be remunerated to the tune of five dollars per head."

You had to be very careful in speaking to whites, and especially white men. My mother said that when a white man sees your teeth he thinks he sees your underclothes.

I had managed in a few tense years to become a snob on all levels, racial, cultural and intellectual. I was a madam and thought myself morally superior to the whores. I was a waitress and believed myself cleverer than the customers I served. I was a lonely unmarried mother and held myself to be freer than the married women I met.

———

Hank was the club's erratic bouncer. Erratic because sometimes he didn't show up, and other times, when his habits hit him, he bounced people onto the sidewalk who had done no more than offend his sensibilities. He spent a few nights monthly in the drunk tank, and was always taken back on his release.

The other waitresses hinted that Hank did a few private jobs for the boss. Secretly I believed the man was afraid of Hank, rightly, for there was no way to anticipate him. He might see in a stranger qualities of great worth, or he might develop an active hate for a person's color.

He had kind of adopted me on my arrival, and at the earliest opportunity I approached him. "Hank, I want to know if you'd look after some business for me?"

In another century that face would have so frightened a slave owner that he would have been compelled to lash the broad back and shackle the wide hands.

"Yeah, li'l sister. What's the matter?"

"You know the two les—bull daggers who come in here?"

"They ain't been messing with you, is they?"

"Oh no." The reverse. "They've asked me to back them in a business. Whorehouse, to be exact. Wednesday to Saturday. And you're the only person I can trust to watch out for my end. I figure to pay you one third of my take."

His mouth hung open. "You're going to be turning tricks?"

"Not me, I'm going to keep on working, but they will. Could you manage the place for me? Watch out for the police and keep track of the money?"

After much repeating myself, he agreed. I created an elaborate system of chits, which would be given to the women and the cabdrivers. At around two-thirty in the morning Hank was to put on a porch light denoting a clear coast, and I would go in and pay off the workers.

I had a vague worry—that a sudden large bank account would put the vice squad on my trail. I wasn't afraid of the police, since I wasn't turning tricks myself, but I was terrified of how a police investigation would influence Mother Cleo. She'd toss me and my baby out of the house with much damning me to the depths of hell. There were other places to live of course, and with the money piling up in secret places I could afford anyone to tend my child, but the fact was that I cared for the Jenkinses and what they thought of me was important.

Their home and their ways reminded me of the grandmother who raised me and whom I idolized. I wouldn't have them offended. When my illicit business reached its peak, I joined their church, and stood in the choir singing the old songs with great feeling.

One afternoon Mother Cleo remarked, "I know something." And smiled a leer. Panic set in.

"What?"

"You doing something." She sang the accusation like schoolchildren promising to tell.

"What? I'm not doing anything." The ready lie at my tongue.

"You got yourself a fella."

Of all things, how could she come up with that? However wrong she was, I perceived she wasn't angry, and it would be safer to lie again.

I asked, "How did you know?" Pleased now that she had caught me.

"'Cause you're coming in later than you used to. Me, I'm a light sleeper. Mr. Henry can sleep till the cows come home, but taking care of children makes me a light sleeper. I hear every footfall. You used to be in around two twenty-five, two-thirty. Now you get in sometimes its three-thirty. Am I right?"

"Yes."

"Well, is he a nice boy? Work where you work, don't he?"

"How do you know so much, Mother Cleo?"

"'Cause anybody else couldn't stay up every night till you get off. If you want to, he can come 'round here to see you."

I started. "Not at night. But in the daytime, I don't mind." That was more like it. With so many unexpected things happening I would be very unhappy to see Mother Cleo's morals slip.

———

For two and a half months I operated at the points of a stylistic triangle, braggadocio (in front of the women) and modest servitude (at the club), and kept wondering what to do with all the cash.

I bought a car which was a model of Detroit genius. A pale-green Chrysler, '39 vintage, convertible. It sported wooden doors and highly polished wooden dashboards. Knobs and buttons were a yellow material like the handles of old-fashioned flatware. I fashioned a sling made out of belts and secured my son, who had begun to walk. We drove around the monotonous streets of San Diego in my beautiful chariot. I had paid cash for it from a dresser drawer of money.

Mother Cleo asked charily, "And where in the world...?"

I had my answer molded. "My boyfriend gave it to me!"

"What'd he do? Steal it?"

"Oh no. He paid cash."

"How come he don't come around?"

"He's going to. I invited him." In fact, I had thought of palming Hank off as the hard-working boyfriend but decided he'd never be able to carry it off.

"Listen here. He ain't a married man, is he?" She began to draw away from me as if I might be a carrier of a loathsome disease.

"No, ma'am. He's not even divorced. I mean, he's never been married."

She calmed down gradually, then her face hardened. "He ain't a white man, is he? I don't 'low white men."

I had to laugh. Of all the tricks who came and went in my establishment, I hadn't even seen one. "No, Mother Cleo, he's not even light-skinned."

274 · *Maya Angelou*

Reluctantly she smiled. "One thing I don't hold with is women messing 'round with married mens. The other is messing 'round with white men. First one the Bible don't like, second one the law don't like."

She could have put her time to greater use concerning herself with my lack of morals rather than with my sexual involvements. Since coming to San Diego I let no attraction penetrate the invisible widow's weeds I had donned. My love was dead, my love was gone, married to some stupid shipfitter and living in the mosquito-ridden swamps of Louisiana. Long die, and stay dead, my love.

CHAPTER 15

During this time when my life hinged melodramatically on intrigue and deceit, I discovered the Russian writers. One title caught my eye. Not because I felt guilty raking in money from the doings of prostitutes but because of the title's perfect balance. Life, as far as I had deduced it, was a series of opposites: black/white, up/down, life/death, rich/poor, love/hate, happy/sad, and no mitigating areas in between. It followed Crime/Punishment.

The heavy opulence of Dostoevsky's world was where I had lived forever. The gloomy, lightless interiors, the complex ratiocinations of the characters, and their burdensome humors, were as familiar to me as loneliness.

I walked the sunny California streets shrouded in Russian mists. I fell in love with the Karamazov brothers and longed to drink from a samovar with the lecherous old father. Then Gorki became my favorite. He was the blackest, most dear, most despairing. The books couldn't last long enough for me. I wished the writers all alive, turning out manuscripts for my addiction. I took to the Chekov plays and Turgenev, but always returned in the late nights, after I had collected my boodle, to the Maxim Gorki and his murky, unjust world.

My dance teacher, who took no personal interest, wore the most outlandish clothes. Her long dark skirt, gathered, fell to just above her ankles. The blouses were of Mexican persuasion and were worn off her thin shoulders. Ropes of colorful beads and thong sandals completed her costume. She looked odd enough for admiration. I copied her clothes, and when not dressed in the white-blouse, black-skirt waitress uniform, I could be seen haunting the libraries, a tall thin black girl in too-long skirts and señorita blouses, which might have been sexy had I had the figure and/or attitude to complement them. Alas, I didn't.

Upon reflection, I marvel that no one saw through me enough to bundle me off to the nearest mental institution. The fact that it didn't happen depended less on my being a good actress than the fact that I was surrounded, as I had been all my life, by strangers. The world of waitress, dreamer, madam and mother might have continued indefinitely, except for another of life's unexpected surprises.

I didn't insist on any rules in my little whorehouse by the side of the road, except one: no all-night dates, no matter what the temptation. I wanted the money without name, the ease without strain. I never wanted any tricks to be in the house after I arrived, hence the signal with Hank.

One evening I sat in a taxi on the darkened street (I never took my automobile to the whorehouse) and waited for the light to go off on the porch. The driver, who also brought trade, and I walked into the house.

I stood in the center of the tiny living room, which smelled of Lysol and smoke and incense, hemmed in by the driver, the women and Hank, and by the furniture, which threatened to oust us all at any moment. Beatrice and Johnnie Mae erased any budding aspirations I had for owning things. Now that they had money, their acquisitive natures came into their own. The total filling up of the living room was so gradual that it was as if the existing furniture gave birth nightly to smaller and even larger images of itself.

Hank passed me the cigar box of money.

"Damn. Turn the damned radio off till we get business settled. You can't hear a shitting thing." I had taken to cursing to round out my image. The two women no longer took any interest in me, except possibly to hate my arrogance and envy my authority. I couldn't care less.

I had not finished recovering their chits and was about to turn to the cabdriver when a drunk, half-dressed white sailor stumbled through the bedroom door. He had nothing on below the blue middy. There was a moment's hush when the women and Hank looked at me. I was hypnotized at the man's nudity and couldn't take my eye's from his white, soft, dangling penis.

Beatrice ran to him. "Honey. I told you to stay—"

"What's going on? Who are all these folks?" His accent was lower Mississippi, and he looked as naked and white and ugly and drunk and nasty as anything I could think of.

Beatrice herded him back to the room.

In those seconds I became a child again. Unreasoning rage consumed me. The low-down sneaky bitches—I had told them to have the place cleared before I got there. They had probably had tricks there every night and I hadn't even questioned them. I could have gone to jail or worse. After all I'd done for them, their whorish hearts were so ungrateful that I had been subjugated to looking at the sickening aspect of a white man's penis.

I turned to Hank, and lumbering toward me, he said, "Rita, swear to God, I thought they was all gone."

Johnnie Mae allowed a little of her jealousy to show. "I don't see nothing wrong myself. You come over here every night collecting money, acting like you somebody's pimp. But you too good to turn a trick. And you keep this big rough sonofabitch watching us all the time. Well, you can kiss my black ass."

Her rudeness didn't surprise me. I would not have moved an eyebrow at anything any more. The drivers stood mesmerized by the event.

I gave the cigar box to Hank. "Hank. Do you want a whorehouse, complete with whores? You've just been given one." I turned to the women, gathering all my injured dignity. "And, ladies, you decided in the beginning that you were going to screw me one way or the other. Look at us now. Who did the screwing?"

Beatrice's voice keened, sharpened and moved through the room like a swinging razor. "If it hadn't been for you, we'd be living like we always did."

"Yes, in the street, or back in some white woman's kitchen."

Johnnie Mae swelled up as if she had taken in more air than it was possible to release. "Be goddam careful how you talk to her, you big-nose bitch."

It was time to go. These lying heathens were not above attacking me. And after all I'd done for them.

"Hank, if you want this place, it's all yours." And one parting shot to the traitors: "At least I'm leaving you better off than I found you. You've got enough secondhand furniture to start you own Goodwill store." And to the cabdriver: "Will you please take me home."

I stood straighter, separating myself from the stench of my present environment, and started out. Johnnie Mae's rage propelled her after me. I reached the door just as she stretched her hand for me. I put on a little speed, not wanting to appear to be running, and escaped down the steps as she and the cabdriver collided in the doorway. He extricated himself in a hurry, more than a little terrified of getting caught between two restless tribes. Johnnie Mae, thwarted, for I had gained the sidewalk, screamed out into the quiet darkness, "You bitch! You think the police don't want to know how you bought that car. You better not drive it again. I'll have the vice squad on your ass."

I don't know how I continued walking to the cab. Her threat and the sound of her screech had stabbed me to the quick as surely as it had pierced the night. The wretch would put the cops on my trail and I'd lose my car, go to jail and be put out of Mother Cleo's. I was sitting in the back of the taxi when a numbing thought sidled across my brain like a poisonous snake. I might be declared an unfit mother and my son would be made a ward of the court. There were cases like that. In the cool early-morning air I began to sweat. The tiny glands in my armpits opened and closed to the pricking of a thousand straight pins.

"Please take me home, and I'm sorry for that terrible outburst." Fear still rode the front seat with the driver and he lost no time depositing me at my destination. I paid him, tipped him grandly and inundated him with praise for his reliability and courtesy, and lack of familiarity. I don't think he heard a word, and before I reached the front door, his tail lights had turned winking around the corner.

During the exotic buying sprees I hadn't thought to get luggage to hold my new acquisitions. I heaped piles of my clothes and my son's into the suitcases Bailey had given me in San Francisco. I had made up my mind that come daybreak, my son and I were going to make a run for it. If the police caught me, they'd catch me at the railway station or on the train, not a sitting duck waiting passively to be arrested. When I had finished cramming as many things as possible into the bags, I sat down to read until daybreak.

Since childhood I had often read until the gray light entered my room, but on that tense night it seemed sleep had allied itself with my enemies, and along with them was determined to overpower me, do me down. I tried sitting in a chair and sitting cross-legged on the bed. A knock awoke me. It was Mother Cleo.

"Rita, you left your light on again. You going to start helping me with the electricity. You don't know how much it cost..." She was moving away from the door, and her words reached down the hall.

I came to full attention and checked my luggage, my money and my story again.

"Mother Cleo, my mother is sick in San Francisco. She telephoned me at the club last night, so I have to go home." I had followed her into the kitchen. She put down her cup and looked at me with such sympathy I almost wished I wasn't lying.

"Oh, you poor thing. She ain't bad off, is she?"

"Oh no, nothing serious." I wanted to calm her fears.

"Well then, you won't be long. You'll leave the baby?"

"Oh no. She wants to see him. And I'll tell you the truth"—as if I could—"I'm not coming back soon."

"Aw. Don't tell me that. I've come to look on you as family."

"Mother Cleo, I appreciate everything you've done for us. And I want you to have this." I laid fifty dollars on the table. "My boyfriend sent it to you as a present."

She beamed and I saw the tears start to form.

"Now, don't cry. We'll come back sometime. I wish you'd bathe the baby while I'm taking a bath, and then we'll hit the highway."

Her last words to me as she and Mr. Henry helped me to the car were attributes to my acting and successful deceit.

"You're just what I wanted for a daughter. You smart and mannerable and truthful. That's what I like most. You living a Christian life. Keep up the good work. God bless you and the child. And your mother."

I tore down the morning streets as if the hounds of hell were coming to collect my soul. The baby responded to the two-wheel curve-taking by giving out air-splitting screams. My "Hush, baby" and "It's all right, baby" could have been unheard whispers. He felt my panic and seemed to want the world to know that he was just as afraid as his mother.

At the train station I wiped the steering wheel and unstrapped the baby. I left the car parked in a No Parking zone, and as far as I know, it is there to this day.

—

I was racing away with my son on my hip and sheer fright in my heart. My general destination was the little village in Arkansas where I had grown up. But the particular goal of the journey was the protective embrace of Mrs. Annie Henderson, the grandmother who had raised me. Momma, as we called her, was a deliberately slow-speaking, right-thinking woman. And above all, she had what I lacked most at the moment. Courage.

CHAPTER 16

There is a much-loved region in the American fantasy where pale white women float eternally under black magnolia trees, and white men with soft hands brush wisps of wisteria from the creamy shoulders of their lady loves. Harmonious black music drifts like perfume through this precious air, and nothing of a threatening nature intrudes.

The South I returned to, however, was flesh-real and swollen-belly poor. Stamps, Arkansas, a small hamlet, had subsisted for hundreds of years on the returns from cotton plantations, and until World War I, a creaking lumbermill. The town was halved by railroad tracks, the swift Red River and racial prejudice. Whites lived on the town's small rise (it couldn't be called a hill), while blacks lived in what had been known since slavery as "the Quarters."

After our parents' divorce in California, our father took us from Mother, put identification and destination tags on our wrists, and sent us alone, by train, to his mother in the South. I was three and my brother four when we first arrived in Stamps. Grandmother Henderson accepted us, asked God for help, then set about raising us in His way. She had established a country store around the turn of the century, and we spent the Depression years minding the store, learning Bible verses and church songs, and receiving her undemonstrative love.

We lived a good life. We had some food, some laughter and Momma's quiet strength to lean against. During World War II the armed services drew the town's youth, black and white, and Northern war plants lured the remaining hale and hearty. Few, if any, blacks or poor whites returned to claim their heritage of terror and poverty. Old men and women and young children stayed behind to tend the gardens, the one paved block of stores and the long-accepted way of life.

In my memory, Stamps is a place of light, shadow, sounds and entrancing odors. The earth smell was pungent, spiced with the odor of cattle manure, the yellowish acid of the ponds and rivers, the deep pots of greens and beans cooking for hours with smoked or cured pork. Flowers added their heavy aroma. And above all, the atmosphere was pressed down with the smell of old fears, and hates, and guilt.

On this hot and moist landscape, passions clanged with the ferocity of armored knights colliding. Until I moved to California at thirteen I had known the town, and there had been no need to examine it. I took its being for granted and now, five years later, I was returning, expecting to find the shield of anonymity I had known as a child.

Along with other black children in small Southern villages, I had accepted the total polarization of the races as a psychological comfort. Whites existed, as no one denied, but they were not present in my everyday life. In fact, months often passed in my childhood when I only caught sight of the thin hungry po' white trash (sharecroppers), who lived sadder and meaner lives than the blacks I knew. I had no idea that I had outgrown childhood's protection until I arrived back in Stamps.

Momma took my son in one arm and folded the other around me. She held us for one sweet crushing moment. "Praise God Almighty you're home safe."

She was already moving away to keep her crying private.

"Turned into a little lady. Sure did." My Uncle Willie examined me with his quiet eyes and reached for the baby. "Let's see what you've got there."

He had been crippled in early childhood, and his affliction was never mentioned. The right side of his body had undergone severe paralysis, but his left arm and hand were huge and powerful. I laid the baby in the bend of his good arm.

"Hello, baby. Hello. Ain't he sweet?" The words slurred over his tongue and out of the numb lips. "Here, take him." His healthy muscles were too strong for a year-old wriggler.

Momma called from the kitchen, "Sister, I made you a little something to eat."

We were in the Store; I had grown up in its stronghold. Just seeing the shelves loaded with weenie sausages and Brown Plug chewing tobacco, salmon and mackerel and sardines all in their old places softened my heart and tears stood at the ready just behind my lids. But the kitchen, where Momma with her great height bent to pull cakes from the wood-burning stove and arrange the familiar food on well-known plates, erased my control and the tears slipped out and down my face to plop onto the baby's blanket.

The hills of San Francisco, the palm trees of San Diego, prostitution and lesbians and the throat hurting of Curly's departure disappeared into a never-could-have-happened land. I was home.

"Now what you crying for?" Momma wouldn't look at me for fear my tears might occasion her own. "Give the baby to me, and you go wash your hands. I'm going to make him a sugar tit. You can set the table. Reckon you remember where everything is."

The baby went to her without a struggle and she talked to him without the cooing most people use with small children. "Man. Just a little man, ain't you? I'm going to call you Man and that's that."

Momma and Uncle Willie hadn't changed. She still spoke softly and her voice had a little song in it.

"Bless my soul, Sister, you come stepping up here looking like your daddy for the world."

Christ and Church were still the pillars of her life.

"The Lord my God is a rock in a weary land. He is a great God. Brought you home, all in one piece. Praise His name."

She was, as ever, the matriarch. "I never did want you children to go to California. Too fast that life up yonder. But then, you all's their children, and I didn't want nothing to happen to you, while you're in my care. Jew was getting a little too big for his britches."

Five years before, my brother had seen the body of a black man pulled from the river. The cause of death had not been broadcast, but Bailey (Jew was short for Junior) had seen that the man's genitals had been cut away. The shock caused him to ask questions that were dangerous for a black boy in 1940 Arkansas. Momma decided we'd both be better off in California where lynchings were unheard of and a bright young Negro boy could go places. And even his sister might find a niche for herself.

Despite the sarcastic remarks of Northerners, who don't know the region (read Easterners, Westerners, North Easterners, North Westerners, Midwesterners), the South of the United States can be so impellingly beautiful that sophisticated creature comforts diminish in importance.

For four days I waited on the curious in the Store, and let them look me over. I was that rarity, a Stamps girl who had gone to the fabled California and returned. I could be forgiven a few siditty airs. In fact, a pretension to worldliness was expected of me, and I was too happy to disappoint.

When Momma wasn't around, I stood with one hand on my hip and my head cocked to one side and spoke of the wonders of the West and the joy of being free. Any listener could have asked me: if things were so grand in San Francisco, what had brought me back to a dusty mote of Arkansas? No one asked, because they all needed to believe that a land existed somewhere, even beyond the Northern Star, where Negroes were treated as people and whites were not the all-powerful ogres of their experience.

For the first time the farmers acknowledged my maturity. They didn't order me back and forth along the shelves but found subtler ways to make their wants known.

"You all have any long-grain rice, Sister?"

The hundred-pound sack of rice sat squidged down in full view.

"Yes, ma'am, I believe we do."

"Well then, I'll thank you for two pounds."

"Two pounds? Yes, ma'am."

I had seen the formality of black adult equals all my youth but had never considered that a time would come when I, too, could participate. The customs are as formalized as an eighteenth-century minuet, and a child at the race's knee learns the moves and twirls by osmosis and observation.

Values among Southern rural blacks are not quite the same as those existing elsewhere. Age has more worth than wealth, and religious piety more value than beauty.

There were no sly looks over my fatherless child. No cutting insinuations kept me shut away from the community. Knowing how closely my grandmother's friends hewed to the Bible, I was surprised not to be asked to confess my evil ways and repent. Instead, I was seen in the sad light which had been shared and was to be shared by black girls in every state in the country. I was young, yes, unmarried, yes—but I was a mother, and that placed me nearer to the people.

I was flattered to receive such acceptance from my betters (seniors) and strove mightily to show myself worthy.

Momma and Uncle Willie noted my inclusion into the adult stratum, and on my fourth day they put up no resistance when I said I was going for a night on the town. Since they knew Stamps, they knew that any carousing I chose to do would be severely limited. There was only one "joint" and the owner was a friend of theirs.

Age and travel had certainly broadened me and obviously made me more attractive. A few girls and boys with whom I'd had only generalities in common, all my life, asked me along for an evening at Willie Williams' café. The girls were going off soon to Arkansas Mechanical and Technical College to study Home Economics and the boys would be leaving for Tuskegee Institute in Alabama to learn how to farm. Although I had no education, my California past and having a baby made me equal to an evening with them.

When my escorts walked into the darkened Store, Momma came from the kitchen, still wearing her apron, and joined Uncle Willie behind the counter.

"Evening, Mrs. Henderson. Evening, Mr. Willie."

"Good evening, children." Momma gathered herself into immobility.

Uncle Willie leaned against the wall. "Evening, Philomena, and Harriet and Johnny Boy and Louis. How you all this evening?"

Just by placing their big still bodies in the Store at that precise time, my grandmother and uncle were saying, "Be good. Be very very good. Somebody is watching you."

We squirmed and grinned and understood.

The music reached out for us when we approached the halfway point. A dark throbbing bass line whonked on the air lanes, and our bodies moved to tempo. The steel guitar urged the singer to complain

> "Well, I ain't got no
> special reason here.
> No, I ain't got no
> special reason here.
> I'm going leave
> 'cause I don't feel welcome here…"

The Dew Drop In café was a dark square outline, and on its wooden exterior, tin posters of grinning white women divinely suggested Coca-Cola, R.C. Cola and Dr Pepper for complete happiness. Inside the one-room building, blue bulbs hung down precariously close to dancing couples, and the air moved heavily like stagnant water.

Our entrance was noted but no one came rushing over to welcome me or ask questions. That would come, I knew, but certain formalities had first to be observed. We all ordered Coca-Cola, and a pint bottle of sloe gin appeared by magic. The music entered my body and raced along my veins with the third syrupy drink. Hurray, I was having a good time. I had never had the chance to learn the delicate art of flirtation, so now I mimicked the other girls at the table. Fluttering one hand over my mouth, while laughing as hard as I could. The other hand waved somewhere up and to my left as if I and it had nothing to do with each other.

"Marguerite?"

I looked around the table and was surprised that everyone was gone. I had no idea how long I had sat there laughing and smirking behind my hand. I decided they had joined the dancing throng and looked up to search for my, by now, close but missing friends.

"Marguerite." L. C. Smith's face hung above me like the head of a bodyless brown ghost.

"L.C., how are you?" I hadn't seen him since my return, and as I waited for his answer a wave of memory crashed in my brain. He was the boy who had lived on the hill behind the school who rode his own horse and at fifteen picked as much cotton as the grown men. Despite his good looks he was never popular. He didn't talk unless forced. His mother had died when he was a baby, and his father drank moonshine even during the week. The girls said he was womanish, and the boys that he was funny that way.

I commenced to giggle and flutter and he took my hand.

"Come on. Let's dance."

I agreed and caught the edge of the table to stand. Half erect, I noticed that the building moved. It rippled and buckled as if a nest of snakes were mating beneath the floors. I was concerned, but the sloe gin had numbed my brain and I couldn't panic. I held on to the table and L.C.'s hand, and tried to straighten myself up.

"Sit down. I'll be right back." He took his hand away and I plopped back into the chair. Sometime later he was back with a glass of water.

"Come on. Get up." His voice was raspy like old corn shucks. I set my intention on getting up and pressed against the iron which had settled in my thighs.

"We're going to dance?" My words were thick and cumbersome and didn't want to leave my mouth.

"Come on." He gave me his hand and I stumbled up and against him and he guided me to the door.

Outside, the air was only a little darker and a little cooler, but it cleared one corner of my brain. We were walking in the moist dirt along the pond, and the café was again a distant outline. With soberness came a concern for my virtue. Maybe he wasn't what they said.

"What are you going to do?" I stopped and faced him, readying myself for his appeal.

"It's not me. It's you. You're going to throw up." He spoke slowly. "You're going to put your finger down your throat and tickle, then you can puke."

With his intentions clear, I regained my poise.

"But I don't want to throw up. I'm not in the least—"

He closed a hand on my shoulder and shook me a little. "I say, put your finger in your throat and get that mess out of your stomach."

I became indignant. How could he, a peasant, a nobody, presume to lecture me? I snatched my shoulder away.

"Really, I'm fine. I think I'll join my friends," I said and turned toward the café.

"Marguerite." It was no louder than his earlier tone but had more force than his hand.

"Yes?" I had been stopped.

"They're not your friends. They're laughing at you." He had misjudged. They couldn't be laughing at me. Not with my sophistication and city ways.

"Are you crazy?" I sounded like a San Francisco–born debutante.

"No. You're funny to them. You got away. And then you came back. What for? And with what to show for your travels?" His tone was as soft as the Southern night and the pond lapping. "You come back swaggering and bragging that you've just been to paradise and you're wearing the very clothes everybody here wants to get rid of."

I hadn't stopped to think that while loud-flowered skirts and embroidered white blouses caused a few eyebrows to be raised in San Diego, in Stamps they formed the bulk of most girls' wardrobes.

L.C. went on, "They're saying you must be crazy. Even people in Texarkana dress better than you do. And you've been all the way to California. They want to see you show your butt outright. So they gave you extra drinks of sloe gin."

He stopped for a second, then asked, "You don't drink, do you?"

"No." He had sobered me.

"Go on, throw up. I brought some water so you can rinse your mouth after."

He stepped away as I began to gag. The bitter strong fluid gurgled out of my throat, burning my tongue. And the thought of nausea brought on new and stronger contractions.

After the cool water we walked back past the joint, and the music, still heavy, throbbed like gongs in my head. He left the glass by the porch and steered me in the direction of the Store.

His analysis had confused me and I couldn't understand why I should be the scapegoat.

He said, "They want to be free, free from this town, and crackers, and farming, and yes-sirring and no-sirring. You never were very friendly, so if you hadn't gone anywhere, they wouldn't have liked you any more. I was born here, and will die here, and they've never liked me." He was resigned and without obvious sorrow.

"But, L.C., why don't you get away?"

"And what would my poppa do? I'm all he's got." He stopped me before I could answer, and went on, "Sometimes I bring home my salary and he drinks it up before I can buy food for the week. Your grandmother knows. She lets me have credit all the time."

We were nearing the Store and he kept talking as if I weren't there.

I knew for sure that he was going to continue talking to himself after I was safely in my bed.

"I've thought about going to New Orleans or Dallas, but all I know is how to chop cotton, pick cotton and hoe potatoes. Even if I could save the money to take Poppa with me, where would I get work in the city? That's what happened to him, you know? After my mother died he wanted to leave the house, but where could he go? Sometimes when he's drunk two bottles of White Lightning, he talks to her. 'Reenie, I can see you standing there. How come you didn't take me with you, Reenie? I ain't got no place to go, Reenie. I want to be with you, Reenie.' And I act like I don't even hear him."

We had reached the back door of the Store. He held out his hand.

"Here, chew these Sen-sen. Sister Henderson ought not know you've been drinking. Good night, Marguerite. Take it easy."

And he melted into the darker darkness. The following year I heard that he had blown his brains out with a shotgun on the day of his father's funeral.

CHAPTER 17

The midmorning sun was deceitfully mild and the wind had no weight on my skin. Arkansas summer mornings have a feathering effect on stone reality.

After five days in the South my quick speech had begun to drag, and the clipped California diction (clipped in comparison) had started to slur. I had to brace myself properly to "go downtown." In San Francisco, women dressed particularly to shop in the Geary and Market streets' big-windowed stores. Short white gloves were as essential a part of the shopping attire as girdles, which denied cleaved buttocks, and deodorant, which permitted odorless walkings up and down the steep hills.

I dressed San Francisco style for the nearly three-mile walk and proceeded through the black part of town, past the Christian Methodist Episcopal and African Methodist Episcopal churches and the proud little houses that sat above their rose bushes in grassless front yards, on toward the pond and the railroad tracks which separated white town from black town. My postwar Vinylite high heels, which were see-through plastic, crunched two inches into the resisting gravel, and I tugged my gloves all the way up to my wrist. I had won over the near-tropical inertia, and the sprightly walk, made a bit jerky by the small grabbing stones, the neat attire and the high headed position, was bound to teach the black women watching behind lace curtains how they should approach a day's downtown shopping. It would prove to the idle white women, once I reached their territory, that I knew how things should be done. And if I knew, well, didn't that mean that there were legions of Black women in other parts of the world who knew also? Up went the Black Status.

When I glided and pulled into White Town, there was a vacuum. The air had died and fallen down heavily. I looked at the white windows expecting to see curtains lose strained positions and resume their natural places. But the curtains on both sides of the street remained fixed. Then I realized that the white women were missing my halting but definitely elegant advance on their town. I then admitted my weariness, but urged my head higher and my shoulders squarer than before.

What Stamps' General Merchandise Store missed in class it made up in variety. Cheap grades of thread and chicken feed, farming implements and hair ribbons, fertilizer, shampoo, women's underwear, and B.V.D.s. Socks, face powder, school supplies and belly-wrenching laxatives were shoved on and under the shelves.

I pitied the poor storekeeper and the shop attendants. When I thought of the wide aisles of San Francisco's Emporium and the nearly heard, quiet conversations in the expensive City of Paris, I gave the store a patronizing smile.

A young, very blond woman's mournful countenance met me in the middle of a crowded aisle. I gave her, "Good morning," and let a benign smile lift the corners of my lips.

"What can I do for you?" The thin face nodded at me like a sharp ax descending slowly. I thought, "The poor shabby dear." She didn't even form her words. Her question floated out like a hillbilly song, "Whakin I dew fer yew?"

"I'd like a Simplicity pattern, please." I could afford to be courteous. I was the sophisticate. When I gave her the pattern number out of my head and saw her start at my Western accent, regained for the moment, I felt a rush of kindness for the sorrowful cracker girl. I added, "If you please."

She walked behind a counter and riffled through a few aging sewing patterns, her shoulders rounding over the drawer as if its contents were in danger. Although she was twenty, or more likely eighteen, her stance and face spoke of an early surrender to the poverty of poor-white Southern life. There was no promise of sex in her hip span, nor flight in her thin short fingers.

"We ain't got it here. But I can put in a order to Texarkana for it for you."

She never looked up and spoke of the meager town twenty-five miles away as if she meant Istanbul.

"I would so much appreciate that." I did feel grateful and even more magnanimous.

"It'll be back in three days. You come in on Friday."

I wrote my name, Marguerite A. Johnson, without flourishes on the small pad she handed me, smiled encouragement to her and walked back into the now-serious noon sunshine. The heat had rendered the roads empty of pedestrians, and it assaulted my shoulders and the top of my head as if it had been lying in wait for me.

The memory of the insensate clerk prodded me into exaggerated awareness and dignity. I had to walk home at the same sprightly clip, my arms were obliged to swing in their same rhythm, and I would not under any circumstances favor the shade trees which lined the road. My head blurred with deep pains, and the rocky path swam around me, but I kept my mind keen on the propriety of my position and finally gained the Store.

Momma asked from the cool, dark kitchen, "What'd you buy, Sister?"

I swallowed the heat-induced nausea and answered, "Nothing, Momma."

———

The days eased themselves around our lives like visitors in a sickroom. I hardly noticed their coming and going. Momma was as engrossed as she'd allow herself in the wonder of my son. Patting, stroking, she talked to him and never introduced in her deep voice the false humor adults tend to offer babies. He, in turn, surrendered to her. Following her from kitchen to porch to store to the backyard.

Their togetherness came to be expected. The tall and large dark-brown woman (whose movement never seemed to start or stop) was trailed one step by the pudgy little butter-yellow baby lurching, falling, now getting himself up, at moments rocking on bowed legs, then off again in the wave of Momma. I never saw her turn or stop to right him, but she would slow her march and resume when he was steady again.

———

My pattern had arrived from old exotic Texarkana. And I dressed for the trek downtown, and checked my hair, which was straightened to within an inch of its life and greased to desperation. From within the Store, I felt the threat of the sun but walked out into the road impelled by missionary zeal.

By the time I reached the pond and Mr. Willie Williams' Dew Drop In, the plastic seemed to have melted to the exact shape of my feet, and sweat had popped through the quarter inch of Arrid in my armpits.

Mr. Williams served me a cold drink. "What you trying to do? Fry your brains?"

"I'm on my way to the General Merchandise Store. To pick up an order."

His smile was a two-line checkerboard of white and gold. "Be careful they don't pick you up. This sun ain't playing."

Arrogance and stupidity nudged me out of the little café and back on the white hot clay. I drifted under the shade trees, my face a mask of indifference. The skin of my thighs scudded like wet rubber as I walked deliberately by the alien white houses and on to my destination.

In the store the air lay heavily on the blades of two sluggish overhead fans, and a sweet, thick odor enveloped me at the cosmetic counter. Still, I was prepared to wander the aisles until the sun forgave our sins and withdrew its vengeance.

A tall saleswoman wearing a clerk's smock confronted me. I tried to make room for her in the narrow corridor. I moved to my left, she moved to her right. I right, she left, we jockeyed a moment's embarrassment and I smiled. Her long face answered with a smile. "You stand still and I'll pass you." It was not a request for cooperation. The hard mountain voice gave me an order.

To whom did she think she was speaking? Couldn't she see from my still-white though dusty gloves, my starched clothes, that I wasn't a servant to be ordered around? I had walked nearly three miles under a sun on fire and was neither gasping nor panting, but standing with the cool decorum of a great lady in the tacky, putrid store. She should have considered that.

"No, you stand still and I'll pass around you," I commanded.

The amazement which leaped upon her face was quickly pushed aside by anger. "What's your name? Where you from?"

A repetition of "You stand still and I'll pass around you" was ready on my tongue, when the pale woman who had taken my order slack-butted down the aisle toward us. The familiar face brought back the sympathy I had felt for her and I explained the tall woman into limbo with "Excuse me, here comes my salesgirl."

The dark-haired woman turned quickly and saw her colleague approach. She put herself between us, and her voice rasped out in the quiet store: "Who is this?"

Her head jerked back to indicate me. "Is this that sassy Ruby Lee you was telling me about?"

The clerk lifted her chin and glanced at me, then swirled to the older woman. "Naw, this ain't her." She flipped the pages of a pad in her hand and continued, "This one's Margaret or Marjorie or something like that."

Her head eased up again and she looked across centuries at me. "How do you pronounce your name, gal? Speak up."

In that moment I became rootless, nameless, pastless. The two white blurs buoyed before me.

"Speak up," she said. "What's your name?"

I clenched my reason and forced their faces into focus. "My name"—here I drew myself up through the unrevenged slavery—"is Miss Johnson. If you have occasion to use my name, which I seriously doubt, I advise you to address me as Miss Johnson. For if I need to allude to your pitiful selves, I shall call you Miss Idiot, Miss Stupid, Miss Fool or whatever name a luckless fate has dumped upon you."

The women became remote even as I watched them. They seemed actually to float away from me down the aisle; and from watching their distant faces, I knew they were having trouble believing in the fact of me.

"And where I'm from is no concern of yours, but rather where you're going. I'll slap you into the middle of next week if you even dare to open your mouths again. Now, take that filthy pattern and stick it you-know-where."

As I strode between the two women I was sheathed in satisfaction. There had been so few critical times when my actions met my approval that now I congratulated myself. I had got them told and told correctly. I pictured the two women's mouths still open in amazement. The road was less rocky and the sun's strength was weakened by my pleasure. Congratulations were in order.

There was no need to stop at Mr. Williams' for a refreshing drink. I was as cool as a fountain inside as I headed home.

Momma stood on the porch facing the road. Her arms hung at her sides and she made no motions with her head. Yet something was wrong. Tension had distorted the statue straightness and caused her to lean leftward. I stopped patting myself on the back and ran to the Store.

When I reached the one-step porch, I looked up in her face. "Momma, what's the matter?"

Worry had forced a deep line down either side of her nostrils past her stiffly held lips.

"What's wrong?"

"Mr. Coleman's granddaughter, Miss June, just called from the General Merchandise Store." Her voice quaked a little. "She said you was downtown showing out."

So that's how they described my triumph to her. I decided to explain and let her share in the glory. I began, "It was the principle of the thing, Momma—"

I didn't even see the hand rising, and suddenly it had swung down hard against my cheek.

"Here's your principle, young miss."

I felt the sting on my skin and the deep ache in my head. The greatest hurt was that she didn't ask to hear my side.

"Momma, it was a principle." My left ear was clogged, but I heard my own voice fuzzily.

The hand didn't surprise me the second time, but the same logic which told me I was right at the white store told me I was no less right in front of Momma. I couldn't allow myself to duck the blow. The backhand swing came down on my right cheek.

"Here's your principle." Her voice had a far-away-tunnel sound.

"It was a principle, Momma." Tears poured down my burning face, and ache backed up in my throat.

The hand came again and again each time I mumbled "principle," and I found myself in the soft dust in front of the porch. I didn't want to move. I never wanted to get up again.

She stepped off the porch and caught my arms. "Get up. Stand up, I say."

Her voice never allowed disobedience. I stood, and looked at her face. It glistened as if she had just dashed a pan of water over her head.

"You think 'cause you've been to California these crazy people won't kill you? You think them lunatic cracker boys won't try to catch you in the road and violate you? You think because of your all-fired principle some of the men won't feel like putting their white sheets on and riding over here to stir up trouble? You do, you're wrong. Ain't nothing to protect you and us except the good Lord and some miles. I packed you and the baby's things, and Brother Wilson is coming to drive you to Louisville."

That afternoon I climbed into a horse-drawn wagon, and took my baby from Momma's arms. The baby cried as we pulled away, and Momma and Uncle Willie stood waving and crying good-bye.

CHAPTER 18

Momma's intent to protect me had caused her to hit me in the face, a thing she had never done, and to send me away to where she thought I'd be safe. So again, the South and I had parted and again I was headed for the cool gray hills of San Francisco. I raged on the train that white stupidity could so dictate my movements and looked unsheathed daggers at every white face I saw.

If the tables could have turned at that instant, I would gladly have consigned every white person living and the millions dead to a hell where the devil was blacker than their fears of blackness and more cruel than forced starvation. But, powerless, I spent the time on the train entertaining the baby when I thought of it, and wondering if I would be met by a warrant for my arrest when I returned to California.

The city didn't even know I had been away, and Mother took me and the baby to a room in her new fourteen-room house as if I had just returned from a long-intended holiday.

I found a job as a short-order cook in a tiny greasy spoon. The men who ate there were defeated leftovers from the now-closed war plants. They slouched into the fifth-rate dingy diner hugging their distress.

The job paid very little and the atmosphere of despair that never lifted depressed me. I left the restaurant each afternoon feeling that the rancid cooking oil and the old men's sadness had seeped into my pores and were crawling through my body.

One afternoon I went into a record shop across the street from the diner and found a woman who was friendly and warm behind the counter. She was white and thirtyish, and didn't condescend to either my color or my youth. When I told her that I liked blues, she pulled out some old Columbia Blue Labels. I said that I also liked jazz, and she suggested recent Charlie "Bird" Parker releases. I let the music wash away the odors and moods of the restaurant, and I left the shop with more records than I could afford. I had agreed with her that I should start collecting the Dial records featuring Bird, Max Roach, Al Haig, Bud Powell, Dizzy Gillespie and others who she said were going to be the "masters." Each payday I kept out enough money to pay my own way at Mother's, and spent the rest on records and books.

Mother was unhappy that my job made me unhappy. She always knew her "daughter had great potential" and was determined that if she had anything to do with it, I was going to realize it.

Weeks later she and I sat in the dining room and picked and poked through the classifieds for my future.

I was nearly nineteen, had a baby, responsibilities and no real profession. I could cook Creole and was a fast, friendly cocktail waitress. Also I was qualified as an absentee madam, but I somehow felt that I simply had not yet "found out my niche" (I had just discovered that phrase and yo-yo'ed it around with frequent and gay abandon).

"Private secretary. If you could type fast enough and do shorthand." Mother was serious. Her pretty face was lined with concentration. "Telephone operator, pays pretty good."

I reminded her that we'd already been through that.

"Key punch. Stenographer. You need training, baby."

She looked at me spot on and added, "Anything worth doing is worth doing well."

I didn't dare remind her that everything I had done had been well done.

"What is Alice doing? What about Jean Mae, and the twins? What are they all doing? Going to college?" Her voice and round black eyes worried me for answers.

Jean Mae, the neighborhood's sepia Betty Grable, had a job hopping cars at a popular drive-in. I hardly had the face, figure or sexuality to be taken in at that restaurant. Alice could be seen nightly whistling down Post Street and up Sutter, her young walk exaggerated, her thin voice insinuating the lone sailor into following three paces behind her to the nearest transient hotel.

The twins married twins, which seemed as appalling to me as streetwalking. I felt there was a closet incest about the whole thing.

The small percentage of classmates who went on to college had become unbearably stuck-up and boring. So I found no inspiration among my peers.

"Companion, Chauffeurette." That I could do. I immediately set a film to flickering on my mind screen. In a snappy uniform, no cap, gray serge and British walker shoes, I drove a man around who was the spitting image of Lionel Barrymore. He always addressed me as "Johnson" and while we liked and respected each other, we took pains never to show it. Late nights, he would call me into the drawing room and I would stand at attention, easily.

"Johnson. Tomorrow's a beaut."

"Yes, sir?"

"We go up to the city, then back to the country club, then the city, then the farm. A little hard on you, I fear."

"It's my job, sir."

"I could count on you to say that, Johnson."

"Yes, sir."

"Good night."

"Good night, sir."

Mother's gaze followed her ringed fingers up and down the page.

"You'd have to live in and it doesn't really pay enough for you to afford a full-time baby-sitter." She flipped the paper closed.

"Take anything that looks like something. You can always quit. Or there's a chance that you won't rise to the challenge and you'll be fired. But the only thing to remember is that 'you were looking for a job when you found that one.' So whoever fires you ain't getting no cherry." She got up and went into the kitchen.

"How about a Dubonnet"—ice already clucked against the sides of glasses—"with a twist of lemon? I'm going to fix myself a Scotch."

When I was around ten in Arkansas, I saw a glamorous actress play a jaunty chauffeurette in a movie. She maneuvered an Oldsmobile with one hand and was as chic as a model. I looked at the paper again and thought about the chauffeuring job. A wisp of nostalgia floated in my heart. The uniform, the easy camaraderie with the staff, the asexuality with my boss, and peace. Just like the Army. Routine, honorable work, hail-fellows well met, good-hearted companions and fair-minded officers. The Army! Just the thing. The idea snap-saluted in my brain. The Army!

I bounded into the kitchen and nearly collided with Mother and her tray of gold and purple drinks. I had developed some grace, quite a lot when I kept my mind on being graceful, but in unguarded moments my body tended to respond giraffe-like to stimuli.

"Mother!" She had righted the threatened glasses and pushed past me for the dining room. "I'm going in the Army!"

She set down the Dubonnet. "You as a sergeant and the baby as a private?"

Her tongue was sharper than the creases in zoot pants and I knew better than to try to best her. I said nothing.

"What would be the value of becoming a WAC?" she asked.

"The Army has all those side benefits and I could learn a trade. There's the G.I. Bill, and when you get out you can go back to school and buy a home at the same time."

"Side benefits" had caused a glint in Mother's eyes.

"Now"—she pushed the wine toward me—"now you have to consider if you're serious. Because if you are, it would be like volunteering for jail. People tell you when to sleep, eat, wake up, work. Personally, I couldn't do it in a million years." Her face frowned revulsion. "But in a way the country would be helping you get a start in life."

Behind her smooth beige forehead, deep thoughts were being turned over, examined and replaced or discarded.

"If you are serious and get in, we'll talk to Mrs. Peabody about taking care of the baby. You could sign up for a two-year tour, save your money, and study languages and advanced typing."

She was talking my future into shape.

"Try out for Officer Candidate School or Officers' Training

Corps. Nothing they could say to you but yes or no. And when you go down there, remember they need you as much as you need them." She saw my disbelief and explained. "The U.S. Army needs nice colored girls, well raised from good families. That's what I meant." She reached for her lipstick tube (never far away). "Government is going to give you an education and a start in life and you're going to give class to that uniform."

"Mother, they would examine me, physically, and find out about the baby."

"You don't have stretch marks and because you breastfed, your breasts never got out of shape." Her words nudged past indifference. "That's not what you ought to be thinking of. No. Decide if you want the Army for two years. Away from your baby and family. Taking orders, and keeping your temper under wraps. That's a decision no one can make for you nor help you make."

She got up from the table and visited one of her flashiest smiles on me.

"I have a date now. We can talk more when you're ready. Remember if you decide for the Army, I'll support you. If you decide to be a whore, all I can say is, be the best. Don't be a funky chippie. Go with class."

She pasted a waxy kiss on my forehead and draped her Kolinsky over her shoulders.

"How do I look?"

"Beautiful."

She tugged the furs into a more casual drape and laughed. "You only say it 'cause it's true."

Her high heels tapped toward the door in drumming rhythm.

CHAPTER 19

The U.S. Recruitment Center hadn't tried hard. The offices were at the foot of San Francisco's Market Street, near the glamorous Ferry Building, but none of the latter's exotica strayed to the prefab white-wash walls of the Center.

A uniformed woman offered me a Dagwood sandwich of brochures and applications and I sat down to read.

Indeed, it sounded like what I needed. Food, shelter, training and comradeship. Two years and I could buy a house for myself and my son. Might find a man, too. After all, there was a conglomeration of men in the Army. All I had to do now was maneuver between outrageous lies and delicate untruths to pass the various tests. (I wasn't concerned about the I.Q., but about the Rorschach.) Had I just wanted to join the regular Women's Army it would have taxed my creative lying skills, but I had gone one further. Mother had said, "Start at the top," so I decided to try out for Officer Candidate School. I thought daily trips to the Center would help my case.

The war's end had left the skeletal WAC staff with little to do except file papers in triplicate and dress up in privilege. For nearly a month I provided diversion. Naturally, the clerks couldn't enjoy my artful dodging as much as I, because they weren't privy to my secrets.

I sidled over the questionnaires and applications, double-checking, double-lying. Married... check one. No. Children... check one. No.

My cavorting brain was of no use to me at the medical examination, though. There the doctors opened my mouth wide (I needed dental work; the Army would pay), thudded and tapped and listened to my strong lungs and courageous heart. All was well.

The gynecologist's table was my Armageddon. There on the cold table, gray steel instruments would probe between my legs and into the unknown territory where my deepest guilts had lodged. I had no more idea of the construction of a woman's regenerative organs than I had of the structure of the moon. Surely, I thought, there would be some scars visible from my son's birth. Some leftover tube hanging down which would signal to the knowledgeable that I was a mother and therefore unfit to serve my country (which by this time I had come to love with a maudlin sentimentality).

"We'll take a few slides." The nurse's face was stony, and the doctor ignored my face, acting as if I was nothing but a thin chest, flat belly and long black legs.

I asked why.

"These are venereal-disease tests." She spoke as if she were weather-watching. I'd gladly have settled for syphilis and gonorrhea. If the Army could take care of my teeth, a couple of injections would cure the diseases.

"The tests will be back in a few days."

I tried to scrape from their faces any information they had gathered. But those faces were trained in suppression. I wanted to shout at their closed ears, "I'll wait. I'll sit in the outer office and wait for the results." But I too had some training—that is, "Never let white folks know what you really think. If you're sad, laugh. If you're bleeding inside, dance."

"I'll be away for a few days," I lied, "but I'll phone as soon as I return." I tried to make it sound as if I would be doing them a favor.

Three or four days jittered by with no pretense at flowing, and then the phone call came.

"Miss Johnson?" I recognized the voice with echoes of starched uniforms and drill squadrons.

"Yes, I'm Miss Johnson." I tried to put "I'm Miss Johnson, so what?" into my own response and failed.

"Sergeant Matthews at the Induction Center."

I know. I know. Go on, dammit.

"I'm calling to tell you you've passed all your tests and have been included in the March–April quota of personnel to enter Officer Candidate School. Is that all right with you?"

I suddenly had dirigible-sized air pockets in my cheeks which prevented me from making any sound except a loud explosion. I nodded into the telephone.

"Will you be prepared to leave the San Francisco area at the beginning of May for Fort Lee, Virginia?"

The air plopped out of my mouth and I jerked the phone away. God knows I didn't want to frighten the sergeant and give her a reason to re-examine my dossier of lies. I turned the sound into a fake cough and brought the mouthpiece back.

"Excuse me. A little spring cough. Oh yes, I can certainly be ready for May first." I was in a little more control, so I added, "I'm most happy to have this opportunity to serve my country and I shall—"

She interrupted, "Yes, well, come down in the next few days and sign the loyalty oath. Good-bye." And hung up.

Now I was ready. Things had arranged themselves in my favor at last. For the next two years I would have the security of purpose and the dignity of being a soldier in good standing in the Army of the United States of America.

Natural restraint and the conceit of sophistication kept me from rushing down immediately to sign the loyalty oath. I was able to keep myself away for two days before I surrendered.

I stood in front of the flag, one hand on the Bible, the other clasped to my breast, and swore I would defend this land from her enemies, etc., etc. The deep motives, the noble intent so moved me that with the least encouragement I would have dissolved in a flood of patriotic tears.

Mother was happy but not surprised at my success story. When I told Bailey that I would soon be going into the Army, he turned a cold stare on me and asked without relishing curiosity, "What the shit for? Men are trying like hell to get out and my sister is dying to get in. You dumb bunny." The air between Bailey and me had coarsened with our growing up and thickened with his cynicism. He could no longer see me clearly and I could not distinguish his black male disappointment in life.

It could not be said that Bailey was living at home, but more accurately that he was based there. He worked as a waiter on the Southern Pacific trains running from San Francisco to Chicago or Los Angeles or Houston.

Few black families are without ties to the U.S. railroads. The early-twentieth-century Negro aristocrats were the families of ministers, morticians, teachers and railroad men. Passes to ride the trains were traded in Southern black areas as easily as legitimate money. And many poor black families ate their beans and greens from good china and used heavy silver from the Union Pacific, Southern Pacific and New York Central.

Bailey was still the plum pretty black color and his teeth shone white like promises. His hair was glossy and his small hands delicate and graceful. But all the gentle reminders of his love for me through our childhood stopped at his eyes. It seemed some confrontation, which he had kept secret, dulled their shine and left them flat and unseeing.

His fast speech, which used to stumble into a stutter with excitement, had slowed, and a songless monotone rasped out his meanings. When he was home from a trip, he never sat around with Mother and me, playing pinochle or coon can, as we used to do, but hurriedly put down his gear and left the house for some mysterious destination. He successfully blocked my prying by saying, "Take care of yourself and your baby and your own business and that'll take all your time."

When I tried to involve Mother in discussion of his whereabouts and how abouts, she said nearly the same thing but generally added, "He's a man. He's got a job and his health and strength. Some people have to make it through life with less." And that was that.

Papa Ford, who had been brought to the new house, sat bowed over his coffee in the warm kitchen.

I asked him, "Papa, what's Bailey doing? Why is he changing so?"

He lifted his head and relished a toothless mouth. Smack. Smack.

"Uh. Uh, girl. Uh, uh." He lowered his head, loving the doom he hinted.

"Papa, what does that mean? Say something."

The passage of years had ground away his emotional-transition apparatus. He would often shift in a moment from a dozing indifference to a fighting fury. He did so then.

"Don't ask so many goddam questions. Keep your goddam big eyes open. You're no shitty-ass baby." A slurp from his mug and he was nearly asleep again.

CHAPTER 20

I had to make arrangements for my personal belongings. I told Mother that when I got out of the Army I would dress in suits, and my cashmere-sweater sets would match kick-pleated Scotch-plaid skirts. I wouldn't be needing the old clothes. Mother had decided they were good enough to be given to charity. I remembered the large St. Vincent de Paul's trucks, backing down our driveway once a year during my teens, collecting Mother's unwanted items. After a brief but pointed sermon when Mother spoke of "those less fortunate than you," I chose the Salvation Army as my beneficiary. Those fresh clean faces in their absurd regalia playing their uninspired music, unheeded, had always depressed me. They had to be the most deserving.

The records would stay in the house. Mother enjoyed Lester Young, Billie Holiday, Louis Jordan, Buddy Johnson and Arthur "Big Boy" Crudup as much as I. She'd play them at her parties and think of me.

I found it hard to think of leaving my books. They had been my elevators out of the midden, and to whom could I entrust such close friends?

The benevolent act of giving away my clothes, however, spilled over into that decision making. Hospitals were the answer. I was certain that lean and lonely tubercular patients would have their spirits lifted reading the *Topper* stories of Thorne Smith, and I had proved it possible to read Robert Benchley's essays and short stories over a hundred times and still laugh. Ann Petry's *The Street*, all Thomas Wolfe,

Richard Wright and Hemingway would be given to an old-folks home. But the Russian writers would be packed away in mothballs and stored in our basement. I would savor the idea of Dostoevsky's, Tolstoy's and Gorki's volumes molding in the dank cellar, wisps of camphor and odors of wet earth floating above them.

I quit my job to spend more time with Guy, to record his cherubic smile and be amazed at the beauty of his coordination. He seldom cried and seemed a budding introvert, for although he never thrust himself from company, he appeared to be equally amused alone. A baby's love for his mother is probably the sweetest emotion we can savor. When my son heard my voice at the downstairs door he'd begin to sing, and when I arrived in his view he'd fall back on his fat legs, his behind would thud to the floor and he'd laugh, his big head rocking up and down.

I knew it would be hard to leave him. Hard on me, but harder on him, for he had no way of understanding that I was gone to prepare a place for us. I hugged his sweetness to me and squeezed my love into his pores. If we were to have a decent life, a small but neat house, good neighborhood and schools, bulky knit sweaters and the expensive tennis shoes I saw large boys wearing, I'd have to get some kind of training and I needed help. Uncle Sam was going to be more a friend to me than any of my bad blood uncles.

With my clothes gone to the Salvation Army and my books packed in wooden boxes downstairs, I spent my remaining time gazing at the training manual and familiarizing myself with creases and salutes and drill formations, how a bunk should be made and how officers were to be addressed.

A week before I was to be inducted, a military voice over the telephone ordered me down to the Recruitment Center.

"I can come this morning or this afternoon."

"This morning! And that's an order, soldier."

"It sounds urgent." Maybe our departure date had been moved up.

"It's more urgent than that. It's about some discrepancy on your documents. We'll see you this morning." Click.

Dammit, dammit and double damn. Probably some ruthless, relentless doctor had re-examined my charts and found that I'd had a baby. And I had sworn that everything I had written was God's own truth. There were laws to punish criminals who lied ("perjury" it was called) on oath. And it must have been worse to lie on oath *and* the flag.

Mother had taken Guy out for the morning, to leave me alone with my army books. I had no one to accompany me. I dressed as I wondered. I shook as I planned. It was pretty certain I wasn't going into the Army, but I might go to jail if the Army wanted to press charges. I should have known better than to lie to the government. People always said Uncle Sam would spend a thousand dollars to get you if you stole a three-cent stamp from him. He was more revengeful than God.

I couldn't run, I couldn't hide. I went to the government building.

On the bus I soft-conned myself. I had done so well on the examinations that if I came clean and explained that I had made solid arrangements for my son's care for two years, they might make an exception. It could be simple, if only I got a kind interviewer and could stop shaking.

"Marguerite Johnson?"

The woman's long thin neck rose out of wide sloping shoulders and her voice skidded like a fire alarm. I would have liked her face softer.

"Yes." Er... "Yes, ma'am." She was an officer. Oh hell, I mean... "Yes, sir."

"Did you or did you not sign the loyalty oath?"

"I did." Did I? I had gone down a few weeks before and sworn to uphold the flag, defend the country and protect my fellow Americans with my life, if need be. I had been so moved by my sincerity that I added to myself, "My country may she always be right but right or wrong, my country." Off we go into the wild blue yonder and the caissons go rolling along.

"Were you or were you not asked if you had ever been a member of the Communist party?"

"I was asked, and I said no." Well, if that was all it was! I felt the blood pushing to open up its old passages and start to flow again.

"You lied, Johnson." The voice sirened up to a screech.

"Lied, sir? No, sir. I've never—"

"This is your signature, Johnson?" She produced the loyalty oath by slight of hand. I didn't need to peer to see the large curving Marguerite Johnson.

"Yes, sir. That is my signature."

She flipped the paper over and grinned her pleasure. "The California Labor School is on the House Un-American Activities list, Johnson. Do you know why?"

"No, sir. I only studied dance and drama there."

"Oh, come now. Don't be stupid. It's a Communist organization and you know it."

"Maybe so, but I have never been a member."

"You went to the school for two years." She had regained her composure, her stiffness.

"But that was when I was fourteen and fifteen. I had just come from the South, and a playground teacher got me a scholarship. It was because I had trouble talking—"

"Communists are ungodly, Johnson. And this man's army fights under God."

I felt as if I were drowning in straw. The light was still visible but no amount of struggling brought me nearer to it.

"Because you were young and, I hope, you're still innocent, the Army is not going to bring charges of falsification against you. But we definitely cannot risk you as a soldier in our army, Johnson. Dismissed."

I was suspended, physically and mentally, for a second.

"Dismissed."

I know I'd have made a good soldier because without the benefit of habit or training, my body turned sharply and walked out into the sunshine.

Mother and the baby were still out when I returned to the big house. Papa Ford was away on his noonday constitutional. The rooms were all dark and cool. I sat at the ornate dining-room table and tried to sort things out.

My clothes were gone, I had no job and I had been rejected by the Army. That damn institution, which accepts everybody (to tell from its soldiers), had turned me down. My life had no center, no purpose. I had to admit, though, that I had lied. Not on the issue they charged against me (hell, I wouldn't have recognized Stalin if he'd been in my class when I was fourteen. Literally, all white folks still looked alike to me: pale and similar), but I had lied about Guy's birth. I wondered if justice was served. If maybe I should just shut up and take my punishment. I needed Bailey. I longed for the old days when I could speak to him and work out my problems.

I got up from the table and opened the door to his room. It had a strange emptiness. Not as if the occupant had just stepped out and was expected back, but as if it had never been occupied and expected nothing. There was a deadness in the air. I turned on the overhead light, went to the windows and pulled up the shades. The gray spring light dared only to enter a yard or so. I decided to change his linen, clean up and put fresh flowers in his room. Meanwhile I would think over my problem.

I stripped the blankets and folded them, then I tugged at the linen. For a moment I was so amazed I forgot my whereabouts. This couldn't be Bailey's bed. He was the model of cleanliness, neatness, decorum. Every member of my family had said at one time or other, "Maya should have been a boy and Bailey a girl. She's so sloppy and he's so neat"—and more to that effect.

The sheets were gray and black with dirt. An odor of perfumed hair oil and must lifted heavily. I tugged at the edges and let the sheets slide to the floor. The pillows rode along on the end of the sheet. As they tumbled, a small round bundle wrapped in brown paper bounced down at my feet.

I opened it without needing to. Thin brown cigarettes were held together with three rubber bands.

Even in his absence, Bailey had helped me. I lighted one of the cigarettes and in minutes was snickering over the stupidity of the Establishment. The U.S. Army with its corps of spies had been fooled by a half-educated black girl. I sat down on Bailey's bed and laughed until I had to fight for my breath.

CHAPTER 21

I took a job as swing-shift waitress in a day-and-night restaurant called the Chicken Shack. The record player blared the latest hits incessantly and the late-night clientele spent their overflow energy loudly in the brightly lighted booths.

Smoking grass eased the strain for me. I made a connection at a restaurant nearby. People called it Mary Jane, hash, grass, gauge, weed, pot, and I had absolutely no fear of using it. In the black ghetto of the forties, marijuana, cocaine, hop (opium) and heroin were only a little harder to obtain than rationed whiskey. Although my mother didn't use anything but Scotch (Black & White), she often sang a song popular in the thirties that at its worst didn't condemn grass, and at its best extolled its virtues.

> Dream about a reefer five foot long
> Vitamin but not too strong
> You'll be high but not for long
> If you're a viper.
>
> I'm the queen of everything
> I got to get high before I can swing
> Light some tea and let it be
> If you're a viper.
>
> Now when your throat gets dry
> you know you're high
> Everything is dandy
> You truck on down to the candy store
> And bust your conk on peppermint candy
>
> Then you know your brown body scent
> You don't give a damn if you don't pay your rent
> Light some tea and let it be
> If you're a viper.

I learned new postures and developed new dreams. From a natural stiffness I melted into a grinning tolerance. Walking on the streets became high adventure, eating my mother's huge dinners an opulent entertainment, and playing with my son was side-cracking hilarity. For the first time, life amused me.

Positive dreaming was introduced on long, slow drags of the narcotic. I was going to do all right in the world, going to have it made— and no doubt through the good offices of a handsome man who would love me to distraction.

My charming prince was going to appear out of the blue and offer me a cornucopia of goodies. I would only have to smile to have them brought to my feet.

R. L. Poole was to prove my dreams at least partially prophetic. When I opened the door to his ring and informed him that I was Rita Johnson, his already long face depressed another inch.

"The ... uh ... dancer?" His voice was slow and cloudy.

Dancer? Of course. I had been a cook, waitress, madam, bus girl— why not a dancer? After all, it was the only thing I had studied.

"Yes, I'm a dancer." I looked at him boldly. "Why?"

"I'm looking for a dancer, to work with me."

I thought he might be a talent scout for a chorus line or maybe the big stage show, featuring colored dancers, called "Change Your Luck."

"Come in."

We sat at the dining-room table and I offered a coffee. He looked me over, one feature at a time. My legs (long), my hips (spare), my breasts (nearly nonexistent). He drank the coffee slowly.

"I've studied since I was fourteen," I said.

If the U.S. Army was going to penalize me for having gone to the California Labor School, it was just possible that someone else would find the time spent there valuable. I was right. His eyes moved from an examination of my body back to my face.

"I'm Poole. From Chicago." His announcement held no boast, and I was sure that represented sophistication rather than false modesty. "I do rhythm tap and I want a girl partner. She doesn't have to do much but flash. Are you agva?" ("Flash" and "A.G.V.A." were words unknown to me.)

I sat quietly and looked at him. Let him figure it out for himself.

"I met the woman at the record shop and she told me about you. Said all you talked about was dancing. She gave me your address.

"Some cats from the Local, musicians, straightened me out with the contracts for a few gigs. Scale is twenty-two fifty, but I'll do a few under scale to get some ends together."

I hadn't the slightest notion of what he was talking about. Scale. Agva. Gigs. Local. Ends.

"More coffee?" I went into the kitchen, walking like a model, chin down and sternum up, and my tail bone tucked under like white women.

I put on a fresh pot of coffee and tried desperately to decide on a role for myself. Should I be mysterious and sultry, asking nothing, answering all questions with a knowing smirk, or should I be the open, friendly, palsy every-boy's-sister girl-next-door type? No decision came to my mind, so I went back into the dining room, my legs stuck together with fine decorum.

"What did you study?"

"Ballet. Modern Ballet and the Theory of Dance." I made it sound like Advanced Thermonuclear Propulsion.

His face fell again.

"Any tap-dancing?"

"No."

"Jazz?"

"No."

"Acrobatics?"

"No." I was losing him, so I jumped in the gap. "I used to win every jitterbug contest. I can do the Texas Hop. The Off Time. The boogie-woogie. The Camel Walk. The new Coup de Grâce. And I can do the split."

With that I stood up, straddle-legged, and looked down into his sad face, then I began to slide down to the floor.

I was unprepared for the movement (I had on a straight skirt), but

R.L. was less ready than I. As my legs slipped apart and down, I lifted my arms in the graceful ballet position number 1 and watched the impresario's face race from mild interest to incredulous. My hem caught mid-thigh and I felt my equilibrium teeter. With a quick slight of hand I jerked up my skirt and continued my downward glide. I hummed a little snatch of song during the last part of the slither, and kept my mind on Sonja Henie in her cute little tutus.

Unfortunately, I hadn't practiced the split in months, so my pelvic bones resisted with force. I was only two inches from the floor, and I gave a couple of little bounces. I accomplished more than I planned. My skirt seams gave before my bones surrendered. Then my left foot got caught between the legs of Mother's heavy oak table, and the other foot jumped at the gas heater and captured the pipe that ran from the jets into the wall. Pinned down at my extremities with the tendons in my legs screaming for ease, I felt as if I were being crucified to the floor, but in true "show must go on" fashion I kept my back straight and my arms uplifted in a position that would have made Pavlova proud. Then I looked at R.L. to see what impression I was making. Pity at my predicament was drawing him up from his chair, and solicitude was written over his face with a brush wider than a kitchen mop.

My independence and privacy would not allow me to accept help. I lowered my arms and balanced my hands on the floor and jerked my right foot. It held on to the pipe, so I jerked again. I must have been in excellent shape. The pipe came away from the stove, and gas hissed out steadily like ten fat men resting on a summer's day.

R.L. stepped over me and looked down into the gas jet. "Goddam." He swiveled over to the window and opened it as wide as it would go, then back down to the stove. Near the wall at the end of the pipe, he found a tap and turned it. The hissing died and the thick sweetish odor diluted.

I had still to extricate my other leg from the avaricious table.

R.L. lifted an edge of the table, and my ankle was miraculously free. I could have gotten up, but my feelings were so hurt by the stupid clumsiness that I just rolled over on my stomach, beat my hands on the floor and cried like a baby.

There was no doubt that R.L. Poole had just witnessed his strangest audition. He could have walked down the hall and out the door, leaving me breathing in the dust of the ancient rug, but he didn't. I heard the chair creak, announcing that he had sat back down.

I was sure he was doing his best to hold in his laughter. I tried for more tears, to irritate him and force him to leave, but the tear ducts had closed and the sound I made was as false as a show girl's eyelashes. Nothing for it but to get up.

I dried my face with dusty hands and lifted my head. R.L. was sitting at the table in the same chair, his head propped up with his hand. The dark-brown face was somber and he said quietly, "Well, anyway, you've got nice legs."

When we went to a nearby rehearsal hall I was amazed to see R.L. Poole move. The wind seemed to make him dance. I pictured his lean bony legs as being attached directly to his sharp shoulders with skeletal pins. For he would hunch his shoulders and glide across the rehearsal-hall floor, his heels and toes tapping below him in a fusillade of small explosions, his arms dangling at his side, his face a pock-marked oval.

He tried to simplify the intricate tap rhythms by singing them to me in a rough, low voice. "Boom, boom, boo rah, boo rah, boo rah, boo rah, brah, brah." Sharp slaps on the floor, dust rising from the old wood.

With the polish of a professional, R.L. made it all appear easy. I telescoped my energy on the gliding steps of the flash, with no less purpose than a ballet student mastering a tour jeté. I would raise my arms shoulder-high, then open them out slowly, take two sliding steps, bend one knee and hold the position. An accomplished flash partner frames and highlights the principal dancer when he is tapping out complex rhythms. To be able to let my body swing free over the floor and the crushing failures in my past was freedom. I thanked R.L. for my liberation and fell promptly in love with him.

CHAPTER 22

I committed myself to a show-business career, and dancing and study-ing dance swallowed me. Charlie Parker's "Cool Breeze" was my prac-tice piece. Flash, slide through the opening riff, then stash during Bird's solo; keeping soft-shoe time by dusting the boards with the soles of my feet, then break during Bud Powell's piano wizardry. Break, cross step. Chicago. Fall. Fall. Break, crossover. Apple. Break. Time step. Slap crossover. Then break and Fall off the Log, going out on the closing riff.

I practiced until my ankles ached, without complaint, and was more than rewarded when R.L. told me one day, "After we break in our act out here, I think we'll go East. Big Time. Join Duke's or Basie's road show."

My concern was not how I'd manage with my son on the Big-time Circuit, but how I could perfect my flash so that R.L. wouldn't go looking for a prettier partner. I used my time at the Chicken Shack to strengthen my ankles. When I was behind the counter I stood on tip-toe, letting one heel down, then raising it, and pressing the other to the floor.

When R.L. decided we were ready to try out our act, I sprang my homemade costume on him. I had gone to a theatrical store and bought a wig, coke feathers, a padded bra and a G-string. I sewed the shiny black feathers on the scanty outfit, then added a few sequins and a little sparkle for show. My costume could be held in one balled fist, and the G-string barely covered my pubic hair and the cleavage of my buttocks.

"Er...no." He lowered his head and searched painfully for the words he wanted. "Uh...Rita...no. That won't...uh...get it... That's...wh...a shake dancer's rig...I mean, I'll show you...Some-thing like a bathing suit...with spangles..."

I stood before him, my oiled skin gleaming, the fluffy wig trembling

with ringlets on my head, withering with disappointment. My costume was a faithful copy of L'Tanya's, the popular interpretive dancer
who was a current favorite at the Champagne Supper Club.

"You'll look...I mean, tap shoes are gonna look...I mean, they
don't go together..."

I remembered. L'Tanya danced barefoot, with a string of little bells
around her ankles and rings on her toes. I reluctantly agreed that my
creation didn't fit a rhythm tap routine but put it away for future use.

R.L. rented a red, white and blue costume for me that was cut like a
one-piece bathing suit. I added a top hat and cane, and we were ready
for our first gig in a small night club down the peninsula. Ah, the smell
of grease paint!

Our routine was honed to a fine point, our flashes and stashes and
hand movements coordinated in machinelike precision. My costume
fit passably well, my hair was done beautifully, and I had on enough
make-up to stave off a winter cold.

The orchestra struck up our music and I led "Poole and Rita" out
on the dance floor.

Dum dum te dum dum dum.

"And now, breaking in their new act, from way out Chicago way—
Poole and Rita!"

I was miraculously in the center of an empty floor, with lights blazing down and I felt nearly naked. Just out of the glare I saw what appeared like a thousand knees and legs around small tables. I couldn't
make out faces in the gloom, but I was sure they were there and probably all staring at me.

R.L. glided onto the floor, tap-tap-tapping away, flashed by me and
I wanted to grab his hand. He pulled away to anywhere, but I was
frozen in the spotlight.

Boom boom boom rah boom rah, boom rah brah, brah.

I realized that I was frightened and I nearly panicked. My God,
what was going to happen? I'd never be able to leave this place. A stake
had been driven down through my head and body, rooting me forever
to this spot.

R.L. flashed by again.

Boom rah boom rah.

If he would only stop that silly tap-dancing and take my hand, we could leave.

He marched up and spoke to me under the music.

"Come on, Rita. Break. Break!"

Break what? I looked at him as if I had never seen him before.

He put his arm around my shoulder like Astaire did Rogers in one of their military parodies.

He looked at me and gave me a push that almost sent me into one of the tables, and hissed, "Break, goddammit, break!"

I broke.

I started dancing all over the place. Tapping, flashing, stashing up and down the floor. I threw in a little Huckle Buck, Suzie Q and trucking. Our routine had completely disappeared, but I was the world's dancing fool. Boogie-woogie, the Charleston. When the band was moving into the last chorus, I was just getting warmed up.

R.L. pursued me across the floor. He finally put his arm around my shoulder again, and by brute force led me off the floor, flashing to the end.

The audience clapped and I pulled away and raced back, booming and boom-rahing. R.L. joined me and again pulled me back to the wings.

I loved it. I was a hungry person invited to a welcome table for the first time in her life.

The costume rental and transportation had diminished our take to fifteen dollars apiece, I was exhausted and had the long bus ride ahead back to the city. But all was better than well. It was supercolossal. I had broken in. I was in show business. The only way up was up.

CHAPTER 23

As I scrambled around the foot of the success ladder, Mother's life flowed radiant. Fluorescent-tipped waves on incoming tides. Men with exotic names, slick hair and attitudes of bored wisdom came into Vivian Baxter's large dark house, stayed awhile and went, making room for their successors.

Good-Doing David, with his silky black skin (Mother always preferred very black men, saying they were the cleanest folks in the world) and silk foulard tie, sat around the kitchen table for a few months. His eyes monitored her movements carefully, and when it was nearly too late she repaid him with a sultry look, thrown over her shoulder, and a smile that promised secret delight. Good-Doing forfeited his tenancy because of a misjudgment in logic. He thought since he was her man, it followed that she was his woman. He shouldn't have been so wrong.

One afternoon a seaman friend called her from the dock, and she invited him over. They maintained a brother/sister relationship.

"John Thomas is coming," she said to me. "Please go get a couple of chickens from the kosher poultry store. Tell them to cut them up." She had pulled out the wooden bowl, and laid her diamond rings in an ashtray. "I'll whip up a few biscuits and give him some fried chicken."

I knew that although the store was only two blocks away, she would have the bread in the oven and the oil heating for the chicken before I returned.

When they said cooking, they called Vivian Baxter's middle name.

When I rushed back into the house, the smell of hot grease met me, and the mixing bowl was washed and draining on the sink. Mother was setting the table for two.

"You have to pick up the baby? Make me a little drink, honey. And see if there's bourbon. John Thomas drinks bourbon. I'll put your chicken on the back of the stove." Her smile was partly for me, partly for the coming visitor and partly for the chicken seasoned, floured and dropping into the boiling skillet.

"You know there's always some in the kitchen for 'grandma 'n de chillun'." Her favorite old-folks line slid into whitefolks vulgarity of the black accent.

I answered the door for Mr. Thomas, and took his herringbone raglan coat and hat.

"Hey, baby, still growing, huh? Where your old ugly mama?" He walked down the hall laughing.

"Let him in, he may be a gambler." Mother's voice clinked like good glass from the kitchen.

Their welcoming laughter mixed as I left the house.

———

The ambulance screamed as it two-wheel-turned the corner from our block. I picked Guy up, not noticing his weight, and ran to our house, where two police cars sat empty, their red eyes turning faintly in the afternoon sunlight.

For the passionate, joy and anger are experienced in equal proportions and possibly with equal anticipation. My mother's capacity to enjoy herself was vast and her rages were legendary. Mother never instigated violence, but she was known not to edge an inch out of the way of its progress. The sound of police and ambulance sirens whine through my childhood memory with dateless frequency. The red lights whirring on top of official cars and the heavy disrespectful footsteps of strange authority in our houses can be brought back clearly in my mind at a beckon.

Inside, Mother was slipping into her suede coat, a quiet smile on her face. She saw me and turned to the brace of policemen who waited for her.

"This is my daughter, Officers. That's who I was waiting for. Baby..." Now for the instructions that I already knew well. "Call the bail bondsman, Boyd Puccinelli. Tell him to meet me at Central Station."

I knew better than to ask what happened. I held the baby tighter.

"It's just a little business with David. Now, don't you worry. I'll be back in an hour."

She checked her make-up in her compact mirror, gave me and the baby a peck on our lips and walked down the steps with the police. Separate and dignified.

Then from the bottom: "Your dinner's in the oven. On low. Oh, and baby, clean up in the bedroom before that stuff dries, please."

There was no sign of Mr. John Thomas in the kitchen. After my son and I had eaten, and I put him down for an afternoon nap, I opened her bedroom door. One chair was on its side, but elsewhere things were in order. As I walked in, the weak winter sunshine paled over dark rust blotches on the rug and showed the lighter red splashes down the sides of the mantel.

Lukewarm soap suds are best to remove bloodstains from furniture. I had nearly finished cleaning up when Mother returned.

"Hi, baby. Any phone calls?"

"No."

"Here, leave that, I'll do the rest. Come on in the kitchen and let me tell you what happened."

Over a fresh drink she gave me what she called a "blow by blow" description.

"John Thomas and I were up to our elbows in fried chicken (I made a gravy longer than I been away from St. Louis for the biscuits) when Good-Doing rang the bell. I let him in and brought him back to the kitchen. He saw John Thomas and stopped shorter than a show horse. Said no, he didn't want to eat. Didn't want a drink, didn't want a chair, so I sat back down and started tending to business. Every time I looked up, I saw he was getting fuller than I was. Finally he said he wanted a few words with me and would I come to the bedroom. I told him to go on, I'd be there. I excused myself from John Thomas and went up the hall.

" 'What's that nigger doing here?' He got ugly in the face and jumped around like a tail on a kite.

"I said, 'You know John Thomas. He's my friend. He's like a brother to me.'

" 'Well, I don't like him eating here. Get him out of the house.'

"I said, 'Good-Doing, don't get it twisted. This is my house and my chicken, and he's my friend.'

"He said, 'Bitch, you supposed to be so bad. You need a good ass-kicking.' "

She looked at me, puzzlement wrinkling her pretty face.

"Baby, I swear to you, I don't know what sent him off, but before I could say anything, he reached in his pocket and pulled out a knife. You know he's got something wrong with the fingers on his left hand, so he bent his head over and was trying to open the knife with his teeth. Now, you can see by that, that he's a fool. Instead of moving away from him I just stepped over to the mantel. I put Bladie Mae in my pocket before I went up to the room. When he came up with his knife half open, I slapped him cross the face with ole Bladie.

"He jumped faster than the blood. Screamed, 'Goddammit, Bibbie, you cut me!'

"I said, 'You goddam right, and you lucky I don't shoot you on top of it.'

"He was holding his face, blood dripping down his hands on to his Hart Schaffner and Marx suit. I gave him a pillow off my bed and told him to sit down. I told him moving around makes the blood pump faster. I came back to the kitchen and told John Thomas to make himself scarce—no point in him being involved—then I called the police and the ambulance."

Mother inspected the contents of her glass, then she took my large hand in her smaller, plump one and ordered my close attention.

"Baby, Mother Dear's going to tell you something about life."

Her face was beautifully calm, all traces of violence lost.

"People will take advantage of you if you let them. Especially Negro women. Everybody, his brother and his dog thinks he can walk a road in a colored woman's behind. But you remember this, now. Your mother raised you. You're full-grown. Let them catch it like they find it. If you haven't been trained at home to their liking tell them to get to stepping." Here a whisper of delight crawled over her face. "Stepping. But not on you.

"You hear me?"

"Yes, Mother. I hear you."

———

There had been some changes at home. Bailey had found his first great love. Eunice was a small, smiling brown-skinned girl who had been our classmate. They had met again, and over the protests of her family, rushed to marry. Bailey, the airy false charmer, had drifted to earth and was happy. He laughed and joked again.

They invited me to their Turk Street apartment, where large Gauguin and Van Gogh prints enlivened the walls and fresh flowers sparkled on waxed tables.

He told funny dirty stories and the three of us laughed into the cheap wine and congratulated ourselves on being smart enough to be young and intelligent. We could see the plateaus of success in our futures. Plateaus where we would wait and rest awhile before climbing higher. When he looked at my 8″ by 10″ professional glossies, he said I had the "biggest nose in show business" but it was prettier than Jimmy Durante's and I ought to be proud.

I tried to punch him, but he laughed and swerved out of the way.

"You'll be the tallest dancer on Broadway. Ha ha." He ran around the table escaping my outstretched hand. "You'll make a million with each leg and a zillion with your nose."

Relief made me laugh out of proportion. Later I kissed them both good night and wished I knew how to thank Eunice for helping Bailey find his sense of humor again.

I walked the dark streets toward home and shivered at Bailey's close escape. Most of his friends, funny and bright during our schooldays, now leaned in nighttime doorways, nodding as their latest shot of heroin raced in their veins. Sparkling young men who were hopes of the community had thrown themselves against the sealed doors set up by a larger community, and not only hadn't opened them, but hadn't even shaken the bolts. The potential sharp-tongued lawyer, keen-eyed scientist and cool-hand surgeon changed his mind about jimmying the locks and took to narcotics so that he could float through the key hole.

Eunice's happy love and soft laughter had come just in time. My brother was saved.

CHAPTER 24

Poole and Rita were booked into the Champagne Supper Club. Pride made me go beserk. I quit my job. How could I exchange the glittering sequined bathing suit and purple satin tap shoes for a waitress apron and old-lady comforts? I wouldn't insult my muse, Terpsichore, by letting even the idea of the Chicken Shack enter into my thoughts.

A two-week engagement in Big Time, and I was ready.

My lights in stars, my name in lights, my name in stars.

For a few months before the opening we worked for whatever money was offered and practiced daily. R.L. showed me increasingly complicated steps. As soon as I learned, he laced them into our routines. When I had no cash, I asked Mother for a loan. I explained that I was investing my time in career preparation, and when the investment paid off she would be with me, holding hands and laughing and reaping the returns.

With characteristic talent, she enlarged my skit into a full-length revue. And she was the star. She reminded me that during the war years, when she had had lots of money and could have afforded to sit back idle, she had studied barbering, cosmetology, ship-fitting, welding, tool-and-dye making, and that the diplomas attesting to her perseverance hung on the walls of her den. She said she had no intention of ever going to work in an airplane factory or barber shop, but if push came to shove (she snapped her fingers), she was qualified. She approved of sticking to an idea until it was definitely proven bad or good.

She lent me the money, without further preachments, and Poole and Rita continued to practice.

Although I lived and ate at home, the small savings I kept in a jar under my bed diminished. My son always seemed to need new clothes; on Sundays I traditionally bought fresh flowers for the house; and then there were the tap shoes. Rehearsing wore out more taps than dancing three times a night in a cabaret.

I approached Bailey for a small advance. He sat, stubble-jawed, on his corduroy sofa, and looked at the adjacent wall.

"I've put Eunice in the hospital. She's very sick."

"What's wrong with her?" I made my voice soft.

"She just had a cold. That's all." But he didn't believe that was all.

"Well, come on. She's young. Nobody dies from a cold." If only I could get him to look at me. I went on making a joke. "They only wish they could."

"Yeah." He put his feet on the cluttered coffee table, leaned back on the sofa and closed his eyes.

"Good-bye, Maya."

"Bailey, it's not that serious." He didn't try to hear me and I could not intrude further by repeating myself.

The apartment stank of dead flowers and dirty dishes. His voice blurred but didn't rise or fall. "I've cut out all the runs except Los Angeles so I can be with her."

The room was oppressive as if a large hand had squeezed the gaiety out of it drop by drop and then released it to resume its former shape.

———

I was getting so I could fairly fly through the routine. My romance with R.L. was danced out in the rehearsal hall, because he made few sexual demands. I gave no arguments to his monthly requests for love-making. After all, he was my teacher and my transportation to Broadway. But I was grateful that they didn't come with greater frequency. An artist, I was certain, protected and preserved his instrument. Pianists, drummers, horn players, saxists all look after their instruments. As a dancer, my instrument was my body. I couldn't just allow a person, anyone, to screw my instrument.

Opening night arrived. Mother had taken a large table for her friends, and Bailey miraculously didn't have to be on the road or at the hospital. The night club, which was large and bedizened with glittering spinning lights, was full.

Excitement made me glow and the lights backstage rubbed away R.L.'s pockmarks. We looked at ourselves in the large mirror. He was absolutely dashing in his powder-blue tuxedo, and I was as glamorous as Esther Williams in my swimsuit. And could dance better, too.

The M.C. called our names, and the band swung into our introduction.

R.L. said in his slow voice, "Okay, Rita, break a leg." Show-business talk. I grinned. "You, too."

And we hit the stage.

The first moment's unreality was caused by the lights. I couldn't see the audience, and I thought about the first time when I panicked and froze to the stage. Maybe this was happening again. Maybe I had frozen, I couldn't tell if I was moving. But suddenly I heard the clap of taps breaking, exploding through the band's arrangement, and I found I was on the far side of the stage and it was time for me to break. I was dancing, my feet and body were doing the right things. With that I let go, just let the orchestra push, prod and pull me. I surrendered every memory I had to oblivion and let myself dance. Each time I danced near R.L., I laughed out loud at the perfect glory of it all. The music was my friend, my lover, my family. It was a pretty day on a San Francisco hill with just enough high to remark on details. It was my son laughing when I entered his room. Great poetry that I had memorized and recited to myself in a warm bath.

The band was playing the closing riffs and R.L. took my hand. We danced to the edge of the stage and bowed. The audience applauded moderately, except for Mother's table and a bravo from where Bailey sat near the door. I never knew whether the great disappointment came from having to stop dancing or from the fact that the audience didn't jump up, run screaming for the stage to touch my victory. But in the dressing room I began to drown in a depression sea. Neither the flowers Bailey sent nor Mother's smile saved me. Two more shows to do that night and by the last one I was questioning whether I was cut out for show biz . . . whether or not it was too coarse for my pure and delicate nature, too commercial for my artistic soul.

All the area's drunks and sporting people caught the last show and I was again intoxicated. They shouted, "Shake it, baby," "Dance, baby, dance," made noise, stumbled around from table to table, and the sense of gay activity helped Poole and Rita and the orchestra to re-create the earlier magic.

The patrons may not really have noticed the very tall, big-nosed dancing fool up there, but their vitality locked me into a love of performing that continued for many years.

Except for a few "casuals" (one-night performances in convention halls), the talent of Poole and Rita was going largely unappreciated. We refused the itinerant offers to perform at stags. I said I would never dance nude for a bunch of white men to gape at me. R.L. agreed and tried to appear possessive, but probably the larger truth was that we couldn't work up a "Beauty and Beast" routine. Neither did I have the attributes to portray Beauty, nor did he have the body to dance Beast. We would have been ludicrous.

The gigs at the Elks were bright splatches in the dull landscape. In black communities there is a counterpart to the white segregated secret society, B.P.O.E. (Benevolent and Protective Order of Elks). We call ours the Improved Benevolent and Protective Order of Elks of the World. I had been initiated into the mysterious organization as a teenager and had once won prizes in its oratorical contest, and now our dance team was hired at the hilarious and good-fun *dansants*.

The middle-aged ladies, usually stout and dressed more attractively than the women whose houses they cleaned, patted me after the shows and admired my leanness.

"Honey, you sure know how to shake that thing." A big pretty laugh. "I used to shake it like that, but them days is gone forever."

Then they would run their palms down my side.

"Bet your momma is proud of you. I bet you she is."

And she was. And I was proud of myself.

"Blue Flame" and "Caravan" were my favorite dance arrangements because R.L. laid out most of the time and I danced barefoot in little balls of blue ostrich feathers and Indian bells at my ankles. I tried to imitate Frances Nealy, a beautiful black woman who had played an Egyptian dancer in a forties technicolor movie. A few Dorothy Lamour hand movements and Ann Miller's leg kicks just added spice.

Then Cotton Candy Adams came to town.

> "Let me be your little dog
> till your big dog come
> Let me be your little dog

till your big dog come
And when your big dog come,
tell him what your little dog done."

R.L.'s words stumbled when he started to tell me about his ex-girl friend and former dancer. "Oh, Rita...she—Candy and I—I mean, she was my old lady...and she, uh, left me. That is, we used to dance together. She came out here—I mean, she said if...When she left me...uh, if I...if she...ever changed her mind, she'd, uh, find me."

"Okay, R.L. She came. Are you all going back together?" I was as snappy as I thought a chorus dancer would be.

"See, Rita, she's a, uh, dancer. I mean, she's great. She used to dance with Parker and Johnson. And she's worked the Orpheum Circuit." He had stopped stuttering. "She brought her costumes. Really flash. Feather fans with rhinestones. See, most of what I taught you—I mean..." Shyness tripped his tongue and he began to stutter again. "Wait till you meet her. She's...You're going to...I think you'll like each other."

"Sure thing, Bozo." I had never called a living soul Bozo. "I'd be delighted to meet her."

Cotton Candy was the picture of every "Daddy's little girl." Her real hair hung down in black waves and dimples punctured her light-brown cheeks. She had a cute walk, which wavered between a wanton strut and a little-girl mince. And then she opened her mouth. "Hi, Rita. R.L. told me about you. You're a dancer."

I didn't know how to hold the shock. Her teeth were rotten and her lips refused to help mold her words. I looked at her eyes and understood. They shone feverishly, yet seemed lifeless. Cotton Candy was a user.

Certainly R.L. knew. After all, he was from Chicago. I couldn't grasp why he would want to get reconciled with her, and I knew from the enchanted way he watched her that that was exactly what he wanted.

"Yes, I'm a dancer. Are you planning to dance in San Francisco?" Might as well have it out in the open.

"Oh yes." Although R.L. was feet from her, she cuddled in his direction. "R.L. and I are going to brush up our old act and get started again." She closed her mouth and dimpled. Her eyes slowly moved to R.L. "Isn't that what you said, Boogie?"

"Yeah. Uh-huh. Yeah. We'll do all the stuff we used to do."

I had to get away immediately. "Well, good luck to you both. Break a leg." I walked away from the lovers before they could see the life leaking out of me.

At home, I paced the floors. Mother had taken my son out and Papa Ford snored in the small back bedroom. I cursed Cotton Candy for coming to San Francisco and consigned R.L. to hell for being stupid enough to take her back. My career was over before it began. My tears came hot and angry. I had dared so many things and failed. There was to be nothing left to do. I had given Curly my young love; he had gone away to marry another woman. The self-defense tactics with the lesbians had gained me a whorehouse, which I had neither the skill nor the courage to keep. I had fled to the home of my youth and had been sent away. The Army and now my dance career, the one thing I wanted beyond all others (needed, in fact) for my son but mostly for myself, had been plucked right out of my fingers. All the doors had slammed shut, and I was locked into a too-tall body, with an unpretty face, and a mind that bounced around like a ping-pong ball. I gave in to sadness because I had no choice.

A few days passed and R.L. didn't come to the house. I telephoned him. He was distracted but promised to drop by and talk about it. I waited past the afternoon hour he mentioned, and long into the night. He never came; he didn't call.

If we had had the opportunity to talk about it, laboriously and painfully, I might have been forever lost in the romance of romance lost. But with no sounding board except my own ears and honest thoughts, I had to stop weeping (it was too exhausting) and admit that Cotton Candy had dibs on him and maybe R.L. felt more loyal to her because she was a user and needed him.

There was nothing about me to bind anyone to me in sympathy. No limp, no habit, crossed eyes or attitude of helplessness. I decided I'd try to sort out my life. I tried to crush the thoughts of self-pity that needled into my brain and told myself that it was time to roll up my costumes, which would eternally have the odor of grease paint in their seams, and put away the tap shoes, which hurt my feet anyway. For, after all, only poets care about what happened to the snows of yesteryear. And I hadn't time to be a poet, I had to find a job, get my grits together and take care of my son. So much for show biz, I was off to live real life.

CHAPTER 25

A friend of Mother's who had a restaurant in Stockton needed a fry cook. I packed the clothes I thought we might need and set out for the eighty-mile journey. I wasn't sure that I'd find pot in the little town, so I stashed a Prince Albert can full, and papers, in the bottom of my suitcase. I refused to cry all the way in the back seat of a Greyhound bus.

Stockton had an unusual atmosphere. Situated in the agricultural San Joaquin Valley, it had long been a center for the itinerant workers, Southerners drawn from depleted farms, Mexicans and Filipinos from their poverty-stricken countries who had raised large families on meager incomes since the early 1900s. World War II had enriched the town's blood by attracting blacks from the South to work at the local dry dock, the shipyards and defense plants in nearby Pittsburg.

When I arrived, there was Wild West rhythm in the streets. Since some of the plants were still running and the police hadn't yet cracked down on crime, prostitutes and gamblers came from San Francisco and Los Angeles on weekends to fleece the willing local yokels.

The restaurant was large, seating seventy-five, and had a steady and regular clientele. But because it was two blocks from Center Street, we got little of the sophisticated walk-in trade. My shift began at four in the afternoon, and I fried hamburgers, pork chops and eggs and ham steaks until midnight. Then, to add juice to my dry life, I would wash up, exchange the sweaty uniform for a clinging one-shoulder deal and high-heeled shoes that hurt my already swollen feet. A slow saunter to Center Street, and a perch at the crowded bar gave me a chance to watch the fascinating city folks, and at the same time haughtily explain to any man fresh enough to approach me that I worked for a living. I wasn't a whore. I told myself that the fact that I might have been mistaken for one, because of my flagrant way of dressing or clinging to a bar alone in a small town at one in the morning, was simply evidence of men trying to read a book by its cover.

———

Big Mary was a large-boned, rough woman from Oklahoma whose husband had died in the tomato fields surrounding Stockton. She was the neighborhood's surrogate mother. She tended children on a daily basis, but when I explained that I needed a weekly arrangement because of my hours, she agreed to let my son live in her house; I could pick him up on my day off. The blood of Indian ancestors pushed her cheekbones up so high that her eyes appeared to be closed, and her skin was the black brown of old polished wood. Mary drank once a month and other arrangements had to be made for all children on that one day. She would dress herself in a clean, loose-fitting cotton dress, and her dead husband's shoes cut out to ease the strain. Sitting at the bar, she'd pull a coffee cup from her purse and order the bartender, "Fill it up!" After drinking the contents, she'd ask the bartender to wash the cup and fill it up again. She would sit, sipping, staring straight ahead, until she had drunk three cups of bourbon. Then she would pay, and without having passed the time of day with anyone, leave the bar as straight as she had entered it.

Her way with children was to feed them well and coddle them. She fell into baby talk whenever children were mentioned, even if none were present.

Her thick Oklahoma accent slurred and her tongue protruded through the evenly shaped, full black lips. I figured that such a display of affection couldn't hurt my son, so I worked without great concern, and devoted myself to the serious business of accumulating a wardrobe.

—

Boys seem to think that girls hold the keys to all happiness, because the female is supposed to have the right of consent and/or dissent. I've heard older men reflect on their youth, and an edge of hostile envy drags across their voices as they conjure up the girls who whetted but didn't satisfy their sexual appetites. It's interesting that they didn't realize in those yearning days past, nor even in the present days of understanding, that if the female had the right to decide, she suffered from her inability to instigate. That is, she could only say yes or no if she was asked.

She spends half her time making herself attractive to men, and the other half trying to divine which of the attracted are serious enough to marry her, and which wish to ram her against the nearest wall and jab into her recklessly, then leave her leaning, legs trembling, cold wet evidence running down her inner thigh. Which one will come to her again, proud to take her to his friends, and which will have friends who only know of her as the easy girl with good (or even bad) poontang?

The crushing insecurity of youth, and the built-in suspicion between the sexes, militate against the survival of the species, and yet, men do legalize their poking, and women do get revenge their whole lives through for the desperate days of insecurity and bear children so that the whole process remains in process.

Alas.

The Poole-Rita partnership, with a little romance on the side, had left me yearning more for the stage and music and bravos of audiences than for a lover's arms.

But as fry cook in a small restaurant in the farm community, my fantasies were little different from any other girl of my age. He would come. He would. Just walk into my life, see me and fall everlastingly in love. I had the affliction suffered by most young women. The sexual excitement of my teens had abated, and I looked forward to a husband who would love me ethereally, spiritually, and on rare (but beautiful) occasions, physically.

He would be a little younger than my father, and handsome in that casual way. His conservative clothes would fit well, and he'd talk to me softly and look at me penetratingly. He'd often pat me and tell me how proud he was of me and I'd strain to make him even prouder. We would live quietly in a pretty little house and I'd have another child, a girl, and the two children (whom he'd love equally) would climb over his knees and I would make three-layer caramel cakes in my electric kitchen until they went off to college.

L.D. Tolbrook was my father's age, my father's color, and was as conservative as a black Episcopalian preacher. He wore tailor-made clothes and his rare smile showed teeth so anxious they clambered over each other. His hands were dainty and his long brown fingers ended with natural-polish manicured nails.

One night he was with a party who had come to the restaurant for a midnight breakfast. I had changed into evening clothes but my replacement hadn't yet come. When the waitress explained the situation to L.D.'s party, he came to the door of the kitchen and said, "Excuse me. I wanted a word with the chef." His voice was soft.

"I'm the swing-shift cook, but I'm off now." I didn't really look at him.

"Well, I understand that." His smile came from a deep well of understanding. "But my party is especially hungry. And we'd take anything you'd give us." He looked at my dress. "I'd make it worth your while to be late to your party."

"I'm not going to a—" Before my mouth could close.

He peeled a ten-dollar bill off his money roll. "Give us bacon and eggs, or ham and eggs. Or anything and any way you fix them. We'll be happy."

I needed the money, so I took it and turned to go back to the dressing room and change my clothes.

"What's your name?"

"Rita."

"All right, Miss Rita. Thank you. We all thank you." He pushed his way through the door.

Though I prided myself on tender sensitivity, I have never known when a great love affair was beginning. Some barricade lies midway my mind, and I'm usually on my back scrutinizing a ceiling before it is borne in on me that this is the man I fantasized in my late-night fingering.

L.D. (Louis David) came the next night a half-hour before midnight, had breakfast and asked for me by name. The waitress brought the message and I went out uniformed and shining with sweat.

He stood. "Miss Rita." He pulled out a chair. "Can you have a seat with me?"

I told him I was still working.

"If you're not busy after, I'd like to invite you for a ride...er, I guess you wouldn't want breakfast." His lips pulled back a little to let me know he'd made a joke.

"No thanks, no breakfast." And, I thought, no ride either. This dry little man couldn't compete with the bar on Center Street.

"I'll tell you how I happened to be here."

He was still standing. My eyes looked straight into his forehead where curly black hair retreated from the advance of scalp.

"After I dropped those people off last night, I went to the gambling shack. Something happened to me. I couldn't keep my mind on the game. Kept forgetting what I was doing. I kept on thinking how sweet it was of you to get out of your nice clothes and fix us something to eat."

His head dropped and his eyes lifted shyly. "I knew it wasn't for the tenner. Something about you told me that." It was time for my eyes to drop.

"So I sat around awhile, then I went on home. This afternoon I got up and went back and cleaned the house out. I won six hundred playing Koch. Then I thought I might pick up that nice lady and spend some of this money on her."

Here he pulled out a roll of money that looked the same as the one he had stripped the night before, but this time I noticed the big diamond ring and his manicured nails. I looked down and was certain the glistening pointed shoes were expensive Florsheims, and the hat lying in the next chair was a Dobbs. Here was the real thing. No loud-talking, door-popping shucker from the Center Street bar, but an established gambler who had Southern manners and city class.

"I thought we might drop in on some of my friends in Sacramento."

The glorious feeling of having caught the big one gently massaged me and diffused in my mind and body. I was lovely when I changed into something sleek and appealing, and said good night to the waitress and the relief cook.

The silver-blue Lincoln struck me as perfect for L.D. It wasn't large or brand-new, but it was rubbing-clean and shining with polish. When we drove away from the lights of Stockton, he found music on the radio and turned it down to a touching purr.

> "I want a Sunday kind of love
> A love to last past Saturday night
> I want to know it's more than
> love at first sight..."

He asked if I was married. Law or common-law? I said no, neither. (I pronounced it 'n eye ther.) He said almost to himself, "I must have got my lucky break. At last."

I leaned back into the real leather seat and grinned for my own enjoyment.

"I have to take care of some business. And I wanted you to come with me. I have to see a lady friend named Clara."

His words never rushed but were selected, chewed over, released into the air as if the best choice possible had been made.

For once being young was fortunate. Everyone had heard the stories about young girls and older men. How older men were good to and generous to and crazy about young girls. I thought to myself, I'd rather be an old man's darling than a young man's slave.

"Clara is a real square shooter. Four square, Rita, like I think you are. Yes sir, honest as the day is long."

Even his idiom was old.

When we drove up to the three-shaded house, he started to get out of the car. "Come on. I'd like you to meet Clara. She's sure to like you..."

I followed him.

The heavy odor of disinfectant in the house was as telltale as a red light over the door. Although memories of my San Diego experience rushed me, I kept my face straight, giving no hint that I knew where we were.

Clara was a small, well-built woman in her thirties. Her heavy make-up mask cracked into seams at her delight.

"Lou!" She backed away from the door and we were right-handed into a dully furnished living room.

L.D. said he had some business to talk over with Clara and excused himself. He offered me a drink but I explained that I didn't drink and received an approving smile for my information.

No sounds reached me from the back of the house. I began wondering: Suppose L.D. was renting a room and instead of coming back himself sent Clara to get me. If she said, "Rita, Lou wants to see you in the back," I wouldn't know how to answer. I wasn't stupid enough to say, "Please tell him that I never go to bed with a man on the first date." She'd laugh me out of the place. There was nothing for it but to submit. But submit in such a way that he'd feel badly and I'd feel nothing. That was my plan.

They were laughing as they came back into the room.

"Clara, you're still ace-high in my book," said L.D. "But we have to get a move-on."

"Aw, Lou, let's sit down for a while. Let me and Rita get acquainted." Her smile wrinkled her whole face and she looked like a rubber doll won at playland.

"This lady worked hard all night and I know she'd like to get home and rest." He looked at me. "I'm sorry. Maybe the next time I'll let you sit around talking women's talk with her. Come on, Rita, we'd better head back to Stockton."

I shook hands with Clara and said, "Thank you, I'm sure . . . See you again . . . I had a very nice time . . . 'Bye."

In the car I hastily discarded my unnecessary defense plans and tried to figure what to expect next. He probably wanted to take me to his place. But as soon as we reached the outskirts of Stockton I was going to ask to be taken home because I had a fearful headache. If he was a real gentleman, he would acquiesce.

We were as quiet on the return drive as the black trees outside the windows. The lights of the town flashed faintly and I prepared my spiel.

"Rita, I've sure appreciated you making this ride with me. I have to go to Sacramento twice a week and it's lonely at night by yourself. I knew you were tired when I asked you, but just like the other night, you showed what a big heart you had. I really appreciate it."

He swung the car into the black area.

"Where do you live?"

Again I had girded myself for no reason. "I have a room at Kathryn's."

"Cooking privileges?" He knew the place.

"Yes."

"Well, sometimes maybe you'll cook me a meal. If you're not too tired."

We were in front of my door and he made no attempt to even kiss me good night.

"Good night, L.D."

"Good night, Rita. I'll see you soon."

The blue car eased down the street and I wondered if in my ignorance I had lost my chance for a life of tender loving being cared for.

The next evening when I left work he was parked outside. He flashed the lights.

"Rita. Good evening. I hope you don't mind, but I wanted to see you again."

Glorious day.

I sat back in the already familiar seat and breathed in his perfume.

"You're so young and fresh. And I sure like the way you talk. So young." He laughed a little. I couldn't remember what I'd talked about the night before, and felt the terrible burden of trying to think up something useful to entertain him.

Young talk to me was silly vacant chatter. I couldn't imagine the drivel of young girls coming out of my head and mouth, but I wanted to amuse, so I decided to tell him one story of my life.

"You know, I love to dance. I've studied since I was fourteen and I've been in show business. I was part of the Poole and Rita dance team."

We had left Stockton streetlights and were on the highway before I noticed.

"We're going down to Tulare; it's not far. Go on, tell me about your dancing. I knew you weren't all that graceful for nothing."

I unreeled imaginary stories of the night clubs I had worked in and the steps I learned and my glamorous costumes. As I talked my career sparkled with success and I was a star of the brightest magnitude, bowing and smiling to a vast audience which would never be satisfied.

In Tulare we visited Minnie, whose house was identical with Clara's, down to the disinfectant and artificial flowers. Minnie lacked Clara's pixie charm and regarded me with the hard eyes of a buyer at a horse auction.

L.D. and Minnie went into a side bedroom and stayed only a few minutes. "Okay, Minnie, see you soon. Let's go, Rita." He had no smile for her and no small talk. I was glad. It was obvious that she wasn't a very nice person. (Nice persons meaning people who tried to draw me out and who found my stolid face and ungiving attitude charming.)

He was either running a lottery or selling the whores dope, and the fact that he never mentioned what his "business" was told me that he thought I was square. It never occurred to me that he might have liked that, so I decided at just the proper time I would tell him that once I had a house in San Diego employing two whores.

That night, I told him about my baby and that he was three years old and how pretty and smart he was. L.D. said nothing until we parked in front of my house.

He twisted in the dark and pulled his roll of money from a side pocket.

"Rita, I don't want you to get me wrong. I'm not trying to buy your affections. But you are alone and have a baby to raise. I'd be less than a man if I didn't try to help you." He folded a bill and pressed it into my hand. "Now, don't say anything. Just use it for yourself and the baby.

"All right, get out now. I won't be able to see you for a few days. There's a big game down in the city. I'll come to the restaurant as soon as I get back."

I wanted to lean over and kiss him, but his aloofness didn't encourage me.

"Good night, L.D., and good luck."

"Thank you, Rita."

I turned the lamp on in my room and looked down at the fifty-dollar bill crumpled in my palm.

It was the first time any man other than Bailey had given me money.

I bought an outfit worthy of a Hollywood siren and toys for my son.

CHAPTER 26

For the next three weeks I rode the California highways with L.D. I met Dimples in Fresno and Helen in Merced and Jackie and Lil in Mendota and Firebaugh, and a few women who had cabins along the road with access to the transient field workers. L.D. continued making generous gifts, saying business was good. I never asked him what business it was and he never offered any information. I didn't have to fend off his advances, since he didn't make any.

Desire for him grew in direct proportion to his indifference. I experimented with every ploy I could dream up. He had revealed to me that he didn't read books, so I tried to impress him with my great love of learning. He liked straight shooters, so one night I told him how much I cared. He had pity for me, an unmarried mother. I cried out my aching loneliness. Nothing fazed him or prodded him into taking me in his arms.

The restaurant had become a larger bore than a lifetime in the Gobi Desert, and I found no enjoyment in my books or playing with my son. All life funneled down to one smile, one man's soft, quiet "Good evening, Rita. How you doing tonight?"

"Here's a hundred dollars." The bills fanned out from his fingers.

"Oh, I couldn't take that much."

"I want you to go shopping and buy some different clothes. You dress too old. You ought to dress your age. You're young. Buy some low shoes and anklets. Some blouses and pretty colored skirts. And put a bow ribbon in your hair."

I hadn't worn socks in years and had hated them then. They made my already long legs look longer. But L.D. asked.

When he saw me in the schoolgirl outfit he said I was his "Bobby Sock Baby" and he was going to give me a special gift. On my next day off he took me to the city.

"This is not business this time. It's just for you. I'm going to give you what you've been wanting."

He smiled and patted my cheek and I would have thought it a privilege to die for him.

San Francisco's South of Market area was a mystery land where homeless drunks loitered before the dirty windows of liquor stores. Pawnshops' glaring signs promised to exchange money out of proportion for goods. People I knew only went South of Market to reach the S.P. railway station or to pay bills at some of the location's loan offices.

L.D. guided his car down the dark streets and I, snuggled at his side, wished the ride would never end. On the highway he had said I was the sweetest little thing he'd ever seen and praised me for wearing the high school clothes that he preferred. I was his Bobby Sock Baby, and he was going to make me so happy I'd cry.

I held precariously to the grateful tears that gathered behind my lids.

When he stopped the car and kissed me gently, long and loving my body pressed to be rid of the prison of skin.

Skid Row's broken glass might have been rose petals, and the arid smell of secondhand alcohol was India's most hypnotizing incense.

L.D. rang the bell at a grille door and called out his name. The door opened automatically and I followed him up dim, carpeted stairs.

When he nodded to me I heeled in the shadows. He walked down the hall where a light gleamed over a half door. I heard whispers, then he came back to me jangling a key. The energy of passion carried me over the room's threshold and threw me across the bed.

L.D. sat patiently beside me and spoke quietly.

"You know I'm much older than you. I'm an old man, so don't expect the same things from me that you get from your young beaus."

Beaus? R.L.? I couldn't matt my allure by telling him there were no beaus, or scream at him to undress or I'd tear his clothes in shreds. I forced my eyes closed and waited.

He kissed me and the tears I had held in the car came unfastened. L.D. held me as if I were made of feather.

"Daddy's baby is scared, huh? Well, Daddy won't hurt his baby. Get undressed and wash up so we can lie down."

"I had a bath before we left Stockton."

He whispered, "Wash over there in that face bowl. Daddy's going to love his baby."

———

I spent the next month metamorphosizing from Miss Insecure to Bobby Sock Baby. Being loved by an older married man gave me a youth I'd never known. I giggled into my Kleenex, fluttered my eyelashes and fairly gamboled over the greensward. At midnight when I doffed the cook's apron and washed my face and arms, I flew, anklets sparking white, into the arms of my garbardined lover. We went to chicken suppers in San Francisco, where I hoped and feared the stubble-bearded gamblers in the back room would recognize me as Vivian's daughter, who made good.

The grass I'd brought from San Francisco was holding out. I disciplined myself. One joint on Sunday and one on the morning of my day off. The weed always had an intense and immediate effect. Before the cigarette was smoked down to roach length, I had to smother my giggles. Just to see the falling folds of the curtains or the sway of a chair was enough to bring me to audible laughter. After an hour the hysteria of the high would abate and I could trust myself in public.

One day off, L.D. took me and my son for a picnic in the country. He had arrived early at my house, but I got ready quickly and we went to pick up the baby.

From the car windows I watched the farm rows. They ran toward the road as if to intercept it. It amused me that the neat lines marched up and fell away, to be replaced by others which in turn were themselves replaced. They had the show business precision of a drill team on parade. The thought of cotton rows practicing routines at night when everyone was asleep tickled my funny bone. A small blob of laughter curdled in the back of my throat and rolled over my tongue. I wanted to explain the joke to L.D., but there was no time. The chuckle was out. My laughter triggered the baby's and he joined me. The whole thing was getting funnier. I tried to control myself, but each time I looked at L.D.'s disapproving face I climbed to a new height of hilarity. When he stopped the car, the contractions were beginning to ease.

We unloaded the car silently and spread a blanket I'd taken from my bed.

When we settled, he said, "You've been smoking gauge, haven't you?"

"Yes." I wasn't ashamed to admit it.

"How long have you been smoking?"

"About a year."

He took my hand and held it tightly. "Do you know that junk can kill your nature?"

I had never heard that. "No."

"Well, let me tell you something. It's gauge that's breaking up my marriage." He stroked my hand. "My silly dilly wife stopped letting me have any and she goes around laughing and giggling all the time. I've told her that I can't go on much longer. I'd hate to lose you too, Rita. Just after I've found you." I thought he was sincere and I was sorry I'd upset him.

I didn't need to think long. The pot had been important when I was alone and lonely, when my present was dull and the future uncertain.

Now I had a man, who talked sweet to me, made excruciatingly good love to me, considered my baby, and was going to make me his wife.

"L.D., when you take me home, I'll throw the rest in the toilet."

He grinned and touched my face. "You're my Bobby Sock Baby. Now let's see what we have to eat."

As we picnicked he continued talking about his wife (I hadn't expected to find My Prince without encumbrances). "She's a millstone around my neck. Sometimes I stay all night in the gambling house just to keep away from her evil mind and sharp tongue."

"Why do you stay with her, L.D.?"

"She's older than I am, and she was good to me once. I never once forget a favor. Can't afford to. Now she's sickly. When I get on my feet, I'm going to send her back home to her folks." He waited a minute, then took my face in his hands. "You're such a sweet baby, Rita. Let's don't talk about it any more." I admired his restraint.

———

The naturally lonely person does not look for comfort in love, but accepts the variables as due course.

I thought I was making him happy. In any case I would have done anything to win a smile or hear him laugh and pat my cheek. The job had become so very tiresome. If I didn't have to work, we could spend more time together. I loved the movies and we'd never been; also I wanted to get into a dance class so I wouldn't get rusty. I knew it was a matter of time before he'd catch on to my hints about the job and order me to quit. I would get an apartment and furnish it with the ragingly popular blond furniture. My bedroom was to tremble with pink frills and lacy ruffles. My son's would be painted yellow and white, with decals of happy animals climbing the walls, expensive toys stacked neatly in a corner, and he would sit at a cute little table learning from clever educative books. Home-baked breads would give the kitchen a solid country air, and after my family had eaten and the baby was fast asleep, I would lie on my scented bed as L.D. loved his baby in the darkness.

Three days passed and L.D. didn't come to the restaurant. I was jittery with worry. He told me where he lived when he told me how hateful and lacking in understanding his wife was, but I didn't know the telephone number. Gamblers protect themselves from borrowers by having unlisted telephones. Before and after work I walked by the gambling joints looking for his car, then past his two-story house, which sat back in a yard of tended rose bushes. Ideas of all sizes and degrees of madness plagued me. He might have had an accident, fatal. Or he might have had a heart attack. Fatal. He might have tired of me and found someone else. I hastily discarded that one. It was better to picture him in a lovely coffin, "his small face narrowed by death and his thin lips at peace."

"Baby, Daddy didn't mean to worry you." Although his face was lined with exhaustion and he hadn't shaved, he looked beautiful. He had driven up just as I walked out of the café, and told me to get in the car.

"Things have been going badly for me. Very badly."

I had no idea how a juvenile bride was to console her man. Should I pinch him and giggle or stroke him like a sister?

"I've been gambling for three days and I lost everything."

Now I could say it. "You've got *me*, L.D."

He didn't hear me.

"I lost over five thousand dollars."

I nearly screamed. There wasn't that much money anywhere except in banks. He could have bought me a house with five thousand dollars.

"And I'm up to my neck. I was trying to win enough money"—he turned away—"to divorce that old hag I'm married to and send her back to Louisiana. Then you and I could be together forever."

I knew it. He did want to marry me. I put my hand on his cheek and pulled him back to face me.

"I don't mind waiting, darling." I had to reassure him, to erase his deep worry. "As long as I know you care."

"But, you see, I may have to go away. I owe the big boys over two thousand dollars. And they don't play."

My God. The mob. I read the papers and had seen enough movies to know they'd take him for a ride and blow his brains out.

"Where would you go?" Anything but to see him killed.

"I used to work for some white folks in Shreveport. Rich ones. I telephoned them and asked for a loan. They said all right, but the wife said I'd have to come back to work for them. Old hot-tailed bitch. I know what she wants."

"What does she want?" I knew and hated her immediately.

"She nearly got me lynched. Says she's in love with me and don't care who knows it. You know how Southern women are."

I didn't know about the women, but I knew L.D. was the greatest lover in the world and if white men were as sad as I'd heard, I could believe the old bitch was in love with him.

"How old is she?"

"Be about twenty-five now, I guess. I haven't seen her for three years."

Old? I thought he had meant wrinkled, yellow-fingernailed old. Why, that bitch probably tried to make him enjoy having sex with her. She probably wriggled and moaned under him just as I did.

"You can't go back there, L.D. You might get killed."

"I've got to do something. This is the time I need a good woman." He had leaned back against the door.

"But I'm a woman, L.D."

"You're a little girl. Sweet as sugar, but a little girl. I mean somebody who can make some money, and in a hurry."

My salary was sixty a week and I paid twenty for the baby-sitter, fifteen for my room, five extra for the baby's milk and laundry. I had the right to take all my meals in the restaurant and that would save cutting into the twenty left. I had enough clothes, thanks to L.D. but what good was twenty dollars against five thousand?

"When Head Up had a little trouble with the Big Boys last month, his wife went to a house in Santa Barbara and made five hundred dollars the first week. In a month he was clear."

"Doing what?"

He still thought I was a square. "But I don't know if I could let anybody I love do that kind of business. I don't think my life is worth a nice woman, my woman, giving up that much of herself."

"L.D., if a woman loves a man, there is nothing too precious for her to sacrifice and nothing too much for him to ask." I had to make him know that I was as capable of doing him a favor as his aging wife. He said nothing.

"Love is blind and hides a multitude of faults. I know what you're talking about, and prostitution is like beauty. It is in the eye of the beholder. There are married women who are more whorish than a street prostitute because they have sold their bodies for marriage licenses, and there are some women who sleep with men for money who have great integrity because they are doing it for a purpose."

"Do you really think that, baby?" His face was beginning to look better.

"Yes, and I'd do it to help you."

He leaned forward and folded me in his arms.

"You sweet child. No, that's wrong. Sweet woman." He pulled away and saw the tears sliding down my face. "What's that for? I didn't ask you to do anything."

"No, I'm just crying out of joy. That you'll let me help you."

"I heard of women like you, but I never thought I'd have one to call my own. My own." He patted me and kissed away my tears.

"Clara. You remember Clara? I think she took to you. I would trust her with you. Clara runs a straight house. No three-way girls and no freak parties." His voice ordered angrily, "I don't want you to get in no freak parties, you understand?"

"Yes, Lou, I understand."

"When this is all over, I want us to be able to get married and I don't want you remembering nothing that I don't do to you. I always want to be able to make you happy, I want you to keep on being my little Bobby Sock Baby."

CHAPTER 27

"You sure are starting at a good time. The radio said rain today."

I sat in an uncomfortable chair and watched the two women.

Clara looked up at me and explained, "Tricks walk in the rain." She laughed. "I'm sure I don't know why. If I was them, I'd rather stay in my own bed." She laughed again. "By myself." Chuckle.

Bea's voice interrupted Clara's amusement. "Goddam. Don't say nothing like that, you'll put the bad mouth on the day. I want to be in bed with ten tricks by noon. It's already nine o'clock and I haven't even broke luck yet."

Carefully applied make-up did not disguise the woman's hard features. When I met her the night before, I had decided she wasn't nearly as nice as Clara, and although I would work with her, we'd never become friends.

"New girl gets to break luck." Clara laid on a little authority. "You know how it goes."

The language was new but its meaning was clear, and I wanted above all things not to appear stupid and not to display my immobilizing nervousness. I tried to concentrate on what the women were doing. Their fingers darted making knots in long strings of heavy white twine.

Bea looked up at me, disdain a mist across her face. "You a cherry, ain't you?"

"Yes." Lying would get me nothing.

"Well, that's a thirty-second business. When you turn the first trick, you'll be a 'ho. A stone 'ho. I mean for life." She grinned sourer than a rotten lemon, but her make-up and jewelry and air of abandoned sex gave her a glint of glamour.

Clara wedged in a peacemaker's tone, "Well, that won't be so bad will it? I mean you're a whore."

"Hell, yes, I'm a damn good one. I'm a mud kicker. In the streets I

make more money by accident than most bitches make on purpose."
She rolled her head and twisted her body. "And it's more action, too. I
mean the lights and tricking all night till the sun comes up."

I wondered why she left the streets.

"I just got too hot. I was getting busted two, three times a week. So
my daddy brought me down to this crib. Let the heat get off. Then I'll
be back switching and bitching and getting merry like Christmas."

They both stood up and shook out strings in their hands. Clara
walked to the living-room door and attached two strings to tacks over
the lintel. She took matches from her robe pocket and lighted the ends
that swung lazily near the floor.

"You burn string in the morning for luck, Rita. When it reaches the
first knot the tricks begin to walk."

Bea had left the room to place string over the other doors.

Clara went back to her uneasy chair.

"Now, Rita, let's have a little talk. You were so tired when L.D.
brought you in last night, I thought I'd wait till morning to tell you
how I run this place." I pulled my attention from the little red mouths
that were nibbling up the string.

"L.D. said your work name was Sugar. I think that goes with you.
You so young and quiet. Now, here's how it goes. In your room you
have a tablet, and when you take a trick he pays me; and after, I sign
your book. If you didn't have a man of your own, I'd give you your
money at the end of the day and you could leave. But what'll happen
is, at the end of the week Lou will come and I'll give it to him. He'll
straighten out your bills, room rent, board and liquor." She caught
herself. "'Course you don't drink and soft drinks are free. Then you
get your day off and get to stay all night with your man.

"All my tricks are Mexican. They're fast but not too clean. Each girl
has her own trick pan and towels. You wash them first and after. Then
you take fresh water and wash yourself good. Since you're a cherry, I
have to tell you Mexicans aren't built very large, but don't open your
legs wide. They are tricks, not your old man, so don't try making love
to them. That's why they call them tricks."

Clara's superstition about the burning string had already disenchanted me, and her conversation on deception of customers erased any respect I had for her. The only way I could be in the business was to give due service for the money paid. I decided privately that I would make each trick (each man) happy and forget the unbearable loneliness that sent him out in the rain searching for love.

"They walk in here," she continued, "and take their choice of you or Bea. L.D. said you shouldn't use make-up and ought to keep on wearing those junie flip clothes. That's all right with me. When you get regulars, Bea is not allowed to pull them, unless you're busy and they can't wait. That's the same with her steadies. Anything you want to know, ask me."

The doorbell rang.

"See, Rita! Look at the string." The red dot had reached a knot on one of the strings. "Trick time."

Bea came running into the room, and the sound of her footsteps was a little more audible than my heartbeat. The moment of truth had gotten stuck in my throat and saliva refused to go around it.

Clara went to open the door.

"Hello, Papa, come in. I've got something special for you today." She stage-whispered, "A school girl."

My God, she was lying. I was already going to be a whore. Take this man's hard-earned money, go to bed with him without love. Why add lying to it?

They came in view. Clara had her arm around the shoulders of a short little fat man who wore matching gray khaki pants and shirt. He looked Indian.

"Sugar, come over and say hello to Papa Pedro."

I walked over as if I were being introduced in my mother's living room.

"Buenos días, Señor Pedro."

His eyes left my flat chest and narrow hips. *"Oh. Hablas español?"*

My mind flinched at his use of the familiar. It should only be used between family members, close friends and lovers, according to my high school teacher.

"Sí. Yo lo puedo hablar."

"Okay, Sugar. Take him in the back and show him a good time."

Bea's voice hacked through from the corner. "Yea, Pedro. If she don't give you enough, you can see me after. Remember the last time?"

His glance didn't stay two seconds in her direction.

Clara took us both by the hand. "Come on, you two. You're wasting time." And drew us to my bedroom door. "Get in there and have fun."

I found my voice. *"Viene con migo, señor."*

He stood in the middle of the floor, looking like a bemused Akim Tamiroff. I had to say something but didn't know how to say "take your clothes off" in Spanish, so I asked how he was. He said well. I pulled off all my clothes during the long pause and he opened his pants. Dignity rode his face bareback.

I washed him and all I remember of my first great slide down into the slimy world of mortal sin is the scratching of the man's zipper on my upper thighs.

———

At sundown Bea washed her face and spent a few minutes in Clara's bedroom. She came out clicking her purse shut.

"I'm nearly shamed to show this little money to my daddy. I've spoiled that man." She looked at me, and without the cosmetic she was ten years younger. "How you feel?"

I didn't know how I felt. I said, "All right, thank you."

"Clara, you ought to get the news over to the camp. Tell them that you got a cherry. Maybe that'll stir up some tricks." She walked to the door, shaking her hips from side to side. "You won't be a cherry long, little girl. Better git it while the gittin's good. See you all in the morning." She slammed the door behind her.

Clara followed and snapped a double lock, then drew a chain across the door.

"Sugar, you better take a long bath. Put some Epsom salts in the water. Take out the soreness."

I said nothing because I thought nothing.

"Don't worry, you didn't do so good today, but then, you're just starting. I'll give you a few tips. Don't take off all your clothes. It takes too long. And remember, the men come here to trick, not to get married. Talk to them dirty but soft. And play with them."

She hmphed to herself.

"You got it easy. I was turned out with white men. They want to talk all the time. They tell you how beautiful you are and how much they love you. And wonder what you're doing being a whore all the time they're jugging in you and paying for it. Then when they get finished they got the nerve to ask you how you liked it. And talk about your freaks! White men can really think of some nasty things to do."

She started to her room and turned. "One thing I can say about my daddy"—her lips prissed and she lifted her nose and wiggled it—"he doesn't want me to do anything freakish. No matter how much money is involved. I like that." She rubbed her hands down her sides complimenting herself. "Better get your bath. Dinner'll be ready soon."

I sat thinking about the spent day. The faces, bodies and smells of the tricks made an unending paisley pattern in my mind. Except for the Tamiroffish first customer, the others had no individual characteristics. The strong Lysol washing water stung my eyes and a film of the vapor coated my adenoids.

I had expected the loud screams of total orgasmic release and felt terribly inadequate when the men had finished with grunts and yanked up their pants without thanks. I decided that being black, I had a different rhythm from the Latinos and all I had to do was let myself learn their tempos.

Clara gave me salts and bath oil and I continued examining the day in fingernailfuls. I was intelligent and I was young. I could teach myself the craft and make loads of money. L.D. might be able to settle his debts before the month was up.

The woman who came in daily at five o'clock to cook reminded me of my grandmother and I had to avert my eyes when she placed dinner on the table.

I reassured myself. I was helping my man. And, after all, there was nothing wrong with sex. I had no need for shame. Society dictated that sex was only licensed by marriage documents. Well, I didn't agree with that. Society is a conglomerate of human beings, and that's just what I was. A human being.

———

For the next week I vied with Bea for the attentions of Pedros, Josés, Pablos and Ramóns. I brushed up on my Spanish and tried with little success to include *tú* in my enticing come-ons. The women's conversations interested me more than the tricks' visits. Men came to Clara's house singly, and rather than having an air of celebration, they all seemed to be ashamed of their own presence and at the same time resigned to be there. I never found one man who considered how I might or might not enjoy those three-minute sojourns in the cell-like room. And for my part, I accepted Clara's signature on my tablet as a symbol of being paid in full.

Bea made an attempt at friendliness one morning. She came into the house early and settled on a stiff chair opposite me.

"Sugar, how do you like it?"

Her voice was kinder than usual, which surprised me, and as I had no ready answer, I muttered, "Well, it's ... a new—"

"New? Screwing ain't new, is it?" She slipped back into sarcasm easily.

"No. That's not what I meant."

"Well, don't worry about it. You'll break in."

"I won't be doing this long." I had to separate myself from the insinuation.

"Like hell. Wait till you make a nice piece of money. Then your daddy will give you a little white girl."

"A what? What would I do with a white girl?"

She laughed a tight little laugh. "Not 'a' white girl. You don't know what 'white girl' is?"

"I don't know what you mean." I was trying to withdraw.

"They call cocaine 'white girl.' Some people call horse 'white girl,' too. I don't mess with heroin, though. It makes me sick. But wait till your daddy gives you some coke. Kiss the baby!" Hugging herself, she coasted away for a second on her thought.

I wouldn't tell her that L.D. didn't even want me to smoke pot, but she seemed to pick the thought out of my mind.

"They won't let you smoke hemp, though. They say it makes a 'ho too frisky. 'Hos get their heads bad and forget about tending to business."

Clara came in bringing coffee, and Bea plunged into conversation with her.

"You know what we did last night? Daddy took me down to a gambling game in Firebaugh... You know who I saw?... Haven't seen that bitch in a month of Sundays..."

I didn't know the people she was talking about and couldn't have cared less what she did the night before, but she had given me something to think about. Since she spoke from experience, she was probably right. But she was talking about pimps and I knew L.D. wasn't a pimp. He was a gambler. I couldn't allow myself to entertain corrosive thoughts. All I had to do was do my best to help him and keep my thoughts clear and unpolluted. I decided I wouldn't even mention the conversation to L.D.

In the long waits between customers, Bea and Clara talked about money, their old men, other whorehouses and their old men and travel to nearby towns and their old men. They both called their men "Daddy," and when speaking of them even when relating the beatings they had received from "Daddy," their voices tightened into lurid imitations of baby talk. Their faces softened and their lips pouted (Clara could wrinkle her nose and wiggle it like a bunny).

I wondered if prostitutes as one suffered from an Electra complex and were motivated by a need to have a daddy, please a daddy and finally make love to a daddy.

"My daddy said he's going to take me to Hot Springs 'for the season.'" Bea sat in her chair by the door and shook her delight.

"Daddy and I went to the Kentucky Derby last year. We had a ball." Clara began to shake her nose. "Everybody was there. I met sports from New York City and Detroit and Chicago."

"My daddy says those Eastern pimps are colder than a whore's heart in Nome. I believe him too. Look at their faces. They chilly. If they don't kill their whores, they make them wish they were dead."

"Well, my daddy didn't never hit me except when I needed it. Oh, he whip my ass then. Better believe it. But no scars. He ain't never left a scar on me."

Bea grinned as if she had outwitted the men. "They ain't crazy. They wouldn't hurt their little moneymakers."

Their conversations were tightly choreographed measures, and since I didn't know the steps, I sat on the sidelines and watched. They would hardly be interested in my dance career, or my son, or the books I'd read. And I flatly, on principle, refused to call L.D. "Daddy." I mean, I protested to myself, my father, Bailey Johnson, Sr., was in San Diego, posturing and er'rering his pretentious butt off. Daddy Clidell was my one-time stepfather, but he and Mother had signed divorce papers. Mother's men, whom I had called Daddy Jack, Uncle Bob or Hanover Daddy, came and went with such regularity that whatever name I tacked on after the paternal title escaped me after a few months. I decided I wouldn't discuss L.D. at all. They were too cynical to understand that we were in love and that after I had helped him out of trouble, after he had a divorce, we were going to be married and live in a dream house with my son and lots of flowers. I would not share my plan with hard-hearted whores.

Despite my youth and high school clothes and stilted Spanish, I wasn't popular at Clara's. The men preferred Bea. She had a swing to her hips and a knowing smile that I couldn't imitate. Then, Mexican farm workers obviously had no erotic fantasies starring black teen-age girls; they came to a whorehouse for a whore, and Bea answered their needs.

———

"Have a good time, you all." Clara waved to L.D. and me from the steps. He didn't acknowledge her but I turned and waved.

In the car he wore the same sour face he'd had when he returned from talking with Clara in her bedroom. Fear that he didn't love me any more iced my bare arms. When I first went to Clara's he had assured me, "Don't worry about going to bed with other men. It'll just make me love you more. You're doing it to help Daddy." He hugged me too. Now I remembered and supposed he had thought so at the time. But when face to face with the reality, he found me disgusting. For the first time since I went to Clara's, I began to feel unclean. I was Lady Macbeth. All the waters in the world wouldn't wash away the fingerprints of the men who had mauled me. I had been stupid to let him talk me into doing something that would turn him from me. He needed love. He needed a good woman to love him, especially now while he was in trouble with the big boys. But instead of using the brain I was inordinately proud of, I had let him down. His life was so unstable (the big diamond ring and expensive car were symbols of insecurity), and when I had a chance to introduce some order into his world I had fluffed it. It was clear I'd never see him again, since waves of hate radiated from him as rhythmically as the heat trembled up from the highway. We rode in silence until we reached Stockton.

"Where do you want to go?" His question popped like a whip.

"To pick up the baby."

The steering wheel almost came off in his hand.

When he parked the car, he made no move toward getting out, so I opened my door and had to ask, "Will you take us for a ride?"

"Close the door, Rita. I better talk to you."

Now it would come. The bad words, the insults, and all rightly placed. I closed the door.

"I talked to Clara. And there wasn't hardly any money at all. I don't think you tried."

"L.D., I did. I tried with all my heart." Relief flooded my brain. If that was all he worried about.

"Clara says you sit around like a judge, never saying anything to them. And that you talk to the tricks in Spanish like a goddam schoolteacher."

"L.D., I'm sorry. I just don't know what to do. But I promise, I'll try harder. Don't be angry, Lou."

"Another thing, you haven't called me Daddy. All the—I'm supposed to be your daddy." He was fierce suddenly. "Remember that."

I said, "Yes, Daddy," and hated it. Later on I'd be able to tell him the

Electra story and explain why I hated my own father, and expand my theory about prostitutes and their men. I knew he wouldn't appreciate being thought a pimp and we'd be able to lose "Daddy" from our vocabulary, unless he allowed my son the right to so address him.

"I can't take you all out today, but here, pay the woman, and here's ten dollars. You all go to a picture show, but don't keep him all night. Take him back to her and I'll come over to your place this evening."

"Yes, Lou." He wasn't angry any longer.

"Daddy?" he prompted.

"Daddy." I smiled and bided my time.

CHAPTER 28

My baby's joy at seeing me instantly erased the odor of disinfectant that had clung to the lining of my nostrils. Clara's house and its inhabitants and its visitors were a puff of smoke sliding behind the farthest hill. I paid Big Mary, and gave no answers to her blunt questions about my new job.

I gathered my son in my arms, and told Mary I'd bring him back in the early evening.

"Ain't you got time for him to spend one night with you? How come you all of a sudden so busy?"

I couldn't explain the tenderness of a great love. And under no pressures could I confide to her the month I planned to spend at Clara's. She'd simply make the common moral judgment, totally missing the finer point of sacrifice and purpose.

The baby, beautiful as a China doll, chattered all the way to the movie, in the movie house and all the way back to my room. He had picked up Big Mary's run-over-shoes accent. I kept repeating the proper pronunciations as he dropped past tenses and plurals. L.D. was right. I had to try harder. My son needed to be with me. I would read to him every day and get the long-playing albums for children of "The Little Prince" and "The Ugly Duckling."

I turned down the path leading to my house, my arms numb to aching with the weight of my son.

"Home, James."

"My name ain't no James."

"My name isn't James."

"No. Yo' name Mother."

"Your name is Mother."

"No, my name ain't no Mother."

When I tried to put him down he folded his legs up under his body and held on to my neck.

"I'm not going to leave you." His heart was thudding on my shoulder, so I carried him into the house.

"Rita." The landlord met me in the hall. "You got lots of long-distance phone calls. From San Francisco. You better call home."

I forced the baby's legs and arms from my side and put him on the floor. He set up an alarm of screaming and I stood at the pay phone waiting for someone to answer.

Papa Ford accepted my collect call. "Girl, I been trying to get you."

Maybe Mother's aim had been good to the extreme and the bail bondsman's magic wouldn't work. I would be very little help, with my own man in trouble at the same time. Of course, there was no contest. Mother came first.

"Your mother's in the hospital."

My Lord. For once she wasn't quick enough. "For what? And how is she?" My calm voice was a lie.

"Operation. Pretty goddam serious. She keeps asking for you. You'd better come home."

I took my son back to Big Mary and told her I had to leave town for a few days. Baxters never tell family business to outsiders, so I left her with no explanation, and my son screaming his motherlessness out, shut up in a back room.

I thought about L.D., but I had no phone number for him, so I asked the landlord to tell him that I had to go to San Francisco... trouble in the family.

I turned my thoughts with the Greyhound, toward San Francisco.

———

My mother's head dipped into the pillow like a yellow rose embedded in a pan of ice. Her forefinger stood sentinel over her red lips.

"Sh. Bailey's over there." A small figure, semaphored on a chaise longue in the corner of the hospital room.

"Eunice died today. He's completely broken up. Today is their one-year anniversary. I got a sedative for him, so he's been asleep for an hour."

Her face and voice showed the strain of worry and illness.

"How are you?"

She dismissed her illness. "Just a female operation. The things I had removed have been used and I wouldn't be needing them again." She still whispered. "I'm glad you came home, though. Bailey needs us. I don't think he'll pull through without one of us around. And I'm going to be in the hospital at least a week. Can you take off from your job?"

"Yes." Sure could.

"Try and wake Bailey up and take him to the house. Have you got somebody good taking care of the baby?"

"Yes, Mother."

"And make him something hot. He hasn't eaten all day. Remember, he's the only brother you've got."

I sat on the seat beside my only brother and gently shook him. He came out of sleep reluctantly. I called his name and he opened his eyes, sat up, looked around. His eyes found Mother, examined the room, came back to me, stunned. He couldn't grasp who he was or where he was.

"My?" His childhood name for me was nearly a cry. His eyes knew something was very wrong, but for the first seconds couldn't remember. The recall split his face open and tears poured down his cheeks.

"Oh my God, My. My. It's Eunice. They've... oh, My."

I took him in my arms and cradle-rocked his body. The sounds of Mother's crying mingled with his muffled moans.

"Let's go home, Bail. Let's just get to the house and we can talk. Let's go home, Bail."

He was eight years old again and trusting. His big wet black eyes looked at me wanting to believe I could do something for his grief. I knew I had no magic, when he most needed me.

"Let's go home, Bail." I could hide the shame of my inadequacy in a skillet, and drown out his sobs in the rattle of pans.

We hugged Mother and they cried together for a moment, but he freed himself without my prodding and came with me to the old high-ceilinged house as obedient as a penitent child.

Grief works its way on people differently. Some sulk, or become morose, or weep and scream a vengeance at the gods. Bailey cried for two hours, unintelligible human sounds growled and gurgled from his throat. Then his face was dry. All tears wasted. And he began to talk.

He ate the food I gave him, automatically, greedily, never stopping or slowing the string of chatter that ran from his mouth.

He told me about Eunice's illness, double pneumonia and tuberculosis, the details of her treatment. The small talk of their sickroom visits. His voice didn't lower and become dramatic when he related how she began to fail. He spoke of the nurse, new on the floor, who barred his way to Eunice's room. "Mrs. Johnson? Mrs. Johnson? Oh, she died this morning. They've taken her away."

He rattled about his new tennis rackets and the better courts in San Francisco. The Southern Pacific dining cars and how hot Arizona was.

I let him talk and didn't try to answer. By morning he began to run down and finally noticed that he was repeating himself. "Oh, My, I told you about that, didn't I?" He drew words around as protection against his news. I gave him a sleeping pill.

"My, you're not leaving me, are you?"

"No."

He balled himself up in Mother's bed and was asleep in minutes.

I awakened to the splash of water and the sound of Bailey singing in the bathroom.

"Jelly, Jelly, Jelly, Jelly stays on my mi-i-nd." He could imitate the bass baritone of Billy Eckstine.

"Jelly Roll killed my pappy, and ran my mammy stone blind."

His voice rolled over joyously in waves. My instant response of elation lasted seconds. He couldn't have made such a quick adjustment. I
joined Papa at the kitchen table and waited.

"Hey, Maya. Fresh coffee? Good morning, Papa Ford." His face was
no wider than my outstretched hand, and the usual rich brown color
was dusty like an old chocolate bar exposed to the light. A smile struggled free and limped across his lips.

"Boy, I sure was upset last night. I hope I didn't worry you too
much. And Mom. Goddam, that was inconsiderate of me to go to her
hospital room screaming and crying."

"It wasn't inconsiderate, Bail, you were upset. You went to your
mother. Where else could you go?"

"Yes, but she's sick herself. And, after all, I'm a man. A man. A man
takes his knocks. He doesn't go running to his mother."

He poured coffee and drank standing, refusing the chair I pulled
out for him.

"Shall I make breakfast for you?" His grin was a little scary, something more than impish, and not yet satanic. "I've learned how to make
Eggs Benedict." He turned to Papa.

"Papa, can you make Eggs Benedict? That's what rich white people
eat."

Papa growled, "I never cooked for white folks, rich or not."

Bailey poked in the refrigerator, and took out eggs and bacon. He
nearly ran to the kitchen closet and was back in a flash with pots, pans,
skillets.

"I'll cook for you, Bailey." Not knowing how to console him. "I
think you need turkey and ham for Eggs Benedict."

He turned on me in red anger. "Will you please leave me alone? I'm
no fucking invalid. I wasn't the one who died, you know."

I liked it better when he cried. I could pet him and talk softly and
feel as if I were effectively coping with his grief.

"I'm Cuban Pete." He started singing in a bad Latin accent, "Oh,
I'm Cuban Pete." He Cesar Romeroed around the table, to the sink,

over to the stove, his grin awful. In a few minutes he placed burned bacon, scrambled eggs and lopsided stacks of hot cakes on the table.

"Get your own silverware. I'm the chef, I'm not the waiter." He straightened up the pancakes with his hands and broke off the ragged edges, trying desperately to make them uniform.

"Sit down, I'll get your plate, Bailey."

"I'm not going to eat right now. But you all enjoy yourself. *Bon appétit.*" He walked out of the kitchen. "I want to hear some music."

In moments, the sound of water splashing in the bathtub mixed with Lester Young's mellow sax reached the kitchen.

Papa Ford frowned. "He's had one bath today, ain't he? He ain't dirty enough for two baths."

"There's nothing wrong with him. He's just nervous." I slammed the sentence out, a barrier against further conversation.

In two days Bailey lost pounds from his already skinny frame and gained in degrees of deception.

Only once did we speak of Eunice.

"If I could have afforded it, I'd have taken her out of San Francisco General and put her in St. Joseph's. People lie who say you die when it's your time to die." He quoted Robert Benton, his favorite at the time. "Hate can be legislated too."

He opened his face by dint of will. "My, I want a favor."

"Anything."

"Eunice's funeral is tomorrow. After that, I never want to hear her name again." He waited.

"All right, Bailey."

"Thank you, My." He closed in upon himself and smiled the new grimace. I lost part of my brother forever.

I didn't report to Mother that the next morning he put on fresh white tennis shorts and shirt, thick white socks and tennis shoes, and walked into the church carrying his new tennis racket.

Papa Ford frowned his disapproval. "Your brother sounds crazy to me. He said he's going to quit his job. This ain't no time to leave the road. Get his meals free. Tips. He can bring home butter and stuff, can't he? Nigger men ain't got but two outs now, as I see it. Keep on sleeping with Old Lady Southern Pacific, or start sleeping in the streets." He smirked. "And he crazy, but he ain't crazy enough for the streets. Shit. He remind me of them Jew boys. He's smart like them. But them Jew boys git some backing to open up some kind of little business. That's how they get their start. Any kind of business he try to start going to be against the law, and he have to be sharper than mosquito shit, too. Keep out of jail. He better stay on the road."

Bailey started staying out all night long, and when he came in, his eyelids were puffy and his movements slow. He walked in pushing before him an odor of unwashed clothes. His eyes were half shut on his secrets. In the afternoons Bobby Wentworth, a former schoolmate now unrecognizable in his thinness and color change, came to the house. He went into Bailey's bedroom walking like a defeated old man and closed the door.

One morning I stood in his empty room over the unmade bed and wondered how I could save my brother. If L.D. and I married soon, he would get us a house large enough for Bailey to have a room. I would nurse him back to health and buy him books and records. Maybe he'd like to go back to school and study law. With his quick brain and silver tongue, he'd be an ace criminal lawyer.

I thought of Grandmother Henderson, who prayed every tribulation into manageable size. I prayed.

Around noon Bailey came home, the unslept night dragging his shoulders down.

I faced him in the hall. "Bailey, what's the matter with Little Bobby?"

His tired face tried to shut me out. "Nothing's the matter with him. Why?"

"He's about the color of mustard and he's got so thin."

"He's just getting down to his fighting weight. Anyway, when are you going back to Stockton? How long can you take off from your job?"

I wasn't sure how much I should tell him. "I'll stay till Mother comes out of the hospital."

"Why?"

"Well, you . . . I mean, I want to be with you."

"I don't need anything. I have told you I'm not an invalid. You'd better get back to Stockton and take care of your own business." It was an order.

I wanted to be sure about his future before I left. "Papa Ford says you're going to quit your job."

"Not going to. I did."

"But what will you do? To live?"

"I'll live." He wasn't bragging, just making a statement.

"But, Bailey, it pays well, doesn't it? I mean, pretty well."

"You're not the one to talk to me about slinging hash. You might be a fry cook the rest of your life, if you're that stupid, but not me."

I refused to bear the insult. "I'm not cooking now, if you want to know. I'm working in a house on the outskirts of Sacramento."

"A what?" He sat up and leaned over to me. "Doing what?"

I knew I had gone too far. I was a boulder rolling down a steep hill and couldn't stop myself.

"What do women do in houses?" The best defense was to be uppity.

"You goddam silly ass. You silly little ass. Turning tricks, huh? My baby goddam sister."

His new temper was cold and sneering. His rages used to be full of fire and crackling; now his diction sharpened and his neck was stiff and he looked down his nose at me. "Who is the nigger?"

"Bailey, it's not like you think."

"Who is the smartass nigger who turned you out?"

"Bailey, he's in trouble and I'm just helping him for a month."

"What's his name?" Although he continued sneering he seemed to thaw a little. "Tell me his name."

"L.D. Tolbrook. And he's old."

"How old?"

"About forty-five."

"What kind of drugs has he given you?"

"You don't understand. He's even stopped me from smoking pot. He's straight and—"

"No pot? Then it's a matter of time before he gives you a noseful of cocaine."

"Bailey." I couldn't bear Bailey's thinking evil about L.D. "He's a ... He's a gambler and he's in trouble with the big boys. So I offered to help him for a month, then we're going to be married."

He leaned into me and spoke gray steel, "You're not going to get married."

"Yes, I am. Yes ..."

"I'll tell you what you're going to do. You are going to go to Stockton and get your baby. Then you're going to find L.D. You're going to tell him he's not to worry about the big boys any more. That he can start worrying about one little boy. Just one. And tell him how little I am. Also tell him that you are my baby goddam sister. Then you're going to get back on the bus and come home. Is that clear, Marguerite?"

I knew the old Bailey could be as violent as Mother, and this new one seemed even more lethal.

"Clear?"

"Yes." That was all I could say. When I arrived in Stockton, I could explain to L.D. that Bailey had misunderstood everything, so for a while I'd go back to San Francisco. When Bailey cooled down, I'd return to him. My absence would make him fonder and I'd have more chance to help my brother pull himself together.

Bailey gave me money for the round trip, and to pay the baby-sitter. I took the afternoon bus to Stockton.

CHAPTER 29

Big Mary's house was near the corner of a typical small-town block, and in the late-afternoon sun the clapboard cottages seemed to be dreaming. I concluded that I must have passed the house when I reached the farthest intersection. My mind was busy with other things, so when I turned and didn't see the house, I decided I was on the wrong street. Another glance at the street names on a sign post assured me that this was the street. Then where was the house? I started back. Here was the little white railroad house. Here was the house with a fenced yard. Here was...but it couldn't be Mary's house. The windows were boarded up and large planks had been nailed in an X across the door.

The two houses flanking Big Mary's were empty. I might have stopped breathing as I walked up and down the creaking steps and tried to peer into windows. The world had suddenly spun off its familiar axis and the rhythm of life slowed to quarter time. The streets and houses, broken toys that lay in overgrown weeds, were monotone in color like objects in an old sepia photograph.

"Who you looking for?"

I turned to face a woman on a porch across the street. Time was in such strange process that I had the opportunity to examine her in minute point. She was fat and white and wore a flowery loose housecoat. From a distance I made out her friendly countenance and the sweat that already dampened semicircles under her arms.

"My baby." But the words wouldn't come. I tried again and the words refused again. I had become paralyzed, literally struck dumb. I stared at the woman in horror.

"Come over here, lady."

She ordered and I had no resistance.

"I know you're looking for Big Mary, aren't you?"

I nodded.

"She moved three days ago. A big truck pulled up and took everything away."

She must have waited for me to question her. After seconds, she continued, "You're the mother, aren't you?"

I nodded.

"There was a big coming and going of the other parents, but I noticed you didn't come for your little boy. Mary and I haven't spoken since she called me a meddling bitch three years ago—she used foul language. But I broke the silence and asked where she was taking the boy. She said you had given him to her. Said you were too busy. I asked where she was going and she told me none of my business. But I know she's got a brother in Bakersfield."

It was a rattling tale told on a radio and I couldn't make it have to do with my life.

"If you want to call the police, come in. I'll give you some lemonade... while you're waiting for them."

The word "police" shook me awake. My brain moved sluggishly. Big Mary had left with my baby and lied as well. Then she kidnapped him. If the police came, they'd question me about my job. A whore (well, I had to admit it) wasn't a fit mother and they'd take him from me and put me in jail.

"I'll call them for you." The woman turned and an oblong of perspiration was dripping down the back of her dress.

Before she reached the door, I forced my voice out. "No thank you. I know where he is, everything's all right."

"Where is he?" The woman's suspicion was nasty.

"I'm going there now. It's over on the south side. By the sloughs." I waved at her. "Thanks anyway," I said and marched down the street.

—

L.D.'s car was parked in front of his house. My scheme was to ring his bell and if his wife answered, tell her I was an old friend and had a message for him from a friend. I'd quickly tell him about Big Mary and the baby and he'd decide what to do. I was proud that I hadn't cried and that I wasn't afraid of his naggish wife.

A pretty, thirtyish, light-brown-skinned woman opened the door. Her long black hair curled around her shoulders, reminding me of a beige Hedy Lamarr.

"You want to see L.D.? What's your name?"

She had the same soft slur that made me love to hear L.D. talk.

"My name is Rita."

"Oh." Her lips firmed on the edges. "So you're Rita. Well, just wait a minute, I'll get Lou."

She closed the door and I waited on the landing, wondering how we'd find my baby.

"Rita." L.D. had opened the door and held it just wide enough for me to see half of his body. "What put it in your head to come to my house?"

I whispered, "I told her I was a friend, L.D. My baby's—"

"Don't you have better sense than to come to my house?"

"I need some help, L.D. I have to talk to you."

He stepped out on the porch and pulled the door closed behind him. His face was inches from me and he spoke through uneven teeth.

"Let me pull your coat, you silly little bitch. This is my house. No 'ho goes to a man's house. You talked to my wife. No 'ho opens her mouth to speak to a man's wife." He curled his mouth and snarled, "Clara's never even met my wife and Clara's been my woman three years. You've been gone a week and you got the nerve...Go to your place. I'll be there when I get time."

He walked back in the house and slammed the door.

I wanted desperately to cry.

I had been stupid, again. And stupidity had led me into a trap where I had lost my baby. I tried to erase L.D. Tolbrook from my mind. Obviously he wasn't very bright. He had had a good woman who would have done anything to help him. And he was too dumb to even have the courtesy to listen to my troubles. And he had lied to me by not telling me that Clara was his woman.

Pity. That he thought outsmarting a young girl, living off the wages of women was honorable. He obviously had been doing it for years. He probably started in the South with white women, thinking that by taking their bodies and their money, he was getting revenge on the white men, who were free to insult him, ignore him and keep him at the bottom of the heap.

Clara must have wriggled her nose off in laughing at my stupidity with her "daddy." And L.D.'s wife probably bought the white piqué dress she wore with money I had made. I detested him for being a liar and a pimp, but more, I hated him for being such an idiot that he couldn't value my sterling attributes enough to keep me for himself alone.

There was no thought of the greed which coerced me to agree with L.D.'s plans in the hope that I'd win, in the end, a life of ease and romance. Like most young women, I wanted a man, any man, to give me a June Allyson screen-role life with sunken living room, and

cashmere-sweater sets, and I, for one, obviously would have done anything to get that life.

I couldn't telephone Bailey or Mother. Even if they had been in the
best of shape, I couldn't admit to them that out of ignorance I'd lost
the baby.

As I walked, my rage at L.D. diminished and I regained some
steadying peripheral vision. Had I melted down on the pavement in
tears of frustration, the action would not have changed the fact that
my baby was still missing. Or the fact that with this latest loss, I was
shatteringly lonely for my baby and his arms hugging my neck. The
weight was on me.

I decided to sleep the night in my old room and leave the next
morning for Bakersfield. The idea that Big Mary might have taken
him on to Oklahoma was squashed over and over in my mind like a
buzzing fly.

———

The small Southern California town on those midnight rides with
L.D. had seemed fanciful and unreal; now from the bus windows it was
drab and seemed overpopulated with mean-faced whites straight out
of my Arkansas past.

A black man gave me a ride to Cottonwood Road.

"If her brother is farming, he got to be living around here somewhere. And you say you don't know his name?"

"No, but I'll find him."

He stopped his old car in front of a café that claimed "Home
Cooking."

"Well, I wish you Godspeed. Try in there. But be careful. These is
some rough folks."

I thanked him and he drove away.

The young waitress shouted over the noisy jukebox and talk, "Anybody here know Mary Dawson?"

Conversation dimmed but no one answered.

She went on, "This woman's looking for her baby."

The faces became friendlier, but still there were no answers.

"Nobody knows her, honey. Try down at Buckets." She directed me to a dirt-floor joint a couple of blocks away.

Old-timey blues whined in the artificial darkness, and one stout bartender walked up and down behind the bar setting up and taking away beer bottles. Every stool was taken by men and women who laughed and talked with the easy familiarity of regulars.

"Mary Dawson? Mary Dawson." The bartender digested the name as he filed my face in his memory bank. "Naw, baby, I don't know no Mary Dawson."

"They call her Big Mary."

"Big Mary. Naw, I don't know no Big Mary."

"She's got my baby. Took him away from Stockton." I felt as if I were blowing my breath against a tornado.

His face softened as suspicion left it. "What she look like?"

"She's as tall as I. As me"—"as I" sounded too dickty—"but bigger, and she has a brother who farms around here. They're from Oklahoma."

A little light winked in his eyes. "Does she drink?"

"Not often, but they say she drinks a lot when she does."

"In a coffee cup?" The smile was abundant.

"Yes." I wanted to hug him.

"That's old John Peterson's sister. Yeah, baby. He lives bout three miles from here."

In the past, whenever I had slipped free of Fate's pressing heel, I gave thanks. This time I promised God a regular church attendance.

"Can you direct me?"

"Aw, you can't walk it. Wait a minute."

He called to a man over at the jukebox. "Buddy."

The man turned and came over to the bar.

"Little lady, Buddy runs a cab service... Buddy, you know where John Peterson's place is?"

Buddy nodded.

"Take her out there, will you?"

Buddy nodded again.

"He'll treat you right, little lady, good luck."

I thanked the bartender and followed Buddy to a dilapidated car. He said nothing on the ride, but my heart beat so that I wouldn't have been able to answer in any case.

He stopped the car on a lonely road surrounded by overturned farmland. A graying clapboard house set deep in a plot of muddy ground.

Buddy nodded toward the house. "That's it. You want me to come back to get you?"

I looked at the house, which seemed left alone, and thought that maybe its occupants had gone to Oklahoma. Then I noticed some movement a few hundred yards from the house. I focused on the movement, trying to determine if the action was caused by a pet or farm animal rooting in the mud.

In a second, my heart squeezed and I screamed. "My baby! That's my baby." One thought shot my legs out of the car and in two steps I was ankle-deep in muck, a new thought sluicing in my mind. Where does he think his mother is?

I picked him up and pressed him close. I felt his body throb and pound with excitement. He stiffened his arms and pushed himself away to see my face. He kissed me and then started crying. The restraint which had held through the long night and the bus trip began to disintegrate. He took a fistful of my hair and twisted and pulled, crying all the time. I couldn't untangle the hair or pull my head away. I stood holding him while he raged at being abandoned. My sobs broke free on the waves of my first guilt. I had loved him and never considered that he was an entire person. Separate from my boundaries, I had not known before that he had and would have a life beyond being my son, my pretty baby, my cute doll, my charge. In the plowed farmyard near Bakersfield, I began to understand that uniqueness of the person. He was three and I was nineteen, and never again would I think of him as a beautiful appendage of myself.

———

Big Mary leaned against the rickety kitchen table. "I didn't mean no harm. I just love him. I take good care of him. You know that."

Her big face crumbled like pastry dough and she trembled. "Why don't you let him stay with me awhile?"

She looked at Guy in my arms and her voice pinched into baby talk. "Pretty, don't you want to stay with Big Mary? Tell your momma you want to stay."

His arms scissored around my neck.

"I'm taking him, Mary."

She couldn't control the tears. "Can't you all stay one night—just one?"

"I have a taxi waiting." I started to the door.

"Well, wait and I'll get his things together."

"No, that's all right, we have to leave."

She made a lunge but stopped before she reached me.

"You don't hate me, do you, Rita? I pray God you don't hate me."

"I don't hate you, Mary."

"He was the prettiest of them all. And you was always going somewhere."

"I understand, Mary. Good-bye. Say good-bye, Guy."

"Good-bye."

Buddy took us to the bus station and my muddy baby and I headed for San Francisco again.

CHAPTER 30

At home, life stumbled on. Mother was again in residence. The record player spun disks ceaselessly, cooking odors wafted through every room, and ice jiggled in glasses like snow bells.

Bailey had given up his apartment and had moved his belongings back into his old room. He told Mother he was job hunting, and paid her room rent "out of savings." He now wore one-button roll suits in dun and charcoal-gray; the modified pegged pants and colorful jerkins were given away. And his smiles were less frequent and different. When Papa Ford said something too ribald or old-fashioned, Bailey seemed not to notice. He never lifted his eyes to check with me, and the teasings about my height and arrogance had stopped.

Since I was job hunting too, I asked where he was looking and for what.

"In the streets. I'm looking for a bank roll, then I'm heading for New York City."

What could he do except wait tables and sing for the family's enjoyment?

"I can use my brain. I've told you 'all knowledge is spendable currency depending upon the market.' There's money to be had, and I intend to have some."

"Bailey, you're not going to pimp, are you?"

"Let me straighten you out. Pimps are men who hate women or fear them. I respect women, and how can I fear a woman when the baddest one I've ever heard of is my mother?"

He looked at me sharply. "And let me tell you another thing, a whore is the saddest and silliest broad walking. All she hopes is to beat somebody out of something, by lying down first and getting up last."

I didn't want to be included in that company, yet I had lived at Clara's.

"I'm not talking about you. There is such a thing as a whore mentality. You can find it in a housewife who will only go to bed with her husband if he buys a new washing machine. Or a secretary who'll sleep with the boss for a raise. Hell, you're both too smart and not smart enough to be a whore. Never. But I don't want you trying it again."

He was seven inches shorter and one year older than I, but as always, he had the last and loudest word. Afterward, as I thought about him, he became even larger in my mind.

He had endured the death of his love and was still going on. Certainly he was limping and using a crutch I didn't approve of, but he hadn't atrophied. He had plans for his future. I reasoned that hard drugs might not be as bad as the people who used them. It was possible that the dirty, ragged, smelly hypes, who were so frightening and repulsive, were naturally slouchy and low-class. There were probably many people who took drugs and never lowered their living standards. I knew from experience that weed wasn't dangerous, so it could follow that heroin and cocaine were victims of rumors spread by the self-righteous. Anyway, man had always needed something to help him through this vale of tears. Fermented berries, corn, rice and potatoes. Scotch or magic mushrooms. Why not the residue of poppies?

The maids and doormen, factory workers and janitors who were able to leave their ghetto homes and rub against the cold-shouldered white world, told themselves that things were not as bad as they seemed. They smiled a dishonest acceptance at their mean servitude and on Saturday night bought the most expensive liquor to drown their lie. Others, locked in the unending maze of having to laugh without humor and scratch without agitation, foisted their hopes on the Lord. They shouted loudly on Sunday morning at His goodness and spent the afternoon preparing the starched uniforms to meet a boss's unrelenting examination. The timorous and the frightened held tightly to their palliatives. I was neither timid nor afraid.

———

I applied for work along Fillmore Street. Neither the local beauty shop nor record store needed a manageress. The realtor said his friend, an Oakland businessman, wanted a cool-headed person to run his restaurant. I bristled with the big-city disdain for small towns; it was generally accepted in San Francisco that Oakland was placed on the other side of the Bay Bridge to accept snide remarks from city so-phisticates. But the chance to rise in the business world to manageress was too tempting to ignore. I didn't entertain the thought that I wouldn't do the job well. After all, although my experience had not in-cluded managing a restaurant, I had successfully lived through some harrowing events and considered myself mature and adult enough for responsibility.

I took the train to Oakland.

James Cain was impressed with what he thought of as my college vocabulary, and the half-carat diamonds flashing in his two front teeth enchanted me. He didn't ask for references and offered seventy-five dollars a week and all my meals.

He was a large, gentle man who smiled a lot at life and kept all the details of his many business affairs in his head. He owned a dry cleaners, a shoe-repair shop, and next door to the restaurant, a gambling house. His clothes were tailor-made, and he wore them with a casual flair. If he had tightened his lips over the diamonds, and if he had lived in another world, he'd have passed for an erudite broker who regularly made killings on Wall Street.

"Cain's" served well-cooked Southern dishes in ample proportions and was popular with the area regulars. Cain had bought three unknown prize fighters and was pushing them toward championship. He wanted to upgrade the restaurant and extend dinner invitations to the successful white fight promoters he met at the gym.

He sat in a red leatherette booth and talked to me. "Ought to have a soup. And a salad. Ought to have a menu, too." When I went to work for him, the day's choices were printed on a child's blackboard near the door.

NECK BONES

SHORT RIBS

HOG MAWS

PORK CHOP

RED SNAPPER

As determined as I was to make good at the job, I couldn't decide what soup or salad would complement those entrées. Soup had been for me, in my Southern youth, an entrée in itself, and salad was mostly potato or slaw. I suggested bouillon. Cain smiled at the sound and told the cook to fix it.

"Tossed salad. Roquefort dressing."

Cain gave the signal to the cook.

I also told him that I had seldom seen hog maws or neck bones featured in white cafés.

The chef was told to cut down on his orders.

"They eat a lot of omelettes, and liver and bacon. I would suggest you stock Chicken à la King."

Cain's keen intelligence had won for him the position of tycoon in Oakland, and he operated on the theory of an equal distribution of labor. He left the menu design and plan to me.

Within a month customers were delivered large menus which offered, in Old English print,

Chicken à la King
Irish Stew
Veal Cutlet
T-bone Steak
Peach Cobbler—Sweet Potato Pie
Ham Hocks and Mustard Greens (a sop which was
   always sold out an hour after opening)

As dining business slackened, I had the opportunity to examine the gamblers carefully. They straggled into the restaurant during the high California mornings, well-cut pants bagging away from their knees; hand-painted silk ties undone and hanging, flapping, forgotten, down their shirt fronts. When their hands shook coffee onto the tablecloths, the waiters brought fresh coffee without condemnation.

The winners and losers looked equally disordered but were distinguishable by their company. Beggars, grifters and petty losers hung on their words, pulled chairs out for them, and shouted at slow-moving waiters for faster service.

The street women who met their men at the dining tables (Cain didn't allow hustling in the restaurant, and no women at all in the gambling room) were of particular interest to me. They came in tired, the night's glamour gone from their faces and the swing from their hips.

The men who drank whiskey for steadiness or diversion took their women's money in the open, counting it out bill by bill, then ordering a flunky to run to the liquor store and quickly bring "a taste." The women's faces surged with pride and defeat. They had proved they were successful and trustworthy whores, but they also knew the men would return to the gambling tables to chance the night's earnings, and the women would be sent home exhausted to empty beds.

A man who got his highs from heavier narcotics never treated his woman so carelessly. He would wait impatiently, drinking heavily sugared coffee. As soon as his woman passed the window, he stood up and paid the small check. The woman waited at the door and the couple walked away eagerly and together. I knew they were hurrying to the fix. I knew that the woman had already made the connection before she came to pick up her man. I knew, and could see nothing wrong. At least they were a couple and depended on each other.

Cain had little time to notice that all was not well at the restaurant, since he spent his days engrossed with his fighters. The operators of his cleaning shop and gambling house were hewing to the traditional lines, and their businesses were booming.

I had to speak to him.

"Mr. Cain, I'm afraid this month we, er, slid back a little."

He thought. "Lost money, huh?"

"Yes. Actually, the menu doesn't seem to appeal to the regulars and there aren't enough of the others to equalize the loss of patronage."

"I see what you mean." And he did. "Let's keep it like you got it for another month. Give those backward Negroes a chance for something better."

He tucked up a large fork of greens, and crumbled corn bread in the pot liquor. "Some people don't appreciate the better things in life."

The second month showed the restaurant deeper in the red, and although I brought Guy to the restaurant daily and fed him T-bone steak while I ate veal cutlet, the chef complained that his refrigerator was jammed with spoiled food.

Mr. Cain told me not to worry. "They scared to go downtown and eat, and when I bring them the same food to their own neighborhood they won't even eat it. That's all right with me. I did my best." He told the cook to clean out the refrigerator and go back to the old menu.

"Can you drive?"

"Yes."

"I want you to take the car and pick up my boxers in the mornings. You drive them to Lake Merrit. They'll get out and run while you follow them. When they go clear around the lake, you pick them up and take them to the gym. Then you pick me up and I'll take you home, then I'll go back to the gym."

Hooray! At last! A chauffeurette.

———

I guided the Cadillac slowly around the dark curves, and the sounds of the three men panting mixed with the soft slaps of the waves. Two boxers were large, muscular heavyweights who gave me unsmiling grunts when I picked them up at the run-down hotel. They sat like huge black monoliths in the back seat, while Billy, a cute little flyweight, joked in the front seat with me.

"Baby, I'll burn 'em up ... with the uppercut. I'll cut their flab ... with a little jab."

Billy reminded me of the old Bailey and I determined to see him fight.

Cain bought me a brown suede suit, and a matching snap-brim hat. My shoes, gloves and purse were suede, and I knew I was as sharp as anyone had a right to be.

I sat up front with him and four other fat old men who smoked cigars and passed fistfuls of money in the glaring lights. The whoosh of sound in the auditorium, and the frenetic activity of people rising and sitting, walking, running, the faces turning like cardboard cutouts, made me think I had been stupid not to have attended a fight before.

The lights dimmed and Billy in white shorts ran down an aisle toward the arena. Another small boxer wearing black trunks kneed his way through the ropes from another aisle.

I turned to Cain, who was negotiating money business with his cronies.

"It's Billy. Why aren't you watching?"

He glanced up at the lighted square and turned back to the sheaf of money in his hands.

He mumbled, "That's just the prelims."

The referee held up both men's hands, and the gong rang. The boxers crouched with their arms tucked into their sides. They began to inch a circle on the floor leaning in and over as if they were trying to identify the different brands of aftershave lotion. Black Shorts, with a rude immediacy, thrust his left fist into Billy's ribs.

Whump.

He withdrew, and while Billy was adjusting, shot his right fist against Billy's cheek.

My scream lofted high and made no indentation on the room's boisterousness.

Billy wobbled for a second, looking for a wall or shoulder to lean against.

"Hit him, Billy." I was standing and ready to climb in the ring.

Black Shorts bounded away and then moved in close. As if responding to a public announcement, the fight fans began to give their attention to the action. Their low thunder diminished and I could hear the boxers' feet sliding across the mat. *Sh-h-h, sh-h-h-whomp.* There is no sound in the world like that of a man storing his fist in the chest of another man. Lions may roar, and coyotes howl, but the vibrations of two human beings struggling for physical superiority introduced to me a nauseating and new terror.

Whump! Whomp! Sh! Sh! Sh! Ooo!

The breath was being pounded out of Billy's little body and I knew it could have been Bailey up there dancing his waltz under the cold eyes of gamblers.

"Stop them, Cain." I turned and leaned over my boss and Billy's owner.

He regarded me as if I were a stranger just gone mad before his eyes.

"What? What? Sit down and cool off." The edges of his teeth showed and his fat face glimmered in the dark.

"Stop them," I said. "That man is beating Billy to death."

"Shut up." I was embarrassing him in front of his friends. "Shut up and sit down."

"You dog. You sadistic dog freak!" The words were accented by the *whomp*s and *sh*s from the ring. "Freak!" I screamed it and turned to run.

Cain grabbed at my arm but I had moved away. The other men were questioning:

"What's the matter with her?"

"She go crazy or what?"

Cain ordered, "Sit down, dizzy bitch."

I was nearly out into the aisle, but I turned and straddled a patron who was by now more interested in our row than in the public contest above.

"Marquis de Sade son of a bitch." I threw my suede purse at Cain and lifted a leg over the patron, freeing myself to reach the aisle. I ran up the corridor to the front door, expecting at any moment to be caught and dragged back to be forced to watch poor little Billy be whomped to death.

I paused to catch my breath and consider the number of pursuers on my trail. The divisions between the rows were empty and the faces, which I expected to have swiveled in my departing direction, still faced forward.

I noticed that the roar was growing and from where I stood I saw the figure in white shorts fold down, knees first, to the canvas. Black Shorts' feet might have been mired in concrete, he stood so certain.

Billy's head crashed forward and the audience screamed its approval. I was right and wrong. Cain was a sadistic bastard. But he wasn't alone. All the bloodthirsty fans were sadistic, too. And so was Billy.

I walked the streets to my house and comforted myself with the knowledge that although my brother was small and agile enough to be a featherweight fighter, no one would ever sit eating hot dogs while he was beaten to death. He shadow-boxed and danced down cruel streets, and his opponents made Black Shorts look less threatening than Papa Ford. I was proud that my brother was living a dangerous life and didn't bow his knee to a living soul.

I knew the job was gone, and even if an apology rectified things with Cain, I couldn't apologize. To hell with him, the job and the fighters. Hooray for my brother.

Cain's letter the next day was as stiff as a short jab: "Rita Johnson, your services will no longer be necessary."

I was in a state again that was blood line familiar. Up a tree, out on a limb, in a pickle, in a mess but I didn't pack my bags (or leave them) and go back to Mother.

Survival was all around me but it didn't take hold. Women nearly as young as I, with flocks of children, were creating their lives daily. A few hustled (I had obviously little aptitude for that); some worked as housemaids (becoming one of a strange white family was impossible. I would keep my negative Southern exposures to whites before me like a defensive hand); some wrestled with old lady Welfare (my neck wouldn't bend for that).

While the total trust of a child can mold a parent into a new form, Guy's big smile (Mother said he laughed an awful lot for a baby) and happy disposition lost its magic to make me happy. He believed in me, but he was a child and I had lost belief in myself.

My head stayed high from habit, but my last hope was gone. Every way out of the maze had proved to be a false exit. My once lively imagination would not come up with one more fantasy. My courage was dwindling. Unfortunately, fortitude was not like the color of my skin, given to me once and mine forever. It needed to be resurrected each morning and exercised painstakingly. It also had to be fed with at least a few triumphs. My strength had fallen away from me as the pert features fade from an aging beauty. I didn't drink and had run out of pot. For the first time in my life I sat down defenseless to await life's next assault.

CHAPTER 31

I had often noticed Troubadour Martin at Cain's. He was extremely tall and dangerously thin. When I used to see him, he reminded me of the phrase often used to describe me, "A long drink of water." He came to my house a week after my job ran out. That was how I'd begun to think of it. His movements were slow and his speech a long time coming. We sat in my living room.

"Hello, Rita."

"Hi, Troub."

Pause.

"Heard you not working for Cain."

"No. The job ran out."

Wait.

"Well, you find anything yet?"

"No, I'm taking a rest."

Hesitation.

"Of course."

Delay.

"Maybe you can help me."

I demurred. This time I didn't intend to jump at the first persuasion. He was black and handsome, and when the light fell right across his face he looked like a thin Paul Robeson. I also knew he wasn't one of the men who sent out for drinks.

"Maybe you know I deal in clothes?"

I knew he was a gambler.

"No."

"I have a connection for ladies' dresses and suits. New." He shook his head before my question. "They're not hot. I run sort of like a catalog business. I'll tell you what I need. See, you won't have to do nothing. I'll bring the things, and ladies can come over here to try them on."

He smiled slowly, and dropped his eyes. I saw the Southern shyness of the man and knew the clothes were stolen.

"You know how you ladies are. Wouldn't like to undress unless there's another lady around."

I didn't know about that. I said nothing.

"And you don't have to sell, I'll do that. I'll give you a percentage of the money. How's that?"

There was nothing to think about. I agreed.

I'd have money coming in and my time would be my own. I could read all day, and take Guy to the park and to movies. I would have the time to teach him to read. And I'd be beholden to no one. Troubadour wasn't interested in me romantically, so I didn't have to concern myself about getting involved with him.

"All right, Troub. When do we start?"

"I'll bring some things around tonight." His words lingered in his mouth. "Uh, Rita, uh, I'm glad to be working with you. Every time I used to see you, I thought to myself, 'That's a real nice lady.' Sure did."

He left me a demure smile.

After two months my closets were filled with expensive two- and three-piece suits. Dresses, sweaters and stockings crammed my drawers, and I spent my days reading Thomas Wolfe and going to the movies with Guy. I had cut down my visits to San Francisco. Mother's house was dim with foreboding tragedy and Bailey still hadn't got his "bankroll together." He was thinner and the new clothes didn't fit. The shirt sleeves slid down to cover half his hands, and his stomach couldn't resist the belt's descent. His color seemed to have faded and his once fast speech had slowed nearly to Troub's rhythm. For her part, Mother talked faster and popped her fingers louder, but her laughter shattered out of her mouth. Unreal.

There was no happiness in the house.

In Oakland, my fantasy settled upon becoming Mrs. Troubadour Martin. He was kind, generous and quiet, and although we made a desultory kind of love a few times, he had never asked for more. The ideal husband.

Troub was definitely strung out on heavy narcotics. Even when I smoked grass, he would take only one or two drags and let me have the rest. I had waited to see when he would try to introduce me to heroin and hadn't been quite sure how I'd respond. Order him out of my house or consider that he made enough money to be able to keep us both high for life? One hit of heroin wouldn't make me an addict. And maybe if I shot it once, he'd know I didn't disapprove and our relationship would be closer. Since he never answered my direct questions about heroin, I schemed to bring about a confrontation.

"Troubadour, I think you'll have to find someone else."

"Why, Rita?" Even shock didn't scurry across his face.

"I think you're keeping something from me. Or have an old lady. And...and I'm beginning to fall for you." It wasn't difficult to make myself cry. All I had to do was think about losing my soft perch, or my brother, or my mother, or old L.D. or the long-lost Curly.

"Rita, I've told you, I don't have any woman."

Tears flowed. "But you never take me with you. I'm not a girl. I want to be your woman. And share everything with you. You don't care about me."

"Yes, I do, Rita. I like you. You're just fine."

"But you don't want me, is that it?"

"No. That's not it." At least he was speaking a little faster.

"Then if you want me, stop hiding what you do. I can take it."

I dried my tears enough to look at him. His eyes squinched together and his jaws clenched. He looked straight at me. "Can you leave the baby for a while? Come for a ride with me."

Here it was. I had to leave Guy alone. Nothing ventured...

Troub pointed the car toward San Francisco.

"Where are we going?" I had expected he was taking me to his room, which was in Oakland near my house. He didn't answer. The Bay Bridge amber lights washed out his brown-earth color and he was a cold, sallow stranger. I couldn't show panic.

"Oh, to the city, huh? That's nice." ("Did I ever tell you I have only a little while to live? I have a brain tumor and the doctors give me six months." I had planned the speech years before to be used if I encountered a rapist or murderer. "They can't operate. Too near the cerebellum.")

Troubadour stared at the streets and chose one. I was dismayed to see that we were on the waterfront. My God, he was a freak of some kind and this was going to be the last few minutes of my life. I still couldn't scream.

He stopped the car on the wharf.

"Come on, Rita."

"But where are we going?"

"I'm going to show you something."

There was an absoluteness about the way he spoke and nodded his head toward the opposite side of the street. A pale sign said "Hotel." I was glad I hadn't screamed. A hotel. Maybe his house was hot and he was bringing me to a hotel to show me the ropes. I followed him through the fog, across four sets of railroad tracks to the hotel.

He walked straight to the desk and told a chalky-white clerk. "Give me the key."

The clerk didn't hesitate and I still followed, a little shaken. Did he keep a room here to act out some extravagant fantasy?

He turned the key in a lock and I went sheeplike into the room.

My first impression was that I was in a city bus station very early in the morning. People sat and lounged on every available place. Three bodies were draped over a bed, men and women sat on the floor, backed by the wall. Two women sat in one chair and all, black and white, were dozing off or waking up or fast asleep. No one noticed our entrance.

Troubadour reached back for me in the dim lamplight.

"Come on." I reeled and tried to shake my sluggish brain awake but it couldn't compute the situation.

It seemed a slow whole minute before the scene registered. This was a hit joint for addicts. Fear flushed my face and neck and made the room tremble before me. I had been prepared to experiment with drugs, but I hadn't counted on this ugly exposure. As I watched the wretched nod and scratch, I felt my own innocence as real as a grain of sand between my teeth. I was pure as moonlight and had only begun to live. My escapades were the fumblings of youth and to be forgiven as such.

I twisted for the door behind me and tried to snatch my hand away, but Troub held on.

"Come on. I want you to see something."

I was afraid to scream and alarm the addicts in their dreaming. If I pulled free and reached the lobby, would the desk clerk know I wasn't going to the police and allow me to go?

Troub tugged at me and we stumbled over outstretched legs toward an open bathroom door.

In the bathroom, Troub removed his jacket and gave it to me. He rolled up his shirt sleeve. Time for Troub and me moved as if we were swimming under water. He took a tablespoon from the sink and a small square of paper from his pocket.

The senses of sound, taste and touch had disappeared, but I had never seen so clearly or smelled so acutely.

The powder was dusted into the spoon and he dribbled a little water over it. He held three matches under the belly of the spoon while the mixture simmered. The sweet smell went into my nose and unlocked my tongue. "Don't do it, Troub. Please don't."

"Shut up and watch me." He tied his arm above the elbow with his tie and tightened it with his teeth. Then he took a syringe from the grimy face bowl and filled it with the hot clear liquid. High-standing keloid scars ran down his inner arm, and the black flesh was purple and yellow in a place, with fresh sores. He pushed the needle into a scar and wiggled it around, then took it out and tried another.

"Please, Troub."

"Shut up and watch this."

The needle pricked one of the soft scabs and rich yellow pus flowed out and down his arm to the wrist.

My tears, which had been terror-frozen, thawed at the sight of the man who had been so nice to me, jabbing and picking in his own flesh, oblivious to the pain and the ugliness.

The needle found its place and blood, mixed with a few drops of heroin, had snaked across his upheld arm. He loosened the tie with his teeth, and as if I had x-ray vision, I watched the narcotic reach his brain. His face muscles slackened and he leaned heavily against the wall.

"Now, you want some?" Slow lips, slow question.

"No."

"You sure? I can cook up for you." His head lolled, but he kept his eyes on me.

"I'm sure. I don't want it."

"Then I want you to promise me you won't use shit. That's why they call it shit. It is. You a nice lady, Rita. I don't want to see you change. Promise me you'll stay like I found you. Nice."

"I promise."

"Let me rest a little in the car, then I'll take you home."

He slumped behind the steering wheel for a half-hour and I watched him.

I thought about the kindness of the man. I had wanted him before for the security I thought he'd give me. I loved him as he slouched, nodding, his mouth open and the saliva sliding down his chin as slowly as the blood had flowed down his arm. No one had ever cared for me so much. He had exposed himself to me to teach me a lesson and I learned it as I sat in the dark car inhaling the odors of the wharf. The life of the underworld was truly a rat race, and most of its inhabitants scurried like rodents in the sewers and gutters of the world. I had walked the precipice and seen it all; and at the critical moment, one man's generosity pushed me safely away from the edge.

He finally awakened and we headed back to Oakland. In front of my house I told him he should take his clothes. I explained that I planned to move back to the city.

He said, "Sell them, you need the money. You've got a baby. There's plenty more stores and plenty more clothes."

The next day I took the clothes, my bags and Guy back to Mother's. I had no idea what I was going to make of my life, but I had given a promise and found my innocence. I swore I'd never lose it again.

SINGIN' AND SWINGIN' AND GETTIN'
MERRY LIKE CHRISTMAS

*For MARTHA and LILLIAN, NED and BEY, for
the laughter, the love and the music*

ACKNOWLEDGMENTS

Thanks to the BELLAGIO STUDY AND CONFERENCE CENTER of the ROCKEFELLER FOUNDATION, particularly BILL and BETSY OLSEN. A special thanks to my friend and secretary, SEL BERKOWITZ.

CHAPTER 1

"Don't the moon look lonesome shining through the trees?
Ah, don't the moon look lonesome shining through the trees?
Don't your house look lonesome when your baby pack up to leave?"

Music was my refuge. I could crawl into the spaces between the notes and curl my back to loneliness.

In my rented room (cooking privileges down the hall), I would play a record, then put my arms around the shoulders of the song. As we danced, glued together, I would nuzzle into its neck, kissing the skin, and rubbing its cheek with my own.

The Melrose Record Shop on Fillmore was a center for music, musicians, music lovers and record collectors. Blasts from its loudspeaker poured out into the street with all the insistence of a false mourner at a graveside. Along one wall of its dark interior, stalls were arranged like open telephone booths. Customers stood playing their selections on turntables and listening through earphones. I had two hours between jobs. Occasionally I went to the library or, if the hours coincided, to a free dance class at the YWCA. But most often I directed myself to the melodious Melrose Record Store, where I could wallow, rutting in music.

Louise Cox, a short blonde who was part owner of the store, flitted between customers like a fickle butterfly in a rose garden. She was white, wore perfume and smiled openly with the Negro customers, so I knew she was sophisticated. Other people's sophistication tended to make me nervous and I stayed shy of Louise. My music tastes see-sawed between the blues of John Lee Hooker and the bubbling silver sounds of Charlie Parker. For a year I had been collecting their records.

On one visit to the store, Louise came over to the booth where I was listening to a record.

"Hi, I'm Louise. What's your name?"

I thought of "Puddin' in tame. Ask me again, I'll tell you the same." That was a cruel childhood rhyme meant to insult.

The last white woman who had asked me anything other than "May I help you?" had been my high school teacher. I looked at the little woman, at her cashmere sweater and pearls, at her slick hair and pink lips, and decided she couldn't hurt me, so I'd give her the name I had given to all white people.

"Marguerite Annie Johnson." I had been named for two grand-mothers.

"Marguerite? That's a pretty name."

I was surprised. She pronounced it like my grandmother. Not Mar-garite, but Marg-you-reet.

"A new Charlie Parker came in last week. I saved it for you."

That showed her good business sense.

"I know you like John Lee Hooker, but I've got somebody I want you to hear." She stopped the turntable and removed my record and put on another in its place.

> "Lord I wonder, do she ever think of me,
> Lord I wonder, do she ever think of me,
> I wonder, I wonder, will my baby come back to me?"

The singer's voice groaned a longing I seemed to have known my life long. But I couldn't say that to Louise. She watched my face and I forced it still.

"Well, I ain't got no special reason here,
No, I ain't got no special reason here,
I'm gonna leave 'cause I don't feel welcome here."

The music fitted me like tailor-made clothes.

She said, "That's Arthur Crudup. Isn't he great?"; excitement lighted her face.

"It's nice. Thank you for letting me hear it."

It wasn't wise to reveal one's real feelings to strangers. And nothing on earth was stranger to me than a friendly white woman.

"Shall I wrap it for you? Along with the Bird?"

My salary from the little real estate office and the dress shop downtown barely paid rent and my son's baby-sitter.

"I'll pick them both up next week. Thank you for thinking of me." Courtesy cost nothing as long as one had dignity. My grandmother, Annie Henderson, had taught me that.

She turned and walked back to the counter, taking the record with her. I counseled myself not to feel badly. I hadn't rejected an offer of friendship, I had simply fielded a commercial come-on.

I walked to the counter.

"Thank you, Louise. See you next week." When I laid the record on the counter, she pushed a wrapped package toward me.

"Take these, Marg-you-reet. I've started an account for you." She turned to another customer. I couldn't refuse because I didn't know how to do so gracefully.

Outside on the evening street, I examined the woman's intention. What did I have that she wanted? Why did she allow me to walk away with her property? She didn't know me. Even my name might have been constructed on the spot. She couldn't have been seeking friendship; after all she was white, and as far as I knew, white women were never lonely, except in books. White men adored them, Black men desired them and Black women worked for them. There was no ready explanation for her gesture of trust.

At home I squeezed enough from the emergency money I kept in a drawer to repay her. Back at the store, she accepted the money and said, "Thanks, Marg-you-reet. But you didn't have to make a special trip. I trust you."

"Why?" That ought to get her. "You don't know me."

"Because I like you."

"But you don't know me. How can you like someone you don't know?"

"Because my heart tells me and I trust my heart."

For weeks I pondered over Louise Cox. What could I possibly have that she could possibly want? My mind, it was certain, was a well-oiled mechanism which worked swiftly and seminoiselessly. I often competed with radio contestants on quiz programs and usually won hands down in my living room. Oh, my mental machine could have excited anyone. I meant anyone interested in a person who had memorized the Presidents of the United States in chronological order, the capitals of the world, the minerals of the earth and the generic names of various species. There weren't too many callers for those qualifications and I had to admit that I was greatly lacking in the popular attractions of physical beauty and womanly wiles.

All my life, my body had been in successful rebellion against my finer nature. I was too tall and raw-skinny. My large extroverted teeth protruded in an excitement to be seen, and I, attempting to thwart their success, rarely smiled. Although I lathered Dixie Peach in my hair, the thick black mass crinkled and kinked and resisted the smothering pomade to burst free around my head like a cloud of angry bees. No, in support of truth, I had to admit Louise Cox was not friendly to me because of my beauty.

Maybe she offered friendship because she pitied me. The idea was a string winding at first frayed and loose, then tightening, binding into my consciousness. My spirit started at the intrusion. A white woman? Feeling sorry for me? She wouldn't dare. I would go to the store and show her. I would roll her distasteful pity into a ball and throw it in her face. I would smash her nose deep into the unasked-for sympathy until her eyes dribbled tears and she learned that I was a queen, not to be approached by peasants like her, even on bended knees, and wailing.

Louise was bent over the counter talking to a small Black boy. She didn't interrupt her conversation to acknowledge my entrance.

"Exactly how many boxes have you folded, J.C.?" Her intonation was sober.

"Eighteen." The boy's answer matched her seriousness. His head barely reached the counter top. She took a small box from a shelf behind her.

"Then here's eighteen cents." She pushed the coins around counting them, then poured them into his cupped palms.

"O.K." He turned on unsure young legs and collided with me. He mumbled "Thank you."

Louise rounded the counter, following the little voice. She ran past me and caught the door a second after he slammed it.

"J.C." She stood, arms akimbo on the sidewalk, and raised her voice. "J.C., I'll see you next Saturday." She came back into the store and looked at me.

"Hi, Marg-you-reet. Boy, am I glad to see you. Excuse that scene. I had to pay off one of my workers."

I waited for her to continue. Waited for her to tell me how precious he was and how poor and wasn't it all a shame. She went behind the counter and began slipping records into paper jackets.

"When I first opened the shop, all the neighborhood kids came in. They either demanded that I 'gi' them a penny' "—I hated whites' imitation of the Black accent—"or play records for them. I explained that the only way I'd give them anything was if they worked for it and that I'd play records for their parents, but not for them until they were tall enough to reach the turntables."

"So I let them fold empty record boxes for a penny apiece." She went on, "I'm glad to see you because I want to offer you a job."

I had done many things to make a living, but I drew the line at cleaning white folks' houses. I had tried that and lasted only one day. The waxed tables, cut flowers, closets of other people's clothes totally disoriented me. I hated the figured carpets, tiled kitchens and refrigerators filled with someone else's dinner leftovers.

"Really?" The ice in my voice turned my accent to upperclass Vivien Leigh (before *Gone With the Wind*).

"My sister has been helping me in the shop, but she's going back to school. I thought you'd be perfect to take her place."

My resolve began to knuckle under me like weak knees.

"I don't know if you know it, but I have a large clientele and try to keep in stock a supply, however small, of every record by Negro artists. And if I don't have something, there's a comprehensive catalog and I can order it. What do you think?"

Her face was open and her smile simple. I pried into her eyes for hidden meaning and found nothing. Even so, I had to show my own strength.

"I don't like to hear white folks imitate Negroes. Did the children really ask you to 'gi' them a penny'? Oh, come now."

She said, "You are right—they didn't ask. They demanded that I 'gi' them a penny.' " The smile left her face. "You say it."

"Give me a penny." My teeth pressed my bottom lip, stressing the *v*.

She reached for the box and handed me a coin. "Don't forget that you've been to school and let neither of us forget that we're both grown-up. I'd be pleased if you'd take the job." She told me the salary, the hours and what my duties would be.

"Thank you very much for the offer. I'll think about it." I left the shop, head up, back straight. I tried to exude indifference, like octopus ink, to camouflage my excitement.

I had to talk to Ivonne Broadnax, the Realist. She was my closest friend. Ivonne had escaped the hindrance of romantic blindness, which was my lifelong affliction. She had the clear, clean eyes of a born survivor. I went to her Ellis Street house, where she, at twenty-five, was bringing up an eight-year-old daughter and a fifteen-year-old sister.

"Vonne, you know that woman that runs the record store?"

"That short white woman with the crooked smile?" Her voice was small and keen and the sound had to force itself past white, even teeth.

"Yes."

"Why?"

"She offered me a job."

"Doing what?" I knew I could count on her cynicism.

"Salesgirl."

"Why?"

"That's what I've been trying to figure out. Why? And why me?"

Ivonne sat very still, thinking. She possessed a great beauty which she carried nonchalantly. Her cupid's-bow lips pursed, and when she raised her head her face was flushed pink and cream from the racing blood.

"Is she funny that way?"

We both knew that was the only logical explanation.

"No. I'm sure that she's not."

Ivonne bent her head again. She raised it and looked at me.

"Did you ask her?"

"No."

"I mean did you ask her for the job?"

"No. She offered it." I added just a little indignation to my answer.

Ivonne said, "You know white people are strange. I don't even know if they know why they do things." Ivonne had grown up in a small Mississippi town, and I, in a smaller town in Arkansas. Whites were as constant in our history as the seasons and as unfamiliar as affluence.

"Maybe she's trying to prove something." She waited. "What kind of pay she offering?"

"Enough so I can quit both jobs and bring the baby home."

"Well, take it."

"I'll have to order records and take inventories and all that." The odor of an improvement in my life had barely touched my nostrils and it made me jittery.

"Come on, Maya" (she called me by the family name). "If you could run a hook shop, you can run a record shop."

Once when I was eighteen in San Diego I had managed a house of prostitution, where two qualified workers entertained and I, as financial backer, took a percentage. I had since layered that experience over and over in my mind with forgiveness and a conscious affectation of innocence. But it was true, I did have a certain talent for administration.

"Tell her you'll take the job and then watch her like a hawk. You know white women. They pull off their drawers, lay down first, then scream rape. If you're not careful, she'll get weak and faint on you, then before you know it you'll be washing windows, and scrubbing the floor." We cackled like two old crones, remembering a secret past. The laughter was sour and not really directed at white women. It was a traditional ruse that was used to shield the Black vulnerability; we laughed to keep from crying.

I took the job, but kept Louise under constant surveillance. None of her actions went unheeded, no conversation unrecorded. The question was not if she would divulge her racism but when and how the revelation would occur. For a few months I was a character in a living thriller plot. I listened to her intonations and trailed her glances.

On Sundays, when the older people came in after church services to listen to the Reverend Joe May's sermons on 78 rpm records, I trembled with the chase's excitement. Large, corseted women gathered around the record players, their bosoms bloated with religious fervor, while their dark-suited husbands leaned into the music, faces blank in surrender to the spirit, their black and brown fingers restive on clutched Bibles.

Louise offered folding chairs to the ladies and moved back behind the counter to her books. I waited for one smirk, one roll of her eyes to the besieged heavens and I would have my evidence that she thought her whiteness was a superior quality which she and God had contrived for their own convenience.

After two months, vigilance had exhausted me and I had found no thread of prejudice. I began to relax and enjoy the wealth of a world of music. Early mornings were given over to Bartok and Schoenberg. Midmorning I treated myself to the vocals of Billy Eckstine, Billie Holiday, Nat Cole, Louis Jordan and Bull Moose Jackson. A piroshki from the Russian delicatessen next door was lunch and then the giants of bebop flipped through the air. Charlie Parker and Max Roach, Dizzy Gillespie, Sarah Vaughan and Al Haig and Howard McGhee. Blues belonged to late afternoons and the singers' lyrics of lost love spoke to my solitude.

I ordered stock and played records on request, emptied ashtrays and dusted the windows' cardboard displays. Louise and her partner, David Rosenbaum, showed their pleasure by giving me a raise, and although I was grateful to them for the job and my first introduction to an amiable black-white relationship, I could exhibit my feelings only by being punctual in coming to the shop and being efficient at work and coolly, grayly respectful.

At home, however, life shimmered with beautiful colors. I picked up my son from the baby-sitter's every evening. He was five years old and so beautiful his smile could break the back of a brute.

For two years we had spun like water spiders in a relentless eddy. I had to be free to work for our support, but the baby-sitters were so expensive I had to have two jobs to pay their fees and my own rent. I boarded him out six days and five nights a week.

On the eve of my day off, I would go to the baby-sitter's house. First he'd grab the hem of my dress, then wrap his arms around my legs and hold on screaming as I paid the weekly bill. I would pry his arms loose, then pick him up and walk down the street. For blocks, as I walked, he would scream. When we were far enough away, he'd relax his strangle hold on my neck and I could put him down. We'd spend the evening in my room. He followed my every turn and didn't trust me to go to the bathroom and return. After dinner, cooked in the communal kitchen, I would read to him and allow him to try to read to me.

The next day was always spent at the park, the zoo, the San Francisco Museum of Art, a cartoon movie house or any cheap or free place of entertainment. Then, on our second evening he would fight sleep like an old person fighting death. By morning, not quite awake, he would jerk and make hurtful noises like a wounded animal. I would still my heart and wake him. When he was dressed, we headed back to the sitter's house. He would begin to cry a few blocks from our destination. My own tears stayed in check until his screams stabbed from behind the closed doors and stuck like spearheads in my heart.

The regularity of misery did nothing to lessen it. I examined alternatives. If I were married, "my husband" (the words sounded as unreal as "my bank account") would set me up in a fine house, which my good taste would develop into a home. My son and I could spend whole days together and then I could have two more children who would be named Deirdre and Craig, and I would grow roses and beautiful zinnias. I would wear too-large gardening gloves so that when I removed them my hands would look dainty and my manicure fresh. We would all play chess and Chinese checkers and twenty questions and whist. We would be a large, loving, hilarious family like the people in *Cheaper by the Dozen*.

Or I could go on welfare.

There wasn't a shadow of a husband-caliber man on my horizon. Indeed, no men at all seemed attracted to me. Possibly my façade of cool control turned them away or just possibly my need, which I thought well disguised, was so obvious that it frightened them. No, husbands were rarer than common garden variety unicorns.

And welfare was absolutely forbidden. My pride had been starched by a family who assumed unlimited authority in its own affairs. A grandmother, who raised me, my brother and her own two sons, owned a general merchandise store. She had begun her business in the early 1900's in Stamps, Arkansas, by selling meat pies to saw men in a lumber mill, then racing across town in time to feed workers in a cotton-gin mill four miles away.

My brother, Bailey, who was a year older than I and seven inches shorter, had drummed in my youthful years: "You are as intelligent as I am"—we both agreed that he was a genius—"and beautiful. And you can do anything."

My beautiful mother, who ran businesses and men with autocratic power, taught me to row my own boat, paddle my own canoe, hoist my own sail. She warned, in fact, "If you want something done, do it yourself."

I hadn't asked them for help (I couldn't risk their refusal) and they loved me. There was no motive on earth which would bring me, bowed, to beg for aid from an institution which scorned me and a government which ignored me. It had seemed that I would be locked in the two jobs and the weekly baby-sitter terror until my life was done.

Now with a good salary, my son and I could move back into my mother's house.

A smile struck her face like lightning when I told her I had retrieved my son and we were ready to come home. There was a glaze over her eyes. It was unnerving. My mother was anything, everything, but sentimental. I admired how quickly she pulled her old self back in charge. Typically she asked only direct questions.

"How long will you all stay this time?"

"Until I can get a house for us."

"That sounds good. Your room is pretty much as you left it and Clyde can have the little room in back."

I decided that a little bragging was in order. "I've been working at the record shop on Fillmore and the people down there gave me a raise. I'll pay rent to you and help with the food."

"How much are they paying you?"

When I told her, she quickly worked out a percentage. "O.K. You pay me that amount and buy a portion of food every week."

I handed her some cash. She counted it carefully. "All right, this is a month's rent. I'll remember."

She handed the money back to me. "Take this downtown and buy yourself some clothes."

I hesitated.

"This is a gift, not a loan. You should know I don't do business slipshod."

To Vivian Baxter business was business, and I was her daughter; one thing did not influence the other.

"You know that I'm no baby-sitter, but Poppa Ford is still with me looking after the house. He can keep an eye on Clyde. Of course you ought to give him a little something every week. Not as much as you pay the baby-sitters, but something. Remember, you may not always get what you pay for, but you will definitely pay for what you get."

"Yes, Mother." I was home.

For months life was a pleasure ring and we walked safely inside its perimeter. My son was in school, reading very well, and encouraged by me, drifting into a love affair with books. He was healthy. The old fears that I would leave him were dissolving. I read Thorne Smith to him and recited Paul Laurence Dunbar's poems in a thick Black Southern accent.

On an evening walk along Fillmore, Clyde and I heard loud shouting and saw a group of people crowded around a man on the corner across the street. We stopped where we were to listen.

"Lord, we your children. We come to you just like newborn babies. Silver and gold have we none. But O Lord!"

Clyde grabbed my hand and started to pull me in the opposite direction.

"Come on, Mom. Come on."

I bent down to him. "Why?"

"That man is crazy." Distaste wrinkled his little face.

"Why do you say that?"

"Because he's shouting in the street like that."

I stooped to my son giving no attention to the passers-by. "That's one of the ways people praise God. Some praise in church, some in the streets and some in their hearts."

"But Mom, is there really a God? And what does He do all the time?"

The question deserved a better answer than I could think of in the middle of the street. I said, "We'll talk about that later, but now let's go over and listen. Think of the sermon as a poem and the singing as great music."

He came along and I worked my way through the crowd so he could have a clear view. The antics of the preacher and the crowd's responses embarrassed him. I was stunned. I had grown up in a Christian Methodist Episcopal Church where my uncle was superintendent of Sunday School, and my grandmother was Mother of the Church. Until I was thirteen and left Arkansas for California, each Sunday I spent a minimum of six hours in church. Monday evenings Momma took me to Usher Board Meeting; Tuesdays the Mothers of the Church met; Wednesday was for prayer meeting; Thursday, the Deacons congregated; Fridays and Saturdays were spent in preparation for Sunday. And my son asked me if there was a God. To whom had I been praying all my life?

That night I taught him "Joshua Fit the Battle of Jericho."

CHAPTER 2

My life was an assemblage of strivings and my energies were directed toward acquiring more than the basic needs. I was as much a part of the acquisitive, security-conscious fifties as the quiet young white girls who lived their pastel Peter Pan–collared days in clean, middle-class neighborhoods. In the Black communities, girls, whose clothes struck with gay colors and whose laughter crinkled the air, flashed streetwise smirks and longed for one picket fence. We startled with our overt flirtations and dreamed of being "one man's woman." We found ourselves too often unmarried, bearing lonely pregnancies and wishing for two and a half children each who would gurgle happily behind that picket fence while we drove our men to work in our friendly-looking station wagons.

I had loved one man and dramatized my losing him with all the exaggerated wailing of a wronged seventeen-year-old. I had wanted others in a ferocious desperation, believing that marriage would give me a world free from danger, disease and want.

In the record store, I lived fantasy lives through the maudlin melodies of the forties and fifties.

"You'd be so nice to come home to."

Whoever you were.

"I'm walking by the river
'cause I'm meeting someone there tonight."

Anyone—that is, anyone taller than I and who wanted to get married. To me. Billy Eckstine sang,

> "Our little dream castle with everything gone
> Is lonely and silent, the shades are all drawn
> My heart is heavy as I gaze upon
> A cottage for sale."

That was my house and it was vacant. If Mr. Right would come along right now, soon we could move in and truly begin to live.

———

Louise Cox and her mother were practicing Christian Scientists. I accepted an invitation to visit their church. The interior's severity, the mass of quiet, well-dressed whites and the lack of emotion unsettled me. I took particular notice of the few Blacks in the congregation. They appeared as soberly affluent and emotionally reserved as their fellow white parishioners. I had known churches to be temples where one made "a joyful noise unto the Lord" and quite a lot of it.

In the First Church of Christ, Scientist, the congregation wordlessly praised the Almighty. No stamping of feet or clapping of hands accompanied the worship. For the whole service, time seemed suspended and reality was just beyond the simple and expensive heavy doors.

———

"Did you like it?"

We sat in Louise's kitchen, eating her mother's homemade-from-scratch biscuits.

"I don't know. I didn't understand it."

After a year of relentless observation, I trusted her to think me unexposed, rather than ignorant.

Her mother gave me a copy of Mary Baker Eddy's *Science and Health*. I began to wrestle with new concepts.

The tough texture of poverty in my life had been more real than sand wedged between my teeth, yet Mary Baker Eddy encouraged me to think myself prosperous. Every evening I went home to a fourteen-room house where my son and seventy-five-year-old Poppa Ford awaited my arrival. Mother usually was out dining with friends, drinking with acquaintances or gambling with strangers. Had she been there, her presence would not have greatly diminished my loneliness. My brother, who had been my ally, my first friend, had left home and closed himself to me. We had found safety in numbers when we were young, but adulthood had severed the bonds and we drifted apart over deep and dangerous seas, unanchored.

In Mother's house, after dinner, I would read my son to sleep and return to the kitchen. Most often, the old man dreamt over an outsized cup of heavily sugared coffee. I would watch his aged ivory face, wrinkled under ghostly memories, then go to my room where solitude gaped whale-jawed wide to swallow me entire.

Science and Health told me I was never alone. "There is no place God is not." But I couldn't make the affirmation real for me.

———

The sailor wandered around the store. He was reading the bulletins and scanning the posters. His dark hair and oval, sensual face reminded me of Italian Renaissance paintings. It was strange to see a white military man in the Black area in broad daylight. I decided that he had gotten lost. He walked to the counter.

"Good morning."

"Have you got 'Cheers'?"

Maybe he wasn't lost, just found himself in our neighborhood and decided to buy some records. "Cheers"? I thought of all the white singers—Jo Stafford, Helen O'Connell, Margaret Whiting, Dinah Shore, Frank Sinatra, Bob Crosby, Bing Crosby and Bob Eberle. Tex Beneke. None had recorded a song entitled "Cheers." I ran my mind over Anita O'Day, Mel Tormé, June Christy. No "Cheers" there. He had looked like a vocal man, but then maybe he was looking for a white Big Band instrumental. Stan Kenton, Neal Hefti, Billy May. No "Cheers" in their catalogs.

"I don't know if we have it. Who cut it?" I smiled. "Cut it" showed that I was so much a part of the record business that I wouldn't say "Who recorded it?"

The man looked at me and said dryly, "Charlie Parker."

Although I lived in a large city, in truth I lived in a small town within that city's preserves. The few whites I knew who were aware of Charlie Parker were my brother's friends and were wrapped away from me in a worldly remoteness. I stumbled to get the record. When I shucked the jacket off he said, "You don't have to play it." He went on, "I'll take 'Well You Needn't' by Thelonius Monk and 'Night in Tunisia' by Dizzy Gillespie."

My brain didn't want to accept the burden of my ears. Was that a white man talking? I looked to see if maybe he was a Creole. Many Negroes from the bayou country could and did pass for white. They, too, had hank-straight black hair, dark eyes and shell-cream skin.

There was nothing like a straight question: "Are you from Louisiana?"

"No, I'm from Portland."

There is a textured grain that colors the Black voice which was missing when he spoke. I wrapped his selections and he paid for them and left. I wondered that he had been neither amiable nor rude and that he didn't remind me of anyone I'd ever met.

My two employers and Louise's handsome friend, Fred E. Pierson, cabdriver and painter, were the only whites I knew, liked and partially understood. When I met Fred, his friendliness had caused my old survival apparatus to begin meshing its gears. I suspected him (perhaps hopefully) of being personally (which meant romantically) interested in me. He helped me to paint the seven downstairs rooms at Mother's house and told me of his great and sad and lost love affair and that he liked having me for a friend.

The next weekend the sailor returned. He browsed for a while, then came to the counter and interrupted my preoccupation with papers.

"Hi."

I looked up as if startled. "Hello."

"Have you any Dexter Gordon?"

"Yes, 'Dexter's Blues'." Another Negro musician.

"I'll take that."

I asked, "How about a Dave Brubeck?"

"No. Thanks, anyway." Brubeck was white. "But anything by Prez? Do you have 'Lester Leaps In'?"

"Yes."

He waited. "Do you know of any jam sessions around here?"

"Oh, you're a musician." That would explain it. Members from the large white jazz orchestras visited Black after-hours joints. They would ask to sit in on the jam sessions. Black musicians often refused, saying, "The white boys come, smoke up all the pot, steal the chord changes, then go back to their good paying jobs and keep us Black musicians out of the union."

He said, "No, I just like jazz. My name is Tosh. What's yours?"

"Marguerite. What kind of name is Tosh?"

"It's Greek for Thomas—Enistasious. The short of it is Tosh. Are there any good jazz clubs here? Any place to meet some groovy people?"

There was Jimbo's, a blue-lighted basement where people moved in the slow-motion air like denizens of a large aquarium, floating effortlessly in their own element.

Ivonne and I went to the night spot as often as possible. She would take money from her catering business and I from my savings; we would put on our finest clothes, and hiding behind dignified façades, enter the always crowded room. Unfortunately, our attitudes were counterproductive. We projected ourselves as coolly indifferent and distant, but the blatant truth was we were out to find any handsome, single, intelligent, interested men.

I told Tosh I didn't know of any places like that in my neighborhood. When he left the store, I was certain he'd find his way to the downtown area, where he would be more welcome.

Louise continued encouraging me toward Christian Science. I gingerly poked into its precepts, unwilling to immerse myself in the depths because, after all, Christian Science was an intellectual religion and the God its members worshiped seemed to me all broth and no bones. The God of my childhood was an old, white, Vandyck-bearded Father Time, who roared up thunder, then puffed out His cheeks and blew down hurricanes on His errant children. He could be placated only if one fell prostrate, groveled and begged for mercy. I didn't like that God, but He did seem more real than a Maker who was just thought and spirit. I wished for a Someone in between.

Louise's partner was Jewish, so I spoke to him of my need and asked him about Judaism. He smiled until he sensed my seriousness, then said he attended Beth Emanu-El. He told me that there was a new rabbi who was very young and extremely modern. A Black singer had recorded "Eli Eli" and I listened to the song carefully. The beautiful high melodies and the low moaning sounded very close to the hymns of my youth. It was just possible that Judaism was going to answer my need. The Torah couldn't be as foreign as *Science and Health.*

For hundreds of years, the Black American slaves had seen the parallels between their oppression and that of the Jews in Biblical times.

> Go down Moses
> Way down in Egypt land
> Tell old Pharaoh
> To let my people go.

The Prophets of Israel inhabited our songs:

> Didn't my Lord deliver Daniel?
> Then why not every man?
>
> Ezekiel saw the wheel, up in the middle of the air.
>
> Little David play on your harp.

The Hebrew children in the fiery furnace elicited constant sympathy from the Black community because our American experience mirrored their ancient tribulation. With that familiarity, I figured Judaism was going to be a snap!

Beth Emanu-El looked like a Tyrone Power movie set. Great arches of salmon-pink rose over a Moorish courtyard. Well-dressed children scuttled from shul and down the wide stairs.

I explained to a receptionist that I wanted to speak to Rabbi Fine.

"Why?" Her question really was, What are you doing within my hallowed halls? She repeated, "Why?"

"I want to talk to him about Judaism."

She picked up the phone and spoke urgently.

"This way." Stiff-legged and stiff-backed, she guided me to the end of a hall. Her gaze rested on me for a still second before she opened the door.

Rabbi Alvin I. Fine looked like a young physical education teacher dressed up for an open house at school. I had thought all rabbis had to be old and bearded, just as all priests were Irish, collared and composites of Bing Crosby and Barry Fitzgerald. He invited me in and offered a seat.

"You want to discuss Judaism?" There wasn't a hint of a snicker in his voice. He could have been asking a question of a fellow rabbi. I liked him.

"I don't know anything about it, so I can't discuss it."

"Do you want to become a Jew?"

"I don't know. I'd just like to read up on your faith, but I don't know the titles of any books."

"What is the faith of your fathers?"

"Methodist."

"And what is it not giving you that you think Judaism would provide?"

"I don't know what Judaism's got."

"Can you say you have applied yourself to a careful study of the Methodist tenets?"

"No."

"Would you say you have totally applied the dictates of the Methodist church?"

"No."

"But you want to study Judaism, an ancient faith of a foreign people?"

He was systematically driving me to defense. If he wanted debate, I'd give him debate.

I said, "I want to read about it, I didn't say I wanted to join your church. I like the music in the C.M.E. Church and I like the praying, but I don't like the idea of a God so frightening that I'd be afraid to meet Him."

"Why does your God frighten you?"

It would sound too childish to say that when my minister threatened fire and brimstone, I could smell my flesh frying and see my skin as crisp as pork cracklings. I told him a less personal truth. "Because I'm afraid to die."

I expected the bromide: If a person lived a good life free of sin, he or she can die easy.

Rabbi Fine said, "Judaism will not save you from death. Visit a Jewish cemetery."

I looked at him and felt the full force of my silliness in being there.

He said, "I'll give you a list of books. Read them. Think about them. Argue with the writers and the ideas, then come back to see me." He bent over his desk to write. I knew I would enjoy talking with him about Life, Love, Hate and mostly Death. He gave me the paper and smiled for the first time and looked even more boyish. I thanked him and left, certain that we would continue our discussion soon. I took a year to buy or borrow and read the books, but twenty years were to pass before I would see Rabbi Fine again.

CHAPTER 3

Tosh became such a regular in the store that his arrivals raised no eyebrows and Black customers even began saying hello to him, although he only nodded a response. He had been discharged from the Navy and found a job in an electrical appliance shop. He had taken a room in the Negro neighborhood and came to the record store every day. We talked long over the spinning records. He said he liked to talk to me because I didn't lie.

I asked how he had come to like Black people so much.

"I don't like Black people," he said, dead serious. "And I don't like Italians or Jews or Irish or Orientals. I'm Greek and I don't like them either."

I thought he was crazy. It was one thing to be introverted, but another to admit to me that he disliked Black people.

"Why do you dislike people?"

"I didn't say I disliked people. Not to like people isn't the same as to dislike them."

He sounded profound and I needed time to mull over that idea.

I asked if he liked children. He said he liked some children.

I told him about my son, how bright he was and pretty and funny and sweet.

"Does he play baseball?"

I hadn't thought about the physical games Clyde could share with a father. A new world appeared with the question. In my next castle-building session, I would dream about a husband who would take our sons to the park to play baseball, football, basketball and tennis, while our daughter and I made cookies and other refreshments ready for their return.

"No, he doesn't play ball yet."

"Let's go to the park on your day off. I'll teach him what I know."

I had not really examined Tosh before. He had thick black hair and the slow, sloe eyes of Mediterranean people. His face was gentle and had an air of privacy. He was handsome, but he fell some distance from the mark I had set for a husband. He was two inches shorter than I and White. My own husband was going to come handsome, six feet three inches and Black. I snatched myself away from the vague reflection and set a date for the three of us to go to Golden Gate Park.

My son and Tosh liked each other. They played handball, and after a picnic lunch, Tosh took a portable set from a package and began to teach my son chess. The day ended at my house, where I introduced Tosh to my mother. She was hospitable, just.

"How did you come to meet Maya? Where are you from?" and "When are you going back?" Tosh held his own before that whirlwind of a woman. He looked directly at her, ignored the implied queries, answering only what he was asked outright. When he left, Mother asked me my intentions.

"He's just a friend."

She said, "Well, remember that white folks have taken advantage of Black people for centuries."

I reminded her: "You know a lot of white people. There's Aunt Linda and Aunt Josie and Uncle Blackie. Those are your friends. And Bailey has those friends Harry and Paul, the table tennis expert."

"That's what I'm saying to you. They are friends. And that's all. There's a world of difference between laughing together and loving together."

A few days later I agreed to allow Tosh to take Clyde out alone. They came to the store as I was leaving and Clyde was full of his afternoon.

"We rode on the cable cars and went to Fisherman's Wharf. I'm going to be a ship's captain or a cable car conductor." His eyes jumped like targets in a game of marbles. "Mr. Angelos is going to take me to the zoo next week. I'm going to feed the animals. I might become a lion tamer." He examined my face and added, "He said I could."

Although Tosh had said nothing romantic to me, I realized that through my son he was courting me as surely as Abelard courted Héloïse. I couldn't let him know I knew. The knowledge had to remain inside me, unrevealed, or I would have to make a decision, and that decision had been made for me by the centuries of slavery, the violation of my people, the violence of whites. Anger and guilt decided before my birth that Black was Black and White was White and although the two might share sex, they must never exchange love. But the true nature of the human heart is as whimsical as spring weather. All signals may aim toward a fall of rain when suddenly the skies will clear.

Tosh grew up in a Greek community, where even Italians were considered foreign. His contact with Blacks had been restricted to the Negro sailors on his base and the music of the bebop originators.

I would never forget the slavery tales, or my Southern past, where all whites, including the poor and ignorant, had the right to speak rudely to and even physically abuse any Negro they met. I knew the ugliness of white prejudice. Obviously there was no common ground on which Tosh and I might meet.

I began to await his visits to the shop with an eagerness held in close control. We went to parks, the beach and dinners together. He loved W.C. Fields and adored Mae West, and the three of us howled our laughter into the quiet dark air of art movie houses.

One night, after I had put my son to bed, we sat having coffee in the large kitchen. He asked me if I could read fortunes and put his hand in mine.

I said, "Of course, you are going to be a great musician and be very wealthy and live a long, rich life." I laid his hand on the table, palm open.

He asked, "Do you see where I'm going to be married?"

I was thrust through with disappointment. While I hadn't ever seen him in the "my husband" role, his attention had been a balm for my loneliness. Now he was saying he was planning marriage. Some childhood sweetheart would arrive on the scene. I would be expected to be kind to her, and gracious.

I looked at the shadowy lines in his hand and spitefully said, "Your love line is very faint. I don't see a happy marriage in your future."

He caught my hand and squeezed it. "I am going to be married, and I'm going to marry you."

The sounds refused to come together and convey meaning. I am going to marry you. He had to be talking about me, since he was addressing me, yet the two words "you" and "marry" had never been said to me before.

Even after I accepted the content of his statement, I found nothing to say.

———

"A white man? A poor white man? How can you even consider it?" Disbelief struggled across her face. My mother's diamond winked at me as her hand flew about in the air. "A white man without a pot to piss in or a window to throw it out."

She was famous for temperamental explosions but she had never been angry enough at me to hurl her full thunderbolt of rage. Now, when I told her of Tosh's proposal, she was accelerating from an "ing bing" (her phrase for a minor riot) to a full-out tantrum. With alarming speed her pretty butter-colored face became tight and reddened.

"Think of your life. You're young. What's going to happen to you?"

I hoped not much more than had happened already. At three years old I had been sent by train from California to Arkansas, accompanied only by my four year-old brother; raped at seven and returned to California at thirteen. My son was born when I was sixteen, and determined to raise him, I had worked as a shake dancer in night clubs, fry cook in hamburger joints, dinner cook in a Creole restaurant and once had a job in a mechanic's shop, taking the paint off cars with my hands.

"Think ahead. What the hell is he bringing you? The contempt of his people and the distrust of your own. That's a hell of a wedding gift."

And, of course, I was bringing him a mind crammed with a volatile mixture of insecurities and stubbornness, and a five-year-old son who had never known a father's discipline.

"Do you love him? I admit I'd find that hard to believe. But then I know love goes where it's sent, even in a dog's behind. Do you love him? Answer me."

I didn't answer.

"Then tell me why. Just why are you going to marry him?"

I knew Vivian Baxter appreciated honesty above all other virtues. I told her, "Because he asked me, Mother."

She looked at me until her eyes softened and her lips relaxed. She nodded, "All right. All right." She turned on her high heels and strutted up the hall to her bedroom.

———

Bailey came to the house at my invitation. He sat in the kitchen with Tosh as I made an evening meal. They spoke about jazz musicians and the literary virtues of Philip Wylie and Aldous Huxley. Tosh had studied literature at Reed College in Oregon and Bailey had dropped out of high school in the eleventh grade. My brother had continued to read, however, spending his days on the Southern Pacific run waiting table in the dining cars and his nights with Thomas Wolfe, Huxley and Wylie. After dinner, Bailey wished Tosh a good night and asked to speak to me. We stood in the dim doorway.

"You invited me over for something more than dinner, didn't you?"
I had never been successful in keeping anything from Bailey.
"I guess so."
"He's in love with you. Did you know that?"
I said he hadn't told me.
Bailey leaned against the door; his dark, round face in the shadow was broken open by a white smile. "A smart man only tells half of what he thinks. He's a nice cat, Maya."
Bailey had been my protector, guide and guard since we were tots, and I knew, despite the disparity in our sizes, that he would remain my big brother as long as we lived.
"Bail, do you think it's all right if I marry him?"
"Did he ask you?"
"Yes."
"Do you want to?"
"Yes."
"What are you waiting for?"
"People will talk about me."
"Marry him, Maya. Be happy and prove them all fools and liars."
He gave me a typically sloppy Bailey kiss on the cheek and left.

———

Tosh and I were married in the Courthouse on a clear Monday morning. To show her displeasure, Mother moved her fourteen rooms of furniture to Los Angeles three days before the ceremony.

We rented a large flat, and on Tosh's orders I quit my job. At last I was a housewife, legally a member of that enviable tribe of consumers whom security made fat as butter and who under no circumstances considered living by bread alone, because their husbands brought home the bacon. I had a son, a father for him, a husband and a pretty home for us to live in. My life began to resemble a *Good Housekeeping* advertisement. I cooked well-balanced meals and molded fabulous jello desserts. My floors were dangerous with daily applications of wax and our furniture slick with polish.

Clyde was sprouting with independence and opinions. Tosh told him often and with feeling that he was absolutely the most intelligent child in the world. Clyde began calling Tosh "Daddy," although I had concocted and given him a dramatic tale during his younger years. The story told how his own father had died on the sands of some Pacific island fighting for his life and his country. I would cry at the telling of the fiction, wishing so hard it had been true.

Tosh was a better husband than I had dared to dream. He was intelligent, kind and reliable. He told me I was beautiful (I decided that he was blinded by my color) and a brilliant conversationalist. Conversation was easy. He brought flowers for me and held my hand in the living room. My cooking received his highest praise and he laughed at my wit.

Our home life was an Eden of constant spring, but Tosh was certain the serpent lay coiled just beyond our gate. Only two former Navy friends (white), one jazz pianist (Black) and Ivonne were allowed to visit our domestic paradise. He explained that the people I liked or had known or thought I liked were all stupid and beneath me. Those I might meet, if allowed to venture out alone, beyond our catacomb, couldn't be trusted. Clyde was the brightest, most winning boy in the world, but his friends weren't welcome in our house because they were not worthy of his time. We had tickets to silent movies and the early talkies, and on some Sundays, took our trash to the town dump. I came to love Tosh because he wrapped us in a cocoon of safety, and I made no protest at the bonds that were closing around my existence.

———

After a year, I saw the first evidence of a reptilian presence in my garden. Tosh told Clyde that there was no God. When I contradicted him, he asked me to prove His presence. I countered that we could not discuss an Entity which didn't exist. He had been a debater at his university and told me that he could have argued either side with the same power; however, he knew for a fact there was no God, so I should surrender the discussion.

I knew I was a child of a God who existed but also the wife of a husband who was angered at my belief. I surrendered.

I tucked away the memory of my great-grandmother (who had been a slave), who told me of praying silently under old wash pots, and of secret meetings deep in the woods to praise God ("For where two or three are gathered together in my name, there am I in the midst of them"). Her owner wouldn't allow his Negroes to worship God (it might give them ideas) and they did so on pain of being lashed.

I planned a secret crawl through neighborhood churches. First I took a nice dress to Ivonne's house and left it, explaining my intent. Then, on at least one Sunday a month, I would prepare a good breakfast for my family and an equally good lie in order to get out of the house. Leaving Clyde at home (he hadn't the experience to lie), I would hurry to Ivonne's, put on the Sunday dress and rush to church. I changed sites each month, afraid that too many repeated visits would familiarize my face and that on some promenade with Tosh I would be stopped by a church member and possibly asked about last week's sermon.

The spirituals and gospel songs were sweeter than sugar. I wanted to keep my mouth full of them and the sounds of my people singing fell like sweet oil in my ears. When the polyrhythmic hand-clapping began and the feet started tapping, when one old lady in a corner raised her voice to scream "O Lord, Lordy Jesus," I could hardly keep my seat. The ceremony drove into my body, to my fingers, toes, neck and thighs. My extremities shook under the emotional possession. I imposed my will on their quivering and kept them fairly still. I was terrified that once loose, once I lifted or lost my control, I would rise from my seat and dance like a puppet, up and down the aisles. I would open my mouth, and screams, shouts and field hollers would tear out my tongue in their rush to be free.

I was elated that I could wallow in the ceremonies and never forsake control. After each service I would join the church, adding my maiden name to the roster in an attempt to repay the preacher and parishioners for the joyful experience. On the street I felt cleansed, purged and new. Then I would hurry to Ivonne's, change clothes and go back to my own clean house and pretty, though ungodly, family.

After watching the multicolored people in church dressed in their gay Sunday finery and praising their Maker with loud voices and sensual movements, Tosh and my house looked very pale. Van Gogh and Klee posters which would please me a day later seemed irrelevant. The scatter rugs, placed so artfully the day before, appeared pretentious. For the first few hours at home I kept as tight a check on my thoughts as I had held over my body in church. By the evening meal, I was ready again for cerebral exercises and intellectual exchange.

CHAPTER 4

During the first year of marriage I was so enchanted with security and living with a person whose color or lack of it could startle me on an early-morning waking, and I was so busy keeping a spotless house, teaching myself to cook and serve gourmet meals and managing a happy, rambunctious growing boy that I had little time to notice public reactions to us. Awareness gradually grew in my mind that people stared, nudged each other and frowned when we three walked in the parks or went to the movies. The distaste on their faces called me back to a history of discrimination and murders of every type. Tosh, I told myself, was Greek, not white American; therefore I needn't feel I had betrayed my race by marrying one of the enemy, nor could white Americans believe that I had so forgiven them the past that I was ready to love a member of their tribe. I never admitted that I made the same kind of rationalization about all the other non-Blacks I liked. Louise was white American (but she was a woman). David was white (but he was Jewish). Jack Simpson, Tosh's only friend, was plain white (but he was young and shy). I stared back hard at whites in the street trying to scrape the look of effrontery off their cruel faces. But I dropped my eyes when we met Negroes. I couldn't explain to all of them that my husband had not been a part of our degradation. I fought against the guilt which was slipping into my closed life as insidiously as gas escaping into a sealed room.

I clung to Tosh, surrendering more of my territory, my independence. I would ignore the straightness of his hair which worried my fingers. I would be an obedient, dutiful wife, restricting our arguments to semantic differences, never contradicting the substance of his views.

Clyde stood flinching as I combed his thick snarled hair. His face was screwed into a frown.

"Mom—ouch—when am I going to grow up—ouch—and have good hair like Dad's?"

The mixed marriage bludgeoned home. My son thought that the whites' straight hair was better than his natural abundant curls.

"You are going to have hair like mine. Isn't that good?" I counted on his love to keep him loyal.

"It's good for you, but mine hurts. I don't like hurting hair."

I promised to have the barber give him a close cut on our next visit and told him how beautiful and rich he looked with his own hair. He looked at me, half disbelieving, so I told him about a little African prince named Hannibal, who had hair just like his. I felt a dislike for Tosh's hair because of my son's envy.

I began scheming. There was only one way I could keep my marriage balanced and make my son have a healthy respect for his own looks and race: I had to devote all my time and intelligence to my family. I needed to become a historian, sociologist and anthropologist. I would begin a self-improvement course at the main library. Just one last church visit, then I would totally dedicate myself to Tosh and Clyde and we would all be happy.

———

The Evening Star Baptist Church was crowded when I arrived and the service had begun. The members were rousing a song, urging the music to soar beyond all physical boundaries.

> "I want to be ready
> I want to be ready
> I want to be ready
> To walk in Jerusalem, just like John."

Over and over again the melodies lifted, pushed up by the clapping hands, kept aloft by the shaking shoulders. Then the minister stepped out away from the altar to stand at the lip of the dais. He was tall and ponderous as befitted a person heavy with the word of God.

"The bones were dry." The simple statement sped through my mind. "Dry Bones in the Valley" was my favorite sermon. The song that whites had come to use in mimicry of the Negro accent, "Dem Bones" was inspired by that particular portion of the Old Testament. Their ridicule—"De toe bone connected to de foot bone, foot bone connected to de ankle bone, ankle bone connected to de..."—in no way diminished my reverence for the sermon. I knew of no teaching more positive than the legend which said that will and faith caused a dismembered skeleton, dry on the desert floor, to knit back together and walk. I also knew that that sermon, properly preached, could turn me into a shouting, spinning dervish. I tried for the first few minutes to rise and leave the church, but the preacher swung his head to look at me each time I poised myself to leave. I sat again. He told the story simply at first, weaving a quiet web around us all, binding us into the wonder of faith and the power of God. His rhythm accelerated and his volume increased slowly, so slowly he caught me off guard. I had sat safe in my own authority in so many churches and waited cautiously for the point in the service when the ignition would be sparked, when "the saints" would be fired with the spirit and jump in the aisles, dancing and shaking and shouting their salvation. I had always resisted becoming a part of that enchanted band.

The minister's voice boomed, "These bones shall walk. I say these bones shall walk again."

I found myself in the aisle and my feet were going crazy under me—slithering and snapping like two turtles shot with electricity. The choir was singing "You brought my feet out the mire and clay and you saved my soul one day." I loved that song and the preacher's voice over it measured my steps. There was no turning back. I gave myself to the spirit and danced my way to the pulpit. Two ushers held me in gloved hands as the sermon fell in volume and intensity around the room.

"I am opening the doors of the Church. Let him come who will be saved." He paused as I trembled before him.

"Jesus is waiting." He looked at me. "Won't somebody come?"

I was within arm's reach. I nodded. He left the altar and took my hand.

"Child, what church were you formerly affiliated with?" His voice was clear over the quiet background music. I couldn't tell him I had joined the Rock of Ages Methodist Church the month before and the Lily of the Valley Baptist the month before that.

I said, "None."

He dropped my hand, turned to the congregation and said, "Brothers and sisters, the Lord has been merciful unto us today. Here is a child that has never known the Lord. A young woman trying to make her way out here in this cruel world without the help of the ever-loving Jesus." He turned to four old ladies who sat on the front row. "Mothers of the Church, won't you come? Won't you pray with her?"

The old women rose painfully, the lace handkerchiefs pinned in their hair shook. I felt very much in need of their prayers, because I was a sinner, a liar and a hedonist, using the sacred altar to indulge my sensuality. They hobbled to me and one in a scratchy voice said, "Kneel, child."

Four right hands overlapped on my head as the old women began to pray. "Lord, we come before you today, asking for a special mercy for this child."

"Amens," and "Yes, Lords" sprang around the room like bouncing balls in a cartoon sing-along.

"Out, Devil," one old lady ordered.

"She has come to you with an open heart, asking you for your special mercy."

"Out of this baby, Devil."

I thought about my white atheist husband and my son, who was following in his nonbelieving footsteps, and how I had lied even in church. I added, "Out, Devil."

The raspy voice said, "Stretch out, child, and let the Devil go. Make room for the Lord."

I lay flat on the floor as the congregation prayed for my sins. The four women commenced a crippled march around my body.

They sang,

> "Soon one morning when death comes walking in my room,
> Soon one morning when death comes walking in my room,
> Oh, my Lord,
> Oh, my Lord,
> What shall I do?"

They were singing of their own dread, of the promise of death whose cool hand was even then resting on their frail shoulders. I began to cry. I wept for their age and their pain. I cried for my people, who found sweet release from anguish and isolation for only a few hours on Sunday. For my fatherless son, who was growing up with a man who would never, could never, understand his need for manhood; for my mother, whom I admired but didn't understand; for my brother, whose disappointment with life was drawing him relentlessly into the clutches of death; and, finally, I cried for myself, long and loudly.

When the prayer was finished I stood up, and was enrolled into the church roster. I was so purified I forgot my cunning. I wrote down my real name, address and telephone number, shook hands with members, who welcomed me into their midst and left the church.

Midweek, Tosh stood before me, voice hard and face stony.

"Who the hell is Mother Bishop?"

I said I didn't know.

"And where the hell is the Evening Star Baptist Church?"

I didn't answer.

"A Mother Bishop called here from the Evening Star Baptist Church. She said Mrs. Angelos had joined their church last Sunday.

She now must pay twelve dollars for her robe, since she will be baptized in the Crystal Pool plunge next Sunday."

I said nothing.

"I told her no one who lived here was going to be baptized. Anywhere. At any time."

I made no protest, gave no confession—just stood silent. And allowed a little more of my territory to be taken away.

CHAPTER 5

The articles in the women's magazines did nothing to help explain the deterioration of my marriage. We had no infidelity; my husband was a good provider and I was a good cook. He encouraged me to resume my dance classes and I listened to him practice the saxophone without interruption. He came directly home from work each afternoon and in the evening after my son was asleep I found as much enjoyment in our marital bed as he.

The form was there, but the spirit had disappeared.

A bizarre sensation pervades a relationship of pretense. No truth seems true. A simple morning's greeting and response appear loaded with innuendo and fraught with implications.

"How are you?" Does he/she really care?

"Fine." I'm not really. I'm miserable, but I'll never tell you.

Each nicety becomes more sterile and each withdrawal more permanent.

Bacon and coffee odors mingled with the aseptic aroma of Lifebuoy soap. Wisps of escaping gas, which were as real a part of a fifty-year-old San Francisco house as the fourteen-foot-high ceilings and the cantankerous plumbing, solidified my reality. Those were natural morning mists. The sense that order was departing my life was refuted by the daily routine. My family would awaken. I would shower and head for the kitchen to begin making breakfast. Clyde would then take over the shower as Tosh read the newspaper. Tosh would shower while Clyde dressed, collected his crayons and lunch pail for school. We would all sit at breakfast together. I would force unwanted pleasantries into my face. (My mother had taught me: "If you have only one smile in you, give it to the people you love. Don't be surly at home, then go out in the street and start grinning 'Good morning' at total strangers.")

Tosh was usually quiet and amiable. Clyde gabbled about his dreams, which had to do with Roy Rogers as Jesus and Br'er Rabbit as God. We would finish breakfast in a glow of family life and they would both leave me with kisses, off to their separate excitements.

One new morning Tosh screamed from the bathroom, "Where in the hell are the goddamn dry towels?" The outburst caught me as unexpectedly as an upper cut. He knew that I kept the linen closet filled with towels folded as I had seen them photographed in the *Ladies' Home Journal.* More shocking than his forgetfulness, however, was his shouting. Anger generally rendered my husband morose and silent as a stone.

I went to the bathroom and handed him the thickest towel we owned.

"What's wrong, Tosh?"

"All the towels in here are wet. You know I hate fucking wet towels."

I didn't know because he had never told me. I went back to the kitchen, not really knowing him, either.

At breakfast, Clyde began a recounting of Roy Rogers on his horse and Red Ryder, riding on clouds up to talk to God about some rustlers in the lower forty.

Tosh turned, looking directly at him, and said, "Shut up, will you. I'd like a little fucking peace and quiet while I eat."

The statement slapped Clyde quiet; he had never been spoken to with such cold anger.

Tosh looked at me. "The eggs are like rocks. Can't you fry a decent goddamn egg? If not, I'll show you."

I was too confounded to speak. I sat, not understanding the contempt. Clyde asked to be excused from the table. I excused him and followed him to the door.

He whispered, "Is Dad mad at me?"

I picked up his belongings, saw him jacketed and told him, "No, not at you. You know grownups have a lot on their minds. Sometimes they're so busy thinking they forget their manners. It's not nice, but it happens."

He said, "I'll go back and tell him 'bye."

"No, I think you should just go on to school. He'll be in a better mood this evening."

I held the front door open.

He shouted, "'Bye, Dad."

There was no answer as I kissed him and closed the door. Fury quickened my footsteps. How could he scream at my son like that? Who the hell was he? A white-sheeted Grand Dragon of the Ku Klux Klan? I wouldn't have a white man talk to me in that tone of voice and I'd slap him with a coffeepot before he could yell at my child again. The midnight murmuring of soft words was forgotten. His gentle hands and familiar body had become in those seconds the shelter of an enemy.

He was still sitting over coffee, brooding. I went directly to the table.

"What do you mean, screaming at us that way?"

He said nothing.

"You started, first with the towels, then it was Clyde's dream. Then my cooking. Are you going crazy?"

He said, "I don't want to talk about it," still looking down into a half-filled cup of near-cold coffee.

"You sure as hell will talk about it. What have I done to you? What's the matter with you?"

He left the table and headed for the door without looking at me. I followed, raising my protest, hoping to puncture his cloak of withdrawal.

"I deserve and demand an explanation."

He held the door open and turned at last to face me. His voice was soft again and tender. "I think I'm just tired of being married." He pulled the door closed.

There is a shock that comes so quickly and strikes so deep that the blow is internalized even before the skin feels it. The strike must first reach bone marrow, then ascend slowly to the brain where the slow-poke intellect records the deed.

I went about cleaning my kitchen. Wash the dishes, sweep the floor, swipe the sputtered grease from the stove, make fresh coffee, put a fresh starched cloth on the table. Then I sat down. A sense of loss suffused me until I was suffocating within the vapors.

What had I done? I had placed my life within the confines of my marriage. I was everything the magazines said a wife should be. Constant, faithful and clean. I was economical. I was compliant, never offering headaches as excuses for not sharing the marital bed.

I had generously allowed Tosh to share my son, encouraging Clyde to think of him as a permanent life fixture. And now Tosh was "tired of being married."

Experience had made me accustomed to make quick analyses and quick if often bad decisions. So I expected Tosh, having come to the conclusion that marriage was exhausting, to ask me for a divorce when he returned from work. My tears were for myself and my son. We would be thrown again into a maelstrom of rootlessness. I wept for our loss of security and railed at the brutality of fate. Forgotten were my own complaints of the marriage. Unadmitted was the sense of strangulation I had begun to feel, or the insidious quality of guilt for having a white husband, which surrounded me like an evil aura when we were in public.

At my table, immersed in self-pity, I saw my now dying marriage as a union made in heaven, officiated over by St. Peter and sanctioned by God. It wasn't just that my husband was leaving me, I was losing a state of perfection, of grace.

My people would nod knowingly. Again a white man had taken a Black woman's body and left her hopeless, helpless and alone. But I couldn't expect their sympathy. I hadn't been ambushed on a dark country lane or raped by a group of randy white toughs. I had sworn to obey the man and had accepted his name. Anger, first at injustice, then at Tosh, stopped my tears. The same words I had used to voice my anguish I now used to fan the fires of rage. I had been a good wife, kind and compliant. And that wasn't enough for him? It was better than he deserved. More than he could reasonably have expected had he married within his own race. Anyway, had he planned to leave me from the first? Had he intended in the beginning to lure me into trust, then break up our marriage and break my heart? Maybe he was a sadist, scheming to inflict pain on poor, unsuspecting me. Well, he didn't know me. I would show him. I was no helpless biddy to be beckoned, then belittled. He was tired of marriage; all right, then I would leave him.

I got up from the table and cooked dinner, placed the food in the refrigerator and dressed in my best clothes. I left the dinner pots dirty and my bed unmade and hit the streets.

The noontime bar in the popular hotel on Eddy Street was filled with just-awakened petty gamblers and drowsy whores. Pimps not yet clad in their evening air of exquisite brutality spent the whores' earnings on their fellow parasites. I was recognized by a few drinkers, because I was Clydell and Vivian's daughter, because I had worked at the popular record shop or because I was that girl who had married the white man. I knew nothing about strong liquor except the names of some cocktails. I sat down and ordered a Zombie.

I clung to the long, cold drink and examined my predicament. My marriage was over, since I believed the legal bonds were only as good as the emotional desire to make them good. If a person didn't want you, he didn't want you. I could have thrown myself and my son on Tosh's mercy; he was a kind man, and he might have tolerated us in his home and on the edges of his life. But begging had always stuck, resisting, in my throat. I thought women who accepted their husbands' inattention and sacrificed all their sovereignty for a humiliating marriage more unsavory than the prostitutes who were drinking themselves awake in the noisy bar.

A short, thickset man sat down beside me and asked if he could pay for my second Zombie. He was old enough to be my father and reminded me of a kindly old country doctor from sepia-colored B movies. He asked my name and where I lived. I told his soft, near-feminine face that my name was Clara. When I said "No, I'm not married," he grinned and said, "I don't know what these young men are waiting for. If I was a few years younger, I'd give them a run for they money. Yes siree bob." He made me feel comfortable. His Southern accent was as familiar to me as the smell of baking cornbread and the taste of wild persimmons. He asked if I was "a, uh, a ah a fancy lady?"

I said, "No." Desperate, maybe. Fanciful, maybe. Fancy? No.

He told me he was a merchant marine and was staying in the hotel and asked would I like to come upstairs and have a drink with him.

I would.

I sat on the bed in the close room, sipping the bourbon diluted with tap water. He talked about Newport News and his family as I thought about mine. He had a son and daughter near my age and they were "some kinda good children" and the girl was "some kinda pretty."

He noticed that I was responding to the whiskey, and came near the bed. "Why don't you just stretch out and rest a little while? You'll feel better. I'll rest myself. Just take off your shoes and your clothes. To keep them from wrinkling up on you."

My troubles and memories swam around, then floated out the window when I laid my head on the single pillow.

When I awakened, the dark room didn't smell familiar and my head throbbed. Confusion panicked me. I could have been picked up by an extraterrestrial being and teleported into some funky rocket ship. I jumped out of bed and fumbled along the walls, bumping until I found the light switch. My clothes were folded neatly and my shoes peeked their tidy toes from under the chair. I remembered the room and the merchant marine. I had no idea what had happened since I passed out. I examined myself and found no evidence that the old man had misused my drunkenness.

Dressing slowly, I wondered over the next move. Night had fallen on my affairs, but the sharp edges of rejection were not softened. There was a note on the dresser. I picked it up to read under the naked bulb that dangled from the ceiling; it said in effect:

Dear Clara,

    I tell you like I tell my own daughter. Be careful of strangers. Everybody smile at you don't have to mean you no good. I'll be back in two months from now. You be a good girl, hear? You'll make some boy a good wife.

Abner Green

    I walked through the dark streets to Ivonne's house. After I explained what had happened, she suggested I telephone home.

"Hello, Tosh?"

"Marguerite, where are you?" The strain in his voice made me smile. He asked, "When are you coming home? Clyde hasn't eaten."

I knew that was a lie.

"Nor have I. I can't eat," he said. I wasn't concerned about his appetite.

I said, "You're tired of being married. Yes? Well, I'll be home when I get there." I hung up before he could say more.

Ivonne said, "Maya, you're cold. Aren't you worried about Clyde?"

"No. Tosh loves Clyde. He'll look after him. He loves me too, but I gave up too much and gave in too much. Now we'll see."

The thought of his loneliness in the large apartment made my own less acute. I slept badly on Ivonne's sofa.

I went home the next day and we resumed a sort of marriage, but the center of power had shifted. I was no longer the dutiful wife ready with floors waxed and rugs beaten, with my finger between the pages of a cookbook and my body poised over the stove or spread-eagled on the bed.

One day my back began to hurt with a sullen ache, the kind usually visited only on the arthritic aged. My head pulsed and my side was punished by short, hot stabs of pain. The doctor advised immediate hospitalization. A simple appendectomy developed complications and it was weeks before I was released. The house was weary with failure— I told my husband that I wanted to go to Arkansas. I would stay with my grandmother until I had fully recovered. I meant in mind, as well as body.

He came close and in a hoarse whisper said, "Marguerite. Your grandmother died the day after your operation. You were too sick. I couldn't tell you."

Ah, Momma. I had never looked at death before, peered into its yawning chasm for the face of a beloved. For days my mind staggered out of balance. I reeled on a precipice of knowledge that even if I were rich enough to travel all over the world, I would never find Momma. If I were as good as God's angels and as pure as the Mother of Christ, I could never have Momma's rough slow hands pat my cheek or braid my hair.

Death to the young is more than that undiscovered country; despite its inevitability, it is a place having reality only in song or in other people's grief.

CHAPTER 6

When our marriage ended completely, a year later, I was a saner, healthier person than the young, greedy girl who had wanted a man to belong to and a life based on a Hollywood film, circa 1940.

Clyde was heartbroken by the separation. He acted as if I were the culprit and he and Tosh the injured parties. His once cheerful face was a muddle of solemnity. He grumbled and whined, asked again and again, "Why did Dad leave us?"

My direct answer of "Because he and I didn't love each other anymore" frightened him, and when he looked at me his eyes held the wonder: Will you stop loving me, too?

I tried to soothe him by explaining that he was my son, my child, my baby, my joy. But his good sense told him that Tosh had been my husband, my love and his father, and I had been able to sever those bonds. What safety was there for him?

A few months before the separation my mother and her close friend, Lottie Wells, returned to San Francisco from Los Angeles.

They opened a café with ten tables and a ten-stool counter where they shared soul-food cooking chores. Lottie was a strong, powerfully built woman the color of freshly made coffee. She spoke softly, hardly above a whisper and was so tender it was impossible to resist loving her. She folded Clyde and me into her care and became our beloved Aunt Lottie.

At first Mother had exhibited no change in her attitude to my marriage, but when she observed my faithful husband, the good provider, and Clyde's love for Tosh, she had said, "O.K., so I was wrong. He's good. I'm big enough to admit my mistake; are you big enough to understand that I only wanted the best for you?" When I told her later that the marriage was at an end, she only said, "Well, as I always say, 'No matter how good a fellow seems on the outside, you have to take him home to know him.' "

Now that I was trying to mend the rift between me and Clyde I appreciated her indifference.

There are few barriers more difficult to breach or more pitiable to confront than that of a child's distrust. I used every wile in the mother's little homemaker kit to win my way back into my son's good graces. I paid attention to his loss and sympathized with him. I taught myself to skate so that we could go to the rink together. At home, I cooked his favorite foods, in portions that would please a cowpuncher and surrendered my reading time to play scrabble and twenty questions and any other diversion he chose. In the street we skipped over cracks in the pavement in a sport he called "no stepping on the lines."

Gradually we rebuilt our friendship.

As that emotional worry diminished, a practical one assumed importance. My pride had not allowed me to ask Tosh for money, but he had left me the small bank account and it was dwindling fast. I had to get a job and one that paid enough so I could afford a baby-sitter. I started looking.

Four dingy strip joints squatted cheek by jowl in San Francisco's International Settlement. The exteriors of the Garden of Allah and the Casbah were adorned with amateur drawings of veiled women, their dark eyes sultry with promise and their navels crammed with gems. The Pirates Cave and Captain's Table advertised lusty wenches and busy serving girls with hitched-up skirts and crowded cleavages, all sketched by the same wishful artist.

I stood on the pavement across from the Garden of Allah. A papier-mâché sultan with a lecherous grin winked atop the one-floor building. Around the doorway old photographs of near-nude women curled under a dirty glass façade. Large letters proclaimed BEAUTIFUL GIRLS! CONTINUOUS ENTERTAINMENT! The advertisement had read: "Female Dancers Wanted. Good take-home pay."

The interior was dimly lighted and smelled of beer and disinfectant. A large man behind the bar asked if I had come to audition. Most of his attention was centered on checking the bottles.

I said, "Yes."

He said, "Dressing rooms downstairs. Go that way."

I followed the path of his arm and descended a narrow stairwell. Women's voices floated up to meet me.

"Eddie's a nice Joe. I used to work here before."

"Yeah. He don't hassle the girls."

"Hey, Babe, who made that costume?"

"Francis."

"Frances?"

"Nah, Fran*cis*. He male, but he's more twat than you."

I allowed the light and sound from an open doorway to direct me. A floor-to-ceiling mirror made the four women seem like forty. They were older than I expected and all white. They were taken aback by my presence. I said hello and received hi's and hello's and then a heavy silence.

They busied themselves professionally, gluing on eyelashes and adjusting wigs and attaching little sequined cones to their nipples. Their costumes were exotic, complicated and expensive. Rhinestones twinkled, sequins shone, nets and feathers and chiffon wafted at each movement. I had brought a full leotard, which left only my hands, head and feet exposed. Obviously I couldn't compete with these voluptuous women in their glamorous clothes. I turned to go. Wrong place, wrong time.

"Hey, where ya going? This is the only dressing room."

I turned back to see a short redhead looking at me.

She said, "My name's Babe, what's yours?"

I stammered. I ran through all my names, Marguerite, Maya, Ritie, Sugar, Rita. The first three were too personal and the others too pretentious, but since I felt least like Rita, I said "Rita."

Babe said, "You'd better get changed. The band will start soon. What's your routine?"

I had no routine. When I read the ad I had expected to audition for a revue and thought a choreographer would give me steps to do, rather like a teacher asking questions in an examination. I said defiantly, "I do modern, rhythm, tap and flash."

Babe looked at me as if I had answered in Latin.

"I mean what's your routine? I'm little Red Riding Hood, see?" She posed, offering her costume for my observation. She wore a red gathered see-through net skirt with folds of the same material draped across her shoulders. Clearly visible beneath the yards of cloth were a red brassiere and a red sequined belt low on her hips; panels of red satin hung from the belt to cover her crotch and the cleavage of her buttocks. A precious little poke bonnet sat on her red curls and at her feet was a cute wicker basket.

I said, "I see." And did.

She pointed to an older blonde, whose breasts hung heavy and uncovered.

"That's Rusty. She's Salome" (she pronounced it "salami"). "She does the Dance of the Seven Veils. That's Jody, she's the Merry Widow. See? Kate is the only one who's not somebody. She does acrobatics. You know? Flips and splits and things like that. So you gotta have a routine."

None of the women looked up.

I said, "Well, I don't have one, so I'd better go home."

She said, "Let me see your costume. Maybe we can make one up."

I was unable to resist Babe's friendliness. Reluctantly I took the balled-up black leotard from my handbag.

"That's it?" Astonishment narrowed her voice into a shriek. The other women looked up for the second time since I'd entered the dressing room.

As usual when I was embarrassed, I responded with an angry stiffness. I said, "Well, I *am* a *dancer*. I might not have a fancy costume, and I may not have a routine, but I can dance. So don't try to make me look small." I looked around at each woman as I fought back mortification. The dancers resumed picking at their flesh privately, like cats licking their fur.

Babe said, "Wait a minute. Don't get your ass on your shoulders. They've never had a colored girl work here. Why don't you try it? I used to work at the Pirates Cave down the street and my best friend was Pat Thomas. She's colored, too."

I thought I am expected to stand here embarrassed and listen to that old "colored best friend" lie again. I rolled my leotard and put it in my bag.

Babe said, "I got an idea. What size are you?"

I told her.

She said, "I've got a G-string and bra made out of rabbit fur. I'll let you wear it, just for the audition, and you can be Jungle Bunny."

That was out, and I told her so emphatically.

She said, "Boy, you sure are sensitive. I didn't mean no harm."

I said, "I didn't mean to scream at you." After all, she had been kind.

"Well, let me think." Her face worked as she looked at me. She shouted, "I know, I know." She bent quickly and began fumbling in an open suitcase on the floor. She pulled out a blue satin set of panties and brassiere. Both pieces were studded with rhinestones and trimmed with blue-dyed feathers. "Try these on."

I undressed while the other women finished their make-up, their faces averted from me. I looked closely at the seat of the panties, and although they seemed clean I didn't pull it too close.

Babe said, "Boy, you got yourself a pretty figure," then she draped yards of blue tulle over me that floated and fell to the floor. "Now you're Alice Blue Gown. That's your routine. You know the song? It's a waltz."

The first tuning-up notes of a rhythm band reached the dressing room and the dancers started like robots jerking to attention. They picked up their purses and rushed to the stairs. Babe trailed them.

She whispered, "They only want four girls and we are five. I hope you get the job. Be real sexy. And don't leave your purse in the dressing room." She turned and raced for the stairs.

The figure in the mirror was strange to me. A long, mostly straight brown body clothed in a cloud of blue gauze. I would never be able to dance with all that material playing around. I took it off, folded it and laid it on Babe's tote bag. I tried to bring the lyrics of "Alice Blue Gown" out of my memory. I couldn't remember and I knew I couldn't waltz without a partner. I went upstairs wearing the bra and G-string.

Four white men sat murmuring in the shadows in the back of the club and four black men were playing "Tea for Two" on the bandstand. Rusty moved across the square polished floor, ridding her body of veils and indifferent to the music. Finally, as the music stopped, she was still as a statue and almost as pale. No hint of sexuality touched her body. And no applause appreciated her performance. She left the stage.

The acrobat took over next as the band began "Smoke Gets in Your Eyes." She wore a tasseled green G-string and brassiere and somersaulted, double-somersaulted, back-flipped, held one leg up over her head, showing the green patch that covered her vagina. As the last notes faded in the air she spun and jumped, ending in a perfect split. She jiggled short rises and allowed the floor to kiss her. There was no response from either the men watching or the men playing.

Jody walked onto the stage to the strains of "Besame Mucho." She wore black tulle, corseted to her body by a sparkling black waist cincher. Her black-stockinged legs and black patent shoes raced across the floor. She rushed from one side to the other, throwing wicked come-hither looks and tossing her wisps of clothes into the audience. When she finished, clad only in a black G-string and bra, she turned her back, pooched her behind up and looked over her shoulder with a pout. The music had ended, but she waited to her own drummer, then went around collecting the discarded clothing and went downstairs.

When Babe walked onto the stage, the four men fell silent. She nodded to the musicians, put one hand on her hip and held her basket aloft with the other.

The band played "All of Me" and the woman became a sexy, taunting twelve-year-old. She pranced about the stage offering illicit sex. She stuck out her tongue in a juvenile tease, then changed the purpose by sliding it around her lips insinuatingly, curling it over the corners. Her eyes were hard and wise and her body ample and rounded. Her breasts jiggled and her hips quivered with promise. She stripped to the red G-string and cones which covered her nipples.

When the music stopped, she stood still, looking out toward the men. Her face wrinkled in a strange smile. She had been sexually exciting and knew it. Within seconds, they began their murmuring again, and Babe collected her discarded clothes and waved at the musicians, who grinned in response. She passed me saying nothing.

I waited in the dark, not quite knowing if I should introduce myself or just go up and start dancing, or be sensible, race downstairs, put my clothes on and go home.

A voice shouted, "Where's the colored girl?"

I nearly answered "Present." I said, "Here."

"Well, let's go," the voice ordered.

I walked onto the stage and the musicians stared their surprise. The drummer beckoned to me.

"Hi, honey. What's your routine?"

Certainly not "Alice Blue Gown."

I said, "I don't know." And added, "I can dance, but I need something fast to dance to."

He nodded. "How about 'Caravan'?"

"That's fine."

He spoke to the other players, counted down four and the music began. I started dancing, rushing into movement, making up steps and changing direction. There was no story, no plan; I simply put every dance I had ever seen or known into my body and onto the stage. A little rhumba, tango, jitterbug, Susy-Q, trucking, snake hips, conga, Charleston and cha-cha-cha. When the music was finished I had exhausted my repertoire and myself. Only after the low talking resumed in the rear did I realize the men had stopped to watch me and that the other women had dressed and were sitting at a small table in the dark.

The drummer said, "Baby, you didn't lie, you can dance." All the brown and black faces smiled in agreement.

I thanked them and went downstairs with pride to change clothes. Babe passed me on the stairs, carrying her bag.

She asked, "How did it go?"

I said, "O.K. What about these things?" meaning her G-string and bra.

She said, "Bring them up with you. I'll just put them in my purse." They would have fit comfortably in a cigarette package.

I said, "O.K. In a minute."

The big bartender stood over the table after I joined the other dancers.

He said, "Rusty, you, and Jody and Kate and—" He turned to me. "What's your name?"

I said, "Rita."

"—and Rita. Start tomorrow." He looked at Babe. "Babe, try again. We had you here last year. The customers like new faces."

He went back to the bar. The three women got up silently and walked over to him. I was embarrassed for Babe, and when I handed the costume to her I wanted to say something kind.

She said, "Congrats. You've got a job. You'd better go over and talk to Eddie. He'll explain everything. How much, hours and the drinks."

I said, "I'm sorry you didn't make it."

She said, "Aw, I expected it. All these guys are down on me since last year."

I asked, "Why?"

She said, "I got married. My old man is colored."

I went to join the others, and the bartender said, "O.K., Kate, you and the other girls know the routine. See you tomorrow night. You."

Although he didn't look at any of us, he meant me. The bartender was a fleshy man with large hands and a monotone voice. His thin, pink skin barely covered a network of broken veins.

"You worked around here before, Rita?" His eyes were focused on the edge of the bar.

"No."

"You been a B-girl?"

"No." I had no idea what he was talking about.

"Salary is seventy-five a week and you work the bar."

I began to get nervous, wondering if I should tell him I knew nothing about mixing drinks.

He continued, "If you hustle you can clear ten, fifteen bucks a night. You get a quarter for every champagne cocktail a customer buys for you and two dollars off every eight-dollar bottle of champagne."

Eddie had given the spiel so often he no longer listened to himself. I began to pick meaning from his litany. I was expected to get men to buy drinks for me and I would get a percentage. Ten extra dollars a night sounded like riches, fur coats and steaks. I rattled around twenty-five cents into ten dollars and choked on the idea of forty cocktails per night. If I told the man I didn't drink, I'd lose the job.

"We use ginger ale and sometimes 7-Up with a lemon twist. And we got the fastest waitresses on the street. Show time is eight o'clock. Six shows a night, six times a week each one of you girls dance fifteen minutes a show." He shifted his head, the spiel was over. I backed away, but he stopped me. "Uh, Rita, you belong to the union?"

"No." I had never heard of a dancers' union or a B-girls' union.

"Soon as we reopen, the AGVA representative'll be down here. Every girl has to belong to the union or we get blackballed. If you want to, we'll advance your initiation fee and you can pay it back in two weekly payments."

"Thank you." I was beginning to like this man who talked like a villainous Edward G. Robinson, yet was too withdrawn to look directly at my face.

"I'm only the manager, but the boss thinks that you shouldn't strip. The other girls are strippers. You just dance. And wear costumes like you wore today." The costume I had borrowed made stripping absolutely unnecessary. "Most girls buy their materials from Lew Serbin's Costume Company down on Ellis Street. Last thing is this, Rita: we've never had a colored girl here before, so people might say something. Don't get upset. If a customer gets out of line with any of the girls in a coming-on way, I take care of that, but uh, if they say something about your color, I can't help that. 'Cause you *are* colored. Right?" He nearly looked at me. "And don't go home with any guy or else the police'll be down and close us up." He turned his back and began typing on the cash register keys.

"See you at seven-thirty tomorrow."

"Thank you."

A showgirl. I was going to be a star shining in the firmament of show biz. Once more adventure had claimed me as its own, and the least I could do was show bravery in my strut and courage in the way I accepted the challenge. It was time to celebrate. No bus could take me back fast enough to Ivonne's house, where I had left my son. I stopped a taxi and gave the driver her address.

Ivonne grinned when I told her of my new profession and laughed outright at the salary.

"Seventy-five bones a week. What are you going to do with all that money? Buy a yacht?"

"It's going to be more than seventy-five." I told her about the drinks and the percentage. Ivonne had the talent of forcing her face absolutely still and looking so intently at an object that her eyes seemed to telescope. She sat a few moments registering my information.

"My. I know you'll try anything once, but be careful. How many Negroes are working down there?"

"Only the guys in the band, as far as I can see. I'm the first Negro dancer they've had."

"That makes it a little different, doesn't it?" Her voice had descended to a tone just above a whisper.

"I don't see that, Vonne."

I had always wanted to believe that things were exactly as they seemed, that secrets and furtive acts and intents always made themselves known somehow. So I acted easily or uneasily on the face rather than the hidden depth of things. "I'm going there to dance and to make some money."

She got up from the sofa and walked toward the kitchen. Our children's laughter floated out from a back bedroom.

"Aleasar made some spaghetti. Let's eat."

We sat down at the wrought-iron dinette table.

I asked, "What worries you about my working down there?"

"I'm not worried, you can take care of yourself." A smile widened her small mouth as much as it could. "All I want to say is what the old folks say, 'If you don't know, ask.' But, don't let anybody make you do something you don't think is right. Your mother already raised you. Stay steady. And if that makes somebody mad, they can scratch their mad place and get glad."

We laughed together. Our friendship was possible because Ivonne was wise without glitter, while I, too often, glittered without wisdom.

CHAPTER 7

The costume store gave me the sense of being in a zoo of dead animals. Rusty bear skins hung on one corner rack; their heads flopped on deflated chests and their taloned paws dragged the floor. Ostrich feathers and peacock plumes in tall bottles were swept in a confined arc by each gust of wind. Tiger skins were pinned flat against the walls and lengths of black feather boa lay curled in a glass-topped counter.

I explained to a heavily made up quick-moving black man that I needed some G-strings and net bras and rhinestones. He flounced around the counter with a feather's grace and scanned my body as if I had offered to sell it and he was in the market.

"Who are you, dear?"

I wondered if it was against the store's policy to trade with just anybody.

"I'm Rita. I'm starting to work tomorrow night at the Casbah."

"Oh no, dear. I mean what's your act? Who are you?"

There it was again. I thought of glamorous Black women in history.

"I'm Cleopatra and ... Sheba."

He wiggled and grinned. "Oh, goody. Two queens."

"And Scheherazade." If I felt distant from the first two, the last one fitted me like a pastie. She also was a teller of tall tales.

"Then you'll need three changes, Right?"

He had begun to jot notes on a pad. I thought of Ivonne's advice and decided that since I really didn't know what I was doing, I'd better ask somebody.

"Listen, excuse me. I've never danced in a strip joint and in fact, the owners don't even want me to strip. They just want me to wear brief costumes and dance."

The man's jerky movements calmed, and when he spoke, some of the theatricality had disappeared from his voice.

"You're new?"

I hadn't thought of myself as new since I was seven years old.

"Well, I'm new in the sense that—"

"I mean, you have no act?"

"Yes. I have no act."

His body took on a stillness as he looked at me. "I will create your costumes. You will be gorgeous."

He brought out beige net bras and G-strings and told me how to dye them the color of my skin by soaking them in coffee grounds. I was to sew brown shiny coq feathers on one set for the Sheba dance, red sequins on another for Scheherazade and gold lamé panels on a G-string for my Cleopatra number. He selected a stuffed cobra, which I was to carry when I portrayed the Egyptian Queen, and ankle bells for Scheherazade. Sheba was to be danced with no frills—a brown doe upon the hills.

He seemed to know so much about show business, I asked if he used to dance.

"I was a female impersonator in New York for years, dear. Just years. When I came out here and found I had gotten older, I got this job, and now I sell pretty things to the pretty young boys."

I paid for the purchases and was grateful that the man hadn't laced sadness in his sad story.

"If you need anything, come back or call me. Ask for Gerry." He flipped away to another customer, then turned his head over his shoulder in my direction and said, "Gerry with a 'G.' " His laughter snapped in the dusty air.

The first shows were anticlimactic. No crowds threw flowers at my bare feet, no deafening bravos exploded when I bowed after dancing for fifteen strenuous minutes. When I realized that I was the only person in the entire night club embarrassed by my near nudity, my embarrassment increased.

My body was all I had to offer and few of the serious-faced men in the audience seemed to notice. There had been scattered applause as the other dancers floated across the stage, flirting with their bodies and snuggling up to the soon-to-be-discarded bits of chiffon. My only applause for the first three performances were the desultory claps from Eddie, who, I decided, was programmed to automatically respond each time an orchestra beat out the closing chord.

The musicians encouraged me as I danced. "Yeah, baby. That's right, shake it!" Their union had ruled that they must have fifteen minutes off each hour, and Eddie arranged for another pianist to come in and play for the acrobat.

Before the next show, Jack, the drummer, came to the dressing room. He had close-set eyes and a sharp countenance, as if his features had run away from his ears to gather at the center of his face.

"Rita, me and the rest of the cats dig you. Just tell us what you want. We can play anything, but all anybody asks for is 'Tea for Two' and 'Lady in Red' and 'Blue Moon' and everything slow. I play so much draggy music, my butt is dragging. One thing I like about you is you don't drag your butt." Then he smiled. His lips parted and a million white teeth gleamed. The abrupt change startled me away from my defenses. I stood watching that sparkling smile, unable to think of an appropriate response. His lips suddenly withdrew from the smile with the finality of a door being slammed.

"Here's the rundown. We'll do 'Caravan' first. Then, 'Night in Tunisia' and 'Babalu.' Then we go back to 'Caravan.' Okay?"

I managed an "O.K." and Jack left the dank dressing room. I had once fallen in desperate love at first sight when I was seventeen. He was a handsome, cocoa-bean-colored man, whose voice was as soft as mink. He had loved me in return and treated me gently. Now, again, there was a dull whirr in my ears and a tightness around my chest and the man wasn't even handsome, might be a brute or happily married and I didn't even know his last name. I only knew he was a drummer and that the sun rose when he smiled.

When Eddie announced my last turn, "Here is Rita as the Arabian princess, Scheherazade," and I went on stage, Jack became the blasé Sultan for whom I danced beautifully. When I finished, there was scattered applause. I turned first to Jack, but he was talking to the pianist. Hastily I remembered my manners, and spun around to bow to the audience. The solemn old men still leaned, hands occupied with diluted drinks. I looked over the audience and found Ivonne sitting alone at one of the tray-sized tables. She smiled and nodded. I smiled back and walked off the stage. Another patter of hands came from a table by the door. I saw two men at a table lighted yellow by the outside amber neons. One looked like a false eye-lashed mannequin; the other was Gerry—spelled with a "G."

For the first week after each show, I raced down the concrete stairs and put on my street clothes. Fully dressed, I tried to disregard the contemptuous looks of the strippers who clattered into the room, flung provocative garments over their naked bodies, then without sitting once, went back to the bar and the clients. I was afraid that I would be speechless if a customer spoke and mortified if he didn't. Furthermore, Jack, whose last name I still didn't know, continued to excite my imagination. I couldn't allow him to see me planted on a barstool guzzling down the fraudulent drinks. So when I danced I refused to look at the audience and kept my eyes half shut and my mind centered on Jack.

"Rita." The bar was empty, except for the musicians packing down their instruments and the strippers waiting for their nightly take. "Rita." Eddie's voice caught me with my hand on the door. I turned.

"Come over here."

I walked back to the bar, the air conditioner had stopped its hum and the room had settled in silence. The women seemed to lean toward me in slow motion and the men on the stage might have been dolls handled by a drowsy puppeteer.

"Rita, we didn't pay your union dues for you to sit downstairs on your can. Do you think that's why we hired you?" He sounded like a teacher admonishing a mischievous child.

"I thought you hired me to dance." My voice would not follow my urging and it came out nearly whining.

A woman snickered in the prurient dark.

"To dance? Dance?" His cough could have been a chuckle. "This here's no concert hall. This ain't the San Francisco Ballet Company."

The pianist laughed out loud. "Lord, ain't that the truth."

Eddie continued, "You want the job?"

Yes. Desperately. I needed the money and I wanted to be near Jack and I loved to dance. I said nothing.

"Tomorrow night, you bring your fanny up here as soon as you change and sit at the bar. First joker that comes in here alone, you ask him for a drink. Or . . ." The unnamed threat hung in my ears. Teacher was brandishing his whipping cane.

"Tomorrow night. One more chance." He began to count bills, thudding his hand on the bar. "Okay, Kate. Here's yours."

Last chance? He didn't know me. There was no chance, absolutely no chance that I'd be there the next night. I went to the door and fumbled at the lock.

"I'll help you, Rita." I turned to see Jack's sharp face cutting through the gloom. My prince, my sultan.

"Thank you."

He opened the door easily. The mustard light from the exterior neon sign robbed him of his own color. He slanted toward me and whispered, "Wait for me. I'll just be a minute."

Standing in the amber doorway, I decided I would call the sitter and tell her I'd be late. Jack would probably take me to breakfast at one of the popular after-hours places and we could talk softly over the loud music. He would smile his break-of-day smile and I would say how much he meant to me. The job was forgotten.

The musicians came out of the club together. Jack was the only one not surprised to find me at the entrance. He said, "You cats go on. I'll meet you at the club. I'm going to walk Rita to a cab." He took my elbow and steered me toward the corner.

"I understand you, Rita." I knew he did. "You think taking B drinks makes you cheap. Well, let me tell you it doesn't. These old guys come in strip joints because they want to look at pretty women. Pretty naked women. Some of them are married, but their wives are old and fat or young and mean. They're not trying to get you to go to bed or anything like that. If they wanted prostitutes, they'd go to whorehouses. They just want to see you and talk to you. Personally, I feel sorry for them. Don't you?" We stopped in front of another darkened night club. If he felt sorry for them, I pitied them to pieces. All I wanted from Jack was to know what he thought I ought to be thinking.

"My wife and I talk about them all the time. She's a waitress in a club like the Garden of Allah and every night she's got some story. I pick her up downtown and she right away starts talking about the guys she's waited on."

A smile began to pull at his face. "Philomena—pretty name, ain't it? She can tell a story that would break your heart. Or else she can make you split your sides. Anyway…" He forced his thoughts back to me. "It's just life, Rita. Just life. Don't be afraid. You're in that joint to make money. So make it." He put his hand on my cheek. "See you tomorrow night." As he turned I caught a side glimpse of his smile. It was all for Philomena and not a wrinkle of it for me.

I spent the next day girding my mind for battle. I loved to dance and I needed to work. I could create steps and develop new choreographies. If men wanted to buy my drinks, I would accept and tell them that the drinks they were paying for were 7-Up or ginger ale. That, along with imaginative dancing, would erase the taint of criminality. Art would be my shield and honesty my spear, and to hell with Jack and his close-set eyes.

The next night Eddie's face moved slowly in surprise when I appeared at the bar. I gave a smile to encourage him.

"Rita. Well. Decided to join the gang, huh?"

I said, "I want the job, Eddie." And kept the grin easy.

"All right. You understand what I told you. Twenty-five cents off every drink and two dollars on a bottle of champagne. There's not many customers yet, but it's early. More'll be coming in soon. You stand a better chance sitting at the bar than at one of the tables. It's too dark for them to see you."

I couldn't afford to ask if he was making a slur at my color. I grinned and waited.

"Want a little drink to warm you up?"

"No, thanks. I'll wait for a customer to buy me something."

I looked around the club. A few men had come in, but the other dancers had already fanned out to sit at their tables. There was a dense romance to the room I hadn't noticed before. The white faces hovered like dully lighted globes and the gloom was fired by glinting rhinestone jewelry. The musicians' stands glittered under red, orange and blue revolving spotlights.

Eddie announced, "And now the Garden of Allah proudly presents Rusty dancing 'Salome and the Seven Veils.' "

Rusty got up from her chair and shrugged off her filmy wrap. She draped it over the customer's lap and stepped up onstage. Her body angled stiffly across the floor in contradiction to the floating chiffon veils.

I hadn't watched any of the women perform since that first day of audition, and so I sat fascinated with Rusty's conception of what was erotically exciting. She glided and stopped, glided and stopped, while her long, lethargic hands draped to the cups of her bra, promising to remove it, then a better idea motivated them to float away and descend to the chiffon at her crotch where they arrived with the same intent. Miraculously a veil would drift off her figure and slowly onto the floor. Rusty's face seemed divorced from the actions of her body. It wore the resignation of a tired traveler on a cross-country bus ride. I knew that that wasn't carnal, but when I turned to get confirmation from the customers, their eyes were focused on the indifferent dancer. They were using her feinting body to erase their present and catapult themselves into a fantasy where sex-starved women lay submissive and split open like red, ripe watermelons.

If I was going to be a success, I had to elicit if not the quality then the same quantity of response.

I had heard all my life that white males, from boyhood to senility, dreamed of slipping into the slave cabin of young "hot mommas" and "ripping off a piece of black tail." My arrogance and my hatred of slavery would not allow me to consciously batten on that image. I decided during Rusty's dance that I would interest the customers in my movements and hold them in the present, even as a tightrope walker hypnotizes an audience.

Eddie announced, "Rita dancing Scheherazade." I stepped upon the stage and into a thousand and one nights. The musicians were forgotten behind me as I moved to the edge of the stage. And the furtive men with their lonely longings became the sultans whom I had to entertain. I watched their faces come alive to me as I pointed and gyrated and swept my arms over my head and out and down to my sides as if I might fly offstage straight to a camel caravan waiting. I convinced myself that I was dancing to save my life, and without knowing why, the audience responded to my predicament. The amount of applause startled me, and even Eddie pursed his lips and nodded as I walked by the bar, headed for the stairs.

The dressing room was empty. I stood amid the costumes and wigs and hair rats considering my success and the next move. There was no time to waste. The men had liked my dance and surely one would buy me a drink. While I toweled my body I planned my strategy. Unlike the other dancers, I would not sit around the bar with kimono or peignoir thrown over my costume. I put on street clothes and went up to the bar.

Eddie showed his pleasure at seeing me by introducing a customer. "Rita, here is Tom. He wants to buy you a drink."

The first conversation was repeated so often, all customers might have been handed questions on slips of paper at the door and been forced to memorize the questions.

"Where'd you learn to dance like that?"

"In school."

"Did you ever make love to a white man?"

"No."

"Would you like to?"

"No. No, I don't think so." Leave room for them to hope. Leave space for me to ask for another drink. "May I have another drink?"

"Sure. Where're you from?"

"N.Y." N.O.Y.B. None of Your Business.

"Long way from home. Don't you get lonely?"

"This drink is called a champagne cocktail and I get twenty-five cents for every one you buy, but really it's only 7-Up. If you buy a bottle of champagne, it'll cost you eight dollars and I'll get two of that. But at least it'll be real champagne and I can sit with you as long as it lasts."

The ploy worked, but my interest was never aroused. The men awoke no curiosity in me. I did not follow them in my mind to their hotel rooms or their loveless homes. They were like markers on a highway, to be used without gratitude and to be forgotten without guilt.

The other dancers did not warm to me, nor I to them. They chatted to each other and kept their conversations and their glances to themselves. They had not forgiven me for that first week when I sat haughtily in the dressing room as they hustled around the bar soliciting drinks. And since they had the toughness without the tenderness I had found in Babe, I ignored them completely. Success at cadging drinks changed my public personality. I became sassy to the customers. Quick, brittle words skipped off my tongue like happy children in a game of tag. Some men liked the flippancy and began to come back to the club not only to watch me dance but to buy drinks, listen to me and talk.

CHAPTER 8

Two months after I began working in the Garden of Allah the composition of the patronage changed. The lonely men whose hands played with their pocketed dreams slowly gave way to a few laughing openfaced couples who simply came in to watch the show.

Occasionally I would be invited to join a table of admirers. They had been told a good dancer was working in a strip joint. I answered their overused question by telling the truth. "I'm here because I have to work and because I love to dance." I also explained about the drinks.

Being so close to the tawdry atmosphere titillated the square couples. I decided they were the fifties version of whites slumming in Harlem's Cotton Club during Prohibition, and while their compliments pleased me, I was not flattered.

Away from the bar my days were cheerful. I was making real money. Enough to buy smart, understated clothes for myself and matching ensembles for Clyde. We spent Saturday afternoons at horror movies, which I loathed. He adored the blood and popping eyes of "the Wolf Man," the screams of "vampire victims" and the menacing camel walk of Frankenstein's monster. He yelled and jumped and hid behind my arm or peeked through his fingers at the grisly scenes.

I asked him why he liked the fearful stories if they frightened him. His reply was a non sequitur. "Well, Mom, after all, I'm only eight years old."

Three months passed and I freely spent my salary and commissions in dining at good restaurants, buying new furniture and putting a small portion away for a trip—Ivonne and I had discussed taking our children on a vacation to Hawaii or New York or New Orleans.

I was young, in good health, and my son was happy and growing more beautiful daily.

One night Eddie paid off the other girls first, saying he wanted to talk to me. After they left, he bellyed up to the bar and cast his glance

on the bandstand where the musicians were stowing away their instruments. When he didn't look at me, I knew it had to be serious.

"Rita, you're making more money than the other girls."

I hoped so.

"...and they say they have a complaint."

"What's the complaint, Eddie?"

"They say you must be promising to sleep with the clients. Otherwise why do you end up every night with four or five bottles of champagne and ten dollars or more in cocktails?"

"Eddie, I don't care whether they like it or not. I haven't promised
anybody anything. I've just made more money. Let's leave it at that,
O.K.?"

"It's not O.K., Rita. They can bring you up on charges with the
union, or even get the club in Dutch. You must be doing something.
No new girl makes this kind of money." His hand covered some dollars on the bar.

My protested innocence was forceful but without explanation. I
could not reveal to him that I told all my customers about the ginger
ale and that they knew the percentage I made from the champagne.

"Please believe me, Eddie. When I leave here, I go straight to my
house and let the baby-sitter take my cab so she can go home. I have a
child at home."

"Rita, it's not me. Far as I'm concerned, you're a straight shooter.
Good people. But these other broads. They, uh, what I mean is they
can give us a bad time. If they want to make real trouble all they have
to do is hint to the right people that girls here accept B drinks." He
wiped at a long-dried spill on the bar and my ears began to burn. "The
State Board of Equalization suspended our license once before."

I had ignored the fact that officers from the Board visited the club
in plain clothes. I told each man who offered me a drink the composition of the drinks and the percentage I would receive. So I had been
dense before, but if I thought fast I could recover.

"Eddie, if they do that—I mean, tell the wrong person—they'll lose
their jobs, too."

He found another spot to rub. "They don't care, not if they get mad enough. They'll just go to work down the street or around the corner. These joints are always looking for experienced girls. And that's what I want to tell you. I'm putting you on notice. Two weeks. You start looking for another place. I'll tell the girls tomorrow night that you're on notice. That ought to make them happy. If you haven't found something in two weeks, I'll try to keep you on a week at a time, but you won't have no trouble finding another job."

Shock made me patient. I stood silent and sheeplike as he counted out my night's money. In the taxi I gathered his words together and poked at them dully. Two weeks' notice. Fourteen days before the good life faded and my son and I would be cut loose to scud again without anchor. The dancers didn't like me and the disaffection was mutual. If they envied the money I made, I was jealous of the whiteness of their skin that allowed them to belong anywhere they chose to go. They could pick up their tassels and pack up their G-strings and go to another job without hesitation, but I remembered Babe. She was as white as they, but just because she slept side by side with her black husband, she was banned from the street. And what about me? I was black all over. No—the strippers felt nothing for me that I didn't feel for them.

I was always tired after the six shows, but this night sleep did not rush to float me out of exhaustion.

The next evening the dressing room was filled with electricity. The women were costumed, but had not made their customary dash upstairs. When I entered, they all turned to look at me. Sour little grins played on their faces. Rusty said, "So, you're leaving, huh, Rita?"

I gaped, surprised for a second. Eddie had told them already. I offered them my most gracious smile, looking into each woman's eyes. "Good evening, ladies. Jody"—turn—"Kate"—turn—"Rusty."

Jody said, "Lovely evening, isn't it?"

My grandmother would have been proud of me. She had purred into my ears since babyhood, "Three things no person worth a hill of beans won't do. One is eat in the street and another is cry in the street.

And never let a stranger get your goat." If they were going to lick their chops over my distress, they would find their tongues stuck to a cake of salt.

Upstairs I greeted Eddie as if he was simply a bartender. I looked away from him quickly and around the club. A few women sat at the tables with male companions. Their two-piece knit dresses and bouffant hairdos were strikingly out of place in the musty club.

I sucked in my breath and followed the opening bars of my music to the stage. Since I was on notice, I could forget the audience and go for myself.

Three fashionably dressed men and a young Marlene Dietrich–looking woman huddled over a table in the center of the room. The woman had a shock of sunlight-yellow hair and brooded over a cigarette holder. The red-haired man had been in before, but had not spoken. Now the four sat watching me as if they were French couturiers and I was wearing the latest creation from Jacques Fath. The more I tried to ignore them, the more they intruded into my mind. Who were they? Some slumming socialites looking for thrills? I tried to give myself to the music, but the group stared so intently that for once the music wouldn't have me, and I stumbled around the floor creating no continuity in my movement and no story in my dance. It occurred to me that they might be talent scouts and maybe I was going to be discovered. I threw that silly thought out of my mind before it could take hold. Lana Turner and Rita Hayworth got discovered, Black girls got uncovered.

I changed downstairs in the empty dressing room and half expected, half wished that the quartet would be gone when I went back upstairs.

"Hello, I'm Don." The redhead grinned and a map of freckles wiggled across his face. "This is Barry."

Barry was a tall, graying man whose smile was distant and distinguished. Don, obviously the major-domo of the group, waved his hand toward a pretty young man whose eyes were beautifully deep.

"This is Fred Kuh, and this"—he gestured like a circus announcer who had saved the lion tamer for the last—"this is Jorie!"

She shook her head and her hair fell back from her face, heavily as if in slow motion. She spoke in a low, theatrical voice.

"Hello. My dear, you dance divinely. Just divine."

Not Marlene Dietrich, I was wrong; she was Veronica Lake with substance, a young Tallulah Bankhead. "And you're so refreshingly young." Her perfume was thick, like the air in Catholic churches.

I said, "I'm twenty-one."

Barry asked if I would have a drink with them and I began my spiel about the B drinks, the percentages and the bad champagne.

Jorie said, "It's true. My Gawd, it's true. You're right on cue. We were told that you'd say that."

"What?"

"You're kind of famous, you know."

Don grinned, "You must be the only open-faced B-girl on the Barbary Coast."

"In San Francisco," said Barry.

Jorie corrected: "In captivity."

They approved of me and I warmed to them. I allowed myself their flattery. It was easy to suppose they liked me because I was honest. I did not want to pry into their acceptance for fear that what I found would be unacceptable to me. Suppose they thought me a clown?

Barry explained that Jorie was a chanteuse, currently starring at the Purple Onion, a nearby night club. He managed the place and was the emcee. Don Curry and Fred Kuh were bartenders and I was welcome anytime I could get away.

These beautiful people and their friends began dropping in each evening and I awaited their arrival. I danced indifferently until I caught a glimpse of their party near the back of the room, then I offered them the best steps I had and as soon as the dance was finished I hurried over. There was no need to butter up the manager or hustle the customers. It gave me a delicious sense of luxury to be sitting with such well-dressed, obviously discriminating people, while the strippers roamed among the tables looking for the odd drink and the lone man.

CHAPTER 9

One evening I was invited to a wine party at Jorie's apartment after closing time. The house sat on a hilly street. A stranger opened the door and took no more notice of me, so I entered and sat on a floor pillow and watched the guests spin around one another in minuet patterns. There were glamorous young men with dyed hair who rustled like old cellophane. Older men had airs of sophistication and cold grace, giving the impression that if they were not so terribly tired they would go to places (known only to a select few) where the conversation was more scintillating and the congregation more interesting.

There were young women who had the exotic sheen of recently fed forest animals. Although they moved their fine heads languorously this way and that, nothing in the room excited their appetites. Unfashionable red lips cut across their white faces, and the crimson fingernails, as pointed as surgical instruments, heightened the predatory effect. Older, sadder women were more interesting to me. Voluminous skirts and imported shawls did not hide their heavy bodies, nor was their unattractiveness shielded by the clanks of chains and ribbons of beads, or by pale pink lips and heavily drawn doe eyes. Their presence among the pretty people enchanted me. It was like seeing frogs buzzed by iridescent dragonflies. The young men, whose names were Alfie, Reggie and Roddy and Fran, hovered around these fat women, teasing them, tickling them, offering to share a portion of their svelte beauty. None of the company spoke to me. That I was one of the three Negroes in the room, the only Negro woman and a stranger as well, was not a sufficiently exotic reason to attract attention.

I sipped the wine and listened to the concert of gossip and bon mots, repartee and non sequiturs.

Don stooped beside me and asked if I was all right and had I met everyone. I told him I was and I had, and added a sincere smile. His high pink color, green eyes and fire-red hair made him the prettiest person at the party, and he had a sense of humor I found missing in the other blades, despite their clacking laughter.

He looked into my eyes and found the lie. He stood and turned quickly. "Everybody!" He spoke just below a shout. "Everybody!" Voices quieted. When the room was still, he spread his arms and fanned his fingers away from his wrists and nodded toward me. "Everybody, this is Rita. She's an artist, a truly tremendous dancer. She is absolutely the world's greatest. I thought you should know."

People peered at me. Most found nothing remarkable about the announcement and, indeed, if at that moment I had executed a tour jeté from a sitting position, it would not have pried them away from their indifference. Only the plum-soft women marked the statement and cared. Each round face softened and smiled on me.

Don dropped his arms and said rather weakly, "Well, I just thought you ought to know." To me he said, "Don't mind these people, Rita. They're only pretending to be blasé because they don't know what else to pretend to be. I'll get you some wine."

One large woman came over to me carrying a pillow. She gracefully settled on the floor at my side, denying her bulk.

"I'm Marge." Then she told me, "And you're Rita."

"That's right."

"And what kind of dancing do you do, Rita?"

"Modern ballet and interpretive." (I knew a shake dancer named L'Tanya who could quiver her hips so fast they disappeared in a blur and she called her performance interpretive.)

Marge's mouth made an O. One young boy who had been courting her wafted over to us. He folded down beside Marge and arched an arm over her round shoulders, his hand dropping on the rise of her breast.

"And what have we here, Mother dear?"

She nearly suppressed a giggle. "Reggie, you're too naughty."

He turned to me, holding his lips tight. "How now, brown cow?"

I knew or should have known it would be a matter of time before some racial remark would be made. Here this chit was calling me a brown cow.

"Rita, this is Reggie. Isn't he a naughty boy? Naughty, naughty." She nearly kitchy-kooed his chin.

I made my diction as prudish as the young man's was prissy. "I haven't the faintest idea whether he's naughty or not. I do know that if he's your son, at least one of you has something to be ashamed of."

Reggie blanched and tightened. "You have a nasty mind to go with that nasty mouth." His voice sharpened with indignation. "What are you doing here, anyway? Who asked you?" He began to tremble.

Marge said, "There's no reason to get excited, Reggie baby. Calm down, hear? Just consider the source." She slipped out of his embrace and put both arms around his back and pulled him over into her lap. "There now, baby, there, there." She pressed chunky fingers on his hair and then looked up at me distraught.

I was thoroughly displeased with myself. I murmured "Sorry" and rose to go, but a door opened behind me and I turned. Jorie stood in the doorway. She wore a long black dress and lights leaped in her hair.

"Well, darlings, aren't you kind. You started without me." She laughed at her own good humor. I liked her more at that moment than I had before. She didn't appear to take herself too seriously. When she saw me she gave a little shriek of delight.

"How marvelous, Rita! You didn't forget. Has everyone met this most divine dancer?"

She came toward me as if she was going to take my hand like a referee and proclaim me champion. She stopped and patted my shoulder. "Have you had wine? Are they treating you all right?"

I told her that they were and, satisfied, she walked on to meet the other guests.

I was in a quandary. Obviously I couldn't leave the moment the hostess made her appearance, and just as obviously I couldn't sit back down on the floor near Marge and Reggie, who had finished ministering to each other's sorrow and were watching Jorie's movements keenly.

I wandered into the kitchen and claimed a drink. I had not drunk much dry wine before that night, but if white people could drink wine like Kool-aid, then there was no reason on God's green earth I could not do the same. The second glass went down smoother than the first and the third more swiftly than the second. Alone, seated in a strange house filled with strangers, I felt as if I were in dangerous waters, swimming badly and out of my depth. I was plankton in an ocean of whales. The image was so good I toasted it with another glass of wine. Loud laughter penetrated the closed door and I wondered how people became so poised, so at ease. Sophistication was not an inherent trait, nor was it the exclusive property of whites. My mother's snappy-fingered, head-tossing elegance would have put every person in the room to shame. If she walked in the house uninvited, even unexpected, in seconds she would have the party clustered around her, filling her glass, listening to her stories and currying for one of her brilliant smiles. My mother was more elegant than Kay Francis and Greer Garson put together, prettier than Claudette Colbert (who I secretly thought was the prettiest white woman in the world) and funnier than Paulette Goddard. Oh, yes. I drank a glass of wine to my mother.

When I found the door leading from the kitchen, I walked back into a near-empty living room. I would have sworn that I had spent no more than fifteen minutes over the wine, but it would have been impossible for the room to clear in that time.

Jorie, Don, Barry and Fred sat in easy chairs listening intently to a record. Gertrude Lawrence or Bea Lillie sang shakily in a reedy voice.

I interrupted, "Oh, hello."

They jumped up, startled into speaking all at once.

"Where have you been?"

"I thought you had gone."

"What were you doing?"

"Where have you been?"

I told them I'd been in the kitchen drinking wine.

Jorie collected herself. "Well, my dear, it's awfully late, but do come and sit a minute."

My progress across the room was not as steady as I wanted, but I proceeded in what I hoped was a dignified manner.

Don got up and led me to a chair.

Barry said, "We're listening to some songs for Jorie's act. She's going to open in New York at the Blue Angel."

Jorie shook out her hair. "My God, I've got to make New Yorkers laugh. That's what I call a challenge. What have New Yorkers got to laugh about?"

I said, "But I thought you were a singer."

Don said, "She's a singer-comedienne. And"—he became protective—"she's bloody brilliant."

Jorie touched Don lightly and smiled, "You don't need to defend me. She didn't say I wasn't bloody brilliant."

Don caught her affectionate tone. "Sorry, Rita, but of course you've never seen Jorie perform, have you?"

Barry said, "And she won't, either. Her working hours, remember? Jorie leaves in three weeks."

At that moment I thought about my job and covered my fear by blurting out, "I'll be able to see you next week. I'm on notice at the club."

"You mean you've been fired?" Disbelief raised Don's voice and widened his eyes.

Jorie said, "But, darling, you're the only talent they've got. I mean. Surely they don't think people come there to see those awful strippers in their awful sequins. I mean."

I explained why I was fired, putting the blame on jealousy.

Barry asked what I'd do next and I could not answer. Only a small savings account stood between me and poverty.

"It's a pity you don't sing," Barry said in his clipped accent. "The Purple Onion needs someone to take Jorie's place."

I had not told them I could sing.

"What about folk songs?" Jorie said. "My dear, everyone, but every single soul today, knows at least one folk song. Of course, it has one thousand verses and lasts for two hours without intermission. I mean."

Everyone laughed and I joined in. Not because I agreed, but because I was pleased to be in such clever company.

I said, "I know a calypso song."

The men exchanged knowing looks with Jorie, then turned to me, straight-faced for a minute, and broke into a mean laughter.

"That's a good one. Oh, Rita, you're good."

They were laughing at me and I was expected to join them. Only the secure can bear the weight of a joke and only the very secure can share in the laughter.

"Do you think calypso music isn't folk music? Folks sing it. Or do you believe because the folks are Negroes their music doesn't count, or that because they're Negroes they aren't folks?"

It was obvious that my anger was unexpected. A pale shock registered on their features. Don's eyebrows rose, making him look like a leprechaun tricked out of his burrow. Barry, having found my loss of control distasteful, averted his eyes. Jorie blinked and winked her false eyelashes. Fred Kuh, who had said little, quietly offered: "No one meant to hurt your feelings, Rita. Jorie has a passion against calypso. That's all there is to it."

"What's wrong with calypso?" I had so strongly pulled anger to me as a defense that I could not shoo it away merely because it was no longer needed.

Fred said, "I think it's because the singers rely more on the beat than on storytelling. And Jorie's concerns are just the opposite."

"Oh, my dear"—Jorie was back with us—"It's the god-awful thump, thump, thump. It's the 'de man,' 'de girl,' 'de boat.' My God, haven't we got beyond 'dis' and 'dat'? Really."

It was a question of how I was to show that I was mollified without seeming to surrender my advantage.

"When you or any white person says 'dis' or 'dat,' it is certain that you intend to ridicule. When a Black person says it, it is because that's the way he speaks. There's a difference." There was a delicious silence. For the moment, I had them and their uneasiness in the palm of my hand. The sense of power was intoxicating.

"You say you dislike calypso and that the songs have no story line. Do you know 'Run Joe' by Louis Jordan?"

Their heads shook, which showed they were not totally immobilized.

"It goes like this." I stood.

> "Moe and Joe ran a candy store
> Telling fortunes behind the door
> The police came in and as Joe ran out
> Brother Moe, he began to shout
>   Run Joe
>   Hey, the man at the do'
>   Run Joe
>   The man he won't let me go
>   Run Joe
>   Run as fast as you can
>   Run Joe
>   The police holding me hand."

I had played Louis Jordan's record until it was gun-metal gray, so I knew every rest and attack of the song. I stretched my arms and waved my hands and body in a modified hula, indicating how fast Joe made his getaway. I tugged away from an imaginary policeman showing the extent of restraint imposed on Moe. I spun in place in the small area, kneeled and bowed and swayed and swung, always in rhythm.

When I finished the song, which seemed to consist of fifty verses, the assembly applauded loudly and their smiles were brilliant.

Jorie lifted a handful of hair and said, "But I mean, pet, you can sing. Have you ever sung before?"

Don said, "It's obvious you have. But professionally?"

When I was growing up in Stamps, Arkansas, Momma used to take me to some church service every day of the week. At each gathering we sang. So I knew I could sing. I did not know how well. Our church was bare because the parishioners were poor and our only musical instruments were tambourines and our voices. I had never sung to piano accompaniment, and although my sense of rhythm was adequate, I had not the shadow of an understanding of meter.

Jorie said, "But, my dear, if you can sing like that you should take my place at the Purple Onion. You'll be a smashing success. I mean they will simply adore you."

"How many songs like that do you know?"

"How many musicians will you need?"

"What about gowns?"

"Can you have an act together in three weeks?"

My God. My world was spinning off its axis, and there was nothing to hold on to. Anger and haughtiness, pride and prejudice, my old back-up team would not serve me in this new predicament. These whites were treating me as an equal, as if I could do whatever they could do. They did not consider that race, height, or gender or lack of education might have crippled me and that I should be regarded as someone invalided.

The old habits of withdrawing into righteous indignation or lashing out furiously against insults were not applicable in this circumstance.

Oh, the holiness of always being the injured party. The historically oppressed can find not only sanctity but safety in the state of victimization. When access to a better life has been denied often enough, and successfully enough, one can use the rejection as an excuse to cease all efforts. After all, one reckons, "they" don't want me, "they" accept their own mediocrity and refuse my best, "they" don't deserve me. And, finally, *I* am better, kinder, truer than "they," even if I behave badly and act shamefully. And if I do nothing, I have every right to my idleness, for, after all, haven't I tried?

Jorie said, "Of course you won't get the mint or probably half of what you're making now. But, my dear, if you're not working after next week, you may as well take this on. For the time being."

They began to make me up. I had to change my name. And wouldn't it be super duper if I had another origin? Something more exotic than tired old Southern Negro. People were tired of the moss hanging from the magnolia trees and the corn pone and the lynchings and all that old stuff. Anyway, I couldn't compete with Josh White, or Odetta, who I thought was the greatest singer of American Negro folk songs, and who worked nearby.

Couldn't we come up with something gayer, less guilt-awakening?

Jorie, Don and Barrie, along with quick assists from Fred, poked around in their imaginations as I sat watching. It was three o'clock in the morning and they were like children amusing themselves with play dough on a rainy day.

Because I was tall, I should be very grand, possibly from a long line of African kings. And could I speak any African?

I had studied African dance with Pearl Primus, but I had never met an African face-to-face. In fact, in the Negro community of 1953 the phrase used to describe a loud and uncaring person was "as uncouth as an African." I had lost a job in a leading dance school in Cleveland because I promised to teach "African primitive dance" to the children of the Black middle class.

No, I did not know any African. But I did speak Spanish. Jorie announced that she had an idea: I could be Cuban. That was it. I could be a Cuban who spoke little English, although I sang in the language. I should be torrid and passionate onstage, but haughty and distant offstage: "Rita, the Cuban Bombshell," the Latin señorita whose father was a Watusi chieftain sold in Cuba.

They were casting me as the star in a drama and I had no real desire to refuse the role. I feebly wondered aloud what would happen if I was discovered a phony. Herb Caen, the acerbic columnist, was a Janus creature, who guarded the local past while guiding the locals' future. He liked Jorie and Stan Wilson and Mort Sahl. But, what if he found that I was a fraud? He could make me the laughingstock of San Francisco.

My new friends countered, "Why should he care? If he did find out and mentioned it, San Franciscans would be amused." People would laugh *with* me, rather than at me. After all, the city had more eccentrics than lights on the Golden Gate Bridge.

I not only agreed to the charade but began adding my own touches. My father, the Watusi chieftain, had not been a slave (ah, to rid myself of that stigma) but was the son of a chief who had sailed to Cuba to retrieve his sister, who had been stolen from Africa. Once there, he had fallen in love with a dark-eyed Spanish girl. He had won her after a bloody duel, married her and she had given birth to my father. They, my very well-to-do parents, had sent me to the United States so that I could see some of the world before I married and settled down in my own well-staffed hacienda.

My audience listened, mouths agape, as I reeled my story before them. Their imaginations had been good, but mine was better. They had been amusing themselves, but I was motivated by the desire to escape.

———

Ivonne sat watching me as I talked. She nodded to indicate not so much that she agreed with me but, rather, that she comprehended what I was saying.

"So I'm going to sing at the Purple Onion. I'll sing calypso songs. Jorie Remus, who is the star there now, and the manager and bartenders are fixing it all up." I sipped the beer I had brought for a celebration. "They're all white, but they're nice. Sort of like foreigners."

She inclined her head.

"I mean they are Americans, but Jorie has lived in Paris. In France. And I guess that's why she's kind of different."

Ivonne drank beer and waited. Our friendship had brought us so close, she sensed that I had something more to say and that what I was saving until last was the most pertinent of my news.

"They remind me of Hemingway and Gertrude Stein and that group that lived in France, you know?"

Because she had not read the books I had read, the names I mentioned did not bring to her visions of the Left Bank and Montmartre. She made no connections with a gay time when America's good white writers sat in places like the Deux Magots dreaming up a literature which would enthrall the world for decades.

My friend was at ease in her silence.

"So they suggested I change my name and . . ." What had been easy to accept in the company of strangers was almost unspeakable now in Ivonne's familiar living room.

I had thought only that an attempt to pass was an acceptance of that which was not true. As I searched for words, it occurred to me that what I was about to do was to deny that which *was* true.

"They suggested that I say I came from Cuba."

Her black eyes and voice were equally cold and hard.

"Oh, Ivonne. For the romance. Just because it'll make me more exotic."

"They want you to stop being Negro ..."

"Oh no, come on."

"And you say these people are free? Free of what? And free for what?"

"You don't understand." I was exasperated with her. She and my mother had more in common than I had with either of them. "And I'm going to sing. I'm going to have a new career."

"You're going to sing Cuban songs? Like Carmen Miranda? With bananas on your head going 'Chi chi boom boom?' " Sarcasm syruped in her voice.

"Listen, Vonne, I'm going to sing calypsos. And I'm going to be good." I didn't relish having to defend myself. She was my friend. We shared secrets and woes and each other's money. We had keys to each other's houses and together watched our children grow.

"Just listen to this." I got up and took a place in front of the coffee table.

> "He's stone cold dead in de market
> Stone cold dead in de market
> Stone cold dead in de market
> I kill nobody but me husband."

My voice faltered and fell. I lifted it into a shout. When it sharpened into a screech I softened it. I fled between and over the notes like a long-distance runner on a downhill patch. When it was all over, I had sung in about three keys and Ivonne leaned back on the nearly paid-for sofa. A small resigned smile played hide-and-seek on her face.

She said, "I'll say this for you, Marguerite Johnson"—no one had called me by that name in years—"You've got a lot of nerve."

And she was right.

CHAPTER 10

North Beach bubbled as noisily and colorfully as the main street in a boom town. Heavy drumbeats thudded out of the doors of burlesque houses. Italian restaurants perfumed the air for blocks while old white-shirted men loudly discussed their bocce games in Washington Square. Pagoda signs jutted from tenements in Chinatown and threatened the upturned faces of milling tourists. One block away on Columbus Avenue, Vesuvio's bar was an international center for intellectuals, artists and young beats who were busily inventing themselves. Next door, Allen Ginsberg and Lawrence Ferlinghetti read their new poetry at the City Lights Bookstore. Two hundred yards down Columbus, the Black Cat bar was a meeting place for very elegant homosexuals who draped themselves dramatically beside the bar and spoke loudly and familiarly of "culture."

The Purple Onion was a basement cabaret which Jorie called *la Boîte* (Don translated that into "the sardine can"). Its walls were painted a murky purple, and although it was supposed to accommodate two hundred people, well over that number crowded into the room the first night I went to catch the show, and the air was claustrophobically close. Jorie in a simply cut, expensive black dress leaned her back against the curve of the piano. She partly sang and partly talked a torch song, waving a cigarette holder in one hand and languorously moving a long chiffon scarf in the other. Her voice scratched lightly over the notes.

> "He's just my Bill
> An ordinary guy
>   you'd see him on the street
>   [*pause*]
> And never notice him."

She looked at the audience directly, shrugging her thin shoulders. Her look said that Bill really was quite awful and she had little understanding of why she herself had noticed Bill. Before our eyes she changed from the worldly-wise woman, disillusioned by a burnt-out love affair, into a "regular" girl who was just one of the folks. The audience howled at the transformation, delighted by having been taken in.

I sat in the rear enthralled. It was hard to believe I was being asked to move into this brilliant woman's place, although my audition had gone well enough. The Rockwell family, led by the elder son, Keith, owned the club, and without much enthusiasm had signed a six-month contract with a three-month option for my services.

Jorie drooped over the piano dripping chiffon, and delivering accented witticisms. Or she would stand still, her shoulders down and her hands at ease and speak/sing a song that so moved her listeners that for a few seconds after she finished, people neither applauded nor looked at one another.

When I went to my first rehearsal, Jorie brought her drama coach to meet me. He was a tall, thin, black-haired man named Lloyd Clark, who spoke elegantly out of pursed lips and threw his fingers out as if he was constantly shooting his cuffs. He was accompanied by a handsome Dutch Amazon, whose blond hair was pulled back and hung in a two-foot ponytail. Her little girl's smile seemed incongruous on a face that could have modeled for a ship's prow.

And she spoke softly. "I'm Marguerite Clark. I'm his wife." There was so much pride in her statement that I would not have been surprised had she hooked her fingers in her armpits and stalked around the room. Lloyd took her adoration as his due and asked me if I had ever worked with a drama coach. I told him that I had not, but that I had studied drama and that I was a dancer.

"Well, first, my dear, you must sing for me." He held a cigarette between his third and fourth fingers, reminding me of a European movie actor. He puffed fastidiously. There was a neatness about the man which showed most prominently in his diction.

"I can't know if I can help you until I have"—each beloved word chosen carefully and handed out graciously, like choice pieces of fruit—"seen you perform."

The piano player, who was white and experienced, intimidated me nearly as much as the drama coach. Earlier in the afternoon he had asked for my sheet music, and when I told him that the songs I intended to sing had hardly been published, he slammed the piano lid down and stood up.

"Do you mean I'm supposed to play without music? Just vamp till ready?"

I did not understand his indignation, nor the sarcasm in his last question. "I've signed a contract and I'm supposed to open in two weeks. What can I do?" I had found that direct questions brought direct answers if they brought answers at all.

"Have some lead sheets written for you," he said indifferently.

"Can you do it? May I pay you to write the lead sheets? Whatever they are."

He gave me a thin smile and, partially pacified, said, "If I can find the time."

He sat again on the bench and opened the piano. "What do you sing?"

I said, "Calypso. 'Stone Cold Dead in the Market.' 'Run Joe,' 'Babalu.' Things like that."

He asked, "What key for 'Stone Cold Dead'?" His fingers ran over the keyboard and I thought of my pervasive ignorance.

"I don't know." The music stopped and the musician leaned his head on the piano. He was so dramatic I thought he should have been the star.

I said, "I'm sorry to be a bother." Usually when one throws oneself at another's feet, one should be prepared to do a fast roll to avoid being stepped on. "But I'd appreciate your help—I'm new."

The pianist rose to the occasion, which, given his sardonic expression earlier, might have come as a bigger surprise to him than to me.

"O.K." He straightened away from the keyboard. "Try this." He started to play and I recognized the tune.

"Yes, that's it."

"I know that's it," he said dryly. "Now how about singing so I can find your key."

I listened carefully, squinting my eyes and tried to find where in all the notes he played I should insert my voice.

"Sing." It was an order.

I started: "He's stone cold dead in de market."

"No, that's wrong. Listen." He played, I listened. I started to sing. He said, "No, wrong again."

Finally by chance I hit the right note. The pianist grudgingly nodded and I sang the song through.

He stood up and bounced a glance off me as he turned toward the bar. "You need music. You really need it."

I watched him order and then gulp down a drink greedily.

And here was Lloyd Clark, tended by his adoring Brünnhilde, telling me to repeat the awkward performance.

Whenever I had danced non-angelically on the point of a pin, I always knew I might slip and break my neck. It could be fatal, but at least all anxiety would cease. Because of that, I often rushed toward holocausts with an abandon that caused observers to think of me as courageous. The truth was, I simply wanted an end to uncertainty.

The pianist responded to my nod and with visible resignation sat at the piano and began to play the song we had tried earlier.

I looked beyond my audience and decided to ignore the musician and his snide attitude. I fastened my mind on the plot. A poor West Indian woman had been threatened by her brutal husband (my mother's father was Trinidadian, and although he was kind he was very severe) and she struck back in self-defense. My sympathies rested with the mistreated woman. So I told the story from her point of view.

Don said, "Great, just great."

Jorie asked Lloyd and the world at large, "Didn't I say she's marvy?"

Lloyd rose smiling, he came toward me offering his hands. "Fab, fab, darling, you're going to be fab. You're marvelously dramatic." He turned to his wife, who was like a tall, white shadow following him. "Isn't she, Marg? Just fab?"

Marguerite gave him a loving smile. "Yes, Lloyd darling." Then to me she said softly, "You're good. So very good. And after you work with Lloyd ... Oh, I can hardly wait." Her voice belied impatience.

"Now, dear, do sit down. Come, we must do some serious talking." Lloyd took my hands. He leaned around me and said to the musician who was beelining for the bar, "Thank you, young man, thank you. And you did it without lead sheets. Brilliant!"

"Now, my dear, sit." He pulled me along to Jorie's table. She patted my cheek and lowered one long-lashed eye slowly, meaning I was in, and hadn't she said so, and I had nothing to worry about and weren't we all so awfully smart. I winked back and grinned.

Marguerite sat so close to Lloyd she was nearly in his lap and Don made congratulatory little noises to me and to himself.

"First, dear, your name," Lloyd said.

"Rita."

"Is that your name? The name you were born with?" Disbelief was evident.

"No, my name is Marguerite."

Marguerite Clark complimented us both. "Oh, isn't that nice?"

"It's all right for you, Marguerite, but it doesn't do anything for her." I had been named for my maternal grandmother, who would not have taken kindly to that statement.

"She needs something more exotic. More glamorous." Lloyd turned to Jorie and Don. "Don't you agree?"

They did indeed.

"A really good name," Don said, "is half the act."

I thought about the popular entertainers who were mentioned in the newspapers weekly. I didn't know if their names were created for show business or if the entertainers had simply been lucky. I said nothing.

"Let's think. Think up some names."

Don went to the bar and brought over a bottle of wine and some glasses.

Thaïs, Sappho, Nana, Lana, Bette, names of heroines from Greek history, world literature and Hollywood were bandied about, but none seemed to please my inventors.

I said, "My brother has always called me Maya. For 'Marguerite.' He used to call me 'My sister,' then he called me 'My,' and finally, 'Maya.' Is that all right?"

Jorie said, "Di-vine. Di-vine, darling."

Don was ecstatic. "It suits you, my dear, oh God, it suits you."

Marguerite waited for Lloyd. He thought, looking at me pointedly, trying to find the name in my face. After a minute, he said, "Yes, you're Maya," as if he was christening me.

Marguerite said, "Lloyd, you're right, darling. She *is* Maya."

Don passed the wine around.

"Maya what?" Jorie looked at Lloyd. "Do deliver us from performers with one name. Hildegarde, Liberace. No, she must have at least two names."

I said, "My married name is Angelos."

Don chewed the words around, tasting them.

"Maya Angelos." Jorie took the name over, weighing it on her tongue. "That's not bad."

Lloyd said, "It sounds too Spanish. Or Italian. No, it won't do." An idea broke his face wide open. "I've got it. Drop the *s* and add a *u*. Maya Angelou." He pronounced it Angeloo. "Of course! That's it!"

Jorie said it was too divine. Don said it was perfection. Marguerite beamed her approval of Lloyd and then of the name.

We all drank wine to toast our success. I had a job, a drama coach, a pianist who was going to provide me with lead sheets, and I had a new name (I wondered if I'd ever feel it described the me myself of me).

We began to prepare for my debut. For three hours each day Lloyd coached me. His instructions included how to stand, how to walk, how to turn and offer my best profile to an audience. He worked over my act as busily as a couturier creating a wedding gown for royalty.

"My dear, but you *must* stand still. Glide out onstage like the *Queen Mary* slipping out of her berth, reach the piano and then stand absolutely, but absolutely, still. After a few seconds look around at your audience and then, only then, at your pianist. Nod your head to him and then you will begin your music. When he finishes his intro, then you will begin to sing."

I found standing still the most difficult of all his instructions. During rehearsal when I was introduced my nerves shivered and the swallows in my stomach did nose dives. I would hear "... and now Miss Maya Angelou," and I would race from the dressing room, down the narrow aisle to the stage and, immediately, without waiting for the music, begin: "Moe and Joe ran a candy store."

"No, my dear. Still. Be totally still. Think of a deep pool."

Again and again I tried until I was able to walk on stage, and, thinking of nothing at all—neither deep pools nor sailing ships—stand absolutely still.

Lloyd said I had to learn at least twelve songs before opening night. I plundered the memories of every acquaintance. Mornings found me in the sheet music shops and record stores, ferreting for material. By midday, I hurried to the pianist's apartment, where we practiced songs over and over until they began to have less meaning than words in a children's game. Afternoons I worked with Lloyd in my house. When he left, I selected some songs to practice in front of Clyde. Although I sang the cute, the humorous songs for his enjoyment and would prance around this way and that, he always watched me with a seriousness that would have impressed a judge. When I finished he would remove his horn-rimmed glasses and look at me speculatively and ask, "Gee, Mom, how can you remember all those words?"

Clyde had become a talker. He talked to me, to the family, to strangers and had long, involved conversations with himself. His discourses ranged over the subjects of his life. He had become a voracious reader, consuming books whole at nearly one sitting, then reliving the plot in his conversations. He read science fiction (he loved Ray Bradbury) and western pulp, his Sunday School lessons, Paul Laurence Dunbar's poems and animal stories and explained to all who would listen that he, Red Ryder and Fluke were going to ride their horses to the moon and talk to God, who was an old Black man who played the guitar. Red Ryder was a Western character from books and Fluke was Clyde's invisible miscreant friend. Fluke made him laugh aloud with his mischievousness. He was able to do things Clyde could not do, and Fluke did them with impunity. If a lamp was overturned and broken, it was because Fluke was walking around on the lamp-shade. When the bathtub ran over and turned the tiled floor into a shallow pool, Fluke had gone to the bathroom after Clyde left and turned the spigot on.

Vainly I tried to explain the difference between lying and making up a story, but decided it was more important that Clyde keep his nonexistent buddy to lessen the loneliness of an only child. I liked to listen from the kitchen when he told Fluke good-night stories and when, in his morning bath, he laughed outright as he warned his friend against indulging in some troublemaking antic.

Francis, the dressmaker, took Gerry's (with a G) ideas and fashioned long, snug dresses out of bolts of raw silk and white corduroy. The gowns were slit on both sides from floor to hip, and underneath I wore one-legged pants of gay batik. When I stood still, the dress material fell gracefully, giving an impression of sober elegance, but when I moved the panels would fly up and it seemed as if one leg was bare and the other tattooed. I wore no shoes. The total effect was more sensational than attractive, but having no illusions about my ability to sing, I reasoned that if I could startle the audience with my costumes and my personality, they might be so diverted that they wouldn't notice.

Opening night, I longed for one of two things. To be dead—dead and forgotten—or to have my brother beside me. Life had made some strenuous demands on me, and although I had never ruled out suicide, no experience so far had shattered me enough to make me consider it seriously. And my brother, Bailey, who could make me laugh at terror or allow me the freedom to cry over sentimental things, was in New York State, grappling with his own bitter reality. So, despite my wishes, I was alive and I was alone.

I watched through a peephole as Barry Drew walked to the stage. He claimed that he was descended from two great theatrical families and had to live up to his heritage.

"And now, ladies and gentlemen"—he rubbed his hands together—"this evening, making her debut at the Purple Onion"—he turned his best side to the light and opened his arms for the world—"Miss Maya Angelou!"

There was some applause, not enough to hearten but not so little I could deny that people were waiting for me.

I counted three and walked slowly down the aisle and onto the stage. I stood still as I had at rehearsal, and a dead calm surrounded me. One second later fear plummeted to my stomach and made my knees weak. I realized that I could not see the people. No one had warned me that a combination of spotlights and nerves would cause blindness. The aisle down which I had walked still lay open and unobstructed. I looked at it once, longingly, then turned to the pianist and nodded. And although I did not know it, another career for me had begun.

———

Popularity was an intoxicant and I swayed drunkenly for months. Newspaper reporters began to ask for interviews and I gave them in an ersatz accent, which was a mélange of the speech of Ricardo Montalban, Jorie Remus and Akim Tamiroff. I was invited to talk on radio and sing on television. Fans began to recognize me in the street and one well-to-do woman organized a ten-member Maya Angelou fan club.

Later I met people who said, "I saw you dance at the Purple Onion." I graciously withheld the information that in fact I was hired at the club as a singer, but the songs had many refrains and such complex rhythms that often I got lost in the plot and forgot the lyrics. So, when the words eluded me, I would admit my poor memory and add that if the audience would bear with me I would dance. The first few times I owned up to a weak memory, Lloyd Clark and Barry Drew frowned disapprovingly, but after the audiences applauded loudly Barry accepted it and Lloyd said, "Wonderful, dear, wonderful. Keep it in. In fact, you should dance more."

I shared the bill with a strange and talented couple. Jane Connell sang scatterbrained ditties, while her sober-side husband Gordon dryly played piano. Their patter was sharp and displayed their Berkeley university background. When they left to join Jorie in New York's Blue Angel, a frowzy blond housewife from Alameda auditioned and was accepted at the club. She brought a wardrobe of silly flowered hats and moth-eaten boas which she flung around her thin neck. Her laugh, which she shared often, was a cross between a donkey's braying and a foghorn. She said she would not change her name because when she became successful she wanted everyone to know it was, indeed, her herself. The name was painted in large white letters outside the club: Phyllis Diller.

CHAPTER 11

Without a father in the house and no other male authority figure in his world, Clyde fell under the spell of uniforms. He began to adore policemen and daydream about becoming a bomber pilot.

"I'll zoom down like this, Mom, brrr and blow their heads off. Boom, boom, boom." He marched and clumped around the house in a poor parody of Gestapo goose-stepping. He saluted walls and chairs and ordered doors to be "at rest, Sergeant Door." He had become enamored of the Air Force and every evening at bedtime he waited in his room for me to hear his prayers and then to sing (he would join in):

"Off we go into the wild blue yonder
Singing songs into the blue..."

Each evening as I left for work, the baby-sitter would say, "Our little soldier is bedded down in his bunk, huh?" I wished I could have cashiered her out of my service with dishonorable discharge.

I was dismayed, but I left him alone until I could decide on the best way to counter his sudden affection for violence. I hoped for divine intercession and bided my time. As his birthday approached he began spending time after school in the local five-and-dime store. He wanted a machine gun or a tank or a pistol that shot real plastic bullets or a BB gun. I took him to the local S.P.C.A. pound and told him he could have an animal. A small dog or any cat he wanted. He wandered around the cages, choosing one dog and then rejecting it when he saw a lonelier-looking cat. He finally settled on a small black kitten with rheumy eyes and a dull, dusty coat. I asked the attendant if the cat was healthy. He said it was, but that it had been taken from its mother too early and abandoned. It needed personal care or the pound would have to destroy it. Clyde was shocked. I could barely get him and his ragged cat out of the building before rage broke through. "Mom, did he mean he would have to kill my cat?"

He was clutching the small animal so tightly I thought he himself might put an end to its miserable life.

"Yes, if no one wanted it, they'd do away with it."

"But Mom, isn't that place called a place for the protection of animals?"

"Yes."

"Well." He thought for a few minutes. "Wow! What sort of person would have a job like that? Going around killing animals all the time."

I saw my opening. "Of course, some people have jobs that order them to go around killing human beings."

The earlier shock was nothing to the sensation that caught and held him. He nearly squeezed the breath out of the kitten. "What? Who? Who kills human beings?"

"Oh, soldiers, sailors. Pilots who use machine guns and bombs. You know. That's mainly what they're hired for."

He leaned back in the car, stroking the kitten. Silent, thinking.

I never mentioned killing again and he never asked for another weapon.

———

Leonard Sillman's Broadway hit *New Faces of 1953* came West in 1954. San Francisco, already the home of irreverent comedians, political folk singers, expensively dressed female impersonators, beat poets and popular cabaret singers, took the witty revue to its heart. Don Curry and I attended an early matinée. When Eartha Kitt sang "Monotonous" in her throaty vibrato and threw her sleek body on a sleek chaise longue, the audiences loved her. Alice Ghostly, with "Boston Beguine," created a picture of a hilarious seduction scene in a seedy hotel lobby where "even the palms seemed to be potted." Paul Lynde, as a missionary newly returned from a three-day tour of the African continent, and Robert Clary, as the cup-sized Frenchman rolling his saucer eyes, turned farce into a force that was irresistible. Ronnie Graham shared the writing and performed in skits with June Carrol.

I left the theater nearly numb. The quality of talent and quantity of energy had drained me of responses.

My family made plans to come to the Onion for an early show. Mother was coming with Aunt Lottie, and they were bringing a few old-time gamblers from the Fillmore district who never left the Negro neighborhood except to buy expensive suits from white tailors. Ivonne was bringing her daughter, Joyce, and Clyde. I reserved front-row seats and then spent a nervous thirty minutes waiting for them to arrive.

The adults had a loud, happy reunion in the front row. A stranger could easily have deduced that they had not seen each other in months or more probably years.

Mother's friends examined Clyde and complimented him on growing so fast. He beamed and threw back his already wide shoulders. Lottie praised Joyce for "turning into a fine young lady" and the conservatively dressed men who generally dealt the poker at the legally illegal gambling houses smiled at everyone and politely ordered drinks for the party. Ketty Lester, a great beauty who hailed from a small Arkansas town thirty miles north of my home, always opened the show. She sang good songs and sang them well. Phyllis Diller followed her and spread her aura of madness over the stage and onto the audience, and then I closed the round's entertainment. The older people were transfixed by Ketty's singing. She sang "Little Girl from Little Rock" and the black people who all had Southern roots acted as if the song had been written expressly for Ketty to sing to them. From the rear of the club, I watched as they smiled and nodded to one another and didn't have to be in hearing distance to know they were exchanging "That's right" and "Sure is" and "Ain't that the truth?"

There was only a minute between the last notes of her encore and Phyllis Diller's introduction. Curiosity kept me standing against the back wall, for I wanted to see how my family would take to the frumpy comedienne. Black people rarely forgave whites for being ragged, unkempt and uncaring. There was a saying which explained the disapproval: "You been white all your life. Ain't got no further along than this? What ails you?"

When Phyllis came out onstage, Clyde almost fell off the chair and Joyce started giggling so she nearly knocked over her Shirley Temple. The comedienne, dressed outrageously and guffawing like a hiccoughing horse and a bell clapper, chose to play to the two children (she had four of her own). They were charmed and so convulsed with laughter they gasped for breath, but being well-brought-up Negro youngsters who were told nice children do not laugh loudly, they put their hands over their mouths.

I slipped into the dressing room, pleased that at last there was something in the show for everyone. Only Ivonne had appeared less than enchanted with the two acts. But then I knew she was waiting for me to sing.

I walked down the aisle to the stage, registering the applause and hoping that my family was not so busy clapping their hands that they were unable to note that other people were applauding as well. I stood quietly, looking out into the audience (I had enlarged on Lloyd's coaching and now took the time to select faces in the pale light). My breath caught audibly as I recognized Alice Ghostly and Paul Lynde at a table midway in the room. Their presence exhilarated me.

I nodded to the three musicians and began my song.

> "I put the peas in the pot to cook
> I got the paper and started to look
> My horse..."

I heard the "shush" and "hush" from somewhere around my kneecaps, but kept on singing.

> "... was running at twenty to one
> So me peas and me rice
> They get..."

The "tsk's" and the "sh's" were coming from my family. I looked down and saw everyone leaning in toward Clyde. His mouth was open and smiling, and then I heard his voice and knew why everyone was admonishing him. He was singing with me—after all, he had heard every song rehearsed a hundred times at home and now he decided to show me that he, too, could memorize the words. It might have been ignored if he had kept up with me, but his words lagged behind mine by at least one beat.

"I put..."
    "*I*"
"...the peas in..."
    "*...put the...*"
"The pot to cook..."
    "*peas in...*"

Absolutely the first time I had a chance to sing for big-time stars and my son was messing it up. I looked at him, hard this time, and he laughed openly. His eyes nearly shut as his face gave way to his own private joke. He acted as if we were playing a game, like twenty questions or top this, and he was enjoying himself so much that I had to forget about the audience and settle for entertaining my son. I tried to slow down my delivery until he could catch up.

When we finished, still a beat apart, I thanked the audience and added that I had had some unexpected but very welcome help. I introduced my son, Mr. Clyde Bailey Johnson. He stood, turned to the audience and bowed, straight-faced, as he had seen his favorite Bud Abbott do in so many films. I gave Clyde a look that in parent/offspring language meant "That was nice, but now we've stopped playing." He translated aptly and was quiet through the rest of my performance.

In the dressing room my family clutched around me, talking in low voices, commending me, relieved that at least I was good enough to spare them embarrassment. They saved their compliments for Ketty and Phyllis, paganly believing that too much praise attracted the gods' attention and might summon their powerful jealousy. They also thought I just might get a swelled head if given too many compliments, so instead they gave me sly looks and furtive pats and when no one was looking the slick old men encouraged me to "keep up the good work." They whispered that Ketty and I were the best on the bill but we had "better be careful" and "take it easy, 'cause white folks get jealous when they see Negroes gettin' ahead."

They left the club, taking with them the familiar nuances and I was somewhat relieved when they had gone. Insecurity can make us spurn the persons and traditions we most enjoy. I had always loved the gamblers when they sat in Mother's kitchen telling tales of the Texas Panhandle and reliving the excitement of boom towns in Oklahoma. But downtown, where educated whites might overhear the Negro grammar and think less of me because of it, I was uncomfortable.

Alice and Paul came to the dressing room and invited me out for a drink. I accepted immediately. We exchanged compliments and during the intermission we sat in an easy friendliness until the next show began. A few nights later Alice brought other members of the company down to catch my show. One singer told me that Eartha was leaving and Leonard Sillman and Ronnie Graham were auditioning dancer/singers to replace her. She had been bound by a contract which had run out at last and was going to open in one of the big-paying Las Vegas hotels. And would I like to try for the part? Naturally I wanted to audition and just as naturally I was petrified.

The theater stage jutted out aggressively into an empty darkness. Sillman sat erect on a straight-backed chair, apart from, yet fearfully a part of, the proceedings.

I was shivering in the wings, thinking of the excitement Eartha brought to her music when a stage manager asked me if I was going to sing "Monotonous." The play on words occurred to me and I did not find it funny. I said yes, but did not add that I would not be singing it like Eartha Kitt. She was overtly sexy and famously sensual. I was friendly, gangly and more the big-sister type. No, I would have no chance if I tried imitating the brown velvet kitten.

When I was called I went out onto the stage and put my hands on my hips and a foot on the chaise longue. I sang a few bars, then swirled around and put the other foot on the chaise longue. I sang and danced, skimming over the stage (a dance teacher had told me when I was fourteen years old that a good dancer "occupies space consciously"), always ending back at the seat with an attitude of haughty boredom. My plan was to capture attention by displaying absolute contradiction. Hot dance and cool indifference.

I waited an interminable two days for Leonard Sillman's "reaction." The phone call came and my heart jumped against my breastbone. I had the job. The famous show-business break had come. Ivonne's friend Calvin bought champagne and we celebrated at her house. I also bought champagne (although I did not care very much for it) and went to Mr. Hot Dogs, where Mom and Lottie and the counter customers helped me to celebrate. I told them that I would join the company for the rest of its tour, then settle down in New York City. My only hesitation was caused by the question of what to do about Clyde. Mom and Lottie said they would take care of him. He could have his breakfast at home as usual and come directly to the restaurant after school, by which time one of them would be going home on the split shift. I accepted that solution, knowing that when I "made it," as I was sure to do, I would rent a large Manhattan apartment and hire a governess for my son. And when I traveled I would take him along with the governess and possibly a tutor.

My life was arranging itself as neatly as a marble staircase and I was climbing to the stars.

Barry Drew met my announcement with an apoplectic explosion. "Oh no, you're not. What? You can't close. What? We have you under contract, you can't walk out on a contract."

I countered that I had already accepted the role, that he had the Kingston Trio and Rod McKuen opening at the club and they were as good or better than I. "I will never have another chance like this again. I don't want to spend my life at the Purple Onion."

He was firm. "You didn't think that when we brought you in here.

You're lucky we didn't offer you a year's contract. You'd have signed your life away to get a job like this."

I cried and begged and hated myself for doing so. He remained unmoved. I ranted about his cruelty, throwing curse words at him like blobs of hot tar, hoping at least to smear his surface.

Barry said coolly, "Sillman not only will not, but cannot, hire you if you break your contract. The union will have you up on charges and you will be blackballed."

He acted as if he himself had founded the union and written its bylaws just to keep restless and irresponsible singers in their places. His contempt was impenetrable. My anger calmed enough for me to see my predicament. I was totally hemmed in and I left the club and headed home, glowering at every passerby and wrapped up close in sullenness.

I expected sympathy from the rest of my family and received it in generous portions. My mother said she was shocked at Barry's behavior, but then as she always said, "The smallest insect makes the most noise," and I should keep that in mind. Aunt Lottie stroked me, gave me tea and as if I were sick, offered to make a nice pot of soup. Ivonne told me on the telephone that I was right to be angry, but to consider that the role in the play simply was not for me and as the saying goes, "You can't miss something you never had."

My pain yielded to the well-worn adages and soft consoling voices. In the absence of anguish I was able to think. It became clear that the roles had been exchanged. Once I had had a need of the Purple Onion facilities and now the Purple Onion had need of my services. The thought that irritated me and planted a seed of disdain was that the managers of the club had not noticed the reversal and had not the grace to appeal to my sense of "Turnabout is fair play."

I had heard the statement made by wistful whites (and had also made it in my youth myself, hoping to prove worthy of acceptance): "There's nothing as loyal as a Negro. Once you make a friend of one, you have a friend for life." Like making a pet of a grizzly bear.

My attitude at the club proved either that the statement was fallacious or that I was not a Negro. I withdrew my affection and kept only the shell of cool courtesy.

CHAPTER 12

"Hello, Mrs. Angelos?"

The telephone had rung on a bleary morning. It was a woman's voice.

"Yes?"

"This is Tennessee Kent at Golden Gate School."

"Yes?" I suppose the wonder in my voice carried over the wires.

"Your son, Clyde, is a student here."

My son's name brought me immediately clear of sleep. "Yes, I know that." Suddenly a clear-headed, responsible mother.

"I think possibly you'd like to come to school and discuss something Clyde has said."

"Is he all right?"

"Oh, yes, don't worry about him."

I did just that as I dressed.

Since our brief period of estrangement, I had worked very hard impressing Clyde that I was reliable, that in any conflict I was on his side. I had not forgotten the importance of my brother's impartial love during my own lonely childhood, and since my son had no sibling, I had to make him know he had support.

I went to the school and found Clyde sitting forlornly on a straight chair in the corridor. I patted his shoulder and stooped to ask what had happened. His eyes were liquid with unshed tears.

He whispered, "I don't know, Mom. They said I said something bad."

"Did you?" He had learned some profanity at a day camp the year before and had been quite proud of it for a few weeks.

"I don't know," he still whispered.

The two women remained seated when I led Clyde into the office. "Good morning, Mrs. Angelos," Miss Kent said. "This is Clyde's teacher, Miss Blum." A stout, middle-aged woman nodded to me seriously. Miss Kent went on, "And maybe it's better to let Clyde sit outside in the corridor while we..."

"No"—I still had my hand on his shoulder—"this concerns him. I want him to hear the discussion."

The teachers exchanged looks. I directed Clyde to a chair and sat beside him.

"Well, maybe Miss Blum will tell you what happened," Miss Kent said.

Clyde's little body was trembling. I patted his knee.

Miss Blum said, "Yesterday was Armed Forces Day and I asked all the children what branch of the service they admired. Some said Navy, others Air Force, others Seabees, but Clyde stood up on his turn and said he'd go to jail first." She looked at him with such venom I wanted to put my body between her look and my son.

Miss Kent said soothingly, "Now, Mrs. Angelos, we know Clyde didn't get that at home. So, we wanted you to know that somewhere, maybe among his friends, he's picking up dangerous thoughts."

I thought immediately about Joseph McCarthy. The witch hunt was in full stride and newspapers carried items about blacklists and jobs being jeopardized. Reputations had been ruined and some people imprisoned because they were suspected of harboring dangerous and treacherous thoughts. My own background was not without incident. When I was nineteen, I had enlisted in the Army and been given a date for induction, but had been summarily rejected because it was discovered that during my fourteenth and fifteenth years I had gone to a school which was on the list of un-American activities.

They said they knew he didn't pick up such thoughts at home.

"Yes, he got that at home, Miss Kent." Oh Lord, my career. What would the Rockwell family do if I was accused of Communist leanings?

"Oh, is that your religious belief?" She was being nice-nasty, giving me a cowardly way out. My son sat beside me, waiting. He had stopped trembling and was holding himself tight, listening to the exchange.

"If you mean do I believe in it religiously, I do."

"Oh, then Clyde was voicing your political views that you hold religiously?"

There was nothing for it but to agree. I said, "That's right."

And that was all Clyde had been waiting for. He bounced up out of his chair, arms stretched and flailing.

"Mom, isn't it true that just because U.S. Steel wants to sell more steel, I shouldn't go and kill some baby Koreans who never did anything to me?"

"Yes, that's true."

"And, Mom, isn't it true that capitalists just make the poor people go and bomb other poor people till they're all dead and live on dead people's money?"

I did not recognize that line, but I said "Yes."

He lifted his arms like a conductor asking a full orchestra for the last chord. "Well, that's all I said."

The teachers sat silent as I stood up.

"Miss Kent, and Miss Blum, I think the session has been emotionally very tiring for Clyde. I'll take him home now and he'll come back to school tomorrow."

They did nothing to hinder our departure.

That afternoon Clyde and I went to a movie that showed ten Disney shorts.

CHAPTER 13

George Hitchcock was a playwright whose play *Princess Chan Chan* was being performed by the Interplayers at a little theater near North Beach. A tall, shambling man with large hands and a staccato laugh, he doubled as an aging character actor. His hair was always dusty because he did not effectively rinse out the white powder.

He watched my show and afterwards asked if he could see me home. I wanted to accept, but wondered what he would think of my living arrangements. I was a glamorous night-club singer, or at least wanted to be considered glamorous, but I still lived at home with my mother. Late evenings I would find her sitting at the dining room table drinking beer and playing solitaire, and definitely not waiting up for me. I was a grown woman and had better know how to look after myself. Just to make sure, she played solitaire until I came home. Her voice would greet the sound of the opening front door. "Hi, baby, I'm in here."

I would say, "Good evening, Mom." And when she lifted her face for a kiss, she'd ask, "How'd it go this evening?" and I'd say, "O.K., Mom." That was what she wanted to hear, and all she wanted to know. Vivian Baxter could and would deal with grand schemes and large plots, but please, pray God, spare her the details.

I invited George home, and on the way, told him about my mother and my son. If he was surprised he didn't show it.

I countered Mom's "Hi, baby. I'm in here" with "I brought a friend home."

George would have had to know my mother to have recognized how startled she was when he walked in. She stopped her laying out of red and black and said, "Welcome," then "How are you tonight?" As if she knew how he had fared the night before.

George seemed at ease.

Mother looked at his worn tweed jacket, rumpled trousers and not quite clean hair and asked, "How long have you known my daughter?"

I knew where she was heading. I said, "We've just met tonight, Mom. George is a writer." That information held her steady for a while.

"He asked me out for a coffee and I thought maybe you'd have a pot on." Coffee was drunk by the potful at breakfast, but never served in my mother's house after morning. "But, of course, we can go down the street to the Booker T. Washington Hotel."

She bounced out of her chair. "Only takes a minute. How about some breakfast?"

I knew the idea of her daughter going into the then swankiest Negro hotel in town, escorted by a raggedy-looking white man would cause hospitality to flow like water.

She invited us into the kitchen.

"What about a little omelette and some bacon?" She turned on the oven and I held out my hand. Whenever she baked biscuits she removed her large diamond rings and put them on my fingers. "And just a few hot biscuits?"

She began the arrangement of bowls and pans and I excused myself and left George to his fate.

When I returned, changed out of evening clothes, the meal was nearly ready and she ordered me to set the table for two, and asked, "So, did you know that George makes a living as a gardener?"

"No, how do you know? Did George tell you that?"

George said, "Yes."

Mom was moving round the kitchen talking, cooking, singing little wisps of songs, the diamond earrings twinkling.

He was hypnotized.

"Put some butter on the table, Maya, please, and did you know he's unmarried and not thinking about getting married in the foreseeable future? Will the strawberry preserves be all right? Get that platter out of the cupboard, will you? Hum, hum..." She whipped up the eggs with a whisk.

"George, how did you come to tell my mother so much of your business?"

He shrugged his shoulders helplessly. "She asked me."

Mother said later that since he was white that was enough to make him unsuitable, but he was also much too old for me. Still I found his company easy and his intelligence exciting. He understood loving poetry, and although I would not show him my own poems, I recited Shakespearean sonnets and Paul Laurence Dunbar late at night in his house in Sausalito.

We shared long walks in Golden Gate Park and picnicked in John Muir woods. His mother was a well-known San Francisco journalist and he told me endless stories of the area and its colorful characters.

A gentle affection, devoid of romance, grew up between us and I enjoyed watching from his window as night faded over the Golden Gate Bridge. I was always back home before daybreak because Clyde expected me at the breakfast table while he chatted about his dreams or Fluke's misdoings.

———

I answered the telephone.

"Meez Angeloo?"

"Yes."

The voice was male and rich and the accent thick and poetic.

"My name is Yanko Varda. I am a painter." He was a well-known figure in San Francisco art circles.

"Yes, Mr. Varda." Why was he calling me?

"No, pleez—Yanko. Just Yanko."

"Yes, Yanko?" Yes, but why was he calling me?

"Meez Angeloo, I have heard so much about you, about your beauty and your talent and your grace. I have decided I must meet this wonderful woman with whom all the men are in love."

I could not think of a soul who was in love with me, but who can resist the suggestion that one has secret admirers?

"How nice of you to say that."

"Not atall. No, not atall. I have decided that I must give a dinner for you so that I myself may see this phenomenon: a beautiful woman with a great mind."

I knew I did not fit his description, but I would have torn my tongue out before I would have denied it.

He set Monday night for dinner and said he lived on a houseboat in Sausalito.

"George Hitchcock will bring you to my boat, which is called the *Vallejo.* I shall prepare, as only I can prepare, an ambrosia fit for a princess, but if you are in fact a queen, as I suspect, I hope you will condescend to take a sip from these humble hands. George will bring you to me. *Au revoir.*"

He sounded like a character in a Russian novel. The embroidery of his language, complex and passionate, enchanted me.

What did one wear to an ambrosial dinner on a houseboat? I selected and rejected every outfit in my closet and finally settled on a flowered dress that belonged to my mother. It was gay but not frivolous, chic but not formal.

George and I drove across the Golden Gate Bridge through a swirling fog and he stopped the car near the water. I stepped out onto wet mud. He rushed around and took my hand. "Follow me, walk on the planks."

Thick boards extended to a small rickety bridge. Lights shone dimly in the mists, but I had to keep my attention on the walkway or I might fall into the sullen-looking water below.

There were turns and steps and more turns. Then George stopped, turned and moved around me in the short space. "Here's where I get off. You go on up these three steps and knock at the door."

I tried to see his face in the overcast night. "What are you talking about?" His features were indistinct.

"I'm not invited tonight. This dinner is just for you."

"Well, wait a minute, I'm not going to ..." I reached for him.

He backed away, laughing, it seemed to me, sardonically. "I'll be back to pick you up at eleven. *Bon appétit!*"

During our short relationship, I had projected an air of independence, kindly but assured, and I could not scream at him or race down the flimsy walkway to clutch his retreating back.

I stood until George melted in the mist, then I turned and looked around. The shape of a large boat seemed to shiver in and out of a dark, misty sky, its windows beaming happily like lights in a giant jack-o'-lantern.

I walked up the remaining stairs wondering if I had been set up for an orgy—or perhaps I was to be an innocent participator in devil worship. I knew you could never tell about white people. Negroes had survived centuries of inhuman treatment and retained their humanity by hoping for the best from their pale-skinned oppressors but at the same time being prepared for the worst.

I looked through the porch door window at a short sturdy man quickly lighting candles in wine bottles, which he put on a long wooden table. No one else was visible, and although he looked strong, I decided I could probably take care of myself if he tried to take advantage of me.

I knocked sharply on the windowpane. The man looked up toward the door and smiled. His face was nearly as brown as mine and a sheaf of gray hair trembled when he moved. He came directly to the door, his smile broadening with each step.

"Rima," I thought I heard him say through the closed door. He pulled the door open and in the same movement stepped away from it and admired me.

"Ah, Rima, it ees you." He could not have been happier.

"No. Uh. My name is Maya."

He was expecting someone else. I quickly traced the days. This was Monday. Had I misunderstood him because of his accent or my excitement? But then, George must have made a mistake too.

"Don't stand there, my dear. Come in. Let me take your coat. Come in."

I walked into the warm kitchen, whose air was dense with the odor of cooking herbs. I looked at my host as he closed the door and hung my coat on a wall peg. His arms were thick and muscled and his neck broad and weather-roughened.

He turned. "Now, Rima, at last you've come to me. Let us drink wine to this meeting."

He seemed so happy, I was truly sorry to disappoint him. "I'm sorry, but I'm Maya Angelou. I'm the singer."

"My dear, I have known since I was a small boy on a hill in Greece that when I met you, you'd never tell me who you were, you would give another name. Equally beautiful and equally mystical. But I would know you by the music in your voice and the shadow of the forest on your beautiful face."

I was completely undone.

Over goblets of wine, he re-created his own version of the Rima legend for me. A creature, half girl and half bird, came periodically to earth assuming full womanly form, singing lilting birdlike melodies and lightening human hearts. Her stays were brief, then she became a bird and flew away to her beloved forest where she was happiest and free. While we ate a thick meat soup, he told me of W. H. Hudson's *Green Mansions* and the heroine, Rima, and said he would lend me the book, since its story was based on my magic.

"I shall address you as Maya in both public and private, for I fear if I continue calling you Rima, you may become annoyed and fly away. But you shall always know that in a small place in my heart I am thanking you for your visit."

The walls were adorned with delicately tinted pastels, and he guided me to each one, explaining, "In this collage I have tried to show a Carthaginian ship, swathed in grace moving from the harbor on its route to pillage another civilization. And here we have the King and Queen of Patagonia before the Feast of Stars." He talked about the beauty of Greece and the excitement of Paris. He was a close friend of Henry Miller and an acquaintance of Pablo Picasso. The time sped by as we ate fruit and cheese and I listened to the stories told in English as ornate as a Greek Orthodox ritual.

"I have a set of young friends who will be embellished by your presence. I beg you to be kind enough to come back to the *Vallejo* on a Sunday afternoon and meet them. We form a party each week and drink wine, eat soup and feast upon the riches of each other's thoughts. Please come—the men will surely worship you and the women will adore you."

George returned for me, and after a ceremonial glass of wine and an embrace from Yanko's leathery arms, he took me back to his house and patiently listened to my story of the evening. He stopped me: "Maya, I believe you're infatuated with Yanko."

"I most certainly am not."

"Many women find him irresistible."

"Probably." And I added without thinking, "but he is old and white."

George got up and turned on the record player.

———

One night at the Purple Onion I bowed to a full house and as I raised my head I heard "Bravo," "Bis," "Bravo." A group of people were standing in the middle of the room applauding, their hands over their heads like flamenco dancers. I bowed again and blew kisses as I had seen it done in movies. They continued applauding and shouting "More!" until the other patrons rose and, joining the group, implored me for another song. I always planned for at least two encores, so it was not the requests that embarrassed me but, rather, the overt display of appreciation which I had never received before. I sang another song and retreated to my dressing room. A waiter brought me a note which informed me: "We are friends. Please join us. Mitch."

I went to the table reluctantly, fearing they might be drunks, out for an evening's hilarity at anyone's expense.

As I approached, the group stood again and began applauding. I was ready to flee to the safety of my dressing room.

A large, dark-haired man offered me his hand.

"Maya, I am Mitch Lifton." He indicated the others individually. I shook hands with Victor Di Suvero and Henrietta, Francis and Bob Anshen, and Annette and Cyril March. "We are friends of Yanko and he suggested that we come to see you. You are absolutely wonderful."

We sat drinking wine and they gave me their particulars. Mitch Lifton's parents were Russian Jews, he was born in Paris, grew up in Mexico and was interested in film. Victor Di Suvero was a descendant of an Italian family that still had businesses in Italy and he was seriously courting the breath-taking Henrietta. Cyril March was a dermatologist from France, and architect Robert Anshen was a Frank Lloyd Wright devotee, whose wife, Frances Ney, gave great parties, kept a wonderful house and her own name. Annette March was an American who spoke French and was a blond, vibrating beauty. I took their cues and told them the things about myself that I thought it wise for them to know.

After my last performance they again stood and shouted their bravos and applauded as if Billie Holiday accompanied by Duke Ellington had just finished singing "I Cover the Waterfront." They left together after reminding me that we all had a date on Sunday, and because I was used to BYOB parties, I asked what I should bring.

"Imagine you're coming to Corfu," Victor said, "and remember that cheese and fruit have never been rejected in the Mediterranean."

———

Gaily colored pennants floated on posts attached to the boat. Cut-glass windows, oddly shaped, broke the monotony of weathered wood. Large pieces of sculpture stood sentinel in the area leading to the bridge in the sunlight. The boat looked like a happy child's dream castle.

Yanko greeted me warmly, but without surprise, allowing me to feel not only welcome but expected. Mitch came forward smiling, followed by Victor. They both embraced me and complimented George on his good luck. The three men fell into a private exchange and I wandered away to observe the gathering.

The party was in lingual swing. European classical music provided a background for tidbits of conversation that drifted clear from the general noise. In one corner Annette and Cyril spoke French to a wild-haired woman who never allowed one sentence to end before she interrupted. A thin, professorial man stroked his goatee and spoke to Yanko in Greek. Bob Anshen waved me over and I stayed awhile listening to him discourse on the merits of solar heating systems. Victor joined the group who warbled in Italian as melodious as a concerto.

Other languages I could not recognize spattered and rattled around the room. One handsome Negro was talking to a group around the long table. When he saw me his face spread in a broad smile and he stood up. If he had started speaking to me in an African language, I would not have been surprised.

"Hello there. How are you?" Straight, university, Urban League, colored, NAACP middle-class Negro accent.

"Fine, thank you."

"My name is Jim, join us."

I had never been found attractive by middle-class Negro men, since I was neither pretty nor fair-skinned, well-off or educated, and since most were firmly struggling up Striver's Row they needed women who could either actually help them or at least improve their visual image.

I sat down and found myself in the middle of a discussion on the recent Supreme Court ruling in *Brown* vs. *Board of Education* that had banned racial segregation in education. Jim and I and a pretty blond woman on the other side of the table argued that not only was the ruling just, it was very late in coming. Our opponents contended for the legitimacy of states' rights. As voices were raised and the selection of words became keener, I noticed that I was less angry than interested. I knew many whites were displeased by the ruling, but I had never heard them discuss it.

One debater was called away; another, bored with the display of passion, said, "You people are too serious," and left to kibbitz a chess game.

Jim impressed me. Hearing his formal accent, I had not expected such resolve. "Where do you live?" Maybe I could invite him to Mother's for dinner.

"We live in Mill Valley. What about you?"

I heard the "we" and restrained myself from a new examination of the room. The place was so crowded I must have overlooked his wife.

"I live in San Francisco."

The blonde who had been on our side in the argument and had made perceptive points in the controversy edged forward on the bench. She leaned toward me.

"San Francisco's not far from Mill Valley. Why don't you come over for dinner?"

Jim said, "And meet our kids." He laughed a little self-consciously. "Jenny is learning how to cook greens and she bakes a mean pan of cornbread."

Jenny blushed prettily.

I said, "Thank you, but I work nights." I had not quite accepted that white women were as serious in interracial marriages as white men.

A statement that had great currency in the Negro neighborhood warned: "Be careful of white women with colored men. They might marry and bear children, but when they get what they want out of the men, they leave their children and go back to their own people." We are all so cruelly and comprehensively educated by our tribal myths that it did not occur to me to question what it was that white women wanted out of the men. Since few Negro men in the interracial marriages I had seen had a substantial amount of money, and since the women could have had the sex without the marriage, and since mothers leave their children so rarely that an incident of child abandonment is cause for a newspaper story, it followed that the logic of the warning did not hold.

I excused myself from the table and went to stand on the deck. The small exclusive town of Tiburon glistened across the green-blue water and I thought about my personal history. Of Stamps, Arkansas, and its one paved street, of the segregated Negro school and the bitter poverty that causes children to become bald from malnutrition. Of the blind solitude of unwed motherhood and the humiliation of prostitution. Waves slapped at the brightly painted catamaran tied up below me and I pursued my past to a tardy marriage which was hastily broken. And the inviting doors to newer and richer worlds, where the sounds of happiness drifted through closed panels and the doorknobs came off in my hands.

Guests began to leave, waving at Yanko, who stood beside me at the rail: "À tout à l 'heure," "Adiós," "Ciao," "Adieu," "Au revoir," "Good-bye," "Ta." Yanko put his hand on my elbow and guided me back inside.

We had become a crowd of intimates around the table. Annette ladled the soup into large bowls and they all talked about sailing plans for next Sunday. If the weather was nice we would leave early so that we could have a full sail in before the Sunday crowd came for open house. Cyril wondered if I would like him and Annette to pick me up, since they also lived in San Francisco. Mitch said he wanted to talk to me about a short film he was going to do. Possibly I would like to narrate it. Victor said he and Henrietta were going to the Matador on Saturday for lunch and I should join them.

They did not question whether I wanted acceptance into their circle. I was chosen and my being a part of the group was a fact; the burden of choice was removed from me and I was relieved.

I told them I had a young son, and before I could ask, Yanko said, "Bring him. The sea is a female. And females desire young and masculine life. Bring him and we shall pacify the mother of us all. Bring him."

One morning we sailed out on a smooth sea. Cyril was at the helm and Victor was regaling us with a gallant tale of medieval conquest. A young Scandinavian was on board, and when Victor was finished he, in turn, told a Viking story of heroic deeds and exploration.

Yanko slapped his forehead and said, "Ah, yes. Now I know what we must do. We must all plan to go abroad and civilize Europe. We must get a large ship and sail down the Thames and cultivate Britain first because they need it most. Then we cross the Channel and bring culture to France. Cyril, you shall be the first mate because you have by nature and training the mechanical mind. Mitch, you shall be the boatswain because of your 'Samson strength'; Maya, you shall be the *cantante*, sitting in the prow singing us to victory. Victor, you shall be second mate because your talent is to organize. Annette, you shall be our figurehead, for your beauty will stun the commoners and enchant the aristocracy. I shall be captain and do absolutely nothing. *Allons, enfants!*"

Yanko allowed me to enter a world strange and fanciful. Although I had to cope daily with real and mundane matters, I found that some of the magic of his world stayed around my shoulders.

CHAPTER 14

If *New Faces of 1953* excited the pulses of San Franciscans, *Porgy and Bess* set their hearts afire. Reviewers and columnists raved about

Leontyne Price and William Warfield in the title roles and praised the entire company. The troupe had already successfully toured other parts of the United States, Europe and South America.

The Purple Onion contract bound me inextricably, but it also held the management to the letter of the law—I could not be fired except after having committed the most flagrant abuses.

On *Porgy and Bess*'s second night I called Barry and said, "I'm off tonight. You may say I'm ill."

"Are you ill?"

"You may say so." And hung up.

I had matured into using a ploy of not quite telling the truth but not quite telling a lie. I experienced no guilt at all and it was clear that the appearance of innocence lay mostly in a complexity of implication.

I went to the theater ready to be entertained, but not expecting a riot of emotion. Price and Warfield sang; they threaded their voices with music and spellbound the audience with their wizardry. Even the chorus performed with such verve that a viewer could easily believe each singer was competing for a leading part.

By intermission I had been totally consumed. I had laughed and cried, exulted and mourned, and expected the second act to produce no new emotions. I returned to my seat prepared for a repetition of great music.

The curtain rose on a picnic in progress. The revelers were church members led by a pious old woman who forbade dancing, drinking and even laughing. Cab Calloway as Sportin' Life pranced out in a cream-colored suit and tried to paganize the Christians.

He sang "It Ain't Necessarily So," strutting as if he was speaking ex cathedra.

The audience applauded loudly, interrupting the stage action. Then a young woman broke away from a group of singers near the wings. She raced to the center of the stage and began to dance.

The sopranos sang a contrapuntal high-toned encouragement and the baritones urged the young woman on. The old lady tried to catch her, to stop the idolatrous dance, but the dancer moved out of her reach, flinging her legs high, carrying the music in her body as if it were a private thing, given into her care and protection. I nearly screamed with delight and envy. I wanted to be with her on the stage letting the music fly through my body. Her torso seemed to lose solidity and float, defying gravity. I wanted to be with her. No, I wanted to *be* her.

In the second act, Warfield, as the crippled Porgy, dragged the audience into his despair. Even kneeling, he was a large man, broad and thick-chested. His physical size made his affliction and his loss of Bess even sadder. The resonant voice straddled the music and rode it, controlling it.

I remained in my seat after the curtain fell and allowed people to climb over my knees to reach the aisle. I was stunned. *Porgy and Bess* had shown me the greatest array of Negro talent I had ever seen.

I took Clyde to the first matinée and he liked the dancing and "the little goat that pulled Porgy off the stage" at the end of the opera.

The Purple Onion had picked up my three-month option and I decided to develop my own material. I began making up music for poems I had written years before and writing new songs that fit the calypso form.

One night the club was filled and more people were waiting outside for the room to clear. I lifted my head from a bow and standing before me was a beautiful Black woman holding a long-stemmed rose. I bowed to her and she returned the bow, continuing to bend until she laid the flower at my feet. She blew a kiss and walked down the aisle to her table. Her friends began applauding again. I was not sure whether it was for me or for her, so I nodded to the musicians and started another encore. Halfway through I recognized the woman. She was the soprano who sang the "Strawberry Song" in *Porgy and Bess*. I almost bit my song in two; all the people at that table were probably from *Porgy and Bess*.

I went directly from the stage to the table and took the rose along.

The group stood and applauded again. I laid the flower on the table and applauded them. The audience, infected, began to applaud us.

"These are the great singers from *Porgy and Bess*," I shouted over the noise. People stood up to look, and soon the whole audience was standing and we were applauding ourselves for our good taste to be alive and in the right place at the right time.

We went to Pete's Pool Room, a large rambling restaurant on Broadway where the beats and artists and big-eyed tourists and burlesque queens went for a breakfast of hard rolls and maybe a game of pool. I wanted to call the whole room to order and present to them the singers from *Porgy and Bess*. We found seats and I heard the names again.

Ned Wright, a tall muscular man of about thirty, said I was excellent and "Don't run yourself down, darling, there are plenty of people in the world who will do that for you."

Lillian Hayman, the dramatic soprano, who was as plump as a pillow and biscuit-brown, laughed often, trilling like a bird and showing perfect white teeth. Chief Bey, the drummer, mumbled in a deep voice that seemed to shake his wiry black frame. Joseph Attles, a tenor, was at forty the oldest of the group. He was tall and very delicately made. A lemon-yellow man, he was understudy for Cab Calloway, who was Sportin' Life, and Joseph James, who sang the role of Jake.

And, of course, Martha Flowers, a great soprano and at that time a Bess understudy. Martha said, "My dear, you stand like an African queen holding off a horde of marauders. All alone." She was short, but as she talked and gestured, body erect, she grew tall before my eyes. I told them how their singing had affected me, and when the opportunity arose, I asked about the dancer.

Martha said, "Leesa Foster, Elizabeth Foster. She is also a soprano and I hear she is going to be one of our Besses." They promised to bring her to the club the next evening.

Martha bettered her promise by bringing not only Leesa Foster but even more people the next night. The voice teacher, Frederick Wilkerson, and two or three other cast members sat with the original group at two tables pushed together. Again they all said they enjoyed my singing, again I demurred, saying that I was really a dancer. Leesa was instantly interested and we spoke of dance schools, teachers and styles. Again we went to Pete's for breakfast. Wilkie, as the voice teacher was called, leaned forward and boomed, "You are singing totally wrong. Totally wrong. If you keep it up you'll lose your voice in five years." He leaned back in his chair and added, "Maybe three years, yes, yes. Maybe three."

His pronouncement pinched my budding confidence. I looked around the table, but no one seemed perturbed by his warning. I asked him what I could do to prevent disaster. He nodded and said in sonorous tones, "You are intelligent, yes I see that. You are intelligent. Get to a voice teacher, a good voice teacher. And study very hard. Apply yourself. That's all." He smacked his lips as if he had just tasted a favorite sweet.

"How can I find a good teacher?"

The singers were as curious about his answer as I. They looked at him.

"Now that's another intelligent question," his voice boomed. "As a matter of fact, I plan to leave *Porgy and Bess* and relocate myself in San Francisco. I am willing to take you as a student if, and only if, you work hard and listen to me. I don't have time for any more students; however, I want to help you. If you don't get help, you not only won't be able to sing, you'll hardly be able to talk."

Robert Breen, *Porgy and Bess*'s good-looking and balding producer, came to the Purple Onion the next evening accompanied by his wife, Wilva, a pleasant little blond woman; the business manager, Robert Dustin; and an attractive, well-built woman who was introduced to me as Ella Gerber, company drama coach. When we shook hands, her dark-lashed eyes studied me.

Breen said he had heard I was a professional dancer. I admitted that.

"We may have an opening soon for a dancer who sings. Would you come to the theater and audition for us?"

I thought about my contract. I would not be free to take the job for nearly three months. Should I tell them? It would be honest and fair to leave the job open for another dancer. I told myself that I loved honesty and openness, not so much for its own sake but for its simplicity—I would be free from apologies, recriminations and accusations. Then I thought of Leesa Foster dancing to the sound of great voices, tossing herself into music and movement as if within that marriage lay all human bliss.

"Would I have to audition to a record or could I work with the company?"

Breen turned his pink, baby-skinned face to Dustin.

"We have a full rehearsal scheduled," Dustin said, "and if you want Maya to try out, that could be arranged."

They looked at me, Ella Gerber's eyes computing the length of my legs, the size of my brain and the amount of my talent.

Breen suggested a date and I agreed. We drank a cold white wine to the audition and they left.

I went to the bar and told Ned about the conversation I had had with Breen. "Dance, darling." He raised his hands to eye level and snapped his fingers. "Dance until they see Nijinsky in a duet with Katherine Dunham." Snap!

———

All the singers were in street clothes, as if they had stopped by the theater en route for something more important. Some stood on the empty stage, others stood in the wings or lounged in the front row of the theater.

Billy Johnson, assistant conductor, waited while the musicians warmed up and tuned their instruments in the orchestra pit. Trills and arpeggios of voices came from backstage.

The stage manager, Walter Riemer, had a flashy smile and was as elegant as John Gielgud, whom he resembled. He took a position just off the stage. "Watch me, dear, when I do this"—he waved his hand like a flag in a high wind—"that's your cue." And he left me.

I sneaked around the curtain and watched as Billy lifted his arms as if he was trying to pull the orchestra out of the pit by invisible strings. The music began to swell, the singers poised.

At a casual indication from Johnson's right hand the voices exploded, ripping shreds in the air.

When Riemer's hand floated my cue, I was laughing and crying at the wonder of it all. I ran on stage, stepping lightly between the singers' notes. If I was supposed to portray a woman carried away by music, blinded and benumbed by her surroundings, enchanted so by the rhythm and melody that she fancied herself a large, gloriously colored bird free to fly rainbows and light up the winds, then I was she.

Three days later, Bob Dustin offered me the job.

I said, as if newly indignant, that the Purple Onion would not let me out of my contract. Dustin commiserated with me and added, "We'll be auditioning people for the next two months. We have to have a lead dancer before we go back to Europe."

Even my imagination had never dared to include me in Europe. Whenever I envisioned foreign countries, I saw them through other people's words or other people's pictures. London to me was as Dickens saw it, a folk song in a cockney accent, Churchill V-ing his fingers, saying, "We shall fight on the beaches," and so forth. Paris, in my mind, rang with the hoofbeats of horse-drawn carriages from the age of Guy de Maupassant. Germany was Hitler and concentration-camp horror or beery burghers in stiff white shirts sitting on benches photographed by Cartier-Bresson. Italy was the hungry streets of *Open City* or curly-haired people singing and eating pasta.

The images had been provided by movies, books and Pathé News, and none included a six-foot-tall Black woman hovering either in the back or in the foreground.

CHAPTER 15

When *Porgy and Bess* left San Francisco I resigned myself to the nightclub routine, and the burden of life was lightened only by twice-weekly sessions with Wilkie and Lloyd and the romping growth of Clyde.

Three days before my contract ran out I received a telephone call from Saint Subber, the Broadway producer, inviting me to come to New York City to try out for a new show called *House of Flowers*. He said Pearl Bailey would be starring and he had heard I was a great deal like her. If I satisfied him and got the role he had in mind, I would play opposite Miss Bailey.

New Yorkers may love their hometown loyally, but San Franciscans believe that when good angels die they stay in northern California and hover over the Golden Gate Bridge. I appreciated the chance to try out for a Broadway show, but the invitation did not make me ecstatic. It meant leaving San Francisco, without the prospect of Europe with *Porgy and Bess*.

Mom and Lottie and Wilkie encouraged me to go. The voice teacher and my mother had found that they had much in common and Mother invited him to move into our house. He came bringing his piano, students, huge rumbling voice and his religious positivism. He could cook nearly as well as the two women and the kitchen rang and reeked with the attempts of three chefs to outtalk and outcook one another.

They would take care of Clyde until I found an apartment and then he could fly to me. Of course I was going to get the part. There was no question of that.

I arrived in New York and went to a midtown hotel which Willkie had suggested. The congested traffic and raucous voices, the milling crowds and towering buildings, made me think of my tiny fourth-floor room at the end of a dark corridor a sanctuary.

I telephoned Saint Subber, who said I must come to his apartment. I wriggled around his invitation, not wishing to face the street again so soon and hesitant about going to a strange man's apartment—especially a New York producer's apartment. Hollywood films had taught me that breed was dangerous: each one was fat, smoked large smelly cigars and all said, "All right, girlie, ya got talent, now lemme see ya legs."

"Mr. Saint Subber"—or was one supposed to call him Mr. Subber?—"I need to have my hair done. May I see you tomorrow?"

He blasted my excuse. "No, no matter, I won't be looking at your hair."

See, my legs. Just as I thought.

"I want to see what you look like." He gave me his address and hung up.

I had come three thousand miles, so surely I had the courage to go a few more blocks.

A uniformed doorman in front of a neat East Side apartment house raised his brows when I told him my destination, but he walked me into the lobby and reluctantly handed me over to a uniformed elevator operator. The operator pulled his face down as if to say "So, hot stuff, huh?" but he said "Penthouse," and we began our smooth ascent. When we stopped he rang a bell and the door opened.

A beautiful blond young man offered me his hand. "Miss Angelou?" He did not look as if my legs would interest him.

"Yes. Mr. Subber?"

The elevator door closed and we were in a beautifully furnished living room.

"No, I'm not Saint. My name is Tom. I'm helping on the production. Please have a seat." He led me to a sofa. "Saint will be with you in a few minutes. What can I get you to drink?"

While he was away I looked at the room and wondered about the tenant. Paintings adorned the walls and flowers were fresh and gay on little tables. A man's voice in argument came through a louvered door.

Tom returned with a gin and tonic in a very tall, extraordinarily thin glass. He asked about my trip and tried to reassure me when I told him I was nervous.

A man rushed through the shuttered door; he was small and thin and his dark hair was cut in a "Quo Vadis."

"Well, that's over. Oh, my God!" He threw himself on a chaise longue and gingerly put both hands to his head. "Oh, God! What do they want? Oh, my head. Virginia!"

A large Negro woman came through another door. She wore the kind of apron I had not seen since I had left the small country town in

Arkansas. It was white, bibbed, starched and voluminous. She went directly to the man and began to massage his temples.

"That's all right, Saint honey, that's all right, you hear. Now don't think about it, honey. Everything's going to be all right."

I could not believe it.

Neither had taken notice of me and I was so enthralled I frankly stared, recording the scene.

Tom and I could have been an audience while two actors performed a scene in experimental theater.

It was decidedly too new, too strange. I started laughing.

The man sat bolt upright. "Who are you?"

"I?" I held the laughter. "I'm Maya Angelou."

"You can't be." He was still sitting straight.

"But I am, I am Maya Angelou." I was willing to swear to it.

"Well, my God, how tall are you?"

"I'm six feet."

"But you can't be!" He seemed sure.

"I am, I am too."

"Stand up. I don't believe it."

I stood up, hoping I had not shrunk in the plane or in the taxi or in the elevator.

"My God, it's true, you're six feet tall."

I laughed because I was happy that at least my height had not betrayed me and because he was funny.

"And a great laugh, too. Oh, my God, I know, you're a Black Carol Channing."

That made me laugh again. He stood up and came to me.

"We'll do your hair red. Will that be all right? Red or blond?"

I said, "I don't think so."

"Oh, you wouldn't like that?" It was a sincere question.

"Noooo." I pictured myself with hair as red as Gwen Verdon's and started laughing again. "No, I don't think it would work."

"All right." He chuckled, too. "We'll think of something else."

I was still laughing.

"What's so funny?"

When I could catch my breath I told him. "I expected you to smoke a cigar and pinch my cheeks, to roll your eyes at me and make some lewd proposition. I've been dreading that all the way from California, and I get here"—the funny bone was struck again—"I get here and...Tom and you and Virginia and my red hair." He, too, began to laugh at the absurd situation. Tom joined in.

Saint Subber said impulsively, "Stay for dinner. Virginia, we'll be another for dinner." For all his theatrics, or maybe because of them, I knew he was a strong man. I had always been more comfortable around strong people.

After a dinner of frogs' legs (I had never eaten them before and had to ask if they were eaten with a knife and fork or with the fingers like spare ribs), he told me to come to the theater the next morning and not to sing any special material, because Truman Capote was going to be at the theater and "Truman hates special material."

I thanked them both for their hospitality and went back to the hotel to telephone Mom. "Do your best tomorrow" she said, "and don't worry. Remember, you've got a home to come back to." I spoke to Clyde, who sounded fine, and hung up and went to bed.

The Alvin Theater was on Broadway and I had been asked to go to the stage door around the corner. I walked quite cheerfully among the crowds on the sidewalk. I had stopped at a music store and bought a copy of "Love for Sale," for no reason except that it had been on display and I had heard it sung so often. If Truman Capote did not like special material, I would sing a standard for him. I noticed only after I had turned the corner at the theater that a line of Negro people stretched around the block headed in the direction I was taking. I exchanged smiles with some of the young standees and gave good mornings to some of the older women with pleasant faces. The line stopped at the stage door. I had never auditioned in New York and thought maybe all Broadway shows had their tryouts in the same theater.

I knocked at the door and Tom opened it. I would not have been surprised if I had been given a number and told to take my place in line. Instead, he said, "Oh, Miss Angelou. Please come in. I'll tell Saint you're here."

He led me to a corner and excused himself. The blurred forms inside the theater became more visible. There were over a hundred Negro people lined up along the backstage wall, waiting, alert.

Tom waved me over and whispered, "Saint will hear you now. Have you your music?"

I said, "Yes."

"Give it to me," he said, "I'll take it to the pianist. Do you want to run over it with her?"

I did not think so—after all, it was only "Love for Sale."

"Just a minute and I'll call your name. Walk right through here." He showed me to the wings and an entrance stage left. "The pianist is in the pit. You nod to her and she'll begin." Just like the old Purple Onion days.

"And there's nothing to worry about." He added, "Truman Capote is out there and Saint and Yip Harburg and Peter Hall. Do your best."

I waited, trying not to think about trying out and thinking about New York. The Apple. I would make it and send for Clyde, then we would spend afternoons in Central Park, perhaps not as nice as Golden Gate Park, but then...I would find a lover, too; among all those millions of people there had to be a man who had been waiting for me to come along and cheer up his life. I would not think about trying out. Just wait until my name was called and then go out and sing.

"Miss Angelou, Maya Angelou."

I walked out in front of the velvet curtain. The lights were bright and hard and white, and the theater seats, only dimly lighted near the stage, darkened into oblivion. I saw a small clump of figures in the distance. On the right side of the orchestra pit a woman sat patiently at a grand piano.

I took my position, thinking of Lloyd Clark: "Stand still, stand perfectly still, darling, still." I stood. Wilkie's teaching ran in my thoughts: "Drop your jaw. Don't try to look pretty by grinning when you sing. Drop your jaw." I dropped my jaw, and then nodded to the pianist, moving nothing but my head.

She stroked out the first notes of my song and I began.

"Love for sale, appetizing young love—"

She stopped.

"Uh, no, uh, I'm playing the verse. If you don't want the verse I'll go right to the refrain."

I had read the verse when I bought the music, but I had never heard it sung.

"Just the 'love for sale' part, please." I thought I heard a titter from backstage, but I could not be sure. She played the first three notes and I began to sing. "Love for sale, appetizing young love for sale." I imagined I was a girl in a trench coat and a beret, standing under a streetlight in old Chinatown in a light rain. Men passed me by after looking me over and I continued my plaintive offer.

I was so engrossed in telling the story that I did not know when the music and I had parted company, or quite how we could get back together. I only knew I was in one key and the piano in another. I looked at the pianist. She began to strike the keys harder, and in a vain attempt to settle correctly I began to sing louder. She lifted her hands and pounded on the piano. I raised my voice and screamed, "If you want to buy my wares" a mile away from what she was playing.

She half rose, crouched over the keyboard. There was a frantic determination in the position of her body, in the bend of her neck. She would get me back on pitch or there would just be splinters left on the piano.

Plunk plunk—she was as loud as I—and I heard a low vocal grumble as she sought to overwhelm my voice into submission. I shouted, "Follow me and climb the stairs." A thin but definite screech slid through my nose. I dropped my jaw to try to force the sound down into the back of my mouth where I could control it. The pianist was standing. Her brow was knit and her teeth bared. She was about to attack the piano for the final chord. I barged in, overtook her and in a second outdistanced her as I yelled "Love for sale."

She flopped on the piano stool exhausted and in defeat.

I was just a little proud that I had gotten all the way through the song. Then I heard the sounds. There were gurgles and giggles from the theater and the muffled bubbling of outright disorderly laughter from backstage.

The flush of heat crawled up my face and spread through my body the instant I realized that I was the object of derision. But I was, I told myself, the person who'd had flowers put at her feet. And I was the entertainer asked to take Eartha Kitt's role in *New Faces.* I was the dancer *Porgy and Bess* wanted to follow the fabulous Lizabeth Foster. And I was being laughed away just because I could not sing "Love for Sale." Well, they need not.

"Excuse me," I said, and looked over the rows of seats toward the indistinct shadows. "I understand that Mr. Capote doesn't like special material. And you've asked me to come out here to show you what I do. I am willing to sing calypso for you or I'd be just as happy to go home."

Indeed, it would be nicer to go back to California. To my mother's big house and good food. To my son, who needed me, and Aunt Lottie, who loved me. Back to the wonderful Purple Onion where my friends would welcome me. The period between becoming a great Broadway star setting New York on its ear and returning to the family's bosom was shorter than the first intervals between the overheard laughter.

There was little sound from the audience. They clapped as if they were wearing furry gloves.

"Yes, Miss Angelou, sing whatever you like."

I said, "I'm going to sing 'Run Joe,' and since I was discouraged from bringing my sheet music, I'll have to sing it a cappella." Wilkie had told me that music sung without accompaniment was called "a cappella."

If I was going home, I had to show them what they were missing, and that I had some place to go.

I gave them the special Saturday-night standing-room-only encore version. The one where I spun around, my body taut. The one where I yelped small noises and sighed like breaking ocean waves.

When I finished, the first applause came from the pianist. She was smiling and clapping so energetically that I surmised that I had rescued her recently endangered belief in the human voice. There was more applause from the audience, and this time it sounded fresh and sincere. I did not know what I was expected to do next. I stood still for a moment, then bowed and rather stiffly turned away.

"Will you wait backstage, Miss Angelou?" Tom's voice sprang through the void.

"Yes, thank you."

Whenever I was embarrassed or felt myself endangered, I relied on my body's training to deliver me. Grandmother Henderson and Grandmother Baxter had drilled my brother and me in the posture of "shoulders back, head up, look the future in the eye," and years of dance classes had compounded the education. I turned and walked to the wings like Cleopatra walking to the throne room (meanwhile clasping the asp in her bodice).

Backstage a few of the hopeful contenders tapped their hands together or snapped their fingers when they saw me. They grinned saucy compliments to me, probably as much for my own sassiness in standing up and talking back as for what they heard of my second song.

Saint Subber, Tom and Truman Capote came backstage and walked over to me.

Saint Subber said, "You've got a certain quality."

Tom's praise was as generous as his manner.

Truman Capote spoke, and I thought for a desperate moment that he was pulling my leg. He said in a faint falsetto, "Miss Angelou, honey, ah love yoah work." He sounded just like a rich old Southern white woman. He reminded me of a Countee Cullen poem:

> She even thinks that up in heaven
> Her class lies late and snores
> While poor Black cherubs rise at seven
> To do celestial chores.

Yet I could not detect a shread of superciliousness on his face or in his soft yielding manner. I thanked him. Tom said he would be in touch with me and I shook hands with the men and left the theater.

Outside I passed the line of people still waiting. They scanned my features intently, trying to read the outcome of my ordeal and thereby prophesy their own. If I was triumphant it meant that success was in the air and might come to them. On the other hand, it could mean that I had just filled the vacancy that they themselves might have taken.

Theirs was a grievous lot. Ten or twenty jobs for two thousand or more trained, talented and anxious aspirants. Another Countee Cullen poem stated that God, should he choose, could explain why he gave the turtle such a strange yet lovely shell, why the spring follows winter, why the snake doffs its skin, "yet," said the poet, "do I marvel at this curious thing, to make a poet Black and bid him sing." And of all things, to bid him sing in New York City.

I thought of *Porgy and Bess*. Of the sixty people who sang and laughed and lived together, the camaraderie and the pride they had in one another's genius. Although I had not heard from the company administrators for three months, I had received cards from Martha Flowers and from Ned Wright. I waited around in my small hotel room and prowled my dingy lobby. I called Mother, who ordered me to keep my chin up, and Clyde, who missed me and gave me news of Fluke's latest adventures. Wilkie reminded me that "In God I live and have my being."

On a Thursday morning I received a note which read: "Miss Angelou, the *House of Flowers* company is happy to inform you that you have been chosen for the part in our production. Please come to the office Thursday afternoon at three to sign your contract."

I shared the news with my family immediately, and when I hung up, the telephone rang again. I thought it was probably Saint Subber calling to congratulate me.

It was Breen's Everyman's Opera Company. Bob Dustin said, "Maya Angelou?"

"Yes."

"This is *Porgy and Bess*. We called your San Francisco number and were told you were in New York."

"Yes."

"We want you for the role of Ruby."

How could there be so much of a good thing?

"But I've just got a part in a new show opening on Broadway."

"Really? Oh, that's too bad. The company is in Montreal now and we leave for Italy in four days."

There really was no contest. I wanted to travel, to try to speak other languages, to see the cities I had read about all my life, but most important, I wanted to be with a large, friendly group of Black people who sang so gloriously and lived with such passion.

"I don't have a passport."

"We are being sponsored by the State Department."

I thought about the school I had attended which was on the House Un-American Activities Committee list.

He said, "Don't worry about your passport. We can get a special dispensation. Do you want to join *Porgy and Bess*?"

"Yes, yes." Yes, indeed.

"Then come to the office and we'll get you straightened out. You'll leave tomorrow afternoon for Montreal."

I telephoned Saint Subber and explained that I had been offered another job. He asked me if I would give up a new Broadway show for a chorus part in a touring company.

I said "Yes."

CHAPTER 16

My mind turned over and over like a flipped coin: Paris, then Clyde's motherless birthday party, Rome and my son's evening prayers said to Fluke, Madrid and Clyde struggling alone with his schoolwork.

I telephoned home again. Mother was pleased and gave me a load of phrases to live by. "Treat everybody right, remember life is a two-way street. You might meet the same people on your way down that you met going up." And "Look to the hills from whence cometh your help." Lottie said she was proud of me and that I had it in me to become great. Wilkie told me to hum a lot, place my voice in the mask and always drop my jaw. And to keep in my heart the knowledge that there was no place where God was not.

I asked to speak with Clyde. Using a tack I loathed, I talked to him as if he was a small child with faulty English. He asked when I was coming home and when was I sending for him. His voice became faint after I said I was not coming the next week but soon. Very soon.

Yes, he'd be a good boy. Yes, he would mind Grandmother and Aunt Lottie. And yes, he knew I loved him. He hung up first.

When I called Ivonne she told me to stop crying, that Clyde had no father, so it was up to me to make a place for both of us, and that that was what I was doing. She said she would go over to the house as usual and see him and take him out. After all, he was not with strangers but with his grandmother—why did I worry?

The past revisited. My mother had left me with my grandmother for years and I knew the pain of parting. My mother, like me, had had her motivations, her needs. I did not relish visiting the same anguish on my son, and she, years later, had told me how painful our separation was to her. But I had to work and I would be good. I would make it up to my son and one day would take him to all the places I was going to see.

I had been given a précis of the DuBose Heyward book on which George and Ira Gershwin had based their opera:

Porgy, a crippled beggar, lives in the Negro hamlet of Catfish Row, North Carolina. He is loved by the town's inhabitants, who eke out their meager living by fishing and selling local produce.

When Crown, a tough stevedore, kills Robbin, Serena's husband, in a crap game, the white police descend upon the hamlet to find the culprit. Sportin' Life, who runs the gambling and other nefarious money-making schemes, escapes into Ruby's house, but Bess, Crown's beautiful and worldly woman, is rejected by the community's women and is nearly captured in the raid. Just as the police dragnet is about to close in on her, Porgy opens the door of his hut and Bess finds safety. Porgy falls in love with Bess and she accepts his love and protection, swearing that she will stay with him forever. Crown escapes from jail and comes to claim Bess at a picnic which Porgy does not attend. Bess is sexually attracted to her old lover and goes away with him for three days. Porgy goes to look for her. When she returns to Catfish Row, Porgy is away and the local women scorn her. Sportin' Life courts her, gives her cocaine and begs her to leave the small town and accompany him to New York, where "I'll give you the finest diamonds on upper Fifth Avenue.

> "And through Harlem we'll go a struttin'
>   We'll go a struttin' and there'll be nuttin'
>   Too good for you."

She cannot resist his entreaty, his style and the drugs. She leaves with him.

Porgy returns and is told of Bess's journey, and against the pleas of his neighbors, calls for his goat, hitches the cart to the animal and sets out to travel to New York to find his Bess.

The naïve story is given dramatic pace by the birth of a longed-for child, a hurricane in which a member of the community is killed and a picnic where Sportin' Life tries to tempt the religious people away from their beliefs.

———

On Friday, breathless, excited and afraid, I arrived at dusk in Montreal.

I was met at the airport, and although it was too early for the cast to assemble, taken directly to the theater. Backstage, men shouted to one another in French and English and hustled around, pulling ropes and adjusting pieces of scenery. When I walked onto the empty set, all the shards of the last two days' tensions fell away. I was suddenly in the papier-mâché world of great love, passion and poignancy.

I was examining Porgy's cabin and the house where Robbin's widow, Serena, sings her mournful aria when the singers began to trickle into the back of the theater.

Ella Gerber saw me slouching upstage in the shadows.

"Oh, Maya, you've arrived!" She came forward. "Here's your script, your hotel and room number. A schedule for rehearsals. I suggest you watch this performance carefully and study your script tonight. You'll be rehearsing tomorrow."

She said I had no dressing room because I would not be performing until we arrived in Italy, but she would tell the cast that I had arrived.

My fears that I had been forgotten turned out to be baseless. When Ella led me down the dressing room corridor, she called out, "Maya's here!"

Martha Flowers ran out into the hall. *"La première danseuse, elle est ici!"*

Lillian Hayman followed smiling, saying "Welcome."

Barbara Ann Webb grinned, spread her arms and made "Hey, girl" sound like "Where have you been so long?" and "Why weren't you here sooner?"

The three women shared a cluttered dressing room and I sat amid the costumes and the disarray of make-up, watching them prepare for the show. Martha was as delicately made as a Stradivarius. Her complexion was the rich brown of polished mahogany and her hands fine and small. She had large bright eyes. Her lips, full and open, revealed even white teeth in the dark face. She called herself, and was called by her friends, "Miss Fine Thing." Rightly.

If Martha was a violin, Lillian Hayman was a cello. She was a medium-brown woman of heavy curves and deep arches. Her dignified posture caused her to be regarded as stout rather than fat, and she moved lightly as if her weight might be only in the eye of the beholder. She had a handsome face softened by a ready warm smile. She was a dramatic soprano and the description was apt.

Barbara Ann Webb, a lyric soprano, was the innocent when I joined the company, and so she remained until I left. She was nearly as large as Lillian, but her curves were younger and more conventionally arranged. A Texan, she had an openness that reminded me of sunshine in movies by Technicolor. Her skin was a shade lighter than a ripe peach, and had she been white, she could have been a stand-in for

Linda Darnell. Throughout ten countries and fifteen cities, those three women became and remained my closest friends.

That first night the chatter in the dressing room wound down and there was a knock at the door.

"Fifteen minutes."

"O.K.," Lillian shouted.

I had heard the announcement of "Half-hour" earlier, but none of the women responded. Now Martha turned away from the mirror and her eyes glazed, began to sing "Do re me fa sol la ti do." I didn't know whether I was expected to say something, then Lillian also dropped her interest in our conversation and an unseeing look came into her eyes, she stretched her lips in a taut, false smile and holding her teeth closed, yelped "Ye, ya, yo, you." Barbara Ann stood and began to sway slowly from side to side. She started to lower and raise her jaw and then sang "Woooo Woooooo."

They took no notice of me, but I couldn't do the same with them. I had never been so close to trained singers and the reverberations shook in my ears. I left the room and walked down the corridor to find my place in the wings. Sounds came out of each door I passed. One baritone roared like a wounded moose, another wailed like a freight train on a stormy night. The tenors yelped in high screeches. There were whines and growls and the siren of an engine on its way to a four-alarm fire. Grunts overlapped the high-pitched "ha ha ho ho's" and the total cacophony tickled me; I could have laughed outright. These exquisite singers who would soon stand on the stage delivering the most lovely and liquid tones had first to creak like rusty scissors and wail like banshees. I remembered that before I could lift my torso and allow my arms to wave as if suspended in water, I had to bend up and down, sticking my behind in the air, plié and relevé until my muscles ached, arch-roll and contract and release until my body begged for deliverance. The singers were not funny. They were working. Preparation is rarely easy and never beautiful. That was the first of many lessons *Porgy and Bess* taught me.

I sat on a stool in the wings and watched the singers respond to the

516 · Maya Angelou

stage manager's shouted "Places, please. Places." They moved directly to their positions in *Porgy's* world. There were a few whispers as the lights began their slow descent to black.

There was applause from in front of the curtain and the lively overture of Gershwin's opera swelled onto the stage. The curtain began sliding open and pastel lights illuminated the set. A group of men, downstage left, were involved in a crap game; some knelt, others mimed throwing dice. Then Ned Wright, as Robbins, threw the dice and sang "Nine to Make, Come Nine." The pure tenor line lifted and held in the air for a second, and in a rush the pageant began.

The sopranos and tenors, bassos and baritones, acted as if they were indeed the poverty-stricken Southern Negroes whose lives revolved around the dirt road encampment of Catfish Row. They sang and listened, then harmonized with each other's tones so closely that the stage became a wall of music without a single opening unfilled.

Their self-hypnotism affected the audience and overwhelmed me. I cried for Robbin's poor widow, Serena, who sang the mournful aria "My Man's Gone Now." Helen Thigpen, a neat little quail of a woman, sang the role with a conviction that burdened the soul. Irene Williams sang Bess, sassily tossing her hips as effortlessly as she flung the notes into the music of the orchestra. Leslie Scott, handsome and as private as an African mask, sang Porgy and in a full, rich baritone. When the first act was over, the audience applauded long and loudly, and I found myself drenched with perspiration and exhausted.

The singers, on the other hand, seemed to step out of the roles as easily as one kicks off too large slippers. They passed me in the wings on their way to the dressing rooms chattering about packing and whether they ought to buy more clothes in Montreal for the European trip.

I didn't like their frivolity. It seemed as if they were being disloyal to the great emotions they had sung about and aroused in me. It wasn't pleasant to discover they were only playing parts. I wanted them to walk offstage wrapped in drama, trailing wisps of tragedy. Instead, Martha came through a parting in the backdrop curtain. Her dark face split in a smile.

"Hey, girl. How do you like it?"

She would not have understood had I said I loved the singing but felt betrayed by the singers.

I said, "I love it."

"Is this the first time you've watched an opera from backstage?"

I told her it was.

The final act was more astounding than the first. I knew now that the actors were not wholly involved in their roles because I had seen the alacrity with which they shuffled off their characters, and yet they caught me again and wove me deftly into the pattern of the play.

The audience jumped to their feet, shouting "Bravo" and clapping their hands, and the company bowed ensemble. Then the chorus members began to peel off the long double lines, leaving a neat arrangement of principal actors, and the audience thundered its approval.

Backstage after the final curtain, singers, stage hands, administrators acted as if the play had never been. The moods they had created, the tears they had wept so copiously and the joy they had reveled in were forgotten.

I wondered if I would make any real friendships or, to be more precise, I doubted that people who could be so emotionally casual had the ability, desire or need to make friendships.

Billy Johnson told me I was expected at the theater the next afternoon for rehearsal. He asked if I could sight-sing and I answered no. Wilkie had encouraged me to study solfeggio so that I would be able to pick up a piece of sheet music and read it as naturally as one reads a newspaper, but I hadn't had the time. Johnson, a prematurely balding white man from Oklahoma, said we'd work it out. That I didn't really have much to learn.

I was assigned to the hotel where Martha and Lillian stayed and we sat late into the night telling our life stories. Martha was the daughter of a preacher in North Carolina. Lillian was choir director of a large church in Jamaica, Long Island. My grandmother had been Mother of the C.M.E. Church in Stamps, Arkansas, so we shared a common religious background.

Rehearsal wasn't as frightening as I had expected. Once Billy Johnson was convinced that the company administrators had actually hired a singer who couldn't read music, he took the situation in hand. He sat at the piano and with one hand played my part. Having been surrounded by the group of highly trained, talented singers, it would be understandable if he had come to believe that not only could all Negroes sing, but they could all sing opera and had perfect pitch. He barely covered his shock at finding that I didn't have a good ear.

His accent was Southern and as refined as oil of wintergreen.

"Well, no, Maya, that's not quite it. Close, but not quite." He played the air again, his fingers stroking the keys daintily. "It's more like this."

After an hour, during which I sang the same tune over and over again, he surrendered gracefully.

"I think you're going to have to put in some work on this before you open with us in Venice."

In the dance sequence I was all right. The rhythm was complex, but I seemed to hear it easily and I danced it freely. Robert Breen had explained that he didn't want the piece to look choreographed. The dancer had to appear so bewitched by the music that she abandoned herself in a glory of dance. I surrendered to the music and allowed it to fashion my performance.

CHAPTER 17

For three days I rehearsed in the afternoons and observed the company from the wings at night. But mornings I spent walking the clean streets of Montreal and listening to the foreign accents and looking at the people.

Among the many perversities in American race relations is the fact that Blacks do not relish looking closely at whites. After hundreds of years of being the invisible people ourselves, as soon as many of us have achieved economic security we try to force whites into nonexistence by ignoring them.

Montreal provided me with my first experience of looking freely at whites. The underground railroad had had Canada as its final destination, and slaves had created a powerful liturgy praising Canada which was sung all over the world. Spirituals abounded with references to the Biblical body of water, the river Jordan. I had been told that Jordan, in our music, meant the Mississippi or the Arkansas or the Ohio River and the stated aim to get to Canaan land was the slave's way of saying he longed to go to Canada, and freedom.

Therefore, Canadians were exempt from many Blacks' rejection of whites. They were another people. I observed their clean streets and the fact that their faces did not tighten when they saw me. The atmosphere was comfortable enough to allow me to try my recently learned French words. Sometimes I was understood.

The hotel lobby looked like a train station. Two children, sixty adults with their suitcases, coats, umbrellas, hats and other paraphernalia were trying to check out and board the two buses that were to take them to the airport.

A scene was played out which I was to see repeated in the capitals of Europe and North Africa. Remaining hotel guests were astounded by the horde of colorful people queuing up to windows, shouting across lines to each other, laughing at the joy of travel and the promise of Europe.

The stars of the company sparkled and attracted. Earl Jackson, our second Sportin' Life, had just joined the troupe when I arrived in Montreal. His wardrobe was as new to the old members as it was to me. He was not a trained singer and the gossip was that he had been hired from the streets of Chicago because he had firsthand information of the role he was to play. He wore a snappy, flashy suit and his hair was as black and slick as his pointy shoes. He knew he was handsome, and because he did not yet belong to any clique, he stood aloof and haughty, as if he were the absolute center of the universe and we were inconsequential people on the periphery.

Leslie Scott dressed expensively and behaved like a classic baritone. His fitted coat had a Persian lamb collar, which was accented by a cashmere scarf. He was a star and made no attempt to play it down.

The women who sang Bess were unfailingly and dramatically attractive. Martha was perfectly made-up and dressed in her dainty coat of many colors; Gloria Davy, tall and Black, held her strangely Oriental beauty contained in distant impassivity. Irene Williams, golden and cheerful, looked as much like Bess in a hotel lobby as she did on the stage. John McCurry, who sang the role of Crown, was six foot six, two hundred and fifty pounds—a booming bass-baritone and the color of a ripe Satsuma plum. His wife was little and as white as he was black. She spoke softly and seldom. Because of the disparity in size, and color, they were called secretly Jack and Jane Sprat.

Most of the tenors who had visited Europe on an earlier tour and had the temperament of their vocal range, wore their coats over their shoulders with a studied indifference and carried walking sticks.

Eloise Uggams and Ruby Green were among the quiet, self-effacing women who looked and acted more like pillars of a religious order than singing members of a flamboyant opera company. Their male counterparts, Joe Jones, Merritt Smith, could have been church deacons, small business owners or solid insurance collectors. They not only didn't seem to belong to the dramatic group but appeared a little ill-at-ease with them in public. The sober members always managed to stand a little apart from the vociferous group as if they were waiting for another train going to a different destination.

The company descended on the airport like an invading horde of Goths on ancient Rome. Some people hummed little airs from *Madame Butterfly* or *Cavalleria Rusticana*. Others continued the conversations they had started on the buses in loud voices to override the general noise. At least five bags were lost, searched for, bemoaned and then found with cries of welcome. After processing about only twenty passports and fifty suitcases, looks passed between the Canadian officials as if they had rehearsed the scene: they raised their eyebrows, shrugged, looked in another direction and waved *Porgy and Bess* company through the turnstile and out of their sight.

The airplane stewardesses found that their aloof manner designed to keep obstreperous passengers in check did not work with their cargo of singers. The sopranos complained that the plane was too cold; the baritones were certain that the overheating was detrimental to their vocal cords; the tenors asked for rock and rye, and said generously they would settle for clover honey and fresh lemon juice. Panic increased among the stewardesses in direct relation to the requests made by their passengers.

When the pilot informed us we were passing over Newfoundland, which meant one hour from Montreal and eight whole hours from Milan, our final destination, the cabin attendants looked dazedly wild-eyed. They withdrew to the front of the plane and remained there, refusing to answer the persistent demands for attention.

Ruby Green was terrified of flying, so I had asked to be her seat companion. I knew that I was always at my best when I was near someone in a worse condition than I. When the plane took off she grabbed the seat arms, tensed her body and, by will alone, lifted the carrier safely in the air. I spoke to her of California, and thinking of Wilkie, reminded her (and myself) that "there was no place God was not." After a few hours she relaxed enough to join the conversation. She said that she had no doubts about God but had no previous knowledge of the pilot, and that throughout three years of traveling with *Porgy and Bess* her serious misgivings about airplane captains had not diminished in the least.

The stewardesses appeared near the front seats. They began hauling out tablecloths and silverware from right to left as fast as possible. Once all our tray tables were down and dressed, they raced back to the minute kitchen stand and grabbed the meals. They handed them rapidly from right to left as quickly and deftly as a Las Vegas gambler deals a deck of cards. When we were all served they returned to their retreat without a single backward glance.

The Milan airport hustle differed only in language from the cacophonous noise of other airports I had known. I busied myself gathering my luggage and staying as close to my friends as possible without appearing to do exactly what I was doing—that is, clinging to their coattails for safety's sake.

The first part of the bus trip from Milan to Venice gave me and my colleagues no time to contemplate the Italian countryside. The driver was determined to show that not only did he know his vehicle and the roads, he was an artist at keeping the two in conjunction even under the most hair-raising circumstances. The bus—extra long and loaded with the entire company and all our baggage, and a guide who thought the language he spoke was English—skidded into curves, screeching like a stuck factory whistle; aimed itself at smaller vehicles as, growling, it leaped and bucked and swung around hills, holding onto the road by two wheels, one wheel, and then simply by sheer memory.

The guide shouted and gesticulated, held his upturned hands away from his body and moved them up and down as if he were weighing two large grapefruit, his head rolling from side to side.

When the bus finally entered a small town, children and dogs became feathers blown out of its path; adults screamed at the driver, who, keeping his foot on the accelerator, turned his head and answered them shout for shout. We stopped at a square in the center of town and relief prevented us from cursing the driver, who stood by the open door, pride in his skill written on his face.

The guide led us to a restaurant and said, "blah, blah, Verona, blah blah." The word "Verona" hit my ears like a clap of remembered thunder. Here was Verona, the home of Romeo and Juliet. The home of the Montagues and Capulets. I walked away from the crowd and looked at the buildings and up at the stone balconies. I placed Juliet above me, imagined her asking "Romeo, Romeo! wherefore art thou, Romeo?" I put her lover in a shadow across the square and allowed him to praise Juliet's beauty and to wish: "O that I were a glove upon that hand, that I might touch that cheek!"

I was really in Italy. Not Maya Angelou, the person of pretensions and ambitions, but me, Marguerite Johnson, who had read about Verona and the sad lovers while growing up in a dusty Southern village poorer and more tragic than the historic town in which I now stood.

I was so excited at the incredible turn of events which had brought me from a past of rejection, of slammed doors and blind alleys, of dead-end streets and culs-de-sac, into the bright sun of Italy, into a town made famous by one of the world's greatest writers. I ran to find Martha and Lillian.

They had saved a chair for me inside the café.

"Martha, did you know this is Verona?"

She looked up from the menu she was studying. "Yes, and it's only twenty miles to Venice."

Lillian said, "My God, if we don't get a different driver, we may never get there."

"Or if we keep this one we'll be there in five minutes." Martha laughed.

I said, "But I mean, this is Verona. Where the—This is the setting for Shakespeare's *Romeo and Juliet.*"

"We all heard it on the bus, Maya." Lillian smiled at me as if I were an excited child. "The guide told us. Weren't you listening?"

Martha pursed her lips, "The Everyman Opera Company goes to the tremendous expense of hiring a guide who speaks an unheard-of language and moves his arms like a semaphore in a strong wind, and our prima ballerina doesn't even listen to him. Alas." She went back to the menu.

Lillian looked at me and shook her head. "Maya, in the next year you'll probably be in the place where Hamlet died, where Othello killed Desdemona or where Cleopatra did herself in with an asp. You're not going to get this excited each time, are you?"

Martha said, "Dear, do let her have her day. After all, this is her first time in Europe." They had both traveled with Gertrude Stein's *Four Saints in Three Acts,* and they acted as if they had chalets in Switzerland and villas in Spain where they took weekend visits. Martha continued, "Let me help you with the menu."

I decided that day never again to let them know how I really felt. If they wanted to play it cool, then I'd show them how to play it cool. I asked for the menu and with my heart beating loud enough for them to hear it, gazed at the list of foods, written in Italian and in a script I'd never seen before. I recognized *uova* as eggs on the basis of my high school Latin and ordered. I knew that I must buy a dictionary the next day and start to teach myself Italian. I would speak the language of every country we visited; I would study nights and mornings until I spoke foreign languages, if not perfectly, at least coherently.

Neither books nor films had prepared me for Venice. I had seen *Blood and Sand*, the Tyrone Power movie, and felt I could walk easily among bullfighters and the beautiful señoritas of Spain. *The Bicycle Thief* and *Open City* gave clear if painful images of Italy after World War II. The Ali Baba and Aladdin's lamp stories, although portrayed by actors with heavy Central European accents, gave me some sense of the Moslem world. But Venice was a fantasia I had not experienced even secondhand. Our bus drove through narrow streets walled by tall buildings. Erratically we burst away from enclosures and saw open water where gondoliers plied their boats with as much élan as our driver conducted his vehicle. Balconies thrust above our heads; vegetable stalls and small shops jutted out beyond the pavement.

Across the square we stopped in a small plaza where there was a hotel. Tables sat out in front of a restaurant. As the company piled out of the bus and began the routine of sorting themselves and their baggage into individual lots, I stood looking at the black-coated waiters who were covering the tables with red checkered cloths.

A few had seen and heard the singers identifying their belongings in loud voices and they had rushed to the restaurant door to call to their fellow workers and Venetian customers. Men and women flowed out of the restaurant and onto the square, their eyes on the crowd of colorful Negroes who hadn't the time or the inclination to give them the slightest thought.

The ogling crowd who waved their hands in a kind of balletic concert were the first large group of native Italians I observed carefully. In Verona I had been too busy coping with my memories and the ancient romance and my own image to really look at the waiters or the other customers. But now, as I stood apart and had the opportunity to take in the whole scene, the Italian faces were contorted with what I took to be revulsion; I concluded that they had never seen so many Black people before and were frightened and repelled.

A tall, tub-chested man in a white coat, who had been standing with the gawkers, said something which brought laughter from the crowd and walked toward the bus. I headed back to where the guide was ineffectually standing guard over a raggle-taggle mound of suitcases and offering his arms and head and torso and garbled tongue as a sacrifice to the god who reclaimed lost luggage. The white-coated man searched among the teeming, shouting singers and settled on John McCurry, who was bent double talking to his wife.

The man stood as if at attention. He spoke to John in Italian, then shot his hand out from waist level. Understandably, John, who had grown up in New York, jumped. The man began to wave his arms, and John, like most of the group who knew Italian from singing Puccini, Rossini, Verdi and Bellini answered him in the poetic language of opera. The man beamed. He turned to the people who waited in the doorway of the restaurant and shouted. They clapped their hands and started toward the bus, talking loudly.

In general, Black Americans do not take kindly to being rushed by a crowd of strange white men. John McCurry was still talking to the man who had acted as scout, but the other singers saw the crowd advancing across the square, and we reacted as if choreographed. We drew in closer to each other, our bags and the bus. The movement was subtle, but it was made with a fair amount of haste. The two small children stood nearer their fathers, who began talking earnestly with their wives. Ned Wright and Joe Attles chose that time to put their arms into the coats which they had always thrown cape-like over their shoulders.

As the group of Italians neared us, their smiles became evident; they were welcoming us to Venice. Our tight group relaxed and the old breezy attitudes returned. We mingled and mixed with the Italians, laughing and shaking hands.

They crowded around John McCurry and shouted, thinking he was the star of the opera. Leslie Scott and Laverne Hutchinson, who alternated in the lead role, were not pleased. John kept saying, *"No, no, io sono* Crown." But because of his size, his wide smile, large bass-baritone voice and probably his impeccable Italian accent, the new fans were certain they were admiring the right person.

Rose Tobias, who handled public relations for *Porgy and Bess,* stepped in to clear up the matter. She was a bright, young New Yorker, confident and pretty. She took Leslie and Laverne by the arms and pulled them into the center of the fray. The Italians were pumping John's hand as if they were priming a well.

Rose, still holding on to her stars, wedged herself between the Italians and John. She shook her head rapidly, causing her heavy blond hair to swirl in the men's faces. She pointed her finger at Laverne and then at Leslie, saying loudly, "Porgy, Porgy." She repeated the action until she was sure that credit went where it was due. She was happy because she had accomplished the task set before her. Rose Tobias was a success as our publicist, even in Italy. It hardly mattered that she didn't speak a word of Italian.

CHAPTER 18

After I registered at the hotel, handed over my passport to the desk clerk and was shown my room, I decided to see Venice on my own. The company manager advanced each singer a portion of salary in lira. I bought a map, a cheap guide to Italian which contained useful phrases and a small Italian-English dictionary, and began my exploration.

The ancient buildings sat closed and remote, holding dead glories within their walls. The canals fanned in every direction from the pavement edge, while red and black gondolas slid along on the water's surface like toy boats sailing on ice. The gondoliers whose crafts were empty sang to amuse themselves or to attract customers. They chanted bits of arias and popular music and their voices pranced over the water, young and irresistible. I wandered, following the map, to the Grand Canal, which in the dusk looked black and oily, and with the lighted gondolas skimming along, it could have been the San Francisco Bay burdened with an array of Chinese junks.

I found the Piazza San Marco, and sat at a small table facing the square. I ordered coffee in my tourist-book Italian and sat watching the people in the grand square and the lights playing on the façade of the Basilica of Saint Mark and dreaming of the age of the doges and the city states of Italy which I had read about. The table I had chosen was in a fairly empty area of the restaurant, but the space was filled rapidly. Voices, suddenly closer, burst through my reverie. I looked around and discovered myself hemmed in by strange faces. I was the focus of at least thirty pairs of eyes. They all seemed to be searching my face—my mouth and nose, hairline and ears—for something precious that had been lost. There was a bizarre sense of being caught in a nightmare dreamed by a stranger.

I looked at my book for the necessary phrase. The waiter came over. "I would like more coffee." He chattered something back to me and nodded toward a group of men among the crowd staring at me. I repeated my request and he may have repeated his answer, because he nodded again toward the men. This time I followed his nod and saw three glasses lifted and smiles directed to me. They were toasting me. Surprise did not prevent me from returning their smile with a cool, restrained one of my own. I inclined my head and the crowd burst into laughter.

One woman asked, " 'St. Louis Blues'?"

One man sitting near me stood up and came very near my table. His black eyes were shining.

"Americano?" He leaned toward me unnecessarily—his voice carried around the restaurant and out into the plaza.

I answered as quietly as my grandmother would have replied if she was trying to show a loudmouth how to behave. "Yes."

His smile widened. "Harlem?"

I nodded again, because I knew what he meant.

He bent his knees and put up his hands in a professional boxer's pose. He jabbed at the air. Everybody laughed. The man withdrew from the position, and looking at me again, asked, "Joe Louis?"

I didn't know how to tell him I knew who Joe Louis was but I didn't know him personally. He repeated, "Joe Louis?"

I put both hands together and raised them over my head in a winner's gesture, and the crowd laughed and raised their glasses again.

It was amazing that the people were all so handsome. Those at one table motioned that I should join them. I only thought about it a second, then went over and sat down in a chair that had been pulled out for me.

Again there was a general noise of approval. As soon as I sat down, men and women at other tables pulled up their chairs. I put my booklet on the table, pointed to it and smiled. A waiter brought a glass and I had a sweet and bitter Campari, which I'd never tasted before. When I grimaced the people wagged their heads and clucked. I looked through the dictionary for the word "bitter"; it wasn't there. A man took the book and began to look for something, but his search was in vain. A woman held her hand out for the book, and when it was passed to her she riffled through the pages and also failed to find what she was looking for. I was given another Campari. As the book traveled from hand to hand we all smiled at each other and the customers talked among themselves. I was having a lovely time and didn't understand a word that was said except *"Americano"* and *"bellissima."*

It was time to go. I smiled and stood up. About thirty people rose and smiled. I shook hands with the people at my table and said *"Grazie."* The others leaned forward, offering their hands and their beaming faces. I shook hands with each one, and walked out onto the square. When I looked back at the lighted café the people were still waving.

The year was 1954, only a decade since their country had been defeated by my country in a war fought for racial reasons as well as economic ones. And, after all, Joe Louis, whom the man seemed so proud to mention, had beaten an Italian, Primo Carnera. I thought my acceptance in the restaurant had been a telling show of the great heart of the Italian people. I hadn't been in Europe long enough to know that Europeans often made as clear a distinction between Black and white Americans as did the most confirmed Southern bigot. The difference, I was to discover, was that more often than not, Blacks were liked, whereas white Americans were not.

I prepared for bed after examining each object in the small bedroom and bath next door. Touching the washstand, the walls and the fine cotton curtains assured me that I was indeed out of the United States. I slept a fitful sleep, longing for my son and feeling nervous because the next evening I would debut in the role of Ruby.

CHAPTER 19

The interior of the Teatro la Fenice was as rococo as the most opulent imagination could have wished. The walls were paneled in rich red velvet interrupted by slabs of white marble and gold mosaic. Heavy crystal chandeliers hung on golden chains. The rounded seats were covered in the same velvet and the wide aisles were carpeted with a deeper red wool.

The dressing rooms had been designed and built by people who possessed a great appreciation for singers and actors. They were large and comfortable to the point of being luxurious. The smaller rooms were furnished with a small sofa, dressing tables and wide lighted mirror and a washstand. And the stars' quarters could have easily passed for superior suites in a first-class hotel.

Irene Williams and Laverne Hutchinson had not been seen all day. In the manner of operatic stars they had been in seclusion. However, singers of the less strenuous roles had walked along the canals and shopped in the small stores. Ned Wright had met a gondolier and arranged a late-night boat ride on the Grand Canal for a few friends. He invited me. I had seen posters of John McCurry and me posted around the city, and as I walked alone in the streets, small boys followed me chanting *"La prima ballerina," "La prima ballerina."* The children's pale-gold complexions and their joyful spirits reminded me of Clyde.

The stars materialized and dress rehearsal began. I was in costume and in place. There was a marked difference between observing the play—carefully scrutinizing each move, paying the closest attention to every note—and being a part of it and having some responsibility for the drama. The poignancy of Porgy's love for Bess and the tragedy of his fate brought tears to my eyes and clogged my throat, so that I could barely push notes out of my mouth. I was certain that in the course of time the play would become stale to me and I would become partially indifferent to its pathos. Over the next year, however, I found myself more touched by the tale and more and more impressed by the singers and actors who told it. The actual performance put dress rehearsal in the shade. The singers sang with fresh enthusiasm as if they had been called upon to create the music on the spot and were equal to the challenge. When Dolores Swann sang "Summertime," the audience was as hushed as the plastic doll that lay in her arms, and when she crooned the last top note the theater exploded with the sound of applause. Serena's lament and the love duet brought the audience to its feet. In the second half, when I finished my dance, the audience cheered again; as I followed the singers to the wings I received kisses and hugs and pats on the back.

Martha caught my hand and said, "Oh, Pavlova, I knew you were the one."

Lillian gave me a grin and said, "You danced your tail off, girl."

The curtain opened and revealed the theatergoers standing in the brightly lit auditorium. They clapped their hands and shouted up a pandemonium: "Bravo," "Bravo." During rehearsal the theater had been like a large inverted rococo snuffbox, but now, filled with beautifully dressed people screaming their appreciation, it was warm and rich and nearly too gorgeous to behold.

The curtains opened and closed and opened and closed and the audience refused to release the stars. Flowers were brought to the stage. I watched from the wings as Irene received bouquets gracefully in her arms until they piled up, threatening to obscure her face. Laverne bowed and smiled, holding on to her hand, then left her alone to take the kudos. When the curtain closed again, they exchanged places and he stood in the center accepting the applause. When the curtain closed for the last time, we hugged each other and danced with ecstasy.

The opening night of our European tour was a smash hit. The Italians were the most difficult audiences to sing for. They knew and loved music; operas, which were mainly for the elite in other countries, were folk music and children's songs in Italy. They loved us, we loved them. We loved ourselves. It was a certainty: if Italy declared us acceptable we could have the rest of Europe for a song.

—

We stayed in Venice for one sold-out week. During that time the stars were feted by city officials and the well-to-do, while the chorus was adored by the ordinary folk. We were hailed in the streets like conquering heroes and given free rides on the canals by gondoliers, who sang strains from *Porgy and Bess*. One owner of a glass-blowing factory presented us with delicate figurines, which we stowed in layers of cotton for our imminent trip to Paris.

I bought a French-English dictionary and packed it with the Italian-English phrase book and other belongings and had them taken to the bus which waited in the square. Fans crowded around us, offering cheeks to be kissed, hands to be shaken and flowers. We exchanged hugs and some tears with people who hadn't known of our existence only seven days before.

When the bus drove toward the station where we were to take a train to Paris, I thought of the city as a larger replica of some of its museums. Venice was itself an object of art, and its citizens the artists who had created it and were constantly re-creating it. I waved my hands, wagged my head and made sorry, sad faces to the well-wishers, as if I was being carried off against my will. Loving Venice and Venetians nearly made me Italian.

The Blue Train sped through Italy. I sat in a compartment with Lillian, Martha and Barbara Ann, listening to them talk about recital salons, and concert halls. Lillian mentioned a voice teacher whom someone in New York had recommended. Martha drew herself up and said the greatest voice teacher in the world was her teacher, in New York, and she wouldn't stand for anyone else messing with her voice. (Operatic singers are fiercely loyal to their teachers.) Lillian told her that was stupid: "Your teacher couldn't be the best vocal teacher in the world because I've heard some terrible stories about her." An argument grew and thrashed around the small space between us. I had nothing to add, since Wilkie was the only voice teacher I'd ever met, and I didn't want to mention his name in case I'd be obliged to defend him. I kept quiet. Barbara Ann said conciliatingly, "Well, you know, it's hard to say who is the best voice teacher in the world. That is until you've heard everyone. There are teachers in Texas no one has ever heard of who are very good." That was for Martha. She turned to Lillian and said, "Just because a person is gossiped about doesn't necessarily mean that the person is guilty." She looked at me for confirmation and added, "I mean, look how they talked about Jesus Christ. Am I right or wrong?"

I said I didn't know, and all three singers turned to me, their questions pouncing on my ears.

"What do you mean you don't know about Jesus?"

"They talked about him like a dog."

"Don't you remember about the Philistines and the Pharisees?"

"Your grandmother would have been ashamed of you."

"What about the money lenders in the temple?"

Martha said, "What about 'buked and scorned?" and then she began to sing: "I been 'buked and I been scorned." Her voice was the most perfect I had ever heard in my life. It was like hot silver being poured from a high place.

Lillian laid her full contralto under the glistening sound:

> "I been 'buked
> And I been scorned
> I been talked about
> Sure as you're born."

Barbara Ann wedged her clear soprano between the other voices, embracing first one tone then the other, getting so near the other trills that her sound almost melted into theirs. The music written hundreds of years before soared in the Italian train, erasing the dispute, and placing us all somewhere between the agony of Christ and the ecstasy of Art.

As the train pulled into the Gare du Nord I heard my name shouted above the clamor of luggage carts and the calls of porters: "Maya Angelou," "*Où est* Mademoiselle Maya Angelou?" I knew I shouldn't have left my son. There was a telegram waiting for me to say he had been hurt somehow. Or had run away from home. Or had caught an awful disease. The train ground to a halt and I forced the conductor aside and opened the door.

Five feet away stood the handsome and rugged Yanko Varda and Annette March, as svelte as a model. They were searching the train and yelling, "Maya Angelou," "Mademoiselle Maya Angelou."

I felt weak with relief. "Yanko, Annette, *je suis ici.*"

We caressed one another like lovers. Annette handed me a basket that held cheese and fruit, a bottle of wine and a loaf of bread. They motioned to me to look back along the track. Victor Di Suvero, Mitch Lifton and Cyril March were handing out similar baskets to some of the singers as they detrained. They said, "Welcome to Paris. This is in honor of Maya Angelou. This is in honor of Maya Angelou. Welcome to Paris."

Yanko called to them, and when they saw me they ran over. Mitch and Victor hugged me and grinned. Cyril, who was always more reserved, gave me the European embrace.

I asked what they were doing in Paris, and they asked me to go with them for a glass of wine. They would explain everything.

I went to Bob Dustin to get the name and address of my hotel and an advance in francs. He agreed to send my baggage along, and my San Francisco friends took me to a sidewalk café.

They had not come to Paris together. Yanko was returning from a trip to Greece.

"Maya, I have found the only beautiful brunette in the world," Victor said. "She is a sculptor, a Greek, a goddess. You will meet her here. She will come to Sausalito. She will light up San Francisco with her black eyes and the men will fall at her feet like Turks. She is Aphrodite."

Victor was en route to Italy on family business. Mitch was on a visit, and the Marches had moved to Paris, where Cyril was practicing medicine. San Francisco papers had run a notice that I had joined *Porgy and Bess*. My friends in Paris had read the company's advance publicity and found when and where we were due to arrive.

I described the fabulous success in Venice, giving myself a little more credit than I deserved. We drank wine, talked about San Francisco and they promised to attend opening night.

CHAPTER 20

Paris loved *Porgy and Bess*. We were originally supposed to stay at the Théâtre Wagram for three weeks, but were held over for months. After the first week I discovered that I couldn't afford to stay in the hotel that had been assigned to me. The policy of the company was to pay the singers half their salary in the currency of the country we were in and the other half in dollars. I sent my dollars home to pay for Clyde's keep and to assuage my guilt at being away from him.

I moved into a small pension near the Place des Ternes, which provided a Continental breakfast with my tiny room. There was a cot-sized bed and just space for me and my suitcase. The family who owned the place and my fellow roomers spoke no English, so perforce my French improved.

One evening after the theater a group of Black American entertainers who lived in Paris came backstage. They enchanted me with their airs and accents. Their sentences were mixed with Yeah Man's and Oo la la's. They fluttered their hands and raised their eyebrows in typically Gallic fashion, but walked swinging their shoulders like Saturday-night people at a party in Harlem.

Bernard Hassel, a tall nut-brown dancer, worked at the Folies-Bergères, and Nancy Holloway, whose prettiness brought to mind a young untroubled Billie Holiday, sang at the Colisée. Bernard invited me to see the night life of Paris.

"*Alors,* something groovy, you know?"

We went to the Left Bank, and he showed me where F. Scott Fitzgerald and Hemingway did some flamboyant talking and serious drinking. The bareness of the bar surprised me. I expected a more luxurious room with swatches of velvet, deep and comfortable chairs and at least a doorman. The café's wide windows were bare of curtains and the floor uncarpeted. It could have been the Coffee Shop in San Francisco's North Beach. High up over the façade hung a canvas awning on which was stenciled the romantic name DEUX MAGOTS.

L'Abbaye was a bar owned by Gordon Heath, a Black American who provided his own entertainment. He sang in a weak but compelling voice and projected an air of mystery. After each song the audience showed their appreciation by snapping their fingers. Heath did not allow hand-clapping.

The Rose Rouge on the Left Bank was closer to my idea of a Parisian night club. It had velour drapes and a uniformed doorman; the waiters were haughty and the customers well-dressed. Acrobats and pantomimists, magicians and pretty half-naked girls kept up a continuous diversion. Bernard introduced me to the handsome Algerian owner, who I immediately but privately named Pepe Le Moko. He said if I wanted to do an act in his club, he'd find a place for me. I said I'd keep it in mind.

Around three o'clock in the morning my escort took me to the Mars Club, which he pronounced "Mairs Cloob" near the Champs-Élysées. It was owned by an oversized American man from New York and specialized in Black entertainment. Bernard pointed out the names printed on the door of people who had worked in the smoky and close room. The only one I recognized was Eartha Kitt. Ben, the owner, repeated Pepe Le Moko's invitation. I said I was flattered and I'd think about it. I knew I wouldn't. Where would I find a musician in Paris who could play calypso accompaniment?

Ben asked, "Why don't you give us a song now?"

I looked at the pianist, who was white and thin and had a long sorry face. He sat playing a quiet moody song. When he finished, Ben called him to the bar and introduced us. "Bobby Dorrough, this is Maya Angelou, she's a singer."

He smiled and his face was transformed. His cheeks bunched under sparkling eyes and his teeth were large and white and even. He said, "Happy to know you, Maya," and the drawl made my skin move along my arms. He couldn't have sounded more Southern white if he had exaggerated.

Ben went to the microphone and announced, "Ladies and gentlemen, we have with us tonight one of the stars of *Porgy and Bess.*"

I was hardly that, but why correct him? I stood and bowed while the audience applauded fiercely.

The pianist said "Welcome to Paris" in a molasses accent. For months I had been away from the sound that recalled lynchings, insults and hate. It was bizarre to find myself suddenly drenched with the distasteful memories in a Parisian *boîte.*

I made myself speak. "Where are you from?"

"I'm from San Antonio." At least he didn't say "San Antone." "Where are you from?"

"San Francisco." I said it so briskly I almost bit my lip.

"Would you like to sing something? I'd be happy to play for you." The graciousness dripped honeysuckle all over the old plantation.

I said, "No. I don't think you can play my music. It's not very ordinary."

He asked, "What do you sing? The blues?" I knew he would think I sang blues. "I play the blues." I was sure he'd say he played the blues.

"No, I sing calypso. Do you also play calypso?" That ought to hold him.

"Yes. I know some. How about 'Stone Cold Dead in the Market'? Or 'Rum and Coca-Cola'?"

I followed him to the piano in a mild state of shock. I told him my key and he was right. He played 'Stone Cold Dead' better and with more humor than my accompanist did at the Purple Onion. The audience liked the song and Bobby applauded quietly. Everything about the man was serene except his piano playing and his smile.

"Want to sing another? How about 'Run Joe'?"

Although that had been the song which started my career and I always used it to close a show or as a dramatic encore, it was not really well known. I was surprised that the pianist knew it. "Yes. I'll sing one more."

He took only a few bars to fall into the mood I was creating and then raced along with me and the story, never drowning my effects but always holding his own. When we finished I felt obliged to shake his hand over the loud applause.

"Aw, Maya, there was nothing to it. You're very good."

Bernard and Ben met me back at the bar. They were still clapping as I approached.

"How about doing one spot a night for me, Maya?" Ben was grinning as he shook my hand. "One show a night. You'll be a sensation in Paris."

Bernard said, "*Chérie*, it'll knock them out."

"But I don't get out of the theater until eleven-thirty." It was nice to be begged to do what I liked to do.

"You could do a show here at twelve-thirty."

I thought about the money. I would be able to move out of the grim little pension that had no luxuries and was minus certain things that I as an American considered necessities. I could afford a room with private bath again and a toilet that wouldn't be at the end of dark stairs. And I could continue sending the same amount of money home. Or, it occurred to me, I could stay where I was—the pension wasn't all that bad—and send more money home. Mom could buy something wonderful for Clyde every other week and tell him I'd sent it. Then perhaps he would forgive my absence.

I asked Ben, "Could you pay me in dollars?"

Ben had been in Paris a long time. His large, round face became wise and hard. "You've got a good connection for exchange?"

I knew some people in the company sold their dollars on the black market and received a higher percentage of francs than banks would give.

I said, "No. I have a son at home. I have to send money for his keep."

His expression softened a little. "Of course, of course, kid, I can give you dollars and you'll be paid every night. That's the way we do it in Paris. You want to talk it over with Bobby? He'll be playing for you."

I waited until the pianist joined us at the bar. "I'm going to start singing here. Ben has offered me a job."

"Well, isn't that nice."

Oh God, I didn't know how I could bear that accent. If he would only play the piano and never speak to me, we'd get along very well.

"When are you going to start?"

Ben asked, "How about day after tomorrow. You could rehearse with Bobby tomorrow and next day and begin that night. How's that, kid?"

That was fine with me and the musician. Bernard bought drinks and we closed the deal by clinking glasses all around.

Bobby Dorrough had a pitch as fine as crystal. I sang snatches of songs to him in the empty bar and as if he were a music machine, the notes went into his ears and immediately his fingers pressed them out of the piano keys. In the first afternoon's rehearsal we ran over my entire repertoire and agreed to spend the next day polishing the numbers. It was nearly dusk when we walked out of the bar.

"Do you want me to get you a taxi, Maya?"

I said, "No, I just live near the Place des Ternes."

"All right then, I'll walk you to your hotel."

"Oh no, thanks. I mean, I feel like walking slowly."

"Well, I wasn't planning to race you down the streets."

"I mean, I'd just as soon walk by myself." I tried to tell him, without hurting his feelings, that I didn't really want to be with him. Suppose some of my friends from the opera met us. I didn't know one person who would be surprised or offended if I was seen with a white man, but neither did I know one who wouldn't be shocked into uncomfortable recall by the Southern accent.

"Would you like to have lunch tomorrow? Before rehearsal?" He was very slow in getting the message.

I said, "No, thank you."

Rejection dawned on him and his pale face flushed with understanding. He said, "All right then, Maya, I'll see you tomorrow."

I walked away, heading toward the Arc de Triomphe.

Martha and Lillian said they'd come down with me to the club. Ned Wright and Joe Attles and Bey promised to drop by for the last show. The news that I had a second job did not displease the company's administration because any publicity I received was good for the opera.

After the midnight show I introduced my friends to the full audience. "Ladies and gentlemen, some members of the *Porgy and Bess* company."

The audience stood up to look at the suddenly modest singers, who refused to rise, but simply nodded grandly from their seats.

I knew what was wrong. I hadn't singled them out and made individual introductions giving their names and the roles they played. "Ladies and gentlemen, I would like you to meet Miss Lillian Hayman, who sings Maria and Serena." She was understudying the two roles. Lillian stood and graciously took the applause. She sat down gratified. "Joseph Attles, Sportin' Life." He stood, waved his long hands and blew kisses. "Ned Wright, Robbins." Ned stood and flashed a smile like a beacon around the room. "And Miss Martha Flowers, Bess." Martha stood up slowly and solemnly. She inclined her head, first to the right, then to the left, then to the audience directly in front. Only after she had bowed did she smile. Her sense of theater was never better—she began the smile slowly, keeping her mouth closed and simply pulling her lips taut. Then she allowed a few teeth to show and gradually a few more, and then more. When her lips were stretched as tight as possible and her teeth glimmering like a row of lights, she snapped her head back and laughed, the high sound tinkling like chimes.

The audience was bewitched. They began to shout, "*Chantez,* Bess. *Chantez, chantez,* Bess."

Martha suddenly became demure, and shaking her head in refusal, draped her small body in her seat. Her action incited the crowd and their clamor rose in volume. At exactly the correct moment, Martha stood up and shyly went to the piano. She leaned and whispered to Bobby. He struck one note and took his hands from the keys.

> "O they so fresh and fine
> And they right off'n the vine."

She was singing the vendor's song a cappella and her voice floated free in the quiet room:

> "Strawberries, strawberries!"

I looked around—everyone was beguiled, including our fellow singers. Martha ballooned her voice, then narrowed it, dipping down into a rough contralto, and then swung it high beyond the lyric soprano into the rarefied air that was usually the domain of divine coloraturas.

For a second after she finished there was no sound. Then people applauded her and began to crowd around her table. She coyly accepted the attention as if she hadn't worked hard for years to earn it.

One of the lessons I learned from *Porgy and Bess* was that jealousy is conceived only in insecurity and must be nourished in fear. Each individual in our cast had the certainty of excellence.

After the din over Martha's singing diminished, I asked Lillian to please sing. She stood up without reluctance and sang,

> "Go way from my window
> Go way from my door
> Go way, way, way from my bedside
> And bother me no more
> And bother me no more."

Her voice was as colorful as Martha's was pure, and the customers were again enchanted. Ned Wright sang a medley of popular songs, beginning with "I Can't Give You Anything but Love," which the French people recognized and loved. Joe Attles gave the audience "St. James Infirmary" and they literally stood in the aisles.

Maya Angelou was a crazy success. A smash hit! The audience thought they had never been better entertained. Ben was certain I would improve business; the bartender and waiters smiled gratefully at me. If I hadn't memorized a story my grandmother told me when I was a knee-high child, I might have become conceited and begun to believe the compliments I did not totally deserve.

The old story came to mind:

Mrs. Scott, a woman well past middle age, fancied young men. She was a great churchgoer and used each religious gathering to search for the objects of her choice. All the young men in her town were aware of her predilections, and she was unsuccessful in snaring them.

One day a new man appeared at the meeting house. He was handsome and although he was adult, he was still young enough to be gullible.

The woman caught him directly after service and invited him to her home for late Sunday afternoon dinner. He accepted gratefully.

She rushed home, killed a chicken and put it on to fry. While the chicken cooked, Mrs. Scott took a small needle from her sewing kit, and putting on her bifocals, picked her way down the lane from her front door. When she reached a tree a hundred yards away, she stuck the needle in the bark and returned to the kitchen to finish preparing the meal.

When the young man arrived, they sat down to a tasty dinner (for Mrs. Scott was an excellent cook), and after they finished, Mrs. Scott invited the man to sit on the porch in the swing, to let his dinner digest. She brought out lemonade and sat with him. Dusk was falling and the shapes of things were blurred.

Mrs. Scott sat bolt upright and turned to the young man. "What on earth is that I see sticking in that tree?" She pointed down the lane to the oak, which was barely a shadow in the darkness.

The young man asked, "What tree, Mrs. Scott?"

"Why, that oak tree at the bottom of the lane." She squinted and bent her neck. "I do believe that's a pin."

The young man, squinting, tried to pierce the gloom.

"Mrs. Scott, I can't hardly see the tree. And you can see something sticking in it?"

"Yes." Mrs. Scott had relaxed her scrutiny. "At first I thought it was a pin, but when I looked for the head it wasn't there—I saw instead a hole. So it's got to be a needle."

The young man turned and looked at Mrs. Scott with admiration.

"You know, ma'am, when you left church this morning, some folks told me to be careful. That you were an old woman who loved young men. But I must say, if you can see the hole in a needle a hundred yards away after the sun has gone down, you're not nearly as old as they say you are."

Mrs. Scott, proud of her compliments and forgetful of her subterfuge, said, "Well, thank you for that. I'll just go and get the needle and show it to you."

She flounced up out of the swing and stepped jauntily down the stairs. When she reached the bottom step she turned to smile at the appreciative young man, and then continuing, she walked two steps and tripped over a cow sitting in the lane.

Yes, I was a success in Paris at the Mars Club. I would have been a fool to have thought the praise was all mine. Ben liked me because I was good enough, but appreciated me because the members from *Porgy and Bess* were likely to drop in and sing for free. Bobby liked me because I was good enough, and he had a chance to play music for which he seldom received requests. The audience liked me because I was good enough, and I was different—not African, but nearly; not American, but nearly. And I liked myself because, simply, I was lucky.

I gave thanks to *Porgy and Bess,* my good fortune and to God. I wasn't about to trip over a cow.

CHAPTER 21

Paris was changing the rhythm of that old gang of mine. Martha took a two-week leave from the company to give a Town Hall recital in New York City. Lillian had said to me often, "I'm so glad I wasn't born here, because I'd never have learned to speak this language," but she had found new French friends and I seldom saw her after the theater. Barbara Ann's husband flew from the United States to be with her, and since they were newly married, they could spare little time for anyone beyond their tight circle of romance. Ned Wright and Joe Attles were bent on a ferocious discovery of Paris. After the final bow they raced from the theater as if an emergency call awaited them. They unearthed little-known restaurants and bars in obscure corners of the city.

From my third-floor (which the French perversely called second-floor) room, I assayed my value to Paris and its promise for me. I had accepted the Rose Rouge offer and become a typical Parisian entertainer. I sang a midnight show at the Mars Club, threw a coat over my sparkly dress, hailed a cab and rode across the Seine to do a second show at the Rose Rouge. My songs were well enough received and fans were beginning to remember me. Some sent notes and occasionally flowers to my dressing room. A few expatriates and two Senegalese students I had met advised me to leave *Porgy and Bess* and make my mark in Paris. The Africans said that in France I would never hear of lynchings and riots. And I would not be refused service in any restaurant or hotel in the country. The people were civilized. And, anyway, the French people loved Negroes. Look at Sid Bechet. Lil Armstrong, a former wife of Satchmo played piano at the Le Jazz Hot and had an avid following. Bambi, a tall, deliciously thin model, could hardly walk the streets in Paris without men following her and raving over her Black beauty. Nancy Holloway and Inez, who owned Chez Inez, sang American songs as well as popular French melodies and were welcomed with hyperbolic Gallic admiration. And, of course, Josephine Baker was a national institution.

I considered the advice seriously. I could find an apartment and send for Clyde. He was bright and would learn the language quickly. He would be freed from growing up under the cloud of racial prejudice that occasionally made every Black childhood sunless. He would be obliged to be good for his own sake rather than to prove to a disbelieving society that he was not a brute. The French students wore short pants and blazers and caps, and I knew my son would look beautiful in his uniform. The prospect looked glorious.

———

A woman asked me to join her table after my show at the Rose Rouge. She welcomed me and introduced me to her friends.

Her voice was tiny but piercing, and a baby-doll smile never left her pink-and-white face, and her eyelids fluttered only a little faster than her hands. She reminded me of Billie Burke and very small door chimes.

"Mademoiselle, do you know who is Pierre Mendès-France?" Smile, blink, rustle.

I said, "Yes, madame. I read the papers."

"I want an affair for him to give." Her English was not broken, it was crippled.

I said in French, "Madame, let us speak French."

She bubbled and gurgled. "*Non. Non.* I love this English for practice to speak."

Alors. She limped along verbally, explaining that she wanted me to sing at a reception which she planned to host. It would be a fund-raising event and they would gladly pay me for my services. I would be expected to sing two songs. Something plaintive that would move the heart, I thought, and loosen the purse strings.

"The blues." Madame said, "Oh, how the blues I love. Will you sing 'St. Louie Blues'?" She started singing the first line: "I hate to see, that evening sun go down."

Her shoulders hunched up to her ear lobes and she made her eyes small and lascivious. Her lips pushed out and I saw the red underlining of her mouth.

" 'I hate to see that evening sun go down.' "

She shook herself and her breasts wobbled. She was imitating her idea of a *négresse*.

I stopped her. "Madame, I know the song. I will sing it at the reception."

She was not fazed by the interruption, but clapped her hands and told her friends to clap theirs. We agreed on a price, and she said, "You are with *Porgy and Bess.* The great opera. If Bess or Porgy or your friends desire to come with you at the reception, they will not be made to pay."

She smiled, laughed, waved her hands and generally jangled like a bunch of keys. I thanked her and left the table.

Since my friends in *Porgy and Bess* were otherwise engaged, I asked the two Senegalese men to escort me to the reception. They were pleased to do so and appeared at the theater's backstage door in tuxedos, starched shirts and highly polished shoes. Their general elegance put me in a party mood. I walked into the salon with a handsome, attentive man on each side, and as we stopped inside the door, I felt that the three of us must have made an arresting tableau.

Madame was informed of my arrival and she floated over in wisps of chiffon, smiling her cheeks into small pink balloons.

"Oh, mademoiselle. How it is kind of you to come." She offered me her hand, but gave her eyes to my escorts. They bowed smartly. "And your friends you brought. Who of you is the Porgy? I do love 'Summertime.' " She had wafted into singing " 'And the living is easy.' "

I said, "No, madame." It was hard to wrest her attention from the two men. "No, madame, they are not with *Porgy and Bess.* These are friends from Africa."

When the import of my statement struck her, the smile involuntarily slid off her face and she recovered her hand from my grasp.

"*D'Afrique? d'Afrique?*" Suddenly there were no bubbles in her voice. M'Ba bowed formally and said in French, "Yes, madame. We are from Senegal."

She looked at me as if I had betrayed her. "But, mademoiselle—" She changed her mind and stood straight. She spoke in French, "Please wait here. I will have someone take you to the musicians. *Bon soir.*" She turned and left.

After I sang, a young woman gave me an envelope with my pay and thanked me warmly. I never saw Madame again.

Paris was not the place for me or my son. The French could entertain the idea of me because they were not immersed in guilt about a mutual history—just as white Americans found it easier to accept Africans, Cubans or South American Blacks than the Blacks who had lived with them foot to neck for two hundred years. I saw no benefit in exchanging one kind of prejudice for another. Also, I was only adequate as an entertainer, and I would never set Paris afire. Honesty made me admit that I was neither a new Josephine Baker or an old Eartha Kitt.

When the *Porgy and Bess* administration informed us that we were moving on to Yugoslavia, I found a woman to give me lessons in Serbo-Croatian and bought myself a dictionary.

Adieu, Paris.

CHAPTER 22

In Zagreb the company was called together to be told that the Yugoslav government and the American State Department wished us to be discreet; we were, after all, guests of the country and the first American singers to be invited behind the iron curtain. We would be driven from the hotel to the theater and back again. We could walk only within a radius of four square blocks of the hotel. We were not to accept invitations from any Yugoslavians, nor were we to initiate fraternization.

The hotel corridors smelled of cabbage and the dust of ages. I found the maid on my floor and asked her in Serbo-Croatian if there was anything interesting to see near the hotel. I had little hope that she would understand me, but she readily answered, "Yes, there's the railroad station." I was elated that the money I had spent on language lessons had not been spent in vain.

I said excitedly, "Madame, I can speak Serbo-Croatian."

She looked at me without curiosity and said, "Yes?" She waited for me to go on.

I repeated, "I learned to speak Serbo-Croatian two weeks ago."

She nodded and waited heavily. No smile warmed her features. I couldn't think of anything to add. We stood in the hall like characters from different plays by different authors suddenly thrust upon the same stage. I grinned. She didn't.

I said, "Thank you."

She said, "You're welcome."

I went to my room taking my confusion along. Why hadn't the woman been amazed to find an American Negro woman speaking Serbo-Croatian? Why hadn't she congratulated me? I knew we were the first Blacks that had stayed in the hotel and possibly the first that had ever visited the town.

At first I concluded that because the maid had never been out of her country and everyone she knew spoke her language, she thought Yugoslavia was the world and the world Yugoslavia. Then I realized that the staff must have undergone intensive indoctrination before our arrival. In the lobby no one stared at us; obviously, we were being studiously and politely ignored. The desk clerks and porters, waiters and bartenders, acted as if the sixty Black American opera singers roamed the halls and filled their lobby every other week. I was certain that we were the only authentic guests in the establishment. The others, who averted their eyes at our approach and buried their heads in their news-papers, seemed less innocent than Peter Lorre in an Eric Ambler movie.

Outside, however, it was a different story. Ordinary citizens crowded three deep to peer into the hotel windows. When one gawker could catch a glimpse of us, he or she nudged the persons nearby and all craned their necks, eyes bulging, and then laughed uproariously, revealing stainless-steel teeth that looked ominous. They had to be talked to sharply like obstreperous children at a summer fair.

Martha, who had rejoined the company, and Ethel Ayler, the new and glamorous Bess, refused my invitation to go for a walk.

Martha leaned back and looked up at me. "But Miss Thing, they think we're monkeys or something. Just look at them. No, my dear, I'm counting on Tito to keep his people outside and I swear Miss Fine Thing will stay inside."

Ethel laughed and agreed with Martha. "They think we're in a cage. I wouldn't be surprised if they threw peanuts at us."

Ned warned me, "I don't think that's the smartest thing you could do. Look at those silver teeth. Those people might start thinking you're a chocolate doll and eat you up. Stay here in the hotel. I'll play you some tonk and buy you a slivovitz."

I hadn't taken Serbo-Croatian lessons just to try out the language on hotel staff who wouldn't even pass the time of day. I walked out of the hotel.

People crowded around me. Short, stocky peasants from the coun-try wore pointed, knitted hats and had eyes that would have been at home in Oriental faces except for their blue color. I spoke to them. "Good afternoon. Please excuse me. Thank you."

It took a few seconds for those nearest me to realize that they could understand me, and then a hilarity exploded that would have been well received at a Fourth of July Shriners' picnic. They shouted and pushed in closer to me. A small surf of panic started to lap at my inner mind. I held it off. I couldn't afford terror to freeze me to the spot or force me to bolt. Hands began to reach for me. They clutched at my sleeve, at my face. I stretched as tall as possible and shouted, "Excuse me, I am going through." I had followed Wilkie's teachings attentively, and if the quality of my singing did not show a marked improvement, the volume at least, had certainly increased.

I boomed again, "Excuse me. I am going through." The noise abated and the country people's mouths gaped. The crowd parted and I strode through their moment of fluster and down the street. I didn't dare turn to see if any had chosen to follow me. Mobs of any color terrified me, and had I seen the mass behind me, without a doubt I would have taken flight and been lost in a second.

When passersby saw me, they stiffened in their tracks as if I were a fairy queen or an evil witch who had the power to suspend their mobility.

I walked into a small store which sold musical instruments. The salesman took one look at me and rushed back to a draped doorway. He shouted, "Come and see this!" Then, as if I had not heard and seen his action, he dressed his face in the universal sales-pitch smile and asked, "How are you? Good morning. May I help you?" He jerked his face away and toward the door again. "Come. Come now." Then back to me with a courteous manner.

I said, "I'd like to buy a mandolin."

He interested me as much as I interested him. It was fantastic that he thought he ceased to exist for me when he removed his attention.

"A mandolin? Certainly." His eyes fled toward the back room. I grabbed his attention: "Here. How much is this one?"

While he removed a mandolin, beautifully inlaid with mother-of-pearl, children began to tumble through the rear door and into the store. They were followed by a heavy woman with a large, florid face. When they saw me they stopped as if they had rehearsed the scene.

The woman directed a question to the man. He looked at her and answered but I couldn't catch the language. They all began to talk at once, the children's voices stabbing in and out of the deeper sounds. I continued examining the mandolin, strumming on it, turning it over in my hands to appreciate its fine woodwork. I ignored them and said to the man that I would like to buy the instrument.

He interrupted the family dialogue and told me the price; I gave him the money. The family had advanced on me. The mother was holding back as many of the children as she could reach while she inched closer to me.

I spoke to her. "Good morning, madame."

She smiled tentatively, but the incredulous look on her face remained.

"Good morning, madame," I repeated, looking directly in her eyes. If they thought I was a talking bear, then they would have to admit that at least I spoke Serbo-Croatian.

Her husband was wrapping my package, so I continued, "How are you, madame?"

Finally, her lips relaxed and opened and I saw the bar of metal that substituted for teeth. She placed herself between me and the children, then said, "Paul Robeson."

It was my turn to be stunned. The familiar name did not belong in Byzantium. The woman repeated, "Paul Robeson," and then began one of the strangest scenes I had ever seen.

She began to sing "Deep River." Her husky voice was suddenly joined by the children's piping "My home is over Jordan." Then the husband teamed with his wife and offspring, "Deep River, Lord." They knew every word.

I stood in the dusty store and considered my people, our history and Mr. Paul Robeson. Somehow, the music fashioned by men and women out of an anguish they could describe only in dirges was to be a passport for me and their other descendants into far and strange lands and long unsure futures.

> "Oh don't you want to go
> To that gospel feast?"

I added my voice to the melody:

> "That promised land
> Where all is peace?"

I made no attempt to wipe away the tears. I could not claim a forefather who came to America on the *Mayflower*. Nor did any ancestor of mine amass riches to leave me free from toil. My great-grandparents were illiterate when their fellow men were signing the Declaration of Independence, and the first families of my people were bought separately and sold apart, nameless and without traces—yet there was this:

"Deep River
My home is over Jordan."

I had a heritage, rich and nearer than the tongue which gives it voice. My mind resounded with the words and my blood raced to the rhythms.

"Deep River
I want to cross over into campground."

The storekeeper and his wife embraced me. My Serbo-Croatian was too weak to carry what I wanted to say. I hugged them again and took up my mandolin and left the store.

———

Porgy and Bess received the expected kudos from sold-out houses in Zagreb, and after a few days we moved on to Belgrade. We had been told that Belgrade was a city that was reasonably cosmopolitan, and we were all eager for the bright lights.

The Moskva Hotel in Red Square was considered a large hotel but it could hardly accommodate our singers, administration and conductors. Bob Dustin, cheery as usual, announced that we would have to triple up, and that if we didn't want to be assigned bed space arbitrarily, we should choose roommates and let him know.

Martha, Ethel Ayler and I agreed to share one of the large high-ceilinged rooms. Ethel had made fast friends with Martha and was an excellent foil for Martha's always sharp, often acid comments. Ethel would smile calmly and say, "Martha Flowers, you are a disgrace. Charming, talented, but a disgrace." Martha would giggle and be coaxed out of her ill-humor.

We had expected three cots in our room, but found one large lumpy bed, a very worn carpet and a single overhead light.

"You mean this is what these people got out of their revolution?" Martha daintily picked her way around the room. "Someone should tell them that they're about due for another." She wrinkled her pretty face in distaste.

Ethel said reprovingly, "Martha, control yourself. Unless you want the NKVD to take you to Siberia. How could you sing with salt in your throat?"

Martha laughed, "Miss Fine Thing can sing anywhere, darling. Even on the steppes of Byelorussia."

Our bags were brought to the room by a porter who didn't raise his eyes. We tried to tip him, but he rushed away as if afraid.

Martha said, "*Regardez ça.* Maya, you speak his lingo, why didn't you tell him we wouldn't bite? Of course; only because he's not cute enough." With the mention of men, Martha and Ethel and I fell into an old conversation which had never concluded and was interrupted only by sleep, performances and forced separation on journeys. The value of men. Their beauty. Their power. Their worth, excitement and attractiveness. Were American Negro men better than Africans? Better companions, better lovers? Yes. No. Whoever had a story to substantiate her point of view told it in detail. Were white American men sexier than French or Italian? Yes. No. We told secrets to each other on trains, ships, in hotel rooms and backstage. I was never loath to exaggerate a tale to make my point, and I'm certain that some of the accounts that were told to me were as fictitious as my own. We were all in our mid-twenties, and given that my two friends had spent ten years cloistered in vocal studios and secreted in institutes of music and I had had fewer romantic experiences than most college coeds, our imaginations got more exercise than our libidos.

Ethel slept in the middle and Martha beside the night table. She jumped when the telephone rang.

"Who on earth, what time is it?" The telephone and Martha's outrage awakened Ethel and me. Something must have happened and Bob Dustin or Ella Gerber wanted the company to gather at once.

Martha sweetened her voice. "Good morning." She sang the greeting.

"Mistress who?" We were all sitting upright in bed. "Mistress Maya Angelou?" Her voice revealed her disbelief. "And you are Mr. Julian? Hold on."

She put her hand over the receiver. "Mr. Julian wants to speak to Mistress Maya Angelou. At eight o'clock in the damned morning. Now, ain't that something?" The phone wire wouldn't extend across the bed. I had to get up in the cold and pad around to the other side.

"Hello?"

"Is this Mistress Maya Angelou?" The question was asked by a voice I had never heard.

"Yes. I am Maya Angelou." I answered to a background of disgruntled noises and curious looks from my roommates.

"Mistress Maya, I am being Mr. Julian. It's that last night I am seeing you dance. I am watching you leap across the stage and looking at your legs jumping through the air and, Mistress Maya, I am loving you." The words ran together like dyes, and it was difficult for me to separate them into comprehension.

"I beg your pardon?"

Martha groaned. "Oh, my goodness, can't he call you after the sun rises? Or does the sun never rise in Yugoslavia?"

"It's I am loving you, Mistress Maya. It's that if you are hearing a man is throwing his body into the Danube today, and dying in the icy water, Mistress Maya, that man is being me. Drowning for the love of you. You and your lovely legs jumping."

"Just a minute. Uh, what is your name?"

"I am being Mr. Julian, and I am loving you."

"Yes, well, Mr. Julian, why do you want to drown? Why would loving me make you want to die? I don't think that's very nice."

Ethel and Martha were both leaning on their elbows watching me.

Martha said, "Would he promise to die before sundown? Do you think he'll do it in time for us to get a little sleep?"

Ethel said serenely, "Now Maya sees what her saintly lifesaving attitude has brought."

"Look, mister."

"It's being Mr. Julian."

"Yes, well, Mr. Julian, thanks for the telephone call—"

"May I please be seeing you? May I please be taking you to one expensive café and watching your lovely lips drinking down coffee with cream?"

"No, thank you. I am sorry, but I have to hang up now."

Martha grumbled, "Hang up, or down. Just let me go back to sleep."

"Miss Maya, if you're not seeing me, if you're not letting me see your lips drinking down coffee with cream, then today, I am sending you my heart."

Oh, my God. The woman who gave me Serbo-Croatian lessons in Paris was a Yugoslavian émigré. After my last class she told me solemnly, "Don't ever in the warmth of passion tell a Yugoslav that you can't live without him. You will find him, his trunks and his family at your door. Ready to move in and improve your life." I had thought she was making a sarcastic joke, for she had said the best thing about Yugoslavia was that she couldn't return to it. When I chided her on exaggeration, she swore that what she said was absolute truth. That Slavs were passionate and so romantic they would gladly mutilate themselves to demonstrate their sincerity. And here this unknown man was threatening to send me his heart.

"Oh, no, Mr. Julian. Please. I beg you. Don't send me your heart."

Martha said, "Tell him to send you his tongue so he'll shut up."

"Mistress Maya. It is that I am sending it to your theater, by hand, this morning. Good-bye, lovely legs leaping." The line went dead.

Martha flopped back on the bed. "Well, thank God for small favors."

Ethel looked at me, waiting to see if I wanted to talk about the phone call.

I said, "I'm going to take a bath."

She said, "O.K. See you," and wiggled down under the heavy quilts.

I was tickled and frightened. "It's I am being Mr. Julian," indeed. He sounded old and rusty—like aged garden furniture, pushed around on concrete. "It's that I'm loving you. I am sending you my heart." Oh no, please.

I walked down the hall to the communal bathroom, thinking about a gory heart wrapped in newspapers waiting in my dressing room.

I stood in the drafty tub sudsing myself and imagined the blood congealed, clotted around the aorta. I dried with the thin towel and assured myself that no one in the world, even in fiction, had ever cut out his own heart. Then I remembered hara-kiri, or the ritual Japanese samurai suicide where the protagonist arranges for friends to help him perform his self-murder. Were the Yugoslavs as dramatic? I prayed not.

Martha and Ethel woke as I was leaving to go downstairs for breakfast.

"Going to meet Mr. Julian, Maya? Going to bring back his heart?"

"I am going to breakfast, ladies. Just breakfast."

"Don't eat braised heart on toast, girl." I could have wrung Martha's silver throat. My appetite fled on the heels of her remark. Downstairs I forced down tea and continually pushed away the bloody pictures which assailed my mind. I couldn't go to the theater early because we were under the same restriction in Belgrade that had obtained in Zagreb. We could walk only in the prescribed four-block area, and buses took us to and from the theater.

I waited throughout the day. Drinking slivovitz and writing letters, forced happy letters, to my family.

Finally, the cast assembled in the lobby and we trooped onto the buses and were driven to the theater.

"Maya, there's something in the dressing room for you."

He did it. The poor bastard. Actually cut out his heart and had it sent to me. I kept my face serene, but my body trembled and the muscles in my stomach were in revolt.

I opened the room door, half braced to see a bloody organ still thumping like a prop in the *Bride of Frankenstein*. A harmless-looking flat package wrapped in gay paper lay on my dressing table. If it was a heart, it had been sliced sliver-thin. I closed the door for privacy and picked up the box. It might have been a See's box of Valentine candies. The note read: "Mistress Maya, here is my heart. I am loving you. I am wishing to see you. Goodbye, my lovely legs. Mr. Julian."

He had to be alive. Otherwise how could he hope to see me? I unwrapped the paper carefully because I might need it again. I pulled the last layer away.

Mr. Julian's heart was a cake. An inedible concoction of flour dough, water and probably concrete. It was a quarter of an inch thick and a little tanner than uncooked biscuit dough. A wisp of paper warned in Serbo-Croatian and French, "DO NOT EAT!" I inspected the thing and decided the warning was entirely unnecessary. Bits of plate glass and small squares of windows were punched down into the cake and there were shreds of paper doilies and tatters of lace which vied for space with dead leaves and dried flowers. The whole thing was sprinkled over with grains of rice, barley and wheat which were glued to the surface.

I swayed somewhere between relief and indignation. At least I didn't have the onus of trying to explain to the Yugoslavian government and the U.S. State Department how a Communist citizen's heart came to be found in my dressing room. On the other hand, what could I do with the putty heart? My luggage was already overweight. I had bought sweaters in Venice for myself and a few presents for my family in Paris. I wanted a few pieces of pottery in Greece and it had been hinted that we were going to Egypt. Certainly I'd find something there to take home. And here I was, saddled with something I did not want or could not give away. There wasn't a soul in the world I disliked enough to give the ugly thing. There was a small catch in the back of the heart which indicated it was meant to hang on the wall. I placed it under my dressing table behind the shoe rack. There would be time enough to deal with it when I had to pack to leave Yugoslavia.

Mr. Julian telephoned every morning at eight o'clock. When I spoke to him sharply, ordering him to cease and desist, he answered, "It's that I'm loving you. It's that I am dying because of you. It's that I'm falling in front of a train."

I asked the desk clerk to stop putting his calls through to our room. The clerk said, "In Yugoslavia, we answer the telephone." Martha refused to answer the ring any longer, for when she told him on the second morning that I was out, he responded with: "In Belgrade? There is no place for her to go. Maybe she is going to the bathroom. I will telephone later." Ten minutes later he said to her, "This is being Mr. Julian. I am wanting to speaking with Mistress Maya Angelou."

Ordinary courtesy bade me to exchange places with Martha so that I could at least answer the telephone.

"Mistress Maya, it's that I am dying."

"All right, Mr. Julian. I can't help that. Only please, don't send me any other parts of your anatomy."

Harsh words did not deter him, nor did kind words give him solace. I answered the telephone each morning and unemotionally, fuzzily and sleepily told him to get lost.

Other members in the cast reported similar conquests. Women fairly hung on the coattails of the bachelor singers, and one evening when Martha was taken to a ballet by an admirer, I left Ethel in the room manicuring her nails and went down to the bath.

When I returned, she was sitting yoga fashion on the bed and a strange man was spread-eagled, face down, on the floor at the foot of her bed.

I stood in the door in mild shock.

Ethel said, "Maya, I've been waiting for you. Help me to get this fool out of the room."

I threw down my towel and soap.

"Mister, mister. Get up." I turned to Ethel who had risen from her lotus position and was standing at the man's feet. "Is he drunk?"

"No, girl, he's crazy."

"O.K. Mister, we're going to put you out in the hall."

His cheek was on the carpet and his eyes wide open. "It is not that I am being drunk. It is that I am loving Mistress Ethel. It is that her love is killing me. It is burning in my heart like a fire."

I said, "O.K. I understand."

Ethel said, "Here, Maya, you take the left foot. I'll take the right. We'll drag him."

The man made no resistance and allowed his body to be scudded across the room. I opened the door and we deposited him, still flat on his stomach, in the hall. Throughout the action, he had continued his litany.

"I am loving Mistress Ethel. I am dying out of love for Mistress Ethel."

We closed the door.

"Ethel, how in the hell did he get in here?"

"There was a knock at the door, and I thought it was you. So I said 'Come in,' and in comes this fool. He takes one look at me and falls flat on the floor. I thought maybe he had died or something so I went around and bent over him. To take his pulse. That's when I saw his eyes were open and he started chanting, 'Mistress Ethel, I am loving you. Dying! Killing myself.' And all that stuff."

"Why didn't you call the desk?"

"I figured you'd be back soon, and he seemed harmless."

We were laughing when we heard Martha's voice at the door and a series of quick raps.

"Hey, open the door. Open up, will you?"

Ethel went to the door and opened it. She called, "Maya, come quick." I raced to Ethel and looked over her shoulder. Martha was trying to disentangle herself from her escort, whose arms were octopusing all over her body.

"Get this fool off me, will you?" Ethel and I grabbed the man and untwined his arms.

"Hey, mister. What do you think you're doing?"

He struggled to regain his hold on Martha. "It's that I am loving Mistress Martha. Mistress Martha, I drink your eyes. I drink your nose."

We freed our friend, and as we gained the security of our room and slammed the door we heard the man's muffled voice. "Mistress Martha, I drink your ears, your nose, your fingers. Mistress Martha, it's that I'm loving you. I am dying."

One evening near the end of our Yugoslavian run, I felt I had danced particularly well, and although I might not have sung the music as written by George Gershwin, my fellow singers had greeted my harmonies with raised eyebrows and approved.

A young couple was directed to my dressing room. The man was a photographer and the woman a dancer. They spoke excellent French and complimented me on my dance. The husband asked to photograph me and invited me to their home the next evening for a pre-Christmas party. They said they would pick me up at the theater and would return me to my hotel after the party.

I considered the invitation. We had been told to stay within the allotted areas and I didn't relish the idea of calling down the wrath of two governments on my head. However, I was myself. That is, I was Marguerite Johnson, from Stamps, Arkansas, from the General Merchandise Store and the C.M.E. Church. I was the too tall, unpretty colored girl who had been born to unhappy parents and raised in the dirt roads of Arkansas and I was for the only time in my life in Yugoslavia. I divined that if I ever became rich and famous, Yugoslavia was not a country I would visit again. Was I then to never see anything more than the selected monuments and to speak to no one other than the tour-guide spies who stuck so close to us that we could hardly breathe? No. I accepted the couple's invitation.

Martha and Ethel warned me at the hotel that I had better not contravene the official orders. I tried to explain my reasons, but they either would not or could not understand. Like all company information, the news that I was going to a private party was common knowledge by noon the next day. Friends stopped by my lunch table cautioning me to change my mind. I thanked them for their advice.

Others came by my dressing room that evening to add their counsel to the general consensus. I was amazed when Helen Ferguson said the couple had invited her too, and that she was going to come along. She was one of the youngest singers in the cast, pretty and so petite she looked like a child. I said, "You know, we're not supposed to go away from the group."

She said, "Listen, I'll never come to Yugoslavia again in my life. I want to talk to some of the people here so I can have some real memories."

We waited outside the stage door and were surprised when a strange young man approached us. "Miss Ferguson? Miss Angelou?"

"Yes."

"Please come with me. I am to take you to the Dovic party."

We followed him around the corner to a flatbed truck which held about thirty people crowded together, laughing and talking. With their help, Helen and I climbed up and joined them. The man slammed the flap, ran around and started the engine, and we were off on our adventure.

The men and women were about our ages and they all spoke some French. They passed bottles of slivovitz around and we drank the fiery liquid and tried to talk over the motor's loud roar. Finally, the crowd began to sing. I couldn't follow the words, but the melodies sounded like Hungarian tziganes. They were heavy and touching. I was so busy listening that I was slow to realize that we had left the lights of Belgrade behind and the old truck was struggling along on a bumpy dirt road. The night was clear and cold, and in the bright moonlight the flat countryside looked familiar, as if I had seen it all before. I had to remind myself that I was behind the iron curtain, not taking an innocent ride in central California. The people could be taking us to Siberia. Helen and I caught each other's looks and laughed, for there was nothing else we could do. The engine began to slow down as we went over an even rougher lane when we finally stopped in front of a large gabled Charles Addams–type house. The crowd of people gave a loud shout and began to jump over the sides of the truck. Helen and I and some of the other women waited until the flap was released.

The Dovic couple came out to welcome us and lead us into an already crowded living room. Helen and I were introduced (the rest seemed to already know each other), and while we were welcomed heartily, no one stared at us as though we were apparitions from a nightmare. I soon felt at ease and got into a discussion on the future of art and its relative value to the masses.

In an adjoining dining room we were given festive foods and drink. My hostess told me she had some records I might like to hear and she called for quiet in the room. People sat down on the floor in groups, sharing bottles of wine and slivovitz. The host put the record on a wind-up record player and Lester Young's saxophone yowled out of the silence. My ears and brain were at extreme odds. I was in Yugoslavia and the ordinary people of the country had no freedom to travel. According to my language teacher in Paris, the common citizen found it impossible to obtain an exit visa or a travel document; they were prisoners in their own land. And outsiders seldom visited the iron curtain countries; few wished to come and fewer were allowed. But I was listening to Lester Young. Helen and I exchanged surprised glances. When the record was over, the host replaced it with a Billie Holiday song and then exchanged that for a Sarah Vaughan, then Charlie Parker.

The host saw my startled expression, and said, "We love music. Everyone at this party is an artist. We are painters, sculptors, writers, singers, dancers, composers. Everything. And we find ways to stay aware of innovations in art everywhere in the world. Bebop was the most important movement in music since Johann Sebastian Bach. How did we get the records?" He smiled and said, "Don't ask." I didn't.

The party was slowing down and I had begun to think of the long, bumpy ride back to the hotel when an old woman emerged from a side door. She wore a chenille bathrobe and slippers to match. She shuffled through the thinning crowd, greeting each person informally and receiving embraces in return. She had to be the grandmother of the house. She had made her way to the center of the living room before she saw me. Her face was immediately struck with panic. She squawked and turned, nearly falling, and headed for the room she had just left.

The host, hostess and other guests came quickly and apologetically to me.

"Miss Angelou, please excuse her. She is eighty years old."

"She is very old and ignorant."

"She has never seen a Black person before."

"She does not mean to hurt your feelings."

I said, "I understand her. If I had lived that long and never seen a white person, the sight of one would give me a heart attack. I would be certain I was seeing a ghost."

"Please. You shouldn't be bitter."

It wasn't my intention to be sarcastic. I was sincere.

The hostess went to the door through which the old woman had disappeared and in a moment the two came out together. The hostess, draping her arm across the woman's frail shoulders, gently guided her toward me. When they were about four feet from where I was sitting, I said in Serbo-Croatian, "Good evening, madame."

She gave me a very faint "Good evening, madame" in return.

I asked, "Will you please sit with me?" The hostess removed her arm and the old woman inched slowly away from her fear and came to join me on the sofa.

I asked, "How are you?"

She whispered, "I am well," and kept her gaze unwavering on my face. She raised a wrinkled hand and touched my cheek. I didn't move or smile. Her hand brushed my hair slightly, then the other cheek. Without shifting her look from me she called her granddaughter.

"Go and bring food and drink."

"But Grandmother, she has already eaten."

"Go."

Mrs. Dovic brought a small meat pie and a shot of slivovitz with the accompanying apricot preserve. I took a bite of the savory and one small spoonful of preserves. Without hesitation I gulped down the jigger of brandy and followed it with another spoonful of preserves.

The old woman smiled and patted my cheek. She began to talk to me so fast I couldn't keep up with her. I laughed and she laughed, showing a full set of the regulation metal teeth. Only after the party relaxed and general conversation resumed did I realize how tense the atmosphere had been. The grandmother patted my cheek again and touched my knee, then she rose laboriously and headed for her room. I called, "Good night, Grandmother," but she didn't respond. The host said, "She has already forgotten you. She is very old. Thank you for being so kind."

We were collecting our coats when the door opened again and the old woman again emerged, but this time followed by an older man. He, too, wore a chenille robe and matching slippers, and sleep had not yet released his face. When I noticed that he did not look around the room for someone or something strange but began greeting the guests closest to him, I knew the old woman was playing a joke on him. He hobbled from one person to another and the old woman stayed close to his side. Suddenly he saw me and almost leaped out of his ninety-year-old antiquity. He screamed and turned as quickly as he could to escape, but the old woman caught his sleeve, and with words I couldn't understand, began to berate him for his ignorance and chide him for being rude.

She guided him to the sofa and made him sit on one side of me while she sat on the other.

"Go bring food and drink."

Again I went through the ritual. When the old man saw I could both eat and drink and I could speak some Serbo-Croatian, he not only decided I was human, he declared me a Yugoslav. Just a very dark one.

"What is your name?"

"Maya."

"A good name."

"Who is your father?"

"Bailey Johnson."

"What a strange name for a Croatian. But I am sure I know him. Who is his father?"

"William Johnson."

"Vilyon? Vilyon? What does he do? I know everybody. I am ninety-three years old. Now tell me, was that Vilyon from Split or the one from Dubrovnik? Tell me."

No one could convince the man that I belonged to a different race and country.

As we headed for the door he said, "Tell Vilyon you have met me. Tell him to come after Christmas. We will talk of the old times."

The desk clerk at the hotel had to unlock the door to let us in. He said, "Miss Angelou. Miss Ferguson. Did you enjoy the party at the Dovic home? Did you enjoy the American records and the food? The old man and woman are very amusing, are they not?"

So much for our sense of freedom.

The next morning a clean-cut American asked to see me. I went to a room in the hotel and listened to a strange white man talk to me as if I were a child.

"You have been asked, Maya, not to wander around Belgrade. The Yugoslavs don't want it. They are a different people from us. They don't understand our ways. You are, after all, a guest in their country. Simple courtesy demands that you honor the wishes of your host."

I said, "I am not the one of the two of us who needs lessons in common courtesy. I did not say one thing last night that I didn't mean, nor that I would be reluctant to repeat. Good morning," and I left.

If *Porgy and Bess* didn't like it, they could find another singer who could dance, or a dancer who could sing. I had already seen Venice, Paris and two towns in Yugoslavia. I could go home to my wonderful son and my night club career.

I never heard any more about the incident, nor did I ask Helen if she had been questioned on our return.

———

"Good morning, Mistress Maya. As you know this is being me, Mr. Julian."

It was also the morning of our closing night in Belgrade.

"Yes, Mr. Julian."

Nothing had deterred him. Neither strong words nor outright insults kept him from telephoning. Martha and Ethel became so used to the ring that it no longer awakened them.

"It's I am loving you yet. It's that when you are leaving tomorrow I am dying."

"Yes, Mr. Julian." The night before, I had joined Joe Jones, Martha, Ethel, Ned and Attles in a slivovitz-and-song fest at a local bar. I felt as if the harsh brandy had baked my brain, and if Mr. Julian could wait until the next morning to die I would best him by twenty-four hours.

"I am not drowning. It is being very difficult for me. Because I am being Yugoslavia's Olympic swimming champion."

Swimming champion? Mr. Julian? Doggone it, I had slipped a bet. His voice had sounded ancient, as if it belonged to a body in the last

stages of deterioration. I liked strong and muscular men. Had I known Mr. Julian was an athlete, I'd have seen him the first time he called.

"I am loving you and wanting to see you, oh ..."

"Maybe I can see you tonight, Mr. Julian." I couldn't make up for the time wasted, but there was no reason I should lose another night.

"Is it true? You will let me take you to one expensive café? And watching you drinking down coffee with cream in your lovely lips?"

"Yes, Mr. Julian." You bet. "After the theater you come to the stage door."

"Mistress Maya, there are always being so many people around your theater. Is it that you can be meeting me one block away?"

"Sure, yes. Of course." It seemed a little late for him to show a shy side.

"One block away near the park. I will be standing. I will be wearing a green suit. I will be smiling. Oh, Mistress Maya, my heart is singing for you. Good-bye, my lovely."

"Good-bye, Mr. Julian."

I hung up the telephone as Martha and Ethel turned over and sat up.

"So, at last. My Lord, we'll get to see this damned Mr. Julian." Martha was grinning and nodding her head.

Ethel said, "Maya, you *are* cold-blooded. You know the man loves you. And you wait until the last night to see him."

Martha added, "It *is* cold—he wants to marry you so you can take him to the States. Now there's no time to get a license. You're just going to use that poor man and toss him away, like a sailor does a woman in a foreign port." She was laughing. "Ohh, you're mean."

I told them both to go to hell and went back to sleep.

Ned met me at lunch. "So you're finally going to see Mr. Julian?"

Annabelle Ross, the coloratura, asked, "Tonight's the night, huh?"

Georgia Burke, the oldest member of the cast and veteran actress, said, "I understand Mr. Julian's finally got lucky. Well, there's nothing like sticking to it, they say."

Barbara Ann sat down at the table. "What made you wait so long, Maya? And what made you change your mind?"

I told her I had thought that he was an ancient lech and I couldn't abide the idea of going out with an elderly stage-door Johnny who would slobber on my cheek and pinch my thighs, but that he had finally told me he was a swimming champion and now I was sorry I waited so long.

She understood and sympathized with me.

An hour later Bey appeared at my door. "O.K., Maya. Got yourself a swimming champion, huh?"

On the way to the theater, a few wags in the back of the bus began to harmonize: "I'd swim the deepest ocean..."

Among the cast no news was private and no affairs sacred.

The audience began applauding in the middle of the finale. They were on their feet, throwing roses and shouting before the curtain fell. We bowed and waved and repeated the bows unremembered times.

Backstage, Marilyn, the wardrobe mistress, was supervising the labeling and packing of costumes. Departures were always her busiest time. She had to tag the clothes that had been torn so they could be sewn or replaced before our next opening night, and to keep separate the pieces due for cleaning and the shoes needing repairs.

As I passed the wardrobe room the door was open on a havoc of disarranged clothes, hats, shoes, baskets and umbrellas. She looked up from her counting. "Going to meet Mr. Julian, huh, Maya?"

My only chance of escaping the curious eyes of my fellow singers was to leave the theater by the front entrance. I gathered my costumes and dropped them in the wardrobe room, as we were required to do. Marilyn's attention was on her work. I slipped past the stage hands who were breaking down the set and stacking scenery. I tiptoed across the stage and jumped from the apron to the theater floor. The lobby was empty and dark as I eased out the door. I had avoided everyone. As I walked to the intersection I looked down the street. I saw a crowd of well-wishers at the stage door; they would keep the company occupied for a least a half-hour. Mr. Julian, I am coming and coming alone. You'll never know what a remarkable feat I have accomplished.

I approached the designated corner, searching for a tall well-built man in a dark-green suit, possibly a tweedy affair. He might be smoking a pipe—pipes and tweeds went so well together.

Mr. Julian wasn't on the corner. I wondered if he had decided, after all, to collect me at the stage door. I crossed the street and stood under the light, planning my next move.

"Mistress Maya?"

I turned, happy to be relieved of the problem. A small, very wiry old man was standing before me. His eyes were large and black and glistening. His bald head looked greased under the streetlight. He was smiling a row of decidedly polished metal teeth. And he wore a Kelly green suit.

"Mistress Maya, it's that I'm being Mr. Julian."

If he was a swimming champion the match took place in 1910.

"Yes, Mr. Julian. How are you?" I offered him my hand and he took it, stroked the back of it, turned it over and kissed the palm.

He mumbled, "I am loving you."

I said, "Yes." And, "How about that coffee?"

If Martha or Ethel or Lillian caught a glimpse of my athletic lover, I'd never be allowed to live it down.

"I can't go far, I must be in the hotel before curfew, you know."

He didn't understand the word "curfew" and I didn't have the time to stand on the corner explaining it.

"Let's go to the café up the street. Is that all right?"

We sat at a small table silently. Each conversational opening I tried was blocked by his statements of undying love. His bright eyes watched me drink coffee. He observed my lips so intently, I had the sensation that his gaze was following each sip slide over my tongue, through the esophagus and into my stomach.

I gulped the last swallow and stood up. "Thank you, Mr. Julian. I must get back to the theater or the bus will leave me."

"I will take you to your hotel." His eyes were begging.

"No, thanks. The buses have to take us. Sorry."

"It's that I will walk you back to the theater. I am loving you."

"Absolutely not! No, thank you. I appreciate the coffee and the thought, but I'd like to remember you right here, having coffee with cream." I didn't offer him my hand again. "Thank you. Please stay. Good-bye, Mr. Julian."

I walked slowly out of the café, but when I closed the door I broke into a run that would have impressed Jesse Owens. The bus was loading as I reached the theater.

As I climbed aboard, Martha said, "Whatever else Mr. Julian is, I can tell he's fast."

Lillian said, "I've got something for you, Maya. You left it in your dressing room and I felt I'd better bring it to you. Your life would not be the same without it."

She handed me a package. It was Mr. Julian's heart.

CHAPTER 23

The singers were hardened to the discomfort of travel and the sense of dislocation. Yet the Yugoslavia trip put an unusual amount of pressure on us all. The cold weather, gray and dreary, and the incommodious hotel with its grim corridors and heavy odors pressed weightily on our spirits. The unhappy people in their ugly, thick clothes and the restrictions on our freedom of movement all combined to make us impatient to put the dour place behind us and to bask in the sunshine of North Africa.

Ethel, Martha, Barbara Ann, Lillian and I crowded our personal belongings into the two overhead racks of our compartment. It was seven o'clock on a dark morning. The cast had begun to assemble at the train station at six and we had boarded the fabled Orient Express as soon as Ella Gerber and Bob Dustin completed their head count and were satisfied that no member of the company was still sleeping at the Moskva. Belgradians crowded around the train steps. Some Yugoslavian women sniffled and dried their eyes as male singers embraced them, checked their watches and boarded the train. A few female singers waved good-bye to some native men, who wept openly.

My friends and I nestled down, anxious for the train to move. We were chatting when a noise alerted us. We looked up to see Mr. Julian standing in the doorway of the compartment, holding a small package. "Mistress Maya?" Tears trickled down his face. "Mistress Maya, I am wishing you joy, happiness and wictory." With that emotional outcry he threw the package in my lap, slammed the door and leaped off the train.

Lillian asked, "*That* was Mr. Julian?"

Ethel said unbelievingly, "No, surely not?"

Barbara Ann asked, "But when was he a swimming champion?"

Martha shifted her small head and said, "He looks like he'd have a hard time floating across a bathtub."

Before I could retort, his face was at the window. He waved his hands in a beckoning motion and the train began to move slowly. Mr. Julian kept up with our window for a while, but as the train gained momentum his face and all the other faces of those left behind began to slide from our view. In a few minutes we were in open country, looking out on lonely farmhouses and sullen fields.

Ned Wright pulled the door open and offered a bottle of slivovitz.

"Here we are, me darlings. Long gone and away. Tito can keep his Yugoslavia. I am meant to sit under sunny skies and sing. What the hell are you crying for, Maya?"

Ethel said it couldn't be for Mr. Julian. "Did you see him?"

Martha laughed, "He looked like a mile of country road in the winter in North Carolina."

I said, "But he persevered. And he was nice. I mean, he never failed to call and he had to get up very early to be at the station before we left. I admire that in anyone."

Ethel asked, "Would you like to go back to Belgrade?"

I didn't have to choose an answer. I said, "No. Pass me the slivovitz!"

The train sped all day through the glowering provinces and we took our meals in an old dining car which smelled like our last hotel. Some of the cast took naps or wrote letters home. We played games of rise and fly bid whist in our compartment with all the passion of addicted gamblers. When the gray afternoon finally surrendered to night, a porter made our beds and we slept.

I awakened to find Martha and Ethel chittering like crickets. The sunlight came boldly through the windows and their faces were lit with a gaiety I hadn't seen for weeks.

"Maya, girl, you're going to sleep all day? Look out the window." Martha edged over and made room for me. The countryside had changed. In one night we had passed from bleak winter to spring. Cows grazed on abundant green foliage and the farmhouses were painted in so many vivid colors the scene resembled a large Matisse painting.

Grownups, smiling broadly, waved at the train, and children bounced, laughing their excitement. The picture touched me so violently that I was startled, and in an instant I realized that I had not seen giddy children since Venice. The Parisian youngsters were so neat in dress and manner they might have been family ornaments created and maintained to adorn. The children I saw in Yugoslavia appeared sensible and level-headed without the buoyancy of childhood. Here were children I could understand. Although their voices didn't carry over the distance and through our windowpane, I was certain they were shouting, yelling and screaming, and I was just as certain that the mothers were saying "Be quiet," "Stop that" and "Hush."

I got up and excused myself. The longing for my own son threatened to engulf me. As I walked down the corridor, controlling the emotional deluge that swelled in my mind, I passed compartments where other members of the company sat close to their windows, absorbed.

We caught brief glimpses of the white buildings and green hills of Athens, then boarded buses which were to take us to the port city of Piraeus. The road was high and winding, and our moods were high. We sang in full voice every song that was suggested and laughed when someone made the wrong harmonic change or forgot the lyrics.

At the waterfront, Dustin doled out cabin assignments and announced that Lee Gershwin was throwing a champagne party on the ship for the entire cast before lunch.

If only Yanko and Victor and Mitch could see me now. I had dredged up some Greek learned during my marriage and greeted the crew members. They were already excited by the cluster of Black people, and when they heard me speaking their language they nearly saluted. Three men left their posts to help me find my quarters, where my suitcases, books and mandolin were already stacked on a table in the single room.

Martha, Lillian, Ethel and Barbara Ann came down the passageway talking about the ship, the champagne party and the handsome Greek sailors.

I stopped them, and said, "Hey, you guys, aren't you surprised that Lee Gershwin is inviting the humble nobodies to her affair?"

Martha said, "Darling, Miss Fine Thing has never been humble, and for your information, she has always been Somebody. She shall grace the motley crew with her presence." She grinned and flung her head back.

Lillian said, "Dearie, there's going to be champagne?" She nodded, answering her own question. "I'm going to drink Madame Gershwin's champagne."

Barbara Ann said smoothly, "Maya, you've never forgiven her for telling you and Joy what to wear in Venice, have you?" She shook her head and managed a sad smile. "And I thought you were supposed to be a Christian. Shame, Maya, shame."

They continued looking for their rooms and left me thinking about Lee Gershwin. She had approached me and Joy in Venice's Saint Mark's Square on our second day in Italy.

"Don't you girls know you shouldn't wear slacks in Italy? The Italians don't like it." Her narrow face was sour with propriety. "Be nice. Remember, we are all ambassadors."

Joy had told her: "One, it's cold. Two, I'm singing every night on a cold stage and changing in a cold dressing room, and three, I'm working six hours a day with the cast on their roles. Four, I shall continue to wear slacks and, if I need it, a parka!"

I simply looked at Lee. If I had given tongue to my voice, I'd have said too much. I simply continued to wear slacks when I thought it necessary, counting on my own sense of propriety to dictate what I should wear where and when. The incident had slipped from my consciousness, but once reminded of it I had to admit that Lee's maternalistic attitude had so infuriated me that, although she traveled with us, I had erased her from my thoughts.

I unpacked the clothes I would need for the three-night, two-day trip to Alexandria and changed into a dress for lunch.

When I walked up the stairs, stewards grinned and spoke to me in Greek, and as I entered the dining room a large, bushy-haired man in a black suit caught my arm.

"Mrs. Angelos?"

"Yes?"

"I am the purser."

I couldn't dredge up one idea of what to expect.

"You speak Greek?" he asked.

"Yes. A little."

"How did you learn?"

"My husband was Greek."

"Ah." And he grinned a broad approval. "Mrs. Angelos, may I make a suggestion?" He turned his large body sideways and spoke out of the side of his mouth as if he were giving me the secret of building an atomic bomb.

"Yes."

"There is a party. A champagne party." He inclined his head toward the tables where members of the cast were already lifting glasses. "We expect a very rough trip to Alexandria. It would be better if you didn't drink today. Or tonight. Not champagne. Not wine. Not water. Eat lightly. Bread. Biscuits. And no drinking."

I thanked him and asked if he had warned anyone else. He smiled, pulling his lips leftward to reveal a solid gold tooth.

He said, "They are opera singers. I wouldn't try to tell them. But you"—again he grinned—"you are nearly Greek"—he took my hand and kissed it—"and you have my sympathy. Good-bye. Remember."

Sympathy? He thought having married a Greek made me deserving of his compassion? Strange.

My friends had saved a chair for me at their table.

"Miss Thing, hold your glass." Martha held the champagne ready to pour.

"No, I'm not drinking." I told them of the warning.

Lillian said, "I've never been seasick in my life.

Martha and Ethel seconded her. They shared the wine and giggled, paying no attention to my admonition. Every table was filled with happy flutters. Even the few nondrinkers were in a party mood. I only half believed the purser, but was glad for an excuse not to participate. I liked to pay for my own drink or at least choose the sponsor who treated me.

"Mother Afrique, your long-lost daughter is returning home..." Lillian was composing another toast and no one was waiting for her to complete it.

"Cheers."

"Salute."

"À votre santé."

"Doz vedanya."

"Skoal."

An officer at the captain's table stood up, kissed the women's hands, bowed to the men and began to pick his way out of the dining room. He was tall and moved gracefully, hardly shaking the braid that looped across his wide shoulders. He turned his head and looked at our table. He had the most sensuous face I had ever seen. His lips were dark rose and pouted, and his nostrils flared as if he were breathing heavily through them. But his eyes were the most arresting feature. They were the "bedroom eyes" sung about in old blues—heavy-lidded, as if he were en route at that moment to the boudoir of the sexiest woman in the world.

"Mart, Ethel, look at that," I said.

My friends, who usually had a high appreciation of male beauty, were so occupied with their party that they gave the officer only a cursory look.

Ethel said, "Yeah, he's cute."

Martha said, "I'll check him out later. Pour a little more of the bubbly into my slipper, please, for I am Queen of the May."

I watched the man leave the dining salon and knew that when the sexy women in our company got around to noticing him, they would take some of the arrogance out of his swinging shoulders and lessen the bounce in his narrow hips.

After lunch I returned to my cabin, leaving the party in full hilarity. By midafternoon when we were well away from the coast of Greece, the ship began to shudder under the attack of a storm. My luggage shot back and forth across the tiny space between my bunk and the wall, and had I not stood up I would have been thrown out of bed. I shoved my bags tightly into the closet and jammed a chair under the closet's doorknob. I took a book and headed for the main deck.

In the passageway I met my suddenly sober and suddenly sick fellow singers. Those who were able to talk said the party had broken up as drinkers and players became too ill to continue; the waiters had removed all bottles and glasses and were tying the tables down.

The dining room was empty and dark, and I struggled, rolling from wall to wall, up the passageway to a small red sign which invited: BAR. The door opened on a small, empty but lighted room. I sat at a table, trying to glue my mind to the plot and away from the roiling sea. After an hour or so, a young crew member came in, saw me and was surprised. He asked if I was all right. I lied and told him in Greek that I was. He looked at me, astonished for a second, then left hurriedly. A few moments later the purser arrived.

"Mrs. Angelos, are you well?"

"Yes, of course." My composure was paper-thin, but it covered the fear.

"You didn't drink. I noticed." He was proud of himself and of me.

"No. I ate bread and a piece of cold chicken."

"Very good. It is going to be worse tonight, but tomorrow will be calmer. You are not to worry. We have a doctor, but he is very busy. Both the opera company and the movie company are sick and he is kept running between the two."

I didn't know about the movie company. "Who are they? From America?"

"No. They are English. Except the star is French. Brigitte Bardot. They are all in their cabins and I don't expect to see either the singers or actors until we reach Alexandria."

He took my hand. "Mrs. Angelos, if you want me, please ring this bell"—he pointed to a button on the wall—"and tell anyone to come for me. I will be with you immediately." He kissed my hand and departed.

A waiter entered and said tea was being served in the dining room. I thanked him and said I wouldn't have anything.

The ship pitched and rolled and quivered and sometimes leaped, seeming to withdraw entirely from the surface of the water. I was frightened at the violence and my inability to control any part of the experience except myself and there was no certainty that my mental discipline would outlast the physical anxiety. But at least I wasn't ill.

The purser pushed his head in the door. "Dinner is being served. I suggest that you eat. Again the plain bread. And again a small piece of meat. No wine. No water." His head disappeared as the vessel rolled over on its side.

Although I had no appetite I decided to continue following his suggestions. The dining room was not quite empty. The captain and his officers sat quietly in their corner; a few teetotalers from *Porgy and Bess* were at separate tables; and two men whose faces I recognized from British movies occupied a table near the wall. I joined Ruby Green and Barbara Ann and ate sparingly.

Barbara asked, "Where have you been? You haven't been sick?"

I told her I'd been reading and I wasn't sick because I didn't drink the champagne.

"You ought to see downstairs. Everybody's sick. I mean, people are moaning like they're dying. The poor doctor no sooner leaves one room than they call him to another. That man's got his work cut out for him. See, here he comes now. Poor thing. Just now getting a chance to eat his dinner."

I looked up, following her gaze, and saw the voluptuous face that had startled me at lunchtime.

"That's the doctor?" I would have more easily believed him to be a gigolo, a professional Casanova.

"Yes. And he's very courteous. He gives the same attention to the men that he gives to the women."

I looked at his retreating back and wondered if Barbara in her naïveté had described the man better than she could have imagined.

After a somber dinner we went below, where the groans of suffering escaped mournfully from each room. I paused before my friends' doors, but I knew I could do nothing for them except sympathize and I could do that without disturbing their agony.

There was a soft rap on my door. When I opened it and saw the purser, I thought he expected me to compensate him for my sound health. I held the door and asked icily, "Yes, what do you want?"

He said meekly, "Mrs. Angelos, I want to show you how to strap yourself in the bed so that you won't fall out and be hurt."

I started to let him in and thought better of it. "No, thanks. I was planning to sleep on the floor. I'll be all right. Thanks, anyway."

He shot his hand in the narrow door opening and grabbed my arm.

"Mrs. Angelos, thank you. You are very sad and very beautiful." He bowed and kissed my hand and released it. I slammed the door. How could he tell I was sad? That was a strange romantic come-on.

I made my actions fit the lie. I stripped mattress and covers from the bed and lay down on the floor to sleep in miserable fits and starts.

The morning was dreary and wet, but the sea was more restrained. The purser was waiting for me outside the dining room door.

"Mrs. Angelos, good morning. You may eat a full breakfast. We will have good weather by evening." He looked at me lovingly, concern seeping out of his pores. "How did you sleep?"

"Beautifully, thank you. Just beautifully."

Some members of our company who had survived the storm exchanged stories of the night before.

"Honey, I was so sick I tried to jump overboard!"

"Did you hear Betty? She prayed half the night, then she got mad and screamed, 'Jesus Christ, this ain't no way for you to act so close to your birthday!' "

My visits to Martha's and Lillian's cabins were not welcome, so I made them brief, staying only long enough to see that although their faces were the color of old leather boots, they would survive. I walked around the ship, enjoying the luxury of solitude. For the first time, there was a tender behind the bar and I ordered an apéritif. The very large British movie actor and his companion came in, ordered and sat near me.

"So you're a sailor too, are you?" The man's gruff voice was directed to me.

"I suppose so."

"But the rest of your company have no sea legs?" He laughed and his eyes nearly closed beneath dark, thick eyebrows.

"Some have been a little sick," I said. The man always played friendly characters, so without knowing his real personality, I felt friendly toward him. "But they're better now."

"My name is James Robertson Justice."

Of course I knew the name and had thought it fitted his giant size and huge laughter. He pointed to his smaller, quieter friend. "And this is Geoffrey Keen."

We talked about opera and movie making and I felt decidedly international. I was on a Greek ship, talking to English movie stars, en route to the African continent.

I ate lunch and dinner alone, but joined Ned Wright and Bey in the bar after dinner. James Robertson Justice was there again and the three men exchanged stories. They all laughed together, but it was not clear if they understood each other. Ned tended to talk and snap his fingers in the air like a flamenco dancer, meanwhile wiggling his head. Bey grumbled in a bass-baritone without moving his lips. Justice spoke in all the British accents, gamboling from upper class, middle class to Welsh and Irish like a skittish lamb on the heath.

I left the men laughing and talking loudly and walked down the passageway. The doctor passed me, lips distended and full, his eyes low and dense.

"Good evening," he said.

I said "Good evening," and wished vainly that he would stop. The purser knocked at my door. I opened it a crack.

"Mrs. Angelos, we will dock at eleven. Everyone will be asked to come to passport control. There will be a crowd. I suggest that you meet me after breakfast, at nine o'clock, and I will see that your passport is stamped first."

"Thank you." I held on to the door. "Thank you very much. Good night." I closed the door firmly.

At nine o'clock the next morning he met me outside the dining room. He took my elbow and guided me to the upper deck. An official handed me my stamped passport and medical documents. The purser led me away.

"Now, Mrs. Angelos, I suggest you get your belongings, not your luggage, but handbags and other things you want to carry. Bring them on deck and then you will not have to stand in line with the others." He kissed my hand and gave me a lingering look.

When the two companies lined up on the main deck and on the stairs leading to the officials' temporary office, I stood beside the rail watching the coast of Africa. The ship was being pulled into the harbor by a small, powerful tugboat.

The sea was a beautiful blue, and the tall white buildings on the shore belied the old statement that all Africans lived in trees like monkeys. Alexandria was beautiful.

I had all my hand luggage and was eager to step out on Egyptian soil. A camera swung from my right side, a shoulder bag from the left. I carried my mandolin and Mr. Julian's heart (I was too ashamed of my treatment of him to throw the thing away), and at my feet was a makeup case and a small box of books.

As the ship neared land, streets and the details of buildings became more visible in the bright sunlight, and I fantasized the Africans who designed the houses and laid out the streets. Tall and dark-brown-skinned. Proud and handsome like my father. Bitter-chocolate black like my brother, lightly made and graceful. Or chunky and muscular, resembling my Uncle Tommy. Thick and sturdy, walking with a roll to their hips like boxers or gandy dancers. The fantasy was mesmerizing, and before I knew it men were lashing the ship to the dock.

Except for their long gowns and little skullcaps, the men did look like my father and brother and uncle, and there appeared to be thousands of them, screaming and shouting and running up and down the pier. From my high perch I tried to distinguish the differences between these Africans who had not been bought, sold or stolen and my people who were still enduring a painful diaspora. But I was either too far away or they moved too fast for my purpose. Still, I was determined and kept my gaze fastened on the area below.

"Mrs. Angelos."

I turned and was face-to-face with the doctor.

"Mrs. Angelos, what are your first impressions of your native continent?"

I retrieved my thoughts and longings and made a snappy remark. "It is colorful. And noisy. And the sun shines on Africa."

He fished two cigarettes from a package and lighted them simultaneously (he had seen *Now Voyager* too, and I wondered how often he had imitated Paul Henreid). He put one between my lips.

"Where are you staying in Alexandria?"

I told him the company was booked at the Savoy.

"Will you honor me with dinner? They have a decent dining room and you won't have to leave your hotel."

I quickly weighed his lips, shoulders, hips and eyes against the chances of finding an interested Egyptian man on the first day. The sea had been smooth for nearly twenty-four hours, which meant that the huntresses were feeling well and would be back in the chase and any available men would be at a premium. "I'd be delighted," I said.

His eyes smoldered wonderful promises; then he tried a smile that was incongruous on the lascivious face. "My name is Geracimos Vlachos. I am called Maki. Expect me at eight o'clock. Until then." He bowed and kissed my hand.

Martha said, "You got him, you fast thing, you. Took advantage of all your sick sisters and snatched that man while everybody was flat on their backs. Dying in the hold."

We were lined up at the rails, ready to disembark.

Lillian nudged us. "Look at the people, will you? Africans. My God. Now I have lived. Real Africans."

Ethel and Barbara were a little more reserved, but just as excited. Our voices nearly equaled in volume the shouts and yells of the dock workers.

I saw that the older singers were as fascinated as we. Katherine Ayres, Georgia Burke, Eloise Uggams, Annabelle Ross and Rhoda Boggs stood facing Bob Dustin, but their eyes continued to steal away to the dock and to the people who were unloading the vessel. When they walked between the gowned stevedores on the way to the buses, their usually reserved smiles broadened into happy grins, and they doled out money, whose value they had not really considered, to the beggars who stretched out their hands.

In the hotel we deposited our hand luggage then raced back to the lobby to look at the Africans. It took less than five minutes to discover that the bellhops, porters, doormen and busboys were black and brown and beige, and that the desk clerk, head waiters, bartenders and hotel manager were white. As far as we knew, they might have all been African, but the distribution of jobs by skin color was not lost on us. The sweetness of our arrival in Africa was diluted, but not totally spoiled.

After all, Gamal Abdel Nasser was the President and every photograph showed him to be brown-skinned. Darker than Lena Horne, Billy Daniels and Dorothy Dandridge. Without a doubt, he was one of us.

We sat in the lounge and ordered drinks. Ned had thrown his cape rakishly across his shoulders and Joe Attles had donned a new and colorful ascot to protect his throat.

Ned asked, "Does anyone want to go with us? We're going to look at The Dark Continent and bring back a sphinx."

We all laughed and clapped our hands. Servants ran out into the lounge and bowed, waiting. We looked at them and each other. If we wore the same clothing no one would be able to say we were not members of the same family, yet we couldn't hold a conversation. (Europeans and white Americans are not surprised to see their lookalikes speaking foreign languages; but except for meeting a few African students in Europe, we had never seen a large group of Black people whose culture, language and life styles were different from our own.)

Martha asked in French if they wanted something. One man answered in French that when he heard us clap our hands, he thought we wanted something. We learned that day, although we slipped up now and then, not to clap our hands at a joke, and that if we wanted to talk across the centuries that separated us from our brothers in Egypt, we had to use French, a language that was beautiful but more attuned to the thin lips of Europeans—it lacked the rhythms of Ned Wright popping his fingers and Martha Flowers swinging her hips. The knowledge made me sullen and I excused myself and went to my room.

The cast assembled for the evening meal. The large dining room was decorated with palm trees and paper ribbons swinging from slow-moving ceiling fans. Alexandria's playboys were present in evening finery, sending champagne to the women and occasionally to a man who caught their fancy. They introduced themselves from table to table, kissed hands, bowed and offered their calling cards. A few women in low-cut satin dresses ogled the male singers; when they netted a man's attention, their red lips split in a smile to welcome a pharaoh. It was sexually stimulating to be the object of such desire, even if the desire was general and the object collective.

I was so busy flirting and watching my friends that I had forgotten about my date with the doctor. He appeared out of nowhere and stood before me.

"Mrs. Angelos, my I present my cousin and cousin-in-law? They live in Alexandria."

I shook hands with a tall, attractive woman and her short, pudgy husband. Maki asked me to join their table. When I excused myself from my friends, they raised their eyes.

We made small talk in a mixture of French and Greek. The tables were cleared, and a small band arranged itself at the back of the room. The men played Greek and Arabic music on instruments I had never seen before. When the belly dancer appeared, tasseled and sequined, our company exploded in approval.

"Yeah, baby. Shake that thing!" And she did. Her hips quivered and trembled and her breasts threatened to jiggle out of the skimpy satin-cup restraints. She bumped so hard she had to be cautioned, "Throw it, but don't throw it away, baby." Her skin was pale brown and her hair straight, and we were all flabbergasted; no white woman we'd ever seen could move that way.

"Shake it, but don't break it."

"It must be jelly 'cause jam don't shake that way."

Later the orchestra played popular songs for dancing and Maki invited me to dance. He held me close and whispered heavily accented words. I gave the appearance of listening, but in fact I was looking around the dance floor for my friends. As busy as they were with their own flirtations they still kept me within sight. I had posed too long as Goody Two-shoes and they weren't going to let me slip without a detailed inspection of my fall. Unity and friendship when needed is reassuring, but sometimes can become an obtrusive and nosy intrusion.

I asked Maki if he knew somewhere else where we might dance. He said he would drop his relatives at their home and we could go to his hotel. "There is an accordion player who specializes in romantic Greek songs. I would like you to hear him."

At once the object of my life was to be in Maki's arms and beyond the scrutiny of my colleagues. I told him I would meet him in front of the hotel. I shook hands with him and his relatives and they rose to go.

Someone at the table said, "Going to let him slide, huh, Maya?"

I said I was going to bed—all the noise had given me a headache. They watched me leave, bemused.

Maki had a taxi waiting, and after we dropped his relatives at their house, near my hotel, we rode in silence for what seemed to be hours. Finally he ushered me into a mean little pension, which would have fitted well on San Francisco's skid row. An unshaven desk clerk handed a key to Maki, who said, "I had forgotten. The accordion player is off tonight. But let us go to my room. I will sing for you."

I considered my options. I didn't know where I was. I didn't speak the language. I was attracted to him. I wasn't married or being unfaithful, for I had no lover. He wouldn't hurt me—after all, he was a doctor, Hippocratic oath and all.

I followed him to the room and his songs were glorious. Early the next morning he said we were only a few blocks from my hotel and he would take a cab and drop me, then return to his ship. I wanted to walk and look at the city. The frivolous night was over; I had enjoyed it. But I needed to think great thoughts about myself and Africa and slavery and Islam; I didn't want a white man at my side—in fact, I didn't want anyone distracting me.

Maki was reluctant to let me go alone. I said, "It's daybreak. And, after all, I am home."

"You do not know this country, Maya."

"I come from this country. I am only returning home."

He said we would meet in two weeks, since his ship was to pick us up again in Alexandria after we finished our run at the Cairo Opera House. He said he loved me and I should think about that; he was married, but would get a divorce and come back to the United States with me; doctors made very good money in the United States and it was difficult to get a visa, but if he was married to an American citizen...

I walked out into a beautiful morning and struggled with a bitter thought. The very country that denied Negroes equality at home provided them with documents that made them attractive abroad. Mr. Julian and Maki, in my case, and hundreds of European men and women who tagged the coattails of Black servicemen and singers and musicians might have found them much less appealing if they claimed West Indian or African citizenship, but since they hailed from "God's country," the "home of democracy" and the richest nation on earth, men were ready to leave their wives and women their husbands for entry into the land of plenty. Avarice cripples virtue and lies in ambush for honesty.

My footsteps disturbed a group of people wrapped in filthy rags and huddled in a doorway. Two small brown children awakened first; they punched and probed in the bundle of clothing until a man's head emerged. When he saw me he began bellowing and a woman sat up-right. I was rooted to the pavement, watching the unfolding scene. The two children, joined by two smaller tykes, made their way to me; the mother and father followed, dragging the tatters of cloth that had once covered them. They encircled me, their hands outstretched. The man and woman clutched their fingers together and brought them to their mouths in a jabbing motion, then they stabbed the bunched hands at their stomachs. They were hungry, but I wasn't sure if it was safe to open my purse. Suppose they grabbed it from me, what could I do?

My inaction called for drama from the adults. The mother grabbed the smallest boy and wedged him between her knees facing me. The father took the child's chin roughly and forced it away from the chest. I looked at the baby's face in the soft morning sunlight. It was a bis-cuit topped with dusty black hair and, like a clean dinner plate, de-void of meaning except for a thick white substance which seeped from the closed eyes and slowly descended the cheeks. The parents held the boy's head for my view as if I had caused the condition, as if I had poked out the eyes with a nail and now I must pay for my deed.

I fished out my advance from my purse and peeled off a bill. When I offered it to the child the man snatched it, and the woman flung her blind offspring behind her dirty skirts and grabbed another boy. They showed me his severed arm. The stump looked as blind and final as the diseased eyes. I gave them another bill. When they began to line up the whole family, I said in French, "I have no more money," and turned to walk toward my hotel.

They followed, running beside and behind me. I opened up my stride, and the man ran in front, talking loudly, gesturing and scream-ing, as if I had just evicted them from their home.

Their noise awakened other beggars who had found sleeping ac-commodations in doorways, on porches and next to roofless buildings. Their supplications, loud and cacophonous, merged; the adults wept and pushed crippled children in my path, ripping the filthy clothes to show the extent of the horror.

Egypt had stumbled under the imperialist and colonial yokes for two thousand years, and finally in 1953 achieved true independence as a republic. But success in gaining self-rule had not yet affected the lives of the poor. Much remained to be done.

I knew that and journalists in the local newspapers knew it, too. I had read magazine articles analyzing the depth of the problems of the country and I was distressed. But sympathy did not lessen my sense of guilt. I was healthy and, compared to the horde of beggars, rich. I was young, talented, well-dressed, and whether I would take pride in the fact publicly or not, I was an American.

The crowd followed me to the hotel where a large uniformed doorman spied me. He rushed to meet me halfway down the block. Then he began screaming and hitting out at the beggars. Occasionally his heavy fists connected and there was a thud of flesh on bone or bone on bone. I called to the man to stop, but he kept flailing his fists and arms until the beggars took to their heels, their shreds of clothing floating behind them like dirty smoke.

"Never mind, mademoiselle. Never mind." His composure was so complete it seemed as if it had never been ruffled. My father had been a doorman in Long Beach, California, during the great depression. I wondered if he had ever had to chase beggars and hobos from the door. Were they Black? Did he feel no more for them than the Savoy doorman felt for his fellow Egyptians?

Martha was sitting in the lobby when I entered. She still wore the dress from the night before. It was impossible to tell whether she had just come in seconds before me or had sat in the same chair all night.

"Good morning, Miss Thing. First night in Africa take the headache away?"

I told her to take a flying leap and went to bed.

CHAPTER 24

We stayed in Alexandria two days before moving on to Cairo, but I would not leave the hotel again and refused to explain my seclusion.

My close friends thought I had fallen in love with the doctor and I accepted their teasing without comment.

We were driven to Cairo, and thrown into another world. More black-skinned people held positions of authority. The desk clerk at the Continental Hotel was the color of cinnamon; the manager was beige but had tight crinkly hair. The woman who supervised the running of the house was small and energetic and her complexion would never have allowed her to pass for white.

Beggars still hounded our footsteps and the audiences which shouted Bravos at our performances were largely European, but I felt I was at last in Africa—in a continent at the moment reeling yet rising, released from the weight of colonialism, which had ridden its back for generations.

We toured the city and went en masse to the pyramids. We rode camels and had our photographs taken in front of the Sphinx, but I couldn't satisfy my longing to breathe in the entire country.

I went again to the pyramids, alone. I used the few Arabic words I had picked up to tell the camel drivers and guides that I wanted to be alone. I took off my shoes and dug my feet into the hot sand.

> Go down Moses, way down in Egypt land,
> Tell old Pharaoh, to let my people go.

A Pharaonic tomb rose above my head and I shivered. Israelites and Nubians and slaves from Carthage and Mesopotamia had built it, sweating, bleeding, and finally dying for the mass of stones which would become in the twentieth century no more than the focus for tourists' cameras.

My grandmother had been a member of a secret Black American female society, and my mother and father were both active participants in the Masons and Eastern Star organizations. Their symbols, which I found hidden in linen closets and night stands, were drawings of the Pyramid at Giza, or Cheops' tomb.

I tried to think of a prayer or at least some dramatic words to say to the spirits of long-dead ancestors. But nothing apt came to mind. When the sun became unbearable, I took a taxi back to town.

North Africa made me more reflective. Other members of the cast reacted similarly to the Egyptian experience.

Ethel and Martha were invited to a private party and they asked Lillian and me to come along. A well-to-do Arab came to the hotel and when he saw that his original invitation had expanded to include four women, he ordered a second horse-drawn carriage. We were driven to a large, lighted villa in Heliopolis, and when we started to climb out of the buggies, he stopped us and shouted at two men who stood by the wide wrought-iron gates. They emerged from the shadows bowing, touching their foreheads and chests like extras in a bad Hollywood film. They were as black as the night which closed in on us.

The host said, "You are not to walk. These servants will carry you." He stepped aside as one of the men walked up to the buggy, his arms outstretched.

Lillian said, "Maya, you let him carry you. I'll walk."

I said, "No. Uh uh. I'll walk with you."

Martha shouted from the other carriage, "Have you ever heard of anything so foul? My dear, Miss Fine's never had to be carried to a party. Come on, Ethel, we'll walk."

We stepped out into mud that oozed up over the tops of our shoes and walked on as if we were doing the most ordinary thing in the world.

We rejected the offer to have house Blacks clean our feet, but accepted towels and wiped away the mud ourselves, chatting vapidly about the pretty villa and the lovely furnishings.

The hosts and other guests were shocked at our refusal to be tended to, not realizing that auction blocks and whipping posts were too recent in our history for us to be comfortable around slavish servants. The party flopped despite flowing champagne and brittle laughter, probably because we couldn't keep our eyes away from the Black men who stood like barefoot sentinels at every door, dressed in old galibiyas, waiting with obsequious smiles on their handsome faces.

When we walked to the door to leave, we found that planks of wood had been laid over the wet walkway that led to the drive. There was only one carriage; we were told that our escort was obliged to stay with the other guests, but that the driver would see us safely back in our hotel.

We were obviously too democratic for the company's comfort and they too feudal for ours.

———

A sign in the hotel elevator read:

Défrisage
MONSIEUR PIERRE
Reservations Made at Hotel Desk

Martha, Ethel, Gloria and I decided to have our hair straightened by chemicals and be rid for a while, at least, of the heavy iron combs heated over cans of sterno that made our hotel rooms smell.

We sat side by side in a luxurious beauty salon and accepted hot cups of sweet black coffee from a young barefoot boy. Monsieur was visibly French: he pooched out his mouth, rolled his eyes and danced pantomimes with his long, thin fingers. Martha and Ethel were lathered down first; then I was taken into a booth. When the assistant put a green foam on my hair, it trickled down to my scalp and began to sting. I tried to sit still and say nothing—after all, my friends were receiving the same treatment without comment—but when my entire head started burning intensely I screamed, "Take it out! Take this out of my hair!"

"Qu'est-ce que vous dites?" Monsieur rounded the corner, pushing the assistant out of the way.

I shouted, "I said take this crap out of my hair."

Ethel said from the next stall, "Oooh, Maya, don't be such a crybaby."

I turned on the water and pushed my head under the faucet. "It's burning me."

The hairdresser, prompted by my loud shouting, hurriedly rinsed out the chemicals. My hair was still wet when I stalked angrily out into the streets, followed by my friends' snickers.

That evening Gloria's hair was so straight and airy that it flew around her head each time she moved. Ethel, Martha and other singers who had endured the process had only to shake their heads and their hair would bounce up and down and sideways with a sinuous smoothness.

A week passed and the hair that moved so freely began to move completely off the women's heads. Bare patches of scalp the size of small coins appeared at first, then enlarged until they could no longer be covered by an adept combing and plastering and pinning of hair from another side of the head.

A few weeks later my mother wrote me, "I read in Dorothy Kilgallen's column that all the young women in *Porgy and Bess* are wearing wigs. What on earth did you do to your hair?" I did my best not to laugh and sent my mother a photograph taken in a coin-operated booth. I was looking into the lens and had both hands to my head, pulling my healthy kinky hair.

———

Undeniably, Egypt impressed every member of the group. Irving Barnes, his wife and eight-year-old-daughter, Gail, spent whole days in museums and art galleries. The child who had put on grown-up airs, throwing her tiny hips as she tried to imitate the strut of a provocative Bess, became a little girl again, intrigued with African toys.

Paul Harris forgot his extraordinary good looks for a while and allowed his plump ego to deflate of its own accord. He semi-adopted two young beggars and they hung around the stage door and the hotel entrance until he emerged. He bought the urchins clothes and shoes and took them to restaurants for belly-distending meals.

Earl Jackson, our street-wise Sportin' Life, underwent the most startling personality change. Where he had used colorful profanity to shock the university-schooled and proper singers, he now substituted kind words, softly spoken. His romantic preferences for the local good-time women shifted and focused on the prim soprano of the group. He was to be found in the wings talking low to Miss Helen Thigpen, or finding a chair for Miss Thigpen in the hotel lobby, or rushing to be first on a bus to save a window seat for the quiet and re-served singer. He had begun to act, for all the world to see, like a man in love. And Thigpen, who had only been excited by recitals and her own repertoire, bloomed under the attention.

We left Egypt undeniably changed. The exposure to extreme wealth and shocking poverty forced the frivolous to be level-headed and encouraged the sober to enjoy what they had taken for granted.

Replicas of the Sphinx and the pyramids were packed along with three-inch busts of Nefertiti and small stuffed camels. Ned acquired a carved walking stick, which he kept at hand for the next six months, and Bey bought a red tasseled fez, which, with the giant congo drum that he never let out of his sight, made him look like a Sudanese musician on a pilgrimage to Mecca.

We boarded our Greek ship in Alexandria and the captain welcomed us. Maki smiled when he saw me, but the purser scowled, glum-browed and mean. He arrived at my cabin a moment after I entered.

"Mrs. Angelos." His voice was nearly closed with accusation.

"Yes?"

"Why did you lie to me?"

"I beg your pardon? I don't lie to anyone." I might not tell the truth, but I did draw the line at outright falsehood.

"You said you were a widow?"

"What? When did I say that?"

"I asked you how you had learned Greek and you said your dead husband taught you." He was pointing his finger at me as if he had caught me stealing the gold out of his mouth.

"I said to you my husband was Greek."

"Exactly." His smile was malevolent with satisfaction. "So he's dead?"

"No. I mean, he was my husband."

"But he's still alive?" Confusion and disappointment shifted his features.

"Very much so."

"Then why did you say he was Greek? Anyone who is Greek will be Greek until he dies."

I thought about that and thought about my husband who had intended to lock me into the apologetic female role, which he understood was proper for wives.

"Yes. You're right. He is Greek and will be that until he dies. But he is no longer my husband." I wanted to apologize to the purser for the misunderstanding, but I couldn't bring myself to ask for pardon.

"Vlachos loves you now?"

God, men talk about women gossiping. "I don't know. I hardly know him."

The frown was gathering again beneath his overhanging brow. "He said you were going to take him to the United States..."

Lillian knocked at the door. "Hey, Maya, let's have a drink."

I opened the door and the purser gave Lillian a little bow, put his hat on and left the cabin.

"Girl, you don't wait, do you? Well, they say there's no time like the present." She laughed.

I knew there was no use explaining the scene, and I knew that even if I stuck to Lillian's side like white on rice, the incident would be company knowledge before dinner.

"Thanks, I'm going to wait. The doctor ought to be coming soon and I have a few thousand words for him."

She blew air out of her cheeks. "Whew. You're a busy lady." She pulled the door slowly, closing it on her grin.

Maki came to the cabin, his eyes wild. "Maya, I have told my wife everything." He reached for me.

I said, "Hold it a minute." I pushed him away. "Listen, I don't know you. You don't know me."

"But I love you. I want to marry you. I will come with you to the United States."

"No, you won't." I opened the door. "You're nice. I guess. But I'm not marrying anyone. And surely not another Greek."

"But I'm in love with you."

592 · *Maya Angelou*

"Really? Could we live in Greece after you married me?"

"You don't understand. Greece is a poor country. In America I could make money and..."

"Mister, my suggestion is that you keep the wife you've got." I walked out into the passageway and held the door open with my foot. "I think you'd better go."

He put his hat on and stepped out of the room. His face was downcast and he was going to say something, but Martha walked by.

"Good morning, Doctor. Good morning, Miss Thing. Still at it, huh?"

I called after her. "Wait, Mart. I'll go up with you."

Except for what I had come to think of as only a reasonable amount of teasing, the rest of the cruise was uneventful.

CHAPTER 25

The opera was well received in Athens. We photographed each other at the Acropolis and drank retsina late at night in small bars. I dodged Maki in the hotel lobby and tore up the letters he sent me without opening them.

I could have been wrong. It was just possible that he did like me a little. But I knew I would never marry again, nor would I be the cause of a marriage breaking up. I couldn't introduce another non-Black to my son and family (although my mother might have accepted this one more heartily because at least he was a doctor). But what made marriage impossible was the fact I would have been embarrassed even if I loved the man (which I didn't). No amount of kindness or fidelity on his part would erase the idea that I had bought a mate with a license that gave me little personal gratification: American citizenship.

We flew from Athens to Tel Aviv. The bright sun that pleased us in Egypt shone on Israel too. The palm trees and white sand and tropical flowers were identical, but the streets were washed clean and there was a total absence of beggars. We were met by English-speaking fans who seemed to have drawn our individual names from lots and immediately became our companions and guides.

The very religious among our company visited Jerusalem, the Wailing Wall, the Mount of Olives and the Dead Sea. The rest were satisfied to buy vials of sand from the Holy Land and agate beads from tourist shops.

Lionel Hampton's band had just finished an engagement in Tel Aviv and we met at a party given by the American embassy and the Israeli government. The *Porgy and Bess* company had not seen such a gathering of American Negroes in months. We fell on the musicians as if they were bowls of black-eyed peas.

In the United States—or anywhere else, for that matter—jazz musicians and opera singers would find few topics of mutual interest. Their vocabularies have no unanimity and even their approach to the common musical scales are as different as odds and evens. But at the foreign official welcoming party we were indisputably siblings.

Helen Ferguson talked with a giant baritone sax player. He bent double to listen to her. Lillian and Ethel laughed with the frenetic drummer who pushed his words over and around a wad of chewing gum.

Gloria Davy and Delores Swan listened attentively as Hamp staccatoed his remarks: "Yeah. Ha, ha. Yeah. Great. Yeah. Great. Ha, ha."

Joe Jones and Merrit were telling stories to the brass section. I had my eyes on Sonny Parker, the male band singer. We had known each other slightly, but never as well as I wished.

"Sonny, who would have thought we'd meet in Israel?" I batted my eyes and tried to convey that I'd be happy to meet him anywhere.

"Yeah, baby. That's life, though. Yeah. Life's like that. Hey, Maya, who is that sharp chick?"

I said, "Barbara Ann Webb," but was too chagrined to add that she was so in love with her husband that when asked how she liked the weather, she would respond with "Richard says..."

I left Sonny and walked around, rustling myself in the sounds and feasting my eyes on the tasty colors of my people.

I met Arik Lavy, who had the tawny hair and open-mouthed laugh of Victor Di Suvero. He introduced himself and his girl friend to me and told me they were both Sabras, persons born in Israel. Each evening in Tel Aviv after the performance I joined them in an open-air café. The Sabras taught me Hebrew folk songs and I sang spirituals in exchange, always thinking that the real Jordan River was only a few miles away and my audience was composed of the very Israelites mentioned in my lyrics.

I made an arrangement with a dance teacher to give classes in modern ballet and African movement for three weeks in exchange for lessons in Middle Eastern dance.

We boarded a plane for Morocco where we would give a concert and continue to Spain. I was downcast at leaving Tel Aviv. I had felt an emotional attachment to Egypt and made an intellectual identification with Israel. The Jews were reclaiming a land which had surrendered its substance to the relentless sun centuries before. They brought to my mind grammar school stories of pioneer families and wagon trains. The dislodged Palestinians in the desert were as remote in my thoughts as the native Americans whose lives had been stifled by the whites' trek across the plains of America.

In Barcelona we were tired. Too many planes, hotel rooms and restaurant meals were exacting a toll on the company's spirits. But the Spaniards had no way of telling the extent of exhaustion the singers experienced. Years of training sustained the quality of performance, and an affection which bordered on kinship reduced the exhibition of ill humor which lay just under everyone's skin.

We went to Lausanne, Switzerland, performed and left, associating the white and icily beautiful town only with one more stop to be checked off our list. Our interests narrowed into petty little concerns and the cities and countries were beginning to melt together.

Genoa was quaint with its narrow streets and sailors—but were sweaters cheaper in Naples? Florence had Michelangelo statues and the Ponte Vecchio, but why didn't the clothes come back from the cleaners really clean?

In Marseilles, Gloria Davy and I tried to lift our spirits. Our birthdays were only two days apart, and we decided to give ourselves a treat. We bought a box lunch and took a small boat to the Château d'If. It turned out to be a dungeon built into the rocks, from which we were told no one had ever escaped, except the fictional Count of Monte Cristo. The guide wanted to show us where prisoners were chained to the walls. We refused and stood aside, gazing wistfully back at the mainland while other tourists ducked their heads and trooped through the small, low opening. I didn't relate the story to my friends because I knew they were too moody to hear another sour tale.

When we reached Turin the company was a drab lot. Merriment had seeped out of our repertoire and we fabricated joy on stage. Sullen and quiet, we went separately to our hotel rooms.

Helen Thigpen announced that she was giving a birthday party for Earl Jackson and everyone was invited. The statement sparked the first light of common interest I had seen in months. We had all noticed that Helen and Earl had become inseparable and had exchanged some character traits. He was more contained and the wise hopping walk had given way to more erect posture, while her reserve had thawed and she smiled more frequently.

Lillian and I made a bet with Martha and Ethel that the lovers were going to announce their engagement at the party. Ned held the bet, declining to join either side.

Helen had taken over the top floor of a restaurant near the hotel. Every table held a bottle of expensive whiskey, and waiters, assigned to our party exclusively, brought food and wine. I sat with Martha and Ethel and her mother, who had just arrived to spend a month with her daughter.

The party began like any party, coolly and dryly at first, but the sounds of a good time increased in direct proportion to the absorption of food and drink. Joy sat down at the piano and Leslie Scott stood to deliver a rich "Blue Moon." We applauded happily. Laverne Hutchinson, without being urged, sang another sentimental song, trying to outdo Leslie. Martha, who was sipping no less steadily than the rest of us, submitted to requests and honored the gathering with a song a cappella. When she finished, another singer took her place. Between songs we talked. People who had found it hard to smile for weeks were suddenly reminding each other of old stories and sharing the hilarious memories. It was a much needed festival.

Rhoda Boggs, at five foot eight inches and nearly two hundred pounds, was called "one of the big women in the company." She wore a mink capelet to all formal affairs, hats that quivered with large silk roses and high-heeled baby-doll shoes, the straps sinking deep into her ankles. She had the lyrical voice and artistic temperament of almost every classical soprano. As the party reached a peak, Rhoda clutched her capelet to her large bosom and started across the small dance floor to share stories with friends at another table. At the same time, Billy Johnson, waspish, impish and balding, decided to traverse the small space en route to another destination. The two collided midway. Rhoda stumbled at the shock while Billy almost fell under the impact. Rhoda was the first to recover. She looked down at the associate conductor as if he were a street urchin laying obstacles in the route of her parade. She rushed to the nearest table.

"Did you see him? Did you see that?" Her indignant voice was sounded like a flute played in anger. "Did you see that he struck Rhoda Boggs?" She went quickly but gracefully to the next table. "Did you see him actually strike Rhoda Boggs? Oh, my dear." She patted her breast and sang a little mean "Where does he live? Oh, where does he stay?" She carried her outrage from table to table, the roses on her hat nodding wildly in agreement at the affront.

Billy Johnson was still wondering in the center of the dance floor when Earl Jackson approached. Rhoda had relayed her news to the hostess and host, and although under Helen's influence Earl had mellowed, it was not safe to think he had ripened.

He caught Billy's lapels and pulled him out of the stupor. "What the hell you trying to do, hittin' that woman? You trying to be funny?"

His voice carried over the room to Rhoda who was fanning her face with her hat. "This is my party, you sonna bitch!"

And then he pushed Billy away with his left hand and slapped him with the right. The loud smack pulled us all to our feet, but Billy Johnson spun and dove a full gainer onto the highly polished wood. All movement and sound were suspended for a second and we heard Billy drawl in his plain Oklahoma accent, "That's the first time a man has really ever hit me."

The moment was so brief, there was no time to decide whether the pronouncement was a complaint or a compliment. Some people laughed out of nervousness, others because it was a funny scene, and a few began to down the last of the free drinks and collect their coats.

Behind my chair I heard a waiter say *"Carabinieri."* I told Ethel to get her mother and I would find Martha, that we should leave at once because the police had been called. I found Martha in a group sympathizing with Rhoda Boggs.

"Mart, we'd better go. The waiters have called the police."

"You're so smart, Miss Thing." Partying and excitement had thickened her tongue.

"Here's your coat." I helped her put it on. "Come on."

I started toward the stairs and she followed me.

"Maya Angelou."

I turned and looked back. Martha was on the landing and I was four steps below her.

"Maya Angelou, you're a smart-ass! Miss Fine Thing doesn't like smart-asses."

Obviously, excitement after such a long period of dullness had intoxicated us all.

I opened my mouth to speak just as she threw the contents of her glass in my face. All the pious self-placating words—"Patience," "Tolerance," "Forgive, for that is the right thing to do"—fled from me as if I had never known them.

I could have gone back up the stairs and stomped her face flat into the floor until her features became part of the parquetry design. But she was so small. Five foot tall and absolutely too small to hit. Yet I couldn't just walk out with the whiskey dribbling down my cheeks and into my collar and down my neck.

I grabbed a handful of the hem of her coat and gave it a lusty jerk. Her feet shot out from under her and she came bumping down the stairs. When she settled, a step below me, I saw that her wig had jumped free from the pins and had been turned askew. Long, black, silky hair covered her face and the wig's part began somewhere behind her left ear.

When I reached the bottom of the stairs I looked back. Ned Wright was bent over the woman. "Oh, my dearie. Someone pushed Miss Fine Thing down the stairs? Do let Uncle Ned help you up."

The soprano had both hands on her wig. In one move she snatched it around straight on her head and composed her face. She smoothed the hair down to her shoulders, fingering the curls that lay on her collar.

"No one pushed Miss Fine Thing," she said, jaw lifted as she struck a pose on the steps. "I fell."

The next day I sat sulking in my room, feeling betrayed and friendless. I told myself the time had come to go home. I missed my son and he needed me. His letters, printed in large letters, arrived regularly, and each one ended: "When are you coming home, Mother? Or can I come to visit you?"

Breen and Bob Dustin had offered to send for him and give me an allowance for his upkeep. But there were many male homosexuals in the company, and while I wasn't afraid that they might molest him I did know he was at an impressionable age. He would see the soft-as-butter men, moving like women, and receiving the world's applause. I wasn't certain that Clyde wouldn't try to imitate their gestures in a childish attempt to win admiration. Everyone wants acceptance.

No matter what it cost in loneliness, I was doing the good-mother thing to leave my son at home. Thus I had soothed my guilt, never admitting that I was reveling in the freedom from the constant nuisance of a small child's chatter. When the travel had been good, it had been very good. I could send money home, write sad and somehow true letters reporting my loneliness and then stay up all night past daybreak partying with my friends. There were no breakfasts to either prepare or worry about. I could wear my hangovers openly, like emblems of sophistication, without fear of judgment.

The truth was, I had used the aloneness, loving it. Of course, I had to work, but dancing and singing every night with sixty people was more like a party than a chore. And I had my friends.

I thought about Martha and knew I'd never speak to her again. Or to Lillian, or Ned, or any of the others. They had been friends before I came along and I was certain they were closing ranks to push me out, even as I sat in the miserable hotel room. I had lunch sent to my room and made up my mind to hand in my resignation. It was time for me to go. The greatest party of my life was over.

That night I barely grumbled hello to the singers backstage, and when we took our places and the overture began, I was working hard at holding back the tears.

The curtain rose on Bey, Ned, Joe Jones, Joe Attles and John Curry shooting dice. Ned, as Robbins, sang his lyrical tenor line, "Nine to make. Come nine," and won the pot. Crown, angered by the game's outcome, took the baling hook and a fight began. In the struggle, Crown stabbed Robbins with the weapon. Robbins screamed as always and turned upstage to face the company. A small gasp of surprise raced around the stage. He had always played the death scene to the audience, milking the moment for every drop of drama. Now he clutched his chest where the hook was supposed to have struck and said aloud, "He struck me. Oooh! He struck me. Did you see that? He struck Ned Wright."

He stumbled across the stage from right to left. He asked Joy Mc-Clain and Delores Swann, "Where does he live? Where is he staying?" He then hurtled over to Freddie Marshall and Ruby Green, "Did you see that? He actually struck me. Oooh weee!"

The company was supposed to be shocked into silence by the murder, and the music rests during the scene, but when Ned began imitating the disaster of the night before, a few soft giggles could be heard onstage.

After thrusting, clutching and stumbling, Ned finally went down to the floor. He then sat up absolutely straight, putting one fist at the back of his head and another to his forehead, gave a vigorous tug, slipping both hands around until they were directly over his ears.

He said prissily, in a loud whisper, "No one struck Ned Wright. I fell." Only then did he lie down and close his eyes.

The giggles might never have increased except that Ned was hunched face down while his body jumped and shook with convulsions, and Bey let out a bass shout of such pure glee that we were all pulled along into uncontrollable laughter.

The conductor looked up from the pit, aghast. He lifted both hands, cueing the singers to begin the dirge; not one voice followed his signal. He lifted his hands higher, imperiously pointing his baton at the stage, but the sopranos had buried their faces in their aprons and the men had covered their mouths with their hats, their shoulders shaking with laughter.

Alexander Smallens' face darkened with fury. He held his baton between his fingers like a pencil and made short stabbing motions at the singers. The orchestra played the entire passage alone. On the cue for the cast to exit stage left in a wild attempt to escape a white policeman who enters stage right, we tripped over each other, falling into the wings.

People leaned on the walls or clung together—some even held on to the curtain—trying to keep laughter under control. Rhoda Boggs wiped the tears from her round face; she managed to steal a breath from her spasms and said, "That Ned Wright. Uh uh. That Ned Wright. He's crazy."

Someone caught me and pulled me around. It was Martha. She looked at me and I wasn't sure if her wide grin was meant to be an attempt to apologize. Suddenly she put her hands on her wig and pulled it askew. Then she shoved it back to the correct position.

"Miss Fine Thing didn't fall. Somebody pushed her."

I bent low, laughing, and she put her arms around my neck. Neither begged the other's pardon. We picked up our friendship as if it had not fallen but had only stumbled. A few weeks later she shed the wig. A

Black beautician in Rome curled her newly grown hair in a high and luxuriant coiffure, and we never mentioned the incident again.

CHAPTER 26

Porgy and Bess was to be the first American opera sung at La Scala. Famous white sopranos, tenors and baritones from the United States had soloed at Milan's renowned opera house; now an entire cast of Negro singers were nervously rehearsing on the legendary stage.

Photographers and journalists lounged around the stage door and waited in our hotel lobbies.

"Miss Davy, how does it feel to be the star of the first...?"

"I am honored, of course, but then, we all work hard. I am just one of the Besses."

"Mr. Scott, are you nervous about singing at La Scala?"

"Nervous? No. I am excited, yes, but then, I am excited each time I sing."

"Miss Flowers, did you ever think you would have the opportunity to sing in Milan? At the world's most prestigious opera house?"

"Certainly. I do believe in the work ethic. Work hard and be prepared. Naturally, we are all pleased."

Oh, I was so proud of them. Their hands were knotted with tension and their brows moist with perspiration, but they acted cool.

We were told that La Scala audiences reacted to singers in the same way patrons of the Apollo in Harlem responded to the acts. That warning didn't need to be spelled out. The Apollo audiences were famous for shouting mediocre performers out of the theater or joining the entertainers on the stage to show them how a dance should be danced and how a song should be sung.

On opening night the backstage silence was unusual and ominous. Dressing-room doors were not only closed but locked. When the five-minute call was given we all went quietly to our places; not even a whisper floated over the dark stage. The rustling audience was stilled by the gradually darkening lights; they applauded the conductor's entrance and the overture began. The cast remained apart and I felt a little afraid. Suppose Gloria lost her voice, or Annabelle couldn't hit her high coloratura note. Just suppose I tripped over someone's foot on my entrance. I was coiled tight like a spring and realized as the curtain rose that every other member of the cast had also wound themselves up taut for a shattering release.

The moment the curtain opened the singers in concert pulled the elegant first-night audience into the harshness of Black Southern life. When Robbins was killed, the moans were real (didn't we all know people who, unable to talk back to authority, killed a friend over fifty cents?). The entrance of the white policeman was met with actual fear (wasn't the law always on the side of the mighty and weren't the jackals always at our heels?). The love story unfolded with such tenderness that the singers wept visible tears. (Who could deny this story? How many Black men had been crippled by the American oppression and had lost the women they loved and who loved them, because they hadn't the strength to fight? How often had the women submitted to loveless arrangements for the sake of bare survival?)

The first smiles of the evening were shared during our bows. We had sung gloriously. Although we faced the audience—which was on its feet, yelling and applauding—we bowed to compliment each other. We had performed *Porgy and Bess* as never before, and if the La Scala patrons loved us, it was only fitting because we certainly performed as if we were in love with one another.

We arrived in Rome on a late spring afternoon. I arranged my bags in the hotel room and went downstairs to find a telephone directory. In Paris, Bernard Hassel had told me to go to Bricktop's if I ever got to Rome. She was a living legend. He said Bricktop, Josephine Baker and Mabel Mercer had been the high-yellow toasts of Europe in the thirties. They hobnobbed with the rich and the royal, and although Mabel had gone to the United States and Josephine was semiretired, Bricktop still owned the most fashionable night club in Rome.

When night fell I walked down the Via Veneto, past the outdoor tables of Doney's Restaurant and into the next block where a small simple sign BRICKTOP'S hung over the door.

I opened the door and found myself standing behind a pudgy broad-shouldered man and a heavily made up woman whose brown hair was frosted blond. A small, very light-skinned, freckled woman with thin red hair stood facing the couple.

"On dit que vous avez bu trop en Cannes. (They say you've been drinking too much in Cannes)*."* She frowned and her French accent was as Southern and sweet as pecan pie.

The man said, "Please, Brickie. I promise not to drink tonight. My word of honor."

Her scowl relaxed when the man's companion added, "I won't let him have a thing, Brickie. We'll just watch the show."

Bricktop called a waiter. "Come here and take King Farouk to a table." My ears almost rejected the name. "But don't give him a drop. Not one *goutte.*"

The couple followed the waiter and Bricktop signaled to me. Her face was closed.

"Are you alone?"

I said, "Yes."

"I'm sorry, miss. But I don't allow ladies in here unescorted." She started to turn away.

I said, "Miss Bricktop, I am sorry too. I have been waiting for six months to come here and meet you." It was flattery, but it was also the truth.

She walked closer to me and stood straight. "What are you doing in Rome?" The question was asked cynically, as if she thought I might be a traveling prostitute, and her eyes said she had heard every version of every lie ever told.

"I'm with *Porgy and Bess.* I am a dancer-singer."

"Uh-huh." I could see her defenses relax. "When did you get in?"

"About two hours ago."

She nodded, appreciating that her place had been my first stop. She turned and lifted her hand. A waiter came scuttling to her.

"Take mademoiselle to a table." She said to me, "Go and sit down. I'll be over to talk to you pretty soon."

The club had thick carpets and heavy chandeliers, and the waiters dressed as handsomely as the customers. Bricktop was a Negro woman away from the United States thirty years, and still her Southern accent was unmistakable. I was even more amazed when she later told me she wasn't Southern at all, but had come from Chicago.

When she finally came to my table, she asked where I was from.

I said, "San Francisco."

"How do you feel, being so far from home?"

I said, "There is no place God is not."

Her face crinkled in a little-girl grin. "Oh, you're going to be my baby. Did you know that I've converted to Catholicism?"

I said I hadn't heard.

She leaned across the table, her eyes sparkling. "I have friends who ask me why. They found out I go to Mass every day and they're shocked. I say, 'Look, for thirty years you saw me running in and out of bars every day and you never tried to stop me and it didn't shock you. Why do you want to stop me now?' " She sat back in the chair and smiled smugly. "Don't you reckon that stopped them?"

She invited me to the club whenever I wanted to come and promised to cook a dinner of black-eyed peas. "I know where to find them in this town. Fact is I know where to find anything and everyone in Rome."

I looked around the room at some famous American and European faces, and at the line of people waiting inside the doorway for tables. I didn't doubt that Brickie had the keys necessary to open the Eternal City.

CHAPTER 27

After a few weeks in Rome I received a disturbing letter from Mother. Wilkie had moved out into his own studio. Lottie was looking for a housekeeping job because Mr. Hot Dog was losing money. And mother was planning to become a dealer in a Las Vegas Negro casino—which meant there would be no one to take care of Clyde, who missed me more than ever. He had developed a severe rash that resisted every medical treatment. I wrote immediately, saying I would be home in a month. I was obliged by union rules to give two weeks' notice, but since we were in Europe, it was only fair to allow the company four weeks to find another dancer-singer.

I went to Bob Dustin and explained that I would be leaving in one month and what a pleasure the tour had been. That evening he came to my dressing room, took a seat and looked at me solemnly.

"I am sorry, but I've got bad news for you. Since you're handing in your notice, we do not have to send you home. You'll have to pay your own way. And you'll have to pay your replacement's fare, first class, from wherever we find her."

The fares could come to over a thousand dollars! I had not seen that amount of cash since the war when I had kept the keys to my mother's money closet.

Bob left me alone with my tears. I told Martha and Lillian, who sympathized but had no money to lend me. Desperation began to build. I had to go to my son, but how could I find the money to do it?

Bricktop answered the private phone number she had given me. "Well, now, stop crying and tell me what's the matter."

I told her how I had left my son and that my family was down on its luck and that I needed to have another job to earn my fare home.

"That's nothing to cry about. I've heard of dancers crying because they were worked too hard, but never because they weren't worked enough. Put your faith in God and come down here this afternoon to rehearse with my pianist. You can start tonight."

For the next two months I not only danced in the opera and sang at Bricktop's but also found daytime employment. Some dancers at the Rome Opera House asked me to give them classes in African movement. I charged them as much as they could afford and watched each penny carefully, so that my bankroll grew. Bricktop fed me often, and once when I was so depressed I could hardly speak she asked me to her house. When I entered the large foyer she lifted her skirt and showed me her knees. The light skin was bruised and scratched.

"I went up the holy stairs on my knees for your son. And I've been lighting a candle and praying to the Holy Mother for him every day. Now, will you please have faith and know that he is all right?"

I counted the money unbelievingly; every penny I needed was there. I made reservations on the *Cristoforo Colombo*. Martha and Ethel, Lillian, Barbara, Bey, Ned, the Joes (Attles and James) gave me a lavish farewell party.

Martha said, "Miss Thing, why don't you fly home? The way you're going it'll take you two weeks to reach California."

I was afraid. If the plane crashed my son would say all his life that his mother died on a tour in Europe, never knowing that I had taken the flight because I was nearly crazy to be with him.

Lillian made a face at Martha. "Let her alone, Miss Fine Thing. She gets these hunches and sometimes they work. Let us not forget about the Cairo and the *défrisage*." We all laughed at the good times in the past which were good enough when they happened but were much better upon reflection.

The nine-day trip from Naples to New York threatened to last forever. I seemed to have spent a month going to bed in the tiny cabin where sleep was an infrequent visitor. Uncomfortable thoughts kept me awake. I had left my son to go gallivanting in strange countries and had enjoyed every minute except the times when I thought about him. I had sent a letter saying I was coming two months before and had felt too guilty to write and explain my delay.

A barely adequate band played music in the second-class salon, and after the third restless night I started singing with them.

A very thin and delicate-looking man from first class introduced himself and sat every evening until the last song had been played and the musicians had covered their instruments. Without the band and his company the trip would have been totally unbearable.

My friend was a chronic insomniac, so we played gin rummy and talked until sunrise. He told me he was a friend of Tennessee

Williams, and we discussed the future of drama. I recited some of my poetry, which he said was promising.

We exchanged addresses at the dock and I took a taxi to the train station. The three-day trip in a coach deposited me tired, frazzled, but happy at the Third and Townsend Station of the Southern Pacific in San Francisco.

CHAPTER 28

Lottie answered the doorbell and gave a shout of welcome. In seconds the family closed around, kissing, stroking and hugging me. They guided me to the sofa, talking and asking questions that they didn't expect to be answered. When I sat down, Clyde jumped into my lap and snuggled his head under my chin. Every minute he would pull away to look at my face, then nestle again against my neck. Mother patted my hair and my cheek and laughed, wiping her eyes.

Lottie said, "She needs a cup of coffee."

"The prodigal daughter," Mother said, "That's who you are. The prodigal daughter returns home."

Lottie, in the kitchen, said, "Oh, baby. We've missed you."

"If we lived on a farm," Mother said, "I'd kill the fatted calf. Oh, yes, baby." She turned to my son. "That's what the mother does when the prodigal daughter returns."

Clyde's arms were wound around my neck.

"Clyde," Mother said.

He murmured into my collar, "Yes, Grandmother?"

"You're too big to sit in your mother's lap. You're a little man. Come on, get up and go find a fat calf. We'll kill it and cook it."

His arms tightened.

I said, "Mother, let him sit here awhile. It's O.K."

The first day was spent dispensing gifts and telling each other snatches of stories. I talked about the company and some of the cities we visited. Mother and Lottie told me about losing the restaurant lease and how Clyde had missed me and how they had taken him to a dermatologist who recommended an expensive allergist, but nothing seemed to help.

Clyde had little to say. The loquacious, beautiful and bubbling child I had left had disappeared. In his place was a rough-skinned, shy boy who hung his head when spoken to and refused to maintain eye contact even when I held his chin and asked, "Look at me."

That evening I went in to hear him say his prayers dully, and when I bent to kiss him good night he clung to me with a fierceness that was frightening. In the very early hours of the morning I heard a faint knock at my door.

I turned on the light and said, "Come in."

My son tiptoed into the room. His face was puffy from crying. I sat upright. "What's the matter?"

He came to my bed and looked at me directly for the first time since my return. He whispered, "When are you going away again?"

I put my arms around him and he fell sobbing on my chest. I held him, but not my own tears.

"I swear to you, I'll never leave you again. If I go, when I go, you'll go with me or I won't go."

He fell asleep in my arms and I picked him up and deposited him in his own bed.

CHAPTER 29

Disorientation hung in my mind like a dense fog and I seemed to be unable to touch anyone or anything. Ivonne was happily married at last; she introduced me to her new husband, but my interest was merely casual. At home I played favorite records, but the music sounded thin and uninteresting. Lottie prepared elaborate meals especially for me, and the food lay heavily on my tongue—it had to be forced down a tight, unwilling throat. Mother and I showed each other the letters we had received from Bailey. The sadness I experienced in Europe when I read the mail had obviously been left abroad, and now rereading his poignant and poetic tales of prison life left me unmoved.

I was aware that I was not acting like the old Maya, but it didn't matter much. My responses to Clyde, however, did alarm me. I wanted to hold him every minute. To pick him up and carry his nine-year-old body through the streets, to the store, to the park. I had to clench my fists to keep my hands off his head and face whenever I sat near him or moved past him.

Clyde's skin flaked with scales and his bedclothes had to be changed each day in an attempt to prevent new contagion. I had ruined my beautiful son by neglect, and neither of us would ever forgive me. It was time to commit suicide, to put an end to accusations and guilt. And did I dare die alone? What would happen to my son? If my temporary absence in Europe caused such devastation to his mind and body, what would become of him if I was gone forever? I brought him into this world and I was responsible for his life. So must the thoughts wind around the minds of insane parents who kill their children and then themselves.

On the fifth day home I had a lucid moment, as clear as the clink of good crystal. I was going mad.

Clyde and I were alone in the house. I shouted at him. "Get out. Go outside this moment."

"Where, Mother?" He was stunned at the violence in my voice.

"Outside. And don't come back, even if I call you. Out."

He ran down the stairs as I picked up the telephone. I ordered a taxi and telephoned the Langley Porter Psychiatric Clinic.

"I am sorry. There's no one here to see you."

I said, "Oh, yes. Someone will see me."

"Madame, we have a six-month waiting list."

"This is an emergency. My name is Maya Angelou. Someone will see me."

I grabbed a coat and went to sit on the steps. Clyde came running around from the backyard when he heard the cab stop. He squinted his eyes as if he were about to cry.

"You're going away?"

I said, "I'm just going to see a friend. You go back in the house. I'll be home in an hour or so."

I saw him watching the taxi until we turned the corner.

The receptionist was not alarmed at my hysteria. "Yes, Miss Angelou. Doctor will see you now, in there." She showed me to a door.

A large, dark-haired white man sat behind the desk. He indicated a seat. "Now, what seems to be the trouble?" He put his hands on the desk and laced his fingers. His nails were clean and clipped short. His good suit was freshly pressed. He looked muscular. I thought he's probably one of the tennis players who drive expensive sports cars and his wife has Black servants who wash her underclothes and bring her breakfast on a tray.

"Are you troubled?"

I started to cry. Yes, I was troubled; why else would I be here? But what could I tell this man? Would he understand Arkansas, which I left, yet would never, could never, leave? Would he comprehend why my brilliant brother, who was the genius in our family, was doing time in Sing Sing on a charge of fencing stolen goods instead of sitting with clean fingernails in a tailor-made suit, listening to some poor mad person cry her blues out? How would he perceive a mother who, in a desperate thrust for freedom, left her only child, who became sick during her absence? A mother who, upon her return, felt so guilty she could think of nothing more productive than killing herself and possibly even the child?

I looked at the doctor and he looked at me, saying nothing. Waiting.

I used up my Kleenex and took more from my purse. No, I couldn't tell him about living inside a skin that was hated or feared by the majority of one's fellow citizens or about the sensation of getting on a bus on a lovely morning, feeling happy and suddenly seeing the passengers curl their lips in distaste or avert their eyes in revulsion. No, I had nothing to say to the doctor. I stood up.

"Thank you for seeing me."

"If you'd like to make another appointment—"

I closed his door and asked the receptionist to call a taxi.

I gave the driver the address of Wilkie's studio. I arrived in the middle of a lesson. He took one look at me and said, "Go into my bedroom. There's a bottle of scotch. I have another student after this one, then I'll cancel for the rest of the afternoon."

I sat on his bed and drank the whiskey neat and listened to the vocalizing in the next room. I didn't know what I was going to say to Wilkie, but I knew I would feel better talking to him than to that doctor, to whom I would be another case of Negro paranoia. I telephoned home and told Lottie where I was and that I'd be home soon.

The piano was finally silent and Wilkie opened the bedroom door. "O.K., old sweet nappy-head thing. Come on and talk to Uncle Wilkie."

I walked out into the studio and collapsed in his arms.

"Wilkie, I can't see any reason for living. I went to a psychiatrist and it was no good. I couldn't talk. I'm so unhappy. And I have done such harm to Clyde..."

He held me until I finished my babbling.

"Are you finished? Are you finished?" His voice was stern and unsympathetic.

I said, "Well, I guess so."

"Sit down at that desk."

I sat.

"Now, see that yellow tablet?" There was a legal-size yellow pad on the blotter. "See that pencil?"

I saw it.

"Now, write down what you have to be thankful for."

"Wilkie, I don't want silly answers."

"Start to write." His voice was cold and unbending. "And I mean start now! First, write that you heard me tell you that. So you have the sense of hearing. And that you could tell the taxi driver where to bring you and then tell me what was wrong with you, so you have the sense of speech. You can read and write. You have a son who needs nothing but you. Write, dammit! I mean write."

I picked up the pencil and began.

> "I can hear.
> I can speak.
> I have a son.
> I have a mother.
> I have a brother.
> I can dance.
> I can sing.
> I can cook.
> I can read.
> I can write."

When I reached the end of the page I began to feel silly. I was alive and healthy. What on earth did I have to complain about? For two months in Rome I had said all I wanted was to be with my son. And now I could hug and kiss him anytime the need arose. What the hell was I whining about?

Wilkie said, "Now write, 'I am blessed. And I am grateful.' "

I wrote the line.

"It's time for you to go to work. I'll call you a cab. Stop at the theatrical agency on your way home and tell them you're ready to go to work. Anywhere, anytime, and for any decent amount of money."

When he walked me to the door he put his arm around my shoulders. "Maya, you're a good mother. If you weren't, Clyde wouldn't have missed you so much. And let Uncle Wilkie tell you one last thing. Don't ask God to forgive you, for that's already done. Forgive yourself. You're the only person you can forgive. You've done nothing wrong. So forgive yourself."

I told the agent I would accept any job and the only stipulation was that I had to have transportation and accommodation for my son. He was surprised at the unusual request, but we signed contracts and I went home.

My lighter mood influenced everyone. I told funny stories about the singers and stopped lying about how miserable I had been.

Mother said, "Well, at least. I knew you had to have some good times."

Lottie was cheered by my new appetite and planned even more elaborate meals for my pleasure. And Clyde began to tell me secrets again. He resurrected Fluke and the two of them held interminable conversations in the house's one bathroom. I took him out of school for a week and we spent days riding bikes in Golden Gate Park and having picnics on the grass.

Before my eyes a physical and mental metamorphosis began as gradually and inexorably as a seasonal change. At first the myriad bumps dried and no fresh ones erupted. His skin slowly regained its smoothness and color. Then I noticed that he no longer rushed panting to my room to assure himself that I was still there. And when I left the house to shop we both took the parting normally, with a casual "See you in a minute." His shoulders began to ride high again and he had opinions about everything from the planning of meals to what he wanted to be called.

"Mother, I've changed my name."

I'm certain that I didn't look up. "Good. What is it today?"

In the space of one month, he had told Fluke and the rest of the family to call him Rock, Robin, Rex and Les.

"My name is Guy."

"That's nice. Guy is a nice name."

"I mean it, Mother."

"Good, dear. It's quite a nice name."

When I called to him later in the day, he refused to answer. I stood in the doorway of his room watching him spraddled on the bed.

"Clyde, I called you. Didn't you hear me?"

He had always been rambunctious, but never outright sassy.

"I heard you calling Clyde, Mother, but my name is Guy. Did you want me?"

He gave me a mischievous grin.

Mother, Lottie and I failed for a time to remember his new name.

"Aunt Lottie, if you want me, call for Guy."

"Grandmother, I have named myself Guy. Please don't forget."

One day I asked him quietly why he didn't like Clyde. He said it sounded mushy. I told him about the Clyde River in Scotland, but its strength and soberness didn't impress him.

"It's an O.K. name for a river, but my name is Guy." He looked straight into my eyes. "Please tell your friends that I never want to be called Clyde again. And, Mother, don't you do it either." He remembered "Please."

Whenever anyone in the family called him Clyde, he would sigh like a teacher trying to educate a group of stubborn kindergarten students and would say wearily, "My name is Guy."

It took him only one month to train us. He became Guy and we could hardly remember ever calling him anything else.

CHAPTER 30

I received a telegram from Hawaii:

OPENING FOR YOU THE CLOUDS. $350 DOLLAR WEEKLY, FOUR WEEKS.
TWO WEEK OPTION. TRANSPORTATION AND ACCOMMODATION YOU
AND SON. REPLY AT ONCE.

The three women who owned the hotel and night club met us at the airport dressed in long, colorful Hawaiian dresses. They were white Americans, but years in the islands had tanned their skins and loosened their inhibitions. Ann, a tall blonde and one-time professional swimmer, smiled warmly and draped fresh leis around our necks. Verne, the shortest of the trio, kissed us, while Betty, handsome and rugged, clapped our backs, grabbed our bags and herded the company into a car.

On the drive to Waikiki I imagined Bing Crosby and a saronged Dorothy Lamour standing under palm trees, singing "Lovely Hula Hands." The air was warm and moist and the perfume of our flowers filled the car. Guy asked how deep I thought the ocean was and if there were any sharks. And did they have any life guards?

The Clouds was near the sea, at an angle from the vast and elegant Queen's Surf Hotel, which jutted pink stucco towers near Diamond Head.

We were shown to our separate rooms with a connecting bath and invited to have our first dinner with my employers.

Guy and I took a walk and happiness wound him up so tight he chattered incessantly. We went along the beach and he ran forward and back, laughing to himself, grabbing my hand to pull me along faster, then letting go in impatience and racing off alone.

After dinner and after his prayers, he told me he had left Fluke at home, because Fluke couldn't swim. I reminded him to wake me in the morning and after we had breakfast I'd change a traveler's check so that he'd have some cash. After he went to sleep, I found Ann and Betty. They showed me the club and we drank and talked late into the night.

I awakened and looked at my watch. It was ten-thirty. I thought the long plane trip had exhausted Guy because he usually got up before seven. There was no answer when I knocked on our connecting door. I tried the knob, but the lock had been turned. I went out and tried the hall door leading to his room. It, too, was locked. I called the maid and explained that my young son was sleeping and I was unable to wake him. She unlocked the door. The room was empty. I didn't panic at first. I thought he had decided to let me sleep and one of the owners had taken him downstairs to eat in the hotel restaurant.

I asked the waiter where I could find my son. He said no children had been in the restaurant that morning. Betty was in her office. She said Verne and Ann were still asleep and she hadn't seen him but I shouldn't worry—he'd probably just gone for a walk.

I thanked her and went back to the rooms. Betty didn't know Guy. He might have decided to spare waking me and he might have gone for a stroll, but there was one sure thing—he would have eaten. Even when he had been seriously upset and physically ill my son's large appetite never slackened. His normal daily breakfast consisted of oatmeal, bacon, eggs, toast, jam, orange juice and milk. On special days he ate hot biscuits and fried potatoes as well.

The maid let me in his room again. The clothes he had worn on the journey were hanging in the closet and his suitcase was open, but the contents looked undisturbed. His pajamas were at the foot of the bed.

Could he have been kidnapped? Why? I had no money. Could some sex maniac have taken my beautiful son? How could he have gotten him out of the hotel naked? Guy would have fought and screamed. I walked down to the beach, but all the children looked like my little boy. They all had tawny skin and dark eyes. I went back to the hotel and called the police.

Two large Oriental men appeared in the lobby. One of them asked, "What was he wearing, Miss Angelou?"

"Oh, nothing as far as I can deduce. All his clothes are in his room."

"What does he look like?"

I showed them a photograph.

"We'll find him, don't worry."

Don't worry?

I went to the bar and ordered gin and nodded when Verne, Betty and then Ann sympathetically repeated, "Don't worry."

This was the way the whole world ended. One child disappears and the sun slips out of the sky. The moon melts down in blood. The earth ripples like a dark ocean. I had another gin and tried to blank out the headlines that rushed behind my eyes: *Child's Body Found in Alley, Boy Kidnapped under Mysterious Circumstances.*

I had just found a seat in the lobby when Guy walked in flanked by the policemen. He had on swim trunks and was completely covered with sand. Weak with relief, I couldn't have stood up even for a moment. He saw me and rushed away from his escorts to stand in front of me.

"Mom"—his voice was loud and concerned—"what's the matter? Are you all right?"

I said yes, I was all right, because I couldn't think of anything else to say.

"Whew!" He blew out his breath. "Gee, I was worried for a minute."

I pulled enough strength from some hidden resource to stand. I thanked the officers and shook hands. They ran their hands over Guy's head, and sand fell to the carpet like brown snow. "Don't worry your mother like that again, hear?"

They left and I fell back in the chair. "Guy, where have you been?"

"Swimming, Mother."

"Where did you get the swimsuit?"

"Grandmother gave it to me. But why were you worried?"

"You didn't have breakfast. That's why."

"But I did."

"The waiter said you hadn't been in this morning."

"I didn't eat here. I ate at the Queen's Surf."

"But you didn't have any money. Who paid?"

"No one. I signed my name."

I was flabbergasted.

"But they didn't know you. I mean, they just accepted your signature?" That was incredible.

He looked at me as if I wasn't quite as bright as he would have liked.

"Mom, you know your name is up on that thing outside?"

I had noticed when we arrived that a large sign proclaimed MAYA ANGELOU. I said, "Yes. I saw it."

"Well, after I finished breakfast I pointed to it and said I would like to sign the check and that Maya Angelou is a great singer and she is my mother."

I nodded.

He was partially right. Although I was not a great singer I was his mother, and he was my wonderful, dependently independent son.

THE HEART OF A WOMAN

I dedicate this book to my grandson,
Colin Ashanti Murphy-Johnson

Special thanks to a few of the many
sister/friends whose love encourages
me to spell my name:
W O M A N

Doris Bullard
Rosa Guy
M. J. Hewitt
Ruth Love
Paule Marshall
Louise Merriwether
Dolly McPherson
Emalyn Rogers
Efuah Sutherland
Decca Treuhaft
Frances Williams
A. B. Williamson
Eleanor Traylor
Ruth Beckford

"The ole ark's a-moverin', a-moverin', a-moverin',
the ole ark's a-moverin' along"

That ancient spiritual could have been the theme song of the United States in 1957. We were a-moverin' to, fro, up, down and often in concentric circles.

We created a maze of contradictions. Black and white Americans danced a fancy and often dangerous do-si-do. In our steps forward, abrupt turns, sharp spins and reverses, we became our own befuddlement. The country hailed Althea Gibson, the rangy tennis player who was the first black female to win the U.S. Women's Singles. President Dwight Eisenhower sent U.S. paratroopers to protect black school children in Little Rock, Arkansas, and South Carolina's Senator Strom Thurmond harangued for 24 hours and 18 minutes to prevent the passage in Congress of the Civil Rights Commission's Voting Rights Bill.

Sugar Ray Robinson, everybody's dandy, lost his middleweight title, won it back, then lost it again, all in a matter of months. The year's popular book was Jack Kerouac's *On the Road,* and its title was an apt description of our national psyche. We were indeed traveling, but no one knew our destination nor our arrival date.

I had returned to California from a year-long European tour as premier dancer with *Porgy and Bess.* I worked months singing in West Coast and Hawaiian night clubs and saved my money. I took my young son, Guy, and joined the beatnik brigade. To my mother's dismay, and Guy's great pleasure, we moved across the Golden Gate Bridge and into a houseboat commune in Sausalito where I went barefoot, wore jeans, and both of us wore rough-dried clothes. Although I took Guy to a San Francisco barber, I allowed my own hair to grow into a wide unstraightened hedge, which made me look, at a distance, like a tall brown tree whose branches had been clipped. My commune mates, an icthyologist, a musician, a wife, and an inventor, were white, and had they been political (which they were not), would have occupied a place between the far left and revolution.

Strangely, the houseboat offered me respite from racial tensions, and gave my son an opportunity to be around whites who did not think of him as too exotic to need correction, nor so common as to be ignored.

During our stay in Sausalito, my mother struggled with her maternal instincts. On her monthly visits, dressed in stone marten furs, diamonds and spike heels, which constantly caught between loose floorboards, she forced smiles and held her tongue. Her eyes, however, were frightened for her baby, and her baby's baby. She left wads of money under my pillow or gave me checks as she kissed me goodbye. She could have relaxed had she remembered the Biblical assurance "Fruit does not fall far from the tree."

In less than a year, I began to yearn for privacy, wall-to-wall carpets and manicures. Guy was becoming rambunctious and young-animal wild. He was taking fewer baths than I thought healthy, and because my friends treated him like a young adult, he was forgetting his place in the scheme of our mother-son relationship.

I had to move on. I could go back to singing and make enough money to support myself and my son.

I had to trust life, since I was young enough to believe that life loved the person who dared to live it.

I packed our bags, said goodbye and got on the road.

Laurel Canyon was the official residential area of Hollywood, just ten minutes from Schwab's drugstore and fifteen minutes from the Sunset Strip.

Its most notable feature was its sensuality. Red-roofed, Moorish-style houses nestled seductively among madrone trees. The odor of eucalyptus was layered in the moist air. Flowers bloomed in a riot of crimsons, carnelian, pinks, fuchsia and sunburst gold. Jays and whip-poorwills, swallows and bluebirds, squeaked, whistled and sang on branches which faded from ominous dark green to a brackish yellow. Movie stars, movie starlets, producers and directors who lived in the neighborhood were as voluptuous as their natural and unnatural environment.

The few black people who lived in Laurel Canyon, including Billy Eckstein, Billy Daniels and Herb Jeffries, were rich, famous and light-skinned enough to pass, at least for Portuguese. I, on the other hand, was a little-known night-club singer, who was said to have more de-termination than talent. I wanted desperately to live in the glamorous surroundings. I accepted as fictitious the tales of amateurs being dis-covered at lunch counters, yet I did believe it was important to be in the right place at the right time, and no place seemed so right to me in 1958 as Laurel Canyon.

When I answered a "For Rent" ad, the landlord told me the house had been taken that very morning. I asked Atara and Joe Morheim, a sympathetic white couple, to try to rent the house for me. They suc-ceeded in doing so.

On moving day, the Morheims, Frederick "Wilkie" Wilkerson, my friend and voice coach, Guy, and I appeared on the steps of a modest, overpriced two-bedroom bungalow.

The landlord shook hands with Joe, welcomed him, then looked over Joe's shoulder and recognized me. Shock and revulsion made him recoil. He snatched his hand away from Joe. "You bastard. I know what you're doing. I ought to sue you."

Joe, who always seemed casual to the point of being totally disin-terested, surprised me with his emotional response. "You fascist, you'd better not mention suing anybody. This lady here should sue you. If she wants to, I'll testify in court for her. Now, get the hell out of the way so we can move in."

The landlord brushed past us, throwing his anger into the per-fumed air. "I should have known. You dirty Jew. You bastard, you."

We laughed nervously and carried my furniture into the house.

Weeks later I had painted the small house a sparkling white, en-rolled Guy into the local school, received only a few threatening tele-phone calls, and bought myself a handsome dated automobile. The car, a sea-green, ten-year-old Chrysler, had a parquet dashboard, and splintery wooden doors. It could not compete with the new chrome of my neighbors' Cadillacs and Buicks, but it had an elderly elegance, and driving in it with the top down, I felt more like an eccentric artist than a poor black woman who was living above her means, out of her element, and removed from her people.

One June morning, Wilkie walked into my house and asked, "Do you want to meet Billie Holiday?"

"Of course. Who wouldn't? Is she working in town?"

"No, just passing through from Honolulu. I'm going down to her hotel. I'll bring her back here if you think you can handle it."

"What's to handle? She's a woman. I'm a woman."

Wilkie laughed, the chuckle rolling inside his chest and out of his mouth in billows of sound. "Pooh, you're sassy. Billie may like you. In that case, it'll be all right. She might not, and then that's your ass."

"That could work the other way around. I might not like her either."

Wilkie laughed again. "I said you're sassy. Have you got some gin?"

There was one bottle, which had been gathering dust for months.

Wilkie stood, "Give me the keys. She'll like riding in a convertible."

I didn't become nervous until he left. Then the reality of Lady Day coming to my house slammed into me and started my body to quaking. It was pretty well known that she used heavy drugs, and I hardly smoked grass anymore. How could I tell her she couldn't shoot up or sniff up in my house? It was also rumored that she had lesbian affairs. If she propositioned me, how could I reject her with-out making her think I was rejecting her? Her temper was legendary in show business, and I didn't want to arouse it. I vacuumed, emptied ashtrays and dusted, knowing that a clean house would in no way in-fluence Billie Holiday.

I saw her through the screen door, and my nervousness turned quickly to shock. The bloated face held only a shadow of its familiar prettiness. When she walked into the house, her eyes were a flat black, and when Wilkie introduced us, her hand lay in mine like a child's rubber toy.

"How you do, Maya? You got a nice house." She hadn't even looked around. It was the same slow, lean, whining voice which had frequently been my sole companion on lonely nights.

I brought gin and sat listening as Wilkie and Billie talked about the old days, the old friends, in Washington, D.C. The names they mentioned and the escapades over which they gloated meant nothing to me, but I was caught into the net of their conversation by the complexity of Billie's language. Experience with street people, hustlers, gamblers and petty criminals had exposed me to cursing. Years in night-club dressing rooms, in cabarets and juke joints had taught me every combination of profanity, or so I thought. Billie Holiday's language was a mixture of mockery and vulgarity that caught me without warning. Although she used the old common words, they were in new arrangements, and spoken in that casual tone which seemed to drag itself, rasping, across the ears. When she finally turned to include me in her conversation, I knew that nothing I could think of would hold her attention.

"Wilkie tells me you're a singer. You a jazz singer too? You any good?"

"No, not really. I don't have good pitch."

"Do you want to be a great singer? You want to compete with me?"

"No. I don't want to compete with anybody. I'm an entertainer, making a living."

"As an entertainer? You mean showing some tittie and shaking your bootie?"

"I don't have to do all that. I wouldn't do that to keep a job. No matter what."

"You better say Joe, 'cause you sure don't know."

Wilkie came to my defense just as I was wondering how to get the woman and her hostility out of my house.

"Billie, you ought to see her before you talk. She sings folk songs, calypso and blues. Now, you know me. If I say she's good, I mean it. She's good, and she's nice enough to invite us to lunch, so get up off her. Or you can walk your ass right down this hill. And you know I'm not playing about that shit."

She started laughing. "Wilkie, you haven't changed a damn thing but last year's drawers. I knew you'd put my ass out on the street sooner or later." She turned to me and gave me a fragile smile.

"What we going to eat, baby?" I hadn't thought about food, but I had a raw chicken in the refrigerator. "I'm going to fry a chicken. Fried chicken, rice and an Arkansas gravy."

"Chicken and rice is always good. But fry that sucker. Fry him till he's ready. I can't stand no goddam rare chicken."

"Billie, I don't claim to be a great singer, but I know how to mix groceries. I have never served raw chicken." I had to defend myself even if it meant she was going to curse me out.

"O.K., baby. O.K. Just telling you, I can't stand to see blood on the bone of a chicken. I take your word you know what you're doing. I didn't mean to hurt your feelings."

I retreated to the kitchen. Wilkie's and Billie's laughter floated over the clangs of pots and the sputtering oil.

I couldn't imagine how the afternoon was going to end. Maybe I'd be lucky; they would drink all the gin and Wilkie would take her to a bar on Sunset.

She sat at the table, gingerly. Each move of her body seemed to be considered before she attempted execution.

"You set a pretty table and you ain't got a husband?"

I told her I lived alone with my son. She turned with the first sharp action I had seen since she came into my house. "I can't stand children. The little crumb-crushers eat you out of house and home and never say, 'Dog, kiss my foot.' "

"My son is not like that. He's intelligent and polite."

"Yeah. Well, I can't stand to be around any of the little bastards. This is good chicken."

I looked at Wilkie, who nodded to me.

Wilkie said, "Billie, I'm going to take you to a joint on Western, where you can get anything you want."

She didn't allow the full mouth of chicken to prevent her from speaking. "Hell, nigger, if I wanted to go to a joint don't you think I could have found one without you? I know every place in every town in this country that sells anything that crosses your mind. I wanted to come to a nice lady's house. She's a good cook, too. So I'm happy as a sissy in a CCC camp. Let me have that drumstick."

While I put away the remaining chicken, she talked about Hawaii.

"People love 'the islands, the islands.' Hell, all that shit is a bunch of water and a bunch of sand. So the sun shines all the time. What the hell else is the sun supposed to do?"

"But didn't you find it beautiful? The soft air, the flowers, the palm trees and the people? The Hawaiians are so pretty."

"They just a bunch of niggers. Niggers running around with no clothes on. And that music shit they play. Uhn, uhn." She imitated the sound of a ukulele.

"Naw. I'd rather be in New York. Everybody in New York City is a son of a bitch, but at least they don't pretend they're something else."

Back in the living room, Wilkie looked at me, then at his watch. "I have a student coming in a half-hour. Come on, Billie, I'll take you back to your hotel. Thanks, Maya. We have to go."

Billie looked up from her drink and said, "Speak for yourself. All I got to do is stay black and die."

"Well, I brought you here, so I'll take you back. Anyway, Maya's probably got something to do."

They both stared at me. I thought for a moment and decided not to lie.

"No. I'm free. I'll take her back to the hotel when she wants to go."

Wilkie shook his head. "O.K., Pooh." His face was saying, "I hope you know what you're doing. Of course I didn't, but I was more curious than afraid.

Billie tossed her head. "So I'll see you when I see you, Wilkie. Hope it won't be another twenty years."

Wilkie bent and kissed her, gave me a very strange look and walked down to his car.

We spent the first few moments in silence. Billie was examining me, and I was wondering what subject I could introduce that would interest her.

Finally, she asked, "You a square, ain't you?"

I knew what she meant. "Yes."

"Then how come you invited me to your house?"

Wilkie really invited her, but I had welcomed his invitation.

"Because you are a great artist and I respect you."

"Bullshit. You just wanted to see what I looked like, up close." She interrupted my denial. "That's all right. That don't hurt my feelings. You see me now, though, you ain't seeing nothing. I used to be a bitch on wheels. Lot of folks thought I was pretty. Anyway, that's what they said. 'Course, you know how folks talk. They'll tell you anything to get what they want. 'Course, there are them that'll just strong-arm you and take it. I know a lot of them, too." Suddenly she withdrew into her thoughts and I sat quiet, not wanting to break into her reverie.

She raised her head and turned half away from me, toward the window. When she spoke it was in a conspiratorial whisper. "Men. Men can really do it to you. Women would too, if they had the nerve. They are just as greedy; they're just scared to let on."

I had heard stories of Billie being beaten by men, cheated by drug pushers and hounded by narcotics agents, still I thought she was the most paranoid person I had ever met.

"Don't you have any friends? People you can trust?"

She jerked her body toward me. "Of course I have friends. Good friends. A person who don't have friends might as well be dead." She had relaxed, but my question put her abruptly on the defense again. I was wondering how to put her at ease. I heard Guy's footsteps on the stairs.

"My son is coming home."

"Oh. Shit. How old you say he is?"

"He's twelve and a very nice person."

Guy bounded into the room, radiating energy.

"Hey, Momhowareya? Whatwereyoudoing? What'sfordinner? CanI goovertoTony's? CanIgoovertoTony'saftermyhomework?"

"Guy, I have a guest. This is Miss Billie Holiday." He turned and saw Billie, but was accelerating too fast to read the distaste on her face.

"Billie Holiday? Oh. Yes. I know about you. Good afternoon, Miss Holiday." He walked over and stuck out his hand. "I'm happy to know you. I read about you in a magazine. They said the police had been giving you a hard time. And that you've had a very hard life. Is that true? What did they do to you? Is there anything you can do back? I mean, sue them or anything?"

Billie was too stunned at the barrage of words to speak.

Guy reached down and took her hand and shook it. The words never stopped tumbling out of his mouth.

"Maybe they expect too much from you. I know something about that. When I come from school the first thing I have to do, after I change school clothes, of course, is go out and water the lawn. Have you not noticed we live on the side of a mountain, and when I water, if there is any wind, the water gets blown back in your face. But if I come in wet, my mother thinks I was playing with the hose. I can't control the wind, you know. Will you come out and talk to me, when I've changed? I'd really like to know everything about you." He dropped her hand and ran out of the room, shouting, "I'll be back in a minute."

Billie's face was a map of astonishment. After a moment, she looked at me. "Damn. He's something, ain't he? Smart. What's he want to be?"

"Sometimes a doctor, and sometimes a fireman. It depends on the day you ask him."

"Good. Don't let him go into show business. Black men in show business is bad news. When they can't get as far as they deserve, they start taking it out on their women. What you say his name is?"

"Guy, Guy Johnson."

"Your name is Angelou. His name is Johnson? You don't look old enough to have married twice."

Guy was born to me when I was an unmarried teenager, so I had given him my father's name. I didn't want Billie to know that much about our history.

I said, "Well, that's life, isn't it?"

She nodded and mumbled, "Yeah, life's a bitch, a bitch on wheels."

Guy burst into the room again, wearing old jeans and a torn T-shirt. "Ready, Miss Holiday? You want to do anything? Come on. I won't let you get wet."

Billie rose slowly, with obvious effort.

I decided it was time for me to step in. "Guy, Miss Holiday is here to talk to me. Go out and do your chores and later you can talk with her."

Billie was erect. "Naw, I'm going out with him. But how the hell can you let him wear raggedy clothes like that? You living in a white district. Everybody be having their eyes on him. Guy, tomorrow, if you mamma will take me, I'm going to the store and buy you some nice things. You don't have to look like you going to pick cotton just 'cause you doing a little work. Come on, let's go."

Guy held the door for her as she picked her way across the room and to the steps. A minute later, I watched from the window as my son directed the hose toward the rose garden and Billie maintained her balance, although the heels of her baby-doll pumps were sinking into the soft earth.

She stayed for dinner, saying that I could drop her off on my way to work. She talked to Guy while I cooked. Surprisingly, he sat quiet, listening as she spoke of Southern towns, police, agents, good musicians and mean men she had known. She carefully avoided profanity and each time she slipped, she'd excuse herself to Guy, saying, "It's just another bad habit I got." After dinner, when the baby-sitter arrived, Billie told Guy that she was going to sing him a good-night song.

They went to his room, and I followed. Guy sat on the side of his bed and Billie began, a cappella, "You're My Thrill," an old song heavy with sensuous meaning. She sang as if she was starved for sex and only the boy, looking at her out of bored young eyes, could give her satisfaction.

I watched and listened from the door, recording every sound, firmly setting in my mind the rusty voice, the angle of her body, and Guy's look of tolerance (he'd rather be reading or playing a word game).

When I dropped her off at the Sunset Colonial Hotel, she told me to pick her up the next morning, early. I was amazed to hear her say that she was having trouble sleeping, so she might as well bring her Chihuahua along and spend the time with me.

For the next four days, Billie came to my house in the early mornings, talked all day long and sang a bedtime song to Guy, and stayed until I went to work. She said I was restful to be around because I was so goddam square. Although she continued to curse in Guy's absence, when he walked into the house her language not only changed, she made considerable effort to form her words with distinction.

On the night before she was leaving for New York, she told Guy she was going to sing "Strange Fruit" as her last song. We sat at the dining room table while Guy stood in the doorway.

Billie talked and sang in a hoarse, dry tone the well-known protest song. Her rasping voice and phrasing literally enchanted me. I saw the black bodies hanging from Southern trees. I saw the lynch victims' blood glide from the leaves down the trunks and onto the roots.

Guy interrupted, "How can there be blood at the root?" I made a hard face and warned him, "Shut up, Guy, just listen." Billie had continued under the interruption, her voice vibrating over harsh edges.

She painted a picture of a lovely land, pastoral and bucolic, then added eyes bulged and mouths twisted, onto the Southern landscape.

Guy broke into her song. "What's a pastoral scene, Miss Holiday?" Billie looked up slowly and studied Guy for a second. Her face became cruel, and when she spoke her voice was scornful. "It means when the crackers are killing the niggers. It means when they take a little nigger like you and snatch off his nuts and shove them down his goddam throat. That's what it means."

The thrust of rage repelled Guy and stunned me.

Billie continued, "That's what they do. That's a goddam pastoral scene."

Guy gave us both a frozen look and said, "Excuse me, I'm going to bed." He turned and walked away.

I lied and said it was time for me to go to work. Billie didn't hear either statement.

I went to Guy's room and apologized to him for Billie's behavior. He smiled sarcastically as if I had been the one who had shouted at him, and he offered a cool cheek for my good night kiss.

In the car I tried to explain to Billie why she had been wrong but she refused to understand. She said, "I didn't lie, did I? Did I lie on the crackers? What's wrong with telling the truth?"

She decided that she didn't want to be taken to the hotel. She wanted to accompany me to the night club and catch my act. Efforts to dissuade her were unsuccessful.

I took her into the club and found her a front-row seat and went to my dressing room.

Jimmy Truitt of the Lester Horton Dance Troupe was in costume for their first number.

"Hey"—Jimmy was grinning like a child—"Billie Holiday is out front. And you can't believe what's happening."

The other dancers gathered around.

"The great Billie Holiday is sitting in the front row, and a little dog is drinking out of her glass." I had gotten so used to Pepe I had forgotten that Billie hardly made a move without him.

The dancers took over the stage, sliding, burning brightly in a Latin routine. When they finished, I was introduced.

After my first song, I spoke directly to the audience.

"Ladies and gentlemen. It is against the policy of the club to mention any celebrity who might be in the audience, for fear that an unseen person might be missed. But tonight I am violating that custom. I think every one will be excited to know that Miss Billie Holiday is present."

The crowd responded to my announcement with an approving roar. People stood cheering, looking around the room for Billie. She looked straight at me, then, picking up Pepe, stood up, turned to the audience and bowed her head two or three times as if she was agreeing with them. She sat down without smiling.

My next song was an old blues, which I began singing with only a bass accompaniment. The music was a dirge and the lyrics tragic. I had my eyes closed when suddenly, like a large glass shattering, Billie's voice penetrated the song.

"Stop that bitch. Stop her, goddamit. Stop that bitch. She sounds just like my goddam mamma."

I stopped and opened my eyes and saw Billie pick up Pepe and head through the crowd toward the women's toilet. I thanked the audience, asked the orchestra leader to continue playing, and headed for the women's lavatory. Twice in one night the woman had upset me. Well, she wasn't going to get away with it. She was going to learn that a "goddam square" could defend herself.

I had my hand on the knob when the door burst open and a very pale middle-aged white woman tore past me.

I entered and found Billie examining herself in the mirror. I began, "Billie, let me tell you something..."

She was still looking at her reflection but she said, "Aw, that's all right about the song. You can't help how you sound. Most colored women sound alike. Less they trying to sound white." She started laughing. "Did you see that old bitch hit it out of here?"

"I bumped into a woman just now."

"That was her. She was sitting on the toilet and when I opened the door, she screamed at me, 'Shut that door.' I screamed right back, 'Bitch, if you wanted it shut, you should have locked the goddam thing.' Then she comes out of there and asked me, 'Ain't you Billie Holiday?' I told her, 'Bitch, I didn't ask you your name.' You should have seen her fly." She laughed again, grinning into the mirror.

I said, "Billie, you know that woman might have been an old-time fan of yours."

She turned, holding on to Pepe and her purse and her jacket. "You know when you introduced me, you know how all those crackers stood up? You know why they were standing up?"

I said they were honoring her.

She said, "Shit. You don't know a damn thing. They were all standing up, looking around. They wanted to see a nigger who had been in jail for dope. I'm going to tell you one more thing. You want to be famous, don't you?"

I admitted I did.

"You're going to be famous. But it won't be for singing. Now, wait, you already know you can't sing all that good. But you're going to be real famous. Well, you better start asking yourself right now, 'When I get famous, who can I trust?' All crackers is bad and niggers ain't much better. Just take care of your son. Keep him with you and keep on telling him he's the smartest thing God made. Maybe he'll grow up without hating you. Remember Billie Holiday told you, 'You can't get too high for somebody to bring you down.' "

Outside, I found a taxi for her. A few months later, she died in a New York hospital. All the jazz and rhythm-and-blues stations had oily-voiced commentators extolling the virtues of the great artist whose like would not be seen or heard again. Jazz buffs with glorious vocabularies wrote long and often boring tributes to the pulchritudinous Lady Day, her phrasing and incredibly intricate harmonics. I would remember forever the advice of a lonely sick woman, with a waterfront mouth, who sang pretty songs to a twelve-year-old boy.

For weeks after Billie's visit, Guy treated me coolly. Neither of us mentioned the shouting scene, but he acted as if I had betrayed him. I had allowed a stranger to shout and curse at him and had not come to his defense. School semester was drawing to a close, and when I asked him whether he wanted to go to summer school or camp, or just stay home and hike the canyons, he answered, from the distance of indifference, that he had not made up his mind.

It was obvious that our home life was not going to return to normal until he aired his grievance.

"Guy, what did you think of Billie Holiday?"

"She was O.K., I guess."

"That's all you thought?"

"Well, she sure cursed a lot. If she curses that way all the time, it's no wonder people don't like her."

"So you didn't like her?"

"Anybody who curses all the time is stupid."

I had heard him use a few unacceptable words when talking in the backyard with his friend Tony. "Guy, don't you use some bad words yourself?"

"But I'm a boy, and boys say certain things. When we go hiking or in the gym. We say things you're not supposed to say in front of girls, but that's different."

I didn't think that this was a time to explain the unfairness of a double standard. He walked to his room, and standing in the doorway without turning back to face me, he said, "Oh yeah. And when I grow up, I'm not going to let anybody—no matter how famous she is—I'm not going to let anybody curse at my children."

He slammed the door.

The Billie Holiday incident had hurt him more deeply than I had imagined. I planned a recovery scheme which would return my son to normal. First I apologized to him, then for the next few days I talked softly, prepared his favorite foods, took him out to the movies and played cutthroat Scrabble with him until I had to leave for work. He was recuperating well when I received a telephone call from his school.

"Miss Angelou, I am a counselor at Marvelland School and we don't think Guy should ride the school bus next semester."

"You don't think . . . What 'we' and why not?"

"The principal, a few teachers and I. We've discussed his actions . . . and we agree—"

"What action? What did he do?"

"Well, he used profanity on the school bus."

"I'll be right there."

"Oh, there's no need—"

I hung up the telephone.

When I walked into the principal's office and saw the welcoming committee, I felt twenty feet tall and as black as midnight. Two white women and a tiny balding white man rose from their seats as I entered.

I said good morning and introduced myself.

"Really, Miss Angelou, the situation did not warrant your making a trip to the school."

The puny-looking man extended his hand. "I'm Mr. Baker, Guy's counselor, and I know he is not a bad boy. Not really."

I looked at the woman who had not spoken. It would be better to let them all have their say.

One woman said, "I teach English, and one of my students reported the incident to me this morning."

"I'd like to know what happened."

The English teacher spoke with deliberation, as if she were testing the taste of the words.

"As I understand it, a conversation had been going on, on a particular topic. When the bus stopped at your corner, Guy boarded it and joined the conversation. He then gave explicit details on that particular subject. When the bus arrived at school, a couple of the girls were crying and they came to me and reported Guy's behavior."

"And what did Guy say? What was his excuse?"

The second woman broke her silence. "We have not spoken to Guy. We thought there was no reason to embarrass him."

"You mean to say you have simply assumed that to be accused is to be guilty. And so you are ready to deny him the right of using the school bus, which is paid for with my taxes, without hearing his side? I want to see Guy. And I want to see him now. I don't know why I thought white teachers would be fair to a Negro child. I want to hear what Guy has to say. And now."

The moment of confrontation brought about an unexpected metamorphosis. The three teachers who had seemed individually small and weak, shifted and swam together coalescing into one unit, three bodies with one brain. Their faces hardened, their eyes hardened.

"We do not interrupt students during class, for anyone. And we do not make a student a special case, just because he happens to be Negro. And we do not allow Negro boys to use foul language in front of our girls."

The two women stood silent and approving.

Mr. Baker spoke for them, as well as for white people everywhere.

The impossibility of the situation filled my mouth with bitter saliva. How could I explain a young black boy to a grown man who had been born white? How could the two women understand a black mother who had nothing to give her son except a contrived arrogance? If I had an eternity and the poetry of old spirituals, I could not make them live with me the painful moments when I tried to prove to Guy that his color was not a cruel joke, but a healthful design. If they knew that I described God to my son as looking very much like John Henry, wouldn't they think me blasphemous? If he was headstrong, I had made him so. If, in his adolescent opinion, he was the best representative of the human race, it was my doing and I had no apology to make. The radio and posters, newspapers and teachers, bus drivers and salespersons told him every day in thousands of ways that he had come from nothing and was going nowhere.

"Mr. Baker, I understand you. Now, I'd like to see Guy." I kept my voice low and under control.

"If we take him out of class, you'll have to take him home. We do not interrupt classes. That is our policy."

"Yes. I'll take him home."

"He'll be marked absent for the day. But I guess that doesn't matter."

"Mr. Baker, I'll take my son home." I had to see Guy, to hear him speak. Nothing would be gained by further conversation. He would have to return to the school, but for the moment, I wanted to know that he was not broken or even bruised.

"I'll wait for him outside. Thank you."

Guy jumped into the car, his face active with concern. "What's the matter, Mom?"

I told him about the meeting with the teachers.

He relaxed. "Aw, gee, Mom, and you came to school for that? It was nothing. Some of those kids are so stupid. They were talking about where babies come from. They said some of the funniest things and they should know better. So I told them about the penis, and the vagina and the womb. You know, all that stuff in my book on the beginnings of life? Well, some of the crazy girls started crying when I said their fathers had done it to their mothers." He began to laugh, enjoying the memory of the girls' tears. "That's all I said. I was right, wasn't I?"

"Sometimes it's wiser to be right in silence, you know?"

He looked at me with the suspicion of youth. "But you always say, 'Speak up. Tell the truth, no matter what the situation.' I just told the truth."

"Yes, honey. You just told the truth."

Two days later, Guy brought home a message which infuriated me. My son was reasonably bright, but he had never been more than a competent student. The letter he brought home, however, stated that due to his wonderful grades, he had been advanced and would be attending another school at the end of the term.

The obvious lie insulted both my son and me, but I thought it wise to remove Guy from the school as soon as possible. I didn't want an already prejudiced faculty and administration to use him as their whipping boy.

I began searching for another school and another house. We needed an area where black skin was not regarded as one of nature's more unsightly mistakes.

The Westlake district was ideal. Mexican, black American, Asian and white families lived side by side in old rambling houses. Neighbors spoke to each other as they mowed their lawns or shopped in the long-established local grocery stores.

I rented the second floor of a two-story Victorian, and when Guy saw the black children playing on our new street, he was giddy with excitement. His reaction made me see how much he had missed the close contact with black people.

"Boy!" He jumped and wriggled. "Boy! Now, I'm going to make some friends!"

CHAPTER 1

For the next year and a half, save for my short out-of-town singing engagements, we lived in the area. Guy became a part of a group of teenagers whose antics were rambunctious enough to satisfy their need to rebel, yet were acceptable to the tolerant neighborhood.

I began to write. At first I limited myself to short sketches, then to song lyrics, then I dared short stories. When I met John Killens he had just come to Hollywood to write the screenplay for his novel *Youngblood,* and he agreed to read some of what he called my "work in progress." I had written and recorded six songs for Liberty Records, but I didn't seriously think of writing until John gave me his critique. After that I thought of little else. John was the first published black author I had really talked with. (I'd met James Baldwin in Paris in the early fifties, but I didn't really know him.) John said, "Most of your work needs polishing. In fact, most of everybody's work could stand rewriting. But you have undeniable talent." He added, "You ought to come to New York. You need to be in the Harlem Writers Guild." The invitation was oblique but definitely alluring.

I had met the singer Abbey Lincoln. We met years earlier and we became friends during the time I stayed in the Westlake district. But she had moved to New York City. Whenever I spoke to her on the telephone, after she stopped praising Max Roach, her love and romantic ideal, she lauded New York City. It was the hub, the absolute middle of the world. The only place for an intelligent person to be, and to grow.

Just possibly if I went to New York, I thought, I could find my own niche, settle down in it and become a success.

There was another reason for wanting to leave Los Angeles. Guy, once so amusing, was growing into a tall aloof stranger. Our warm evenings of Scrabble and charades were, for him, a part of the long ago. He said the childhood games simply did not hold his attention. When he obeyed my house rules, he did so with the attitude that he was just too bored to contest them.

I didn't understand, at the time, that adolescence had invaded him and deposited its usual hefty burden of insecurity and apprehension. My wispy sometimes-lover, who lived nearby, was too tediously pious to help me comprehend what was happening to my son. Indeed, his reverence for Eastern religions, a vegetarian diet and sexual abstinence rendered him almost, but not quite, incapable of everything except deep conversations on the meaning of life.

I called my mother and she answered after the first ring.

"Hello?"

"Lady?"

"Oh hello, baby." She spoke as crisply as a white woman.

I said, "I'd like to see you. I'm going to move to New York and I don't know when I'll come back to California. Maybe we could meet somewhere and spend a couple of days together. I could drive north, part of the way—"

She didn't pause. "Of course, we can meet, of course, I want to see you, baby." Six feet tall, with a fourteen-year-old son, and I was still called baby. "How about Fresno? That's halfway. We could stay at that hotel. I know you read about it."

"Yes. But not if there's going to be trouble. I just want to be with you."

"Trouble? Trouble?" The familiar knife edge had slipped into her voice. "But, baby, you know that's my middle name. Anyway, the law says that hotel has to accept Negro guests. I'll swear before God and five other responsible men that my daughter and I are Negroes. After that, if they refuse us, well..."—she laughed hopefully and high-pitched—"well, we'll have a board to fit their butts."

That part of the conversation was finished. Vivian Baxter sensed the possibility of confrontation and there would be no chance of talking her out of it. I realized too late that I should simply have taken the Southern Pacific train from Los Angeles to San Francisco and spent the two days in her Fulton Street house, then returned to pack for my continental move.

Her voice softened again as she relayed family gossip and set a date for our meeting in the middle of the state.

———

In 1959, Fresno was a middling town with palm trees and a decidedly Southern accent. Most of its white inhabitants seemed to be descendants of Steinbeck's Joads, and its black citizens were farm hands who had simply exchanged the dirt roads of Arkansas and Mississippi for the dusty streets of central California.

I parked my old Chrysler on a side street, and taking my overnight case, walked around the corner to the Desert Hotel. My mother had suggested that we meet at three, which meant that she planned to arrive at two.

The hotel lobby had been decorated with welcome banners for a visiting sales convention. Large florid men mingled and laughed with portly women under low-hanging chandeliers.

My entrance stopped all action. Every head turned to see, every eye blazed, first with doubt, then fury. I wanted to run back to my car, race to Los Angeles, back to the postered walls of my house. I straightened my back and forced my face into indifference and walked to the registration desk. The clock above said two forty-five. "Good afternoon. Where is the bar?" A round-faced young man dropped his eyes and pointed behind me.

"Thank you."

The crowd made an aisle and I walked through the silence, knowing that before I reached the lounge door, a knife could be slipped in my back or a rope lassoed around my neck.

My mother sat at the bar wearing her Dobbs hat and tan suede suit. I set my case down inside the door and joined her.

"Hi, baby," her smile was a crescent of white. "You're a little early." She knew I would be. "Jim?" And I knew she'd already have the bartender's name and his attention. The man grinned for her.

"Jim, this is my baby. She's pretty, isn't she?"

Jim nodded, never taking his eyes away from Mother. She leaned over and kissed me on the lips.

"Give her a Scotch and water and another little taste for yourself." She caught him as he started to hesitate. "Don't refuse, Jim. No man can walk on one leg." She smiled, and he turned to prepare the drinks.

"Baby, you're looking good. How was the drive? Still got that old Chrysler? Did you see those people in the lobby? They're so ugly they make you stop and think. How's Guy? Why are you going to New York? Is he happy about the move?"

Jim set my drink down and lifted his in a toast.

Mother picked up her drink. "Here's looking at you, Jim." And to me. "Here's a go, baby." She smiled and I saw again that she was the most beautiful woman I had ever seen.

"Thanks, Mother."

She took my hands, put them together and rubbed them.

"You are cold. Hot as it is, your hands are freezing. Are you all right?"

Nothing frightened my mother except thunder and lightning. I couldn't tell her that at thirty-one years old, the whites in the lobby had scared me silly.

"Just fine, Mother. I guess it's the air conditioning."

She accepted the lie.

"Well, let's drink up and go to our room. I've got some talk for you."

She picked up the bills from the bar, counted them and pulled out two singles.

"What time do you come on, Jim?"

The bartender turned and grinned. "I open up. At eleven every morning."

"Then, I'll break your luck for you. Scotch and water, remember. At eleven. This is for you."

"Oh, you don't have to do that."

Mother was off the stool. "I know. That's why it's easy. See you in the morning."

I picked up my suitcase, followed her out of the dark bar into the noisy lobby. Again, the buzz of conversation diminished, but Mother never noticed. She switched through the crowd, up to the desk.

"Mrs. Vivian Baxter Jackson and daughter. You have our reservation." My mother had married a few times, but she loved her maiden name. Married or not, she often identified herself as Vivian Baxter.

It was a statement. "And please call the bellboy. My bag is in my car. Here are the keys. Set your bag down here, baby." Back to the registration clerk. "And tell him to bring my daughter's case to our room." The clerk slowly pushed a form across the counter. Mother opened her purse, took out her gold Sheaffer and signed us in.

"The key, please." Again using slow motion, the clerk slid the key to Mother.

"Two ten. Second floor. Thank you. Come on, baby." The hotel's color bar had been lifted only a month earlier, yet she acted as if she had been a guest there for years. There was a winding staircase to the right of the desk and a small group of open-mouthed conventioneers standing by the elevator.

I said, "Let's take the stairs, Mother."

She said, "We're taking the elevator," and pushed the "up" button. The waiting people looked at us as if our very presence had stripped everything of value from their lives.

When we got out of the elevator, mother took a moment, then turned and walked left to 210. She unlocked the door and when we entered, she threw her purse on the bed and walked to the window.

"Sit down, baby. I'm going to tell you something you must never forget."

I sat on the first chair as she opened the drapes. The sunlight framed her figure, and her face was indistinct.

"Animals can sense fear. They feel it. Well, you know that human beings are animals, too. Never, never let a person know you're frightened. And a group of them...absolutely never. Fear brings out the worst thing in everybody. Now, in that lobby you were as scared as a rabbit. I knew it and all those white folks knew it. If I hadn't been there, they might have turned into a mob. But something about me told them, if they mess with either of us, they'd better start looking for some new asses, 'cause I'd blow away what their mammas gave them."

She laughed like a young girl. "Look in my purse." I opened her purse.

"The Desert Hotel better be ready for integration, 'cause if it's not, I'm ready for the Desert Hotel."

Under her wallet, half hidden by her cosmetic case, lay a dark-blue German Luger.

"Room service? This is two ten. I'd like a pitcher of ice, two glasses, and a bottle of Teachers Scotch. Thank you."

The bellboy had brought our bags, and we had showered and changed.

"We'll have a cocktail and go down for dinner. But now, let's talk.

Why New York? You were there in '52 and had to be sent home. What makes you think it has changed?"

"I met a writer, John Killens. I told him I wanted to write and he invited me to New York."

"He's colored, isn't he?" Since my first marriage to a Greek had dissolved, Mother had been hoping for a black son-in-law.

"He's married, Mother. It's not like that."

"That's terrible. First ninety-nine married men out of a hundred never divorce their wives for their girl friends, and the one that does will probably divorce the new wife for a newer girl friend."

"But really, it's not that way. I've met his wife and children. I'll go to New York, stay with them for a couple of weeks, get an apartment and send for Guy."

"And where will he stay for two weeks? Not alone in that big house. He's only fourteen."

She would explode if I told her I planned for him to stay with the man I was leaving. Vivian Baxter had survived by being healthily suspicious. She would never trust a rejected lover to treat her grandson fairly.

"I've made arrangements with a friend. And after all, it's only two weeks."

We both knew that she had left me and my brother for ten years to be raised by our paternal grandmother. We looked at each other and she spoke first.

"You're right. It is only two weeks. Well, let me tell you about me. I'm going to sea."

"To see. See what?"

"I'm going to become a merchant marine."

I had never heard of a female merchant seaman.

"A member of the Marine Cooks and Stewards Union."

"Why?" Disbelief raised my voice. "Why?" She was a surgical nurse, a realtor, had a barber's license and owned a hotel. Why did she want to go to sea and live the rough unglamorous life of a seaman?

"Because they told me Negro women couldn't get in the union. You know what I told them?"

I shook my head, although I nearly knew.

"I told them, 'You want to bet?' I'll put my foot in that door up to my hip until women of every color can walk over my foot, get in that union, get aboard a ship and go to sea." There was a knock at the door. "Come in."

A uniformed black man opened the door and halted in surprise at seeing us.

"Good evening. Just put the tray over there. Thank you."

The bellboy deposited the tray and turned.

"Good evening, you all surprised me. Sure did. Didn't expect to see you. Sure didn't."

Mother walked toward him holding money in her hand.

"Who did you expect? Queen Victoria?"

"No. No, ma'am. I mean... Our people... in here... It's kinda new seeing us... and everything."

"This is for you." She gave him the tip. "We are just ordinary guests in the hotel. Thank you and good night." She opened the door and waited. When he walked out mumbling good night, she closed the door with finality.

"Mom, you were almost rude."

"Well, baby, I figure like this. He's colored and I'm colored, but we are not cousins. Let's have a drink." She smiled.

During the next two days, Mother showed me off to some old card-playing friends she had known twenty years earlier.

"This is my baby. She's been to Egypt, all around Milan, Italy, and Spain and Yugoslavia. She's a singer and dancer, you know." When her friends were satisfactorily impressed with my accomplishments, Mother made certain of their wonder by adding, "Of course, I'll be shipping out myself in a few days."

We hugged in the empty lobby of the Desert Hotel; the convention had ended the day before our departure.

"Take care of yourself. Take care of your son, and remember New York City is just like Fresno. Just more of the same people in bigger buildings. Black folks can't change because white folks won't change. Ask for what you want and be prepared to pay for what you get." She kissed me and her voice softened to a whisper. "Let me leave first, baby. I hate to see the back of someone I love."

We embraced again and I watched her walk, hips swaying, into the bright street.

———

Back at home I collected myself and called Guy, who responded by coming into the living room and then walking back to lean against the doorjamb.

"Guy, I want to talk to you. Please sit down." At this stage, he never sat if he could stand, towering above the boredom of life. He sat, obviously to pacify me.

"Guy, we're going to move." Aha, a flicker of interest in his eyes, which he quickly controlled.

"Again? Okay. I can pack in twenty minutes. I've timed myself." I held on to the natural wince that struggled to surface.

In his nine years of schooling, we had lived in five areas of San Francisco, three townships in Los Angeles, New York City, Hawaii and Cleveland, Ohio. I followed the jobs, and against the advice of a pompous school psychologist, I had taken Guy along. The psychologist had been white, obviously educated and with those assets I knew he was also well-to-do. How could he know what a young Negro boy needed in a racist world?

When the money was plentiful, we lived in swank hotels and called room service. At other times we stayed in boardinghouses. I strung sheets as room dividers, and cooked our favorite food illegally on a two-burner hot plate. Because we moved so often, Guy had little chance to make or keep friends, but we were together and generally we had laughed a lot. Now that post-puberty had laid claim to him, our friendly badinage was gone and I was menacing him with one more move.

"This is the last time. Last time, I think."

His face said he didn't believe me.

"We're going to New York City." His eyes lit up again and just as quickly dulled.

"I want to leave Saturday. John and Grace Killens are looking for an apartment for us. I'll stay with them and in two weeks you'll join me. Is that all right?" Parent power becomes so natural, only children notice it. I wasn't really asking his permission. He knew it and didn't answer.

"I thought I'd ask Ray if he'd like to stay in the house with you for two weeks. Just to be company for you. That O.K. with you?"

"That's perfectly all right, Mother." He stood up. He was so long, his legs seemed to start just at his arm sockets. "If you'll excuse me."

Thus he ended our unsatisfactory family chat. I still had to speak to my gentleman friend.

As we sat close in the morning's sunshine, Ray's handsome yellow face was as usual in benign repose.

"I'm leaving Saturday for New York."

"Oh? Got a contract?"

"No. Not yet."

"I don't think that I'd like to face New York without a contract..."

Here it was.

"Just Guy and I are going. We're going to stay."

His whole body jumped, the muscles began to skitter around his face. For the first time I thought that maybe he cared for me. I watched him command his body. After long minutes his fists fell open, the long fingers relaxed and his lips lost their hardened ridges.

"Is there anything I can do to help you?"

He consented to stay in the house and send Guy to me in two weeks. After, he might take the house himself, otherwise he would close it. Of course, we would remain friends.

CHAPTER 2

John and Grace Killens lived with their two children and his mother in a roomy brownstone in Brooklyn. They accepted me as if I were a friend returning from a long journey. John met me at the door. "Girl, you finally got out of the country. Kick the mud off your shoes, come inside and make yourself at home."

Grace was quieter. "Welcome to New York. I'm glad you came."

Their hospitality was casual, without the large gestures that often discomfort a guest. The first days of my stay were filled with learning the house and studying the personalities of its inhabitants. John genuinely enjoyed being passionate. He was good-looking, and his dark-brown eyes in a light-brown face could alternately smolder or pierce. He talked animatedly, waving his hands as if offering them as gifts to his listeners.

Grace was pretty and petite, but she never allowed John's success or the fact that she was his great love interfere with independent thought.

John's mother, Mom Willie, who wore her Southern background like a magnolia corsage, eternally fresh, was robust and in her sixties. She was one of the group of black women who had raised their children, worked hard, fought for her principles and still retained some humor. She often entranced the family with graphic stories set in a sullen, racist South. The tales changed, the plots varied; her villains were always white and her heroes upstanding, courageous, clever blacks.

Barbara, the younger of the Killens children, was a bright tomboy who spoke fast and darted around the house like a cinnamon-colored wind. Her brother, Jon, larger and more gentle, moved slowly, spoke seldom and seemed to have been burdened with the responsibility of pondering the world's imponderables.

Everyone except Jon, whose nickname was Chuck, talked incessantly, and although I enjoyed the exchange, I found the theme inexplicably irritating. They excoriated white men, white women, white children and white history, particularly as it applied to black people.

I had spent my life on city front steps, in country backyards, kitchens, living rooms and bedrooms, joining in and listening to the conversations of black people, but I had never heard so much attention given to the subject of whites.

Of course, in Arkansas, when I was young, black children knowing that whites owned the cotton gin, the lumber mill, the fine houses and paved streets, had to find something which they thought whites did not possess. This need to have something all one's own coincided with the burgeoning interest in sex. The children sang, beyond the ears of adults and wistfully:

> "Whites folks ain't got the hole...
> And they ain't got the pole...
> And they ain't got the soul...
> To do it right... real right... All night."

In the ensuing years in California the jokes came scarcer and the jobs grew meaner. Anger was always present whenever the subject of whites entered our conversations. We discussed the treatment of Rev. Martin Luther King, Jr., the murder of Emmett Till in Mississippi, the large humiliations and the petty snubs we all knew were meant to maim our spirits. I had heard white folks ridiculed, cursed and envied, but I had never heard them dominate the entire intimate conversation of a black family.

In the Killens' home, if entertainment was mentioned, someone would point out that Harry Belafonte, a close family friend, was working with a South African singer, Miriam Makeba, and South Africa was really no different from South Philly. If the West Indies or religion or fashion entered the conversation, in minutes we were persistently examining the nature of racial oppression, racial progress and racial integration.

I fretted at the unrelenting diatribe, not because I disagreed but because I didn't think whites interesting enough to consume all my thoughts, nor powerful enough to control all my movements.

I found an apartment in the Killens' neighborhood. I spent the days painting the two bedrooms and sprucing up the furniture I bought in secondhand stores, and returned each night to sleep at the Killens' house.

One evening after the rest of the family had gone to bed, I sat up having a nightcap with John. I asked why he was so angry all the time. I told him that while I agreed with Alabama blacks who boycotted bus companies and protested against segregation, California blacks were thousands of miles, literally and figuratively, from those Southern plagues.

"Girl, don't you believe it. Georgia is Down South. California is Up South. If you're black in this country, you're on a plantation. You have to deal with masters. There might be some argument over whether they are vicious masters, but be assured that they all think they are masters... And if they think that, then you'd better believe they think you are the slave. Maybe a smart slave, a pretty slave, a good slave, but a slave just the same."

I reminded John that I had spent a year in New York, but he countered, "You were a dancer. Dancers don't see anything except other dancers. They don't see; they exist to be seen. This time you should look at New York with a writer's eyes, ears and nose. Then you'll really see New York."

John was right. Seven years earlier, when I studied in New York, my attention was unequally distributed between the dance studio where I was studying on scholarship, my son and my first, disintegrating marriage. Truly I had had neither the time nor mind to learn New York.

John's eyes were blazing, and although I was his only audience, he was as intense as if he were speaking to a filled room.

"I tell you what to do. Go to Manhattan tomorrow. Go first to Times Square. You'll see the same people you used to see in Arkansas. Their accents might be different, their dress might be different, but if they are American whites, they're all Southern crackers. Then go to Harlem. Harlem is the largest plantation in this country. You'll see lawyers in three-piece suits, real estate brokers in mink coats, pimps in white Cadillacs, but they're all sharecropping. Sharecropping on a mean plantation."

I intended to see Harlem with John's advice in mind, but Guy arrived before I had the opportunity. I picked him up at the airport, and when he walked into the house I saw that he was already too large for the living room. We had been separated a month and he seemed to have grown two inches taller and years away from me. He looked at the hastily painted white walls and the Van Gogh prints I had chosen and matted.

"It's O.K. It looks like every other house we've lived in."

I wanted to slap him. "Well, it's a little better than the street."

"Oh, Mother, come now. That wasn't necessary." The superiority in his voice was an indication of how he had been hurt by our separation.

I grinned. "O.K. Sorry. How about the desk? You always said you wanted a big office desk. Do you like it?"

"Oh sure, but you know I wanted a desk when I was a little kid. Now..."

The air between us was burdened with his aloof scorn. I understood him too well.

When I was three my parents divorced in Long Beach, California, and sent me and my four-year-old brother, unescorted, to our paternal grandmother. We wore wrist tags which informed anyone concerned that we were Marguerite and Bailey Johnson, en route to Mrs. Annie Henderson in Stamps, Arkansas.

Except for disastrous and mercifully brief encounters with each of them when I was seven, we didn't see our parents again until I was thirteen.

Our reunion with Mother in California was a joyous festival, studded with tears, hugs and lipsticked kisses. Under and after the high spirits was my aching knowledge that she had spent years not needing us.

Now my angry son was wrestling with the same knowledge. We had been apart less than a month—he had stayed an unwelcome guest in his own home, while I had gloried in every day of our separation.

He covered the hurt with a look of unconcern, but I knew his face better than my own. Each fold, every plane, the light or shadow in his eyes had been objects of my close scrutiny. He had been born to me when I was an unmarried adventurous seventeen-year-old; we had grown up together. Since he was fatherless most of his fourteen years, the flash of panic in his eyes was exchanged for scorn whenever I brought a new man into our lives. I knew the relief when he discovered the newcomer cared for me and respected him. I recognized the confusion that changed his features each time the man packed to leave. I understood the unformed question. "She made him leave. What will she do if I displease her too?" He remained standing, hands in his pockets, waiting for me to convince him of the stability of my love. Words were useless.

"Your school is three blocks away, and there's a large park almost as nice as the one on Fulton Street."

At the mention of the San Francisco park where we picnicked and he learned to ride a bike, a tiny smile tried to cross his face, but he quickly took control and sent the smile away.

"...and you liked the Killens children. Well, they live around the corner."

He nodded and spoke like an old man. "Lots of people are different when they're visiting than when they're at home. I'll see if they're the same in New York as they were in California."

Youthful cynicism is sad to observe, because it indicates not so much knowledge learned from bitter experiences as insufficient trust even to attempt the future.

"Guy, you know I love you, and I try to be a good mother. I try to do the right thing, but I'm not perfect"—his silence agreed—"I hope you'll remember whenever I've done something that hurts you that I do love you and it's not my intention..."

He was studying my face, listening to the tone of my voice.

"Mom..." I relaxed a little. "Mother" was formal, cold, disapproving. "Mom" meant closeness, forgiveness.

"Mom, I know. I know you do the best you can. And I'm not really angry. It's just that Los Angeles..."

"Did Ray do anything...mistreat you?"

"Oh no, Mom. He moved about a week after you left."

"You mean you lived alone?"

Shock set my body into furious action. Every normal function accelerated. Tears surfaced and clouded my vision. Guy lost half his age and suddenly he again was a little boy of seven who slept with a butcher's knife under his pillow one summer at camp. What did he slip under his pillow in Los Angeles while I partied safely in New York?

"My baby. Oh honey, why didn't you tell me when I phoned? I would have come back."

Now his was the soothing voice. "You were trying to find a job and a house. I wasn't afraid."

"But Guy, you're only fourteen. Suppose something had happened to you?"

He stood silent and looked at me, evaluating my distress. Suddenly, he crossed the room and stopped beside my chair. "Mom, I'm a man. I can look after myself. Don't worry. I'm young, but I'm a man." He stood, bent and kissed me on the forehead. "I'm going to change the furniture around. I want my desk facing the window." He walked down the hall.

The black mother perceives destruction at every door, ruination at each window, and even she herself is not beyond her own suspicion. She questions whether she loves her children enough—or more terribly, does she love them too much? Do her looks cause embarrassment—or even more terrifying, is she so attractive her sons begin to desire her and her daughters begin to hate her. If she is unmarried, the challenges are increased. Her singleness indicates she has rejected, or has been rejected by her mate. Yet she is raising children who will become mates. Beyond her door, all authority is in the hands of people who do not look or think or act like her and her children. Teachers, doctors, sales clerks, librarians, policemen, welfare workers are white and exert control over her family's moods, conditions and personality; yet within the home, she must display a right to rule which at any moment, by a knock at the door, or a ring of the telephone can be exposed as false. In the face of these contradictions, she must provide a blanket of stability, which warms but does not suffocate, and she must tell her children the truth about the power of white power without suggesting that it cannot be challenged.

"Hey, Mom, come and see."

Every piece of furniture was in a new place, and the room looked exactly the same.

"Like it? After dinner, I'll play you a game of Scrabble. Where is the dictionary? What are we having for dinner? Does the television work? Gee, I'm famished."

My son was home and we were a family again.

—

The Harlem Writers Guild was meeting at John's house, and my palms were sweating and my tongue was thick. The loosely formed organization, without dues or membership cards, had one strict rule: any invited guest could sit in for three meetings, but thereafter, the visitor had to read from his or her work in progress. My time had come.

Sarah Wright and Sylvester Leeks stood in a corner talking softly. John Clarke was staring at titles in the bookcase. Mary Delany and Millie Jordan were giving their coats to Grace and exchanging greetings. The other writers were already seated around the living room in a semicircle.

John Killens walked past me, touching my shoulder, took his seat and called the meeting to order.

"O.K., everybody. Let's start." Chairs scraped the floor and the sounds reverberated in my armpits. "As you know, our newest member, our California singer, is going to read from her new play. What's the title, Maya?"

"*One Love. One Life.*" My usually deep voice leaked out high-pitched and weak.

A writer asked how many acts the play had. I answered again in the piping voice, "So far only one."

Everyone laughed; they thought I was making a joke.

"If everyone is ready, we can begin." John picked up his note pad. There was a loud rustling as the writers prepared to take notes.

I read the character and set description despite the sudden perversity of my body. The blood pounded in my ears but not enough to drown the skinny sound of my voice. My hands shook so that I had to lay the pages in my lap, but that was not a good solution due to the tricks my knees were playing. They lifted voluntarily, pulling my heels off the floor and then trembled like disturbed Jello. Before I launched into the play's action, I looked around at the writers expecting but hoping not to see their amusement at my predicament. Their faces were studiously blank. Within a year, I was to learn that each had a horror story about a first reading at the Harlem Writers Guild.

Time wrapped itself around every word, slowing me. I couldn't force myself to read faster. The pages seemed to be multiplying even as I was trying to reduce them. The play was dull, the characters, unreal, and the dialogue was taken entirely off the back of a Campbell's soup can. I knew this was my first and last time at the Guild. Even if I hadn't the grace to withdraw voluntarily, I was certain the members had a method of separating the wheat from the chaff.

"The End." At last.

The members laid their notes down beside their chairs and a few got up to use the toilets. No one spoke. Even as I read I knew the drama was bad, but maybe someone would have lied a little.

The room filled. Only the whispering of papers shifting told me that the jury was ready.

John Henrik Clarke, a taut little man from the South, cleared his throat. If he was to be the first critic, I knew I would receive the worst sentence. John Clarke was famous in the group for his keen intelligence and bitter wit. He had supposedly once told the FBI that they were wrong to think that he would sell out his home state of Georgia; he added that he would give it away, and if he found no takers he would even pay someone to take it.

"*One Life. One Love?*" His voice was a rasp of disbelief. "I found no life and very little love in the play from the opening of the act to its unfortunate end."

Using superhuman power, I kept my mouth closed and my eyes on my yellow pad.

He continued, his voice lifting. "In 1879, on a March evening, Alexander Graham Bell successfully completed his attempts to send the human voice through a little wire. The following morning some frustrated playwright, unwilling to build the necessary construction plot, began his play with a phone call."

A general deprecating murmur floated in the air.

"Aw, John" and "Don't be so mean" and "Ooo Johnnn, you ought to be ashamed." Their moans were facetious, mere accompaniment to their relish.

Grace invited everyone to drinks, and the crowd rose and started milling around, while I stayed in my chair.

Grace called to me. "Come on, Maya. Have a drink. You need it." I grinned and knew movement was out of the question.

Killens came over. "Good thing you stayed. You got some very important criticism." He, too, could slide to hell straddling a knotted greasy rope. "Don't just sit there. If they think you're too sensitive, you won't get such valuable criticism the next time you read."

The next time? He wasn't as bright as he looked. I would never see those snooty bastards as long as I stayed black and their asses pointed toward the ground. I put a nasty-sweet smile on my face and nodded.

"That's right, Maya Angelou, show them you can take anything they can dish out. Let me tell you something." He started to sit down beside me, but mercifully another writer called him away.

I measured the steps from my chair to the door. I could make it in ten strides.

"Maya, you've got a story to tell."

I looked up into John Clarke's solemn face.

"I think I can speak for the Harlem Writers Guild. We're glad to have you. John Killens came back from California talking about your talent. Well, in this group we remind each other that talent is not enough. You've got to work. Write each sentence over and over again, until it seems you've used every combination possible, then write it again. Publishers don't care much for white writers." He coughed or laughed. "You can imagine what they think about black ones. Come on. Let's get a drink."

I got up and followed him without a first thought.

Ten different conversations were being held in the kitchen.

The writers were partying. Gone were the sober faces and serious eyes. As John Clarke and I entered, another writer spoke to me. "So, Maya, you lived through your baptism. Now you're a member of the flock." Sarah, a pretty little woman with fastidious manners, put her hand on my arm. "They were easy on you this evening, dear. Soft, you might say. Because it was your first reading. But you'll see, next week you watch how they treat Sylvester."

Paule Marshall, whose book *Brown Girl, Brown Stones* was going to be made into a television movie, smiled conspiratorially. "See, I told you, it wasn't too bad, was it?" They had stripped me, flayed me, utterly and completely undone me, and now they were as cheery as Christmas cards.

I sipped the cool wine and thought about the evening's instruction. Because I had a fairly large vocabulary and had been reading constantly since childhood, I had taken words and the art of arranging them too lightly. The writers assaulted my casual approach and made me confront my intention. If I wanted to write, I had to be willing to develop a kind of concentration found mostly in people awaiting execution. I had to learn technique and surrender my ignorance.

John Killens interrupted my thoughts. "Maya, how long will it take you to rewrite that play?"

I hadn't decided on a rewrite, or even whether I would attend another Guild meeting.

"I need to know so I can schedule your next reading."

"I'm not sure. Let me think about it."

"There are a lot of people ready to read. You'd better decide, otherwise you'll have to get in line."

"I'll call you tomorrow."

John nodded and turned away. He lifted his voice. "O.K., everybody. What about Cuba? What about Castro? Are we going to sit back and watch the United States kick Castro's ass, like its been kicking our ass, and say nothing?"

In the second following John's question, the air held quiet, free of chatter. Then voices rose.

"All black people ought to support Castro."

"Cuba is all right. Castro is all right."

"Castro acts like he grew up in Harlem."

"He speaks Spanish, but it could be niggerese."

John waited until the voices fell.

"There's no time like right now. You know about the slave who decided to buy his freedom?" Small smiles began to grow on the black, brown and yellow faces. Grace chuckled and bit into her cigarette holder.

"Well, this negero was a slave, but his owner allowed him to take jobs off the plantation at night, on weekends and holidays. He worked. Now, mind you, I mean, he would work on the plantation and then walk fifteen miles to town and work there, then walk back, get two hours' sleep and get up at daybreak and work again. He saved every penny. Wouldn't marry, wouldn't even take advantage of the ladies around him. Afraid he'd have to spend some of his hard-earned money. Finally, he saved up a thousand dollars. Lot of money. He went to his master and asked how much he was worth. The white man asked why the question. The negero said he just wanted to know how much slaves cost. The white man said he usually paid eight hundred to twelve hundred dollars for a good slave, but in the case of Tom, because he was getting old and couldn't father any children, if he wanted to buy himself, the master would let him go for six hundred dollars.

"Tom thanked the slave owner and went back to his cabin. He dug up his money and counted it. He fondled and caressed the coins and then put them back in their hiding place. He returned to the white man and said, 'Boss, freedom is a little too high right now. I'm going to wait till the price come down.'"

We all laughed, but the laughter was acrid with embarrassment. Most of us had been Toms at different times of our lives. There had been occasions when the price of freedom was more than I wanted to pay. Around the room faces showed others also were remembering.

"There is a Fair Play for Cuba organization. An ad is going to be taken out in the daily newspapers. The ad will cost money. Anyone who wants to sign it can find the form in the living room. Put your name down and if you can afford to, leave some money in the bowl on the cocktail table."

A few people began to move hurriedly toward the front room, but John stopped them.

"Just a minute. I just want to remind you all that if your name appears in the ad this afternoon, you can bet ten thousand dollars and a sucker that by nightfall it'll be in the FBI files. You'll be suspect. Just remember that."

John Clarke coughed his laugh again. "Hell, if you're born black in the United States, you're suspect of being everything, except white, of course." We laughed, relieved at the truth told in our own bitter wit. I thought of lines in Sterling Brown's poem "Strong Men":

> We followed away, and laughed as usual.
> They heard the laugh and wondered.

Just before I left the house, I signed the already-filled application form.

Paule Marshall stopped me at the door. "I really want to hear your rewrite. You know, lots of people have more talent than you or I. Hard work makes the difference. Hard, hard unrelenting work."

The meeting was over. Members were embraced, kissed lips or cheeks and patted each other. John Killens offered to drive me home.

Grace hugged me and whispered. "Ya did good, kid, and I know you were scared witless."

When John parked in front of my house, I gathered my papers and asked, "What's the hardest literary form, John?"

"Each one is the hardest. Fiction is impossible. Ask me. Poetry is impossible. Ask Langston or Countee. Baldwin will say essays are impossible. But everyone agrees, short stories are so impossible, they almost can't be written at all."

I opened the car door, "John, put me down for a reading in two months. I'll be reading a new short story. Good night."

I thought about my statement as I walked up the stairs. I had gathered from the evening's meeting that making a decision to write was a lot like deciding to jump into a frozen lake. I knew I was going in, so I decided I might as well try what John Killens suggested as the deepest end: the short story. If I survived at all, it would be a triumph. If I swam, it would be a miracle. As I unlocked my door, I thought of my mother putting her age back fifteen years and going into the merchant marines. I had to try. If I ended in defeat, at least I would be trying. Trying to overcome was black people's honorable tradition.

CHAPTER 3

There is an awesome reality to Rent Day. It comes trumpeting, forcing the days before it into a wild scramble. My rent day seemed to
come due every other day, and Guy always needed just one more pair
of jeans. The clothes I had to have were eternally in the cleaners, and
staples disappeared from my kitchen with an alarming regularity.

I could get a job singing, but I didn't have an agent. Harlem theatrical representatives sought light-skinned Cotton Club–type beauties
for their traveling revues. Midtown white agents would only book unknown black entertainers for out-of-town or night gigs, stag parties or
smokers. I knew one white New York club owner who had been a loyal
friend to me, but with my recently acquired new level of black dignity
I refused to go pleading to him for work.

I found a job on my own. The little club on the Lower East Side was
a joint where people came when they didn't have any other place to
go. There was a long bar, diluted drinks, dinner-plate-sized tables and
no dressing rooms (I changed in the women's toilet) and the work itself embarrassed me.

I sang in the club for two miserable months. People I admired were
doing important things. Abbey and Max Roach were performing jazz
concerts on liberation themes. Lorraine Hansberry had a play on
Broadway which told some old truths about the black American
Negro family to a new white audience. James Baldwin had the country in his balled fist with *The Fire Next Time*. Killens' *And Then We
Heard the Thunder* told the uncomfortable facts about black soldiers in
a white army. Belafonte included the South African singer Miriam
Makeba in his concerts, enlarging his art and increasing his protest
against racial abuse. And I was still singing clever little songs only
moderately well. I made the decision to quit show business. Give up
the skintight dresses and manicured smiles. The false concern over
sentimental lyrics. I would never again work to make people smile

inanely and would take on the responsibility of making them think. Now was the time to demonstrate my own seriousness.

Two weeks after my firm decision, I received an offer to appear at the Apollo Theater, and the idea of rejecting the invitation never occurred to me. The Apollo, in Harlem, was to black entertainers the Met, La Scala and a Royal Command Performance combined. Pearl Bailey, Dizzy Gillespie, Count Basie, Duke Ellington had played on that stage.

Frank Schiffman, the manager, sat in the darkened theater listening to rehearsal. Tito Puente's big band with Willie Bobo and Mongo Santamaria dropped dancing notes in the air like dust particles in a windstorm.

Schiffman sat rigid in the first row. I rehearsed my songs with the band, spurred on by the timbales of Willie Bobo and Mongo Santamaria's conga. I enlarged on my initial interpretation of the music, singing better than I was usually capable of. Schiffman didn't move or speak until I started to rehearse "Uhuru," an audience-participation song which I used as an encore.

"No audience participation in the Apollo." His voice was as rusty as an old iron bar.

"I beg your pardon?" Always get siditty when you're scared, was my policy. "Were you speaking to me?"

"Yeah, no audience participation in the Apollo."

"But that's my act. I always use 'Uhuru' as an encore. The word means freedom in Swahili. Babatunda Olatunje, the great Nigerian drummer, taught it to me—"

"No audience participation—."

"Is that your policy, Mr. Schiffman? If so..."

A few musicians rustled sheet music; others talked in Spanish.

"It's not a policy. The only policy in the Apollo is 'Be Good.' I'm telling you no audience participation because Apollo audiences won't go along with it. You'll die. Die on the stage if you try to get this audience to sing with you." He gave a little laugh and continued, "Most of them can sing better than you anyway."

A few musicians who understood English laughed. Many people

could sing better than I, so Schiffman had told me nothing I didn't already know.

"Thanks for your advice. I'm going to sing it anyway."

"It'll be a miracle if they don't laugh you off the stage." He laughed again.

"Thank you." I turned back to the orchestra. "I don't have sheet music, but the song goes like this..."

I didn't expect Schiffman to know that my life, like the lives of other black Americans, could be credited to miraculous experiences. But there was one other thing I was sure he didn't know. Black people in Harlem were changing, and the Apollo audience was black. The echo of African drums was less distant in 1959 than it had been for over a century.

One Hundred and Twenty-fifth Street was to Harlem what the Mississippi was to the South, a long traveling river always going somewhere, carrying something. A furniture store offering gaudy sofas and fake leopard-skin chairs shouldered Mr. Micheaux's book shop, which prided itself on having or being able to get a copy of any book written by a black person since 1900. It was true that sportily dressed fops stood on 125th and Seventh Avenue saying, "Got horse for the course and coke for your hope," but across the street, conservatively dressed men told concerned crowds of the satanic nature of whites and the divinity of Elijah Muhammad. Black women and men had begun to wear multicolored African prints. They moved through the Harlem streets like bright sails on a dark sea.

I also knew that fewer people giggled or poked the sides of their neighbors when they noticed my natural hair style.

Clever appliance-store owners left their TV sets on the channels broadcasting U.N. affairs. I had seen black people standing in front of the stores watching the faces of international diplomats. Although no sound escaped into the streets, the attentive crowds appeared. I had waited with a group of strangers one night near St. Nicholas Avenue. The mood was hopeful, as if a promise was soon to be kept. The crowd tightened, pulled itself closer together and toward the window, as a small dark figure appeared on all the screens at once. The figure was that of an African wearing a patterned toga, striding with theatrical dignity toward the camera. The sidewalk audience was quiet but tense. When the man's face was discernible and the part in his hair distinct, the crowd began to talk.

"Hey, Alex. Hey, brother."

"He's a good-looking thing."

"That African walk like God himself."

"Humph. Ain't that something."

The man's mouth moved and the crowd quieted, as if lip reading. Although it was impossible to understand his message, his air of disdain was not lost on the viewers.

One fat woman grinned and giggled, "I sure wish I knew what that pretty nigger was saying."

A man near the back of the crowd grunted. "Hell. He's just telling all the crackers in the world to kiss his black ass."

Laughter burst loudly in the street. Laughter immediate and self-congratulatory.

Schiffman had been in Harlem since the beginning of the Apollo. He had given first contracts to a number of black performers who went on to become internationally famous. Some people in the area said he was all right, and he had black friends. He understood who was running numbers, who was running games and who was square and respectable. But he wasn't black. And he was too mired in the Harlem he had helped to fashion to believe that the area was moving out of his control and even beyond his understanding.

"Uhuru" was definitely going to be my encore.

Fortunately my first show was at one o'clock on a Monday afternoon. About forty people sat staggered in an auditorium which could hold seven hundred. Tito Puente's big band echoed in the room with the volume of an enlarged symphony orchestra. The comedian delivered his jokes for his own amusement, and the small audience responded as if he were a favorite nephew entertaining in the family living room. The tap dancer sent a private message in heel-and-toe code, and the audience sent back its answer in applause. The male singer sang a Billy Eckstein–like arrangement and he was well received.

I walked onto the stage wearing my sky-blue chiffon gown and the blue high heels, dyed to match.

The first few calypso songs elicited only polite responses, but when I sang a Southern blues, long on moaning and deep in content, the audience shouted back to me, "Tell the truth, baby." And "Sing, tall skinny mamma. Sing your song." I was theirs and they were mine. I sang the race memory, and we were united in centuries of belonging. My last song was "Baba Fururu," a Cuban religious song, taught to me by Mongo Santamaria a year earlier when I had joined Puente on a tour of six Eastern theaters. Speaking only a few words of English, Mongo taught me the song syllable by syllable. Although he couldn't translate the lyrics, he said the song was used in black Cuban religious ritual.

That first Apollo audience consisted of grandparents, raising the children of their own absent children, and young women on welfare, too good to steal and too timid to whore, and young men, made unnecessary.

The Afro-Cuban song ignored hope and laid itself down in despair. The blue notes humped themselves and became the middle passage. They flattened and moaned about poverty and how it felt to be hated. The Apollo audience shouted. They had understood. When I returned and announced that my encore was another African song, called, in Swahili, "Freedom," they applauded, ready to go with me to that wished-for land.

I explained, "If you believe you deserve freedom, if you really want it, if you believe it should be yours, you must sing:

> "*U hu uhuru* oh yea freedom
> *U hu uhuru* oh yea freedom
> Uh huh Uh hum"

Willie Bobo, Mongo and Juliano set four-four, five-four and six-four times on conga, timbales and caracas, and I started singing. I leaned back on the rhythms and began

> "*O sawaba huru*
> *O sawaba huru*
> *O sawaba huru*"

I joined the audience on the refrain:

> "Oh yea, oh yea freedom
> uh huh
> uh hum
> uh hum
> uh hum."

The audience sang passionately. They were under my voice, before my voice. Understanding beyond my own understanding. I was the singer, the entertainer, and they were the people who were enduring. They accepted me because I was singing the anthem and carrying the flag.

By evening of the first day, I saw the power of the black grapevine. During the six o'clock show someone screamed from the audience, "Sing Freedom, Sing Freedom." It was my encore, so I had to sing the routine of planned songs. The audience clapped until I returned. I began, "If you believe you deserve freedom. If you…"

> "Uh huh *uhuru* yea freedom
> uh huh *uhuru* yea freedom
> uh huh *uhuru* yea freedom
> uh huh, oh yea free-dom."

The audience had it and gone.

"Just a minute. Some of you all know the song, but let me explain it to the folks who don't know."

A voice from the audience screamed. "All right, but don't wait for slowpokes. We ready to sing."

I continued with my explanation and the drums began. The audience pounded out the rhythm, moving it, controlling and possessing the music, the orchestra and me.

> "Uh, uh, oh huh.
> O yea, freedom,
> Uh huh. Uh huh"

As the song ended the small crowd thundered a hot appreciation. Even as I bowed, I knew the applause was only in a small part for me. I had been merely the ignition which set off their fire. It was our history, our painful passage and uneven present that burned luminously in the dark theater.

For six days and three shows per day, the tumultuous response was repeated. On the last day of the run, John and Grace brought Guy, Barbara and Chuck Killens. I watched the three teen-agers from a curtain peephole. The comedian's routines were beyond their understanding, the singer's laments about unrequited love didn't catch their concern. The tap dancer made his complicated routine seem too easy. When I went on stage the exoticism of seeing a familiar person in an unfamiliar setting did not hold their attention past the first few minutes. Before I finished my first song, I looked down and saw the three mumbling among themselves. When I finished, however, the children joined energetically with the audience on "Uhuru," not so much singing the music as screaming the words. Guy's cracking lopsided voice pierced high above the ensemble sound. Schiffman had been right and wrong. Some people sang better than I, but no one laughed me off the stage.

After the Killens and Guy left my dressing room, I prepared for the last show. I knew I would never again make an appearance as a singer. There was only one Apollo Theater, and no other place had the allure to melt my resolve. While the run had given me stature among my New York acquaintances, its real value was in the confidence it gave me. I had not won world-wide fame, or gained stunning wealth, but I was leaving show business at the right time: stepping down from the pinnacle of the Apollo stage. And an I-told-you-so imp had grinned behind my eyes all week long. Apollo audiences had been filling Frank Schiffman's ears with "Oh yea, oh yea, freedom," so he hadn't spoken to me since opening night. It was going to be an hallelujah time when he gave me my check. I finished the set and waited in the wings while the audience yelled for my return. I went back to the microphone and began, "Thank you, ladies and gentlemen. This last piece needs audience participation. It is a song from Africa. It's called 'Uhuru,' which means freedom. I'd like the people of this side of the theater to sing, *uh uhuru,* oh yea freedom"—the drums began to roll in a quick promise—"and this side..."

"Damn, why don't you do your act, girl? If you can't sing, come back on Wednesday. That's amateur night."

The man's voice came from the balcony, strident and piercing the dark theater like an unexpected light. My heart thumped, and I couldn't think of a thing to say. A few giggles from around the room encouraged him.

"Anyway"—his voice was meaner and louder—"anyway, if you like Africa so much, why don't you go back there?"

The only thing I knew was I would never get off the stage. Hell's eternity would find me rooted in front of the mute microphone, my feet glued to the floor. The baby-blue spotlight blinding me and holding me forever in that place. A grumble began in the balcony and was joined by sounds of displeasure on the main floor. I still couldn't move. Suddenly a lemon-sour voice from the front rows shouted, "Shut up, up there, you bastid. I paid money to come in here."

Some "yeahs" and "that's rights" popped up in the theater.

They angered my detractor. He shouted, "Go to hell, you old bitch. I paid for this shit too."

"Aw, cool it, goddammit. Let the woman sing," a man's bass voice ordered from the rear. "Yeah." Another man spoke from the balcony and sounded dangerously near to the heckler. "Yeah, you don't like it. Get your ass down on the stage and do what you can do."

That was it. Either there would be a bloody fight with cutting and shooting or the heckler was going to come on the stage, take the microphone and make me look even more foolish than I thought I was. I was surprised to realize that the drummers were still playing.

The woman, my first defender, lifted her voice...

"Freedom, freedom, freedom."

She was in tempo but the melody was wrong.

More voices joined, "Freedom, Freedom." The drums rolled on like an irate river. "Freedom, Freedom." The singers in the audience increased. "Freedom." The entire main floor seemed to have joined the drums. They had taken my side and taken the song away from me.

The bass voice cut through the music, "Sing girl, goddammit, sing the goddam song."

I sang "*O sawaba huru, O sawaba huru.* Oh yea. Oh yea, freedom." We didn't sing the song Olatunji had taught me, but we sang loudly and gloriously, as if the thing we sang about was already in our hands. My closing show reminded me of Mother's advice: "Since you're black, you have to hope for the best. Be prepared for the worst and always know that anything can happen."

When Schiffman gave me my check, we both grinned.

CHAPTER 4

I thought Godfrey Cambridge was one of the prettiest men I had ever seen. His features had the immutability of a Benin mask, and his white teeth were like flags of truce. His skin was the color of rich black dirt along the Arkansas River. He was tall and big and spoke English with the staccato accent of a New York–born descendant of West Indian parents. He was definitely the one.

He was introduced to me at a Greenwich Village party. He said that he was an unemployed actor, and because I mistook his curiosity for romantic interest, I pursued. We exchanged phone numbers and when I called and invited him to dinner, he accepted. Guy and Godfrey became a team in the first ten minutes. Guy enjoyed Godfrey's funny stories about his job as a taxi driver and his adventures auditioning for white musicals. We ate a four-course meal (I always used my cooking to enhance my sex appeal) and laughed a lot. After Guy went to bed, Godfrey and I sat in the living room listening to records and drinking cognac-laced coffee. To my disappointment, the jokes continued. Godfrey talked about crazy passengers, egotistic actors and tyrannical directors, and each story led to a punch line which begged for laughter. The stories became more forced and time moved haltingly. Despite my availability, my cooking and my willingness, together we ignited no passionate fires.

When I let him out of the house, he gave me a brother's kiss and I scratched him off my list as a possibility.

———

The Harlem church was full, with standees in the rear. A few white people sat in the middle rows, stiffly, not moving, not turning to look at the black people, who buzzed like hived bees. Godfrey and I had come to hear Rev. Martin Luther King, Jr. He had just been released from jail, and was in New York to raise money for the Southern Christian Leadership Conference and to make Northerners aware of the fight being waged in Southern states.

Five black men marched in single-file onto the rostrum, their solemnity a perfect foil for the raucous welcome of the audience.

The host minister introduced Wyatt Walker, a Baptist preacher whom I thought too handsome for virtue and too young for wisdom.

He spoke, in a purely Baptist voice, of Alabama and the righteous struggle for justice. Fred Shuttlesworth, another attractive minister, was introduced. I wondered if the SCLC had a policy of keeping the ugly preachers at home and sending only the good-looking ones to the North. Shuttlesworth leaned his thin body over the podium, jutting a black hawklike face at the audience. His words were sharp and his voice accusatory. He became a hatchet of a man. Chopping away at our geographic security. What were we doing in New York City, while black children were being set upon by dogs, black women were raped and black men maimed and killed? Did we think New York City could escape the righteous wrath of God? This was our chance to join the holy crusade, pick up the gauntlet flung down in hate, carry it through the bloody battleground to the region of peace and justice and equality for all. The audience stood up and the Reverend Shuttlesworth sat down.

Ralph Abernathy was introduced next. He moved slowly and quietly toward the podium. He stood a few seconds, looking down at his hands, which rested on top of the desk. His speaking voice was a surprise and his delivery a shock. He didn't have the fire of Walker or the anger of Shuttlesworth. His message was clear and quick, and in an unnerving way, the most powerful. The South was in a phase of change, and everyone must pay for change because everyone will benefit from change. As Christians, we all should be ready for change because if we think about it, Jesus was the greatest changer in history. He changed the idea of an eye for an eye, and a tooth for a tooth. He ran the moneylenders from the temple because they were cheating the people and taught forgiveness even of one's enemies. Rev. Abernathy reminded the audience that only with God could we develop the courage to change the unchangeable. When he moved, ponderously, slowly to his seat, there was a long moment when the audience sat still. Because his words had not been coated with passion or fashioned in eloquent prose, they took longer to swallow. The host minister rose again, and all rustling stopped. The room held its breath.

The preacher told us what we already knew about Martin Luther King, the dangers he had experienced and the triumphs he had won. The listeners didn't move. There was a yawping expectancy under the stillness. He was here, our own man, black, intelligent and fearless. He was going to be born to us in a moment. He would stand up behind the pulpit, full grown, and justify the years of sacrifice and the days of humiliation. He was the best we had, the brightest and most beautiful. Maybe today would be the day we would find ourselves free.

The introduction was over and Martin Luther King, Jr., rose. The audience, collectively, lost its composure, pews scraped against the floor as people stood, rearing back, pushing, leaning forward, shouting.

"Yes, Lord. Come on, Dr. King. Just come on."

A stout short woman in red, standing next to me, grabbed me around the waist and squeezed. She looked at me as if we were old friends, and whispered, "If I never drew another breath, I could die happy."

She released me and caught the arm of a man on her right, pulling the arm to her breast, cradling it and whispering, "It's all right, now. He's right here and its all right."

Martin Luther King, Jr., stood on the dais, away from the podium, allowing the audience full view of his body. He looked at the audience, smiling, accepting the adulation but strangely apart from it. After a minute, he walked to a position behind the podium and raised both hands. It was at once a surrendering and a quelling gesture. The church became quiet, but the people remained standing. They were trying to fill their eyes with the sight of the man.

He smiled warmly and lowered his arms. The audience sat immediately, as if they had been attached by invisible strings to the ends of his fingers.

He began to speak in a rich sonorous voice. He brought greetings from our brothers and sisters in Atlanta and in Montgomery, in Charlotte and Raleigh, Jackson and Jacksonville. A lot of you, he reminded us, are from the South and still have ties to the land. Somewhere there was an old grandmother holding on, a few uncles, some cousins and friends. He said the South we might remember is gone. There was a new South. A more violent and ugly South, a country where our white brothers and sisters were terrified of change, inevitable change. They would rather scratch up the land with bloody fingers and take their most precious document, the Declaration of Independence, and throw it in the deepest ocean, bury it under the highest mountain, or burn it in the most flagrant blaze, than admit justice into a seat at the welcome table, and fair-play room in a vacant inn.

Godfrey and I slid close, until our shoulders and thighs were touching. I glanced at him and saw tears glistening on his dark face.

Rev. King continued, chanting, singing his prophetic litany. We were one people, indivisible in the sight of God, responsible to each other and for each other.

We, the black people, the most displaced, the poorest, the most maligned and scourged, we had the glorious task of reclaiming the soul and saving the honor of the country. We, the most hated, must take hate into our hands and by the miracle of love, turn loathing into love.

We, the most feared and apprehensive, must take fear and by love, change it into hope. We, who die daily in large and small ways, must take the demon death and turn it into Life.

His head was thrown back and his words rolled out with the rumbling of thunder. We had to pray without ceasing and work without tiring. We had to know evil will not forever stay on the throne. That right, dashed to the ground, will rise, rise again and again.

When he finished washing us with his words, caressing our scarred bodies with his optimism, he led us in singing "Oh, Freedom."

Strangers embraced tightly; some men and women wept openly, choking on sobs; others laughed at the waves of spirit and the delicious tide of emotion.

Godfrey and I walked from Harlem to the Hudson River in near-silence. From time to time, he would throw his arm around my shoulder, or I would take his hand and squeeze it. We were confirming. We sat on a bench overlooking the sluggish water.

"So what's next? What are we going to do about it?" Godfrey beat me to the question and I had no answer. "We got to do something. Reverend King needs money. You know damn well we're not going down to Hang 'em High and let some cracker sheriff sap up on our heads. And we're not going to no Southern jail; so what are we going to do?"

He was asking the wind, the dark river and himself. I answered, "We could get some actors and singers and dancers together." Years before, Hollywood musicals had shown how young talented unknowns put on gloriously successful shows with no money, and although I was over thirty years old, I still believed in the youthful fantasy.

Godfrey said, "We can put on a show, maybe run it through the summer." When he grinned at our future success, he showed that he was as youthful and fanciful as I.

Godfrey had a friend, Hugh Hurd, an actor who knew everybody and had fabulous organizational skills. He would talk to Hugh. There were a lot of singers from *Porgy and Bess* who hadn't worked since the opera folded, and I agreed to talk to them.

It occurred to us that we should get permission from the people at the SCLC in order to raise money in their name. Godfrey said since I was the Christian, I ought to be the one to make the contact.

Within one hour our plans were laid. I would write a show, Godfrey would do a funny skit, and he and I would produce it. Hugh Hurd, if he agreed, would direct it. We would pay the performers and ourselves union scale, and all other monies would go to the SCLC. We had no idea where the show would be held, who would perform, how much we would charge or even whether the religious organization would welcome our intentions. There was a lot to do and we had to get started.

The SCLC offices were on 125th Street and Eighth Avenue in the center of Harlem. I had telephoned and made an appointment to speak to Bayard Rustin. When I walked up the dusty stairs to the second floor, I rehearsed the speech I had tried out on John Killens. "Mr. Rustin, I want to say first that not only do I and my colleague, Godfrey Cambridge, appreciate and laud the activities of Reverend Martin Luther King and the SCLC, we admire your own work in the field of race relations and human rights." John had told me that Bayard Rustin had led protest marches in the United States during the forties, worked to better the condition of the untouchables in India, and was a member of the War Resisters' League. "We want to show our appreciation and support by putting on a show here in New York. A show which will highlight the meaning of the struggle and, at the same time, raise money for the Southern Christian Leadership Conference." He couldn't possibly refuse the offer.

At the head of the stairs, a receptionist, sitting behind a warped wooden desk, told me that Mr. Rustin had been called away on an emergency mission, but Stanley Levison would see me. I was stopped. Could I still use my speech? Levison sounded Jewish, but then John Levy and Billy Eckstein were black men with Jewish names.

The woman spoke on the telephone and then pointed to a door. "Mr. Levison will see you now."

He was short, stockily built, well dressed and white. I had come to talk to a black man about how I and Godfrey, also black, could help ourselves and other black people. What was there to say to a white man?

Stan Levison waited. His square face blank, his eyes direct, unapologetic.

I began. "I am a singer. That is, I was a singer, now I'm a writer. I want to be a writer..." My poise was gone and I hated myself. How could I dream of confronting an entire country of bigots, when facing a lone white man threw me into confusion.

"Yes, and how can the SCLC help you?" He saw my indecision. In desperation, I leaped into my prepared speech. "I want to say first, that not only do I and my colleague, Godfrey Cambridge..."

"Oh the comedian, Cambridge. Yes, I've heard him." Levison leaned back in his chair.

"...appreciate and support..." I cut out the part about Bayard Rustin and finished with "and raise money for the SCLC."

Levison moved forward. "Where will the play be shown?"

"Uh." Dammit, caught again. If only Bayard Rustin had been in the office, I could have counted on a few minutes during which he would thank me for realizing who he was, and appreciating what he had done.

"We don't have a theater yet, but we will have one. You can bet your life we will get one." Insecurity was making me angry.

"Let me call in someone. He's a writer and might be able to help you." He picked up the telephone. "Ask Jack Murray to step into the office, please." He hung up the phone and asked, with only a little interest, "And what do you know about the SCLC?"

"I was at church yesterday. I heard Dr. King."

"Oh yes. That was a great meeting. Unfortunately, we didn't take in the money we expected."

The door opened, and a little man wearing brown slacks and an open shirt and sports jacket walked in, in a hurry. "Jack Murray" had sounded black, but he was as white as Stanley Levison.

"Yeah, Stanley. What is it?"

Levison stood, and waving his arm in my direction, said, "This is Miss Angelou. Maya Angelou. She had an appointment with Bayard, but he was called away. She's got an idea. Maya, this is Jack. He also works with the SCLC."

I stood and offered my hand to Murray, and watched a little-boy's smile cross his middle-aged face.

"Glad to know you, Miss Angelou. What's your idea?"

I explained that we wanted to stage a play, a kind of revue, using whatever good talent available, and that we planned to develop the show on the theme of liberation.

Stanley Levison laughed for the first time. "I was right to call in Jack. Do you know anything about *Pins and Needles*?" I didn't, so he told me that Jack Murray had been involved with *Pins and Needles* in the thirties and it became a Broadway show, but based on the problems of the working class.

"Do you have a theater?" Again, I had to confess that we, my colleague and I, hadn't got that far.

"How large is the cast? How long do you need for rehearsal?" His tone was friendly, but if I admitted that so far our plans had only gone as far as an emotional conversation on the banks of the Hudson, the two white men would think me childish.

I said, "We have a number of actors and on-call singers. My friend is out making contacts." I blathered on about the need to keep the cast good, but small, so that there would be a substantial amount of money left over for the Southern Christian Leadership Conference.

When Jack Murray got a chance to speak, he repeated, "How long will you need for rehearsal?" I spoke the first thought that offered itself to me. "Two weeks."

Stanley coughed. "That's a very short rehearsal period, isn't it?"

I looked at him and he seemed as solid as a bank building. Maybe he was right. Two weeks might not be enough time, but my ego was at stake.

"We're going to use black entertainers. Professional people." It was my intention to stop the irritating interrogation and put the two white men back in the white race where they belonged.

Stanley cleared his throat and chuckled, "Oh, Miss Angelou, you're surely not trying to tell us that Negro entertainers don't need the same time as white entertainers because they are just naturally endowed with talent?"

That was exactly what I had said, and exactly what I meant. But it sounded wrong coming out of the mouth of a white man. Arrogance prevented me from retraction and was about to lead me into a corner from which there was no escape.

"Black entertainers have had to be ten times better than anyone else, historically..."

Jack Murray's voice floated softly into my tirade, "Miss Angelou, I assure you, you don't have to convert the converted. Historically, the exploited, the enslaved, the minority, has had to strive harder and be more qualified just in order to be considered in the running. Stanley and I understand that. That's why we are full-time volunteers at SCLC. Because we understand."

I was grateful that his words were apt and his voice soothing; in the next eighteen months I was to find myself frequently in debt to Jack Murray for throwing life lines to me as I floundered in seas of confusion or frustration.

"Do you know the Village Gate?" Every performer in the United States had heard of the Greenwich Village night club where Lenny Bruce, Nina Simone and Odetta might be found playing on the same night.

Murray said, "Art D'Lugoff owns it and he's an okay guy. He usually has a few unbooked days during the summer. After your plans are a little further along, maybe we could have a little meeting with Art. How soon do you expect to be ready?"

"All we needed was permission from your organization. We'll be ready in a few days. When can I see Mr. Rustin?"

There was something wrong with asking white men for permission to work for my own cause.

Levison looked at me and without answering, picked up the telephone. "Has Mr. Rustin come in? Good. Let me speak to him."

I waited while he continued. "Bayard, I've got a young woman in here who is going to put on a play to raise money for the organization... Right. She had an appointment. She's coming in to see you now."

I shook hands with both men and walked out of the office. Stanley

Levison didn't say "wants to put on a play" but "is going to put on a play." An oblique permission, admittedly, but it was what I came for.

Bayard Rustin stood, shook my hand and welcomed me.

"Miss Angelou? Ah hum, sorry I wasn't here when you arrived. Stanley says you have a play. Have a seat. Care for coffee? Have you got money for your production? Cash? A theater? What is the play's message? While we at SCLC are grateful for all efforts, understandably what the play says or doesn't say can be of more importance than the money it raises. You understand that?" Words stepped out of his mouth sharply, fast, clipped in the accent of a British Army sergeant. He was tall, lean, dark brown and good-looking.

I explained again, revealing a little more to Bayard than I had to Stanley or Jack. Neither Godfrey nor I had any experience at producing a show, but we knew people and if the SCLC gave us the go-ahead, that's exactly what we would do. I added that Jack Murray had offered to intercede with Art D'Lugoff, and if that worked, we would use the Village Gate as a theater.

Bayard nodded and told me he'd have to see the script first and, if it was acceptable, the SCLC would approve and even lend us its mailing list.

The telephone rang before I could express my excited thanks. After speaking briefly into the receiver, he stood and offered his hand to me.

"Miss Angelou, an important call from Atlanta. Please excuse me. Get the script in to me as soon as possible. Thank you and good luck."

He was sitting back down even as we shook hands, his attention directed to the telephone.

I was out on the street. Burning to talk to Godfrey. We had permission, maybe we had a theater, we had the desire and the talent. Now all we needed was a cast, musicians and a script. I stopped on the corner of 125th Street. Hell, how did one write a script?

Godfrey brought Hugh to a diner on Broadway where we had scheduled our meeting. Hugh substantiated Godfrey's confidence; he acted efficient. His skin was the color of an unbroken coconut, and he looked just about as hard to crack.

His attitude was in contradiction to his youth, but Godfrey later explained to me that Hugh's parents, West Indians, also owned liquor stores, and Hugh had grown up coping with stock, greedy salesmen, shifty employees and drunken customers.

"Naturally," he "supported Martin Luther King. Any black man who didn't deserved to be thrown in an open ditch and covered with shit." Of course he would direct the show, but he needed absolute autonomy. Certainly he would work for scale and if things went well, he might contribute his salary to the SCLC, and where the hell was the script?

After a week, our plans were gelling. Godfrey had lined up actors. I telephoned singers and dancers, Hugh arranged with musicians, but we still had no script. I had sat late into the night trying to pick plots out of the air. We needed a story which had the complexity of *Hamlet* and the pertinence of *A Raisin in the Sun*. Facile ideas came swiftly and had to be discarded without regret. My characters had the predictability of a B cowboy movie and the naïveté of a Sunday School play.

Godfrey, Hugh and I met Jack Murray down at the Village Gate. Art D'Lugoff, reminding me of a tamed California bear, said we could use the theater on Sundays, Monday and Tuesday nights. We had to pay the lighting technician unless we furnished our own, but D'Lugoff would contribute the room free. By the way, what was the play about and could he see the script?

Guy had found a part-time job in a bakery nearby, and dawns found him showering and dressing, and me sitting at a typewriter, constructing plot after unacceptable plot and characters so unreal they bored even me.

One morning, Guy stood looking over my shoulder at the blank page in the typewriter.

"Mom, you know, you might be trying too hard."

I turned quickly and blurted, "This is important. It's for Martin L. King, for the SCLC, for black people everywhere. I can't possibly try too hard."

He stepped back, hurt by my brusqueness. "Well, I'm just reminding you of something you said all the time. 'If it don't fit, don't force it.' Bye, I'm going to work."

I hadn't spanked him since he was seven years old. Now that he was a tall fifteen-year-old the temptation to slap the water out of him was almost irresistible.

John Killens was expectedly sympathetic and, unfortunately, un-helpful. "You've got a theater and no cash, a cause and no play. Yep. Your work is cut out for you. Good luck. Keep trying."

Time and need had me in their clutches. Entertainers who had been contacted were calling Hugh or Godfrey every day; they in turn, telephoned me, asking when we could start auditions. I wasn't work-ing, so at fifteen Guy was the only breadwinner. His money provided food, and John and Grace lent me money for rent so that I didn't have to touch my small savings account. I needed the American Guild of Variety Artists scale I would receive once the play was on.

Desperation had triumphed the day Godfrey stopped by my house. He had dropped off a fare in the next block and decided to ring my bell and see if I was in.

When I opened the door and saw his face, I started crying. He stepped into the foyer and took me in his arms.

"I've had women scream when they saw me, and some broads laugh when I come up on them all of a sudden, but I never had anybody break down and start crying." He was patting my shoulder. "You're a first, baby. I appreciate what you're doing. You're a first. Cry on. Cry your heart out. I'm enjoying this."

I had to laugh.

"No, keep on crying. I'll write you down in my diary. I've heard of women who cry when a man leaves, but you cry when..."

Laughter defeated my tears. I led him into the living room and went to the kitchen for coffee. I washed my face and composed myself. The tears had been as much a surprise to me as they were to Godfrey.

"Godfrey, I can't write the play. I don't even know where to start."

"Well, hell, you start with Act I, Scene I, same way Shakespeare started."

My throat hurt and tears began to well up behind my eyes.

"I can't write the damn thing. I've agreed to do something I can't do."

"Well, don't do it, then. Nobody's going to die if you don't write the damn play. Fact is, it might be better if you didn't write a word. There's a lot of people who would be grateful not to have to sit through one more bad play. Personally, I wish a lot of playwrights would have said just what you said. 'I can't write the damn thing.' " He laughed at himself.

"But what can we do? The SCLC is waiting. Art D'Lugoff is waiting. Hugh and the entertainers are ready. And I'm the bottleneck."

He drank the coffee and thought for a minute. "We'll let the entertainers do their acts. Most of them have been out of work so long, they'll jump quicker than a country girl at a hoedown. You don't have to write a play. If you've got a skit or two, you can give it to them. We'll do a cabaret kind of thing. That's all."

When I realized that Godfrey's idea was workable, the burden of tension left my body and for the first time in weeks I relaxed and my brain started to function.

"We could ask them for songs and dances and turns particularly black."

"The old Apollo routines. Something like Redd Foxx and Slappy White. You know: 'I'm Fox' and the other one says, 'I'm White,' then Foxx answers, 'You're either a fool or you're color blind.' "

The ideas were springing. There was no reason to worry. We would have a show. We would raise money. The reputation I didn't even have was not going to be ruined.

Godfrey looked at his watch. "Gotta go. Some fool without a dime in his pocket is waiting to get me to take him to the Bronx." He got up. "This stop was okay. I helped a damsel in distress. Maybe my next fare will pay me in Canadian dimes."

We stood at the door and I looked at the rusted and dented taxi, illegally parked in front of my house.

"You could have got a ticket."

He said, "That would have been the only thing given to me today. You're okay now. We've got a show. A cabaret." He had the taxi door open.

I shouted, "We'll call it 'Cabaret for Freedom.' O.K.?"

"Yeah, that sounds serious. Entertaining and serious. Just what we ought to be. See you."

Straight out of the movies. We were the talented unknowns, who with only our good hearts, and those of our friends, would create a show which professional producers would envy. Our success would change the hearts of the narrow-minded and make us famous. We would liberate the race from bondage or maybe we would just go on and save the entire world.

At dress rehearsal, Guy and Chuck sat with me in the shadows of the Village Gate. Singers and dancers moved across the stage, making themselves familiar with the boards, and the microphone. Godfrey stood under the lights near the stage, and Hugh Hurd sat in the rear, clothed in the importance of being the director.

Jay "Flash" Riley started his comedy routine. His face and body jumped and skittered and his eyes opened and shut in rhythm; his lines were funny and unexpected, so the boys beside me howled in appreciation. Later a female singer, Leontyne Watts, sang a sultry, moaning song for a man loved and lost, and I identified with her song.

Although I had not really loved and lost, I was lonely and even missed the pedestrian love affair I left in Los Angeles. Godfrey and I were being molded into a friendship which had no room for romance. John Killens was concretely married; John Clarke had another interest and was, in any case, too hard for my liking. Sylvester Leeks had hugged me often, but never asked for my phone number. If I had the chance, I could moan some salty songs. I had been living with empty arms and rocks in my bed. I was only saved from utter abstinence by accidentally running into a musician who remembered me from my touring days. He lived on the Upper West Side and, once a week, I would visit his studio apartment. Because of the late hours of his job, he slept until after two. He told me he preferred me to catch him as he was waking. It kept him from having to make up the sofa twice and take two showers in the same day. I always left satisfied, so I was glad to oblige. We were not only not in love and just slightly in like, our weekly ferocious rendezvous stopped just short of doing each other bodily harm.

CHAPTER 5

On opening night, customers took every seat in the cavernous Village Gate. The Harlem Writers Guild members, their families and friends had arrived, and after wishing me luck, took seats near the stage. I imagined them, after the house lights dimmed, taking copious and critical notes in the dark. John and Grace Killens filled tables with their famous friends. Sidney and Juanita Poitier and Danny Barajanos, Lorraine Hansberry, Bob Nemiroff, Ossie Davis and Ruby Dee, an editor from the *Amsterdam News,* New York's black newspaper, a Brooklyn lawyer and a few politicians from Harlem.

Backstage the cast assembled, nervous over the presence of celebrities and excited with the expected opening night jitters. Bayard Rustin spoke to the performers in his tight, clipped voice, explaining the importance of the project and thanking them for their art and generosity. Godfrey made jokes about the opportunity to work, to be paid, and to do some good, all at the same time. I quoted Martin Luther King, "Truth dashed to earth shall rise again," and then Hugh Hurd asked us to leave so that he could give his cast a last-minute pep talk.

The show began and the performers, illuminated with the spirit, hit the stage and blazed. Comfortable with the material of their own routines, comedians made the audience howl with pleasure and singers delighted the listeners with familiar romantic songs. The revue, which is what the show had become, moved quickly until a scene from Langston Hughes's *The Emperor of Haiti* brought the first note of seriousness. Hugh Hurd, playing the title role, reminded us all that although as black people we had a dignity and a love of life, those qualities had to be defended constantly.

Orson Bean, the only white actor in the cast, shuffled up to the microphone and began what at first seemed a rambling remembrance. In minutes, the audience caught his point and laughed in appreciation. Leontyne Watts sang a cappella, "Sometimes I Feel Like a Motherless

Child," and everyone knew that the words meant that oppression had made orphans of black Americans and forced us to live as misfits in the very land we had helped to build.

The entire cast stood in a straight line and sang "Lift every voice and sing…"

The audience stood in support and respect. Those who knew the lyrics joined in, building and filling the air with the song often called "The Negro National Anthem."

After the third bow, Godfrey hugged me and whispered, "We've got a hit. A hit, damn, a hit."

Hugh Hurd said, "He's standing up out there."

Godfrey said, "Hell, man, everybody who's got feet is standing up."

Hugh said, "Aw, man. I know that. I mean Sidney. Sidney Poitier is standing up on the table." A few of us rushed to the sidelines, but were unable to see through the crush of people still crowding toward the stage.

The next afternoon, Levison, Godfrey, Hugh, Jack Murray and I met in Art D'Lugoff's office. We sat tall on the dilapidated chairs, proud of the success of Cabaret for Freedom.

Art said that not only could we use his night club without charge for five weeks, he would make his mailing list available. Stanley accepted the offer but said unfortunately there was no one in the SCLC office to take advantage of it. The small paid staff was swamped with organizational work, sending out direct-mail appeals, and promoting appearances of visiting Southern ministers. That was unfortunate because the mailing list included people out in Long Island and up in New Rochelle. People who wouldn't ordinarily hear of our revue, but who would support it and maybe even make contributions to SCLC if they could be contacted. Godfrey, Hugh and I looked at each other. Three white men were willing to lay themselves out for our cause and all I was ready to do was sing and dance, or at best, encourage others to sing and dance. The situation was too historic for my taste. My people had used music to soothe slavery's torment or to propitiate God, or to describe the sweetness of love and the distress of lovelessness, but I knew no race could sing and dance its way to freedom.

"I'll take care of it." I spoke with authority.

Stanley allowed a little surprise into his voice. "Are you volunteering? We can't afford to pay a salary, you know."

Hugh said, "I'll help any way I can." He understood that we just couldn't let the white men be the only contributors.

Godfrey smiled. "And, you know, me too."

Jack said, "You'll have to draft a release and you can type it on stencils. We've got a mimeograph machine in the office."

Stanley continued, "We can provide paper and envelopes, but you'll have to address the envelopes by hand. Some of the money you've already made can be used for postage. We can't use the franking machine for your project, I'm sorry, but we'll be glad to help you."

I had no idea of how to work a mimeograph machine, nor did I know what a stencil or franker was. The only thing I had understood, and which I knew I could do was address envelopes by hand. Again, and as damn usual, I had opened my mouth a little too wide.

Art shook hands and told me to pick up the mailing list the next day at a midtown address.

Outside in the afternoon sunshine, Stanley and Jack thanked us all again, and said they'd see me the next day. They hailed a taxi.

Godfrey, Hugh and I went to a bar across the street. Hugh said, "You were right, girl. I was proud of you and you know I meant what I said. I'll be up there to help whenever I can."

"Yeah." Godfrey paid for the drinks. "But you got to understand. I'm not going to address no envelopes. If I did, my handwriting is so bad, the post office would send the mail to the Library of Congress for framing and posterity. I'll drive you anywhere you want to go. I'll help you stuff the envelopes and I'll come over to your house and have dinner."

I told them I had never worked a mimeograph machine. Hugh asked if I could type a stencil. When I admitted that my two-finger typing had been limited to an occasional letter, they looked at me with wry alarm.

"You've got a hell of a lot of nerve. You volunteered to 'take care of it' and you don't know shit." Hugh spoke more with admiration than anger.

"She knows she's got to do it. Come hell or the Great Wall of China. She's got to do it. I'm betting on you, kid." Godfrey called out to the bartender, "Play it again, Sam. For my buddies and me."

I wrote a simple announcement of Cabaret for Freedom listing the actors, the producers and the director. The mimeograph machine was much simpler than I expected. I took Guy to the office with me the first day, and he explained how the machine worked. The stencils were a little more complicated, but after a while, I realized that all I had to do was take my time, admittedly a lot of time, typing the script. Soon Godfrey was taking hundreds of envelopes to the morning and afternoon post.

The Village Gate filled to capacity to see our revue. The actors were happy and after they were paid, some took bills from their pockets, offering the money to the SCLC.

"Did a gig last week. King needs this five dollars more than I do."

"I put my money where my mouth is. It's not much but..."

Time, opportunity and devotion were in joint. Black actors, bent under the burden of unemployment and a dreary image of cinematic and stage Uncle Tom characterizations, had the chance to refute the reflection and at the same time, work toward the end of discrimination.

After Cabaret for Freedom, they would all be employed by suddenly aware and respectful producers. After Martin Luther King won freedom for us all, they would be paid honorable salaries and would gain the media coverage that their talents deserved.

"Give me that check. I'm going to sign it over to the SCLC. I'm sticking this week."

It was the awakening summer of 1960 and the entire country was in labor. Something wonderful was about to be born, and we were all going to be good parents to the welcome child. Its name was Freedom.

Then, too soon, summer and the revue closed. The performers went back to the elevator-operating or waiting-on-tables jobs they had interrupted. A few returned to unemployment or welfare lines. No one was hired as a leading actor in a major dramatic company nor as a supporting actor in a small ensemble, or even as a chorus member in an Off-Off-Broadway show. Godfrey was still driving his beat-up cab, Hugh continued to work split shifts in his family's liquor stores, and I was broke again. I had learned how to work office machines, and how to hold a group of fractious talented people together, but a whole summer was gone; I was out of work and Guy needed school clothes.

During the revue's run, Guy had been free to spend his part-time salary on summer entertainment. He and Chuck Killens spent fortunes at Coney Island. They pursued the mysteries of pinball machines and employed the absence of adults to indulge in every hot-dog and spun-sugar fantasy of childhood.

Although Godfrey collected me when he could and took me to Harlem or delivered me back to Brooklyn, the money used for other transportation and the lunches at Frank's on 125th ate away at my bankroll. Rent was due again.

Grossman, a night-club owner from Chicago, phoned. Would I be interested in singing in his new club, the Gate of Horn? I kept the relief out of my voice with great effort. Two weeks at a salary which would pay two months' rent and pay for Guy's back-to-school clothes.

After I accepted the offer, with secret but abject gratitude, I began to wonder what to do with Guy.

Grace and John offered to let him stay at their house, but Guy wouldn't hear of that. He had a home. He was a man. Well, nearly, and he could look after himself. I was not to worry about him. Just go and work and return safely.

I called a phone number advertised in the Brooklyn black newspaper. Mrs. Tolman answered. I explained that I wanted someone who would come for three hours a day in the afternoon. Just cook dinner for my fifteen-year-old, clean the kitchen and make up his room.

I diminished her reluctance by saying that I was a woman alone, raising a boy, and that I had to go away for two weeks to work. I asked her over to the house to see how respectful my son was. I implied that he was well raised but didn't say that outright. If I was lucky, when I returned from Chicago, she'd use those words herself.

Despite the harshness of their lives, I have always found that older black women are paragons of generosity. The right plea, arranged the right way, the apt implication, persuade the hungriest black woman into sharing her last biscuit.

When I told Mrs. Tolman that if I didn't take the job in Chicago, I wouldn't be able to pay my rent or buy shoes for my son, she said, "I'll take the job, chile. And I'm going to take your word that you've got a good boy."

Convincing Guy that we needed a housekeeper demanded at least as much finesse. After I told him about Mrs. Tolman, I waited quietly for the minutes he needed to explain how well he could look after himself and how she was going to get in the way and how well he could cook and that he wouldn't eat a bite of her food and after all, what did I think he was? A little baby? And "Oh please, Mother, this is really boring."

"Guy, Mrs. Tolman is coming because of the neighborhood. I've been looking at it very carefully."

Against his will, he was interested.

"I'm convinced that a few professional burglars live down the street. Too much new furniture going in and out of the house. If those people don't see an adult around here, they may take advantage of the hours when you're away and clean us out."

He got caught in the excitement of the possibility of crime.

"You think so? Which people? Which house?"

"I'd rather not point the finger without knowing for sure. But I've been watching closely. Mrs. Tolman will come around three, she'll be gone by six. Since she's going to be here, she'll cook dinner for you and wash your clothes. But that's a front. She's really here to make the burglars think our house is always occupied."

He accepted the contrived story.

John understood Guy's display of independence, and told me it was natural. He urged me to go to Chicago, sing, make the money and come home to New York where I belonged. He would keep an eye on my son.

———

The modest Gate of Horn on Chicago's Near North Side was located only a few blocks from the plush Mr. Kelly's. The Gate had in warmth what Mr. Kelly's had in elegance. I arrived in the middle of the Clancy Brothers' rehearsal. Mike was at the microphone checking the sound system.

"Is this loud enough" Too loud? Can you hear us or are we blowing the ass back out of the room?"

The Irish accent was as palpable as mashed potatoes and rich as lace.

After the sound was adjusted, the brothers and Tommy Makem sang for their own enjoyment. Their passion matched the revolutionary lyrics of their songs.

> "... The shamrock is forbid by law
> to grow on Irish ground."

If the words Negro and America were exchanged for shamrock and Irish, the song could be used to describe the situation in the United States.

The Clancy Brothers already had my admiration when we met backstage.

Amanda Ambrose, Oscar Brown, Jr., and Odetta came to opening night. We sat together and made joyful noises as the Irish singers told their stories.

The two weeks sped by, punctuated by telephone calls to Guy, who was understandably "doing just fine," and to John Killens, who said everything was smooth. Oscar Brown and I spent long afternoons volleying stories. He was writing a play, *Kicks & Co.*, for Broadway and I bragged that I had just come from a successful run of Cabaret for Freedom, which I partly wrote and co-produced.

We set each other afire with anger and complimented ourselves on our talent. We were meant for great things. The size and power of our adversaries were not greater than our capabilities. If we admitted that slavery and its child, legal discrimination, were declarations of war, then Oscar and I and all our friends were generals in the army and we would be among the officers who accepted the white flag of surrender when the battle was done. Amanda's husband, Buzz, inspired by the fever of protest, made clothes for me based on African designs. Odetta, newly married, and radiant with love, was off to Canada. Before she left she gave me an afternoon of advice. "Keep on telling the truth, Maya. Stay on the stage. I don't mean the night-club stage, or the theatrical stage. I mean on the stage of life." And my Lord she was beautiful.

"And remember this, hon, don't you let nobody turn you 'round. No body. Not a living ass."

Closing night had been a hilarious celebration. The Clancy Brothers' fans had found room to accept my songs, and the black people who had come to hear me had been surprised to find that not only did they enjoy the Irish singers' anger, they understood it. We had drunk to each other's resistance.

The next morning Oscar stood with me in the hotel lobby as I waited to pay my bill.

A uniformed black man came up to me.

"Miss Angelou? There's a phone call for you from New York."

Oscar said he'd keep my place in the line and I went to the phone.

"Maya?" John Killens' voice was a spike, pinning me in place. "There's been some trouble."

"Trouble?" Somewhere behind my kneecaps there was a place that waited for trouble. "Is Guy all right?" The dread, closer than a seer's familiar, which lived sucking off my life, was that something would happen to my only son. He would be stolen, kidnapped by a lonely person who, seeing his perfection, would be unable to resist. He would be struck by an errant bus, hit by a car out of control. He would walk a high balustrade, showing his beauty and coordination to a girl who was pretending disinterest. His foot would slip, his body would fold and crumple, he would fall fifty feet and someone would find my telephone number. I would be minding my own business and a stranger would call me to the phone.

"Hello?"

A voice would say, "There's been trouble."

My nightmare never went further. I never knew how serious the accident was, or my response. And now real life pushed itself through the telephone.

"Guy is okay." John Killens' voice sounded as if it came from farther than New York City. "He's here with us. I'm just calling to tell you not to go to your house. Come straight here." Oh, the house burned down. "Was there a fire? Is anything left?" I had no insurance.

"There wasn't a fire. Don't worry. Just come to my house when your plane arrives. I'll tell you when you get here. It's nothing serious." He hung up.

Oscar Brown was at my side. His green eyes stern. He put his hand on my shoulder.

"You O.K.?"

"That was John Killens. Something's happened."

"Is Guy O.K.? What was it?"

"Guy's O.K., but John wouldn't say."

"Well, hell, that's a bitch, ain't it? Calling up saying something's wrong and not saying..." He went over and picked up my bags.

"You pay your bill, I'll bring the car to the front door."

The drive to the airport was an adventure in motoring and a lesson in conversational dissembling. Oscar made erratic small talk, driving with one hand, leaning his car around corners, passing motorists with such speed that our car threatened to leave the road entirely. His chatter was constantly interrupted with "Guy's O.K. Now, remember that." He would turn to look at me. Fixing a stare so intense it seemed hypnotic. Noticing that he was conducting a car, he would swivel his head occasionally and give a moment's attention to the road.

At the airport, he held me close and whispered. "Everything's going to be O.K., little mother. Call me. I'll be at home waiting."

I dreaded the flight. Afraid that I would begin to cry and lose control. Afraid that the plane would crash and I would not be around to look after Guy and take care of the unknown problem.

"Well, and isn't it the wonder of Maya?" The accent was unmistakable. I raised up and looked in the seat behind me. Mike Clancy was grinning over a glass of whiskey with Pat next to him. Liam and Tommy were seated across the aisle.

"You thought you could lose us, did you? Never, little darling. We have sworn to follow you to the ends of the earth. How's about a tipple to cinch the agreement."

I said I'd order something when the stewardess came around.

There was no need to wait. Mike had prepared against the eventuality of a stingy attendant or a plane run by teetotalers. He reached under the seat and when he straightened up, he was holding a bottle of whiskey. Pat pulled a glass from the pocket of the seat in front of him.

Mike said, "If you insist on frivolities such as ice and water, you'll wait until the serving lady comes. If not, I'll start pouring now and you tell me when to stop."

I didn't wait.

The trip was riotous. Many passengers were incensed that four white men and a black woman were laughing and drinking together, and their displeasure pushed us toward silliness. I asked Liam to translate a Gaelic song that I had heard him sing a cappella. He said he'd sing it first.

His clear tenor floated up over the heads of the already-irate passengers. The haunting beauty of the melody must have quelled some of the irritation, because no one asked Liam to shut up.

Mike tried in vain to start conversations with two stone-grey men who sat behind him, but they retained their granite aloofness.

As the plane landed in New York, we sang a rousing chorus of "The Wearing of the Green."

The Clancys offered to share a taxi into the city, but I said I was going to Brooklyn.

Brooklyn and Guy. My heart dropped and I sobered. The company and the drink had erased Guy and the problem from my mind.

I thanked them and got into a taxi with my bags and a load of new guilt.

What a poor kind of mother I was. Drinking and laughing it up with a group of strangers, white men at that, while my son was in some kind of trouble.

When the taxi arrived at John's house, I was abject as well as apprehensive.

Grace hugged me and smiled. "Welcome home, Maya." Her smile told me things couldn't be too bad. Mom Willie called from the dining room, "That her?" I answered and she walked into the foyer. She was looking serious and shaking her head. Her look and gesture said, "Well, boys will be boys, and that's life." That was a relief. I asked where Guy was. Grace said he was upstairs in Chuck's room but John wanted to speak to me first.

Mom Willie gave me coffee as John explained what happened. A group of boys had threatened Guy and John heard about it and decided Guy would be safer at his house until I returned.

I nearly laughed aloud. Only a disagreement among kids.

John continued, "The boys are a gang called the Savages. They killed a boy last month, and as he lay in the funeral home, the Savages went in and stabbed the body thirty-five times."

Oh my God.

"They terrorize everybody. Even the cops are scared of that bunch. When I heard that Guy had offered to fight them, I drove over to your house and got him. He didn't want to go. He had stuck all your butcher knives in the curtain at your door and told me he was waiting for them to come back. I said, 'Boy you'd better get your butt in this car.' I told the woman downstairs to tell the gang, when they came back, that his uncle came to get him."

Mom Willie spoke first. "Well, honey, raising boys in this world is more than a notion. Ask me about it. While they're young, you pray you can feed them and keep them in school. They get up some size and you pray some crazy white woman don't scream rape around them and get them lynched. They come of age and white men call them up to go fight, and you pray they don't get killed over there fighting some white folks' war. Naw. Raising a black boy makes you sit down and think."

John had respectfully waited for his mother to finish her remembrances. "I'll get Guy now." He went to the stairs and called, "Guy, come down. Your mother's here."

I heard the heavy steps rushing down the stairs and I wanted to stand, but my body wouldn't obey. Guy bounded into the kitchen and the sight of him brought tears to my eyes.

"Hi, Mom. How was the trip?" He bent down and kissed my cheek. "Gee, it's great to have you home." He read my face and stopped smiling. "Oh, I guess Mr. Killens told you about the little incident. Well, it wasn't really serious, you know." He patted my shoulder as if he were the reassuring parent, and I the upset child.

"What happened, Guy? How did you get involved with a gang like that? What—"

"I'll discuss that with you. Privately, please." He was back on his dignity, and I couldn't deflate him. Whatever the story, I had to wait until we were alone.

John understood and said he'd drop us off at home. Guy shook his head. "Thanks, Mr. Killens. We'll walk." He turned to me. "Where are your bags, Mom?"

I nodded toward the entry and he walked away.

Grace said, "He wants to be a man so much, my God. It would be funny if it wasn't so serious."

John said, "Everything in this society is geared to keeping a black boy from growing to manhood. You've got to let him try for himself."

I joined Guy at the door and we said good night to the Killens.

We walked through the dark streets, and as Guy asked about Oscar Brown and other Chicago friends, I saw phantoms of knife-wielding boys jumping from behind trees, hiding behind cars, waiting in gloomy doorways.

I asked Guy to tell me about the incident, adding that Brooklyn was more dangerous than New York City. He said, "Let's wait till we get home. But I'll tell you this, Mother." A pronouncement was on its way. "I don't want you to think about moving. I'm living here and I have to walk these streets. If we moved, the same thing could happen and then we'd move again. I'm not going to run. 'Cause once you do, you have to keep on running."

We walked the rest of the way in silence.

He made a pot of coffee for me and I sat waiting until he was ready to talk.

We sat opposite each other in the living room and I tried to keep serenity on my face and my hand on the coffee cup.

It had all begun with the housekeeper. One day, the week before, Mrs. Tolman had brought her granddaughter to our house. Susie was fifteen, cute and eager. She and Guy talked while Mrs. Tolman cooked and cleaned. The next day Susie came back with her grandmother. Again the teenagers talked and this time they played records. On the third morning, Susie came alone. They played records and, this time, they danced together in the living room. Susie said she liked Guy, really liked him. Guy told her that he was already dating a girl but that he appreciated Susie's honesty. She became angry and Guy explained that he and his girl friend didn't cheat on each other. Susie said Guy was stuck-up and thought he was cute. They had an argument and Guy put her out of the house.

I wondered if he meant he had asked her to go. He said no. He walked to the door and opened it and *told* her to get out.

He continued explaining that today when the bell rang, he opened the door and a fellow about eighteen was standing there. He said his name was Jerry and he was Susie's boyfriend. He said he was the chief of the Savages and he had just heard that Guy had hit Susie. Guy told him that was a lie. He balled up his fist and said, "If I ever hit anybody with this, no one has to ask if I hit them." He went on to explain to Jerry that Susie was angry because of a little run-in they had. He told Jerry to remember the old line about a woman scorned. Jerry had never heard the phrase and told Guy that he and his friends would be back in the afternoon and Guy could explain it then.

As soon as Jerry left the doorstep, Guy called Chuck Killens and told him about his visitors and asked him to come over and bring his baseball bat. He then went to the kitchen and gathered all my knives and placed them strategically in the lace curtain at the front door. He figured that with Chuck swinging the bat, and him parrying with a large knife and a cleaver, they could hold off at least eight of the Savages.

When I asked if he had heard of the gang before, he answered, "Everybody knows the Savages; a few of them even go to my school."

"How large is the gang?"

"Only fifteen active members. But when they have a rumble, they can get about thirty together."

And this crazy young army was threatening my son. He saw my concern.

"I'll handle it, Mom. We're going to live here and I'm going to walk the streets whenever I want to. Nobody's going to make me run. I am a man."

He kissed me good night and picked up the coffee cup. I heard him moving in the kitchen. In a few seconds, his bedroom door closed, and I remained, glued to my chair in the living room. After an hour or so, the bloody pictures of my son's mutilated body began to disappear. I went to the kitchen and filled the ice bucket, got a pitcher of water and the Scotch bottle. I brought my collection to the living room and sat down.

First I had to understand the thinking of the Savages. They were young black men, preying on other young black men. They had been informed, successfully, that they were worthless, and everyone who looked like them was equally without worth. Each sunrise brought a day without hope and each evening the sun set on a day lacking in achievement. Whites, who ruled the world, owned the air and food and jobs and schools and fair play, had refused to share with them any of life's necessities—and somewhere, deeper than their consciousness, they believed the whites were correct. They, the black youth, young lords of nothing, were born without value and would creep, like blinded moles, their lives long in the darkness, under the earth, chewing on roots, driven far from the light.

I understood the Savages. I understood and hated the system which molded them, but understanding in no wise licensed them to vent their frustration and anger on my son. Guy would not countenance a move to safer ground. And if I insisted, without his agreement, I could lose his friendship and thereby his love. I wouldn't risk that; yet something had to be done to contain the lawless brood of alienated teenagers.

As the sun's first soft light penetrated the curtains, I telephoned my musician lover in Manhattan. I told him quickly what had happened and what I needed. I had awakened him, but he heard my need and said he'd get up and be at my house in an hour or less.

He stood in the doorway, refusing my invitation to come in for coffee. He handed me a small box, a big grin, and wished me luck. Guy arose, showered, dressed, had a glass of milk, refusing breakfast. He ran out of the house, to warm up before a morning basketball game. He seemed to have forgotten that the Savages were out to get him. I calmed my fears by telling myself that fellows like the Savages were mostly night creatures, and that in the early mornings the streets were at their safest.

At nine o'clock, I telephoned Mrs. Tolman and told her I'd like to come over and pay her. She said she'd be waiting.

I took the pistol out of its fitted box and slipped it in my purse. The three blocks between our houses were peopled with workers en route to jobs, men washing cars and children running and screaming in such normal ways. I felt I had gone mad and was living in another dimension, removed totally from the textured world around me. I was invisible.

Mrs. Tolman introduced me to her buxom daughter, who was breast-nursing a baby. The woman said yes when I asked if she was also Susie's mother.

I gave Mrs. Tolman cash, counting out the bills carefully, using the time to pacify my throat so that my voice would be natural.

"Mrs. Tolman, is Susie here?"

"Why, yes. They just got up. I heard them laughing in her room."

Mrs. Tolman was happy to oblige.

Susie stood in the doorway leading to the kitchen. Her face was still sultry from sleep and she was pretty. If I had been lucky enough to have a second child, she could have been my daughter.

"Susie, I've heard about you, and I'm happy to meet you."

"Yeah," she mumbled, not too interested. "Nice to meet you too." I caught her as she was turning to go.

"Susie, your boyfriend is Jerry?" She perked up a little. "Yeah, Jerry's my boyfriend."

Mrs. Tolman giggled. "I'll tell the world."

"Where does he live? Jerry."

"He lives down the street. In the next block." She was pouting again, uninterested.

I spoke again, fast, collecting her thoughts.

"I have something for him. Can we go together to his house?"

She smiled for the first time. "He's not there. He's in my room."

Her mother chuckled. "Seem like that's where he lives."

"Could he come out? I'd like to have a few words with him."

"O.K." She was a sweet play pretty, in her baby-doll shortie night-gown and her hair brushed out around her face.

I sat with only a silly smile, looking at the nursing mother and the old woman who was pressing out the money in her lap.

"Here he is. This is Jerry." A young man stood with Susie in the doorway. A too-small T-shirt strained its straps against his brown shoulders. His pants were unbuttoned and he was barefoot. I took in his total look in a second, but the details of his face stopped and held me beyond my mission. His eyes were too young for hate. They glinted with promise. When he smiled, a mouthful of teeth gleamed. I jerked myself away from enchantment.

"Jerry. I'm Miss Angelou. I'm Guy's mother." He closed his lips and the smile died.

"I understand that you are the head of the Savages and you have an arrangement with my son. I also understand that the police are afraid of you. Well, I came 'round to make you aware of something. If my son comes home with a black eye or a torn shirt, I won't call the police."

His attention followed my hand to my purse. "I will come over here and shoot Susie's grandmother first, then her mother, then I'll blow away that sweet little baby. You understand what I'm saying? If the

Savages so much as touch my son, I will then find your house and kill everything that moves, including the rats and cockroaches."

I showed the borrowed pistol, then slid it back into my purse.

For a second, none of the family moved and my plans had not gone beyond the speech, so I just kept my hand in the purse, fondling my security.

Jerry spoke, "O.K., I understand. But for a mother, I must say you're a mean motherfucker. Come on, Susie." They turned and, huddling together, walked toward the rear of the house.

I spent a few more minutes talking to Mrs. Tolman about the trip and the weather.

We parted without mentioning my son, her granddaughter or my trim Baretta, which lay docile at the bottom of my purse.

Guy brought afternoon heat into the house along with gym clothes for the laundry. He was grinning.

"We won the game. I made ten shots." I acted interested. "I'm getting pretty good. Coach says I'm among his best athletes." He feinted and jumped.

"Good, dear. Oh, by the way, did you see any of the Savages at school?"

He stopped dribbling an imaginary ball and looked at me, surprised, as if I had asked if he had seen an extraterrestrial.

"Yeah. Sure I saw the guys this morning. I walked to school with some of the members. We talked." He started toward his room, protecting his masculine secrecy.

"Excuse me, but please tell me what you talked about. I'd really like to know."

"Aw, Mom." He was embarrassed. "Aw, I just made up something. I said my gang in California always fought to the death, but never on hearsay. And I said I'd meet him and one other person on neutral ground. With knives or fire or anything. I said I wasn't about to run. I told you, Mom, that I'd handle it." He grinned. "What's for dinner?"

I had to laugh. He was definitely my son, and following my footsteps, bluffing all the way.

I had only threatened the young vultures hovering over my son;

Guy had offered to literally fight fire with fire. Fortunately we were believed—because maybe neither of us was bluffing.

———

Revolución had accepted my short story. That it would appear only in Cuba, and probably in Spanish, did not dilute the fact that I was joining the elite group of published writers. The Harlem Writers Guild celebrated. Rosa Guy, a founding member, who had been in Trinidad when I joined the group, had returned and offered her house for the week's reading and a party in my honor.

Rosa was tall, beautiful, dark-brown and fiery. She danced, argued, shouted, laughed with an exciting singleness of mind. We were alike in boldness and fell quickly into a close friendship. She had been born in Trinidad, and although she had lived in New York City since she was seven years old, her speech retained a soft Caribbean slur.

CHAPTER 6

I made my way through the busy streets of Harlem, dressed in my best and wearing just enough make-up. Along the way, I received approval from lounging men or passers-by.

"Hey, baby. Let me go with you."

"Oowee, sugar. You look good to me."

"Let me be your little dog, till your big dog come."

I smiled and kept walking. The compliments helped to straighten my back and put a little swing to my hips, and I needed the approval.

I was en route to the SCLC to meet Bayard Rustin. I had seen him a few times at fund-raising parties since the closing of Cabaret for Freedom, but we had not had a private meeting since the first time in the organizational offices, and I imagined a thousand reasons why I had been asked to return.

The receptionist told me Mr. Rustin was waiting. He stood up and leaned over the crowded desk, offering me his hand.

"Maya, thank you for coming. Have a seat. I'll call Stan and Jack."

I sat and ran through my mind all the possibilities. There was a discrepancy in the figures from Cabaret for Freedom. They wanted me to produce another revue. They wanted me to write a play about Martin Luther King and the struggle. They didn't know I couldn't type, so they were going to offer me a job as secretary. They needed volunteers and...

Stan and Jack came in smiling (that could mean that the receipts had been O.K., but I wasn't sure).

We all shook hands, exchanged the expected small greetings and sat down.

Bayard said, "You speak first, Stanley."

Stan Levison cleared nonexistent phlegm from his throat. "Uh, Maya, you know we're proud and pleased at the way you handled Cabaret for Freedom."

Jack interrupted. "The content was brilliant. Just brilliant. The performers..."

Stanley harrumphed and continued, "We think you've got administrative talent." He looked at Bayard.

Just as I thought. I was going to be offered a typing job.

Bayard spoke. "We are going to have a shift in the organization and we're going to need someone, a trustworthy person, reliable, and someone who knows how to get along with people." He looked over at Jack.

It was Jack's turn. "We watched how you dealt with that cast. You kept order; and if anybody knows, I know the egos of actors. You never raised your voice, but when you did speak everyone respected what you had to say."

He nodded to Stanley, who began to speak immediately.

"You understand what the struggle is about. You did say you grew up in the South, didn't you?"

I nodded. Stamps, Arkansas, with its dust and hate and narrowness was as South as it was possible to get.

"We are sorry to say that Bayard is going to be leaving the SCLC."

I looked at Bayard. His long, handsome face was lined, and his eyes appeared troubled.

Oh, he was sick. He had to be sick to leave an organization he loved so dearly and had worked for so diligently. I was so saddened by my speculation that I did not connect Bayard's leaving and my invitation to the office.

"I'm going for a short rest." Distance was already in Bayard's voice, confirming my assessment. "And I'll be joining A. Phillip Randolph and the Brotherhood of Sleeping Car Porters." His face said he was already there.

I said, "I'm sorry to hear that, Bayard. Is there anything I can do?"

"Yes." Bayard was back with us, connected again to the office conversation. "We're looking around for someone to take my place. I suggested that you were capable."

Only shock, which held me viselike, prevented me from jumping and running out of the office and down the street. Take Bayard Rustin's place. He had worked for the Quakers, led marches in Washington, D.C., during the forties, had been to India and worked with the Untouchables. He was educated, famous, and he was a man.

I didn't say anything because I couldn't speak.

Stanley said, "When Bayard came up with your name, we were quite surprised. But we've thought about it and come to an agreement. You're the person we would all like to run the office."

Jack nodded a slight happy smile to me.

Bayard said, "The position that's being offered to you, Maya, is coordinator for the SCLC. Of course, that's a little like an umbrella. Many chores fall under its spread."

I blurted out stupidly, "I can't type."

The men laughed, and I could have kicked myself for giving them the chance to patronize me.

Jack said, "You'll have a secretary to do your typing." He laughed again. "And answer your telephone."

Stanley said, "Now, let's talk salary. You know the SCLC is in need of money and always will be, so we are able to pay only a living wage."

I was torn. I could think of nothing more gratifying than to work for Martin Luther King, and the Lord knew I needed a living wage. But maybe bodaciousness was leading me to a dangerous height where I'd find breathing difficult. And another nagging uneasiness intruded upon my excitement: Suppose I was being used to force Bayard out of his position.

I gathered myself and stood. "Gentlemen, thank you. I am honored by your invitation. I'd like to think about it. I'll telephone you tomorrow." And I was out the door, down the stairs and back to the safety of Harlem streets.

John Killens agreed to meet me at a downtown hotel where he had taken a room to do a rewrite. We sat in the hotel dining room.

"If you feel that way, call Bayard. Ask him directly. He's a man. Personally, I don't believe he'd have suggested you if he didn't want you to take the job."

"All right, but what is a coordinator? Can I do it? I'd rather not try than try and fail."

"That's stupid talk, Maya. Every try will not succeed. But if you're going to live, live at all, your business is trying. And if you fail once, so what? Old folks say, Every shuteye ain't sleep and every goodbye ain't gone. You fail, you get up and try again."

He could talk, he was already a success. I wasn't convinced.

"Anyway, coordinator is a nice way of saying fund-raiser. You'll be putting on affairs and sending out mailing lists and speaking and arranging speaking engagements to raise money. There's no mystery to that. And if you're not going to sing again 'ever in life,' then this sounds like your best bet."

Bayard met me between appointments. "If you take the position or if you refuse it, I'm leaving. Understand now, I will always support Martin. Even with my life. But it's time for a move."

He stood beside my barstool at Frank's Restaurant on 125th Street. "I've worked with Randolph for many years and he wants to build a new organization for union workers. I'm not leaving the war, just joining another battle. Take it. You'll do a good job." He patted my shoulder and walked out, taking his mystery and leaving me still not quite decided.

———

I heard on the morning radio that some black youngsters had sat down at a dining-room counter in North Carolina and that Martin was in jail again. The telephones rang constantly and the office swirled with activity. Hazel Grey, who had come to work as my assistant, was allotting chores to volunteers as I walked in. She looked up from her desk.

"Maya, the printing returned and a bunch of kids from Long Island are coming over this morning to stuff envelopes."

"Good." I walked into my office. Hazel followed. "They're coming from an all-white school."

"Why? Who invited them and how old are they?"

"High school students. Boys and girls. Their counselor called; he's coming with them." That white youngsters were going to brave Harlem was in itself startling, but that a white adult, in a responsible position, not only agreed, but was willing to officiate in the unusual situation was befuddling. It looked as if the world that would never change was changing.

I had a brief meeting with the black volunteers.

"You're going to have some help in an hour or two with jobs you've been unable to complete."

A grandmother from a local church said, "Bless the Lord."

I went on, "Thirty young people are on their way, and we have to decide on how they can help us. We may not have this opportunity again. Now, you tell me what needs to be done."

"The mimeograph machine needs to be moved away from the window. The sunshine is melting the ink."

"I wish somebody would take all that junk out of the back office."

"Somebody ought to file that stack of papers in the hall."

"We need the steps cleaned. Don't look right to come to Martin Luther King's office and have to walk up dirty steps."

The counselor looked like an old Burgess Meredith. He was dressed in grey and looked as grey as a winter sky. His casualness was studied and his contrived shamble attractive. He was shorter than most of his charges.

"Miss Angelou, these students have been excused from their classes. In support of the students sitting in in North Carolina, they chose to give the day to the Martin Luther King organization. We are ready to do whatever job you assign us."

He stood in the middle of the youthful energy like a dull drake among a brood of white ducklings.

I called in the volunteer captains and introduced them. Hazel and I sat through lunch in my office. We chuckled over the white youngsters who were scrubbing the steps and sweeping the floor and doing the jobs for us which were being done in their homes and in their streets by black women and men. We knew that what we were seeing was a one-time phenomenon, so were determined to enjoy it.

The children and their counselor filed in to say goodbye. They accepted my thanks and the thanks of the SCLC. I made a little speech about the oneness of life and the responsibility we all had to make the world livable for everyone. They left and we turned up the volume on the news station. Martin was still in jail. The police had dragged the blacks out of the diner. The North Carolina black community was angry, but nothing had happened yet. The office was drifting back to normal when Hazel buzzed my phone.

"Hey, Maya. Got something else for you. Are you ready?"

"Yes."

"Two groups of whites are coming tomorrow and a high school class from an integrated school. Have we got work for them?"

I listened, speechless.

Hazel laughed, "I asked you if you were ready."

The weeks ran together, the days raced. White and black people were changing as Martin Luther King traveled to and from jail and across the United States, his route covered by the national media. Malcolm X could be seen stripping white television reporters of their noise on the evening news. In Harlem, the Universal Negro Improvement Association formed in the twenties by Marcus Garvey was being revived, and the Ethiopian Association was coming back to life.

White movie stars attracted by Harry Belafonte and Sidney Poitier were lending their names to the struggle, and their sincerity stood up against the most suspicious scrutiny. One evening at Belafonte's house, Shelley Winters explained why she was glad to contribute her money and her time to the SCLC.

"It's not that I love Reverend King or all black people or even Harry Belafonte. I have a daughter. She's white and she's young now, but when she grows up and finds that most of the people in the world are black or brown or yellow, and have been oppressed for centuries by people who look like her, she's going to ask me what I did about it. I want to be able to say, 'The best I could.' " I was still suspicious of most white liberals, but Shelley Winters sounded practical and I trusted her immediately. After all, she was a mother just like me, looking after her child.

At home Guy talked about the movement. I was pleased that he and Chuck had joined a youth group of the Society Against Nuclear Energy, and I gave him permission to participate in a march protesting nuclear war.

Avoiding the evening subway rush, I always stopped in a bar near the 125th Street stop of the A train. The place was rough because its bartender and regulars were living lives of little gentleness.

The ice would slide away in my glass while street-wise men and world-wise women marveled over the nation's excitement.

"You see them Negroes in North Carolina. They mean business."

"Charlie better straighten up. We're tired of this shit."

"Man, that Martin Luther King. He's not a man made of blood."

"He's a fool. Love your enemies? Jesus Christ did that and you saw what happened to him."

"Yeah, they lynched him."

"Black people ought to be listening to Malcolm X. He's got it right. Crackers are blue-eyed devils."

"I don't go for that hate talk. Negroes ain't got time to be hating anybody. We got to get together."

I returned from lunch. In the outer office Millie Jordan was working over a table of papers. Hazel was busy on the telephone. I walked into my office and a man sitting at my desk, with his back turned, spun around, stood up and smiled. Martin King said, "Good afternoon, Miss Angelou. You are right on time."

The surprise was so total that it took me a moment to react to his outstretched hand.

I had worked two months for the SCLC, sent out tens of thousands of letters and invitations signed by Rev. King, made hundreds of statements in his name, but I had never seen him up close. He was shorter than I expected and so young. He had an easy friendliness, which was unsettling. Looking at him in my office, alone, was like seeing a lion sitting down at my dining-room table eating a plate of mustard greens.

"We're so grateful for the job you all are doing up here. It's a confirmation for us down on the firing line."

I was finally able to say how glad I was to meet him.

"Come on, take your seat back and tell me about yourself."

I settled gratefully into the chair and he sat on the arm of the old sofa across the room.

"Stanley says you're a Southern girl. Where are you from?" His voice had lost the church way of talking and he had become just a young man asking a question of a young woman. I looked at him and thought about the good-looking sexy school athlete, who was invariably the boyfriend of the high-yellow cheerleader.

I said, "Stamps, Arkansas. Twenty-five miles from Texarkana."

He knew Texarkana and Pine Bluff, and, of course, Little Rock. He asked me the size and population of Stamps and if my people were farmers. I said no and started to explain about Mamma and my crippled uncle who raised me. As I talked he nodded as if he knew them personally. When I described the dirt roads and shanties and the little schoolhouse on top of the hill, he smiled in recognition. When I mentioned my brother Bailey, he asked what he was doing now.

The question stopped me. He was friendly and understanding, but if I told him my brother was in prison, I couldn't be sure how long his understanding would last. I could lose my job. Even more important, I might lose his respect. Birds of a feather and all that, but I took a chance and told him Bailey was in Sing Sing.

He dropped his head and looked at his hands.

"It wasn't a crime against a human being." I had to explain. I loved my brother and although he was in jail, I wanted Martin Luther King to think he was an uncommon criminal. "He was a fence. Selling stolen goods. That's all."

He looked up. "How old is he?"

"Thirty-three and very bright. Bailey is not a bad person. Really."

"I understand. Disappointment drives our young men to some desperate lengths." Sympathy and sadness kept his voice low. "That's why we must fight and win. We must save the Baileys of the world. And Maya, never stop loving him. Never give up on him. Never deny him. And remember, he is freer than those who hold him behind bars."

Redemptive suffering had always been the part of Martin's argument which I found difficult to accept. I had seen distress fester souls and bend peoples' bodies out of shape, but I had yet to see anyone redeemed from pain, by pain.

There was a knock at the door and Stanley Levison entered. "Good afternoon, Maya. Hello, Martin. We're about ready."

Martin stood and the personal tenderness disappeared. He became the fighting preacher, armed and ready for the public fray.

He came over to my desk. "Please accept my thanks. And remember, we are not alone. There are a lot of good people in this nation. White people who love right and are willing to stand up and be counted." His voice had changed back to the mellifluous Baptist cadence raised for the common good.

We shook hands and I wondered if his statement on the existence of good whites had been made for Stanley's benefit.

At the door, he turned. "But we cannot relax, because for every fair-minded white American, there is a Bull Connor waiting with his shotgun and attack dogs."

I was sitting, mulling over the experience, when Hazel and Millie walked in smiling.

"Caught you that time, didn't we?"

I asked her if she had set up the surprise. She had not. She said when Martin came in he asked to meet me. He was told that I was due back from lunch and that I was fanatically punctual. He offered to play a joke by waiting alone in my office.

Millie chuckled. "He's got a sense of humor. You never hear about that, do you?"

Hazel said, "It makes him more human somehow. I like a serious man to be able to laugh. Rounds out the personality."

Martin King had been a hero and a leader to me since the time when Godfrey and I heard him speak and had been carried to glory on his wings of hope. However, the personal sadness he showed when I spoke of my brother put my heart in his keeping forever, and made me thrust away the small constant worry which my mother had given me as a part of an early parting gift: Black folks can't change because white folks won't change.

During the next months, Mother's warning dwindled further from my thoughts. The spirit in Harlem was new and old and dynamic. Black children and white children thronged the streets, en route to protest marches or to liberation offices, where they did small but important chores. Black Nationalists spoke on street corners, demanding freedom now. Black Muslims charged the white community with genocide and insisted on immediate and total segregation from the murdering blue-eyed devils. Wells Restaurant and the Red Rooster served the best soul food and offered great music at evening sessions to parties of blacks and whites and visiting African diplomats. The Baby Grand, where Nipsy Russell had played for years, had closed, but the Palm Café was a haven for hard drinkers and serious players. The *Amsterdam News* was vigilant in its weekly attack against the "forces of evil," and G. Norwood, one of its social and political columnists, kept the community informed on who was doing what, to whom and with how much success.

The national mood was one of action, and the older groups, such as the NAACP and the Urban League, were losing ground to progressive organizations. Young blacks had begun calling Roy Wilkins a sellout Uncle Tom and Whitney Young, a dangerous spy. Only Martin and Malcolm commanded respect, and they were not without detractors.

—

The Harlem Writers Guild meeting at Sarah Wright's house was ending. As we were saying goodbye, Sarah's phone rang. She motioned us to wait and answered it. When she hung up, she said excitedly that the Cuban delegation to the United Nations, led by President Castro, had been turned out of a midtown hotel. The group was accused of having brought live chickens to their rooms, where they were to use them in voodoo rites. The entire delegation had been invited to the Teresa Hotel in Harlem.

We all shouted. Those few writers and would-be writers who were not members of Fair Play for Cuba nonetheless took delight in Fidel Castro's plucky resistance to the United States.

In moments, we were on the street in the rain, finding cabs or private cars or heading for subways. We were going to welcome the Cubans to Harlem.

To our amazement, at eleven o'clock on a Monday evening, we were unable to get close to the hotel. Thousands of people filled the sidewalks and intersections, and police had cordoned off the main and side streets.

I hovered with my friends on the edges of the crowd, enjoying the Spanish songs, the screams of "*Viva* Castro," and the sounds of conga drums being played nearby in the damp night air.

It was an *olé* and hallelujah time for the people of Harlem.

Two days later, Khrushchev came to visit Castro at the Teresa. The police, white and nervous, still guarded the intersection of 125th Street and Seventh Avenue, which even in normal times was accepted as the most popular and possibly most dangerous crossroad in black America.

Hazel, Millie and I walked down a block from the office, pushing through the jubilant crowd. We watched as Castro and Khrushchev embraced on 125th Street, as the Cubans applauded and the Russians smiled broadly, showing metal teeth. Black people joined the applause. Some white folks weren't bad at all. The Russians were O.K. Of course, Castro never had called himself white, so he was O.K. from the git. Anyhow, America hated Russians, and as black people often said, "Wasn't no Communist country that put my grandpappa in slavery. Wasn't no Communist lynched my poppa or raped my mamma."

"Hey, Khrushchev. Go on, with your bad self."

Guy left school, without permission, to come to Harlem with a passel of his schoolmates.

They trooped into the SCLC office after the Russian and Cuban delegations had left the neighborhood for the United Nations building.

Millie called and told me my son was in the back, stamping envelopes.

Surprise and a lack of sensitivity made me confront him before his friends.

"What are you doing here? You're supposed to be in school."

He dropped the papers and said in a voice cold and despising, "Do you want to speak to me privately, Mother?"

Why couldn't I know the moment before I had spoken what I knew as soon as my question hit the air. I turned without apology and he followed.

We stopped and faced each other in the hallway.

"Mother, I guess you'll never understand. To me, a black man, the meeting of Cuba and the Soviet Union in Harlem is the most important thing that could happen. It means that, in my time, I am seeing powerful forces get together to oppose capitalism. I don't know how it was in your time, the olden days, but in modern America this was something I had to see. It will influence my future."

I looked at him and found nothing to say. He had an uncanny sense of himself. When I was young I often wondered how I appeared to people around me, but I never thought to see myself in relation to the entire world. I nodded and walked past him back to my office.

Abbey, Rosa and I decided what was needed was one more organization. A group of talented black women who would make themselves available to all the other groups. We would be on call to perform, give fashion shows, read poetry, sing, write for any organization from the SCLC to the Urban League that wanted to put on a fund-raising affair.

CHAPTER 7

For six months I had been coordinator of the SCLC. I knew how to contact reliable philanthropists, the first names of their secretaries, and which restaurants the donors used for lunches. I carried a briefcase, and sat on subways, sternly studying legal papers. I was called Miss Angelou in my office and took copious notes in business conferences with Stan Levison and Jack Murray. Martin Luther King was sacred and fund-raising was my calling. Days were crammed with phone calls, taxi rides and serious letters reminding the mailing list that freedom was costly and that a donation of any amount was a direct blow against the citadel of oppression which held a helpless people enthralled.

After a day of such heart-stirring acts, I would travel back to my apartment. Somewhere after sunset and before I reached Brooklyn, the glorious magic disappeared. When I stepped off the subway at Park, I was no longer the bright young woman executive dedicated to Justice, Fair Play for Cuba and a member of the Harlem Writers Guild. I was an unmarried woman with the rent to pay and a fifteen-year-old son, who had decided that anything was better than another dull evening at home with Mother. Secretly, I agreed with him.

Tony's Restaurant and Bar on nearby Sterling Place became a sanctuary. It was not so dull that it attracted churchgoing families exclusively, nor so boisterous as to promise company combined with danger to unescorted women.

The first time I went into Tony's, I chose a barstool and ordered a drink, offering my largest bill, and invited the bartender to take out enough for one for himself. (Vivian Baxter told me when I was seventeen and on my own that a strange woman alone in a bar could always count on protection if she had treated the bartender right.)

He poured out my second drink loosely, allowing the gin to spill over the measuring jigger, then he told me his name.

Teddy was a small, neat man, his light toast-colored skin pulled tight across his face. He had large, slow eyes, which raked the bar while his little hands snapped at bottles, glasses and ice, and he talked with everyone along the counter, stepping into and out of conversations without losing a name or mixing up a drink.

"New in the neighborhood?" He carried drinks to the end of the bar, collected money, rang the register and asked, "Where're you from?"

"Are you a working girl or do you have a job?"

The softness of his voice belied the fact that he was asking if I was a prostitute. I knew better than to act either ignorant or offended. I said my name was Maya. I was from California and I had a job in Manhattan, lived alone with my teenage son three blocks away.

He returned from the other end of the bar carrying a drink.

"This one's on me, Maya. I want you to feel at home. Come in anytime."

I left a good tip, thanked him and decided to return the next evening.

Within a month, Teddy and I had a sly joking relationship, and the regulars nodded to me coolly but without hostility.

Appearances to the contrary, there is a code of social behavior among Southern blacks (and almost all of us fall into that category, willingly or not) which is as severe and distinct as a seventeenth-century minuet or an African initiation ritual. There is a moment to speak, a tone of voice to be used, words to be carefully chosen, a time to drop one's eyes, and a split-second when a stranger can be touched on the shoulder or arm or even knee without conveying anything more than respectful friendliness. A lone woman in a new situation knows it is correct to smile slightly at the other women, never grin (a grin is proper only between friends or people making friendship), and nod to unknown men. This behavior tells the company that the new woman is ready to be friendly but is not thirsting after another woman's mate. She should be sensual, caring for her appearance, but taking special care to minimize her sexuality.

The big man and I had noticed each other several times, but, although he was always alone, he had never spoken to me. One evening I walked into the bar and settled myself on a corner stool. Teddy served me my first drink and called me the Harlem Girl Friday. Then the man called from his stool at the bar's extreme end.

"Hey, Bar, that one's on me."

Teddy looked at the man, then at me. I shook my head. Teddy didn't move, but his eyes swung back to the man, who nodded, accepting my refusal.

Accepting the first drink from a strange man is very much like a nice girl having sex on a first date. I sat waiting for the second offer.

"My name is Tom, Maya, why won't you have a drink with me?"

I hadn't seen him move and suddenly he was close enough for me to feel his body heat. He spoke just above a whisper.

"I didn't know you, I didn't know your name. A lady can't drink with a nameless man." I smiled, pressing my cheek muscle down to show the hint of a dimple.

He was a reddish-tan color which Southern blacks called mariney. His face was freckled and his smile a blur of white.

"Well, I'm Thomas Allen. I live on Clark off Eastern Parkway. I'm forty-three and unmarried. I work in Queens and I work hard and I make pretty good money. Now you know me." He raised his voice, "Bar, give us another one like that other one," then dropped his voice. "Tell me, why are you all alone? Have the men gone blind?"

Although I knew it was an expected move in the courting game, flirting made me uncomfortable. Each coy remark made me feel like a liar. I wiggled on the stool and giggled and said, "Oh, stop."

Thomas was smooth. He led, I followed; at the proper time he withdrew and I pulled forward; by the end of our introductory ceremony, I had given him my address and accepted an invitation to dinner.

We had two dinner dates, where I learned that he was a bail bondsman and divorced. I went to his house and received lavish satisfaction. After a few nights of pleasure I took him home to meet my son.

He was Tom to his friends, but to establish myself as a type different from the people he knew, I called him Thomas. He was kind to me, always speaking gently, and generous to Guy. We were a handsome trio at the movies, at the zoo, and at Coney Island. His family treated me with courtesy, but the looks they traded with each other spoke of deep questions and distrust. What did I want with their brother? A grown woman, who had been in show business and the Good Lord knew what else. Her teenage son, whose sentences were threaded with big words, who talked radical politics and went on protest marches. What was Tommy going to do with them? And for goodness' sake, she wasn't even pretty, so what did he see in her?

If they had asked me, instead of each other, I could have informed them with two words: sex and food.

At first, my eagerness in the bedroom shocked him, but when he realized that I wasn't a freak, just a healthy woman with a healthy appetite, he was proud to please me. And I introduced him to Mexican and French menus, spreading glories of food on my dining-room table. We enjoyed each other's gifts and felt easy together. I had only one regret. We didn't talk. He never introduced a subject into our evenings and answered with monosyllables to any questions asked.

After the most commonplace greetings, our conversations were mostly limited to my shouting in his bedroom and his grunts at my dining-room table. He treated my work at the SCLC as just another job.

A large donation or a successful money drive would send me away from the office sparkling. Thomas would accept the news with a solemn nod, then thump the newspaper, so that I would know he was really busy reading. His replies to questions about the quality of his workday were generally given in a monotone.

"It was O.K."

Were any interesting people arrested?

"No. Just the same old whores and pimps and murderers."

Aren't some of those criminals dangerous?

"Walking down the street is dangerous."

Wasn't he ever afraid of gun-toting criminals?

"I've got a gun too, and a license to carry it."

But for my arrogance, our relationship would never have progressed beyond the reach of our carnal appetites.

The Writers Guild had met at Rosa's apartment and people were arranging rides to a late-night party in Harlem. I declined, saying Thomas was coming to take me home.

Someone suggested I bring him to the party, but before I could respond, another writer asked if it was true that fella was a bail bondsman. He was a bail bondsman, so what? The woman said, "Humph," and hunched her shoulders. "Well, I hope you're not getting serious about him. Because he sure as hell wouldn't be welcome in my house. They're as bad as cops. Living on poor folks' misery."

I had no time to think of the consequences of what I was going to say. The woman, of course, was not my friend, but even a polite acquaintance would not have tried to embarrass or challenge me in public. She had never bought me a pound of dried lima beans and was utterly unable to make me ugly up my face between the sheets. She could blow it out of her behind.

"I'm marrying him, and I'm tearing up your invitation to the wedding."

John Killens turned. "What the hell you say?"

Rosa, who knew all my secrets, widened her eyes and asked, "Since when?"

I dealt with all the questions with a coolness I didn't feel.

It was true that Thomas had not asked me to marry him, and Guy had no special regard for him. I knew I wasn't in love with him, but I was lonely and I would make a good wife. I could cook, clean house and I had never been unfaithful, even to a boyfriend. Our lives would be quiet.

I was getting used to the idea and even liking it. We'd buy a nice house out on Long Island, where he had relatives. I would join a church and some local women's volunteer organizations. Guy wouldn't mind another move if he was assured that it was definitely the last one. I would let my hair grow out and get it straightened and wear pretty hats with flowers and gloves and look like a nice colored woman from San Francisco.

When I told Thomas that I wanted to get married, he nodded and said, "I've been thinking about that myself. I guess it's time."

Guy accepted the news gravely. After a few seconds of silence, he said, "I hope you'll be happy, Mother." He turned away, then back again, "We'll be moving again, won't we?"

I lied about my daydreams, reminding him that Thomas had a large apartment only blocks from our house, which meant that he wouldn't have to change schools again. I thought to myself, maybe we wouldn't buy our house on Long Island until Guy went away to college.

My announcement was cheerfully received at the office. Hazel hugged me and said, "There's nothing like having a good man." She was happily married, so I expected her response.

Abbey looked at me quizzically. "Maya Angelou, I hope you know what you're doing."

"I don't, but I'm going to pray a lot."

She laughed and promised to pray with me. She was diligently minding her new marriage, keeping her penthouse immaculate and recording complicated music with Max.

Rosa was practical. "He's not jealous, is he? If you marry a jealous man, life will be hell." I told her he wouldn't have any reason for jealousy.

Rosa was writing every day, coping with her large rambunctious family, being courted by handsome African diplomats and working in a factory to pay her rent.

My two closest friends were too busy with the times and their own lives to talk me out of my rash decision.

Thomas gave me an engagement ring and said we'd marry in three months. We would be married in Virginia, his home state, in the church where his parents were married. Then we would drive to Pensacola, Florida, because he always wanted to fish in the Gulf of Mexico. Guy would stay with his family while we were away.

Obviously he didn't require my agreement, since he didn't ask for it. The decision to marry me automatically gave him authority to plan all our lives. I ignored the twinge which tried to warn me that I should stop and do some serious thinking.

I had never seen Virginia or Florida. Travel was a lovely thing to look forward to.

Time and opportunity were remolding my life. I closed my lips and agreed, with a new demureness.

CHAPTER 8

One Monday morning Hazel told me that over the weekend she had heard a South African freedom fighter speak. He was so thorough and so brilliant that even the biggest fool in the world had to see that Apartheid was evil and would have to be brought down. His name was Vusumzi Make (pronounced Mah-kay).

A few volunteers, standing in the outer offices, had also heard the speaker. They joined in the conversation with added compliments.

"The smartest and calmest African I've ever heard."

"A little fat, but cute as he wants to be."

"Reminded me more of Dr. King than anybody I've ever seen."

I asked his name again.

Hazel said she had written it down and that the man was in the United States to petition at the United Nations against South Africa's racial policy. He was speaking again later in the week. Maybe we could attend the lecture together. I said maybe.

A mound of cardboard boxes stood against my office wall. I opened them all. Each contained a beautiful piece of luggage and a note: "Best Wishes to My Bride." I carried pleasure to my desk.

Frank Sinatra, Peter Lawford, Joey Bishop and Sammy Davis, Jr., had agreed to give a benefit performance for the SCLC at Carnegie Hall. Jack O'Dell, a highly respected organizer, had joined the organization, and he was breaking down the hall's seating. Stanley, Jack, Jack Murray and I had to separate sections and price seats.

Hotel accommodations had to be arranged for the famous "Rat Pack" and its entourage. Musicians' union officials had to be contacted and tickets drafted and ordered. High-paying patrons needed to be solicited and church groups contacted and asked to take blocks of seats.

We were working late on Friday afternoon when Hazel said she had to go. She reminded me that Make was speaking and she was meeting her husband across town early so they could get good seats. (She knew my being able to go along was out of the question.)

As she left, I asked her to take notes for me and tell me all about it on Monday.

Work took over my weekend. I saw Guy only during the few hours on Saturday when he came to the office to join other black and white young volunteers. Thomas was working a night shift, so I took a late-night subway to Brooklyn and walked the quiet streets home. Guy's note on the dining-room table informed me that he was at a party. "Home at 12:30 A.M." Twelve-thirty was absolutely the limit. After all, he was barely fifteen. I was strict and he was usually agreeable. I would lie across my bed with a book and stay awake to make sure that he honored his note.

Morning found me in the same position and Guy sleeping innocently in his bedroom.

Make had been more eloquent than the previous time. Hazel said a heckler had asked why sixteen million Africans allowed three million whites to control them, reminding Make that we black Americans were only a tenth of the United States population, but we had stood up and fought back ever since we were brought here as slaves.

Hazel said Make was devastating. First, he spoke of the black American struggle. He knew the history better than most black Americans. He talked about Denmark Vesey and Gabriel, and all the known leaders of slave rebellions. He quoted Frederick Douglass and Marcus Garvey. He said that Dr. DuBois was the father of Pan-Africanism, having attended the Pan-African Congress in Paris in 1919, where he stated clearly the idea of a free and united Africa. Make then, systematically, explained how Africa was bludgeoned by slavery, having her strongest sons and daughters stolen and brought to build the country of the slaves. He spoke of colonialism, the second blow that brought the continent to abjection. He said the spirit of Africa lives, but it is most vital in its descendants who have been struggling away from the motherland. At home, in South Africa, the people needed help and encouragement from those of us who, knowing slavery firsthand, had found the oppressor to be a formidable but opposable foe.

I made a note to go to hear Make the next time he spoke. Again, my responsibilities crowded out my intention. John Killens phoned on Thursday morning.

"Maya, I heard Make last night. Kind of expected to see you there."

I explained that we were nearing the Carnegie Hall date.

"Well," he said, "if you're free tomorrow night, come over to my place. Grace and I have asked a few people over to meet him."

"I'm working late tomorrow night, too."

"Come anytime. We'll get started around eight. We'll probably be going on until one or two. Make is the representative of the Pan-African Congress. That's the radical organization, but he's coming with Oliver Tambo, the head of the African National Congress. The ANC is to the PAC what the NAACP is to the Black Muslims. The two get along, though. Try to make it."

Before leaving for work the next morning, I woke Guy and asked him to go to John's for dinner, and said I would meet him there at nine-thirty.

Chagrin at being a capricious and too-often-absent mother would get me to the Killens' house.

I left the office a little early, and after John opened the door, I walked through the milling crowd of acquaintances and strangers to find Guy, Chuck, Barbara and Mom Willie in the kitchen. Guy looked up, then back at his watch and grinned.

Mom Willie offered me food, but I declined and said I'd better go shake hands with the honored guests.

Guy said, "He's going to knock you out, Mom. We talked a little. He's more brilliger than the slighy toves." Guy was working so hard to appear grown-up, I was surprised to hear him use his favorite childhood phrase. Make had made my reserved son relax and talk like a child again.

I went to the living room and greeted Paule and John Clarke, Sarah Wright and Rosa.

The air in the room crackled like static. John Killens introduced me to a small, trim dark man.

"Maya Angelou, meet Oliver Tambo, a warrior from South Africa." Tambo shook my hand and bowed.

John continued, "And come here and meet Vusumzi Make, another South African warrior."

Make's appearance surprised me. I had imagined him very tall and older. He was three inches shorter than I and his baby face was surrounded by fat. He had broad shoulders and a wide waist, all encased in a beautifully cut pin-stripe suit, and he was in his early thirties.

"Miss Angelou. Glad to meet you. You represent the black hero Martin King, as I represent the South African black hero Robert Sobukwe. Hazel Grey has been telling me about you. If we had not met I would have known you anyway. I've met Guy."

His accent was delicious. A result of British deliberateness changed by the rhythm of an African tongue and the grace of African lips. I moved away after smiling, needing to sit apart and collect myself. I had not met such a man. He was intense and contained. His movements were economical and delicate. And he didn't seem to know that he was decidedly overweight. John's introduction was probably apt. He was a warrior, sure of his enemies and secure with his armament.

Rosa left her African diplomat to join me on the couch. "You met Make. He'd been asking to meet you. Take it easy, kid." She smiled for me alone and went back to her escort.

Paule Marshall stood in front of me. "Listen, Maya Angelou. What did you do to Make? He says he wants to know you better."

I told her I only said hello.

She said, "Must have been a hell of a hello. He asked me how well I knew you and if you were married." Paule laughed and flicked her eyes. "I didn't say a word. It's up to you."

John and Grace corralled their guests back to the living room, where everyone found seats. After the chairs and sofas filled, people rested on footstools or wedged themselves between couches on the floor. John introduced Oliver Tambo, who talked about South Africa, the ANC and its leader, Chief Albert Luthuli, in terse and controlled anger.

We applauded the man and the cause that brought him to the United States. Then John introduced Mr. Make, and my love no longer was in the hands of Thomas Allen.

Make started talking from a seated position, but passion lifted his voice and raised him out of the chair. He had been a defendant charged with treason in the trials after the Sharpville Massacre. The Africans, ANC and PAC members, along with people who belonged to neither organization, had met in 1958 to oppose oppression in their country. They had been inspired by Martin Luther King and the SCLC. (He looked over at me and nodded.) They had been encouraged by Malcolm X and the Muslims to set themselves apart from their oppressors.

When he finished, he asked for questions and sat down, dabbing at his face with a cloud of white handkerchief.

My first reaction was to wish I could be the white cloth in his dark hand touching his forehead, digging softly in the corners of his lips. Intelligence always had a pornographic influence on me.

He asked for questions and was immediately satisfied.

"Which organization was the most popular in South Africa?" Was he really flirting with me?

"Did Luthuli and Sobukwe get along?" Did fat men make love like thin ones?

"When would the average South African become politically aware?" Was he married?

"What could we, as black Americans, do to speed along the struggle?" How long was he going to stay in New York?

Make and Tambo shared the questions, volleying answers back and forth with the ease of professional tennis players.

Make turned. "Doesn't Miss Angelou have a question?" Stage experience kept me from squirming. All attention shifted to me and I shoved my real questions to the back of my head and asked, "Mr. Make, would it be possible to solve the South African problem with an employment of nonviolence?"

He stood and walked to my corner. "That which works for your Reverend King cannot work in South Africa. Here, whether it is honored or not, there is a Constitution. You at least have laws which say, Liberty and justice for all. You can go to courts and exact an amount of success. Witness your Supreme Court ruling of 1954. In South Africa, we Africans are written out of all tenets dealing with justice. We are not considered in the written laws dealing with fair play. We are not only brutalized and oppressed, de facto, we are ignored de jure."

He was standing over me, and I felt lucky. Fortunate to be a black American, and in comparison to him and his people, only slightly impaired by racism. But even more so fortunate. His eyes were on me and I would have had to be thicker than raw pigskin to know that something about me hooked him.

I folded my arms and sat back as he used the time to develop his statement. He finished to standing applause, and was wrapped around in seconds by a group of excited people.

We caught sight of each other through the shifting bodies but he never returned to my corner. After another drink, I went to collect Guy; my days started early and Guy had his bakery job again.

At the door, Make stopped us.

"Miss Angelou, just a minute. Guy, I would be honored to see your mother home."

Make knew that asking Guy's permission would please us both. My son smiled, loving the Old World formality, straight out of the Three Musketeers and the Corsican brothers.

"Thank you, Mr. Make. I am seeing her home."

I could have pinched him until he screamed.

Make said, "Of course, thank you anyway." The big lunk almost bowed from the waist. "I hope we'll meet again, Miss Angelou. Good night. Good night, Guy."

He walked away and we went out the door.

"He doesn't know that you're engaged, or he wouldn't have asked to take you home." Guy chattered all the way. "But he's really smart. He's from the Xhosa tribe. You know, Miriam Makeba's click song; well, that's his language. He was a barrister, that's a lawyer, before he was placed in exile and escaped from South Africa."

"When did he tell you all that?"

"He came into the kitchen and talked to Chuck and Barbara and me. He just walked in, introduced himself and sat down."

Most politicians I had met, excluding Martin Luther King, thought talking to children a waste of their adult time. I was liking the African more and more. And obviously I'd never see him again, and if we did meet, Thomas and my looming marriage stood between us.

The next morning, Paule rang to say she was giving a little party that evening and I had to come. I had another late night at work and once I got to Brooklyn and changed, I really wouldn't be up to going back to Manhattan. She urged me to stop by after work, reassuring me that the party was to be very casual. I said I'd drop in.

Late that afternoon I called John to say how much I enjoyed meeting Make, adding that he was very impressive. He agreed and said I'd get to see him again that night at Paule's. The party was being given for Oliver Tambo and Make. I mulled over the possibilities for hours. If we met and he pursued, would I have the strength to resist and did I really want to? Of course, last night was over, and he might bring a woman to Paule's. If he persisted and if I surrendered, I'd have to break off with Thomas, and my dream of quiet security would evaporate. Make would leave the country and I'd be back to where I was, or even worse. I'd be lonely and broken-hearted.

I took a train directly to Brooklyn. It was Friday night. Guy gulped down his food and gave me a kiss. He was off to a party, but would be in by twelve-thirty.

After a shower, I settled in my bed with a book, a drink and a package of cigarettes. The ghost of Paule's party invaded the room. Specters of laughing black people, shouting and arguing, crowded around my bed. Make was in the middle of the throng, his pretty full-moon face intense, his accent curving words into new shapes, his logic unarguable. If I went to the party... I called Thomas. He didn't answer. I did have a nice, rather new outfit that I could wear, and open high-heel sandals. Actually, it wouldn't take long to dress and if I took a subway to Times Square, I could change to the AA local and get off three blocks from Paule's building. Within a half-hour, I was ringing

her doorbell. Inside, the men and women crowded together in jubilation. The record player was on to a moderate volume, and jazz music
weaved among the voices.

I headed toward the living room, pushing through the crowded
hallway. As I passed the kitchen, off to my left, I heard Make's voice.

"Miss Angelou." He came to me, grinning a white-teeth welcome.
"I had just about given you up." He took my hand. "Paule said you'd
come from work. But I suppose you went home to freshen up."

I nodded and excused myself, saying I had to see Paule. In fact, I
had to get away from the man's electricity. Sparks seemed to be shooting from him to my nipples and my ears. My underarms tingled and
my stomach contents fell to my groin. I had never fainted in my life,
but at that moment I felt I was sinking into a warm black and friendly
pool.

Paule laughed when she saw me. "I know you didn't wear that to
work. You're setting out to get him, aren't you, Maya Angelou?"

I got huffy and denied her accusation. "I'm going to be married,
Paule. I'm no chickenshit floozy."

Her ready temper answered, "Well, excuse the hell out of me." She
went to join other guests. I was a fool. I lied and offended my friend at
the same time. Make made no further attempt to talk to me.

The music was stopped and Tambo's voice could be heard as the
talking quieted. He spoke briefly, repeating the speech of the night
before. Ken Marshall asked Make to say a few words, and he walked
to the center of the living room. I didn't listen to his words but used
the time to study his body. He had closely cut, soft crinkled hair and
an even dark-brown skin. Big round black eyes, which moved slowly,
taking in the details of his listeners. There were a few hairs on his
chin, which he fingered with small hands as he talked. His chest
bloomed above an indented waist, then his hips widened out in a
nearly feminine voluptuousness. Fat thighs touched, under the
sharply creased trousers, and his small feet were encased in highly
polished shoes. I completed the investigation and decided Make was
the ideal man.

I gave him a few sultry looks, and when his back was turned, I raced downstairs and stopped a cab. I justified the expense of a taxi ride to Brooklyn by telling myself I was paying for my honor.

The American Society for African Culture had its annual black-tie ball on Saturday night in the ballroom of a midtown hotel, and as co-ordinator for the SCLC, I was expected to attend. Thomas was working late, so Rosa and her escort met me in Manhattan. Her African diplomat wore embroidered pants and a matching voluminous over-shirt which reached the floor. The man was blue-black and spectacular. His unquestionable dignity gave lie to the concept that black people were by nature inferior. His presence alone refuted the idea that our descendants had been naked subhumans living in trees three centuries before, when the whites raided them on the African continent. That elegance could not have been learned in three hundred years.

The dance auditorium was filled with black women made up and coiffed and beautiful in Dior and Balenciaga gowns or in dresses run up by local seamstresses. African women floated, serene-faced in their colorful national dress, and a few whites mingled with black men in tuxedos or outfits like that worn by Rosa's friend. I left my friends to check in at the table reserved for the SCLC. The Greys were watching the dancing couples, and when I greeted them, Hazel jumped.

"Oh, there you are. So you met him after all." I knew who she meant. "He was over here a few minutes ago, asking for you."

I saw him coming across the dance floor, like an ocean liner plying through tugboats toward a pier. He asked me to dance.

He moved surprisingly well for his bulk, and his enjoyment of the dance made him seem less serious. He pulled me to him, and I felt the hardness under the layers of surrounding fat. He laughed.

"You're afraid of me, aren't you? A big girl like you, an American so-phisticate, frightened by a little black man from The Dark Continent."

"Why should I be afraid of you?"

He was still laughing. "Maybe you think I'll think you are a missionary and I'll eat you."

"I don't think that. Anyway, if more Africans had eaten more missionaries, the Continent would be in better shape."

He stopped dancing and looked at me with approval. "Miss Angelou, you have every reason to be alarmed. I intend to change your life. I am going to take you to Africa."

I drew my body straight and made my face uninviting. "Mr. Make, I am going to be married in two months. So your plan is impossible."

"I have heard that, but where is the elusive groom? I've seen you three times and, except for your son, you've been without male companionship."

I defended Thomas. "My fiancé is working."

"And what does this diligent man do?"

He was smirking. He knew the answer to his question.

"He's a bail bondsman. And I'm going to see him after the dance tonight."

Make grabbed my hand and led me back to my table. He pulled out my chair and after I sat, he leaned to me and whispered, "I owe it to our people to save you. When you see your bloody fiancé, tell him that I'm after you and that with me every day is Saturday Night and I'm black and I'm dangerous."

He left and my heart threatened to stop.

I went home early and alone. Guy was asleep and the house was cavernous.

Thomas answered the telephone. Had I enjoyed the fancy-dress ball? No, he was too tired to come and pick me up. No, I shouldn't call a taxi. After all, we'd see each other the next day. He was taking me to the movies.

Sleep didn't come to me willingly. Thoughts raced, chasing each other like lively children in a game of tag. Marry a man I hadn't even slept with and go to Africa. Leave Martin King and my own struggle. But all the black struggles were one, with one enemy and one goal. Thomas would shoot me with his service pistol. Why did Make want me? He didn't know me or my background. But then, I didn't know him either. What about Guy? Surely Make didn't expect me to leave my son. A chance for Guy to finish growing up in Africa. Suppose the man was too fat to make love. I knew of black women who had maimed husbands who refused them sex. I wouldn't go to that extreme; on the other hand, I didn't think I would stay with a man who couldn't satisfy me. Speculation was a waste of time. I was going to marry Thomas, and we'd live a nice complacent life in Brooklyn.

The next night the movie was deadly boring. I got up on the pretext of wanting a soft drink and I sat in the lobby smoking and wondering what Make was doing. Patrice Lumumba was in New York. Rosa was going to meet him and his assistant Thomas Kanza. Abbey and Max were performing in the Village. Malcolm X was speaking at a public meeting in Harlem, and somewhere Make was showering his listeners with glittering words. Guy was attending a youth rally in Washington Square Park. The world was on fire.

Thomas headed the car toward his street.

"I don't feel like going to your house," I told him.

He looked over at me, but I kept my face straight ahead.

"Are you all right? It's not that time of month, is it?"

"No. I just want to go home."

No, he hadn't offended me. No, I wasn't sick.

I told him we were living in exciting times and that because of the United Nations, Africans and oppressed people from all over the world were making New York the arena where they fought for justice.

"I haven't lost anything in Africa and they haven't lost anything in our country. They can all go back where they came from as far as I'm concerned. Anyhow, I get all the excitement I need in my job and I don't want to hear about politics at home."

It was a long speech for Thomas and a disastrous one for our relationship. I could imagine future aborted conversations when I would be silenced. Days, weeks, months would pass with neither of us going beyond small talk.

I prepared dinner at home and waited alone for Guy to return.

The next days brought bouquets of mixed flowers and vases of red roses to cover my desk and make me feel like a desirable courtesan. The accompanying cards read "From Vusumzi Make to Maya Angelou Make." Hazel looked worried and Millie grinned as if she and I were sharing a secret.

Thomas chose the same time to have more wedding presents delivered. Young, shabbily dressed men hauled boxes up the stairs and deposited them in the outer offices. "Tom to Maya." I opened the cartons to find an expensive record player covered in smooth leather and two more pieces of matching luggage. It was a flattering present, but I couldn't dispel the idea that the set was stolen property.

I refused Make's daily invitations to lunch and declined Thomas' offer to visit his apartment.

Confusion had me spread-eagled. I couldn't run nor could I dodge.

Office politics were further irritations. Despite the long hours and what I thought of as my diligent commitment, two more men had been brought in to help in the running of the organization. I had had nothing to say about their employment.

After a business lunch with the president of a national Negro women's club where we discussed the selling of a large block of tickets, it was suggested that I report the results to the office newcomers. When I refused to do so, insisting on my own autonomy, loyalties began to shift. Welcoming smiles faded or gleamed sunshine-bright. Small groups of workers crowded the desks of the new arrivals, while Hazel and Millie used every slight occasion to enter my office, bringing me news or coffee, fresh papers or mail.

CHAPTER 9

Thursday morning I agreed to meet Make for lunch a few blocks from my office. I would explain to him why he had to accept my rejection.

Wells Restaurant, pride of Harlem, on 132nd Street and Seventh Avenue, had been popular since the twenties, when it was a favorite stop on the route of whites, visiting what many called "Nigger Heaven."

The food had remained good, the menus still listed white items such as steaks and lamb chops, but its main offerings, fried chicken, smothered pork chops, short ribs and biscuits catered to the local palates.

Make stood as I entered. He wore yet another well-tailored suit and custom-made shirt. I didn't need to look at his shoes to know they were shining like new money. He began talking before I sat down.

He was pleased that I had overcome my timidity. My coming showed I had courage, a virtue which we both knew was a prerequisite in the struggle. He had talked to Paule Marshall, by telephone, and told her that his intention was to marry me and take me to Africa. I couldn't focus on the menu, but we ordered lunch. He continued talking and I ate food I could neither see nor taste.

He had been jailed for political action in South Africa. When the government released him, the police took him to an isolated desert area near South-West Africa and left him there, hundreds of miles from the nearest human beings. A city-bred man, with no knowledge of open country, he had scrabbled over rocky ridges and found water. He pulled caterpillars from shrubs and ate them (they taste a lot like shrimp). He encountered a group of Hottentot hunters and because he could speak a little of their language, they gave him dried meat and a small water pouch. Keeping away from large towns and following the stars, he walked out of South Africa into Bechuanaland. The Boers' control and spies had pervaded that country as well, so he kept to the forest. He made a slingshot and killed small animals and ate them raw, or cooked when it was safe enough to light a fire. Their skins padded his worn-out shoes or were laid inside his shirt for warmth. Days passed when the only things he saw moving were the vultures that lazed high in the sky above him. He walked through South and North Rhodesia, making sparse contacts with revolutionaries he had heard about, who were themselves in hiding or on the run. He took his first breath of freedom when he crossed into Ethiopia.

"I was the first Pan-African Congress member to escape. But, Miss Angelou, when I left exile without water or food, I intended to reach Ethiopia. When I knew I was coming to the yew ess, I came with the intention of finding a strong, beautiful black American woman, who would be a helpmate, who understood the struggle and who was not afraid of a fight. I heard about you and you sounded like the one. I met Guy and I was impressed with his manliness and intelligence, obviously your work, and then I saw you."

He reached across the table and took my hand. His little brown fingers tapered down to small white nails. I tried to picture those exquisite hands carrying caterpillars, wiggling to his mouth.

"You are exactly what I dreamed on my long march. Tall and clear-eyed. Needing to be loved. Ready to fight and needing protection. And not the protection of a bloody bail bondsman."

Oh Lord, that reminded me.

"Mr. Make, I agreed to have lunch with you to tell you I am going to marry the bloody bail bondsman."

He leaned his bulk back in the chair and his face darkened and clouded over with resignation.

"You are breaking my heart. I am an African with large things to do. I have left my father and mother in Jo'Burg, and given the ordinary run of time, I shall never see them again. Unless the revolution takes place during my lifetime, I shall never see the land again. To an African, the family and the land...I need you. I want to marry you."

"I'm sorry." And God knew I meant that.

"I shall finish at the U.N. tomorrow. On the next day, I shall fly to Amsterdam, an open city, where I am told whiskey is cheap and a variety of entertainment is available to a lonely man."

I saw those delicate hands sliding over white women's bodies and in their long, lank hair. But I couldn't imagine him kissing the white lips.

"I shall stay in Amsterdam four or five days and then I shall go to Copenhagen, another open city. My desire for you is total, Miss Angelou. I want your mind, and spirit and your body. After all, I may be an African with a mission, but I am also a man. I must attend a conference in London in ten days, but before the conference, I must try to drive thoughts of you out of my mind." He stopped talking and I waited in the silence for a second before I excused myself and went to the toilet.

Wells had wasted none of its elegance on the women's room. There were two small cubicles for toilets and a small outer area which was only large enough for two people.

A woman bumped into me on her way out. She saw the tears on my face.

"Hey, are you O.K? You sick?"

I shook my head and walked through the open door. She poked her head in. "You sure you don't need any help?"

I shook my head again and thanked her.

The little mirror over the washstand was vague with dust but I looked in it and saw misery in sharp outline. If I went through with the wedding to Thomas, I would load our marriage with such disappointment, the structure couldn't stand. He was too good a man to abuse, yet I knew that I would never forget or forgive the facts. Because of him, I would have lost Make, a life of beckoning adventure and Africa. Africa. I would hate him for that. And Make. Make needed me. I would be a help to him. I was brave. Abbey had once told me I was too crazy to be afraid. I would be a fool to let Make go to a bunch of whorish white women in Amsterdam. In fact, I might be betraying the entire struggle. I wouldn't do that. And then Guy. Guy would have the chance to have an African father. There could be no greater future for a black American boy than to have a strong, black, politically aware father. His being African would add an enriching spice.

Admitting for the first time a decision I had made at the fancy-dress ball, I would accept Make's offer.

I called Abbey from a pay phone. She answered.

"Just wanted to make sure you were there."

"What's happening?"

"Nothing yet, I'll call back."

"Are you all right?"

"Yeah. Really. I'll call you in a few minutes."

Make stood again as I reached the table. I sat down and took the napkin in my hands. The words refused to get themselves in order.

"Mr. Make, I'll do it. I'll do it. I'll go with you."

His face broke open. A brown moon splitting, showing its white core. The room was filled with large even teeth and shining round eyes.

"I'll marry you, Miss Angelou. I'll make you happy. We will be known as the happiest family in Africa." He came around the table and pulled me to my feet to kiss me. I noticed other customers for the first time and drew away.

Make laughed, turning to the tables of black people openly watching us.

"It is all right. She has just said she'll marry me."

Applause and laughter. The folks liked a happy story.

He held my hand as if I had just won a race, "This is the joining of Africa and Africa-America! Two great peoples back together again."

I tried to sit back down. He was going to make a speech. A laugh rumbled up his chest and between the perfect teeth.

"No. I claim my engagement kiss."

His lips were full and soft. Shaken by the physical touching, we took our seats again. The woman who had offered to help me in the toilet came to our table.

"Honey, I should have known you weren't crying out of sadness." She smiled. "You all have a drink with us. We've been married eighteen of the best years of my life."

A man's voice shouted across the room, "Ernestine, just offer the folks a drink and come on back and sit down."

The woman grinned. "See how nice we get along? He orders. I obey. Sometimes."

Make and I laughed as she strutted back to her table.

After a few nervous minutes of finding no way to say all the things which needed to be said, I asked Make if he was free for the afternoon. He said he was. I excused myself and went to the telephone.

"I've done it this time, Ab."

"Done what?"

"It. I've told Vusumzi Make I'll marry him."

"Who?" Her voice was strong with shock.

"A South African freedom fighter. He's brilliant, Abbey, and pretty. Beautiful, in fact. And we've fallen in love."

"Well, hell, Maya Angelou, what about Thomas?"

"I want to talk to you about that."

"Seems like to me, you'll have to talk to Thomas."

At the moment that chore didn't seem so onerous.

"I wish you'd come down to Wells and meet him and take him to your house. I have to go back to the office, but I'll come over after work. Will you?"

She didn't use a second to deliberate.

"Of course I'll come. Are you going to wait or do I just walk in and ask for the African who's going to marry Maya Angelou?"

I told Make that my friend, Abbey Lincoln, was coming to pick him up.

He recognized her name immediately and began to tell me how the Max Roach/Abbey Lincoln records were smuggled into South Africa and then passed around like the hot revolutionary material they were. He knew the title of every track and most of the words to all their songs. The man, indeed, was a wonder.

When I looked through the window and saw Abbey double-parking her Lincoln sedan, we left the restaurant. Abbey got out of the car and shook hands with my latest fiancé. They drove away and the rest of the afternoon passed like film in slow motion starring a stranger. I answered telephones, signed letters, spoke to volunteers, but my mind hovered somewhere between the Serengeti plains, Thomas' apartment in Brooklyn and the sweet scent of patchouli which rose each time Mr. Make shifted his heavy body.

Max and Mr. Make were talking and Abbey was preparing dinner when I arrived at the Columbus Avenue apartment. Abbey shouted a welcome from the kitchen and both men embraced me.

Make said proudly, "Ah, here is my beautiful wife."

Max nodded. "Maya, you got yourself one this time. Yeah, you got yourself a man."

I sat through dinner in a stupor. Max and Abbey's place was no more real than my office had been. A man I had met exactly one week earlier was grinning possessively at me across the table. Max, who had seen enough of life to be healthily suspicious, approved of the stranger. Later when I helped Abbey dry the dishes, she said that she thought I was better suited to the unknown Make than to the known Thomas. And anyway, I was just wild enough to make it work.

Make slipped close to me over the ribbing of the corduroy couch.

"I am tired, and would like to rest. Max has said I might stretch out in that room." I was supposed to agree. I did want to grab his hand and lug him to bed, but I said, "Mr. Make, I…"

"Please, we are going to be married, call me Vus."

"Vus, I'm obliged to clear up the matter with Thomas." Make leaned against the back of the sofa and kept quiet for a few minutes.

"Yes. I agree. But when you talk to him I want to be present. He might be difficult."

"I'll speak to him alone tomorrow night. And then…"

"Shouldn't I come with you? It might be dangerous."

I refused his offer. Talking with Thomas was my responsibility. My pompous idiocy had gotten me into the mess, and rash emotion was further complicating the jumble. And I felt a little excitement at the coming confrontation.

"Then I shall be the one to talk to Guy. I'm going to be his father and we must begin our relationship properly."

Vus put me into a taxi heading for Brooklyn.

Guy had rocks in the jaws and flint in his eyes. He had called the office and had been told that I had left early. He went to the Killens and they had no news of my whereabouts. Thomas hadn't heard from me and Paule Marshall didn't know where I was. He couldn't find Abbey's number. He chided me. It wasn't fair to insist that he be considerate and phone home if I was going to treat him with casual indifference. It was nearly eleven o'clock.

Three men looked to me for proof of devotion.

My son expected warmth, food, housing, clothes and stability. He could be certain that no matter which way my fortune turned he would receive most of the things he desired. Stability, however, was not possible in my world; consequently it couldn't be possible in his. Too often I had had to decline unplayable hands dealt to me by a capricious life, and take fresh cards just to remain in the game. My son could rely on my love, but never expect our lives to be unchanging.

Thomas wanted equilibrium, also. He was looking for a nice wife, who was a good cook and was neither so pretty or so ugly that she drew attention to herself. I tried his number again. I had to tell him that he hadn't yet found his mate. He didn't answer the ring.

Vus saw me as the flesh of his youthful dream. I would bring to him the vitality of jazz and the endurance of a people who had survived three hundred and fifty years of slavery. With me in his bed he would challenge the loneliness of exile. With my courage added to his own, he would succeed in bringing the ignominious white rule in South Africa to an end. If I didn't already have the qualities he needed, then I would just develop them. Infatuation made me believe in my ability to create myself into my lover's desire. That would be nothing for a stepper.

At dawn Thomas answered the telephone. He said he would pick me up from the office and collect the wedding gifts. We would stop at my house and after dinner with Guy, we would go back to his apartment for "a little you-know-what."

The day jerked itself to evening in stops and starts. Time either wouldn't move at all or it raced like a whirlwind.

At last, and too soon, Thomas stood in my office doorway, smiling, showing his death-white teeth.

"Hey, baby, where's the stuff?"

I said "Hi" and pointed him to the cartons against the wall. While I was saying good night to the office staff, he carried the gifts downstairs, and when I joined him on the pavement he was loading them in the trunk of his car.

He was still smiling. I wondered how could anybody say goodbye to a smiling man.

"You like the luggage, baby?"

"Yes. Where did you buy it?"

The question wiped the smile from his face. "Why?"

"Oh, in case I want to add to the set."

He relaxed and the smile returned as full as it was before. "I got them from a fellow I know. And if you want some more, I'll get them for you."

I had suspected that the bags were stolen when they appeared in my office in supermarket cardboard boxes, and Thomas now confirmed my suspicions. I needed all the hurt feelings I could muster for the imminent farewell scene, so I kept quiet and waited.

At home, Guy watched television and Thomas read the sports pages while I cooked dinner. I knew that but for my shocking plans, we were acting out the tableau of our future. Into eternity. Guy would be in his room, laughing at *I Love Lucy* and Thomas would be evaluating the chances of an athlete or a national baseball team, and I would be leaning over the stove, preparing food for the "shining dinner hour." Into eternity.

We ate without excitement and Guy said good night, going back to his room.

Thomas rose to bring in the luggage but I stopped him.

"I have some talk for you. Why don't we have a drink?"

I began talking slowly and quietly. "I've met a South African. He escaped over the desert. He kept himself alive by eating worms. The whites sent him out to die but he survived. He has come to the United States and he deserves our support." I looked at Thomas, who had become a terrapin, his large head withdrawn into his shoulders, his eyes steady and unblinking.

I continued my story, saying that the man was inspired by Dr. Martin Luther King and had come to petition the United Nations on behalf of his people. I used small words and short sentences as if I were telling a fairy tale to a child. Thomas was not enthralled.

I said, "A large conference is going to be held in London, where other people who have escaped from South Africa will meet and form a joint freedom-fighting organization." So far I was telling the truth. But since I didn't have the courage to tell Thomas I was leaving him, I knew I was building up to a lie.

The man in front of me had turned into a big red rock, and his freckles blotched dark brown on his face.

"Indians from the South Africa Indian Congress and Africans from both South Africa and South-West Africa will take two weeks to work out an accepted charter. As we know, " 'In unity there is strength.' "

There was no light in Thomas' eyes.

We sat in dangerous silence.

I balled up my nerve. "They...Anyway, this African I've just met has asked me to attend the conference. They want a black American woman who can explain the philosophy of nonviolence." I was getting there.

Thomas twitched his shoulders, raised his body an inch, then slid deeper into the chair. His eyes still reflected nothing.

"I have decided to accept the invitation and deliver a paper on Martin Luther King."

The invention came as a wonderful surprise. I had been searching all day and during the preparation of dinner in vain for a way to say what I had to say, and nothing had come to me. Obviously, apprehension had sharpened my imagination.

"I don't know how long I'll be gone, but I may go to Africa after that."

Thomas, in an unexpectedly fast move, sat up straight. He looked at me, his face wise and hard.

"You got another nigger." He hadn't raised his voice. "All that shit was to tell me you got yourself another nigger."

The moment I dreaded and had lied to avoid had arrived.

"Say it. Say it in plain words. Say, 'Thomas' "—he mimicked my speech—" 'Thomas, I got myself another nigger.' Say it."

He was the interrogator and I was the suspect.

"Well, he's not a nigger."

"He's African, ain't he? Then, he's a nigger just like me and just like you. Except you try to act like a goddam ofay girl. But you just as much a nigger as I am. And so is your goddam holy Martin Luther King, another blackass nigger."

He knew I loathed that word and didn't allow its use in my home. Now each time he said "nigger" he sharpened it and thrust it, rapier-like, into my body.

"Thomas"—I forced a sweet calm into my voice—"Thomas, there doesn't seem to be anything more to say."

He denied that we had come to the end of our conversation and the end of the relationship. I was acting above my station, putting on airs like my siditty friends who were talking about freedom and writing stupid books that nobody read. Thinking I was white, raising my son to use big words and act like a white boy. His sister had told him to watch out for me. I didn't mean him no good. I thought I was better than his family.

I didn't move, even to pick up my drink. He spoke, letting the profanity and his dislike of me fill the room.

He would be surprised if that African didn't leave me stranded in London or in Africa, and I'd come back, dragging my ass, trying to make him feel grateful for a chance to fuck me. Well, don't think that he'd be around. Forget his phone number. In fact, tomorrow, he would have his phone number changed.

I noted with relief that he was already talking about tomorrow. His shoulders fell and he leaned back against the chair, his energy spent. I still didn't move.

He rose and walked out of the room and I followed. He was so large, he filled the entry. In a sharp move, he jerked back the curtain which covered the oval window at the door.

"Come here." I was afraid to refuse, so I wedged myself close to him. "Look at that woman."

Across the street a lone black woman walked under hazy streetlight carrying two full shopping bags. I didn't know her. Thomas reached into his jacket and pulled out his gun.

"You know something? I could blow that broad's head off, and I wouldn't do a day."

He put the pistol back into its holster, opened the door and walked down the steps to his car.

I made another drink and thanked God for blessing me yet one more time. I had hurt Thomas' ego but I had not broken his heart. He wasn't injured enough to attack me, but he would never want to see me again.

———

Stanley and Jack Murray accepted my news without surprise. They said they had not expected me to stay. They felt that since I was an entertainer, I would leave the organization whenever I was offered a good night-club contract or a part in a Broadway play. That's why they had brought in other dedicated workers to take over my job. I didn't bother to tell them how wrong they were.

Grace Killens laughed at me.

"You met him last week at our house, didn't you? And this week you're going to marry him. The Wild West Woman." She laughed and laughed.

John took the news solemnly. Concern tightened his face and squeezed his voice into sharpness.

"He's serious about the struggle, but what else do we know? Are you going to be a second or third wife? How is he planning to look after you? Don't forget Guy. You're putting him under a strange man's roof and he's almost a man himself. How does he feel about that?"

Because he was the most important, I had left Guy for the last. Vus had said he wanted to be the first to talk to him and I was happy to accept the much-vaunted masculine camaraderie. Let men talk to men. It was better for a woman, even a mother, to stand back, keep quiet and let the men work out their mannish problems.

Guy was spending the night with Chuck, and Abbey and Max were performing, so Vus and I were given the use of their apartment. He prepared an elaborate dinner of roast beef and sautéed vegetables and poured a delicious wine. I learned that night that he was an expert in extending pleasure.

At the dining table he spread before me the lights and shadows of Africa. Glories stood in thrilling array. Warrior queens, in necklaces of blue and white beads led armies against marauding Europeans. Nubile girls danced in celebrations of the victories of Shaka, the Zulu king. The actual earth of Africa was "black and strong like the girls back home" and glinted with gold and diamonds. African men covered their betrothed with precious stones and specially woven cloth. He asked me to forgive the paucity of the gift he had for me and to understand that when we returned to Mother Africa he would adorn me with riches the likes of which I had never imagined. When he led me into the darkened guest room and placed a string of beads around my neck, all my senses were tantalized. I would have found the prospect of a waterless month in the Sahara not only exciting, acceptable. The amber beads on my nut-brown skin caught fire. I looked into the mirror and saw exactly what I wanted to see, and more importantly what I wanted him to see: a young African virgin, made beautiful for her chief.

The next afternoon I told Guy that the South African we had met at the Killens' house was coming around for dinner. He took the news so casually I thought that perhaps he had forgotten who Make was. He went to his room and began playing records as I fumbled setting the table.

When the doorbell rang, Guy popped out of the back room like a bottle cork and spun through the kitchen.

"I'll get it."

Before I could set the stove burners to safe levels, I heard the rumble of voices, speaking indistinguishable words.

I reached the living room just as Vus was beginning to lower himself into Guy's favorite chair. He stood again and we shook hands. I offered him the so much more comfortable sofa. Guy shook his head and smiled wanly. "This is comfortable, too, Mom."

Since early childhood, Guy had made certain pieces of furniture his private property. In preschool years and until he was eight or so, each night he would lasso chairs or tables with toy ropes before going off to bed, and he would warn his "horses" to stay in the corral. Although he grew out of the fantasy, his sense of property possession remained and everyone respected it.

Vus sat down in Guy's chair, and I thought he was getting off to a miserable start.

Guy offered to bring drinks, and the second he left the room Vus said, "There is no reason to be nervous. We are both men. Guy will understand." I nodded. Vus thought he understood, but I wondered how much of my son's temperament would really escape him.

I sat primly on the sofa across the room. Guy walked in carrying a napkin-covered tray, ice, glasses and a bottle of Scotch.

"Mom, something smells like its sticking." He walked to Vus. "How do you like your drink?"

Vus stood and mixed his own drink from the tray in Guy's hands. The two of them seemed absorbed in an atavistic ritual. I had ceased to be the center of attention.

"Well, I'll go tend to the dinner."

Vus looked up over his drink. "Yes. Guy and I must talk." Guy nodded as if he already knew something.

"Guy, will you please come to the kitchen for a moment?"

He hesitated, reluctant to leave our guest.

"Now, Mom?"

"Yes. Please."

We stood beside the warm stove and I opened my arms to embrace him. He stepped back, wary.

"Please come. I just want to hug you."

His eyes darted and he looked young and defenseless. Unwilling, he walked into my embrace.

"I love you. Please know that." I hadn't meant to whisper.

He extricated himself and went to the door. His face suddenly sad and old.

"You know, Mom. That sounds just like goodbye."

The sensuality between parents and children often is so intense that only the age-old control by society prevents the rise of sexuality. When a single parent is of the opposite sex the situation is more strained. How to feel love and demonstrate affection without stirring in the young and innocent mind the idea of sexuality? Many parents, alarmed at the dreadful possibility of raising incestuous thoughts in their children's minds, withdraw, refusing all physical contact and leaving the children yearning and befuddled with ideas of unworthiness.

Guy and I had spent years skating the thin ice.

During his twelfth summer, we attended a party in Beverly Hills. The children's party had been catered at one end of an Olympic-sized swimming pool, and I drank Margaritas with the adults at the pool's other end.

That evening, when we returned to our house in Laurel Canyon, Guy startled me.

"You know, Mom. Everyone talks about Marilyn Monroe's body. But we were watching today and all the guys said you had a prettier shape than Marilyn Monroe.

After he went to bed, I sat pondering my next move. He was old enough to masturbate. If I began to figure in his sexual fantasies he would be scarred and I would have added one more weight to an already difficult life.

That night I went through my wardrobe separating away the provocative dresses and choosing the staid outfits which were more motherly. The next day I stopped at the Salvation Army with a large package, and never again bought a form-fitting dress or a blouse with a plunging neckline.

I continued preparing the prenuptial feast, assuring myself that Guy would take the news calmly.

When I set the dining table, I consciously deadened my ears and hummed a song out loud. I was getting a husband, and a part of that gift was having someone to share responsibilities and guilt.

They came to the table and I saw from Guy's face that Vus had not told him of our marriage plans.

We sat to dinner and I ate straw.

The conversation swirled around me, making no contact: Soccer was as violent a sport as American football. Sugar Ray Robinson was a gentleman, but Ezzard Charles was of the people. Malcolm X had the right ideas but Martin Luther King was using tactics which had only been effective in India. Africa was the real "Old World" and America was aptly described by George Bernard Shaw, who said that it was "the only country which had gone from barbarism to decadence without once passing through civilization."

Guy was relaxed and entered into the exchange with his own young wit. They made each other laugh and my stomach churn.

I gathered the dishes, and when Guy rose to help clear the table, Vus stopped him.

"No, Guy, I must speak to you about our future. And I shall speak now. May we go into your room?"

A shadow of panic rushed into Guy's eyes. He turned to me peering, quickly trying to scan my thoughts. In a second he collected himself.

"Of course. Please. Come this way."

He led the big man into his bedroom; after they entered, the door slammed.

I made a clatter of dishes and a rattle of pans, slamming them together and jingling the flatware into cacophonous harmonies, trying to drown out my own thoughts and any sounds which might slide under Guy's door and slither across the kitchen floor and float up to my ears.

Suppose Guy rejected the man and our plans. He could refuse. Because the white world demonstrated in every possible way that he, a black boy, had to live within the murdering boundaries of racial restrictions, I had raised him to believe that he had a say in the living of his life, and that barring accidents, he should have a say in the dying of his death. And now, so armed, he was able to shape not only his future, but mine as well.

The kitchen was clean, every glass dried and the dishes put away. I sat with a cup of coffee at the kitchen table, controlling the opposing urges to walk without knocking into Guy's room or grab my purse and haul out the front door, running to Ray's and a triple Scotch on the rocks.

Laughter from behind the door brought me back to reality. Guy had accepted Vus, which meant I was as good as married and on my way to live in Africa.

They emerged from the room, broad grins stretched their faces. Guy's high-yellow color was reddened with excitement and Vus looked satisfied.

"Congratulations, Mom." This time Guy opened his arms offering me safe sanctuary. "I hope this will make you very happy."

I stood in Guy's arms and Vus laughed. "Now you'll have two strong men to take care of. We three will be the only invaders Mother Africa will willingly take to her breast."

The evening filled with laughter and plans. When Vus left for Manhattan, Guy spoke candidly.

"You would never have been happy with Mr. Allen."

"How do you know?"

"I know."

"Yes, but how? Because he's a bail bondsman?"

"No, because he didn't love you."

"And Mr. Make does?"

"He respects you. And maybe for an African, that's better than love."

"You know a lot, huh?" I didn't try to conceal my pride.

"Yeah. I'm a man."

———

The next few days glittered, as friends, recovered from shock at my hasty decision, strung out a Mardi Gras of parties. Rosa threw a Caribbean fete, where her African, black American and white liberal friends argued and laughed over plates of her famous rice and beans. Connie and Sam Sutton, an unpretentious intellectual couple, invited academic colleagues to a quiet dinner, which in time turned into a boisterous gathering. All over New York City strangers hugged me, patted my cheeks and praised my courage. Old friends told me I was crazy while struggling to control their admiration and envy.

At the end of the string of parties, Vus and I left for England, leaving Guy in the home of Pete and T. Beveridge, who lived a few blocks from my Brooklyn house.

We sat on the plane holding hands, kissing, seeing our future as a realm of struggle and eternal victory. Vus said we would marry in Oxford, such a pretty little town.

I explained that I wanted to have my mother and son present at my wedding and asked if we could wait. He patted my cheek and said, "Of course. In London we will say we married in America. When we return to New York we will say we married in England. We will have our wedding according to your wishes and whenever you say. I am marrying you this minute. Will you say yes?"

I said yes.

"Then we are married."

We never mentioned the word marriage again.

CHAPTER 10

London air was damp, its stone buildings old and grey. Colorfully dressed African women on the streets reminded me of tropical birds appearing suddenly in a forest of black trees. Vus and I moved into a one-room apartment which the PAC kept near Finsbury Park.

For the first few days, I was happy to stay in bed after Vus left for the conference. I read, rested and gloated over how well fortune was finally treating me. I had a brilliant and satisfying man, and I was living the high life in London, a mighty long way from Harlem or San Francisco's Fillmore District. Evenings, Vus entertained me with a concert of stories. His musical accent, his persuasive hands and the musk of his aftershave lotion, hypnotized me into believing I lived beside the Nile and its waters sang my evensong. I stood with Masai shepherds in the Ngorongoro crater, shooing lions away from my sheep with a wave of an elephant hair whisk. Morning love-making and evening recitals lost none of their magic, but the time between the two events began to lengthen. When I told Vus that I was not used to having so much time on my hands, he said he would arrange for me to meet some of the other wives of freedom fighters attending the conference.

Mrs. Oliver Tambo, the wife of the head of the African National Congress, invited me to lunch. The house in Maida Vale was neat and bright, but the sensation of impermanence in the large rooms was so strong that even the cut flowers might have been rented. She welcomed me and the other guests cordially but with only a part of her attention. I didn't know then that all wives of freedom fighters lived their lives on the edge of screaming desperation.

As we sat down at the table, the telephone rang constantly, interrupting the conversation we were trying to establish. Mrs. Tambo would lower one side of her head and listen and most often allow the rings to wear themselves to silence. A few times she got up, and I could hear the one-sided sound of a telephone conversation.

Lunch was slow-cooked beef and a stiff corn-meal porridge called mealy. She told me that she had gone to the trouble of preparing South African traditional food so that I would not be shocked when I met it again. I didn't tell her that in the United States we ate the same thing and called it baked short ribs and corn-meal mush.

A startlingly beautiful woman spoke to me. Her skin was blue-black and smooth as glass. She had brushed her hair severely, and it lay in tiny ripples back from a clean, shining forehead. Her long eyes were lifted above high cheekbones and her lips formed themselves in a large black bow. When she smiled, displaying white even upper teeth but bare lower gums, I knew she was from Kenya. I had read that the women of that country's Luo tribe have their bottom four teeth extracted to enhance their beauty. She was bright and tough, describing Europe's evil presence in Africa.

Mrs. Okalala from Uganda, a squat tugboat of a woman, said she found it ironic, if not downright stupid, to hold a meeting where people discussed how to get colonialism's foot off the neck of Africa in the capital of colonialism. It reminded her of an African saying: Only a fool asks a leopard to look after a lamb.

Two Somali women wrapped in flowing pink robes smiled and ate daintily. They spoke no English and had attended the lunch for form's sake. Occasionally they whispered to each other in their own language and smiled.

Ruth Thompson, a West Indian journalist, led the conversation, as soon as lunch was finished.

"What are we here for? Why are African women sitting eating, trying to act cute while African men are discussing serious questions and African children are starving? Have we come to London just to convenience our husbands? Have we been brought here only as portable pussy?"

I was the only person shocked by the language, so I kept my reaction private.

The Luo woman laughed. "Sister, you have asked, completely, my question. We, in Kenya, are women, not just wombs. We have shown during Mau Mau that we have ideas as well as babies."

Mrs. Okalala agreed and added, "At home we fight. Some women have died in the struggle."

A tall wiry lawyer from Sierra Leone stood. "In all of Africa, women have suffered." She picked at the cloth of her dress, caught it and dragged it above her knees. "I have been jailed and beaten. Look, my sisters. Because I would not tell the whereabouts of my friends, they also shot me." She wore a garter belt and the white elastic straps on her left leg evenly divided a deep-gouged scar as slick and black as wet pavement. "Because I fought against imperialism."

We gathered around her, clucking sympathy, gingerly touching the tight skin.

"They shot me and said my fighting days were over, but if I am paralyzed and can only lift my eyelids, I will stare the white oppressors out of Africa."

The spirit of overcoming was familiar to me, also. In my Arkansas church we sang,

> "I've seen starlight
> I've seen starlight
> Lay this body down
> I will lay down in my grave
> And stretch out my arms."

Nineteenth-century slaves who wrote the song believed that they would have freedom and that not only would souls cross over Jordan to march into glory with the other saints, but the grave itself would be unable to restrict the movement of their bodies.

When the lawyer dropped the hem of her dress all the women wrapped her 'round with arms, bodies and soft voices.

"Sister, Mother Africa is proud of you."

"A true daughter of a true mother."

The Somali women had also touched the scar. They spoke unintelligible words of sorrow and stroked the Sierra Leonian woman's back and shoulders.

Mrs. Tambo brought out a large bottle of beer. "This is all there is in the house."

The lawyer took the bottle with both hands and raised it to the sky. "The mother will understand." She turned and handed the beer to Mrs. Okalala. "Auntie, as the elder, you must do the honor."

I followed the general movement and found myself with the women bunched together in the center of the small living room. The woman faced us, solemnly.

"To talk to God I must speak Lingala." Except for the Somali women and me, all the women nodded.

She began to speak quietly, near a moan. Her tempo and volume increased into a certain chant. She walked around in rhythm and dribbled beer in the four corners of the room. The women, watching, accompanied her in their languages, urging her on, and she complied. The Somali women's voices were united into the vocal encouragement. I added "amens" and "hallelujahs," knowing that despite the distances represented and the Babel-like sound of languages, we were all calling on God to move and move right now. Stop the bloodshed. Feed the children. Free the imprisoned and uplift the downtrodden.

I told about black American organizations, remembering the Daughter Elks and Eastern Stars, Daughters of Isis and the Pythians. Secret female organizations with strict moral codes. All the women in my family were or had been members. My mother and grandmothers had been Daughter Rulers and High Potentates. Oaths were taken and lifelong promises made to uphold the tenets and stand by each sister even unto death.

The African women responded with tales of queens and princesses, young girls and market women who outwitted the British or French or Boers. I countered with the history of Harriet Tubman, called Moses, a physically small woman, slave, and how she escaped. How she stood on free ground, above a free sky, hundreds of miles from the chains and lashes of slavery and said, "I must go back. With the help of God I will bring others to freedom," and how, although suffering brain damage from a slaver's blow, she walked back and forth through the lands of bondage time after time and brought hundreds of her people to freedom.

The African women sat enraptured as I spoke of Sojourner Truth. I related the story of the six-foot-tall ex-slave speaking at an equal rights meeting of white women in the 1800s. That evening a group of white men in the hall, already incensed that their own women were protesting sexism, were livid when a black woman rose to speak. One of the town's male leaders shouted from the audience: "I see the stature of the person speaking and remark the ferocious gestures. I hear the lowness and timbre of the speaker's voice. Gentlemen, I am not convinced that we are being addressed by a woman. Indeed, before I will condone further speech by that person, I must insist that some of the white ladies take the speaker into the inner chamber and examine her and then I will forbear to listen."

The other men yelled agreement, but the white women refused to be a party to such humiliation.

Sojourner Truth, however, from the stage took the situation in hand. In a booming voice, which reached the farthest row in the large hall, she said:

"Yoked like an ox, I have plowed your land. And ain't I a woman? With axes and hatchets, I have cut your forests and ain't I a woman? I gave birth to thirteen children and you have sold them away from me to be the property of strangers and to labor in strange lands. Ain't I a woman? I have suckled your babes at this breast." Here she put her large hands on her bodice. Grabbing the cloth she pulled. The threads gave way, the blouse and her undergarments parted and her huge tits hung, pendulously free. She continued, her face unchanging and her voice never faltering, "And ain't I a woman?"

When I finished the story, my hands tugging at the buttons of my blouse, the African women stood applauding, stamping their feet and crying. Proud of their sister, whom they had not known a hundred years before.

We agreed to meet often during the conference and share our stories so that when we returned to our native lands we could take back more than descriptions of white skins, paved streets, flushing toilets, tall buildings and ice-cold rain.

A year would pass before I actually went to Africa, but that afternoon in Oliver Tambo's English apartment, I was in Africa surrounded by her gods and in league with her daughters.

The conference ended and Vus had to go to Cairo on PAC business. He took me to London's Heathrow airport and handed me a pile of English pounds.

"Find a good apartment, in Manhattan, and furnish it well. It must be large and central." I was unhappy at the prospect of going back to New York alone, but he assured me that he would return in two weeks or at most a month. After he concluded his business in Egypt he might have to go to Kenya. The thought of his exotic destinations cheered my spirit and strengthened my resolve. I was happy to return to New York and the task of finding an apartment which would fit his exquisite taste.

In one week I found an apartment in Manhattan on Central Park West, packed books and hired a mover. On our moving day, Guy and I sat among the boxes in the Brooklyn living room. He wanted me to tell him about London again. I described the speakers talking in the rain at Hyde Park Corner and the solemn guards at Buckingham Palace, but he wanted to hear about the Africans.

"Tell me how they looked. How did they walk? What were they called?"

The names were beautiful. "There was Kozonguizi and MakeWane, Molotsi, Mahomo."

Guy sat quietly. I knew he was running the sounds through his mind. After a moment he said, "You know, Mom, I've been thinking of changing my name. What do you think?"

What I thought was that my marriage to Vus had affected him deeply, but I said nothing.

"Johnson is a slave name. It was the name of some white man who owned my great-great-grandfather. Am I right?"

I nodded and felt ashamed.

"Have you chosen a name?"

He smiled, "Not yet. But I'm thinking about it. All the time."

Guy spent the next few weeks adjusting to his new school, and I used the time seeing my friends and trying to beautify the apartment.

The Harlem Writers Guild members and Abbey listened attentively to my description of Africans in London. They nodded, appreciating the freedom fighters' dedication. They smiled at me, proud that I had been so close to the motherland.

Before Vus returned, I painted the kitchen and put brightly colored wallpaper in the bathroom. The apartment was crisp and elegant.

Vus came home like a soldier returning from a conquered battlefield. His sagas of Cairo were heroic. He had drunk coffee with President Nasser and talked privately with his assistant. Egyptian officials supported the African struggle for freedom, and soon he would take Guy and me to live in Cairo. Excitement shook away Guy's just-forming adult postures. He jumped up, wiggling.

"We're going to Egypt? I'll see the pyramids? Boy, I'm going to be riding camels and everything."

Vus chuckled, happy to be the cause of such elation. Guy finally took his thrills to bed and I rushed into Vus's waiting arms.

—

The next morning my interior decorating met with stony disapproval. The old sofa was wrong for a man in my husband's position and the secondhand-store bedroom set definitely had to go.

"I am an African. Even a man sleeping in the bush will lay fresh leaves on the ground. I will not sleep on a bed other men have used."

I didn't ask him what he did in hotels. Certainly he didn't call the manager and say, "I want a brand-new mattress. I am an African."

I said, "But if we're going to Egypt we shouldn't buy new furniture."

He answered, "The things we buy will be of such quality they will have a high resale value. And anyway, we're not moving immediately."

I followed him meekly around a furniture store where he selected an expensive bed, a teak coffee table and a giant brown leather sofa.

He paid in cash, pulling bills from a large roll of money. The source of Vus's money was a mystery. He evaded my questions with the agility of an impala. There was nothing for me to do but relax and accept that he knew what he was doing. My son and I were in his care and he looked after us well. He was an attentive father, making solo visits to Guy's school and sitting with him late evenings over textbooks. They laughed often and affectionately together. When other Africans visited, Vus would insist that Guy sit in on the unending debates over violence and nonviolence, the role of religion in Africa, the place and the strength of women in the struggle. I tried to overhear their interesting conversations, but generally I was too busy with household chores to take the time.

It seemed to me that I washed, scrubbed, mopped, dusted and waxed thoroughly every other day. Vus was particular. He checked on my progress. Sometimes he would pull the sofa away from the wall to see if possibly I had missed a layer of dust. If he found his suspicions confirmed, his response could wither me. He would drop his eyes and shake his head, his face saddened with disappointment. I wiped down the walls, because dirty fingerprints could spoil his day, and ironed his starched shirts (he had his shoes polished professionally).

Each meal at home was a culinary creation. Chicken Kiev and feijoda, Eggs Benedict and Turkey Tetrazzini.

A good woman put ironed sheets on the beds and matched the toilet paper to the color of the bathroom tile.

I was unemployed but I had never worked so hard in all my life. Monday nights at the Harlem Writers Guild challenged my control. Heavy lids closed my eyes and the best reading of the best writing could not hold my exhausted attention.

"A bride, you know." Everyone would laugh, except Rosa, who knew how hard I was trying to be a good housewife.

"That African's got her jumping." Hands clapped at the humor of it all. But they were speaking more truth then they knew. When I wasn't home tired I was as tight as a fist balled up in anger. My nerves were like soldiers on dress parade, sharp, erect and at attention.

We were living luxuriously but I didn't know how much cash we had, nor could I be sure that the bills were paid. Since I had been sixteen, except for three married years between, I had made and spent my own money.

Now I was given a liberal food and house allowance and a little cash for personal expenditure (taxis and Tampax). Vus collected and paid the bills. The novelty was not amusing and my heart was not at peace.

Members of the South Africa United Front were invited to India to meet Krishna Menon. When Vus left I fumbled around the house for a few days, seeing no one but Guy, trying to accommodate an uncomfortable sense of uselessness. When every window was polished and every closet as orderly as department-store racks, I decided to go to Abbey's house. The most called-upon prerequisite of a friend is an accessible ear.

"He doesn't want me to work, but I don't know what's going on and it's making me feel crazy."

Abbey brushed the nap of her long-haired sofa. "You wanted a man, Maya Angelou. You've got one." She just didn't know how seriously upset I was.

"But, Ab, I didn't give over my entire life. You know that's not right."

She locked her jaws and stared at me for a long time. When she spoke, her voice was hard and angry. "A man's supposed to be in charge. That's the order of nature." She was raising an argument which we had debated for years.

My position had always been that no one was responsible for my life except me. I was responsible for Guy only until he reached maturity, and then he had to take control of his own existence. Of course, no man had ever tried to persuade me differently by offering the security of his protection. "Well, then, I must be outside of nature. 'Cause I can't stand not knowing where my air is coming from."

Abbey made a clucking sound with her tongue, and said, "The worst injury of slavery was that the white man took away the black man's chance to be in charge of himself, his wife and his family. Vus is teaching you that you're not a man, no matter how strong you are. He's going to make you into an African woman. Just watch it." She dismissed the discussion and me. But she didn't know the African women I had met in London or the legendary women in the African stories. I wanted to be a wife and to create a beautiful home to make my man happy, but there was more to life than being a diligent maid with a permanent pussy.

CHAPTER 11

The Cultural Association for Women of African Heritage had its second meeting at Abbey's luxury penthouse apartment on Columbus Avenue. Several weeks before, we had agreed on a charter, a policy statement and a name: CAWAH. It sounded exotic. We agreed. The newly founded organization included dancers, teachers, singers, writers and musicians. Our intention was to support all black civil rights groups. The charter, as drawn up by Sarah Wright and signed unanimously by the membership, stated that since the entire power of the United States was arrayed in fury against the very existence of the Afro-Americans, we, members of CAWAH, would offer ourselves to raise money for, promote and publicize any gathering sincerely engaged in developing a just society. It further stated that our members, multitalented, would agree, after an assenting vote, to perform dance concerts, song fests, fashion shows and general protest marches.

Abbey's living room filled with strident voices. Should we or should we not insist that every member show her commitment to being black by wearing unstraightened hair. Abbey, Rosa and I already wore the short-cut natural, but it was the other women, with tresses hanging down like horse's manes, who argued that the naturals should be compulsory.

"I've made an appointment for next Friday. I'm having all this shit cut off because I believe that I should let the world know that I'm proud to be black." The woman placed her hands on the back of her neck and lifted years of hair growth.

I said, "I don't agree." I would miss seeing her long black pageboy.

Abbey said, "I don't agree either. Hair is a part of woman's glory.

She ought to wear it any way she wants to. You don't get out of one trick bag by jumping into another. I wear my hair like this because I like it and Max likes it. But I'd dye it green if I thought it would look better."

We all laughed and put that discussion aside, addressing ourselves to plans for an immense fashion show based on an African theme and showing African designs. Abbey said, "In Harlem, I'm sick of black folks meeting in white hotels to talk about how rotten white folks are." So Rosa and I were assigned to find a suitable auditorium for the affair.

Rosa and I met on 125th Street and the first thing she said was "Lumumba is dead." She continued in a horror-constricted voice, saying that she had learned of the assassination from Congolese diplomats, but that there would be no announcement until the coming Friday when Adlai Stevenson, the United States delegate to the United Nations, would break the news.

I said nothing. I knew no words which would match the emptiness of the moment. Patrice Lumumba, Kwame Nkrumah and Sékou Touré were the Holy African Triumvirate which radical black Americans held dear, and we needed our leaders desperately. We had been abused, and so long abused, that the loss of one hero was a setback of such proportion it could dishearten us and weaken the struggle.

We were walking aimlessly, in a fog, when the sound of people talking, moving, shouting, broke into our stupor. We allowed ourselves to be drawn to the corner where the Nation of Islam was holding a mass meeting.

The street corner wriggled with movement as white policemen nervously guarded the intersection. A rapt crowd had pushed as close as possible to the platform where Malcolm X stood flanked by a cadre of well-dressed solemn men. Television crews on flatbed trucks angled their cameras at the crowded dais.

Malcolm stood at the microphone.

"Every person under the sound of my voice is a soldier. You are either fighting for your freedom or betraying the fight for freedom or enlisted in the army to deny somebody else's freedom."

His voice, deep and textured, reached through the crowd, across the street to the tenement windows where listeners leaned half their bodies out into the spring air.

"The black man has been programmed to die. To die either by his own hand, the hand of his brother or at the hand of a blue-eyed devil trained to do one thing: take the black man's life."

The crowd agreed noisily. Malcolm waited for quiet. "The Honorable Elijah Muhammad offers the only possible out for the black man. Accept Allah as the creator, Muhammad as His Messenger and the White American as the devil. If you don't believe he's a devil, look how he's made your life a hell."

Black people yelled and swayed. Policemen patted their unbuttoned holsters.

Rosa and I nodded at each other. The Muslim tirade was just what we needed to hear. Malcolm thrilled us with his love and understanding of black folks and his loathing of whites and their cruelty.

Unable to get close to the platform, we pushed ourselves into Mr. Micheaux's bookshop and watched and listened in the doorway.

"Talk, Malcolm."

Malcolm roared back, his face a golden-yellow in the sun, his hair rusty-red.

"If you want to live at any cost, say nothing but 'yes, sir' and do nothing except bow and scrape and bend your knees to the devil. But if you want your freedom, you'd better study the teachings of the Honorable Elijah Muhammad, and start respecting your women. Straighten out your home affairs and stop cheating on your wives. You know who you're really cheating?"

Female voices shot up like arrows over the crowd. "Tell these fools, brother Malcolm." "Tell them to stop acting like little boys." "Explain it. Explain it on down." "Break it down."

Malcolm took a breath and leaned toward the microphone. "You are cheating your fathers and mothers and grandfathers and grandmothers and-you-are-cheating-Allah."

A man on the platform lifted his hands, showing copper palms, and chanted in Arabic.

After a burst of applause, Malcolm paused and looked solemnly at the crowd. People stopped moving; the air became still. When he spoke again his tone was soft and sweet.

"Some of you think there are good whites, don't you? Some good white folks you've worked for, or worked with or went to school with or even married. Don't you?"

The listeners exchanged a grumble of denial.

Malcolm continued speaking low, nearly whispering. "There are whites who give money to the SCLC, the NAACP and the Urban League. Some even go so far as to march with you in the streets. But let me tell you who they are. Any white American who says he's your friend is either weak"—he waited for the word to have its effect and when he spoke again his voice growled—"or he's an infiltrator. Either he'll be too scared to help you when you need help or he's getting close to you so he can find out your plans and deliver you back in chains to his brothers."

The street corner exploded with sound as anger and recognition collided. When Malcolm finished speaking the crowd yelled their approval of the fire-hot leader. Rosa and I waited in the bookstore until most of the people left the corner.

We walked without speaking to Frank's Restaurant. Again there was no need to talk. Malcolm's words were harsh, but too close to the bitter truth to argue. Our people were alone. As always, alone. We could not expect protection from whites even if they happened to be our relatives. Slave-owning fathers had sold black sons and daughters. White sisters had put their black sisters in slave coffles for a price.

Rosa and I drank at the bar, not looking at each other.

"What can we do?"

"What do you think?" Rosa turned to me sadly as if I had failed her. She had been counting on me to be intelligent. She continued, frowning, "What the shit do you think? We've got to move. We've got to let the Congolese and all the other Africans know that we are with them. Whether we come from New York City or the South or from the West Indies, that black people are a people and we are equally oppressed."

I ordered another drink.

The only possible action that occurred to me was to call the members of CAWAH and throw the idea out for open discussion. Among us we would find something to do. Something large enough to awaken the black American community in New York.

Rosa didn't think much of my idea but she agreed to go along.

About ten women met at my house. Immediately the tone was fractious and suspicious. How did Rosa know Lumumba was dead? There had been no announcement in the newspapers.

Rosa said she had gotten her news from reliable sources.

Some members said that they thought our organization had been formed to support the black American civil rights struggle. Weren't we trying to swallow too much, biting into Africa? Except for Sékou Touré and Tom Mboya, when had the Africans backed us?

One woman, a fashion model, hinted that my husband and Rosa's diplomat boyfriend made us partial to the African cause. Abbey said that was a stupid attitude, and what happens in Africa affects every black American.

One woman said the only thing Africans had really done for us was to sell our ancestors into slavery.

I reminded the conservatives in our group that Martin Luther King had said that he found great inspiration and brotherly support on his recent trip to Africa.

Rosa spoke abruptly. "Some of us are going to do something. We don't know just what. But all the rest of you who aren't interested, why'n the hell don't you get your asses out and stop taking up our time?"

As usual when she got excited, her West Indian accent appeared and the music in her voice contradicted the words she chose.

Abbey got up and stood by the door. A rustle of clothes, the scraping of shoes, and the door slammed and six women were left in the living room.

Abbey brought brandy and we got down to business. After a short, fierce talk our decisions were made. On Friday, we would attend the General Session of the United Nations. We would carry black pieces of cloth, and when Adlai Stevenson started to make his announcement on Lumumba's death, we six women would use bobby pins and clip mourning veils to the front of our hair and then stand together in the great hall. It wasn't much to do but it was dramatic. Abbey thought some men might join us. She knew Max would like to come along. Amece, Rosa's sister, knew two West Indian revolutionaries who would like to be included. If men joined us, we would make elasticized arm bands, and at the proper moment, the men could slip the black bands up their sleeves and stand with the women. That was the idea. No mass movement but still a dramatic statement.

As the meeting was coming to end, I remembered a piece of advice Vus had given a few young African freedom fighters:

"Never allow yourself to be cut off from the people. Predators use the separation tactic with great success. If you're going to do something radical go to the masses. Let them know who you are. That is your only hope of protection."

I quoted Vus to the women and suggested that we let some folks in Harlem know what we intended to do. Everyone agreed. We would go to Mr. Micheaux; he could pass the word around Harlem faster than an orchestra of conga drums.

The next afternoon we went back to the bookstore, where posters of blacks covered every inch of wall space not taken up by shelves: Marcus Garvey, dressed in military finery, drove forever in an open car on one wall. W. E. B. DuBois gazed haughtily above the heads of book browsers. Malcolm X, Martin Luther King and an array of African chiefs stared down in varying degrees of ferocity.

Mr. Micheaux was fast moving, quick talking and small. His skin was the color of a faded manila envelope. We stopped him on one of his spins through the aisles. He listened to our plans impatiently, nodding his head.

"Yeah. The people ought to know. Tell them yourselves. Yeah, you tell them." His short staccato sentences popped out of his mouth like exploding cherry bombs. "Come back this evening. I'll have them here. Not nigger time. On time. Seven-thirty. You tell them."

He turned, neatly avoiding customers in the crowded aisle.

A little after seven o'clock at the corner of Seventh Avenue, we had to push our way through a crowd of people who thronged the sidewalks. We thought the Muslims, or the Universal Improvement Association, were holding a meeting, or Daddy Grace and his flock were drumming up souls for Christ. Of course, it was a warm spring evening and already the small apartments were suffocating. Anything could have brought the people into the streets.

Mr. Micheaux's amplified voice reached us as we neared the bookstore.

"A lot of you say Africa ain't your business, ain't your business. But you are fools. Niggers and fools. And that's what the white man wants you to be. You make a cracker laugh. Ha, ha." His voice barked. "Ha, ha, crackers laugh."

Because of my height, I could see him on a platform in front of the store. He held on to a standing microphone and turned his body from left to right, his jacket flapping and a short-brim brown hat shading his face from view.

"Abbey, these people"—the human crush was denser nearer to the bookstore—"these people are here to hear us."

She grabbed my hand and I took Rosa's arm. We pressed on.

"Some of your sisters are going to be talking to you. Talking to you about Africa. In a few minutes, they're gonna tell you about Lumumba. Patrice Lumumba. About the goddam Belgians. About the United Nations. If you are ignorant niggers, go home. Don't stay. Don't listen. And all you goddam finks in the crowd—run back and tell your white masters what I said. Tell 'em what these black women are going to say. Tell 'em about J. A. Rogers' books, which prove that Africans had kingdoms before white folks knew how to bathe. Don't forget Brother Malcolm. Don't forget Frederick Douglass. Tell 'em. Everybody except ignorant niggers say 'Get off my back, Charlie. Get off my goddam back.' Here they come now." He had seen us. "Come on, Abbey, come on, Myra, you and Rosa. Come on. Get up here and talk. They waiting for you."

Unknown hands helped us up onto the unstable platform. Abbey walked to the microphone, poised and beautiful. Rosa and I stood behind her and I looked out at the crowd. Thousands of black, brown

and yellow faces looked back at me. This was more than we bargained
for. My knees weakened and my legs wobbled.

"We are members of CAWAH. Cultural Association for Women of
African Heritage. We have learned that our brother, Lumumba, has
been killed in the Congo."

The crowd moaned.

"Oh my God."

"Oh no."

"Who killed him?"

"Who?"

"Tell us who."

Abbey looked around at Rosa and me. Her face showed her nervousness.

Mr. Micheaux shouted. "Tell 'em. They want to know."

Abbey turned back to the microphone. "I'm not going to say the
Belgians."

The crowd screamed. "Who?"

"I won't say the French or the Americans."

"Who?"

It was a large hungry sound.

"I'll say the whites killed a black man. Another black man."

Mr. Micheaux leaned toward Abbey. "Tell 'em what you all are
going to do."

Abbey nodded.

"On Friday morning, our women and some men are going to the
United Nations. We are going to sit in the General Assembly, and
when they announce the death of Lumumba we're going to stand up
and remain standing until they put us out."

The crowd agreed loudly.

"I'm coming."

"I'll be there."

"Me too."

"Yeah, stand up and be counted."

"That's right!"

A few dissenting voices were heard.

"Bullshit. Is that all?"

"They kill a man and you broads are going to stand up? Shit." And, "They'll shoot your asses too! Yes, they will."

The opposition was drowned out by the larger encouragement.

Mr. Micheaux took the microphone.

"Come here, Myra." The little man could spell my name but he never pronounced it correctly. "You talk."

He turned to the crowd. "Here's a woman married to an African. Her husband just barely escaped the South African white dogs. Come on, Myra. Say something."

I repeated what had already been said at least once. Repetition was a code which everyone understood and appreciated. We had a saying: "Make everything you say two-time talk. If you say it once, you better be able to repeat it." Black ears were accustomed to the call and response in jazz, in blues and in the prose of black preachers.

Mr. Micheaux took the microphone from me and called Rosa.

She looked out at the faces and spoke very quickly.

"We'll be there. Any of you who wants to come will be welcome. We are going to meet at eight-thirty in front of the U.N. We'll make up extra veils and arm bands and our members will be waiting to distribute them. Come all. Come and let the world know that no longer can they kill black leaders in secret. Come."

She gave the microphone to Mr. Micheaux and beckoned to me and Abbey. We were helped off the stage. The crowd parted, and made an aisle of sounds.

"We'll be there."

"Eight-thirty on Friday."

"See you, sister. See you at the U.N."

"God bless you."

We sat quiet in the taxi and held on to each other. The enormity of the crowd and its passionate response had made us mute. We agreed to meet the next day.

I went back to an empty house. Guy's dinner dishes drained on the sideboard and a note propped on the dining-room table informed me that he was attending a SANE meeting and to expect him at ten-thirty.

Rosa phoned. We had to draw money from CAWAH. Her niece Jean was going downtown to a fabric outlet in the morning. She would buy black tulle and elastic. Rosa would pick up bobby pins from Woolworth's. We ought to meet at her house to make the arm bands and stick the pins in the veils. I agreed and hung up. Abbey phoned. Would I call women of CAWAH and would I check with the Harlem Writers Guild, and just to be on the safe side, wouldn't it be a good idea to make up a hundred veils and arm bands? I agreed.

Guy came home, full of his meeting. SANE was planning a demonstration on Saturday in New Jersey. He and Chuck would like to go. If the Killens and I gave permission for them to miss a school day, they would join a march on Friday, walking across the George Washington Bridge. He would be O.K., Mom. They would carry sleeping bags, and a lot of peanuts, and after all, hadn't I said I wanted him to be involved? "Dad," would certainly agree if he wasn't in India. My generation had caused the atomic bomb to be dropped on Hiroshima, the year he was born. So he could say correctly that he was an atomic baby. He and Chuck had talked. The bomb must never be used again. Human beings had been killed by the hundreds of thousands, and millions mutilated, and did I want to see the photographs of Hiroshima again?

I gave him permission to go to New Jersey.

Jean, Amece and Sarah cut the bolt of black tulle. Rosa sewed strips of elastic to half the large squares while Abbey and I gathered bobby pins into the remainder.

Jean pinned a veil to her hair and the stiff material stood out like a softly pleated fan. Her eyes and copper-colored skin were faintly visible through the material. She looked like a young woman, widowed by an untimely accident. We looked at her and approved. Our gesture was going to be successful.

On Friday morning, I stepped over Guy's sleeping bag, which he had laid open on the living-room floor. It wouldn't be kind to awaken him, since he would be sleeping rough that evening after his march.

He knew I had planned to leave the house early for the United Nations. I placed a five-dollar bill on the plaid sleeping bag and left the apartment.

Abbey's house was a flurry of action. CAWAH women were busy, drinking coffee, laying the veils in one box, talking, putting the arm bands in another box, eating sweet rolls a teacher had brought, smiling and flirting with Max, who walked around us like a handsome pasha in a busy harem. We left for the elevators, carrying the boxes, and jumpy with excitement.

Max and Abbey could take four in their car. The rest would find taxis. We agreed to meet on the sidewalk in front of the U.N. Amece and Rosa had the veils, so they rode with Max. The teacher, the model, Sarah and I would travel together. Jean and the other friends would get their own taxis. Finding a cab so early on Friday on New York's Upper West Side was not easy. Business people had radio-controlled taxis on regular calls, and many white drivers sped up when black people hailed them, afraid of being ordered north to Harlem and/or of receiving small tips.

At ten minutes to nine our taxi turned off 42nd Street onto First Avenue. Sarah and I screamed at the same time. The driver put on brakes and we all crashed forward.

"What the hell is going on here?" The cabbie's alarm matched our own. People stood packed together on the sidewalk and spilled out into the street. Placards stating FREEDOM NOW, BACK TO AFRICA, AFRICA FOR THE AFRICANS, ONE MAN, ONE VOTE waved on sticks above the crowd.

We looked out the windows. Thousands of people circled in the street and all of them were black. We paid and made our way to the crowd.

"Here she is. Here's one of them."

"Sister, we told you we'd be here. Where you been?"

"How do we get inside? The police said…"

"They won't let us in."

The shouts and questions were directed at me. I began a chant and used it moving through the anxious crowd: "I'll see about it. I'll take care of it. I'll take care of it. I'll see about it." Not knowing whom to see, or really how I would take care of anything.

Rosa was waiting for me in front of the severely modern building by the large glass doors.

"Can you imagine this crowd? So many people. So many." She was excited and her Caribbean was particularly noticeable. "And the guards have refused entrance."

"Rosa, you said you'd get tickets from the African delegations."

"I know, but only the Senegalese and my friend from Upper Volta have shown up." She had to shout, because the crowd had begun to chant.

She leaned toward me, frowning, "I've only got seven tickets." The people on the sidewalk shouted. "Freedom!" "Freedom!" "Lumumba! Lumumba!"

She said, "Little Carlos is here. The Cuban, you know. He took the tickets and went in with Abbey, Max, Amece and others. He'll bring the tickets back and take in six more. It's the only way." Carlos Moore was an angry young man who moved through Harlem's political sky like a luminous meteor.

I looked over at the black throng. Many had never been in midtown Manhattan, thinking the blocks south of Harlem as dangerous as enemy territory and no man's land. On our casual encouragement, they had braved the perilous journey.

Carlos came trotting through the double doors. "Sister, you have arrived." He grinned, his little chocolate face gleeful. "I am ready for the next group. Let's go! Now!"

I turned, and without thinking about it, plucked the first people in the crowd.

"Give me your placards. You're going in." I held the ungainly weighted sticks and Carlos shouted to the chosen men and women. "Follow me, brothers and sisters. Stay close to me." They disappeared into the dim foyer, and I redistributed the placards.

Rosa had walked away into the crowd. I took her example and moved through the people near the building.

"What's going on, sister?"

"The crackers don't want to let us in, huh?"

"We could break the motherfucker wide open."

"Shit, all we got to do is die. And we gonna do that any goddam way."

I stopped with that group. "Nothing could please the whites more than to have a reason to shoot down innocent black folks. Don't give them the pleasure."

An old woman grabbed my sleeve. "God will bless you, honey. If you keep the children alive."

She sounded wise and was about the age of my grandmother. "Yes, ma'am. Thank you." I took her hand and pulled her away from the seething mass. She would go in with the next group. We walked to the steps together. I turned and raised my voice to explain what had obviously happened.

Informers had alerted the police that Harlem was coming to the U.N. So security had been increased. In order to get into the building we had to exercise restraint. The cops were nervous, so to prevent some trigger-happy idiot from shooting into the crowd, we had to remain cool.

The people assented with a grace I found assuring. The old woman and I reached the top steps as Carlos came through the doors. "Six more. And we move. Now!"

Carlos gathered the next five people along with the old lady and led them into the building.

For the next thirty minutes, as Carlos siphoned off groups of six and led them into the building, more cadres of police arrived to stand armed and confused on the sidewalks and across the street, while plain-clothed white men took photographs of the action.

A marcher grabbed my sleeve. "What you folks think you're doing? You told us to come down here and now you can't get us in." The man was furious. He continued, "Yeah, that's black folks for you. Running around half shaved and grinning."

I wanted to explain how some fink had put us in the cross, but Rosa appeared, taking my other sleeve.

"Come on, Maya. Come on now." Her urgency would not be denied. I looked at the angry man and lied. "I'll be right back."

Inside the gleaming hall, unarmed security guards stood anxiously at their posts. Near the wide stairs leading to the second floor, Carlos was hemmed in by another group of guards.

"I've got my ticket. This is mine." Frayed stubs protruded from his black fist. "They were given to me by a delegate."

Rosa and I pushed into the circle, forcing the guards away. Rosa took his arm. "Come on, Carlos, we've got to go."

We walked together straight and moderately slowly, controlling the desire to break and run, keening into the General Assembly.

Although we were beyond the guards' hearing, Carlos whispered, "The Assembly has started. Stevenson is going to speak soon."

Upstairs, more guards stood silent as we passed. Two black men were waiting by the entry to the hall, anxiety flushing their faces.

"Carlos! We thought they had you, man."

"They'll never have me, mon. I am Carlos, mon."

His assurance had returned. Rosa smiled at me and we entered the dark, quiet auditorium. Miles away, down a steep incline, delegates sat before microphones in a square of light, but the upper balcony was too dim for me to distinguish anything clearly.

After a few seconds, the gloom gave way, and the audience became visible. About seventy-five black people were mixed among the whites. Some women had already pinned veils over their faces.

Amece, Jean and the teacher sat together. Max and Abbey were across the aisle near Sarah and the model. An accented voice droned unintelligibly.

"Uh, uhm, mm, um."

The little white man so far away leaned toward his microphone, his bald forehead shining-white. Dark-rimmed glasses stood out on the well-known face.

A scream shattered his first word. The sound was bloody and broad and piercing. In a second other voices joined it.

"Murderers."

"Lumumba. Lumumba."

"Killers."

"Bigoted sons of bitches."

The scream still rode high over the heads of astounded people who were rising, clutching each other or pushing out toward the aisle.

The houselights came on. Stevenson took off his glasses and looked to the balcony. The shock opened his mouth and made his chin drop.

A man near me screamed, "You Ku Klux Klan motherfuckers."

Another yelled, "Murderers."

African diplomats were as alarmed as their white counterparts. I was also shaken. We had not anticipated a riot. We had been expected to stand, veiled and mournful, in a dramatic but silent protest.

"Baby killers."

"Slave drivers."

Terrorized whites in the audience tried to hustle away from the yelling blacks. Security guards rushed through the doors on the upper and lower levels.

The garish lights, the stampede of bodies and the continuing high-pitched scream were overpowering. My knees weakened and I sat down in the nearest seat.

A woman in the aisle beside me screamed at the guards, "Don't dare touch me. Don't put your hands on me, you white bastard!"

The guards were shouting, "Get out. Get out."

The woman said, "Don't touch me, you Belgian bastard."

Below, the diplomats rose and formed an orderly file toward an exit.

When the piercing scream stopped I heard my own voice shouting, "Murderers. Killers. Assassins."

Two women grappled with a guard in the aisle. Carlos had leaped onto a white man's back and was riding him to the floor. A stout black woman held the lapels of a white man in civilian clothes.

"Who you trying to kill? Who you trying to kill? You don't know me, you dog. You don't know who you messing with."

The man was hypnotized and beyond fear, and the woman shook him like a dishrag.

The diplomats had vanished and except for the guards the whites had disappeared. The balcony was ours. Just as in the Southern segregated movie houses, we were in the buzzards' roost again.

Rosa found me and I got up and followed her. We urged the people back to the safety of the street. The black folks strode proudly past the guards, through the hall and out the doors into sunshine.

The waiting crowd, enlarged by latecomers and more police, had changed its mood. Insiders had told outsiders that we had rioted, and now an extravagant disorder was what the blacks wanted, while the law officers yearned for vindication.

"Let's go back in." "Let's go in and show them bastards we mean business." "This ain't no United Nations. This is just united white folks. Let's go back in."

A cadre of police stood on the steps, their eyes glittering. By law, they were forbidden inside the U.N. building, but they were eager to prevent our reentry.

Some folks screamed at the silent seething police.

"You killed Lumumba too. You shit."

"I wish I had your ass on 125th Street."

"Take off your pistol. I'll whip your ass."

Carlos rushed to me.

"We're going to the Belgian Consulate. Walk together." Rosa's voice was loud. "Forty-sixth Street. The Associated Press Building. Let us go. Let's go."

The crowd began to move between a corridor of police which stretched to the street. Up front, someone had started to sing.

"And before I'll be a slave, I'll be buried in my grave..."

The song rippled, now high, now low. Picked up by voices and dropped but never discarded.

"And go home to my God and be free."

Mounted police, sitting tall on hot horses, looked down as we crossed First Avenue, singing.

Rosa and I were walking side by side in the last group as we turned into 43rd Street. I said, "That scream started it. Wonder who screamed."

She frowned and laughed at the same time. "Amece, and she almost killed Jean."

The marchers around us were singing

> "No more slavery,
> No more slavery,
> No more slavery over me."

Rosa continued, "Amece said she looked down and saw Stevenson and thought about Lumumba. She reached to caress her daughter, but Jean jumped and Amece screamed. Unfortunately, she had her arm around Jean's neck. So when Jean jerked, Amece tightened her grip and kept screaming. Nobody was going to hurt her baby. So she screamed." Rosa laughed. "Nobody but Amece. She nearly choked Jean to death."

The crowd was trooping and chanting.

Six mounted police climbed the sidewalk and rode through the stragglers. People jumped out of the way as the horses bore down on them.

A wiry black man unable to escape was being pressed against the wall of a building. I flung myself toward him slapping horses, jutting my elbows into their flanks.

"Get away. Move, dammit."

The man was flat against the wall, ignoring the horses, staring up at the policemen. I reached him and took his hand.

"Come on, brother. Come on, brother."

We walked between the shifting horses and back to Rosa, who had halted the group.

Rosa was grinning, her face filled with disbelief. "Maya Angelou, I thought you were scared of animals. You went into those horses, kicking ass!"

She was right. I had never owned a pet. I didn't understand the intelligent idiocy of dogs or cats; in fact, all animals terrorized me. The day's action had taken away my usual self and made me uncommon. I was literally intoxicated with adventure.

We approached the corner of 46th and Sixth Avenue, and the intersection reminded me of a South American news telecast. For the moment, heavily armed police and angry people seemed to neutralize the scene. Bright sunlight left no face in shadow and the two groups watched each other warily, moving dreamily this way and then that. That way and this. Policemen's hands were never far from their pistols, and plain-clothed officers spoke into the static of walkie-talkies. Black demonstrators edged along the sidewalk, rumbling and carrying battered and torn placards.

Police cars were parked double in the street and a captain walked among his men, talking and looking obliquely at the crowd, trying to evaluate its mood and its intention.

When Rosa dashed away from me and into the shuffling crowd, a beribboned officer came over.

"You're one of the leaders?" His pink face was splotched with red anger.

Following the Southern black advice "If a white man asks you where you're going, you tell him where you've been," I answered, "I'm with the people."

"Where is your permit? You people have to have a permit to demonstrate."

Three black men suddenly appeared, placing themselves between the policemen and me.

"What do you want with this black lady?"

"Watch yourself, Charlie. Don't mess with her."

Instantly more police surrounded my protectors, and black people from the dragging line, seeing the swift action, ran over to encircle the newly arrived police.

I had to make a show of confidence. I looked into the officer's face and said, "Permit? If we left it to you whites we'd be in the same shape as our folks in South Africa. We'd have to have a permit to breathe."

A man standing by my side added, "Naw. We ain't got no damn permit. So you better pull out your pistols and start shooting. Shoot us down now, 'cause we ain't moving."

The policemen, eager to accept the man's invitation, snorted and fidgeted like enraged horses. The officer reigned them in with his voice. He shouted, "It's all right, men. I said, it's all right. Back to your stations."

There was a brief period of hateful staring before the cops returned to the street and we rejoined the larger group of black people shuffling along the pavement.

Rosa found me. "Carlos is inside." Her eyes were narrowed. "Somebody said he's been in there over a half-hour. The Belgian Consulate is on the eleventh floor. Maybe the cops have got him."

The knowledge of what police do to black men rose wraithlike before my eyes. Carlos was little and pretty and reminded me of my brother. The cops did have Bailey and maybe he was being clubbed or raped at that very minute. I saw a horrifying picture of Bailey in the hands of madmen but there was nothing I could do about it.

I could do something about Carlos.

I said, "I'm going in. You keep the people marching."

I searched the faces nearest me.

Vus once told me, "If you're ever in trouble, don't under any circumstances ask black middle-class people for help. They always think they have a stake in the system. Look for a *tsotsi,* that's Xhosa for a street hoodlum. A roughneck. A convict. He'll already be angry and he will know that he has nothing to lose."

I continued looking until I saw the man. He was taller than I, railthin and the color of bitter chocolate. One deep scar ran from the flange of his left nostril to his ear lobe and another lay between his hairline and his left eyebrow.

I beckoned to him and he came toward me.

"Brother, my name is Maya. I think Carlos Moore is in this building somewhere. He's the leader of this march. The cops may have him and you know what that means."

"Yeah, sister, yeah." He nodded wisely.

"I want to go in and see about him and I need somebody to go with me."

He nodded again and waited.

"It'll be dangerous, but will you go?"

"Sure." The planes on his face didn't change. "Sure, Sister Maya. Let's go." He took my elbow and began to propel me to the steps.

I asked, "What's your name?" He said, "Call me Buddy."

Rosa's voice came to me as we went through the revolving doors. "Be careful, Maya."

The lobby was busy with police, guards and milling white men. Although my escort was pushing me quickly toward the bank of elevators, I had time to look at the building's directory. Above the eleventh-floor listing of the Belgian Consulate were the words AMERICAN BOOK COMPANY, 10TH FLOOR. A flat, florid police officer stepped in front of me and my companion.

"Where are you going?"

The *tsotsi* spoke. "None of your goddam business."

I poked his side and said sweetly, "I'm going to the American Book Company."

The cop and the *tsotsi* stared knowingly at each other. Loathing ran between the two men like an electrical current.

"And you. Where do you think you're going?"

"I'm going with her. Every step of the way."

The cop heard the challenge and narrowed his eyes and I heard the protection and felt like a little girl. The pudgy cop followed us to the elevators and I pushed the tenth-floor button, holding on to the black man's hand. The ride was tense and quick. We walked out into the hall and turned to watch the officer's face until the doors closed.

I said, "Let's find the stairs."

Around the corner we saw the exit sign.

"Buddy, you go through and let the door close, then see if you can open it again."

He walked out onto the landing and waited until the door slammed shut. I stepped back as he turned the knob and opened the door from his side.

"Come on. Let's get up there."

We raced up the steps to the eleventh floor. He grabbed the knob, but the door wouldn't open.

"That cracker cop. He beat us to it. Stay here."

He turned and trotted up another flight. I heard him mutter. "This damn door is locked too."

He came down the steps heavily.

"What you wanna do now?"

I couldn't think at the moment. I had only a vague plan to reach the eleventh floor and "see about Carlos." My mind had not budged beyond the possibility of achieving that feat. I looked stupidly at Buddy, who was waiting for an answer. After a few seconds, my voice surfaced. "I guess there's nothing else to do but go back to the street. I'm sorry."

I expected to see disgust or at least derision on my accomplice's face, but he displayed no emotion.

"All right, sister. Let's go."

We walked back down to the tenth floor and I pushed the door, but it resisted. I must have gasped, because he pushed me aside and grabbed the knob. "Let me do it." He took the knob and leaned his body against the metal panel, but the door wouldn't give. Panic accelerated my blood. Like an idiot I had given myself to death. The cops could open the door any minute and blow my brains out. No one would see and no one would be able to protect me. I saw an image of my son in his classroom. Who would tell him, and how would he handle the news? My new husband would receive a telegram in India. What would he think of a wife so frivolous as to commit suicide? My poor mother... The man beside me, whom fear had caused me to forget, took my shoulders in his hands.

"Sister. Sister. You ain't got nothin' to worry about. I'm here."

He released me and stood on the landing's edge. "They'll have to walk over my dead body to get to you."

Buddy ran down the steps. I heard him stop on the ninth floor, then his footsteps descended and stopped again and again. In a few seconds he called, "Sister Maya, come on. I got a door. Come on." I met him on the sixth-floor landing. My heart was fluttering so I could hardly catch my breath. The hallway and the elevator looked to me like Canada must have to escaping slaves. We were in the lobby before my embarrassment returned. My hand on his arm turned him around. "Buddy, I apologize for panicking a while ago. I'm going to tell my husband about you."

He looked at me, and shook his head. "Sister, in this country a Negro is always about to get killed, so that ain't nothing. But you tell your husband that a black man was ready to lay down his life for you. That's all."

He took my elbow and guided me past the still-waiting police and to the door. I walked right into Rosa's arms.

"Girl, what happened? Carlos came out just after you went in. A bunch of us were getting ready to go get you." We hugged tightly. I said, "Rosa, you've got to meet this brother," but when I turned to introduce Buddy, he had disappeared into the thinning crowd.

Rosa continued, "You were in there nearly twenty minutes." That was astounding news. I had been bold, blatant and audacious. I had been silly, irresponsible and unprepared. My body had been enclosed with panic and my mind immobilized with fear. A stranger had shown the courage of Vivian Baxter and the generosity of Jesus. And all that had happened in twenty minutes.

Television and radio reporters were walking among the remaining protesters seeking interviews.

One woman spoke into a microphone. "Yes, we're mad. You people pick us off like we're jack rabbits. You dad-gummed right, we're mad." A man walking behind her added, "Lumumba was in the Congo. The Congo is in Africa and we're Africans. You get that?"

CAWAH members had agreed to make no public statements, so we turned our faces when the journalists approached. The line of marchers was exhausted. People had begun to peel away. Their shoulders sagged and they walked heavily. They knew that their latest protest had done no good. They had been Joshua's band, shouting and screaming, singing and yelling at the walls, but Jericho had remained upright, unchanged.

That night I went to Rosa's for dinner and to watch the evening news. The cameras caught black bodies hurtling out of the U.N. doors, and marchers chanting along 46th Street.

Angry faces in profile glided across the screen, shouting accusations. When an unknown, well-dressed man came into view, and speaking pompously, said that he took full responsibility for the demonstration, Jean responded by calling him a sap sucker and turning off the television.

The echo of the day's excitement and the wonder of CAWAH's power to bring all those people from Harlem kept us quiet for a few minutes. When conversation did return we talked about our next moves. The day had proven that Harlem was in commotion and the rage was beyond the control of the NAACP, the SCLC or the Urban League. The fury would turn on itself if it was not outwardly directed. There would be an increase of stabbings and shootings as black people assaulted each other, discharging tension, and blindly looking for a surcease of pained lives.

Rosa and I said, "the Black Muslims" and grinned, because we thought alike and at the same time. Of course, the Muslims, with their exquisite discipline and their absolute stand on black-white relations, would know how to control and use the ferment in Harlem. We should go straight to Malcolm X and lay the situation in his lap. It would be interesting to see what he would do. And it would be a relief to shift the responsibility.

The next day, Guy jumped with excitement. "Mom, you're great. Really great. I wish I had been there. Boy, I wish I could have seen Stevenson's face. Boy, that's fantastic."

John Killens phoned. "Why didn't you let me know you people were going to have a riot? I'm always ready for a riot. You know that, angel."

When I explained that we had only expected a few people, he grunted and said we had fallen into the same trick bag whites are in. We underestimated the black community.

Two days later, Rosa and I walked into the Muslim Restaurant. Making the appointment had been the easiest part. I simply telephoned the Mosque and asked if Mr. Malcolm X could spare a half-hour for two black ladies. After a brief pause I was given a time and a place. Putting my thoughts in respectable order was more difficult, because after I knew Malcolm would see us I became appalled at our presumption.

We told a waitress that we had come to see Mr. Malcolm X. She nodded and walked away, disappearing through a door at the end of the long counter. We stood nervously in the center of the room. In a moment Malcolm appeared at the rear door. His aura was too bright and his masculine force affected me physically. A hot desert storm eddied around him and rushed to me, making my skin contract, and my pores slam shut. He approached, and all my brain would do for me was record his coming. I had never been so affected by a human presence.

Watching Malcolm X on television or even listening to him speak on a podium had been no preparation for meeting him face to face.

"Ladies, *Salaam aleikum.*" His voice was black baritone and musical. Rosa shook hands, and I was able to nod dumbly. Up close he was a great red arch through which one could pass to eternity. His hair was the color of burning embers and his eyes pierced. He offered us a chair at a table and asked a nervous waitress for tea, which she brought in trembling cups.

Rosa was more contained than I, so she began explaining our mission. The sound of her voice helped me to shake loose the constriction of muteness. I joined the telling, and we distributed our story equally, like the patter of a long-time vaudeville duo.

"We—CAWAH..."

"Cultural Association of Women of African Heritage."

"Wanted to protest the murder of Lumumba so we—"

"Planned a small demonstration. We didn't expect—"

"More than fifty people—"

"And thousands came."

"That told us that the people of Harlem are angry and that they are more for Africa and Africans"

"than they ever let on..."

Malcolm was leaning back in his chair, his chin tilted down, his attention totally ours. He straightened abruptly.

"We know of the demonstration, but Muslims were not involved. New York *Times* reporters telephoned me and I told them, 'Muslims do not demonstrate.' And I'll tell you this, you were wrong."

Rosa and I looked at each other. Malcolm X, as the most radical leader in the country, was our only hope, and if he didn't approve of our action then maybe we had misunderstood everything.

"You were wrong in your direction." He continued speaking and looking straight into our eyes. "The people of Harlem are angry. And they have reason to be angry. But going to the United Nations, shouting and carrying placards will not win freedom for anyone, nor will it keep the white devils from killing another African leader. Or a black American leader."

"But"—Rosa was getting angry—"what were we supposed to do? Nothing? I don't agree with that." She had more nerve than I.

"The Honorable Elijah Muhammad teaches us that integration is a trick. A trick to lull the black man to sleep. We must separate ourselves from the white man, this immoral white man and his white religion. It is a hypocrisy practiced by Christian hypocrites."

He continued. White Christians were guilty. Portuguese Catholic priests had sprinkled holy water on slave ships, entreating God to give safe passage to the crews and cargoes on journeys across the Atlantic. American slave owners had used the Bible to prove that God wanted slavery, and even Jesus Christ had admonished slaves to "render unto their masters" obedience. As long as the black man looked to the white man's God for his freedom, the black man would remain enslaved.

I tried not to show my disappointment.

"Thank you. Thank you for your time. Mr. X—oh, I don't know your last name. I mean, how should you be addressed?"

"I am Minister Malcolm. My last name is Shabazz. But just call me Minister Malcolm."

Rosa had stood, irritation on her face.

Malcolm said, "I know you're disappointed." His voice had softened and for a time the Islamic preacher disappeared. "I'll tell you this. By twelve o'clock, some Negro leaders are going to be like Peter in your Christian Bible. They will deny you. There will be statements given to the press, not only refuting what you did, but they will add that you are dangerous and probably Communists. Those Negroes"—he said the word sarcastically—"think they're different from you and that the white man loves them for their difference. They will sell you again and again into slavery. Now, here's what we, the Nation of Islam, will not do. We will not ask the people of Harlem to march anywhere at any time. We will not send black men and black women and black children before armed and crazy white devils, and we will not deny you. We will do two things. We will offer them the religion of Islam the Prophet Muhammad and the Honorable Elijah Muhammad. And we will make a statement to the press. I will say that yesterday's demonstration is symbolic of the anger in this country. That black people were saying they will not always say 'yessir' and 'please, sir.' And they will not always allow whites to spit on them at lunch counters in order to eat hot dogs and drink Coca-Colas." He stood; our audience was over. Suddenly he was aloof and cool, his energy withdrawn. He said, *"Salaam aleikum"* and turned to join a few men who had been waiting for him at the counter.

We left the restaurant in a fog of defeat. Black despair was still real, the murders would continue and we had just used up our last resource. When Rosa and I embraced at the subway there was no elation in our parting.

That evening the radio, television and newspapers bore out Malcolm's predictions.

Conservative black leaders spoke out against us. "That ugly demonstration was carried out by an irresponsible element and does not reflect the mood of the larger black community."

"No good can come from yesterday's blatant disrespect at the U.N."
"It was undignified and unnecessary."

Malcolm X was as good as his word. He said, "Black people are letting white Americans know that the time is coming for ballots or bullets. They know it is useless to ask their enemy for justice. And surely whites are the enemies of blacks, otherwise how did we get to this country in the first place?"

CHAPTER 12

Vus was back in New York, a little heavier and more distracted. He said the Indian curries had been irresistible and his meetings succeeded but raised new questions which he had to handle at once. He was out of the house early and came home long after dark. Guy was engaged in the mysteries which surround fifteen-year-old boys: The cunning way girls were made. The delicious agony of watching them walk. The painful knowledge that not one of the beauteous creatures would allow herself to be held and touched. Except for the refrigerator, the telephone was his only important link to life. One morning I realized that weeks had passed since I had participated in a conversation with anyone. When Max invited me over to read a script with Abbey, I accepted gladly. He had composed the music for Jean Genet's play, *The Blacks*, which was to open Off-Broadway in the late spring. When I walked into their apartment, a small group of musicians was tuning up beside the piano. I was introduced to the production team.

Sidney Bernstein, the producer, was a frail little man, who sat smiling timidly, his eyes wandering the room unfocused. The energetic and intense director, Gene Frankel, snapped his head from right to left and back again in small jerks, reminding me of a predatory bird, perched on a high bluff. The stage manager, Max Glanville, a tall sturdy black man, was at ease in the room. He sat composed while his two colleagues twitched. When Frankel said he was ready to hear the music, there was impatience in his voice.

Sidney smiled and said there was plenty of time.

Abbey and I sat opposite each other holding copies of the marked script. We divided the roles evenly and when the music began, we read, sometimes against the music, over it, or waited in intervals as the notes took center stage. Neither of us was familiar with the play, and since its structure was extremely complex, and its language convoluted, we read in monotones, not even trying to make dramatic sense. Finally, we reached the last notes. The evening had seemed to be endless. Gene Frankel was the first to stand. He rushed up to Max, took his hand, looked deep into his eyes, "Great. Great. Just great. We've got to be going. O.K. Thank you, ladies. Thank you. Great reading." Frankel turned around like a kitten trying to catch its tail. "O.K., Sidney? Let's go. Glanville." He turned again. "Musicians? Oh yeah, thanks, guys. Great."

In a second he was at the door, his hand on the knob. Sidney went to the musicians, shaking hands, giving each a bit of a wispy grin. He thanked Max and Abbey and me. "The music was perfect." Glanville looked at his white partners slyly and smiled at us. His leer said he was leaving with them only because he had to, and we would understand.

"O.K., folks. Thanks. Thanks, Max. We'll be talking to you." When the door closed behind them I laughed, partly out of relief. Max asked what was funny. I said the play and the producers.

"You mean you didn't understand it." All of a sudden he was angry and he began to shout at me. He said *The Blacks* was not only a good play, it was a great play. It was written by a white Frenchman who had done a lot of time in prison. Genet understood the nature of imperialism and colonialism and how those two evils erode the natural good in people. It was important that our people see the play. Every black in the United States should see it. Furthermore, as a black woman married to a South African and raising a black boy, I should damn well understand the play before I started laughing at it. And as for ridiculing the white men, at least they were going to put the play on, and all I could do was laugh at them. I ought to have better sense.

The musicians made a lot of noise packing up their instruments. Abbey sat quiet, looking at Max; I got up and gathered my purse. I wanted at least to reach the door before the tears fell.

"Good night."

Abbey called, "Thanks, Maya. Thanks for reading." I was nearly at the elevator before I heard a door and Max's voice at the same time.

"Maya, wait." He walked toward me. I thought that he was sorry to have spoken so harshly. "Take this." He handed me a wrapped package. "Read it." He was nearly barking. "Read it, understand it. Then see if you'll laugh." I took the manuscript and he spun around and went back into his apartment.

Vus studied political releases, Guy did schoolwork and I read *The Blacks*. During the third reading, I began to see through the tortuous and mythical language, and the play's meaning became clear. Genet suggested that colonialism would crumble from the weight of its ignorance, its arrogance and greed, and that the oppressed would take over the positions of their former masters. They would be no better, no more courageous and no more merciful.

I disagreed. Black people could never be like whites. We were different. More respectful, more merciful, more spiritual. Whites irresponsibly sent their own aged parents to institutions to be cared for by strangers and to die alone. We generously kept old aunts and uncles, grandparents and great-grandparents at home, feeble but needed, senile but accepted as natural parts of natural families.

Our mercy was well known. During the thirties Depression, white hobos left freight trains and looked for black neighborhoods. They would appear hungry at the homes of the last hired and the first fired, and were never turned away. The migrants were given cold biscuits, leftover beans, grits and whatever black folks could spare. For centuries we tended, and nursed, often at our breasts, the children of people who despised us. We had cooked the food of a nation of racists, and despite the many opportunities, there were few stories of black servants poisoning white families. If that didn't show mercy, then I misunderstood the word.

As for spirituality, we were Christians. We demonstrated the teachings of Christ. We turned other cheeks so often our heads seemed to revolve on the end of our necks, like old stop-and-go signs. How many times should we forgive? Jesus said seven times seventy. We forgave as if forgiving was our talent. Our church music showed that we believed there was something greater than we, something beyond our physical selves, and that that something, that God, and His Son, Jesus, were always present and could be called "in the midnight hour" and talked to when the "sun raised itself to walk across the morning sky." We could sing the angels out of heaven and bring them to stand thousands thronged on the head of a pin. We could ask Jesus to be on hand to "walk around" our deathbeds and gather us into "the bosom of Abraham." We told Him all about our sorrows and relished the time when we would be counted among numbers of those who would go marching in. We would walk the golden streets of heaven, eat of the milk and honey, wear the promised shoes and rest in the arms of Jesus, who would rock us and say, "You have labored in my vineyard. You are tired. You are home now, child. Well done." Oh, there was no doubt that we were spiritual.

The Blacks was a white foreigner's idea of a people he did not understand. Genet had superimposed the meanness and cruelty of his own people onto a race he had never known, a race already nearly doubled over carrying the white man's burden of greed and guilt, and which at the same time toted its own insufficiency. I threw the manuscript into a closet, finished with Genet and his narrow little conclusions.

Max Glanville called two days later.

"Maya, we want you in the play." The play? I had jettisoned Genet and his ill-thought-out drama.

Glanville's voice reached through the telephone. "There are two roles and we're just not sure which one would suit you best. So we'd like you to come down and read for us."

I thanked him but I said I didn't think so and hung up. I reported the call to Vus only because it gave me a subject to introduce into dinner conversation. However, he jarred me by laughing. "Americans are either quite slow or terribly arrogant. They do not know or care that there is a world beyond their world, where tradition dictates action. No wife of an African leader can go on the stage." He laughed again. "Can you imagine the wife of Martin King or Sobukwe or Malcolm X standing on a stage being examined by white men?" The unlikely picture made him shake his head. "No. No, you do not perform in public."

I had already refused Glanville's invitation, but Vus's reaction sizzled in my thoughts. I was a good actress, not great but certainly competent. For years before I met Vus, my rent had been paid and my son and I had eaten and been clothed by money I made working on stages. When I gave Vus my body and loyalty I hadn't included all the rights to my life. I felt no loyalty to *The Blacks,* since it had not earned my approval, yet I chafed under Vus' attitude of total control. I said nothing.

Abbey had been asked to take a role in the play. I told her that Vus had said he wouldn't allow me to. She said Max thought the play was important, and since Vus respected Max, maybe they ought to talk. Abbey hung up and in moments Max called, asking for my husband.

I heard Vus hang up the telephone in the living room. He walked into the kitchen. "I'm meeting Max for a conference." Every meeting was a conference and each conversation a discussion of pith. I nodded, and kept on washing dishes.

Vus came home and asked for the manuscript. I recovered the play from the back of the closet and gave it to him. Guy and I played Scrabble on the dining-room table while Vus sat under a lamp in the living room. He would rise from time to time and pass through to the kitchen getting a fresh drink. Then he would return silently to the sofa and *The Blacks.*

Guy went off to bed. Vus still read. I knew he was going back and forth through the script. He hardly looked up when I said good night.

I was in a deep sleep when he shook me awake. "Maya. Wake up. I have to talk to you." He sat on the side of the bed. The crumpled pages were spread out beside him.

"This play is great. If they still want you, you must do this play." I came awake like my mother—immediately and entirely aware.

I said, "I don't agree with the conclusion. Black people are not going to become like whites. Never."

"Maya, you are so young, so, so young." He patronized me as if I were the little shepherd girl and he the old man of Kilimanjaro.

"Dear Wife, that is a reverse racism. Black people are human. No more, no less. Our backgrounds, our history make us act differently."

I grabbed a cigarette from the night stand, ready to jump into the discussion. I listed our respectfulness, our mercy, our spirituality. His rejoinder stopped me. "We are people. The root cause of racism and its primary result is that whites refuse to see us simply as people."

I argued, "But the play says given the chance, black people will act as cruel as whites. I don't believe it."

"Maya, that is a very real possibility and one we must vigilantly guard against. You see, my dear wife"—he spoke slowly, leaning his big body toward me—"my dear wife, most black revolutionaries, most black radicals, most black activists, do not really want change. They want exchange. This play points to that likelihood. And our people need to face the temptation. You must act in *The Blacks*."

He continued talking in the bed and I fell asleep in his arms.

The next morning Abbey and I went down to the St. Mark's Playhouse on Second Avenue. Actors sat quietly in the dimly lit seats, and Gene Frankel paced on the stage. Max Glanville had seen us enter. He nodded in recognition and walked to the edge of the stage. He stopped Gene in mid-step and whispered. Frankel lifted his head and looked out.

"Maya Make. Maya Angelou Make. Abbey Lincoln. Come down front, please." We found seats in the front row.

Glanville came back and sat down. "Abbey, we want you to read the role of Snow. But, Maya, we've not decided whether you should do the Black Queen or the White Queen."

I said, "Of course the Black Queen."

"Just read a little of both roles." He got up and went away, returning with an open manuscript.

"Read this section." He flipped pages. "And then read this underlined part."

I stepped up on the low stage and without raising my head to look at the audience began to read. The section was short and I turned the script to the next underlined pages and recited another monologue without adding vocal inflection.

There was scattered applause when I finished and a familiar husky voice shouted, "You've got all the parts, baby." Another voice said, "Yes, but let's see your legs."

Godfrey Cambridge flopped all over a seat in the third row and Flash Riley sat next to him.

I joined them and we talked about Cabaret for Freedom, while Frankel, Bernstein and Glanville stood together on the stage muttering.

Frankel shouted, "Lights" and the house lights came on. He walked to the edge of the stage. "Ladies and gentlemen, I'd like to introduce you to each other, and please mark your scripts. Godfrey Cambridge is Diouf. Roscoe Lee Browne is Archibald. James Earl Jones is Village. Cicely Tyson is Virtue. Jay Riley is the Governor, Raymond St. Jacques is the Judge. Cynthia Belgrave is Adelaide. Maya Angelou Make is the White Queen. Helen Martin is Felicity, or the Black Queen. Lou Gossett is Newport News. Lex Monson is the Missionary. Abbey Lincoln is Snow and Charles Gordone is the Valet. Max Roach is composer, Talley Beatty is choreographer and Patricia Zipprodt is costume designer. Ethel Ayler is understudying Abbey and Cicely. Roxanne Roker understudies Maya and Helen."

I looked around. Ethel and I exchanged grins. We had been friends years before during the European tour of *Porgy and Bess.*

Frankel continued, "We've got a great play and we're going to work our asses off."

Rehearsals began with a playground joviality and in days accelerated into the seriousness of a full-scale war. Friendships and cliques were formed quickly. The central character was played by Roscoe Lee Browne, and within a week he became the chief figure off stage as well. His exquisite diction and fastidious manners were fortunately matched with wit. He was unflappable.

James Earl Jones, a beige handsome bull of a man watched Frankel with fierce stares, reading his lips, scanning his hairline and chin, ear lobes and neck. Then suddenly James Earl would withdraw into himself with a slammed-door finality.

Lou Gossett, lean and young, skyrocketed on and off the stage, innocent and interested. For all his boyish bounding he had developed listening into an art. Cocking an ear at the speaker, his soft eyes caring and his entire body taut with attention.

Godfrey and Jay "Flash" Riley competed for company comedian.

When Flash won, Godfrey changed. The clowning began to disappear and he sobered daily into a drab, studious actor.

Cicely, delicate and black-rose beautiful, was serious and aloof. She sat in the rear of the theater, her small head bent into the manuscript, saving her warmth for the character and her smiles for the stage. Raymond, looking like a matinee idol, and Lex were old-time friends. They studied their roles together, breaking each other up with camped-up readings. Helen and Cynthia were professionals; just watching them, I knew that they would have their lines, remember the director's blocking and follow the steps of Talley's choreography without mistakes in a shorter time than anyone else. Charles Gordone, a finely fashioned, small yellow man, made slight fun of everything and everyone, including himself as another target for sarcasm.

There was some resistance to Frankel's direction on the grounds that, being white, he was unable to understand black motivation. In other quarters there was a submission which bordered on obsequiousness and which brought to mind characterizations of Stepin Fetchit.

Each day, tension met us as we walked into the theater and lay like low morning fog in the aisles.

Abbey and I, with the solidarity of a tried friendship, read and studied together, or joined by Roscoe, lunched at a nearby restaurant where we discussed the day's political upheavals. We three would not have called ourselves solely actors. Abbey was a jazz singer, I was an activist, and although Roscoe had played Shakespearean roles and taught drama, he had also been a sprinting champion and an executive with a large liquor company. Early on, we agreed that *The Blacks* was an important play but "the play" was not the only thing in our lives.

My marriage was only a few months old, Vus was still an enigma I hadn't solved and the mystery was sexually titillating. I was in love. Guy's grades had improved but he was seldom home. When I offered to invite the parents of his new friends over for dinner, he laughed at me.

"Mom, that's old-timey. This isn't Los Angeles, this is New York

City. People don't do that." He laughed again when I said people in N.Y.C. have parents and parents eat too.

"I haven't even met most of those guys' folks. Look, Mom, some of them are seventeen and eighteen. How would I look if I said, 'My mom wants to meet your mom'? Foolish."

The Harlem Writers Guild accepted that most of my time would be spent at the theater, but that did not release me from my obligation to attend meetings and continue writing.

By the first week's end, Frankel had completed the staging and Talley was teaching the actors his choreography. The set was being constructed and I was laboring over lines.

Raymond, Lex, Flash, Charles and I played the "whites."

We wore exaggerated masks and performed from a platform nine feet above the stage. Below us, the "Negroes" (the rest of the company) enacted for our benefit a rape-murder by a black man (played by Jones) of a white woman (a masked Godfrey Cambridge). In retaliation we, the colonial power—royalty (the White Queen), the church (Lex Monson), the law (Raymond St. Jacques) the military (Flash Riley) and the equivocating liberal (Charles Gordone)—descended into Africa to make the blacks pay for the crime. After a duel between the two queens, the blacks triumphed and killed the whites one by one. Then in sarcastic imitation of the vanquished "whites," the black victors ascended the ramp and occupied the platform of their former masters.

The play was delicious to our taste. We were only acting, but we were black actors in 1960. On that small New York stage, we reflected the real-life confrontations that were occurring daily in America's streets. Whites did live above us, hating and fearing and threatening our existence. Blacks did sneer behind their masks at the rulers they both loathed and envied. We would throw off the white yoke which dragged us down into an eternal genuflection.

I started enjoying my role. I used the White Queen to ridicule mean white women and brutal white men who had too often injured me and mine. Every inane posture and haughty attitude I had ever seen found its place in my White Queen.

Genet had been right at least about one thing. Blacks should be used to play whites. For centuries we had probed their faces, the angles of their bodies, the sounds of their voices and even their odors. Often our survival had depended upon the accurate reading of a white man's chuckle or the disdainful wave of a white woman's hand. Whites, on the other hand, always knew that no serious penalty threatened them if they misunderstood blacks. Whites were safely isolated from our concerns. When they chose, they could lift the racial curtain which separated us. They could indulge in sexual escapades, increase our families with mulatto bastards, make fortunes out of our music and eunuchs out of our men, then in seconds they could step away, and return unscarred to their pristine security. The cliché of whites being ignorant of blacks was not only true, but understandable. Oh, but we knew them with the intimacy of a surgeon's scalpel.

I dressed myself in the hated gestures and made the White Queen gaze down in loathing at the rotten stinking stupid blacks, who, although innocent, like beasts were loathsome nonetheless.

It was obvious that the other actors also found effective motivation. The play became such a cruel parody of white society that I was certain it would flop. Whites were not so masochistic as to favor a play which ridiculed and insulted them, and black playgoers were scarce.

James Baldwin was a friend of Gene Frankel's and he attended rehearsals frequently. He laughed loudly and approvingly at our performances and I talked with him often. When I introduced him to Vus they took to each other with enthusiasm.

At dress rehearsal, on the eve of opening night, black friends, family and investors who had been invited hooted and stamped their feet throughout the performance. But I reckoned their responses natural. They were bound to us, as fellow blacks, black sympathizers or investors.

Vus and Guy grinned and assured me that I was the best actor on the stage. I accepted their compliments easily.

On the morning of opening night, the cast gathered in the foyer, passing jitters from hand to hand, like so many raw eggs. I looked around for Abbey but she hadn't arrived.

When we walked into the dark theater, Gene Frankel bellowed from the stage.

"Everybody down front. Everybody."

He was having a more serious nervous attack than we who had to face the evening audience. I snickered. Roscoe Brown turned to me and made a face of arch innocence.

We filled the front rows, as Frankel paced out the length of the stage. He stopped and looked out at the actors.

His voice quivered. "We have no music. No music and Abbey Lincoln will not be opening tonight. Max Roach has taken his music out of the show."

He threw out the information and waited, letting the words rest in our minds.

Anxious looks were exchanged in the front row.

"Abbey's understudy is ready. She's been rehearsing all morning."

We turned and saw Ethel sitting poised stage left. Frankel added, "We can go on. We have to go on, but there is a song and the dance, for which we don't have a damn note."

Moans and groans lifted up in the air. We had endured the work, the late nights and early mornings of concentration, the long subway trips, the abandoned families, Talley Beatty's complex choreography and the director's demanding staging.

Max Roach was a genius, a responsible musician and my friend. I knew he had to have a reason.

I got up and went outside to the public telephone.

Max answered, sounding like a slide trombone. "The son of a bitches reneged. We had an agreement and the producers reneged on it."

"And Abbey is out of the play?"

"You goddam right."

"Well, Max, you won't hate me if I stay?"

"Hell no. But my wife will not get up on that stage."

Frankel had said we would open with or without the music.

I asked, "Max, would it be all right if I wrote the tunes? We can get along with two tunes."

"I don't give a damn. I just don't want to have that bastard using my music."

"I'll still be your sister."

Max was an attentive brother but he could be a violent enemy.

"Yeah. Yeah. You're my sister."

The telephone was slammed down.

If I stopped to think about my next move, I might convince myself out of it. Black folks said, "Follow your first mind."

I beckoned Ethel from the aisle. She rose and we walked into the lobby. Ethel had musical training and I had composed tunes for my album and for Guy. Together we could easily write the music for just two songs.

Ethel had the air of a woman born pretty. The years of familial adoration, the compliments of strangers, and the envy of plain women had given her a large share of confidence.

"Sure, Maya. We can do it. It's just two songs, right? Let's get to the piano."

We walked down the stage to where Frankel was in conference with Talley and Glanville.

"We'll write the music."

"What?"

"We'll write it this afternoon."

I added, "And teach it to the cast."

Frankel nearly jumped into Sidney Bernstein's arms. "Did you hear that?"

Bernstein smiled and waggled his head happily.

"I heard. I heard. Let's let them do it. If they say they can do it, let's let them do it. Nice girls. Nice ladies. Let them do it."

Sidney's small frame shook with eagerness. "Dismiss the cast. Let them have the theater."

Frankel nodded.

Ethel and I sat close on the piano stool. The old *Porgy and Bess* companionship was still good between us. We agreed that the key of C, with no flats or sharps, would be easier for nonsinging actors to learn.

Ethel played a melody in the upper register and I added notes. We spoke the lyrics and adjusted the melody to fit. Within an hour, we had composed two tunes. The cast returned from the break. They stood around the piano and listened to our melodies. I turned at the first laughter, ready to defend our work, but when I looked at the actors I saw that their laughter was with me and themselves. Ethel Ayler and I had not done anything out of the ordinary. We had simply proved that black people had to be slick, smart and damned quick.

That night the play began on a pitch of high scorn. The theater became a sardonic sanctuary where we sneered at white saints and spit on white gods. Most blacks in the audience reacted with amusement at our blasphemous disclosures, although there were a few who coughed or grunted disapproval. They were embarrassed at our blatancy, preferring that our people keep our anger behind masks, and as usual under control.

However, whites loved *The Blacks*. At the end of the play, the audience stood clapping riotously and bellowing, "Bravo," "Bravo." The cast had agreed not to bow or smile. We looked out at the pale faces, no longer actors playing roles written by a Frenchman thousands of miles distant. We were courageous black people, looking directly into enemy eyes. Our impudence further excited the audience. Loud applause continued long after we left the stage.

We howled in our dressing rooms. If the audience missed the play's obtrusive intent, then the crackers were numbly insensitive. On the other hand, if they understood, and still liked the drama, they were psychically sick, which we suspected anyway.

We were a hit, and we were happy.

Blacks understood and enjoyed the play, but each night in the theater whites outnumbered my people four to one, and that fact was befuddling. Whites didn't come to the Lower East Side of New York to learn that they were unkind, unjust and unfair. Black orators, more eloquent than Genet, had informed white Americans for three centuries that our living conditions were intolerable. David Walker in 1830 and Frederick Douglass in 1850 had revealed the anguish and pain of life for blacks in the United States. Martin Delaney and Harriet Tubman, Marcus Garvey and Dr. DuBois, and Martin King and Malcolm X had explained with anger, passion and persuasion that we were living precariously on the ledge of life, and that if we fell, the entire structure, which had prohibited us living room, might crumble as well.

So in 1960, white Americans should have known all they needed to know about black Americans.

Why, then, did they crowd into the St. Mark's Playhouse and sit gaping as black actors flung filthy words and even filthier meanings into their faces? The question continued to stay with me like a grain of sand wedged between my teeth. Not painful but a constant irritant.

At last, a month after we had opened, I was given an answer. That evening the cast had changed into street clothes and gathered in the lobby to meet friends. A young white woman of about thirty, expensively dressed and well cared for, grabbed my hand.

"Maya? Mrs. Make?" Her face was moist with tears. Her nose and the area around it, were red. Immediately, I felt sorry for her.

"Yes?"

"Oh, Mrs. Make." She started to sob. I asked her if she'd like to come to my dressing room. My invitation was like cold water on her emotion.

She shook her head, "Oh no. Nothing like that. Of course not, I'm all right."

The rush of blood was disappearing from her face, and when she spoke again her voice was clearer.

"I just wanted you to know ... I just wanted to say that I've seen the play five times." She waited.

"Five times? We've only been playing four weeks."

"Yes, but a lot of my friends ..."—now she was in control of herself again—"a lot of us have seen the play more than once. A woman in my building comes twice a week."

"Why? Why do you come back?"

"Well"—she drew herself up—"well, we support you. I mean, we understand what you are saying."

The blur of noise drifted around us, but we were an isolated inset, a picture of American society. White and black talking at each other.

"How many blacks live in your building?"

"Why, none. But that doesn't mean..."

"How many black friends do you have? I mean, not counting your maid?"

"Oh," she took a couple of steps backward. "You're trying to insult me."

I followed her. "You can accept the insults if I am a character on stage, but not in person, is that it?"

She looked at me with enough hate to shrivel my heart. I put my hand out.

"Don't touch me." Her voice was so sharp it caught the attention of some bystanders. Roscoe appeared abruptly. Still in character, giving me a little bow, "Hello, Queen."

The woman turned to leave, but I caught her sleeve. "Would you take me home with you? Would you become my friend?"

She snatched her arm away, and spat out, "You people. You people." And walked away.

Roscoe asked, "And pray, what was that?"

"She's one of our fans. She comes to the theater and allows us to curse and berate her, and that's her contribution to our struggle."

Roscoe shook his head slowly. "Oh dear. One of those."

The subject was closed.

CHAPTER 13

The lipstick smudge was not mine, nor did the perfume come from my bottles. I laid Vus's shirt across the chair and hung his suit from the doorknob. Then I sat down to wait for him to come from the shower.

We had not discussed infidelity; I had simply never thought of it.

But the third time Vus's clothes were stained with the evidence of other women's make-up I had to face the possibility.

He came into the bedroom, tying the belt of his silk paisley dressing gown.

"Dear, shall we go out to breakfast? I have a meeting downtown. We could go to Broadway and then—".

"Vus, who is the woman? Or rather, who are the women?"

He turned to me and dropped his hands to his side. His face as blank as a wooden slat.

"Women? What women?" The round eyes which I loved were glazed over, shutting me out. "What stupidness are you talking about?"

I kept my voice low. I was asking because I was my mother's daughter and I was supposed to be courageous and honest. I didn't want an honest answer. I wished for him to deny everything, or to hand me any contrived explanation.

"The lipstick. It's fuchsia. It's not mine. This time the perfume is Tweed. I have never worn that scent."

"Ah," he smiled, stretching and opening his fine lips, allowing me a flash of even teeth. "Ah, my darling, you're jealous." He walked over and took my hands and pulled me up from the chair. He held me close and his belly shook against mine. He was laughing at me.

"My darling wife is a little jealous." His voice and body rumbled. He released me and looked into my eyes.

"My dear, there are no other women. You are the only love in my world. You are the only woman I've ever wanted and all that I have."

That was what I wanted to hear, but as a black American woman, I had a history to respect and a duty to discharge. I looked at him directly.

"Vus, if you fell in love with Abbey, or Rosa or Paule, I could understand. I would be hurt but not insulted. They are women who would not intend to hurt me, but love is like a virus. It can happen to anybody at any time. But if you chippie on me, you could get hurt, and I mean seriously."

Vus pulled away. We were face to face, but he had withdrawn into his privacy.

"Don't you ever threaten me. I am an African. I do not scare easily and I do not run at all. Do not question me again. You are my wife. That is all you need to know."

He dressed and left without repeating his breakfast invitation.

I walked around the house thinking of my alternatives. Separation was not possible. Too many friends had advised me against the marriage, and my pride would not allow me to prove them right. Guy would never forgive me if I moved us one more time and I couldn't risk losing the only person who really loved me. If I caught Vus flagrantly betraying me, I would get a gun and blow his ass away or wait until he slept and pour boiling lye in his mouth. I would never use poison, it could take too long to act.

I hung his suit near an open window and washed the lipstick stain from his shirt.

There was a sad irony in the truth that I was happier in the dusty theater than in my pretty apartment on Central Park West.

Despite the clash of cultures, Guy and Vus were building a friendship. My son was making a strenuous effort to understand the ways of "Dad." He was interested in knowing what it must have been like to be a black male growing up in Africa. Vus was pleased by Guy's interest and accepted his free, curious upbringing, although it was alien to his own. When Guy questioned his stepfather's announcements, Vus took the time to explain that an African youngster would never ask an adult why he had done or said a certain thing. Rather, African youths courteously accepted grown-up statements, then went off on their own to find the answers that suited them. They sat together, laughing, talking and playing chess. They were pleased with the dinners I prepared, but when I called their attention to the fresh flowers on the table or a new dress I was wearing, their reactions were identical.

"How very nice, my wife."

"Lovely, Mom. Really very lovely."

"Guy, your mother makes a beautiful house for us."

They treated me as if I were the kind and competent family retainer.

Guy had forgotten the years when I had encouraged him to interrogate me, question my rules, try to pick apart my every conclusion.

There had been no father to bring balance into the pattern of my parenting, so he had had the right to question and I had the responsibility of explaining. Now Vus was teaching him to be an African male, and he was an apt student. Ambiguity stretched me like elastic. I yearned for our old closeness, and his dependence, but I knew he needed a father, a male image, a man in his life. I had been raised in a fatherless home, so I didn't even know what fathers talked about to their daughters, and surely I had no inkling of what they taught their sons.

I did know that Guy was treating me in a new and unpleasant way. My face was no longer examined for approval, nor did he weigh my voice for anger. He laughed with Vus, and consulted Vus. It was what I said I wanted, but I had to admit to myself that for my son I had become only a reliable convenience. A something of very little importance.

At home, Vus read American, European and African papers, clipping articles which he later copied and sent to colleagues abroad. He spent mornings at the United Nations, buttonholing delegates, conspiring with other African freedom fighters and trying to convince the press that South Africa in revolution would make the Algerian seven-year-war appear like a Sunday School picnic. He talked to everyone he thought influential—bankers, lawyers, clergymen and stockbrokers. I decided to accept that the make-up which smudged his collars and the sweet aromas which perfumed his clothes came from brushes with the secretaries of powerful men.

I started going to the theater early and returning home reluctantly.

Backstage, Roscoe Lee Browne and I acted out a two-character drama which brought color into my slowly fading life. Our strongest expressions were silent, and physical touching was limited to scrupulous pecks on each other's cheeks. More picturesque than handsome, his attentions held no threat or promise of intimacy. Although the other cast members appeared oblivious to the measure of my misery, he noticed but was too discreet to embarrass me with questions.

When I sat in my dressing room, working the crossword puzzle, or pressing a poem into shape, Roscoe's light step would sound beyond the door.

"Hello, my dear. It's outside. By the door."

I would jump to catch the sight of him, but the hallway was always empty, save a neat posy resting against the wall, or one flower wrapped in flimsy green paper.

The constancy and delicacy of Roscoe's concern made him the ideal hero for fantasy and the necessary contrast to my real life. He was all pleasure and no offense, excitement without responsibility. If we had embraced or if we once discussed the torment of my marriage, our private ritual of romance would have failed, overburdened by ordinariness. If one is lucky a solitary fantasy can totally transform one million realities.

My controlled paranoia prevented me from realizing the seriousness of a phone call I received one evening.

When I picked up the receiver, a man's throaty voice whispered "Maya Make? Vusumzi Make is not coming home."

The statement surprised me but I wasn't alarmed. I asked, "Did he ask you to tell me that? Why didn't he call? Who are you?"

The man said, "Vusumzi will never come home again." He hung up the telephone.

I walked around the living room trying to sort out the message. The English was labored but I could not place the origin of the heavy accent. Vus knew so many foreigners, the man could have been from any country in the world. He also knew many women, and just possibly an African diplomat suspected that his wife and Vus were having an affair. He telephoned, not so much to threaten Vus, as to awaken my suspicions. He had wasted his money and his time. When I left for the theater, Vus hadn't returned home.

During the play the memory of the telephone call lay just under the remembered lines. Helen Martin and I were engaged in the play's final duel when the idea came to me that Vus might be in danger. The angry husband could have already hurt him. Maybe he had been caught with the man's wife and had been shot or stabbed. I finished the play, and only Roscoe took notice of my distraction. Each time I looked at him, he raised an eyebrow or pursed his lips, or gave me a questioning glance.

After the final ensemble stare into the audience, I turned and rushed for my dressing room, but Roscoe caught up with me in the corridor behind the stage.

"Maya, are you all right?"

The care on his face activated my tears. "It's Vus. I'm worried."

He nodded. "Oh yes, I see." He couldn't possibly see and I couldn't possibly tell him. We walked into the lobby en route to the dressing rooms, and Vus stepped out of the crowd of playgoers.

"Good evening, my dearest." He was whole and he was beautiful.

Roscoe smiled as they shook hands. He said, "Mr. Make, our Queen is a great actress. Tonight she excelled herself." He inclined his head toward me and walked away. I knew that Vus didn't approve of public displays of emotion, so I hugged him quickly and went to change into street clothes.

I couldn't hold my relief. In the taxi I rubbed his large round thigh, and put my head on his chest, breathing in his living scent. "You are loving me tonight." He chuckled and the sound rumbled sweetly in my ear.

He made drinks at home and we sat on the good sofa. He took my hand.

"You are very nervous. You have been excited. What happened at the theater?"

I told him about the telephone call and his face changed. He began chewing the inside of his bottom lip; his eyes were deep and private.

I faked a light laugh and said, "I thought some irate husband had caught you and his wife *in flagrante*, and maybe he ..."

I shut up. I sounded silly even to myself. Vus was far away.

When he spoke his voice was cold and his speech even more precise than usual.

"We must have the number changed. I'm surprised it took them so long."

I didn't understand. He explained. "That was someone from the South African police. They do that sort of thing. Telephone the wives of freedom fighters and tell them their husbands or their children have been killed." He grunted, "I guess I should be insulted that they are just beginning on you. It indicates that they have not been taking me seriously." He turned his large body to face me. "Tomorrow, I'll have the number changed. And I will step up my campaign."

The telephone incident brought me closer to the reality of South African politics than all the speeches I had heard. That voice stayed in my ear like the inane melody of a commercial jingle. When I least expected it, it would growl, "Maya Make? Vusumzi Make will never come home again."

I wanted to stay at Vus's side, go everywhere with him. My concern followed him in the street, in taxis, trailed him into the U.N. Even when we were at home, I wasn't satisfied unless we were in the same room. Vus's attempts to reassure me were futile. Worry had come to live with me, and it sat in the palms of my hands like beads of sweat. It returned even as I wiped it away.

The second telephone call came about two weeks later.

"Maya Make? Do you know your husband is dead?" The voice was different but the accent was the same. "His throat has been cut." I slammed down the telephone, and a second later I picked it up and screamed obscenities over the buzz of the dial tone. "You're a lying dog. You racist, Apartheid-loving, baby-killing son of a bitch." When I replaced the telephone, I had used every profane word I knew and used them in every possible combination. When I told Vus he said he'd have the number changed again. He worried that such tactics threw me. I could expect those and worse. I decided if the phone calls continued, I would handle them and keep the news to myself.

Having a live-in father had a visible effect on my son. All his life Guy had been casual to the point of total indifference about his clothing, but under Vus's influence, he became interested in color-coordinated outfits. Vus took him to a tailor to be fitted for two vested suits. He bought splendid shoes and button-down shirts for my fifteen-year-old, and Guy responded as if he had been waiting for such elegance all his life.

The telephone calls resumed. I was told that I could pick up my husband's body at Bellevue, or that he had been shot to death in Harlem. Whenever I was home alone, I watched the telephone as if it were a coiled cobra. If it rang, I would grab its head and hold on. I never said hello but waited for the caller's voice. If I heard "Maya Make," I would start to quietly explain that South Africa would be free someday and all the white racists had better be long-distance swimmers or have well-stocked life rafts, because the Africans were going to run them right to the ocean. After my statement I would replace the receiver softly and think, That ought to get them. Usually, I could spend an hour or so complimenting myself on my brilliant control, before worry would snake its way into my thoughts. Then I would use the same telephone to try to locate Vus.

Mburumba Kerina, of the South-West Africa People's Organization, was his friend and lived in Brooklyn. I would call and Jane, Kerina's black American wife, would answer.

"Hi, Jane. It's Maya."

"Oh hello, Maya. How are things?"

"O.K. and with you?"

"Oh nothing. And with you?"

"Nothing." Then she would shatter my hopes that my husband was at her house. "How is Vus?"

"Oh fine. And Mburumba?"

"Just fine. We ought to get together soon."

"Yes, very soon. Well, take care."

"You too. Bye."

"Bye."

Jane never knew how I envied her unusual assurance. She was younger than I and had been working as a guide at the U.N. when she met Kerina. They fell in love and married, and she settled into the nervous life of a freedom fighter's wife as coolly as if she had married the minister of a small-town Baptist church.

When I found Vus after numerous phone calls, I gave reasons contrived for my interruptions.

"Let's go to dinner after the play."

"Let's go straight home after the play."

"Let's go to a bar after the play."

Vus was a master of intrigue, so I suppose that I never fooled him with my amateur cunning, but he was simply generous enough to pretend. One afternoon I answered the telephone and was thumped into a fear and subsequent rage so dense that I was made temporarily deaf.

"Hello, Maya Make?" Shreds of a Southern accent still hung in the white woman's voice.

"Yes? Maya Make speaking." I thought the woman was probably a journalist or a theater critic, wanting an interview from Maya Angelou Make, the actress.

"I'm calling about Guy." My mind shifted quickly from a pleasant anticipation to apprehension.

"Are you from his school? What is the matter?"

"No, I'm at Mid-town Hospital. I'm sorry but there's been a serious accident. We'd like you to come right away. Emergency ward."

She hung up. I grabbed my purse and the keys, slammed the door, raced down the stairs and was standing on the pavement before I realized I didn't know the address of the hospital. Fortunately, a taxi had stopped by a traffic light. I ran over and asked the driver if he knew where the Mid-town Hospital was located. He nodded and I got into the cab and said, "Please hurry. It's my son."

My watch said it was eleven, so Guy was in school and couldn't have been hurt in a traffic accident. Maybe there had been a gang fight. The cabbie cut in front of cars, causing other drivers to honk their horns and screech their tires, but it seemed that time and the taxi were crawling.

I paid with bills I never saw and ran through the doors of the Emergency entrance. A young black nurse at the desk looked at me wearily.

"Yes?"

I told her that my son had been hurt, and I wanted to know how badly, and where was he and could I see him? I told her his name, and she began to run her finger down a list. She continued examining the next page. She didn't find Guy's name. I told her I had received a phone call. She said they had not admitted a Guy Johnson and was I sure of the hospital? I heard the caller's voice. "I'm at Mid-town Hospital . . ."

She was lying. She was in the South African service. The thoughts slammed into my consciousness like blows to the heart. For the first time since I heard "I'm calling about Guy" I became aware of thinking.

I went to a pay phone and called Guy's school. After a few minutes I learned that he was in history class.

I walked up Central Park West toward the apartment, too angry to savor relief. I thought of the greedy immorals who lay claim to a people's land by force, and denied the existence of other human beings because of their color. I had opposed the racist regime on principle because it was ugly, violent, debasing and murderous. My husband had his own reasons for trying to bring down the government of Verwoerd and I had supported him. But as I walked under the green trees, and smelled the aroma of young summer flowers, I felt a spasm of hate constrict my throat and tighten my chest. To break a mother's heart for no gain was the most squalid act I could imagine. My defiance from now on would be personal.

———

Ethel Ayler had a co-starring role in a new Broadway play, so she was leaving *The Blacks.* We talked backstage on her last night.

Ethel said, "Maya, Sidney ought to pay us something for our music." I agreed.

We had tried to squeeze money out of the producer on three or four occasions, but each time we mentioned being paid for composing the two songs, he had laughed and invited us to lunch or dinner. Now when Ethel was closing we decided to make a last attempt. We changed clothes quickly and rushed into the lobby, where we saw Sidney Bernstein standing alone.

Ethel and I walked over to him. Ethel said, "Sidney, you know this was my last night. I start rehearsing *Kwamina* tomorrow."

Sidney turned and gave Ethel an insipid little smile, "Yeah, Ethel, congratulations. I hope it'll be a hit."

I said, "So does she, Sidney. But we want to talk to you about money. You have to pay us something for composing the music for this show."

He raised his chin and looked in my face. He didn't even try to dilute his scorn.

"Get off my back, will you? You didn't compose anything. I saw you. You just sat down at the piano and made up something."

Ethel and I stared at him, then at each other. The people Sidney had been waiting for arrived, collected him and, laughing, walked down the stairs.

I saw Ethel control her features. She closed her lips and made her eyes vacant. When she shrugged her shoulders I thought I knew what she was going to say.

"He's a fool, Maya. Forget him." I had anticipated correctly. She held her cosmetic case delicately in her left and waved at me elegantly with her right. "Take it easy, Maya. Let's keep in touch." She walked away. A Broadway success was her future, so she could ignore Sidney Bernstein's unfairness. However, I couldn't. And the statement that I had composed nothing, I had simply sat down at the piano and made the music up, clogged the movement of my brain.

Vus and James Baldwin were waiting at the bottom of the stairs, so I dropped the befuddlement on them.

What did it mean? The stupid bastard was of a piece with the other arrogant thieves who took the work of black artists without even threatening them with drawn pistols. I wasn't locked into *The Blacks*.

Vus still paid most of the bills, so I wasn't dependent on the job, and since I had no theatrical ambition I didn't have to be afraid that the producers would bad-mouth me off and on Broadway. Vus and Jim stayed quiet.

Vus took my shoulders in his hands and pressed his thumbs into the soft muscles at the joint of my arms. The pain made me forget about Sidney Bernstein, Ethel Ayler, the music and *The Blacks*. I stopped crying and he released me.

"My dear. You will never return to this theater. You have just closed."

I looked at Jim Baldwin. Vus's statement was as shocking as Bernstein's rejection. I knew that Jim would understand that I couldn't simply not return to the theater. He would explain that as a member of Equity, the theatrical union, I was obliged to give at least two weeks' notice. Jim was silent. Although we three stood in arm's reach of each other, he watched Vus and me as if we were screen actors and he was sitting apart in a distant auditorium.

I said, "I can't close without giving notice. My union will have me up on charges. Bernstein can sue me..."

Vus walked away to the pavement's edge and hailed a taxi. I whispered to Jim, "Tell him I can't do that. Please explain. He doesn't understand."

Jim grinned, his big eyes flashing with enjoyment. "He understands, Maya. He understands more about what Bernstein has done than you. Don't worry, you'll be all right."

We crowded into the back seat of the cab. Vus leaned toward the driver.

"Take us, please, to the nearest Western Union office."

The driver hesitated for a few seconds, then started his motor and drove us to Broadway. On the ride, Vus and Jim leaned across me, agreeing on the bloody arrogance of white folks. It was ironic that the producer of a play which exposed white greed so eloquently could himself be such a glutton. Whether we were in the mines of South Africa, or the liberal New York theater, nothing changed. Whites wanted everything. They thought they deserved everything. That they wanted to possess all the materials of the earth was in itself disturbing, but that they also wanted to control the souls and the pride of people was inexplicable.

We walked into the Western Union office. Jim and I stood talking while Vus filled out a form.

He handed it to the telegraph operator. When the man finished copying the message, Vus paid and then, taking the form back, he walked over to us and read aloud: "Mrs. Maya Angelou Make will not be returning to *The Blacks* or the St. Mark's Playhouse. She resists the exploitation of herself and her people. She has closed. Signed, Vusumzi Linda Make, Pan African Congress, Johannesburg, South Africa. Currently Petitioner at United Nations."

Vus continued. "That will be the last you will hear of those people, my dear. Unless Bernstein wants an international incident."

Jim laughed out loud. "See, Maya Angelou, I told you, you have nothing to worry about."

We walked out of the office, and linking arms, strolled into the nearest bar.

The fat Xhosa, the thin New Yorker and the tall Southerner drank all night and exchanged unsurprising stories on the theme of white aggression and black vulnerability. And somehow we laughed.

I sat beside the telephone the next day. The hangover and drama of leaving the show made me quick and ready to blast the ears of Bernstein, or Frankel or Glanville or anyone who would dare call me about Vus's telegram. The telephone never rang.

CHAPTER 14

Black and white activists began to press hard on the nation's conscience. In Monroe, North Carolina, Rob Williams was opposing a force of white hatred, and encouraged black men to arm and protect themselves and their homes and families. Mae Mallory, a friend from the U.N. protest, had joined Rob. Julian Mayfield, the author of *The Big Hit* and *Grand Parade*, wrote a stinging article on Williams' position and then traveled South to lend his physical support. Stokely Carmichael and James Foreman founded a new group, Student Nonviolent Coordinating Committee, an offshoot of the Southern resistance organizations, and were taking the freedom struggle into hamlets and villages, where white hate was entrenched and black acceptance of inferior status a historic norm. Malcolm X continued to appear on national television. Newspapers were filled with reports of tributes to Martin Luther King and editorials honoring his nonviolent ideology. The white liberal population was growing. White students joined black students in Freedom Rides traveling on public conveyances to Southern towns which were racist strongholds.

Ralph Bunche was the U.S. ambassador to the U.N. and had received the Nobel Prize for his work as mediator in the Palestine conflict. When his son was denied membership in the all-white Forest Hills Tennis Club, Dr. Bunche made a statement which revealed his insight. The internationally respected representative, who had a complexion light-colored enough to allow him to pass for white, said, "I know now that until the lowliest Negro sharecropper in the South is free, I am not free."

Ossie Davis' play *Purlie Victorious* opened on Broadway, and his wife Ruby Dee, as the petite Lutie Belle, had white audiences howling at their own ignorance and greed. Paule Marshall's *Soul Clap Hands and Sing* was published, and readers were treated to well-written stories of black hope, despair and defeat. John Killens' *And Then We Heard the Thunder,* exposed the irony of black soldiers fighting for a white country in a segregated army. Baldwin's *The Fire Next Time* was an unrelenting warning that racism was not only homicidal but it was also suicidal. In Little Rock, Daisy Bates had led nine children into a segregated white high school and when the Arkansas governor, Orval Faubus, ordered local police to prevent the students' entry, President Dwight Eisenhower sent federal troops to keep the peace.

Harry Belafonte and Miriam Makeba were performing fund-raising concerts for the freedom struggle. Max and Abbey traveled around the country doing their "Freedom Now Suite."

Guy was totally occupied with school, SANE, Ethical Culture and girls. Vus traveled to and from East Africa, West Africa, London and Algeria, and I sat at home. I had no job and only the spending money Vus had left. My departure from the SCLC had been so hasty, I was embarrassed to go back and offer my services even as a volunteer. I was not a Muslim nor a student, so there was no place for me either in Malcolm X's organization or in SNCC. I withdrew from my friends and even the Harlem Writers Guild.

At last Vus returned from his latest extended trip. As usual, he brought gifts for me and Guy, and stories which had us tense with excitement and open-mouthed with admiration. My present was a blouse and an orange silk sari. He was delicate and assured when he wrapped the cloth around my hips and draped the end over my shoulders. I didn't ask where or how he had learned the technique. I was becoming a good African wife.

We walked into the lobby of the Waldorf-Astoria Hotel and the quiet was intimidating. Tuxedoed white men held the elbows of expensively dressed white women, and they made no noise as they glided over the carpeted floor. I held on to Vus's arm and, dressed in my orange sari, stretched my head and neck upward until I added a few more inches to my six-foot frame. Vus had taught me a little Xhosa, and I spoke clearly and loudly in the click language. When we entered the elevator I felt all those white eyes on my back. I was an African in the bastion of white power, and my black King would protect me.

The Sierra Leone's ambassador's suite was festive with brown- and black-colored people in African dress and the melodies of Ghanaian High Life music. Vus took me to the ambassador, who was standing with a group of women near the window.

The ambassador saw Vus and beamed. "Ah, Mr. Make. Welcome. Ladies, I would like you to meet our revolutionary brother from South Africa, Vusumzi Make." Vus smiled and bowed, the light catching his cheekbones, and causing his hair to glisten.

He straightened up and spoke, "Your Excellency, I present my wife, Maya Angelou Make."

The ambassador took my hand. "She is beautiful, Make." He also bowed. "Madam Make, we have heard of you in Africa. Mr. Make has done the continent a great service. Welcome."

I shook hands with the ambassador and each of the women and suddenly found the crowd had dispersed. I saw Vus near a table where a uniformed bartender mixed drinks. The ambassador was dancing with a pretty little woman in a very low-cut cocktail dress and I was left at the window. A roving waiter offered a tray of drinks. I chose a glass of wine and looked down on the lights of New York.

Strange languages swirled around me, and the smell of a spice, known among Arkansas blacks as bird pepper, became strong in the room. I stopped the waiter and took a glass of Scotch from his tray. Vus had taken over from the ambassador and now he was dancing with the little sexy woman, holding her too close, gazing too deeply in her eyes. I found the waiter in a group of laughing guests, took another Scotch and went back to the window to drink and think.

I had a fresh haircut and was wearing the prettiest outfit I owned. I could speak French and Spanish very well and could talk intelligently on a number of subjects. I knew national politics intimately and international subjects moderately well. I was married to a leading African freedom fighter and had daubed French perfume on my body, discreetly. Yet, no one talked to me. I had another drink.

The lights on the street had begun to blur, but I could see clearly that Vus was still dancing with the woman. I would have known what to do if the party had been given by Afro-Americans, or even if there had been a few Afro-American guests. Or if the African guests had all been female. But Vus was successfully teaching me that there was a particular and absolute way for a woman to approach an African man. I only knew how a wife addressed an African husband. I didn't know how to start a conversation with a male stranger, but I did know I was certainly getting drunk. If I could eat soon, I could stop the fast-moving effect effect of alcohol on my brain and body. I headed for the kitchen.

I nearly collided with the ambassador. He backed away and smiled. "Madam Make, I hope you're enjoying yourself."

I made myself smile. "Thank you, Your Excellency," and continued.

A black woman in a housedress was bent over, taking baking tins from the oven. When she straightened and saw me, she made her face and voice flat.

"Can I help you, ma'am?" Her Southern accent was strong.

"I just wanted a bite of something. Anything."

"Ma'am, they will be serving in a few minutes."

"Are you the ambassador's wife?" My question might have sounded stupid, considering the way she was dressed. But I knew that sometimes the chores of party-giving could increase so that guests arrived before the last tasks were done and the hostess had the time to change.

The woman laughed loudly. "Me? God, no. Madam Ambassador? Me?" She laughed, opening her mouth wide, her tongue wiggled. "No, ma'am. I am a Negro. I am the cook." She turned back to the stove, her body shaking with glee. She muttered. "Me?"

I waited until she turned to me again.

"May I give you a hand? I am also a cook." The laughter left her face as she examined me. Her gaze slid from my hair and gold earrings, to my necklace and dress and hands.

"No, honey. Maybe you can cook, but you ain't no cook."

I pulled out a chair from the dinette table and sat down. She was right about my profession, but we were both black, both American, and women.

I said, "I'm married to an African, who is out there dancing the slow grind with some broad. And nobody's talked to me. So..."

She put her hands on her hips and shook her head. She said, "Honey, mens, they ain't gone change. You need a little sip." A drink was the last thing I needed, but she reached down alongside the refrigerator and pulled out a bottle of gin from her purse. She poured lavishly into a coffee cup. I took it while she sloshed a little gin into her cup and raised it to me.

"Honey, we women got to stick together. I mean." She swallowed the gin, made a face and growled and I followed her example.

"Sit down and take it easy." She turned and stirred a pot of bubbling sauce, still talking to me over her shoulder.

"What you going to do about it? You welcome to sit in here, but sooner or later, you're going to have to go out there and face him. But help yourself to the gin."

I did.

The cook was ladling chili into a large Chinese bowl when Vus came through the kitchen door. The steam and the booze unfocused my eyes. When I saw him loom through the mist, I started laughing. He reminded me of Aladdin's Djinn, only bigger.

Maybe the cook's gin bottle was a lamp, and I had certainly been rubbing it.

Vus stood over me, asking what I was laughing about. But each time I inhaled so that I could explain, Vus seem to grow larger as if he were somehow connected to my breathing, and laughter would contract my chest and I couldn't say a word.

Vus walked out of the room, and the cook came to me.

"That was your husband?" I nodded, still laughing.

"Well, child, you better get to stepping. He's fat. When a fat man gets mad, huh. I don't care if he's African or not. Ain't no fat man in the world wants to be laughed at." She handed me my purse. The sound of her voice had a small sobering effect, but when I tried to tell her why I had been laughing, I began to giggle again.

"You better go out of here, child, before that man comes back. I saw his face and it wasn't funny."

Finally, her advice reached my active brain. I got up, thanked her and walked from the kitchen through the living room door out into the hall. I pressed the elevator button and as the doors opened Vus burst out of the apartment, saw me and came running down the hall, shouting, telling me to wait. We both stepped into the half-filled elevator.

Vus began to talk. I was his wife, the wife of an African leader. I had embarrassed him. Sitting in the kitchen, getting drunk with the cook. When he tried to talk to me, I had laughed in his face. No African lady would bring such disgrace on her husband. I looked at the other people in the elevator, but they averted their white faces. As neither Vus nor I existed in their real world, they simply had to wait until we reached the ground floor and then our sounds and shadows would disappear.

Vus kept up his tirade as the elevator stopped on our descent, picking up people from other floors. When we reached the lobby, the other passengers scattered like snowflakes. I walked, with my head high, toward the front entrance. Vus was following me, talking, ranting, saying what shame I had brought onto his head, to his name, to his family. What a disappointment I was. How disrespectful I was to a son of Africa.

Deciding not to go out into the street, I turned sharply from the revolving doors and headed back to the elevators. Vus's voice, which had been a rumbling monotone, suddenly lifted.

"Where are you going? Not back to the party. I forbid you. You are my wife. We are going home." At the elevator, I made a quick pivot and walked in the direction of the registration desk, Vus following in my wake, still talking.

The desk clerks, dressed as formally as expensive morticians, thrust long mournful faces at me. I walked past them haughtily. Vus grabbed for my arm but only brushed my sleeve. I snatched away from him and lengthened my stride. When I reached the front doors the second time I looked over my shoulder and saw that his face was bathed in sweat. With an oblique turn, I dodged a small group of white men entering the lobby and increased my speed. Vus's breath came harder and his sentences were short explosions. "Stop! Foolish woman! Moron! Idiot!" I might be all those things or none, but he wasn't going to catch me. I began to sprint. I ran around the sofas, making guests draw their legs out of the way. Vus was lumbering less than a foot behind me. A desk clerk's face suddenly appeared at my side, anxious and gulping. We could have been two underwater swimmers in a clear pool. With just a little energy, I quickly outdistanced him. Vus shouted, "Don't touch her. She's my wife." He stressed the possessive.

A conservatively dressed black man stood in my way. I ran straight toward him but at the last second I veered, and he pulled his attaché case up, and cradled it in his arms. I heard his sigh of relief after I passed him.

When I reached the bank of elevators again, I looked back. Vus was nearly in arm's reach. The desk clerk followed him, and behind the desk clerk, a uniformed policeman and a grey-suited man, whom I took to be the manager, brought up the rear. The cop's presence gave me added energy. This seemed as good a time as I was ever likely to get. I would show that if I didn't have to dodge bullets, if it was a fair race, just me and him, I could outrun any New York policeman. I hitched my purse in my armpit and stretched my legs.

Shouts floated around the lobby "Stop her!" and Vus's "Don't touch her" and "Who is she?"

Startled guests stood together under the crystal chandelier, as we wound through the lobby. I screamed back, "All of you can go to hell."

An empty revolving-door section was moving slowly, so I dove into it and pushed quickly. I heard a thud, and when I stepped out onto the pavement, I looked through the side window. I saw Vus, the clerk and the policeman had hit the door at the same time and tumbled into a heap on the floor. At that moment I turned and saw a woman get out of a taxi. Before she could slam the door, I ran and jumped into the cab.

It wouldn't be wise to go home, so I gave the driver Rosa's address on Riverside Drive.

I sat drinking black coffee and watching Rosa laugh at my description of the race in the Waldorf-Astoria lobby. I had sobered. My actions were unforgivable. I had shown all those white folks that black people had no dignity. I had embarrassed my husband, who was risking his life for our people. He had called me an idiot and he was right. Rosa kept laughing, but for me there was nothing funny anymore.

Vus telephoned the next morning and came to collect me.

He brought flowers for Rosa and perfume for me. We kissed; he declared his love. He didn't mention my outrageous display and I said nothing about his vulgar flirtation. We were completely reconciled.

—

The sheriff's deputies appeared armed and solemn at my apartment one winter afternoon. When they were assured that I was Mrs. Make, one man handed me a piece of paper while the other tacked a notice on the front door. They moved with the precision of practice and were gone before I could sort out my questions. I stood in the hall reading the form and then looked at the notice. We had been evicted for nonpayment of the rent. We had to be out of the apartment in twenty-four hours, or the sheriff's deputies would put our furniture on the street.

Guy was still at school. Vus was at the U.N. I calmly made a pot of coffee and sat down in the kitchen to think. I had never been put out of a house in all my life. My mother would throw one of her famous tantrums if she heard about my eviction. My son was certain to be embarrassed and made more insecure. My friends would pity me and my enemies would shake their heads and smirk.

I read the form again. I was holding the third and last notice, which meant that Vus had collected the other two and said nothing to me. Then the responsibility was his. I had played the cared-for housewife, who made no money. I hadn't asked for the position, but had accepted the role marriage had forced upon me. I convinced myself that I was without blame, and the total responsibility of how and where Guy and I lived lay in Vus's lap.

I could borrow money from the Killens or my mother or Rosa, but according to the eviction notice it was too late to pay back rent. We had no recourse save to vacate the premises.

I went to the local supermarket and collected cartons. When I returned the eviction notice seemed to have become enlarged. It covered the door from ceiling to floor. After rereading it, I went inside and began packing. I put all our clothes in suitcases and the steamer trunk I had brought from California. I culled the best pots and skillets from kitchen cupboards and placed them in cardboard boxes. The furniture, the expensive sofa, good beds and chairs had been Vus's selection, so their disposal or arrangement could wait.

There was a frantic sound of the scraping of the key and the jerking open of the door. Guy and Vus arrived together. They crowded each other in the foyer.

Guy spoke first. "Mom, did you see this door? Did you see the ...?" I sat on the sofa watching them untangle themselves. Vus came into the living room followed by Guy. "Have you spoken to anyone?"

It was a strange question. I didn't know what he meant, so I shook my head. When Guy asked me, not Vus, what we were going to do, I knew that although I had relinquished my responsibility, and although Guy had seemed to accept Vus as head of our family, in a critical moment he turned back to me.

Vus asked Guy to please go to his room. For the first time in months, Guy studied my face. I nodded and he went into his room reluctantly and left his door ajar.

Vus sat down with a heaviness which could not be credited to his bulk alone.

His first statement struck me as being as strange as his first question. "I have a lot of money, so there's nothing to worry about."

In a few hours, we would be on the street. It was enough that we would have no place to sleep, but our address and telephone number would cease to belong to us. In fact, we were soon to lose everything which identified us to our community except our names, and Vusumzi Make sat facing me, saying, "There's nothing to worry about."

The tiny lines around his eyes deepened and he began to pull viciously at the hairs on his chin. He didn't hear me offer to make a drink or a fresh pot of coffee, so I didn't repeat the offer.

After a few minutes he hauled himself out of the chair and picked up his brief case. He turned at the door and looking in my direction, but without actually looking in my eyes, spoke. "As I say, there is nothing to worry about." He opened the door, walked out, and eased it closed, quietly.

Guy came out of his room, agog with worry.

"Mom, what's going to happen? The thing said twenty-four hours. Where are we going? How did this happen? What did you do?"

The sight of my long tall beautiful boy brought back the memory of an ancient incident.

My then husband, Tosh, Guy, who was seven, and I were riding in our truck one lovely Sunday morning. We had just finished our weekly outing at the San Francisco city dump where Tosh and Guy threw office trash and home garbage onto the acrid ever-going burning heap of refuse. We had been in a high mood on the return home. Guy made puns and Tosh laughed at them. I felt secure. I had a loving husband and my husband had a job. My son, who was healthy and bright, received love and the necessary, to me, amount of chastisement. What more could I, a young uneducated black girl expect? I was living in my earthly paradise.

We waited at the intersection of Fulton and Gough for the lights to change. Suddenly, a car lurched into the passenger side of the truck. I was thrown forward, my forehead struck the windshield and my teeth crunched against the top of the cab's dashboard. When I regained consciousness, Tosh was blowing his breath in my face and murmuring. I asked about Guy and Tosh said that as the car hit, I grabbed for Guy and folded him in my arms. Now he was standing on the corner unhurt.

I got out of the truck and walked over to my son, who was being consoled by strangers. When I bent down at his side, he took one glance at my battered face and instead of coming into my arms, he began to scream, strike out at me and back away.

Tosh had to come to talk him into the taxi. For days, he moped around the house avoiding my gaze. Each time I turned quickly enough to catch him looking at me, I shivered at the hateful accusation in his eyes.

We had not caused the accident. Tosh had been the driver, and I was the most injured person. But I was the mother, the most powerful person in his world who could make everything better. Why had I made them worse? I could have prevented the accident. I should not have allowed our truck to be at that place at that time. If I hadn't been so neglectful, my face would not have been cut, my teeth would not be broken and he would not have been scared out of his wits.

Now, eight years later, Guy was asking himself why had I, by neglecting my duty, why had I put his pride in jeopardy? Had I thought that being married removed my responsibility to keep the world on its axis and the universe in order?

Guy stood flexing and tightening his fists, as if he were squeezing and releasing, then squeezing the questions again. I remained quiet, relishing a small but savory knot of satisfaction. He had shifted his loyalty to Vus, leaving me only the leftovers of attention. Now in the crisis, I became the important person again.

When he realized that I was not going to speak, he sat down on the sofa beside me. Suddenly I didn't know what to say. If, when he reentered the room, I had given an explanation or posed a few alternatives, our lives would have continued in the same rhythms indefinitely. But I had waited too long to speak.

I watched my son. When he slid on the sofa, opened his long arms to embrace me and said, "It'll be okay, Mom. We'll live through this one, too," I began to cry. My teenager was growing up.

Vus returned after nightfall. He had arranged for the sale of our furniture, and a mover would arrive the next morning to take our personal belongings to a hotel where he had rented and paid for a furnished apartment. He had also started the ball rolling for us to go to Egypt. He delivered the news to me but winked at Guy and cocked his head. Guy looked back at Vus with a blank stare and said, "That's great, Dad," and walked into his room.

For three weeks, in the musty hotel off Central Park West, we lived a life alien to everything I had known. Retired people, sick and discarded, shuffled along the hallways, whispering passionately to themselves. At all hours they inched frail feet along the lobby's worn carpet. They never looked up, or spoke to anyone, just continued traveling, staying close to the walls, their heads down, pushing the dank air.

Guy began to speak in a lower register and Vus and I whispered even in the bedroom. Our comings and goings were furtive and quiet. Only Rosa visited me during those weeks. I didn't want anyone else to know that we had moved underground and joined a pack of tragic moles.

I kept telling myself it was only for three weeks. A person could stay on a torture rack, or fast, for three weeks. It was just as well that we left New York with no fanfare, and no sad farewells. Vus went to Egypt to prepare a place for us while Guy and I traveled to San Francisco. I needed to see my mother. I needed to be told just one more time that life was what you make it, and that every tub ought to sit on its own bottom. I had to hear her say, "They spell my name W-O-M-A-N, 'cause the difference between a female and a woman is the difference between shit and shinola."

At the airport she looked worn, although she was wearing too much nut-brown powder and the lipstick was so thick that when we kissed hello, our lips made a sucking sound. Her happiness at seeing us was brief.

On the way home she confirmed the suspicions which arose the moment I had seen her. She drove her big car poorly and talked about trifling matters. Vivian Baxter was very upset.

She settled Guy into his old room on the downstairs floor of the big Victorian house, and asked me to join her in the kitchen. She began to talk, over tall and strong drinks.

She had sent me a photograph of her new husband. He was a dark-brown good-looking man, and she had raved about him in her letters to me. They had sailed together and played on the beaches of Tahiti and Fiji and in the bars of Sydney, Australia. Their marriage sounded like a frolic: Two lovers in a boat put out on a calm sea. But as she talked, seated at her kitchen table, I saw that the relationship was floundering, and she was straining every muscle to keep it afloat.

"He means well, baby, and he tries to do well, but it's the drink. He just doesn't know how to control it."

Her face was sad and her voice trembled as she put fresh ice and Scotch in our glasses. Her husband was away on a long trip and she was finding it hard to manage her loneliness.

The next few weeks brought a change in our relationship which I never expected: We reversed roles. Vivian Baxter began to lean on me, to look to me for support and wisdom, and I, automatically, without thinking about it, started to perform as the shrewd authority, the judicious one, the mother. Guy was disconcerted by the new positions in the family. He became rigidly courteous, smiled less and assumed a sober stateliness which sat awkwardly on the shoulders of a teenage boy.

Vus called from Cairo to say that our tickets were waiting at a local travel agency, and it was impossible to hide my relief.

When I told Mother that we would be leaving soon, she came out of her doldrums for a few hours of celebration. She was thankful, she said, not only for my support but that she had raised a woman who could stand up to a crisis. She reminded me that there were too many old females and not nearly enough women. She was proud of me and that was my going-away gift.

We left San Francisco with her assurance that she would work out the difficulties in her own life and we were not to worry. Her last bidding was not easily carried out. I sat through the entire journey, from San Francisco to Los Angeles to London to Rome, with the concern for my mother riding in my lap. Only when we left Rome's Fiumicino Airport did I start to think about Egypt, Vus and the life my son and I were beginning.

Whether our new start was going to end in success or failure didn't cross my mind. What I did know, and know consciously, was that it was already exciting.

CHAPTER 15

Our plane landed at Cairo on a clear afternoon, and just beyond the windows, the Sahara was a rippling beige sea which had no shore. Guy and I went through customs, each peering through a frosted glass for a sight of Vus.

Barefoot men in long soiled nightdresses walked beside us, talking Arabic, asking questions. When we shook our heads and shrugged our shoulders, gesturing our lack of understanding, they fell about laughing, slapping their sides and doubling over. Laughter in a strange language has an unsettling effect. Guy and I walked close together, shoulders touching, into the main terminal.

The room was cavernous, and nearly empty, and Vus was not there. A porter asked in his version of English if we wanted a taxi. I shook my head. I had money, nearly a thousand dollars in travelers' checks, but I wasn't about to get into a taxi in an unknown country. Then I realized with a numbing shock that I had no address. I couldn't take a taxi if I wanted it.

I thought about Guy and caught the gasp before it could surface.

"Mom, what are we going to do? You gave Dad the arrival time, didn't you?"

"Of course. We'll just go over there and sit down." I didn't comment on the accusation in his voice, but I recorded it. We had lugged our baggage through a group of laughing porters and janitors when two black men in neat Western suits approached.

"Sister Maya? Sister Make?"

I nodded, too relieved to speak.

"Welcome to Cairo. And Guy? Welcome."

We shook hands and they mentioned their multisyllabic names. Vus was in a meeting with a high official and would join us as soon as possible. He had asked them to pick us up and bring us to his office.

They helped us into a ramshackle Mercedes Benz as if they were placing royalty in a state carriage. My son and I rose to the occasion. Neither of us said a word when, on the outskirts of Cairo, the driver neatly swerved to avoid hitting a camel, although I did push my elbow into Guy's side as we passed the beautiful white villas of Heliopolis. The shiny European cars, large horned cows, careening taxis and the throngs of pedestrians, goats, mules, camels, the occasional limousine and the incredible scatter of children made the streets a visual and a tonal symphony of chaos.

When we entered the center of Cairo, the avenues burst wide open with such a force of color, people, action and smells I was stripped of cool composure.

I touched the man in the front passenger seat and shouted at him, "What's going on? Is today a holiday?"

He looked out the open windows, and turned back to me shaking his head.

"The crowd? You mean the crowd?"

I nodded.

"No." He smiled. "This is just everyday Cairo."

Guy was so happy, he laughed aloud. I looked at the scene and wondered how we were going to enjoy living in a year-long Mardi Gras.

Emaciated men in long tattered robes flailed and ranted at heavily burdened mules. Sleek limousines rode through the droppings of camels that waved their wide behinds casually as they sashayed in the shadow of skyscrapers. Well-dressed women in pairs, or accompanied by men, took no notice of their sisters, covered from head to toe in voluminous heavy black wraps. Children ran everywhere, shouting under the wheels of rickety carts, dodging the tires of careening taxis. Street vendors held up their wares, beckoning to passers-by. Young boys offered fresh-fruit drinks, and on street corners, men stooped over food cooking on open grills. Scents of spices, manure, gasoline exhaust, flowers and body sweat made the air in the car nearly visible. After what seemed to be hours, we drove into a quiet, by comparison, neighborhood. Our escorts parked the car, then led us through a carefully tended front garden and into a whitewashed office building. They placed our luggage by the door of the lobby, then shook hands with Guy and me, and assuring us that Vus would arrive soon, left us in the lobby.

Africans came and went, nodding to us in passing. Just as exhaustion began to claim my body, Vus entered through the open doors. He shouted when he saw us, and came rushing to hold me and Guy in his arms. He grinned freely, and he looked about ten years old. I had no doubt, for the moment, that we were going to make each other frivolously happy. Cairo was going to be the setting for two contemporary lovers.

Vus released me and hugged Guy, chuckling all the while. He was a sexy brown-skin Santa Claus, whose love and largesse were for us alone.

"Come, let's go home. We live across the street." I spoke to Guy and pointed to the luggage. Vus shook his head and said, "They will be brought to us." We walked through the garden, arms linked, and headed for number 5 Ahmet Hishmat.

Vus led us up the stairs of the large marble-fronted building. On the steps, a black man dressed in dirty clothes grinned and bowed: "Welcome, Mr. Make." Vus put some coins in the man's outstretched hand and spoke to him in Arabic. As we walked into the building's cool dark corridor, Vus told us the man was Abu, the *boabab* or doorman, and he would deliver our bags. At the end of the corridor, he unlocked a carved door and we entered a luxurious living room. A gold-and-red-striped satin sofa was the first object which caught and held my attention.

A muted tapestry hung on the wall above another rich-looking sofa.

In the middle of the room a low table of exquisite parquetry rested on an antique Oriental rug.

Vus wondered aloud if I liked the room and Guy made approving sounds, but I couldn't imagine how a landlord could leave such important and expensive pieces in a rented apartment.

Guy shouted from a distance. "You should see this, Mom."

Vus took my elbow and directed me into the next room, where a Louis XVI brocaded sofa and chairs rested on another rich rug. The dining room was filled with French antique furniture. The large bedrooms held outsize beds, armoires, dressing tables and more Oriental rugs.

I grinned because I didn't know what else to do. When we reached the empty kitchen, a little sense returned to me.

A soot-encrusted lamp sat on a ledge with stacked plates, a pile of cheap cutlery and thick glasses.

Vus coughed, embarrassed. "They use this"—indicating the lamp— "to cook on. It's a Sterno stove. Uh...I didn't get around to fixing up the kitchen yet. Anyway, regular stoves are very, very expensive. I thought I'd wait until you arrived."

"You mean, we own all that crap?" I must have shouted because Guy, who was crowded into the small room with us, frowned at me, and Vus gave me a haughty, angry look.

"I have tried to make a beautiful house for you, even to the point of ignoring my own work. Yes, I've postponed important PAC affairs to decorate this apartment, and you call it crap?" He turned and walked through the door. Guy shook his head, disgusted with my lack of gratitude and grace, and followed Vus out of the kitchen. Their silent departure succeeded in humbling me. Vus was a generous man. Indeed, I had only seen that kind of furniture in slick magazine advertisements, or in the homes of white movie stars. My husband was lifting me and my son into a rarified atmosphere, and instead of thanking him for the elevation, I had been sour and unappreciative.

A profound sense of worthlessness had made me pull away from owning good things, expensive furniture, rare rugs. That was exactly how white folks wanted me to feel. I was black, so obviously I didn't deserve to have armoires, shiny with good French veneer, or tapestries, where mounted warriors waged their ancient battles in silk thread. No, I decided to crush that feeling of unworthiness. I deserved everything beautiful and I merited putting my long black feet on Oriental carpets as much as Lady Astor. If Vus thought he wanted his wife to live beautifully, he was no less a man (and I had to get that under the layers of inferiority in my brain) than a Rockefeller or a Kennedy.

The luggage had been placed in the middle of the floor of the first living room. I heard Vus's and Guy's voices from the balcony, so I went to join them with a smile warm enough to melt the snows on Mount Everest.

"This is the most gorgeous house I've ever seen." Vus nodded and smiled at me as if I were a recalcitrant child who had recovered her good manners following a foolish tantrum. Guy grinned. He had known his mother would come through. We stood looking down on the back of a man who was bent weeding what Vus said was our private garden. We had a doorman and our own gardener. That information was a fair-sized lump, but I swallowed it.

The first weeks in Cairo were occupied with introductions to freedom fighters from Uganda, Kenya, Tanganyika, North and South Rhodesia, Basutoland and Swaziland. Diplomats from already-independent African countries dropped by our apartment to meet Vus Make's American wife, who was trying to be all things to everybody.

Jarra Mesfin, from the Ethiopian Embassy, and his wife Kebidetch Erdatchew came early and stayed late. Joseph Williamson, the Chargé d'Affaires from Liberia, and his wife A. B. invited us to the Residency.

I was the heroine in a novel teeming with bejeweled women, handsome men, intrigue, international spies and danger. Opulent fabrics, exotic perfumes and the service of personal servants threatened to tear from my mind every memory of growing up in America as a second-class citizen.

Vus, Guy and I had lunch near the pyramid of Giza, where we watched camel riders lope around the bottom of the Sphinx. Car radios, nearly turned to their highest pitch, released the moaning Arabic music into the dusty air.

I had hired Omanadia, a short stubby older woman from Sudan, as cook-housekeeper after Vus said my reluctance to have a servant in the house was not proof of a democratic spirit, but rather of a bourgeois snobbism, which kept a good job from a needy worker. Anyway, she was a cook and knew how to manage the little Sterno lamp which remained my only stove.

Guy was enrolled in the American College at Mahdi, and was picked up daily in a bus for the fifteen-mile ride out of Cairo to his school. He might have felt the need to show off for his schoolmates and new teachers, or the abrupt cultural change may have prompted him, but whatever the reason or reasons, he did extremely well in his studies. There was no need to urge him to do his homework, and the mood which had visited him in the more recent months in New York and San Francisco was dispelled. In Cairo, he had a clarity, was cheerful, garrulous and my young son again. We engaged each other in a contest to see who would have the largest Arabic vocabulary and speak with the best accent.

There was an Afro-Asian Solidarity Conference in downtown Cairo and Vus thought I'd like to attend.

The sight of the huge auditorium made me catch my breath. Long tables, banked at an easy incline, held headsets and microphones, and men of every color, wearing various national outfits, wandered the aisles, conversing loudly in many languages strange to my ear. The arrangement of seats, the microphones and the multinationals reminded me of the General Assembly of the United Nations, my heart thumped and I reached for Vus, who, hating public displays of attachment unless he initiated them, stepped away, but stayed close enough to whisper.

"They don't make you nervous, do they?"

I straightened myself and pulled as far from him as he had withdrawn from me. "Not at all. I don't frighten easily."

That was more mouth than truth, but I put my head up and walked down into the mingle of men. Vus caught my arm and stopped me.

"I want to introduce you to your fellow countryman." I looked around to see a thin young man, dressed in a well-cut suit, smiling at me. He was of one piece. His eyes were almond shaped, his face long and gently molded into an oval, his smile was long and thin, and he was the color of a slightly toasted almond. Vus said, "This is David DuBois. He is a journalist in Cairo, and my very good friend. David, meet my wife, Maya."

His first words were a healing balm spread on an ache I had not distinguished. "Hello, Maya Angelou Make. I've heard about you. All Egypt will be happy to welcome you. And they say you can sing, too."

The voice of an adult American black man has undeniable textures. It has a quality of gloss, slithery as polished onyx, or it can be nubby and notched with harshness. The voice can be sonorous as a bass solo or light and lyrical as a flute. When a black man speaks in a flat tone, it is not only intentional but instructional to the listener.

I had forgotten how much I loved those sweet cadences. I said, "I surely want to thank you. I'm glad to be here."

We smiled at each other and embraced. Maybe he had missed hearing a black American woman's voice.

———

The cocktail parties at home increased. Vus had to make contacts, and he also had to entertain them, their wives and friends. When he was in Cairo, the house throbbed with activity. I learned to cook elaborate dinners without pork and served chilled fruity unalcoholic punches when our guests were Moslem. Roast hams, rice with ham, spinach with salt pork and peas with pig knuckles, with Scotch and gin, were served to African and European guests.

I began to notice the undeniable link between Vus's journeys and our entertainment schedule. When he returned from Algeria, which was independent and militantly anticolonial, his spirits were high and he strutted through the house with an air of insouciance. At those times, he wanted to be alone with me and Guy. He would describe the successful Algerian revolution as if the seven-and-a-half-year rebellion had taken place in South Africa rather than at the continent's most northerly tip. Guy would listen, his eyes gleaming, his face immobile, as Vus told us proudly of his conversations with Ben Bella or Boumedienne. Trips to Ghana also resulted in proud reports of the

Nkrumah government and homey conversations. We three would play Scrabble and listen to music. Then in our dim bedroom, he would take me into his arms delicately. My body was the prayer wheel where he placed all his supplications. Love-making became a high celebration, rich and sacred, a sacramental communion.

Conversely, when he had traveled into southern Africa, without passports or documents, when he doffed the tailored suits and hand-made shoes, and wore the open sandals and blankets of tribesmen in order to reach a stranded party of escapees, he returned to Cairo quickened, tense with wakefulness. The whites of his eyes were always shot with red lines, and his attention was abstracted with what he had seen, and where he had been.

He was hardly in the house before he would pick up the telephone.

"Are you free this evening? Come over. My wife will cook her famous Afro-American food. We'll drink and eat. Come."

The invitation would be repeated several times before he would ask if I had something I could prepare in a hurry. Invitees would troop into the apartment, eat and drink copiously, talk loudly with each other and leave. Occasionally during the gatherings, David DuBois and I would find a quiet corner and talk about our folks back home.

David's journalistic assignments involved all of Europe, Africa and Asia, and marriage had broadened my interests to include the mercurial politics of those areas as well. However, while the conversations around us swelled with concern over Goa and India, Tshombe and the Belgian-owned Union Minière, the Lebanon and Middle East crisis, we wondered how the black parents in America could let their little children walk between rows of cursing, spitting white women and men, en route to school? What would happen to the children's minds when uniformed police sicked dogs on them just because they wanted to get to class?

At a certain point, we always stopped the self-pitying and reassured ourselves that our people would survive. Look what we had done already.

David and I would begin to hum softly, one of the old spirituals.

(He always insisted on starting with his favorite, "Glory, Glory, Hallelujah, When I Lay My Burden Down.")

Surely exhibitionism was a part of our decision to sing in a room of talkers, but a deeper motivation was also present. The lyrics and melody had the power to transport us back into a womblike familiarity. Admittedly, Africa was our place of genesis, long, long ago, but more recently, and more dearly known were the sounds of black America. When David and I lifted the song, diplomats and politicians, women on the make, and men on the run, freeloaders and revolutionaries, stopped haranguing, flirting, jibing, imploring, pontificating, explaining, and turned to listen. First half-heartedly, informed by the knowledge that we were airing melodies written by the last large group of people enslaved on the planet, courtesy forced them to attend. After a few verses, the music made its own demands. They could not remain ignorant of its remarkable humanity. I could not read their minds, but their faces were wide open with allegiance to our songs. Vus, conscious of their attentiveness, paid tribute to our survival and by joining in helped David and me to reestablish for ourselves a connection to a bitter, beautiful past.

CHAPTER 16

Omanadia came to the balcony on a lovely summer afternoon.

"Madame?"

I had arisen from a nap in the cool bedroom. I felt refreshed and indulgent. "Yes, Omanadia?" She could not have the rest of the day off, if that was what she wanted. I needed a little more pampering.

"Madame, I stopped the rug man again. You were sleeping."

"What rug man?" I was awake, but slow.

"The man collecting for the rugs. He hasn't been paid for two months. And the two furniture collectors." She laughed roguishly. "The other maids down the street tell me when they're on Ahmet Hishmat, so I don't open the door."

Because of her age and sharp tongue, Omanadia was the bane and the pet of shopkeepers, younger servants and doormen. She knew all the gossip and most of the facts concerning people in our neighborhood.

"Omanadia, how much do we owe?"

She tried to keep a straight face, but her eyes danced. "How much, madame? But Mr. Make would not like me to say. He is the man, madame."

"How much, Omanadia?"

She made her fingers an abacus. We had only paid a tenth of the price on the rugs. We owed over half the cost of the bedroom furniture. We had not paid anything on the embroidered bed linens or towels. The two living rooms and the dining-room set were way overdue for payment, and our rent was two months in arrears. I thanked her and told her to take the rest of the afternoon off.

The specter of the New York City deputy sheriff stood in the doorway, hid just behind the heavy drapes, waited nearly visible in my well-tended flower garden. Eviction in New York was bad, but at least I was at home, where my friends would have helped if I called on them. And always there was Mom. I could have gathered my son and flown back to San Francisco. But if we were thrown out into the streets of Cairo ... along with the other homeless waifs, whom could I ask for help? When I was young, poor and destitute I had resisted welfare in the U.S. I certainly wasn't about to ask for assistance in a country which was having trouble feeding its own nationals.

I had to get a job.

David answered his telephone and when I said I had an emergency, he agreed to meet me at a tearoom in downtown Cairo.

The restaurant was luminous with crystal chandeliers, polished mahogany counters and jeweled women drinking Turkish coffee from dainty china cups. It was the wrong setting for my pitiable tale.

David had chosen a table in the center of glitter, and when he held out a chair for me, I decided to lie—to tell him the emergency was contrived, that I just wanted a chance to get out of the house. Or that I was planning a banquet and couldn't decide on a menu. He ordered whiskey and I prattled about embassy parties, and dinner near the pyramids, and how well I was learning Arabic, and how Guy was settling down in his new school.

I noticed he hadn't smiled once. When I finally stopped chattering, he asked quietly, "The emergency. What is the emergency?"

"Nothing really." We had had no time to build a friendship. I was about to use him simply because we were both black Americans. My mother's saying, "We're colored but we're not cousins," echoed in my mind. I shouldn't presume that our uniqueness gave me license to ask him for a favor.

"Does it have to do with Vus?" He looked at me directly and I thought, Doesn't everything have to do with Vus?

I said, "I'm getting a little bored sitting at home. I've worked all my life. So really, I thought maybe you might know how I could get a job. Just to have something to do."

He relaxed and grinned. "You want a job? Nice women don't work in Cairo. I thought you knew that. Why don't you join one of the women's organizations? Or set up a club among the wives of African diplomats. You could write some articles for black American newspapers. The *Amsterdam News* or something. Nothing to do?" He laughed. "Girl, I thought you were serious."

I was more than serious, I was desperate. And putting on silly airs, I had appeared to David like the frivolous women I scorned.

"David, I'm broke. Every piece of furniture in that house was bought on installment. The rent is past due, and Guy's school fees are in arrears. I don't have enough money to go back home and I can't stay here unless I get a job." The smile faded from his face and he nodded. "O.K., O.K. I figured it was something like that. Maybe. Maybe, I can get something for you. I'll do what I can. What about Vus? Will he let you work?"

"If I can get a job, I'll handle the rest of it. I've been through too much to turn back now. I've been a frycook, a waitress, a strip dancer, a fund-raiser. I had a job once taking the paint off cars with my hands. And that's just part of it."

David shook his head. "Black women. Huh, huh. O.K. Let's have another drink. I'll call somebody I know this afternoon."

I left the restaurant emboldened by alcohol and a lot of boastful conversation and I felt as secure as the cared-for women still pointing honey-filled baclavas into their red mouths.

Two days later, David took me to meet Zein Nagati, president of the Middle East Feature News Agency. Dr. Nagati was a very large handsome man in rumpled tweeds who had the air of a university professor.

He spoke rapidly, never repeating himself, as if he was used to talking to efficient shorthand secretaries.

He had started a magazine called the *Arab Observer*. It was not strictly speaking an official organ of the Egyptian government; that is, it did not come directly under the heading of the Ministry of Information. Its editorial position, however, would be identical with the national politics. He was hiring a Hungarian layout artist, and already had twelve reporters working. DuBois said I was an experienced journalist, wife of a freedom fighter and an expert administrator. Would I be interested in the job of associate editor? If so I should realize that since I was neither Egyptian, Arabic nor Moslem and since I would be the only woman working in the office, things would not be easy. He mentioned a salary that sounded like pots of gold to my ears and, standing, he reached for my hand.

"Very good, Mrs. Make. You'll begin on Monday. I'll be there to introduce you, and DuBois can show you around. *Salaam.*"

He picked up his brief case, inclined his head to me, shook hands with David and left the room.

I wanted to speak but I felt I had fallen into a deep trench with steep muddy sides.

When I regained a degree of consciousness, David was talking.

"You won't find it that hard. I'll help. Call me at any time. You've done reporting, and you've run offices. Anyway, you wanted a job."

He offered to show me his office, which was in the same building, and then take me to lunch. I followed him meekly, but I don't remember seeing his desk or meeting any other person. We went to the Cairo Hilton, but I could have eaten air sandwiches and a salad made of clouds. My thoughts nibbled on David's exaggerations to Dr. Nagati based on the lies I had told him. And the larger chunk in my throat which prevented me from swallowing solid food consisted of wondering what cleverness I could devise which would allow me to tell Vus and keep both the job and my husband.

David dropped me off at Ahmet Hismat and patted me on the shoulder. "Girl, you realize, you and I are the only black Americans working in the news media in the Middle East?"

I gave him a phony smile and got out of the taxi with that new mind full of responsibility.

In the United States, when I faced any new situation I knew what to do. I had half educated myself by spending nights and long days in libraries. I had given my son a fair smattering of general information from borrowed books. But in Egypt I faced the dilemma without help. Only the American Embassy would have a collection in English, and since I had spoken so harshly to Africans about the United States' racist policy, going there was out of the question.

I fingered the books Vus and I had brought from the States. George Padmore's *Africa and World Peace*, DuBois' *Souls of Black Folks*, collections of Langston Hughes's and Paul Laurence Dunbar's poems and Baldwin's *Nobody Knows My Name*.

The Baldwin book gave me heart. Nobody seemed to know my name either. I had been called everything from Marguerite, Ritie, Rita, Maya, Sugar, Bitch, Whore, Madam, girl and wife. Now in Egypt I was going to be called "associate editor." And I would earn the title, if I had to work like a slave. Well not quite, but nearly.

Guy brought home another notice for fees from school, and I told him I had made arrangements to pay. The evidence of his complete trust was the fact that the question on his face disappeared in seconds.

Vus returned on Sunday morning, rested and handsome. He was the only person I ever knew who could finish a ten-hour plane trip looking as fresh as new money. We exclaimed over our gifts; he brought a Zulu necklace for me and a chess set for Guy. We had a large Sunday dinner, and Guy left for the movies with some school friends.

We spent a lovely hour in the bedroom, reacquainting our bodies, and then I brought hot tea and cakes to the living room. Vus joined me in his robe and slippers.

I began cautiously.

"I saw David DuBois. We went to tea."

"Oh great. How is he?"

"I asked him to help me find a job."

Vus sputtered, then rubbed his mouth with a napkin.

His next reaction startled me. He began to laugh. At first a few chuckles but they increased to a hearty guffaw, then he lost his breath again. When he calmed down his first words were "You black women. Who knows what to do with you?" His laughter was more restrained. "Black and American. You think you can come to Egypt and just go get a job? That's foolish. It shows the nerve of the black woman and the arrogance of the American. I must say, my dear wife, those are not very attractive qualities. Don't pout, Maya, you know I love you. There are simply some things which do not become you. I gave you Gamal Nasser's book, didn't you read it? The UAR is committed to upgrading its citizens economically as well as politically. As my wife, and a foreigner as well, you would never find a job. Besides, I look after you. I like you to look after me and Guy, and ..."—here he rubbed his chin lovingly—"and maybe we'll have a child, a little brother for Guy."

There is a silent scream, which tears through the veins, separating the muscles, pinching the nerves, yet the body seems to remain immobile. We had never talked about having children. I had one son. I seemed to have given an order to my body that one was enough, because although I used no contraceptives, I had only been pregnant the one time.

He was still playing with his chin, pulling at the sparse hairs.

"Vus, the rent is past due. The collectors have been here for payment on the furniture and the rugs. Guy's school has sent two notes home. I've fired the gardener and paid Omanadia out of my food money. I have to go to work."

"But I will see that everyone is paid. I always do, don't I?" I wouldn't answer and I wouldn't remind him of the New York eviction.

He raised his voice. "I don't throw away money, you know that. I only receive an allowance for the office and living expenses. Travel is costly. Printing charges are high. I must keep up my appearance. And so must you. We are freedom fighters. We are not beggars."

Craft and cunning were necessary and even as I schemed, I doubted if I was smart enough.

"Vus, you say you need me. You need a woman, not just a hostess. Your struggle is my struggle. I need to be more involved than serving dinner to refugees and keeping your house."

He started to interrupt but I continued. "If I work, you can spend the living allowance on the office. Instead of a quarterly newsletter, you could send out a monthly. We would be able to buy some warm coats for the new escapees. My salary could take care of the house expenses."

He listened and his eyes shone for a second, then the light went out.

"Darling, you are a wonderful woman. Excuse the harsh words. You're not arrogant. You are thoughtful. I appreciate your idea. But it's not possible. You'll never find work in Cairo."

"Vus, I have a job. Associate editor of the *Arab Observer*. I start to-morrow."

I watched the disbelief on his face turn to anger, then to rage.

"You took a job without consulting me? Are you a man?"

He stood and began to pace over the expensive rug. His tirade carried him from the sofa to the entry, over to the large chair and back to stand in front of me. His vilification included my insolence, independence, lack of respect, arrogance, ignorance, defiance, callousness, cheekiness and lack of breeding. I sat, watching him, listening and thinking. He was right. Somewhere in his swarm of words he had my apt description. I also understood that maybe I had gone too far. Even

an American black man would have found such a headstrong wife unsuitable, and how much more an African husband, steeped in a tradition of at least the appearance of male authority. I realized that I had
handled the thing badly. I should have been more delicate. I should
have allowed Vus time to see me depressed and mournful. Then he
could have coerced from me the reason for my mood. I could have so
manipulated the situation, that he would, himself, have suggested that
maybe I should find a little something to do. A small part-time job.
Perhaps a little secretarial work in the afternoon. With the awareness
of my unfortunate mismanagement came the shocking knowledge
that I was no longer in love.

The man standing over me venting his fury, employing his colorful
vocabulary was no longer my love. The last wisps of mystery had disappeared. There had been physical attraction so strong that at his approach, moisture collected at every place where my body touched
itself. Now he was in hand's reach, and tantalization was gone. He was
just a fat man, standing over me, scolding.

His anger was finally spent, his energy flagged. I waited until he
backed away and sat down in the chair facing me. He was exhausted
from the outpouring of reproach and I was benumbed by the loss of
love. We sat looking at each other, at the floor, at the tapestries, at each
other again.

He was the first to speak. His voice was soft.

"You must call David and explain that you acted as an American
woman, but that I returned home and reminded you that now you are
an African wife."

I knew that neither threats nor inducements would cause me to
give up the job.

I made my voice silken soft. "I have given my word. Not only to
David but to Dr. Zein Nagati. He is a friend of Gamal Abdel Nasser
and he knows that I am your wife. He said they need me. It might reflect badly on your name if I withdraw now."

Vus stood again. "You see? You see how your foolish headstrong
American ways have endangered the struggle?"

He tried to build up to the earlier anger but was too tired to do so.

He went back to the bedroom and reappeared dressed. He walked past me and out of the house, slamming the door.

I stayed in the pretty living room, thinking. I had a son to raise, and a lovely house. I had a job for which I was unqualified. I had an angry husband, whom I no longer loved. And I was in Cairo, Egypt, where I had no friends.

The doorbell rang, and thinking Vus had stalked out leaving his keys, I opened it. David DuBois stood smiling in the dim light. I grinned because he looked like Deliverance itself.

"Girl, I thought you might be getting nervous about tomorrow. So I came 'round to tell you everything's going to be all right."

We sat in the living room talking lightly about journalism and expectations. I wanted to unburden my aggravation. To tell him that I not only didn't know how to be an associate editor, but that my husband was bitterly opposed to my being anything but his obedient wife.

Vus walked in on our inane chatter. When he saw David his face lightened, the heavy cheeks lifted and he smiled delightedly.

They embraced as he called David "My brother." David must have noticed that he didn't speak to me.

"Vus, you must be proud of your wife. I mean about the job."

Vus cooled, and drew himself inward. "Job?" He said the word as if he had never used it before.

David looked at me, caught the misery which I didn't try to hide. He turned back to Vus. "When you were away she telephoned me. I took her out to tea and she said you were working so hard, stretching yourself so thin, that she was beginning to worry about your health. She said that as your wife she had to carry some of the load. That no one man could continue to do all you do without help."

Vus's body began to relax. His shoulders eased down to their natural position, a slow smile began to slacken his tightened features.

With words David was stroking away his hostility. "She said that most African men, in your position, would never allow their wives to work, but that you were a revolutionary, and that the success of the African conflict was your goal. And you meant to reach it by any means necessary."

Vus nodded. "True. True."

David was persuasive, convincing and a liar. He was also my supportive, fast-thinking inventive brother.

I was surprised to find when Vus and I went to bed, that being in the arms of a stranger in no way lessened my physical pleasure.

Vus insisted on accompanying me downtown to the *Arab Observer* offices. When we entered the enormous loftlike room, David called from a far corner. He greeted Vus first, then me. He introduced Vus first to my colleagues, and all the men shook hands, asked after each other's health and thanked God in Arabic. I was outside their ceremony like a foundling on an orphanage doorstep. After they finished saluting and bowing and grinning, David beckoned to me and I was presented.

Although I sensed little cordiality, I relaxed, because at least the men were not antagonistic. Vus's presence had assured them that I was not an audacious woman challenging their male community. I belonged to a man who, probably in straitened circumstances, was putting his wife to work. By introducing Vus first, David had followed established ritual and dissipated the hostility before it could collect.

I had to admit that although Vus's decision to escort me to my job (my father never accompanied me on the first day of school) infuriated me, his attendance had been a godsend.

I was shown my desk and a servant brought us all small cups of coffee from a brazier near the window. The coffee-drinking ceremony finally finished, Vus shook hands again with all the men, nodded to me and left the office. David stayed a few minutes, then shook hands around the room. When he took my hand, he said quietly, "You've made a good impression. I'll call you later."

I had said nothing, done nothing, shown no intelligence, wit or talent. Was I to assume that was the good impression?

Ignorance held me in my chair for at least an hour. Men, whose names I had already forgotten, or hadn't heard clearly at the first introduction, passed my desk, their hands full of papers and their eyes averted. The servant brought me cup after cup of sweet sluggish coffee, which I drank dutifully.

Suddenly there was a great sound of swishing papers, thumping feet, the tacking of typewriters. Dr. Nagati had arrived. He bobbed his head to the now industriously bustling reporters and came directly to my desk.

"Mrs. Make?" I stood.

"How are you getting on? David was here? You've been introduced? Good." He raised his voice, and speaking in Arabic, caused the employees to gather around him. Again, I stood outside the circle of men, not understanding as he continued to speak in an explosive tone. He slid into English without changing the force of speech.

"Mrs. Make?" It was a shouted order to come to attention, in a full-dress parade.

"Yes, Dr. Nagati?" I edged through the passage now made for me to face the great man. He looked down at me and tried a smile, which failed.

"This man handles British news. This one is in charge of European, this one is editor of Soviet news, this one American, this one Asian, and you will write about Africa. You will also look at all their copy, and they will look at yours. The *Arab Observer* will be a weekly, starting next week. We print in the basement of this building. You will go downstairs now with me and meet the typesetters."

Without another word, he walked away. It only took me a second to realize that he expected me to follow.

We walked into the dimly lit and dusty room on the lower floor. Dr. Nagati raised his voice, hollering in Arabic. Men in traditional galabias appeared like phantoms out of the gloom. All at once bright lights exposed the farthest recesses.

I was introduced in English as Mrs. Make, the new associate editor. The men shook my hand and welcomed me in Arabic. I smiled and wished Dr. Nagati would stay in the building forever, or at the very least return with me to the upstairs offices. We took our leave of the printers, and he talked until we reached the door leading out of the building. The magazine must be ready for distribution next week. It must have grace and be beautiful. Its news must be timely and accurate. I must remember that although none of the men had worked with women before, except possibly secretaries, they were all cultured and capable. Speaking of secretaries, he would be sending a few over later in the week.

"Goodbye, Mrs. Make. I'm sure you'll do well." He pushed the door open and disappeared through it, while my mouth was hanging open wide enough to allow in a swarm of flies.

I directed myself back to my desk. At least I knew that I was expected to cover the African affairs. It would be necessary to collect all newspapers, magazines, journals and essays. A large map and a set of the Oxford English Dictionary would help. Now, now that I no longer desired Vus, I needed him. Every fact he'd ever learned was filed neatly in his orderly brain. He knew tribes, leaders, topography, weather and the political stances of all countries on the continent.

Two reporters, the coffee bearer and I reached my desk at the same time. The server set down the small cup and walked away, as both the journalists drew up chairs. When I sat down, they told me their names again, and began to chat with me, quite cozily. We agreed tacitly that our first introduction had never happened. They offered to show me the Telex machine and how I could acquire background material on any news release. They proposed that I move my desk into the adjoining room, where there was a library with hundreds of books in English. The grin began in my stomach or behind my kneecaps or under my toenails. It undulated in sweet waves, overrunning my body with warmth and well-being. I thought of Brer Rabbit. Like all Southern black children, I had heard folk tales since my early youth, and a favorite came back to me as I sat in that wide-open newsroom in Cairo.

For years Brer Rabbit had been stealing carrots from a garden, and after many attempts, after many elaborate but ineffectual snares, the owner of the plot finally succeeded in catching him.

The man was red as blood with anger. He shook the rabbit until his tail nearly fell off. He said, "Rabbit, I've got you now. And I'm going to do the worst thing in the world to you. I mean the baddest thing. I mean the meanest thing. I'm going to make you cry and scream and wish that God never put breath in your body."

The rabbit started crying. "Please, Mr. Farmer. Don't do the worst thing to me. Do anything but that. But I don't think you know what the worst thing is. So just do me as you want to do me." The rabbit started shuffling and grinning. "But don't do the worst thing."

The farmer looked at the rabbit suspiciously. He asked, "What is the worst thing?" Rabbit said, "I won't tell you." The farmer began to lie. "You can tell me, little rabbit. I won't do it. I promise you."

The rabbit began to relax. He asked the farmer. "Do you swear if I tell you, that you won't do it to me?"

The farmer put his hand on his heart and swore. The rabbit relaxed even more.

He said, "Farmer, you've got a big black iron pot. You can fill it with lard and light a fire under it and cook me in boiling oil, and I wouldn't care."

The farmer was doubtful, but the rabbit kept talking. "You can skin me alive and use my fur to make a coat for your little girl, and that would be all right with me." The farmer looked at the rabbit with disbelief, but the rabbit continued. "You can cut off all my feet and give them to your friends for good luck and I'd like that. But the worst thing..."

The farmer was getting excited. "Tell me, little rabbit, what is the worst thing?"

The rabbit began to tremble, his voice got so little the farmer could barely hear him. "See that briar patch over there?" He pointed to a clump of nettles, "Please don't throw me over there." The farmer's face became hard. He asked the rabbit, "Are you sure that's the worst thing?" Rabbit said, "They stick in my sides like burning needles, they pop in my eyes like thorns, they hold me like chains and lash my body like whips. Please don't throw me in the briar patch."

The farmer picked up the rabbit by the ears, he lifted him high in the air and he began to swing him around over his head, all the time asking, "Are you sure?" And the rabbit answered, crying, "It's the worst thing!"

Finally, when the farmer had the rabbit turning at a fast speed, he pointed him toward the briar patch and let go. Brer Rabbit landed on his feet. His eyes were dry and bright. His ears perked up and waved.

Brer Rabbit grinned at the farmer, his teeth shining white as buttermilk. He said, "Home, at last. Home at last. Great God Almighty, I'm home at last."

I smiled sweetly as the men shoved and pulled my desk into the library. When they left, and I stood before the crowded bookshelves, reading unfamiliar titles and the names of authors unknown to me, still I felt just like Brer Rabbit in the briar patch.

CHAPTER 17

For two weeks I stayed in the room, using each free moment to cull from the shelves information about journalism, writing, Africa, printing, publishing and editing. Most of the books had been written by long-dead authors and published years before in Britain; still, I found nuggets of useful facts.

The arrival of secretaries forced me back into the larger room with my male colleagues, but by that time I had a glimmering of journalistic jargon. I began to combine a few news items taken directly from the Telex, and insert some obscure slightly relevant background information. Then I would rehead the copy and call it my own.

I stayed at the *Arab Observer* for over a year and gradually my ignorance receded. I learned from Abdul Hassan how to write an opinionated article with such subtlety that the reader would think the opinion his own. Eric Nemes, the layout artist, showed me that where an article was placed on a page, its typeface, even the color of ink, were as important as the best-written copy. David DuBois demonstrated how to select a story and persevere until the last shred of data was in my hands. Vus supplied me with particulars on the politically fluid, newly independent African states. I received a raise from Dr. Nagati, the respect of my fellow workers and a few compliments from strangers.

Weekdays began with a family breakfast served by Omanadia. Vus read the newspaper, Guy's face was buried in a book and I scanned work I always brought to the table. Often after we left the house, going separate ways, I would think that we had again lost the art of talking together. We had ceased to find amusement in one another.

Guy's life was becoming intricately complicated. He was asked to cope with adolescent sexuality, the enigmatic Arabic language, a body which seemed to be stretching to touch the clouds and another joyless home. In attempting to protect himself he withdrew into books or threw himself into the wild, raucous Cairo streets.

I offered to give parties for his Arabic friends so that he could spend more time in the house. He refused politely but coolly, saying that neither he nor his acquaintances wanted to be shut up indoors. They'd rather be in the *souks* and back streets, the old town and the great Al Tahrir Square, and don't worry about him, he was just fine.

Neither of us could successfully masquerade our unhappiness from the other. We had been too close, too long. We accepted with mutual respect the other's pretense at contentment.

Vus's work doubled.

The number of men escaping from South Africa was escalating. Some only reached Northern Rhodesia, where they stayed hidden until arrangements could be made for their further escape. A few men lodged in Ethiopia, but they had to be moved, and Vus's responsibility was to find friendly nations where the now-homeless wanderers could stay. All needed clothes, food, housing. Some wanted military training, while others asked for medical or legal education. Vus's concern in their behalf never wavered.

Although the romance in our marriage had evaporated, I still admired and appreciated him. I even loved him, I simply was not in love with him. There was ample evidence that he had other romantic interests anyway. Often, he returned home very late, reeking of perfume, heavy lidded and offering no explanation. On a few evenings, he didn't return at all. I said nothing. I had my work, my house and had made two friends. A.B. Williamson, the round pretty wife of the Liberian Chargé d'Affaires, and Kebidetch Erdatchew, wife of the Ethiopian Embassy's First Secretary. On the surface, we seemed to have nothing in common save our gender and blackness. Kebidetch was thin, small and married to a son of the royal Selassie House. She was as beautiful as antique gold and as reserved as a vault and lent credence to the common African saying that the loveliest women on the continent were to be found in Ethiopia.

Her own beauty was legendary. One day in Addis Ababa, the regal Jarra Mesfin saw her from a passing car and determined, at that hasty glance, that he would find her, woo her and wed her. The ensuing courtship and marriage became the subject of popular songs sung in the streets and cafés of Ethiopia. Seven years later, they still shared languid looks across crowded rooms. They were childless and lived in Zamalek in a quiet luxurious apartment, with an ancient manservant they had brought from Ethiopia.

A.B. (friends called her Banti) had been raised in the underdeveloped Grand Bassa region of Liberia. Her family sent her to Monrovia, the capital city, for further education. Her pert looks and witty good humor won her friends and marriage to a bright young lawyer, whose career was just beginning to rise.

The couple lived in the Ambassador's Residence with their own three children, Banti's younger sister, the teenage daughter of a friend, two Liberian maids, a nanny, an Egyptian laundryman, a doorman and a cook. The building shivered with sound. Noisy children played tag games on the graceful staircase. West African High Life music boomed from the large record player, young girls giggled over young-girl secrets in the ceremonial drawing room, and Banti moved her short chubby body through the house, her laughter adding one more spice to the already aromatic cacophony.

Kebi, Banti and I met several times at diplomatic receptions, and at my house during one of our costly parties, but we didn't cross the threshold from courteous acquaintance into friendship until one night at the Liberian Residence when an overflow of visitors filled every inch of space in the building's first floor. African, Asian and European diplomats with their wives mingled with Egyptian government officials and their wives. Waiters, hired for the occasion, prodded through the throng, shoving trays of drinks toward the crowded guests.

I was sitting with a Yugoslavian woman in the informal lounge when I heard Vus's voice part the general murmur of the crowd in another room.

"I speak for the Xhosa, the Zulu, the Shona and the Lesotha. You are a foolish people. Foolish." I jumped up, and remembering my manners just in time, excused myself. (Vus was cozying up the Yugoslavians at that time.) I nudged my way through the flock of people. Vus's tone was becoming louder.

"A foolish, small-minded greedy nation. You are mean and stupid. Stupid." I had arrived sooner than I expected, because as I pushed forward, people nearer the action pulled away, impossibly dispersing. I saw Vus standing face to face with a white man, whose red cheeks and popped eyes were his only evidence of life. He stood stone-stiff; he might have died erect, and been left on the spot to be viewed like a statue. Vus's face, however, was alive with contempt, and his right arm was raised. He was poking the white man's chest with his forefinger.

"Tell them, tell the savages of your country, that Mother Africa will no longer allow them to suck from her breast."

I knew that Vus was intoxicated with either alcohol or rage or a dangerous combination of the two. All sounds had diminished to a low, steady, disapproving undertone. I felt as powerless as if I were mute or hypnotized.

"I speak for Southern Africa. For South-West Africa. For Mozambique, Angola..."

"And Ethiopia." The sound came from the rear, and grew louder as the speaker neared Vus. "He speaks for the Amharas and the Gullas and for the Eritreans." Jarra appeared, having pressed his way through the pack of bodies. He stood beside Vus. There was another movement, I saw another separation and Kebi appeared to stand near Jarra. Her movement gave me the courage to edge nearer Vus, but we acted with different motives. She was displaying her support of Jarra; I was hoping that my presence would provoke Vus into gathering his control. We five stood in the center of the room, like warring tribes in a forest clearing, and we had reached a stalemate. Joe Williamson's already high-pitched voice soared over the crowd.

"Brothers. Brothers." Joe stepped up to Vus and Jarra, daintily, like a proud bantam rooster. "Argument is one thing. Riot is another. This is not an occasion for either."

Without changing tone he spoke in Liberian patois, "Ole man say in my country, 'Hurry, hurry, get dere tomorrow. Take time, get there today.' Or better yet, 'We come to party to show our teeth. We go to war to show our arms.' "

Vus turned to look at Joe, and I held my breath. Joe was the doyen of the African diplomatic corps; he had been supportive of Vus and all the other freedom fighters and was highly respected in Cairo, and I liked him. If Vus turned on Joe, I could cross him off our list of acquaintances, because Vus's tongue could be sharp as an assagai, and Joe was a proud man. Vus smiled and shook his head. He said, "Bro Joe, you should be president of this entire continent."

Jarra, taking his cue from Vus's relaxation, said, "Speak for the rest of Africa, Vusumzi, not Ethiopia. However, maybe the emperor will make him a *ras*." They laughed.

The gathering seemed to exhale at the same time. All of a sudden, music could be heard. The knots of people disbanded. Vus, Joe and Jarra walked away together and the man who had been the object of Vus's tirade disappeared. Only Kebi, Banti, who had been standing behind her husband, and I were left in the middle of the floor. Kebi looked at us, lifted her eyebrows and gave a tiny shrug of her frail shoulders. Banti put her hands on her hips and grinned roguishly. I thought of us as foot soldiers, bringing up the rear in a war whose declaration we had not known, left on the battlefield after a peace was achieved, in which we had not participated. I laughed out loud. Banti and Kebi chuckled. We moved nearer and, smiling, touched each other's shoulders, arms, hands and cheeks. Brought to friendship by the frustrated lashing out of one man, a near-stranger's defense of the first man, and by the clever, humorous mediation of a third man, we three women were to be inseparable for the next year and a half.

I never learned what fuse ignited the conflagration. At home, Vus answered my query: "He was wrong, and too cowardly to say what he meant."

"Did he insult you? I mean us, the race?"

"Not directly. Like most white racists, he was paternalistic. I would have preferred he slap me than that he talk down upon me. Then I could retaliate in kind."

I totally agreed. Some whites, in black company, beset by the contradiction between long-learned racism and the demands of courtesy, confusedly offend listening blacks. The stereotypical "Some of my best friends..." and other awkward attempts at what they think to be civility, elicit from black people an outburst of anger whites can neither comprehend nor avoid.

———

An inability to speak fluent Arabic and the difference in cultures made friendships with Egyptian women difficult. The secretaries in my office were neither brave enough (I understood that as a six-foot-tall black American female editor, I was somewhat of an oddity) nor had the time (many had taken jobs to help their needy parents and siblings) nor were interested enough (some were already betrothed and were working to pay for their trousseaus) to respond to my friendly overtures.

I had heard of Hanifa Fathy and noted the respect with which her name was spoken. Hanifa Fathy, the poet. Then, Hanifa, wife of a judge. It was unusual to hear an Egyptian woman's marital alliance not reported as her first accomplishment. When we finally met at a conference, I was surprised to find her pretty. I had never heard her looks described. She wore her light-brown hair long, in the manner of Lauren Bacall, and her strong feminine features reminded me of the bold American actress.

When we shook hands (her handshake was firm), she said she had been reading my work in the *Arab Observer* and was determined that we should meet. I accepted her invitation to meet some Egyptian female writers, scholars and teachers.

In Hanifa's modish living room, I met Egyptian women who had earned doctorates from European universities, and serious painters and talented actresses, but I found them too trained, too professionally fixed, to welcome the chummy contact of friendship. Hanifa, however, was warm and witty. We spent gossipy Saturday afternoons on the veranda of the Cairo country club.

My marriage had shape, responsibility and no romance, and although I was working ten hours a day at the *Arab Observer,* my salary slipped away like sand in an hourglass. There was never enough. Vus needed more clothes, more trips, more parties. Guy needed more clothes and more allowance. I needed more of everything, or at least I wanted an increase of the things I had and the possession of things I had never owned.

On the face of it, things looked bad, but I couldn't escape from a cheeriness which sat in my lap, lounged on my shoulders and spread itself in the palms of my hands. I was, after all, living in Cairo, Egypt, working, paying my own way. My son was well. Then there were David DuBois, Banti, Kebi and Hanifa.

I had the possibility of a brother and three sisters. It could have been much worse.

Banti gave a hilarious party, to which only women were invited. The occasion was a celebration of the birthday of a great Liberian female doctor. Elaborate food and a variety of drinks were served by uniformed attendants. The living room was decorated as if for a supreme Embassy function, and a trio of musicians played familiar melodies.

Wives and secretaries from the African embassies and a sprinkling of Egyptian women and I felt deliciously important. We ate, talked, drank and half the invitees finally danced, moving individually, across Banti's polished hardwood floor. Each woman observed the steps of her own country. Kebi, with her hands on her hips, slid her feet in tiny patterns, meanwhile raising first one shoulder, then the other, and rotating the shoulders in sensuous undulation. Banti and Mrs. Clelland from the Ghanian Embassy danced High Life, stepping lightly, with knees slightly bent, pushing their backsides a little to the left, a little to the right and directly behind themselves. I combined some Twist with the Swim and received approving laughter and applause from the nondancers who sat on the sidelines.

The party was nearing its end when a young woman took the floor. She wore West African national dress. The long printed skirt and matching blouse hugged a startling body. She had wide shoulders, large erect breasts, billowing hips and the waist of a child. All the dancers backed away and found seats, as the beautiful woman moved to the music. She swiveled and flourished, jostled and vibrated, accompanied by the audience's encouragement and laughter.

"Swing it, girl. Swing it."

"Show that thing, child. Show it."

"Whoo. Whoo."

She made her face sly, knowing, randy, and her large hips fluttered as if a bird, imprisoned in her pelvis was attempting flight.

The viewers' delight reminded me of the pleasure older black American women found in other women's sexiness. Years before when I had been a shake dancer, some ladies used to pat my hips and exclaim, "You've got it, baby. Shake it. Now, shake it." Their elation was pure, sensual and approving. If they were old they looked on female sensuality as an extension of their own, and were reminded of their youth. Younger women recollected the effects of their last lovemaking or were prompted by womanish sexuality into pleasant anticipation of their next satisfying encounter.

I was tickled that African women and black American women had the custom in common.

When the music and dancing were finished I joined the women who crowded around the dancer, patting, stroking her and laughing.

"I am from Northern Nigeria." Her voice was soft and she kept her eyes lowered, respecting the age and positions of the older women. "I am an unmarried girl with a good dowry. I'm here to stay with Egyptian friends and study Arabic."

Her name was Mendinah and she was obviously looking for a husband.

We complimented her on her beauty and welcomed her to Cairo, and I secretly wished her luck.

CHAPTER 18

One week later Vus returned from Addis Ababa. He asked what had happened in his absence. I reported on my work and that David had found another way for me to supplement my salary. I had agreed to write commentary for Radio Egypt, and I would be paid four pounds for a review and an extra pound for each one I narrated.

Guy had earned acceptable grades on recent tests and had generously spent more time at home while Vus was away. I also told Vus about the women's party and Mendinah. He accepted my news and told me drily of his trip. The once-exotic names no longer titillated me, and Vus had long since stopped trying to enchant me with tales of his perilous exploits. We returned to the sequence of our lives. Work occupied our days, and parsimonious love-making ended some stolid nights.

The news spread in the African diplomatic corps that Mendinah was a slut, a hussy, a whore, a home-breaking harlot. The rumor was hot oil poured into the ears of the African women who had admired her. She had sought appointments with four ambassadors. Three had reported to their wives that the pretty woman offered them her favors in return for money. In weeks she had cut a lascivious swath between members of the diplomatic corps and their wives. Her name became an alarm, forcing my female friends to assemble and close ranks against the dangerous intruder.

She would never be invited to another woman's home. She would be turned away from every door, and not addressed on the street. The husbands who had fallen for her charms would be dealt with in the privacy of their marriages, but her blatant disrespect of the African wives had to have public penalty.

Two months passed and for the African community Mendinah disappeared, lost her name, had no presence. Then one evening, an

Egyptian woman, close acquaintance of the African women, gave a party. Vus and I arrived late. When we entered the first room, the informal lounge, Banti, Kebi and seven ladies already sat on the sofas, their multicolored dresses radiant against dark-brown skin. They greeted Vus, who responded and continued into the salon, where more guests stood talking. I stopped to exchange regards with my friends and the other ladies I had come to know and like.

Our small talk was suddenly pierced by "Good evening, Mrs. Make." The sound was disquietingly familiar. I looked up and saw Mendinah in the arched doorway leading to a hall passage. She was standing by a record player. I nodded to her and she lifted the machine's arm, stopping the music. When she turned her fabulous body to face me, I saw again the cunning face, the small hint of cruelty.

"Mrs. Make, Mr. Make has been trying to reach me all day long. He called all over Cairo trying to get my number." Her words, voice and intent were pitiless and for seconds my heart opposed its natural function.

She poked her voice easily through my entire body. "When he finally reached me, he said he had to talk to me, to see me about something very important." As she glanced at the seated women, I gritted my teeth and held on to the sternness of my long-dead grandmother.

"I refused to let him come to my apartment." Her eyes hurriedly returned to fasten on me. "Then he said it had to do with you. That you needed someone to help you at the office. I have been looking for a job, you know." Again, her eyes rushed to the African women, and quickly back to me.

Nothing happened. No angel came to take me up to a deserved heaven. No one shook my shoulder to awaken me from the immobilizing nightmare. No one moved. I raked through my mind, gathering every shred of skill, art and craftiness and stepped toward her.

"Mendinah?" I kept my voice soft and haughty. She looked up into my face as I approached.

"I am Mendinah, Mrs. Make." The tone of her response was sassy.

"And were you willing to work for me? At a very high salary? With an allowance for rent and possibly your own car? Were you willing?"

Deceit left her face, and suddenly she became a young girl, who could have been my baby sister. Her defenses were down, she was vulnerable and I thrust at her with all my will.

"Unfortunately the job has been filled, but if it had not, dear Mendinah"—I was still speaking low—"you would never do. You are ignorant and you are a tramp." I gave her a filthy smile and walked past her into the salon.

Luckily a row of chairs was lined against a near wall. I went directly to a seat. Wind and pride had left my body. My stomach felt empty and my head light. I sat erect from habit and early training. Banti and Kebi rushed in and took seats beside me. Banti took my right hand and Kebi the other.

They both murmured consolation.

"You were wonderful, sister, wonderful." That was Banti.

"You made me proud of you, Maya." Kebi squeezed my hand.

"You looked like a queen mother."

"A princess."

"Don't cry. Not now. You have handled it. It is over."

Banti leaned toward me, forcing me to look in her serious face. "Sister, you will be avenged. Not to worry. You know what old man say in my country?" She had slipped from standard English into the melodic Liberian country accent. "Old man say, 'If you mess with Jesus Christ, God will make you shit.' "

She nodded her head, asserting her own affirmation.

The blasphemy and humor struck me at the same time. I was shocked and tickled. To arrange in the same sentence God, Jesus Christ, righteousness, revenge and the word "shit" was so incongruous I was startled away from the humiliation of Mendinah's announcement.

Both friends' faces were solemn with concern, both heads bobbed in agreement with Banti's old man's wisdom. At last I nodded, smiled and rose. Vus was standing alone near a distant window.

"Ah, my dear. Nice party, isn't it?"

"Vus, who is that girl playing records over there?"

He turned and looked straight at Mendinah, whose profile was distinct against the white walls.

Vus shook his head, "I don't know. No." Shaking his head, his eyes dark with puzzlement.

"Vus, you know her. Don't lie. At least don't lie."

He twisted toward me, sudden recognition smoothing the planes of his face. "Oh, say, is that that Mendinah you were telling me about?"

I wanted to slap him until he snapped and split open like popcorn.

I walked away. I wasn't sure what God would do if someone messed with His only Son, nor how I would fare when I dropped the obeisant attitude of an accepting wife and allowed my black American female-ness to emerge.

The silent ride home seemed endless. Vus drove slowly, letting the old rickety car choose its own speed.

When we were at last in the apartment, I checked Guy's room, and found him asleep. That part of my life was comfortably accounted for. Now all I had to do was face my lover and one-time love, whom I heard dragging furniture around in the living room. I went into our bedroom and stood in the dark, wondering how to begin.

"Maya. Maya, don't go to bed yet." I walked out and down the hall. The big man sat composed, and had arranged a chair to face him.

"Sit down here, Maya. I want to talk to you about Mendinah. Mendinah and all the others."

There was a moment's relief. At least I didn't have to start the conversation. That brief easement was pushed away with an abysmal fear. If he insisted that I accept his infidelity, I'd have to leave him. Condoning it would increase the misdeed. I had heard of men who brought other women into their homes, into the beds they shared with their wives. If Vus was planning such flagrancy, I would have to pick up my son and my heels, and get on the road, one more time.

I sat facing him, our knees touching.

"I am a man. An African man. I am neither primitive nor cruel. A nation of interlopers and most whites in the world would deny me on all counts, but let me deal with each of those stated conditions." It was going to be a long night.

"A man requires a certain amount of sexual gratification. Much more than a woman needs, wants or understands."

"That's a lie, Vus. You're not a woman, how do you know what I need?"

"I do not choose to argue a point which cannot be proved, but which is tacitly agreed upon. I will continue. As an African man, in my society, I have the right to marry more than one woman."

"But that is not true in my society and you knew that when we met."

"I met you in the U.S."—he smiled—"but now we are in Africa."

Was he implying that geography affected his gonads? I reminded him that he had been unfaithful in New York.

He looked shocked. "You have no evidence of that." He was almost correct. I had only the lingering scent of perfume, and the unforgotten cosmetics on his clothes.

When I said nothing, he relaxed and leaned back in his chair, spreading his vast thighs. "To an African man, the act of sex is only important as long as it lasts. It is not the factor which holds a family together. It pleases and relieves tension, so that one can get about the business of living."

I asked with sarcastic sweetness, "And what about African women? Don't they want pleasure and release?"

He frowned, offended. "Haven't I always satisfied you? Have I ever left you wanting? I have come home many nights, physically drained, and abstracted with my work, but I have done my duty to you. Deny that if you can."

The conversation was getting away from me. Onus and guilt were shifting into my lap, where they surely didn't belong.

"I don't love you anymore, Vus." It was the truth, but I used it not for declaration, so much as to startle him and take back a little advantage.

He stayed at ease. "I know that, my dear. I've known it for a long time. Nor am I, any longer, in romantic love with you. However, we respect and admire each other. We have the asset of mutual goals: the struggle for freedom, loyalty to Mother Africa." He paused for a second, then went on in a softer voice. "And Guy's future as an African man."

At that second, I hardened my heart. I didn't believe all the legitimizing drivel Vus concocted about African male infidelity and I would not allow him to teach such nonsense to my son.

"What about Mendinah? Tell me about her. Tell me why you put my name into your mouth, when all you wanted was to get her in bed?"

"I apologize to you for that. Sincerely." His quick mind served him quickly. "Although I did hear you say you wished there was another black woman in your office."

There have always been, for me, periods in arguments when my thoughts swirl around in semi-solid circles, leaving no protruding phrase for my mind to grab. I am rendered mute until the eddying jumble slows down and I am able to pick out enough words to form a first sentence. The moment had come. Ideas rushed around like crazed children in a mad tag game. Vus was African and his values were different from mine. Among the people I knew, my family and friends, promiscuity was the ultimate blow in a marriage. It struck down the pillars of trust which held the relationship aloft. It was also physically dangerous. Venereal diseases could easily be the result of indiscreet momentary gratification. It was disloyal and, finally, unfriendly. Nor was it a characteristic solely of African men. From the beginning of human history, all societies had tried to cope with the custom. The Judeo-Christian Bible forbade adultery, for both sexes. Usually, however, women paid the highest price, losing their hair to rough barbers, or their lives to an affronted community that stoned them to death.

In the United States white men, with the implements of slavery and racial oppression, had taken from black men their names, languages, power, wives, daughters, innate senses of self-value, their confidence. Because they had been unable, however, to kill the sexuality, white men began to envy it, extol it, adore and fear it. A number of black men, finding that they had one thing left which was beyond the reach of their enemies' grasp commenced to identify themselves, to themselves, as sexual masters, possessors of the big dicks, the artful penises, the insatiable lust. White men greedily and enviously agreed. White women, in secret fantasies and rare public displays, yearned over the huge private parts. Some black women agreed that black men had rapacious appetites, and allowed their husbands and lovers the freedom of the fields. Some other women, with knives and guns, boiling water, poison and the divorce courts proved that they did not agree with the common attitude.

"Mendinah. It is said that she is a sexual glutton. Women like that are only good for one, at most two experiences." He had been talking for some time. I suddenly remembered the drone of his voice. "The men who have spoken about her consider her a pretty but temporary vessel."

I nodded, assured. I had finally found my words.

"I'm leaving you, Vus. I'm not sure when or where I'm going. But I'm leaving you."

His face didn't change from the placid sheet of control when I got up and went to bed.

Banti's telephone call at my office came unexpectedly. I had gone to her house early the morning following the Mendinah incident and told her of my plans to leave Vus. Her response had been that of a wife who had a faithful husband. "Sister, you have been a giant. Everyone admires your patience. Truly, you have proved yourself." With my decision made, the burden of tolerance lifted and the approval of my friend, I had gone to work buoyant.

"Sister," I heard her say on the telephone, "Joe and I want you to come to us, this evening. After dinner. Nine o'clock. Will you?"

I agreed. The day rushed along. Entire paragraphs leaped out of my typewriter, needing little, if any, revision.

Vus didn't appear for dinner, so Guy and I ate alone. He was reading, so was happy to hear that I had an appointment and he would have the house quiet and to himself.

The heavy door of the Liberian Residency was opened by a servant. I stepped into the foyer and heard a cloud of low voices. Banti hadn't advised me to dress for a party. But then, the tone wasn't party-like. I walked past the doorman two paces, and I was at the door of the salon, where a multitude of faces peered at me.

It was a surprise birthday party, months off schedule and lacking the gaiety of a fete.

About twenty people sat in a crescent of chairs. Kebi, Jarra and Banti were together. I hastily examined the familiar faces and felt that I had stumbled, unluckily, into a secret ritual or a dangerous kangaroo court.

No one smiled, not even my friends, and the awkward moment could have lasted forever. Joe Williamson's high melodic voice preceded his presence.

"Sister Maya. We are waiting for you. Come in. Come in. Abdul will bring you a drink. Come, you are to sit beside Brother Vus."

My eyes followed the general indication of his right hand. Vus sat, stiff and sober at the center of the row of chairs. I knew that I was befuddled, thrown and totally mystified, so I smiled and obeyed Joe's directive, finding an empty seat beside my husband. The low thrumming of voices did not stop. I leaned toward Vus and whispered, "What is this? What's happening?"

He gave me a calm look and said, "This is all for you." There was only weariness in his tone.

"Brothers and sisters." Joe walked in the center of the floor. "You know why you are here." I was handed a drink of Scotch. "Our sister from across the seas, and across the centuries, is planning to leave our brother from South Africa."

Damn. Vus knew it, I knew it, and I had told Banti a few hours earlier. I gazed at the African men and women, and found that the information was not news to them. No eyes widened, no jaws tightened at the announcement.

"Our sister and her son have returned to Africa. We all know that she has worked very hard and that she feels herself an African." A mumble of agreement followed his statement.

"Our South African brother wages a fight for all of us. No day passes but that he is on the battlefield. No night comes without Vusumzi Make at the gun, threatening the fortress of white oppression." Another rumble of accord lifted and floated in the room.

"Now, I, the brother to all of you, have called for palaver. Neither of these young people have family in Egypt, outside this small community. So I have asked you so that we can examine the points and weigh the matter." Panic was rising in my mind and paralyzing my legs.

Joe said, "I will ask this side of the room to argue for our sister, Maya, and this side for our brother, Vus."

I shook myself away from the numbing shock and stood up.

"Excuse me, Joe, but I'm not on trial. I'm going home." Joe spoke to me over the undertone of disapproval.

"Sister, you are going to stay in Africa. You have a son and a name. If you can sit through this palaver, the outcome will be news in Africa. You know, Maya, our people do not count on papers or magazines to tell us what we need to know. There are people here from Ghana, Mali, Guinea, Nigeria, Ethiopia and Liberia. Sister, try hard and sit down."

Years before I had understood that all I had to do, really had to do, was stay black and die. Nothing could be more interesting than the first, or more permanent than the latter. In truly critical moments I reminded myself of those discoveries. I walked back and sat down beside Vus, who had become a large, black stranger.

Joe Williamson placed a dining-room chair in the middle of the half-circle, talking all the while.

"The group from Maya, going right, will defend our brother. People left of Vus will support our sister. And please remember, folks, we are the only family they have in this strange land."

I looked to my right, and my heart raced. My friends, Banti, Kebi, Margaret Young, a Nigerian close friend, and Jarra would be arguing for Vus. I turned and looked across to the other side and saw three infamous lechers, a few old indifferent men and three women whom I didn't know well. My team looked hopeless.

Joe took his seat and spoke to me.

"Sister, tell your complaint. Tell your side."

Black Americans had no custom of publicly baring the soul. In old-time churches, people used to rise and complain about the treatment they had received from fellow members, but those conferences had died out, leaving only the memory in ribald jokes.

Mrs. Jackson stood up in church and reported, "Reverend, brothers and sisters. I accuse Miss Taylor of going 'round town saying my husband has a wart on his private part." The congregation's "uh huh huhs" sounded like drumrolls. Miss Taylor got up and said, "I have to speak to clarify what I said. Brothers and sisters, I did not say that Mr. Jackson had a wart on his private part. I never did. 'Cause I never saw it. What I said, and this is all I said, was it felt like it was a wart."

There was no precedent in my life for airing private affairs. I held myself still and erect.

Joe repeated, "Sister, tell your part. Why do you find our brother impossible as a husband?"

I looked at Joe, then at my dear friends, lined up in Vus's defense. Banti, Kebi and Margaret know all my complaints, I had cried in their arms, and laid my head on their laps uncounted times. Now they sat with straight flat faces, as if we were strangers. I turned to look at the company gathered in my behalf. Their faces were also cold, unsupportive and strange. I was alone again, but then, since I was already black, all I had to do was die.

I said, "The man stuffs his thing in any opening he finds. I am faithful, he is not."

A few coughs fell from the mouths of my squad, and Vus's troop twitched and cleared their throats.

"I slave my ass off." (African women hardly ever used profanity in mixed company, but I wasn't strictly an African, and, after all, they had gathered to hear me speak and I was a black American. Mentioning slavery in present African company was a ploy. Their forefathers had been spared, or had negotiated for the sale of my ancestors. I knew it and they knew it. It gave me a little edge.)

"I put money into the house. At ten o'clock I go alone to the Broadcast Building to narrate an essay, and I'm paid one pound. Vus spends money as if we are rich. He expects me to be faithful and steady and he comes home smelling of cheap perfume and a whore's twat." They may not have heard the word before but everyone knew what it meant.

I reveled in the rustle of discomfort. They asked me and I told them.

Joe Williamson clapped his hands. "All right, Sister Maya has spoken. I call upon Vus's defense." In a snap, queries were directed at me.

"Have you kept yourself clean?"

"Do you refuse your husband his marital rights?"

"You are an American, after all; how well can you cook African food?"

"Do you curse and act unbecoming?"

"Do you try to dominate the man?"

"Do you press him to have sex when he is tired?"

"Do you obey him? listen to him carefully?"

I answered every question with openness and sass. The sooner they rejected me, the sooner this odd ritual would be over. I would be free or get whatever was coming to me.

When I finished responding, Joe turned to my squad. Their interrogation of Vus was weak and without heart.

"Do you love her?"

"Have you provided for her?"

"Do you satisfy her?"

"She had a child when she came to you. Have you tried to give her more children?"

"Do you want her?"

Vus answered honestly and quietly.

There was a hiatus when he finished while Joe called for drinks for the crowd. We remained seated, holding fresh icy glasses.

Joe began to prance in the clear plot of floor. Dainty, sure and masculine.

"It seems to me, brothers and sisters, that Maya is in the right. Her objection is stronger than our brother's reply. I suggest that in this palaver our brother is the loser."

He turned to Vus's supporters.

"Do you agree?" When the heads nodded, for the first time that night friendliness and smiles returned to the faces of my confidantes.

Joe went to stand in front of Vus, an arm's reach away.

"Bro Vus, it is decided that you are in the wrong, and Sister Maya is in the right. Do you agree?"

Vus lowered his large head in assent.

Joe bowed, taking the agreement, and continued.

"You must provide drink for everyone who has met here tonight. You must bring a lamb or goat for us all to chop." A rampage of laughter followed the pronouncement but was quelled with Joe's next words: "And our sister has the right to leave you."

Silence settled on the shoulders of the listeners. Falling from the air like particled smog.

Joe faced me. "Sister, you have done well. You have sat through African palaver and you have won. Now you may leave."

I was wrung dry by the ritual and only a little pleased by Joe's statement that now I had the right to leave. I never thought I needed anyone's approval but my own.

Joe stepped up to me, close enough for me to see clearly the whites of his eyes.

"Now, sister, now that the triumph is in your hands, now that people from six countries agree that you can leave your husband, and no guilt will fall on your head. Now. Now in your position of strength, we throw ourselves on your mercy." The group responded with jubilant laughter.

"We ask you, from your righteous pinnacle, would you please give the man one more chance?"

I looked at Banti, who instructed me with a nod. Kebi gave me a small smile. Margaret Young, my Nigerian friend, lifted her perfect eyebrows. I should say yes. I hadn't decided where to go, I had no date to leave, and if Joe was right, which I suspected, if I acted graciously, my name in Africa would be golden.

"Stay six months. Sister, give the man six months."

I looked at Vus. He was anxious. I knew immediately that his concern had less to do with me than it had to do with his repute. He had never knowingly or wittingly mistreated me. I could stay with him six months.

I said, "I will stay."

Chairs scraped the floor. Vus took me in his arms, and whispered. "You are a generous woman. My wife."

Joe Williamson shouted, "This time, we party. We wait for the fatted calf, but now we drink and celebrate the reunion of our brother and sister. We toast Mother Africa, who needs all her children."

CHAPTER 19

Guy graduated from high school and then took a knapsack and joined Egyptian friends for a trek in the Sahara. My friendship with Kebi and Banti became stronger. More women were hired in my office and some found my presence incongruous and unacceptable. I spoke halting Arabic, smoked cigarettes openly, was not a Muslim, and was an American on top of that. On the day when President Kennedy and Khrushchev had their confrontation over the independence of Cuba, in the hours when the next world war hung like an unpaid debt over our heads, no one spoke to me. The male employees ignored me; as if by a time warp we were all returned to my first day at the *Arab Observer*. The women were openly hostile. Papers which they needed to bring to my desk were handed over by the coffee server or the copy boy. Actions by people thousands of miles away, men who didn't know I was alive and whose sympathy I would never expect, influenced my peace, and rendered me odious. Kennedy was an American, and so was I. I didn't have the language to explain that being a black American was qualitatively different from being An American. I worried like everyone else, but made myself scarce in the office.

Vus was trying and so was I, but neither of us was able to infuse vitality into our wilting marriage. He steadily gained weight as I became thinner. Indifference became the mattress we lay on, so our sexual sharings disintegrated into unsatisfying periods of hasty and uncomfortable rubbings.

I had promised to stay for six months and we both felt the time was dragging.

Banti and Kebi found excuses to send their drivers to my house bearing food and crates of liquor. Accompanying notes stated that they had overordered or simply had no more storage room.

I became more dependent on our friendship. I spent nearly every evening in the company of one or the other or both of the sisterly women. When we talked, they told amusing tales of home, of their families, of the husbands they loved, of the children, of a merciful God and sometimes of their private fantasies. Vus was never mentioned.

After five months I began to think about my future and Guy's placement in an African school. Ghana's university was known to be the best institution of higher learning on the continent. I thought I'd be very lucky to enroll him there. I had no contacts in Ghana, but I did have Joe Williamson as a brother. I went to him.

"Joe, I'm leaving."

He showed no surprise.

"I want to go to West Africa. I want to place Guy in the University of Ghana and I need a job."

He nodded.

"And I need your help."

He nodded again and said he had been expecting my decision and had prepared for it. There was an offer of a job from the Liberian Department of Information, based on a white paper on Liberia which I had written for the United Arab Republic. He got up from his desk and hugged me.

"Sister, you will be an asset to Liberia."

Vus accepted my departure with undisguised relief. We had worn our marriage threadbare, and it was time to discard it. He would get tickets on United Arab Airlines. He had friends in Ghana we could stay with for a few days. If I got into trouble I could always count on him. I could have any of the furniture, which was now paid for, sent on to Liberia.

I thanked him for the plane arrangements and refused the furniture. I knew that other women would be in the house before the sheets lost my body's heat. He grinned and hugged me.

I had taken Guy into my confidence as far as was possible with a proud, distant seventeen-year-old boy. He knew that for the past year

I had been unhappy. After the palaver, I had told him we would remain in Cairo for at least six more months, and he would have time to finish school.

He wanted to have a party. All his friends would come. Would Vus and I leave him the house for a few hours? Would Omanadia cook chicken and lamb and rice her special way? Maybe he could borrow records from the Williamsons and wouldn't it be all right if he served a little beer? His sudden jollity made me perceive how much he had been affected by our pleasureless home. I realized that it had been a long time since I had seen that wide innocent smile, or his fine dark eyes shine.

Banti and Joe gave us a farewell party. Kebi and Jarra prepared an authentic Ethiopian dinner for a merry crowd. David DuBois took us all out to an opulent restaurant near the pyramids. I had a goodbye lunch with Hanifa Fathy and her friends, and the day finally arrived to leave Cairo.

———

Guy held my hand on the plane. He leaned near and whispered, "It'll be O.K., Mom. Don't cry. I love you, Mom. Lots of people love you."

I made no attempt to explain that I was not crying because of a lack of love, or certainly not the loss of Vus's affection. I was mourning all my ancestors. I had never felt that Egypt was really Africa, but now that our route had taken us across the Sahara, I could look down from my window seat and see trees, and bushes, rivers and dense forest. It all began here. The jumble of poverty-stricken children sleeping in rat-infested tenements or abandoned cars. The terrifying moan of my grandmother, "Bread of Heaven, Bread of Heaven, feed me till I want no more." The drugged days and alcoholic nights of men for whom hope had not been born. The loneliness of women who would never know appreciation or a mite's share of honor. Here, there, along the banks of that river, someone was taken, tied with ropes, shackled with chains, forced to march for weeks carrying the double burden of neck irons and abysmal fear. In that large clump of trees, looking like wood moss from the plane's great height, boys and girls had been hunted like beasts, caught and tethered together. Sacrificial lambs on the altar of greed. America's period of orgiastic lynchings had begun on yonder broad savannah.

Every ill I knew at home, each hateful look on a white face, each odious rejection based on skin color, the mockery, the disenfranchisement, the lamentations and loud wailing for a lost world, irreclaimable security, all that long-onerous journey to misery, which had not ended yet, had begun just below our plane. I wept. Guy rose from time to time to bring fresh Kleenex, and I didn't dare speak to him of my thoughts. I would not make a sound. If I opened my mouth, I might not be able to close it again. Screams would pierce the air and I would race the aisles like a mad thing.

I cramped my lips together until the seam between them meshed, and allowed, as my only expression, the warm tears gliding like honey down my face.

—

The airport at Accra sounded like an adult playground and looked like a festival. Single travelers, wearing Western suits or dresses which would be deemed fashionable in New York, were surrounded by hordes of well-wishers, swathed in floral prints or the rich plaid silk of Kente cloth. Languages turned the air into clouds of lusty sound. The sight of so many black people stirred my deepest emotions. I had been away from the colors too long. Guy and I grinned at each other and turned to see a sight which wiped our faces clean. Three black men walked past us wearing airline uniforms, visored caps, white pants and jackets whose shoulders bristled with epaulettes. Black pilots? Black captains? It was 1962. In our country, the cradle of democracy, whose anthem boasted "the land of the free, the home of the brave," the only black men in our airports fueled planes, cleaned cabins, loaded food or were skycaps, racing the pavement for tips. Guy nudged me and I turned to see another group of African officers walking unconcerned toward the gate which opened out on the tarmac.

Ghana was the place for my son to go to college. My toby (the Southern black word for a lucky talisman), had "hunched me right." Guy would be able to weigh his intelligence and test his skills without being influenced by racial discrimination.

We passed through customs, delighted to have our bags examined by black people. Our taxi driver was black. The dark night seemed friendly to me, and when the cab's lights illuminated a pedestrian, I saw a black face. By the time we reached the address Vus had given me, a knot in my stomach, which had bunched all my remembered life, had unfurled. I realized I hadn't seen a white face for over an hour. The feeling was light and extremely strange.

We stopped in front of a rambling white bungalow, which looked eerily fluorescent in the black night. A short reserved man answered Guy's knock. He welcomed us in and told us that he was Walter Nthia, and after embracing us both, showed us to rooms in the rear of the house. I joined him quickly in the living room to assure him that we didn't plan to stay long. I needed no more than a week to get my son's schooling arranged and get him a place to stay on campus, and I had to hurry on to Liberia, where I had a job waiting in the Department of Information.

Walter said Bro Vus was the pride of the PAC, and that my reputation had preceded me. We could stay as long as necessary. He was an economist, working for the Ghanaian government, was divorced and lived alone. He didn't entertain much, but he had asked a few South Africans and black Americans resident in Ghana to come that evening to greet us.

The visitors came together. There was a tall thin Yoruba man and his Canadian wife, who were introduced as Richard and Ellen, a South African man, whose name I could not decipher, and three black Americans. Frank, with his coppertone skin, smile of spaced teeth and merry eyes, hugged us as if we were cousins. Vickie Garvey was short, pretty. Her black hair lay in soft curls and she shook hands firmly, and spoke directly. Alice Windom took my heart the moment I saw her. She spoke in a Midwestern accent, and laughed as if she had a small cough. Her skin was dark-brown dusted black and her black eyes looked bluntly, unblinking. She had the prettiest legs I've ever seen.

We drank the brought gin, and I told them what I knew about Egypt. When I started talking I noticed that because of my friends and my husband, I knew more about Liberia, Ethiopia, South Africa and Tanzania than I knew of Cairo. They were all interested in politics and when they began speaking of Kwame Nkrumah, the President of Ghana, the Osagyefo, their eyes glistened and their speech was filled with glowing compliments.

"Why are you going to Liberia? It's backward. Stay in Ghana." Alice's question and invitation were seconded.

"Yes. Ghana is the place."

"Kwame Nkrumah is man pass man. Iron cut iron."

Guy caught on and explained, "He is a man who surpasses other men. An iron so strong that it cuts iron."

Frank clapped Guy on the shoulder. "You're smart, little brother. I'm glad you're going to stay, at least."

Vickie asked if I knew Julian Mayfield and if I knew that he and his wife lived in Accra. Julian, James Baldwin, Rosa Guy, John Killens and I had spent many nights until dawn, arguing, drinking, explaining and complaining in Paule Marshall's apartment.

Alice said I had been invited to Julian's house the next evening.

Richard and Ellen added little to the general conversation except to invite me and Guy to a picnic, two days later. They said everyone would be there. The man hadn't charmed me and his wife was dry as old bread. I declined their offer saying we were too tired. But Guy spoke up. "Mother has spoken for herself. I'll be happy to go."

Everyone in the room, including me, knew that I had been out of line. My son was bigger than anyone there, and nearly grown, and I had acted as if he were still a little boy. In the silence in which I left them, Richard, Ellen and Guy made their arrangements. They could come by early in the morning of the picnic. He didn't need to bring anything. All he had to do was be ready.

Frank promised to come and take me and Guy to Julian's house the next day. When they all left I was a little envious. They were in an exciting country at an exciting time. Kwame Nkrumah was the African hero. He had wedded Marxism to the innate African socialism, and was as loved by black people all over the world as he was hated and feared by whites in power. But Joe Williamson had called in debts to get me a job in Monrovia, and I had given my word that I would go there and make him proud. I couldn't change my fate.

Julian Mayfield had the looks to flutter a young girl's heart. He was tall, broad, black, witty, handsome and was married. Anna Livia Cordero Mayfield was a small dark-eyed beautiful Puerto Rican medical doctor, who was as opinionated as a runaway train on a downhill slope.

Our reunion was feverish with greetings and news. We retold old stories and exchanged new tales. Anna Livia gave me the names of people to see at the university. Julian promised to accompany me to the offices. We ended the evening howling at Julian's outguessing the American vigilantes, and making his circuitous way to African asylum. The crowd found Guy's importuning intelligence amusing, although I did not, and Julian said I could go to Liberia with a free mind. He would keep an eye on my son. He added, "Now, listen, boy, Ghanaian young folks call everybody six months older than themselves auntie or uncle. I'll look after you, but big and rusty as you are, don't you ever make the mistake of calling me 'Uncle Julian.' I'll be your big brother, and that's all." We all laughed and hugged and chose hours and dates to meet again.

Frank deposited us at Walter's. Guy and I said curt good nights. I had been less than pleased at his arrogant insistence into the adult conversation. He was displeased at my displeasure.

When I awakened the next morning, his bedroom was empty. Richard and Ellen had gathered him for their picnic, and Walter had left the house.

I spent the day examining Guy's clothes. Separating the things which could be mended, setting aside the jeans which were only good for dust cloths. I hung up his two good suits, in preparation for our trip to the university. I only unpacked two dresses and my underclothes. I would be leaving in such a short time, I would save the African three-piece outfits Banti had given me. She had vouched that by wearing them, I would travel through Liberian society as a Liberian.

I cooked, ate, folded clothes, read the titles in Walter's bookcase until dark.

At about six o'clock, I began to feel uncomfortable, edgy. I felt as if

I had forgotten a commitment or stepped on and crushed some precious thing. I went into the kitchen and found Walter's bottle of gin. I was accustomed to drinking in company, but drinking alone had never appealed to me. I poured a small jelly glass to the rim with gin.

I was sipping the strong liquor when the doorbell rang. Alice Windom stood on the steps, with Frank standing behind her.

"Hey, Maya. I guess we're first. The rest will be here in a little while." I admitted them into the house and poured glasses of fruit juice, since neither of the two drank alcohol. I saw my gin glass was empty and refilled it.

We sat relaxed in the living room. Frank, unable to keep his eyes from Alice's face, or body or legs, talked about the picnic in episodes.

"Plenty food. Lots of good food. Right, Alice?"

She didn't quite smile, just adjusted her jaw muscles and showed a little teeth.

"Folk enjoyed themselves, had a good time. Right, Alice?"

She offered another friendly grimace to the room.

I asked, "What time do you think Guy will come home?"

Alice answered. "We passed them at Winneba. Richard got drunk at the picnic, so Guy was driving. They should be here in the next few minutes."

My mind adapted to her statement. If Guy was driving, everything was all right. His first driving lessons had been taken in a tired Citroën, along the crowded streets of Cairo. There was no question that he could handle a car.

Tires gusted on the driveway.

Alice said, "Here they are. They've arrived."

The old Arkansas toby, unimpressed by spanned oceans, quivered under my skin. I rose immediately and went to Guy's room and collected his passport. Across the tiny hall I found my passport and money and waited while Alice opened the door.

A short exchange of mumbles wavered down the passageway. Suddenly a voice cut through.

"Where is his mother? Isn't his mother here?"

I slid our passports and the English pounds I had collected into my bra and stepped out into the hall. Ellen was in the living room, tousled and covered with blood. When she saw me she screamed.

"Maya, it wasn't our fault. Nobody else was hurt, and anyway he's still alive." I understood every word and intent of her hysteric speech, and continued walking until I stood close to her red-spotted face. I came from a race used to violence and habituated to loss.

"Where is my son, Ellen? I need to go there now." I used the control I remembered in my grandmother's voice when she heard of a lynching.

Ellen was sobbing on Alice's shoulder. "He's in Korle Bu Hospital. But I swear, he was still breathing."

When we got into the car I asked Ellen to stop whimpering. It was neither her life nor her son. We rode to the hospital quickly, and in a quiet broken only by Ellen's intermittent snuffles and snorts.

Korle Bu's emergency ward was painfully bright. I started down the corridor and found myself in a white tunnel, interrupted by a single loaded gurney, resting against a distant wall. I walked up to the movable table and saw my son, stretched his full length under white sheets. His rich golden skin paled to ash-grey. His eyes closed and his head at an unusual angle.

I took my arm away from Alice's grasp and told Ellen to stop her stupid snuffling. When they backed away, I looked at my son, my real life. He was born to me when I was seventeen. I had taken him away from my mother's house when he was two months old, and except for a year I spent in Europe without him, and a month when he was stolen by a deranged woman, we had spent our lives together. My grown life lay stretched before me, stiff as a pine board, in a strange country, blood caked on his face and clotted on his clothes.

Richard came up behind me and grabbed my shoulders. I turned and nearly suffocated in the breath of old whiskey and rotten teeth.

"Maya, it was not my fault."

He slurred the words out of wet dripping lips. My control fled. I reached for him, for his throat, his eyes, his nose, but before I could get my hands on him, I felt hands stroking my back, holding my waist.

"Sister, please. Please. Exercise patience."

I turned to see a strange couple, old and sweet-faced with wisdom. They continued. "This is your son?" I nodded. "Sister, we found him on the side of the road. We brought him to Korle Bu."

Their kindness cracked my armor. I screamed and they gathered me in their arms. "Sister, look at him. He's still breathing."

They forced me to face the long body and I saw the chest rising and falling in calm rhythm.

"Sister, please say thanks to God." The woman still held my waist and the man held my hands.

"He was hit by a truck. His car was stopped, the motor was off. If he had been moving, your son would be dead."

"We arrived and the folks in the car had pulled him out and laid him beside the road."

"We saw the wreck and picked him up and brought him to Korle Bu."

"Now thank God that he's alive."

I looked over at my unconscious son and said, "I thank God. And I thank you."

The couple embraced me, and walked over to my baby. A nurse appeared. "Who is responsible here?"

I said, "I am responsible. I am his mother."

She was efficient and without tenderness. "You both are black American?" I nodded, wondering if our place of birth would have as negative an impact in Ghana as our color had in our homeland. She rattled her spiel, "He must have X-rays. One of our X-ray technicians is also a black American. I will call him, but you must register down the hall and make payments at the cashier's desk."

I didn't want to leave Guy unattended in the hall. I looked for the Ghanaian couple but they had disappeared.

"I'll stay with him, Maya." Alice put her hand on my arm. Her face was just solemn enough to let me know she was serious, but not so gloomy as to add to my building hysteria.

I finished the registration and hastened after a line of people who paraded behind my son's gurney. The X-ray technician and I exchanged names. He pointed the cart on which Guy lay toward a door.

We entered. The drunken Richard, his apologetic mousy wife, Alice and a few whose faces I didn't know, lounged against the wall. The technician dismissed all the visitors except Alice and me.

"I'll need someone to hold him and to position him. He's unconscious, but I've got to X-ray his whole body."

Alice and I slid Guy's heavy body onto a new table. We shifted him, turned him, placed his arms neatly at his sides, arranged his legs, positioned his head until every inch of his body had been exposed to the baleful eye of the X-ray machine. We pushed him back onto the rolling tray, and I asked the technician to step aside.

"How long will he be unconscious?"

"I can't tell you. I think he's in shock. But he may be in a coma. The picture will be back tomorrow. Come back in the morning. Maybe there'll be some news." Two nurses met us at the door and wheeled Guy quickly down the hall. I started to follow, but Alice touched my arm.

"Let them have him. They'll make him comfortable. That's their business."

I watched the gurney disappear, carrying away the closest person in the world to me.

I went back to Walter's house and made a pot of coffee. I drank cup after cup, cooling the boiling liquid with gin. Alice went home, Walter went to bed, but at dawn I found a phone directory and called a taxi.

In the clear day, the hospital looked like a normal hospital. I was shown to Guy's room, he recognized me and my spirits soared.

"Hi, Mom, what happened?"

His voice was faint and his skin the color of a hot-house lemon.

I told him about the accident, but before I could finish the story, he had drifted back into unconsciousness. I sat for an hour, willing him to awareness, wiping his face with the edge of his pillow case. Worrying if he was going to die, and wondering how I could go on, where I could go, what I would have to live for if he died.

A doctor met me outside the room.

"You are Mrs. Angelou?" (I had written my old name on the admission form.)

"Yes, Doctor, how is he? Will he live?"

"He has a broken arm, broken leg and possible internal injuries. But he is young. I think he will come through."

I spent the day in Guy's room, watching him slide in and out of consciousness. When I took a taxi to Julian's house, it was because the nurses had pointedly asked me to leave. Visiting hours were posted and everyone had to observe them.

Anna Livia opened the door, and I collapsed in her arms. She had heard about the accident and when the hysteria dissipated, she said that although she was not assigned to Korle Bu Hospital, she would make a visit to Guy that evening. I should go get a night's sleep. She dropped me at Walter's house. The door leading to Guy's room looked ominous, still I knocked, hoping to hear him say, "Yes, Mom. I'm busy. I'll be out in a minute."

I turned and sat down on my borrowed bed. The next thing I knew, Walter was shaking my shoulder. "Sister Maya. Sister. Dr. Codero is on the telephone."

I followed him, fumbling my way down the hall. I didn't know any Dr. Codero, nor did I recognize the man who awakened me or even the house I was reeling through.

"Hello. Maya Angelou here." That was the way Vus answered the phone, with his full name.

"Maya, it's Anna Livia. I had some new X-rays done. They've been developed. I'm at Korle Bu now. The accident was more serious than the other doctors thought. Guy's neck is broken."

The crash, my pale son, his awful clammy skin, my love for him, all rushed into my brain at once.

"In three places. I have ordered him moved. He is going to be put in a body, arm and leg cast. Are you there, Maya?"

I was nowhere. Certainly nowhere I had ever been before. I said, "Yes, of course."

She explained that she had contacts at a military hospital and when the plaster hardened he would be taken there. He was quite tense, so it was better that I held off my visit until he calmed down.

I said, "I'm on my way."

She meant well, but she didn't know my son. She didn't know the cocky boy who had to live daily with his father's rejection, or the young man who had lived with the certainty of white insolence and the unsureness of moving from school to school, coast to coast, and was made to find his way through another continent and new cultures. A person whose only certitude lay in the knowledge that Mom, effective or not, was never too far away.

"I'm on my way."

I waited in the halls and yard and canteen of the hospital while the plaster hardened, then joined my son in the ambulance for his transfer. The still-damp cast emitted a sour odor, but my sedated son looked like a pale-yellow angel in a long white gown.

CHAPTER 20

Accra became a wondrous city as Guy's health improved. The sprawling Makola market drew me into its heaving perfumed bosom, and held me there for hours. Black women, sitting before stalls, offered for sale peanuts, peanut butter, wax-printed cloth, cutlery, Pond's face cream, tinned milk, sandals, men's pants, hot pepper, pepper sauce, tomatoes, plates, palm oil, palm butter and palm wine.

The open-air shopping center, alive with shouted language and blaring music, its odors and running children, its haggling customers and adamant saleswomen, made America's great department stores seem colorless and vacant by contrast.

I walked around and around Flagstaff House and the Parliament, where black people sat debating the future plans for their own country. I felt heady just being near their power. When Guy was out of danger, I wrote to Mother. I told her of the accident and explained that I had held off writing because there was nothing she could have done except help me to worry.

She sent me a large sum of money and said if I wanted her to come, she'd be in Africa before I knew it.

Guy would be in the hospital for one month, then he'd have to recover at home for three months. I moved into the YWCA, and wrote to Joe and Banti Williamson. Going to Liberia had to be canceled. I would find a job and stay in Ghana. Anna Livia allowed me to use her kitchen to cook daily meals for Guy. I hitch-hiked, found rides, or took the mammy lorry (a jitney service) to the hospital. My money was leaking away and I had to find work. Guy would be released, and I had to have a home for him to come to.

Julian suggested that I meet Efuah Sutherland, poet, playwright and head of Ghana's theater. She received me cordially. We sat under a fixed awning at her house, drinking coffee and looking out on the grassy slope of her inner compound.

Yes, she had heard of me. And she knew of my son's accident. This was Africa. News traveled.

Efuah was black and her slim body was draped in fine white linen. In respose, her face had the cool beauty found in the bust of Nefertiti, but when she smiled, she looked like a mischievous girl who kept a delicious secret.

I explained my need for work, and listed my credentials. She arranged for me to meet Professor J. H. Nketia, ethnomusicologist and head of the Institute of African Studies. Dr. Nketia called his staff together: Joseph de Graaf, professor of drama, Bertie Okpoku, dance professor, and Grace Nuamah, dance mistress. He introduced me, and said they would talk together and let me know very soon.

Efuah phoned before the week was out. I had a job at the University of Ghana as administrative assistant. Since I had no academic degrees, I couldn't be processed through the usual channels. Which meant that I could not expect to receive the salary other foreigners were paid. I would be paid as a Ghanaian, which was a little more than half the foreign wage. (I was later informed that non-Ghanaians received more money because they had to pay twice as much as nationals for everything.)

I tried to speak, but Efuah continued. "An instructor we know is on leave for six months. We have arranged for you to have his house."

I cried out gratefully and Efuah's cool voice brushed my ear. "Sister, I am a mother, too." She hung up.

I collected the trunk which I had left at Walter's, the suitcases I had stowed in the YWCA's storeroom and the bag I had been living out of, and moved into a nicely furnished house on campus.

When I picked up Guy from the hospital, he reminded me of a big tree about to fall. He had grown another inch and put on a few pounds from inactivity. The cast, which covered his head and spread out over his shoulders like a monk's cowl, was grey with dirt, but he had to wear it another three months.

We celebrated his homecoming with roast chicken and dressing, our favorite food. He was in high spirits. He had lived. Anna Livia said he was mending well. He'd made a few friends in the hospital and soon he'd be enrolled in the university. The next day I took his diploma and report cards to the Registrar's office and was told bluntly that my son could not enter the university. He was not qualified. The University of Ghana had been modeled on the British system. Students had to have completed the sixth form—or as Americans call it, junior college. I was dismissed peremptorily.

That was unacceptable. Guy had been through as much as I could handle.

Conor Cruise O'Brien was vice-chancellor of the University, and Nana Kobina Nketsia IV, a paramount chief, was former vice-chancellor. I made an appointment to see Dr. O'Brien, and Efuah introduced me to the Nana.

I pleaded and talked, moaned and whined, said I wasn't asking for a scholarship or any financial aid. I would pay tuition and for his books. After weeks of haunting the offices, collaring the men in halls, catching up with them on the campus paths, I was finally told that they had decided it was not fair to penalize students coming from American schools.

They had arranged a three-part test. Guy would be expected to take the examination on Monday at nine o'clock.

I took Guy the news, and since I hadn't told him of the trouble, he took it casually. "O.K., Mom. I'll be ready."

Monday morning my desk felt like sponge and the papers on it were unintelligible. I looked at my watch every five minutes. Efuah passed and stopped to chat, but I was too distracted to keep up my end of the conversation.

At last, Guy came loping across the campus, his cast helmet looking almost white under the noonday sun. I forced myself to remain seated. He entered my tiny office, taking up its spare room.

"Finished." His complexion looked healthy, and his eyes were free of worry.

"How did you do?"

"Great. I won't get the results for a couple of days. But I did great. Mom, do you know that Conor Cruise O'Brien is the same man who headed the U.N. Congo project?"

I knew.

"Well, one of my questions was 'What role has the European in African development?' " He chuckled with pleasure. "Well, I'll tell you. I ate Dr. O'Brien up in little pieces. I read his book *To Katanga and Back* in Cairo."

He leaned over and kissed my cheek. "I'm going to meet some guys in the Junior Common Room."

Speechless, I watched him bound away. I had tommed, mewled and begged to get him registered, and in an attempt to show how manly he was, the smartass had bungled everything. I allowed myself to relish the fury.

After an hour, when I could walk without my knees wobbling and speak without yelling, I crossed the campus and found Dr. O'Brien in the Senior Common Room. I grinned for him and was prepared to shuffle and scratch. My people had written the book on dealing with white men.

I spoke out of a mealy mouth. "Dr. O'Brien, Guy told me how he answered one of those questions. You haven't had a chance to see his exam yet…"

"Oh, but I have, Miss Angelou. His answers are fine. His registration papers will be sent to your office. We want minds like that in the university."

I grinned again and backed away.

Sooner or later, I was going to have to admit that I didn't understand black men or black boys and certainly not all white men.

Guy was moving into Mensa Sarba Hall. I had seen his room in the dormitory and it looked too small and too dark, but he loved it. For the first time in his life, he was going to live alone, away from my persistent commands. Responsible to himself and for himself. My reaction was in direct contrast with his excitement. I was going to be alone, also, for the first time. I was in my mother's house at his birth, and we had been together ever since. Sometimes we lived with others or they lived with us, but he had always been the powerful axle of my life.

He dragged the old trunk toward the door, but I stopped him.

"Don't lift heavy things like that. You could hurt yourself. I want you to be careful. Remember your neck."

He put the trunk down and turned. "Mom, I know I'm your only child and you love me." His face was quiet and his voice calm. "But there's something for you to remember. It is my neck and my life. I will live it whole or not at all."

He pulled me to him and wrapped his arms around me. "I love you, Mom. Maybe now you'll have a chance to grow up."

A car horn honked outside. Guy opened the door and called. "Come on in. I'm ready." Two Ghanaian young men leaped on the porch, shouting, and blustered into the room. When they saw me, they composed themselves.

I offered them a drink, a beer, some food. I wanted to delay the departure. All refused. They had to return the car to their uncle, and Guy had to begin his new life.

They shared Guy's possessions, trundling the boxes, grips and trunk into a new Mercedes Benz. Guy gave me one more squeeze, then they piled into the car and drove away.

I closed the door and held my breath. Waiting for the wave of emotion to surge over me, knock me down, take my breath away.

Nothing happened. I didn't feel bereft or desolate. I didn't feel lonely or abandoned.

I sat down, still waiting. The first thought that came to me, perfectly formed and promising, was "At last, I'll be able to eat the whole breast of a roast chicken by myself."

ALL GOD'S CHILDREN NEED
TRAVELING SHOES

*This book is dedicated to
Julian and Malcolm and all the fallen ones
who were passionately and earnestly
looking for a home.*

SWING LOW, SWEET CHARIOT,
COMING FOR TO CARRY ME HOME.

ACKNOWLEDGMENTS

A special thank you to RUBEN MEDINA and ALAN PALMER for their brotherly love and laughter through many years. Thanks to JEAN AND ROGER GENOUD for their camaraderie during our strange and rich years, to SEYMOUR LAZAR for belief in my youthful ambition, and to Shana Alexander for talking to me about the mystery of return. Thanks to ANNA BUDU-ARTHUR for being a constant Sister.

The breezes of the West African night were intimate and shy, licking the hair, sweeping through cotton dresses with unseemly intimacy, then disappearing into the utter blackness. Daylight was equally insistent, but much more bold and thoughtless. It dazzled, muddling the sight. It forced through my closed eyelids, bringing me up and out of a borrowed bed and into brand new streets.

After living nearly two years in Cairo, I had brought my son Guy to enter the University of Ghana in Accra. I planned staying for two weeks with a friend of a colleague, settling Guy into his dormitory, then continuing to Liberia to a job with the Department of Information.

Guy was seventeen and quick. I was thirty-three and determined. We were Black Americans in West Africa, where for the first time in our lives the color of our skin was accepted as correct and normal.

Guy had finished high school in Egypt, his Arabic was good and his health excellent. He assured me that he would quickly learn a Ghanaian language, and he certainly could look after himself. I had worked successfully as a journalist in Cairo, and failed sadly at a marriage which I ended with false public dignity and copious secret tears. But with all crying in the past, I was on my way to another adventure. The future was plump with promise.

For two days Guy and I laughed. We looked at the Ghanaian streets and laughed. We listened to the melodious languages and laughed. We looked at each other and laughed out loud.

On the third day, Guy, on a pleasure outing, was injured in an automobile accident. One arm and one leg were fractured and his neck was broken.

July and August of 1962 stretched out like fat men yawning after a sumptuous dinner. They had every right to gloat, for they had eaten me up. Gobbled me down. Consumed my spirit, not in a wild rush, but slowly, with the obscene patience of certain victors. I became a shadow walking in the white hot streets, and a dark spectre in the hospital.

There was no solace in knowing that the doctors and nurses hovering around Guy were African, nor in the company of the Black American expatriates who, hearing of our misfortune, came to share some of the slow hours. Racial loyalties and cultural attachments had become meaningless.

Trying utterly, I could not match Guy's stoicism. He lay calm, week after week, in a prison of plaster from which only his face and one leg and arm were visible. His assurances that he would heal and be better than new drove me into a faithless silence. Had I been less timid, I would have cursed God. Had I come from a different background, I would have gone further and denied His very existence. Having neither the courage nor the historical precedent, I raged inside myself like a blinded bull in a metal stall.

Admittedly, Guy lived with the knowledge that an unexpected and very hard sneeze could force the fractured vertebrae against his spinal cord, and he would be paralyzed or die immediately, but he had only an infatuation with life. He hadn't lived long enough to fall in love with this brutally delicious experience. He could lightly waft away to another place, if there really was another place, where his youthful innocence would assure him a crown, wings, a harp, ambrosia, free milk and an absence of nostalgic yearning. (I was raised on the spirituals which ached to "See my old mother in glory" or "Meet with my dear children in heaven," but even the most fanciful lyricists never dared to suggest that those cavorting souls gave one thought to those of us left to moil in the world.) My wretchedness reminded me that, on the other hand, I would be rudderless.

I had lived with family until my son was born in my sixteenth year.

When he was two months old and perched on my left hip, we left my mother's house and together, save for one year when I was touring, we had been each other's home and center for seventeen years. He could die if he wanted to and go off to wherever dead folks go, but I, I would be left without a home.

The man who caused the accident stood swaying at the foot of the bed. Drunk again, or, two months later, still drunk. He, the host of the motor trip and the owner of the car, had passed out on the back seat leaving Guy behind the steering wheel trying to start the stalled engine. A truck had careened off a steep hill and plowed into Richard's car, and he had walked away unhurt.

Now he dangled loosely in the room, looking shyly at me. "Hello, Sister Maya." The slurred words made me hate him more. My whole body yearned for his scrawny neck. I turned my face from the scoundrel and looked at my son. The once white plaster that encased his body and curved around his face was yellowing and had begun to crumble.

I spoke softly, as people do to the very old, the very young, and the sick. "Darling, how are you today?"

"Mother, Richard spoke to you." His already deep voice growled with disapproval.

"Hello, Richard," I mumbled, hoping he couldn't hear me.

My greeting penetrated the alcoholic fog, and the man lumbered into an apologetic monologue that tested my control. "I'm sorry, Sister Maya. So sorry. If only it could be me, there on that bed ... Oh, if only it could be me ..."

I agreed with him.

At last he had done with his regrets, and saying good-bye to Guy, took my hand. Although his touch was repulsive, Guy was watching me, so I placed a silly grin on my face and said, "Good-bye, Richard." After he left, I began quickly to unload the basket of food I had brought. (The teenage appetite is not thwarted by bruises or even broken bones.)

Guy's voice stopped me.

"Mother, come so I can see you."

The cast prevented him from turning, so visitors had to stand directly in his vision. I put the basket down and went to stand at the foot of the bed.

His face was clouded with anger.

"Mother, I know I'm your only child, but you must remember, this is my life, not yours." The thorn from the bush one has planted, nourished and pruned, pricks most deeply and draws more blood. I waited in agony as he continued, eyes scornful and lips curled, "If I can see Richard and understand that he has been more hurt than I, what about you? Didn't you mean all those sermons about tolerance? All that stuff about understanding? About before you criticize a man, you should walk a mile in his shoes?"

Of course I meant it in theory, in conversation about the underprivileged, misunderstood and oppressed miscreants, but not about a brute who had endangered my son's life.

I lied and said, "Yes, I meant it." Guy smiled and said, "I know you did, Mother. You're just upset now." His face framed by the cast was beautiful with forgiveness. "Don't worry anymore. I'm going to get out of here soon, then you can go on to Liberia."

I made bitterness into a wad and swallowed it.

I puckered and grinned and said, "You're right, darling. I won't be upset anymore."

As always, we found something to laugh about. He fumbled, eating with his unbroken left hand and when he did have the food firmly in his grasp, he pretended not to know how to find his mouth. Crumbs littered his gown. "I'll figure it out, Mom. I promise you I won't starve to death." We played word games, and the visiting hours went by quickly.

Too soon I was back on the bright street with an empty basket in my hands and my head swimming in the lonely air.

I did know some people who would receive me, but reluctantly, because I had nothing to offer company save a long face and a self-pitying heart, and I had no intention of changing either. Black Americans of my generation didn't look kindly on public mournings except during or immediately after funerals. We were expected by others and by ourselves to lighten the burden by smiling, to deflect possible new assaults by laughter. Hadn't it worked for us for centuries? Hadn't it?

On our first night in Ghana, our host (who was only a friend of a friend) invited Black American and South American expatriates to meet us. Julian Mayfield and his beautiful wife Ana Livia, who was a medical doctor, were known to me from New York and the rest were not. But there is a kinship among wanderers, as operative as the bond between bishops or the tie between thieves: We knew each other instantly and exchanged anecdotes, contacts and even addresses within the first hour.

Alice Windom, a wit from St. Louis, and Vicki Garvin, a gentle woman from New York City, were among the Americans laughing and entertaining in the small living room. In the two years which had passed since Guy had been in the company of so many Black Americans, he had grown from a precocious adolescent into an adept young man. He bristled with pleasure, discovering that he could hold his own in the bantering company.

Each émigré praised Ghana and questioned my plans to settle in Liberia. There was no need to tell them that I hungered for security and would have accepted nearly any promised permanence in Africa. They knew, but kept up the teasing. One asked, "You remember that Ray Charles song where he says, 'When you leave New York, you ain't going nowhere'?"

I remembered.

"Well, when you leave Ghana, going to Liberia, you ain't going to Africa, in fact you ain't going nowhere."

Although I knew Liberians who were as African as Congo drums, I honored the traditional procedure and allowed the raillery to continue.

Alice advised, "Honey, you'd better stay here, get a job and settle down. It can't get better than Ghana and it could be a lot worse." Everyone laughed and agreed.

The fast talk and jokes were packages from home and I was delighted to show the group that I still knew how to act in Black company. I laughed as hard as the teasers and enjoyed the camaraderie.

But Guy's accident erased all traces of their names, their faces and conviviality. I felt as if I had met no one, knew no one, and had lived my entire life as the bereft mother of a seriously injured child.

Tragedy, no matter how sad, becomes boring to those not caught in its addictive caress. I watched my host, so sympathetic at the outset, become increasingly less interested in me and my distress. After a few weeks in his house, his discomfort even penetrated my self-centeredness. When Julian and Ana Livia Mayfield allowed me to store my books and clothes at their house, I gave my host only perfunctory thanks, and moved into a tiny room at the local YWCA I focused my attention on myself, with occasional concentrations on Guy. If I thought about it I was relieved that no one anticipated my company, yet, I took the idea of rejection as one more ornament on my string of worry beads.

One sunny morning Julian stood waiting for me in the YWCA lobby. His good looks drew attention and giggles from the young women who sat on the vinyl chairs pretending to read.

"I'm taking you to meet someone. Someone you should know." He looked at me without smiling. He was tall, Black, tough and brusque.

"You need to have someone, a woman, talk to you. Let's go." I withdrew from his proprietary air, but lack of energy prevented me from telling him that he wasn't my brother, he wasn't even a close friend. For want of resistance, I followed him to his car.

"Somebody needs to tell you that you have to give up this self-pity. You're letting yourself go. Look at your clothes. Look at your hair. Hell, it's Guy whose neck was broken. Not yours."

Anger jumped up in my mouth, but I held back the scorching words and turned to look at him. He was watching the road, but the side of his face visible to me was tense, his eyes were unblinking, and he had pushed his full lips out in a pout.

"Everybody understands... as much as anyone can understand another's pain... but you've... you've forgotten to be polite. Hell, girl, everybody feels sorry for you, but nobody owes you a damn thing. You know that. Don't forget your background. Your mother didn't raise you in a dog house."

Blacks concede that hurrawing, jibing, jiving, signifying, disrespecting, cursing, even outright insults might be acceptable under particular conditions, but aspersions cast against one's family call for immediate attack.

I said, "How do you know my business so well? Was that my daddy visiting your mother all those times he left our home?"

I expected an explosion from Julian. Yet his response shocked me. Laughter burst out of him, loud and raucous. The car wobbled and slowed while he held tenuously to the steering wheel. I caught his laughter, and it made me pull his jacket, and slap my own knee. Miraculously we stayed on the road. We were still laughing when he pulled into a driveway and let the engine die.

"Girl, you're going to be all right. You haven't forgotten the essentials. You know about defending yourself. All you have to do now is remember... sometimes you have to defend yourself from yourself."

When we got out of the car Julian hugged me and we walked together toward The National Theatre of Ghana, a round, white building set in an embrace of green-black trees.

Efua Sutherland could have posed for the original bust of Nefertiti. She was long, lean, Black and lovely, and spoke so softly I had to lean forward to catch her words. She wore an impervious air as obvious as a strong perfume, and an austere white floor-length gown.

She sat motionless as Julian recounted my dreadful tale and ended saying that my only child was, even as we spoke, in the Military Hospital. When Julian stopped talking and looked at her pointedly, I was pleased that Efua's serene face did not crumble into pity. She was silent and Julian continued. "Maya is a writer. We knew each other at home. She worked for Martin Luther King. She's pretty much alone here, so I have to be a brother to her, but she needs to talk to a woman, and pretty soon she'll need a job." Efua said nothing, but finally turned to me and I had the feeling that all of myself was being absorbed. The moment was long.

"Maya," she stood and walked to me. "Sister Maya, we will see about a job, but now you have need of a Sister friend." I had not cried since the accident. I had helped to lift Guy's inert body onto the x-ray table at the first hospital, had assisted in carrying his stretcher to an ambulance for transfer to another hospital. I had slept, awakened, walked, and lived in a thick atmosphere, which only allowed shallow breathing and routine motor behavior.

Efua put her hand on my cheek and repeated, "Sister, you have need of a Sister friend because you need to weep, and you need someone to watch you while you weep." Her gestures and voice were mesmerizing. I began to cry. She stroked my face for a minute then returned to her chair. She began speaking to Julian about other matters. I continued crying and was embarrassed when I couldn't stop the tears. When I was a child, my grandmother would observe me weeping and say, "Be careful, Sister. The more you cry, the less you'll pee, and peeing is more important." But the faucet, once opened, had to drain itself. I had no power over its flow.

Efua sent Julian away with assurances that she would return me to the hospital. I looked at her, but she had settled into herself sweetly, and I was freed to cry out all the bitterness and self-pity of the past days.

When I had finished, she stood again, offering me a handkerchief.

"Now, Sister, you must eat. Eat and drink. Replenish yourself." She called her chauffeur, and we were taken to her home.

She was a poet, playwright, teacher, and the head of Ghana's National Theatre. We talked in the car of Shakespeare, Langston Hughes, Alexander Pope and Sheridan. We agreed that art was the flower of life and despite the years of ill-treatment Black artists were among its most glorious blossoms.

She knew the president and called him familiarly "Kwame."

She said, "Kwame has said that Ghana must use its own legends to heal itself. I have written the old tales in new ways to teach the children that their history is rich and noble."

Her house, white as chalk and stark, had rounded walls which enclosed a green lawn. Her three children came laughing to greet me, and her servant brought me food. Efua spoke in Fanti to the maid, and a mixture of Fanti and English to the children.

"This is your Auntie Maya. She shall be coming frequently. Her son is ill, but you shall meet him, for he will soon be released from the hospital."

Esi Rieter, the oldest, a girl of ten, Ralph, seven, and the five-year-old, Amowi, immediately wanted to know how old my son was, what was his illness, did I have other children, what did I do. Efua sent them away assuring them that time would answer all questions.

I ate as I had cried, generously. After the meal, Efua walked me to the car.

"Sister, you are not alone. I, myself, will be at the hospital tomorrow. Your son is now my son. He has two mothers in this place." She put her hand on my face again. "Sister, exercise patience. Try."

When the driver stopped at the hospital, I felt cool and refreshed as if I had just gone swimming in Bethesda's pool, and many of my cares had been washed away in its healing water.

The hospital acquired color, there was laughter in its halls and Guy's good humor stopped being contrived. He and the doctors, surprisingly, had been right. Recovery was evident in the ways of his hands and in his lumbering, cast-top-heavy lurching up and down the corridors.

Outside, the sun, which had pounced, penetrating and hostile, now covered me with beneficial rays, hoisting me out of depression and back on my feet, where my new mood told me I deserved to be.

I smiled at strangers and took notice of buildings and streets. Weeks passed before I was conscious that I had let go of misery.

The visit to Efua, and Julian's reluctant but sincere offer to be my brother had been very strong medicine.

I was impatient to get my life in order. Obviously, I wouldn't go to Liberia, so... I had to find a job, a car and a house for Guy to come to while he continued recuperating. I needed to get my hair cut, a manicure, a pedicure. My clothes were disgraceful.

Flashes of panic occurred and recurred. Was it possible that during the two-month depression, I had damaged my determination? The only power I had ever claimed was that I had over myself. Obviously, I had come perilously close to giving it away to self-pity.

I thought about Julian's hard words, "Your mother didn't raise you in a dog house." His intuition had come understated.

My mother, that pretty little woman with a steel chest, had taught me and my brother Bailey that each person was expected to "paddle his own canoe, stand on his own feet, put his own shoulder to the wheel, and work like hell." She always added, "Hope for the best, but be prepared for the worst. You may not always get what you pay for, but you will definitely pay for what you get." Vivian Baxter had axioms for every situation, and if one didn't come to mind when she needed it, she would create a better one on the moment.

I had been a pretty good student, ingesting and internalizing her advice, so now I pushed away the gnawing fear that I might have lost some of my vital willfulness.

I looked at the disheveled mess I had been living in and at my nearby neighbors. To my surprise, many of the women who had been at that first-night party and who had faithfully attended Guy's hospital room, lived down the hall from me. I was also amazed to learn that mops, brooms, pails and other cleaning implements were available for the free use of the center's guests.

Alice and Vicki watched me emerge from the bonds of my chrysalis and accepted me with no comment, save an easy teasing. While I swabbed my small floor and washed my clothes Alice said, "I would offer to help you Maya, but somehow I didn't inherit any of the race's domestic talents."

Vicki offered, but I knew the work was cathartic, so I washed walls, polished door knobs and the tiny window. The scales and stench of defeat floated into the pail's dirty water.

The YWCA residents forgave me my drunken spree with hopelessness and we began to spend time together in the building's cafeteria and on the streets filled with views I had not seen. Alice took me to Black Star Square to see the monumental arch, named in part for the newspaper founded in the United States by the ex-slave and abolitionist, Frederick Douglass.

Vicki and Sylvia Boone rode with me to Flagstaff House, the seat of government. Seeing Africans enter and leave the formal building made me tremble with an awe I had never known. Their authority on the marble steps again proved that Whites had been wrong all along. Black and brown skin did not herald debasement and a divinely created inferiority. We were capable of controlling our cities, our selves and our lives with elegance and success. Whites were not needed to explain the working of the world, nor the mysteries of the mind.

My visits to the hospital diminished to one daily appearance and Guy's gladness made me young again.

Efua introduced me to the chairman of the Institute of African Studies at the university and pleaded with him to hire me. She had told him that I had been on my way to a job in Liberia until my seventeen-year-old son had been involved in an accident, adding that I had to stay in Ghana until he fully recovered. She smiled at him and said I was already trying to hear Fanti, and would make a good Ghanaian.

Professor J. H. Nketia, one of Ghana's leading scholars, was so un-pretentious as to be unsettling. He listened with patience to Efua, then asked me, "Can you type?" When I said only a little, but that I could file and write, he gathered his chin in a stubby brown hand and smiled. "Can you start on Monday?" He told me I would be paid on the Ghanaian scale and he would arrange for me to get a small car. I knew that the proffered job spoke more of his own compassion and his af-fection for Efua than of a need for my services.

Foreign employees at the university earned high salaries, compared to the national average wage, and very liberal compensations. They were given housing allowances, tuition or aid for their offspring's edu-cation, transportation allowances and a perk charmingly referred to as dislocation allowance. They had been recruited in their own coun-tries, and hired for their academic credentials and experience. Save for two youthful years at night school, I had only a high school education.

I challenged myself to do whatever job assigned to me with intense commitment and a good cheerfulness.

A professor went on leave and I moved into his house for three months. When Guy was released from the hospital he settled into our furnished, if temporary, home.

The community of Black immigrants opened and fitted me into their lives as if they had been saving my place.

The group's leader, if such a collection of eccentric egos could be led, was Julian. He had three books published in the United States, had acted in a Broadway play, and was a respected American-based intellectual before an encounter with the CIA and the FBI caused him to flee his country for Africa. He was accompanied in flight and supported, in fact, by Ana Livia, who was at least as politically volatile as he.

Sylvia Boone, a young sociologist, had come to Africa first on a church affiliated tour, then returned with sophistication, a second Master's degree and fluent French to find her place on the Continent. Ted Pointiflet was a painter who argued gently, but persistently that Africa was the inevitable destination of all Black Americans. Lesley Lacy, a sleek graduate student, was an expert on Marxism and Garveyism, while Jim and Annette Lacy, no relation to Lesley, were grade school teachers and quite rare among our group because they listened more than they talked. The somber faced Frank Robinson, a plumber, had a contagious laughter, and a fierce devotion to Nkrumah. Vicki Garvin had been a union organizer, Alice Windom had been trained in sociology. I called the group "Revolutionist Returnees."

Each person had brought to Africa varying talents, energies, vigor, youth and terrible yearnings to be accepted. On Julian's side porch during warm black nights, our voices were raised in attempts to best each other in lambasting America and extolling Africa.

We drank gin and ginger ale when we could afford it, and Club beer when our money was short. We did not discuss the open gutters along the streets of Accra, the shacks of corrugated iron in certain neighborhoods, dirty beaches and voracious mosquitoes. And under no circumstances did we mention our disillusionment at being overlooked by the Ghanaians.

We had come home, and if home was not what we had expected, never mind, our need for belonging allowed us to ignore the obvious and to create real places or even illusory places, befitting our imagination.

Doctors were in demand, so Ana Livia had been quickly placed in the Military Hospital and within a year, had set up a woman's clinic where she and her platoon of nursing sisters treated up to two hundred women daily. Progressive journalists were sought after, so Julian, who wrote articles for American and African journals, also worked for the *Ghana Evening News.* Frank and his partner Carlos Allston from Los Angeles founded a plumbing and electric company. Their success gave heart to the rest. We had little doubt about our likability. After the Africans got to know us their liking would swiftly follow. We didn't question if we would be useful. Our people for over three hundred years had been made so useful, a bloody war had been fought and lost, rather than have our usefulness brought to an end. Since we were descendants of African slaves torn from the land, we reasoned we wouldn't have to earn the right to return, yet we wouldn't be so arrogant as to take anything for granted. We would work and produce, then snuggle down into Africa as a baby nuzzles in a mother's arms.

I was soon swept into an adoration for Ghana as a young girl falls in love, heedless and with slight chance of finding the emotion requited.

There was an obvious justification for my amorous feelings. Our people had always longed for home. For centuries we had sung about a place not built with hands, where the streets were paved with gold, and were washed with honey and milk. There the saints would march around wearing white robes and jeweled crowns. There, at last, we would study war no more and, more important, no one would wage war against us again.

The old Black deacons, ushers, mothers of the church and junior choirs only partially meant heaven as that desired destination. In the yearning, heaven and Africa were inextricably combined.

And now, less than one hundred years after slavery was abolished, some descendants of those early slaves taken from Africa, returned, weighted with a heavy hope, to a continent which they could not remember, to a home which had shamefully little memory of them.

Which one of us could know that years of bondage, brutalities, the mixture of other bloods, customs and languages had transformed us into an unrecognizable tribe? Of course, we knew that we were mostly unwanted in the land of our birth and saw promise on our ancestral continent.

I was in Ghana by accident, literally, but the other immigrants had chosen the country because of its progressive posture and its brilliant president, Kwame Nkrumah. He had let it be known that American

Negroes would be welcome to Ghana. He offered havens for Southern and East African revolutionaries working to end colonialism in
their countries.

I admitted that while Ghana's domestic and foreign policy were
stimulating, I was captured by the Ghanaian people. Their skins were
the colors of my childhood cravings: peanut butter, licorice, chocolate
and caramel. Theirs was the laughter of home, quick and without ar-
tifice. The erect and graceful walk of the women reminded me of my
Arkansas grandmother, Sunday-hatted, on her way to church. I listened to men talk, and whether or not I understood their meaning,
there was a melody as familiar as sweet potato pie, reminding me of
my Uncle Tommy Baxter in Santa Monica, California. So I had finally
come home. The prodigal child, having strayed, been stolen or sold
from the land of her fathers, having squandered her mother's gifts and
having laid down in cruel gutters, had at last arisen and directed herself back to the welcoming arms of the family where she would be
bathed, clothed with fine raiment and seated at the welcoming table.

I was one of nearly two hundred Black Americans from St. Louis,
New York City, Washington, D.C., Los Angeles, Atlanta, and Dallas
who hoped to live out the Biblical story.

Some travelers had arrived at Ghana's Accra Airport, expecting
customs agents to embrace them, porters to shout—"welcome," and
the taxi drivers to ferry them, horns blaring, to the city square where
smiling officials would cover them in ribbons and clasp them to their
breasts with tearful sincerity. Our arrival had little impact on anyone
but us. We ogled the Ghanaians and few of them even noticed. The
newcomers hid disappointment in quick repartee, in jokes and
clenched jaws.

The citizens were engaged in their own concerns. They were busy
adoring their flag, their five-year-old independence from Britain and
their president. Journalists, using a beautiful language created by wedding English words to an African syntax, described their leader as
"Kwame Nkrumah, man who surpasses man, iron which cuts iron."
Orators, sounding more like Baptist southern preachers than they
knew, spoke of Ghana, the jewel of Africa leading the entire continent

904 · *Maya Angelou*

from colonialism to full independence by the grace of Nkrumah and God, in that order. When Nkrumah ordered the nation to detribalize, the Fanti, Twi, Ashanti, Ga and Ewe clans began busily dismantling formations which had been constructed centuries earlier by their forefathers. Having the responsibility of building a modern country, while worshipping traditional ways and gods, consumed enormous energies.

As the Ghanaians operated an efficient civil service, hotels, huge dams, they were still obliged to be present at customary tribal rituals. City streets and country roads were hosts daily to files of celebrants of mourners, accompanied by drums, en route to funerals, outdoorings (naming ceremonies), marriages or the installations of chiefs, and they celebrated national and religious harvest days. It is small wonder that the entrance of a few Black Americans into that high stepping promenade went largely unnoticed.

The wonder, however, was neither small nor painless to the immigrants. We had come to Africa from our varying starting places and with myriad motives, gaping with hungers, some more ravenous than others, and we had little tolerance for understanding being ignored. At least we wanted someone to embrace us and maybe congratulate us because we had survived. If they felt the urge, they could thank us for having returned.

We, who had been known for laughter, continued to smile. There was a gratifying irony in knowing that the first family of Black Americans in Ghana were the Robert Lees of Virginia, where the first Africans, brought in bondage to the American Colonies in 1619, were deposited. Robert and Sarah Lee were Black dentists who had studied at Lincoln University in Pennsylvania with the young Kwame Nkrumah, and had come in 1957 to Ghana to celebrate its just won independence. They returned a year later with their two sons to become Ghanaian citizens.

The Lees and the presence of W.E.B. Du Bois and Alphaeus Hunton nearly legitimized all of us.

Dr. Du Bois and his wife Shirley Graham had been personally invited by the President to spend the rest of their lives in Ghana. Dr.

Hunton had come from the United States with his wife Dorothy to work with Dr. Du Bois on the ambitious Encyclopedia Africana.

The rest of the Black Americans, who buzzed mothlike on the periphery of acceptance, were separated into four distinct groups.

There were over forty families, some with children, who had come simply and as simply moved into the countryside hoping to melt onto the old landscape. They were teachers and farmers.

The second group had come under the aegis of the American government and were viewed with suspicion by Ghanaians, and Black Americans stayed apart from them as well. Too often they mimicked the manners of their former lords and ladies, trying to treat the Africans as Whites had treated them. They socialized with Europeans and White Americans, fawning upon that company with ugly obsequiousness.

There was a minuscule business community which had found a slight but unsure footing in Accra.

Julian's circle had stupendous ambitions and thought of itself as a cadre of political émigrés. Its members were impassioned and volatile, dedicated to Africa, and Africans at home and abroad. We, for I counted myself in that company, felt that we would be the first accepted and once taken in and truly adopted, we would hold the doors open until all Black Americans could step over our feet, enter through the hallowed portals and come home at last.

Guy, wearing a metal and leather neck brace, enrolled in the university and moved happily into Mensah Sarbah Dormitory Hall. I was surprised and delighted to find that being alone brought a deeply satisfying bliss. I hummed, sang to myself, strutted, cooked and entertained for a month before the professor returned and claimed his house.

The YWCA wasn't as sterile on my second stay. I had a job, a car, some money and amusing friends.

All meals were served in the ground floor dining room under the watchful eyes of Directress Vivian Baeta, the daughter of a Ghanaian clergyman. Miss Baeta was young and pleasant, but a little too correct for our tastes. She frowned upon loud voices and noisy laughter and most diners, often white collar workers from nearby office buildings who filled the restaurant each mealtime, acceded to her wishes. The Black American residents, however, having no living room save Julian's side porch, used the dining room as a place to gather, to talk, to argue and maybe to flirt with male friends before returning to the celibate cells on the second floor.

Although we tried to respect Miss Baeta's desires, passion dictated the volume of our conversations. The directress's disapproving look fell upon us frequently.

One lunch time Vicki, Alice and I were occupying our usual table when a voice louder than any tone we had ever used split the quiet air.

"No rye?" Again, "No rye? What fa country you peepo got? No rye?" A huge, six-foot-tall woman was standing at a window table. She wore West African cloth, her head tie was large and beautifully wrapped, and she was angry.

"You peepo! You Ghanaians. You got yourself your Kwame Nkrumah, but you got no rye. Last night, you give the peepo cassava. Breakfast you give us garri. Lunch you give us yam. Still no rye." She was complaining specifically to the persons in charge who were nowhere to be seen. Miss Baeta had poked her head into the dining room, seen the irate woman, and had hastily withdrawn. Other diners put their heads dangerously close to their plates as if searching for some microscopic intruder in their food.

The woman continued. "I come to you peepose country from Sierra Leone where we serve rye. I know this country is proud Ghana, but it still is Africa and you don't give me rye. You think you England? You think you German? Where is the rye?"

The woman was demanding rice and I quickly sympathized with her. The grandmother who raised me was a firm believer in rice. The only white newspapers which reached our house were brought at grandmother's request by maids oncoming from work. Momma was a good cook who experimented with the exotic recipes she found in the White papers. She would prepare Italian spaghetti, macaroni and cheese, scalloped potatoes, O'Brien potatoes, creamed noodles, but still she served rice with each meal. The family was not obliged to eat the rice if we were pleased with the other starches, but Momma never felt the table was properly set until the filled rice bowl was placed in its usual spot.

The African woman was screaming, "You peepo, you got your Black Star Square. You got your university, but you got no rye! You peepo!" She began to laugh sarcastically, "You make me laugh. Pitiful peepo. Pitiful. No rye, no pride. Ha, ha. See me, Sierra Leone woman, laugh. Ha, ha. Ha, ha!"

I went through the private doors into the kitchen. The cook was sitting on a stool drinking a soda. I said, "Uncle, please excuse me." He looked up frowning, apparently expecting one more complaint.

"Uncle, there is a woman out there who is dying for rice."

He shook his head. "Rice tonight. For dinner. Rice tonight."

I said in a sweet voice, "Oh please, Uncle. She must have rice. Please."

He said, "She must wait, or go somewhere else. Rice tonight."

I was defeated. I turned to leave, then turned back. "The woman will go back to her home thinking Ghanaians are mean."

"Let her go. Rice tonight! Anyway, where is she from?" He wasn't really interested. I had my hand on the door. I said, "Sierra Leone."

The cook jumped off the stool. "Why didn't you say that? You said 'a woman.' I thought you meant a Black American. Sierra Leone people can't live without rice. They are like people from Liberia. They die for rice. I will bring her some."

The woman was still standing and talking to the air, although weakly, when the cook passed through the dining room bearing a large platter of rice. He placed it on the woman's table without a word, and she sat down speechless, her eyes hungrily counting the white grains.

When the cook reached the kitchen door the room exploded in applause.

The University of Ghana with its white buildings and red tiled roofs loomed like a chimera atop Legon's green hills. The Moroccan architecture of arches, wide, low steps and loggia gave the institution an unusually inviting warmth. African students and faculty paraded the halls and grounds in distinctive and often colorful outfits.

Women often wore short cotton skirts and blouses or the richly patterned long national dress, consisting of provocatively cut peplum blouses and long, tight skirts meant to accent small waists and abundant hips.

Some men wore the northern territory woven smocks which were highlighted with bright embroidery, while some others favored Western slacks and short sleeved shirts. Moslems from Nigeria or Cameroon wore the Grand Bou Bou: twelve yards of fine cotton fashioned into pants, shirts and a matching floor length over-smock. Despite the hot weather there were a few African professors who elected to wear the Cambridge or Oxford school gowns over woolen pants, buttoned down shirts and ties. Some wore Nehru jackets made popular by President Nkrumah. It was not surprising to see a lecturer in national dress on Monday, a casual smock and slacks on Tuesday, and worsted tweed on Wednesday. Ghana's colorful cloth was sold in every marketplace, so status could not be determined by clothes. Thus the market woman, the bank teller and the student might wear the same pattern on any morning and nothing was thought of the coincidence. A fragrance of flowers permeated that riot of color, sound and activity provoking all the senses into constant exercise.

My office door opened onto a grassy courtyard and the windows looked out onto a dance pavilion. Students, faculty, tradesmen, market women selling roasted peanuts and plaintain, visitors and administrators were in constant view. Astonishingly, in that strain of energy projects were designed and work was completed.

Efua wrote and directed plays. The handsome Joe de Graft taught acting, and occasionally graced the stage with a quite heroic presence. Bertie Okpoku and Grace Nuamah taught the traditional dances of the Ashanti, Ewe, and Ga people. Professor Nketia, with disarming gentleness, controlled all the artistic temperaments while teaching music, music theory, music history, and African musicology.

I worked wherever I was needed. Professor wrote *Kple, Music of the Gods,* a book on the liturgy of the Ewe, and despite my scanty knowledge of typewriters, I was asked to type the manuscript, and did so. Reports on students' development, their absences and illnesses were kept in my files. Sometimes I handled theatre reservations or sold tickets at the box office in town. When Ireland's Abbey Theatre director, Bryd Lynch, came to teach at Legon, she chose to present Bertolt Brecht's *Mother Courage* in full production, and I was chosen to play the title role.

My son was growing into manhood on the university campus, under my eye, but not my thumb. Ana Livia and Julian, Efua and her children, my housemates and our lusty friends provided recreation enough. At last life was getting itself in joint.

Vicki, Alice and I had decided to share a house, and the pretty white bungalow we found was a proud prize. There were three bedrooms (Vicki characteristically offered to take the smallest), a commodious living room and dining room. The kitchen was a disappointment to me, but my housemates, who claimed no interest in cooking, hardly noticed its meagre appointments.

Vicki Garvin was a pretty little yellow woman, always immaculately groomed with tiny, graceful hands. She had been a national union organizer in the United States and was highly respected in American and European labor circles, and had come to Africa in the legion of hopeful returnees. She was strong-nerved, but years of unsuccessful bargaining with American bosses and reluctant workers had left cynicism in her voice and her face was quick to adopt a shadow. She had a Bachelor's degree in English, a Master's degree in economics and years of experience.

She had gone first to Nigeria, but after a bitter reception, or rather, a bitter rejection, had been encouraged to believe that she would easily find creative work in the progressive country of Ghana.

For months she carried her qualifications as burnt offerings to labor and trade union offices, and when not ignored outright she was told "the big man," meaning the boss, "is travelling. Come again." When Vicki did find work it was as a typist in a foreign embassy. She refused rancor, saying that right now "Ghana needs its jobs for Ghanaians, but someday...."

Alice Windom, the youngest in the bungalow, was also the most explosive. She was a dark mahogany color, had a wide open smile and the prettiest legs in Accra. Men used to sit in our living room, oblivious to the exquisite conversation of three bright women, too busy ogling and loving Alice's legs. Alice had degrees from an Ohio university and a Master's from the prestigious University of Chicago. Her argumentative talents, so recently exercised in the school environments, were as pointed as broken bones.

She had come from a family of university professors, and had debated with her siblings for dominance. Neither visitors nor the other bungalow inhabitants could best her in verbal contests. During her last school years, she had vowed to save her money and come to Ghana to live forever. Her field was sociology and her dream was to belong to a community of African social workers. She searched in associations and congresses and committees, but her diligence went unrewarded. Alice became a receptionist in a foreign embassy.

As was expected, Alice was not as casual as Vicki on being denied a chance to work in her field of interest. "Damn, these Africans in personnel are treating me like Charlie did down on the plantation." There was never a suggestion that she might leave Ghana for greener pastures.

It was agreed in the house that as far as work was concerned, I was the most fortunate. As administrative assistant at the University of Ghana, I had direct contact with African students, faculty, administrators and small traders. While the job was a blessing, the pay was not bounteous.

I received no housing, tuition, or dislocation allowances. On the first day of every month, when the small manilla envelopes of cash were delivered to the offices, I would open mine with a confusion of sensations. Seventy-five pounds. Around two hundred dollars. In San Francisco, my mother spent that amount on two pairs of shoes. Then I would think, seventy-five pounds, what luck! Many Ghanaians at the university would take home half that much with gratitude. My feelings slid like mercury. Seventy-five pounds. Sheer discrimination. The old British philosopher's packet was crammed with four times that, and all I ever saw him do was sit in the Lecturers' Lounge ordering Guinness stout and dribbling on about Locke and Lord Acton and the British Commonwealth.

I would count out the paper money, loving the Black president's picture. Thirty pounds for rent; thirty for my son's tuition, being paid on the installment plan; ten for beer, cigarettes, food. Another five for the houseman who my friends and I paid fifteen pounds per month to clean the bungalow.

A grown man could live on fifteen pounds, and there I was being a simpering ass. I was my mother's daughter. When I left her house at seventeen, she had said, "I'm not worried about you. You'll do your best, and you might succeed. And remember, as long as you're making a living for yourself you can take care of your baby. It's no trouble to pack double." All I had to do was find extra work.

The editor's office of the *Ghanaian Times* had all the excitement of a busy city intersection. People came, left, talked, shouted, laid down papers, picked up packages, spoke English, Fanti, Twi, Ga and Pidgin on the telephone or to each other.

T. D. Kwesi Bafoo perched behind his desk as if it was the starting mark for a one hundred yard sprint. At a signal he would leap up and hurl himself past me, through the crowded room and out of the door.

His cheeks, brows, eyes and hands moved even before he talked.

I said, "I am a journalist. I've brought some examples of my work. These are from the *Arab Observer* in Cairo." He waved away my folder and said, "We know who you are. A good writer, and that you are a Nkrumaist." I was certainly the latter and not yet the former.

As he stuffed papers into a briefcase he asked, "Can you write a piece on America today?"

"Today? Do you mean right now?"

He looked at me and grinned, "No. America today. America, capitalism and racial prejudice."

"In one article?" I didn't want him to know the request was implausible.

He said, "A sort of overview. You understand?"

I asked, seriously, "How many words, three thousand?"

He answered without looking at me, "Three hundred. Just the high points."

The seething energy would no longer be contained. Bafoo was on his feet and around the desk before I could rise.

"We'll pay you the standard fee. Have it here by Friday. I have another meeting. Pleasure meeting you. Good-bye."

He passed and disappeared through the door before I had gathered my purse and briefcase. I imagined him running up to the next appointment, arriving there in a heat, simmering during the meeting, then racing away to the next, and on and on. The picture of Mr. Bafoo so entertained me that I was outside on the street before the realization came to me that I had another job which paid "the standard fee." I was earning that at the university. In order to afford luxuries I had to look further.

The Ghana Broadcasting office was as to the *Times* newspaper office what a drawing room was to a dance hall. The lobby was large, well furnished and quiet. A receptionist, pretty and dressed in western clothes, looked at me so quizzically, I thought perhaps she knew something I needed to know.

She frowned, wrinkling her careful loveliness. "Yes? You want to talk to someone about writing?" Her voice was as crisp as a freshly starched and ironed doily.

I said, "Yes. I am a writer."

She shook her head, "But who? Who do you want to talk to?" She couldn't believe in my ignorance.

I said, "I don't know. I suppose the person who hires writers."

"But what is his name?" She had begun to smile, and I heard her sarcasm.

"I don't know his name. Don't you know it?" I knew that hostility would gain me nothing but the front door, so I tried to charm her. "I mean, surely you know who I should see." I gave her a little submissive smile and knew that if I got a job I'd never speak to her again.

She dismissed my attempt at flattery by saying curtly, "I am the receptionist. It is my job to know everyone in the building," and picked up the morning paper.

I persisted, "Well, who should I see?"

She looked up from the page and smiled patronizingly. "You should see who you want to see. Who do you want to see?" She knew herself to be a cat and I was a wounded bird. I decided to remove myself from her grasp. I leaned forward and imitating her accent. I said, "You silly ass, you can take a flying leap and go straight to hell."

Her smile never changed. "American Negroes are always crude."

I stood nailed to the floor. Her knowledge of my people could only have been garnered from hearsay, and the few old American movies which tacked on Black characters as awkwardly as the blinded attach paper tails to donkey caricatures.

We were variably excited, exciting, jovial, organic, paranoid, hearty, lusty, loud, raucous, grave, sad, forlorn, silly and forceful. We had all the rights and wrongs human flesh and spirit are heir to. On behalf of my people, I should have spoken. I needed to open my mouth and give lie to her statement, but as usual my thoughts were too many and muddled to be formed into sentences. I turned and left the office.

The incident brought me close to another facet of Ghana, Africa, and of my own mania.

The woman's cruelty activated a response which I had developed under the exacting tutelage of masters. Her brown skin, curly hair, full lips, wide flanged nostrils notwithstanding, I had responded to her as if she was a rude White salesclerk in an American department store.

Was it possible that I and all American Blacks had been wrong on other occasions? Could the cutting treatment we often experienced have been stimulated by something other than our features, our hair and color? Was the odor of old slavery so obvious that people were offended and lashed out at us automatically? Had what we judged as racial prejudice less to do with race and more to do with our particular ancestors' bad luck at having been caught, sold and driven like beasts?

The receptionist and I could have been sisters, or in fact, might be cousins far removed. Yet her scorn was no different from the supercilious rejections of Whites in the United States. In Harlem and in Tulsa, in San Francisco and in Atlanta, in all the hamlets and cities of America, Black people maimed, brutalized, abused and murdered each other daily and particularly on bloody Saturday nights. Were we only and vainly trying to kill that portion of our history which we could neither accept nor deny? The questions temporarily sobered my intoxication with Africa. For a few days, I examined whether in looking for a home I, and all the émigrés, were running from a bitter truth that rode lightly but forever at home on our shoulders.

The company of my companions, Guy's returning robust health, and Efua's friendship weened me away from my unease and the questions. I would not admit that if I couldn't be comfortable in Africa, I had no place else to go.

I turned my back to the niggling insecurities and opened my arms again to Ghana.

I wanted my hair fixed Ghanaian fashion and didn't want to spend time in a hot beauty shop. I made an appointment for a home visitor.

The laughing Comfort Adday was a stenographer as well as a beautician. She told me "Sistah, I don't work. My fingers work. Work is for farmers. As for my part, I try hard to stay away from farms." She pulled patches of my hair and wound them with coarse black thread. "I have to save myself for later. For children. Then when I get ready, for a husband."

Peals rang over my head as she seemed to wrench my hair out of its roots. "You only have the one boy, eh?" I tried to nod, but my head was in a vise. I mumbled, "Yes." She said, "But my deah," laughter... "You know they say 'one child is no child.'"

I had heard the saying but couldn't nod and chose not to mumble again. Comfort continued, making her voice low and suggestive, "And they say, too, 'if you don't use it you'll lose it.'" Here her laughter rose and her hands pulled, jerking me nearly to a standing position. "You're not a chicken, you know, Sistah." I was over thirty. "Not to say you are too old to lay eggs." She tugged a scrap of hair and luckily left my head attached to my neck. "But you keep waiting, your egg maker will grow grey." Her laughter exceeded all earlier efforts, "and any chicks that come," tug, wrestle, jerk, "will walk out fully dressed, playing the drums." Jubilation at her own wit and wisdom bent her body in half, but her fingers never ceased pulling my hair or coiling the black thread against my scalp.

"Sistah, look at yourself." She released me. Her face, the color of ancient bricks, was groomed with a proud smile. I went to the mirror. Long, black spikes jutted from my head in every direction, and long strings hung to my shoulders. It was a fashion worn by the pickaninnies whose photographs I had seen and hated in old books. I was aghast. No wonder she had laughed so heartily. I quickly searched her face for ridicule, but respect for her work was all I found.

I stuttered. "But, I wanted, . . . I didn't want . . ." I could neither go in the street with that hairdo, nor was I capable of unwinding the cord that now shone on my hair with an evil gleam. For some unknown reason the beautician had chosen to teach me a lesson on the foolishness of trying to "go native."

"Sistah, now sit down, let me finish."

"I thought you were finished." My voice came weakly and was drowned out by her great laughter. "Oh sistah, oh my deah." She had to hold her stomach which threatened to shake itself loose from her body. "Oh Sistah. I just told you that I knew you weren't a spring chick. If I let you go out like that, they'd catch both of us and put us in the silly folks hospital."

The agony of laughter left her face slowly. "No sistah, my deah, only young girls whose time has not come can wear their hair like that."

She gathered the dangling strings and pulled them tightly together. Her fingers moved quickly over my head. After a few minutes she picked up scissors from a stool and with a few snips, removed the last hanging strings.

"Now look. See yourself, and tell me."

I looked in the mirror and was relieved that I looked like every other Ghanaian woman. My hair was pulled tightly into small neat patches and the triangular designs of tan scalp and black hair was as exact as the design in tweed cloth.

"Sistah, you have given me such a good laugh, I shouldn't charge you." Comfort was washing her combs and rolling her scissors and thread in a cotton white cloth. I knew that last statement was only for show.

In just six months I learned that Ghanaian women might take in orphans, give generously to the poor, and feed every person who came to their houses. They could allow their men certain sexual freedom, but they were very strict in money matters. When it came to finances "Ghana women no play, oh," had been said to or around me hundreds of times.

I paid Comfort.

She said, "I will come again in two weeks. Oh, how I like to laugh with you."

I didn't want to wonder whether she was sincere, but I noticed that I hadn't laughed even once.

A Black couple who had just arrived in Africa sat in our living room explaining their presence on the Continent.

"Because of Nkrumah" (The man pronounced the President's name NeeKrumah) "and Sékou Touré, we decided it was either Ghana or Guinea. We have come to Mother Africa to suckle from her breasts." The man spoke so vigorously his Afro trembled and his long neck carried his head from side to side. He wore a brightly colored African shirt and reminded me of a large exotic bird.

Alice spoke angrily, "Hell man, you ought to be ashamed of yourself. Talking about sucking from Africa's breasts. When you were born Black in America, you were born weaned."

I said, "Africa doesn't need anybody as big as you pulling on her tits."

Vicki said, "And that's an ugly metaphor."

The man was sparring quickly. "The Zulus use it."

"But you're a Black American," I reminded him.

"Yeah. Well, who is to say my ancestors weren't Zulus?"

In just a few months our living room had begun to compete with the Mayfield side porch for popularity. Late nights found us drinking beer and fastidious over even the smallest points in a conversation.

Alice earned her reputation as the most formidable disputant. Having spent her working hours answering telephone calls and receiving embassy visitors, she looked eagerly toward the evenings and weekends. Then she could exercise her sharp mind and quick tongue on anyone within hearing range.

The wise Vicki said, "What Africa needs is help. After centuries of slavers taking her strongest sons and daughters, after years of colonialism, Africa needs her progeny to bring something to her."

Alice grinned, warming up. She said, "I've never seen Africa as a woman, and somewhere I resent the use of any sexual pronoun to describe this complex continent. It's not he or she. It is more an it."

The visitors looked disapprovingly at us all. The need to believe in Africa's maternal welcome was painfully obvious. They didn't want to know that they had not come home, but had left one familiar place of painful memory for another strange place with none.

The woman, whose large natural matched her husband's, sat like a broken doll. Her brown face was still, her dark eyes flat and staring. I would not have been too surprised had she cried, "Maa Maa, Maa Maa" in a tiny toy voice.

Alice said, "The Sahara continues to eat up arable land at a frightening rate, and nomadic people continue to herd cattle which eat every blade of grass that pops up. What the continent needs is about five hundred artesian well diggers and about five hundred agronomists. That would have been a gift to bring."

"I belong here. My ancestors were taken from this land." The visitor was fighting back.

"Of course, you're right." Vicki's voice was soothing. "And under ideal conditions you could return and even lay claim to an ancestral inheritance. But Alice has a good point. The continent is poor, and while Ghanaians have wonderful spirits, thanks to themselves and Kwame Nkrumah, they are desperate."

I asked, "What did you do at home? What is your work?"

The man was still silent, and I had spoken only to put sound into the sad silence.

Vicki offered advice, "Ghana would be easier than Guinea, unless you speak French."

The woman's voice was a surprisingly rich contralto. "He worked in the Chicago stockyards, and I was a Bunny."

She got our total and immediate attention. Although she wore no makeup and a sleeved dress of a demure cut, it was easy to imagine her in a bunny costume. She muttered just above a whisper, "We've been saving for two years."

Her husband stood up scowling, "Don't tell them anything, Hon. It's just like Negroes. They are here, in their own place, and they don't want us in. Just like crabs in a bucket. Pulling the other one down. When will you people learn? Let's go."

They would have been surprised to learn that we were no less annoyed with them than they with us. They were just two more people in an unceasing parade of naïve travelers who thought that an airline ticket to Africa would erase the past and open wide the gates to a perfect future. Possibly we saw our now seldom expressed hopes in the ingenuous faces of the new arrivals.

Vicki waved her small hands. "Wait a minute. You don't understand."

"Come on, Hon. The taxi driver was wrong."

I asked, "What taxi driver?"

The woman answered, "We don't know his name. He was driving us around and when he found out we were Americans, he said he was going to take us to a Black American home. That's how we got here."

We looked at each other knowing the danger of getting a reputation of inhospitability in this country, where we were striving for welcome.

Alice lit a fresh cigarette from an old one. "I guess because we talk so much, folks have the idea that we know something, so Black Americans come here or to Julian Mayfield's house. We weren't trying to discourage you from staying in Ghana. We just wanted to prepare you for what you might, no, what you will encounter so you won't be disappointed."

Vicki added, "Sort of immunizing you before you get the disease."

I added, "We're trying to explain that if you expect Africans to open their arms and homes to you, you'll be in for a terrible shock. Not that they will be unkind. Never unkind, but most of them will be distant. One problem, of course, is our inability to speak the language. Without a language it is very difficult to communicate." The man's anger had propelled him to the door. I touched his sleeve and said, "Don't rush off. Have dinner with us."

All people use food for more reasons than mere nutrition, and I was hoping that in the present case it would work to calm our visitors' ruffled feathers.

The husband acted as if he still wanted to leave, but was persuaded by his wife to stay.

As I had hoped, they relaxed during dinner and allowed themselves to be charmed by Alice, who worked at being her clever best. She made them laugh at her Chicago stories, Vicki related tales of Paul Robeson, and I talked about my years in show business.

We stood at the door saying good-bye when the man, all seriousness again, shook Alice's hand. "I think we'll go to Guinea. If we have to learn a foreign language to be accepted in Africa, we may as well learn French."

The woman waved. "We certainly appreciate the dinner and your advice. Hope we meet again."

That they had missed our clearly made points boded well for them. They just might succeed in their search for the illusive Africa, which secreted itself when approached directly, like a rain forest on a moonless night. Africa might just deliver itself into their hands because they matched its obliqueness.

The telephone call brought unsettling news. The secretary's voice simply said, "You are wanted at the *Ghanaian Times.*" I sped to the office building, accompanied by nervous excitement. Had my article been accepted, or had the editor discovered what I already knew; that in order to write about the United States, capitalism and racial prejudice one needed a lifetime, three hundred thousand words, and a lot of luck?

T. D. Bafoo was on his feet when I arrived at his desk.

"Maya!" He waved my pages at me and as usual spoke in short explosions. "This is good, Sister! You Black Americans know a thing or two, don't you?" He spoke too quickly for me to respond.

"We will have a new baby, you know?" I didn't.

"And we will invite you to the outdooring, in the country."

An outdooring is the first African rite of passage. It always begins at dawn, eight days after the child's birth, and gives family and friends a chance to see and welcome the newest soul.

"I am asking Alice, Vicki, and Julian and others! Come! Black Americans must see how we salute life! Party! We have a great party for life!

"Come to my house, here tonight in Accra. Greet my wife. I will tell you how to come to us in Kanda."

I thanked him, took his address, smiled and was again left standing as he hurried away.

The modesty of T. D.'s pretty bungalow was surprising. He was a Big Man, and even in Nkrumah's best of all worlds, Big Men often lived in coarse ostentation. Some owned huge castle-like houses and were driven by chauffeurs through the streets of Ghana in Mercedes-Benzes and limousines. Although most cabinet ministers, members of Parliament, government administrators, and wealthy businessmen wore the common matching shirt and pants which had been popularized by the President, their wealth and power were not held in secret. Wives, mistresses, girlfriends, and female relatives were known to wear heavy gold necklaces and bracelets to market and to import expensive furniture from Europe. It was not unknown for some Big Men and their women to treat the servant class as slaves. They were generally unpopular, and in safe company they were ridiculed, but their power was threatening and little was said of them in public.

A smiling T. D. met me at the door. "Sister, come, come inside. You are finally here. You are at home, and meet my wife. Come, we will eat foo foo and garden eggs." Although he still spoke as if he needed to cram everything into one sentence, he was a quieter man in his own house.

His wife was a tall, brown woman with an earnest face and a beautiful voice, and was very pregnant. She smiled and took my hand.

"Sister Maya. *Akwaba.* Welcome. I am making chicken for you, since you can't eat fish."

T. D. grinned, "Sister, news travels in Ghana. We know everything or nothing. Come, we will have beer. What do you like?"

Beer preferences were fiercely defended or opposed. The two vying brands were Star and Club.

"I'm a Club person myself." I spoke as proudly as I had heard Ghanaians do.

"Ye! Ye! I knew you were okay. I am Club too. All Star drinkers are untrustworthy. Differences between good and bad beer drinkers are stronger than the imperialist introduced divisions between Africans. Don't you think so, Sister?" T. D. laughed like a boy and took me into his study. "We will drink in here." He spoke to his wife, "Join us when you can."

We sat down in a room crowded with books and papers and magazines. Mrs. Bafoo spoke from the doorway, "Kwesi, are you going to give Sister Maya your famous speech? You would do better if you stand on the chair." She entered carrying beer and laughing.

T. D. had the grace to drop his head. When he looked at me his eyes were sharp with mischief. "Sister, I am Fanti. This woman is a nurse, but she is also an Ewe. A terrible mixture. Nurses think they know the body and Ewes think they know the mind. Oh boy, what have I married?"

I spent the afternoon eating with my fingers and listening to T. D.'s political discussions. I experimented with my Fanti, much to the amusement of my hosts, and found that while I had a reasonable vocabulary, my melody was not in tune. T. D. suggested I pick up Ewe, but when I heard Mrs. Bafoo sing-speak her language, I decided I would continue struggling to master Fanti.

The couple, throughout the evening, tenderly but relentlessly teased each other about their mixed marriage, laughing at their differences, each gibe a love pat, sweetly intimate.

I left after nightfall with directions to T. D.'s country place, and the feeling that maybe the new friendship would lead me behind the modern face of Ghana and I could get a glimpse of Africa's ancient tribal soul. That soul was a skittish thing. Each time I had approached it, bearing a basket of questions that plagued me, it withdrew, closed down, disguising itself into sensual pleasantries. It had many distracting guiles.

The musical names of Ghana's cities were lovely on the tongue and caressing to the ears; Kumasi (Koo mah see), Koforidua (Ko fo rid you ah), Mpraeso (Um prah eh so). Ghanaians boasted that Accra and Sekondi were old towns showing proof of trade with Europeans in the fifteenth century. I loved to imagine a long-dead relative trading in those marketplaces, fishing from that active sea and living in those exotic towns, but the old anguish would not let me remain beguiled.

Unbidden would come the painful reminder—"Not all slaves were stolen, nor were all slave dealers European." Suppose my great-grandfather was enslaved in that colorful town by his brother. Imagine my great-grandmother traded by her sister in that marketplace.

Were those laughing people who moved in the streets with such equanimity today descendants of slave-trading families? Did that one's ancestor sell mine or did that grandmother's grandmother grow fat on the sale of my grandmother's grandmother?

At first when those baleful thoughts interrupted my pleasant reveries I chased them away, only to learn that they had the resistance of new virus and the vitality to pop into my thoughts, unasked, at odd and often awkward times.

So I had been intrigued watching T. D. and his wife using their tribal differences to demonstrate their love. Getting to know them might lay to rest the ugly suspicion that my ancestors had been weak and gullible and were sold into bondage by a stronger and more clever tribe. The idea was hideous, and if true, I was forced to conclude that my own foreparents probably abstained from the brutish sale of others simply because they couldn't find tribes more gullible and vulnerable than they. I couldn't decide what would be the most appalling; to be descended from bullies or to be a descendant of dupes.

The Bafoos' love could erase the idea that African slavery stemmed mostly from tribal exploitation.

On a midmorning break I went into the Senior Common Room. My entry made no impact on the confident people who continued their conversation, offering their voices to each other as beautiful women offer their hands to homely suitors.

The Englishman was speaking desultorily through a thin nose, "I understand their anger. I do think it is unattractive, but I understand it."

A Yugoslav woman, too intellectual for cosmetics, argued without passion, "But they have been treated like beasts."

The Englishman was a little petulant, "That doesn't give them the right to act bestial."

A Canadian attempted to bring balance. "While it isn't a laudable response, it is understandable. The effects of cruel treatment die slowly."

The Englishman said, "Look here, they've been there three hundred years, why the devil are they starting up now?" He raised his voice and ordered, "Another beer, Kojo. Fact, beer all around."

He was an irritated Ronald Colman in an old movie. I sat in a corner drinking tepid beer, knowing I had walked in on a theatrical set and that I would be wise to either sit quietly or exit stage left.

The Ghanaian steward, old and doddering, understood "all around" did not include me, so he took bottles to the large table and went back to his stool behind the counter.

The Senior Common Room at the Institute of African Studies was reserved for professors, lecturers and some administrators. Although it was filled with ancient furniture and a persevering odor of beer, some employees from other faculties at Legon University preferred it to their own lounges. I supposed its popularity could be credited to the nearby Faculty of Music and Dance. At any moment in the day pretty girls and half-dressed men rushed past its door en route to dance classes. Master drummers gave demonstrations hourly outdoors behind the building. Singers practicing in the high-pitched Ghanaian tones could be heard in the area stereophonically. The lounge itself was stuffy, but the surrounding area was fresh and appealing.

The German professor from another department spoke loudly, "Old Man," he said, attempting a British accent, "it's understandable that you're tired of unrest. Your empires have exhausted you."

The Englishman answered, "I don't know about my empire," he pronounced it "empiah," "but agitation becomes a bore after a while."

The Yugoslav woman was ready for a fight. "But not to the agitators."

The Canadian spoke and the room was no longer a set, nor were the people characters I could laugh at or ignore. He said calmly, "But American Negroes are not the masses. They are only about ten percent of the U.S. population."

They were talking about Black Americans. I was sure that the recent riot in Harlem which had been front-page news in Ghana had stimulated the discussion. I focused to listen and to find a place to enter.

"More beer, Kojo, please." The Yugoslav woman's voice was as neat as her body and clothes were abandoned. "I put it to you that the American Negroes are fed up with the system because Democracy does not work. They feel that they are proof."

The old long-snout Briton popped up, "Democracy was never created for the lower classes. Everyone knows that. Just like at Ghana."

As I was gathering a response to singe their ears, a Ghanaian professor of English walked in. He went to the crowded table and said, "Hello, old chums." Without turning to face the steward, he raised his voice. "Beer all around, Kojo." He pulled out a chair and sat. "You were saying 'just look at Ghana.' What about my country?"

I let my preparation scatter. Here was the proper person who would have the arch counterstatement.

The Englishman was already bored with the conversation, but he forced himself to respond. He said, "Democracy which has never worked anyway, was never intended for the masses. And I gave Ghana as evidence."

The African accepted his beer, and without a glance at the steward, poured a glass and drank.

"Hum," he licked his lips. "Delicious. We may not make a great democracy, but no one can complain that we don't make a good beer. What?"

The Europeans laughed and the African joined in. They had assassinated my people as well as my new country. I looked at the steward, but his face was passive and his eyes focused on the open door.

I raised my voice and said, "Obviously you people think you've got all the answers. Well, you should wait until someone who really cares asks you a question. You don't know a damn thing about Black Americans, and I resent every stupid thing you've said."

It wasn't going well at all. My brain was not responding properly. I needed to be sharp, cutting, and politely rude in order to reach their hardened ears, and all I had done was blubber.

I said, "You people are idiots, and you dare speak of Ghana. You rejects." I was surprised to find myself standing and my voice loud and screeching. "You left your old cold ass countries and came here where you've never had it so good. Now you've got servants and can bathe more than once a month. It's a pity more of you don't take advantage of the opportunity. You stinking bastards."

Rage piloted me to the door. "And don't say a word to me, I'll slap the water out of all of you."

I always knew that fury was my natural enemy. It clotted my blood and clogged my pores. It literally blinded me so that I lost peripheral vision. My mouth tasted of metal, and I couldn't breathe through my nostrils. My thighs felt weak and there was a prickling sensation in my armpits and my groin. I longed to drop on the path to my office, but I continued ordering my reluctant body forward.

"Professor?" A soft voice turned me around. The steward was there smiling as if I was a child who had acted mischievously.

He asked, "Professor, why you let them disturb your heart?"

I stuttered, "They were——" I knew the steward was uneducated, but surely he understood the rude scene that had occurred.

"They were insulting my people. I couldn't just sit there."

His smile never changed. "And your people, they my people?"

"Yes, but——I mean American Blacks."

"They been insulted before?"

"Yes——but..."

"And they still live?"

"Yes, but...they also insulted Ghana, your country."

"Oh Sister, as for that one, it's nothing."

"Nothing?" He was not only uneducated, I thought he was stupid as well.

He said, "This is not their place. In time they will pass. Ghana was here when they came. When they go, Ghana will be here. They are like mice on an elephant's back. They will pass."

In that second I was wounded. My mind struck a truth as an elbow can strike a table edge. A poor, uneducated servant in Africa was so secure he could ignore established White rudeness. No Black American I had ever known knew that security. Our tenure in the United States, though long and very hard-earned, was always so shaky, we had developed patience as a defense, but never as aggression.

I needed to know more. I said, "But that African. He is a part of that group."

"No, Sistah. He is a part of Africa. He just a Beentoo."

Beentoo was a derisive word used for a person who had studied abroad and returned to Ghana with European airs. The steward continued, "He's been to the United Kingdom. Been to the United States. In time, that posing will pass. Now he is at home, and home will take him back."

He reached out his arm and touched my shoulder. "Don't let them trouble your heart. In a way you are a 'Beentoo' too. But your people ... they from this place, and if this place claims you or if it does not claim you, here you belong."

He turned and shuffled back to the lounge.

The steward, Otu, and I were in the kitchen. Since I prepared all the food, he was second cook. He washed and diced vegetables, cleaned the utensils as I finished using them and generally made my job easy.

"Auntie?" It was a name of respect.

"Uncle," I responded respectfully.

"There is a boy, Kojo, who would like to speak to you."

"What does he want?"

"Oh, Auntie, should I know?"

Otu didn't look at me directly and I knew the conversation promised to be as formal as a Japanese tea ceremony.

"Otu, if you do not know, I shall not know. Then I cannot speak to the boy."

My friendship with Efua, reading Ghanaian short stories and the Fanti I had learned provided me with some insight into the circuitous conversational form.

"Auntie, if I am to say that which I do not know, I will serve neither you, the boy, nor myself." He stopped talking so abruptly I could almost see the period at the end of his sentence. Obviously, we had to start again.

"Uncle?"

"Auntie?"

"This boy who wants to see me, is a nice boy?"

"Yes, Auntie. His family is good. His father and uncles are from my village."

"Kojo is his name?"

"Yes, Kojo."

"And how can I help Kojo, Uncle?"

"Ah Auntie, it is known that you are good." I had found the right key. "This boy would like to work for you, Auntie."

For me? There was nothing I needed done, and if there was I had no money to pay anyone to do it.

"Otu, there is no job here. Please tell him."

"Auntie, he has not asked me for a job. He has asked to speak to you."

Oh, the tortuous subtlety of language. "There is no point..." Otu turned, and standing stock-still, looked at me.

I was beaten. I said, "Well, tell him to come around, I will speak to him."

"Yes, Auntie." Otu seldom smiled, but a quick change on his face told me of his pleasure.

"I will get him."

"No, Otu, let's finish dinner. Maybe tomorrow."

"He is just there, Auntie." I followed his nodding head and saw a small figure pressed against the screen door.

"Kojo." Otu's voice was strong with authority. "Kojo, bra."

The door opened and a boy of about fourteen stepped timidly into the room. His smile was both deferring and mischievous. He had heard the entire conversation and knew how I had been maneuvered by Otu.

"Kojo, this is Auntie Maya."

Respectfully, he dropped his eyes, but not before I saw the glint of amusement.

He whispered, "Evening, Auntie."

"Kojo, I'm sorry, but I have no job for you."

"Oh." His head was still bowed.

"Ka. Ka. Ka." Otu spat out the Fanti word meaning speak.

Kojo lifted his eyes and I noticed his resemblance to my beloved brother. He shared with Bailey a rich, dark brown color, small hands and a perfectly round head.

He said, "Auntie, I can do anything. I can shop, and save you money at Makola Market, and even in Bokum Square." Those were the two largest markets in Accra, where the intimidating market women haggled customers to desperation, and they did present a challenge to me.

The boy continued, "I hear Ga and Hausa. I can clean, and I am learning to tailor."

The timidity had been a disguise, he was as lively as young yeast.

"But I shop and I have a dressmaker."

Otu was quietly putting pans away.

"Auntie, I can be your 'small boy.' I can bring you beer and wash your car, and if Wofa Otu will teach me, I can laundry. Auntie, I don't want money. No salary. Just dash."

In West Africa, while tips were not compulsory, they were expected and were called dash.

"Otu?"

"Auntie?"

"Can you use a small boy?"

The older man answered as if I had asked a silly question. "Auntie, all children are serviceable. Everyone can use a small boy."

"Kojo, I will take you." The boy's smile made me gasp. His straight white teeth clenched and I saw Bailey's smile.

"Where will you sleep?"

"Near, Auntie. Near. I have another uncle who has a place for me. But morning, I will be here. All day and evening. Thank you, Auntie. Thank you, Wofa."

He turned and ran out the screen door, slamming it behind him. I glanced at Otu quickly, hoping to catch a certain knowing look, but his face was expressionless.

Alice and Vicki accepted Kojo and within weeks he seemed a part of the household. He was in the way when I wanted to cook, in the living room dusting furniture which Otu had just polished, sitting in my parked car playing with the steering wheel and smiling, always smiling that Bailey smile.

"Auntie," Otu was helping me prepare dinner.

"Otu."

"Auntie, that small boy, Kojo, wants to speak to you."

"Well? He speaks to me all the time."

"He thought, Auntie, that he would speak to you after dinner."

I suppose I should have known that something important was coming, but I did not.

Alice and Vicki were out and I was sitting drinking Nestlé's coffee in an easy chair when Kojo whispered from the dining room, "Auntie, is it time to talk to you now?"

"Come in, Kojo, don't hang about out there."

He stood a few steps from me, his head bowed.

"Kojo, look at me. Don't pretend shyness. I know you."

"Auntie." The sweet smile and soft voice were softening me for whatever was to come.

"Auntie, you see, I am a small boy." Everyone could see that.

"And I need to go to school."

Of course. How could I have not noticed that summer was ending and he would have to return to his village?

"Yes, Kojo. Certainly you need an education. When will you be leaving?"

"Well, Auntie, the school I want is here, in Accra, just near to this place." He waited and my brain laboriously began to work. He wanted me to send him to school and to pay his fees. I had been set up.

"Auntie, I have my school fees and they have accepted me. Only I want to continue to be your small boy." Again I had misjudged the child. He was not manipulating me. He liked me. I let him know of my relief.

"Well, of course, Kojo, if you are able to do your school work and still be my small boy, you are welcome. I like you too, Kojo." When he left we were both smiling broadly.

Two weeks later he brought a letter addressed to me. The headmaster asked for my presence to discuss Kojo's courses. The meeting was so long and detailed I was exhausted when I finally arrived late at the university. Kojo had brought good grades from his village school, but he had not studied certain required subjects. The headmaster explained that the boy would need a great deal of help at home and he was so lucky to have educated Aunties.

Three evenings each week, Alice, Vicki or I sat with Kojo at the dining table conjugating verbs, dividing sums and making maps to scale.

At times an annoying thought would buzz in my head; my son was finally grown up and at college. While packing his clothes for the university, I included my last nights of poring over homework and worrying about grades. I locked into his cases the years of concentrating over childish penmanship and memorizing the capitals of countries and their chief exports. I had been freed. Now, with Kojo's eagerness the old became new and I was pinched back into those familiar contractions. His young laughter, high-pitched and honest, and his resemblance to Bailey enchanted me away from resistance. I resumed the teaching-mother role automatically and easily, save for the odd uncomfortable moment when I felt trapped in a déjà vu.

The music of the Fanti language was becoming singable to me, and its vocabulary was moving orderly into my brain.

Efua took me to a durbar, a thanksgiving feast in Aburi, about thirty miles from Accra. Thousands of gaily dressed celebrants had gathered, waving, singing and dancing. I stood on the edge of the crowd to watch the exotic parade. Hunters, rifles across their shoulders, marched in rhythm to their own drummers. Soldiers, with faces set in grim determination, paced down the widened roads behind their drummers while young girls screamed approval. Farmers bearing scythes and fishermen carrying nets were welcomed loudly by the throng.

The annual harvest ritual gave each segment in the society its opportunity to thank God and to praise its workers and their yield.

I was swaying to the rhythm when the drums stopped, and the crowd quieted. The restless air steadied. A sound, unlike the other sounds of the day, commenced in the distance. It was the harsh tone of hundreds of giant cicadas grinding their legs together. Their rasping floated to us and the crowd remained quiet but edgy with anticipation. When men appeared out of the dust scraping sticks against corrugated dry gourds, the crowd recovered its tongue.

"Yee! Yee! Awae! Awae!"

The scrapers, like the paraders who preceded them, gave no notice to the crowd or to the small children who ran unceremoniously close to their serried ranks.

Rasp, Rasp. Scrape! Scrape, Scour, Scrunch, Scrump. Rasp, Rasp! Scree! The raspers faded into a dim distance.

The deep throb of royal drums was suddenly heard in the distance and again the din of celebration stopped. The people, although quiet again, continued to move, sidle, exchange places and wipe their brows. Women adjusted the clothes which held babies securely to their backs.

Rambunctious children played tag, men and women waved at each other, smiled, but kept looking toward the sound of the drums.

Efua touched my shoulder and offered me a large white handkerchief.

I said, "Thank you, but I'm all right." She kept her hand extended. I took the handkerchief.

Men emerged out of the dim dust. One set had giant drums hefted onto their shoulders, and others followed in splendid cloth, beating the drums with crooked sticks. The powerful rhythms rattled my bones, and I could feel the vibrations along the edges of my teeth.

People began clapping, moving their feet, their hands, hips and heads. They shouted clamorously, "Yee! Yee! Aboma!" And there was still a sense of anticipation in the turbulence. They were waiting for a climax.

When the first palanquin hove into view, I thought of a Chinese junk on the Yangtze (which I had never seen), and a ten ton truck on a California freeway (which I knew well). Long poled hammocks, sturdy as Conestogas, were carried by four men. In the center of each conveyance sat a chief, gloriously robed in rich hand-woven Kente cloth. At his side (only a few chiefs were female) sat a young boy, called the Kra, who, during an earlier solemn ceremony, had received the implanted soul of the chief. If the chief should die during the ritual, there would be no panic, for his people would know that his soul was safe in the young boy's body and, with the proper ritual, could be placed into the body of the chief's successor.

The drums beckoned, the kings appeared, and the air nearly collapsed under the weight of dust and thudding drums and shouting jubilation.

Each chief was prouder than the one preceding him. Each dressed in more gold and richer colors. Each black beyond ebony and shining with oil and sweat. They arrived in single file to be met by the adoring shouts of their subjects. "Na-na. Na-na." "Yo, Yo, Nana." The shouting united with the thumping of the drums and the explosion of color. Women and men bounced up and down like children's toys, and children not tall enough to see over the crowd were lifted by the nearest adults to see their passing royalty.

A flutter of white billowed over that excited scene. Thousands of handkerchiefs waving from thousands of black hands tore away my last reserve. I started bouncing with the entranced Ghanaians, my handkerchief high above my head, I waved and jumped and screamed, "Na-na, na-na, na-na."

The sunlit dance floor seethed with wiggling bodies. Benson's High Life Orchestra played the popular tune "Wofa No, No." After dancing for a half hour, I was resting at my table in preparation for another spree. On Ghana's dance floors, women and men could dance alone or with members of the same sex without causing the slightest notice. As I looked around at the mostly empty tables, I saw a man in a white lace Grand Bou Bou whose size was startling. His back was turned so his face was not visible, but he sat so high above the surface of his table he had to be over six and a half feet tall. He had broad shoulders and a very thick neck.

I didn't want to be caught staring if he turned, but I did cut my eyes in his direction often, hoping to see his face. When the orchestra finished playing, three women and a small man returned, laughing, to his table. The big man stood and roared, "Bienvenue. C'était bien?" He turned and I saw that his face had the regularity of a perfect square. Every feature was of the proper size and in the proper place. He looked like romantic drawings of ancient African kings on caparisoned horses. He would have been at home surrounded by voluminous tents, talking birds and camel caravans. He remained standing while the women sat. He pulled the smaller man away from the table and bent his great bulk to speak privately and briefly. When he fin-

936 · *Maya Angelou*

ished he spoke to the women and they gathered their stoles and purses and followed him as he made a path through the tables to the door. I watched the small man walk toward my table. In a wee corner of my mind I hoped that he was headed for a destination beyond me.

He stopped and gave me a slight bow. "Mademoiselle?"

I nodded.

"May I take a little of your time?"

I nodded again. He sat nicely on the edge of a chair.

"My name is Mamali, and I have a friend." His quiet voice and manner gave him a ministerial air.

"Yes?"

"May I ask your name and if you are married?"

My answers were as direct as his questions.

"Is it possible that you noticed the large man who sat at that table?"

I reined in wild horses and answered with calm dignity, "I noticed him."

"He is my friend. He is Sheikhali, and he has asked me to ask you if you will dine with him tonight." He took out a note pad and pen.

The horses were surging again. I said, "But I don't know him. Who is he? Where does he live? Where would we dine?"

"Miss Angelou, he is from Mali. He imports thoroughbred horses and was formerly the largest importer of beef to Ghana. When he visits Accra for business purposes, he generally stays at my residence, but he has a place and I am certain that he would take you to a very fine restaurant."

"But is he married?" He had treated the three laughing women with the indulgence of a benevolent Pasha.

Mamali looked up from his note pad, "All personal questions must be directed to himself. If you agree to dine, I will need your address. He will come for you at nine o'clock."

I hoped that I wasn't accepting too quickly, but how could one know the peculiarities of a culture glimpsed largely in a technicolor fantasy?

My disappointment at finding the house empty was enormous. I needed Alice and Vicki to counsel me on what to wear. I needed to share my excitement over Sheikhali and most crucial, I needed them to see him and let him see them. Suppose he kidnapped me and sold me to an Arab trader? My apprehension was not bootless. During my stay in Cairo I knew ambassadors from sub-Saharan Africa who rushed to Arab countries to negotiate for the release of their nationals stolen and placed for sale on the still active slave market.

It was most important that Sheikhali see my friends and understand that they were intelligent, worldly Americans who could call out the American Army to rescue me. When that last idea came to me I had been searching my closet for an elegant, rich but simple dress. I stopped and sat on the bed, imagining the American government, which had been a participant in both my people's enslavement and emancipation, sending troops to rescue me from one more auction block.

At the knock I opened the door and my knees weakened. Sheikhali filled up the whole outdoors. He wore yards of blue silk embroidered with real gold, a small blue lace cap draped itself jauntily over his brow.

"Miss Angelou?"

"Please come in."

His presence ate up every inch of space, and there was hardly any air left for me to breathe.

I said calmly, "Please sit down. My friends will be here soon."

He sat, stretching long legs out into the center of the room.

"Your...uh...friends?... Your friends to eat? You, me, restaurant?"

His English was terrible. I asked in French, if he would prefer to speak French.

When Sheikhali smiled, I knew I had earned one more star for my heavenly crown. His black lips opened gradually and his teeth shone as diamonds spied through the darkness of a deep pocket.

"You speak French, too?" He used the familiar "tu," and I was pleased.

I explained that I wanted to let my friends know where I was going and with whom. He nodded, the smile still on his face. "Write them a note. Tell them Sheikhali is taking you to L'Auberge Restaurant in his avion d'argent."

Ghanaians called the 1963 Coupe de Ville Cadillac with its high standing fins and prohibitive cost "money with wings," so I was not surprised to hear Sheikhali call his car a silver airplane. I wrote two notes for my housemates, and allowed the gallant caliph to usher me into his silver American chariot.

In the restaurant he waved away the waiter and the menu and spread his hands like large palmetto fans on the tablecloth.

He spoke to me, "We will have coquille St.-Jacques, trout, and beef steak. I suppose you drink wine?" I hesitated. Clearly he was not used to dissent. In the car I had been as demure as an African violet, but now I had to speak. I said, "Thank you, but I don't eat fish or seafood. I'd like steak and vegetables." A tinge of surprise widened his eyes, then he smiled.

"American women. It is said that you know much. I see you (again the familiar 'tu') know what you will and will not eat. And wine, will wine please you?"

As a Muslim, he was not supposed to drink alcohol. I refused the wine. His look was piercing.

He clapped his hands and the waiter scurried to his side.

"Mademoiselle will have steak, vegetables and wine. Good wine." He continued ordering his own meal. I looked around the restaurant, trying not to think about the man or the rest of the evening and my good or bad luck at catching his attention.

"Mademoiselle Angelou," his voice was a soft rumble, "May I call you Maya?" He was already using "tu," so I said yes, and he took the conversation by force.

Although he often visited France he had never been to the States, and was it true that after slavery White Americans gave their money to the Blacks and now all Blacks were rich? I don't think he heard my gasped denial. And why wasn't I married? I was tall and young and pretty. Had all the men in Ghana gone blind? I murmured against the flattery, but he touched my hand very gently, "Don't you want children? You must not wait long, for a woman can live without a husband, but everyone must have at least one child." He was obviously concerned.

"I have a son."

"In America?"

"No, my son is here at the university." He was too dignified to display his surprise, but I saw the flicker cross his face.

"You have a child at the university, but then how old are you?" I said, "I'll tell you my son's age. He is eighteen. But my mother says a woman who will tell her own age will tell anything." For the first time, I heard him laugh. He slapped his leg and nodded approval.

"I like a funny woman. Pretty women are seldom funny. I like you." And I liked him. He was certainly the most sublimely handsome man I had ever seen. I knew that if the purple was visible in his blue-black skin under artificial light, he would be stunning in direct sunlight.

I asked, "Tell me about yourself. Everything but your age."

He smiled, and as I drank wine he told me of his youth.

He was the first son of a fourth wife. His father, who sired thirty-two children, had given most of his attention to the first sons. He had married Sheikhali's mother, the youngest wife, in his old age. She had been catered to and petted by her husband and all his wives because she had brought a whisper of youth back to the aging man, but after Sheikhali's birth, the old man sickened and died, and nearly all his goods had been shared by the older wives and their offspring.

When he was ten years old, he joined other young men and began herding cattle. They walked cows and goats through rain forests, across the savannahs, and over the desert, protecting them from wild animals, venomous snakes, and severe weather. By thirteen, after his initiation into manhood, he was made leader of the drive and became sole supporter of his mother, her mother and family.

I told him, "I compliment you. You've had a hard youth, but now you have become a rich man."

"I was a man at thirteen. I am still a man. Nothing has changed."

Maybe it was that balance of maleness and manliness which intrigued me. I had long known that there were worlds of difference between males and men as there were between females and women. Genitalia indicated sex, but work, discipline, courage and love were needed for the creation of men and women.

Dinner was finished and I couldn't remember the taste of anything I had eaten.

"Now, we go to the hotel." He clapped his hands again.

I tensed. How dare he assume that he could take me to dinner and then immediately to bed. I was no prude and the thought of those large arms around me did make my breath quicken, but I needed some soft talk, some endearments, a few "honeys" and "darlings."

He pulled a tooled leather bag from his smock and gave bills to the waiter.

"For you. Now help the mademoiselle." The waiter pulled my chair and when I stood I saw Sheikhali was already at the door. He could hurry all he wanted, I followed idly, selecting the best way to reject an invitation which had not yet been offered.

We were in the car before any apt words came to me. Just as I formed a disclaiming and apologetic sentence, he began to sing. The tone was naturally deep and the melody haunting. I didn't understand the words, but the meaning was clear.

I was being serenaded. Possibly in his culture a serenade was equal to an evening of sweet talk and all the blandishments one could wish.

He parked at the Continental Hotel, and helped me out of the car.

"This is the best dance band in Accra, but if you prefer we can go on to the Star Hotel. Benson is playing there tonight."

I shook my head and he took the gesture to mean I didn't choose the Star Hotel. In fact, I was physically responding to my ignorance. He had mentioned hotel, and I had immediately assumed that he was planning an erotic tryst and had just talked myself out of and into agreement.

I didn't have to act demure when we entered the lobby. Embarrassment had made me truly docile. Sheikhali laughed when he danced and oh, the man could move. He lifted his arms and yards of blue silk billowed. He spun around and the lights glinted off the gold threads. His cap, still on his head, was the only non-moving part of the whirling mountainous man. Years of dance classes and professional dancing did not allow me to keep pace with Sheikhali. At the end of the first song he glided close and gathered me in his arms.

"You move like a night wind. A soft night wind. I like you."

We spent hours dancing and looking at each other. He whispered a translation of the song he had sung in the car: "A man loved a woman for her large eyes, for her hair that moved like a hive of bees, for her hands and sweet voice. And she answered him with a promise of eternal faithfulness." When he clapped his hands and drew out his money pouch, I was sorry the evening was over.

"We can go to the Star Hotel if you like, or I can take you home." He looked down at me from an enormous height. "Or since I have an apartment in this hotel, we can go there and rest for a time."

Happily, I chose the apartment.

Sheikhali was exotic, generous and physically satisfying, but we had trouble translating ourselves to each other. My upbringing had not fitted me for even a pretended reticence. As a Black American woman, I could not sit with easy hands and an impassive face and have my future planned. Life in my country had demanded that I act for myself or face terrible consequences.

Three days after our meeting, I returned home to find a grinning Kojo and a large white refrigerator standing in my living room.

Kojo rubbed the enamel and said, "Auntie, it's for you."

"For me? From where?"

"Briscoe's, Auntie. It came today." He grinned. Admiring me as much as the refrigerator. "The Mali man sent it."

I read the tag attached to the door of the appliance. *"For Mrs. Maya Angelou. From Mr. Sheikhali."* I said, "But I have a refrigerator."

"I know, Auntie, but the Mali man said you could have two."

"It's silly. I'll send it back." Consternation wiped away Kojo's grin. "Oh, Auntie. You'll hurt the Mali man."

"Tomorrow I will call Briscoe's and have someone come here and pick it up. Nobody has enough food for two refrigerators."

"But please, Auntie." He was pleading as if he was the donor, or even worse the recipient.

"I will do so, tomorrow." His little shoulders fell and he turned, mumbling, and walked into the kitchen.

That next evening Kojo met me at the door.

"Auntie, Briscoe came and got your refrigerator." His voice accused. He shook his head sadly. "Poor Mister Mali man."

Sheikhali was disappointed that I refused his gift, but he offered to pay my rent and give me money for my car. When I explained that I was a woman used to working and paying my own bills, he stared at me in a questioning silence.

One late evening, in his hotel room, he told me he would marry me and take me to Mali. I would learn his language, Fufulde, and teach his children proper French and English.

"What children? You have children?" I was standing at the window, looking down on the lighted gardens.

"I have eight children, from two women. But only one wife. You will like her. She is a good woman. Tall like you." He sat on the bed, looking like a black Buddha, his wide shoulders outlined by a white sleeveless undershirt.

"You will be my second wife. I will build you a beautiful house and you will be happy."

The unusual proposal nearly made me laugh.

"But if you have one wife who is good, why do you want to marry me? And you already have children. What do you want with me?"

I sat beside him on the bed.

"If I need more children I will take a young girl because you and my wife will have no more babies. But you, you are kind and educated. My wife is also kind, but she is like me, she has no education. My family will accept you. I will send to America for your parents and I will bring your son to Mali. Thus our families will marry."

He had taken my life and the lives of my entire family, except my brother, into his plan. There was no way to explain that not one of us could live within his embrace. He laughed when I thanked him, but refused.

"Women always say no. I will find out what you want, and then I will ask again."

My emotions, raised on the romance of Hollywood films, might have faltered had he pleaded love, but his offer had the crispness of a business negotiation, and I had no difficulty in refusing to participate in the transaction.

Kojo had been my "small boy" for two months. He had settled into his school routine and was usually available for small chores and swift errands.

"Auntie?" His downcast eyes and softened voice made me tense. He wanted something. "Kojo, what is it now? Clothes? Shoes? A new school?"

"Auntie, there are some people to see you." He stayed so far beyond the door only a quarter of his body was visible.

"People? Where? What do they want?"

He whispered, "In the backyard, Auntie."

No visitor had ever come to my back door. I hurried through the kitchen and opened the screen. The yard was filled with people dressed in rich cloth and gold. A very old man, leaning on a carved stick, was surrounded by two middle-aged couples, some young adults, and a few teenagers.

A middle-aged man spoke, "Good afternoon, Auntie. We would speak to you." I reproached Kojo for allowing the people to stand in the backyard, and said to the man, "Thank you. Kojo will take you around to the front. Please come inside."

Kojo giggled, and keeping his eyes down, slithered around me and out into the yard.

I went back through the house and opened the door. The people filed into the living room, each shaking my hand and murmuring a name I couldn't quite comprehend. I offered the available chairs, and the older people sat leaving one chair for me. The younger visitors remained standing. I had no idea what the occasion was, but the formality of my visitors was clearly ritualistic.

I called Kojo to bring beer. When one woman complimented me on the prettiness of the living room, the crowd agreed quietly. A man admired a Kofi Bailey print of Kwame Nkrumah which hung on a far wall. There were faint approving sounds "Osagyefo." "Man pass man."

After the beer was served and Kojo left the room, the old man cleared his throat.

"Auntie, we have come to thank you for Kojo. We are his family. These are his brothers and sisters." The teenagers bobbed and smiled. "His uncles and aunts are here and there is his mother and his father. I am the great-grandfather of Kojo, and we thank you."

The family was nodding and smiling. I looked toward the kitchen door, expecting to catch a glimpse of a peeping Kojo, but there was none.

The old man continued, "We have come by lorry from Akwapim, and we have brought thanks."

By their bearing, clothes and jewelry, it was evident that Kojo's family was high-born and well-to-do. If they had travelled from Akwapim by lorry to thank me, it was also clear that they treasured the boy.

"Speak, Mother." Great-grandfather stretched his hand to a woman sitting to his right.

"Auntie," the woman was twice my age. "The boy, Kojo, is good and he might become better. All the mothers cherish him." Here the women gave an amen corner response. "He has grown in our family and in our village, so he was sent to the town. And proof of his goodness is he found you and your Sisters." A new rumble of agreement trembled in the room.

The old man stretched his hand to a tall man who resembled Kojo. "Speak, Father."

"Auntie, we have family here in the town, but none has the Brioni education." In Akan languages Brioni meant White. "Our chief and our grandfather told us if Kojo was to become better, he must have that understanding. Now we have talked to his headmaster. We have spoken to his teachers, and we have listened to your steward who is our cousin. Without payment and without knowing his family, you, Auntie, and your Sisters are teaching our Kojo the Brioni ways of thinking, and so..." His voice trailed away.

The old man spoke. "Bring the thanks."

The lounging teenagers came away from the wall. The older repeated, "Bring the thanks." When they walked out, I smiled, but could think of nothing to say, and since none of the Ghanaians I had met indulged in small talk, it wasn't surprising that the room became quiet. I was not immodest enough to think we deserved thanks, and I knew my housemates would be embarrassed when I related the episode. I kept smiling. The youngsters brought in a crate of vegetables, then another and another, and it seemed they would never stop. They packed crates against crates until the floor was covered.

The old man pointed to a box of eggplant. "Here are garden eggs. Here onions, plantain, pineapples, cassava, yam, coco yam, mango, paw paw, and outside in ice we have brought you snails." He meant the land mollusk which was as large as a kitten and which even starvation could not force down my throat. My jaws ached from smiling.

He continued, "We want you to know that Kojo did not come from the ground like grass. He has risen like the banyan tree. He has roots. And we, his roots, thank you."

The old man braced his cane against the floor and pulled himself nearly erect. The other visitors and I arose.

"Kojo's family has many farms, Auntie." That was obvious. "And while we are not trying to repay you and your Sisters, every month we will send you thanks according to the season."

Each person shook my hand and filed out of the house. The grin on my face had become painfully permanent, and I grinned until I watched Kojo bouncing in the street before his adoring family. They patted him, brushed his clothes, stroked his face, all talking at once. I waited behind the screen until they bade their final good-byes and left him looking like a forlorn puppy against the fence.

"Kojo." He jumped and turned to me.

"Kojo, come this instant."

The boy walked to the house, trying without immediate success to exchange the intoxicating security of being loved with his usual disguise of the befuddled youth. By the time he reached the door and opened the screen, he was timid, young Kojo, my small boy and servant.

"Kojo, why didn't you tell me?"

"Tell you what, Auntie?"

It would sound silly to reproach the boy for not telling me that he had family and that his family was wealthy. And even more stupid, to blame him for being loved.

I lied. "Why didn't you tell me that your family was coming?"

"Oh that, Auntie? I knew they would come someday. I just didn't know when." He looked at me out of Bailey's eyes and grinned. "Auntie, after I take these thanks to the kitchen, may I make you some tea? White tea with lots of sugar?"

"Yes, thank you, Kojo." The visit had been brief but arduous. I had been taken further on my search for Africa and, at least, I had grinned throughout the entire journey.

"Yes, Kojo, I would love some tea with milk, no sugar." I had a half bottle of gin under my bed. Gin with hot tea was just what I needed.

I lay on my bed drinking for myself and for all the nameless orphans of Africa who had been shunted around the world.

I drank and admitted to a boundless envy of those who remained on the continent, out of fortune or perfidy. Their countries had been exploited and their cultures had been discredited by colonialism. Nonetheless, they could reflect through their priests and chiefs on centuries of continuity. The lowliest could call the name of ancestors who lived centuries earlier. The land upon which they lived had been in their people's possession beyond remembered time. Despite political bondage and economic exploitation, they had retained an ineradicable innocence.

I doubted if I, or any Black from the diaspora, could really return to Africa. We wore skeletons of old despair like necklaces, heralding our arrival, and we were branded with cynicism. In America we danced, laughed, procreated; we became lawyers, judges, legislators, teachers, doctors, and preachers, but as always, under our glorious costumes we carried the badge of a barbarous history sewn to our dark skins. It had often been said that Black people were childish, but in America we had matured without ever experiencing the true abandon of adolescence. Those actions which appeared to be childish most often were exhibitions of bravado, not unlike humming a jazz tune while walking into a gathering of the Ku Klux Klan.

I drank the gin and ignored the tea.

Ghana was flourishing. The National Council of Ghana Women, which included representatives of all the clans, was beginning to prove that centuries-old tribal mistrust could be erased with intelligence and determination. The Cacao Marketing Board reported huge profits from the country's major export. Large shining office buildings rose in the cities and the land was filled with happiness.

People stopped in the street and said to passersby, "Oh, but life is sweet, oh, and the air is cool on my skin like fresh water."

The shared joy was traceable to President Nkrumah, who had encouraged his people to cherish their African personality. His statements were memorized and repeated in the litany of teachers and students: "For too long in our history Africa has spoken through the voice of others. Now what I have called the African Personality in international affairs will have a chance of making its proper impact and will let the world know it through the voices of its sons." When he declared that West Indians and Black Americans were among Africa's great gifts to the world, the immigrant community gleamed with gratitude.

For the first time in our lives, or the lives of our remembered families, we were welcomed by a president. We lived under laws constructed by Blacks, and if we violated those laws we were held responsible by Blacks. For the first time, we could not lay any social unhappiness or personal failure at the door of color prejudice.

We shadowed Nkrumah's every move, and read carefully his speeches, committing the more eloquent passages to memory. We recounted good gossip about him, loving his name, and furiously denied all negative rumors.

Because we were still American individualists, bred in a climate which lauded the independent character in legend and lore, and because we had been so recently owned, we could not be easily possessed again, therefore we tried rather to possess the charismatic leader. His private life belonged to us. When photos of his Egyptian wife appeared in the papers, we scanned her features and form with a scrutiny bordering on the obsessive.

We, the Revolutionist Returnees, danced the High Life at the Lido, throwing our hips from side to side as if we would have no further use for them, or we would sit together over Club beer discussing how we could better serve Ghana, its revolution and President Nkrumah. We lived hard and dizzyingly fast. Time was a clock being wound too tight, and we were furiously trying to be present in each giddy moment.

Then, one day the springs burst and the happy clock stopped running. There was an attempt on the President's life, and the spirit of Ghana was poisoned by the news. Fortunately, the President was uninjured, but the citizens did not escape. Makola and Bokum markets lost their usual last-day-Mardi Gras air, and the streets were stricken dumb. The African professors, unspeaking, sent messages of befuddlement to each other by their sad eyes and the shaking of their heads. Even the European faculty at Legon spoke in murmurs.

Government officials, always concerned over foreign intervention and interior espionage, were sharpened in their paranoia and began to search for spies in all corners of the country. Representatives of The Young People's Corps wrote articles, were put on the alert, and those tender faces, filled with anger and suspicion, mirrored the country's tragedy.

Some newspaper articles suggested that no true Ghanaian could possibly be involved in the scurrilous assault on the President, so obviously the search should concentrate on foreign infiltrators. Nearly all noncitizens fell under some measure of suspicion. The British, former colonial rulers, though still covertly admired, were exempt from accusations because they were considered to be mere representatives of a fading Empire.

After a few days of general inflammatory accusation, the finger of suspicion pointed toward the Soviets. Whispers and rumors suggested that those Communists, with their oblique but decided expansionist aims, had tried to kill the President in order to throw Ghana, the Light of Africa, into chaotic darkness. That swell of conjecture abated quickly. Then, the newspaper brought heady news to me. At last there were denunciations of American capitalism, American imperialism, American intervention and American racism. At last, the average Ghanaian would realize that we, the band of disenchanted Blacks, were not fabricating the tales of oppression and discrimination. Then they, not the politicians or intellectuals, they, the farmers and tradespeople and clerks and bus drivers, would stop asking us, "How could you leave America? Don't you miss your big cars?" and "Do you live in Hollywood?" Before I could really sit down and enjoy the feast of revenge, the shadow of the pointing finger moved.

A high-ranking pundit said, "America can use its Black citizens to infiltrate Africa and sabotage our struggle because the Negro's complexion is a perfect disguise. Be wary, Africa, of the Peace Corps Blacks, the AID Blacks, and the Foreign Service Blacks." He suggested finally, that Africans should approach all American Blacks with caution, "if they must be approached at all."

We saw ourselves as frail rafts on an ocean of political turbulence.

If we were not welcome in Ghana, the most progressively Black nation in Africa, where would we find harbour? Naturally we sought to minimize the impact of that painful advice. A few Revolutionists joined the witch hunt, tearing away, with loud protestations, all historical ties to the newly accused. They hoped to deflect suspicion from themselves and to inch closer to the still unrealized goal of acceptance. Many of us kept silent, heads erect and eyes forward, hoping to become invisible and avoid the flaming tongues. Failing the success of that maneuver, we prayed that the assault would pass soon, leaving no scar and little memory.

As usual, I drove each day from my house in Accra to the university, seven miles away, but the distance became painfully perverse. At times, I felt I would never arrive at my destination. Roadblocks delayed progress. They were manned by suddenly mean faced soldiers, their guns threatening and unusual in a country where policemen were armed only with billy sticks. Further on the same drive, it would seem that my arrival at the University at Legon was too imminent. Before I could collect enough composure to calm my face and steady my hands, I would be on campus, where students dropped their eyes at my approach, and professors pointedly turned their backs.

As the Black American community trembled beneath the weight of unprovable innocence, the investigation progressed in all directions. Suspects were imprisoned, and rumors flew like poison arrows around the country. Some Americans and other foreigners were deported, slowly the barbs ceased, the cacophony of distrust quieted. Life returned. The roll of drums and the sound of laughter could be heard in the streets. None of the Revolutionist Returnees had been directly accused, and we were still grateful to be in the motherland, but we had been made a little different, a little less giddy and a lot less sure.

For two weeks I worked myself into a trembling frenzy at the in-town National Theatre. While Efua directed an English translation of a Chinese play, I had helped to sew costumes and coach the student actors. I pulled and pushed the bleachers in the open air auditorium which had to be rearranged constantly. Rickety sets, made by students with no theatrical background, were ever in need of strengthening. Someone had to synchronize the taped music with the onstage action, and a person was needed in the box office. I chose to try to be all things to all the people at all times. The play's pomp and pageantry had been a great success. Ghanaians finding a similarity between the ancient Chinese spectacle and their own traditional dramas kept the theatre filled. I was shaky with exhaustion, but I held on to the idea of returning soon to the university, and that steadied me.

On a quiet Monday morning I parked my car at the Institute of African Studies and sat watching the sun light up the green lawns stretching upward to the white shining buildings. The campus was quiet. I was happy to be back in its peaceful atmosphere.

I started walking to the Faculty of Music and Dance and met Bertie Okpoku, the director of dance.

"Hey, Maya, you finally decided to come home?"

We shook hands and ended the gesture with a traditional finger snap which signified best wishes, and walked together exchanging news until I reached my office.

"Oh, yes." His face became solemn. "One bad thing happened. Sister Grace lost her whole pay packet last week." He shook his head. "Everybody in the Dance department has been affected. So don't expect much laughter around here." Grace Nuamah was the country's chief traditional dancer, a small, thick set, middle-aged woman who performed a welcoming dance at all state functions and important ceremonies. She was an Ashanti woman, with a ready smile, a soft voice, and a hilarious sense of humor. Grace supported herself, nieces and nephews, and was generous with her friends, so the news of her loss saddened my morning, and when I opened the office door and saw the desk piled a foot high with papers, I was suddenly tired. I sat down to examine the stack and it seemed that each student at Legon needed assistance of some sort, and needed me to furnish it. One student wanted a transfer, another additional financial support, while some simply needed excuses from school to take care of familial responsibilities. Each petition had to be checked against the applicant's file and the mid-morning sun was beating into my office before I noticed the passage of time.

I thought I would complete one more paper before a break. I lifted a form letter and a small brown manilla envelope caught my eye. It read, "Grace Nuamah." I opened it to find a roll of Ghanaian pounds stuffed inside. Happy surprise made me give an involuntary shout. I was living close to economic catastrophe, and I knew how precious the salary was for Grace.

She was demonstrating a dance step to her class when I entered the rehearsal hall. The students saw me first, and she, following her distraction, saw me and stopped the class. We walked together out of the door.

She said, "Sister, welcome back from the town. We missed you, oh."
I said, "Sister Grace, Bertie told me about your pay—"
She interrupted, "Into each life some rain must fall." Africans whose own lore and literature are rich with proverbs also make frequent use of English axioms.

I told her that I had found something highly unusual on my desk and showed her the envelope.

She said, "But Sister, it's your pay packet." I said that my salary had been delivered to me in Accra and offered the envelope. There was not a hint of recognition on her face as she took the packet and began to read. "Well, then ..." She narrowed her eyes against the bright sunlight. "Oh, Sister! Oh, Sister!" Stretching her arms over her head, she jumped up. "Oh, Sis-ter, Sis-ter. Hey, thank you, oh."

Students and musicians and workers, hearing her loud shouts, came running. She said in Ashanti, "Sister is blessed. She found my money. Sister is blessed." The smiles and pats and hugs would have been worth contriving a recovery of Grace's loss.

She said, "Sister, I will repay you." I told her that I was repaid, but she insisted. "Sister, I shall repay you."

Throughout the day, people stopped in my office to shake my hand, rejoicing in Grace's good fortune.

Two weeks passed and the memory of the incident waned. University life with its steady routine restored my energies and I felt so good I decided to give myself the treat of having a proper lunch. Like all faculty members, I had been assigned to take meals in one of the university's eight halls, but it was only on the rare occasion that I visited Volta Hall High Table. The dining room was vast and tiered and quiet. Following the British academic arrangement, students sat at Low Table about four feet beneath the long high row where faculty sat facing them. I joined the members at High Table, without speaking, for we knew each other only casually, and there was no love lost or found between us.

Although the African food had been anglicized, it was delicious. A Ghanaian lamb curry, cooked with a minimum of spices, was served and was accompanied with diced papaya, fresh pineapple, tomatoes and mango. I offended the steward by asking for fresh red pepper.

The steward answered with an imitative British accent, "Oh, but Madam, we don't serve that." I knew that students brought their own pepper to the dining room and I was also certain that the steward had had his own cache stored in the kitchen.

When I suggested that maybe he could find a little for me, the White professors looked at me and sniffed disapproval. So typical, their faces seemed to say. So crude a palate and coarse a taste, so typical.

I said loudly, but with courtesy, "If you can't get some for me, I'm sure one of the students would gladly bring pepper to High Table." The steward frowned and reminded me of many American Negroes in the early fifties, who were enraged whenever they saw a natural hair style in public. They felt betrayed, as if the women wearing the frizzy coiffure were giving away secrets; as if they were letting White folks know that our hair wasn't naturally straight. I had seen Black people curse each other on New York City subways and had seen women snubbed in streets throughout the United States because they dared to reveal their Negro-ness.

The steward, infuriated, said "I will find pepper. I will bring pepper to you, Madam."

I ate slowly, relishing every fiery mouthful, ignoring the departure of the faculty. Innate obstinacy made me order and eat a dessert which I did not want and which the steward did not wish to provide.

Coffee was served in the Senior Common Room, and I took a seat by the window and listened to the conversation in progress.

"It was really a little serio-comedic drama. We had traveled about fifty miles into the interior and at nightfall John stopped and let down the flaps of the Land Rover, so we crawled in the back to go to sleep."

A woman's voice cut through the air, "You and the mosquitoes, I don't doubt."

"Oh no, we had netting. Anyway, just as we were drowsing, we heard a voice, 'Ko koko koko ko koko ko.'"

West African houses in the interior are often made of thatch or non-resonant land-crete, so a visitor seeking entrance, unable to rap on a responding door, would politely stand outside and make the sound of knocking, "ko ko ko, ko ko ko."

The storyteller continued, "John lifted the flap and an African stood there dripping wet, wearing a sarong and waving his hand at us."

At nightfall, a farmer home from his fields would take the akatado, the shawl of his wife's dress, and go to the bathhouse. After washing, the man would drape himself in cloth before returning for the evening meal.

"John made me put my slacks back on and we got out of the Rover."

One of the listeners hugged himself and chortled, "Better you than me."

The woman continued, "We didn't see that we had a choice. Anyway, we had thought we were miles from civilization, but we followed the man through a few yards of jungle and there was a village."

The same woman with the keen voice said, "Personally, wild elephants could not have made me leave that car."

"Well, the man took us to the chief, and he had someone serve us tea with whiskey in it. Pretty terrible, actually, but we drank it. Then an interpreter arrived and the old man, toothless and quite ragged, looked directly at us as he spoke his dialect."

I thought of the unpleasant irony that Africans and Asians always speak dialects, rarely languages, while Europeans speak languages and almost never dialects.

The woman continued, "The interpreter said, 'the chief says, you are human beings. I can see that, because I am a human being.' "

There was a little laughter in the Common Room.

She went on quoting the old African. " 'God made daylight so that human beings can be busy outside tending their farms, fishing, and doing all the things for which they need light. God also gave human beings this head,' " she pointed a thin finger at her own head, " 'so that they would have enough sense to make indoors. Human beings sleep indoors at night, for God made night so that animals can search for their food, and breed, and have their young.' " The woman paused, then added, "Well, I thought that was poetic. Then he sent us to a hut where ledges had been built in the walls. We were given mats to sleep on. I guess it was a kind of guest house. John said the people who had lived there before had died of mosquito bites. Anyway, we slept in our clothes and in the morning a woman was cooking over a fire just outside and she gave us yams and crab stew about seven-thirty in the morning. Imagine crab stew at seven-thirty in the morning. When we tried to give her a tip, she refused, and beckoning us to follow, took us back to the old man and the translator was called again. He stood before the chief who looked at us and shook his head as if we were naughty children. When he stopped talking, the translator said, 'The chief says "you are human beings. I can see that. God has chosen to make you without a proper skin. I do not question why. I accept. We brought you inside and slept you and fed you because you are humans. You cannot pay us. We did not make you human. God did that. You are traveling in a strange land. What less could we do? If I came to your land, and was outside, you would have to do the same for me. Could I pay you? No. For you did not make me. God did that.' "

A man with a mouthful of coffee sputtered, "Can't you just imagine the old codger caught in a revolving door in New York expecting somebody to help him because God made him?"

There was a round of self-conscious laughter.

An English woman stood, dropped her napkin and spoke in a low voice. "Even if that story is true you should never tell it again. You and your husband sound like ungrateful clods, and the African has the grace of Saint Augustine. I must say that I don't pity you. I don't pity Africa. I pity Europe. What poor representatives she has sent abroad. I am here to give three seminars. I must say I'll be relieved to go. You are an embarrassment."

The woman left and there was more soft embarrassed laughter. I sat watching the little group, wondering and curious to see what they would do and even more interested to learn what I would do.

"Well, must be going."

"I, too. See you at seven?"

"Of course."

"Ciao."

"Ta."

And they were gone. I looked at the steward, but his face had no more expression than a black billiard ball. I gathered my belongings and left the Common Room walking in an air of pleasant pride. I had not let my heart be troubled, I had not spoken idiotically, and I was overjoyed that the English woman whom I had seen only once had stood up and talked back. It was sad that she was leaving, and I wouldn't have the chance to know her.

On an early morning the small figure of a woman stood in my office door. I was used to being at the institute long before other faculty members, so I supposed the figure to be a student, but as I neared I recognized Grace Nuamah.

Her smile was white and wide and a wonderful morning treat. "Sister Maya, welcome. Sister Maya, I came early to ask you to come to lunch with me today." It wasn't yet eight o'clock. "I wanted to ask you before you made other plans. A special friend of mine is preparing food. And Sister, there will be no fish."

Grace and I left Legon under the blistering midday sun.

"Sister, I am still thanking you. We're going to Ring Road and then over to Asylum Down."

I asked whose house we were visiting. Her smile was sassy. She said, "Someone who knows how much I am in your debt. Just you wait and see."

After we reached Accra, the drive was short. Following her directions, I stopped the car in front of a large impressive house surrounded by palms and a beautifully kept flower garden. Grace laughed with happy anticipation.

"Just you wait, Sister Maya."

Her expectation was contagious, and I became excited. The door was closed, which was unusual in Ghana, and meant that the house was air conditioned.

A servant greeted us. Seeing Grace, he grinned, "Ooo, Auntie, welcome." He spoke Ashanti, so I assumed our hosts were also from the north. In the foyer, I was introduced and the servant nodded solemnly to me, but gave his smile back to Grace.

"He is expecting you, Auntie Grace. Please come and sit; I will bring beer."

We followed him into the richest living room I had seen in Ghana.

Over-stuffed sofas were discreetly placed on Oriental rugs. Ornate sconces hung on walls covered with flocked paper. Crystal and silver sat on highly polished tables and recorded music issued softly into the room.

When Grace and I were alone, I asked, "Who are these folks?" Grace, still grinning, said, "Just you wait."

We were sipping beer from German steins when a side door opened and a slim man of medium height wearing a suit, shirt and tie entered the room. He moved like a dancer and spoke in a rich baritone voice.

"Oh, little Grace. So you have come. What honor you bring to my humble house."

He took Grace's hands and drew her up from the sofa. She purred like a stroked kitten. He said, "You have stayed away entirely too long. If our relationship is in jeopardy, the crime must be on your head and it is you who will pay."

He was laying it on and Grace was loving it, twisting her short body from side to side, taking one hand then the other from his grasp to put over her mouth as she smiled coquettishly. Their chatter and gestures came to an abrupt stop and Grace said, "Brother, I have brought my friend." They both turned to look at me, and I knew at once that I had been a spectator at a ritual which had been choreographed for my enjoyment.

"Sister Maya, this is my dear friend Abatanu." Now the man smiled for me. His teeth were white as if they had just been painted.

He reached for my hands and I stood.

"Miss Angelou, you have made a great impression on Grace, and she is not easily impressed. Welcome."

He held my hands a moment too long, and looked just a little too deeply into my eyes. I decided in those first moments that I didn't like his type. His suaveness was too practiced and his sophistication too professional. When he led the conversation to my background, my family, and where I lived in the States, Grace became silent, allowing us to get acquainted. Although I knew how to equivocate and to flirt by oblique responses, the man's manner so put me off that I answered politely, but directly. Only a charlatan or a fool will ignore rejection, and Mr. Abatanu was neither.

When we sat down to lunch, he spoke only to Grace, and although she repeatedly tried to include me in their conversation, he would have none of it. Grace saw her match-making intentions foiled by our mutual lack of interest, and tried every gambit to sow interest between me and my host, but at last admitting failure, we finished the meal amid awkward silences.

My departure was plain. I shook hands with Abatanu and he soberly accepted my thanks for lunch. Grace said she'd join me in the car, so I went outside and didn't have long to wait.

"Sister." Hurt and reprimand vied for prominence in her voice. "Sister," she shook her head, "Oh, Sister, and I was trying to thank you. He is a fine man, educated man, rich man, and he loves women, oh."

"Grace, I was glad to meet him, so I thank you."

"No, Sister, you didn't like him and when he saw that, he stopped liking you."

"Sister Grace, he never started liking me."

"I told you I would thank you, and you probably thought I forgot, but I have been talking to Abatanu for weeks about you, and when finally I had everything arranged you didn't like him. Oh, pity, Sister. Pity."

It was hot. I was driving and more than a little irritated that I had spent an entire afternoon bored. I said, "Sister Grace, not to be rude, but if he is so fine, why don't you have him?"

My question surprised her and drove the frown from her face. She laughed and put her hand lightly on her breast.

"Me? Me? Oh no! When you have a big beautiful gold nugget, you don't melt it down to play with it. You might lose it. A wise person puts the nugget in a strong box and saves it for an important occasion. Sister Maya, I've been saving him a long time, and I was giving him to you."

She stayed quiet for a while as I drove through heavy afternoon traffic, then she gave a great sigh and asked the breeze, "And what about him? Oh, what does he think?"

Years before I memorized a George Eliot quote, "I never feel sorry for conceited people, supposing they carry their comfort around with them." Abatanu had enough comfort to cushion him from a drop higher than the one I furnished for him. I said nothing. Grace sighed again and said, "An African woman would have appreciated the gift and accepted it."

I hadn't been expecting her to give me a teddy bear or a talking doll. I gave my attention to the highway, hurrying back to Legon. When we stopped, I got out and took Grace's hand. "Sister, I truly appreciate your thinking so kindly of me, and I'm grateful for your generosity."

Grace would not or could not surrender her distress.

"Sister, I knew Americans were different, but. . . ." She shook her head, patted my shoulder, and I stroked her arm. We stood looking at each other with nothing more to say.

Sheikhali was late again. I had been dressed and waiting for two hours. His tardiness had become so frequent that even as I prepared for a rendezvous I did so slowly, knowing there would be no need to rush.

Our date was for seven. At nine-thirty I got into my car and drove to the Star Hotel.

The head waiter took me to a pleasant table for two, overlooking the dance floor. Hurt pride rather than hunger or my wallet made me order a bottle of wine and a three-course dinner. I had nearly finished choking down the unwanted food when Sheikhali arrived.

He wore a flowing white robe and red tasseled fez. He was followed by the small Mamali who wore a matching outfit. They strode to my table. Sheikhali called for another chair and the two men sat down.

"Maya. I went to your house. It was dark. Even the servants refused to answer." I decided not to tell him that both Otu and Kojo were away.

"I went to the Continental Hotel, the Lido, L'auberge. Am I a man to chase a woman? Look at me." Anger had furrowed his face and tightened his throat. "My French is not good enough. I have brought Mamali to speak for me."

For the first time Mamali spoke, "Good evening, Sister. Sheikhali has asked me to translate for him. He will speak Fufulde. I will translate into French."

Mamali spoke with warmth, but his posture and words were formal. Sheikhali leaned back in his chair and looked at Mamali.

"Bon?"

Mamali nodded, the big man coughed and began. His language was melodic and his voice soft. He stopped.

Mamali said, "I have walked thousands of miles through forest storms, and I know under which tree to stand when the rains fall; a certain tree can change the mind of the winds. I know."

Mamali stopped so that Sheikhali could resume. He spoke for a long time. When his voice fell, the attentive Mamali spoke again.

"I know the desert. I find my way through sand that burns and sun that bites, and I am never lost. I look at a cow. I feed a horse. I know them. I look at the moon and read the weather. You know books. Me, I know life. I have never been into one school. Not one. You read. I can write my name. So you know schools, but I know man, woman, cow, horse, desert, jungle, sun and moon. Who is smart, you or me?"

I said nothing.

Sheikhali turned and spoke to me directly. "I will marry you, for you are a good woman. In Mali the women will teach you to be better. If you are intelligent enough, you will learn enough. Because of me, you will be respected. But you must lose this White woman way of..." He said a word to Mamali, who translated. "Impatience." Sheikhali continued, "Your father will come from America and we will talk." For a second I tried to imagine Bailey Johnson, Sr., who was at least as proud as Sheikhali and as stiff as a penguin, leaving his perfectly furnished home in San Diego, California, to come to Africa, which he thought was populated by savages. It was impossible to picture my fastidious father even considering a prospective son-in-law who had grown up sleeping on the ground, surrounded by cattle.

I said, "I can't marry you. I can't go to Mali. Thank you, but...I can't."

He turned quickly to Mamali and spoke in Fufulde. Mamali dropped his eyes. When he spoke it was with regret.

"If you say no again, I will stop trying. I am a man, not a boy to be played with. This last time, will you...?"

"No. I cannot."

Sheikhali stood a mile above my head and smiled. His even teeth glistened.

"You are still a good woman, but you are not so intelligent. You are a functionaire. Only a functionaire." He spat out the words, turned and followed by Mamali, left the restaurant.

In French the word for civil servant did not sound as lifeless as in English.

Each morning Ghana's seven-and-one-half million people seemed to crowd at once into the capital city where the broad avenues as well as the unpaved rutted lanes became gorgeous with moving pageantry: bicycles, battered lorries, hand carts, American and European cars, chauffeur-driven limousines. People on foot struggled for right-of-way, white-collar workers wearing white knee-high socks brushed against market women balancing large baskets on their heads as they proudly swung their wide hips. Children, bright faces shining with palm oil, picked openings in the throng, and pretty young women in western clothes affected not to notice the attention they caused as they laughed together talking in the musical Twi language. Old men sat or stooped beside the road smoking home-made pipes and looking wise as old men have done eternally.

The too sweet aromas of flowers, the odors of freshly fried fish and stench from open sewers hung in my clothes and lay on my skin. Car horns blew, drums thumped. Loud radio music and the muddle of many languages shouted or murmured. I needed country quiet.

The Fiat was dependable, and I had a long weekend, money in my purse, and a working command of Fanti, so I decided to travel into the bush. I bought roasted plaintain stuffed with boiled peanuts, a quart of Club beer and headed my little car west. The stretch was a highway from Accra to Cape Coast, filled with trucks and private cars passing from lane to lane with abandon. People hung out of windows of the crowded mammie lorries, and I could hear singing and shouting when the drivers careened those antique vehicles up and down hills as if each was a little train out to prove it could.

I stopped in Cape Coast only for gas. Although many Black Americans had headed for the town as soon as they touched ground in Ghana, I successfully avoided it for a year. Cape Coast Castle and the nearby Elmina Castle had been holding forts for captured slaves. The captives had been imprisoned in dungeons beneath the massive buildings and friends of mine who had felt called upon to make the trek reported that they felt the thick stone walls still echoed with old cries.

The palm tree–lined streets and fine white stone buildings did not tempt me to remain any longer than necessary. Once out of the town and again onto the tarred roads, I knew I had not made a clean escape. Despite my hurry, history had invaded my little car. Pangs of self-pity and a sorrow for my unknown relatives suffused me. Tears made the highway waver, and were salty on my tongue.

What did they think and feel, my grandfathers, caught on those green Savannahs, under the baobab trees? How long did their families search for them? Did the dungeon wall feel chilly and its slickness strange to my grandmothers who were used to the rush of air against bamboo huts and the sound of birds rattling their grass roofs?

I had to pull off the road. Just passing near Cape Coast Castle had plunged me back into the eternal melodrama.

There would be no purging, I knew, unless I asked all the questions. Only then would the spirits understand that I was feeding them. It was a crumb, but it was all I had.

I allowed the shapes to come to my imagination: children passed tied together by ropes and chains, tears abashed, stumbling in dull exhaustion, then women, hair uncombed, bodies gritted with sand, and sagging in defeat. Men, muscles without memory, minds dimmed, plodding, leaving bloodied footprints in the dirt. The quiet was awful. None of them cried, or yelled, or bellowed. No moans came from them. They lived in a mute territory, dead to feeling and protest. These were the legions, sold by sisters, stolen by brothers, bought by strangers, enslaved by the greedy and betrayed by history.

For a long time, I sat as in an open-air auditorium watching a troop of tragic players enter and exit the stage.

The visions faded as my tears ceased. Light returned and I started the car, turned off the main road, and headed for the interior. Using rutted track roads, and lanes a little larger than foot paths, I found the River Pra. The black water moving quietly, ringed with the tall trees, seemed enchanted. A fear of snakes kept me in the car, but I parked and watched the bright sun turn the water surface into a rippling cloth of lamé. I passed through villages which were little more than collections of thatch huts with goats and small children wandering in the lanes. The noise of my car brought smiling adults out to wave at me.

In the late afternoon, I reached the thriving town that was my destination. A student whom I had met at Legon had spoken to me often of the gold-mining area, of Dunkwa, his birthplace. His reports had so glowed with the town's virtues, and I had chosen that spot for my first journey.

My skin color, features and the Ghana cloth I wore made me look like any young Ghanaian woman. I could pass if I didn't talk too much.

As usual, in the towns of Ghana, the streets were filled with vendors selling their wares of tinned pat milk, hot spicy Killi Willis (fried, ripe plaintain chips), Pond's Cold Cream and anti-mosquito incense rings. Farmers were returning home, children returning from school. Young boys grinned at mincing girls and always there were the market women, huge and impervious. I searched for a hotel sign in vain and as the day lengthened, I started to worry. I didn't have enough gas to get to Koforidua, a large town northeast of Dunkwa, where there would certainly be hotels, and I didn't have the address of my student's family. I parked the car a little out of the town center and stopped a woman carrying a bucket of water on her head and a baby on her back.

"Good day." I spoke in Fanti, and she responded. I continued, "I beg you, I am a stranger looking for a place to stay."

She repeated, "Stranger?" and laughed. "You are a stranger? No. No."

To many Africans only Whites could be strangers. All Africans belonged somewhere, to some clan. All Akan-speaking people belong to one of eight blood lines (Abosua) and one of eight spirit lines (Ntoro).

I said, "I am not from here."

For a second fear darted in her eyes. There was the possibility that I was a witch or some unhappy ghost from the country of the dead. I quickly said, "I am from Accra." She gave me a good smile. "Oh, one Accra. Without a home." She laughed. The Fanti word *Nkran*, for which the capitol was named, means the large ant that builds ten-foot-high domes of red clay and lives with millions of other ants.

"Come with me." She turned quickly, steadying the bucket on her head and led me between two corrugated tin shacks. The baby bounced and slept on her back, secured by the large piece of cloth wrapped around her body. We passed a compound where women were pounding the dinner foo foo in wooden bowls.

The woman shouted, "Look what I have found. One Nkran has no place to sleep tonight." The women laughed and asked, "One Nkran? I don't believe it."

"Are you taking it to the old man?"

"Of course."

"Sleep well, alone, Nkran, if you can." My guide stopped before a small house. She put the water on the ground and told me to wait while she entered the house. She returned immediately followed by a man who rubbed his eyes as if he had just been awakened.

He walked close and peered hard at my face. "This is the Nkran?" The woman was adjusting the bucket on her head.

"Yes, Uncle. I have brought her." She looked at me, "Good-bye,

Nkran. Sleep in peace. Uncle, I am going." The man said, "Go and come, child," and resumed studying my face. "You are not Ga." He was reading my features.

A few small children had collected around his knees. They could barely hold back their giggles as he interrogated me.

"Aflao?"

I said, "No."

"Brong-ahafo?"

I said, "No. I am——." I meant to tell him the truth, but he said, "Don't tell me. I will soon know." He continued staring at me. "Speak more. I will know from your Fanti."

"Well, I have come from Accra and I need to rent a room for the night. I told that woman that I was a stranger..."

He laughed. "And you are. Now, I know. You are Bambara from Liberia. It is clear you are Bambara." He laughed again. "I always can tell. I am not easily fooled." He shook my hand. "Yes, we will find you a place for the night. Come." He touched a boy at his right. "Find Patience Aduah, and bring her to me."

The children laughed and all ran away as the man led me into the house. He pointed me to a seat in the neat little parlor and shouted, "Foriwa, we have a guest. Bring beer." A small Black woman with an imperial air entered the room. Her knowing face told me that she had witnessed the scene in her front yard.

She spoke to her husband. "And, Kobina, did you find who the stranger was?" She walked to me. I stood and shook her hand. "Welcome, stranger." We both laughed. "Now don't tell me, Kobina, I have ears, also. Sit down, Sister, beer is coming. Let me hear you speak."

We sat facing each other while her husband stood over us smiling. "You, Foriwa, you will never get it."

I told her my story, adding a few more words I had recently learned. She laughed grandly. "She is Bambara. I could have told you when Abaa first brought her. See how tall she is? See her head? See her color? Men, huh. They only look at a woman's shape."

Two children brought beer and glasses to the man who poured and handed the glasses around. "Sister, I am Kobina Artey; this is my wife Foriwa and some of my children."

I introduced myself, but because they had taken such relish in detecting my tribal origin I couldn't tell them that they were wrong. Or, less admirably, at that moment I didn't want to remember that I was an American. For the first time since my arrival, I was very nearly home. Not a Ghanaian, but at least accepted as an African. The sensation was worth a lie.

Voices came to the house from the yard.

"Brother Kobina," "Uncle," "Auntie."

Foriwa opened the door to a group of people who entered speaking fast and looking at me.

"So this is the Bambara woman? The stranger?" They looked me over and talked with my hosts. I understood some of their conversation. They said that I was nice looking and old enough to have a little wisdom. They announced that my car was parked a few blocks away. Kobina told them that I would spend the night with the newlyweds, Patience and Kwame Duodu. Yes, they could see clearly that I was a Bambara.

"Give us the keys to your car, Sister; someone will bring your bag."

I gave up the keys and all resistance. I was either at home with friends, or I would die wishing that to be so.

Later, Patience, her husband, Kwame, and I sat out in the yard around a cooking fire near to their thatched house which was much smaller than the Artey bungalow. They explained that Kobina Artey was not a chief, but a member of the village council, and all small matters in that area of Dunkwa were taken to him. As Patience stirred the stew in the pot, which was balanced over the fire, children and women appeared sporadically out of the darkness carrying covered plates. Each time Patience thanked the bearers and directed them to the house, I felt the distance narrow between my past and present.

In the United States, during segregation, Black American travelers, unable to stay in hotels restricted to White patrons, stopped at churches and told the Black ministers or deacons of their predicaments. Church officials would select a home and then inform the unexpecting hosts of the decision. There was never a protest, but the new hosts relied on the generosity of their neighbors to help feed and even entertain their guests. After the travelers were settled, surreptitious knocks would sound on the back door.

In Stamps, Arkansas, I heard so often, "Sister Henderson, I know you've got guests. Here's a pan of biscuits."

"Sister Henderson, Mama sent a half a cake for your visitors."

"Sister Henderson, I made a lot of macaroni and cheese. Maybe this will help with your visitors."

My grandmother would whisper her thanks and finally when the family and guests sat down at the table, the offerings were so different and plentiful it appeared that days had been spent preparing the meal.

Patience invited me inside, and when I saw the table I was confirmed in my earlier impression. Ground nut stew, garden egg stew, hot pepper soup, kenke, kotomre, fried plantain, dukuno, shrimp, fish cakes, and more, all crowded together on variously patterned plates.

In Arkansas, the guests would never suggest, although they knew better, that the host had not prepared every scrap of food, especially for them.

I said to Patience, "Oh, Sister, you went to such trouble."

She laughed, "It is nothing, Sister. We don't want our Bambara relative to think herself a stranger anymore. Come, let us wash and eat."

After dinner I followed Patience to the outdoor toilet, then they gave me a cot in a very small room.

In the morning I wrapped my cloth under my arms, sarong fashion, and walked with Patience to the bath house. We joined about twenty women in a walled enclosure that had no ceiling. The greetings were loud and cheerful as we soaped ourselves and poured buckets of water over our shoulders.

Patience introduced me. "This is our Bambara sister."

"She's a tall one all right. Welcome, Sister."

"I like her color."

"How many children, Sister?" The woman was looking at my breasts.

I apologized, "I only have one."

"One?"

"One?"

"One!" Shouts reverberated over the splashing water. I said, "One, but I'm trying."

They laughed. "Try hard, sister. Keep trying."

We ate leftovers from the last night feast and I said a sad good-bye to my hosts. The children walked me back to my car with the oldest boy carrying my bag. I couldn't offer money to my hosts, Arkansas had taught me that, but I gave change to the children. They bobbed and jumped and grinned.

"Good-bye, Bambara Auntie."

"Go and come, Auntie."

"Go and come."

I drove into Cape Coast before I thought of the gruesome castle and out of its environs before the ghosts of slavery caught me. Perhaps their attempts had been halfhearted. After all, in Dunkwa, although I let a lie speak for me, I had proved that one of their descendants, at least one, could just briefly return to Africa, and that despite cruel betrayals, bitter ocean voyages and hurtful centuries, we were still recognizable.

The worthy Otu dropped his customary aplomb and rushed nimbly into the kitchen.

He whispered, "Madame, Nana's driver is here. Madame, I didn't know you knew Nana. His driver has come to get you. He is waiting in the car. It's Nana's Mercedes outside."

He was shaken by excitement and awe and the dual assault made him accusatory.

He peered discourteously into my face, "Madame," [the friendly title "Auntie" was forgotten] "do you know the Nana?"

"Yes." I gave him the answer dryly, shielding my own surprise.

One evening, months before, I had met the chief at Efua's house and had spoken to him about Guy's entrance into the university.

Although Conor Cruise O'Brien was then head of the University of Ghana, Nana Nketsia had been the first African Vice Chancellor, stepping down for O'Brien at his own decision.

The Ghanaian academic system, following its British model, accepted students who had completed a Sixth Form, which was equal to an American two-year junior college course. Guy had only completed high school, but I explained to the Nana that at home he would be qualified to enter our best institutions. My argument, assisted by the pathos of a mother appealing for a sick and hospitalized son, won the day.

Weeks later I was informed that Guy would be accepted if he passed an entrance examination. I had not seen the Nana since that first meeting, but I had heard much about him. He was an Ahanta Paramount Chief who, in ancient times, would have had absolute power. The modern Nana was fiercely political. He had been the first Ghanaian chief to be arrested for resisting British colonialism and had been educated in Britain, coming down from Oxford with double firsts, equal to the American summa cum laude. He was an adviser to President Nkrumah and Ambassador Plenipotentiary. Along with those staggering credits, Nana was handsome.

If Otu was shocked by the unheralded appearance of the Chief's driver, I was stunned.

I waged a small war in my closet, selecting and rejecting what was to be worn to a chief's house. As I walked outside, Otu, who had become a stranger, stood at sharp attention, his arms at his side, his eyes down.

"Good evening, Madame." As if I didn't have sufficient nervousness, he transferred his tension to me, and I barely greeted the driver who held the car door open.

The drive was too short to clear my mind. I had never been face to face with royalty and didn't know the protocol. I suspected that I had been sent for to discuss some incident pertaining to the presence of Black American residents, and I was nervous. I knew I was given to dramatic overstatement, or was known to waffle about repetitiously. To further complicate matters, I was sincere. Sincerity badly stated elicits mistrust.

The driver stopped before a mansion, which in the dark, surrounded by even darker trees, appeared ominous. Light came from a few windows, and the small fires of servants were visible in the compound beyond the house. Muffled drums could be heard from a distant hill. I noticed only a few cars parked along the street when I got out of the car. I asked the driver if the Nana was giving a party.

He shook his head and gave me an impish smile. "Auntie, I do not hear your language."

The driver opened the front door for me and I walked into a woodland fantasy.

The large living room was furnished with rich sofas, burl tables and was interrupted by a wide-branched tree that grew up through the ceiling. African mats were thrown on the tiled floor, and in a distant corner two men sat talking under lamp light.

The chauffeur disappeared after he ushered me through the door, and the men seemed to take no notice of me. I stood unsure in the shadows and struggled with a decision. What was the proper way to address a chief, and more hazardous, what would he think of me if I violated some unknown but sacred taboo?

In Egypt I had seen well-dressed and urbane diplomats prostrate themselves before a visiting Hausa chief, and I had read that the Akan chiefs were believed to be the living embodiment of all the Fantis and Ashantis who had ever lived; therefore, their leaders' physical bodies were sacred.

Admittedly, my ancestors had come from Africa, but I was my own person from St. Louis, Arkansas and California, a member of a group which had successfully held a large and hostile nation at bay. Anyway, I had been minding my own business in my own house. I hadn't asked to come to pay homage to anybody.

I walked past the tree over the slippery mats and into the light.

"Nana? I am Maya Angelou. You sent for me?"

Both men looked up and their smiles were quick. They had been aware of my entrance and of my hesitation all along.

"Miss Angelou. Welcome to my home. Please meet Mr. Kwesi Brew." The chief wore a white Northern Territory smock. His black skin, white teeth and red tongue made for an unutterable drama.

Kwesi Brew rose and shook my hand. I had read his lyrical poetry and knew that he was Minister of Protocol in charge of State formalities, so I was not prepared for his boyishness.

"Sister, so I am getting to meet the very famous Maya Angelou. Too many people in the country say good things of you. Can you be that good?"

"Mr. Brew, I am happy. It is always a pleasure to meet a poet."

He was caught off-guard, but recovered in an instant. "Oh, Miss Angelou, you don't mean you have wasted time reading my sad little efforts?"

"Mr. Brew, I am certain that your poem, 'If this is the time to conquer my heart, do so now,' is neither little nor is it sad."

A delighted laugh popped out of his mouth. "Oh, oh, Nana. This one! This lady. But she's quick, oh!"

Nana nodded, smiling, "Kwesi, sit. Maya. May I call you Maya?" I nodded.

"Maya, sit. Welcome to the Ahenfie. That means the house of the Nana, and what will you have to drink?"

I said I had no preference, and he shook his head. "A woman like you should always have a preference." I thought of my grandmother. If I responded to a question of choice by saying, "I don't care," she would give me a look identical to the one I had just seen on Nana's face. Then she would warn me that "Don't care ain't got no home."

I told Nana, "I'll have gin and ginger." He said, "You can have schnapps. Schnapps is the proper drink for serious conversation." Immediately I drew up, stiffened my spine. "I'm sorry, I don't drink schnapps. If you don't have gin and ginger, I will have water."

Kwesi laughed, "Oh, Nana, I had better be your Ocheame." He turned to me still smiling, but with a formal air. "Sister, anything you want to say to the Nana, say it to me. I will be your correspondent. Speak only to me." He had the posture and only needed the livery to be taken for the chief's spokesman.

"Please, Ocheame, I would like to have a schnapps. It is good for me." Nana smiled, acknowledging my tact, and called for drinks.

I had never heard such a voice. In ordinary conversation it had been deep and mellifluous, but raised to a shout, it rattled and clattered and clanged like a cowbell played by a madman.

"Kwame, take whiskey and bring it." He shouted, or yelled in Fanti, and I imagined that every mote of dust in the room quivered into action. I must have jumped because Kwesi put his hand on my arm and grinned. "My chief's got some voice, huh?"

When drinks were placed before us, Nana poured a libation on the tiles and said a prayer to the old ones. It was done as perfunctorily as grace is said at an informal family table. He drank first then in an ordinary voice he said, "Maya, we have been talking about the Afro-Americans. Osagefo knows America. He said that in the United States he was not an African from the Gold Coast. Whites only saw the color of his skin and treated him like a nigger."

Kwesi added, "Aggrey of Africa also lived in the United States for a while. You know who he was, don't you, Sister?"

Nana intruded, "Dr. Kwegyr Aggrey from Ghana earned a doctorate from Columbia University and taught in North Carolina. He understood racism and he loved his Black skin. He said, 'If I died and went to heaven and God asked me would I like to be sent back to earth as a White man' "—Nana's voice was thundering again—" 'I would say no, make me as Black as you can and send me back.' " The klaxon trumpeted. "Aggrey of Africa said, 'Make me completely Black, BLACK, BLACK.' "

That was the spectacular language, the passion of self-appreciation. I had traveled to Africa to hear it, and hear in an African voice, and in such a splendor of sound.

The gold chain on the chief's black chest was cruelly bright. "Aggrey speaks for me. Aggrey speaks for Africa. We are Black, BLACK! And we give no explanation, no apology."

The warmth flowed through me and I had to hold on, close my teeth, contract my muscles or I would have become an embarrassing quiver of gratitude.

Kwesi Brew lifted his glass. "I propose a toast, Nana. A toast." He bounded up and I quickly stood to clink his glass. I expected Nana to join us, but the chief remained seated, although he held his glass aloft.

Kwesi said, "To the African Personality." I gestured with my glass and repeated, "To the African Personality." Nana roared, "To the African Personality," and we drank.

I realized that I had not seen the tribal leader on his feet since my arrival. His bare muscled arms were robust and his skin was as smooth as black flannel, but maybe he was ill.

Kwesi saw my concern and shook his head, "Sister, Nana does not stand. In our tradition everyone stands for the Nana, but the Nana, spiritual and moral leader of Ahanta people, stands for no one. It would mean that all the Ahantas are standing and no one is great enough to command such tribute, you understand? Na Na. Ena ena. Mother of his people, father of his country."

The chief busied himself during that explanatory speech. He twisted the knobs on the radio at his side and sipped from his glass of schnapps.

"But Sister"—Kwesi poured drinks for the two of us—"We, you and I, are lowly mortals, not saints like our chief."

Nana roared a cautionary "Kwesi," and Kwesi laughed. "Nana, you are my chief, and if I make a mistake I am certain you will overlook it." Nana smiled and beckoned Kwesi to sit down again.

He spoke in a moderate voice, "You are my poet, and maybe Ocheame, but you are not my jester. Sit, now and let me talk more to this lady."

Kwesi and I sat obediently upon the sofas like scolded children.

"Efua speaks of you as a sister. T. D. Bafoo, our enfant terrible, claims you are his relative. Even Kofi Batcha and others supported your membership in the Ghana Press Club. Julian Mayfield was the only Black American there until you came."

Nana listed each commendation as if he were reading from a plaque soon to be presented to me.

He continued, "It is known that your salary at the University is less than any amount paid to a non-Ghanaian. It is also known that your son studies at Legon and that you receive no financial assistance for his education."

His monologue was leading toward a sweet haven of help. I knew now why I had been sent for. The Chief and the Chief of Protocol were about to announce that I had been allotted a fabulous raise. A smile slipped out of my control, but Nana was not watching me, and Kwesi, who had not taken his gaze from my face, smiled back. "You are a mother and we love our mothers." Nana had reached a rhythm reminiscent of preachers in Southern Black churches. There would be no turning back.

"Africa is herself a mother. The mother of mankind. We Africans take motherhood as the most sacred condition human beings can achieve. Camara Laye, our brother, has said, 'The Mother is there to protect you. She is buried in Africa and Africa is buried in her. That is why she is supreme.' "

Kwesi was accompanying Nana with his voice, "Ka, Nana, Ka, Nana, Ka, Nana."

I had been forgotten for the while as the men performed a concert of sound, passion and music. Years of discomfort on the hard seats of the Christian Methodist Church in Arkansas had given me the talent to appear attentive while my real thoughts were focused in the distance.

What was I going to do with the money? Would I pay off the car or Guy's tuition or buy gold? I decided that if the university had displayed such patience so far, it could wait a little longer for Guy's tuition and my car payment, and I would have a gold necklace. I would have a necklace made of gold the color of sunrise and it would make my brown skin voluptuous, and I would at last buy a small piece of Kente cloth, red, gold and blue. I would ask the seamstress to make me a skirt so tight that it would mould my behind into a single roundness, and I would have to take mincing and coquettish steps.

Nana's sermon on the saintliness of Motherhood was falling, the tempo had slowed, Kwesi's encouragements had ceased. When Nana stopped talking there was a moment of respectful quiet.

I said, "Nana, I appreciate hearing that Africans cherish their mothers. It confirms my belief that in America we have retained more Africanisms than we know. For also among Black Americans Motherhood is sacred. We have strong mothers and we love them dearly."

Kwesi put his glass down. "Sister, I do not wish to contradict you, but isn't it true that the most common curse word among Americans imputes that the offender is the offspring of a female dog?"

What would he have said had he wanted to contradict me?

I said, "Brother, I was speaking not of Americans but Black Americans. We're not the same; we're more like you, if you haven't noticed."

Nana laughed, "She's got you, Kwesi." Kwesi kept his diplomatic smile and plunged directly to my heart.

"But, Sister, isn't it true that Black Americans and Black Americans alone, of all the people in the world, created a curse word which suggests that the accursed has known his own mother? Known her, that is, in a biblical sense?"

My rapier brain parried, "Yeah, yes, well, not really. I mean, I don't know.... Possibly in some other language..." I was falling and Nana became my net. He said, "Kwesi, you know that the oppressed person, if convinced that he is worthless, looks to strike the person dearest to him. Oscar Wilde reminded us that we always hurt the thing we love. So it is human all over the world." He laughed, "Even in Harlem. Maybe especially Harlem. That is why we must do something special for our people in the diaspora. You in America have labored long and done well. Look at your schools, Fisk, Tuskegee, Atlanta University. You were slaves and now you head universities. Horace Mann Bond and St. Clair Drake are friends of mine." I had been ready to leave. After Kwesi spoke of the vulgarity heard so frequently in our neighborhoods, I was prepared to disappear in shame, but the mention of our schools and scholars was redemptive.

I smiled, "Oh yes, not all Blacks hate themselves."

Nana said, "We are well aware of that" (He often used the royal "we") "and now ... I asked you here to see if you are interested in a job in Kaneshie."

So I wasn't being offered a raise. All that daydreaming about gold had been a waste of time.

I said, "Kaneshie? That sounds lovely." It was horrible. Kaneshie was a bush town, 150 miles from Accra.

I continued, "But I am quite happy at Legon, and I think I am of use there. Kaneshie? They say it's beautiful country up there, but—"

Nana interrupted, "This job pays double your present salary and you will be provided with a bungalow and a new car."

Kwesi said, "Now that's looking after our people in the diaspora."

A move was not necessarily a negative thing. A house of my own in the heavily wooded area up north could be quite inviting, and with a new car I could drive to Accra in a few hours, and I could still buy that red-gold necklace and even a full kente cloth.

Kingdoms may fall and love may leave, but a dogged survival instinct is loyal to the end. I had never been promised nor (despite my secret hopes) did I expect certainty. I knew that God was in His heaven and anything might happen to His world. Kaneshie was the center of the diamond industry, and as I thought about it, it began to increase in promise. Rumors had it that people walking around might stumble upon diamonds laying in the road. I had not been a particularly lucky person, but just possibly I would find a lovely diamond to go with my gold necklace.

I said, "Nana, the idea interests me. What would be my duties?"

He answered, "You would do much as you are currently doing. Run the office. You can type of course?" He didn't wait so I didn't have time to lie. "And, I suppose, familiarize yourself with the working of a mine. Know the laborers, the output, the World Bank prices. This sort of thing. I'm sure you could do that."

I had always liked the idea of being someone's girl Friday. It promised responsibility with good pay and was a sort of marriage without sex.

"I'd be pleased to give it a try, and thanks to the person who mentioned me for the job."

Kwesi looked at me and wagged his head forward, then smiled and said, "Nana, I believe we have had a most fruitful meeting. Maya will do well in Kaneshie. It might be a little lonely at first, but your people will be coming up to see you and you will make friends. Now, Sister, do tell me how did you come to read my poetry?"

Nana said, "Kwesi, one minute. Poets are worse than prime ministers, always looking for ears. Maya, I'm going to send for my children. They should meet you."

Kwesi laughed, "Of course. The Budu-Arthur tribe. They are wonderful, and they are many."

Nana lifted his voice and hurled it into the universe.

"Children, come. Araba, Adae, Abenaa, Abaa, Ekua and Kwesi Budu-Arthur. Come, come and greet your American Auntie."

The clarion voice, enunciating the names with such force, prepared me for a schoolroom of children arriving in martial drill. Instead, a tall, slim, beautiful girl of fifteen entered the lighted area.

"Poppa, you wanted me?" Her voice lovely and musical.

Nana said, "Araba, yes, I want you and the others. Miss Angelou, this is my oldest child. Araba Budu-Arthur, Miss Angelou."

As he spoke, more children drifted in, talking among themselves. When five of them had gathered, Nana looked up and asked, "And Adae? As usual I must ask. And Adae?"

Four young voices answered him, but no meaning could be extracted from the din. When the noise reached a peak, another girl entered to stand with her siblings. Adae was nearly as tall as Araba, but while her older sister displayed a solemn dignity, Adae seemed to move even standing still. The children stood together like an often rehearsed theatrical troupe, their eyes focused on me.

I said, "I'm pleased to meet you all." Adae turned to her siblings and said knowingly, "That's the way American Negroes speak. They say 'you all.' " She faced me again, while her brothers and small sisters examined me with obvious curiosity.

Adae said, "I'm pleased to meet you, Maya. Very pleased."

Keeping my voice low, I said, "As you have noticed, I am an American Negro, and among my people children do not call their elders by their first names. A fifteen-year-old girl [Adae was 15] would call me Mrs. Angelou, or if she liked me and I agreed she would address me as Auntie Maya. I will accept either." Adae looked at her older sister then at the young children. She looked at me for a very long minute.

"Very well, I don't know you yet, but I'll probably like you, so we will call you Auntie Maya. Do you agree?" She left me no time to respond. She nodded and said, "Good-bye, Auntie Maya. Good-bye, everybody." The four smaller children, as if on a signal, chorused, "Hello and good-bye, Auntie. Good-bye, everybody," and running, followed Adae from the room.

Nana, who had been silent during the exchange, spoke to Araba who was standing calmly before me. "And you, Araba, do you have something clever to say to Auntie Maya?" Her voice was as smooth as cream, and her smile was gentle. "Auntie, Adae knows that African children behave as you described Black American children do. She was acting the way European kids act at our school. Please overlook her, she's really a very nice person." Araba excused herself with the grace of a kindly monarch taking leave of adoring subjects. Kwesi and Nana smiled at each other.

Kwesi said to me, "That is the Budu-Arthur brood. There is no way to tell what they will become, but I'd wager Adae will be president of the world and Araba will be its queen."

Nana shook his head and laughed to himself proudly, "My children." Then he looked over at me, "I do hope Adae didn't annoy you. It is through the eyes of strangers that a parent can see their children as people."

I denied any annoyance and said I'd like to see the children alone.

He agreed, then ordered the driver in one shout and modulated to continue speaking to me. "You will hear from me when an appointment is arranged." He offered me his hand, and I was tempted to kiss it, but checked myself just in time. I grasped his hand and shook it firmly.

"Thank you, Nana."

"Don't thank me, but when you go to Kaneshie let them know that your heart and head are concentrated on Africa and not, like most Americans, on Coca Cola and Cadillacs." Nana added, "And Maya, take your C.V."

The driver had come in. I asked, "C.V.?"

He said, "Curriculum vitae. Your schools, degrees and work history. Good night. Kwesi will see you to the car."

Kwesi was at my side being solicitous, the driver was standing beside the car, and I was laughing weakly. Kwesi noticed me trembling when he embraced me and probably credited my nervous response to meeting the great man.

"Sister, we must talk. You must come to me and my wife Molly. We will feed you and definitely no fish. Ha, ha."

If everyone knew my dietary restrictions, why didn't Nana know that I had not been to college? I should have said so on the spot. During the drive home, I berated myself for the show of cowardice. Obviously the temptation of a good job, large salary and European-style benefits were enough to send my much vaunted morality scurrying. It wasn't pleasant to admit that I was no more moral than the commercial bandits upon whom I heaped every crime from slavery to Hiroshima.

As soon as I reached my house, I decided that when Nana telephoned I would tell him to offer the job to Alice or Vicki. Then I pillowed myself in goodness and slept righteously.

When our grinning faces appeared at Julian's door, he tried waving his arms to distract us, but only succeeded in agitating the tell-tale odors of sage, oregano and fried pork. He had received another package of sausage from Washington, D.C. The Revolutionist Returnees had gotten wind of its arrival and converged on the Mayfield home in private cars, taxis and on foot. Julian, who was no more or less generous than the next person, put on a gruff face and said he was working and we had to leave, but when he saw we wouldn't be run off, he gave in and laughed. "Which one of you nuts was spying on the airport?"

Ana Livia brought a platter of sausage patties to the porch, and we fell upon it with a savor unrelated to hunger. Homesickness was never mentioned in our crowd. Who would dare admit a longing for a White nation so full of hate that it drove its citizens of color to madness, to death or to exile? How to confess even to one's ownself, that our eyes, historically customed to granite buildings, wide paved avenues, chromed cars, and brown, black, beige, pink and white-skinned people, often ached for those familiar sights?

We chewed the well spiced pork of America, but in fact, we were ravenously devouring Houston and Macon, Little Rock and St. Louis. Our faces eased with sweet delight as we swallowed Harlem and Chicago's south side.

"All we need now is a plate of grits." That from Lesley Lacy who had probably never eaten grits in his life.

Julian brought out a bundle of week-old dailies from the States and dealt parcels out to us as if they were large floppy cards. He saved a magazine and held it above his head. "Here's my article on Baldwin in *Freedomways.*"

Nobody Knows My Name, James Baldwin's book, had passed through so many hands its pages were as fluffy as Kleenex and had caused fierce arguments. Some detractors denounced Baldwin as a creation of White America, adding that he had been constructed by the establishment for the establishment. His supporters argued that if White America had been smart enough to make a James Baldwin, obviously there would have been no need to create one. In New York City, Sylvester Leaks had disappointed some of his fans by attacking Baldwin. We in Ghana knew that Julian had written an article in support of the controversial author.

Julian, in his most roguish tone, said, "I'll put the magazine here.

No tearing, scratching or biting, first come and all that shit." Alice moved like a whip, snatched up the magazine, which meant that she would take it home and that Vicki or I would be next in command.

Ana Livia spoke and took our total attention by announcing, "Dr. Du Bois is sick. Lucid, but very sick. He said he has stopped learning and it is time for him to go." Our small crowd made a large noise of protest. Du Bois was ninety-six years old, and frail, but we wanted him to live forever. He had no right to his desire for death. We argued that great men and women should be forced to live as long as possible. The reverence they enjoyed was a life sentence, which they could neither revoke nor modify.

When the discussion reached a noise level that prohibited all understanding, Julian said he had read about a march to Washington, D.C., to be led by Martin Luther King, Jr. The news of Dr. Du Bois' deteriorating health was driven away by an immediate buzzing of sarcastic questions.

"King leading a march. Who is he going to pray to this time, the statue of Abe Lincoln?"

"Give us our freedom again, please suh."

"King has been in jail so much he's got a liking for those iron bars and jailhouse food."

The ridicule fitted our consciousness. We were brave revolutionaries, not pussyfooting nonviolent cowards. We scorned the idea of being spat upon, kicked, and then turning our cheeks for more abuse. Of course, none of us, save Julian, had even been close to bloody violence, and not one of us had spent an hour in jail for our political beliefs.

My policy was to keep quiet when Reverend King's name was mentioned. I didn't want to remind my radical friends of my association with the peacemaker. It was difficult, but I managed to dispose of the idea that my silence was a betrayal. After all, when I worked for him, I had been deluded into agreeing with Reverend King that love would cure America of its pathological illnesses, that indeed our struggle for equal rights would redeem the country's baleful history. But all the prayers, sit-ins, sacrifices, jail sentences, humiliation, insults and jibes had not borne out Reverend King's vision. When maddened White citizens and elected political leaders vowed to die before they would see segregation come to an end, I became more resolute in rejecting nonviolence and more adamant in denying Martin Luther King.

Someone made the suggestions that although we were radicals, as Black Americans we should support our people in the States and form a march sympathetic to the Washington march. As products of a picketing, protesting era, we unanimously and immediately agreed. Of course, we would march on the American Embassy with placards and some appropriate shouts. Julian would investigate Ghana's policy on marches and secure permits if needed. Lesley would inform the Ghanaian students at the university who might like to join. Each of us excitedly chose assignments, feeling ourselves back on familiar ground. When it came to action we were in the church where we had been baptized. We knew when to moan, when to shout and when to start speaking in tongues.

Since Dr. Du Bois was too old and ill to accompany us, Julian would ask Dr. Alphaeus Hunton. Dr. Hunton was co-director with Dr. Du Bois of the Encyclopedia Africana, and would represent the older, more sober, more thoughtful segment of the Black American residents. We also decided to do more than march. Hundreds of thousands were expected at the Washington gathering and Mahalia Jackson was to sing and Dr. King would speak. Our community couldn't even count on one hundred people, so we decided to write a stinging protest declaration and form a committee which would present it to the American ambassador inside the embassy. Our arrangements were made and agreed upon, and we broke up our meeting, our heads filled with a new and exciting charge and our fingers still smelling of spicy pork sausage.

The Washington March was to begin at 7:00 A.M. on August 27. Because of the seven-hour time difference, we planned to begin our supportive march at midnight on the twenty-sixth in the park across from the embassy.

The crowd, much larger than any of us expected, stumbled around in the dark greeting and embracing. I heard American voices which were new to me, and saw Guy arrive laughing with a group of young Ghanaian friends. At eighteen, he had a long history of marches, having participated in political protests since he was fourteen.

Alice and her Rhodesian friend appeared carrying sticks which had oiled rags wrapped tightly at one end. They would be lighted as we began our vigil.

Farmers and junior high school teachers, Black Americans on holiday in Accra, and some Peace Corps volunteers swelled the ranks. We had begun to wonder about Julian, who was late. Those of us close to him knew that was unusual, since he was always punctual in political matters.

The general atmosphere was festive, with little bursts of laughter exploding in the humid darkness. We had lighted some fire sticks when Julian arrived. He called a few of us away from the crowd.

"Dr. Du Bois is dead." His face in the flickering light was grey-black and his voice was flat. "I don't think we should inform everyone, but you all should know."

Alice, pragmatic and direct, said, "Well, what timing. He had a full and useful life and I think we should tell everybody. They'll feel more like marching."

We agreed and fanned out carrying the important news to the congregation. Sound became muffled as if Dr. Du Bois himself had appeared and ordered immediate quiet from the group. Suddenly someone whose voice I didn't recognize began singing, "Oh, oh, Freedom, oh, oh, Freedom, oh, oh, Freedom over me.

> And before I'll be a slave
> I'll be buried in my grave
> And go home to my God
> And be free."

There were a few mumbles of opposition in the crowd. "This is a political demonstration. Why are they singing that Ole' Time Religion stuff?"

The detractor was drowned out as voices joined the soloist. We were singing for Dr. Du Bois' spirit, for the invaluable contributions he made, for his shining intellect and his courage. To many of us he was the first American Negro intellectual. We knew about Jack Johnson and Jesse Owens and Joe Louis. We were proud of Louis Armstrong and Marian Anderson and Roland Hayes. We memorized the verses of James Weldon Johnson, Langston Hughes, Paul Laurence Dunbar and Countee Cullen, but they were athletes, musicians and poets, and White folks thought all those talents came naturally to Negroes. So, while we survived because of those contributors and their contributions, the powerful White world didn't stand in awe of them. Sadly, we also tended to take those brilliances for granted. But W.E.B. Du Bois and of course Paul Robeson were different, held on a higher or at least on a different plateau than the others.

We marched and sang thinking of home and the thousands who were marching in Washington, D.C., and many of us held in our minds a picture of the dapper little man, sporting a vandyke beard, perfectly groomed, who earned a Harvard doctorate before the end of the 1800's and who said in 1904, "The problem of the twentieth century will be the problem of the color line."

Dawn drifted in on a ragged file of damp and worn out marchers. During the early morning hours, a West African tropical downpour had drenched us and sent us scurrying to cars and trees and doorways.

The African marchers said they could have forewarned us. They knew that a driving rain always followed the death of a great soul.

I asked, "God weeps?"

"Of course not. It is the way the spirits welcome a great soul to the land of the dead. They wash it first."

We had walked in the dark, through the flickering light of oil sticks, protesting American racism and extolling the indomitability of the human spirit.

But daylight brought a hard reality. We were in fact marching against the American Embassy. It was a large impressive building made more impressive by the marines who lay belly down on its rooftop pointing shining guns in our direction.

Our lines had diminished through the night. People who had jobs or children or appointments or reservations had slipped away. Although there had been an agreement that we would march in relays, I was happy that none of the Revolutionist Returnees had left. Julian was still trudging along like Sisyphus on his unending climb. Bobby and Sarah Lee walked together chatting in the way of old marrieds, calm as if out for a morning stroll. Lesley and Jim Lacy remained, their faces still showing youthful anger. Vicki, Alice, Kofi Bailey, Guy, a few Black Americans I didn't know and some Ghanaians continued walking. Everyone stopped, as if on signal, when two soldiers came out of the embassy door carrying a folded American flag. They stepped smartly to the flag pole, ignoring us, and began the routine movements of raising the banner.

Someone in our group shouted, "This isn't Iwo Jima, guys." Another screamed, "You haven't taken Bunker Hill, you know. This is Africa."

The incident fed energy to our tired bodies and we began to laugh. One of the soldiers was Black and during the ceremony, no doubt nervous, the soldiers fumbled and the flag began to sag toward the ground. It was the Black man who hurriedly caught the cloth and folded it lovingly into the White soldier's arms.

Some of us jeered, "Why you, brother? What has that flag done for you?"

"Brother, why don't you come over here and join us?"

"That flag won't cover you in Alabama."

The soldiers finished attaching the flag and began drawing the ropes. As the flag ascended, our jeering increased. A careful listener could have heard new vehemence of our shouts. We were scorning the symbol of hypocrisy and hope. Many of us had only begun to realize in Africa that the Stars and Stripes was our flag and our only flag, and that knowledge was almost too painful to bear. We could physically return to Africa, find jobs, learn languages, even marry and remain on African soil all our lives, but we were born in the United States and it was the United States which had rejected, enslaved, exploited, then denied us. It was the United States which held the graves of our grandmothers and grandfathers. It was in the United States, under conditions too bizarre to detail, that those same ancestors had worked and dreamed of "a better day, by and by." There we had learned to live on the head of burnt matches, and sleep in holes in the ground. In Arkansas and Kansas and Chattanooga, Tennessee, we had decided to be no man's creature. In Dallas we put our shoulders to the wheel, and our hands in God's hand in Tulsa. We had learned the power of power in Chicago, and met in Detroit insatiable greed. We had our first loves in the corn brakes of Mississippi, in the cotton fields of Georgia we experienced the thundering pleasure of sex, and on 125th Street and 7th Avenue in Harlem the Holy Spirit called us to be His own.

I shuddered to think that while we wanted that flag dragged into the mud and sullied beyond repair, we also wanted it pristine, its white stripes, summer cloud white. Watching it wave in the breeze of a distance made us nearly choke with emotion. It lifted us up with its promise and broke our hearts with its denial.

We hurled invectives against the soldiers' retreating backs, knowing that the two young men were not our enemies and that our sneers did not hide our longing for full citizenship under that now undulating flag.

In the early afternoon, Julian, Alice, Jean Pierre, Dr. Hunton and I walked past the nervous eyes of guards and into the embassy. The calm first secretary, standing in for the absent ambassador, accepted our written protest and told us he would see that it got into the hands of the proper authorities. He smiled and said a chummy, "My wife is marching in Washington with Reverend King. I wish I could be there." The ceremony was unsatisfactory. We joined the once again large crowd of marchers and explained what we had done, and the march was over.

I went home alone, emptied of passion and too exhausted to cry.

Malcolm had arrived at midday in Accra, and by evening the May-fields' house was filled with expatriates eager to meet and listen to him. We sat on chairs, stools, tables and hunched on the floor, excited into a trembling silence.

"I am still a Muslim. I am still a minister and I am still Black." The golden man laughed, and lamplight entangled itself in his sandy beard.

"My trip to Mecca has changed many other things about me. That is what the Hadj is supposed to do, and when I return to America I will make some statements which will shock everybody." He rubbed his beard and his eyes were quick with humor. "Of course, I suppose people would be really shocked, if Malcolm X wasn't shocking."

The crowd responded in quick unison like a laugh track for a television comedy. Those who knew him were surprised at Malcolm's light-heartedness.

When I met him two years earlier, he had been the bombastic spokesman for Elijah Muhammad's Nation of Islam. Clean shaven and dark-suited, he sizzled proudly on street corners and from television screens, as he called Whites "Blue-eyed devils" and accused America of totalitarian genocide.

Just as Jomo Kenyatta was Kenya's "Burning Spear," so Malcolm X was America's Molotov cocktail, thrown upon the White hope that all

Black Americans would follow the nonviolent tenets of Dr. Martin Luther King. "Freedom at any cost" had been his rallying cry. He had been the stalking horse for the timid who openly denied him but took him, like a forbidden god, into their most secret hearts, there to adore him.

The living room and side porch were filled with an attentive and shocked audience, as Malcolm, still at ease, sat describing his recent pilgrimage to Mecca.

"Brothers and Sisters, I am pleased to see you all here in the homeland and bring you news which won't come as news to you from that place you left. The situation has not lightened up. Black people are still marching, sitting in, praying in and even swimming in."

We all knew that the Muslims had shown disgust with the Black American integrationists.

He continued, "And White Americans are still saying that they don't want Blacks in their restaurants, churches, swimming pools and voting booths. I thought I'd bring you familiar news first. Now this is new news." Those of us on the floor and those who had found chairs leaned eagerly toward Malcolm.

"I have had to rethink a number of things." He said that though his basic premise that the United States was a racist country held true, he no longer believed that all Whites were devils, nor that any human being was inherently cruel at birth. "On this journey to Mecca, I met White men with blue eyes, who I can call brother with conviction. That means that I am forced to reconsider statements I have made in the past and I must have the courage to speak up and out about those reconsiderations."

His possession of language had not diminished, nor had his magnetic aura lessened. We sat enthralled at what he said and how he said it.

"I am not in favor among the followers of the Honorable Elijah Muhammad, and this new statement will anger them more, but our people are in need of truth and I have tried and will continue to try to speak only truth to the people. The teaching of the Honorable Elijah Muhammad enabled me to break the noose that ignorance and racism put around my neck, and I will always thank Allah and the Honorable

Elijah Muhammad for that. But a person must make the effort to learn, and growing is the inevitable reward of learning."

He never mentioned the Islamic leader's name without the salutary designation, and although he was speaking to a very informal gathering in a homey living room, save for the lowered volume of his voice, he might well have been addressing an audience of thousands in Harlem.

Julian asked him to tell us why he came to Ghana.

Malcolm set his tea cup on a nearby table and, lacing his long fingers, began a sawing motion with them which was his only physical indication of tension.

After Mecca he had stopped in Cairo and met Egyptian government officials and David Du Bois, and had gone to Nigeria to confer with other African politicians. He needed as many governmental contacts as possible so that when he took the case of the Black American before the General Assembly of the United Nations, he could be sure at least of some African and maybe other nationals' support.

Every complexion of political persuasion was present in Julian's house that evening. There were true revolutionaries, counter-revolutionaries, petit bourgeois, capitalists, communists, hedonists, socialists, humanitarians and aging beatniks. When Malcolm mentioned arguing for our people before the United Nations, we shouted spontaneously and with one voice of approval. He said, "If our cause was debated by all the world's nations, it would mean that finally, we would be taken seriously. We could stop courting the 'fair-minded white people in the U.S.' as Martin Luther King called some of his constituents. America would be forced to face up to its discriminatory policies. Street protests and sit-ins would be as passé as auction blocks and as unnecessary as manumission papers. If South African Blacks can petition the U.N. against their country's policy of apartheid, then America should be shown on the world's stage as a repressionist and bestial racist nation."

A single question arose from that diverse group, and Alice put it into words. "Do you want us to arrange for you to meet Ghanaian officials and to see President Nkrumah?"

The serious scowl left Malcolm's brow. He looked around at the company, spending a few seconds on each face. Then he smiled.

"Black Americans! You all are really something." He laughed aloud. "You people just got here and already you know the President."

His laughter rang high, giving us license to join him and forget that of the forty or so people gathered, only Julian had actually met President Nkrumah and, although we all sported posters and drawings of the handsome leader, most of us had never even seen him in the flesh.

In the now relaxed atmosphere, Malcolm furnished us stories of his journey. Some were just funny and others were funny and bitter.

"I was waiting at the Nigerian Airport when a White man came up and spoke to me. He offered his hand so I shook it. Then he grinned and said, 'I've admired you, Mr. X, truly admired you.' I asked him, 'Would you have shaken my hand in New York?' He went red as a fire engine and said, 'I don't suppose so.' So I asked why he felt it was all right to do so in Africa, and that man had the nerve to get indignant. He said, 'Well, we're both Americans!' "

Our merry response was totally lacking in merriment. We laughed, as usual, because of the truth in the incident and because there was nothing else to do about it.

When Malcolm followed Ana Livia to the buffet dinner in the dining room, a few people sat pooling knowledge like children gathering pennies to buy a special treat.

"How well do you know Kofi Batcha?"

"And surely..., the Minister of Defense can be approached."

"I think he owes me one."

"If you can't be sure, he certainly won't remember."

"He should meet Nana Nketsia."

"T. D. Bafoo will be of help."

"Efua Sutherland can open some doors."

"How about Geoffrey Bing?"

"He's White, old, out of favor, and going senile."

"But he knows where the bodies will be buried and who will dance on whose grave."

"What about Michael Dei-Anan?" We agreed to contact the poet-statesman who always had an available ear for a Black American.

In one week we were able to introduce Malcolm to Ghanaian Cabinet Ministers, the African and European Diplomatic Corps as well as the Cuban and Chinese ambassadors. Julian, Ana Livia, Lesley and I were his chauffeurs, while Vicki was secretary.

The Ghana Press Club gave a party in Malcolm's honor, a mighty unusual action for that band of journalists. We arrived to warm hand-shakes, drum rolls, shouts of praise and music from the open air dance floor. Malcolm accepted the greetings with appreciation and then sat at a table and absorbed himself in the people dancing nearby. I thought he was enjoying the spectacle of pretty women and suave men moving sensually to the rhythms of the High Life, West Africa's most popular dance, but I noticed his hands were in his lap and he was lacing his fingers, first this way, then the other, then this way, then....

When the High Life Orchestra took its break, a Ghanaian journalist asked Malcolm to speak. He neither rushed nor lagged through the festive party air, but at the microphone, under the stars, Malcolm began soberly.

"First, Brothers and Sisters, thank you for inviting me to the Ghana Press Club. I do not want you to think that because I have been sitting quietly, that I do not appreciate your invitation. The fact is, I am in no mood to dance. I think of our brothers and sisters at home, squirming under the heel of racial oppression, and I do not care to dance. I think of our brothers and sisters in the Congo, squirming under the heel of imperialist invasion, and I do not care to dance. I think of our brothers and sisters in Southern Africa squirming under the heel of apartheid, and I do not care to dance."

The crowd was not pleased to have their gaiety censored, and a few disapproving murmurs could be heard. They were drowned out by the strong voices of T. D. Bafoo, Kofi Batcha, Cameron Duodu and Nurru Bello Damz who were standing at their respective tables.

"Hear! Hear! Hear, Hear!" And "Speak! Speak!"

Fortunately, Malcolm's speech was brief, and when the orchestra returned the celebrants crowded again onto the floor, dancing, flirting, wiggling and inviting. Obviously they sympathized with the African struggle everywhere, naturally they supported the aspirations for freedom, but their country was in their own hands. President Nkrumah was the "Mass pass Mass," the person who surpassed others, and their revolution was a success.

"Ye. Ye." The time had come to dance.

Alice looked at Malcolm, then wagged her head at me, and I thought of my grandmother who said, "If you want to know how important you are to the world, stick your finger in a pond and pull it out. Will the hole remain?"

When Malcolm met Nana Nketsia the two men acted magnetized. I had not heard Nana speak so quietly nor seen Malcolm listen so deeply. Each man grew in the other's presence and when I took Malcolm to his hotel, he said, "Now I have met African royalty. A chief. True, true. He knows his people and he loves them, and they love him." Malcolm's face wore a mask of wistfulness so telling I had to look away.

Lesley arranged for him to speak at Legon University, and that night the auditorium was filled with students, lecturers and some townsfolk. Since Malcolm was the guest of the young Marxist League, the organization's representative spoke first. The young man quoted

Karl Marx with such force, he seemed to have taken on his subject's persona. The crowd became impatient, but Malcolm sat on the stage calmly listening to the speaker.

Guy had given me the honor of agreeing to sit near me. He and his Ghanaian friends were equally anxious for the Marxist to leave the podium so that Malcolm could speak, and they began to murmur. I coughed to get Guy's attention, but he looked at me and frowned. His scowl said, "Don't reprimand me in public. Don't embarrass me." He was right. He was nineteen and each of us had labored with some success to create new ways to talk to each other. Nature was guiding his hands to loosen the maternal bonds, and although I felt if I was freed from the stay of motherhood, I might fly away like a feather in the wind, with trepidation, I too tried to let my child become his own man.

Finally, Lesley Lacy introduced Malcolm and immediately his oratorical skill captured the audience. The years in prison, in mosques, on street corners, at college lecterns and before television cameras had produced a charismatic speaker who could play an audience as great musicians play instruments. He spoke moderately loud, then thundered, whispered, then roared. He used the imagery of Black American Baptist preachers and the logic of university intellectuals. He spoke of America, White and Black Americans, racism, hate and the awful need to be treated as humans.

When he finished the audience rose. A group of students which included Guy, began to chant the football cheer, "Asante Kotoko."

Malcolm quieted the crowd and asked for questions.

He met each question squarely. The audience applauded. A faculty member asked why Malcolm incited people to violence. Why did he preach violence? He answered, "I am responding to violence. If your house is on fire and I come to warn you, why should you accuse me of setting the fire? You should thank me for my concern. Maybe you can put out the fire before it is too late."

The Africans relished Malcolm's use of proverbs. His answers were as considered and detailed as his address had been. Then a student stood, "Mr. Malcolm X, what I don't understand is why you call yourself Black. You look more like a White man than a Negro." The young man sat down and a few embarrassed titters and some disapproving groans could be heard on the dark floor.

At first Malcolm laughed. He opened his mouth wide and laughed loud and long.

"Little brother, I've been waiting for that question since I landed in Africa, and while many people thought it, you're the first person who had the nerve to ask. I commend your courage. Well, let's look at it. At home, that is, in that place where I was born, I've been called by Whites a yellow nigger, a light-skinned nigger, a red uppity nigger, a fair-skinned seditious nigger, but never until now have I been called a White man. I mean, Whites who should know their own have never made the mistake of overlooking my African blood. It is a strange sensation to have to explain, in Africa, the effects of slavery, and maybe the young man who asked the question is the only person who really needs an explanation, but if there are others, I suggest that you all listen carefully.

"As slaves, we were the property of slave masters. Our men were worked to death, our women were raped, then worked to death, and many of our children were born looking like me. The slave master fathers denied their children, but fortunately we retained enough Africanisms to believe that the mother's child was our child, no matter who or what the father had been.

"Before I became a Muslim, when I was hustling on the streets of America, because of my color, Black people called me mariney, and Detroit Red. Some even cussed me out and called me unprintable names, but nobody tried to give me away to White folks. I was accepted. Now, my point is, if Whites who should know don't claim me, and Blacks who should know do claim me, I think it's clear where I belong. I am a Black man. Notice, I don't say Black American, I don't consider myself a democrat, a republican, or an American. I am a Black Muslim man of African heritage. Next?"

Black Americans led the applause and soon the entire audience was standing, clapping and laughing its approval.

Malcolm's time was perforated in orderly sections like postage stamps. He went to see Lesley at Legon, visited with Sarah and Bobby Lee in their home, called upon Alphaeus and Dorothy Hunton and still had energy many evenings to fill Julian's living room with a fluency of strong language and his always unexpected humor.

We congratulated ourselves on our successes, but commiserated over our largest failure. Despite all our efforts we were not able to get Malcolm an audience with Kwame Nkrumah.

Some thought that the President's reluctance to meet the radical Black leader stemmed from a desire to stay in America's good graces. That idea was argued down since Nkrumah's policies tended decidedly toward nonalignment. There were as many Russians in Ghana as Americans, and they seemed to be treated equally.

Julian tried to reach Shirley Graham Du Bois, but she was not available. Mrs. Du Bois could have arranged a meeting in seconds. She and the president were family-close. It was said that Nkrumah called her "little mother," and that she telephoned him each night at bedtime. Ana Livia, the late Doctor Du Bois' doctor, telephoned her and even went to the Du Bois home, but Shirley was as elusive as smoke in a high wind. I accused her of being deliberately inaccessible, but after my friends said that my paranoia had gotten out of hand again, I kept my thoughts to myself.

The Nigerian High Commissioner, Alhadji Isa Wali, invited Malcolm to lunch and a few of us tagged along. We sat in the Residency dining room, watching our leader work a subtle charm on the already enchanted diplomat.

It was clear that Malcolm had a number of integrated personae. None was contradictory to the others, but each was different. When he sat with me after a long day of interviews and meetings, he was a big brother advisor, suggesting that it was time for me to come home. "The country needs you. Our people need you. Alice and Julian and Max Bond and Sylvia, you should all come home. You have seen Africa, bring it home and teach our people about the homeland." He talked of his family. "Betty is the sweetest woman in the world, and the girls. Did I show you these pictures?" Each time I would deny that I had seen the photographs and each time he would point out and name his daughters.

In the late evenings, he was like a traveling salesman or a soldier on duty, a family man, sadly away from those he loved most.

But in the larger formal company of Black American expatriates, he told humorous stories about Whites and about himself. He entertained easily and was quick to laugh.

On stages, he spoke fiercely against oppression and for revolution. "I am neither a fanatic nor a dreamer. I am a Black man who loves justice and loves his people."

And with the Nigerian High Commissioner, who at five feet stood fourteen inches shorter than Malcolm, he was a large attentive son, explaining himself endearingly to his small father.

"We have much work to do at home. Even as you have your work here in Africa. We are lambs in a den of wolves. We will need your help. Only with the help of Africa and Africans can we succeed in freeing ourselves." His voice was soft, his volume low, still he spoke with force.

After lunch we gathered on the veranda so that Alice could take her photographs for history. The ambassador presented Malcolm with a grand bou bou, which he quickly put on. The rich robe which had fallen to the floor when worn by High Commissioner Alhadji Isa Wali came just below Malcolm's knees. Both men laughed at the difference in size, but the ambassador said, "Some are big, some are small, but we are all one."

The Chinese Residency was festive with lights and music on Malcolm's last night in Ghana and our jollity matched the atmosphere. Vicki was being courted by the Chinese delegation. They offered her a trip to China and an opportunity to stay there and teach. Alice had applied for a job with the E.C.A., based in Addis Ababa, and her chances looked good.

We wore our prettiest dresses and best smiles and when we entered the large salon our hosts greeted us as if they had hardly been able to await our arrival. (After a few minutes I noticed that they greeted each new guest as generously.) Julian and Ana Livia were already there with Malcolm mingling in the crowded room. Drinks were brought on large trays and a pretty variety of foods waited on buffets.

The Cuban ambassador and his glamorous wife were talking earnestly with Malcolm when Shirley Du Bois entered. She was a medium-sized, light brown-skinned woman with large eyes, a long attractive face and the confidence of Mount Kilimanjaro. After being welcomed by those in her path, she walked immediately to Malcolm and, taking him by the arm, guided him to a corner where they sat.

The guests swirled around each other, exchanging conversational partners as if they were participants in a jamboree. After nearly an hour, Shirley and Malcolm emerged from their retreat and rejoined the party.

Shirley said loudly, "This man is brilliant. I am taking him for my son. He must meet Kwame. They have too much in common not to meet." On that decisive statement she took her leave. Malcolm spent a few more minutes talking with our hosts, then Julian said since Malcolm was to travel the next morning he would drive him to the Continental Hotel.

I was in a rage when I drove my housemates home.

"Are you ready for Shirley Du Bois? 'I'm taking him for my son.' Hell, before she wouldn't even see him. I can't stand that." Alice and Vicki let me rant alone. I didn't mind that they acted indifferent to Shirley's belated acceptance of Malcolm, I was enjoying my anger.

We were ready for bed when the telephone rang. Alice answered it, while Vicki and I stood by nervously. No one in Accra telephoned after eleven o'clock, save to announce a crisis.

Alice hung up the phone and turned to us. She was somewhere between laughing and crying.

"Kwame Nkrumah will see Malcolm at nine o'clock in the morning. Julian is taking him to Flagstaff House."

Vicki whooped and hollered, "Success! Success!" She grabbed me, then Alice, then me again. Alice was a little stunned and I was furious.

I said, "Shirley went straight home and called the President and told him he had to see Malcolm. She could have done that a week ago, but no."

Alice agreed, but Vicki said, "Better late than never. You all ought to be celebrating, I say."

For me sleep was difficult that night. My bed was lumpy with anger and my pillow a rock of intemperate umbrage.

The next morning we met Malcolm after his visit with President Nkrumah. The bright sunshine, the bougainvillaea and the singing birds around the hotel didn't brighten my countenance. I claimed to be saddened by Malcolm's pending departure, but in fact my heart was still hardened to Shirley Du Bois. Rather than inquire about the Nkrumah interview, I stood apart pouting, while Alice snapped photos and Julian put Malcolm's luggage in the car. A convoy of limousines glided up importantly to the hotel's porte-cochere. Small flags waved from the hoods of luxury cars, which meant that each car carried an ambassador.

Alice said there must be some diplomatic meeting, and began to pose Malcolm and Julian for a picture. As she finished, the Nigerian High Commissioner approached.

"My people, good morning. Brother Malcolm, morning. A few of us have come to accompany you to the airport." The gesture was so unexpected that even Malcolm was speechless.

The Nigerian diplomat continued, "The Chinese, Guinea, Yugoslav, Mali, Cuban, Algerian and Egyptian ambassadors are here. Others wanted to come but national matters detained them. We will pull up and onto the road as you will want to ride with your friends. We will follow."

Julian was the first to speak to Malcolm after the High Commissioner left us.

"Man, we ought to pay you for this visit. You've given this poor group of Black exiles some status. Forty-five minutes with the president and now a convoy of limousines to see you to the airport. Man! We were living here before, but after your visit we have really arrived."

We were all laughing with pleasure when we heard the familiar sounds of Black American speech. We turned around and saw Muhammad Ali coming out of the hotel with a large retinue of Black men. They were all talking and joking among themselves. One minute after we saw them, they saw Malcolm.

The moment froze, as if caught on a daguerreotype, and the next minutes moved as a slow montage. Muhammad stopped, then turned and spoke to a companion. His friends looked at him. Then they looked back at Malcolm. Malcolm also stopped, but he didn't speak to us, nor did any of us have the presence of mind to say anything to him. Malcolm had told us that after he severed ties to the Nation of Islam, many of his former friends had become hostile.

Muhammad and his group were the first to turn away. They started walking toward a row of parked cars. Malcolm, with a rush, left us and headed toward the departing men. We followed Malcolm. He shouted, "Brother Muhammad. Brother Muhammad."

Muhammad and his companions stopped and turned to face Malcolm.

"Brother, I still love you, and you are still the greatest." Malcolm smiled a sad little smile. Muhammad looked hard at Malcolm, and shook his head.

"You left the Honorable Elijah Muhammad. That was the wrong thing to do, Brother Malcolm." His face and voice were also sad. Malcolm had been his supporter and hero. Disappointment and hurt lay on Muhammad's face like dust. Abruptly, he turned and walked away. His coterie followed. After a few steps they began talking again, loudly.

Malcolm's shoulders sagged and his face was suddenly gloomy. "I've lost a lot. A lot. Almost too much." He led us back to my car. "I want to ride with Maya and Julian. We'll meet at the airport." Alice and the other friends rode with Ana Livia and three six-footers tried to be comfortable in my little Fiat. Even when we saw the diplomat's limousines following us, the heavy mood seemed destined to stay.

Malcolm broke the silence. "Now, Sister, what do you think of Shirley Du Bois?" The question gave me a chance to articulate my anger, and I let loose. I spoke of her lack of faith, her lack of identity with Black American struggle, her isolation from her people, her pride at sitting in the catbird seat in Ghana. Malcolm let me continue until my tirade wound down.

"Now, Sister, I thought you were smart, but I see you are very childish, dangerously immature." He had not spoken so harshly before to anyone in Ghana—I was shocked.

"Have you considered that her husband has only been dead a few months? Have you considered that at her age she needs some time to consider that she is walking around wounded, limping for the first time in many years on one leg?"

Tears were bathing my face, not for the sad picture Malcolm was drawing of Shirley, but for myself as the object of his displeasure.

Julian, from his uncomfortable seat in the back of the car, put his hand on my shoulder gently, "Keep your eyes on the road."

Malcolm said, "Sister, listen and listen carefully. Picture American racism as a mountain. Now slice that mountain from the top to the bottom and open it like a door. Do you see all the lines, the strata?" I could hardly see the road ahead, but I nodded.

"Those are the strata of American life and we are being attacked on each one. We need people on each level to fight our battle. Don't be in such a hurry to condemn a person because he doesn't do what you do, or think as you think or as fast. There was a time when you didn't know what you know today." His voice had become more explanatory and less accusatory.

"When you hear that the Urban League or the NAACP is giving a formal banquet at the Waldorf-Astoria, I know you won't go, but don't knock them. They give scholarships to poor Black children. One of those recipients might become a Julian Mayfield, or a Maya Angelou, or a Malcolm X. You understand?"

I would have died rather than say I disagreed. I said, "I will think about that."

He said, "I can't ask anymore. I admire all of you. Our people can be proud. Julian will tell you about my meeting with Nkrumah. I wanted to ride with you to encourage you to broaden your thinking. You are too good a woman to think small. You know we, I mean in the United States and elsewhere, are in need of hard thinkers. Serious thinkers, who are not timid. We are called upon to defend ourselves all the time. In every arena." Malcolm had lost his harshness and seemed to be reflecting rather than addressing either me or Julian.

Julian asked him if Muhammad's actions at the hotel came as a surprise, and Malcolm did not answer directly. "He is young. The Honorable Elijah Muhammad is his prophet and his father, I understand. Be kind to him for his sake, and mine. He has a place in my heart."

At the airport, the ambassadors and other well-wishers swooped him away. Alice had time to arrange him for one last photo and we all shook his hand and hugged him.

Julian said in a forbidding tone, "Man, I don't like to see you traveling alone. You know there's a price on your head."

Malcolm smiled. "No one can guard anyone's life. Not even his own. Only Allah can protect. And he has let me slide so far." He smiled for us all and then was gone.

The letdown affected our speech. There seemed to be no words to describe what we were feeling. We regarded each other with embarrassment. Malcolm's presence had elevated us, but with his departure, we were what we had been before: a little group of Black folks, looking for a home.

I still found myself grinning when I came unexpectedly upon a clasp of confident Ghanaian children whispering in Ga or Fanti, their little legs shining and shimmering like oiled eels; my breath still crowded in my throat at the sight of African soldiers, chests thrust forward, stiffened legs and behinds high like peacocks' tails. The forests had lost none of their mystery and the bush villages were still enchanting. But Ghana was beginning to tug at me and make me uncomfortable, like an ill fitting coat.

The job at the diamond mine had been filled before I was obliged to test my morality or lie about my academic background. Nana had become a close and generous friend who continued seeking a better paying position for me, and I spent good times with his children and friends. I was welcome in many Ghanaian homes and had sufficient male company to satisfy my needs and vanity. My housemates and the other Revolutionist Returnees provided opportunities for strong political debate and laughter, but I had to admit that I had begun to feel that I was not in my right place. Every moment in Ghana called attention to itself and each social affair was self-conscious. When I went dancing, between the beats and during the steps, I thought, "Here I am, Maya Angelou, dancing in Africa. I know I'm having a good time." Shopping in the crowded streets I thought, "This is me at last, really me, buying peppers in Makola market, aren't I lucky?" I decided that I was too aware of my location; not just in Accra, or in Adabraka, or Asylum Down.

I needed to get away from Africa and its cache of subtle promises and at least second-hand memories. I blamed the entire continent and history for my malaise when the real reason was more pointedly specific and as personal as a migraine.

Guy was troubling me. I was questioning my worth as a mother, and since I had been a parent over half my life, I thought if I failed in that role, success in any other area would have very little meaning.

One evening, a Ghanaian friend had come bringing gin and a terrible piece of gossip. He opened the fresh bottle, poured a few drops on the ground for the spirits, then we seated ourselves and drank comfortably.

"Sister, I have bad news about your son." My first thought was that he had been in another accident. As soon as that idea came it vanished; I would have been telephoned.

"What news, Brother?" I stayed seated in a fake serenity.

"It is said that he has a girlfriend."

I laughed, "Well, I hope so."

"Don't laugh, Sister. This certain friend is thirty-six years old and is an American and works for the American Embassy."

As I was asking, "What?" thoughts tumbled over themselves in my mind.

The woman was a year older than I. Couldn't she find any lover older than my nineteen-year-old son? An American government employee? Ghanaians were still a little suspicious of all Americans, especially Black diplomats and employees in the embassy. I had just been made a member of the Ghana Press Club. Undoubtedly, suspicion would fall on me if the gossip was true.

"Brother, I thank you for the information. I will see to my son. Shall we freshen our drinks?"

I would not allow my informant to warn me that young men in love are like elephants in rutting time, difficult to dissuade. I knew that I could always talk to Guy.

The next day I took a break from a play in production after a student told me that my son was outside. Guy and I stood on the lawn in front of the National Theatre.

He appeared two inches taller than he had been the week before, and I had not noticed that he had grown a moustache.

"I am told that you have a girlfriend."

He had the nerve to be annoyed with me and, worse, to show his annoyance. "Mother, did you actually call me into town to talk about that?"

"I am told that she is thirty-six years old, and works for the American Embassy."

"Yes?" When a nineteen-year-old decides to clothe himself in dignity, nothing but pity or abject fear can penetrate his armor. I was too angry to ask for sympathy and obviously Guy had moved beyond fear of my disapproval.

"Is it true?"

"Oh, Mother, really. Don't you think it's time I had a life of my own?"

How could his life be separate from my life? I had been a mother of a child so long I had no preparation for life on any other level. As usual, anger, my enemy, betrayed me. I looked up at the young golden brown giant towering above my head.

"I will knock you down, Guy. Right here in front of God and everybody. Knock you down, do you hear?" I hadn't struck him since he was seven years old and had told me that I was too big to hit a small child.

"I will knock you down and I mean it."

His smile came from his new grown-up and distant place, and cut my heart to shreds.

He patted my head, "Yes, little mother. I'm sure you will." Then he turned and walked away.

When he closed up and left me no entry, a sense of loss rendered me momentarily unstable.

His existence had defined my own. As a child his sense of humor, attraction for puns and affection for me had lightened the single parent burden. He learned to read early because I loved to read, and I taught him to recite the poetry I had memorized in my own youth. When my seven-year-old son stood before me, beating the bones of his young chest, disclaiming, "It matters not how dark the night, how charged with punishments the scroll, I am the master of my fate, I am the captain of my soul," I saw myself, as if thrown upon a screen, clearly brave, clearly sure, sculpting a good life from resistant stone.

As my mother had done for me, I told him jokes and encouraged him to laugh at life and at himself. The Black child must learn early to allow laughter to fill his mouth or the million small cruelties he encounters will congeal and clog his throat.

Guy had been a good student, but did not develop into excellence because of our brief stays in cities where we lived. When he graduated from high school at the American College in Cairo, he told me he had gone to nineteen schools in eleven years. I was sorry to think that I hadn't noticed, but realized at the time I couldn't have changed our movements or destinations.

I had begun dancing or singing for a living when he was seven, and contracts took me from San Francisco to New York, and all the cities between the coasts. My family and even school administrators disapproved of what they thought was my vagabond life, but I was unable to live their ideals. I had no formal education, and no training other than in dance.

Once I was called to a Los Angeles school by the child psychologist. She was a White woman, in a white smock, in a white office.

"Miss Angelou, Guy is not doing well in school because he is hyperactive. I believe that comes from being moved around so frequently."

I sat still, looking at her, knowing that nothing she could say would influence the lives my son and I would lead.

She leaned back and pronounced, "He needs to stay put. He needs an established home life. I know that you are an entertainer and have to travel in your work, but maybe you could leave him with someone in your family. Your mother would look after him, perhaps?"

My mother, whom I loved dearly, had left me with my paternal grandmother from the time I was three until my thirteenth year. She had matured since then and become my reliable friend and a doting mother, but Guy was my responsibility and my joy.

I said nothing. The psychologist became uncomfortable as I sat silent. "He needs security, Miss Angelou. Stability will give him that security."

I stood and spoke. "Thank you for your concern and your time, Doctor, but I am his security. Wherever we go, we go together. Wherever he is he knows that that six-foot-tall Black woman is not too far away. What I don't furnish in stability, I make up in love. Good day."

We left a few weeks later for Chicago, another apartment hotel and another school.

His teens had not been easy for either of us. As he grew older, he began to withdraw, and because I didn't understand that an avalanche of sexuality had fallen upon him, I felt betrayed at his withdrawal. In our worst moments however, we had been saved by love and laughter.

But now, here in Ghana where neither of us was threatened by racial hate, where we both had separate and reasonably good lives, where it seemed we could both be happy, he had moved beyond my reach and into the arms of a cradle robber. Speaking to the woman would be a mistake. If she agreed to end the relationship, Guy would hate me for taking away his play pretty, and if she refused, we would have a fist fight.

I needed to get away from him and myself and the situation. Maybe to Europe, or Asia. I never thought of returning to America.

The cable from New York City shook the blues away. It read: "Berlin Volksopera wants original company Blacks, four days, stop. Venice Biennale, three days, stop. Ticket paid, plus salary. Can you come?" It was signed: Sidney Bernstein. Three years earlier, I had been a member of a cast which successfully presented Jean Genet's scathing play in New York City. At first, I gave little thought to either the play or the other actors. I was ecstatic with the thought of separating myself from Guy and his brand new grown-up ways.

I rushed to talk to Alice, who was brimming with her own excitement. She had accepted the job in Ethiopia and had decided to stop in Egypt on her way to Addis Ababa. A conference of nonaligned countries would be meeting in Cairo. By adding a little money to my prepaid ticket I could meet her there after I left Venice. The prospect of seeing Joe and Bahnti Williamson again was exhilarating. The Liberian couple had been brother and sister to me during my stay in Egypt. David Du Bois, the son of Shirley Graham and stepson of Dr. Du Bois, also lived in Cairo and we had been very close friends. A visit to Cairo sounded like the real answer to the malaise which had descended around me. When I learned that Julian and Ana Livia were also going to attend the Cairo conference, it was clear that I would accept Bernstein's offer and rearrange my ticket to stop in Egypt on my return to Ghana.

I took delight from the flicker of worry which crossed Guy's face. I had told him that I was leaving for Germany and Italy and Egypt. He recovered too soon to please me.

"Have a wonderful time, Mom. A wonderful time."

Since the Ghanaian pound could not be exchanged on the international market, I swapped my cash with a friend for his Nigerian pounds and packed my new flamboyant African clothes and my gifts of gold jewelry. I was going to meet a group of sophisticated New York actors, some of whom were my friends, and I meant to strut.

I became nervous only when I thought of the years since I had been on the stage. (Playing *Mother Courage* in Ghana's National Theatre didn't really count.) The other actors, all brilliant and ferociously ambitious, had moved around New York City's theatres, competing with professionals and growing with each role. Their names and work had become known and lauded. I decided to spend two days in Frankfurt, boning up on the play, or those actors would run me off the stage.

The trip on Lufthansa was a test in discomfort. The flight stewards spoke excellent English and were solicitous without being intrusive, but I kept my eyes on the script in my lap, and let my mind wander from the German accents to John Hersey's book *The Wall* which had gripped me with horror in my youth. I listened to the speech of the passengers returning to their fatherland and remembered the black and white photographs of emaciated human beings rescued from Auschwitz. It was distressing. In Ghana I worked hard at forgiving those African chiefs who collaborated in the slave trade centuries before, but couldn't find it in my heart to exonerate the stewardesses who were toddlers at the time of the Holocaust. Prejudice is a burden which confuses the past, threatens the future, and renders the present inaccessible.

I rehearsed in a small pension in Frankfurt until the lines came automatically to my mind and my tongue. I had learned years before that if I was to act in a play it was wise to memorize every part, even the scenes in which I did not appear. The resulting confidence would spill over into my own role.

Berlin, with its cold temperature, its high-rises, wide, clean avenues and White, White people was exactly what I wanted to see and where I needed to be. I began to relax even as I was being driven from the airport to the Hilton Hotel. When I arrived at my destination I found wide, carpeted corridors, a large, well-furnished bedroom and a bathroom white as a Protestant heaven.

I thought of some Africans I had met who so loved the glories of Europe, they were too immobilized to construct a splendid African future.

This was easy to understand. Europe had ruled long, had brought to Africa a language, a religion, modern ideas of medicine, and its own pervading self-love. How could one suggest in one's own secret heart that Whites were not gods, descending from heaven, and like gods, bringing bounty on one hand and brutality on the other? That was the way of the gods.

After a bath, I dressed in my most glorious pale lavender silk Grand Bou Bou, and went down to meet the cast.

Raymond St. Jacques was still so handsome he looked as if he had been sculpted, then cast in copper. Cecily Tyson was smaller than I remembered and much more glamorous. We embraced and laughed at finding ourselves, of all places, in Germany. Godfrey Cambridge had been unable to come to Berlin because he was in a Broadway show, but Lex Monson and Jay Flash Riley pulled me off the floor with their embraces, and the young Lou Gossett, one half legs and the other smiles, bounced up and down to see me. James Earl Jones and I exchanged our customary cool salutes. Years before in New York City we had worked successfully creating a distance which time had not narrowed.

"Lady! Ah, my Lady!" A sonorous voice completed the welcome I had been seeking. Roscoe Lee Browne entered the rehearsal room and I nearly shouted. He had lost none of his princely air nor elegant good looks. He laughed outright when he saw me, and he spoke to me as he spoke to all women; as if we were Fairie Queens.

We embraced and walked away from the cast and began to tell each other of our current lives. We went to a bar and ordered drinks. Roscoe had heard rumors of my recent divorce, and was genuinely sorry to find that they were founded on fact. He asked about my acceptance in Ghana, adding that he had known President Nkrumah when they had both studied at Lincoln University.

I had prepared a tale for the cast, which had Africans and Black Americans lovingly striding arm in arm up a golden staircase to an all sepia paradise inhabited with black-robed Black saints strumming on ebony harps. I had no need to lie to Roscoe, who would have seen through the fiction anyway.

"We have it good, very good, or bad. Heartbreakingly bad."

Roscoe made his face long. "Africans find it hard to forgive us slavery, don't they?" He took my hand and said, "I thought you would have known that. My dear, they can't forgive us, and even more terrible, they can't forgive themselves. They're like the young here in this tragic country. They will never forgive their parents for what they did to the Jews, and they can't forgive the Jews for surviving and being a living testament to human bestiality." He patted my hand. "Now, dear lady, tell me the good side—but first let me hear the story you're going to tell everyone else."

He laughed when I said I'd spare him the part about all of the Black Americans climbing aboard a chariot and humming our way to heaven.

He said, "Not unless they cast me as De Lawd." It was wonderful to laugh again, and particularly sweet to laugh Black American rueful laughter in Germany.

The Blacks translated into German became *Die Negers*. Posters were on bold display throughout Berlin which made the cast snicker behind Black hands. Lex said, "It's a good thing they're speaking German. The first American cracker that comes up to me and says 'I saw you in *de Niggers*' is going to get a nigger beating that'll make him do a million novenas." That was particularly funny coming from Monson who played the Catholic priest in the play, coached the actors in church liturgy and whose youth as a devoted acolyte still influenced his adult mannerisms.

Helen Martin, who had the role of the Black Queen and whose sharp tongue was an instrument to be avoided, said, "I hope these Germans don't think they're getting away with something. We know who they are and what they're saying. I hope I don't have to read them the real Riot Act before it's finished."

I listened and participated in the sardonic responses and realized again the difference between the Black American and the African. Over centuries of oppression we had developed a doctrine of resistance which included false docility and sarcasm. We also had a most un-African trait: we were nearly always ready and willing to fight. Too frequently we fought among ourselves, rendering our neighborhoods dangerous to traverse. But Whites knew that our bellicosity could disperse into other places, on jobs, in elevators, on buses, and in social gatherings.

Single White men seldom physically threatened single Black men, saying "You know they will cut you."

An ancient joke among Blacks told of a bigot who was chided by his friends for calling all Blacks "niggers."

"But that's what they are," he announced.

"What do you call the minister of the venerable White Rock Baptist Church?"

The bigot answered, "A nigger."

"And the president of the Black university?"

"A nigger."

"And the award-winning scientist?"

"A nigger," was the reply.

"And that Black man standing over there watching us with a knife in his hand?"

"Oh, I call him, 'Sir.' "

Black American insouciance was the one missing element in West Africa. Courtesy and form, traditional dignity, respectful dismissal and history were the apparent ropes holding their society close and nearly impenetrable. But my people had been unable to guard against intrusions of any sort, so we had developed audacious defenses which lay just under the skin. At any moment they might seep through the pores and show themselves without regard to propriety, manners or even physical safety. I had missed those thrilling attitudes, without being aware of their absence.

Rehearsals went smoothly. The actors were unselfconscious and professional. An uninformed observer would have been flabbergasted at the difference between the rehearsal cast who moved with an easy grace through the staging and the same cast which burst onto the stage opening night.

Throughout practice each of us had concentrated on our lines and movements, noticing our colleagues for physical and spoken cues, but on the afternoon before opening, the usual excitement was heightened by Jay Flash Riley who lighted the tinder for a group explosion.

Jay, in his outlandish military costume, and wearing the caricatured mask of a White colonial soldier, popped his head in each dressing room and speaking in an exaggerated guttural accent said, "Remember Jesse Owens!" We all laughed, but we all remembered. In Germany, during the 1936 Olympics, the Black runner, Owens, representing the United States, had won four gold medals and shattered Adolf Hitler's dictum that the Aryan race was superior. The

German audience reportedly booed Owens, and Hitler refused to allow the winner to accept the medal from his hands.

There was no mention of Jay's statement, but we left our dressing rooms determined to show the Germans that while we were only eight people, we were serious actors and angry Blacks, and we could call the entire Allied army back and put it onto the stage, and whip them one more time.

After numerous bravos and standing ovations, we attended a reception in the theatre's modern gleaming lobby. The strain of opening night and my efforts to hold my own with those actors exhausted me, and I was tired to the point of perversity.

A blond, trim man with two women approached me and gave a neat little bow. "Madame Angelou, you are a great artist." He told me his name was Dieter, and added that he was an architect. "I want to introduce my wife and mother. We would like to invite you to supper."

He presented the women who complimented me in dainty English. "It is our honor, Madame."

"Our country is uplifted by your visit."

They looked like three dolls from a porcelain collection.

"We would like you and any friends of yours to come to an après-theatre club. There is a jazz orchestra."

Irascibility prompted me. I said, "I am too tired tonight, but I'd love to come to your house tomorrow. I've never been in a German home." Surprise at my request held their attention for brief seconds. Then the women looked at the man, who nodded. "That will be possible, Madame. We will prepare breakfast. I will pick you up here at 10:00 A.M. Please feel free to ask anyone you like." He handed me his card and I shook hands with the women. The man kissed the air above my hand and saluted me with a discreet click of his heels.

"Until tomorrow, Madame."

Roscoe had left the reception early, and I didn't think any other actors would be amused to see strange Germans en famille. A young and very handsome Jewish man wearing a yarmulke was standing alone by a bar. I went to him and began a conversation. His name was Torvash, and he was an Israeli actor on tour, and had enjoyed our performance. I asked about Arik Lavy, a Sabra singer I had known years earlier in Tel Aviv. The actor knew him. He laughed easily and was pleasant to talk with. I relaxed and told him of my invitation, adding that I certainly was expected to bring along another Black from the cast. He looked at me sharply, "You're not inviting me, I hope?"

That must have been in intention from the moment I saw his yarmulke, but I said nothing.

"To a German home? I do not mean to be rude, but why do you think they invited you?"

"They really asked me to a night club. They planned to make a grand entrance. When Black people are scarce, we're in style." His laugh was quick and pretty.

"Did you tell them you would ask me?"

"I hadn't seen you then."

He thought a minute. "I'll come along. It should be interesting."

We shared a drink, agreed on the time to meet and bade each other a good night.

I slept poorly, unable to shake the feeling that I had forced an invitation, then taken advantage of it. An act, not criminal, but not quite savory.

I awakened with the Fifty-first Psalm reciting itself in my head. "Have mercy upon me, O God, according to Thy loving kindness; according to the multitude of Thy tender mercies, blot out mine transgressions."

As I prepared for the morning's appointment, I assured myself that the situation could not possibly end negatively. We were after all, decades away from Germany's evil days, and if my host, my escort and I weren't good people, at least we were sophisticated.

I put on a bib of filigree gold and a grand bou bou of lace, whiter than ice, and went down to meet my host. He stood in the middle of the glass and chrome lobby talking to a child. The merry-go-round of people spinning near him did not draw his attention. The boy, a miniature color drawing of Dieter, and dressed like him in pressed pants, blue worsted jacket, white open-neck shirt and ascot, was admiring his surroundings. I didn't really want to interrupt their conversation, but I said, "Good morning."

"Oh, Madame Angelou." He appeared pleased to see me.

"May I present my son, Hans?" The child, who was about ten, stiffened, said in heavily accented English, "How do you do?" bowed and clicked his little heels.

Oh Lord, I had lucked upon a right one. I did what any or most of my people do when they really have no alternative, I laughed.

"Madame Angelou, have you friends coming, too?"

"Well, not a friend exactly, but I met an Israeli actor last night and since we were both alone, I invited him to escort me to breakfast." There was only a slight focusing of his eyes on me, which was followed by a gracious smile.

"Wonderful. I suppose you met Torvash. I saw him here last night. He is a very popular comedian-mime. He tours Europe each year and it's nearly impossible to get tickets to his concerts. Oh, here he is now."

Torvash arrived quickly as if spun off the eddy of people. We shook hands. The two men greeted each other. Little Hans bowed when he was introduced, and suddenly we were both forgotten. The two men swept into a German conversation. I imagined their words probing like dentists' picks. Their eyes were darting, searching.

The boy and I followed the men to a car parked in the driveway, and when the back door was opened for us by a doorman I made no protest, although I expected to be offered a seat up front. After all, I was the invited guest, but the men claimed each other's attention so thoroughly, small graces went begging.

They talked until Dieter stopped the car beside a large, very modern two-story house. We descended and walked on pavement among shaped shrubs and entered the house from the side door, and Hans rushed up the stairs.

Dieter shouted to his wife and led us downstairs. I sent Torvash a few suggestive looks, but he didn't respond.

The basement was a huge dining room dominated by an oversize round table which was set with silver, napkins and glasses. When I looked away from the table, I saw full bouquets of cut flowers in crystal vases on small tables, in the empty and dust-free fireplace and in corners. A screened double door led to a rear garden.

Dieter's wife was giving the room last minute domestic attention. She stopped to shake my hand and welcome me then stepped past me and extended her hand to Torvash. I watched her face tense then relax in less than a second, and we were given seats at the table. Dieter said he was going to bring beer, and his wife excused herself, saying she had to get to the kitchen.

I took advantage of our first moments alone.

"Well, what do you think?"

Torvash shook his head sadly. "He was probably a Nazi. That's what I think."

We might have come from the same small southern town, or urban ghetto or East European village. I shook my head and clicked my tongue. He imitated the gesture and made a bitter face.

"Do you want to leave?" I was ready to walk out with him.

"No. We will see this to the end. I understand you asking me, I don't understand why he asked you." At that moment the entire family entered carrying trays of food.

Dieter set bottles of beer in the table's center, his wife placed whole loaves of bread and large mounds of butter on a side buffet. Hans brought a tray of sausages and went back through the door bringing a roasted ham. Dieter's mother-in-law came smiling, and set potato salad in front of Torvash.

"Good morning, this is for you." She spoke in German, and Torvash stood to shake her hand. After I spoke to her she centered her concern on her Israeli guest. The night before she had appeared to be a contained, conservative, quiet, middle-aged German woman, but she bloomed for Torvash and couldn't stop talking, and giggling, and flirting. She had lost a sense of her age and place.

Dieter interrupted.

"Mother." He smiled, but spoke sternly and she arose, flushing, and left the table.

Dieter said to me, "You see, we didn't know who your guest would be, but it's no problem. We have made arrangements for him."

Torvash said, "Sorry for any inconvenience." Dieter said, "A guest in our home is no inconvenience." His wife smiled and added, "I had salmon all ready." She bobbed her head, "We have one more trip and then we can begin to eat." Again the family trooped out of the room.

I said, "Torvash, you've made a conquest."

He didn't raise his eyes from the table. "Jews are for German women as Blacks are for nice White women in the States. They dream of us, the untouchables, and maybe we dream of them. But we are unsafe, except as toys."

I had seen some White women in the United States flirt so outrageously with Black men in public that they reminded me of dogs in heat. But after rubbing against the men, rolling their eyes and licking their lips, if the Black man asked for dates and persisted, the women would not only refuse, but would become angry that the men were forgetting their manners. It was a cruel minuet danced between spike-heeled women and barefoot men.

The family returned bringing hard boiled eggs, salmon, pickles, mayonnaise, mustards and relish, and I ate without a blessing but with gusto. Dieter must have spoken sharply to his mother-in-law in the kitchen, for she never said another word—just kept her eyes on the table, attacking the food angrily.

Between bites we engaged in nerve dulling small talk. I told the listeners where I was from, Torvash listed the cities on his tour, Dieter related in detail the incidents of his visits to the United States, and his wife smiled a lot. Hans and his grandmother ate.

A middle-aged couple came through the garden door and were introduced as neighbors who had been invited to join us for beer.

Their surprise when they were introduced made it obvious that they had expected to meet Die Negers, but not the Jew. Flushed, they sat near Dieter and spoke to me in good but halting English. After another inestimable spate of uninteresting conversation, I asked for a joke.

I said, "I collect jokes. I believe that if you know what a person eats, how and if he prays, how he loves and what makes him laugh, you can claim to understand him, at least a little. I'll tell you a Black American story and you tell me a German one." Immediately I began to recount a Brer Rabbit tale from my childhood which showed the hare defenseless and threatened. As always, in African and Afro-American folktales, the seemingly weak animal with the sharpest brain outwits its well-armed adversary. I left the listeners without a doubt that the vulnerable trickster represented my people and the heavily equipped opponent was the White race. The tale always drew agreeing laughter from Blacks, but the only response I got from that company was a few polite chuckles. We drank more beer and I prodded them for a story.

"Just so I can say I have really met Germans and heard their humor."

The visitors and Dieter spoke to each other, obviously making suggestions which one or the other would reject. Dieter said, "Get Torvash to tell an Israeli joke. He must know millions. He comes from a people known for their black humor." He smiled, "No pun intended." Torvash spoke, looking directly at me. "I do know a story. It's not an Israeli one, nor is it, strictly speaking, a German story, but rather German and Jewish. If that's all right?" The air tightened in the room and there was a barely audible gasp from Dieter's mother-in-law.

I said, "Please tell it. I'm sure everyone wants to hear it."

When I looked at Dieter and his neighbors I knew how wrong I was.

Their faces were stricken with white surprise, but Dieter recovered. He said, "By all means. A German and Jewish story? Do tell it."

Torvash leaned back in his chair and began in a soft voice.

"There was a Jewish man during World War II who had a sixth sense and would have premonitions whenever the Brown Shirts or SS troops were going to make a raid. He would leave the place moments before the soldiers would arrive. It was a gift he had."

I scanned the faces at the table. They had turned mottled grey, like certain Italian marble, and their bodies were held stiffly, not unlike marble statuary.

Torvash continued smoothly as if telling a fairy tale to enchanted children. "The man had gone on like that for three years, but one day his talent deserted him and he was caught."

It seemed that Torvash and I were the only people breathing air.

The rest had their lips slightly parted, but there was no visible contracting of their nostrils or chests.

"And the soldiers took the Jew to an SS officer who began to interrogate him. The officer said, 'I know you are the one who has been escaping us all these years. You think you are clever.'" Torvash had straightened up in his chair. His face was suddenly seamless and his eyes were like stones. He had become the Nazi officer. "'I will see how clever you are. I shall ask you one question. If you answer correctly, I will let you immigrate. If you are wrong...'" The actor paused and looked at Dieter. "You know."

I answered, surprising myself by saying, "I know. Go on."

Torvash resumed his performance as the German. "One of my eyes is false. It was made for me by the world's greatest false eye maker. It cost me a fortune. If you can look at my eyes and tell which one is false, you will be allowed to leave Germany."

Then the actor's shoulders slumped and pulled forward, his face lengthened and began to shake, his eyes opened in fear and his lips were suddenly loose. He was the terrified Jew in the clutch of fear.

"I know, sir, I know. I know because the false one looks so human."

Torvash dropped the old man's face as if it had been a mask and said, "My father, who survived, said that was a popular story in his concentration camp."

It seemed to me that no one moved, or coughed, or even breathed. I know that the story had fallen from my ears, down into my chest, and I found it hard to fill my lungs.

Dieter recovered first. "Yes, I have heard that one myself. Now," he rose, "if I could have some help we will have dessert."

He refused his neighbor's offer to help clear the table. "No, just family. You stay and entertain our guests." Dieter's wife, her face free of emotion, began to remove plates and silverware with remarkable efficiency. In moments, Torvash, the neighbors and I were seated before a table which showed no evidence of ever having been used.

"I wish you had not told that story." The neighbor's voice was just above a whisper. His wife nodded, her mouth grim. "Yes, you see Dieter has a false eye, but you couldn't know that."

The family trooped noisily back to the table smiling and bringing fruit, bowls of whipped cream, tarts, cheeses and more beer. To my surprise they seemed at ease, as if in leaving the room for a few minutes they had obliterated their own awful history.

Dieter sat down and handed out dessert while his wife poured coffee into ornate, yet fragile cups.

We all murmured appreciation for the beautifully presented sweets and the abundance of the meal. I refused to examine Dieter's eyes. When each plate was laden and the last coffee poured, Dieter leaned back into his chair and spoke, "We have a story. A German folktale." The pronoun hinted at collusion, and I looked at Torvash who kept a placid face.

"This story is very old and most German children hear it before they reach their teens."

Despite the obliqueness or childishness of a folktale, I knew it could be used to serve the teller's end. Apprehension stirred on my neck and arms.

Dieter's face was rosy with anticipation. "Ready? Shall I tell it?" Everyone, including Torvash, agreed. I settled back hoping to enjoy the story.

Dieter coughed and began, "Once a German worker was on his way to the factory. It was a bitter, cold morning, and the worker was hurrying along when he saw a small bird on the ground, too cold to move. The worker picked up the bird and felt a small heart beat. He held the bird cupped in his hands and breathed hard, blowing warm air on the little bird."

He mimicked the action, his face shining with concentration. "And because of the schnapps he had just drunk with coffee and the warm breath, the bird began to liven, to stir. The worker repeated blowing and blowing and the little bird opened both eyes. But just then, the factory bell rang. The worker was puzzled. What could he do? He had to get to the factory, but he couldn't put the bird back down to finish freezing to death. He looked around, and a cow had just passed and left a large pat on the ground. Steam was rising from the pat. The worker said, 'Oh, that's what I will do.' So he walked over and pushed the little bird down into the hot pat of cow dung, and went to work. That is the end of act one."

I looked at the company and saw all the faces beaming except that of my escort, whose skin was the color of tallow.

"The second act finds the bird recovered. He sticks his head up and out of the dung and loudly, very loudly begins to peep. 'Peep, peep, peep.' That's the end of the second act. Third act: A wolf in the forest has hunted for days for food and found nothing. He is starving. He hears 'peep, peep, peep,' and walks to the pat of cow dung, and sees the bird and opens his mouth, and gobbles the bird down like this."

Dieter spreads his mouth open and shows how the wolf swallowed the bird.

"And that is the end of the third act, and the end of the story, except that there are three morals. One..." Dieter turns just a little to face Torvash, "Remember, he who puts you in the shit is not necessarily your enemy. And two, he who takes you out is not necessarily your friend." Dieter stood from his chair and leaned his back against the wall. "And the most important moral of all is..." He raised his voice into a shout, "Once you find yourself in the shit, keep your big mouth shut."

Everything began to swell at once. My heart was too full of blood, and the blood was pounding too fast in my ears. The people at the table were suddenly huge, white papier mâché–like unpainted figures in a Mexican parade. Torvash became all Jews, and it seemed the necktie he wore was strangling him. The odors of fresh strawberries and burnt sugar mixed with the smell of beer and sausages. I almost toppled over the table as I ran for the door. The garden was as neat as a living room, and I searched for a covert corner to vomit up all the hate I had just ingested. I hung over a row of yellow flowers willing to drown them in bile, but nothing came except a salty hot water that I dribbled into the asters.

When I returned to the room, the people were sitting in their same chairs and speaking German softly. Dieter stood as I approached the table. "Oh, my dear Mrs. Angelou, I suppose your constitution is not used to such a heavy German breakfast. Do you feel better now?"

The SS officer and the Jew, the bird, the pile of cow dung, and the starving wolf had disappeared. The two men were like champion boxers who, having delivered smashing blows, had returned to their corners for relief. Dieter was again the solicitous host and Torvash had his normal look of bemusement. The others were calm.

"I'd like to go to my hotel. Thank you for everything."

"Oh, but I must show you my collection of African art."

"Really, I'm not feeling well. I must—" I nodded to the visitors and to Dieter's wife. "Sorry, but I must."

"Then we will leave through the other way. You can see some of the art on the way out. Are you ready?" Torvash shook hands around the room and we went up the few stairs to a side door through which we had entered. Dieter said, "Come this way," and we followed.

The white walls on either side of the hall were crowded with African masks. Dieter described them as we passed. "This is Bambara, this is Fon. Here are Yoruba burial urns. This is Ashanti. I have a large collection of Ashanti gold weights in the other room. If you'd like to see..."

I mumbled, "Not this time. I must take my medicine every four hours." The lie came so unexpectedly even I believed it.

"Well, the next time you come to Berlin..." He pointed, "Here are some Benin bronzes on that wall."

We had reached the front door, so I opened it and walked out into the sunshine.

We sat in the car. I was again in the back seat. Dieter turned his torso around to speak to me. "Since you live in Ghana, I thought you might like to do some trade for me. Of course I have an agent here in Berlin, but his prices are very high and I am certain the Africans don't see even one percent of that money. Maybe you could do something for me."

"I don't trade. I particularly don't trade in African art."

Torvash turned slightly, his light eyes glowing amber and his lips pulled into a smile.

Dieter said, "I am a serious collector, and if you could get some old

Ashanti carvings and maybe some Bambara for me or masks from Sierra Leone...I'd pay you very well. Very well."

I didn't need to look at Torvash, I was certain that his smile was widening.

"I don't trade, Dieter, and I'd really like to get to my hotel."

There was little conversation, only some muttering from the front seat which I ignored. I sat trying to hold my mind together, trying to keep it blank.

At the hotel Dieter was still polite. He bowed over my hand and thanked me for a superb morning. He and Torvash shook hands. They were like two acquaintances who had shared a taxi. There was no admittance that each had walked uninvited into the other's most private place, and shone a painful light.

Dieter drove away and I turned to the Israeli. "I'm sorry. I started something I didn't expect."

"At least we know why you were invited."

I nodded. "He wanted me to exploit the African sculptors. I didn't expect that."

"I think you should examine your reason for accepting the invitation." Torvash took my hand. "Neither you nor I can afford to be so innocent. Not here in Germany or anywhere in this world, unless we admit that we want the return of slavery and the concentration camps." He gave me a sad smile and walked away down the street.

I told only Roscoe about the incident. He said, "Excellent stories. Exceptional and expectable. But you are the most interesting element of the tale. The Israeli knew, and you should have known what would happen. Be careful, dear girl, that Africa doesn't take away all your cynicism. You have become dangerously young."

The play's exquisite writing gathered me and the actors into itself, and we, becharmed, did its bidding without protest. The script vilified all Whites, and we used each opportunity to shout profanities at the German audience which accepted each calumny as if they either didn't comprehend our meanings, or thought of our diatribes as the insignificant mouthings of insignificant clowns.

I wondered how well another play with other actors would have fared. Would the audience have stood and thrown roses if the actors had been Jewish, re-enacting a scene in Dachau? I knew the answer and I disliked the Germans for pandering to us, and I disliked myself and the cast for being bullies.

When I realized that I wanted to apologize to my friends, all Jews and even the Germans, I knew that Africa had creolized me. I was neither meat nor fowl nor good red herring. My native sassiness which had brought me from under the heels of brutes, had been softened by contact with the respectfulness of Ghanaians, yet, unlike them I did not belong to a place from which I could not be dislodged. I had put on just learned airs along with my African cloth, and paraded, pretending to an exotic foreign poise I had not earned nor directly inherited.

In the actors' company I laughed or shook my head or grunted because I knew the cues and sounds necessary for acceptance, but I had become something other, another kind of person. The New York actors were concerned with what plays were going into production, what roles were going to be filled, and how on earth or on any other planet could a Black actor, talented and trained, exact success from a resistance race and a difficult profession. They were quick and pretty and clever, and when the brief tour concluded they would return home where their restless striving would be not only understood, but expected. The European trip had simply taken them from the arena for a brief respite, but even as they rested they honed their reflexes and practiced their footwork.

We left Berlin for Italy, without regret or hesitation. The actors were looking forward to yet another stage, and I was eager to see Venice again.

Once we arrived in the city of canals, I learned that we were to perform in the lush Teatro La Fenice. I remembered the first time I had seen the jewel box of a theatre.

Ten years earlier when *Porgy and Bess* had played there and Venice was the first European city I had ever seen, I walked its narrow streets and created a fictional connection between myself and its past. I had been a lover of a doge, a sister to Othello and Correggio's generous patron. For a short while I let my Black American history sink beneath the surface of the city's sluggish water. All the citizens of Venice had been our friends. Gondoliers on the Grand Canal had saluted us with arias from the opera and children followed the cast singing their heavily accented version of "Summertime."

The surface of Venice had not changed. The same birds flew their same swooping patterns over the same tourists in the unchanging San Marco Square. But when "The Blacks" arrived in the floating city, some citizens, angered by the worldliness of presentations at the Venice Biennale, had taken their protests to the streets. As we prepared to enter the theatre we met angry people shouting, "We do not want your filth in Venice." Our Italian sponsors shrugged their shoulders and told us the demonstrators were religious fanatics and we should ignore them.

Some of my colleagues were disposed to follow that advice, but I found it hard to pretend indifference.

Raymond and Lex saw my nervousness and assured me that I had nothing to worry about.

Raymond said, "Queenie, if they touch one hair on your natural, they'll sing 'O Sole Mio' in another key and out of another hole. Come on, let's go!" We put our heads up and marched in as if the Pope had given us the pretty little theatre just because we were so righteous.

The audience applauded Genet and the audacious cast. The next few days passed without particular interest. My thoughts had turned to Egypt. I was about to walk on the streets where a good marriage went bad, and sit in parlors where my ex-husband and I had worn veiled but angry looks.

There were no last minute tearful departures among me and the cast. Everything we had had to share had been exchanged. Their eyes were filled with excitement for the next play, or for Hollywood, for success which was waiting for them to claim it. Roscoe saw me to the launch which was the first leg of my journey to Cairo. At the wharf he held me, then pulled away.

"Be careful, sweet lady. You went to Africa to get something, but remember you did not go empty handed. Don't lose what you had to get something which just may not work. And I have heard, 'If it don't fit, don't force it.' Bad grammar, but sound advice." In honor of his wisdom, he raised one eyebrow and I raised two. There was nothing to add, so we embraced and left each other with a laugh.

From the airplane window sunlight on the Sahara made the sandscape look like a lumpy butterscotch ocean.

The Williamsons sent their limousine to collect me from the Cairo airport. Two of their children accompanied the driver. Although Baby Joe and Edwina, four and six years old, had grown up from infancy in Egypt with Arabic nannies and Egyptian children, they still had the manners and even the accents of the children I had come to know in Ghana. They greeted me with hugs, then sat dignified in the car seats, waiting for me to begin the conversation. They responded to my questions directly and briefly.

Yes, their parents were well. Yes, they were enjoying school. Yes, they had lots of friends. Yes, their Arabic was good. Edwina, suddenly excited, asked, "Auntie Maya, do you know the Old Man is here?"

Liberians affectionately called their president, William V. S. Tubman, "Old Man." Edwina told me that he was "very good and smokes more cigars than Daddy and they are bigger, too." Baby Joe explained, "But he is the President." Once they had broken the mold of proper childish behavior, they would not put it together again. They chattered about parties and punishments, and what friends were visiting from Liberia. I was told that Edwina was reading well, and I had to listen to Baby Joe say his ABC's. They spoke about their mother's pregnancy with a charming naturalness. Baby Joe wanted another sister. "Edwina can be not good, you know." Liberians rarely accuse a person of being overtly bad, but they use the opprobrium of being "not good."

I arrived at the residency. Bahnti Williamson was waiting. "Ooh, Auntie Maya, welcome home."

She smiled, showed a pretty set of small, white teeth, and stretched her arms to me. "Ooh, Auntie Maya, how we have been anxious to see you. Ooh, Auntie." She turned her baby-filled belly to the side so that we could embrace, and I felt at home.

During the nearly two years when I had lived in Cairo with a teenage son I scarcely understood, and a husband I understood too well, Bahnti and her husband Joe, Jarra and Kebidetch Mesfin, an Ethiopian couple, and David Du Bois, had given me their laughter, love, company and very little advice.

Bahnti and I entered the residency, which had the air of a Liberian village during feast day. Henry, the Williamsons' oldest son, Bahnti's younger sister, cousins, Liberian visitors and wives of African diplomats stationed in Cairo crowded around embracing me and shaking my hand. After we sat together eating "country chop" (a spicy African stew) and toasted my arrival, Bahnti took me to a guest room where she explained that Joe was almost too busy to come home.

The president had brought a large retinue of cabinet members to attend the conference of nonaligned countries, and Joe, as Liberian Ambassador, had to be available to the delegation every minute. She said that she had hardly been able to await my arrival. There was no one to help in the preparations for the president's visit to the residency, which would take place in two days. I allowed myself to forget the twenty or more relatives, friends and servants who hovered over her like drone bees around the queen, preening her and making her comfortable.

"Sister, Ooh Auntie Maya, if you hadn't come, I would never receive the 'Old Man.'" African and southern Black American women can exude a charm which acts as a narcotic on their targets. The living room had seemed perfect when I entered, but if Bahnti asked me, I was willing to repaint, hang new wallpaper or simply move the furniture.

We sat on her balcony at sunset with frosty drinks. Bahnti told plain stories with such humorous embellishment that I would choke on laughter. Each time a spasm would shake my body, Bahnti would throw her hands in the air and say, "Oh Sister Maya, oh Auntie, you are the funny one. Old Man say in my country laughter is better than rice. Now Sister, you must listen. Joe has told President Tubman about you, and he has promised that you will sing for him day after tomorrow night."

I choked again, "What? Sing? Sing what?"

"Oh, but Auntie, you know Old Man studied in the states and he loves the Negro Spirituals. Auntie, you used to sing them to us and the children. So Old Man is expecting to sing 'Swing Low, Sweet Chariot' with you."

I drank and considered the request. There was no chance that I would refuse it, but at least I wanted Bahnti to know that what she was asking of me was not a small thing.

Many years had passed since I had sung in night clubs for a living, and although I had had moderate success I never had illusions about my musical or vocal talents. I succeeded because I wore exotic costumes and told interesting stories against a musical background.

I said, "Sister Alzetta." Calling her by her given name was one way to let her know how seriously I regarded her request. "I hope you have not led the president to think I am a Miriam Makeba. She is a singer, I just sometimes carry the tune."

My statement must have also tickled the unborn baby, because Bahnti held her stomach as she laughed. "Oh Auntie, Old Man knows how great Miss Makeba is, but he can't fold up his tongue to sing those click songs. He's going to sing 'Swing Low, Sweet Chariot' with you just as he learned it in the South of America. Not in South Africa. Hoo, hoo."

I explained that I was going to meet Black American friends from Ghana who were attending the conference.

Her laughter still echoed in my mind as I was driven by her chauffeur to the Cairo Hilton. Julian, Alice and I sat in the air-conditioned restaurant ordering hot dogs, hamburgers and french fries. Ana Livia had joined colleagues from her country who formed the Puerto Rican Delegation of Petitioners. Julian, as a member of the Ghana Press

Delegation, had sat in on a few of the nonaligned conference meetings, and he was full of news.

As soon as I could break into his speech, I told them of my assignment to sing with President Tubman and how nervous I was. Their laughter rivaled Bahnti's.

Julian recovered first. "So, Maya Angelou, you've made it all the way from Arkansas to Africa so that you can perform for a president? You couldn't get to the White House so you aimed for the Black House. Okay, I'm proud of you."

Alice said Liberia had been settled by freed American slaves, and their descendants still formed the elite so maybe I was related to the president. There was no reason to be nervous. I should just consider that maybe I was singing at a family reunion.

I went with them to meet David, who was in his usual state of overcommitment. He worked as a journalist at the Egyptian News Service as well as a stringer for international news services.

After a hearty and genial greeting, we began a garrulous chatter of conversation which sense would hardly penetrate. David spoke glowingly of Malcolm X's recent visit to Cairo, and wanted to know what we could do to protect him when he returned. Alice announced that she had taken the E.C.A. job in Addis Ababa, and asked who did we know in Ethiopia. I wanted suggestions for my presidential command performance. Julian wanted to hear about the conference, the conferees, and every detail of their plans.

None of us really expected the other to respond to our statements. It was enough to make the pronouncements and ask the questions in a friendly atmosphere. We knew that ultimately, each of us would be obliged to carry out our own assignments and find our own solutions. The brief gathering was nurturing and when the commotion abated we parted quite satisfied.

The Liberian Residency was festooned with flags and garlands. The family and family friends waited impatiently. Servants wearing new clothes and rehearsed into numbness stood at military attention in the foyer, and the children, quieted by the importance of the occasion, formed their own small line inside the salon.

Beyond the open door, along the steps and down the walk to the entry gatehouse, Egyptian and Liberian soldiers, their weapons at the ready, awaited President Tubman. The unnatural and uncomfortable silence was broken by the arrival of cars and the shouted orders of Army officers. Joe left the family rank and descended the stairs to meet a group of beribboned and laughing men.

William V. S. Tubman was surrounded by his court of cabinet ministers, but he was clearly visible, and after the phalanx had climbed the stairs, he entered the building arm in arm with Ambassador Williamson. Although he wore a tuxedo heavily adorned with medals and ribbons, he looked like an ordinary man that one might meet in church or in the Elks Hall or in any Black American community. That impression was short-lived—for after he embraced Bahnti and the other family members, Joe presented me. "Mr. President, this is our friend, the American singer Maya Angelou." The force of the man was befuddling. I didn't know whether to bob or curtsy.

"Oh, Miss Angelou, I have been looking forward to this evening. To have some of A. B.'s good Liberian chop and some Negro spirituals. Welcome." He and his energy passed me and I felt as if a light had been turned off. He was a president with a royal aura.

People born into democracies and who have learned to repeat, if not to practice, the statement that all men are created equal think themselves immune to the power of monarchies. They are pridefully certain that they would never tug their forelocks nor would their knees ever bend to a lord, laird or feudal master. But most have never had those beliefs put to test. Being physically close to extreme power causes one to experience a giddiness, an intoxication.

At that moment, I wanted to be close to President Tubman's aura, encompassed by, warmed, and held forever in its rich embrace.

At formal dinner, I was seated far away from the important officials, but close enough to observe them entertaining their leader. Each person had a story, told in the unique Liberian accent, and as each story concluded, President Tubman approved the telling by adding an appropriate proverb for each tale. The cabinet ministers and diplomats beamed with pride and laughed easily with and for their "Old Man."

When dinner was finished, Joe led the guests into the decorated salon. As President Tubman sat in a thronelike chair flanked by his suddenly serious attendants, Bahnti looked at me and raised her eyebrows. Joe introduced me, saying although I was a singer and writer, much more important I was the auntie of his children, a daughter of Africa and his chosen sister.

"Mr. President, excuse me." I was standing in the center of the salon. "I have never sung for a president. In fact, I've never met a president before."

William Tubman laughed and rolled his giant cigar between his fingers. "My child," he chuckled and his retinue chuckled, "My child, I am just a common garden variety president. Sing!" I began a traditional blues in a comfortable tempo. The president snapped his fingers and the guests slowly followed his example. When I finished the song the applause was loud and long.

"Now, my child, sing 'Swing Low, Sweet Chariot.' "

I began the old song, softly. "Swing Low, Sweet Chariot, Coming for to carry me home." The president's baritone joined. "Swing Low, Sweet Chariot, Coming for to carry me home."

Other voices picked a harmonic path into the song, and I heard Bahnti's high soprano waver, "If you get there before I do, Coming for to carry me home, Tell all my friends I'm coming too, Coming for to carry me home." They sounded neither like Whites nor like Black Americans, but they sang with such emotion that tears filled my eyes. Save for a few Egyptian government officials and me, all the singers were African. I knew from the dinner conversation that not one of them was fired with religious zeal, so for what chariot were they calling and what home could they possibly miss? I dropped my voice and gave them the song.

They were Americo-Liberians. Possibly five generations before, an ancestor—an American slave—had immigrated to Africa to marry into one of the local tribes. Now, after a century of intermarriage, they sat in beribboned tuxedos in this formal salon, drinking French champagne, models of the international diplomatic community. In their own land they owned rubber plantations and rice and coffee farms, and in their homes they spoke Bassa and Kru and Mandinke and Vai as easily as they spoke English.

Still, their faces glowed as they picked up the melody.

> See that host all dressed in red,
> Coming for to carry me home.
> It looks like a band that Moses led,
> Coming for to carry me home.

They were earnest and their voices were in tune, but they could not duplicate the haunting melody of our singing. While it is true that not all Black Americans can sing or dance, those who do create tones so unique that they are immediately identifiable. Of all Africans I had heard, only the Zulus, Xhosas, and Shonas of South Africa produced the velvet and wistful sounds which were capable of reaching the ear and heart with an undeniable message of pain.

Did it mean that only the African, and only the African living in total despair, pressed down by fate, refused, rejected and abandoned could develop and sing this kind of music?

The strains faded away and beautiful smiles accompanied the audience's applause. In the absence of my creative ancestors who picked that melody out of cotton sacks, I humbly bowed my head.

When Guy met me at the airport with chocolates (expensive) and a lovely piece of African cloth which he himself had chosen at the market, I was quick to think that my absence had made his heart grow fonder. His face was young with trust again, and he was laughing again—hearty, open laughter. I concluded that my decision to stay as long as possible with Bahnti and Joe had been wise, for my son had come back from that adolescent region where the barriers were so dense and high, they kept out prying eyes and even light.

He carried my bags into the house and the aroma of fried chicken met me at the door. I knew that dish was beyond Otu's talent and since Alice and Vicki were gone... I looked questioningly at Guy.

He smiled and hugged me. "I cooked it, Mom. I know you hate airplane food."

The tears on my face surprised me and distressed Guy.

We had not used weeping to manipulate each other. I apologized and Guy said, "Maybe this is not the time to talk to you."

I insisted that the time to talk was when one had something to say. I sat, still in my traveling clothes, while Guy spoke as carefully as if he was reading a prepared treatise.

He declared his gratitude for all I had ever done. He announced that I was an excellent mother. He said no parent could have been more patient, more generous or more loving. I began to contract, to tighten my muscles and my mind for the blow which I knew was coming. Because it was not a wallop, it slipped up on and into me like a whisper.

"Mom," he looked like the sweet boy I had such joy raising. "Mom, I've thought about this seriously and continuously since you left. You have finished mothering a child. You did a very good job. Now, I am a man. Your life is your own, and mine belongs to me. I am not rejecting you, I'm just explaining that our relationship has changed...."

He was not pulling at the apron strings, he was carefully and methodically untying the knots and raveling the very thread.

"I have not decided just what I want to do. Whether I shall stay in Ghana and finish at the university, or go to another country to finish my education. In any case, I shall apply for scholarship so you can be free of the burden of my tuition."

Now the entire apron was a pile of lint and I was speechless. He talked, beckoning me into his thoughts, but I was unable to follow him. I didn't know the road.

At the end of his speech, he hugged me again and thanked me again, and saying he had plans for dinner, went out the door.

I walked around the empty house trying to make sense of the sentences which tumbled over themselves in my brain.

"He's gone. My lovely little boy is gone and will never return. That big confident strange man has done away with my little boy, and he has the gall to say he loves me. How can he love me? He doesn't know me, and I sure as hell don't know him."

Efua appeared at my door, drawn, her usual healthy skin the color of gun metal. When she entered the house I saw her trembling hands. I knew better than to ask any questions. At the proper time she would say why she had come to me.

When I returned from the kitchen with cool beer, she was more composed but she was still standing in the middle of the living room.

"Sister, have you seen it? Have you seen the paper?" I said no, and wondered if the president had been assassinated. I implored her to sit, but she shook her head.

"Today's paper. Second page."

A presidential assassination would have claimed front page.

"Sister Efua, please come, and sit and let me pour you beer."

She remained erect, but shaking, oblivious to my entreaties.

"No one has claimed him. No one has come. Oh my Africa! What is happening to you? Oh my Africa."

The dramatic cries overwhelmed my suddenly very small living room. She could have filled a Greek theatre stage.

"Oh my Africa! Where are you going?"

I poured a glass of beer for her and placed it on a table beside a chair. I took mine to another seat and waited.

"Oh. Oh. My country. My people."

The moans began to fade and Efua finally came aware of her location. She gave me a wan smile. "Sister, excuse me, but I suppose you might not understand. A man, an Ashanti, a Ghanaian died two days ago. His body was lain in the morgue. No one has come for him."

She had her gaze on me, but the vacant eyes were staring and I was not being recorded in her vision.

"Do you know what that means?"

I shook my head.

"Africa is breaking. That body in the morgue is a stone from Africa's mountain. He belongs someplace. The day he was given a name he was also given a place which no one but he himself can fill. And after his death, that place remains his, although he has gone to the country of the dead. His family and clan will honor his possession of that place and cherish him. Never in Ghana has a body lain unclaimed for two days. That is why the newspaper has reported it. It should have been on the front page. Headlines. Africans must be shocked into realizing what is happening to them. To us."

She shook her head and gathering her cloth around her shoulders, walked through the doorway. I followed. She stood on my porch, turning her head slowly, looking from left to right to left at the houses and cars in my street. When she spoke her voice was low, nearly a moan. "Everybody in these cities should be made to go live in his native village for one year, barefoot and in rags. We have begun to think like Europeans. Sister, mind you, our gods will become angry. I would be afraid to anger Jesus Christ, but I confess, the thought of angering African gods absolutely terrifies me."

She leaned to kiss me farewell and walked down to her car where the chauffeur stood holding the door for her.

The visit muddled me. Efua, the model of containment, had been weeping not over the death of a stranger, but because other people who were also strangers had not come for his remains. As usual, as if I had been sent to the continent on assignment, I placed the African and Black American cultures side by side for examination. In Ghana, one unclaimed corpse merited principal news coverage, and Efua's emotional response, while in America, Black bodies still quick with life demanded no such concern. Too often among ourselves, since lives were cheap, dying was cheaper. Since the end of slavery, Black Americans running or walking, hitchhiking or hoboing from untenable place to unsupportable place, had died in fields, in prisons, hospitals, on battlegrounds, in beds and barns, and if pain accompanied their births, only the dying knew of their deaths. They had come and gone unrecorded save in symbolic lore, and unclaimed save by the soil which turned them into earth again.

I thought of the African gods whom Efua was loath to anger and decided that they must have been bristling with rage for centuries. How else explain the alliance of African greed and European infamy which built a slave stealing-selling industry lasting for over three centuries? Weren't the African gods showing their anger when they allowed the strongest daughters and sons to be carried beyond the seas' horizon? How much had they been provoked to permit disease and droughts and malnutrition to lay clouds of misery on the land? I agreed with Efua. I certainly would not like to see the gods of Africa anymore riled up than they were already.

The evening paper reported the family had come from the north to collect the body. Ghanaians breathed more easily, and so did I.

Misery is a faithful company keeper, and Comfort was dissolving under its attention. I watched for three months as her laughter diminished then disappeared along with about thirty pounds of sensuous curves. There was no jollity in her face, nor was there any strength in her hands. When she strung my hair, the movement on my head could have been caused by two sleepy snails going to rest.

"No, Sistah, I am not sick. Just weary."

We had come to know each other well enough for me to use an admonishing tone. "Sister, you have wearied yourself into bad health. You're so weak now you can hardly pull the comb through my hair."

Months before she would have blamed my hair, saying that it had a mind of its own and I should have the impertinence beaten out of it.

She said only, "I am getting weaker each day." She paused, then said, "It's the woman. She's doing it."

I asked, "What woman? Doing what?"

Even Comfort's voice was being erased. She said in a whisper, "His old wife is using some bad medicine on me. First she gave permission for us to be friendly, then when she saw how he loves me, she said 'no.' "

"Friendly? Comfort, did she think you would be just friends with her man? Plain friends?"

"She knew we were loving. Why else would my mother speak to her mother? And she agreed. Then... and then she saw that we were more than loving. We were... he liked me. That's when she promised I would lose. Lose everything. My looks, my weight. I would lose him and my mind. Oh, Sistah, she has power medicine. I might even lose my life."

"Did she give you something to drink?" I thought of arsenic.

"No, I eat at home. I have a cousin and a servant from my village who look after me. No. I have taken nothing that she has touched." She pulled a stool and sat beside me. I remarked that she looked like a little girl.

She said, "Sistah, I feel old, but I think she is taking old age from me."

Had she talked to the woman herself? Maybe if she went to the woman...

Comfort began to shudder and I apologized for the suggestion. She waved a bony hand at me.

"No, Sistah Maya, now you see my trouble?" She shivered and her eyes were filled with despair.

"The woman came to me. To my house. My steward let her in. Sistah, I went in to her. I was surprised. She is old. Once she looked fine, but now...Oh age...I will not live to see what it can do to me." She was near to tears, so I encouraged her to continue with her story.

"Well, Sistah, you know I was fat and fine as cocoa butter, and the man was loving me. Anyway, when she came to my house I asked her what she wanted...not sweetly, and she said she wanted to ask me two questions. God forgive me, but I was crazy. I didn't offer her a drink. I wouldn't even sit down. She is old, Sistah, and I still stood looking down on her." Comfort shook her head, wanting not to believe her own rudeness. She continued.

"She was wearing an old mourning cloth; she said, 'My first question is, do you know what love costs?' And I told her," Comfort crossed her hands atop her head, "I am not a market woman, so I do not think of everything in money terms. Then she said, 'My last question is, are you ready to pay anything for love?' A spell must have been on me then, because I lost all my training. I talked. I raised my voice. I said I wasn't so old and ugly I had to buy love, and I felt sorry for anybody who had to do so.

"Then I made my biggest mistake, because she stood up and said, 'You feel sorry for the person who bought love? Is that true?' She was looking at my mouth, and I laughed and chipsed. Sistah, I sucked my teeth at that woman. Even I can't believe I did that. The old woman wrapped her mourning cloth tight around her and said, 'You will lose. You will lose all,' and then she walked out of my house. Oooh, and Sistah, see me now? The man will not come to me. My flesh is falling away. Do your people have medicine? Power medicine?"

I asked her if she had seen a doctor, and she shook her head, "European doctors have nothing to help my condition. Don't you Black Americans have medicine?"

Many Black-owned newspapers in the United States carried announcements in the classified sections of magic practitioners.

> Get your man back!
> High John the Conqueror Roots

No one I knew admitted to using their services.

I had to tell Comfort that my people had no reliable medicine except that they had learned in school.

She said she had been to many African doctors and found no one able to move the terrible curse. She had even spent a week in Larteh, a town which hosts hundreds of practitioners, but had had no success. Her last hope was to travel to another country.

"Sistah, I have heard of a woman in Sierra Leone. She is very very good. I must go and stay two weeks, cleansing myself, and then she will see me. I must pay her in pure gold."

I said, "I don't have gold, but let me lend you some money."

Weakness made her old, robust smile gentle, "Sistah, thank you, but my uncle is a goldsmith, and I have plenty of trinkets. What I want is to go and come. I want us to sit out in your compound on a Saturday. I want my strength back so that when I put my hands on your head you will know that Comfort has her hands on your head, and I want you to make me laugh. Oh Sistah, I cannot say how much I want to laugh."

We embraced when she left and she promised to see me again in two months. Fine, fat and laughing.

Two weeks later a friend of Comfort's came to my door.

"Sister Maya, I have come with very sad news. Our Sister, Comfort, died in Sierra Leone. She had not been there a week. Sorry to bring this news, but I knew you would want to know. She so loved to laugh with you."

Malcolm was a prompt and exciting correspondent, using the mails to inform, instruct, and encourage us. His letters were weighty with news and rich in details of his daily life. The United States was on the brink of making great changes, and the time was ripe for the Organization of Afro-American Unity. His family was wonderful and it just might be increasing. Death threats were proliferating in his post box and he changed his telephone number frequently to protect his wife from vulgar and frightening callers.

Some of his letters were plain directives:

> A young painter named Tom Feelings is coming to Ghana. Do everything you can for him. I am counting on you.
>   The U.S. State Department is sending James Farmer to Ghana. The Ambassador will pick out special people for him to see and special places he should go. I want you all to collect him and show him around. Treat him as you treated me. I am counting on you.

There were good people working for the OAAU, full of energy and enthusiasm, but none had the organizational skills to set up and run an efficient office. What they needed was an experienced coordinator.

He didn't mention that I had worked as Northern Coordinator for Martin Luther King's SCLC. By omitting the reminder, he forced me to speculate upon my possible value to the organization. I went to Julian for advice. He said, "I suspect we'll all be home soon. Africa was here when we arrived and it's not going anywhere. You can always come back."

Alice's letter from Ethiopia pushed me closer to my decision. She wrote that Malcolm came through Addis, looking good but harried and still traveling without a companion. "If he gets that OAAU in shape, he'd be sure to have people around him. Like you and Julian, I'm worried for his safety."

My Ghanaian friends said they would be sorry to see me go, but they understood that my people's struggle came first.

I thought long and carefully before I came to a final decision.

My son convinced me, and had nearly succeeded in convincing himself, that he was a grown man. He was either doing brilliant work at the university or, when he was distracted, none at all. He was a character in a drama of his own composition, and was living the plot as it unfolded. Even if he forgot his lines, his mannishness wouldn't allow him to accept prompting.

When I told him I was thinking of returning to the United States, he had smiled broadly.

"Yes, Mom. It is time for you to go back home."

His only frown came when I said I would pay up his tuition and leave him a solid bank account.

"I'm really sorry I have to take your money, Mother, but some-day…someday." Visions of future affluence danced in his eyes. The little boy and even the rambunctious teenager had strutted upon the stage and exited. This new leading man did not need a mother as supporting actress in his scene. He welcomed having the stage to himself at last.

It seemed that I had gotten all Africa had to give me. I had met people and made friends. Efua, Kwesi Brew, T. D. Bafoo and Nana had woven themselves as important strands into the fabric of my life. I had gotten to know and love the children of Africa, from Baby Joe to the clever Kojo, the bouncing Abena, the grave Ralph and the ladylike Esi Rieter. They had given me their affection and instructed me on the positive power of literally knowing one's place. Sheikhali had provided African romance, and Comfort's life and her death had proved the reality of African illusion. Alice and Vicki and Julian and Ana Livia would return to the United States someday and we would stir up our cauldron of old love and old arguments, and not one whit of steam would have been lost during our separation. I had seen the African moon grow red as fire over the black hills at Aburi and listened to African priests implore God in rhythm and voices which carried me back to Calvary Baptist Church in San Francisco.

If the heart of Africa still remained allusive, my search for it had brought me closer to understanding myself and other human beings. The ache for home lives in all of us, the safe place where we can go as we are and not be questioned. It impels mighty ambitions and danger-ous capers. We amass great fortunes at the cost of our souls, or risk our lives in drug dens from London's Soho, to San Francisco's Haight-Ashbury. We shout in Baptist churches, wear yarmulkes and wigs and argue even the tiniest points in the Torah, or worship the sun and refuse to kill cows for the starving. Hoping that by doing these things, home will find us acceptable or failing that, that we will forget our awful yearning for it.

My mind was made up. I would go back to the United States as soon as possible.

Nana Nketsia was traveling to Lagos by car and when he invited me and his two oldest daughters to accompany him as far as the Togo border, I accepted gratefully. Now that I had decided to leave Africa, I realized I had not seen Eastern Ghana.

Araba rode with me and Adae got into her father's car. Three hours after we left Accra we arrived at the small but busy town of Aflao. Nana beckoned me to follow and led me to a large two-story stone house at the end of a quiet lane.

"We will stay here for the night, and at dawn my driver and I will continue to Lagos. Come inside, I want you to meet our host, the customs officer." A servant responded to Nana's knock and his daughters, Nana and I were shown into a daintily furnished sitting room. Before we could choose seats a young girl around Araba's age entered through a side door. She smiled and extended her hands and made a little curtsy to Nana.

"Nana, welcome. I am Freida, Adadevo's daughter. He is still at the office. I will make you comfortable."

Nana introduced Araba, Adae and me, and Freida bobbed prettily, accepting the introduction. She supposed we would be weary after such a long journey and offered to show us to our rooms. Nana was put on the ground floor, and I was given a second floor guest room. Araba and Adae were to share a room near Freida.

Although I was used to the dignity of African girls, I was taken aback by Freida's grown-up composure at sixteen. She was a practiced hostess. I surmised that she was an only child of a single parent and circumstances had forced her to grow up quickly and very well. Nana carried his shortwave radio to his quarters and I retired to my room.

For the next hours as the girls giggled down the hall, I thought of my impending departure and the Organization of Afro-American Unity. There had been no mention of salary or responsibilities. I knew that I would be paid the minimal wage and would be asked to raise money, organize files, recruit members, stuff envelopes, draft news releases, type, file and answer the telephone. Those were the usual chores that go begging in understaffed and underfinanced civil rights organizations.

It would be good to see my family and old friends. Suddenly I was excited at the prospect of being back in New York City, and back in the fray.

Araba broke into my thoughts. "Auntie Maya, Mr. Adadevo is here, and dinner is served." I prepared myself and joined the group in the dining room.

Mr. Adadevo was a tall, dark brown man of pleasing appearance, and when he spoke his voice sang with the melodic Ewe accent. The girls sat together at dinner, using English to talk across their language barrier while Nana and Mr. Adadevo spoke of portentous matters of State. The hours of assessment in the guest room had drained my energy, and I was glad there was no general conversation which could command my participation.

At an early hour, I asked to be excused, honestly claiming exhaustion.

The bed, sleep and I met together and I rose at dawn to go downstairs and bid Nana a safe journey. He promised that he would return to Ghana before my departure.

When Mr. Adadevo entered the kitchen the day was bright and I was having yet another cup of instant coffee. He ate quartered oranges and asked me why I was only then visiting this area. I made a courteous reply, then he asked if I would like to see the nearby town of Keta only thirty miles away. Without any real interest I again answered courteously.

"That would be nice. We should start back to Accra by early afternoon." He assured me that we would have plenty of time and left to rouse the still sleeping girls.

It was decided that we would take his large car. Araba, Adae and Freida sat in the back, and Mr. Adadevo, his driver and I occupied the front seat.

The countryside was beautiful, but not unusually so. My eyes had become accustomed to coconut trees and palms, and bougainvillaea growing freely on country roads and city streets. A quiet murmur reached me from the back seat and since neither Mr. Adadevo nor his driver spoke, I was lulled by the car motor and the moist warm air into a near torpor.

Suddenly, I jerked alert and looked ahead. We were approaching a sturdy and graceful bridge. My heart began to race and I was struggling for breath. I gasped, "Stop, stop the car. Stop the car." The driver consented. I was sitting next to the window, so I opened the door and quickly stepped to the ground. I spoke through the back window.

"Get out, girls. Come. You, too, Freida. We are going to walk across this bridge." Although they were stunned by my behavior, they obeyed, and I said to the startled Adadevo, "We will join the car on the other side." I walked briskly apart from my charges who were unsettled by my actions and tittering nervously. My pretended concern over the waterscape and the overgrown river banks caused me to turn my head often, as if looking for a particular object or view. In fact, I was more jittery than the teenagers. I could not explain my behavior. I only knew that the possibility of riding across that bridge so terrified me that had the driver refused to stop, I would have jumped from the still moving car.

Mr. Adadevo was standing at the end of the bridge, and after he saw the passengers safely in the back seat, he took my arm and drew me aside.

"Why were you afraid? I have rarely seen such terror. Do you know anything about this bridge?" I shook my head.

"Have you ever heard of the Keta bridge?" I shook my head again. I had never heard the area mentioned. "The old bridge, I should say

bridges," his face was solemn, "were infamous for being so poorly constructed that in any flood they would crumble and wash away. People
in conveyances of any kind lost their lives, so a century ago passengers
in palanquins used to stop and get down in order to walk across. In a
crisis, only people on foot could hope to reach the other side." I felt a
quick chill. He asked, "Are you sure someone didn't tell you that
story?" I said, "I must have read it somewhere." I apologized for startling him and knew without question that I had no inkling of the
bridge's history.

After my inexplicable outburst, there was a new tension in the car.
No sounds came from the back seat, but Mr. Adadevo began speaking
immediately after the bridge episode and didn't stop until we reached
Keta.

He talked about Accra, of Ghana's growth, of the wisdom of
Kwame Nkrumah. He said he admired the American Negro athletes
and Dr. Martin Luther King. He spoke of his region, describing it in
detail, its fishing and copra industries, its markets and major towns,
and its religion.

I half heard his crooned chant as I was more engrossed in examining my actions at the bridge.

"There is a lagoon behind Keta and of course the ocean before it,
and that has caused the people of the town a great problem. For after
the work of enlarging the ports of Tema and Sekondi-Takowadi, the
ocean has reacted by backing up onto Keta. They have already lost
over two miles of the town. The people are being squeezed by two
forces of water. The town will disappear in time and the people have
nowhere to go."

When I heard the dire story, I again surprised myself. I felt as if I
had just been told a beloved relative was dying. Tears came to my eyes
and threatened to run down my face. I dreaded the possibility of crying before strangers, but even more awful was the prospect of allowing Nana's daughters to see me out of control. The motto of their
family was "royalty does not weep in the street," and I had spent a
great effort showing them that although I was born from slaves, I was
descended from kings.

I took a handkerchief and faked a cough.

Araba leaned foward, "Auntie, are you all right?"

I told her I thought I was reacting to the dust, and she was satisfied.

Adae, asserting her intelligence and explaining me to her new friend, said "Auntie is very sensitive. She has allergies." I was grateful for their presence, for without them I might have bent over my lap and let the emotion of loss drain out of me in rivers of tears. I swallowed the knots in my throat over and over and wondered if I was losing my mind. What did that bridge and the sea's encroachment on Keta have to do with me?

Adadevo was still talking as the car turned through the narrow streets of the old town. Although we could not see the ocean, suddenly I knew or felt that the next turn would give us a panoramic view of the surf. I held onto myself and hoped that the presentiment would prove false.

Mr. Adadevo said, "Now here is the sea. You call it the Atlantic Ocean. We have another name for it in Ewe."

The driver parked at the side of Keta's market and Mr. Adadevo asked me to come and meet his sister, who had a stall on the market's periphery. We walked in file with Freida and the driver carrying large empty straw baskets.

Mr. Adadevo's sister was tall and thin and resembled Efua. When we were introduced, I found that she spoke very scanty English and I expected that she would speak French.

The Ewe tribe which occupied Togo and the eastern area of Ghana had been a German colony in the nineteenth century, but after Germany's loss of World War I, the allied victors took away Germany's mandate and gave the area to France. French became the province's official language in 1920, so I offered to speak French with my host's sister, but her French was only a little better than her English. We smiled at each other and shook our heads in exasperation. She spoke rapid Ewe with her brother and niece, while Araba and Adae looked on.

I waved good-bye, anxious to climb into the raised market which was issuing sounds of trade and merriment.

The narrow stairs were bounded by wooden walls, making the entrance dim. I was looking down, making certain of my footfall, when a voice above me drew my attention. I looked up to see an older woman, unusually tall, blotting out the light behind her. She spoke again and in a voice somewhat similar to my own, but I was unable to understand her.

I smiled and, using Fanti, said regretfully, "I am sorry, Auntie, but I don't speak Ewe." She put her hands on her wide hips, reared back and let loose into the dim close air around us a tirade of angry words. When she stopped, I offered, in French and in a self-deprecating tone, "I am sorry, Auntie, but I don't speak Ewe."

She clapped her hands close enough to my face for me to feel the rush of air, then she raised her voice. My ignorance of the meaning of her words did not prevent me from knowing that I was being denounced in the strongest possible language.

When I could wedge myself into her explosion, I spoke in English nearly whining, "Auntie, I am sorry, but I do not speak Ewe."

It seemed the walls would collapse. The big woman took a step down to me, and I backed down two steps. There was no room on the stairs for me to pass her, and I wouldn't have had the nerve to try to force my way beyond that now enraged giant frame. Her invective was coming faster and louder. I knew that my luck had to have totally deserted me to allow me to meet a mad woman on darkened stairs who I could neither placate nor threaten.

Mr. Adadevo spoke behind me, and I turned only slightly, afraid to leave my back unprotected.

"Mr. Adadevo, would you please talk to this Auntie. I can't make her understand."

The woman fired another salvo, and Mr. Adadevo stepped up and placed himself between me and my assailant. He spoke softly in Ewe. I heard the word "American" while I was watching the woman's face. She shook her head in denial. My protector spoke again, still softly. I heard "American Negro." Still the woman's face showed disbelief.

Mr. Adadevo looked at me and said, "Sister, she thinks you are someone else. Do you have your American passport with you?"

I hadn't seen my passport in two years, but I remembered having an old California driver's license, which had its identifying photograph. I took the wrinkled, but still slick paper from my wallet and gave it to Mr. Adadevo. He handed the document to the woman who strained to see in the darkness. She turned and walked up the stairs into the light. Mr. Adadevo followed and I followed him.

There, the woman, who was over six feet tall, stood peering at the flimsy piece of paper in her dark hand. When she raised her head, I nearly fell back down the steps: she had the wide face and slanted eyes of my grandmother. Her lips were large and beautifully shaped like my grandmother's, and her cheek bones were high like those of my grandmother. The woman solemnly returned the license to Mr. Adadevo who gave it back to me, then the woman reached out and touched my shoulder hesitantly. She softly patted my cheek a few times. Her face had changed. Outrage had given way to melancholia. After a few seconds of studying me, the woman lifted both arms and lacing her fingers together clasped her hands and put them on the top of her head. She rocked a little from side to side and issued a pitiful little moan.

In Arkansas, when I was a child, if my brother or I put our hands on our heads as the woman before me was doing, my grandmother would stop in her work and come to remove our hands and warn us that the gesture brought bad luck.

Mr. Adadevo spoke to me quietly, "That's the way we mourn."

The woman let her arms fall and stepping up to me, spoke and took my hand, pulling me gently away. Mr. Adadevo said, "She wants you to go with her. We will follow." The girls and the driver had climbed the stairs and we entered the crowded market. I allowed myself to be tugged forward by the big woman who was a little taller than I and twice my size.

She stopped at the first stall and addressed a woman who must have been the proprietor. In the spate of words, I heard "American Negro." The woman looked at me disbelieving and came around the corner of her counter to have a better look. She shook her head and, lifting her arms, placed her hands on her head, rocking from side to side.

My companions were standing just behind me as the vendor leaned over the shelf where tomatoes, onions, and peppers were arranged in an artistic display. She began speaking, and raking the produce toward the edge.

Mr. Adadevo said something to the driver who came forward and placed each vegetable carefully into his basket. My host said, "She is giving this to you. She says she has more if you want it."

I went to the woman to thank her, but as I approached she looked at me and groaned, and cried, and put her hands on her head. The big woman was crying too. Their distress was contagious, and my lack of understanding made it especially so. I wanted to apologize, but I didn't know what I would ask pardon for.

I turned to Mr. Adadevo and asked if they thought I looked like someone who had died.

He answered and his voice was sad, "The first woman thought you were the daughter of a friend. But now you remind them of someone, but not anyone they knew personally."

My guide now pulled me through a press of bodies until we came to a stall where the owner sold yams, cassava and other tubers. Her wares were stacked on the ground in front of the stall and rose in piles around the stool she occupied. My escort began her litany to the saleswoman. Somewhere in the ritual she said "American Negro" and the woman repeated the first stall owner's behavior. Freida began putting yams and cocoa yams and cassava into her basket. The two women were rocking and moaning.

I said, "Mr. Adadevo, you must tell me what's happening."

He said, "This is a very sad story and I can't tell it all or tell it well." I waited while he looked around. He began again, "During the slavery period Keta was a good sized village. It was hit very hard by the slave trade. Very hard. In fact, at one point every inhabitant was either killed or taken. The only escapees were children who ran away and hid in the bush. Many of them watched from their hiding places as their parents were beaten and put into chains. They saw the slaves set fire to the village. They saw mothers and fathers take infants by their feet and bash their heads against tree trunks rather than see them sold into slavery. What they saw they remembered and all that they remembered they told over and over.

"The children were taken in by nearby villagers and grew to maturity. They married and had children and rebuilt Keta. They told the tale to their offspring. These women are the descendants of those orphaned children. They have heard the stories often, and the deeds are still as fresh as if they happened during their lifetimes. And you, Sister, you look so much like them, even the tone of your voice is like theirs. They are sure you are descended from those stolen mothers and fathers. That is why they mourn. Not for you but for their lost people."

A sadness descended on me, simultaneously somber and wonderful. I had not consciously come to Ghana to find the roots of my beginnings, but I had continually and accidentally tripped over them or fallen upon them in my everyday life. Once I had been taken for Bambara, and cared for by other Africans as they would care for a Bambara woman. Nana's family of Ahantas claimed me, crediting my resemblance to a relative as proof of my Ahanta background. And here in my last days in Africa, descendants of a pillaged past saw their history in my face and heard their ancestors speak through my voice.

The first woman continued leading me from stall to stall, introducing me. Each time the merchant would disbelieve the statement that I was an American Negro, and each time she would gasp and mourn, moan and offer me her goods.

The women wept and I wept. I too cried for the lost people, their ancestors and mine. But I was also weeping with a curious joy. Despite the murders, rapes and suicides, we had survived. The middle passage and the auction block had not erased us. Not humiliations nor lynchings, individual cruelties nor collective oppression had been able to eradicate us from the earth. We had come through despite our own ignorance and gullibility, and the ignorance and rapacious greed of our assailants.

There was much to cry for, much to mourn, but in my heart I felt exalted knowing there was much to celebrate. Although separated from our languages, our families and customs, we had dared to continue to live. We had crossed the unknowable oceans in chains and had written its mystery into "Deep River, my home is over Jordan." Through the centuries of despair and dislocation, we had been creative, because we faced down death by daring to hope.

A few days later at Accra's airport I was surrounded by family and friends. Guy stood, looking like a young lord of summer, straight, sure among his Ghanaian companions. Kwesi Brew, T. D. Bafoo and their wives were there to bid me farewell. Efua and her children, Nana's brood of six, Grace Nuamah and other colleagues from Legon, Sheikhali and Mamali, and some Nigerian acquaintances milled through the crowd. Julian hugged me, "Be strong, girl. Be very strong." Nana's car appeared on the tarmac, and coming through a private door he joined the well-wishers. I drank with each party, and gave and received generous embraces, but I was not sad departing Ghana.

Many years earlier I, or rather someone very like me and certainly related to me, had been taken from Africa by force. This second leave-taking would not be so onerous, for now I knew my people had never completely left Africa. We had sung it in our blues, shouted it in our gospel and danced the continent in our breakdowns. As we carried it to Philadelphia, Boston and Birmingham we had changed its color, modified its rhythms, yet it was Africa which rode in the bulges of our high calves, shook in our protruding behinds and crackled in our wide open laughter.

I could nearly hear the old ones chuckling.

A SONG FLUNG UP TO HEAVEN

Dedicated to
Caylin Nicole Johnson
Brandon Bailey Johnson
and to my entire family
wherever and whoever
you are

ACKNOWLEDGMENTS

I thank seven of my living teachers:

The Reverends

Frederick Buechner
Eric Butterworth
Serenus T. Churn, Sr.
H. Beecher Hicks
Barbara King
Cecil Williams
Andrew Young

CHAPTER 1

The old ark's a-movering
a-movering
a-movering
the old ark's a-movering
and I'm going home.
—Nineteenth-century American spiritual

The old ark was a Pan Am jet and I was returning to the United States. The airplane had originated in Johannesburg and stopped in Accra, Ghana, to pick up passengers.

I boarded, wearing traditional West African dress, and sensed myself immediately, and for the first time in years, out of place. A presentiment of unease enveloped me before I could find my seat at the rear of the plane. For the first few minutes I busied myself arranging bags, souvenirs, presents. When I finally settled into my narrow seat, I looked around and became at once aware of the source of my discomfort. I was among more white people than I had seen in four years. During that period I had not once thought of not seeing white people; there were European, Canadian and white American faculty at the university where I worked. Roger and Jean Genoud, who were Swiss United Nations personnel, had become my close friends and in fact helped me to raise—or better, corral—my teenage son. So my upset did not come from seeing the white complexion, but rather, from seeing so much of it at one time.

For the next seven hours, I considered the life I was leaving and the circumstances to which I was returning. I thought of the difference between the faces I had just embraced in farewell and those on the plane who looked at me and other blacks who also boarded in Accra with distaste, if not outright disgust. I thought of my rambunctious nineteen-year-old son, whom I was leaving with a family of Ghanaian friends. I also left him under the watchful eye and, I hoped, tender care of God, who seemed to be the only force capable of controlling him.

My thoughts included the political climate I was leaving. It was a known fact that antigovernment forces were aligning themselves at that very moment to bring down the regime of Kwame Nkrumah, Ghana's controversial, much adored but also much hated president. The atmosphere was thick with accusations, threats, fear, guilt, greed and capriciousness. Yet at least all the visible participants in that crowded ambience were black, in contrast to the population in the environment to which I was returning. I knew that the air in the United States was no less turbulent than that in Ghana. If my mail and the world newspapers were to be believed, the country was clamoring with riots and pandemonium. The cry of "burn, baby, burn" was loud in the land, and black people had gone from the earlier mode of "sit-in" to "set fire," and from "march-in" to "break-in."

Malcolm X, on his last visit to Accra, had announced a desire to create a foundation he called the Organization of African-American Unity. His proposal included taking the plight of the African-Americans to the United Nations and asking the world council to intercede on the part of beleaguered blacks. The idea was so stimulating to the community of African-American residents that I persuaded myself I should return to the States to help establish the organization. Alice Windom and Vickie Garvin, Sylvia Boone and Julian Mayfield, African-Americans who lived and worked in Ghana, were also immediate supporters. When I informed them that I had started making plans to go back to America to work with Malcolm, they—my friends, buddies, pals—began to treat me as if I had suddenly become special. They didn't speak quite so loudly around me, they didn't clap my back when laughing; nor were they as quick to point out my flaws. My stature had definitely increased.

We all read Malcolm's last letter to me.

Dear Maya,

I was shocked and surprised when your letter arrived but I was also pleased because I only had to wait two months for this one whereas previously I had to wait almost a year. You see I haven't lost my wit. (smile)

Your analysis of our people's tendency to talk over the head of the masses in a language that is too far above and beyond them is certainly true. You can communicate because you have plenty of (soul) and you always keep your feet firmly rooted on the ground.

I am enclosing some articles that will give you somewhat of an idea of my daily experiences here and you will then be better able to understand why it sometimes takes me a long time to write. I was most pleased to learn that you might be hitting in this direction this year. You are a beautiful writer and a beautiful woman. You know that I will always do my utmost to be helpful to you in any way possible so don't hesitate.

Signed
Your brother Malcolm

I looked around the plane at the South African faces and thought of Vus Make, my latest husband, from whom I had separated. He and members of the Pan-African Congress and Oliver Tambo, second in command of the African National Congress, really believed they would be able to change the hearts and thereby the actions of the apartheid-loving Boers. In the early sixties I called them Nation Dreamers. When I thought of Robert Sobukwe, leader of the Pan-African Congress who had languished for years in prison, and Nelson Mandela, who had recently been arrested, I was sure that they would spend their lives sealed away from the world. I had thought that, despite their passion and the rightness of their cause, the two men would become footnotes on the pages of history.

Now, with the new developments about to take place, I felt a little sympathy for the Boers, and congratulated myself and all African-Americans for our courage. The passion my people would exhibit under Malcolm's leadership was going to help us rid our country of racism once and for all. The Africans in South Africa often said they had been inspired by Martin Luther King, Jr., and the Montgomery bus boycott of 1958. Well, we were going to give them something new, something visionary, to look up to. After we had cleansed ourselves and our country of hate, they would be able to study our methods, take heart from our example and let freedom ring in their country as it would ring in ours.

Sweet dreams of the future blunted the sharp pain of leaving both my son and the other important man in my life. Given enough time, Guy would eventually grow up and be a fine man, but my romantic other could never fit into my world, nor I into his.

He was a powerful West African who had swept into my life with the urgency of a Southern hurricane. He uprooted my well-planted ideas and blew down all my firmly held beliefs about decorum.

I had been in love many times before I met him, but I had never surrendered myself to anyone. I had given my word and my body, but I had never given my soul. The African had the habit of being obeyed, and he insisted on having all of me. The pleasure I found with him made me unable, or at least unwilling, to refuse.

Within a month of conceding my authority over myself and my life to another, I realized the enormity of my mistake. If I wanted chicken, he said he wanted lamb, and I quickly agreed. If I wanted rice, he wanted yams, and I quickly agreed. He said that I was to go along with whatever he wanted, and I agreed. If I wanted to visit with my friends and he wanted to be alone but not without me, I agreed.

I began to feel the pinch of his close embrace the first time I wanted to sit up and read and he wanted to go to bed.

And, he added, I was needed.

I agreed.

But I thought, "Needed?" Needed like an extra blanket? Like air-conditioning? Like more pepper in the soup? I resented being thought of as a thing, but I had to admit that I allowed the situation myself and had no reason to be displeased with anyone save myself.

Each time I gave up my chicken for his lamb, I ate less. When I gave up a visit with friends to stay home with him, I enjoyed him less. And when I joined him, leaving my book abandoned on the desk, I found I had less appetite for the bedroom.

"You Americans can be bullheaded, stupid and crazy. Why would you kill President Kennedy?" He didn't hear me say, "I didn't kill the president."

My return to the United States came at the most opportune time. I could leave my son to his manly development hurdles; I would leave my great, all-consuming love to his obedient subjects; and I would return to work with Malcolm X on building the Organization of African-American Unity.

By the time we arrived in New York, I had discarded my vilification of the white racists on the plane and had even begun to feel a little more sorry for them.

I was saddened by their infantile, puerile minds. They could be assured that as soon as we American blacks got our country straight, the Xhosas, Zulus, Matabeles, Shonas and others in southern Africa would lead their whites from the gloom of ignorance into the dazzling light of understanding.

The sound in the airport was startling. The open air in Africa was often loud, with many languages being spoken at once, children crying, drums pounding—that had been noise, but at New York's Idlewild Airport, the din that aggressively penetrated the air, insisting on being heard, was clamor. There were shouts and orders, screams, implorings and demands, horns blaring and voices booming. I found a place beside a wall and leaned against it. I had been away from the cacophony for four years, but now I was home.

After I gathered my senses, I found a telephone booth.

I knew I was not ready for New York's strenuous energy, but I needed to explain that to my New York friends. I had written Rosa Guy, my supportive sister-friend, and she was expecting me. I also needed to call Abbey Lincoln, the jazz singer, and her husband, Max Roach, the jazz drummer, who had offered me a room in their Columbus Avenue apartment that I had refused. But most especially, I had to speak to Malcolm.

His telephone voice caught me off guard. I realized I had never spoken to him on the telephone.

"Maya, so you finally got here. How was the trip?" His voice was higher-pitched than I expected.

"Fine."

"You stay at the airport, I'll be there to pick you up. I'll leave right now."

I interrupted. "I'm going straight to San Francisco. My plane leaves soon."

"I thought you were coming to work with us in New York."

"I'll be back in a month . . ." I explained that I needed to be with my mother and my brother, Bailey, just to get used to being back in the United States.

Malcolm said, "I had to leave my car in the Holland Tunnel. Somebody was trying to get me. I jumped in a white man's car. He panicked. I told him who I was, and he said, 'Get down low, I'll get you out of this.' You believe that, Maya?"

I said yes, but I found it hard to do so. "I'll call you next week when I get my bearings."

Malcolm said, "Well, let me tell you about Betty and the girls." I immediately remembered the long nights in Ghana when our group sat and listened to him talk about the struggle, racism, political strategies and social unrest. Then he would speak of Betty. His voice would soften and take on a new melody. We would be told of her great intelligence, of her beauty, of her wit. How funny she was and how faithful. We would hear that she was an adoring mother and a brave and loving wife.

Malcolm said, "She is here now and making a wonderful dinner. You know she is pretty and pregnant. Pretty pregnant." He laughed at his own joke.

I said, "Please give her my regards. I must run for my plane. I'll call you next week."

"Do that. Safe trip."

I hurriedly telephoned Max Roach and Abbey Lincoln to say that I was home. They also offered to pick me up from the airport, but I told them I would phone them next week from San Francisco.

Rosa Guy listened to my explanation and understood. Our conversation was brief.

I thought of calling James Baldwin, who had become a close friend. We met in Paris in the 1950s when he was writing and I was the principal dancer in the opera *Porgy and Bess*. We became closer in 1960 when I lived in New York. Jimmy was familiar with the work of Jean Genet, and when I played the White Queen in the Genet drama *The Blacks*, he spent long evenings helping me with the role. I didn't telephone him because I knew he could persuade me to stay in New York for at least a day. His physical smallness, his sense of humor and his love for me reminded me so much of my brother, Bailey, that I could never completely resist him.

CHAPTER 2

My mother met me at the San Francisco airport. She was smaller and prettier than she had been in my memory. She kissed me and said, "Describe your luggage to the skycaps, they will bring your bags to the car." The porters had eyes only for my mother. They danced attendance to her, like a male corps de ballet around the première danseuse, and she didn't even seem to notice. Mother rushed us to the car and my heart leaped to find Bailey sitting in the backseat. He had flown in from Hawaii to meet me and at once began talking and asking questions.

Mother said, "She grew prettier. You're a good-looking woman, baby."

Bailey said, "Yeah, but good looks run in this family. She didn't have anything to do with that. Tell me about Guy."

Mother said, "I read in the papers that you were coming back to work with Malcolm X in some new organization. I hope not. I really hope not." She paused and then continued, "If you feel you have to do that—work for no money—go back to Martin Luther King. He's really trying to help our people. Malcolm X is a rabble-rouser."

My breath left me and I couldn't seem to get it back. Just as suddenly, I had enough air, and as I opened my mouth to respond, Bailey touched my shoulder and I turned to him. His face was solemn as he wagged his head. I closed my mouth.

Although less than two years older than I and barely five feet four, my brother had been my counselor and protector for as long as I could remember. When we were just three and four, our parents separated. They sent us, unaccompanied, from California to our paternal grandmother and uncle, who lived in Stamps, a small Arkansas hamlet. Since the adults were strangers to us, Bailey became head of a family that consisted of just us two. He was quicker to learn than I, and he took over teaching me what to do and how to do it.

When I was seven, our handsome, dapper California father arrived in the dusty town. After dazzling the country folk, including his mother, his brother and his children, he took Bailey and me to St. Louis to live with our mother, who had moved back to Missouri after their divorce. He wasn't concerned with offering us a better life, but rather, with curtailing the life my mother was living as a pretty woman who was single again.

My grandmother bundled us and a shoe box of fried chicken into my father's car and cried as she waved good-bye. My father drove, hardly stopping until he delivered us to my mother in St. Louis.

For the first few months we were enraptured with the exotic Northern family. Our maternal grandmother looked white and had a

German accent. Our grandfather was black and spoke with a Trinidadian accent. Their four sons swaggered into and out of their house like
movie toughs.

Their food astonished us. They ate liverwurst and salami, which we
had never seen. Their sliced bread was white and came in greasy, slick
waxed paper, and after eating only homemade ice cream, we thought
there could be nothing greater than enjoying slices of multicolored
cold slabs cut from a brick of frozen dessert. We delighted in being
big-city kids until my mother's boyfriend raped me. After much persuasion (the man had warned me that if I told anyone, he would kill
my brother), I told Bailey, who told the family. The man was arrested,
spent one night in jail, was released and found dead three days later.

The police who informed my grandmother of the man's death, in
front of me, said it seemed he had been kicked to death.

The account staggered me. I thought my voice had killed the man,
so I stopped speaking and Bailey became my shadow, as if he and I
were playing a game. If I turned left, he turned left; if I sat, he sat. He
hardly let me out of his sight. The large, rambunctious big-city family
tried to woo me out of my stolid silence, but when I stubbornly refused to talk, Bailey and I were both sent back to Arkansas. For the
next six years, my brother was the only person for whom I would bring
my voice out of concealment. I thought my voice was such poison that
it could kill anyone. I spoke to him only rarely and sometimes incom-
prehensibly, but I felt that because I loved him so much, my voice
might not harm him.

In our early teens we returned to our mother, who had moved back
to California. Our lives began to differ. Just as Bailey had shadowed me
earlier, he now seemed set on opposing each move I made. If I went to
school, he cut class. If I refused narcotics, he wanted to experiment. If
I stayed home, he became a merchant marine. Yet despite our dissim-
ilar routes and practices, I never lost my complete trust in Bailey.

And now, as I sat in my mother's car being bombarded by the met-
ropolitan flash and my mother's attack on Malcolm, I held my peace;
Bailey encouraged me to do so, and I knew he would be proven right.

My mother's Victorian house on Fulton Street was exactly as it had been when I left four years earlier. She had bought new rugs and added or changed some furniture, but the light still entered the tall windows boldly, and the air still held the dual scent of Tweed perfume and a slight hint of gas escaping from a very small aperture.

I was encouraged to put my bags in my old bedroom and then to join Mother and Bailey in the vast kitchen for a sumptuous welcome-home.

Mother told racy stories, and Bailey regaled me with Hawaiian songs and then gave me his interpretation of an island man's hula. Mother brought out a recipe for Jollof rice that I had sent her from Ghana. She unfolded the letter and read, "Cook about a pound of rice, sauté a couple or three onions in not too much cooking oil for a while, then put in three or four or five right-sized tomatoes..."

At this point in her recitation, Bailey began laughing. He was a professional chef in a swank Hawaiian hotel. The approximation of ingredients and cooking time amused him.

"Dice some cooked ham in fairly large-sized pieces," my mother continued, "and include with salt and cayenne pepper any leftover fried chicken into the tomato sauce. Heat through, then mix in with rice. Then heat quite a while."

We all laughed when Mother said she had followed the recipe exactly and that the dish was a smashing success.

Bailey then told us stories about the tourists and their dining orders at his Waikiki hotel: "I'd like fried chicken and biscuits." "Y'all have any short ribs and corn bread?"

Mother telephoned friends, who dropped by to look at me and Bailey. Many spoke of us as if we weren't in the room.

"Vivian, she looks so good. I know you're proud." And "Well, Bailey didn't grow any more, but he sure is a pretty little black thing."

The entire weekend was a riot of laughter, stories, memories awakened and relished in the bright sunlight. The specter of my distant son cast the only shadow. His arrogance and intractability were discussed, and my family put his behavior in its proper place.

My mother said, "He's a boy."

I said, "He thinks he is a man." Mother said, "That's the nature of the group. When they are boys, they want to be treated like men, but when they are gray-haired old coots, they go around acting like boys." No one could argue with that. "Don't worry about him. You have raised him with love. The fruit won't fall too far from the tree."

The finality in her tone told me she was finished with the subject, but I wondered—what if the fruit fell and was picked up by a hungry bird? Wasn't it possible that it could end up on a dung heap far away from the mother tree?

These were the bleak moments in my homecoming that could not be brightened by Bailey's quick wit or my mother's hilarious homilies.

I had been a journalist in Cairo, and Guy had finished high school there. We moved to Ghana, and when he recovered from a devastating automobile accident, he entered the university. Classrooms were not large enough to hold all of him. When I talked to him about the importance of grades, he patted my head and said, "I understand your interest, little Mother, but those are my concerns and my business. I'll take care of them."

For two years, Guy weaned himself away from my nurture. He broke dates with me, and when I surprised him with an unannounced visit, he firmly let me know that I was not welcome.

When I chose to return to the U.S. to work with Malcolm, I paid Guy's tuition through his graduating year. I told him he could have all the freedom he required. In fact, I said I would give him Ghana.

The paramount chief Nana Nketsi IV assured me that he would pay sharp attention to Guy; and the Genouds, who were childless, assured me that Guy would be like a son to them. They promised to give me a monthly report on how he was faring, so I should feel at ease.

Of course I didn't. From the moment I bought my ticket, guilt called out my name.

Guy was nineteen, and I, who had been his shade since he was born, was leaving him under the broiling African sun. Each time I would try to speak with him about his future, he would cut me off. When I tried to talk about my departure, he curtly told me that indeed I should go home, to go and work with Malcolm. Guy was a man who was trying to live his own life.

CHAPTER 3

The golden morning was definitely a San Francisco Sunday. I dressed quickly and left the house. I had been home less than forty-eight hours, and already I had a creeping sensation that I should be moving on. My mother was comfortably encircled by her ring of friends and Bailey, who had shown me on Friday night how Hawaiian men enjoyed themselves, and on Saturday night how San Franciscans still did their weekend partying, was planning to return the next week to the Hawaiian Islands.

The streets were empty. San Franciscans who hadn't gone to church were sleeping off Saturday-night parties. I walked through parks and trudged up hills. At every peak, I was struck by the beauty that lay invitingly at the foot of the hill.

I had not consciously considered a destination, but I found myself at the end of Golden Gate Park's panhandle, and I realized that my mother's close friend lived nearby.

Aunt Lottie Wells had come to San Francisco from Los Angeles ten years earlier. She joined the family, became my friend and helped me to raise Guy. Her house was a smaller version of Mother's home. Fresh-cut flowers were everywhere, reposing on highly polished tables beneath glistening mirrors.

She said she knew I would visit her, so she hadn't gone to church. She had a pan of biscuits in the oven and was ready to fold over one of her light-as-air omelettes. Lottie smiled, and I was glad that the spirit of wanderers, which lived with me, had brought me to her home.

Her telephone rang as we were sitting down to the table. She answered it in the hall.

She returned. "It's Ivonne for you," she said, grinning. "She called your house and your mother told her you would probably stop by here."

Ivonne was my first adult friend, and I knew we would spend some delicious hours talking about ourselves, the men we loved and the ones who got away. We had never been slow to give each other advice, although I didn't remember either of us being quick to hearken to the other's counsel.

I picked up the phone. "Hey, girl. Where are you? How are you doing?"

"Maya, girl, why did you come home? Why did you come back to this crazy place?"

There was no cheer in her voice.

"I came back because I think I have something to do."

She said, "These Negroes are crazy here. I mean, really crazy. Otherwise, why would they have just killed that man in New York?"

I took the phone away from my ear and looked at it. I cradled it in my hands, looking at its dull black surface; then I laid it down on the hall table. Instead of returning to the dining room, I walked into a bedroom and locked the door.

I didn't have to ask. I knew "that man in New York" was Malcolm X and that someone had just killed him.

CHAPTER 4

Bailey's anxious voice awakened me.

"My. My. Open this door. Open it now."

At times when my life has been ripped apart, when my feet forget their purpose and my tongue is no longer familiar with the inside of my mouth, a touch of narcolepsy has befriended me. I have fallen asleep as an adored lover told me that his fancy had flown. When my son was severely injured in the automobile crash, I couldn't eat and could barely talk, but I could fall asleep sitting on the straight-back metal hospital chairs beside his door.

This time I woke up in a strange room knowing everything. I was still in Aunt Lottie's house, and Malcolm was dead. I had returned from Africa to give my energies and wit to the OAAU, and Malcolm was dead.

"Open this door, My. Wake up and open the damn door or I'll break it down."

He would. I turned the lock.

He looked at my face. "I'm sorry, baby. Go in the bathroom and wash up. I'm taking you somewhere. Somewhere important. Go on."

My bloated face and swollen eyes told me I had cried, but I didn't remember and didn't want to remember.

Bailey waited in the hall, holding my purse and jacket.

"Here, take this. Put this on. Say good-bye to Aunt Lottie."

She took me in her arms. "So sorry, baby. So sorry."

My eyesight and my equilibrium failed me, so Bailey guided me down the hills. He always knew when and when not to talk. He remained silent as we walked out of the residential district and on to the Fillmore area. There, all the people who had been absent from the streets earlier were now very much present, but in ordinary ways. Shouts, conversation and laughter seemed to cascade out of every door. Customers left and entered grocery stores, absorbed in conversation. Men stood in front of saloons engaged in dialogue so private it needed to be whispered. I was shocked to see life going on as usual.

I said to Bailey, "They don't know."

Bailey grunted. "They know. They don't care."

"What do you mean they don't care? I can't accept that. When they know that Malcolm has been killed, the people will riot. They'll explode."

Bailey deftly steered me through the open door of the smoky Havana Bar, where the jukebox music vied with customers' voices.

I looked into the grinning faces and was stumped. In Ghana, I had read that the mood of unrest here was so great that the black community was like a powder keg that would take very little to detonate. But only hours after their champion had been killed, black men and women were flirting and drinking and reveling as if nothing had happened. Bailey ordered two drinks, and when the bartender slid them in front of us, my brother touched me with his elbow and asked the bartender, "Hey, man, you hear what happened to Malcolm X?"

The bartender made a swiping gesture with the bill Bailey had laid down.

"Well, hell, man. They shot him. You know they say, you live by the sword, you die by the sword."

He added ignorance to ignorance by pronouncing the "sw" in sword like the "sw" in the word "swear."

"How dare you... don't you know what Malcolm X has done?"

Bailey took my arm. "Thanks, man. Keep the change."

In seconds I was outside in the clear air, and Bailey was propelling me along Fillmore Street.

"Come on. We're going to Jack's Tavern."

That historic saloon had been my mother's hangout for years. The clientele tended to be older, more established, more professional. They would know the importance of Malcolm's life and most certainly the importance of his death. I needed to be there quickly, so I began to walk a little faster.

Bailey said, "Don't set yourself up to be knocked down. Keep your expectations in control."

The night before, I had told him of my disappointment with Mother. She didn't appreciate or even understand Malcolm and the struggle of black people for equality.

I asked, "Does she think she's liberated?"

Bailey said, as if he had always known it, "Some folks say they want change. They just want exchange. They only want to have what the haves have, so they won't have it anymore. Now, Mom is not like that. She just wants to be left alone. She thinks if no one gets in her way, she can get her freedom by herself. She doesn't want even Martin

Luther King to tell her where her liberation lies—and certainly not Malcolm X."

When we walked into Jack's Tavern, we were greeted by Mother's friends.

"Well, Vivian's children came from the ends of the earth to see about their old mother."

Another voice came from near the bar: "Better not let Vivian hear you call her old."

Someone answered, "If anybody tells her I said it, I'll deny it to my dying day."

"How are you all doing?"

One of the oldest regulars told the bartender, "Set them up. Their money's no good in here."

I was relieved to find Trumpet still tending bar. He had been a pal of mine during the lean days when I was studying and teaching dance, trying to raise my son, keep my love affairs intact and live on one grain of rice and a drop of water. We had spent long hours as buddies, talking about the ways of the world.

I said, "Trumpet, I know you heard about Malcolm."

"Naw, baby. When did you come home? Good-looking old tall long-legged girl."

"Trumpet, Malcolm is dead. Somebody shot him."

Trumpet stood up straight. "Really? No, that's awful. Awful news. Sorry to hear that. When did you get home? How was Africa?"

Bailey said to me, "Get your drink. Let's sit down at a table."

I followed him. He must have seen that at the moment, I was quite soberly going mad.

"You know, of course, that you can't go back to New York. With Malcolm dead, there is no OAAU, and you can't start one or restart his on your own. You wouldn't know who to trust. Accusations are going to be flying thick as grits, and that is no place for you."

Bleakness and grief welled up in me, and I started to cry.

Bailey said, "Stop that. What happened to you in Africa? Did you forget? You can't let people see you cry in public. That's like laying your head down on a chopping block in the presence of an executioner.

"Now, you want the black people to rise up and riot. Don't count on it. Nothing's going to happen right away. I mean nothing. But after a while, a white man is going to step on a black woman's toe, and we'll have a civil war again."

I asked, "What can I do? I don't want to go back to Africa. You say don't go to New York. I hate San Francisco right now."

"Come back to Honolulu with me. Aunt Leah is there. You can stay with her for a while."

My mother's only sister was an evangelist in Oahu, and I didn't take much comfort in Bailey's invitation.

"You can go back to singing in nightclubs. A lot of new places have opened since you were last there."

He continued talking, but I stopped listening and began concentrating on regaining my self-control.

"Maya. Maya." He spoke softly, and for the first time his voice was heavy with sympathy. "Baby, let me tell you what's going to happen. In a few years, there are going to be beautiful posters of Malcolm X, and his photographs will be everywhere. The same people who don't give a damn now will lie and say they always supported him. And that very bartender, the one with the sword"—Bailey mispronounced the word as the bartender had done—"he will say, 'Malcolm was a great man. I always knew he was a great man. A race man. A man who loved his people.' "

I looked at my brother, who was always the wisest person I knew, and wondered if he could possibly be wrong this time.

When we returned home Mother had the grace to give me her sympathy.

"I didn't care for his tactics, but nobody should be shot down like a yard dog. I know he was your friend, baby, and I'm sorry. I want you to know I'm sorry he was killed."

It took me two days to reach Ghana by telephone, and when I did, Guy's voice was hardly audible. He spoke through the crackle of international static.

"I hope you'll enjoy Hawaii, Mom. I was sorry about Malcolm." Then he said, "I am very well. I'm doing fine, and school is fine."

What else could or would he say?

"I've been back to the hospital, and I can play football now."

In the automobile crash years earlier, Guy had broken his neck and spent six months in a torso cast. He healed, but I doubted seriously that he had been given medical clearance to play any full-contact sport.

"Yes, Mother, of course I miss you."

He didn't.

"Mom." His voice began to fade, but for the first time I heard my son's true voice. "Mom, I'm really sorry about Malcolm. We held a vigil in Accra… Really, really sorry."

Thousands of air miles and millions of Atlantic waves sandwiched my son's voice, and I could no longer hear him, but I was satisfied. We had lived so close together that through his normal teenage bravado and his newly learned air of male superiority, I could translate him into my mother language fluently. Despite the static and the pauses when the line went dead, despite the faintness of his voice and the loud buzzing that never stopped, the call was, for me, a huge success.

I learned from what he said and what he didn't say that he was living the high life, the very high life. In fact, he was glad that he had been invited to the world party and that there was no mother around to give him curfew hours. He was going to school and enjoying the competition and the open forum for debate, because he was always eager for argument. He missed me, but not in the sense that he wished me back in Ghana. He missed me just because I had left a vacuum. He was glad for the opportunity to furnish the vacuum with his own chosen baubles.

Generally, he was happy in his fortified city of youth. And if a cold breeze blew over the ramparts, he had his bravado to keep him warm.

He was sincerely sorry about Malcolm. He was so near the sacred and fearful grail of black manhood that any man of color who faced the threat of life with courage, and intellect, and wit, was his hero. He included among his paladins Mahatma Gandhi, Paul Robeson, Nelson

Mandela, Mao Tse-tung, Hannibal, Robert Sobukwe and Martin Luther King, Jr. However, Malcolm X topped the list. Guy himself had lost an ideal, so he felt sincere sympathy for me. He knew I had lost a friend.

CHAPTER 5

The San Francisco streets bore out Bailey's predictions. Life was so mundane that I was plunged into despair.

Why were black people so indifferent? Were we unfeeling? Or were we so timid that we were afraid to honor our dead? I thought what a pathetic people we were.

American blacks were acting as if they believed "A man lived, a man loved, a man tried, a man died," and that was all there was to that.

Papers ran pictures of the handsome Malcolm before the assassination alongside the photo of his bloody body, with his wife, Betty, leaning over her beloved on her knees, frozen in shock.

If a group of racists had waylaid Malcolm, killed him in the dark and left his body as a mockery to all black people, I might have accepted his death more easily. But he was killed by black people as he spoke to black people about a better future for black people and in the presence of his family.

Bailey rescued me. He had returned to Hawaii and found a nightclub that was offering me a job singing. He had lined up a rhythm section and had talked Aunt Leah into letting me stay with her until I could find a place.

Mother admitted, "Yes, I phoned your brother. You were prowling around the streets and the house like a lame leopard. Time for you to straighten up and get back into the whirl of life."

She lived life as if it had been created just for her. She thought the only people who didn't feel the same were laggards and layabouts.

One would have to be a determined malcontent to resist her sincere good humor. She played music, cooked wonderful menus of my favorite foods and told me bawdy jokes, partly to entertain and partly to shock me out of my lethargy. Her tactics worked.

We packed for Hawaii with great joviality. Mother bought me beautiful expensive Western clothes. I began to look forward to the trip. With her powerful personality, she had pulled me out of the drowning depths and onto a safe shore. I had not forgotten Malcolm, nor was I totally at ease about Guy, but some of my own good humor had returned, and I was ready to search for a path back into life.

CHAPTER 6

The exterior of Aunt Leah's house was middle-class Southern California ranch-style stucco. The inside was working-class anywhere. A large, light beige sofa and matching chair were dressed in fitted, heavy plastic covers; a curved blond cocktail table bore up a crouching ceramic black panther. The drapes, which remained closed during my entire stay, were a strong defense against the persistent Hawaiian sunlight. Well-worn Bibles lay on all surfaces, and pictures of Jesus hung on all the walls. Some images were of the Saviour looking benignly out of the drawing, and others were the tortured visages of Him upon the cross.

Having spent a month in my mother's tuneful and colorful house, I felt that I had left reality and entered surreality.

My aunt was religious, and she lived her religion. Her response to "Good morning, how are you?" was "Blessed in the Lord, and Him dead and crucified."

Her husband, named Al but called "Brother"—tradition dictated that I call him "Uncle Brother"—was a big, good-looking country man who adored his wife. He had come from the Arkansas Ozarks with the strength of John Henry, a sunny disposition and very little education. He was working as a laborer when he and my aunt met. She encouraged him to return to school and helped him with his books. By the time they moved to Hawaii, he had become a general contractor who could read a sextant and was building high-rise hotels.

His presence made the house bearable because he didn't take anything too seriously, even my aunt. There was always a shimmer in his eyes when he looked at her: "Yes, baby. Yes, baby, I thanked the Lord, too, but I know the Lord is not going to lay one brick for me. He is not going to plaster one wall. He's counting on me to do that for Him. So I got to go."

CHAPTER 7

There is reliable verity in the assurance that once one has learned to ride a bicycle, the knowledge never disappears. I could add that this is also true for nightclub singing.

Rehearsing with a rhythm section, putting on a fancy, shiny dress and makeup and stepping up to the microphone was as familiar to me as combing my hair. To my surprise, I remembered how to step gracefully out of a song after I had blundered into it in the wrong key, and how to keep an audience interested even when the tune was a folk song with thirty-nine verses.

Within a few weeks at the Encore in Hawaii, I was drawing a good crowd that was eager to hear my style of singing calypso songs in a pseudo-African accent.

The love songs of the Gershwins and Duke Ellington and the clever calypso lyrics were my reliable repertoire. I sang to drum, bass and piano accompaniment, and in each set I included one African song that I translated so loosely the original composer would not have recognized it.

The club orchestra played Hawaiian music, which pleased sailors, businessmen and families. They not only enjoyed the music, they joined in on the audience-participation numbers and would sally forth to the dance floor and treat themselves and the establishment to a hula, samba, rumba, jitterbug, cha-cha or even a tap dance.

I would go home to Aunt Leah's around three A.M., and the sensation was as if I had just left Times Square and stepped onto the dock of the bay at the back of the moon.

Auntie didn't believe in much volume, so music from her radios was hardly audible; every now and again the name of Jesus could be heard from a broadcast sermon. Nor did she approve of air-conditioning. Uncle Brother had installed first-rate units in the house, but Aunt Leah was Calvinistic. She was certain that too many physical comforts in this life would cut down on benefits for the Christians lucky enough to get into heaven, or might even make it too difficult to get in at all. The house was dark, and the air was heavy and stayed in one place. With its sluggish mood, it should have been an ideal location in which to indulge a hearty dose of self-pity. But somehow, piety had claimed every inch of air in that house.

Gloom definitely could not find a niche at the nightclub. It was impossible to think about the life Guy might be living, or Malcolm's death, or the end of yet another of my marriages made in heaven while I was onstage singing "Stone Cold Dead in the Market" or the Andrews Sisters' irresistible song "Drinking Rum and Coca-Cola."

Offstage, the other entertainers were so busy flirting outrageously, fondling one another or carrying arguments to high-pitched and bitter ends that there was no room in which I could consider my present and my past.

I wanted a place where I could languish. I found a furnished flat, moved in, seated myself, laced my fingers and put my hands in my lap and waited. I expected a litany of pitiful accounts to come to mind, a series of sad tales. I was a woman alone, unable to get a man, and if I got one, I could not hold on to him; I had only one child (West Africans say one child is no child, for if a tragedy befalls him, there is nothing left), and he was beyond my reach in too many ways. I expected a face full of sorry and a lap full of if-you-please. Nothing happened. I didn't get a catch in my throat, and there was no moisture around my eyes.

Didn't I care that I had been a bad mother, abandoning my son, leaving him with a meager bank account and up to his own silly teenage devices? He'd go through that money like Grant went through Richmond, and then what? I thought I should be crying. Not one tear fell.

A kind of stoicism had to have been in my inheritance. My inability to feel enough self-pity to break down and cry did not come from an insensitivity to the situation but rather, from the knowledge that as bad as things are now, they could have been worse and might become worser and even worserer. As had happened so many times in my life, I had to follow my grandmother's teaching.

"Sister, change everything you don't like about your life. But when you come to a thing you can't change, then change the way you think about it. You'll see it new, and maybe a new way to change it."

The African-American leaves the womb with the burden of her color and a race memory chockablock with horrific folk tales. Frequently there are songs, toe-tapping, finger-popping, hand-slapping, dancing songs that say, in effect, "I'm laughing to keep from crying." Gospel, blues, and love songs often suggest that birthing is hard, dying is difficult and there isn't much ease in between.

Bailey brought some paintings to my new apartment. Certainly I couldn't change history; however, I could trust Bailey to have thought out some of my future.

"Remember what I told you about Malcolm? These same people who didn't appreciate him will revere him in ten years, and you will get in deep trouble if you try to remind them of their earlier attitude.

"Guy is a man-boy. Bright and opinionated. You raised him to think for himself, and now he's doing just that. That's what you asked for, and that's what you've got. When he gets his stuff together, he's going to be a man of principle. Don't worry, he's your son.

"As for you, you'll make a living singing. But that's about all. Nobody knows what you're going to do or who you're going to be. But everybody thinks you're going to do wonderful things. So let's have a drink, and you get busy doing whatever you're s'posed to do."

He was right. I would only eke out a living as a singer. The limited success I had, which Bailey recognized, stemmed from the fact that I didn't love singing. My voice was fair and interesting; my ear was not great, or even good, but my rhythm was reliable. Still, I could never become a great singer, since I would not sacrifice for it. To become wondrously successful and to sustain that success in any profession, one must be willing to relinquish many pleasures and be ready to postpone gratification. I didn't care enough for my own singing to make other people appreciate it.

After six months, the audiences, whose sizes had been respectful, became smaller. A musician told me where my customers had gone.

"There's a real singer down at the Aloha Club, and she's packing them in every night."

On my break I went to the rival club to see my competition. The singer rocked me back in my chair. She was as tall as I, good-looking and very strong. But mainly, she could sing. She had a huge, deep voice, and when she walked on the stage, she owned it. When she nodded to her musicians to start, she reminded me of Joshua and the Battle of Jericho.

> "Then the lamb, ram, sheep horns began to blow
> The trumpets began to sound
> Joshua commanded the children to shout
> And the walls came tumblin' down."

The singer stepped up to the microphone unsmiling, wagged her head once to the right and then to the left, the orchestra blared and so did she. Her big dramatic voice windsurfed in that room and walls came tumbling down.

The protective walls I had built around myself as a singer, those that allowed me to sing for convenience, to sing because I could and to sing without rejoicing in the art, all caved in as if obeying the urgency of a load of dynamite.

Listening to Della Reese, I knew I would never call myself a singer again, and that I was going to give up Hawaii and my job at the Encore. I would return to the mainland and search until I found something I loved doing. I might get a job as a waitress and try to finish a stage play I had begun in Accra. I had notebooks full of poems; maybe I'd try to finish them, polish them up, make them presentable and introduce them to a publisher and then pray a lot.

When I thanked Della Reese, I did not mention exactly what she had done for me. I should have said "You've changed my life" or "Your singing made the crooked way straight and the rough road smooth." All I said was "I needed your music, and thank you for giving it so generously." Miss Reese gave me a cool but gracious reply.

The next day I had a meeting with the family in Hawaii and called my mother in San Francisco to tell her that I was moving to Los Angeles. Some former gaping wounds had healed and I was eager. The time had come to return to the mainland, to get a job—to reenter real life.

Uncle Brother gave me the keys to an old Dodge he and Aunt Leah had left in Los Angeles. "It runs when it wants to and goes where it likes, but it ought to serve you till you can do better."

He and Bailey and Aunt Leah, against her better judgment, came down to closing night. My aunt sat primly throughout the whole show, her arms wrapped around her body, or she laid her hands in her lap and kept her gaze upon them.

I had planned to leave Hawaii the next day, so my last show was not only a farewell to the Encore but to my family and to the few acquaintances I had made on Waikiki Beach. As I prepared to go onstage, I thought about the haven Hawaii had been. I had arrived on the island in a fragile and unsteady condition. The shock of Malcolm's murder had demoralized me. There seemed to be no center in the universe, and the known edges of the world had become dim and inscrutable.

Leaving Guy in Africa had become a hair shirt that I could not dislodge. I worried that his newly found and desperate hold on his mannishness might cause him to say or do something to irritate the Ghanaian authorities.

I had brought anxiety and guilt to Hawaii, but each month the worries had abated. Friends in New York informed me that Malcolm's widow, Betty, had given birth to healthy twins, and although his dream of an organization of African-American unity would not be realized, his family was hale and his friends were true. The actors and writers Ossie Davis and Ruby Dee, attorney Percy Sutton and Alex Haley, who had written Malcolm's biography, were among the steady pillars holding the Shabazz family aloft.

I heard from friends in Ghana that Guy began behaving much better after I left. Often people in general, and young people in particular, need the responsibility of having to depend upon themselves for their own lives.

So I was leaving Hawaii a lighter and brighter person. I was going to Los Angeles, and although I did not know what I would do or whom I would find there, life was waiting on me and it wasn't wise to test its patience.

For that last show on the last night, I decided not to sing but to dance.

I asked for the music, then invited it to enter my body and find the broken and sore places and restore them. That it would blow through my mind and dispel the fogs. I let the music move me around the dance floor.

I danced for the African I had loved and lost in Africa, I danced for bad judgments and good fortune. For moonlight lying like rich white silk on the sand before the great pyramids in Egypt and for the sound on ceremonial fonton-fron drums waking the morning air in Takoradi.

The dance was over, and the audience was standing and applauding. Even Aunt Leah finally looked up and smiled at me.

Bailey hugged me and gave me a wad of money.

"You're good." He pointed to my heart. "You'll go far." He said I had what I needed to face another unknown.

I was off to California.
Aloha.

CHAPTER 8

There is about Los Angeles an air of expectation. Not on the surface, where the atmosphere is lazy, even somnolent, but below the city's sleepy skin, there is a suggestion that something quite delightful might happen and happen soon.

This quiet hope might be the detritus of so many dreams entertained by so many hopefuls as they struggled and pinched and dieted and preened for Hollywood cameras. Possibly those aspirations never really die but linger in the air long after the dreamers have ceased dreaming.

The days in Los Angeles were beautiful. The soft, wavering sunlight gave a filtered golden tint to the streets.

The inhabitants of the working-class neighborhood were obviously house-proud. Little bungalows were cradled confidently on patches of carefully tended lawn, and wind chimes seemed to wait for the breeze on every porch.

I longed for one of those tidy and certain houses. If I could live in a house like that, its absolute rightness of place would spill over and the ragged edges of my life would become neat to match the house.

Frances Williams was the very person I needed. I had known her a decade earlier, and she knew everyone else very well. She was active in Actors' Equity and had connections in both black and white churches.

Fran, as she was called, counseled on the mystery of the theater, on its power and beauty, and gave good advice to anyone smart enough to listen.

She was a large woman with a lusty voice not unlike a cello, and she had a great love of the theater. She and her brother, Bill, lived in a large house at the rear of a corner lot. The house and all the grounds were often pressed into service when Fran directed experimental theater. She had acted in forty movies and had worked as an extra in over a hundred more. When I looked her up, she had exactly what I needed: a place to live and the possibility of a job.

There were two vacant apartments. Each had one room that served as living room, bedroom and study, and each had a large, commodious kitchen. I took one apartment, and Fran told me that the actress Beah Richards took the other.

The apartment was small and dark and humid, so I bought gallons of white latex paint and a stack of rollers and brushes. I painted every inch of visible wall and the entire floor bone-white. I went over the floor with a few coats of adobe enamel. In the lean years before Guy encountered puberty, he and I learned by trial and error how to antique furniture from Salvation Army stores and even how to repair the odd chair or sofa that seemed destined for a junkyard.

I had become such a regular in all Salvation Army and Goodwill stores that salespeople saved certain choice pieces for me. "Maya, how are you? Have I got a fabulous nightstand for you." "Have I got a great dresser for you."

In Los Angeles I bought orange, rust and brown burlap and draped the material casually at windows. I made huge colorful floor pillows and piled them on the floor. Van Gogh and Matisse posters enlivened the walls.

I stacked painted wood planks on bricks to form bookcases and burned cheap candles in Chianti and Mateus wine bottles. When the melted wax nearly covered the bottles, I put fresh candles in them and placed them around the room for light and esoteric effect.

At little expense, and out of a crying need, I had a house; now I needed a job. The money I brought from Hawaii was sifting through my fingers like fine sand.

Again Fran had the answer. Having lived in Los Angeles since the 1950s, she knew every corner where black people lived. Having worked on their campaigns, she called every elected official by his or her first name.

"This job is called Random Research. You won't be paid much, but you are on an honor system. No one will be going behind you to check on your honesty. You will be given a questionnaire and a district. You will go to every fourth house and ask the housewife the questions on your form."

"What questions?"

"What cereal does your family prefer? What soap powder do you use? What peanut butter do you buy? Like that."

The salary was pitifully low, but the job was blissfully simple. I had started working on my stage play. Random Research would allow me time to develop my characters and plot. I would ask questions of the housewives, but between houses and women and questions and answers, I would let my characters play out plot possibilities. They would find their own voices and design their own personalities.

Watts was my assigned locale, and I was disappointed to find it had lost its air of studied grace. I had known the area when it had a kind of staid decorum, a sort of church-ladies-display-at-a-Sunday-afternoon-tea feeling. The houses were all of the proper size, none so large as to cause envy, none so small as to elicit pity.

Years earlier, the lawns were immaculate, grass was trimmed to an evenness and flowers were carefully placed and lovingly tended. There had not been many people on the street. A drive through residential Watts was like driving through a small town in a 1940s Hollywood movie. There were always the odd teenagers pumping themselves up on Schwinns, but they could have been extras in the film, save that these bikers were black, as were the women who called them home for supper: "Henry, Henry..."

The Watts I visited in 1965 was very different. The houses were still uniform and similarly painted, and the lawns still precise, but there were people everywhere.

On my visit to Watts to orient myself for the new job, I passed groups of men in T-shirts or undershirts, lounging on front porches and steps. Their talk was just a little louder than usual, and they didn't stop their conversation or lower their voices when I came into view.

Although I was never pretty, my youth, a good figure and well-chosen clothes would usually earn a clearing of the throat, or at least a veiled sound of approval. But the men in this Watts didn't respond to my presence.

"Good morning, I am working for a company that wants to improve the quality of the goods you buy. I'd like to ask you a few questions. Your answers will ensure that you will find better foods in your super-market and probably at a reduced price."

The person who wrote those lines, for interviewers to use with black women, knew nothing of black women. If I had dared utter such claptrap, at best I would have been laughed off the porch or at worst told to get the hell away from the woman's door.

Black females, for the most part, know by the time they are ten years old that the world is not much concerned with the quality of their lives or even their lives at all. When politicians and salespeople start being kind to black women, seeking them out, offering them largesse, the women accept the soft voices, the simpering statements, the often idle promises, because those are likely to be the only flatter-ing behavior directed to them that day. Behind the women's eyes, however, there is a wisdom that does not pretend to be unaware; nor does it permit gullibility.

Martin Luther King, Jr., once related a story that demonstrated just how accurate the black woman was at assessing her location in the scheme of things and knowing how to handle herself wherever she was.

He told us about an older black woman who had worked for a white woman in Alabama, first as her laundress, then as her maid, then as her cook and finally as her housekeeper. After forty years, the black woman retired, but she would go to visit her former employer occa-sionally.

On one visit, her employer had friends over for lunch. When the employer was told that Lillian Taylor was in the kitchen, she sent for her. Lillian went into the living room and greeted all the women, some of whom she had known since their childhoods.

The white woman said, "Lillian, I know you've heard of the bus boycott."

"Yes, ma'am, I've heard of it."

"Well, I want to know, what do you think of it? Are you supporting it?"

"No, ma'am. Not one bit. Not one little iota. And I won't let none of mine support it, either."

"I knew you'd be sensible, Lillian, I just knew it in my bones."

"Yes, ma'am, I won't touch that bus boycott. You know my son took me to live with him and his family (he won't let me even lift a finger), and he works for the power company way 'cross town from our house. I told him, 'Charles, don't you have anything to do with that bus boycott. You walk to work. Stay all the way out of that bus boycott.' And my grandchildren, they go to school way over on the east side, I told them the same thing: 'Don't have anything to do with that boycott. You walk to school.' And even today, when I wanted to come over and visit you, I got a lady from my church to bring me. I wasn't going to touch that boycott. Sure wasn't."

The room had become quiet, and Lillian Taylor said, "I know you have plenty help now, but do you want me to bring you all more coffee?"

She went to the kitchen and was followed by the white woman's daughter.

"Lillian, why do you treat my mother like that? Why not just come out and say you support the boycott?"

Lillian said, "Honey, when you have your head in a lion's mouth, you don't snatch it out. You reach up and tickle him behind his ears and you draw your head out gradually. Every black woman in this country has her head in a lion's mouth."

I knew that a straight back and straight talk would get the black woman's attention every time.

"Good morning. I have a job asking questions."

At first there would be wariness. "What questions? Why me?"

"There are some companies that want to know which products are popular in the black community and which are not."

"Why do they care?"

"They care because if you don't like what they are selling, you won't buy, and they want to fix it so you will."

"Yeah, that makes sense. Come on in."

I was never turned away, although most times the women were abstracted. Few gave me their total attention. Some complained that their husbands were around all day.

"I work nights, and usually I come home and sleep a few hours, then get up and have time to fix up my house. But with him not working, he's home all day, bringing his friends in and all that."

Or they complained that the men weren't around.

"I don't know where he's spending his time. He's not working, he's not at the job and he's not at home... makes me a little suspicious."

Listening to the women brought me more squarely back to the U.S.A. The lilt of the language was so beautiful, and I was heartened that being away from the melody for a few years had not made one note foreign to me.

The women ranged from college graduates to those who would find it challenging to read the daily newspaper, yet the burdens of their conversations were the same.

Those who worked or needed medical attention or collected supplemental food stamps were dependent on private cars. Public transportation was so poor that if a woman had to use it in order to be at work by eight-thirty A.M., she would have to leave home at five A.M.

Those who worked as housekeepers, maids and cooks shopped on their way home from their jobs in the stores used by their employers. The goods were fresher, of better quality and remarkably cheaper.

I had gone to Watts to fulfill the demands of my job and had gotten so much more. The women opened their doors and minds to me. Even as I asked about dishwashing Dove and Bold and Crisco and Morton salt, I found hardworking women and hard-thinking women. Indirectly, I met their men, whose jobs had disappeared and who found they were unable to be breadwinners in their own homes.

Some men, embarrassed at their powerlessness, became belligerent, and their wives' bodies showed the extent of their anger. Some, feeling futile, useless, left home, left the places where they read disappointment in every face and heard shame in every voice. Some drank alcohol until they reached the stage of stupor where they could not see or hear and certainly not think.

On the surface, Watts still appeared a pretty American dream, wide thoroughfares, neat lawns, nice bungalows. Those factors were facts, but there is always a truth deeper than what is visible.

Without work and steady salaries, the people could not envision tomorrows. Women and men, furious with themselves and each other, began to abandon the children. They didn't leave them in baskets on doorsteps, they abandoned them in the home. Dinners together became fewer because the father was seldom there and the mother was busy reviewing where she went wrong, or prettying up to set out her lures again.

The bootless children, with discipline removed, without the steadying hand of a present parent who cared, began to run like young tigers in the streets. First their need drove them to others like themselves, with whom they could make a family. Then their rage made the newly formed families dangerous. Gangs of abandoned children bullied their way up and down the sidewalks of Watts, growing bolder and angrier every day.

They left the schools in record numbers. What could school offer them that could be of use? Education, so they could get jobs? But their parents had had jobs that were taken away. Their parents had believed in the system, and see them now? Empty uncaring husks of the people they once were. No. School promised nothing, nothing save a chance to lose the families they had just made and needed so desperately.

CHAPTER 9

The uproar in Watts taught me something I had not known. Odor travels faster and farther than sound. We smelled the conflagration before we heard it, or even heard about it. The odor that drifted like a shadow over my neighborhood was complex because it was layered. Burning wood was the first odor that reached my nose, but it was soon followed by the smell of scorched food, then the stench of smoldering rubber. We had one hour of wondering what was burning before the television news reporters arrived breathlessly.

There had been no cameras to catch the ignition of the fire. A number of buildings were burning wildly before anyone could film them. Newscasters began to relay the pictures and sounds of the tumult.

"There is full-blown riot in Watts. Watts is an area in southeast Los Angeles. Its residents are predominately Negroes." Pictures were interspersed with the gasps of the newscasters.

That description was for the millions of whites who lived in Los Angeles but who had no idea that Watts existed and certainly no awareness that it was a parcel of the city and only a short ride from their own communities.

Policemen and politicians, all white, came on the television screens to calm down the citizenry in the unscathed regions.

"You have nothing to fear. The police have been deployed to Watts, and in a few hours we will have everything under control."

Those of us who watched the action live on television over the next few days knew that the officials were talking out of their hats.

The rioters had abandoned all concern for themselves, for their safety and freedom. Some threw rocks, stones, cans of beer and soda at police in cars and police on foot. Heavily burdened people staggered out the doors of supermarkets, followed by billows of smoke. Men and women carried electrical appliances in their arms, and some pushed washers and dryers down the middle of the street.

However, nothing—not the voices trained to relay excitement nor the images of unidentifiable looters entering and leaving unlighted shops—could capture the terrifying threat of a riot like the stench of scorched wood and burning rubber.

Radios blared, "Watts is on fire." Television cameras filmed a group of men turning over a car and a young woman throwing a bottle at a superstore window. The glass seemed to break in slow motion. In fact, throughout the duration of the explosion, every incident shown on television seemed acted out at a pace slower than real time.

Sirens screamed through the night, and television screens showed gangs of young men refusing to allow fire trucks a chance to put out fires.

"Burn, baby, burn." The instruction came clear over the radios: "Burn, baby, burn." Certain political analysts observed that the people were burning their own neighborhood. Though few houses were set afire, the rioters considered the stores, including supermarkets, property of the colonialists who had come into the neighborhood to exploit them and take their hard-earned money.

Two days passed and I could wait no longer. I drove to Watts and parked as near the center of the uprising as possible, then I walked. The smell had turned putrid as plastic furniture and supermarket meat departments smoldered. When I reached a main street, I stopped and watched as people pushed piled-high store carts out of burning buildings. Police seemed to be everywhere and nowhere, watching from inside their cars.

A young boy, his arms laden, his face knotted in concentration, suddenly saw me.

"You want a radio?"

I was amazed that there was no guilt in his voice. I said, "No, not yet. Thanks anyway."

Ordinarily I would have read in the boy's face, or felt, an "Uh-huh, this woman knows I've been stealing." There would have been at least an ounce of shame. But his approach had been conspiratorial, as if to say, "We're in this together. I know you not only know what I am doing, you approve of it and would do it yourself if you could."

Smoke and screams carried in the air. Someone behind me was cursing long, keen streaks of profanity. It became hard to discern if the figures brushing past me were male or female, young or old.

The farther I walked, the more difficult it was to breathe. I had turned and started back to my car when a sound cut the air. The loud whine of police sirens was so close it stabbed into my ears. Policemen in gas masks emerged out of the smoke, figures from a nightmare. Alarm flooded me, and in a second I was dislocated. It seemed that the sirens were in my nose, and smoke packed my ears like cotton. Two policemen grabbed a person in front of me. They dragged the man away as he screamed, "Take your hands off me, you bastards! Let me go!"

I ran, but I couldn't see the pavement, so it was nearly impossible to keep my footing. I ran anyway. Someone grabbed for me, but I shrugged off the hand and continued running. My lungs were going to burst, and my calves were cramping. I pushed myself along. I was still running when I realized I was breathing clean air. I read the street signs and saw that I was almost a mile away from my car, but at least I wasn't in jail. Because I had run in the opposite direction from where I had parked, I would have to circle Watts to find my car, but at least I wasn't in Watts.

When I returned home, the television coverage was mesmerizing. The National Guard was shown arriving in Watts. They were young men who showed daring on their faces but fear in their hearts. They were uncomfortable with new, heavy responsibilities and new, heavy guns.

After three days the jails began to fill. The media covered hundreds of looters being arrested. Frances Williams said that the rumor in the neighborhood beauty salons and barbershops was that the police were arresting anyone black and those suspected of being black.

Watts was all anyone could think of. The fact of it, the explosion of anger, surprised and befuddled some: "I've driven through Watts many times. It's very nice." Some people were furious: "The police should have the right to shoot at will. If a few of those looters were shot, the rest would get the message soon enough." Watts went on burning. It had not had enough, and I hadn't had enough.

Curiosity had often lured me to the edge of ruin. For years, I had known that there is nothing idle about curiosity, despite the fact that the two words are often used in tandem. Curiosity fidgets, is hard to satisfy, looks for answers even before forming questions. Curiosity wants to behold, to comprehend, maybe even to become.

Two days after my tentative foray into the war zone, I had to go again, but this time I wouldn't allow fear any control over me. This time I would not run.

The combustion had spread, so my previous parking space was now only a block from the riot. I parked there anyway and walked directly into the din.

Burglar alarms continued to ring in the stores that had no front doors or windows. Armed civilians stood in front of ravaged businesses, guarding against further looting. They were heckled.

"Hey brother, you guarding Charlie's thing. You must be a fool."

"I sure wouldn't risk my life for somebody else's stuff. If they care that much for it, they ought to come down here and look after it themselves."

"Ain't that much money in the world make me lose my life..."

The National Guard was heckled, too, but not as pointedly.

"Hey, man, you drew some lame duty."

"Don't you feel like a fool standing in front of a supermarket?"

I heard this in front of a pawnshop: "Hey, man, don't you feel stupid keeping people from stealing something that was already stole in the first place?"

The soldiers worked at keeping straight faces.

The devastation was so much broader. On the second day of the riot, and my first day visiting Watts, there was a corridor of burned-out buildings and cars, but on the fourth day, the corridor had widened substantially.

That night I sat down at my kitchen table and wrote on a yellow pad my description of the events I had seen in Watts and the uprising as it was reported on television.

> *Our*
> YOUR FRIEND CHARLIE *pawnshop*
> *was a glorious blaze*
> *I heard the flames lick*
> *then eat the trays*
> *of zircons*
> *mounted in red-gold alloys*
> *Easter clothes and stolen furs*
> *burned in the attic*
> *radios and TVs*
> *crackled with static*
> *plugged in*
> *only to a racial outlet*
>
> *Hospitality, southern-style*
> *cornpone grits and you-all smile*
> *whole blocks novae*
> *brand-new stars*
> *policemen caught in their*
> *brand-new cars*
> *Chugga chugga chigga*
> *git me one nigga*
> *lootin' n burnin'*
> *he won't git far*
>
> *Lighting: a hundred Watts*
> *Detroit, Newark and New York*
> *Screeching nerves, exploding minds*
> *lives tied to*
> *a policeman's whistle*
> *a welfare worker's doorbell*
> *finger*

Spirit walked with me on my second visit to the exploding section of Watts. I became invisible in the black community. I had to stop and stand still when I realized that no one seemed to see me. When I had visited Watts on the first day of my new job, no one spoke to me or commented on my presence, but I was seen. This time I could have been in a white neighborhood. When a black person appears in a white part of town, there is a moment of alarm, but if the black doesn't appear threatening, he is erased from the white mind immediately.

In the black community, a black person is always given her humanity.

On this visit to Watts, the responses were different. Neither the looters, the police, the spectators nor the National Guard took notice of me. A group of young men was bouncing a car filled with white passengers whose faces looked like Halloween masks through the car windows. Terror bulged from their eyes, and if the windows had been open, I would have heard the screams pouring out of their wide, gaping mouths.

A phalanx of police slipped by me and were upon the rioters quickly and quietly. The officers began handcuffing the offenders, and I turned my attention to the now settled car. Its inhabitants were exchanging smiles that I didn't read as smiles of relief, but rather of satisfaction. They had come to Watts to get a thrill, and hadn't they done just that?

The newly arrested men were marched close enough for me to touch them, but neither they nor the police regarded me.

I came upon some people who were sauntering down the main street, casually taking in the sights. They were so at ease in that uneasy time and place that it was obvious they lived in the neighborhood. Their concentration was on the stores and the burned-out shells of buildings, so they didn't see me.

The havoc now had areas of calm, and either I brought serenity with me or it found me wherever I was. I watched as people sifted through debris. Each whole cup or unbroken plate was treated as a treasure. A woman smiled with pleasure when she found a matched pair of shoes. A man passed me carrying a pair of well-worn pants and grinning.

On the first day of insurgency, people of all ages allowed their rage to drive them to the streets. But on the fourth day, the anger of the older citizens was spent. I read sadness and even futility on their faces. But I saw no one attempt to dissuade the younger rioters from their hurly-burly behavior.

People in front of and behind me were taken to jail, and I was ignored. Admittedly, I didn't curse or shout at the law enforcers, nor did I carry anything that even faintly resembled loot, but that had not influenced the police earlier. People on their way to or from work had been apprehended.

The night before, I had remembered one of my mother's statements: "Nothing's wrong with going to jail for something you believe in. Remember, jail was made for people. Not horses." That is when I had decided I would return to Watts ready to be arrested.

Three police vans were filled and driven away as I stood on the corner of 125th and Vermont. I headed back to my car with an equal mixture of disappointment and relief.

The upheaval continued in volume and drama for five days, and although the violence waned, the frustration was as pervasive as ever. Politicians and community representatives met and held press conferences. Viewers were told that a plan for Watts was being hammered out.

The ash had not yet settled on every car and windowsill before the streets were filled with tourists who came to look at Watts. Journalists from France, England and the Soviet Union were shown on television interviewing people in Watts. They asked any question that came to mind: "Why did Watts burn?" "Why did you burn your own neighborhood?" "Isn't America supposed to be the melting pot?" "Were you trying to get the heat up to melting temperature?"

The people answered with anything that came to their minds.

"It burned down before I noticed."

"I didn't have a job, so I burned down Watts."

"I didn't have anything else to do, so I burned a store."

The journalists were being treated with the old-as-slavery response: "If a white man asks where you're going, you tell him where you've been."

A white man asks, "Where are you going, boy?" Your response should be, with much head scratching and some shuffling, "You know, boss, I was down that street over there by that big old tree, you know, and I saw something 'twas hard to look upon..."

"I didn't ask where you were, I asked where are you going."

"Yes sir, that's what I'm trying to tell you. If you had seen what I've seen...I don't...if they're...couldn't have been a half a mile away. I had to get out of there, or I don't know what would have happened."

The white man would usually respond, "Oh, you're a fool. I'm not going to waste any more time on you." The white man walks away, and the black man is pleased that no secrets were revealed or any lies told.

But talking drums of the black community carried the message loud and clear. The rebellion reached some important ears, and things were going to change. Community spokespersons said what was needed most was a medical clinic so that sick people didn't have to travel two or three hours just to see a doctor.

The unemployed wanted jobs, the underemployed wanted better jobs.

Who would answer all the questions, fulfill all the requests? Would anyone? Could anyone? History had taught the citizens of Watts to hope for the best and expect nothing, but be prepared for the worst.

A shaft of sunlight penetrated the gloom of cynicism when Budd Schulberg, an award-winning writer, went to Watts and founded the Watts Writers Workshop. People who didn't know his name would bless him forevermore.

"He's a Hollywood writer, you say?"

"And he's coming to Watts?"

"Here's one white man who's putting his body where his mouth is. I like that. I sure do."

Some women, mostly white, largely the wives of film moguls, banded together to form an organization, Neighbors of Watts. They went to the area to ask the women how they could be of help.

Mrs. Violetta Robinson, often called the Mother of Watts, told them what the women of Watts needed—an accredited, well-funded child-care center so that they could leave their children and go to work with clear minds. Something of slavery lurked in the shadows of that request. Slave mothers, up before sunrise and sleeping after dark, went to the canebrakes and cotton fields with minds less clouded with concern because they knew a woman, Aunt Susie, Aunty Mae, Aunt Carrie, would be looking after all the children. They took satisfaction in the fact that "Aunt Susie loves children." The children "just love Aunty Mae." "Aunt Carrie won't stand for no foolishness from the children, but she would feed them herself. She won't let them eat from a trough like hogs as some did on other plantations." Sometimes the children's plates were corn husks or cabbage leaves; still, each child ate with clean fingers and from a clean surface.

One hundred and fifty years later, black women still needed that same assurance.

My landlady, who knew everything, said the Neighbors of Watts were going to provide a child-care center. She also said a medical institute was going to be built in Watts, and that it would be named for Charles Drew, a great African-American doctor who developed a technique to separate out plasma from whole blood.

A French journalist telephoned me and said James Baldwin had given him my name and number. I agreed to an interview. He sat, contained, on my studio bed-cum-sofa.

"We French, we have never, never, never had slavery, so we feel we don't understand the American racism."

Maybe it was that third "never" that made me pick him up and dust him off.

"What did you call Haiti? A resort?"

Suddenly his English failed him. "Haiti? *Est-ce que tu a dit Haiti?*"

I said, *"Oui."*

He said, "I meant in France. *Nous* have *jamais* had *esclavage* on the land of France."

I said, "You were the rulers of Haiti and Martinique—and Guadeloupe. None of the Africans went there on the *Ile de France.* They were taken there on slave ships."

He said he was beginning to understand the rage a little. If people like me were so angry, how much angrier were those who had less than I?

I looked at the man, his beret, his neat little dancing hands, and looked at my studio apartment with its furniture from Goodwill and its prints from Woolworth's. I had less than many others I knew, but if he thought I was well-off, then nothing I could say would help him understand Watts. If he had visited the area one day before it exploded, if he had gone to the right bar or pool hall or community center, he could have met someone who heard his accent and, realizing he was a stranger, might have invited him home.

He could have been sitting in a well-furnished house dining on great chicken and greens, receiving all the kindnesses. Then he really would have been befuddled if, on the following day, he heard of the conflagration and had seen his host of the day before struggling with the heavily armed police.

But I could not needle him. He was not going to comprehend the anger and disappointment in Watts, and further provoking him was not going to make me feel better. Like many of my ancestors, I settled back to tell him some of what he wanted to hear and some of what I wanted to say.

Surely he returned to Paris with some truth and some fiction. Surely he wrote an account of the Watts riot allowing his readers to hold on to the stereotypes that made them comfortable while congratulating themselves on being in possession of some news.

CHAPTER 10

Frank Silvera was exactly what is meant in South America by the word *mestizo.* His ancestors were African and Spanish, and he was a light-skinned black man who could play a Mexican father to Marlon Brando's Zapata. A black man who could play an Italian father to Ben Gazzara in *A Hatful of Rain* on Broadway. A black man who could play the title role of Shakespeare's *King Lear.*

Silvera had a theater company in Los Angeles that he named the Theatre of Being or, as the member actors called it, Tee Oh Bee. Beah Richards, my next-door neighbor, was the star of the company, with Vantile Whitfield and Dick Anthony Jones as resident leading men.

Beah, with her success on and off Broadway and particularly in James Baldwin's *The Amen Corner,* was a legend in the African-American community. At the time I met her, she was often called our greatest stage actress, vying only with Ruby Dee for that honor.

Frank decided to stage *Medea* at his Theatre of Being. Naturally, Beah would take the title role. And just as naturally, she would take it beyond all real or imagined limits. When Frank announced the project, Beah and I and a few friends celebrated. In the middle of that evening's festivities, problems were mentioned. Beah didn't drive. I offered to take her to the theater each day, and she said she would pay for the gas.

The role of the nurse had not been filled. I joined the line of actors auditioning, and, using a Langston Hughes poem and a Shakespearean sonnet, I was given the role of the nurse.

I knew I was adequate, but I was never sure if Frank hired me because of my talent or to ensure that Beah had a way to get to the theater.

Frank and Beah shared a profound mutual admiration. She would speak, and he would either laugh uproariously or stroke his chin and pace the floor, lost in a deep brown study.

Rehearsals further increased my insecurity. I would stand backstage as Frank consistently positioned Beah center stage under the bright beams. Of course she was the star, but the role of the nurse was not irrelevant, and he never called on me. I began to smart in the shadows. I went to a bookstore and bought Euripides' version of *Medea,* as well as every book I could find about Medea, Jason, the *Argo* and the Golden Fleece.

There was a neighborhood bar next to the theater. I informed the stage manager that I could be found in the bar whenever I was wanted. Each day I would drop Beah off, greet folks in the theater, then go to sit at a table in the dimly lit bar. I worked out who the nurse was and why she was so loyal to Medea.

In my created version of the play's history, Nurse had been the midwife at Medea's birth. Nurse had a baby just after Medea was born, but Nurse's baby died. Medea's mother, not wanting the brother, persuaded Nurse to become a nurse cow and give to Medea the dead child's milk.

In the bar, I built my character, her whims and her whimsy. I decided early on that Nurse thought of Medea as her own daughter and doted on the girl. As Medea grew into womanhood, Nurse cherished her, idolized her and followed her everywhere, walking as precisely as possible in her footsteps. When Medea married Jason, Nurse attended the ceremony. When Medea stole the fleece of pure gold from her father, the king, because Jason asked her to do so, Nurse helped her. Nurse later escaped the king's rage by joining Medea on the Argonauts' ship, the *Argo*. Nurse was crippled by arthritis because she often slept on the ground. She didn't mind the discomfort as long as she was near Medea. She had grown old and dotty in service to Medea, who took Nurse's worship as her due. Maddened by rage at Jason's growing coldness toward her, Medea killed their two sons. Nurse knew of the murders but gave Medea no rebuke, saying, "She did what any woman would have done if provoked."

I began taking license with the simply told story of passion and horror. Since I was not directed, I had to create situations that would explain why the character I was playing could condone even the most base actions of Medea. I did not propose to comprehend Medea's mind, or how love and idolatry could lead to theft and murder, but I did find that Nurse had a fair voice, and singing was the only pleasure she had that didn't stem from Medea.

I got some stage gray hair and ghoulish makeup, and a week before opening, when I was invited to join rehearsal, I brought the gray-haired, limping, singing nurse onto the stage. Beah and Frank were amazed, and neither was too pleased, but we were too close to opening for Frank to redirect me.

The play opened to baffling reviews. Some critics loved it, while others loathed it. Some thought it modern and wonderfully acted, and some thought it stagey and mannered. All lauded Beah Richards, and a few had kind words for the elderly actress whom no one knew but who played the nurse so well.

CHAPTER 11

Sid's Café and Bar was a popular hangout for people from New Orleans. The owner, Jase, and his wife, Marguerite, were highly respected cooks of Louisiana food, and the bar was always filled with bright laughter and loud talk. Jase and Marguerite liked and welcomed me, so Sid's became my base.

One evening a group of four in the red booth at the front of the café were particularly interesting. The two women were as loud and fierce as the men, yet no one used profanity. They saw me watching, and one man beckoned me over.

"Hey, are you alone?"

I said, "Yes."

"Well, join us."

"Yes, come on." I sat. "Are you from New Orleans?"

"No."

"Well, we are. Where did you run away from?"

"I came here from Hawaii, and before that, San Francisco, and before that, Ghana in West Africa."

"Hey, all right. You will fit right in with me. I am one crazy lying nigger, too. My name is Phil. What's yours?"

"My name is Maya, and I am neither a nigger nor a liar."

One woman said, "That's right. Speak up for yourself. This fool calls himself a nigger, and he'd put his fist through the face of the first white man using that word."

"I can say it 'cause I am me. I don't mean any harm."

I said, "But you're calling yourself a despicable word, and surely you are not despicable."

Phil said, "I believe you were in Hawaii and Africa. You sound a little like a teacher I had in Baton Rouge."

I said, "I thought you were from New Orleans."

Phil said, "Told you I was a lying nigger. I can be ornery, too."

I said, "Maybe I'd better go back to my table."

Everyone spoke at once.

"No. Stay with us."

"Tell us about Africa."

"No, I want to hear about Hawaii."

"Don't mind Phil. He really doesn't mean any harm, and we do laugh a lot."

I enjoyed the group's company, and after I had been around them a few weeks, Phil used the racial slur less. When he did slip, he would pop out his eyes and look straight at me.

One morning they came to my house. I offered them Mogen David and Mateus wine. We sat around the kitchen table drinking and telling stories.

Phil suggested that we go for a ride. We agreed, although we were all too old to be joyriding, since the youngest of us had to be at least thirty.

There were no dissenters. We all piled into Phil's run-down car and said things like:

"Home, James, and don't spare the horses."

"Driver, follow that cab."

"There's a tenner in it for you if you keep him in sight."

We were in high spirits as we crossed railroad tracks and heard a train whistle blow. We began to imitate the sound. After a second, Phil backed up until our car sat on the tracks. He turned off the motor.

I couldn't see the train, but judging by the sound of the whistle, it was just around a curve in the tracks.

I shouted, "Move the car. Move the damn car." I was sitting in the backseat. Phil turned his head to look at me and grinned.

I pushed on the back of the front passenger seat, but the woman in it had gone to sleep. Another voice joined mine as the train rounded into view. "Move, man, what the hell?" I had begun to scream. "You are going to get us killed."

The motor turned over, and the car slid off the tracks seconds before the train sped behind us.

The two passengers in the backseat with me cursed Phil roundly, but I couldn't speak. I had been frightened mute again, just like twenty-five years earlier, when I had been so terrorized that I had chosen to become mute.

This time I had no choice. Words simply would not come. Phil stopped the car on the corner by my house.

"You want to get out here?"

I nodded.

The woman sitting next to him awakened grouchy. "What's going on?" She frowned and leaned forward. I crawled out around her. When I was standing beside the car, I realized that I had urinated. My clothes were wet and crumpled.

When Phil waited for me to walk away, I decided he must have known I had been scared enough to pee on myself. I could not stand there all day, so I crossed the street in front of the car to give him a good chance to see me.

His laughter did not surprise me. "I scared the piss out of her. Look. Yes, I did ... Maya, come back and clean up my car. Come back, I won't do it again."

I continued walking to my house. He drove slowly beside me, laughing, urging me to get back in the car. His taunting did not embarrass me. The level of my fear totally outweighed everything he said.

He didn't drive off until I walked up the steps to my house.

As I showered, the terror released me. In clean, dry clothes, I sat down and thought about the horrible incident. I remembered Phil's self-description when I first met him, and I realized that I had learned at least one important lesson. Believe people when they tell you who they are. They know themselves better than you. The racial pejorative might not have applied to him. I didn't know him well enough to know if he was or wasn't a liar, but I found out he was certainly mean and he was ornery.

CHAPTER 12

The telephone voice startled me.

"Hello, is this my Maya?"

Shock closed my throat.

"Hello, Maya, speak to me. This is your husband."

He wasn't my husband, but he was my great love and my greatest fear, and I had left him in Africa. "Hello," I answered, reluctantly.

"I am here." He couldn't be. I looked at the door. "I am in New York City. I have come to the States to collect you. God gave you to me. Remember?"

I couldn't speak.

He was the man I felt had taken the heart out of my body and worn it boldly on his shoulder like an epaulette, and I had adored him.

He said, "Do you still love me?"

I finally asked, "Are you really in New York City?"

He continued, as was his way. "Of course you love me. I am coming to California to collect you and take you back to Africa."

I told him that I had made a life for myself in Los Angeles and I was not going anywhere.

We had both worked on trying to establish a relationship in Ghana. He was loud, bombastic and autocratic. But he loved me and found me funny and sexy, and he said I was brilliant. He was astonishingly hand-some, and his upbringing as a young royal gave him an assurance that I had found irresistible. We might have succeeded at being together, but I had no precedent for being who he wanted me to be. I did love him, but that had not been enough. He needed to be worshiped. Being an American, a black American woman, being Vivian Baxter's daugh-ter, Bailey Johnson's sister and Guy Johnson's mother, I was totally un-prepared to worship any mortal.

We had argued loudly and reconciled feverishly so many times that I knew our lives would always follow that pattern. I had come to that realization at the same time that my son had found "mother" to be a useless word, so I was often addressed as "Yeah."

I had left Africa to him and to my African love. And now my lover was on the same continent, and I had no place to run.

I called my mother for her strength and guidance. Her voice was warm and loving.

"Baby, it's a big world, and Los Angeles is a big city. He can come. Los Angeles can hold both of you."

She hadn't heard him roaring at me, or me screaming back at him.

"Oh yes," she went on, "I spoke to Guy the other day. He's about finished at school, and I think I hear homecoming in his talk."

"Oh?"

"Yes, he'll want to come home when he finishes. But he's out of money."

"Mom, I left him enough to live on, so if he's squandered—"

She said, "He's my grandson. I won't see him needy."

"That's between you and your grandson, but when he is ready to come home, I'll give you the money for his fare. Just don't let him know."

Mother said, "I understand," and she did.

———

The African arrived and filled my little studio apartment with his loud voice and his maleness. His sexuality was so evident that I thought everyone could perceive it.

He charmed my landlady and my neighbor. When he told them that he had come to take me back to Africa, they both offered to help me pack.

My body was in a state of utter bliss, but I could not mask my displeasure that he wanted to be waited upon as if he were an invalid: "Get this." "Fetch that." "Make food for me."

I knew English was not his first language; still, I had to tell him that "fetch" was an old-fashioned word used during slavery and I would not respond favorably to it.

On some evenings I wondered what I would do without him. On some evenings we talked about my concerns and he listened. On some evenings he held me and let me cry about Malcolm.

I would moan and say, "Black men shot him, what's the matter with us?"

"You are human. That is a historic problem. Remember, Cain killed Abel. His brother."

"But what will our people do? It took a long time to make Malcolm."

"You've got a long time. Some say that the American Negro represents the best the African can hope for."

He looked at my surprise.

"I agree in part. Sold by your people, brought here as slaves. Slavery lasted nearly three hundred years, and ten, twenty years after it was abolished, you had schools. Colleges. Fisk, Howard, Tuskegee. And even today, look at you, you are everywhere in this country. You will be all right." He patted me and hugged me.

When he was good, he was very very good. Ah. But when he was bad...

———

I went to my friend the actress Nichelle Nichols. We had become friends ten years earlier, during the filming of *Porgy and Bess.*

She was beautiful even when scowling. "Girl, tell him he is in America now, and we believe in one person, one vote. Anyway, bring him over for dinner. I'll have a little bee for his bonnet."

After fifteen minutes, I saw that dinner at Nichelle's was a bad idea. He spoke of Mother Africa and her children everywhere, and Nichelle was spellbound.

As we left, she whispered to me, "You're so lucky."

CHAPTER 13

Los Angeles, seen through my lover's eyes, was more colorful than I had realized, more variegated. He saw Watts as a community of great interest. After he observed many black families trying to restore their neat neighborhoods, he said, "But these people are fastidious."

I was surprised at his surprise. He explained, "Until recently in Africa all we saw of American Negroes was Rochester with Jack Benny, and Stepnfetchit, and athletes like Joe Louis and Jackie Robinson. I haven't seen it, but I understand Harlem is a hellhole."

"Harlem is beautiful."

In every conversation with him, I put on my armor of defense, whether I needed it or not, and whether or not my point of view was defensible.

"There are a few ugly places," I admitted, "but there are many ugly places in Africa."

We visited black-owned bookstores that featured books by blacks and about blacks.

He bought out entire shelves' worth and asked me to pay. The money was his, but he asked me to carry it, saying that he could not understand paper money without a black man's face on it.

I sidestepped a full-out argument by not reminding him that the Ghanaian pound, with Kwame Nkrumah's face on it, was only ten years old.

I was in a labyrinth, going somewhere without knowing my destination or even when I might arrive. I still loved him and wanted him, but there were parts of his life I could not even begin to fathom.

Sometimes, when I answered my telephone, a woman's voice would ask for him. She was calling from New York.

My lover explained, "She is a very old black lady, and she was helpful to me when I stopped at the United Nations."

Her voice didn't sound old, and he laughed with her on the telephone as if she were a girl.

"Her name is Dolly McPherson, and she is a very powerful old woman. She is an official at the Institute of International Education."

Our final argument came unexpectedly over Doris Day and Rock Hudson. We had gone to a movie in which they starred. He was totally silent as I drove home. He didn't speak when we got out of the car or when we entered the house. He was pouting. I didn't know why, and I was certainly not going to ask. I hated the torture of the silent treatment that he used when he was displeased.

I went straight to the kitchen and began warming the food I had cooked earlier. When the table was set with my good china and dinner placed on my best tablecloth, I went into the living room, where he sat like a Yoruba carving.

"Dinner is ready."

He looked up at me, his eyes glinting and his face in a monumental scowl.

"Why can't we be like them?"

"Like whom?"

"Those two actors in the film."

"Doris Day and Rock Hudson?"

"I don't know their names, but why can't we be to each other the way they are?"

"Are you serious?"

"Do you think I am playing?"

"Those are actors. They are not real. I mean, the roles are just roles. You know that."

He had graduated from England's top university with the highest academic degree and he was one of the most educated persons I had ever known. He was being perverse.

Perversity is contagious. I asked, "You want me to become a perky little blond woman? Is that what you want? You have little chance of getting that from me."

He said, "You American Negroes. I never know if you are just stupid or merely pretending." He looked at me pityingly.

Cursing has never been one of my strong suits, but I gathered a few sordid words and started throwing them around. The louder I became, the more scornful his look, and the louder I became.

I picked up my car keys and my purse and went into the kitchen. I took the corners of the tablecloth and let the food and plates and silverware and glasses fall down in the center. I dragged the whole thing to the living room.

"Here's dinner if you want it. I'm leaving."

Anger and frustration rode with me all the way to Nichelle's house.

"Well, Maya, you're always welcome to stay here, but you know how I feel about your marriage."

We weren't married. In Ghana we had done a little homemade ritual in the presence of a few friends. There had been no public ceremony, no authority to sanction our being together, no license assuring us of society's agreement. We had said some words, made some promises and poured schnapps on the ground.

I called my mother in San Francisco, who said that Bailey was visiting. I spoke to my brother and told him of my predicament. He listened and said that they would both be in Los Angeles the next day. I told them that I was spending the night with Nichelle and gave them the phone number and address.

They arrived at Nichelle's house in the morning in a rental car and I filled them in over coffee. I mentioned the African's cold treatment and how it drove me mad. They both understood. I said nothing about the curse words.

Mom said, "Well, let's go over and meet this man who wants to take you back to Africa."

Bailey rode in my car. He had been my closest and dearest friend all my life. "My, how is it? What do you want?"

"I want him to go back to Africa. He brings no peace, and I can't seem to manufacture any while he is around. He should go."

Bailey said, "Then he will go, and go today. Somewhere."

My brother was black and beauteous. He had given me my name, protected me, educated me and told me when I was twelve that I was smart. He had added that I was not as smart as he was, but I was smarter than almost everyone else. He was, at his tallest, five feet four inches tall.

The African had showered and changed, but the soiled tablecloth remained on the floor.

He shook hands with Bailey and embraced my mother.

Mother looked at the litter on the floor and turned to me.

"I left it here last night."

Mother said, "Aha."

I nodded to Bailey. He helped me carry the sour-smelling bundle back to the kitchen. Mother sat down, and as Bailey and I left the room, I heard her say, "Now, what's going on between you and my baby?"

Bailey asked me, "Where are his clothes? Does he have enough money to leave?" I pointed to a closet and told him that the African had plenty of money. I added, "He said he had brought a lot because he was going to carry me back to Africa."

Bailey said, "The hell. Did he think he had to pay a bride-price?"

That was my brother. He could make me laugh even in the grimmest situations.

"He's been talking about going to Mexico City. Kwesi Brew is Ghana's ambassador to Mexico, and Kwesi and his wife, Molly, love him. They dote on him."

Bailey said, "From what I see, he can take a lot of doting."

He watched as I cleared up the mess. "You are really your mother's daughter. He doesn't know he is lucky that you didn't dump that dinner on his head."

I told him that if I had done that, I thought the African would have hit me.

Bailey responded instantly, "He'd have only one time to do that. Next time he'd draw back a stub. Let's go see what your mother is doing."

My little mother sat in the one upholstered chair as primly as an old-fashioned schoolteacher. Her legs were crossed at the ankles. Her purse and gloves lay in her lap.

"Well, baby, this gentleman has reported you to me. He said you used profanity last night."

The African blurted out, "She used words I never even heard Negro sailors use when their ships docked in Ghana's port city of Tema. Her mouth should be washed out. You should do that."

Mother said, "Oh, I would never do a thing like that. Never. People use profanity because they have limited vocabularies or because they are lazy or too frustrated to search for the words they want. My daughter has an extensive vocabulary and doesn't have a lazy bone in her body. So she cursed out of frustration. Why were you frustrated, baby?"

Bailey spoke before I could answer. "Excuse me, Mom, but I'd like to speak to him." He turned to the African. "Would you come with me for a walk around the block?"

The African assented. When they were both on the steps, Bailey stuck his head back in the door.

"Pack his clothes."

Mother watched as I folded the flamboyant African robes into a trunk.

"Your brother said you didn't sound right on the telephone. That's why we are here."

"I wasn't right. I won't deny I was happy to see him, but I can't stand his rudeness in my face all the time."

"Wasn't he rude in Africa?" Although it was ten A.M., she was making herself a Scotch. She had told me years earlier that the time to drink was when you wanted it and could afford to buy it for yourself.

"It wasn't so bad there. First he had his business to focus his attention. He had his children, and I had my own house. And here he's only got me. So since he can't stand anyone around me, I've become the whipping boy."

Mother sucked her teeth loudly. "Well, you sure as hell weren't raised to be that for anybody. But it's all right. Your brother will take care of it."

The two men walked back into the house laughing uproariously and patting each other on the back.

"I want you to come to Africa yourself, Bailey, see how we live, eh."

Bailey said, "You bet. I'll probably be there before Maya gets back." He noticed my suitcase on the floor. He asked, "Oh, you've been packing?"

I said, "Yes, this is mine. I'm going back up to San Francisco with you and Mom." I wanted to save my lover's face. "I packed for him, too." I pointed to the luggage in the corner. "He's been talking to friends in Mexico City."

The African said, "That's where I'm going, and I'm going today. I will telephone Kwesi Brew. He will meet me."

I offered to make breakfast. Bailey shook his head. "I'm taking him to a great breakfast place in Venice. You need to make reservations for one from Los Angeles to Mexico City." Bailey and Mother went into the kitchen so my lover and I could have privacy. We embraced emotionally.

"You could come with me..."

I was already missing him. I said, "Not now, later. But why did you decide so suddenly to go?"

"Your brother. He talked to me, man to man. There seems to be something in my personality that rubs you the wrong way, and I may threaten, or at least weaken, your decision to return to me and Africa. So, at his suggestion, I am leaving you some space. He really loves you. You are lucky. But he understands me, and that's more important. He has retained more of the African spirit than you or your mother."

I could have kicked him. He was doing the very thing that had run me away from him in Africa. He so routinely disparaged other people's importance that he didn't notice he was degrading me.

"You can come to Mexico or I'll come back here. I mean to take you back."

Bailey said he would telephone about the reservation. I wished my love a safe journey and asked to be remembered to Kwesi and Molly Brew.

He was gone.

———

Bailey and Mother left that same day, but not before ragging me about the inane predicament I had created for myself.

"It's time for the troubleshooters to move on. You must not think you can call out the troops at each rumor of war."

I didn't call them to come. Or perhaps I did. Desperation may have been in my voice, must have been there, but I did not ask outright that they come to Los Angeles to rescue me. I was a woman, not a child. My name was spelled double-you oh em a en.

No, I didn't ask, but I was extremely glad they had come.

CHAPTER 14

Despite acres of ravaged city blocks and hulks of burned-out cars, Los Angeles seemed to have settled back into a satisfied-with-itself air. The cauldron still simmered in a few quarters, but the energy was spent and it would not boil over again anytime soon.

I had finished writing my play, and I asked Frank Silvera for advice. "Find a producer and give it to him. It will be his job to find the money, the theater, a director and a cast."

I said to him that he had not had to use those tactics; he had done everything himself.

He reminded me that he was the owner, producer and director of Tee Oh Bee.

I searched diligently for a producer, but there was a dearth of them

interested in a new play by an unknown playwright who also happened to be black and female. Few would even read the manuscript.
Coming out of the shadow of the Watts revolt, they thought the plot
would lean heavily on racial unrest.

My plot in "All Day Long," admittedly slight, was based on one day
in the life of a poor thirteen-year-old black boy who was relocated to
the North. Among his many travails were the difficulty of understanding the Northern accent and comprehending how a sofa could
secretly contain a bed larger than any he had ever seen.

In my play, the boy worked through his befuddlement at flushing
toilets (where did it all go?), the mystery of a refrigerator that stayed
cold without a block of ice in it and the gift of fresh water that came
through hardened silver tubes. A slim idea, but I remembered my own
stupefaction when Bailey and I returned to California as teenagers
after ten years in the rural South. In Arkansas we had drawn water
from a well, and for baths we had heated it on a wood-burning stove.
We slept on mattresses stuffed with feathers from chickens we raised
and killed and ate, and used a shack away from the house as a toilet.

So a foldout sofa and an indoor toilet had been miracles of moder-
nity to me. I found no one interested enough to produce "All Day
Long."

Back to the library. I had to learn how to produce. All I discovered
there was that producing meant having money, and most of the people I knew had very little; the few who were well-off weren't interested in my play.

Kwame Nkrumah, the president of Ghana, was deposed while on a
visit to China. It appeared that the time was out of joint, which meant
that even if I wanted to return to Africa, Ghana was out of the question for me. I had been a devout Nkrumaist.

In just two years, Malcolm had been murdered and the Watts conflagration had left a roster of arrestees, hundreds homeless and many
hurt. My once great love affair hadn't worked out the second time, and
now a person I had supported and admired was in exile from his country. I knew how Africans build their lives around their land, their fam-

ilies and friends. I wept for Kwame Nkrumah, for Ghana, for Africa, and some tears were for me.

CHAPTER 15

I sensed my friend Nichelle pulling away from me. I knew I was tenderhearted and a little paranoid, but I felt that she disapproved of me for sending the African away. I thought that she believed I was too hasty in letting go of the man who seemed to her to have been so desirable for me. He had status, intelligence, money and charisma. I might not do better than that anywhere.

Beah Richards was my neighbor, and we were friendly but never close friends. Professor M. J. Hewitt, a beautiful green-eyed friend with whom I was close, had found a great love and gone off to South America with him.

I noted the signs and determined that the time had come for me to be moving on.

My deliberations were focused on where to go. San Francisco didn't beckon, Hawaii held nothing for me. I began to look at New York.

I telephoned Bailey, who had moved back from Hawaii to San Francisco. "Of course, go to New York. As long as you don't get involved in the politics."

Mother came to the phone and said, "That's all right. But don't forget you can always come home."

A letter from the African's elderly lady friend in New York helped me decide definitely that I should head back East. Dolly McPherson wrote:

Dear Miss Angelou,

I am going into the hospital for surgery. I'll probably take a month to completely recover, but if you want to come to New York, I'll try to help you get settled. Possibly I can help you find employment if you need it.

Our African friend told me so much about you I can hardly wait to get to know you. If you'd like to send me your resume, I'll be glad to look it over and see how I might be of help.

> Yours,
>
> Dolly McPherson

The friendliness in the letter made me bless the sweetness of old black women. I began to look forward to meeting her. I was sure she would invite me to her church. And of course I'd be glad to go.

I had started packing and deciding to whom I would give away household goods when Rosa Guy telephoned me from New York. She was my friend from the Harlem Writers Guild, and she had finished her book *Bird at My Window.* She wanted to come to California and promote it. I told her that if she could come soon, I would arrange a book signing and introduce her to bookstore owners. One week later Rosa arrived in Los Angeles wearing her New York air as casually as a well-worn cape that fitted her perfectly. She told me how all our New York City friends were faring, and the conversation made me think more about that hard and demanding and most glamorous city in the world.

Her novel of a dysfunctional relationship between a mother and son was gripping and sold well at the black-owned Aquarian bookstore. She could take a California success story back to New York.

Rosa was delighted when I told her that I was planning to return to New York. "Certainly, come to New York, you can stay with me. I have a big apartment uptown."

Abbey Lincoln and Max Roach had moved from Columbus Avenue to Central Park West. Their new apartment had an extra room. Abbey offered it to me over the telephone. Now I had two places I could stay.

Couples rarely know how much their togetherness shuts others out, and even if they did, there would be nothing they could do, save make everyone painfully self-conscious.

Rosa always had a string of devoted gentlemen friends, but since I had known her, she had not been the other half in a double arrangement—which seemed to say "We are together and you, third person, are invisible most of the time."

I accepted Rosa's offer and continued packing.

Everything said about the capricious nature of life and the best-laid plans is patently true. Just as I chose a departure date, my door-bell rang. When I opened the door, Bailey stood on the landing, his face grave.

"Baby, Guy returned to San Francisco three days ago, and I've come for you. He's in the hospital. He is in serious condition but not a life-threatening one. Get what you need." Surprise, whether good or bad, can have a profound effect on the body. Some people faint, some cry aloud. Bailey caught me as my knees buckled. He helped me back in the room to a chair.

Rosa asked what happened.

Bailey said, "Guy was sitting in a parked car that was hit by an out-of-control truck. Mother wanted to telephone you and tell you to fly up to San Francisco. I said no, that I would drive down and get you." He turned to Rosa. "Do you want to come with us, or will you wait till Maya gets back?"

Rosa said she was already packed and could fly home out of San Francisco as easily as out of Los Angeles. She would come with us.

In a few ragged minutes we were walking to Bailey's car. He handed me his car keys. "You drive."

"No, you know me. I might fall asleep."

"I drove all night to get here. Take the keys. You have me and your good friend in the car and you are trying to get to your son. Just remember."

I took the keys.

My passengers never awakened even when I stopped for gas.

Seven hours later I parked in front of Mother's house in San Francisco, and they woke up as if by plan.

Mother was waiting.

"He is stable. I've been talking to the doctors." She showed Rosa to a guest room and encouraged her to get some rest, adding that we would return soon. Mother drove her large car to the hospital.

Guy was ashen and looked like a grown man in the hospital bed. He was awake.

"Hello, my son."

"Hello, Mom."

He was stiff in our embrace. "I can't move much. My neck. It's broken again."

Suddenly I felt guilty. I had not been in the truck that hit him. In fact, I was not even in the same city where the accident occurred, and yet I felt guilty.

When something goes wrong with offspring, inevitably the parent feels guilty. As if some stone that needed turning had been left unturned. In the case of a physical handicap, the mother feels that when her body was building the infant, it shirked its responsibility somewhere.

I stood looking at my son, wondering where I had failed. I knew I would stay near until he recovered. I also knew that staying around Vivian Baxter would be strengthening.

She had a litany of morale-building sayings. "Keep your eyes on the road, your hand on the plow, your finger in the dike, your shoulder to the wheel, and push like hell." My mother would issue the statements as if from the godhead, and it was up to the hearer to fathom the meaning.

After a few days, Rosa left San Francisco for New York.

I visited Guy every day and watched as he slowly revived. I was right in my earlier observation. He was a grown-up stranger who reminded me of my son.

He said the University of Ghana had given him all it had to give. No, he wasn't sorry to leave Ghana, and although he had made some enemies, he had also made some friends he would keep for his lifetime.

As soon as he was well, he'd find work. Of course he would. He had had his first job at thirteen as a stacking boy in a Brooklyn bakery.

He would stay with his grandmother when he was released from the hospital. She would give him a roomful of her aphorisms. "Take care of your own business. Everybody else's business will not be your business." "Look to the hills from whence cometh your help." "You can tell a person by the company he keeps." "Never let your right hand know what your left hand is doing." Always adding that "each tub must sit on its own bottom."

I left San Francisco when I saw Guy sitting up like a golden prince and being served like a king in my mother's house.

CHAPTER 16

Leaving Los Angeles was harder than I expected.

Human beings are like some plants. If we pause a few seconds in our journey, we begin setting down roots, tendrils that entangle other people as we ourselves are entangled.

Don Martin and Jimmy Truitt of the Lester Horton Dance School had been especially kind to me. When I took classes with them, they were careful not to let me appear ungainly, although I was fifteen years older than the other students. They deserved the courtesy of a farewell.

I was indebted to the Tee Oh Bee people as well as to Seymour Lazar, a Hollywood lawyer who had been generous with his advice and who gave me a nearly new car when mine refused to run another mile.

M. J. Hewitt had returned copper-colored from her South American trip and was full of stories I longed to hear. My friend Ketty Lester, a nightclub entertainer who sang as if she had a wind chime in her mouth, had to receive a good-bye.

I asked the help of Frances, Nichelle and Beah, and together we gave me a going-away party that spilled out of my house into Beah's, then into the big backyard where ripe figs from a huge tree made walking messy.

I looked at Los Angeles anew and saw the fun I was having. I thought that leaving the town just as I was beginning to appreciate it might not be the best idea I had ever had. Then I remembered another of Vivian Baxter's truisms: "Take as much time as you need to make up your mind, but once it is made up, step out on your decision like it's something you want."

After I had survived the ugly rebellious years of "What can she possibly know that I don't?" I had followed my mother's advice to the letter and had not found her in error even once. I telephoned Guy to ask, "Are you going to be all right?" His tone was sincerely tender. "Mom, stop worrying. I'm your son and I'm a man."

When I pulled together the money I had been saving, it proved enough to get me to New York and keep me for at least two months. I'd have a job by that time.

CHAPTER 17

Rosa's Upper West Side apartment was luxurious. The rooms were large and the ceilings so high that the place reminded me of the Victorian houses of San Francisco. The furniture was comfortable and the kitchen extraordinary, with the huge pots and outsize pans of a serious cook who was also a dedicated party giver.

People loved Rosa's parties for the food and her ability to make each person feel that with her or his arrival, the party could begin.

We quickly agreed that I would share expenses and cooking as long as I was there but that I would be looking with focused attention for my own apartment.

I had been in New York less than a week when Rosa decided to give a party. I asked if I could invite Dolly McPherson. Since she was an elderly woman, I wanted to ask her for around seven-thirty.

"Your friends won't be coming till around nine or ten. We'll have a drink and then she can get home before it's too late."

Rosa said that was all right with her.

African friends from the United Nations kept Rosa's liquor cabinet filled with a full complement of the most desired spirits, but she always insisted on buying her own wines. I was assisting with the cooking of banquet dishes when the doorbell rang.

I said to Rosa, "That must be Miss McPherson."

I had only to open the door to see how wrong I was. A beautiful young dark-brown-skinned woman wearing a lime-green dress stood before me.

Maybe one of Rosa's early guests. I said, "Good evening."

She said, "I am here to see Miss Angelou."

I said, "I am Miss Angelou."

She said, "You can't be. I mean, I am here to see the older Miss Angelou, maybe your mother."

I said, "I am the only Miss Angelou here."

We stared at each other for a few seconds.

I asked, "Are you Miss McPherson?"

She nodded, and we started to laugh at the same time.

She said, "The old goat."

We were still laughing when we sat down in the living room.

She asked, "What did he tell you about me?" I told her that the African had said she was an old but very intelligent woman who had been helpful to him.

"He could rightly say that. He courted me seriously and spent quite a few nights at my apartment."

It was my turn to say, "The old goat. And what did he tell you about me?"

"That you were very old and that you owned a house where you let rooms. He said you were one of those African-Americans who felt they had found something in Ghana, and you always had a soft spot for Africans in general and Ghanaians in particular."

Now I wanted to use a word more descriptive of the African than "goat," but the situation seemed so funny to me, and to Dolly as well, that even over drinks and throughout the party, whenever I caught her eye, we were both rendered speechless by laughter. We were both intelligent women who had been had by the same man. In more ways than one.

CHAPTER 18

I knew there would be no peace for me until I visited the Audubon Ballroom. Until I let the grisly scene play out in front of me.

The dance hall and theater had been famous for decades. When I had gone visiting in the fifties, I often imagined Langston Hughes and Arna Bontemps and Zora Neale Hurston dancing the Charleston to the big-band music of Jimmy Lunceford, Count Basie and Duke Ellington.

Time passed and took away the popularity of orchestra music, the big bands and public dancing. When I went on my nostalgic walk to the ballroom in 1967, New York City had begun the process of condemning the Audubon. Its meager reserve was realized from renting the premises to organizations, conventions, councils and committees.

On February 21, 1965, the Organization of African-American Unity had rented the ballroom for a fund-raiser. Malcolm X had been the speaker.

I approached the building slowly. The windows were dusty and the doors barred. As I tried to peer into the vast emptiness, the questions that crouched just beyond my conscious mind came full force.

Had I stayed in New York when I returned from Ghana, would I have been sitting with Betty Shabazz and her children?

Would I have heard the final words of Malcolm X?

Would I have heard the shots puncture the air?

Would I have seen the killers' faces and had them etched in my mind eternally?

I could see no shadow inside; no chimera arose and danced.

I walked away.

CHAPTER 19

I had sung in Jerry Purcell's swank supper club once, and although I was not looking for nightclub work, I telephoned him. He invited me for dinner. We had been good friends, and I thought he might have some idea where I could find work. We met at his Italian restaurant, the Paparazzi.

He was still a big, movie-star-handsome man who walked as if he were heavier from his waist down than from his waist up. We greeted each other as old friends. I told him I was staying with a friend and that I was still writing poetry, but I longed to write plays and my money was disappearing faster than I had expected.

At that moment Jerry began to grow angel's wings. He said, "I'm in management now, and I am doing well."

He rose often from the table to greet customers and to speak to his staff, but he always returned, smiling. He was more affable than I remembered.

I said good-bye after lunch, and he handed me an envelope, saying that his office number and the name of his personal secretary were enclosed. He said I should find my own apartment and that if I needed anything, I should phone his secretary. He said, "Bring your friends here. Whenever. Just take the bill, add your tip and sign it."

He sent a waiter with me to hail a taxi. I sat back in the seat and opened the envelope. The number and the secretary's name were there, along with a large amount of cash.

For the next two years Purcell treated me like a valued employee. Save for the odd temporary office job and the money I made writing radio spots for Ruby Dee and Ossie Davis, I depended upon his largesse. He didn't once ask anything and seemed totally satisfied with a simple thanks. I did write a ballad based on *Portnoy's Complaint* for a singer Jerry managed. And I wrote twelve astrological liner notes for a series of long-playing albums he was planning to release.

When I tried to explain how his generosity afforded me the opportunity to improve my writing skills, he shrugged his shoulders and said, "I manage artists who make more in one night than you have ever made in a year. Yet I know no one more talented than you."

His patronage was a gift as welcome as found money bearing no type of identification.

CHAPTER 20

New York was vigorous, and its inhabitants moved quickly. Everyone was always going somewhere determinedly. There seemed to be no question or doubt about their destination. New Yorkers knew they were going to arrive, and no one had better get in the way.

In order to join New York's ebb and flow, I had to spend some time listening to the sounds, watching the streams of people coursing east and west and north and south. When I thought I had my balance, I dared to look for an apartment.

There are only so many times in life when our good fortunes and bad fortunes intersect. At such junctions, it is wise to pray, and failing that, keep the passport up-to-date and have some cash available.

The first few days, the city seemed an ice rink, and I was a novice wobbling on weak ankles. I continued going out each day to follow up on tips and hunt down newspaper listings.

I had wanted a flat in a brownstone, or at least a large apartment in one of the older buildings on Riverside Drive. Life offered me a one-bedroom apartment in a brand-new building on Central Park West. It was painted white, and its best feature was a long living room with big windows and a view of the park.

The place was clinical and so different from what I wanted that I thought bad fortune had caught me and I would be forced to live, at least for a while, in a cold and sterile environment. But life proved itself right and me wrong. Friends began giving me fine things for the apartment.

I was having dinner in a Harlem restaurant when a good-looking amber-colored man introduced himself. That is how I met the handsome Sam Floyd, who had the airs of a meticulous fop and the mind of an analytical scientist. He was one of James Baldwin's closest friends and, after a few months, became a close friend to me. His quick but never cruel wit lifted my spirits on many lean and mean days. I invited him to my empty apartment. He said, "People think New Yorkers are cold, but that is only when they are prevented from helping people who really don't need help. I have a small rug for you." We laughed. After we discovered that we really liked each other, we spent time together at least once a week.

Sam was only partially right. As soon as it became known that I had an empty apartment, I began to receive good and even great furniture. A desk came from Sylvia Boone, who had just returned from Ghana. The composer Irving Burgee, who had written calypso songs for Harry Belafonte, was the most financially successful member of the Harlem Writers Guild, and when he heard that I had a new apartment, he gave me a sleek table and an upholstered chair.

CHAPTER 21

Dolly McPherson and I were becoming good friends. Obviously we never revealed to anyone how we met. Either or both of us could have taken umbrage, and perhaps we did privately. But there was no reason to be angry with each other. Dolly had no way of knowing that when the man was with me, he acted as if he were my husband. And I couldn't know that when he wasn't with me, I aged about forty years and became an old black American lady who let rooms.

Dolly and I liked each other's ability to laugh at a circumstance that neither of us could undo. I met her family. Dolly's youngest brother, Stephen, looked so much like Bailey that I could hardly speak when we met.

Stephen was my brother's height and skin color, and was a brilliant research scientist. Like Bailey, Stephen had the wit to make me laugh at the most inane jokes and even at inappropriate times.

I wrote to Mother, "You didn't give me a sister but I found one for myself. As soon as possible I want you to come to New York and meet her."

Dolly and I started spending time in an antique shop on the Upper West Side.

Bea Grimes had the only black-owned secondhand store on Broadway. I liked that she was a big country woman with a colorful vocabulary and her own business. She thought of me as being a lot like her, except I had a little more learning and owned practically nothing.

She and Dolly and I often sat talking in the musty crowded back of her shop. She found out that I hardly knew the difference between a Meissen cup and a Mason jar, but she did, and sitting in the gloom, often with a drink in a paper cup, she schooled me on what to look for in ceramics, china, and silver.

"What kind of silver you got?"

I told her that I had no silver.

"No silver? No silver?"

"My mother has silver. I'll be forty on my next birthday. It's too early for me."

Bea clucked her tongue and shook her head. "You ought to have bought yourself something silver on your thirtieth birthday. Even a silver spoon. You can't be a lady with no silver." She asked, "What you got sitting on your buffet?"

I hesitated.

Dolly said, "Oh, Bea, she doesn't have a buffet."

"Child, I'd better come around and see your place. I'm going to get you set up. You need some help."

1130 · *Maya Angelou*

Bea sold me an Eames chair for thirty dollars and a nineteenth-century Empire sofa for a hundred.

Bea needed to be needed and in fact liked the needing. She sat in that miasmic atmosphere surrounded by goods that had belonged to someone else who must have found pleasure in preserving them, might have even doted on them. Now they were abandoned to the often careless fingers of customers whose greatest interest was in haggling with the store owner to get a bargain price.

"These young white kids nearly give away their parents' and grandparents' things. You want to see something? Someday I'll take you to an estate sale. The heirs act like they don't care how much money they get. Main thing to them is get rid of this old stuff. Make you think seriously about dying, don't it?"

Thanks to Bea Grimes in particular and a host of friends in general, I was able to turn the clinical-looking apartment into a lush experience. Pale lilac silk drapes at the window, a purple wool sofa, one new pale green Karastan rug from Stern's, a reputable record player and I was ready to show off my home.

The Harlem Writers Guild members, along with Sam Floyd, James Baldwin, Connie Sutton and her husband, Sam, and the artist Joan Sandler, came to party. In fact, Jimmy's whole family came to party.

When I looked around, there were over fifty people in my suddenly small apartment, and they were having a New York good time. James Baldwin and Julian Mayfield and Paule Marshall were discussing the political responsibilities of writers. John Killens, the founder of the Harlem Writers Workshop, waded in with Alexander Pushkin. Ivan Dixon, the screen actor, on a visit from California, and M. J. Hewitt were sitting on the floor near the piano in deep conversation while Patty Bone, who had been Billie Holiday's accompanist, played a Thelonious Monk tune.

Sam Floyd and Helen Baldwin, Jimmy's sister-in-law, helped me in the kitchen. I used the make-do tip that my mother had taught me: "If more people come than expected, just put a little more water in the soup." She believed it was all right to turn away people for cocktails but bad luck to turn anyone away from a dinner party.

The party finally wound down and released its hold on the revelers. The food had been enjoyed and the drink had been served generously, yet there were leftovers sufficient for the next day's dinner and no one faced the grayness of dawn totally besotted.

CHAPTER 22

Jimmy Baldwin was a whirlwind who stirred everything and everybody. He lived at a dizzying pace and I loved spinning with him. Once, after we had spent an afternoon talking and drinking with a group of white writers in a downtown bar, he said he liked that I could hold my liquor and my positions. He was pleased that I could defend Edgar Allan Poe and ask serious questions about Willa Cather.

The car let us out on Seventy-first Street and Columbus Avenue, but I lived on Ninety-seventh and Central Park West. I said, "I thought you were taking me home." He said, "I am, to my home."

He started calling as he unlocked the front door. "Momma, Paula, Gloria, Momma?"

"James, stop that hollering. Here I am." The little lady with an extremely soft voice appeared, smiling. She looked amazingly like Jimmy. He embraced her.

"Momma. I'm bringing you something you really don't need, another daughter. This is Maya."

Berdis Baldwin had nine children, yet she smiled at me as if she had been eagerly awaiting the tenth.

"You're a precious thing, yes you are. Are you hungry? Let Mother fix you something."

Jimmy said, "I'll make us a drink. We won't be staying long."

Mother said, "You never stay long anywhere."

Their love for each other was like a throb in the air. Jimmy was her first child, and he and his brothers and sisters kept their mother in an adoring family embrace.

When we reached the door, I said, "Thank you, Mrs. Baldwin."

She asked, "Didn't you hear your brother? He gave you to me. I am your mother Baldwin."

"Yes, Mother Baldwin, thank you." I had to bend nearly half my height to kiss her cheek.

CHAPTER 23

I was job hunting persistently. Gloria, Jimmy Baldwin's sister, had told me that Andrea Bullard, an editor at *Redbook,* had learned that a job was going to become available at the *Saturday Review* and the administrators would be looking for a black woman.

I applied for a position in editing. Norman Cousins talked to me, and on a Friday afternoon, he asked that I write précis on five major articles taken from international journals and bring them to him on Monday by noon.

I said I would, but I was so angry that Dolly's office could hardly hold me.

"Obviously he doesn't want me for the job. If in fact there's a job at all."

Dolly said, "But you have had an interview with Cousins. There must have been something."

I told her, "Maybe there was something about me he didn't like. Maybe I was too tall or too colored or too young or old—"

Dolly interrupted, "Suppose it's none of those things?"

"Dolly, when an employer sets an impossible task for a want-to-be employee, he does it so that he is freed from hiring that particular employee and yet can say he did try. 'I did…but I couldn't find anyone capable of doing the work.' "

Dolly said, "You can do it, I know, and I'm going to help. Decide on the five journals and I'll ask my secretary to help over the weekend. We can't let this chance get away." She went on, "He's going to have to tell you to your face you are not what he wants." She began to move rapidly around her office, gathering papers.

I could hardly refute her statement. I knew I should never ask anyone to fight my battles more passionately than I. So I agreed to write the précis.

"International journals?" She called her secretary. "Mrs. Ford, I need five journals. Miss Angelou is going to do some research and writing tonight and tomorrow. I will also need your help on Sunday."

The secretary stood in the room, somber and contained.

"Intellectual journals from five countries. Thank you." Mrs. Ford left and returned with her arms filled. I was given *The Paris Review, The Bodleian, The Kenyan,* an Australian magazine and a German magazine.

The weekend was a flurry of encyclopedias and yellow pads. I sat on the floor with *Roget's Thesaurus,* the King James Bible and several dictionaries.

On Sunday, Mrs. Ford came to Dolly's apartment and typed my handwritten summaries. Dolly read them and declared, "This is as good as or better than anything they print in the darn magazine."

For Dolly, that was strong talk.

There are some people who are fastidious about the language they use, possibly because of their upbringing. Dolly and I could be alone in an empty apartment, yet if Dolly said "hell," she always spelled it.

Now she was still irate. She said, "If the editor had enough damned nerve to ask you for that much work in two days, you have enough damned nerve to write the pieces and deliver them in person before noon on Monday."

On Monday morning I stepped crisply into the office of the *Saturday Review.*

"I have an appointment with Mr. Cousins."

The receptionist said, hardly looking up, "He's not here."

"But I'm supposed to give him some digests. May I see his secretary?"

"She's not here, either. You can just leave them there."

She never once really looked at me, but I had the sensation that she had looked and seen right through me. At first glance, I appeared a nice-looking woman in her late thirties, well dressed, carefully coiffed, with more than enough confidence.

But the receptionist knew that I didn't belong there and she did. To her I was just another colored girl out of my place. Dangerously, her knowledge almost became my knowledge. I laid the pages on the desk and somehow got to the elevator as quickly as possible.

CHAPTER 24

Jimmy Baldwin had visited me the night before and our conversation had turned into a loud row. I was not surprised to hear his voice on the telephone.

"Hey baby, are you busy?"

"Not too busy, why?"

"I'm coming to pick you up. I'll be in a taxi. I want to talk to you."

We didn't speak in the cab. The argument had been over the Black Panthers in general, of whom I approved, and Eldridge Cleaver in particular, who I thought was an opportunist and a batterer.

Jimmy had said, "You can't separate Cleaver from the Panthers. He is their general."

I had argued that Huey Newton was the general and Eldridge was a loudmouth foot soldier.

The Black Panthers had earned respect in the African-American community. They had started a school where the students were given free breakfasts and professional tutoring. They were courteous to women and addressed one another with kindness. Even the most arch-conservative privately admired their trim Panthers' uniforms topped by rakishly worn berets. The people were happy to see them stride through the neighborhood like conquering heroes accepting greetings.

Eldridge had a different air. It was as if he were years older than the others. When I saw him on television, he seemed more inimical and bitter than the other Panthers. They were angry, enraged and determined to do something about the entrenched racism, but he was aloof and chilly.

Jimmy had said, "Why are you skirting the issue? You don't like Cleaver because you don't like what he said about me."

"That's true. But that's not all."

"Yeah?" He had smiled, and his fine hands flew around in the air like dark birds. He knew me very well. "You can't stand hearing anyone insult or even talk about your friends."

I had not responded. Not only was it true, I thought, but it was a good way to be.

When the cab stopped now on Forty-fourth Street, off Broadway, I asked, "We had to come to a transient hotel?"

He paid the driver. "It's sleazy, I know that, but I used to hang out here years ago. I come here a lot of times when I want to think." I was pleased that he would want me around while he thought.

It was early afternoon outside, but the dim bar and the reek of spilled beer and urine made me think of midnight in a low-down and dusty dive during prohibition.

Jimmy's eyes had no more time than mine to grow accustomed to the gloom, but he led me directly to the bar. Obviously he was familiar with the place.

He pulled out a stool. "Baby, you order drinks, I've got to make a phone call."

I ordered two Scotches and thought about the mind's whimsy. James Baldwin, whose writing challenged the most powerful country in the world, who had sat down with the president and who spoke French as if he had grown up on the streets on Montmartre, came to this dank dive to think.

I was absorbed in thought myself when a person moved too close to me.

"Hello. My name is Buck. Let me buy you a drink."

I looked up to see a huge man standing about an inch away from me.

I pulled back and said, "Thank you, but I'm with someone."

He grunted. "Well, he's not your husband."

"Oh really, how did you come to that conclusion?" I flinched a second after I asked the question. I really didn't want him to answer, in case his response would be too telling.

He stuck out his arm and shook his hand on a limp wrist. "He's one of those, you know."

"What I do know is that I am with him. So you'd better go to your seat before he comes back."

Jimmy did walk and gesture with feminine grace, but I couldn't allow the intruder to get away with his insinuations.

Buck was still talking when Jimmy returned. My eyes had grown used to the light given off by neon signs behind the bar. Jimmy saw the man, sized up the situation and neatly stepped between the offender and me.

He looked up into the intruder's face. "You've been looking after her for me, haven't you?"

Before Buck could answer, Jimmy said, "Thank you, you son of a bitch. Now you are dismissed."

Jimmy's ferocity shocked me, and my jaw dropped. It dropped farther when the man turned, unspeaking, and walked away.

Jimmy sipped his drink. "Well, baby, I'm going to California. I've decided that I should help Eldridge Cleaver."

Hearing his plans kept me speechless.

"I know you say you hate him, but he is a thinking black man, and he is in trouble because he is thinking and is talking about what he thinks. He needs our help."

I said, "Well, I thought about it, and what he wrote about your homosexuality in his stupid book was so vulgar that I'd rather hang him than help him."

"*Soul on Ice* is a very important book, and you have to remember, the son always kills the father."

The statement was intriguing. I mulled it over as Jimmy gathered his thoughts.

"I met Richard Wright in Paris and got to know him sufficiently," he said. "Everything about Wright that I disliked I wrote about in my essay 'Alas, Poor Richard.' Many Wright devotees were as angry with me then as you are now with Eldridge."

"I'm not a devotee." I hastened to put myself in a clearer light. "I love you, true, but I'm not a damned devotee. I am a careful reader, and I know the difference between your critical evaluation of Wright's post–*Black Boy* work and the hatchet job Cleaver did on you. Not on your work but on you, on your character."

"Maybe he couldn't find enough about my work to attack. Sometimes people assail the homosexual because they think that by flailing the gay boy, they can reduce that same tendency they suspect in themselves. It's difficult being different."

"Well, do you suppose if I know that, it will make it easier for me to see you go to California to help Cleaver?"

"Baby, understand when I say I am going to help Eldridge, and I hope I do, that I am really going for myself. Because it is the right thing for me to do. Understand?"

My own obstinacy would not allow me to concede quickly and admit that I did understand, and that I even hoped that if I found myself in the same or a similar circumstance, I would behave as wisely.

"Understand?"

More at that moment than ever before, he reminded me of Bailey. They were two small black men who were my big brothers.

I said, "I'm just afraid for you out there with those roughnecks."

"I am a roughneck, too. Grow up. Being black and my size on the streets of Harlem will make a choirboy a roughneck. But do you understand why I'm going?"

I said, "Yes."

CHAPTER 25

Jerry Purcell's East Side apartment was the epitome of elegance. I was invited to dinner, and I took Rosa with me. She marveled at the luxury and whispered, "And he's a bachelor?"

I told her, "Yes." Years earlier he had fallen for and married a movie starlet, but the marriage didn't last.

Jerry's partner, Paul Robinson, who was always at his side, was great company and could have been a professional comedian. Because he reproduced so accurately any accents relevant to his hilarious stories, he was irresistible.

I was pleased that Jerry was there to meet my friend and even more pleased that they seemed to like each other.

Jerry had sent out for food, and his housekeeper served us in the dining room.

Rosa came back from a trip to the bathroom. She whispered to me, "Girl, the faucets are gold."

I said, "Probably gold plate."

She lifted her shoulders and asked, "So?"

I saw her point. Anybody wealthy enough to have gold-plated bathroom fixtures was *wealthy*.

Jerry had asked me to bring some poems.

After I read them and received compliments, we played backgammon with much merriment. Jerry nodded at me. "Let me speak to you."

I followed him into a small sitting room.

"You're a good poet, and you might become great. You could become bigger than you imagine. Don't sell out, if I ever hear of you selling out..."

"How could I sell out? To whom would I sell out and what would I sell?"

"I mean, don't be stupid and use drugs."

I was flabbergasted. The night, which had been one of laughter and teasing, had turned into a drug-counseling session.

"There is no chance that I will ever use anything. I've learned a painful lesson from my brother."

"Okay. I had to say that. I've made a decision. I'm going to give you a monthly allowance. Continue working on your play and writing poetry."

He patted me on the back, and we returned to the living room. Amazement showed on my face.

Rosa asked, "Are you all right?"

I nodded. "It's probably time for us to go home."

Jerry turned to Paul. "Paul, will you drop Maya off when you go? Rosa's going to stay here a while. That's all right, Maya? If Paul takes you home?"

I looked at Rosa, who looked at Jerry, then back at me. She said, "I'll go with Maya," but the regret in her voice was palpable.

I couldn't get out of the apartment soon enough.

Paul Robinson said to Rosa, "He really fell for you. And you seemed to find him interesting."

Rosa said, "He's a nice man. I like him."

I asked, "But when did you know you liked him? I hardly heard you say two words to each other."

Rosa said, "I could be wrong, but I think I like him. No, I know I do."

There is a language learned in the womb that never needs interpreters. It is a frictional electricity that runs between people. It carries the pertinent information without words.

Its meanings are "I find you are incredibly attractive. I can hardly keep my hands off your body.

"And I am crazy to touch you, to kiss your mouth, your eyes."

The couple may have been introduced in a cathedral or a temple, but these are among the luscious thoughts each body sends to the other.

Some folks are born with more of that idiom than others. My body has always been slow-witted when it comes to that language. It neither speaks it fluently nor comprehends it clearly.

CHAPTER 26

The African was back. He telephoned from Ghana.

"I am not coming for you this time. You had your chances. Many chances. Now I am convinced that you do not love Africa. You do not love Ghana. I am not coming for you. I am coming to teach at one of your important universities. But I will bring you something. You are so American now. Would you like a car?"

His voice was so loud, he hardly needed a telephone.

I asked, "Why would you bring a car from Ghana? I'm living in New York. That is just down the street from Detroit. That's where they make cars."

"Maya, your tongue is too sharp, I've told you time and time again. You must watch out for your tongue."

But my tongue was all I had, all I had ever had. He had the stature, the money, his country, his sex, and now he was coming to my country to teach in an "important university" where I had never been. When it came to parrying, he had his armament, but I also had my weapon.

"I shall stay with the second secretary, who has a place near the United Nations, but I'd like to see you. Just for two hours. I'd like to invite some people I've not seen since my last visit." (I doubted that Dolly would be among the group.)

"How many should I prepare for?"

"Few. I think about ten."

That meant at least twenty.

"I'd be pleased to have them in my place."

"Then it's done. My host will bring me, so I suppose that makes us twelve. You can accommodate twelve?"

"Well, of course, when are you planning to come?" I expected to hear him say within the next month or so.

He said, "I'm traveling tomorrow. I'll spend a day in the U.K. and I'll be in New York on Friday. Can you see me then?"

"Um, yes. Yes. Of course." There would be time.

"Around three?"

"Three is fine."

A smile slowly moved across my face. I hugged myself with delight and telephoned Dolly.

We splurged on a bottle of good Spanish sherry and sat in her living room.

She said, "Of course he would never imagine that we'd meet."

I told her, "He's coming with some diplomats. We shall have to be careful."

She said, "I know you don't want to embarrass him."

"I certainly do want to embarrass him, but to himself, not to others."

Dolly grinned. I said, "I don't want to put his whole business in the street, but I have to get him back for 'She is an old American Negro who lets rooms...'"

Dolly said, "What about 'She is very, very old but very intelligent,' after whispering in my ear that I was very beautiful and that I had the skin of a young country girl?"

"He said that?"

"Many times."

"Oh, we must make him sweat, if only for a minute. He's got to sweat."

Our plans were concluded among peals of laughter and squeals of satisfaction, and for the next few days we had broad smirks on our faces.

Jimmy and Sam Floyd came for drinks.

Jimmy asked, "What's going on? You are the veritable cat who has lured the canary into its gullet."

"All I can tell you is it's not an innocent, hopeless, defenseless canary. If anything, I may be the house cat who plans to swallow down the lion."

"Be careful, baby. Learn from nature. How many times have you seen or heard of a tabby bearding a lion in its den?"

"I have not heard that, but I have heard of a pussy that dared to look at a queen."

My answer caught him, and he laughed loudly. "Okay. Okay. I still say be careful, baby, and let me know how it turns out."

Sam Floyd enjoyed the repartee with Jimmy. He laughed his little-boy coughing laugh and lit another Gauloise.

"That was quick and good, but I'm with Jim. Be careful. A big cat isn't swallowed down easily, and it can turn awfully fast. It's known for that."

I advised Dolly to put her clock in her purse (she never wore a watch) because we had to time her entrance to the minute. Drinks and groceries had to be bought and food had to be prepared.

In African homes and most African-American homes, the host expects, and is expected, to offer food and beverage to guests. The provisions may be as meager as a piece of fruit and a glass of water, but they must be offered.

The sight of him at my door made me lean against the jamb. He was as beautiful as ever and as black as ever. His skin shone as if it had just been polished, and his teeth were as white as long-grain rice.

Seeing me had some effect on him, too, for he rocked back and forth a few times before he entered the apartment.

We embraced but held ourselves in check. There were too many hard words like shields across our chests, and his escort entered close behind him and stood silent as we greeted each other.

I brought out schnapps, and although I expected it, I flinched when the African poured a few drops for the elders onto my Karastan rug.

We spoke of old friends and new woes. He had not gone to Guinea, where President Nkrumah lived in exile. He said lies and gossip and rumors filled the papers and radio reports. There had been an intimation that he supported the rebels who overthrew President Nkrumah.

"Maya, you yourself know that to be a lie. I was in Mexico with Kwesi Brew when the coup took place. And even so, I was always a Nkrumaist. They called me a verandah boy, meaning one who stood on the verandah talking about independence and then worked to kick the colonials out of our country. We were among the group who brought him to power."

I couldn't imagine anyone ever calling him a boy, even when he was twelve years old.

The doorbell rang, and in minutes my living room was furnished with people in rich robes and colorful caftans. Different languages sang in the air. I poured drinks, and although I had a pot of chili and rice, the company was satisfied with the fruit and cheese spread on the buffet next to the silver.

At exactly five minutes to four, while the company was engrossed in the African's conversation, I quietly went to the door and unlocked it. I picked up a glass of wine and went back to my seat.

At one minute to four, I interrupted the African. "Excuse me, but I and the other women here have a burning question I have been meaning to ask. I know you can answer."

He obligingly turned to me.

"Will you speak of fidelity? Is the African man more faithful than the European man? And what makes him so?"

He cleared his throat and spoke. "Yes, that is a lady's question, but having said that, it still deserves being answered." I might have kicked him had I not tasted the promised revenge on my tongue.

"The African man is more faithful than the European, not because he loves his woman more than the European loves his woman but because he loves himself more than the European man loves himself."

Dolly walked in the door. Only a few heads turned.

"You see, the African man is supposed to know where he is at all times. If he is in the wrong place, he knows that, and he has to leave…"

Dolly walked up to his chair and laid a hand on his shoulder. "Hello there."

He turned and looked up. It took him a second to register her face and another to remember where he was. He looked at me. The first question was, Did I see her, too? The second was, Did I know who she was? Really? The third was, How did she get here?

Dolly said coyly, "Won't you stand for me?"

He bounded out of his chair like a man half his age.

"Miss McPherson? Of course it's Miss McPherson."

Dolly said, "You can still call me Dolly."

"Of course, Dolly." Although her appearance benumbed him, he was able to operate in the familiar. He made small, small talk until he could recover.

"How have you been? Of course you've heard about what is going on in my country."

The joke had gone on long enough. From Dolly's face, I learned that she, too, had lost her taste for it.

I said, "Dolly, come to the kitchen, please." To the African, I said, "If you will rejoin the guests, we'll be right back."

In the kitchen, Dolly laughed and said, "He didn't know what to do."

I said, "Or who to do it to." We both laughed.

She asked, "Do you think anyone had any idea?"

"Certainly not. You were a pretty woman greeting a handsome man you had known somewhere else." I added, "Known in the biblical sense."

She laughed. "Girl, you ought to be ashamed of yourself."

We had given the African at least five moments of unease, which satisfied our appetites, and no one but he had been the wiser.

"He's lucky you're not mean," Dolly said.

"I think I'm lucky he found you and not some easy lady in the local bucket of blood."

She asked, "Who's to say he didn't find her, too?"

"Girl, you ought to be ashamed of yourself."

Back in the living room, the African had finished regaling his subjects with stories of current goings-on in Africa. He was standing.

"Maya, I must be going. My host needs to go to an appointment, and I shall accompany him. Tomorrow I shall continue my journey to

Connecticut. Thank you for this brief respite at your place. Miss McPherson, oh, Dolly, you must tell me how you met. I'll come back to New York if Miss Angelou invites me."

He pointed to my bedroom and said to me, "I shall need just a second of your time. May we go in here?"

We walked in and I closed the door.

"Maya, you are in danger."

"What?"

"You have become someone else in New York. Someone I don't know."

"What do you mean?"

"Did I ever try to make you a laughingstock in my country?"

"No, but most of the time you treated me as if I were an empty-headed flunky."

"I may have been wrong, but at least I was being myself. This setup here is beneath you. You have tried to belittle me. That is beneath the Maya I know and still love."

He turned and walked back into the living room, saying, just loud enough for me to hear, "Pale hands I loved beside the Shalimar."

I had told him once that if I ever became so angry with him that I wouldn't speak, he could whisper that line of poetry written by Laurence Hope and I would melt into the palm of his hand.

In the living room he spoke in Fanti to the people: "Let us leave these ladies and go attend to our business."

He turned to me and said in English, "I am going now, Maya, God bless you."

I saw hurt and embarrassment in his face. I had meant to prick him, not to pierce him.

I responded with the Fanti departure phrase, *"Ko ne bra,"* which means "Go and come," but I knew he would never come back again.

I looked at Dolly, who was looking as crestfallen as I felt.

"Well, sister, we couldn't swallow the big cat easily. He seems to have stuck in our throats."

She said, "Yes, I know."

CHAPTER 27

It was 1968, and the site was Carnegie Hall. Ossie Davis was to be master of ceremonies, Pete Seeger would sing, James Baldwin would spear up the audience and Martin Luther King, Jr., would conclude the evening. The concert was planned to recognize the hundredth anniversary of the birth of W. E. B. DuBois. The historian had died in Ghana five years earlier at the age of ninety-five.

Jimmy had taken a box for family and friends, so Sam Floyd and Dolly and I joined the Baldwins and the baritone Brock Peters and his wife, Deedee.

The occasion was serious, but the people were lighthearted as they glittered in the lobby of Carnegie Hall.

When Ossie Davis appeared onstage in a sleek tuxedo that fitted him everywhere, the audience was eager for him. Ossie glowed with grace and pleased the patrons with his easy wit. Next, Pete Seeger, the well-known folksinger, arched his long, lean body around his guitar and sang:

> *"Where have all the flowers gone?*
> *Long time passing . . ."*

The crowd showed their appreciation by asking for an encore.

James Baldwin flew onto the stage, talking before he even reached the microphone. The audience expected his machine-gun ack-ack way of speaking. There were shouts of approval at the end of each sentence. He flailed at this country that he loved, explaining that it could do better and had better do better or he could prophesy with a sign, water now but fire next time. He spoke to and for the people as if they were his family and they loved him. His rashness tickled them and his eloquence stroked them.

Everyone in the hall waited out a long moment before Ossie reappeared. As if by an agreed-upon signal, we all held our breath.

Ossie's voice was filled with joy and respect. He said simply, "Ladies and gentlemen, Reverend Dr. Martin Luther King."

And he was there, smiling, nodding, waving a hand, an average-size, average-looking, average black man upon whom hung the dreams of millions.

He waited a while as the throng quieted, and then his voice filled the hall, filled our ears, filled our hearts.

When he began, his passion slowly wound his audience into a nearly unbearable tautness. A dramatic orator, King lured us back to the nineteenth century and into the mind of a young man who had been born black only a few years after the abolition of the slave trade, yet whose exquisite intelligence and courage allowed him to become the first African-American to earn a doctorate from Harvard University in 1895.

Martin King could have been describing a contemporary, or a relative, he spoke so knowingly of W. E. B. DuBois. We listeners bonded resolutely, because King showed us how we were all related to one another and that we shared the same demons and the same divines. He cemented the bonding by telling us that DuBois had included all of us, no matter our color, status or age, into his dream of a fair and workable future.

The melody in Martin King's speech changed subtly. Those familiar with the oratorical style of black preachers knew he had begun his finale.

Mother Baldwin stretched out her legs, feeling for her shoes. Brock got up, as did Jimmy Baldwin and his brother David. I looked down on the main floor and was reminded of a black Baptist church on a Sunday morning when the preacher has told the parishioners the old story in a new way. Each time I looked, more people had risen, so that by the time Reverend King said his last word, everyone was standing.

The spontaneous response was tumultuous and the mood even

more joyous than it had been in the early evening. Martin Luther King, Jr., never disappointed. The people had enjoyed the grace of Ossie Davis, the music of Pete Seeger, the excitement of James Baldwin. Then Martin King had held high his rainbow of good wishes for all the people, everywhere.

The Baldwin party was walking down the corridor from the box when Reverend King appeared.

Everyone complimented him. Mother Baldwin received a hug and praise for her son.

"I know you're proud of this fellow, aren't you, Mother?"

Berdis Baldwin blushed as if we were at Jimmy's christening and the preacher had declared her son to be the most wonderful child he had ever seen.

Martin King said to me, "And you, Maya. I wanted to talk to you. What are you doing now?"

I said I was writing a play.

"Can you put a bookmark on a page and give me one month of your time? This poor people's march we are girding up for is not a black march or a white march. This is the poor people's march. I want us to stay in Washington, D.C., until legislation is passed that will reduce the poverty in our rich country. We may have to build tent cities, and if so, I want to be able to do that."

"But what can I ..."

More people had joined our group of Baldwins and friends.

"I need someone to travel this country and talk to black preachers. I'd like each big church to donate one Sunday's collection to the poor people's march. I need you, Maya. Not too many black preachers can resist a good-looking woman with a good idea."

Mother Baldwin said, "That's the truth."

Martin went on, "Also, when anyone accuses me of just being non-violent, I can say, 'Well, I don't know. I've got Maya Angelou back with me.' "

Jimmy said, "Yes. Of course she will do it."

I saw, or thought I saw, how Reverend King was planning to expand the reach and influence of the Southern Christian Leadership Conference.

He asked for only one month. I said, "Yes, but only after my birthday. I have to give a party to explain to these hard-nosed New Yorkers why I'm going back to the SCLC. They think I'm much more of an activist, a real radical."

"What I'm planning is really radical. When is your birthday?"

I said, "April fourth."

We both nodded.

CHAPTER 28

Guy had been Western Airlines' first black junior executive. He had declared he would keep the job for a specified time then go to Europe. His eighteen-month stay in the U.S. was up. He had bought a used Land Rover and was headed to London to pick it up. He had set aside one day to visit me in New York.

I decided to give a party and invite all the men who had advised and/or cautioned me when Guy was a rambunctious teenager. Since I was a single woman raising a black boy in the United States, I had asked a group of male friends to tell me when they thought I was treating Guy in a way that might endanger his sense of himself.

Many times after gatherings, I would receive phone calls. "Hey, Maya, Guy was playing chess and you made him leave the game. That wasn't hip."

"But it was just a game, and we had someplace to go."

"When a boy is playing a man, it's never just a game. It is about his manhood. He's always testing it."

Or: "You made Guy get up and give his seat to a woman. That wasn't hip."

"But it was courteous. I have to teach him courtesy."

"Yeah, but you didn't give him a chance to do the right thing on his own. You have to trust his upbringing."

I had listened and learned, and despite the past three or four rocky years, Guy had grown into a very nice young man. I wanted to show him off to my friends.

Coming from the supermarket I met Hercules, a freedom fighter from Rhodesia whom Guy and I had known in Cairo.

My mind was so filled with Guy's arrival that I didn't remember that in Cairo Hercules had tried to be Guy's buddy, and although I was married, he had attempted to seduce me.

Hercules asked how I was and how Guy was.

I told him Guy was in New York for just one day and that I was giving a party for him that night. I gave Hercules the address and told him he would be welcome.

When I entered the apartment, Guy had a wall-size map spread on the floor.

"Here, Mom, here's where I want to go."

It was the Sahara Desert.

I thought he was going back to Ghana, where we had friends.

"No, I'm going to have a photographic safari service from Mauritania back to Morocco."

My only child? My beloved son with whom I was now well pleased? My heart fell in my chest, but I said nothing. The red and green lines on the map seemed to be moving.

"I've planned it out with friends. We're going to meet up in Spain so we can run with the bulls in Pamplona, then we'll take this road to the Mediterranean and ferry over to Morocco."

He looked at me very quickly, as if he had been thinking aloud and suddenly remembered that I was present.

"Mom, you're afraid." It was not a question, he had read fear on my face.

"Yes. I am."

He said, "I understand, but you needn't be. I am free, and I have you to thank for that."

I didn't dare question; nor did I dare let him see my fear again. I asked him to help me put away the groceries and to second my cooking.

We fell into a rhythm that we had begun to develop when he was ten, except now he was adept. No onions went scooting across the floor, no fingers had to be washed, kissed and bandaged.

I admired the man, but I did miss the boy.

The party was merrily rolling along. Friends who hadn't seen one another in too long a time were having a reunion. I didn't know any young girls to invite as company for Guy, but Dolly asked over a new teacher who was on her first job. Guy came to the kitchen. "Mom." He was displeased. "Mom, Hercules is here."

The look on his face shook my memory loose. Of course, all the hosts in and around Cairo had stopped inviting Hercules. Housekeepers' young daughters were claiming they had been raped or impregnated by him, and since he had taken up drink, his language was often foul.

I shook my head and said to Guy, "I forgot. I was thinking about you and forgot."

He wagged his head and pitied his old doddering mother. I was thirty-nine.

I listened to the discussion between Jimmy Baldwin and Max Roach. They were talking about South Africa.

Hercules came up to me. "Sister Maya, thank you for inviting me." I said "Yes" coolly.

He said, "I brought my girlfriend. Let me introduce her."

He introduced me to a woman standing at his side. I admit that my displeasure with myself, and the memory of Hercules's behavior in Egypt, kept me from acknowledging the guest warmly. I said a perfunctory hello and went to join another small group.

I was looking for a way to get into the heated discussion among John Killens and Julian Mayfield and Rosa Guy when Hercules's woman tugged my sleeve.

"Is it my whiteness that makes you uncomfortable?" She could not have startled me more if she had poured her drink on the rug.

I collected myself sufficiently. "Of course not. Look around, there are Sam and Connie Sutton, and Roger and Jean Genoud. You are no more white than they, and they are at home here. Please, help yourself to a drink."

I moved to a less troublesome area and caught up on the laughter that was loud in the room.

Later, Dolly, Guy and I laid out the food on the buffet and the dining table. I stood with serving spoons in hand and said in a loud voice, "Grub est servi."

The line was taut and furiously fast at first, then, when it slackened, some people who had eaten jumped back in line for seconds.

I said, "Please, let everybody get served once before seconds are handed out."

Hercules's lady friend, who was back in line, said, "This is not the democratic way. First come, first served. Can you really hold a place in line for someone who is not here?"

I said, "Yes, I can. Because this is my house. I wouldn't tell you how to run it at your house."

Hercules said, in support of his lady, "She is right. This is not the democratic way."

My patience with them and with myself was as brittle as melba toast. I said, "You, who have needed a passbook to move from one district in Johannesburg to another, are to tell me about democracy?"

She said, "You people, you kill me. You don't realize that English is not his first language."

I was ready to evict her at "you people," but I was serving a plate. When I finished dishing up food, I said to Hercules, "Take her out of my house. She may be indulged and famous as a rude guest in other people's home, but she gets put out of mine."

Suddenly the laughter had stopped, and all was quiet. I had not raised my voice, but I knew everyone present had heard me.

I couldn't take back a single word, and in that moment I hated myself and the woman. I sounded like a bully, and I truly abhorred bullies.

"Out." It was too late. "Out."

The woman's departing statement cut me more deeply than she could have ever imagined. "People think you're so kind. They should see you as you are. A great bully."

I said nothing, and in a few minutes, noise returned and the party pitch reestablished itself.

Guy left early to see the teacher home. Some friends said, "You showed wonderful restraint. She came out to be trouble."

Others didn't mention the incident. When I was totally alone, I sat down and wondered how else I could have handled that awful situation. I found no answer, so I started to clean the apartment. I emptied ashtrays and washed glasses. I took trash to the garbage chute. Little by little, I cleaned and polished my house till it glistened.

As I finished, Guy rang the bell. He entered and stood at the door, observing the clean apartment.

"I meant to be back in time to help you."

"Oh no, as you see . . ."

"Mom, I'm going to make us both a drink." I sat down to await the service.

He brought two filled glasses into the living room. He lifted his to me, I lifted mine to him.

"Mom, if you ever speak to a woman I bring to your house as you spoke to that woman, I will sever our relationship."

I looked at my son sitting aloof like a high-ranking judge on a lofty seat. His words alone constituted a body blow, and his posture added weight to the statement. I thought of carrying him on my hip all over the world, of sleeping in hotel rooms separated by a sheet hanging across the middle of the room to give each of us privacy. I thought of how I had raised him and saw that he was right.

I said, "Of course, you are absolutely correct. You are obliged to protect anyone you bring out anywhere. If the person is under your umbrella, you are supposed to defend her or him. It would kill me if you severed our relationship. But let me tell you this. If you bring someone to my house that stupid, it is likely that I will speak to her as I spoke to that woman. And severing our relationship will be your next job."

He looked at me for a long minute, then got up and came to the sofa to sit beside me.

He opened his long arms. "I love you, Mom, you're a gas. I truly love you."

CHAPTER 29

John Patterson was my across-the-hall neighbor, and we shared the same birthday.

I spent the morning cooking for my party. He was planning to celebrate with his fiancée, a beautiful fawnlike girl half his age.

When I could safely leave my pots for a few minutes, I went to his apartment for a glass of wine and for our opportunity to congratulate each other.

I cheered him for his impending marriage, and he saluted me for taking on a thirty-day job that would give me the chance to visit the major American cities. I always added "and churches."

I didn't have my itinerary, but I told John that I thought I had to go to Atlanta first for meetings with Reverend King and the leaders of the SCLC.

I admitted to Dolly that I had trepidation about the trip, and even some fear over how the ministers in the different churches would take to me and to Reverend King's plans. So much depended upon my doing well.

Dolly said, "If the Reverend King thinks you can do it, that's enough for me. And don't believe that the whole thing depends on you. You're not the only fish in the sea. He's got others. Anyway, you will do wonderfully."

A sister always knows how to set you down, and a true sister lets you down easily.

My apartment smelled like I was readying for a Christmas feast. I was really putting on the dog. Stepping out. All the Harlem Writers

Guild members were coming. I invited Jerry Purcell and his partner, Paul Robinson, and some of the regulars from Terry's Pub, the local bar.

I cooked Texas chili without the beans, baked ham and candied yams, rice and peas for the West Indian palate, macaroni and cheese and a pineapple upside-down cake.

I looked the apartment over and was proud. The food was prepared, ice buckets were filled, glasses were sparkling and the daffodils were as perky as their name.

The telephone ring surprised me.

"Maya?" It was Dolly.

"Yes?"

"Have you listened to the radio or television?"

I said no.

"Maya, please don't turn either of them on. And don't answer the phone. Give me your word."

"I give you my word."

"I'm on my way."

I made a drink and sat down, trying to guess what could have happened that could cause her such alarm.

Dolly stood at my door, her face ghastly with news.

I said, "Come in. Nothing could be that bad."

It was that bad and worse.

She said, "Martin Luther King was shot. Maya, he's dead."

Some words are spoken and not heard. Because the ears cannot accept them, the eye seems to see them. I saw the letters D E A D. Who was dead? Who was dead now? Not Malcolm again. Not my grandmother again. Not my favorite uncle Tommy. Not again.

I didn't realize I was talking, but Dolly grabbed me and held me.

"Maya, it's Martin King. Reverend King."

"Stop talking nonsense. Stop it." When I really heard her, the world capsized. If King was dead, who was alive? Where would we go? What was next? Suddenly I had to get out.

I didn't take my purse or keys or turn off the stove or the lights or tell Dolly where I was going.

John was locking his door. We looked at each other.

He asked, "Where are you going?"

I said, "Harlem."

He said, "Me, too."

He didn't speak as we walked to Harlem. I turned my thoughts over as one turns pages in a book. In the silence I spoke to myself, using the time to comprehend the emptiness.

That great mind, which considered adversity and said, This too shall pass away, had itself passed away.

That mellifluous voice, which sang out of radios and televisions and over altars and pulpits, which intoned from picket lines and marches and through prison bars, was stilled. Forever stilled.

That strong heart which did beat with the insistence of a kettle drum was silent. Silenced.

———

Waves of noise of every kind flooded down 125th Street. There was an undulation of raw screams, followed by thuds like the sound of buffaloes running into each other at rutting time. I never discovered what or who caused that particular dissonance, but the sheer jangle of glass breaking was obvious.

When John ran into friends and they fell into a sobbing embrace, I walked on alone.

There were noticeable differences between this current turmoil and the Watts uprising. In Los Angeles, rage had ruled. There, the people acted out of a pent-up anger over past slights and historic cruelties. On the evening of April 4, 1968, a lamentation would rise and hold tremulously in the air, then slowly fall out of hearing range just as another would ascend.

Strangers stopped in front of strangers and asked, "Why? Why?"

"You know? You know."

Then strangers hugged strangers and cried.

A television in the window of an appliance store played tapes of Martin King speaking. No sound accompanied the pictures, but people stood silent, five deep in front of the shop window, as the uproar swirled unnoticed around them. I joined the watchers for a few moments and heard the moan behind me.

Rosa Guy emerged from the crowd. We stood looking at each other. We embraced and said nothing. When we released each other, we continued our separate ways.

A man, naked to the waist, walked out of a building with a conga drum strapped to his body. He waddled toward me, the head of the drum protruding from under his arm. He passed me shouting, not singing, unintelligible words.

I went into a lighted diner and sat at the far end of the counter. Only one other customer was in the place. He was leaning over so far his head was on the counter.

I waited for a few minutes for a waitress, and when none appeared, I called out, "Can I get some service?"

The man raised his head. "If all you want is coffee, you can get it yourself."

I went behind the counter and lifted the coffeepot and looked at the man. "May I help you?"

"No, baby, nobody can help me. Nobody can help nobody. You know this is all about Malcolm."

"What?"

I expected to hear the awful despair at Martin Luther King's death. Malcolm's name shocked me.

"Malcolm?"

"See, they killed him not far from here, and we didn't do anything. Lot of people loved Malcolm, but we didn't show it, and now even people who didn't agree with Reverend King, they out here, just to show we do know how to care for somebody. Half of this is for Malcolm X, a half for Martin King and a half for a whole lot of others."

I laid my own head on the counter weighted with new realization.

A man lived. A man loved.

A man tried, and a man died.

And that was not all there was to that. And it never was.

CHAPTER 30

Death of a beloved flattens and dulls everything. Mountains and sky-scrapers and grand ideas are brought down to eye level or below. Great loves and large hates no longer cast such huge shadows or span so broad a distance. Connections do not adhere so closely, and important events lose some of their glow.

Everywhere I turned, life was repeating itself. The photograph of Coretta Scott King, veiled and standing with her children, reminded me of the picture of Jacqueline Kennedy with her children. Both women were under the probing, curious and often sympathetic eye of the world. Yet each stood as if she and her children and her memories lived together in an unknowable dimension.

On radio and in newspapers, Martin King's name was linked again and again with the name Malcolm X. As if the life and death of one confirmed the life and death of the other.

Depression wound itself around me so securely I could barely walk, and didn't want to talk.

I went to Dolly's apartment. I didn't want my absence to alarm her.

"I'm going to hibernate for a few weeks."

She asked, "What do you mean?"

"I'm going to stay alone. I will not be seeing anyone. I just need to seek balance."

Dolly said, "I understand. But listen, I'm going to bring you some food. And you're going to have to talk to me once a day. I don't care what you say, just don't stop talking. Okay?"

Jerry Purcell sent an employee who knocked on my door loudly and repeatedly. When I opened it, he handed me a package wrapped in tinfoil.

"Jerry said that you would get a plate every other day. If you're not here, I'll leave it by the door."

Jimmy Baldwin pried me loose from my despair. "You have to get out of here. Get dressed. I'm taking you somewhere."

Exactly what Bailey had said and done when Malcolm was killed.

"Put on something that makes you feel pretty." I remembered the old saying, which was a favorite of my Arkansas grandmother. "It's hard to make the prettiest clothes fit a miserable man."

Jimmy said, "Some friends have invited me to dinner, you will enjoy them. They are both funny, and you need to laugh." We were in front of the building before Jimmy said, "This is Jules Feiffer's apartment."

Judy opened the door and welcomed us. Although I had not formed a picture of the Feiffers, I was unprepared for her beauty. She could have been a movie actress. Jules also surprised me. He looked more like a young, intense college professor than one of the nation's funniest, most biting cartoonists.

They both hugged Jimmy, and the three of them laughed aloud as if they had heard a funny story when they last parted and had not had time to finish their laughter.

The Feiffers' pretty ten-year-old daughter joined us in the living room. When Jimmy embraced her and asked after her school, she answered easily, showing the poise of a person twice her age.

We adults finished our drinks and moved into the dining room. We told and heard great stories over a delicious dinner. Jimmy talked about being a preacher in Harlem at fourteen years old. He may have lost some of his evangelical drama, but it returned that night in force. He preached a little and sang in a remarkably beautiful voice. His story was funny and touching. When we laughed, it was always with him and with the people he spoke of, never at them.

Jules talked about school and his college mates. His tale was told with wit so dry that when we laughed, we thought we breathed in dust.

Judy kept the glasses filled and added the appropriate response whenever it was needed. She said, "Nothing funny ever happened to me until I met Jules."

When my time came, I thought of the saying "You have to fight for the right to play it good." I described Stamps, Arkansas. Although there is nothing amusing about racial discrimination, the oppressed find funny things to say about it.

"The white folks are so prejudiced in my town, a colored person is not allowed to eat vanilla ice cream.

"And when a white man heard a black man singing 'My Blue Heaven,' he called the KKK. They visited the offender and told him that the Molly in the lyric was a white woman, and they wanted to hear how he would sing the song now that he had new information."

I sang what the black man supposedly sang:

> *"Miss Molly and y'all*
> *I ain't in that stuff at all*
> *Y'alls happy in y'alls*
> *Blue heaven."*

There was very little serious conversation. The times were so solemn and the daily news so somber that we snatched mirth from unlikely places and gave servings of it to one another with both hands.

The evening was full. I was on the street before I realized how much I had relaxed in the Feiffers' home. I told Jimmy I was so glad to laugh.

Jimmy said, "We survived slavery. Think about that. Not because we were strong. The American Indians were strong, and they were on their own land. But they have not survived genocide. You know how we survived?"

I said nothing.

"We put surviving into our poems and into our songs. We put it into our folk tales. We danced surviving in Congo Square in New Orleans and put it in our pots when we cooked pinto beans. We wore surviving on our backs when we clothed ourselves in the colors of the rainbow. We were pulled down so low we could hardly lift our eyes, so we knew, if we wanted to survive, we had better lift our own spirits. So we laughed whenever we got the chance.

"Now, how does your spirit feel?"

I said, "Just fine, thank you."

CHAPTER 31

They were from Northern California and looked the part. Jon wore a loose-knit tan sweater with leather elbow patches and tan pants. Verna, a small, neatly made woman, sat comfortably in a light-colored Chanel suit, and Steve wore black slacks and a black V-neck sweater over a white turtleneck shirt that filled in the V.

They had gotten my address from Enrico Banducci, who owned the Hungry I in San Francisco. Enrico and I liked each other, so we had kept in touch over oceans and continents.

"Ms. Angelou, we know you are a writer and, we are told, a very good one."

"Yes."

"Do you have anything published?"

I didn't think it wise to say I had a short story published in *Revolución*, Cuba's premier magazine.

I said, "Ah." Then I added, "I have written some short essays that Ruby Dee and Ossie Davis read on a national radio station."

"We'd be glad to see them."

"Yes, they could tell us a lot about your style."

"When I heard you were looking for a writer, I put a few in my attaché case." I had borrowed the attaché case from Sam Floyd. "Please tell me what kind of writer are you looking for."

Jon leaned back and said, "We think it's past time for our station to do some programs on African-American culture and history. We were told that you have lived in Africa, and you might be the very person to bring it together for us."

Steve said, "We need an insider's view." Well, I certainly was inside.

"I am writing a play now, but I do have some ideas for a documentary."

"Would the subject of African-American culture be of interest to you?" Steve asked.

"Of course!"

Steve flinched. I did not intend to speak so abruptly, but the question was so inane it caught me off guard.

"Of course," I said more softly. "In fact, in Ghana I was struck by how much of what I thought was Afro-American culture really had its origin in Africa. Now I know I should have anticipated that, but I did not."

Jon asked, "Do you think you have enough material?"

"How long do you want the program?"

"No, no," Verna said, "not a program, we want a series. Ten one-hour programs. Can you do that?"

"Certainly. Surely. I just misunderstood. Ten one-hour programs?" I wondered if there was that much material in the whole world. "Yes. I can do that."

"We will be seeing other writers, but who is your agent?"

Would they even consider me if I admitted I had no agent?

"I have a manager. He acts as my agent." Having a manager might make me seem an important writer. "I'll give you his address and telephone number."

I wrote down Jerry Purcell's phone number. "He's away today, but I'm sure you can reach him tomorrow at this number."

I needed the day to find Jerry before they talked to him. I had to tell him that he was my manager.

For over an hour we talked about San Francisco and the state of the Broadway stage and PBS in general and their station KQED in particular and the United States and Africa. That was the kind of conversation I liked to have, rambling, tumbling, wandering off from one subject onto another.

Their humor pleased me. I forgot where I was and why I was there. When they stood, I remembered and immediately wondered if I had talked too much and overstayed my welcome. We shook hands all around, and Jon said, "We will speak to your manager, and you will hear from us before the week is out."

Yes, I did like them, and I hoped they liked me.

Three days later Jerry telephoned. "I got good money for you, so you'll be going out to San Francisco."

I whooped all the way to the library.

With time and a kindly librarian, any unskilled person can learn how to build a replica of the Taj Mahal. I pored over books about television documentaries. I read instructions on how to write television plays and accounts of producing and directing television.

I studied hard and memorized phrases and words I had never used. Boom and speed and camera angle, tripod and seconds and reverses. After a week I had an enlarged vocabulary. When I wasn't reading about television, I was writing for television.

I thought that I would learn on the job, but I would learn quicker and more easily if I had some of the language.

I designed a series called *Blacks. Blues. Black.* We were blacks in Africa before we were brought to America as slaves, where we created the blues, and now we were painfully and proudly returning to being upstanding free blacks again.

The program would show African culture's impact on the West. As host, I would introduce the lyricism of poetry and the imagery of prose. In one program I would have B. B. King playing blues and church choirs singing spirituals and gospel songs. There would be African, African-American and modern ballet dance, and I would point out their similarities. The art of African sculpture would be shown as the source and resource of many Western artists' creativity. I would place Fan, Ashanti and Dogon masks alongside the works of Picasso, Klee, Modigliani and Rouault.

It was thrilling to think of returning to San Francisco, with something to do and the faith that I would do a good job.

CHAPTER 32

I was so excited that the telephone call hardly penetrated.

"My name is Robert Loomis, and I am an editor at Random House. Judy Feiffer spoke of you. She said you told wonderful stories."

"How nice of her. James Baldwin and her husband told the best."

"I am calling to ask if you'd like to write an autobiography."

I said, "No, thank you. I am a poet and playwright."

He asked, "Are you sure?"

"Yes, quite. In fact, I'm leaving in a few days to write and host a television series for PBS in San Francisco. I'll be there for a month or more."

"May I have a California number for you?"

I gave him Aunt Lottie's San Francisco telephone number and my mother's number in Stockton, California, where she had moved.

"I'm pretty certain that I will not write an autobiography. I didn't celebrate it, but I have only had my fortieth birthday this year. Maybe in ten or twenty years." We both laughed and said good-bye.

In San Francisco I collected dancers and singers and musicians and comedians. I went to churches and synagogues and community centers. On the day of the first shoot, Bob Loomis telephoned again.

"Miss Angelou, I'm calling to see if you've had a change of mind, if you are certain that you don't want to write an autobiography for Random House."

I said, "Mr. Loomis, I am sure that I cannot write an autobiography. I am up to my lower jaw in this television series. When I come back to New York, I'd like to talk to you about a book of poetry."

He said, "Fine," but there was no eagerness in his voice. "Good luck to you."

———

In San Francisco I was pleased that all the pieces were falling into their proper places. The ministers I approached were agreeable, the choir conductors were talented and willing. I borrowed an entire collection of Makonde sculpture from Bishop Trevor Hoy at the Pacific School of Religion and church officials allowed me to film their services. I took television crews into elementary schools and people's private homes.

Blacks. Blues. Black was well received. The *Sun Times,* the local black newspaper, gave it a rousing review. Rosa Guy and Dolly came out for the premiere.

People who had looked askance when I began the series were now standing in line to participate. Schools had adopted the programs, and I was told that some preachers were using my subjects as topics for their sermons in San Francisco.

On my last day, Robert Loomis called again. I have always been sure that he spoke to James Baldwin. He said, "Miss Angelou, Robert Loomis. I won't bother you again. And I must say, you may be right not to attempt an autobiography, because it is nearly impossible to write autobiography as literature. Almost impossible."

I didn't think. I didn't have to. I said, "Well, maybe I will try it. I don't know how it will turn out, but I can try."

Grandmother Henderson's voice was in my ear: "Nothing beats a trial but a failure."

"Well, if you'd like to write forty or fifty pages and send them to me, we can see if I can get a contract for you. When do you think you can start?"

I said, "I'll start tomorrow."

CHAPTER 33

Rosa and Dolly and I traveled to Stockton to spend a last weekend with my mother before returning to New York.

She cooked and laughed and drank and told stories and generally pranced around her pretty house, proud of me, proud of herself, proud of Dolly and Rosa.

She said black women are so special. Few men of any color and even fewer white women can deal with how fabulous we are.

"Girls, I'm proud of you."

In the early morning, I took my yellow pad and ballpoint pen and sat down at my mother's kitchen table.

I thought about black women and wondered how we got to be the way we were. In our country, white men were always in superior positions; after them came white women, then black men, then black women, who were historically on the bottom stratum.

How did it happen that we could nurse a nation of strangers, be maids to multitudes of people who scorned us, and still walk with some majesty and stand with a degree of pride?

I thought of human beings, as far back as I had read, of our deeds and didoes. According to some scientists, we were born to forever crawl in swamps, but for some not yet explained reason, we decided to stand erect and, despite gravity's pull and push, to remain standing. We, carnivorous beings, decided not to eat our brothers and sisters but to try to respect them. And further, to try to love them.

Some of us loved the martial songs, red blood flowing and the screams of the dying on battlefields.

And some naturally bellicose creatures decided to lay down our swords and shields and to try to study war no more.

Some of us heard the singing of angels, harmonies in a heavenly choir, or at least the music of the spheres.

We had come so far from where we started, and weren't nearly approaching where we had to be, but we were on the road to becoming better.

I thought if I wrote a book, I would have to examine the quality in the human spirit that continues to rise despite the slings and arrows of outrageous fortune.

Rise out of physical pain and the psychological cruelties.

Rise from being victims of rape and abuse and abandonment to the determination to be no victim of any kind.

Rise and be prepared to move on and ever on.

I remembered a children's poem from my mute days in Arkansas that seemed to say however low you perceive me now, I am headed for higher ground.

I wrote the first line in the book, which would become *I Know Why the Caged Bird Sings.*

"What you looking at me for. I didn't come to stay."

A NOTE ON THE TYPE

The principal text of this Modern Library edition
was set in a digitized version of Janson, a typeface that
dates from about 1690 and was cut by Nicholas Kis,
a Hungarian working in Amsterdam. The original matrices have
survived and are held by the Stempel foundry in Germany.
Hermann Zapf redesigned some of the weights and sizes for
Stempel, basing his revisions on the original design.